The Cambridge Handbook of Human Affective Neuroscience

Neuroscientific research on emotion has developed dramatically over the past decade. The cognitive neuroscience of human emotion, which has emerged as the new and thriving area of "affective neuroscience," is rapidly rendering existing overviews of the field obsolete. This handbook provides a comprehensive, up-to-date, and authoritative survey of knowledge and topics investigated in this cutting-edge field. It covers a range of topics, from face and voice perception to pain and music, as well as social behaviors and decision making. The book considers and interrogates multiple research methods, among them brain imaging and physiology measurements, as well as methods used to evaluate behavior and genetics. Editors Jorge Armony and Patrik Vuilleumier have enlisted well-known and active researchers from more than 20 institutions across three continents, bringing geographic as well as methodological breadth to the collection. This timely volume will become a key reference work for researchers and students in the growing field of neuroscience.

Jorge Armony holds the Canada Research Chair in Affective Neuroscience in the Department of Psychiatry at McGill University. He is also a researcher at the Douglas Mental Health University Institute and a member of the International Laboratory for Brain, Music, and Sound Research (BRAMS). Dr. Armony's research focuses on the neural mechanisms of emotional processing across modalities, including the interactions of these mechanisms with other cognitive functions in healthy individuals as well as in patients suffering from psychiatric and neurological disorders.

Patrik Vuilleumier is a professor at the University of Geneva Medical School, where he leads the Laboratory for Neurology and Imaging of Cognition and directs the Geneva Neuroscience Center. Dr. Vuilleumier was part of the interdisciplinary team that helped shape the Swiss National Center of Competence in Research in Affective Sciences. Dr. Vuilleumier's research focuses on the influence of emotion processing on perception, attention, and action, using functional neuroimaging techniques and neuropsychological studies of brain-damaged patients.

The Cambridge Handbook of Human Affective Neuroscience

Edited by

JORGE ARMONY

McGill University

PATRIK VUILLEUMIER

University of Geneva

CAMBRIDGE
UNIVERSITY PRESS

University Printing House, Cambridge CB2 8BS, United Kingdom

One Liberty Plaza, 20th Floor, New York, NY 10006, USA

477 Williamstown Road, Port Melbourne, VIC 3207, Australia

314–321, 3rd Floor, Plot 3, Splendor Forum, Jasola District Centre, New Delhi – 110025, India

103 Penang Road, #05–06/07, Visioncrest Commercial, Singapore 238467

Cambridge University Press is part of the University of Cambridge.

It furthers the University's mission by disseminating knowledge in the pursuit of
education, learning and research at the highest international levels of excellence.

www.cambridge.org
Information on this title: www.cambridge.org/9780521171557

© Cambridge University Press 2013

First published 2013
5th printing 2022

Printed in the United Kingdom by TJ Books Limited, Padstow Cornwall

A catalog record for this publication is available from the British Library.

Library of Congress Cataloging in Publication data

The Cambridge Handbook of Human Affective Neuroscience / [edited by] Jorge Armony, Patrik Vuilleumier.
  p. ; cm.
Handbook of human affective neuroscience
Includes bibliographical references and index.
ISBN 978-1-107-00111-4 (hardback) – ISBN 978-0-521-17155-7 (pbk.)
1. Affective neuroscience.   2. Emotions.   I. Armony, Jorge, 1965–   II. Vuilleumier, Patrik, 1965–   III. Title:
Handbook of human affective neuroscience.
[DNLM: 1. Emotions. BF 531]
QP360.C337   2013
612.8–dc23   2012030622

ISBN 978-1-107-00111-4 Hardback
ISBN 978-0-521-17155-7 Paperback

To the memory of
David Servan-Schreiber, superb colleague and
generous friend who introduced me to, among many
other things, the field of Human Affective
Neuroscience (JA)
Jon Driver, a truly inspiring mentor whose
guidance and friendship have been a unique
experience that is still very much alive in my work (PV)

Contents

Color plates follow page 380.

List of Contributors

ADAM K. ANDERSON, University of Toronto

JORGE ARMONY, McGill University

ANTHONY P. ATKINSON, Durham University

SONIA BISHOP, University of California

CAROLIN BRÜCK, University of Tübingen

ROBERTO CABEZA, Duke University

FRANCES S. CHEN, University of Freiburg

HUGO D. CRITCHLEY, University of Sussex

MAURICIO R. DELGADO, Rutgers University–Newark

RICARDO DE OLIVEIRA-SOUZA, D'Or Institute for Research and Education (IDOR)

GREGOR DOMES, University of Freiburg

JUDITH DOMÍNGUEZ-BORRÀS, University of Geneva

JOSEPH E. DUNSMOOR, Duke University

THOMAS ETHOFER, University of Tübingen

DOMINIC S. FARERI, Rutgers University–Newark

LESLEY K. FELLOWS, McGill University

SOPHIE FORSTER, University of California

KATHERINE GARDHOUSE, University of Toronto

NATHALIE GEORGE, GHU Pitié-Salpetriere

JAY A. GOTTFRIED, Northwestern University Feinberg School of Medicine

JUNG EUN HAN, McGill University

AHMAD R. HARIRI, Duke University

NEIL A. HARRISON, University of Sussex

MARKUS HEINRICHS, University of Freiburg

ALISHA C. HOLLAND, Boston College

ANDREAS KEIL, University of Florida

ELIZABETH A. KENSINGER, Boston College

JOHANNA KISSLER, University of Bielefeld

OLGA KLIMECKI, Max Planck Institute for Human Cognitive and Brain Sciences

STEFAN KOELSCH, Free University of Berlin

SYLVIA D. KREIBIG, Stanford University

BENJAMIN KREIFELTS, University of Tübingen

ROBERT KUMSTA, University of Freiburg

KEVIN S. LABAR, Duke University

EAMON J. MCCRORY, University College London

APRAJITA MOHANTY, Stony Brook University

JORGE MOLL, D'Or Institute for Research and Education (IDOR)

JOHN P. O'DOHERTY, California Institute of Technology

LETICIA OLIVEIRA, Universidade Federal Fluminense

MIRTES PEREIRA, Universidade Federal Fluminense

LUIZ PESSOA, University of Maryland, College Park

K. LUAN PHAN, University of Illinois at Chicago

PIERRE RAINVILLE, University of Montreal

DAVID SANDER, University of Geneva

ANNETT SCHIRMER, National University of Singapore

CATHERINE L. SEBASTIAN, Royal Holloway, University of London

TANIA SINGER, Max Planck Institute for Human Cognitive and Brain Sciences

CHANDRA SEKHAR SRIPADA, University of Michigan

PEGGY L. ST. JACQUES, Harvard University

ESSI VIDING, University College London

PATRIK VUILLEUMIER, University of Geneva

DIRK WILDGRUBER, University of Tübingen

AMY WINECOFF, Duke University

ROLAND ZAHN, University of Manchester

Introduction

Understanding human emotion and the mechanisms underlying its generation or expression has been a central preoccupation of thinkers for millennia. Yet, its scientific study, particularly from a biological perspective, is quite recent, especially in comparison to that of other mental processes, such as vision, language, attention, or memory. Despite this late start, neuroscientific approaches to emotion have experienced a dramatic growth over the past decade. This has led to the birth of the new area of affective neuroscience, which has extended the field of cognitive research initiated in the previous decade. This new development was in large part due to important advances in the use of noninvasive functional neuroimaging techniques – such as positron emission tomography (PET), electroencephalography (EEG), magnetoencephalography (MEG), and, particularly, functional magnetic resonance imaging (fMRI). Together with refinements in more traditional methods, such as lesion studies, behavioral measures, and physiological recordings, the new techniques helped scientists make subjective and "private" affective processes more "visible" and amenable to experimental research in humans.

Largely building on previous research in neurophysiology, human affective neuroscience research began by focusing on the so-called basic emotions, particularly fear, mostly through visual stimuli (e.g., facial expression). However, as illustrated in the wide range of topics covered here, emotion research now covers different sensory modalities, processes, interactions with other systems, as well as individual differences. Emotion is now an accepted component of many "unrelated" disciplines, such as social psychology, economics, marketing, politics, and philosophy.

This book is intended to provide a wide yet comprehensive, up-to-date, and authoritative review of the cognitive neuroscience of human emotion that is both rigorous and accessible. Naturally, to keep the book manageable and of a reasonable size, we had to make some difficult choices in terms of its contents. Rather than choosing a few snippets from the entire field of affective neuroscience, we decided to focus on a specific area within the field. With this in mind, we explicitly left out nonhuman animal work. This does not mean in any way that we underestimate the importance of this research. Indeed, as stated in many of the chapters, research in experimental animals has been critical in providing the framework in which human affective neuroscience has developed; the authors were encouraged to highlight corresponding links with animal and biological sciences whenever possible. However, adding this perspective to the book would have required substantial coverage of molecular and cellular techniques that go beyond the aims of a single book. We also left out more clinically oriented research, such as emotional dysfunction in psychiatric and neurological disorders, although several of the chapters, especially those in the *Individual Differences* section, are highly relevant to this important area of knowledge.

One of the key features of this volume is that all the invited authors are established, yet young researchers – the Generation X of human affective neuroscience research – representing more than 20 institutions across three continents. They are some of the most active researchers who have contributed to the field and are still doing so.

The volume's 28 chapters are organized into seven independent yet complementary sections. We believe that this organization of topics will help readers gain a broad and structured view of the field.

Section I provides an introduction to the study of emotion from a cognitive neuroscience perspective. It is followed by a methodology section (Section II) that presents some of the most effective and widely used approaches to measure emotional responses. It describes the various techniques in a rigorous yet accessible manner, with particular emphasis easy-to-follow on affective neuroscience research – highlighting the advantages and limitations of each approach and providing concrete examples to help the reader appreciate these issues.

Section III consists of six chapters covering emotional perception and expression across different modalities (visual, auditory, olfactory, and somatosensory) and different domains within a given modality (e.g., auditory: voices and music; vision: faces and bodies). We decided to take this approach rather than, say, dividing the section according to the basic emotions, because most researchers, and thus their work, tend to focus on one of these domains but often encompass several emotions and/or processes. Thus, this structure, although somewhat arbitrary (because emotion is typically multimodal) will be most helpful to readers and reflects the current mainstream directions in human affective neuroscience.

Section IV follows with a description of how emotion and cognition interact. In this large and ever growing field, we focus on some of the most studied topics; namely emotion-attention interactions, emotion regulation, and decision making. Because of its importance and the large literature associated with it, interactions between emotion and learning and memory are covered in a separate section (Section V); its three chapters cover implicit and explicit aspects of memory, aversive learning, and reward learning. Chapters in Section VI address recent research in the so-called higher emotions, including morality, empathy, and other social emotions. Finally, Section VII covers some of the most studied individual differences – namely sex and gender, anxiety, age, and genotype – in emotional processing.

This book is particularly aimed at scientists and students of all levels (undergraduate, graduate, and postdoctoral) from psychology, neuroscience, and cognitive science, as well as people from other disciplines – including medicine, biology, computer science, economics, sociology, and political science – who have an interest in the relation between emotion and their area of study or research. In addition, this book should be useful to more clinically oriented professionals, including physicians and therapists, who are interested in gaining a better understanding of the neurobiological bases of human emotions.

Section I

INTRODUCTION TO HUMAN AFFECTIVE NEUROSCIENCE

CHAPTER 1

Models of Emotion

The Affective Neuroscience Approach

David Sander

Since its emergence in the 1990s (e.g., Davidson & Sutton, 1995; Panksepp, 1991), affective neuroscience has considerably extended our knowledge of the emotional brain. However, affective neuroscience research has only started to influence interdisciplinary models of emotion. The scientific object of affective neuroscience is "affect," which many disciplines share. Yet the way that affective neuroscience approaches affect and emotion is unique. For historical reasons and because of epistemological boundaries, psychological, neuroscientific, computer-based, and philosophical models of emotion have developed relatively independently from each other during most of the 20th century. Today, however, there is hope that the interdisciplinary nature of affective neuroscience will be able to constrain such varied models of emotion by bridging the gaps among different disciplinary approaches to emotion. Various debates that exist between and within disciplinary approaches to emotion could also benefit from the search for converging behavioral, computational, and neural evidence that is characteristic of affective neuroscience.

In this context, the overall aim of this chapter is to consider major current models of emotion by using an affective neuroscience approach. It provides a global survey of historical and conceptual issues that have guided scientific inquiries about emotion and presents the major theoretical foundations for more experimental work described in the following chapters. Although the scope of affective neuroscience research is not limited to emotion but includes other affective phenomena such as moods, preferences, and affective dispositions, this chapter examines models of emotion because they are more typically the focus of affective neuroscience research.

After having introduced what is implied by an affective neuroscience approach to models of emotion, I address terminological and taxonomy-related issues and suggest what seems to be a relatively consensual definition of emotion. Next, I outline the major models of emotion in modern research and the contrast in their focus on different phenomena: expression, action tendencies, bodily reaction, feeling, and cognition. Finally, as a brief conclusion, I illustrate the potential of the affective neuroscience approach to constrain theoretical models of emotion by considering more particularly the case of the amygdala.

The Affective Neuroscience Approach

In this chapter, affective neuroscience is defined in reference to cognitive neuroscience, similarly to the way in which cognitive sciences have been used as a reference for the development of affective sciences (see Sander & Scherer, 2009, for an overview of affective sciences).

Affective sciences can be seen as either integrated in or as complementary to cognitive sciences, depending on how one conceives the relationship between affect and cognition (see Forgas, 2008; Hilgard, 1980; Moors, 2007). Indeed, a traditional conceptual debate is whether affective processes are a type of cognitive process or whether they are qualitatively different in nature. This controversy is fundamental for contemporary models of emotion and is therefore addressed in this chapter. However, this debate seems to be quite independent from the approach of affective neuroscience. Indeed, there does not seem to be any reason for thinking that consideration of affective neuroscience either as a discipline on its own or as a "cognitive neuroscience of affect" modifies its approach.

In fact, the very reason for the growing importance of affective neuroscience was the recognition that emotion can be usefully studied by using the concepts and methods of cognitive neuroscience, leading to the "cognitive neuroscience of emotion" (for discussion see, e.g., Lane & Nadel, 2000; Ochsner & Schacter, 2000; Sander & Koenig, 2002). For instance, when Davidson and Sutton (1995) pointed to affective neuroscience as an emerging discipline, they argued that studies on emotion require a careful dissection of emotional processes into elementary mental operations, which is similar to the approach of cognitive neuroscience.

With respect to models of cognition, one strength of cognitive neuroscience is that

it relies on the so-called cognitive neuroscience triangle (see, e.g., Kosslyn & Koenig, 1992). Indeed, rather than relying on a single approach to cognition (e.g., brain mechanisms) or even on two approaches (e.g., brain and psychological mechanisms), cognitive neuroscience also relies on a third approach – the computational approach – to constrain models. Computational analysis has been important for the development of models of traditional domains of cognitive neuroscience such as perception, attention, memory, and action (Kosslyn & Koenig, 1992; Marr, 1982) and has also, more recently, been considered as important for models of social cognition (see Mitchell, 2006) and emotion (see Moors, 2007; Sander & Koenig, 2002). Inspired by David Marr's seminal work on levels of analysis (Marr, 1982), cognitive neuroscience defines computational analysis as a logical exercise aimed at determining what processing subsystems are necessary to produce a specific behavior, given specific input (Kosslyn & Koenig, 1992). Such computational analysis is important for producing explicit models of the mind in the form of functional architectures that could, in principle, be simulated by artificial neural networks or other computer-based models.

The view that incorporating emotion in computational models would be beneficial to our understanding of the mind has preceded the emergence of affective neuroscience, and very influential scholars in artificial intelligence such as Herbert Simon and Marvin Minsky have strongly emphasized the importance of taking emotion into account in models of the mind (e.g., Minsky, 1986; Simon, 1967). For instance, Minsky (1986, p. 163) strongly emphasized the critical role of emotion in models of artificial intelligence by arguing that "the question is not whether intelligent machines can have any emotions, but whether machines can be intelligent without any emotions." Such a pioneering perspective, according to which emotion should be modeled in artificial intelligence, was instrumental in creating a new field of research called "affective computing" (see Picard, 1997).

Affective computing can be defined as the type of computing that relates to, arises from, or deliberately influences emotion and other affective phenomena (Picard, 2009). In that regard, a close consideration of affective computing can be viewed as being the basis for the implementation of emotions as adaptive mechanisms in autonomous agents (e.g., Cañamero, 2009), not only in robotics but also for software agents such as embodied conversational agents (e.g., Pelachaud, 2009). The basis of affective computing resides in the establishment of computational models of emotion (Fellous & Arbib, 2005; Petta & Gratch, 2009) that are based on both psychological (Gratch & Marsella, 2005) and neuroscience (Taylor & Korsten, 2009) constraints. For instance, with respect to connectionist models of emotional processing (see Roesch, Korsten, Fragopanagos, & Taylor, 2010), the most classic example is the work of Armony and colleagues. In their pioneering work, Armony and colleagues proposed a computational connectionist model of fear conditioning, constrained by what was then known about the neuroanatomy and neurophysiology of fear learning, in particular by modeling both cortical and subcortical pathways to the amygdala (Armony, Servan-Schreiber, Cohen, & LeDoux, 1995). However, this model was strongly inspired by the functional neuroanatomy of fear learning, and it is therefore unclear how it could be extended to other emotions and to aspects other than emotional learning.

Affective neuroscience and affective computing converge toward the importance of considering biological, psychological, and computational constraints in modeling emotion (see, e.g., Roesch et al., 2011). This convergence is consistent with the notion outlined earlier that the task of affective neuroscience is the same as that of cognitive neuroscience; namely, to "map the information-processing structure of the human mind and to discover how this computational organisation is implemented in the physical organization of the brain" (Tooby & Cosmides, 2000, p. 1167). A critical advantage of adopting a complete affective neuroscience approach is that it invites affective scientists to develop functional architectures that are sufficiently explicit to derive competing hypotheses that can be subject to computational simulations, conceptual analyses, and empirical experiments. As discussed in the next section, this advantage brought by explicit models is particularly salient in emotion research where definitional issues are still highly debated.

What Is an Emotion?

Fehr and Russell (1984) highlighted the difficulty in producing an explicit definition of emotion when they wrote that "everyone knows what an emotion is, until asked to give a definition. Then, it seems, no one knows" (p. 464). Definitions of emotion vary not only as a function of disciplines or approaches but also across history and culture. Scholars have emphasized the need to consider whether there is a history of emotion; that is, an understanding as to how emotions and the concept of emotion may have changed over historical time (see Konstan, 2009). As Konstan described it, the English term "emotion" is relatively recent and has only been used more often than, for instance, "passion," "affection," and "sentiment" in the past 200 years. Long before this period, other terms that closely correspond to "emotion" can also be found, such as the ancient Greek term *pathos*. In fact, Aristotle's definition of *pathê* as "those things on account of which people change and differ in regard to their judgments, and upon which attend pain and pleasure" (Rhetoric, Book 2, Chapter 1, 1378a) can be considered as one of the first influential explicit definitions of emotion (see Konstan, 2009). This definition was influential not only because it suggested a link between emotion and judgments but also because it already contained the dimension that almost all current models consider necessary: *valence* (here, "pain and pleasure"; see Colombetti, 2005, for a review). A history of emotion can be drawn from the time of Aristotle's definition (see, e.g., Konstan, 2009) that considers how definitions have evolved and whether emotions have changed over historical time; for example, whether today's emotions of "shame" or "anger" are the same as those described by ancient Greeks, Mesopotamians, or other civilizations.

Of course, the difference mentioned here in terms of time can also be investigated in terms of space. Although the differences found over the centuries cannot be directly investigated by affective neuroscience, the cultural differences that are observed today are a classical topic of emotion psychology (see e.g., Tsai, Knutson, & Fung, 2006) and have begun to be investigated from an affective neuroscience approach – as suggested, for instance, by the publication of a special issue on *Cultural Neuroscience* in the journal *Social Cognitive and Affective Neuroscience* (see Chiao, 2010). Reviewing historical and cultural effects on emotion would go far beyond the scope of this chapter, but, as it will be discussed later, the question of whether emotions are a universal phenomenon or whether they vary as a function of time and space is fundamental for many theories in affective sciences.

The Variety of Definitions of Emotion

"What is an emotion?" is not only the title of one of the most widely cited articles on emotion (James, 1884) but is also a current conceptual question in emotion research that seems to correspond to a never ending attempt to define emotion (see, e.g., Duffy, 1934; Frijda, 2007; Gendron & Feldman Barrett, 2009; Kleinginna & Kleinginna, 1981; Russell & Barrett, 1999; Scherer, 2005). Certainly, what affective neuroscience can significantly contribute to this effort is an understanding of emotion as a scientific concept, in particular by offering functional architectures of emotional processes in the form of explicit models.

A necessary step in modeling emotion is to acknowledge the variety of definitions that scholars have given to emotion. In a tour de force, Kleinginna and Kleinginna (1981) reviewed almost 100 definitions of emotion found in the literature and categorized them in 10 specific lists that emphasized various aspects of emotion: (1) affective definitions (emphasizing feelings of arousal and/or hedonic value); (2) cognitive definitions (emphasizing appraisal and/or labeling processes); (3) external stimuli definitions (emphasizing external emotion-generating stimuli); (4) physiological definitions (emphasizing internal physical mechanisms of emotion); (5) expressive behavior definitions (emphasizing externally observable emotional responses); (6) disruptive definitions (emphasizing disorganizing or dysfunctional effects of emotion); (7) adaptive definitions (emphasizing organizing or functional effects of emotion); (8) multi-aspect definitions (emphasizing several interrelated components of emotion); (9) restrictive definitions (distinguishing emotion from other psychological processes); and (10) motivational definitions (emphasizing the relationship between emotion and motivation).

In affective neuroscience, scholars also disagree on how to define an emotion. For instance, let us consider the definitions offered by two of the most influential scholars of current research on the emotional brain, Damasio (1998) and LeDoux (1994). LeDoux (1994, p. 291) highlighted the fact that emotions cannot be unconscious when stating that "in my view, emotions are affectively charged, subjectively experienced states of awareness. Emotions, in other words, are conscious states." According to Damasio (1998, p. 84), "the term emotion should be rightfully used to designate a collection of responses triggered from parts of the brain to the body, and from parts of the brain to other parts of the brain, using both neural and humoral routes." Therefore, Damasio certainly does not exclude the possibility that what he calls an emotion can be unconscious. Distinguishing between emotion and feeling, Damasio (1998, p. 84) also stated that "the term feeling should be used to describe the complex mental state that results from the emotional state." It is likely that such a *mental state* is conceptually closer to what LeDoux called an emotion, although Damasio called it a feeling rather than an emotion.

The Specificity of Emotion

The distinction between *emotion* and *feeling* mentioned earlier is just one of many conceptually useful distinctions that can be made in the category of affective phenomena. In fact, the term "emotion" is often considered in a framework that includes other less studied affective phenomena such as mood, motivation, drive, desire, preference, attitude, valenced reaction, passion, sentiment, affect, core affect, arousal, affective style, or affective reactivity. Some of these concepts are more scientifically defined because they have been coined to refer to a specific new concept and therefore suffer less than others from having a "folk" meaning (e.g., *affective style*, see Davidson, 1992; *core affect*, see Russell & Barrett, 1999). Attempts to define these constructs have sometimes led to extreme positions. For instance, Duffy questioned the specificity of emotion and argued that "for many years the writer has been of the opinion that 'emotion' as a scientific concept is less than useless" (Duffy, 1941, p. 283). She argued that, because emotion can be reduced to other constructs, there is no need to create a specific term for emotional states.

More recently, Brehm (1999) argued that emotion can be reduced to motivational states. Indeed, some question the boundaries between emotion and motivation. For instance, because Rolls (1999) included thirst or sexual behavior as emotions in his book *The Brain and Emotion*, Phillips (1999) proposed that it might have been more appropriate to title this book "The Brain and Motivation."

Motivation is typically considered as being related to emotion, but most scholars would agree on the need to distinguish between these two constructs (for discussion, see, e.g., Frijda, 1986, 2007). For instance, motivation can be considered both as a determinant and as a constituent of emotion. As a determinant, motivation is often considered causal for the elicitation of emotion because events that are relevant for major motivations of the individuals (e.g., needs or goals) are indeed those that typically elicit emotions (see Moors, 2007). As a constituent of emotion, motivation is often considered as being expressed in action tendencies (e.g., approach or avoidance) that indeed motivate a change in the relation between the individual and the event (see Frijda, 1986). A definition highlighting the specificity of emotion is suggested later.

Taxonomies of Emotion

Not only can emotion be distinguished from other affective phenomenon but also within the category of "emotion," various subcategories have been proposed. To the best of my knowledge, no full taxonomy of emotion has achieved consensus, but some categories are recognized as conceptually useful. Taxonomies of emotion are based on various features, and categories often overlap so that they should not be seen as describing mutually exclusive categories of emotion, but rather as describing ways in which emotions are categorized in various research traditions. Indeed, a given emotion (e.g., anger) can belong to many categories.

Basic Emotions

As an example of a category that is defined by the type of emotion, the so-called basic emotions category is very common in current affective neuroscience research (for review, see Ortony & Turner, 1990). This category, which is conceptually similar to the categories of "primary," "discrete," or "fundamental" emotions, acknowledges the fact that, according to many researchers, a small set of emotions – typically between 2 and 10 – are more elementary than others. This concept of "basic emotions" is key to the development of the basic emotion theory that is discussed later (see the section, "Is Emotion an Expression?"). The following emotions are often considered as being "basic": anger, disgust, fear, enjoyment, sadness, and surprise (see Matsumoto & Ekman, 2009).

In this theory, the adjective "basic" is used to express three postulates (see Ekman, 1992). First, it is used to convey the notion that "there are a number of separate emotions which differ one from another in important ways" (Ekman, 1992, p. 170). Second, it is used to indicate that "evolution played an important role in shaping both the unique and the common features which these emotions display as well as their current function" (Ekman, 1992, p. 170). Finally, the term also often refers to the notion that nonbasic emotions are made up of blends of basic emotions (e.g., Tomkins, 1963).

Of note, the notion of basic emotions is anchored in the philosophical history of psychology; for instance, Descartes (1649, Art. 69) distinguished among six primary emotions (admiration, love, hatred, desire, joy, and sadness) and assumed that all other emotions either belonged to these families or were blends of these primary emotions.

Most of the work in affective neuroscience in the last decade has consisted of searching for discrete dedicated brain systems underlying each and every basic emotion, using as evidence either neuropsychological double dissociations (see Calder, Lawrence, & Young, 2001) or brain imaging results (see Vytal & Hamann, 2010). As discussed later (see the section, "Is Emotion an Expression?"), this view has been strongly challenged by both conceptual analyses and empirical results.

Positive versus Negative Emotions

Another example of a category that is defined by the type of emotion is the common valence-based distinction between "positive" and "negative" emotions. For instance, Tomkins' (1963) influential contribution to affective sciences was a book divided into two volumes, the first volume concerning *positive affects* and the second one on *negative affects*. Although the type of valence used to distinguish between so-called positive emotions and negative emotions is often not clear (see Colombetti,

2005), it is often the feeling component that is considered: An emotion is positive when "it feels pleasant" or negative when "it feels unpleasant." This valence-based distinction has been key to the development of the circumplex/bidimensional theories of emotion that are discussed later (see in particular the section, "Is Emotion a Feeling?"). Of course, the valence dimension is not restricted to the feeling component; eliciting events are sometimes categorized as positive or negative in terms of their appraised intrinsic pleasantness or goal conduciveness (e.g., Scherer, 2001). There is not always congruence between the appraised valence of an event and the valence of the feeling. For instance, although the emotion of "interest" is considered as positive in terms of feeling, it can also be elicited by appraised negative stimuli (e.g., disgusting stimuli can elicit interest; see Silvia, 2006b).

Although feelings are often considered to be either positive or negative, some scholars have argued that evaluations of events can be ambivalent (see Cacioppo & Berntson, 1994). This means that one can feel *both* good *and* bad about an event, rather than good *or* bad about it (see Larsen, 2007). Depending on the aspect of the event that is appraised, the very same event can be appraised as positive or negative, meaning that if two aspects are appraised simultaneously by two dissociated evaluative channels, both positive and negative feelings could be elicited (for discussion, see Cacioppo & Berntson, 1994). For instance, having a sexual relationship with someone else than one's significant other can be appraised as positive in the sense that it elicits pleasure, but as negative because it interferes with moral concerns of the individual. Ambivalent attitudes have been considered as evidence for the separability of positive and negative substrates and the view that mixed emotions could be jointly elicited. For instance, it has been suggested that individuals can feel *both* happy and sad at the same time while viewing tragicomic movies (Larsen, McGraw, & Cacioppo, 2001).

In affective neuroscience, the notion that brain systems could be differentially involved in the processing of positive and negative stimuli is grounded in various research traditions. For instance, understanding the brain mechanisms involved in a pain/aversion system versus a pleasure/reward system (see Haber & Knutson, 2010; Lieberman & Eisenberger, 2009) has been a major aim of affective neuroscience. Lieberman and Eisenberger (2009) suggested that the "pain network" consists of the dorsal anterior cingulate cortex, insula, somatosensory cortex, thalamus, and periaqueductal gray (see Chapter 9), whereas the "reward network" consists of the ventral tegmental area, ventral striatum, ventromedial prefrontal cortex, and the amygdala (see Chapter 19).

Another related tradition is illustrated by the work of Berridge and colleagues, who distinguish between brain mechanisms subserving the processes of "liking" versus "wanting" (see, e.g., Berridge & Robinson, 2003). This trend of research led to the suggestion that there exist several "hedonic hotspots" in the brain, including regions of the nucleus accumbens and the ventral pallidum that are involved in the liking process, whereas the dopamine system, often considered to mediate pleasure, would, in fact, mediate a particular form of wanting for reward called "incentive salience" (see Berridge & Robinson, 2003). This distinction between liking and wanting could also lead, in principle, to ambivalent processes, given that, for instance, individuals could like what they do not want or want what they do not like, consistent with the notion that people can come to both want something more and like it less (Litt, Khan, & Shiv, 2010).

Such a distinction between liking and wanting speaks in favor of the importance of distinguishing different types of valences in affective neuroscience, as is the case in other disciplines (see Colombetti, 2005). This approach can have considerable effects on the literature on preferences, values, and decision making, as discussed, for instance, in the neuroeconomics literature, because it may represent a complementary approach to the one advocating that all valenced processes are transferred into a common currency (see Chapter 17).

Another research tradition that has influenced an affective neuroscience account of the opposition between positive and negative emotions is grounded in investigations of functional hemispheric asymmetry (see the next section). The so-called valence hypothesis of hemispheric asymmetry posits that there is a center for positive feelings in the left hemisphere and a center for negative feelings in the right hemisphere (e.g., Ahern & Schwartz, 1979). This hypothesis is highly debated, and several alternatives have been suggested in the literature (for discussions, see Gainotti, 2000; Killgore & Yurgelun-Todd, 2007). For instance, the so-called right-hemisphere hypothesis suggests that all emotion-related mechanisms are more lateralized in the right hemisphere.

Approach-Related versus Avoidance-Related Emotions

An alternative to the "valence hypothesis" described earlier is the account of "anterior brain asymmetry," as mainly tested by Davidson and colleagues. Davidson and Irwin (1999) proposed the existence of an approach system that facilitates appetitive behavior and generates some approach-related positive emotions such as pride or enjoyment. These kinds of emotions would be generated in the context of moving toward a goal. Such a system would be lateralized toward the left hemisphere. These authors also postulated a second system that would, however, be lateralized toward the right hemisphere. This system facilitates withdrawal and generates some withdrawal-related negative emotions such as fear or disgust.

An opposition between approach and avoidance behaviors in the emotional response is very often proposed and is supposed to have a strong phylogenetic basis (see Schneirla, 1959). Most theories of emotion acknowledge action tendencies to approach pleasure and avoid pain, and this concept originates in philosophical writings.

For instance, Hobbes (1651/1985, p. 119) suggested a dissociation between these two behaviors as they relate to desire when he wrote that "this Endeavour, when it is toward something which causes it, is called Appetitive.... And when the Endeavour is [away] from... something, it is generally called Aversion. These words Appetite, and Aversion... signify the motions, one of approaching, the other of retiring."

A particularly interesting aspect of the hemispheric asymmetry hypothesis is that it does not overlap with the valence hypothesis, because it claims that a negative but approach-related emotion such as anger would be lateralized over the left hemisphere (for a discussion and review of empirical evidence, see Carver & Harmon-Jones, 2009). The "approach versus avoidance" partition is important because it allows the distinction of a valence-based dissociation from an action-tendencies-based dissociation.

Self-Reflexive (or Self-Conscious) Emotions

A typical example of a distinction based on the type of object that elicits the emotion is the category of so-called self-reflexive emotions such as shame, embarrassment, guilt, or pride. A specific feature of this category is that the object of the emotion is the self, rather than the eliciting event. For instance, one feels ashamed *about oneself*, but one feels afraid *about a snake*. As discussed by Fontaine (2009), scholars often refer to this category to describe emotions in which the self rather than a survival concern is at stake. In this regard, in addition to the two particularly well studied self-reflexive emotions of shame and guilt (Deonna & Teroni, 2008; Tangney & Dearing, 2002), other emotions for which the self is at stake could therefore be included (e.g., humiliation, gratitude, envy, or jealousy; see Fontaine, 2009).

These emotions, sometimes also called "self-conscious emotions" or "moral emotions," are increasingly being investigated in affective neuroscience, given the recent rise of interest and research on nonbasic emotions (e.g., Takahashi et al., 2009) on one hand and on the self (e.g., Powell et al., 2009) on the other (see Chapter 21). Affective neuroscience could certainly play a key role in understanding the specificities of subtypes of self-reflexive emotions (e.g., Basile et al., 2011) by providing empirical evidence that can constrain debates concerning the differences and similarities of emotions such as shame and guilt (see Deonna & Teroni, 2008; Wagner, N'Diaye, Ethofer, & Vuilleumier, 2011).

Aesthetic Emotions

A second example of a distinction that is based on the type of object that elicits the emotion is the category of aesthetic emotions. These emotions are typically elicited when people engage with artworks or with objects or scenes in nature (see Robinson, 2009). There is a debate whether aesthetic emotions are a special type of emotion or whether this category should be mainly defined by the fact that it is elicited by artwork (see Robinson, 2005).

Some appraisal accounts of aesthetic emotions have been suggested (e.g., Silvia, 2006a). Such an approach is useful for analyzing two critical issues in the study of aesthetic emotions. First, given that appraisal mechanisms are key to explaining individual differences, this approach can be used to explain why people have different emotions in response to the same work of art. Second, it can be used to explain how expertise determines aesthetic emotions (see Silvia 2006a, 2009).

The investigation of aesthetic emotions has somewhat favored positive emotions over negative emotions, but the emotions elicited by works of art are not limited to positive emotions (e.g., an emotion elicited by a work of art appraised as "ugly"). Although the growing field of neuroesthetics, which aims at understanding the neurobiological basis of aesthetic experience (see Zeki, 2001), has focused on the visual arts, auditory art has also been investigated, with a particular focus on how music elicits emotion (see Chapter 12).

Make-Believe Emotions

Emotions that are elicited by fiction (e.g., literature or movies) are sometimes called "make-believe emotions" (or "as-if-emotions" or "quasi-emotions") because the individual knows or believes that the triggering event is unreal (see Säätelä, 1994). For instance, if the emotion of fear has evolved so that humans can react in an adapted way to danger (e.g., when survival is at stake), why would we be afraid of a monster on a screen, and would this fear be similar to that we experience when confronted with real danger (see Gibson, 2009; Mulligan, 2009; Walton, 1978)? The fact that we can experience an emotion although the eliciting event is known to be unreal has been called "the paradox of fiction" and is the subject of one of the major debates in modern research on the links between fiction and emotion (see Gibson, 2009).

If make-believe emotions were to be qualitatively different from genuine emotions, this would have quite an impact on affective neuroscience research. Most of the research in affective neuroscience has been conducted with laboratory material that is fictional in the sense that the participant knows that the given event does not really happen (e.g., pictures, movies, faces, or voices). This issue is less pronounced when real stimuli such as snakes (Nili, Goldberg, Weizman, & Dudai, 2010) are physically presented.

It is possible that many of the core emotional processes are similarly activated by artificial and real events, but it is certainly the case that, to elicit full-blown emotions in the scanner, more realistic procedures such as those manipulating social interactions or using games will be less likely to elicit make-believe than genuine emotions. For instance, making the participant believe that a depicted event in a picture is fiction rather than a real event significantly changes prefrontal cortex responses to this emotional picture (e.g., Vrticka, Sander, & Vuilleumier, 2011).

Counterfactual Emotions

Counterfactual emotions are emotions such as regret, disappointment, or envy that are elicited by counterfactual thinking; that is, thinking about the alternatives to what has actually happened (see Coricelli & Rustichini, 2010; Roese, 1994). For instance, the appraisal that one made the wrong choice between two alternatives may lead to regret because one is able to think about what would have happened if only a better alternative choice had been made (see Dijk & Zeelenberg, 2005).

The emotions that arise by comparing factual and counterfactual events have been mainly investigated in the context of decision making in which alternative options are possible. In affective neuroscience, the counterfactual emotion that has been most studied is regret; the orbitofrontal cortex has been shown to have a critical role in the processing of regret-related outcomes in a decision-making task (e.g., Camille et al., 2004; Coricelli et al., 2005). It has also been shown that there is an enhanced amygdala response to regret-related outcomes when these outcomes are associated with self-blame (Nicolle, Bach, Frith & Dolan, 2011).

Social Emotions

Social emotions are those emotions that are typically elicited by social situations (e.g., shame, embarrassment, envy, jealousy, admiration, guilt, gratitude, Schadenfreude, and pity), often when other human agents are present or imagined (see Hareli & Parkinson, 2009). Such emotions can serve, for instance, to regulate social behavior, elicit social attitudes in others, or achieve social goals. The emergence of the field of so-called social neuroscience shows how much interest the affective neuroscience community has developed for social emotions (see Chapters 21–23).

Research on social emotions has led to the proposal of fine-grained distinctions between emotions such as shame and guilt (see the earlier section on self-reflexive emotions) or jealousy and envy. For instance, in terms of differences between envy and jealousy, Parrott and Smith (1993) suggested that envy is characterized by feelings of inferiority, longing, resentment, and disapproval of the emotion but that jealousy is characterized by fear of loss, distrust, anxiety, and anger.

A related research question concerns how emotions are modulated by the social context. For instance, fear, which is not a "social emotion" – in the sense that it is not typically elicited by social events – can still be modulated by how other individuals appraise the danger that elicited fear. For example, if a baby is hesitating to cross a visual cliff because he is afraid to fall and his mother expresses fear on her face, then the baby will be less likely to cross than if his mother smiles (see Sorce, Emde, Campos, & Klinnert, 1985). More generally, the notion of "social appraisal" illustrates the fact that the way an individual appraises an event can be modulated by how other individuals appraise the very same event (see Manstead & Fischer, 2001). Results suggest, for instance, that social appraisal influences the recognition of facial expressions of emotion (Mumenthaler & Sander, 2012). Studies that have compared how the brain computes social versus nonsocial emotional information suggest that some regions that are critical for emotional processing are also involved in the processing of social relevance (see Norris et al., 2004; Scharpf, Wendt, Lotze, & Hamm, 2010; Vrticka et al., 2011).

Moral Emotions

Moral emotions are those emotions that are elicited by moral evaluations. As described by Mulligan (2009), such emotions possibly rely on various moral phenomena such as moral norms (e.g., one ought not to tell lies), moral obligations (e.g., to look after one's aged parents), moral right and wrong (e.g., murder), moral values (e.g., goodness), and moral virtues (e.g., courage). Various classifications of moral emotions have been suggested (see Haidt, 2003; Mulligan, 2009; Tangney, Stuewig, & Mashek, 2007). For instance, one can distinguish together

with Haidt (2003) four types of moral emotions: (1) those that are self-conscious (e.g., shame and guilt); (2) those that are other-condemning (e.g., contempt, anger, and disgust), (3) those that are elicited by the suffering of others (e.g., compassion), and (4) those that are other-praising (e.g., gratitude and elevation).

In addition to the study of moral emotions, affective neuroscience research has considered moral judgments as a way to study the affective determinants of morality; for instance, by using moral dilemmas (e.g., Greene et al., 2001; see Chapter 21).

Epistemic Emotions

Some emotions such as interest, confusion, surprise, or awe particularly relate to knowledge and learning, and are, for this reason, sometimes called "epistemic" (or "knowledge") emotions (Morton, 2010; Silvia, 2010; de Sousa, 2008).

For instance, the emotion "interest" plays a key role in exploration, learning, growth of knowledge, and the development of expertise in many domains (Silvia, 2006b). The appraisal structure of interest has been studied, and results suggest that the events that elicit interest are those that are appraised as *novel and complex, but comprehensible* (Silvia, 2006b).

Although epistemic emotions have not been the focus of much research in affective neuroscience, related aspects such as novelty processing have indeed been extensively investigated, with a key role attributed to the amygdala for the processing of new and unfamiliar stimuli (e.g., Blackford, Buckholtz, Avery, & Zald, 2010) – possibly relating to a role of the amygdala in uncertainty and ambiguity processing (see Whalen, 1998).

As noted by Morton (2010), even emotions that are not directed at knowing (i.e., nonepistemic emotions) can lead to epistemic consequences. For instance, fear certainly leads to an increase in vigilance and attention to the threat, as well as the aim of better knowing the situation to discover possibilities for escape.

To conclude this section on the taxonomies of emotion, one can note that the described categories are not mutually exclusive. For instance, anger can be described as a typically *basic, negative, approach-related,* often *social,* and sometimes *moral* emotion. These taxonomies of emotion are possibly useful ways to consider the various types of emotions and to simplify this variety. Another, certainly more productive, way of reducing the complexity is to develop models of emotion aimed at representing the current knowledge of the functional architecture of emotion and to allow testable predictions to be derived. At the origin of the current models, one finds debates concerning definitions of emotions.

Definitions of Emotion and the Origin of Current Models

The period that was arguably the most influential for current models and debates in affective sciences was the second part of the 19th century. Indeed, most of the current models of emotion can be traced to – at least – this period and to the work of Darwin, Dewey, Irons, James, Lange, Spencer, and Wundt to cite some of the most influential scholars.

This period was not only critical for debates concerning *what an emotion is* but it was also fundamental for preparing the emergence of neuroscientific accounts of emotion. For instance, when Peper and Markowitsch (2001) considered the pioneers of affective neuroscience, they pointed to those who described early concepts of the emotional brain during that period: Exner's (1894) suggestion of an aversiveness processing center in the brain, Freud's (1895/1953) neuron network theory of emotional memory, and Waynbaum's (1907/1994) general emotion center.

In fact, the typical neuroscientific accounts of emotion that today are considered as classical (e.g., the existence of a limbic system) were launched by a reaction to a very specific and controversial account of emotion, the so-called James-Lange theory of emotion. This account focused on the general framework that was common to the theories as proposed by James (1884) and Lange (1885). The main thesis defended by these scholars can be summarized by James's (1884, p. 189) definition of emotion, which certainly has been the most widely cited definition of emotion since: "Bodily changes follow directly the PERCEPTION of the exciting fact, and that our feeling of the same changes as they occur IS the emotion." For instance, Cannon's (1927) neuroscientific theory of emotion was a direct reaction to James's definition of emotion and gave rise to the very influential thalamic theory of emotion (see also Cannon, 1931), setting the stage for contemporary debates on the respective roles of the central nervous system and the peripheral nervous systems in emotion (see Damasio, 1998; Chapter 3).

Partly on the basis of Cannon's work in insisting on the role of the thalamus and hypothalamus in emotion (see Lashley, 1938), Papez (1937) produced the first explicit proposal of a cerebral circuit as a mechanism of emotion by also adding the hippocampus and the cingulate cortex to it. Relying in particular on Cannon's and Papez's works on brain regions involved in emotion and on Broca's (1878) work on the anatomical description of a "great limbic lobe," MacLean (1952) proposed a concept that has been extremely influential in the field: the limbic system. An important extension of Papez's model was MacLean's inclusion of the amygdala as part of the limbic system, following, for instance, the work of Kluver and Bucy (1939).

However, the very notion of the limbic system as being the unitary basis of the emotional brain has been strongly questioned and criticized (see Calder et al., 2001; LeDoux, 1991). Although the thalamic theory, Papez's circuit, and the limbic system are certainly no longer considered prevailing brain-based models of emotion, they had a critical influence on what became affective neuroscience a few decades later.

This contribution was particularly critical in the classical debate between the peripheralists and the centralists. Indeed, whereas the so-called peripheralists relied on James's (1884) definition and argued that the critical source of emotion was to be found in the peripheral nervous system, the so-called centralists relied on Cannon's (1927) reaction to James's definition of emotion and argued that the critical source of emotion was to be found in the central nervous system.

In parallel with this debate, the age of behaviorism was flourishing, particularly in the United States. The legacy of behaviorism for current definitions, models, and methods is particularly strong in investigations of the emotional brain. For instance, the fear-conditioning experiments that Watson used to test conditioned emotional reactions in a human infant (Watson & Rayner, 1920) have been the fundamental basis for the development of much of the work that has led to our understanding of brain circuits involved in fear learning in humans and animals, which has often been considered as a royal road for increasing knowledge concerning the emotional brain more generally (Hartley & Phelps, 2010; LeDoux, 1996). In fact, the legacy of behaviorism to studies of the emotional brain goes beyond classical conditioning to include operant conditioning with concepts that link emotion to motivation, such as those of "reward" and "punishment." In that respect, many researchers who investigate emotions in the brain still use concepts and methods inherited from behaviorism, with a typical example being the model of emotion suggested by Rolls that focuses on the role of reinforcement (see, e.g., Rolls, 2007). Indeed, according to Rolls (2007, p. 72), "emotions may be defined as states elicited by reinforcers (rewards and punishers)."

Understanding the brain mechanisms underlying reinforcement learning and, in particular, identifying the reward circuit in the brain have been major research questions (see Haber & Knutson, 2010; Lieberman & Eisenberger, 2009) since the landmark study of Olds and Milner (1954), who showed that rats would work for electrical stimulation in several parts of their brain.

In addition to this behaviorist legacy, another critical epistemological development of the last century that has strongly shaped affective neuroscience is the cognitive revolution. Although behaviorism never dominated in Europe, the importance that this approach had in the United States meant that a cognitive approach to the mind was considered as being a revolution (see Miller, 2003). This revolution, which took place mainly in the 1950s, certainly influenced the emergence of models of emotion that considered cognition as a critical aspect of emotion (e.g., Arnold, 1960; Lazarus, 1966; Schachter & Singer, 1962).

The approach of considering the cognitive mechanisms underlying the process of emotion elicitation (i.e., appraisal), as well as the process of emotion categorization (i.e., labeling), allowed the development of many influential cognitive models of emotion in the 1980s (e.g., Frijda, 1986; Lazarus, 1984; Ortony, Clore, & Collins, 1988; Roseman, 1984; Scherer, 1984). Such models were considered cognitive because they defined emotion as caused by cognitive appraisals (e.g., Lazarus, 1966) or as labeled by cognitive categorization (e.g., Schachter & Singer, 1962).

A Typical Definition of Emotion

Is there a minimal consensus for a definition of emotion? A review of recent major models of emotion indicates that there is indeed consensus on four key criteria: (1) Emotions are multicomponent phenomena; (2) emotions are two-step processes involving *emotion elicitation* mechanisms that produce *emotional responses*; (3) emotions have relevant objects; and (4) emotions have a brief duration compared with other affective phenomena.

EMOTIONS ARE MULTICOMPONENT PHENOMENA

The three current dominant models of emotion – basic emotion models, circumplex/bidimensional models, and appraisal models – all seem to consider that an emotion is not unitary but rather has several components. This idea is not particularly recent (e.g., Irons, 1897) but has become more and more consensual in the last decades (see Kleinginna & Kleinginna, 1981). For instance, as a major representative of the circumplex/bidimensional (valence and arousal) theories of emotion, Russell (2009, p. 1259) emphasizes the concept of "components" when describing the role of psychological construction as follows:

Psychological construction is not one process but an umbrella term for the various processes that produce: (a) a particular emotional episode's 'components' (such as facial movement, vocal tone, peripheral nervous system change, appraisal, attribution, behaviour, subjective experience, and emotion regulation); (b) associations among the components; and (c) the categorisation of the pattern of components as a specific emotion.

This notion that an emotional episode is formed by various components also serves as a basis for basic emotion theories. For instance, as major representatives of basic emotion theories, Matsumoto and Ekman (2009, p. 69) recently emphasized the notion of multiple integrated responses when describing emotion elicitation as follows: "If the perceived schemas do not match those in the emotion schema database, no emotion is elicited and the individual continues to scan the environment. A match, however, initiates a group of responses, including expressive behaviour, physiology, cognitions, and subjective experience.... In our view, the term 'emotion' is a metaphor that refers to this group of coordinated responses."

From another basic emotions perspective, Panksepp (2005) also considered the multifaceted nature of emotion: "I use the term emotion as the 'umbrella' concept that includes affective, cognitive, behavioral, expressive, and a host of physiological changes" (p. 32). Interestingly, the notion of a coordinated and integrated response is also shared with the third major family of models of emotion – appraisal models. To the best of my knowledge, every appraisal theory of emotion agrees with the idea that emotions are multicomponent phenomena,

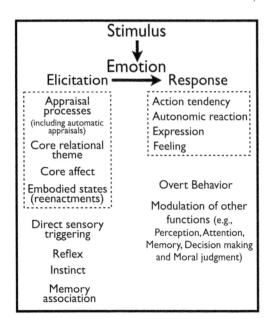

Figure 1.1. Mechanisms involved in emotion elicitation and its effects on the emotional response. Effects of emotion on behavior and on other psychological functions are also represented. Dashed lines surrounding some mechanisms indicate that these mechanisms are considered in some theories to be part of the emotion process.

and this aspect has particularly been emphasized in the component process model of emotion proposed by Scherer (1984, 2009; see the later discussion).

Taken together, the major theories of emotion acknowledge the existence of five components: (1) appraisal, (2) expression, (3) autonomic reaction, (4) action tendency, and (5) feeling. These components are discussed in detail in the section, "Theories of Emotion and Emotion Components." As depicted in Figure 1.1, whereas the appraisal component is typically considered responsible for *emotion elicitation*, the four other components are typically considered as comprising the *emotional response*.

EMOTIONS ARE TWO-STEP PROCESSES (EMOTION ELICITATION AND EMOTIONAL RESPONSE)

There is more to emotion than the elicited emotional response: There is also the emotion elicitation mechanism. Indeed, although one may not think of this first elicitation step as being part of an emotion, one feature of contemporary models of emotion is to consider *emotion elicitation* as not being antecedent to emotion, but as being constitutive of emotion. A useful analogy can be made with memory. Indeed, memory could easily be considered as corresponding mainly to remembering: Memory is at work when one remembers something. But according to most contemporary models, there is more to memory than what is actually remembered: There are also the encoding and consolidating mechanisms. Although the process of *encoding* could easily be seen as separate from – and antecedent to – memory, it is typically considered as constitutive of memory. Considering this analogy, elicitation is to emotion what encoding is to memory: its first constitutive step.

Among the five components described earlier, there are debates regarding which components should be considered as belonging to the emotion elicitation phase or to the emotional response phase. In fact, it has been suggested that, as a process, emotion elicitation is modulated by rapid emotional responses through feedback connections from the initial emotional responses that may further activate emotion elicitation mechanisms (see Sander, Grandjean, & Scherer, 2005). As depicted in Figure 1.1, the five components described earlier are typically categorized as being involved either in emotion elicitation (appraisal component) or in the emotional response (action tendency, autonomic reaction, expression, and feeling components).

Although appraisal dimensions (including automatic appraisals) are considered in most theories to be the major determinants of emotion elicitation (see the section, "Is Emotion a Cognition?"), other mechanisms have also been suggested to be involved in emotion elicitation. Indeed, some models suggest that core relational themes, core affects, embodied states, direct sensory triggering, reflexes, instincts, or memory associations can elicit emotions.

Appraisal dimensions. Mainly conceived as an extension of the two appraisal dimensions proposed by Lazarus (primary appraisal and secondary appraisal), a detailed set of criteria has been developed by appraisal theorists to subserve the subjective interpretation of the personal significance of events (for a review, see Scherer & Ellsworth, 2009). As described by Scherer and Ellsworth (2009), these criteria include "the novelty or familiarity of objects or events; their intrinsic pleasantness or unpleasantness; their significance for the individual's needs or goals; their perceived causes (self, another person, or circumstances); the individual's ability or power to influence or cope with the consequences of the event, including the level of uncertainty; and the compatibility of the event with social or personal standards, norms, or values."

The number and order of these dimensions (i.e., criteria) vary in different models. They assume that the level of processing of these dimensions is typically automatic (see Moors, 2009), but could also take place voluntarily. An affective neuroscience approach to appraisal mechanisms is relatively recent (see Brosch & Sander, in press; Sander et al., 2005) as compared with other theoretical traditions. For instance, studies using electroencephalography have tested the temporal order of some of these criteria (e.g., Grandjean & Scherer, 2008). Other studies and conceptual analyses have pointed to a role of particular brain structures in some of these criteria; for instance, the amygdala is suggested to be critically involved in relevance detection (see Cristinzio et al., 2010; Sander, Grafman, & Zalla, 2003; and the concluding section). In fact, some of the earlier mentioned cognitive mechanisms (e.g., novelty detection) have been the focus of intense empirical research in cognitive neuroscience (see, e.g., Kumaran & Maguire, 2007), but typically without links being directly made to emotion elicitation.

According to appraisal theories of emotion, the appraisal component is a constitutive (rather than antecedent) component of the emotional experience (see Moors, in press). The combination of appraisal outputs is the core of emotional experience and determines the response profiles of the other components that are later integrated.

Core relational themes. Smith and Lazarus (1990) suggested that events could be rapidly categorized into specific "core-relational themes" that would then elicit corresponding emotional responses. This appraisal approach to emotion is therefore a more categorical conceptualization of emotion-eliciting appraisals than the appraisal dimensions suggested in most appraisal models (see Smith & Kirby, 2009). According to this more "molar" approach, each distinct emotion has its own distinct core relational theme that represents a particular type of adaptational relationship with one's circumstances (see Smith & Kirby, 2009). For instance, according to Smith and Lazarus (1990), taken together, the appraisals of high motivational relevance, high motivational incongruence, and other-accountability correspond to the core relational theme of "other-blame," which evokes anger. These core relational themes therefore correspond to high level of appraisals that elicit specific emotions.

Core affects. Non-appraisal-driven elicitation mechanisms have also been suggested in the literature. For instance, the construct "core affect" has been created to describe "a neurophysiological state consciously accessible as a simple primitive nonreflective feeling most evident in mood and emotion but always available to consciousness. Although one feeling, it can be characterized by two pan-cultural bipolar dimensions: pleasure–displeasure (valence; feeling good versus bad) and activation (arousal; feeling energetic versus enervated)" (Russell & Feldman Barrett, 2009, p. 104).

Although a core affect could be understood as a result of appraisals that elicit hedonic and arousal responses, it is conceptualized instead as a component of emotion that is modulated by the affective quality of an object but is "free-floating (i.e., not about something)" (Russell & Feldman Barrett, 2009, p. 104), in the sense that a core affect is not directed at any particular eliciting event.

Embodied states (reenactments). Building mainly on the embodied cognition tradition and on simulation-based accounts of emotion recognition, embodiment has been suggested to be a key element to be considered when investigating emotion elicitation (see, e.g., Niedenthal, 2007).

Generally speaking, the very notion of "embodied cognition" considers that so-called high-level cognition is grounded in the reactivation of previous experiences in bodily-related systems such as sensory and motor mechanisms (see Niedenthal & Barsalou, 2009). In this regard, Niedenthal and Barsalou (2009) suggested that embodiment refers to reenactments that can span the range from cortical reactivation of modality-specific areas; to internal bodily activity associated with arousal, heart rate, and breathing; to actions in the musculature. The embodied cognition approach can be potentially strong in explaining how a current situation can induce an embodiment that is based on past experiences and thereby elicit current emotions.

Direct sensory triggering. "Can untransformed, pure sensory input directly generate emotional reactions? The answer is likely to be yes" (Zajonc, 1984, p. 122). As expressed here by Zajonc, the view that exteroceptive sensory processing can directly elicit an emotion is quite common and has been expressed by researchers of various traditions (e.g., James, 1884; Lang & Bradley, 2009; Lange, 1885; Zajonc, 1980).

For instance, in James's famous definition of emotion, most readers focus on the notion that the emotion is the feeling of the bodily changes as they occur, but the first part of James's definition addresses the question of what elicits these changes: "Bodily changes follow directly the PERCEPTION of the exciting fact." One way to interpret this statement is to consider that there is no room for cognitive appraisal because the reaction *directly* follows the *perception*. However, the word "perception" may have been used here by James in a broader sense than one of "direct sensory triggering," as indeed seems to be demonstrated by other pieces of James's writings (e.g., James, 1894; see Ellsworth, 1994, for discussion).

A very similar position was presumably suggested by Lange (1885, p. 673): "If I begin to tremble because I am threatened with a loaded pistol, does first a psychical process occur in me, does terror arise, and is that what causes my trembling, palpitation of the heart, and confusion of thought; or are these bodily phenomena produced directly by the terrifying cause, so that the emotion consists exclusively of the functional disturbances in my body?"

Here, again, most readers focus on the notion that the bodily phenomena are now suggested to be the cause rather than the consequence of emotion. When Lange wrote that "bodily phenomena produced directly by the terrifying cause," it is not fully clear whether the word "directly" referred to sensory processing or to other automatic (possibly cognitive) processes.

Because James's and Lange's definitions insist on a *direct* elicitation of the bodily response, the study of which brain mechanisms are involved in emotion elicitation has led to results that have often been interpreted as indicating a possible direct sensory triggering of emotion. Zajonc was particularly influential in that respect. For instance, describing the multilevel model of processing from the stimulus presentation to sensation to affect and to cold cognitions, Zajonc (1980, p. 171) claimed that "an affective reaction always directly follows the sensory input." In particular, from the neuroanatomical work suggesting the existence of a direct pathway from the retina to the hypothalamus (see, e.g., Moore, 1973) in the mammalian visual brain, Zajonc (1984, p. 119) argued that "these findings would imply that pure sensory input requiring no transformation into cognition is capable of bringing about a full emotional response involving visceral and motor activity."

More contemporary versions of this notion strongly rely on the presumed existence of a subcortical "direct" pathway to the amygdala (see LeDoux, 1996). Indeed, experiments on auditory fear conditioning in rats have shown the existence of a direct subcortical pathway from the auditory thalamus to the amygdala, in addition to the more indirect cortical pathway (see LeDoux, 1996).

Although uncontroversial anatomical evidence is lacking in humans, functional evidence suggests that a colliculo-pulvinar-amygdala subcortical pathway is involved in coarse and fast processing of visual stimuli in humans (e.g., Morris, DeGelder, Weiskrantz, & Dolan, 2001; Vuilleumier, Armony, Driver, & Dolan, 2003; see Vuilleumier, 2005). A recent model has raised the question of whether such a pathway might be better conceptualized as a two-stage architecture – rather than a dual route – according to which coarse and fast modes of processing first occur in magnocellular pathways and then are complemented by slower parvocellular visual pathways (see Chapter 14).

The notion of a very rapid and coarse processing to the amygdala – whether it corresponds to a direct anatomical pathway or a first stage of processing – is typically interpreted as accounting for the direct sensory triggering of emotion. If one admits that direct sensory processing can elicit full-blown emotions, a key question is whether this is the rule or the exception (see Leventhal & Scherer, 1987; Robinson, 1998). It is possible that covert activation may not induce any subjective feeling state, but may still modulate indirect responses such as startle (Anders, Weiskopf, Lule, & Birbaumer, 2004), or support intuition based on interoceptive signals (Katkin, Wiens, & Öhman, 2001).

Reflexes. A similar perspective to that just described concerning the possible direct sensory triggering of an emotional response argues for the existence of emotional reflexes. For instance, Lang and Bradley (2009, p. 334) wrote that "emotional reflexes are physiological or behavioural reactions evoked automatically in humans by affectively evocative stimuli." The very notion of "reflexes" typically insists on the absence of interpretation between the presence of a stimulus and the production of an emotional response. Such reflexes are presumed to be adaptive mechanisms that prepare for survival by heightening sensory intake (e.g., as in the extra widening of the pupil to a threat or to attractive stimuli) through a range of autonomic and somatic changes (Lang & Bradley, 2009). A reflexive view of amygdala function has also been put forward by Vuilleumier (2009).

Instincts. The concept of "instinct" is certainly not a modern one in affective neuroscience; it has been used by scholars such as James (1890) to conceptually analyze what is an emotion. Most of the issues described earlier in the subsections "Direct Sensory Triggering" and "Reflexes" also apply to instincts because they are often thought to be particular kinds of reflexes that are motivational constructs necessary for survival, which are automatically triggered by direct sensory processing (see James, 1890, Chapter 24; see Lang, 1994, for discussion).

Memory associations. A very popular idea in affective sciences is that associative learning, including conditioning, can "provide" an emotional value to an event. The role of associations in emotion elicitation has been suggested by various and relatively independent traditions of research. For instance, the notion that a previously neutral stimulus can acquire an emotional value if associated, through classical conditioning, with an aversive stimulus is the basis of the behaviorist approach to emotion (see Watson & Rayner, 1920) and is one of the most popular paradigms used in the affective neuroscience literature (i.e., the fear-conditioning paradigm).

From another perspective grounded in cognitive psychology, Bower (1981) adapted the associative network theory of memory to model the effects of mood on memory. As described by Bower (1981, p. 129), "in this theory, an emotion serves as a memory unit that can enter into associations with coincident events. Activation of this emotion unit aids retrieval of events associated with it; it also primes emotional themata for use in free association, fantasies, and perceptual categorization."

Focusing on anger, Berkowitz (1990) endorsed a related approach, what he has called a "cognitive-neoassociationistic" perspective to emotion. According to this perspective, specific ideas, memories, feelings, and expressive-motor reactions are associated in the form of an "emotion-state" network. Given the spreading of activation in such networks, the activation of any node (e.g., a particular memory) can elicit an activation of an associated node (e.g., a particular feeling).

Recently, although from a different perspective, Bar (2009) suggested a direct bidirectional link between moods and associative processing. Indeed, this author has suggested that positive mood promotes associative processing and that associative processing promotes positive mood. A key network proposed to be involved in this link is the contextual associations network, which includes the medial temporal lobe, the medial parietal cortex, and the medial prefrontal cortex. For instance, according to Bar (2009), the ruminations that are typically produced during a negative mood are promoted by hyper-inhibition of the medial prefrontal cortex on the medial temporal lobe. In contrast, during a positive mood, the medial prefrontal cortex provides less constrained inhibition of the medial temporal lobe, thereby allowing broad associative activation rather than rumination.

Another theoretical framework that is mainly based on the formation of memory associations is the "somatic marker hypothesis" proposed by Damasio (1994, p. 174): "Somatic markers [SMs] are a special instance of feelings generated from secondary emotions. Those emotions and feelings have been connected by learning to predicted future outcomes of certain scenarios. When a negative SM is juxtaposed to a particular future outcome the combination functions as an alarm bell. When a positive SM is juxtaposed instead, it becomes a beacon of incentive." Therefore, according to this hypothesis, the association of an event to a negative or a positive somatic marker would determine, at least partly, its emotional value. Functioning as a convergence zone, the ventromedial prefrontal cortex is proposed to play a key role in the creation and activation of these associations (see Damasio, 1994).

Of note, the role of associations in emotion elicitation has been suggested not only for vision but also for other sensory modalities, particularly for olfaction (see Chapter 10) and music (see Chapter 12).

From a theoretical perspective, a key conceptual question is the type of eliciting mechanism that can be considered as being constitutive of emotion. To the best of my knowledge, multilevel appraisal dimensions, core relational themes, core affects, and embodied states have been considered as being components of emotions. Affective neuroscience methods (see Chapters 2–6), in particular those allowing high temporal resolution, could be a great help in explaining how elicitation mechanisms shape the components of the emotional response (i.e., action tendency, autonomic reaction, expression, and feeling).

EMOTIONS HAVE RELEVANT OBJECTS

All research traditions on emotion – even those that are not based on appraisal theories – point to a link between an emotion and the significance (also called importance or relevance in its broad sense) of the eliciting situation for the organism. For instance, as LeDoux (1989) puts it, "The core of the emotional system is a network that evaluates (computes) the biological significance of stimuli." Of course, it is critical to define what is meant by "significance" in the various theories that highlight this concept.

Most theories consider at least evolutionary significance as a key dimension, with the notion that events that are survival related in terms of promoting secure conditions or avoiding aversive conditions are particularly prone to eliciting emotions (e.g., Bradley, 2009; Ekman, 1992; Frijda, 1986; Lazarus, 1991; Ohman & Mineka, 2001; Panksepp, 1991; Sander et al., 2003).

The notion of *relevance*, as it has been used in various theories of emotion, not only captures the dimension of evolutionary sig-

nificance but also refers to other types of concerns. For instance, Frijda (1986, 2007) has discussed the notion that emotions are elicited by events that are relevant to major concerns of an individual. Concerns are psychological representations that underlie or overlap with other motivational constructs such as needs, goals, desires, and values. As broadly defined, a concern is a disposition to desire the occurrence or nonoccurrence of a given kind of situation. As proposed by Frijda, "source concerns" refer to general kinds of goals and satisfaction (e.g., security), whereas "surface concerns" are defined by such goals and satisfactions for a particular person, object, or state of affairs (e.g., attachment to a political party).

A consensual definition of relevance detection that considers both the notions of "biological significance" (e.g., LeDoux, 1989) and of "primary appraisals" (e.g., Lazarus, 1991) would consider that an object or situation is appraised as relevant for an individual if it increases the probability of satisfaction or dissatisfaction toward a major concern of the individual. In parallel with a concern-based definition of relevance, some theories have focused more on the types of appraisal criteria that could be involved in a relevance dimension. For instance, Scherer (2001) has suggested that the novelty check, the intrinsic pleasantness check, and the goal/need relevance check all contribute to relevance detection.

As the relevance of the eliciting situation is supposed to be a sine qua non condition of emotion elicitation, understanding its determinants is critical for all theories of emotion. Whether a theory refers to stimulus significance primarily in terms of (1) pleasure and arousal (e.g., Bradley, 2009); (2) biological and evolutionary considerations (e.g., LeDoux, 1989; Öhman & Mineka, 2001); (3) primary appraisal (e.g., Lazarus, 1991); (4) dynamics of appraisal checks (e.g., Scherer, 2001); or (5) concerns (e.g., Frijda, 2007), all approaches seem to agree that emotions do indeed have relevant objects: Only those specific events that are detected as relevant elicit emotions.

EMOTIONS HAVE A BRIEF DURATION COMPARED WITH OTHER AFFECTIVE PHENOMENA

The duration of an emotion has not been studied systematically (for a discussion, see Verduyn, Van Mechelen, & Tuerlinckx, 2011), and, to the best of my knowledge, no affective neuroscience study has investigated this issue. Recent work has begun to investigate subsequent changes in brain activity induced by transient emotions (Eryilmaz, Van De Ville, Schwartz, & Vuilleumier, 2011), but it did not probe emotion or mood after the transient episodes. A key difficulty in the empirical study of emotion duration is whether what is measured is a new emotional episode (e.g., elicited by thinking again about the eliciting situation, which might often be the case for sadness) or is directly elicited by the very first appearance of the eliciting situation. In contrast to other affective phenomena such as moods, preferences, affective styles, and dispositions, emotions are typically considered as being brief episodes with a quick onset and a brief duration (see, e.g., Ekman, 1992; Scherer, 2005). Such an episode involves many components of the organism and is therefore costly in terms of cognitive and physiological resources (see Levenson, 2011).

To conclude, it seems that there is a consensus in defining an emotion as *an event-focused, two-step, fast process consisting of (1) relevance-based emotion elicitation mechanisms that (2) shape a multiple emotional response (i.e., action tendency, autonomic reaction, expression, and feeling).*

Both emotion elicitation and emotion response mechanisms can modulate overt behavior, as well as many psychological functions such as perception, attention, learning, memory, decision making, and moral judgment (see Chapters 14 and 17–21).

Theories of Emotion and Emotion Components

"It is the theory that decides what we can observe." – Albert Einstein

As mentioned in the previous section, a consensual and critical characteristic of emotions concerns their multifaceted nature: Emotions are not unitary reactions, but rather are multicomponent processes. Major theories of emotion have primarily focused on different components of emotion. I discuss the major current theories of emotion in this section by referring to the suggested components of emotion in which each one is particularly interested.

Is Emotion an Expression?

Darwin's seminal work on the expression of emotion (Darwin, 1872/1998) is often considered as the origin of many scientific endeavors on emotion. Inspired by Darwin's analysis of the evolution and functions of the expression of emotion, many scholars have considered expression (e.g., facial, vocal, and postural) as a key facet of emotion (see Chapters 7, 8, and 11). In particular, in interpreting Darwin, Tomkins (1963) has argued that the primary site of the affect is the face and has created the influential notion of "affect programs" (see also Griffiths, 1997).

According to Tomkins (1963), the notion of "innate affect programs refer to what is inherited as a subcortical structure which can instruct and control a variety of muscles and glands to respond with unique patterns of rate and duration of activity characteristic of a given affect." This idea that specific affect programs are stored in the human brain and trigger specific expressions (see Figure 1.2) was instrumental in the way that two scholars – both students of Tomkins – formalized their theories of emotion: the basic emotion theory developed mainly by Paul Ekman and the differential emotion theory developed mainly by Carroll Izard.

The idea of *fundamental* or *basic* emotions is not specific to this Darwin-inspired approach and can be found in various traditions. For instance, as highlighted earlier, Descartes (1649, Art. 69) had already distinguished among six primitive emotions. Another clear example is found in Irons, who described seven emotions,

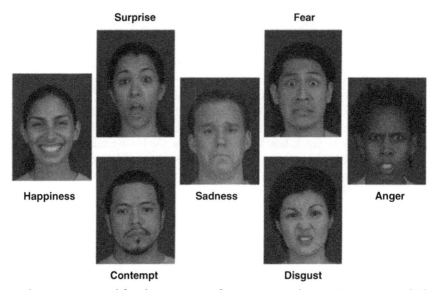

Surprise   Fear

Happiness   Sadness   Anger

Contempt   Disgust

Figure 1.2. The seven universal facial expressions of emotion according to Matsumoto and Ekman (2009). This figure is reproduced by permission of Oxford University Press.

"each ... qualitatively distinct from the others" (1897, p. 645).

Theorists differ on the number and nature of basic emotions that they propose, but typically include the following six emotions: anger, joy, sadness, fear, disgust, and surprise (see Ortony & Turner, 1990). The emotion of contempt is also sometimes included in the list (see Figure 1.2; Matsumoto & Ekman, 2009).

Basic emotions are typically characterized in this tradition as innate, easy, categorical, and immediate (see Russell, Bachorowski, & Fernandez-Dols, 2003). As depicted in Figure 1.3, the basic emotion system is responsible for both emotion elicitation (through perception and schema production, as well as schema evaluation based on pattern matching with an emotion schema database) and emotional responses (emotional responding, cognition, physiology, subjective experience, and expressive behavior).

Although both Ekman (e.g., Ekman, 1972) and Izard (e.g., Izard, 1971) have strongly focused on facial expressions of emotion (see Figure 1.2), the study of responses in the autonomic nervous system was also considered relatively early on as indicating the existence of basic emotions (for discussion, see

Cacioppo et al., 2000; Kreibig, 2010; Levenson, 2011; Rainville, Bechara, Naqvi, & Damasio, 2006; see Chapter 3).

The hypothesis that basic emotions rely on specific brain activities has been explicitly proposed by Ekman (1999, p. 50): "There must be *unique* physiological patterns for each emotion, and these CNS patterns should be specific to these emotions not found in other mental activity." Based (often implicitly) on this notion, a large body of affective neuroscience research has attempted to identify specific brain regions implementing distinct basic emotions. For instance, with respect to sadness, Panksepp (2003) suggested the existence of a "human sadness system" that is based on those structures subserving animal separation distress (the anterior cingulate, ventral septal, and dorsal preoptic areas; the bed nucleus of the stria terminalis; the dorsomedial thalamus; and the periaqueductal central gray area of the brainstem). Various investigations also revealed a crucial involvement of the insula and basal ganglia in disgust (see Calder et al., 2001). With respect to fear, Mineka and Öhman (2002) proposed that "the amygdala seems to be the central brain area dedicated to the fear module." Of note, according to this "fear module" model, fear

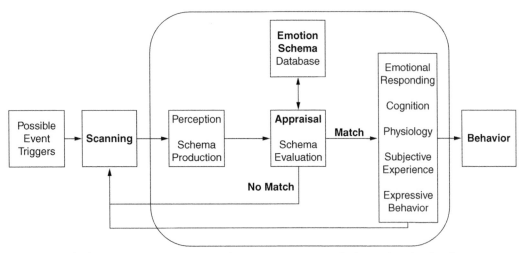

Figure 1.3. The basic emotion system according to Matsumoto and Ekman (2009). This figure is reproduced by permission of Oxford University Press.

elicitation would not require any cognitive processing, and the only emotional response that would require a cognitive appraisal is the feeling component (experienced fear).

Neuroimaging experiments and meta-analyses have further promoted the notion of dedicated brain systems for basic emotions. For instance, Murphy, Nimmo-Smith, and Lawrence (2003) conducted a meta-analysis that provided partial support for affect program emotion accounts. The activation distributions associated with three basic emotions differed significantly, with fear being associated with the amygdala, disgust with the insula and globus pallidus, and anger with the lateral orbitofrontal cortex. However, no difference was found in the activation distributions for happiness and sadness.

Phan, Wager, Taylor, and Liberzon (2002) also used a meta-analytic procedure to test for differential activations as a function of basic emotions. Although many activations were widely distributed over the brain, these authors noted that sadness was particularly associated with the subcallosal anterior cingulate cortex, that both disgust and happiness were particularly associated with the basal ganglia, and that fear was particularly associated with the amygdala, but no evidence was found for anger.

On the basis of another meta-analysis, Vytal and Hamann (2010) explicitly argued that neuroimaging results support the existence of discrete neural correlates of basic emotions. In this meta-analysis, the authors considered activation likelihood maps representing regional activity that was consistently associated with each basic emotion (see Vytal & Hamann, 2010, p. 2870). The authors concluded that the most prominent clusters are located as follows: (1) for happiness, in the right superior temporal gyrus (BA 22) and left anterior cingulate cortex (BA 24); (2) for sadness, in the left caudate head, left medial frontal gyrus (BA 9), and right inferior frontal gyrus (BA 9); (3) for anger, in the left inferior frontal gyrus (BA 47) and right parahippocampal gyrus (BA 35); (4) for fear, in the bilateral amygdala, right cerebellum, and right insula; and (5) for disgust, in the bilateral insula (BA 47). Of course, such findings do not exclude the possibility of finding more fundamental dimensions or components that constitute the various emotions and are differentially organized for specific emotions (for discussion, see Hamann, 2012).

A limitation of meta-analyses is the difficulty in distinguishing among the emotional components in the series of studies included; this limitation corresponds to the amalgamation between what is presented to the participant and the various components. For instance, when a participant is presented with an angry face or an angry voice, one can wonder whether it is the neural basis of anger or mainly the neural basis of fear (as elicited by being confronted by an angry person) that is revealed.

In addition, because most studies have focused on the *perception* of facial expressions of emotion, very little is known about the brain mechanisms responsible for the *production* of facial expressions (see Korb & Sander, 2009; Morecraft, Stilwell-Morecraft, & Rossing, 2004; Rinn, 1984). For instance, even the anatomical substrates of spontaneous versus voluntary facial expressions remain unclear (see Korb & Sander, 2009). Evidence from brain-damaged patients has suggested a double dissociation, with voluntary expressions depending on cortical structures but spontaneous expressions depending on subcortical structures; however, other studies have indicated that areas of the cingulate cortex may be relevant for spontaneous facial movements as well (see Korb & Sander, 2009).

When considering the production of an expression, a critical issue is to understand *what* is expressed. Although this section on expression describes in detail the basic emotion theory, other theories of emotion have also considered the component of expression. For instance, researchers used predictions derived from appraisal theories of emotion to develop an alternative approach to facial expression (e.g., Scherer, 1992; Smith, 1989; Smith & Scott, 1997). The issue of mental activity driving particular muscle activity was addressed by Darwin (1872/1998), who interpreted the frown produced by the innervation of the corrugator supercilii as a sign of "something difficult or displeasing encountered in a train of thought or in action" (p. 222; see also Pope & Smith, 1994). Moreover, Duchenne (1876/1990) attributed a special role in thought-related expressions to the superior part of the *musculus orbicularis oculi* (which he called the "muscle of reflection"). Along the same line, it has been proposed that the facial expression of a given emotion expresses a differential response pattern based on a series of appraisal outcomes (see Sander, Grandjean, Kaiser, Wehrle, & Scherer, 2007).

From another perspective – strongly contrasting with the basic emotion theory – is the proposal that specific emotions often do *not* cause expressions; expressions are, rather, social messages directed to the receiver that do not necessarily correlate with specific emotions (see Russell et al., 2003). This approach, which emphasizes the psychological construction of emotion expression by relying on the existence of strong contextual and cultural effects, is particularly defended by scholars adopting circumplex theories of emotion (e.g., Barrett, 2009; Russell et al., 2003; see the later section "Is Emotion a Feeling?").

Affective neuroscience research will be critical in the future in comparing these alternatives, in particular if robust methods are developed to measure brain activity while participants produce expressions of emotion. Techniques with a high temporal resolution will certainly be particularly suited for investigating the dynamics of expression production.

Is Emotion an Action Tendency?

Emotions prepare and guide actions (e.g., Frijda, 1986). In his *theory of emotion*, Dewey (1895, p. 17) considered emotions to imply "a readiness to act in certain ways" and suggested that "anger means a tendency to explode in a sudden attack, not a mere state of feeling."

To some degree, emotion expressions can be conceived of as particular types of actions that are guided by motivations to act – with a specific relational aim – on the world. The emotion component that is supposed to serve action, in a coherent manner with the expression component described earlier, can be referred to as the "action tendency" component.

Arnold (1960) first explicitly used the notion of action tendency as a central element of felt emotion; this concept was then particularly developed in the emotion theory proposed by Frijda (1986, 2007) to

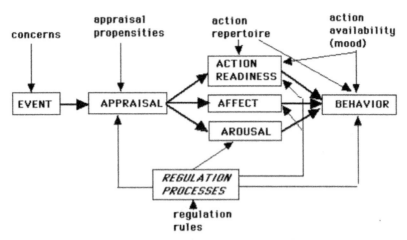

Figure 1.4. The emotion process as proposed by Frijda (2007). This figure is reproduced by permission of Taylor & Francis.

describe the internal motive states that are hypothesized to underlie a felt urge, the felt direction of that urge (e.g., toward or away from), and the "aboutness" of that urge (Frijda, 2009b). Such action tendencies (e.g., approach, avoidance, being with, interrupting, dominating, submitting) are also thought to underlie overt behavior such as running away or physically approaching a stimulus (Frijda, 2009b).

As a motivational process, an action tendency is a state of "action readiness" (see Figure 1.4) that prepares the body to act with specific relational aims (e.g., exuberance, as in joy, determines a diffuse openness to contacts; hostility, as in anger, determines stopping or hurting the antagonist; see Frijda, 2009a).

Two opposing key action tendencies have been the focus of much research in affective neuroscience: approach versus withdrawal. As described by Gable and Harmon-Jones (2008, p. 476), "approach motivation refers to an urge or action tendency to go toward an object, whereas withdrawal motivation refers to an urge or action tendency to move away from an object" (see also the earlier section, "Approach-Related versus Avoidance-Related Emotions").

Consideration of an action tendency is extremely important conceptually because it allows a distinction between the "approach versus avoidance" dimension and

the "positive versus negative" dimension. Although such a distinction was not explicit in the early work of Davidson, the view that Davidson's model mainly reflected action tendencies rather than the valence of feelings has received support from the study of anger. Indeed, evidence is accumulating that anger is an approach-related emotion and that the left-sided approach system is consistently involved in anger (see Carver & Harmon-Jones, 2009).

The view that these hemispheric asymmetry results are best accounted for as a function of approach and avoidance action tendencies has been challenged with, for instance, the hypothesis that a promotion regulatory focus would be associated with greater left frontal activity, whereas a prevention regulatory focus would be associated with greater right frontal activity (see Amodio, Shah, Sigelman, Brazy, & Harmon-Jones, 2004). Another alternative account relates the left anterior region to behavioral activation, independent of the direction of behavior (approach or withdrawal), and the right anterior region to goal-conflict-induced behavioral inhibition (Wacker, Chavanon, Leue, & Stemmler, 2008).

It has been suggested that the distinction between "approach processes" and "avoidance processes" should not be confounded with the distinction between "positive

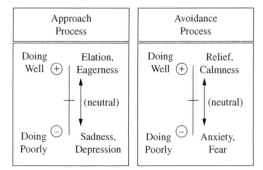

Approach Process		Avoidance Process	
Doing Well (+)	Elation, Eagerness	Doing Well (+)	Relief, Calmness
—	(neutral)	—	(neutral)
Doing Poorly (−)	Sadness, Depression	Doing Poorly (−)	Anxiety, Fear

Figure 1.5. Bipolar affect dimensions according to Carver and Scheier (1998). This figure is reproduced by permission of Cambridge University Press.

emotions" and "negative emotions" because both approach and avoidance processes can lead to both positive and negative emotions (e.g., Carver, 2004). Not only do action tendencies correspond to the motivational aspect of the emotional response but they may also play a role in self-regulation and in modulation of the elicited emotions.

For instance, as depicted in Figure 1.5, Carver and Scheier (1998; see also Carver, 2004) proposed that approach processes yield negative affects such as sadness or depression when progress is inadequate, but yield positive affects such as eagerness, happiness, or elation when progress exceeds the criterion. According to these authors, avoidance yields negative affects such as anxiety or fear when progress is inadequate but yields positive affects such as relief, calmness, or contentment when progress exceeds the criterion.

Such a perspective highlights the critical notion of *goals* in affective neuroscience. For instance, Davidson (1994) made a distinction between "pre-goal attainment affect" and "post-goal attainment affect," arguing that only pre-goal attainment positive affect engages the prefrontal cortex (in particular, the left-sided part). In contrast, post-goal attainment positive affect (e.g., contentment) does not engage the dorsolateral prefrontal cortex. Therefore, positive achievement-related emotions do not necessarily rely on the left-sided prefrontal approach system, although they can elicit broad sympathetic activation (see

Kreibig, Gendolla, & Scherer, 2010). More generally, the notion of *goal* is particularly critical because it represents the junction between motivation and emotion: Emotions are elicited by goal-relevant events, and emotions support goal attainment by producing goal-related action tendencies.

Is Emotion a Bodily Reaction?

Among the many scientific debates in affective sciences, two intense and long-lasting debates during the last century have largely shaped current perspectives of emotion: the James/Cannon debate and the Zajonc/Lazarus debate. The implications of these two debates are still with us today, and they have a strong impact on human affective neuroscience. As noted earlier, the debate that is arguably the clearest historical foundation of contemporary affective neuroscience is Cannon's reaction to James's theory of emotion.

Indeed, if the basis of emotion is to be found in the central nervous system rather than in the peripheral nervous system, then it is fully legitimate to have scholars such as Papez, MacLean, or Panksepp search for emotional systems in the brain, leading to the current, sophisticated models of the cerebral basis of emotion. Of course, affective neuroscience does consider the peripheral nervous system as important for emotion (see Chapters 3 and 9). In fact, to the best of my knowledge, all current major theories of emotion consider changes in the body as an aspect of emotion. However, the *role* and the *specificity* of the bodily reaction in emotion remain two issues that are very much debated.

A seminal debate concerns the *role* of the bodily reaction during an emotional episode: Some scholars argue that it is the perception of this reaction that elicits the emotion (including the feeling; see Damasio, 1994; James, 1884; Prinz, 2004), whereas others instead suggest that this reaction is part of the elicited emotional response (see Cannon, 1927; Frijda, 1986; Scherer, Schorr, & Johnstone, 2001).

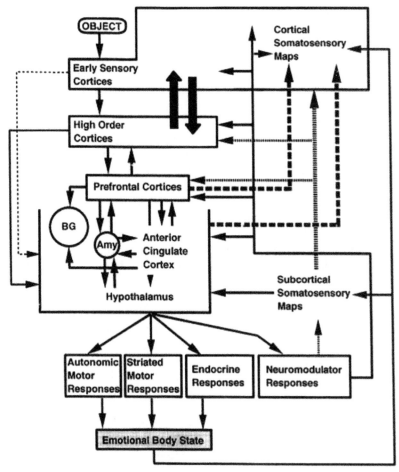

Figure 1.6. Flow diagram involving emotion processing structures according to Damasio (1998). This figure is reproduced by permission of Elsevier.

Of note, James himself claimed that both his and Lange's theory concerned emotional consciousness (rather than emotion; see James, 1884, p. 516). Although most theoretical approaches agree that the bodily reaction is involved in the elicitation of a conscious feeling, the debate mainly concerns whether the bodily reaction is also more generally fundamental for all other components of emotion (see Chapter 3).

If one accepts the view that it is the bodily reaction that elicits the emotion, then one must explain what elicits the bodily reaction in the first place. If the mechanisms suggested to elicit the bodily reaction are also those that typically elicit an emotional response, the debate then seems to be mainly a semantic one. However, if what

elicits the bodily reaction is considered instead to be limited to reflexes (for discussion, see Lang & Bradley, 2009), instincts (for discussion, see Lang, 1994, p. 217), pure sensory processes (see Zajonc, 1984), or semantic memory associations (e.g., Bower, 1981) – without room for evaluative interpretation in the elicitation process – then a substantial theoretical debate remains.

James's approach was extremely influential for current research in affective neuroscience, in particular for the notion that bodily changes are primary to other emotional components. This perspective has given rise to neo-Jamesian theories of emotion (e.g., Damasio, 1994; Prinz, 2004). For instance, according to Damasio (1998) and as depicted in Figure 1.6, many brain systems are involved in the production and then the representation of an "emotional body state." A critical role has been attributed to subcortical but also cortical (SI, SII, and the insular cortex) somatosensory maps as representing the bodily response (see Chapter 9).

The idea that specific emotional body states could be represented in long-term memory systems in the brain has been used as a counterargument to the classical criticisms according to which bodily feedback is not sufficiently specific and, in particular, is too slow to be primary to an emotional experience. Indeed, as argued by Niedenthal (2007), theories of embodied cognition avoid such criticisms because they consider the modality-specific brain systems that store the representations of bodily reactions, rather than possible "online" actual bodily reactions. Such a notion is, for instance, central to Damasio's model of emotion in which the "as-if body loop" system implements "the simulation, in the brain's body maps, of a body state that is not actually taking place in the organism" (Damasio & Damasio, 2006, p. 19). According to these authors, such a simulation process indicates that the as-if loop system is what the mirror-neuron system achieves conceptually.

It is worth noting that James's definition of emotion was restricted to what he called *standard* emotions (e.g., surprise, curiosity, rapture, fear, anger, lust, greed), which he assumed to have *distinct bodily* expressions. Therefore, other emotions – perhaps aesthetic, epistemic, or self-reflexive emotions – do not necessarily follow his definition.

This distinction raises an important implication of James's theory on bodily reactions for current psychophysiological and affective neuroscience research: Even according to James, some emotions have a distinct bodily expression, whereas others do not. This would mean that the bodily expression is primary only for some types of emotion, which, in fact, is consistent with the basic emotion theories (see Levenson, 2011; see also the earlier section, "Is Emotion an Expression?").

Research concerning the existence of patterns of bodily reactions that are specific to basic emotions is not conclusive (for reviews, see Cacioppo et al., 2000; Kreibig, 2010; Levenson, 2003; Chapter 3). Most of the research has compared bodily reactions evoked for different basic emotions and found that response patterns can discriminate among those emotions, which is consistent with most theories of emotion (although not for some constructivist approaches to emotion such as the conceptual act model; Barrett, 2009). Of course, finding that two basic emotions can be distinguished from each other by the pattern of bodily reaction they elicit does not conceptually show autonomic specificity nor demonstrate that there are no more fundamental dimensions underlying these differences (e.g., the dimensions of approach versus avoidance could explain observed differences for anger versus fear).

Observing such differences is critical for any functional perspective of emotion, but the question remains about what causal mechanisms determine the (specific) bodily reactions. For instance, both "affect program" and "appraisal" approaches predict some functional specificities in the bodily reaction, but disagree on the underlying eliciting mechanisms.

Another consequence of James's theory relates to bodily feedback theories of emotion, in particular, the "facial feedback theory," according to which contracting facial muscles that are normally recruited in given facial expressions (e.g., zygomaticus major) can elicit or, at least, intensify the congruent emotion (see Soussignan, 2002). This effect has been shown to occur even if participants are apparently not aware that their emotions are under study and believe that they are instructed to contract their muscles for other reasons (see Soussignan, 2002).

Indeed, a modulatory effect of such contractions on emotion intensity seems to indicate that the bodily reactions are integrated in the brain during the emergence of an emotional experience (Figure 1.7). Affective neuroscience research into the role of bodily reactions and representations in emotion has considerably strengthened the explanatory power of embodiment and the models based

Simulation of Smiles (SIMS) Core Model

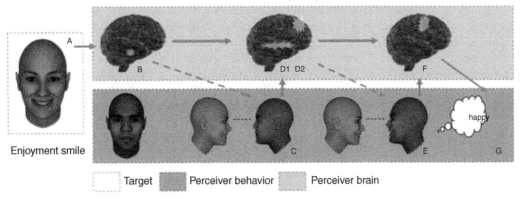

Figure 1.7. The Simulation of Smiles Core Model proposed by Niedenthal, Mermillod, Maringer, and Hess (2010). This figure is reproduced by permission of Cambridge University Press.

on that concept (see, e.g., Niedenthal, 2007; Niedenthal et al., 2010; Prinz, 2004). Figure 1.7 illustrates the SIMS model proposed by Niedenthal et al. (2010) for an enjoyment smile, for which eye contact plays an important role in leading to the recognition that the person feels happy (for details concerning this model, see Niedenthal et al., 2010, p. 428).

A key question concerning embodiment and, more generally, the bodily reaction in emotion concerns its very nature: Does this reaction correspond to specific patterns of bodily changes associated with particular situations or instead to a general arousal that is contextually interpreted? Jamesian and basic emotion theories argue in favor of the existence of specific patterns for some emotions (e.g., for "standard emotions" [James, 1884] or for "basic emotions" [Levenson, 2011]). However, scholars in affective neuroscience such as Davidson, Gray, LeDoux, and Panksepp have argued that it is unlikely that autonomic nervous system activity would show emotion-specific response patterns, and so the focus should be on research on the central nervous system (see Ekman & Davidson, 1994, p. 261). The difficulty of observing a specific bodily reaction for a specific emotion is consistent with the fact that many theories have the tendency to use the general construct of "arousal" to refer to the bodily reaction during an emotion.

For instance, Schachter and Singer (1962) considered the states of physiological arousal that are found in emotion to be general patterns of excitation of the sympathetic nervous system (see also Reisenzein, 2009). When a stimulus elicits an arousal (as is typically the case during many emotions), the notion of "phasic" arousal can be applied to describe increases in arousal over a period of a few seconds to a few minutes (Fowles, 2009).

Although the concept of arousal is indeed tightly linked with bodily reactions, it is in fact a much wider construct used for research not only on emotion (e.g., Bradley, 2009; Duffy, 1957; Russell & Barrett, 1999; Schachter & Singer, 1962) but also on attention (see Robertson & Garavan, 2004), performance (e.g., Yerkes & Dodson, 1908; see Aston-Jones & Cohen, 2005), memory (see McGaugh, 2006), and personality (e.g., Eysenck, 1967; Gray, 1987). For instance, Gray's (1987) early model of the systems involved in emotion included a nonspecific arousal system (NAS), which, together with the behavioral approach system (BAS) and the behavioral inhibition system (BIS), is responsible for approach- and "stop"-related behaviors. With respect to personality, for instance, according to Wallace, Bachorowski, & Newman (1991), the neuroticism construct can be conceived as reflecting the lability or reactivity of the nonspecific arousal system proposed by Gray. As described in the next section, the usefulness of the notion of a general arousal system has been strongly challenged over the years (see Neiss, 1988; Robbins, 1997), but it is still one of the most widely used constructs in affective neuroscience.

Is Emotion a Feeling?

Until the 20th century, most theories of emotion – including those of James and Wundt – were in fact theories of *feeling* (i.e., emotional experience or emotional consciousness; see Reisenzein & Döring, 2009). Many theories still equate emotion with feeling, but major efforts have been made to distinguish the two (see Frijda, 2007; Reisenzein & Döring, 2009; Scherer, 2005).

Research on the feeling component has been considered as potentially important in affective neuroscience to separate the mechanisms involved in feeling from those involved in other emotional components (see, e.g., Damasio, 1998; LeDoux, 2007). This distinction is consistent with various considerations that focus on the emotional experience rather than on other emotional reactions. As discussed earlier (see the section, "What Is an Emotion?"), this distinction can integrate James's perspective with other perspectives, because James's definition of emotion was, in fact, a definition of the *emotional consciousness* (i.e., the feeling). That such an emotional consciousness integrates the bodily reaction is compatible with most current theories of emotion. The fact that the feeling component is necessarily conscious can be a matter of conceptual discussion (see Grandjean, Sander, & Scherer, 2008), but the terms "feeling," "emotional consciousness," or "emotional experience" are typically used interchangeably in the literature. In addition, the literature tends to consider emotional consciousness as emerging from the interaction among emotional components (typically appraisal, expression, action tendency, and the autonomic reaction) or dimensions (typically valence and arousal).

The relative importance of the different components in various emotional experiences (see Frijda, 2005) and their specific content (for review, see Lambie & Marcel, 2002) continue to be the subject of debate. For instance, Frijda (2005, p. 494) discussed the structure of emotional experience and argued that "it generally contains conscious reflections of the four major nonconscious components of the process of emotions: affect, appraisal, action readiness, and arousal. In addition, it may include the emotion's felt 'significance." Panksepp (2005, p. 32) considered that "primary-process affective consciousness emerges from large-scale neurodynamics of a variety of emotional systems that coordinate instinctual emotional actions."

From another theoretical perspective, Grandjean et al. (2008) have suggested that a feeling is a complex dynamic phenomenon that implies neuronal synchronizations at different levels; they have conceptualized "the process of an emergent conscious feeling as the result of synchronizations of different subsystems at different levels" (p. 493; see also Scherer, 1984). Using a similar approach, Thagard and Aubie (2008, p. 811) argued that "conscious emotional experience is produced by the brain as the result of many interacting brain areas coordinated in working memory."

Some regions of the brain have been particularly linked to the feeling component of emotion, such as the anterior cortical midline structures (Heinzel, Moerth, & Nothoff, 2010). Whether the amygdala is involved in the feeling component is a question that is still strongly debated (for discussion, see Feinstein, Adolphs, Damasio, & Tranel, 2010).

Most of the conceptualizations of the feeling component in the literature are based on a dimensional perspective, largely on Wundt's model, which classifies feelings along three dimensions: (1) pleasantness–unpleasantness, (2) excitement–inhibition, and (3) tension–relaxation (see, e.g., Wundt, 1905). In a similar tradition, Osgood and colleagues' work on the dimensions underlying affective meaning suggested the existence of three basic dimensions: arousal, valence, and potency (Osgood, May, &

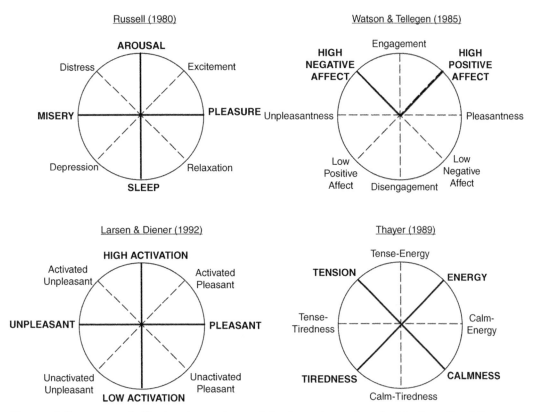

Figure 1.8. Four types of affective circumplex models of emotion as described by Russell and Barrett (2009). This figure is reproduced by permission of Oxford University Press.

Miron, 1975; see also Russell & Mehrabian, 1977).

Further research by Russell and others concentrated on two dimensions of the three, which led to the suggestion of a circumplex model of affect (Russell, 1980). As depicted in Figure 1.8, various dimensions have been suggested to anchor the so-called affective circumplex. Such an approach reduces emotion to nonemotional elements that can be felt on their own as distinctive dimensions (see Russell, 2005). The two dimensions of arousal and valence are typically considered constitutive of the circumplex model, but other related variants exist (see Figure 1.8 and Barrett & Russell, 2009).

Other traditions that have focused more on the physiological response than on the feeling component have also highlighted the role of arousal and valence as key dimensions to organize the emotional potential of stimuli (see Bradley & Lang, 2009).

Intense debates concern whether arousal and valence should really be considered as the two major dimensions (see, e.g., Fontaine, Scherer, Roesch, & Ellsworth, 2007) and whether these dimensions should be considered as unidimensional continua (see, e.g., Robbins, 1997, for arousal, and Cacioppo & Berntson, 1994, for valence).

As mentioned earlier (see the section, "A Typical Definition of Emotion"), current leading versions of the circumplex model are framed in the context of the construct called "core affect;" that is, the neurophysiological state that is always accessible as simply feeling good or bad, energized or enervated. For instance, Russell (2005) argued that core affect provides the emotional quality for any conscious state. Linking this model to affective neuroscience research, Posner, Russell, and Peterson (2005) relied on Russell (1980)'s model in suggesting that "all affective states arise from two fundamental neurophysiological systems, one related to valence (a pleasure–displeasure continuum) and the other to arousal, or alertness" (p. 716). According to these authors, these two neurophysiological systems would be independent and subserved largely by subcortical structures.

In particular, they conclude that the mesolimbic system may "represent a neural substrate for the valence dimension proposed by the circumplex model of affect" (p. 722). With respect to the pathways of the "arousal network," the authors highlight the critical role of the reticular formation that receives information from the amygdaloreticular pathways. The authors also describe how the descending tracts from the reticular formation form the spinoreticular pathways that modulate muscle tone and activity in the sweat glands. An integrated representation of the activity within these two neurophysiological systems – valence and arousal – would be the basis for a conscious emotion.

With a similar approach, Barrett, Mesquita, Ochsner, and Gross (2007) considered the neurobiology of core affect to be mediated by two related functional circuits. The first one subserves the representations of sensory information about a stimulus and involves connections among the basolateral complex of the amygdala, the central and lateral aspects of the orbitofrontal cortex, and the anterior insula. The second circuit subserves the stimulus's somatovisceral impact and involves reciprocal connections between the ventromedial prefrontal cortex – including the closely related subgenual anterior cingulate cortex – and the amygdala, which together modulate the visceromotor (i.e., autonomic, chemical, and behavioral) responses. The resulting core affective state would be available to be experienced and could contribute directly to the contents of conscious experience.

Importantly, although arousal is often conceptualized as a psychophysiological reaction in the body that can be measured with an index of sympathetic nervous system activity (see Schachter & Singer, 1962, for discussion, and Chapter 3), it is also sometimes conceptualized as synonymous with vigilance and typically measured with electroencephalography-related measures (see Jones, 2003; Paus, 2000).

In arguing in favor of the general psychological significance of the concepts of "arousal" or "activation," Duffy (1957, p. 265) considered that "the terms 'activation' and 'arousal' . . . refer to variations in the arousal or excitation of the individual as a whole, as indicated roughly by any one of a number of physiological measures (e.g., skin resistance, muscle tension, EEG, cardiovascular measures and others). The degree of arousal appears to be best indicated by a combination of measures."

As is apparent in that description, the concept of arousal has a somewhat ambiguous status. This ambiguity has remained in affective neuroscience, and this concept's explanatory power has been diminished over the years by the fact that, as analyzed by Robbins (1997, p. 58), "the arousal construct is not well supported empirically." For instance, Robbins (1997) argued that the various indices of arousal do not intercorrelate to a high degree, as would be expected of a unitary construct, and that manipulations of arousal, whether pharmacological or psychological, do not interact in a manner suggestive of an underlying unidimensional continuum.

Frijda (1986, p. 168) distinguished among three response systems that embrace the concept of arousal or activation: autonomic arousal, electrocortical arousal, and behavioral activation. In addition, whereas modulations of arousal were first thought to be mediated by a diffuse network of neurons in the brainstem (the reticular formation), further research into the chemical identification of discrete neural systems and the distribution of their projections to the forebrain suggested that the reticular formation might not subserve a "general" arousal system (Robbins, 1997). Robbins (1997) argued that these findings raised doubts in the utility of arousal-like constructs and therefore the notion of a unique arousal system is neither conceptually useful for psychological theories nor consistent with neuroscience research (see also Neiss, 1988). However, the usefulness of a general arousal construct, at least as a "heuristic," has been defended (see Robertson & Garavan, 2004), and the notion of an arousal dimension is still central to many theories of the emotional experience.

The importance of the arousal construct in affective neuroscience has been reinforced by the intensive use of stimuli varying in terms of subjective ratings of arousal (and valence and domination; see Bradley & Lang, 2009). For instance, Anderson et al. (2003) considered that an affective experience is determined by the two primary dimensions of valence and arousal, and they investigated how the human brain processes olfactory stimuli that vary in terms of valence and intensity. The authors used the term "intensity" to refer to "arousal" (Anderson & Sobel, 2003, p. 582) because they used olfactory stimuli for which stimulus intensity appears to be strongly correlated with indices of arousal (see Bensafi et al., 2002).

Anderson et al. (2003) showed that more intense odors activated the amygdala more, independently of the valence of odors (i.e., for both pleasant and unpleasant odors). In contrast, regions of the orbitofrontal cortex were associated with valence, independent of intensity. These findings were interpreted as suggesting that the affective representations of intensity and valence draw on dissociable neural substrates (see also Hamann, 2003, 2012).

With a similar design – but adding the critical condition of so-called neutral olfactory stimuli – Winston, Gottfried, Kilner, and Dolan (2005) questioned this conclusion by arguing that the amygdala is not sensitive to intensity per se, but is sensitive to intensity only when stimuli are either positive or negative. Such results therefore challenged the view that the amygdala is specifically involved in coding the intensity (or arousal) dimension.

Although not explicitly equating intensity with arousal, Small et al. (2003) manipulated the intensity and valence of taste; they observed that amygdala activity was driven by stimulus intensity regardless of valence and that variation in valence elicited

responses in the anterior insula/operculum, extending into the orbitofrontal cortex.

A few brain imaging experiments have investigated the neural systems subserving the dimensions of valence and arousal with the same conceptual framework that is at the origin of the circumplex model of emotion – that the arousal is a property of the feeling, but not of the presented stimulus. Gerber et al. (2008) presented participants with faces that varied in valence and arousal. Surprisingly, the authors found that activity in the amygdala and in the thalamus was stronger for low-arousal faces than for high-arousal faces. The authors interpreted this finding as being consistent with the fact that low-arousal faces are more ambiguous and salient than high-arousal faces. The authors also observed that the more negatively valenced the faces, the more active the dorsal anterior cingulate cortex and the inferior parietal cortices.

Posner et al. (2009) presented participants with those emotion words that are typically used in the circumplex model. These authors were then able to identify regions that correlated positively or negatively with valence ratings and with arousal ratings. Of note, no particular relation was observed between activity in the amygdala and arousal ratings.

Using the same theoretical approach, Colibazzi et al. (2010) investigated the neural systems subserving valence and arousal during the experience of induced emotions. In this study, rather than presenting isolated faces, pictures, words, or odors, the authors explicitly requested participants to use a validated scenario in order to feel emotions that, indeed, were reported by the participants to vary as a function of felt valence and felt intensity. The amygdala was found to code for the arousal dimension, with more amygdala activity associated with more felt arousal regardless of valence. Costa et al. (2010) reported similar findings.

In fact, evidence from various lines of research indicates important similarities and overlaps in the brain mechanisms involved in the processing of positive and negative stimuli. For instance, Leknes & Tracey

(2008) pointed to a common neurobiology for pain and pleasure by highlighting those brain systems that appear to be common to the processing of painful versus pleasant sensations.

The two dimensions of emotional experience that are the focus of this section – valence and arousal – are often considered in the literature as building blocks of the phenomenology of emotions (with respect to the valence dimension, see also the earlier section "Positive versus Negative Emotions"). However, as highlighted in previous sections, it has also been suggested that feeling is shaped by felt action tendencies, felt motor expressions, and felt bodily reactions (i.e., bodily feelings that are more specific than a felt arousal). A key proposal of some cognitive approaches to emotion is that, as discussed in the next section, cognitive processes also shape feeling, being both causal in emotion elicitation and constitutive of the feeling.

Is Emotion a Cognition?

The consideration that emotions are types of cognitions may seem paradoxical for research traditions that emphasize a clear dissociation between emotion and cognition (e.g., LeDoux, 1993; Zajonc, 1984). In fact, the opposition of cognition and emotion in contemporary research in cognitive sciences and affective sciences has crystallized long-standing debates in many disciplines and approaches in which rational thinking is opposed to emotional reactions (for discussion, see de Sousa, 1987; Elster, 1996; Forgas, 2008; Kirman, Livet, & Teschl, 2010; Sander & Koenig, 2002).

Historically, partitioning the mind into several entities has been a powerful way to generate theories about how the mind works. As analyzed by Hilgard (1980), the most prevalent partition since the 18th century has been the tripartite classification of mental activities into cognition, affection, and conation. Such a tripartite vision of the mind has certainly facilitated the distinction – perhaps artificial – between cognitive neuroscience and affective neuroscience.

A review of traditions that have considered emotion and rationality as antagonists would go beyond the scope of this chapter (for discussions, see, e.g., Hilgard 1980; Kirman et al., 2010). However, it is important to note that some scholars have highlighted that emotions can be conceived of as being rational. For instance, de Sousa (2009) emphasized that a crucial role of emotions in rationality is that of defining the goals of action. In addition, the view that emotions can serve decision making (e.g., de Sousa, 1987, Frank, 1988) has been acknowledged by scholars in affective neuroscience who have highlighted the role of the emotional brain in decision-making processes.

Another critical debate relating to major theories of emotion – one that has perhaps been as important for contemporary research as the James versus Cannon debate – is the Zajonc versus Lazarus debate. In the 1980s, Robert Zajonc and Richard Lazarus proposed contrasting perspectives regarding the relationship of emotion and cognition (e.g., Lazarus, 1982, 1984; Zajonc, 1980, 1984). Whereas Zajonc defended the two ideas that (1) emotion and cognition are separate and that (2) emotion is primary to cognition, Lazarus advocated that (1) cognitive appraisal is an integral feature of emotion and that (2) cognition is primary to (the other aspects of) emotion.

As highlighted earlier (see the section, "A Typical Definition of Emotion"), according to Zajonc, "an affective reaction always directly follows the sensory input" (1980, p. 171) without the need for cognition to intervene. As depicted in Figure 1.9 (see also Figure 1.1), this would mean that, perhaps because of the early amygdala reaction, emotional responses may occur directly as *untransformed sensory* information (Zajonc, 1980, 1984).

In this context, the first question highlighted in Figure 1.9 is that of the existence of a *dichotomy* between sensory processing and cognitive processing. Where does cognition start in the flow of information processing that is elicited by a stimulus? For instance, Zajonc considered a dichotomy between the effects of untransformed sensory information

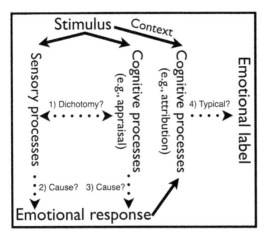

Figure 1.9. Some key questions in the "emotion versus cognition" debate.

on one hand and the effects of cognition on the other, with cognition defined as processes that must involve some minimum *"mental work"* (Zajonc, 1980, 1984).

One could argue that the question of whether sensory processing is cognition (i.e., involves "mental work" in Zajonc's terminology) is a definitional one, and so the "dichotomy" issue highlighted in Figure 1.9 is mainly conceptual. The endorsement of such a dichotomy goes beyond Zajonc and similar research traditions. In fact, it relates to the definition of cognition given by Neisser (1967) in the first cognitive psychology textbook: "The term 'cognition' refers to all processes by which the sensory input is transformed, reduced, elaborated, stored, recovered, and used." However, even if one considers that the dichotomy between "sensation" and "cognition" is valid, there is no logical reason to take such a dichotomy as evidence for a dichotomy between "emotion" and "cognition."

Let us consider two types of sensation: exteroceptive sensory processing and interoceptive sensory processing. There is no reason to equate exteroceptive sensory processing with emotion (for a discussion, see also Parrott & Schlukin, 1993a). Of course, interoceptive sensory processing raises a different issue that concerns whether emotion should be considered as a *bodily sensation* (see the section, "Is Emotion a Bodily Reaction?").

The second question highlighted in Figure 1.9 is more prone to empirical investigation: Can "pure" sensory processing cause an emotion? Such an issue is discussed earlier (see the section, "A Typical Definition of Emotion"), and to the best of my knowledge, there is no evidence showing that a pure sensory process can indeed cause an emotion as typically defined. This question is very different from the question of automaticity. Evidence suggests that emotion elicitation can be unintentional, unconscious, efficient, and fast (i.e., automatic, see Moors, 2009; Moors & De Houwer, 2006; Vuilleumier, 2005). But does automaticity mean "pure sensory processing"? A simple counterexample is at hand: reading. Indeed, the process of reading is automatic but no one would claim that reading is not a cognitive process.

Lazarus's appraisal theory of emotion would fully accept that automatic cognition can elicit emotions, but that noncognitive mechanisms cannot. Therefore, whereas Zajonc would typically respond "yes" to the question of causality highlighted in Figure 1.9, Lazarus would typically respond "no." According to Lazarus, cognitive appraisals are necessary for emotion elicitation and are constitutive of emotions. Such a perspective is the landmark of so-called appraisal theories of emotions. Although it is not often referred to, it is interesting to note that Lazarus considered a possible exception in the case of specific instances of fear. This exception concerned phylogenetically based triggers of fear. He wrote that "perhaps humans are 'instinctually' wired to react with fear to spiders, snakes, or strangeness" (Lazarus, 1982, p. 1021).

An analysis of all the arguments from Zajonc and Lazarus is beyond the scope of this chapter, but both authors would certainly agree that some reactions that are sometimes associated with emotions can be triggered in the context of sensorimotor processes. For instance, the startle response that can accompany emotions is typically not considered as an emotion but rather as a reflex (see Ekman, Friesen, & Simons, 1985); it could, however, be understood in a sensorimotor framework. Taste-driven facial expressions in newborns (for discussion, see Erickson & Schulkin, 2003) also correspond to affective reactions that could be understood with such an approach (see also Leventhal & Scherer, 1987).

As introduced earlier, Zajonc insisted on two neuroscientific arguments to support the notion of direct sensory triggering of emotion: (1) the existence of a retino-hypothalamic tract, allowing the organism to generate an emotional reaction from a purely sensory input, and (2) the fact that an amygdala response to faces is supposed to indicate the possibility of a noncognitive response to faces. As is apparent from these arguments, an appeal to the brain was very important for Zajonc in arguing that cognition is not needed to elicit emotions.

Indeed, a few years later, an affective neuroscience approach was applied to this debate (see LeDoux, 1989, 1993; Parrott & Schulkin, 1993a,b). The general line of argument developed by LeDoux was similar to that developed by Zajonc. LeDoux (1989, 1993) proposed that cognitive computations are distinct from affective computations. Cognitive computations would be performed in a system centered on the hippocampus with the goal of "the elaboration of stimulus input and the generation of 'good' stimulus representations" (LeDoux, 1993, p. 62). In contrast, affective computations would be performed in a system centered on the amygdala; the goal of affective (or emotional) computations would be "the evaluation of the significance of the stimulus (determination of the relevance of the stimulus for individual welfare)" (LeDoux, 1993, p. 62).

According to LeDoux, affective computations could be performed on cognitive representations, the main difference being the *goal* of the computation. This functional perspective not only advanced the proposal of a dissociation between an affective and a cognitive system but it also supported Zajonc's claim concerning the primacy of affect by relying on the rapid subcortical pathway involving the amygdala and bypassing the cortex (see Chapter 15).

The view of the amygdala as a *sensory* gateway to emotion has been influential (Aggleton & Mishkin, 1986) and is consistent with perspectives suggesting that pure sensory processing can elicit emotions. However, Parrott and Schulkin (1993a,b) argued against this view by proposing, along lines inspired by Lazarus, that cognition and emotion are best understood as inseparable processes, not merely as interacting ones. They used cognitive neuroscience evidence to argue for top-down modulations of sensory processes and suggested that the most relevant distinction would be between "emotional cognition" and "nonemotional" cognition.

Whether one adopts a perspective that considers cognition and emotion as antagonists (e.g., LeDoux, 1993) or instead as inseparable (e.g., Parrott & Schulkin, 1993a,b) largely depends on the definitions of both emotion and cognition that one adopts (see Leventhal & Scherer, 1987; Moors, 2007). In a tour de force, Moors (2007) produced a taxonomy of definitions for cognitive processes and discussed how various types of definitions affect debates concerning the emotion-cognition relationship. Such a taxonomy allowed Moors (2007) to distinguish between nine accounts of cognition. She concluded that if one defines cognitive processes as those that mediate between variable input-output relations by means of representations, then one must admit that cognition is often involved in emotion.

Even LeDoux, who has advocated that the process of stimulus evaluation is affective rather than cognitive, explicitly considered that "the processes involved in stimulus evaluation could, if one chose, be called cognitive processes" (1989, p. 271). Therefore, with respect to the third question highlighted in Figure 1.9, there seems to be a consensus that cognition *can* cause emotion. Appraisal theories of emotion claim not only that cognition can cause emotion but also that cognitive appraisal is the *typical* cause of emotion, with other causes being atypical. The suggestion that cognitive processes that evaluate the subjective meaning of an event are the origin of emotion is a royal road to consider and explain individual differences in emotion (see Chapters 22 and 24–28).

Appraisal is one type of cognition that is much investigated in emotion research. As depicted in Figure 1.9, a second type of cognition – one that is different from appraisal – is often referred to in theories of emotion. First mainly considered in the framework of the so-called bifactorial theory of emotion (Schachter & Singer, 1962), this second type is today most evident in constructivist theories of emotion (e.g., Barrett, 2009; Russell, 2009). Although Schachter and Singer's (1962) cognitive theory of emotion was based not on the typical process of emotion generation, but rather on atypical cases in which arousal is unexplained (see Reisenzein, 1983), current constructivist theories have thought to extend this type of cognitive attribution and interpretation to typical cases of emotion elicitation (e.g., Barrett, 2009; Russell, 2009).

As highlighted in the fourth question of Figure 1.9, the aim of this second type of cognition is to label an emotion as a function of both the emotional response and the context in which the stimulus appears. The emotional response corresponds mainly to *arousal* in Schachter's theory and to a blend of *arousal and valence* (i.e., core affect) in Russell and Barrett's theory.

The two types of cognitions involved in the process, and described in Figure 1.9, are well captured by the following example provided by Schachter and Singer: "Imagine a man walking alone down a dark alley, a figure with a gun suddenly appears. The perception-cognition 'figure with a gun' in some fashion initiates a state of physiological arousal; this state of arousal is interpreted in terms of knowledge about dark alleys and guns and the state of arousal is labeled 'fear'" (p. 380).

The appraisal-type of cognition here corresponds to the perception-cognition "figure with a gun" that initiates, in some fashion, a state of physiological arousal. This fits with the proposed role of appraisal in the elicitation of an emotional response, and it is likely that the use of the term "perception-cognition" by Schachter and Singer reflects

the complexity of the dichotomy issue highlighted in the first question of Figure 1.9. The attribution-type of cognition here corresponds to the interpretation of the state of arousal in terms of knowledge. This interpretation attributes the origin of the felt arousal to the appraised stimulus in context, which allows labeling of the felt arousal (see Reisenzein, 2009). As phrased by Schachter and Singer (1962), "it is the cognition which determines whether the state of physiological arousal will be labeled as 'anger,' 'joy,' 'fear,' or whatever" (p. 380).

This view is a neo-Jamesian one, but with a major difference in that according to James, the bodily response was specific for many emotions, whereas Schachter instead considered a general undifferentiated response (see Ellsworth, 1994). Among current constructivist approaches, this notion was well captured by Posner et al. (2005), according to whom "the circumplex model of affect proposes that all affective states arise from cognitive interpretations of core neural sensations that are the product of two independent neurophysiological systems" (p. 715).

Appraisal theories of emotion also acknowledge the importance of the context by considering that a stimulus is always appraised contextually and as a function of the currents needs, goals, and values of the individual. The appraisal process is often thought to fully determine the emotional response, including the feeling and the attached label (see Sander et al., 2005). This perspective leaves room for reappraisal and for interactive processing between components, without postulating an attribution-type of cognition in addition to an appraisal-type of cognition.

On the basis of philosophical approaches to emotion that have highlighted the role of subjective evaluation in emotion elicitation, scholars such as Arnold and Lazarus have pioneered the development of psychological models of emotion that consider appraisal processes as the key determinants of emotion (see contributions in Scherer et al., 2001). Appraisal models of emotion

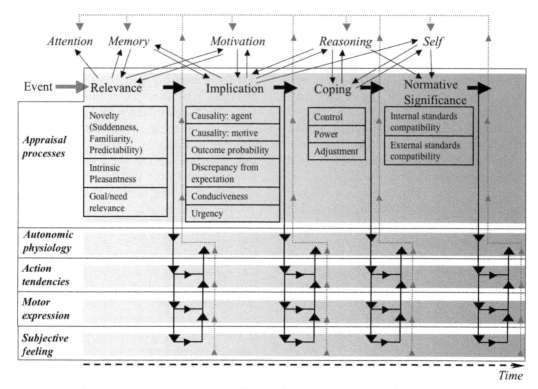

Figure 1.10. The emotion process as proposed by Sander, Grandjean, and Scherer (2005). This figure is reproduced by permission of Cambridge University Press.

typically consider that appraisal (1) is causal in emotion elicitation; (2) is constitutive of (not only antecedent to) emotion (i.e., the combination of appraisal outputs is key for emotional experience); and (3) determines the response profiles of the other components that are later integrated.

Because an individual's appraisal of an event is a function of the specific *relation* between the individual and the event, the construct of a "core relational theme" has been proposed at a relatively molar level. As mentioned earlier, a core relational theme corresponds to the central person-environment relationship that underlies each type of emotion (see e.g., Lazarus, 1991 pp. 121–24; Smith & Lazarus, 1990). As described in Lazarus (1991, p. 122), examples of these themes are "a demeaning offense against me and mine" (for anger); "having experienced an irrevocable loss" (for sadness); or "making reasonable progress

toward the realization of a goal" (for happiness).

At a more dimensional or molecular level, process-oriented models have been suggested to account for the functional dynamics of the emotion components. As an example, Figure 1.10 provides the component process model of emotion – a functional architecture of emotion in which the emotion components and their interactions are described (Scherer, 2001; see also Sander et al., 2005).

According to this model, cognitive appraisal is seen both as a cause and as a component of emotion (on this issue, see Lazarus, 1991, pp. 172–74). The appraisal component interacts with various cognitive systems to drive variations in the four components of the emotional response (autonomic physiology, action tendencies, motor expression, and subjective feeling (see the section, "A Typical Definition of Emotion").

In the component process model of emotion, for instance, Scherer has proposed that the appraisal dimensions (called stimulus evaluation checks) are organized in terms of achieving four appraisal objectives:

(1) How relevant is this event for me? Does it directly affect me or my social reference group? (relevance); (2) What are the implications or consequences of this event and how do these affect my well-being and my immediate or long-term goals? (implications); (3) How well can I cope with or adjust to these consequences? (coping potential); (4) What is the significance of this event with respect to my self-concept and to social norms and values (normative significance (Sander et al., 2005, p. 319).

These appraisal processes interact with many cognitive functions, and, as depicted in Figure 1.10, there is a bidirectional influence between them.

Electroencephalography has been used to investigate the temporal dynamics of the appraisal processes, and results suggest that different appraisal checks have specific brain state correlates that occur rapidly. For instance, Grandjean and Scherer (2008) manipulated three appraisal processes (novelty, intrinsic pleasantness, and goal conduciveness) and obtained results using topographical and wavelet analyses suggesting that the effects of these processes occur in sequential rather than parallel fashion.

These effects are predicted to differentially affect the emotional response components (for a review, see Scherer, 2009). For instance, Lanctôt and Hess (2007) found that facial reactions to the intrinsic pleasantness manipulation were faster than facial reactions to the goal conduciveness manipulation. With respect to autonomic physiology, Delplanque et al. (2009) observed that earlier effects on heart rate occurred in response to novelty detection than in response to pleasantness manipulation.

Most appraisal models of emotion suggest that appraisal processes function at multiple levels of processing (see Leventhal & Scherer, 1987; Teasdale, 1999). In particular, the automaticity of appraisal processes is an important topic of research in the field (for a discussion, see Brosch, Pourtois, & Sander, 2010; Coppin et al., 2010; Cunningham & Zelazo, 2007; Moors, 2010; Robinson, 1998).

The notion that emotional stimuli are prioritized by the attention system has been supported by many research trends in affective neuroscience (see Vuilleumier, 2005; Chapter 14). Evidence suggests that the appraisal of relevance (rather than, e.g., threat detection) might be critical for emotional attention (e.g., Brosch, Sander, Pourtois, & Scherer, 2008). Indeed, stimuli that are appraised as relevant, in a potentially automatic way, would then drive attention and may also modulate perception, memory, decision making, and moral judgment.

An in depth investigation of the "appraising brain" using affective neuroscience concepts and methods would certainly allow a new perspective to understanding the various functions of the neural mechanisms composing the emotional brain (see Brosch & Sander, in press). Most appraisal models agree that relevance detection is a sine qua non condition for emotion elicitation. The suggestion of a process that evaluates the affective relevance of an event is consistent with growing evidence indicating shared brain systems for the processing of both pleasant and unpleasant stimuli (see Leknes & Tracey, 2008). The suggestion that the amygdala is critical for relevance detection rather than being specific for threat processing, valence-based evaluation, or intensity coding is an affective neuroscience proposal that has directly linked appraisal models of emotion with brain systems (Sander et al., 2003).

Evidence that the amygdala is critical for relevance detection is accumulating, with results indicating that this region is indeed sensitive to novelty (e.g., Blackford et al., 2010), needs (e.g., Piech et al., 2009), goals (e.g., Cunningham, Van Bavel, & Johnsen, 2008), and values (e.g., Brosch, Coppin, Scherer, Schwartz, & Sander, 2011). Because the amygdala has also been considered in other lines of research to be central for a fear module or for the arousal dimension, investigating the function of the amygdala seems to reveal the potential of affective neuroscience to test models of emotion.

Conclusion: Investigating the Human Brain to Test Models of Emotion

In 1928, Claparède wrote that "the psychology of affective processes is the most confused chapter in all psychology" (p. 124). During the last few decades, affective psychology and, more generally, the affective sciences have developed considerably. Affective neuroscience has been instrumental in this development. I hope to have shown in this chapter that an affective neuroscience approach could decrease the "confusion" highlighted by Claparède (1928) by increasing conceptual clarity and hypothesis-driven empirical testing of models of emotion.

Key constructs such as basic emotion, emotion expression, approach, avoidance, action tendency, embodiment, bodily reaction, arousal, valence, feeling, or appraisal have all already been the focus of affective neuroscience research. However, the potential of affective neuroscience goes beyond a focus on such constructs and can be considered as the royal road to put theories of emotion to the test. Indeed, most current theories of emotion make predictions as to how brain mechanisms compute emotional information. Therefore, affective neuroscience research can be used to comparatively test models of emotion. For instance, studies exploring the specific function of the amygdala can directly speak to models of emotion in the following ways: (1) If the amygdala is specific to a "fear module," then it provides evidence for a basic emotion model; (2) if the amygdala is specific to the arousal dimension, then it provides evidence for circumplex models of emotion; and (3) if the amygdala is specific to relevance detection, then it provides evidence for appraisal models of emotion. Many other examples of how affective neuroscience research can constructively contribute to debates on current theories of emotion can be found throughout this volume.

Outstanding Questions and Future Directions

- Does the brain implement modules for basic emotions or do all emotions emerge from covariations of the same brain networks underlying specific components?
- Will the current conceptual distinction between *emotion* and *feeling* significantly contribute to the resolution of the debate concerning a potential *causal* role of the bodily reaction in emotion? Given its ambiguity, will the global concept of "arousal" be refined in future affective neuroscience research?
- If one admits that automatic processing can be cognitive, will affective neuroscience bring evidence supporting the notion that pure sensory processing (i.e., not cognitive according to Zajonc) is sufficient to elicit full-blown emotions?
- How will research on "typical" cognitive systems further integrate the affective neuroscience approach? Ongoing research has already highlighted the role of emotion in perception, attention, memory, decision making, and moral judgment. Other research on error monitoring and goal-directed behavior also increasingly integrates affective neuroscience data and approach.
- How will computer simulations that are based on computational models contribute to testing affective neuroscience models?
- Is emotion regulation a specific process or is it inherent to the emotion process? Affective neuroscience will help test whether regulatory mechanisms are outside emotion or take place within emotion processes.

References

Aggleton, J. P., & Mishkin, M. (1986). The amygdala: Sensory gateway to the emotions. In R. Plutchik & H. Kellerman (Eds.), *Emotion: Theory, research and experience* (Vol. 3, pp. 281–99). Orlando: Academic Press.

Ahern, G. L., & Schwartz, G. E. (1979). Differential lateralization for positive vs. negative emotion. *Neuropsychologia, 17*, 693–98.

Amodio, D. M., Shah, J. Y., Sigelman, J., Brazy, P. C., & Harmon-Jones, E. (2004). Implicit regulatory focus associated with resting frontal cortical asymmetry. *Journal of Experimental Social Psychology, 40*, 225–32.

Anders, S., Weiskopf, N., Lule, D., & Birbaumer, N. (2004). Infrared oculography - validation of a new method to monitor startle eyeblink amplitudes during fMRI. *Neuroimage, 22*(2), 767–770.

Anderson, A. K., Christoff, K., Stappen, I., Panitz, D., Ghahremani. D.G., Glover, G., ... Sobel, N. (2003). Dissociated neural representations of intensity and valence in human olfaction. *Nature Neuroscience, 6*(2), 196–202.

Anderson, A.K., & Sobel, N. (2003). Dissociating intensity from valence as sensory inputs into emotion. *Neuron, 39*(4), 581–83.

Armony, J. L., Servan-Schreiber, D., Cohen, J. D., & LeDoux, J. E. (1995). An anatomically constrained neural network model of fear conditioning. *Behavioral Neuroscience, 109*(2), 246–57.

Arnold, M. B. (1960). *Emotion and personality.* New York: Columbia University Press.

Aston-Jones, G., & Cohen, J. D. (2005). An integrative theory of locus coeruleus-norepinephrine function: Adaptive gain and optimal performance. *Annual Review of Neuroscience, 28*, 403–50.

Bar, M. (2009). A cognitive neuroscience hypothesis of mood and depression. *Trends in Cognitive Sciences, 13*, 456–63.

Barrett, L. F. (2009). Variety is the spice of life: A psychological constructionist approach to understanding variability in emotion. *Cognition and Emotion, 23*, 1284–1306.

Barrett, L. F., Mesquita, B., Ochsner, K. N., & Gross, J. J. (2007). The experience of emotion. *Annual Review of Psychology, 58*, 373–403.

Barrett, L. F., & Russell, J. A. (2009). The circumplex model of affect. In D. Sander & K. Scherer (Eds.), *The Oxford companion to emotion and the affective sciences* (pp. 85–88). New York: Oxford University Press.

Basile, B., Mancini, F., Macaluso, E., Caltagirone, C., Frackowiak, R. S., & Bozzali, M. (2011). Deontological and altruistic guilt: Evidence for distinct neurobiological substrates. *Human Brain Mapping, 32*(2), 229–39.

Bensafi, M., Rouby, C., Farget, V., Bertrand, B., Vigouroux, M., & Holley, A. (2002). Autonomic nervous system responses to odours: The role of pleasantness and arousal. *Chemical Senses, 27*(8), 703–9.

Berkowitz, L. (1990). On the formation and regulation of anger and aggression: A cognitive-neoassociationistic analysis. *American Psychologist, 45*(4), 494–503.

Berridge, K. C., & Robinson, T. E. (2003). Parsing reward. *Trends in Neurosciences, 26*(9), 507–13.

Blackford, J. U., Buckholtz, J. W., Avery, S. N., & Zald, D. H. (2010) A unique role for the human amygdala in novelty detection. *Neuroimage, 50*(3), 1188–93.

Bower, G. H. (1981). Mood and memory. *American Psychologist, 36*, 129–48.

Bradley, M. (2009). Natural selective attention: Orienting and emotion. *Psychophysiology, 46*, 1–11.

Bradley, M., & Lang, P. (2009). Eliciting stimulus sets (for emotion research). In D. Sander & K. R. Scherer (Eds.), *The Oxford companion to emotion and the affective sciences* (pp.137–38). New York: Oxford University Press.

Brehm, J. W. (1999). The intensity of emotion. *Personality and Social Psychology Review, 3*, 2–22.

Broca, P. (1878). Anatomie comparée des circonvolutions cérébrales: Le grand lobe limbique et la scissure limbique dans la série des mammifères. *Revue d'Anthropologie, 7*, 385–498.

Brosch, T., Coppin, G., Scherer, K. R., Schwartz, S., & Sander, D. (2011). Generating value(s): Psychological value hierarchies reflect context dependent sensitivity of the reward system. *Social Neuroscience, 6*, 198–208.

Brosch, T., Pourtois, G., & Sander, D. (2010). The perception and categorization of emotional stimuli: A review. *Cognition and Emotion, 24*(3), 377–400.

Brosch, T. & Sander, D. (in press). The appraising brain: Towards a neuro-cognitive model of appraisal processes in emotion. *Emotion Review.*

Brosch, T., Sander, D., Pourtois, G., & Scherer, K. R. (2008). Beyond fear: Rapid spatial orienting towards emotional positive stimuli. *Psychological Science, 19*(4), 362–70.

Cacioppo, J. T., & Berntson, G. G. (1994). Relationship between attitudes and evaluative space: A critical review, with emphasis on the separability of positive and negative substrates. *Psychological Bulletin, 115*, 401–23.

Cacioppo, J. T., Berntson, G. G., Larsen, J. T., Poehlmann, K. M., & Ito, T. A. (2000). The psychophysiology of emotion. In R. Lewis &

J. M. Haviland-Jones (Eds.), *The handbook of emotion* (2nd ed., pp. 173–91). New York: Guilford Press.

Calder, A. J., Lawrence, A. D., & Young, A. W. (2001). Neuropsychology of fear and loathing. *Nature Reviews Neuroscience, 2*, 352–63.

Camille, N., Coricelli, G., Sallet, J., Pradat-Diehl, P., Duhamel, J. R., & Sirigu, A. (2004). The involvement of the orbitofrontal cortex in the experience of regret. *Science, 304*, 1167–70.

Cañamero, L. (2009). Autonomous agent. In D. Sander & K. R. Scherer (Eds.), *The Oxford companion to emotion and the affective sciences* (pp. 67–68). New York: Oxford University Press.

Cannon, W. B. (1927). The James-Lange theory of emotions: A critical examination and an alternative theory. *American Journal of Psychology, 39*, 106–24.

Cannon, W. B. (1931). Again the James-Lange and the thalamic theories of emotion. *Psychological Review, 38*, 281–95.

Carver, C. S (2004). Negative affects deriving from the behavioral approach system. *Emotion, 4*(1), 3–22.

Carver, C. S., & Harmon-Jones, E. (2009). Anger is an approach-related affect: Evidence and implications. *Psychological Bulletin, 135*, 183–204.

Carver, C. S., & Scheier, M. F. (1998). *On the self-regulation of behavior*. New York: Cambridge University Press.

Chiao, J. Y. (2010). At the frontier of cultural neuroscience: Introduction to the special issue. *Social Cognitive and Affective Neuroscience, 5*(2–3), 109–10.

Claparède, E. (1928). Feelings and emotions. In M. Reymert (Ed.) *Feelings and emotions – The Wittenberg Symposium* (pp. 124–39). Worcester, MA: Clark University Press.

Colibazzi, T., Posner, J., Wang, Z., Gorman, D., Gerber, A., Yu, S., . . . Peterson, B.S. (2010). Neural systems subserving valence and arousal during the experience of induced emotions. *Emotion, 10*, 377–89.

Colombetti, G. (2005). Appraising valence. *Journal of Consciousness Studies, 12*(8–10), 103–26.

Coppin, G., Delplanque, S., Cayeux, I., Porcherot, C., & Sander, D. (2010). I'm no longer torn after choice: How explicit choices can implicitly shape preferences for odors. *Psychological Science, 21*, 489–93.

Coricelli, G., Critchley, H. D., Joffily, M., O'Doherty, J. P., Sirigu, A., & Dolan, R. J. (2005). Regret and its avoidance: A neu-roimaging study of choice behavior. *Nature Neuroscience, 8*, 1255–62.

Coricelli, G., & Rustichini, A. (2010). Counterfactual thinking and emotions: Regret and envy learning. *Philosophical Transactions of the Royal Society B 365*(1538), 241–47.

Costa, V. D., Lang, P. J., Sabatinelli, D., Versace, F., & Bradley, M. M. (2010). Emotional imagery: Assessing pleasure and arousal in the brain's reward circuitry. *Human Brain Mapping, 31*(9), 1446–57.

Cristinzio, C., N'Diaye, K., Seeck, M, Vuilleumier, P., & Sander, D. (2010). Integration of gaze direction and facial expression in patients with unilateral amygdala damage. *Brain, 133*, 248–61.

Cunningham, W. A., Van Bavel, J. J., & Johnsen, I. R. (2008). Affective flexibility: Evaluative processing goals shape amygdala activity. *Psychological Science, 19*, 152–60.

Cunningham, W. A., & Zelazo, P. D. (2007). Attitudes and evaluations: A social cognitive neuroscience perspective. *Trends in Cognitive Sciences, 11*, 97–104.

Damasio, A. R. (1994). *Descartes' error: Emotion, reason, and the human brain*. New York: Putnam.

Damasio, A. R. (1998). Emotion in the perspective of an integrated nervous system. *Brain Research Reviews, 26*(2–3), 83–86.

Damasio, A. R., & Damasio, H. (2006). Minding the body. *Daedalus, 135*(3), 15–22.

Darwin, C. (1998). *The expression of the emotions in man and animals*. London: Murray. (Original work published 1872)

Davidson, R. J. (1992). Emotion and affective style: Hemispheric substrates. *Psychological Science, 3*, 39–43.

Davidson, R. J. (1994). Asymmetric brain function, affective style and psychopathology: The role of early experience and plasticity. *Development and Psychopathology, 6*, 741–58.

Davidson, R. J., & Irwin, W. (1999). The functional neuroanatomy of emotion and affective style. *Trends in Cognitive Science, 3*, 11–21.

Davidson, R. J., & Sutton, S. K. (1995). Affective neuroscience: The emergence of a discipline. *Current Opinions in Neurobiology, 5*, 217–24.

Delplanque, S., Grandjean, D., Chrea, A., Coppin, G., Aymard, L., Cayeux, I., . . . Scherer, K. R. (2009). Sequential unfolding of novelty and pleasantness appraisals of odors: Evidence from facial electromyography and autonomic reactions. *Emotion, 9*(3), 316–28.

Deonna, J. A., & Teroni, F. (2008). Differentiating shame from guilt. *Consciousness and Cognition* 17(4), 1063–1400.

Descartes, R. (1649). *Les passions de l'âme.* Paris.

de Sousa, R. (1987). *The rationality of emotion.* Cambridge, MA: MIT Press.

de Sousa, R. (2008). Epistemic feelings. In G. Brun, U. Doguoglu, & D. Kuenzle (Eds.), *Epistemology and emotions* (pp. 185–204). Surrey, UK: Ashgate.

de Sousa, R. (2009). Rationality. In D. Sander & K. R. Scherer (Eds.), *The Oxford companion to emotion and the affective sciences* (p. 329). New York: Oxford University Press.

Dewey, J. (1895). The theory of emotion. (2) The significance of emotions. *Psychological Review,* 2, 13–32.

Dijk, E. van, & Zeelenberg, M. (2005). On the psychology of 'if only': Regret and the comparison between factual and counterfactual outcomes. *Organizational Behavior and Human Decision Processes,* 97(2), 152–60.

Duchenne, G. B. A. (1990). *Mécanisme de la physionomie humaine: Ou, analyse électrophysiologique de l'expression des passions* [The mechanism of human facial expression] (R. A. Cuthbertson, Ed. & Trans.). Cambridge: Cambridge University Press. (Original work published 1876)

Duffy, E. (1934). Is emotion a mere term of convenience? *Psychological Review,* 41, 103–4.

Duffy, E. (1941). An explanation of "emotional" phenomena without the use of the concept "emotion." *Journal of General Psychology,* 25, 283–93.

Duffy, E. (1957). The psychological significance of the concept of "arousal" or "activation." *Psychological Review,* 64, 265–75.

Eysenck, H. J. (1967). *The biological basis of personality.* Springfield, IL: Charles C. Thomas.

Ekman, P. (1972). Universals and cultural differences in facial expression of emotion. In J. R. Cole (Ed.), *Nebraska symposium on motivation* (pp. 207–83). Lincoln, NE: University of Nebraska Press.

Ekman, P. (1992). An argument for basic emotions. *Cognition and Emotion,* 6, 169–200.

Ekman, P. (1999). Basic emotions. In T. Dalgleish & M. Power (Eds.), *Handbook of cognition and emotion* (pp. 45–60). Chichester, UK: Wiley.

Ekman, P., & Davidson, R. J. (1994). Afterword: Is there emotion-specific physiology? In P. Ekman & R. J. Davidson (Eds.), *The nature of emotion: Fundamental questions* (pp. 261–62). New York: Oxford University Press.

Ekman, P., Friesen, W. V., & Simons, R. C. (1985). Is the startle reaction an emotion? *Journal of Personality and Social Psychology,* 49(5), 1416–26.

Ellsworth, P. (1994). William James and emotion: Is a century of fame worth a century of misunderstanding? *Psychological Review,* 101(2), 222–29.

Elster, J. (1996). Rationality and the emotions. *Economic Journal,* 1386–97.

Erickson, K., & Schulkin, J. (2003). Facial expressions of emotion: A cognitive neuroscience perspective. *Brain and Cognition,* 52(1), 52–60.

Eryilmaz, H., Van De Ville, D., Schwartz, S., & Vuilleumier, P. (2011). Impact of transient emotions on functional connectivity during subsequent resting state: A wavelet correlation approach. *Neuroimage,* 54(3), 2481–91.

Exner, S. (1894). *Entwurf zu einer physiologischen Erklärung der psychischen Erscheinungen* [Outline of a physiological explanation of mental phenomena]. Leipzig: Franz Deuticke.

Fehr, B., & Russell, J. A. (1984). Concept of emotion viewed from a prototype perspective. *Journal of Experimental Psychology: General,* 113, 464–86.

Feinstein, J. S., Adolphs, R., Damasio, A., & Tranel, D. (2010). The human amygdala and the induction and experience of fear. *Current Biology,* 21(1), 34–38.

Fellous, J.-M., & Arbib, M.A. (2005). *Who needs emotions? The brain meets the robot.* New York: Oxford University Press.

Fontaine, J. R. J. (2009). Self-reflexive emotions. In D. Sander & K. R. Scherer (Eds.), *The Oxford companion to emotion and the affective sciences* (pp. 357–59). New York: Oxford University Press.

Fontaine, J. R., Scherer, K. R., Roesch, E. B., & Ellsworth, P. (2007). The world of emotions is not two-dimensional. *Psychological Science,* 18(2), 1050–57.

Forgas, J. P. (2008). Affect and cognition. *Perspectives on Psychological Science,* 3(2), 94–101.

Frank, R. (1988). *Passions within reason.* New York: Norton.

Fowles, D. C. (2009). Arousal. In D. Sander & K. R. Scherer (Eds.), *The Oxford companion to emotion and the affective sciences* (p. 50). New York: Oxford University Press.

Freud, S. (1953). Project for a scientific psychology. In *The standard edition of the complete psychological works of sigmund Freud* (Vol. 1). London: Hogarth Press. (Original work published 1895)

Frijda, N. H. (1986). *The emotions.* Cambridge: Cambridge University Press.

Frijda, N. H. (2005). Emotion experience. *Cognition and Emotion,* 19, 473–98.

Frijda, N. H. (2007). *The laws of emotion.* Mahwah, NJ: Erlbaum.

Frijda, N. H. (2009a). Action readiness. In D. Sander & K. R. Scherer (Eds.), *The Oxford companion to emotion and the affective sciences* (p. 1). New York: Oxford University Press.

Frijda, N. H. (2009b). Action tendencies. In D. Sander & K. R. Scherer (Eds.), *The Oxford companion to emotion and the affective sciences* (pp. 1–2). New York: Oxford University Press.

Gable, P. A., & Harmon-Jones, E. (2008). Approach-motivated positive affect reduces breadth of attention. *Psychological Science,* 19, 476–82.

Gainotti, G. (2000). Neuropsychological theories of emotion. In J. C. Borod (Ed.), *The neuropsychology of emotion* (pp. 214–38). New York: Oxford University Press.

Gendron, M., & Feldman Barrett, L. (2009). Reconstructing the past: A century of ideas about emotion in psychology. *Emotion Review,* 1(4), 316–39.

Gerber, A. J., Posner, J., Gorman, D., Colibazzi, T., Yu, S., Wang, Z., . . . Peterson, B.S. (2008). An affective circumplex model of neural systems subserving valence, arousal, and cognitive overlay during the appraisal of emotional faces. *Neuropsychologia* 46, 2129–39.

Gibson, J. (2009). Fiction and emotion. In D. Sander & K. R. Scherer (Eds.), *The Oxford companion to emotion and the affective sciences* (pp. 184–85). New York: Oxford University Press.

Grandjean, D., Sander, D., & Scherer, K. R. (2008). Conscious emotional experience emerges as a function of multilevel, appraisal–driven response synchronization. *Consciousness & Cognition,* 17(2), 484–95.

Grandjean, D., & Scherer, K. R. (2008). Unpacking the cognitive architecture of emotion processes. *Emotion,* 8(3), 341–51.

Gratch, J., & Marsella, S. (2005). Lessons from emotion psychology for the design of lifelike characters. *Applied Artificial Intelligence,* 19(3–4), 215–33.

Gray, J. A. (1987). *The psychology of fear and stress.* New York: Cambridge University Press.

Greene, J. D., Sommerville, R. B., Nystrom, L. E., Darley, J. M., & Cohen, J. D. (2001). An fMRI investigation of emotional engagement in moral judgment. *Science,* 293, 2105–8.

Griffiths, P. E. (1997). *What emotions really are: The problem of psychological categories.* Chicago: University of Chicago Press.

Haber, S. N., & Knutson, B. (2010). The reward circuit: Linking primate anatomy and human imaging. *Neuropsychopharmacology,* 35, 4–26.

Haidt, J. (2003). The moral emotions. In R. J. Davidson, K. R. Scherer, & H. H. Goldsmith (Eds.), *Handbook of affective sciences* (pp. 852–70). Oxford: Oxford University Press.

Hamann, S. (2003). Nosing in on the emotional brain. *Nature Neuroscience,* 6(2), 106–8.

Hamann, S. (2012). Mapping discrete and dimensional emotions onto the brain: controversies and consensus. *Trends in Cognitive Sciences,* 16(9), 458–466.

Hareli, S., & Parkinson, B. (2009). Social emotions. In D. Sander & K.R. Scherer (Eds.), *The Oxford companion to emotion and the affective sciences* (pp. 374–75). New York: Oxford University Press.

Hartley C. A., & Phelps E. A. (2010). Changing fear: The neurocircuity of emotion regulation. *Neuropsychopharmacology,* 35(1), 136–46.

Heinzel, A., Moerth, S., & Northoff, G. (2010). The central role of anterior cortical midline structures in emotional feeling and consciousness. *Psyche,* 16(2), 23–47.

Hilgard, E. R. (1980). The trilogy of mind: Cognition, affection, and conation. *Journal of the History of Behavioral Sciences,* 16, 10717.

Hobbes, T. (1985). *Leviathan.* England: Penguin Classics. (Original work published 1651)

Irons, D. (1897). The primary emotions. *Philosophical Review,* 6, 626–45.

Izard, C. E. (1971). *The face of emotion.* New York: Appleton-Century-Crofts.

James, W. (1884). What is an emotion? *Mind,* 9, 188–205.

James, W. (1890). *The principles of psychology.* New York: Dover Publications.

James, W. (1894). The physical basis of emotion. *Psychological Review,* 1, 516–29.

Jones, B. E. (2003). Arousal systems. *Frontiers in Bioscience,* 8, 438–51.

Katkin, E. S., Wiens, S., & Ohman, A. (2001). Nonconscious fear conditioning, visceral perception, and the development of gut feelings. *Psychological Science,* 12(5), 366–70.

Killgore, W. D. S., & Yurgelun-Todd, D. A. (2007). The right-hemisphere and valence hypotheses: Could they both be right (and sometimes left)? *Social, Cognitive and Affective Neuroscience,* 2(3), 240–50.

Kirman, A., Livet, P., & Teschl, M. (2010). Rationality and emotions. *Philosophical Transactions of the Royal Society B*, 365(1538), 215–19.

Kleinginna, P. R. Jr., & Kleinginna, A. M. (1981). A categorized list of emotion definitions with suggestions for a consensual definition. *Motivation and Emotion*, 5, 345–79.

Kluver, H., & Bucy, P. C. (1939). Preliminary analysis of the function of temporal lobe in monkeys. *Archives of Neurology and Psychiatry*, 42, 979–1000.

Konstan, D. (2009). History of emotion. In D. Sander & K. R. Scherer (Eds.), *The Oxford companion to emotion and the affective sciences* (pp. 206–7). New York: Oxford University Press.

Korb, S., & Sander, D. (2009). Neural architecture of facial expression. In D. Sander & K. R. Scherer (Eds.), *The Oxford companion to emotion and the affective sciences* (pp. 173–75). New York: Oxford University Press.

Kosslyn, S. M., & Koenig, O. (1992). *Wet mind, the new cognitive neuroscience*. New York: Free Press.

Kreibig, S. D. (2010). Autonomic nervous system activity in emotion: A review. *Biological Psychology*, 84, 394–421.

Kreibig, S. D., Gendolla, G. H. E., & Scherer, K. R. (2010). Psychophysiological effects of emotional responding to goal attainment. *Biological Psychology*, 84, 474–87.

Kumaran D., & Maguire E. A. (2007). Which computational mechanisms operate in the hippocampus during novelty detection? *Hippocampus*, 17(9), 735–48.

Lambie, J. A., & Marcel, A. J. (2002). Consciousness and the varieties of emotion experience: A theoretical framework. *Psychological Review*, 109(2), 219–59.

Lanctôt, N., & Hess, U. (2007). The timing of appraisals. *Emotion*, 7, 207–12.

Lane, R., & Nadel, L. (2000). *Cognitive neuroscience of emotion*. New York: Oxford University Press.

Lang, P. J. (1994). The varieties of emotional experience: A meditation on James–Lange theory. *Psychological Review*, 101(2), 211–21.

Lang, P., & Bradley, M. (2009). Reflexes (emotional). In D. Sander & K. R. Scherer (Eds.), *The Oxford companion to emotion and the affective sciences* (pp. 334–36). New York: Oxford University Press.

Lange, C. G. (1885). The mechanism of the emotions (Benjamin Rand, Trans.) Reprinted from The classical psychologists, pp. 672–84, by B. Rand (Ed.), 1912.

Larsen, J. T. (2007). *Ambivalence*. In R. F. Baumeister & K. D. Vohs (Eds.), *Encyclopedia of social psychology*. Thousand Oaks, CA: Sage.

Larsen, J. T., McGraw, A. P., & Cacioppo, J. T. (2001). Can people feel happy and sad at the same time? *Journal of Personality and Social Psychology*, 81, 684–96.

Lashley, K. S. (1938). The thalamus and emotion. *Psychological Review*, 45(1), 42–61.

Lazarus, R. S. (1966). *Psychological stress and the coping process*. New York: McGraw-Hill.

Lazarus, R. S. (1982). Thoughts on the relations between emotion and cognition. *American Psychologist*, 37(9), 1019–24.

Lazarus, R. S. (1984). On the primacy of cognition. *American Psychologist*, 39, 124–29.

Lazarus, R. S. (1991). *Emotion and adaptation*. New York: Oxford University Press.

LeDoux, J. E. (1989). Cognitive-emotional interactions in the brain. *Cognition and Emotion*, 3, 267–89.

LeDoux, J. E. (1991). Emotion and the limbic system concept. *Concepts in Neuroscience*, 2, 169–99.

LeDoux, J. E. (1993). Cognition versus emotion, again – this time in the brain: A response to Parrott and Schulkin. *Cognition and Emotion*, 7(1), 61–64.

LeDoux, J. E. (1994). Emotional processing, but not emotions, can occur unconsciously. In P. Ekman & R. J. Davidson (Eds.), *The nature of emotion: Fundamental questions* (pp. 291–93). New York: Oxford University Press,

LeDoux, J. E. (1996). *The emotional brain*. New York: Simon & Schuster.

LeDoux, J. E. (2007). Unconscious and conscious contributions to the emotional and cognitive aspects of emotions: A comment on Scherer's view of what an emotion is. *Social Science Information*, 46, 395–404.

Leknes, S., & Tracey, I. (2008). A common neurobiology for pain and pleasure. *Nature Reviews Neuroscience*, 9, 314–20.

Levenson, R. W. (2003). Autonomic specificity and emotion. In R. J. Davidson, K. R. Scherer, & H. H. Goldsmith (Eds.), *Handbook of affective sciences* (pp. 212–24). New York: Oxford University Press.

Levenson, R. W. (2011). Basic emotion questions. *Emotion Review*, 3, 379–86.

Leventhal, H., & Scherer, K. (1987). The relationship of emotion to cognition: A functional approach to semantic controversy. *Cognition and Emotion*, 1(1), 3–28.

Lieberman, M. D., & Eisenberger, N. I. (2009). Pains and pleasures of social life. *Science*, 323, 890–91.

Lindquist, K. A., Wager, T. D., Kober, H., Bliss-Moreau, E., & Barrett, L. F. (2012). The brain basis of emotion: A meta-analytic review. *Behavioral and Brain Sciences*, 35, 121–143.

Litt, A., Khan, U., & Shiv, B. (2010). Lusting while loathing: Parallel counterdriving of wanting and liking. *Psychological Science*, 21(1), 118–25.

MacLean, P. D. (1952). Some psychiatric implications of physiological studies on frontotemporal portion of limbic system (visceral brain). *Electroencephalography and Clinical Neurophysiology*, 4, 407–18.

Manstead, A. S. R., & Fischer, A. H. (2001). Social appraisal: The social world as object of and influence on appraisal processes. In K. R. Scherer, A. Schorr, & T. Johnstone (Eds.), *Appraisal processes in emotion: Theory, research, application* (pp. 221–32). New York: Oxford University Press.

Marr, D. (1982). *Vision: A computational investigation into the human representation and processing of visual information*. New York: W. H. Freeman.

Matsumoto, D., & Ekman, P. (2009). Basic emotions. In D. Sander & K. R. Scherer (Eds.), *The Oxford companion to emotion and the affective sciences* (pp. 69–73). New York: Oxford University Press.

McGaugh, J. L. (2006). Make mild moments memorable: Add a little arousal. *Trends in Cognitive Sciences*, 10, 345–47.

Miller, G. A. (2003). The cognitive revolution: A historical perspective. *Trends in Cognitive Sciences*, 7(3), 141–44.

Mineka, S., & Öhman, A. (2002). Phobias and preparedness: The selective, automatic, and encapsulated nature of fear. *Biological Psychiatry*, 52(10), 927–37.

Minsky, M. (1986). *The society of mind*. New York: Simon and Schuster.

Mitchell, J. P. (2006). Mentalizing and Marr: An information processing approach to the study of social cognition. *Brain Research*, 1079, 66–75.

Moore, R. Y. (1973). Retinohypothalamic projection in mammals: A comparative study. *Brain Research*, 49, 403–9.

Moors, A. (2007). Can cognitive methods be used to study the unique aspect of emotion: An appraisal theorist's answer. *Cognition and Emotion*, 21(6), 1238–69.

Moors, A. (2009). Automatic appraisal. In D. Sander & K. R. Scherer (Eds.), *The Oxford companion to emotion and the affective sciences* (pp. 64–65). New York: Oxford University Press.

Moors, A. (2010). Automatic constructive appraisal as a candidate cause of emotion. *Emotion Review*, 2, 139–56.

Moors, A. (in press). On the causal role of appraisal in emotion. *Emotion Review*.

Moors, A., & De Houwer, J. (2006). Automaticity: A theoretical and conceptual analysis. *Psychological Bulletin*, 132, 297–326.

Morecraft, R. J., Stilwell-Morecraft, K. S., & Rossing, W. R. (2004). The motor cortex and facial expression: New insights from neuroscience. *Neurologist*, 10, 235–49.

Morris, J. S., DeGelder, B., Weiskrantz, L., & Dolan, R. J. (2001). Differential extrageniculostriate and amygdala responses to presentation of emotional faces in a cortically blind field. *Brain*, 124(6), 1241–52.

Morton, A. (2010). Epistemic emotions. In P. Goldie (Ed.), *The Oxford handbook of philosophy of emotion* (pp. 385–400). New York: Oxford University Press.

Mulligan, K. (2009). Moral emotions. In D. Sander & K. R. Scherer (Eds.), *The Oxford companion to emotion and the affective sciences* (pp. 262–65). New York: Oxford University Press.

Mumenthaler, C., & Sander, D. (2012). Social appraisal influences recognition of emotions. *Journal of Personality and Social Psychology*. doi:10.1037/a0026885

Murphy, F.C., Nimmo-Smith, I., & Lawrence, A. D. (2003). Functional neuroanatomy of emotions: A meta-analysis. *Cognitive, Affective, & Behavioral Neuroscience*, 3(3), 207–33.

Neiss, R. (1988). Reconceptualizing arousal: Psychobiological states in motor performance. *Psychological Bulletin*, 103(3), 345–66.

Neisser, U. (1967.) *Cognitive psychology*. New York: Appleton-Century-Crofts.

Nicolle, A., Bach, D. A., Frith, C., & Dolan, R. J. (2011). Amygdala involvement in self-blame regret. *Social Neuroscience*, 6(2), 178–89.

Niedenthal, P. M. (2007). Embodying emotion. *Science*, 316, 1002–5.

Niedenthal, P. M., & Barsalou, L. W. (2009). Embodiment. In D. Sander & K. R. Scherer (Eds.), *The Oxford companion to emotion and the affective sciences* (p. 140). New York: Oxford University Press.

Niedenthal, P. M., Mermillod, M., Maringer, M., & Hess, U. (2010). The Simulation of Smiles (SIMS) model: Embodied simulation and the meaning of facial expression. *Behavioral and Brain Sciences*, 33(6), 417–33.

Nili, U., Goldberg, H., Weizman, A., & Dudai, Y. (2010). Fear thou not: Activity of frontal and temporal circuits in moments of real-life courage. *Neuron*, 66(6), 949–62.

Norris, C. J., Chen, E. E., Zhu, D. C., Small, S. L., & Cacioppo, J. T. (2004). The interaction of social and emotional processes in the brain. *Journal of Cognitive Neuroscience*, 16, 1818–29.

Ochsner, K. N., & Schacter, D. L. (2000). A social cognitive neuroscience approach to emotion and memory. In J. C. Borod (Ed.), *The neuropsychology of emotion* (pp. 163–93). New York: Oxford University Press.

Öhman, A., & Mineka, S. (2001). Fears, phobias, and preparedness: Toward an evolved module of fear and fear learning. *Psychological Review*, 108(3), 483–522.

Olds, J., & Milner, P. (1954). Positive reinforcement produced by electrical stimulation of septal area and other regions of rat brain. *Journal of Comparative Physiology and Psychology*, 47, 419–27.

Ortony, A., Clore, G. L., & Collins, A. (1988). *The cognitive structure of emotions*. New York: Cambridge University Press.

Ortony, A., & Turner, T. J. (1990). What's basic about basic emotions? *Psychological Review*, 97, 315–31.

Osgood, C. H., May, W. H., & Miron, M. S. (1975). *Cross-cultural universals of affective meaning*. Urbana: University of Illinois Press.

Panksepp, J. (1991). Affective neuroscience: A conceptual framework for the neurobiological study of emotions. In K. Strongman (Ed.), *International reviews of emotion research* (pp. 59–99). Chichester, UK: Wiley.

Panksepp, J. (2003). Feeling the pain of social loss. *Science*, 302, 237–39.

Panksepp, J. (2005). Affective consciousness: Core emotional feelings in animals and humans. *Consciousness and Cognition*, 14(1), 30–80.

Papez, J. (1937). A proposed mechanism of emotion. *Archives of Neurology and Psychiatry*, 38, 725–43.

Parrott, W. G., & Schulkin, J. (1993a). Neuropsychology and the cognitive nature of the emotions. *Cognition & Emotion*, 7, 43–59.

Parrott, W. G., & Schulkin, J. (1993b). What sort of system could an affective system be? A reply to LeDoux. *Cognition & Emotion*, 7, 65–69.

Parrott, W. G., & Smith, R. H. (1993). Distinguishing the experiences of envy and jealousy. *Journal of Personality and Social Psychology*, 64, 906–20.

Paus, T. (2000). Functional anatomy of arousal and attention systems in the human brain. *Progress in Brain Research*, 126, 65–77.

Pelachaud, C. (2009). Embodied conversational agent. In D. Sander & K. R. Scherer (Eds.), *The Oxford companion to emotion and the affective sciences* (pp. 139–140). New York: Oxford University Press.

Peper, M., & Markowitsch, H.J. (2001). Pioneers of affective neuroscience and early concepts of the emotional brain. *Journal of the History of the Neurosciences*, 10, 58–66.

Petta, P., & Gratch, J. (2009). Computational models of emotion. In D. Sander & K. R. Scherer (Eds.), *The Oxford companion to emotion and the affective sciences* (pp. 94–95). New York: Oxford University Press.

Phan, K. L., Wager, T., Taylor, S. F., & Liberzon, I. (2002). Functional neuroanatomy of emotion: A meta-analysis of emotion activation studies in PET and fMRI. *Neuroimage*, 16(2), 331–48.

Phillips, A. G. (1999). "The Brain and Emotion" by Edmund T. Rolls. *Trends in Cognitive Sciences*, 3(7), 281–82.

Picard, R. (1997). *Affective computing*. Cambridge, MA: MIT Press.

Picard, R. W. (2009). Affective computing. In D. Sander & K. R. Scherer (Eds.), *The Oxford companion to emotion and the affective sciences* (pp. 11–15). New York: Oxford University Press.

Piech, R. M., Lewis, J., Parkinson, C. H., Owen, A. M., Roberts, A. C., et al. (2009) Neural correlates of appetite and hunger-related evaluative judgments. *PLoS One*, 4(8), e6581.

Pope, L. K., & Smith, C. A. (1994). On the distinct meanings of smiles and frowns. *Cognition and Emotion*, 8, 65–72.

Posner, J., Russell, J. A., Gerber, A., Gorman, D., Colibazzi, T., Yu, S., . . . Peterson, B. S. (2009). The neurophysiological bases of emotion: An fMRI study of the affective circumplex using emotion-denoting words. *Human Brain Mapping*, 30, 883–95.

Posner, J., Russell, J. A., & Peterson, B. S. (2005). The circumplex model of affect: An integrative approach to affective neuroscience, cognitive development, and psychopathology. *Development and Psychopathology*, 17, 715–34.

Powell, L. J., Macrae, C. N., Cloutier, J., Metcalfe, J., & Mitchell, J. P. (2009). Dissociable neural substrates for agentic versus conceptual representations of self. *Journal of Cognitive Neuroscience*, 22(10), 2186–97.

Prinz, J. J. (2004). *Gut reactions: A perceptual theory of emotion*. New York: Oxford University Press.

Rainville, P., Bechara, A., Naqvi, N., & Damasio, A. R. (2006). Basic emotions are associated with distinct patterns of cardiorespiratory activity. *International Journal of Psychophysiology*, 61, 5–18.

Reisenzein, R. (1983). The Schachter theory of emotion: Two decades later. *Psychological Bulletin*, 94, 239–64.

Reisenzein, R. (2009). Schachter-Singer theory. In D. Sander & K. R. Scherer (Eds.), *The Oxford companion to emotion and the affective sciences* (pp. 352–53). New York: Oxford University Press.

Reisenzein, R., & Döring, S. (2009). Ten perspectives on emotional experience: Introduction to the special issue. *Emotion Review*, 1, 195–205.

Rinn, W. E. (1984). The neuropsychology of facial expression: A review of the neurological and psychological mechanisms for producing facial expressions. *Psychological Bulletin*, 95, 52–77.

Robbins, T. (1997). Arousal systems and attentional processes. *Biological Psychology*, 45(1–3), 57–71.

Robertson, I. H., & Garavan, H. (2004). Vigilant attention. In M. S. Gazzaniga (Ed.), *The cognitive neurosciences* (pp. 631–640). Cambridge, MA: MIT Press.

Robinson, J. (2005). *Deeper than reason: Emotion and its role in literature, music, and art*. New York: Oxford University Press.

Robinson, J. (2009). Aesthetic emotions (philosophical perspectives). In D. Sander & K. R. Scherer (Eds.), *The Oxford companion to emotion and the affective sciences* (pp. 6–9). New York: Oxford University Press.

Robinson, M. D. (1998). Running from William James' bear: A review of preattentive mechanisms and their contributions to emotional experience. *Cognition and Emotion*, 12, 667–96.

Roesch, E. B., Korsten, N., Fragopanagos, N., Taylor, J. G., Grandjean, D., & Sander, D. (2011). Biological and computational constraints to psychological modelling of emo-

tion. In P. Petta et al. (Eds.), *Handbook for research on emotions and human-machine interactions* (pp. 47–65). Berlin: Springer-Verlag.

Roesch, E. B., Korsten, N., Fragopanagos, N., & Taylor, J. G. (2010). Emotions in artificial neural networks. In K. R. Scherer, T. Baenziger, & E. B. Roesch (Eds.), *Blueprint for affective computing: A sourcebook* (pp. 194–212). New York: Oxford University Press.

Roese, N. J. (1994). The functional basis of counterfactual thinking. *Journal of Personality and Social Psychology*, 66, 805–18.

Rolls, E. (1999). *The brain and emotion*. New York: Oxford University Press.

Rolls, E. T. (2007). A neurobiological approach to emotional intelligence. In G. Matthews, M. Zeidner, & R. D. Roberts (Eds.), *The science of emotional intelligence* (pp. 72–100). Oxford: Oxford University Press.

Roseman, I. J. (1984). Cognitive determinants of emotions: A structural theory. In P. Shaver (Ed.), *Review of personality and social psychology* (Vol. 5, pp. 11–36). Beverly Hills, CA: Sage.

Russell, J. A. (1980). A circumplex model of affect. *Journal of Personality and Social Psychology*, 39, 1161–78.

Russell, J. A. (2005). Emotion in human consciousness is built on core affect. *Journal of Consciousness Studies*, 12, 26–42.

Russell, J. A. (2009). Emotion, core affect, and psychological construction. *Cognition & Emotion*, 23(7), 1259–83.

Russell, J. A., Bachorowski, J., & Fernandez-Dols, J. M. (2003). Facial and vocal expressions of emotion. *Annual Review of Psychology*, 54, 329–49.

Russell, J. A., & Barrett, L. F. (1999). Core affect, prototypical emotional episodes, and other things called emotion: Dissecting the elephant. *Journal of Personality and Social Psychology*, 76, 805–19.

Russell, J. A., & Feldman Barrett, L. (2009). Circumplex models. In D. Sander & K. R. Scherer (Eds.), *The Oxford companion to emotion and the affective sciences* (pp. 85–88). New York: Oxford University Press.

Russell J. A., & Mehrabian, A. (1977). Evidence for a three-factor theory of emotions, *Journal of Research in Personality*, 11(3), 273–94.

Säätelä, S. (1994). Fiction, make-believe and quasi emotions. *British Journal of Aesthetics*, 34, 25–34.

Sander, D., Grafman, J., & Zalla, T. (2003). The human amygdala: An evolved system for relevance detection. *Reviews in the Neurosciences*, 14(4), 303–16.

Sander, D., Grandjean, D., Kaiser, S., Wehrle, T., & Scherer, K. R. (2007). Interaction effects of perceived gaze direction and dynamic facial expression: Evidence for appraisal theories of emotion. *European Journal of Cognitive Psychology*, 19(3), 470–80.

Sander, D., Grandjean, D., & Scherer, K. R. (2005). A systems approach to appraisal mechanisms in emotion. *Neural Networks*, 18, 317–52.

Sander, D., & Koenig, O. (2002). No inferiority complex in the study of emotion complexity: A cognitive neuroscience computational architecture of emotion. *Cognitive Science Quarterly*, 2, 249–72.

Sander, D., & Scherer, K. R. (Eds.). (2009). *The Oxford companion to emotion and the affective sciences*. New York: Oxford University Press.

Schachter, S., & Singer, J. (1962). Cognitive, social, and physiological determinants of emotional state. *Psychological Review*, 69(5), 379–399

Scharpf, K. R., Wendt, J., Lotze, M., & Hamm, A. O. (2010). The brain's relevance detection network operates independently of stimulus modality. *Behavioural Brain Research*, 210(1), 16–23.

Scherer, K. R. (1984). On the nature and function of emotion: A component process approach. In K. R. Scherer, & P. Ekman (Eds.), *Approaches to emotion* (pp. 293–317). Hillsdale, NJ: Erlbaum.

Scherer, K. R. (1992). What does facial expression express? In K. Strongman (Ed.), *International review of studies on emotion*, (Vol. 2, pp. 139–65). Chichester, UK: Wiley.

Scherer, K. R. (2001). Appraisal considered as a process of multi-level sequential checking. In K. R. Scherer, A. Schorr, & T. Johnstone (Eds.), *Appraisal processes in emotion: Theory, methods, research* (pp. 92–120). New York: Oxford University Press.

Scherer, K. R. (2005). What are emotions? And how can they be measured? *Social Science Information*, 44(4), 695–729.

Scherer, K. R. (2009). The dynamic architecture of emotion: Evidence for the component process model. *Cognition & Emotion*, 23(7), 1307–51.

Scherer, K. R., & Ellsworth, P.C. (2009). Appraisal theories. In D. Sander & K. R. Scherer (Eds.), *The Oxford companion to emotion and the affective sciences* (pp. 45–49). New York: Oxford University Press.

Scherer, K. R., Shorr, A., & Johnstone, T. (Eds.). (2001). *Appraisal processes in emotion: Theory, methods, research*. New York: Oxford University Press.

Schneirla, T. C. (1959). An evolutionary and developmental theory of biphasic processes underlying approach and withdrawal. In M. R. Jones (Ed.), *Current theory and research in motivation* (pp. 1–49). Lincoln: University of Nebraska Press.

Sergerie, K., Chochol, C., & Armony, J. L. (2008). The role of the amygdala in emotional processing: A quantitative meta-analysis of functional neuroimaging studies. *Neuroscience and Biobehavioral Reviews*, 32, 811–30.

Silvia, P. J. (2006a). Artistic training and interest in visual art: Applying the appraisal model of aesthetic emotions. *Empirical Studies of the Arts*, 24, 139–61.

Silvia, P. J. (2006b). *Exploring the psychology of interest*. New York: Oxford University Press.

Silvia, P. J. (2009). Aesthetic emotions (psychological perspectives). In D. Sander & K. R. Scherer (Eds.), *The Oxford companion to emotion and the affective sciences* (p. 9). New York: Oxford University Press.

Silvia, P. J. (2010). Confusion and interest: The role of knowledge emotions in aesthetic experience. *Psychology of Aesthetics, Creativity, and the Arts*, 4, 75–80.

Simon, H. A. (1967). Motivational and emotional controls of cognition. *Psychological Review*, 74(1), 29–39.

Small, D. M., Gregory, M. D., Mak, Y. E., Gitelman, D., Mesulam, M. M., & Parrish, T. (2003). Dissociation of neural representation of intensity and affective valuation in human gustation. *Neuron*, 39, 701–11.

Smith, C. A. (1989). Dimensions of appraisal and physiological response in emotion. *Journal of Personality and Social Psychology*, 56, 339–53.

Smith, C. A., & Kirby, L. D. (2009). Core relational themes. In D. Sander & K. R. Scherer (Eds.), *The Oxford companion to emotion and the affective sciences* (pp. 104–5). New York: Oxford University Press.

Smith, C. A., & Lazarus, R.S. (1990). Emotion and adaptation. In L. A. Pervin (ed.), *Handbook of personality: Theory and research*, (pp. 609–37). New York: Guilford Press.

Smith, C. A., & Scott, H. S. (1997). A componential approach to the meaning of facial expressions. In J. A. Russell & J. M. Fernandez-Dols (Eds.), *The psychology of facial expression* (pp. 229–54). New York: Cambridge University Press.

Sorce, J. F., Emde, R. N., Campos, J. J., & Klinnert, M. D. (1985). Maternal emotional signaling: Its effect on the visual cliff behavior of one-year-olds. *Developmental Psychology*, 21, 195–200.

Soussignan, R. (2002). Duchenne Smile, emotional experience, and automatic reactivity: A test of the facial feedback hypothesis. *Emotion*, 2(1), 52–74.

Takahashi, H., Kato, M., Matsuura, M., Mobbs, D., Suhara, T., & Okubo, Y. (2009). When your gain is my pain and your pain is my gain: Neural correlates of envy and schandenfreude. *Science*, 323, 937–39.

Tangney, J. P., & Dearing, R. L. (2002). *Shame and guilt*. New York: Guilford Press.

Tangney, J. P., Stuewig, J., & Mashek, D. J. (2007). Moral emotions and moral behavior. *Annual Review of Psychology*, 58, 345–72.

Taylor, J. G., & Korsten, N. (2009). Connectionist models of emotion. In D. Sander & K. R. Scherer (Eds.), *The Oxford companion to emotion and the affective sciences* (pp. 96–97). New York: Oxford University Press.

Teasdale, J. (1999). Multi-level theories of cognition and emotion relations. In T. Dalgleish & M. Power (Eds.), *Handbook of cognition and emotion* (pp. 665–82). Chichester, UK: Wiley.

Thagard, P., & Aubie, B. (2008). Emotional consciousness: A neural model of how cognitive appraisal and somatic perception interact to produce qualitative experience. *Consciousness and Cognition*, 17, 811–34.

Tomkins, S. S. (1963). *Affect imagery consciousness*: Vol. II. *The negative affects*. New York: Springer.

Tooby, J., & Cosmides, L. (2000). Toward mapping the evolved functional organization of mind and brain. In M. S. Gazzaniga (Ed.), *The new cognitive neurosciences* (2nd ed., pp. 1167–78). Cambridge, MA: MIT Press.

Tsai, J. L., Knutson, B., & Fung, H. H. (2006). Cultural variation in affect valuation. *Journal of Personality and Social Psychology*, 90, 288–307.

Verduyn, P., Van Mechelen, I., & Tuerlinckx, F. (2011). The relation between event processing and the duration of emotional experience. *Emotion*, 11(1), 20–28.

Vuilleumier, P. (2005). How brains beware: Neural mechanisms of emotional attention. *Trends in Cognitive Sciences*, 9(12), 585–94.

Vuilleumier, P. (2009). The role of the human amygdala in perception and attention. In P. J. Whalen & E. A. Phelps (Eds), *The human amygdala* (pp. 220–49). New York: Guilford.

Vuilleumier, P., Armony, J. L., Driver, J., & Dolan, R. J. (2003). Distinct spatial frequency sensitivities for processing faces and emotional expressions, *Nature Neuroscience*, 6(6), 624–31.

Vrticka, P., Sander, D., & Vuilleumier, P. (2011). Effects of emotion regulation strategy on brain responses to the valence and social content of visual scenes. *Neuropsychologia*, 49(5), 1067–82.

Vytal, K., & Hamann, S. (2010). Neuroimaging support for discrete neural correlates of basic emotions: A voxel-based meta-analysis. *Journal of Cognitive Neuroscience*, 22(12), 2864–85.

Wacker, J., Chavanon, M. L., Leue, A., & Stemmler, G. (2008). Is running away right? The behavioral activation-behavioral inhibition model of anterior asymmetry. *Emotion*, 8(2), 232–49.

Wagner, U., N'Diaye, K., Ethofer, T., & Vuilleumier, P. (2011). Guilt-specific processing in the prefrontal cortex. *Cerebral Cortex*, 21(11), 2461–2470.

Wallace, J. F., Bachorowski, J., & Newman, J. P. (1991). Failures of response modulation: Impulsive behavior in anxious and impulsive individuals. *Journal of Research in Personality*, 25, 23–44.

Walton, K. (1978). *Fearing fictions. Journal of Philosophy*, 75, 5–27.

Watson, J. B., & Rayner, R. (1920). Conditioned emotional reactions. *Journal of Experimental Psychology*, 3, 1–14.

Waynbaum, I. (1994). The affective qualities of perception. *Journal de la Psychologie Normale et Pathologique*, 4, 289–311. (Original work published in 1904) [English translation in Niedenthal, P.N., & Kitayama, S. (Eds.), *The heart's eye*. New York: Academic Press, pp. 23–40].

Whalen, P. J. (1998). Fear, vigilance, and ambiguity: Initial neuroimaging studies of the human amygdala. *Current Directions in Psychological Science*, 7(6), 177–88.

Winston, J. S., Gottfried, J. A., Kilner, J. M., & Dolan, R. J. (2005). Integrated neural representations of odor intensity and affective valence in human amygdala. *Journal of Neuroscience*, 25, 8903–7.

Wundt. W. (1905). *Grundriss der Psychologie* [Fundamentals of psychology] (7th rev. ed.). Liepzig: Engelman.

Yerkes, R. M., & Dodson, J. D. (1908). The relation of strength of stimulus to rapidity of habit-formation. *Journal of Comparative and Neurological Psychology*, 18, 459–82.

Zajonc, R. B. (1980). Feeling and thinking: Preferences need no inferences. *American Psychologist*, 35, 151–75.

Zajonc, R. B. (1984). On the primacy of affect. *American Psychologist*, 39(2), 117–23.

Zeki, S. (2001). Artistic creativity and the brain. *Science*, 293(5527), 51–52.

Section II

MEASURING EMOTIONAL RESPONSES

CHAPTER 2

Objective and Subjective Measurements in Affective Science

Katherine Gardhouse & Adam K. Anderson

Emotions are complex, multidimensional phenomena that agitate our physiology, behavior, and cognition. Emotions participate in and out of awareness, informing decision making, attitudes, and moods. They can be expressed in a variety of ways or even be withheld across time if we so choose. Because of the complex emotional lives of humans, affective neuroscience is riddled with problems of measurement. Although emotional phenomena are interconnected, the science and accompanying measures developed to study the constellation of properties associated with affective experience are strictly defined. Two broad categories of measures are used in the science of affect: objective and subjective measures. There is value in creating a dichotomy between subject and object when studying emotion scientifically because, as we discuss later, these measures offer different tools for investigation. Although we define measurements with these categorical labels, there is no clear dividing line in the human experience that justifies the use of only one of these metrics. This is because the physiology and qualia (i.e., qualitative properties of

experience) associated with any emotional experience are inextricably linked. No one tangible component will sufficiently capture the essence of an emotional experience because emotions are by their nature multifaceted. Therefore it is important to use objective and subjective measures in combination to uncover the correlations among the neurocognitive, physiological, behavioral, and phenomenological reality of emotional events.

It remains the goal in affective neuroscience research to integrate as many measures as possible when attempting to gauge affective experience. Of course the ability to take measurements is generally limited by the laboratory or contextual environment of the research. As such, we need to be deliberate when developing experimental paradigms to ensure that we capture the nature of emotions to the best of our ability. This chapter examines the value of objective and subjective measures used in affective neuroscience. Although we do not argue for the use or importance of one type of measure over another, we begin by outlining the differences between them. We focus on examples from our own research that showcase the use of these response indices, illustrating how objective and subjective measures operate uniquely and offer opportunities to investigate the properties of emotion from different vantage points. Finally, we address some limitations to measurement and comment on innovative work that is pushing research forward by combining measures with inventive methods.

Objective versus Subjective Measures

Objective measurement is a cornerstone of science. Objectivity allows for precise measurement, analysis, and replication of experiments to such a degree that when the experimental context is duplicated, different investigators can observe the same results. The science of psychology is the application of the scientific method to mental events such as emotion. In emotion research there are many objective measures that can be recorded in finite units and that require minimal interpretation on the part of the researcher. These include measures of global behavior (e.g., approach, withdrawal), skeletomotor activity (e.g., facial expressions), autonomic physiology (e.g., electrodermal activity), and neurological patterns (e.g., electrical current, blood oxygen supply). Objective measures expand our methodological horizon and assist with the development of emotion theory, adding to our understanding of emotion by increasing our ability to identify and predict states. However, it is important to note that the investigation will be limited if we do not include measures of subjectivity. In this regard, psychological sciences are unique in comparison to many of the "hard" sciences in that they do not depend entirely on objective measures, but measure such fanciful matters as thoughts and emotions.

Subjective measures, unlike objective measures, are not as easily quantified because they consist of qualitative descriptions collected from participants' reflections on their own feeling states. Because these reports are self-reflecting inner accounts of

emotions, they require interpretation and categorization from the investigator. That being said, researchers strive to measure subjective states as objectively as possible so as to assess the experiential content of another person's mind with a high degree of insight and consistency. Investigations carried out in affective neuroscience use methods such as self-report, emotive language and expressions, descriptions of feelings and so on to collect accounts of emotional experience. We can record how participants feel during experimentation and compare accounts across experimental groups using standardized evaluations, correlate these findings with objective measures, and track fluctuations in emotional experience to monitor the inner emotional lives of our subjects.

Objective Measures

A wide variety of objective measures are used in the modern affective neuroscience laboratory. Most were not available or did not even exist a half-century ago. The increasing quality of the technology used to measure physiological reactions has essentially defined the field of affective neuroscience to date. During episodes of emotional arousal we can monitor – via muscle and gland fluctuations – peripheral-physiological reactions, including heart rate, respiration, electromyography (EMG) recordings during facial expressions, transient dilation of the pupils, electrodermal activity through the skin (see Chapter 3), or even temperature changes of body parts through thermography. We can also monitor neurological perturbations using electroencephalographic (EEG) rhythms and event-related potentials (ERPs), magneto-encephalography (MEG), functional magnetic resonance imaging (fMRI), and positron emission tomography (PET; see Chapters 4–5). Objective measures facilitate extraordinary examinations of emotional experience that could not be obtained through subjective measures alone. Even when subjective reports are thoroughly explored and divulged, the acting, feeling subject is not privy to a great deal of the underlying components comprising a particular emotional experience. Objective measures can be instrumental in gaining access to those components. Our lab has employed a number of objective measurement strategies to investigate the functional basis of emotional expression and experience.

Respiration

When our lab set out to investigate why specific facial expressions appear the way they do (Susskind et al., 2008), objective measures provided important insights that would not have been accessible via subjective report alone. In particular, there is not a great deal that individuals can subjectively report when asked why they contort their face the way they do during a disgust reaction. Whether they make this expression for social or other purposes, it is an automatic reaction about which we can only subjectively hypothesize. Or, like many of our students did in response to that very question, you might just contort your face to display confusion and shrug your shoulders. Although we produce facial expressions all the time, they are not shaped consciously. Even if there is a one-to-one mapping between subjective experience and expression, which is highly debatable, subjective reports do not provide meaningful information on the question of why expressions appear as they do.

Using respiratory measures, however, helped provide support for a theory originally proposed by Darwin. Darwin hypothesized that facial expressions evolved to regulate our perception before they served as nonverbal social communication signals (Darwin, 1872/1998). For example, although the facial expression of fear has been adapted as a social signal to alert other conspecifics of danger, the role of fearful facial expressions would have originally optimized sensory exposure to the environment. If this is the case, it is likely that different facial expressions originally served to modify sensory systems in order to control exposure to

environmental stimuli (Pieper, 1963). Using objective measures to investigate the production of emotional expressions can thus shed light on the evolutionary basis of our very complex social display system.

We chose to focus on fear and disgust expressions because a statistical model of expression appearance (Dailey, Cottrell, Padgett, & Adolphs, 2002; Susskind, Littlewort, Bartlett, Movellan, & Anderson, 2007) revealed that fear and disgust have opposite shape and surface reflectance features (see Figure 2.1). Because fear expressions are associated with increases in behavioral and neural markers of perception and attention (e.g., Anderson, Christoff, Panitz, De Rosa, & Gabrieli, 2003), it might be the case that sensory acquisition is augmented during fearful events. Disgust expressions (eye closing, brow lowering), being opposite in structural form to fear expressions (eyelid opening, raised eyebrows; Susskind et al., 2008) and associated with sensory rejection (Rozin & Fallon, 1987), may by contrast serve to diminish sensory exposure. To test this hypothesis, we monitored air intake while participants posed fear and disgust facial expressions. We measured changes in nasal inspiratory capacity, one of the most basic and primitive forms of sensory intake (Zelano & Sobel, 2005), to test objectively whether facial expressions alter the sensory interface by augmenting or diminishing sensory exposure.

Participants were directed to make facial expressions of fear and disgust while nasal respirometry, nasal temperature, and abdominal-thoracic respiratory measures were collected during a controlled instructed breathing cycle. We measured inspiratory volume by a flow meter attached to a facemask and placed a nasal thermistor under the right nostril to measure temperature. Two strain gauges attached around the chest and the abdomen measured respiration. Expression configuration had a significant effect on air intake, which increased linearly from disgust, to neutral, to fear. Despite an equal duration of inspiration, fear was associated with an increase in air velocity and volume relative to neutral

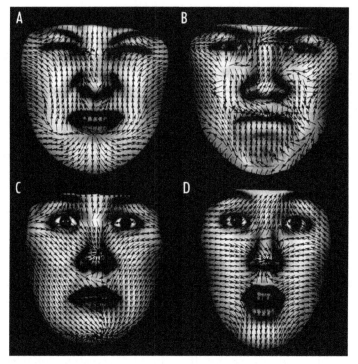

Figure 2.1. (A) Disgust, (B) anger, (C) fear, and (D) surprise facial expression prototypes. The facial action patterns depicted by the arrows represent vector flow fields of the skin surface contortions found from a mean group of each facial expression.

expressions. By contrast, disgust was associated with diminished air velocity and volume relative to neutral. In addition to respiratory measures, we also measured visual field size, finding an increase during fearful expressions and reduced size during disgust expressions, as indexed by detection of eccentric targets. Taken together, these findings provide evidence of a multimodal sensory augmentation during fear and a sensory reduction during disgust.

The overall augmentation found in inspiratory capacity and visual field size during expressions of fear compared to the diminished sensory capacity associated with disgust expressions suggests that emotional facial configurations do not only act as communication signals but also may have evolved to alter sensory intake, thereby serving an egocentric function regulating the receptors on the face. This link between form and function is not strongly supported using subjective measures because expe-

rience may not offer much insight into how such innate physiological aspects of emotional response and display originated. Indeed, fear and disgust are not opposites in the domain of subjective emotional experience. In contrast, the objective measures provide insight into why these specific facial expressions are constructed in particular configurations. After completing these experiments, our lab went on to explore how these adaptive expressions have been adopted into the complex human socioemotional world using objective measures to track facial muscle activity.

Facial Muscle Activity

This research lends support to the theory that facial expressions had evolved to regulate sensory intake (Darwin, 1872/1998; Susskind et al., 2008), but then these sensory gatekeepers were further adapted to serve as social signals as well; the emotional states behind these expressions may also participate in complex socioemotional interactions (Ekman 1973; Marsh, Ambady, & Kleck, 2005). Our lab set out to address the question of whether the complex social sense of morality is also based within the evolutionary context of basic oral disgust (see Chapman, Kim, Susskind, & Anderson, 2009). Oral disgust is a basic emotional response that is found in some of the most ancient organisms on the planet. For example, sea anemones will spit out toxic substances immediately after ingestion (Garcia & Hankins, 1975). More highly evolved animals such as rats have developed elaborate social mechanisms to prevent ingesting dangerous substances. If one rat is sick, other rats will pick up the scent of recently consumed foods and, by this social exchange, avoid that food in any future encounter (Galef, 1985). Does such an ancient and engrained response system influence our own complex sense of disgust in moral decision making? Is morality based in the evolutionarily ancient precursor of the disgust response? Immoral acts undoubtedly elicit strong negative emotions (Rozin, Lowery, Imada, & Haidt, 1999). Moreover, past research has found that, when negative emotions such as disgust are evoked, reactions to moral transgression are heightened (Schnall. Haidt, Clore, & Jordan, 2008). Yet does this effect occur because disgust is a precursor for responses to immoral acts, or is it just an effect of emotional arousal in general?

Neurological evidence associates insular activation with oral disgust (Phillips et al., 1997). Why not measure insular response patterns during oral disgust and then compare them with reactions to moral transgressions? Would a similar neurological pattern in these two experiences inform us about the relationship of these two phenomena? As much as these types of findings are of interest, they do not enlighten this particular discussion in a concrete manner. The insula has been associated with numerous cognitive and emotional responses, including interoceptive awareness and anxiety, anger, and uncertainty (e.g., Simmons, Matthews, Paulus, & Stein, 2008). At present, it is difficult to determine what specific emotional state activates the insular cortex in response to a moral transgression, or any emotion for that matter.

In an attempt to directly test the relationship between morality and disgust we used measures that, unlike insular activation, are more uniquely correlated with the disgust experience. Given our evidence for the sensory functional origins of facial expression appearance, we set out to find a precise facial muscle or set of muscles that would respond uniquely during the consumption of disgusting substances. We used electromyography (EMG) to assess the facial expression of participants while they drank unpleasant tasting (bitter, salty, sour) liquid (see Figure 2.2). EMG provides an excellent objective measure because it precisely measures the muscle activity via electrodes attached to the skin. We focused on measuring the activation of the levator labii muscle on the face, which is thought to be characteristic of the disgust expression (Ekman, Friesen, & Hager, 2002). This muscle raises the upper lip and is associated with nose wrinkling that, as we discussed earlier, might have evolved to help reduce further chemosensory exposure to toxic substances (Susskind et al., 2008).

We found that levator labii region activation was strongly correlated with responses to only the unpleasant tasting substances, not to pleasant liquids over similar intensity, and thus it appeared to index aversive gustatory experience. We went on to test levator labii activation while participants viewed emotionally arousing photos and found that the degree of disgust to disgusting pictures (related to contamination; for example, vomit, bathroom images), but not the degree of sadness to sad pictures, was associated with activation of the levator labii muscle. This objective measure proved to be a useful index to test basic oral disgust and then further to monitor responses to more complex reactions to photographs. As such, the levator labii response demonstrated both specificity for disgust and continuity across disgust triggers, from basic distaste to more complex contamination disgust.

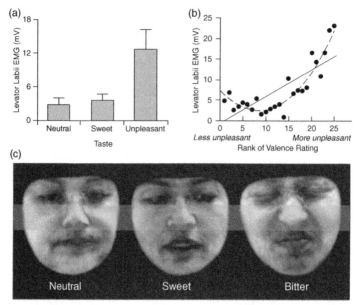

Figure 2.2. (A) Mean levator labii region EMG response evoked by ingestion of neutral, sweet, and bitter liquids. (B) Correlation between valence (positive vs. negative) ratings and levator labii region EMG response. Points on the plot show this average EMG response by rank; higher rank indicates greater unpleasantness. (C) The five most expressive individuals' facial expressions were averaged to prepare a model-generated expression during tasting neutral, sweet, and bitter solutions. The upper lip and nose areas are highlighted to show the action of the levator labii muscle (upper lip raise and nose wrinkle) across conditions.

Having demonstrated the reliability of the levator labii as an indicator of the disgust experience, we extended our research to test sociomoral transgressions. We used the ultimatum game, which requires participants to split a sum of money between themselves and the other player. The proposer decides how she would like to divide the money between herself and the responder. If the responder rejects an offer, then neither player gets any money. Players typically reject offers of less than 30%. One possible explanation is that we all have a strong sense of fairness (Rabin, 1993). It feels unfair to offer the other player no money, but our self-interest ensures that we keep a bit more than half. Likewise it seems unfair if we receive much less than half, and therefore some moral principle causes the responder to reject unfair offers even at his own expense (i.e., he receives nothing rather than the offered amount). Given that fairness is central to human morality (Sokol & Ham-

mond, 2010) we examined the facial motor activity associated with violations of fairness using this paradigm. We found that levator labii region EMG activity was elicited significantly by unfair offers. Specifically, there was a marked increase in self-reported disgust to unfair offers, which was paralleled by a parametric increase in levator labii region activity as offers became increasingly unfair. Furthermore, both the degree of experienced disgust and the corresponding levator labii activity predicted rejection of unfair offers, suggesting that our sense of morality and moral behavior has a basis in disgust.

However, other research examining expression recognition has proposed that there are three subtypes of the disgust facial expression: one in response to oral disgust, the second to nasal disgust, and the third to moral violations. The third is associated strongly with the upper lip curl produced by the levator labii, but this expression was also judged as signaling anger (Rozin,

Lowery, & Ebert, 1994). However, it is known that verbal reports often confuse anger and disgust (Nabi, 2002). Therefore it is important to note that, throughout our investigation we measured subjective reports of disgust in response to distaste, visual disgust, and moral transgressions using facial expression matching rather than verbal labels. At each level of our investigation the subjective measures confirmed that disgust was the emotion that participants associated with each experience, not anger. Moreover, the subjective reports were consistent with the objective data, such that higher ratings of disgust correlated with levator labii movement, whereas other emotional ratings did not. So why bother with the objective measures if subjective reports can confirm our findings so easily? In this particular case, self-reports may have been insufficient to make strong conclusions. Language can both limit and extend the meaning of a situation, and in the case of the word "disgust," it is not always clear whether this linguistic term incorporates other emotions, such as anger, into its meaning as well (Nabi, 2002). Thus, verbal self-report measures of subjective experience alone would not be diagnostic of "pure" disgust. Together participants revealed both objective and subjective signs of disgust that were associated with the degree of unfairness in the Ultimatum Game. From this, we proposed that our moral capacity is based in ancient evolutionary precursors related to disgust and distaste. The objective measures allowed us to draw a direct link between facial motor activity evoked by bad tastes to highly complex social and moral judgments.

Autonomic Activity

We used electrodermal activity (EDA) to assist in an investigation of the psychological and physiological underpinnings of the emotional enhancement of memory (EEM). Although humans are able to report that emotional events hold privileged positions in memory, whether it is a graduation, a surprise birthday party, a wedding, or a birth (e.g., Berntsen & Rubin, 2004), uncov-

ering the mechanisms responsible for such a memory boost has been more challenging. In this research, the question being asked was geared toward understanding the role of the amygdala in emotional memory enhancement. To begin our investigations, we relied on subjective reports of affect (arousal and valence) and memory to evaluate stimuli known to recruit amygdala activity. Although subjective measures only brought us so far in this investigation, by adding objective measures of EDA we were able to gain insight regarding the role of physiological activity in relation to subjective experience, autonomic activity, and amygdala activation.

Past neuroimaging research has shown that greater amygdala activation during emotional, relative to neutral, events is associated with enhanced episodic memory (e.g., Adolphs, Tranel, & Buchanan, 2005; Kensinger & Corkin 2004). In considering the role of the amygdala in EEM, we wanted to use stimuli known to reliably recruit the amygdala. We know that the identification of fearful faces is disrupted in patients with amygdala damage (e.g., Adolphs, Gosselin, et al. 2005), and because research has found fearful faces, compared to neutral, happy, angry, sad, or disgusted faces, to be especially linked to amygdala activation (Anderson et al., 2003), we used fearful faces to test the involvement of the amygdala in EEM. If amygdala activation is sufficient to enhance episodic memory, then EEM should be present for fearful faces relative to neutral faces because only fearful faces engage the amygdala. Moreover, because fear faces have been shown to induce even greater activation of the amygdala than negatively arousing scenes, we might predict even more pronounced memory for fearful faces.

However, we did not find that fearful faces were subject to reliable EEM across a variety of delays relative to aversive scenes (e.g., photographs of mutilated bodies, horrible car crashes, etc.), which were better remembered (Anderson, Wais, & Gabrieli, 2006). Relative to fearful faces, aversive scenes specifically enhanced the experience of remembering rather than familiarity, consistent with prior findings (Kensinger & Corkin, 2004). Because the heightened amygdala activation is strongly associated with fearful faces, we argued that amygdala activation was necessary but not sufficient for EEM. Although participants' subjective memory reports gave an indication that there is more than amygdala activity at play in EEM, to better understand the role of the amygdala we decided to assess objective measures of autonomic activity.

To further probe EEM, we then used EDA to test differences in peripheral sympathetic arousal while participants looked at fearful faces and at aversive scenes. Aversive scenes, but not fearful faces, resulted in a significant increase in autonomic arousal responses relative to neutral events (Anderson et al., 2006). The effect of emotion on EDA paralleled that of memory; remember that responses for negative scenes were significantly higher than for neutral scenes and fearful faces. This parallel dissociation in memory and sympathetic arousal is evidence that additional sympathetic activity is required in tandem with amygdala response to ensure robust EEM.

There are many potential differences between the aversive scenes and the fearful faces that may explain the selective memory enhancement, one being that, with amygdala activation, a certain level of adrenomedullary activation and associated central arousal might be needed to enhance memory. This finding is consistent with research that has proposed that peripheral and central stress hormones are required for EEM (e.g., Okuda, Roozendahl, & McGaugh, 2004), which fearful faces might not summon to the same degree. Our heightened memory for major emotional events in our lives would thus reflect a brain (amygdala)-body (systemic arousal) interaction. Using the objective measures of EDA allowed us to make inferences about this interaction that would not have been possible by observing amygdala activation alone.

And it appears that there is a unique interaction of amygdala and autonomic arousal during fear presentation. A study by Williams et al. (2005) measured skin conductance response (SCR) and blood-oxygen-level-dependent (BOLD) activity using fMRI while participants viewed faces expressing danger. SCR provides a measure of autonomic arousal. They found that there were distinct responses to fear, anger, and disgust. Fear was found to produce enhanced arousal with amygdala activity, whereas anger and disgust elicited anterior cingulate and insular activity, respectively. The corresponding arousal onset for anger was rapid with slow recovery, whereas disgust showed a delayed onset of SCR arousal. Fear was shown to uniquely draw autonomic arousal with amygdala activity. The pairing of the objective autonomic and neural measures in this study showed that each emotional experience produces a distinctive neural and visceral reaction in the body that may be the support of enhanced emotional memory.

Central Nervous System Measures

Technologies used in neuroimaging research inform theoretical debates by providing information that other physiological measures may not be sensitive enough to detect and that investigators are unable to decipher using subjective reports. An example of one such debate surrounded the nature of how arousal and valence operate. Although it was the consensus that emotional episodes do vary subjectively in arousal and valence (e.g., Cacioppo & Bernston, 1994), it remained a question of how these components interacted during emotional experiences. Although it has been suggested that valence and arousal influence experience separately (Russell, 1980), it is difficult to isolate physiological correlates to verify this assumption because subjective reports generally produce correlations between the two dimensions (Lang, Greenwald, Bradley, & Hamm, 1993). Valence and arousal generally function in parallel such that as a stimulus becomes increasingly negative it also becomes more subjectively intense and physiologically arousing. For example, when you hear a really unpleasant sound (i.e., negative valence), as the intensity (e.g., volume=arousal) increases, you are likely to rate the noise as more unpleasant.

To probe these dimensions, we needed to find a way to manipulate the phenomenal aspects of valence and arousal separately, and we aimed to verify the independence of these two components objectively. We used measures of olfaction to more cleanly isolate valence and arousal, and we were then able to assess their brain substrates (Anderson et al., 2003). Four stimuli were used to dissociate the valence and arousal dimensions: high- and low- concentration odorants of citral (pleasant) and valeric (unpleasant) acid were prepared. The intensity of these stimuli correlates with subjective arousal ratings (Bensafi et al., 2002) and can be dissociated from stimulus valence (Doty, 1975), which allowed us to avoid linguistic complications because participants were able to identify changes in these variables very definitively. We found that intensity of response correlated with amygdala response, while valence did not. The right medial orbitofrontal gyrus activity, a region highly associated with affective and olfactory processing (Rolls, 2001), correlated with valence but not intensity.

These findings support our theoretical understanding of emotional experience, confirming that arousal and valence are neurally dissociable dimensions comprising our affective perceptions, even though they are often correlated in subjective experience. These results direct our attention to areas of the brain that are uniquely involved in the intensity and hedonics of sensory experience. Importantly, these objective manipulations (i.e., molecular structure and molar concentration) of chemosensory compounds gave us insight into the dimensional basis for affective experience that one's own consciousness has difficulty interpreting. That is not to say, however, that subjective measures lack merit, but in specific instances objective measures provide information that subjective measures simply cannot.

Subjective Measures

Although the role of subjective measures in neuroscience research is essential, this was not always the general consensus. There was an extensive period in psychology's history when objective measures ruled the land. During the behaviorism movement, founded in the belief that all psychological processes are observable, psychology was more or less defined as an objectively based "hard" science. Research focused on using strict behavioral measures such as reaction times and response patterns to study mind. In present-day research we can effectively measure observable emotional reactions in numerous ways, and although we place importance on these objective measures, it is no longer the case that objective measures take precedence in affective research. The general consensus is that there is a great deal missing if the inner mental life of participants is not explored because subjective measures provide information that cannot be gleaned from objective measures alone.

Self-Report

A standard method used to monitor subjective experience during an experiment is self-report. More or less all subjective measures are of the self-report variety, presented in different formats or approached with different questions in mind. One way this can be done is with standardized indices that require participants to answer questions about themselves using a Likert-type rating scale (e.g., 1 = not at all aroused, 7 = extremely aroused). These rating scales provide only a rough indication of how a participant is feeling, but can be very useful because they supply an introspective account of the mental states of participants. For example, when conducting an fMRI study, rating scales provide subjective data without requiring the participant to talk in the scanner. Participants can respond to questions that appear on a screen by pressing corresponding buttons on a control box. Mood checklists are another form of self-report comprising a series of descriptors – happy, nervous, fearful, and so on – that subjects can use to indicate their feelings. These checklists can be used with different time frames in mind (e.g., present, over the last week, in general) to help assess moods, attitudes, and dispositions, respectively. Subjective experience can also be measured by asking open-ended questions that allow participants to answer in detail using their own words and descriptions through speech or writing. These open-ended questionnaires and interviews (e.g., the Structured Clinical Interview for DSM-IV; First, Gibbon, Hilsenroth, & Segal, 2004) require more time and interpretation on the part of the investigator, which renders them less available to objective scrutiny, but provide deeper insight to experience.

Questionnaires (e.g., the Positive Affect Negative Affect Schedule [Watson, Clark & Tellegen, 1988], Beck Depression Inventory [Beck, Steer, & Brown, 1996]) are useful tools because they have been meticulously developed to address specific situations or groups and are used to assess a wide range of affect-related states and traits. In conjunction with other objective neural measures they make for a powerful suite of tools to investigate affective functions. (For other issues related to anxiety questionnaires, see Chapter 24.)

For example, when investigating the influence of mindfulness meditation training on emotional experience in individuals with subsyndromal complaints of depression and anxiety, we assessed acute emotional states and neural reactivity during sadness provocation, as well as used the Beck Depression Inventory (BDI), the Beck Anxiety Inventory (BAI), and the Symptom Checklist 90 Revised (SCL-90-Revised) to evaluate individual traits of depressive affect, anxiety, and psychopathology, respectively (Farb el al., 2010). Analysis of these set of questionnaires confirmed that all participants showed moderate levels of depression and anxiety. The experimental group completed an 8-week mindfulness training course, whereas the control group was waitlisted for the course, and all partici-

pants then completed an fMRI scan. During the scan, sad and neutral video clips were shown and subjective measures were administered intermittently throughout. Participants rated their mood after watching each clip on a 5-point Likert-type scale (1 = not sad at all; 5 = extremely sad). This procedure provided us with an online index of each participant's mood and allowed us to track fluctuations of mood with corresponding neural changes in response to the film clips. Indeed sad film clips reliably induced a dysphoric mood when compared to neural clips. Correlation analyses of these questionnaires (BDI, BAI, and SCL-90-R) found that only BDI scores signaling depressive traits were reliably correlated with right insula activation. You can see in Figure 2.3 that higher BDI scores were associated with greater deactivations in these regions in response to sadness provocation (Farb et al., 2010). Although both the experimental group and the control group responded with similar reports of sad mood to the film clips, those who underwent mindfulness training demonstrated less neural reactivity to sadness provocation than the control group, in particular in cortical midline activations as well as less deactivations of right midinsular regions related to objective body states.

The self-report indices used in the scanner (i.e., sadness ratings) correlated with activation along the posterior and anterior regions of the cortical midline, as well as in left-lateralized language and conceptual processing centers (Farb et al., 2010). These neural patterns have been previously associated with increased self-focus, cognitive elaboration, and problem solving that would be typical of reappraisal processes, which support healthy assessment and self-reflection (Ray, Wilhelm, & Gross, 2008). The significant neural differences found after mindfulness training provide support that this practice might reduce rumination and cognitive reactivity, processes that are known to predict depressive relapse (Segal et al., 2006). The use of questionnaires and self-report in this study provided critical information

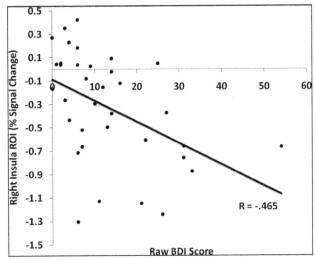

Figure 2.3. The percentage signal change in the right insula of controls and mindfulness participants correlate with Beck Depression Inventory (BDI) scores such that greater BDI-II scores predict greater reductions of right insula activity in the region of interest (ROI).

regarding the emotional state of participants before and after mindfulness training (see Table 2.1), and they allowed online tracking of emotional responses while the participants were in the scanner. As sadness ratings were held equal across groups, it was possible to attribute neural differences between the mindfulness group and the control group to changes in cognitive processes in response to sadness appraisals, because emotional reactivity was similar between groups. The subjective measures thus painted a more complex picture.

Table 2.1. Levels of Depression and Anxiety in Control and MT Patients

Variable	Age	(±SD)	Gender (M/F)	BDI-II	(±SD)	BAI	(±SD)	SCL-90R	(±SD)
Both groups at pretraining						.opt			
Control	42.00		4/12	20.56	(13.10)	.opt13.38	(8.49)	79.88	(50.41)
MT	45.55		5/15	23.35	(13.92)	.opt16.35	(12.66)	108.25	(66.52)
$t(34)$	0.94	Ns		0.62	ns	.opt 0.84	ns	1.45	ns
MT group training effects (pre- vs. post-MT)						.opt			
Posttraining				6.58	(5.67)	.opt 9.79	(9.82)	55.63	(50.13)
Difference score				-15.84	(11.04)	.opt-5.32	(6.64)	-47.00	(39.44)
$t(19)$				6.25	$p<.001$	.opt 3.49	$p<.003$	5.19	$p<.001$

Note. MT=mindfulness training.

Self-Report of One's Own Emotional Awareness

Another example of how subjective measures significantly inform investigations of affect is the role that subjective measures have played in the longstanding debate about the degree to which emotionally salient stimuli require awareness to be processed. At one point the prevailing notion was that they did not (for reviews see Tsuchiya, 2009). But this notion has been challenged by reexamining the measures typically used to gauge awareness of a stimulus. When more sensitive measures are used many participants are actually aware to some degree, for example, of fearful faces flashed at latencies previously thought to be outside of awareness (Pessoa, Japee, Sturman, & Ungerleider, 2006).

Until recently a stimulus was only considered consciously perceived when participants were able to assess their current mental state and report affirmatively on it. It was assumed that if there is any awareness, participants should be able to introspect and provide confirmation on whether or not they have become aware of a stimulus' presence. By this definition anything that does not permeate the introspective barrier, and is thus not reported, is not consciously perceived (Merikle, Smilek, & Eastwood, 2001). However, levels of consciousness are not so cleanly divided. At what point does one become aware of a stimulus in the environment or of percolating sensations from inside the body? Blindsight patients have no conscious experience of seeing and they do not engage with their environment naturally (Pegna, Khateb, Lazeyras, & Seghier, 2004). Yet we know from blindsight studies that these patients do in fact "see." They can correctly use information gained from vision (e.g., avoid walking into an object), although they will report that they do not see anything. There are also examples of when conscious experiences of our own bodies are not even true in reality. For example, in dummy hand experiments participants wear virtual reality goggles and stare at a dummy hand, while their real hand is hidden from view.

When the dummy hand and their own out-of-view hand are touched or moved, the participant experiences an illusion of ownership over the dummy hand (Slater, Spanlang, Sanchez-Vives, & Blanke, 2010). Emotional contagion also occurs unconsciously, causing humans to adopt emotional states from others without being aware of this exchange, like when one unconsciously mimics the facial expression of someone else in pain (Bavelas, Black, Lemery, & Mullett, 1986).

These conundrums highlight the wide variation in levels of processing that blurs the lines between aware and unaware (see also Chapter 14). The awareness of an organism can range from alert wakefulness, to drowsiness, sleep, dream-states, anesthetic awareness, and comatose states, all of which maintain some level of awareness. Measuring the critical point when awareness is turned on is a difficult challenge. Although we can use objective measures to gauge awareness by measuring correct behavioral responses and neurological patterns when stimuli are flashed on a screen, these measures have led neuroimaging researchers to conclude that emotional faces are unconsciously perceived because the amygdala is activated when participants do not respond behaviorally to the emotional faces presented (e.g., Liddell et al., 2005; Whalen, 1998). This research suggests that participants are unaware of backwardly masked emotional faces shown for 30 ms or less. This might be considered the threshold of visual awareness. Further research has suggested that this is not the case, however, because the objective measures used were not sensitive enough to tease apart the awareness level of participants (Pessoa, Japee, & Ungerleider, 2005; Pessoa et al., 2006).

In one study, participants were asked to first respond objectively whether or not a fearful face was present on the display screen (correct or incorrect behavioral response), and second, to subjectively rate the confidence of their answer (Pessoa et al., 2005). They found 7 of 11 participants detected fearful-face targets at 33 ms and 25 ms, and 2 participants were even able to detect 17-ms latencies based on confidence ratings. This use of confidence ratings arguably provides a subjective index of the participants' own assessment of their performance (Kolb & Braun, 1995). Participants indicated whether they were guessing or not. Response confidence and accuracy should provide an index of awareness such that higher confidence ratings should correlate with correct responses more often than with incorrect responses if participants have some awareness of the face (Pessoa et al., 2006). Using these measures together, a "hit" is recorded with a correct response and high confidence, and a "miss" when there is a correct response with low confidence. A "false alarm" refers to an incorrect trial with high confidence, and a "correct rejection" refers to an incorrect trial with low confidence (Pessoa et al., 2006). These can then be used to calculate the distribution of correct and incorrect responses to both fear faces and nontarget neutral faces.

One extremely innovative advantage provided by this use of subjective measure is that it provides a method we can use to assess the content of awareness as well as the experience of the response (Pessoa, 2008). At shorter durations (< 30 ms) participants are able to reliably detect fearful faces, and at longer presentation intervals (>30 ms) participants were able to produce accurate discriminations consistently. This division provides a more accurate understanding of awareness, outlining a zone when subjects are objectively aware but subjectively unaware (Kolb & Braun, 1995). They are likely able to make correct responses above chance, but not have confidence to indicate that they know the response was accurate. This could be referred to as the unaware perception zone (e.g., Pessoa et al., 2006), and it delineates a spectrum of awareness that is not based on an absolute threshold, dividing awareness from unawareness (Macmillan & Creelman, 2005). This dissociation increases our ability to understand different levels of emotional processing, providing a realistic index of perception that is not accessible via objective measures. Under these more rigorous testing conditions, it has been shown that amygdala activation to fear faces is associated with subjective awareness (Pessoa et al., 2006).

Complicating matters is research that suggests the amygdala plays some modulatory role in awareness itself (see also Chapter 14). For instance, we have shown that emotionally arousing events are associated with enhanced perceptual awareness (Anderson, 2005). That is, under conditions of reduced attention during dual target rapid serial visual presentation, there is a transient "attentional blink," lasting a few hundred milliseconds, during which incoming stimuli have difficulty reaching awareness. When emotionally arousing events are presented within the blink period, they tend to survive the blink (Anderson, 2005). Patients with bilateral and unilateral amygdala lesions have been shown to exhibit other impairments associated with amygdala damage, such as impaired fear conditioning and reduced EEM, but they did not demonstrate the arousal modulation of the attentional blink (Anderson & Phelps, 2001). That is, emotionally arousing stimuli did not survive the blink any more than did neutral ones. Further, it was shown when stimuli were made more perceptually salient, they also survived the blink more readily, and this finding was intact following amygdala damage, suggesting that the amygdala plays an important role in emotional salience. Rather than concluding that the amygdala does not depend on attention or awareness for the extraction of emotional/motivational salience, these results indicate that feedforward perceptual representations arrive at the amygdala which in turn influence awareness. Thus the amygdala is not just dependent on awareness but also modulates it. Therefore amygdala activation may be both a cause and a consequence of awareness.

Classification of Emotions

With subjective indices of emotion comes unavoidable categorization. The feeling state of an individual ultimately has to be pegged down with some description, and using words to describe such complex experiences is no simple matter. For the sake of scientific rigor, how do we best capture and define emotional states? There are theories for both basic and complex categories of emotion. Basic emotions are considered biologically determined, whereas complex emotions may be susceptible or related to cultural climates. Paul Ekman (1973) uncovered a set of universal facial expressions that correspond to the same emotional experience across cultures and used this set to establish a model for emotion classification. His model included six basic emotion states of anger, disgust, happiness, fear, surprise, and sadness. These facial expressions provide an objective index of the underlying experiences, but only as they pertain to those six emotional states. As you are well aware, we have many more emotional words to describe how we feel and many more feeling states then just those six, but they do not all come with their own facial signature. Some expressions too, may be adapted to other feelings because of cultural norms. Later in his career, Ekman extended the basic model to include complex emotional states that do not necessarily have corresponding facial expressions (Ekman, 1992). Whether complex emotions such as hatred, shame, anxiety, or jealousy are unique unto themselves, or whether they are combinations of the six basic categories is a discussion of much interest, and choosing the appropriate model to develop an experiment is paramount. To best capture the nature of a state many researchers opt not to use discrete categories, but rather adopt dimensional approaches using ratings of arousal (e.g., intensity) and valence (i.e., pleasant vs. unpleasant), for example (Russell, 1980). Robert Plutchik developed the three-dimensional model that combines basic and complex categories of emotion with dimensional theories of emotions. In his model eight basic emotions that are evolutionarily based and cause either approach or withdrawal can be influenced by different intensities to produce the complex and primarily human-based, emotions (Conte & Plutchik, 1981). For example, the basic approach experience of joy can become more or less intense to form ecstasy or serenity respec-

tively, whereas the withdrawal experience of fear can become more or less intense to form terror or shyness, respectively. How these semantic definitions map out to match objective neurological measures is a very complicated matter and one that we return to later in our discussion. Are these categories doing a sufficient job in isolating an experience that is a unique emotion, or are elements of the experience being lost in between categories?

To complicate the categorization of emotions further there are states and traits to consider as well; time is an interesting variable when thinking about emotional classification. Are you showing a momentary emotional state or a more prolonged mood, or are your feelings attributed to your disposition or personality? Should transient emotions be measured and regarded differently from lasting experiences like that of depression or love? Regardless of the nature of emotions being experienced, when it comes to subjective measurement of emotional states, it is imperative that these details are definitively considered and controlled for in experimentation. Carefully defining your region/emotion of interest and focusing on it while eliminating and controlling for other possible confounds will help with the murky waters of emotions and our corresponding terminology. Doing so can ultimately allow researchers to have meaningful conversations about investigations of the same topic. For example, as is the case for disgust research, disgust and anger can easily be intertwined or confused. This is evident when following Russell's two-dimensional model of affect (Russell, 1980) that focuses on arousal and valence. When assessed with these dimensions in mind, disgust and anger are very closely related and could meet the same criterion during analysis. As a result it is important to find unique markers of each in order to dissociate the two and to find ways to ensure that participants can indicate this distinction accurately. Some of these considerations reemerge in the following discussion of current limitations to measurement in the field.

Limitations to Measurement and Research Solutions

The human affective experience cannot be fully described by correlating electro-neurobiological signals with emotional experiences. In part this is because qualitative properties of experience exist for which we have no clearly defined biological markers, and also because of the complexity of the systems interacting during any given emotional event. The search for neural correlates of experience has been a widely debated issue in neuroscience (e.g., Chalmers, 2000). One line of theoretical neuroscience is rooted in reductive materialism. Here it is believed that brain states are equivalent to mental states and that all mental states have biological counterparts. If this is the case, our emotional experience of sadness, for example, will have a marker that is distinct from any other event (Crick & Koch, 1990). Other scientists are less interested in searching for correlates of emotion because they see the experience of mind as a dynamic process based in an interaction of brain, body, and environment well beyond the confines of neurological markers alone (Alter, 2005; Chalmers, 1995). In such a case, the neural reactions are still necessary for experience, but are not sufficient to describe it in its entirety.

Undoubtedly, neuroimaging techniques can reveal brain regions that are correlated with specific behaviors or cognitive processes, but these techniques may be limited because they cannot speak directly to the causal relations between discrete brain structures and their putative functions. This caveat is particularly significant in neuroimaging studies of affective functions. To begin with, a great deal of neuroimaging work relies on "reverse inference." We speculate about the involvement of an affective process (e.g., sadness) from the activity of a particular brain region (e.g., the amygdala). Although this has been very informative, it has limited validity because the relationship is only correlational (D'Esposito, Ballard, Aguiree, & Zarahn, 1998). Furthermore, affective functions are poorly defined,

and thus isolating different components of affective behavior and then relating them to the extensive constellation of observed brain activations are not often accomplished (Anderson, 2007).

For example, there has been an ongoing debate as to how emotional expressions are processed in the brain (i.e., how you would view the face of another), and the debate has been difficult to resolve because of conflicting neuro-correlational findings that lend support to each side. Neuropsychological evidence from patient studies initially led researchers to believe that expression processing is executed by a discrete, categorical analysis in which each emotional expression is uniquely processed by a specific brain region, with distinct physiological signatures and correlates. This is known as the basic prototype theory of emotion (Ekman, 1973). From this, emotional experience and expression have been characterized as a set of specific types, such as fear, anger, sadness, or happiness (Ekman, 1992). Neuropsychological and neuroimaging data provide evidence consistent with neurally localized representations of facial expressions. Damage to the amygdala differentially impairs fear recognition while leaving other distinct emotions, such as disgust recognition, largely intact. By contrast, damage to anterior insula differentially impairs disgust recognition while leaving fear recognition intact (Phillips et al., 1998). Convergent evidence from functional neuroimaging demonstrates that fear expressions maximally activate the amygdala, whereas disgust expressions maximally activate the anterior insula (Anderson et al., 2003; Phillips et al., 1998). Patient studies have implicated a basal ganglia-insula system in disgust recognition dysfunction in Parkinson's and Huntington's diseases (Suzuki, Hoshino, Shigemasu, & Kawamura, 2006). Anger recognition may involve the ventral striatum (Calder, Keane, Lawrence, & Manes, 2004), and deficits in anger recognition have been linked to Parkinson's disease (Lawrence, Goerendt, & Brooks, 2006). These data provide strong evidence consistent with the notion that facial expression recognition is supported by distinct expert systems that process specialized information and result in selective deficits when damaged (e.g., Downing, Jiang, Shuman, & Kanwisher, 2001).

However, on the other side of the debate, the dimensional circumplex model of affect posits that emotions are fuzzy categories clustered on axes such as valence, arousal, or dominance (e.g., Russell, 1980). In this case, isolated and specialized brain regions would not facilitate facial expression processing, but rather multiple neurophysiological systems integrate information to form an interpretation of the face and of emotional experience (Russell, 1980). These systems would participate when processing multiple facial expressions, instead of solely being dedicated to one type of expression recognition. There is behavioral evidence consistent with the dimensional circumplex representation theory, whereby certain emotion types are closer (e.g., anger and disgust) than others (sadness and happiness) in emotion space (e.g., Haxby et al., 2001). This evidence suggests that expression judgments tend to overlap, indicating that emotion categories are not entirely discrete and independent. In contrast with the dimensional circumplex theory, the basic prototype account does not address the similar relationships between the basic emotions, because it does not explain clustering between expression types (for review on this debate, see Lindquist et al., 2011; Vytal & Hamann, 2010).

Again, there is neural evidence that supports this theory as well. Consistent with the circumplex model, patients with selective impairments in facial expression recognition following amygdala damage maintain a largely intact capacity to judge similarity between expression classes (Hamann & Adolphs, 1999), which may result from the profile of activation across the remaining spared neural systems. These profiles, whether facial, auditory, or somato-visceral, may be integrated in a convergence zone, such as the right somatosensory cortices (Adolphs, Damasio, Tranels, Cooper, & Damasio, 2000). Con-

trary to the emotion-specific impairments of prototypes described earlier, studies have also shown that regions "specialized" for a specific facial expression also demonstrate reliable responses to other expressions. For instance, regions of the anterior insula responsive to disgust are also responsive to fear in faces (e.g., Anderson et al., 2003), and conversely, the amygdala can reveal robust responses to expressions of disgust (Anderson et al., 2003), anger (Wright, Martis, Shin, Fischer, & Rauch, 2002), and sadness (Blair, Morris, Frith, Perrett, & Dolan, 1999). Although a brain region may be maximally responsive to a specific emotion, these nonmaximal responses to other expressions may have important functional significance for expression recognition. The degree to which a particular individual perceives anger and disgust in the same expression, or detects similarity between sadness and fear, may reflect the combinatorial response across independent neural systems.

Thus recognition of facial expressions seems to have been characterized in two seemingly incompatible ways, and it is clear from these two viewpoints that the neural correlates of recognition behavior are very multifaceted. In an attempt to explore facial expression processing our lab used computational modeling to address this theoretical debate (Susskind et al., 2007). Progress in the field of machine learning offers an innovative opportunity to test the computational consequences of different representational theories and can lend support to researchers by providing deeper insight to help them untangle the relations among behavioral, neuropsychological, and neuroimaging data. Progress in computer facial expression analysis has just begun to contribute to an understanding of the information representations and brain mechanisms involved in facial emotion perception by integrating and closely comparing human recognition data with machine-based approaches (see also Chapter 7). To test the theories of expression recognition described earlier, our lab measured computer model judgments and compared these to human subject judgments of facial expressions to examine the extent to which recognition of emotional expressions directly reflects the statistical structure of facial images (Susskind et al., 2007, 2008).

Computer models were optimally trained to make distinct judgments of basic prototype facial images by analyzing the structure of expressions. After training, both human and model judgments had accurate discrimination, such that fear ratings were highest for fearful faces, and disgust ratings were highest for disgust expressions, and so forth. Because the computer model judgments were highly correlated with human judgments for these basic expressions, we then went on to test whether these distinct internal representations would support similarity judgments between the distinct prototypical expressions. We found that the computer model also performed comparably to human observers when making similarity judgments between distinct basic emotions such that anger and disgust were found to be more similar than anger and surprise, for example. That the computer models were trained to make expert judgments on basic emotions, and were then also able to make judgments of similarity in affective expression across different facial prototypes, demonstrates that no explicit understanding of dimensions (i.e., valence, arousal, or dominance) is required. For instance, the observation that individuals expressing disgust may portray feelings of anger but little happiness can be computed from the similarity of structural features. These findings suggest that, rather than being competing models, basic and dimensional aspects of expressions, as well as hypothetically emotional experience, can be gleaned from the same underlying representational systems.

In combination with neural and behavioral evidence, emergent similarity between humans and computers seen by using the computer model suggests that expression recognition in the brain may depend on detecting important component or structural features (e.g., eye opening in surprise and fear), and not basic emotion proto-

types or dimensions such as valence/arousal. Opposed to the basic prototype theory and the dimensional circumplex account, this can better be described as the component process model of emotion (Scherer, 1984, 2001), which emphasizes that expression configurations are composed of subunits, with appraisals being associated with specific physical features of the face (e.g., eye opening) that may be common across basic expressions (e.g., fear and surprise). This evidence suggests that underlying expression similarity can be achieved in humans by visual feature analysis such that facial displays of basic emotions are not entirely independent, but portray related states sharing components of an expression (Scherer, 1984).

This research approach provides crucial objective information to expand our understanding of correlating brain regions at work in the processing of emotional events. Using innovative methods such as computational modeling alongside neurophysiological correlative data can bolster our theoretical understanding of the brain's role in evaluating emotional events and generating emotional experience.

Limitations of Subjective Measures

Subjective reports can be gathered in numerous ways, and it is important to note that the administration of self-reports should be done carefully to increase the generalizability of results. But even when carefully administered, self-reports are susceptible to a number of confounds, including social desirability effects, response bias, distortions due to social stereotypes, or personal defense and avoidance (Eriksen, 1960; Holender, 1986). This susceptibility is particularly pronounced for emotion research because the questions asked can be very personal, sensitive, or uncomfortable. Although self-report indices receive criticism for these reasons, they are invaluable to affective research because they provide insight into personal experience and serve as control parameters to track individual differences. These measures can be correlated with objective measures to increase the predictive power of results and support relationships found between mental and neural activity.

Linguistic and Phenomenological Limitations of Subjective Measures

Although humans have the ability to self-reflect, raw emotional subjectivity is ineffable. We cannot fully describe the feeling of grief when a loved one dies, the joy that a parent experiences holding his or her newborn child, the hurt of a break-up or divorce, or the anger of abuse. When describing all of the details of an emotional experience there are limitations to how effectively we can communicate our abstract feelings when we are required to do so using concrete language. Even the most carefully designed self-reports used in scientific studies reduce emotional experience to finite terms. When self-reports are subjected to statistical analyses, the depth of the emotion being described is limited. A major concern with most self-report measures is the unavoidable reliance on language (Eriksen, 1960). In using semantically based tools, we are confronted with a convoluted and complex linguistic challenge because not only does language fail to directly communicate experience but also the questions asked and answers given can be interpreted in many ways by both the participant and the researcher. It is not always easy to express a feeling, and sometimes it is not even clear to the subjects how they themselves feel. Language has evolved to describe a vast array of specific feeling states, but it is worth considering whether some things cannot be said. "Any patch of sunlight in a wood will show you something about the sun which you could never get from reading books on astronomy" (C. S. Lewis, 1963, *Letters to Malcolm*, p. 91).

Emotional states are often described with terminology using discrete categories (e.g., arousal: sleepiness vs. wide awake, valence: pleasure vs. displeasure). Difficulty arises in using categorical labels of specific emotions (e.g., sad, happy, angry, and disgusted) because it is often the case that more than one label applies to an emotional state, or more than one emotional state can be described with the same label. To circumvent this issue, in our lab we typically do not ask participants to pick only one category to match the feeling they are experiencing. Instead participants are presented with seven canonical emotional facial expressions (disgust, fear, sadness, surprise, and happiness) and are asked to rate, using a Likert scale, how their own feelings matched each of the photographs (Chapman et al., 2009). This method helps tease apart the interrelated categorical system and provides participants with a much more versatile index.

In addition to linguistic challenges, it is also difficult to measure the experience of affect because there exist so many contributing factors to any given experience. For example, the most detailed description of how someone feels pain cannot ensure a comprehensive understanding of that experience of pain because it is influenced by one's own pain tolerance, past experience of pain, expectation, attention toward the infliction, and distress (Moseley, 2007). Even when two individuals share the exact same experience, how they perceive and respond to it will differ because of a vast number of differences in personality, history, emotional state, and the like, and these countless contributing influences make it impossible to know exactly how perceptions vary.

Although subjective experience is unique, the feelings we have are not like anything else we would quantitatively measure. It is not like anything else at all – except that is, the next person's subjective experience. It is at least similar to other subjective experiences. Humans make the assumption that others experience the world – have passions, motivations, thoughts, and reflections – in similar ways to their own. All humans share this thing that cannot be said, cannot be fully described, but can only be experienced. Humans have the ability to relate to the minds of others, to empathize another's experience (see Chapter 23). We can know to some degree how it feels to be in the shoes of another. This adds power to subjective measures. Empathy allows subjective reports to have deeper insight because, although the mind is not physically measurable at present, it is not forbidden territory because we can share experiences, histories, recollections, concerns and outlooks between minds. It is our hope that we can use our experiential findings in tandem with objective measures to verify intuitions we have regarding the emotional state of participants with fact.

In our own work, we have attempted to find some objective measures of subjective self-reports of emotional experience. Given the central role of the amygdala in human affective neuroscience, one of the most under-investigated questions is whether amygdala lesions are associated with altered emotional experience. Although there is ample evidence that amygdala activation is correlated with emotional experience, whether the amygdala is necessary for the subjective experience of emotions is unclear because amygdala recruitment may represent one of many information-processing functions correlated with emotional experience, such as memory modulation or motivational salience. Indeed, if emotional experience was substantially altered following amygdala damage, then any effects on information processing, such as the emotional modulation of memory and attention, could and likely would be secondary to this primary deficit. In our own examinations of this issue, we assessed emotional states and traits in individuals with bilateral and right or left amygdala damage, following unilateral temporal lobectomy (Anderson & Phelps, 2000). In our most detailed examinations, we assessed subjective experience through a daily "diary" in which individuals made reports on positive, negative, and arousing everyday experiences. Patients with amygdala damage had simi-lar intensity and frequency in their reports of daily emotional events as that of control participants.

One complicated possibility is that patients with amygdala damage are describing "as if" experiences, so that their self-report is inaccurate. They may be describing their experiences in a prototypical way that reflects how they ought to feel, instead of how they really feel, or they may lack the ability to gauge the intensity of their emotions the same way as controls might. We wanted our self-report measure to have indices that are not accessible to subjects' explicit knowledge of how emotions work, making it more difficult to "fake" a genuine emotional experience. To do so we examined the covariance structure of emotional experiences. Lay knowledge suggests that positive and negative valence load oppositely on a single dimension. We found, like others, that positive and negative experiences are independent dimensions (Watson, Clark, & Tellegen, 1988), and this underlying emotional covariance structure was present in patients with amygdala damage as well, suggesting intact emotional experiential structure. This covariance structure may represent an objective index of subjective emotional experience, which was found to be intact following amygdala lesions. In a separate study, we also assessed objectively the facial expressions of amygdala-lesioned patients who displayed internally felt emotions on their face through a relived emotions paradigm (Anderson & Phelps, 2000). Under those circumstances, these patients demonstrated robust and reliably decoded expressions of various emotions including fear, yet could not recognize that expression on another person's face. Although more data and studies on a variety of patients are clearly needed on this issue, these findings suggest that the amygdala may be important for some aspects of emotional awareness but not others. Getting to the bottom of such a question takes creative consideration as we strive to verify subjective measures and ensure their accuracy.

Bridging the Gap between Objective and Subjective Observations

Merging Measures: Neurophenomenology

Research investigations in affective neuroscience are often designed to minimize dependence on subjective reports by attempting to control participants' affective experiences using paradigms that reliably evoke emotional states of interest. However, this approach has limitations when we attempt to assess spontaneous emotional experience, and it can be too strict when measuring complex emotional experiences. There are times when subjective reports are less informative to the paradigm, and it is entirely appropriate to manipulate and measure emotional responses objectively; for example, when mapping out the receptive field properties of amygdala neurons using fearful faces as stimuli, it is not obvious from introspection that there is crucial importance in the eyes (Whalen et al., 2004) and thus subjective reports lack relative input. But when we start to look at high-level emotional experiences, such as trauma or depression, too great a focus on measuring experience objectively and the need to be completely formulaic in our assessments can prevent us from assessing real, deeply passionate experience. Subjective measures can assist in allowing us more flexibility in emotional paradigms of this sort (Lutz & Thompson, 2003).

An interesting challenge for affective neuroscience is to find new ways to integrate experiential measures with objective physiological measures. Recent research assessing mind wandering integrated both metrics using a neurophenomenological approach. Mind wandering is generally thought to consist of internally focused reflections on future endeavors and unresolved issues (Gusnard & Raichle, 2001). A series of neuroimaging studies have unveiled what is referred to as the default network, which appears to be activated when individuals let their thoughts wander away from the task at hand. The default network includes ventral ACC, posterior cingulate/precuneus,

and temporoparietal cortex regions (Mason, Van Horn, Wegner, Grafton, & Macrae, 2007). Although mind wandering is not strictly speaking an affective process, it most certainly can involve emotional thoughts. Rumination in depression is an obvious example of when mind wandering may be heavily riddled with affect. In addition, research by Eryilmaz and colleagues (2011) has found that emotional arousal does in fact affect the default network by increasing activity of the ventral ACC, insular cortex, and their coupling. After emotion induction by watching fearful, joyful, and neutral movies, participants showed subsequent changes in self-referential thoughts during rest.

But how does one measure mind wandering effectively? Christoff, Gordon, Smallwood, Smith, and Schooler (2009) used subjective measures in conjunction with fMRI to investigate the neurophenomenology of mind wandering and found that activation of the default network is more pronounced when participants are unaware that their thoughts were drifting away from a task they were completing while in the scanner. This awareness of one's own mental state is often referred to as meta-awareness (Schooler & Schreiber, 2004). As such, when participants did not have meta-awareness of the fact that they were mind wandering (i.e., they were not consciously aware that they were mind wandering), the default network was even more pronounced than when participants were consciously aware of their mind wandering. "Experience sampling," an online self-report regarding current mental states (Kahneman, Krueger, Schkade, Schwarz, & Stone 2004), was used to investigate the cognitions of participants throughout the task.

To measure experience sampling while in the scanner, participants performed a relatively simple go/no-go task by indicating when a target appeared on screen or not. The task chosen was previously found to correlate with a high degree of mind wandering (Smallwood, Baracaia, Lowe, & Obonsawin, 2003). While they were doing this task, experience sampling was administered intermittently by presenting the participants with thought probes (Antrobus, 1968). These thought probes asked participants to rate, on a 7-point Likert scale, whether or not they were on- or off-task and whether they were aware that they were on- or off-task. Participants were trained to do experience sampling before the experiment began, and awareness was defined as the experience of recognizing that their thoughts were drifting away from the task before they were asked (Schooler, Reichle, & Halpern, 2004). If they did not recognize that their thoughts were drifting until the thought probe inquired, then they could respond that they were unaware. Importantly, this self-report method provided a deep relationship between neural networks and experience because the subjective measures targeted mind wandering directly. The researchers correlated "off-task" and "on-task" moments with neural activity by analyzing the 10-second interval immediately preceding the probe. Behavioral measures were also analyzed by tracking the number of incorrect responses on the task, which was previously found to correlate with mind wandering (Cheyne, Carriere, & Smilek, 2006). As mind wandering increases, errors increase.

The use of experience sampling diverged from previous work in mind wandering because most prior neuroimaging studies indirectly equated mind wandering with resting periods between tasks. It was assumed that during task performance, participants were less likely to let their thoughts drift, and once the task had ended, the incidence of mind wandering would increase (Mason et al., 2007). However, by using experience sampling these researchers were able to index mind wandering more accurately while it occurred during an online task, and they could even assess when subjects had a meta-awareness that they were off-task or not. This innovative use of a subjective measure of meta-awareness, in combination with behavioral and neuroimaging data, allowed the researchers to identify activation of the executive network, which includes regions of lateral prefrontal cortex and dorsal ACC, not detected

in earlier studies, as well as the default network during reported periods of mind wandering. The researchers argued that designs that merge self-report and behavioral/neurological measures will play a critical role in advancing our understanding of the neurophenomenology of subjectivity because they provide a more direct link to experience during online measures of brain function (Christoff et al., 2009). Future research that investigates deeply experiential aspects of the human emotional life will benefit from employing a network of measures to provide a more in-depth understanding of the neurophenomenology of emotion.

Conclusion: Objective and Subjective Measures

A central challenge for theory and research in emotion continues to be the development of comprehensive methods that account for the array of activity among numerous systems and, ultimately, that integrate these recorded measures. Of course, it would be optimal to measure every aspect of emotion. Although emotional complexity currently defies exhaustive measurement, it is imperative that researchers not limit themselves by focusing on only one type of measurement, because objective and subjective measures offer unique insight and can be very powerful when used in parallel. At present, one cannot measure activity in brain structure (e.g., the amygdala), and diagnose a particular affective experience. Similarly, one cannot rely solely on reports of affective experience to characterize underlying neural configurations. The challenge before affective neuroscientists is to include and integrate multiple indices from both subjective and objective categories of measurement to best capture the mental and neural bases of emotional life.

Outstanding Questions

- Will evidence presented from fMRI data be able to tease apart different models of emotions, including whether basic emotions exist or whether they are supported by overlapping systems described best by dimensional accounts?

- Can fMRI reveal the constituent appraisal processes thought to underlie the generation of emotions?
- What possibilities do new technologies that record daily experiences offer future studies of real-world emotional experiences?
- Although much of the research we discussed in this chapter is based on group mean data, are there potentially more important individual differences in emotions that have not yet been explored? How do culture and genetics interact to make up an individual's emotional competence?
- In what new ways might we use computer modeling to explore emotion space, and how will these analyses modify psychological theories of emotion?

References

Adolphs, R., Damasio, H., Tranel, D., Cooper, G., & Damasio, A. R. (2000). A role for somatosensory cortices in the visual recognition of emotion as revealed by three-dimensional lesion mapping. *Journal of Neuroscience*, 20(7), 2683–90.

Adolphs, R., Gosselin, F., Buchanan, T. W., Tranel, D., Schyns, P., & Damasio, A. R. (2005). A mechanism for impaired fear recognition after amygdala damage. *Nature*, 433, 68–72.

Adolphs, R., Tranel, D., & Buchanan, T. W. (2005a). Amygdala damage impairs emotional memory for gist but not details of complex stimuli. *Nature Neuroscience*, 8, 512–18.

Alter, T. (2005). The knowledge argument against physicalism. In the *Internet Encyclopedia of Philosophy*. Retrieved from http://www.iep.utm.edu.

Anderson, A. K. (2005). Affective influences on the attentional dynamics supporting awareness. *Journal of Experimental Psychology: General*, 134(2), 258–81.

Anderson, A. K. (2007). Seeing and feeling emotion: The amygdala links emotional perception and experience. *Social, Cognitive, & Affective Neuroscience*, 2, 71–72.

Anderson, A. K., Christoff, K., Panitz, D., De Rosa, E., & Gabrieli, J. D. (2003). Neural correlates of the automatic processing of threat facial signals. *Journal of Neuroscience*, 23, 5627–33.

Anderson, A. K., & Phelps, E. A. (2000). Expression without recognition: Contributions of the human amygdala to emotional communication. *Psychological Science*, 11, 106–11.

Anderson, A. K., & Phelps, E. A. (2001). Lesions of the human amygdala impair enhanced perception of emotionally salient events. *Nature*, 411, 305–9.

Anderson, A. K., Wais, P. E., & Gabrieli, J. D. (2006). Emotion enhances remembrance of neutral events past. *Proceedings of the National Academy of Sciences*, 103, 1599–1604.

Antrobus, J. S. (1968). Information theory and stimulus-independent thought. *British Journal of Psychology*, 59, 423–30.

Bavelas, J. B., Black, A., Lemery, C. R., & Mullett, J. (1986). "I show how you feel": Motor mimicry as a communicative act. *Journal of Personality and Social Psychology*, 50 (2), 322–29.

Beck, A., Steer, R. A., & Brown, G. K. (1996). *Manual for the Beck Anxiety Inventory-ii*. San Antonio, TX: Psychological Corporation.

Bensafi, M., Rouby, C., Farget, V., Bertrand, B., Vigoroux, M., & Holley, A. (2002). Autonomic nervous system responses to odors: The role of pleasantness and arousal. *Chemical Senses*, 27, 703–9.

Berntsen, D., & Rubin, D.C. (2004). Cultural life scripts structure recall from autobiographical memory. *Memory and Cognition*, 32, 427–42.

Blair, R. J., Morris, J. S., Frith, C. D., Perrett, D. I., & Dolan, R. J. (1999). Dissociable neural responses to facial expressions of sadness and anger. *Brain: A Journal of Neurology*, 122(Pt. 5), 883–93.

Cacioppo, J. T., & Bernston, G. G. (1994). Relationships between attitudes and evaluative space: A critical review with emphasis on the separability of positive and negative substrates. *Psychological Bulletin*, 115, 401–23.

Calder, A. J., Keane, J., Lawrence, A. D., & Manes, F. (2004). Impaired recognition of anger following damage to the ventral striatum. *Brain*, 127(9), 1958–69.

Chalmers, D. J. (1995). Facing up to the problem of consciousness. *Journal of Consciousness Studies*, 2(3), 200–219.

Chalmers, D. J. (2000). What is a neural correlate of consciousness? In T. Metzinger (Ed.), *Neural correlates of consciousness: Empirical and conceptual questions* (pp. 17–40). Cambridge, MA: MIT Press.

Chapman, H. A., Kim, D. A., Susskind, J. M., & Anderson, A. K. (2009). In bad taste: Evidence for the oral origins of moral disgust. *Science*, 323(5918), 1222–26.

Cheyne, J. A., Carriere, J., & Smilek, D. (2006). Absent-mindedness: Lapses of conscious awareness and everyday cognitive failures. *Consciousness and Cognition: An International Journal*, 15(3), 578–92.

Christoff, K., Gordon, A. M., Smallwood, J., Smith, R., & Schooler, J. W. (2009). Experience sampling during fMRI reveals default network and executive system contributions to mind wandering. *Proceedings of the National Academy of Sciences*, 106(21), 8719–24.

Conte, H. R., & Plutchik, R. (1981). A circumplex model for interpersonal personality traits. *Journal of Personality and Social Psychology*, 40(4), 701–11.

Crick, F., & Koch, C. (1990). Towards a neurobiological theory of consciousness. *Seminars in Neuroscience*, 2, 263–75.

Dailey, M. N., Cottrell, G. W., Padgett, C., & Adolphs, R. (2002). EMPATH: A neural network that categorizes facial expressions. *Journal of Cognitive Neuroscience*, 14, 1158–73.

Darwin, C. (1998). *The expression of the emotions in man and animals*. New York: Oxford University Press. (Original work published 1872)

D'Esposito, M., Ballard, D., Aguirre, G. K., & Zarahn, E. (1998). Human prefrontal cortex is not specific for working memory: A functional MRI study. *Neuroimage*, 8, 274–82.

Doty, R.L. (1975). An examination of relationships between the pleasantness, intensity and concentration of 10 odorous stimuli. *Perception and Psychophysiology*, 17(5), 492–96.

Downing, P. E., Jiang, Y., Shuman, M., & Kanwisher, N. (2001). A cortical area selective for visual processing of the human body. *Science*, 293(5539), 2470–73.

Ekman, P. (1973). *Darwin and facial expression: A century of research in review*. New York: Academic Press.

Ekman, P. (1992). An argument for basic emotions. *Cognition and Emotion*, 756(3–4), 169–200.

Ekman, P., Friesen, W., & Hager, J. C. (2002). *Facial action coding system*. Salt Lake City: Research Nexus.

Eriksen, C. W. (1960). Discrimination and learning without awareness: A methodological survey and evaluation. *Psychological Review*, 67(5), 279–300.

Eryilmaz, H., Van De Ville, D., Schwartz, S., & Vuilleumier, P. (2011). Impact of transient emotions on functional connectivity during subsequent resting state: A wavelet correlation approach. *Neuroimage*, 54(3), 2481–91.

Farb, N. A., Anderson, A. K., Mayberg, H., Bean, J., McKeon D., & Segal, Z. V. (2010). Minding one's emotions: Mindfulness training alters the neural expression of sadness. *Emotion*, 10(1), 25–34.

First, M. B., Gibbon, M., Hilsenroth, M. J., & Segal, D. L. (2004). The Structured Clinical Interview for DSM-IV Axis I Disorders (SCID-I) and the Structured Clinical Interview for DSM-IV Axis II Disorders (SCID-II). In M. J. Hilsenroth, D. L. Segal, & M. Hersen (Eds.), *Comprehensive handbook of psychological assessment, Vol. 2: Personality assessment* (pp. 134–43). Hoboken, NJ: Wiley.

Galef, B. G. (1985). Direct and indirect behavioral pathways to the social transmission of food avoidance: Experimental assessments and clinical applications of conditioned food aversions. *Annals of the New York Academy of Sciences*, 443, 203–15.

Garcia, J., & Hankins, W.G. (1975). The evolution of bitter and the acquisition of toxiphobia. In D. A. Denton & J. P. Coghlan (Eds.), *Olfaction and taste V* (pp. 39–45). New York: Academic Press.

Gusnard, D. A., & Raichle, M. E. (2001). Searching for a baseline: Functional imaging and the resting human brain. *Nature Reviews Neuroscience*, 2, 685–94.

Hamann, S. B., & Adolphs, R. (1999). Normal recognition of emotional similarity between facial expressions following bilateral amygdala damage. *Neuropsychologia*, 37(10), 1135–41.

Haxby, J. V., Gobbini, M. I., Furey, M. L., Ishai, A., Schouten, J. L., & Pietrini, P. (2001). Distributed and overlapping representations of faces and objects in ventral temporal cortex. *Science*, 293(5539), 2425–30.

Holender, D. (1986). Semantic activation without conscious identification in dichotic listening, parafoveal vision, and visual masking: A survey and appraisal. *Behavioral and Brain Sciences*, 9(1), 1–66.

Kahneman D., Krueger A. B., Schkade D. A., Schwarz, N., & Stone, A. A. (2004). A survey method for characterizing daily life experience: The day reconstruction method. *Science*, 306, 1776–80.

Kensinger, E. A., & Corkin, S. (2004). Two routes to emotional memory: Distinct neural processes for valence and arousal. *Proceedings of the National Academy of Sciences*, 101, 3310–15.

Kolb, F. C., & Braun, J. (1995). Blindsight in normal observers. *Nature*, 377, 336–38.

Lang, P. J., Greenwald, M. K., Bradley, M. M., & Hamm, A. O. (1993). Looking at pictures: Affective, facial, visceral and behavioral reactions. *Psychophysiology*, 30, 261–73.

Lawrence, A. D., Goerendt, I. K., & Brooks, D. J. (2006). Impaired recognition of facial expressions of anger in Parkinson's disease patients acutely withdrawn from dopamine replacement therapy. *Neuropsychologia*, 45(1), 65–74.

Lewis, C. S. (1963). *Letters to Malcolm chiefly on prayer*. New York: Harcourt.

Liddell, B. J., Brown, K. J., Kemp, A. H., Barton, M. J., Das, P., Evian, A., Williams, G., & Williams, L. M. (2005). A direct brainstem–amygdala–cortical 'alarm' system for subliminal signals of fear. *Neuroimage*, 24(1), 235–43.

Lindquist, K. A., Wager, T. D., Kober, H., Bliss-Moreau, E., & Feldman Barrett, L. (2011). *The brain basis of emotion: A meta-analytic review*. Cambridge, MA: Harvard University Press.

Lutz, A., & Thompson, E. (2003). Neurophenomenology: Integrating subjective experience and brain dynamics in the neuroscience of consciousness. *Journal of Consciousness Studies*, 10, 31–52.

Macmillan, N. A., & Creelman, C. D. (2005). *Detection theory: A user's guide* (2nd ed.). Mahwah, NJ: Erlbaum.

Marsh, A. A., Ambady, N., & Kleck, R. E. (2005). The effects of fear and anger facial expressions on approach- and avoidance-related behaviors. *Emotion*, 5, 119–24.

Mason, M. F., Van Horn, J. D., Wegner, D. M., Grafton, S. T., & Macrae, C. N. (2007). Wandering minds: The default network and stimulus-independent thought. *Science*, 315, 393–95.

Merikle, P. M., Smilek, D., & Eastwood, J. D. (2001). Perception without awareness: Perspectives from cognitive psychology [Special issue]. *Cognition*, 79(1–2), 115–34.

Moseley, G. L., (2007). Reconceptualising pain according to its underlying biology. *Physical Therapy Review*, 12, 169–78.

Nabi, R. L. (2002). Cognition. *Emotion*, 16, 695.

Okuda, S., Roozendaal, B., & McGaugh, J. L. (2004). Glucocorticoid effects on object recognition memory require training-associated emotional arousal. *Proceedings of the National Academy of Sciences*, 101, 853–58.

Pegna, A. J., Khateb, A., Lazeyras, F., & Seghier, M. L. (2004). Discriminating emotional faces without primary visual cortices involves the right amygdala. *Nature Neuroscience*, 8, 24–25.

Pessoa, L. (2008). On the relationship between emotion and cognition. *Nature Reviews Neuroscience*, 9(2), 148–58.

Pessoa, L., Japee, S., Sturman, D., & Ungerleider, L. (2006). Target visibility and visual awareness modulate amygdala responses to fearful faces. *Cerebral Cortex*, 16(3), 366–75.

Pessoa, L., Japee, S., & Ungerleider, L. (2005). Visual awareness and the detection of fearful faces. *Emotion*, 5(2), 243–47.

Phillips, M. L., Young, A. W., Senior, C., Brammer, M., Andrews, C., Calder, A. J., . . . David, A. S. (1997). A specific neural substrate for perceiving facial expressions of disgust. *Nature*, 389(6650), 495–98.

Phillips, M. L., Young, A. W., Scott, S. K., Calder, A. J., Andrew, C., Giampietro, V., et al. (1998). Neural responses to facial and vocal expressions of fear and disgust. *Proceedings of the Royal Society of London. Series B: Biological Sciences*, 265(1408), 1809–17.

Pieper, A. (1963). *Cerebral function in infancy and childhood*. New York: Consultants Bureau.

Rabin, M. (1993). Incorporating fairness into game theory and economics. *American Economic Review*, 83(5), 1281–1302.

Ray, R. D., Wilhelm, F. H., & Gross, J. J. (2008). All in the mind's eye? Anger rumination and reappraisal. *Journal of Personality and Social Psychology*, 94, 133–45.

Rolls, E. T. (2001). The rules of formation of the olfactory representations found in the orbitofrontal cortex olfactory areas of primates. *Chemical Senses*, 26, 595–604.

Rozin, P., & Fallon, A. E. (1987). A perspective on disgust. *Psychological Review*, 94, 23–41.

Rozin, P., Lowery, L., & Ebert, R. (1994). Varieties of disgust faces and the structure of disgust. *Journal of Personality and Social Psychology*, 66, 870–81.

Rozin, P., Lowery, L., Imada, S., & Haidt, J. (1999). The CAD triad hypothesis: A mapping between three moral emotions (contempt, anger, disgust) and three moral codes (community, autonomy, divinity). *Journal of Personality and Social Psychology*, 76, 574.

Russell, J. A. (1980). A circumplex model of affect. *Journal of Personality and Social Psychology*, 39, 1161–78.

Scherer, K. R. (1984). On the nature and function of emotion: A component process approach. In K. R. Scherer & P. Ekman (Eds.), *Approaches to emotion* (pp. 293–317). Hillsdale, NJ: Erlbaum.

Scherer, K. R. (2001). Appraisal considered as a process of multi-level sequential checking. In K. R. Scherer, A. Schorr, & T. Johnstone (Eds.), *Appraisal processes in emotion: Theory, methods, research* (pp. 92–120). New York: Oxford University Press.

Schnall, S., Haidt, J., Clore, G. L., & Jordan, A. H. (2008). Disgust as embodied moral judgment. *Personality and Social Psychology Bulletin*, 34, 1096.

Schooler, J. W., Reichle, E. D., & Halpern, D. V. (2004). Zoning out while Reading: Evidence for Dissociations between Experience and Metaconsciousness. In D. T. Levine (Ed.,), *Thinking and seeing: Visual meta-cognition in adults and children.* (pp. 203–26). Cambridge, MA: MIT Press.

Schooler J.W., Schreiber C.A. (2004). Experience, meta-consciousness, and the paradox of introspection. *Journal of Conscious Studies*, 11, 17–39.

Segal, Z., Kennedy, S., Gemar, M., Hood, K., Pedersen, R., & Buis, T. (2006). Cognitive reactivity to sad mood provocation and the prediction of depressive relapse. *Archives of General Psychiatry*, 63, 749–55.

Simmons, A., Matthews, S. C., Paulus, M. P., & Stein, M. B. (2008). Intolerance of uncertainty correlates with insula activation during affective ambiguity. *Neuroscience Letters* 430, 92.

Slater, M., Spanlang, B., Sanchez-Vives, M. V., & Blanke, O. (2010). First person experience of body transfer in virtual reality. *PLoS ONE* 5(5): e10564.

Smallwood, J. M., Baracaia, S. F., Lowe, M., & Obonsawin, M. (2003). Task unrelated thought whilst encoding information. *Consciousness and Cognition*, 12, 452–84.

Sokol, B. W., & Hammond, S. I. (2010). A moral theory: What's missing? *Journal of Applied Developmental Psychology*, 31(2), 192–94.

Susskind, J., Lee, D., Cusi, A., Feinman, R., Grabski, W., & Anderson, A. K. (2008).

Expressing fear enhances sensory acquisition. *Nature Neuroscience*, 11(7), 843–50.

Susskind, J. M., Littlewort, G., Bartlett, M. S., Movellan, J., & Anderson, A. K. (2007). Human and computer recognition of facial expressions of emotion. *Neuropsychologia*, 45, 152–62.

Suzuki, A., Hoshino, T., Shigemasu, K., & Kawamura, M. (2006). Disgust specific impairment of facial expression recognition in Parkinson's disease. *Brain: A Journal of Neurology*, 129(Pt, 3), 707–17.

Tsuchiya, N., Moradi, F., Felsen, C., Yamazaki, M., & Adolphs, R. (2009). Intact rapid detection of fearful faces in the absence of the amygdala. *Nature Neuroscience.* 12(10), 1224–25.

Vytal, K., & Hamann, S. (2010). Neuroimaging support for discrete neural correlates of basic emotions: A voxel-based meta-analysis. *Journal of Cognitive Neuroscience*, 22(12), 2864–85.

Watson, D., Clark, L. A., & Tellegen, A. (1988). Development and validation of brief measures of positive and negative affect: The PANAS scale. *Journal of Personality and Social Psychology*, 54, 1063–70.

Whalen, P. J. (1998). Fear, vigilance, and ambiguity: Initial neuroimaging studies of the human amygdala. *Current Directions in Psychological Science*, 7(6), 177–88.

Whalen, P.J., Kagan, J., Cook, R. G., Davis, F. C., Kim, K., Polis, S., . . . Johnstone, T. (2004). Human amygdala responsivity to masked fearful eye whites. *Science*, 306(5704), 2061.

Williams, L. M., Das, P., Liddell, B., Olivieri, G., Peduto, A., Brammer, M. J., & Gordon, E. (2005). BOLD, sweat and fears: fMRI and skin conductance distinguish facial fear signals. *NeuroReport*, 16(1), 49–52.

Winkielman, P. W., & Schooler, J. W. (2009). In F. Strack & J. Förster (Eds.), *Social cognition: The basis of human interaction*. Philadelphia: Psychology Press.

Wright, C. I., Martis, B., Shin, L. M., Fischer, H., & Rauch, S. L. (2002). Enhanced amygdala responses to emotional versus neutral schematic facial expressions. *Neuroreport*, 13(6), 785–90.

Zelano, C., & Sobel, N. (2005). Humans as an animal model for systems-level organization of olfaction. *Neuron*, 48, 431–54.

CHAPTER 3

A Two-Way Road

Efferent and Afferent Pathways of Autonomic Activity in Emotion

Neil A. Harrison, Sylvia D. Kreibig, & Hugo D. Critchley

Definitions of Emotion

How to conceptualize and define emotion remains an active debate (Scherer, 2005) and is of considerable importance, because different concepts of emotion contribute to divergent interpretations of research findings (see, e.g., the natural kinds debate; (Feldman-Barrett, 2006; Izard, 2007). In the interaction of emotion and physiology, two important conceptualizations can be distinguished: efferent (outwardly conducting nervous impulses to an effector organ) and afferent (inwardly conducting impulses toward the central nervous system) effects of the autonomic nervous system (ANS) in emotion.

A prevalent view that emphasizes the role of efferent outflows of ANS activity conceptualizes emotion as a multicomponent response, elicited by appraising an event as relevant to personal goals, needs, or values, with coordinated effects on subjective feeling, physiology, and motor expression (Scherer, 2009; see also Chapter 1). This

definition emphasizes the multiple components that constitute an emotional response, including emotional feelings, physiological reactivity, and instrumental and expressive behavior, as well as the central orchestration of the response.

In contrast, emphasizing the role of afferent input from the ANS, Scherer (2004, p. 139) suggested that subjective emotional feelings reflect a "multimodal integration of synchronized changes in component processes." Thus, feelings are viewed as a central representation of the appraisal-driven changes occurring in emotion; this conception assumes a feedback mechanism from the various response components. Although the afferent and efferent definitions of emotional response are not mutually exclusive, the large majority of research on emotion has been based on the efferent conceptualization. The following sections draw on research findings in support of each conceptualization. However, we first consider the anatomy and central control of the ANS.

Anatomy and Central Control of the Autonomic Nervous System

The anatomical structure of the ANS and its central control constitute the basis for understanding autonomic effects of emotion.

Anatomy of the Autonomic Nervous System

To understand the functional complexity of the ANS and appreciate the basis of earlier misinterpretations of its functional architecture requires a brief overview of its conceptual origins. Langley (1900) coined the term *autonomic nervous system* to refer to the system of motor neurones and their axonal connections that carry signals from the central nervous system (CNS) to all innervated tissues and organs, except striated muscles. Langley also initiated the current division of the ANS into sympathetic, para- (meaning by the side of or alongside) sympathetic, and enteric components, a differentiation that importantly was based predominantly on *neuroanatomical*, not functional, considerations. Following this innovation, preganglionic cell bodies originating in the intermediate zone of the thoraco-lumbar spinal cord (and their axonal connections) were assigned to the sympathetic nervous system, whereas preganglionic cell bodies originating in the distal zones of the cranio-sacral spinal cord (including brainstem dorsal motor nucleus of the vagus, nucleus ambiguus, superior and inferior salivary nuclei, and Edinger-Westphal nuclei and their axonal connections) were assigned to the parasympathetic nervous system.

Sympathetic and parasympathetic nervous systems are also differentiated according to several other anatomical features. For example, sympathetic preganglionic axons are typically short and project through the spinal cord ventral roots to synapse with postganglionic neurons in either the para- or prevertebral ganglia or through the hypogastric nerves to the pelvic splanchnic ganglia. Parasympathetic preganglionic axons, by contrast, are typically long and project through the third (oculomotor), seventh (facial), and ninth (glossopharangeal) cranial nerves to synapse with postganglionic neurons in ganglia associated with the intraocular smooth muscles and glands of the head; via the tenth (vagus) nerve to ganglia associated with thoracic and abdominal organs; and through the pelvic splanchnic nerves to ganglia associated with pelvic organs.

These anatomical differences, however, should not be confused with differences in specificity of *function*. For example, despite being considerably longer than parasympathetic postganglionic neurons, sympathetic postganglionic neurons show a similar degree of specificity and do not branch in their projection course to target tissue (Pick, 1970). Instead, both sympathetic and parasympathetic neurons display tight target specificity, multiply branching only when close to their specific target cells (Pick, 1970). As shall be seen in the section, "The Autonomic Nervous System and Patterned Physiological Responses," although use of the terms "sympathetic" and "parasympathetic" nervous systems has utility on an anatomical basis, their use in a global sense to define sympathetic and parasympathetic *functions* has the potential to generate misunderstandings and create a false impression of the functional architecture of the ANS. It also demonstrates the fallacy of using individual convenience measures, such as skin conductance change, as unitary indices of overall sympathetic tone, which is discussed in more detail later.

Central Autonomic Network

Homoeostatic control and integration across these functionally discrete autonomic pathways are supported by a hierarchy of direct and indirect central synaptic connections, called the central autonomic network, which has been identified principally through the application of modern tract tracing techniques (Janig, 2006; Saper, 2002). Broadly, this network includes direct connections with autonomic premotor neurons within the ventromedial and ventrolateral medulla, ventrolateral pons, and lateral and paraventricular hypothalamus, and indirect connections with the periaqueductal gray (PAG), parabrachial, and Kolliker-Fuse nuclei in the brainstem, the central nucleus of the amygdala and anterior cingulate, insula, and medial prefrontal cortices. Sympathetic nuclei in the paraventricular hypothalamus interact with homeostatic (e.g., thermoregulatory) hypothalamic centers and in the dorsal pons they lie in close proximity to ascending neuromodulator pathways (dopamine, 5-HT, acetylcholine, and noradrenaline) implicated in cortical arousal and motivation. Interactions between medullary, pontine, and hypothalamic centers may also support the generation of distinct autonomic response patterns evoked differentially across physiological or behavioral challenges described in the section, "Functional Architecture of the Autonomic Nervous System"(Saper, 2002).

Noradrenergic projections to the thalamus and cortex of locus coeruleus (noradrenergic cell group A6 and A4) are further implicated in mediating central arousal and alertness, enhancing attention, and the sensory processing of emotionally valenced stimuli and other environmental challenges. The locus coeruleus and caudal noradrenergic cell groups in the lateral tegmentum influence efferent sympathetic drive via brainstem and descending spinal projections (Svensson, 1987). Similarly, within the brainstem efferent parasympathetic centers (nucleus ambiguus and dorsal motor nucleus of the vagus, Edinger-Westphal nucleus, and salivatory nucleus) interconnect with the solitary nucleus and area postrema, in which visceral afferent and blood-borne signals are relayed (Blessing, 1997). Descending influences from prefrontal and limbic cortices (cingulate, medial temporal, and insula) and the amygdala on autonomic control, mediated by hypothalamic and brainstem centers, have also been demonstrated (Asahina, Suzuki, Mori, Kanesaka, & Hattori, 2003; Kaada, 1951; Mangina & Beuzeron-Mangina, 1996).

Low-level autonomic challenges have been used to detail the proximate, typically brainstem, mechanisms engaged in autonomic regulation. However, description of the central autonomic network has necessitated an approach that encompasses psychological and behavioral interactions with the internal bodily state. One common approach has been to simultaneously perform functional brain imaging while recording changes in one or more autonomic parameters; for example, heart rate (Wager et al., 2009), blood pressure (Critchley, Corfield, Chandler, Mathias, & Dolan, 2000; Gianaros et al., 2005), or skin conductance response (Critchley, Elliott, Mathias, & Dolan, 2000) induced with a variety of different experimental paradigms (e.g., mental arithmetic or isometric exercise). Studies using this type of approach have suggested a key role of the mid/dorsal anterior cingulate in modulating peripheral sympathetic responses across a broad variety of contexts, with activity in this region appearing to reflect the integration of bodily state with behavioral engagement (volitional, attentional demanding, requiring awareness). Differences in the location of this midline cortical activity appear to reflect both the characteristics of the experimental task (cognitive, perceptual, motivational) and the different axes of measured autonomic response (Critchley, 2009).

This type of approach has also helped illustrate the different temporal profiles of individual components of the central autonomic control network. For example, using a skin conductance biofeedback paradigm, Nagai and colleagues trained participants to volitionally increase and decrease their sympathetic tone (Nagai, Critchley, Featherstone, Trimble, & Dolan, 2004). As described earlier, short-term phasic fluctuations in sympathetic activity (corresponding to sympathetic skin conductance responses, SCRs) were coupled to enhanced activity in dorsal anterior cingulate and insular cortices and in subcortical regions including the thalamus. However, longer term tonic drifts in skin conductance level (SCL) correlated negatively with a region of the ventromedial prefrontal cortex (vmPFC), extending to the subgenual cingulate. Interestingly, this region is part of the "default mode

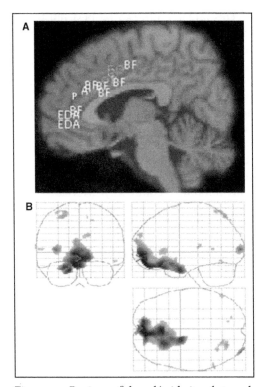

periphery, whereas the vmPFC and sub-genual cingulate inversely reflect sympathetic tone and may also reflect effects mediated parasympathetically. To date, however, functional imaging studies have been more variable than studies relating the ACC to autonomic control in showing the reactivity of brainstem centers supporting the proximate regulation of sympathetic response, though there is accumulating evidence highlighting the importance of dorsal pontine regions, including the PAG.

Efferent Effects of Autonomic Nervous System Activity in Emotion

Differentiated autonomic activity between types of emotion presupposes that the ANS is capable of producing a variety of responses. We thus first look at this prerequisite before considering the possible relations between emotion and physiological response and empirical findings of autonomic response in emotion. This efferent perspective reflects the causal direction of the influence of emotion on physiology.

The Autonomic Nervous System and Patterned Physiological Responses

Critical to the debate surrounding the existence of emotion-specific physiological patterning is the question of whether the ANS would, in principle, even be capable of producing specific patterned responses. Cannon (1931), in his influential five-point critique of the James-Lange theory (discussed in more detail in the section on visceral afferent neurons), mentioned as one objection that the ANS is simply too slow and too undifferentiated to produce the type of patterned physiological responses postulated to occur in the various emotions. Sixty years later, Levenson (1988) reconsidered this critique and came to the conclusion that, in fact, the ANS is capable of producing such differentiated responses. A wealth of empirical data (reviewed later) demonstrating the ability of the ANS to generate highly differentiated and specific responses across multiple

Figure 3.1. Regions of dorsal/mid-cingulate and vmPFC that predict task-evoked increases and decreases in sympathetically mediated autonomic activity. A: Regions of dorsal anterior/mid-cingulate that predict task-evoked increases in sympathetically mediated autonomic activity. BF=biofeedback experiment; EDA=electrodermal activity, P=pupillary response; colored letters=cardiovascular responses, BP=mean arterial blood pressure. B: Regions of vmPFC that predict decreases in tonic sympathetic (skin conductance) level during performance of a skin conductance biofeedback task.

network," which deactivates when people are engaged in arousing externally directed behavior suggesting a coupling with anti-sympathetic effects on bodily state (see Figure 3.1).

On the basis of these and other findings, Critchley has proposed a heuristic model suggesting a functional topography within the anterior cingulate cortex related to autonomic control (Critchley, Wiens, Rotshtein, Ohman, & Dolan, 2004). In this model, dorsal anterior/mid cingulate activity particularly reflects sympathetic effects in the functionally distinct channels have helped solidify Levenson's conclusion (Janig, 2006) and have led to a reconceptualization of the ANS as a system consisting of multiple functionally discrete pathways, rather than as a bipolar system operating in an undifferentiated all-or-nothing manner. Additionally, autonomic regulation of mechanical aspects of sensory organs, such as the eye and ear, assists attentional focusing on emotionally salient environmental stimuli, whereas regulation of immune responses to host infection or bodily injury (Tracey, 2002) implicates the ANS in the regulation of emotional and behavioral sickness responses (Harrison et al., 2009).

Functional Architecture of the Autonomic Nervous System

Empirical data from anatomical, neurophysiological (Janig, 2006), and neurochemical (Gibbins, 1995) studies in animals and humans have shown that pre- and postganglionic neurons of both the sympathetic and parasympathetic nervous system link together in *functionally distinct pathways* that exert precise actions on their selective target tissues. Collectively these data have helped undermine a number of previous false assumptions; for example, that (1) sympathetic preganglionic neurons diverge widely and synapse with postganglionic neurons with multiple diverse functions and (2) that adrenaline and noradrenaline released physiologically from the adrenal medulla act to uniformly enhance the effects of sympathetic postganglionic neurons. These data have helped dispel the belief that the sympathetic nervous system operates in a monolithic all-or-nothing fashion (Cannon, 1931) and have instead enabled its reconceptualization as a system composed of multiple discrete functional subunits, each of which displays a characteristic pattern of discharge that is dependent on the structure of central circuits and the synaptic connections of these circuits with different groups of afferent input. Taken together, this structure makes a large degree of functional specificity possible.

This architecture can be best illustrated by closer inspection of a few of these discrete functional subunits. For example, two distinct classes of sympathetic vasoconstrictor neurons have been identified. The first, sympathetic *muscle vasoconstrictor neurons*, are noradrenergic axons associated with small and large arteries, which play a critical role in modulating blood pressure in response to ongoing environmental demands. They are spontaneously active and under powerful inhibitory control by arterial baroreceptors, shown by their rhythmic inhibition with each heart beat (Wallin & Fagius, 1988). They are activated by nociceptors on the body surface and distention-sensitive receptors in the bladder and colon and are inhibited by low-threshold mechanoreceptive afferents from the skin. Their activity is also modulated by breathing, but is unaffected by activation of central thermoreceptors (Janig, Sundlof, & Wallin, 1983). *Cutaneous vasoconstrictor neurons*, by contrast, play a role in thermoregulation. They too are spontaneously active; however, unlike muscle vasoconstrictor neurons they show absent or only weak modulation by arterial baroreceptors (Blumberg, Janig, Rieckmann, & Szulczyk, 1980). Unlike muscle vasoconstrictor neurons, they are inhibited by stimulation of nociceptors and other bodily afferents (e.g., trigeminal nasal afferents), whereas stimulation of low-threshold skin mechanoreceptor afferents leads to their excitation (Blumberg et al., 1980). These neurons are not sensitive to breathing, but do show inhibition in response to warming of the spinal cord (Janig, 2006), consistent with their role in thermoregulation (see Figure 3.2).

In addition to these two distinct classes of sympathetic vasoconstrictor neurons, a number of other, functionally distinct sympathetic *non-vasoconstrictor* pathways have also been described. For example, two separate sympathetic pathways to the adrenal medulla have been identified, one mediating the release of adrenaline and the other the release of noradrenaline (Vollmer, 1996). These pathways again show specific functional fingerprints. For example, adrenergic

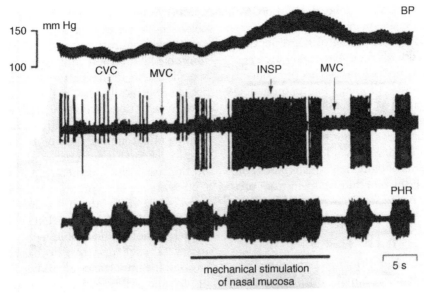

Figure 3.2. Different subclasses of autonomic neurons show distinct patterns of functional reflex activity. The figure shows changes in blood pressure and firing rate in three different types of sympathetic preganglionic neurons across time and in response to mechanical stimulation of the nasal mucosa (labeled at the bottom). The top row shows changes in diastolic and systolic blood pressure. The middle row shows activity in three neuronal types – cutaneous vasoconstrictor (CVC), inspiratory (INSP), and muscle vasoconstrictor (MVC) neurons – in an anaesthetized cat. Each neuron can be distinguished by its distinctive discharge shape. The bottom row shows activity in the phrenic nerve (active during inspiration). Before stimulation the CVC neuron is active in expiration but not inspiration, the MVC neuron is active in inspiration but not expiration, and the INSP neuron is almost silent. Noxious mechanical stimulation of the nasal mucosa can be seen to inhibit activity in the CVC neuron, activate the MVC neuron in inspiration as well as expiration (which continues even after nasal stimulation has ceased), and activate the INSP neuron only in inspiration. Note the increase in blood pressure (BP) correlated with the continuous muscle vasoconstrictor discharge. Reproduced with permission from W. Janig, *The integrative action of the autonomic nervous system*, Cambridge University Press, 2006.

pathways are strongly activated by hypoglycemia, whereas noradrenergic pathways are not (Morrison & Cao, 2000). Discrete functional ANS subunits have also been described in individual metabolic pathways; for example, lipolysis (Bartness, Shrestha, Vaughan, Schwartz, & Song, 2010; Morrison, 2001), liver gluconeogenesis (Shimazu & Fukuda, 1965), and insulin and glucagon release (Bloom & Edwards, 1975). Similarly with regard to the pelvic organs, at least three functionally distinct types of sympathetic non-vasoconstrictor motility-regulating neurons have been described (Janig, 2006). Type 1 neurons are excited during contraction/distension of the urinary bladder, but inhibited during colonic contraction/distension. Type 2 neurons, in contrast, are inhibited during contraction/distension of the urinary bladder, but excited by contraction/distension of the colon, whereas type 3 neurons are activated only by distension of the anal canal. None displays respiratory rhythmicity or baroreceptor responsivity, again suggesting both differential regulation of these discrete functional subunits by central circuits and the synaptic connections of these circuits with different groups of afferent input.

Complementing this neurophysiological evidence for discrete functional ANS subunits, histochemical investigations of sympathetic pre- and postganglionic neurons have shown that functionally distinct autonomic neurons (defined by their target tissue) may, on occasion, also be differentiated by the profile of neuropeptides co-localized with their classical neurotransmitter. This finding has led to the concept of neurochemical coding of autonomic neurons (Furness, Morris, Gibbins, & Costa, 1989). Together these multiple, functionally discrete pathways enable the ANS to support the differing allostatic and metabolic requirements of individual organs across the broad repertoire of human behavior, providing the hardware necessary for emotion-specific autonomic responding.

What Is the Relationship between Physiological Responses and Emotion?

Conceptually, the range of potential relationships between emotion and discrete physiological responses extends from a tight one-to-one mapping to a null-relationship (i.e., complete independence; Cacioppo & Tassinary, 1990). Although these extreme positions are now rarely endorsed, several contrary positions on the issue of emotion-specific physiological patterning are still currently presented in the literature (Kreibig, 2010). The diversity of these positions can perhaps best be appreciated through closer inspection of a few examples. First, on the basis of the great heterogeneity of emotion-specific physiological responses found in meta-analytical studies (Cacioppo, Berntson, & Larsen, 2000), Feldman-Barrett has argued that "it is not possible to confidently claim that there are kinds of emotion with unique and invariant autonomic signatures" (Feldman-Barrett, 2006: 41). Instead, she has proposed that patterns of physiological response follow more general dimensions of threat and challenge and positive versus negative affect. Further, she has argued that because ANS activity is mobilized in response to the metabolic demands associated with actual or expected behavior and because different behaviors have been shown to be neither emotion specific nor context invariant (Lang, Bradley, & Cuthbert, 1993), emotion-specific autonomic patterns are therefore improbable.

Conversely, Stemmler has argued that given the specific functions of individual emotions for human adaptation it would be improbable for there not to be emotion-specific activation patterns (Stemmler, 2004). Specifically, he has reasoned that because emotions are associated with distinct goals, they require a differentiated patterning of autonomic activity to enable distinct behavioral preparation and protection of the organism. Further, given that the CNS is organized to produce integrated patterns of response rather than single isolated changes (Hilton, 1975), it is likely that individual physiological variables will contribute to several such patterns; he has therefore stressed the importance of studying patterns of physiological response, rather than single isolated variables (Stemmler, 2004).

Results of meta-analyses of physiological responding in emotion, however, have suggested an intermediate position (Cacioppo et al., 2000). Although these studies have identified some reliable differences in the pattern of ANS responses to specific emotions, they have also revealed context-specific effects. In other words, patterns of ANS activity differ not only between emotions but also according to the particular emotion induction paradigm used. In one particularly influential review, Cacioppo et al. found that valence-specific patterning was more consistent than emotion-specific patterning. In particular, negative emotions were associated with greater autonomic responses than positive emotions. However, as has been recently noted (Kreibig, 2010), this meta-analysis had an unequal representation of positive (one) and negative (five) emotions, which likely significantly biased these findings. Supporting this critique, a recent comprehensive review of the literature on physiological responding in emotion, which did include multiple positive emotions (affection, amusement, contentment, happiness, joy, pleasure, pride, and surprise), also identified a greater degree of emotion-specific physiological patterning (Kreibig, 2010). This more recent finding is also consistent with those of several other review articles that typically acknowledge that discrete emotions may differ in *patterns* of autonomic responses evoked, even if not on *individual* variables (Mauss & Robinson, 2009).

Thus, current positions range from highly specific ANS patterning to distinct emotions, through intermediate degrees of patterning (in which emotion-specific patterning of responses is also sensitive to the method of emotion induction), to a dimensional organization of autonomic patterns. Common to each of these positions, however, is an acknowledgment that patterns of physiological response do show differences across either emotional categories or emotional dimensions. We now turn to reviewing the empirical evidence for patterned autonomic responses between distinct emotions.

Patterned Autonomic Responses to Distinct Emotions

In this section we review the literature relating to physiological responses to the five basic emotions of fear, anger, disgust, sadness, and happiness, based on a recent comprehensive review of the literature (Kreibig, 2010). Where possible, we have attempted to synthesize the literature and start each subsection with a summary of the characteristic patterns of autonomic responses associated with that distinct emotion. It should, however, be noted that many of the physiological responses reported here represent the modal findings across published studies. These responses are rarely unanimously reported in the literature. We also discuss conflicting findings that prevent identification of a modal response or that illuminate potential influences of induction conditions. For a discussion of response patterns for other emotions (e.g., anxiety, embarrassment, amusement, joy, pride, and relief) and a comprehensive listing of studies, see Kreibig (2010).

The measures reported in the literature are largely based on cardiovascular, respiratory, and skin conductance responses. However, where available, we have also integrated the smaller literature on physiological responses in other autonomic axes, such as

pupil dilation, core temperature, and gastric rhythmicity. Given the frequently significant context-specific effects on patterns of observed autonomic responses, we have also included a description of the induction paradigms used in each study discussed and their likely influence on the pattern of ANS responses observed. This section does not attempt to provide an exhaustive review of the literature but rather summarizes and highlights the most salient studies.

Fear

Studies of fear have used a number of different fear-induction paradigms, including presentation of threatening pictures or film clips, personalized recall, standardized imagery, and even real-life manipulations, such as threat of electric shock. Overall, studies on autonomic responses to fear have identified a broad pattern of sympathetic activation, including increased heart rate, myocardial contractility, vasoconstriction, and electrodermal activity (Kreibig, 2010). Of note, however, in contrast to responses to anger, the majority of studies investigating changes in peripheral resistance have demonstrated a fear-associated *reduction* in peripheral vascular resistance (Stemmler, Heldmann, Pauls, & Scherer, 2001). This broad increase in cardiac and electrodermal measures of sympathetic activation has also been shown to be accompanied by a decrease in vagal influences on the heart (Rainville, Bechara, Naqvi, & Damasio, 2006) and by an increase in respiratory activity associated with a decrease in blood carbon dioxide levels (Kreibig, Wilhelm, Roth, & Gross, 2007); in particular, the increase in respiratory rate is secondary to a reduction in expiration time (Etzel, Johnsen, Dickerson, Tranel, & Adolphs, 2006; Kreibig et al., 2007).

A large number of studies investigating physiological responses to fear (and indeed to other emotions) have recorded only one or two channels of physiological responses, typically effects on heart rate and skin conductance responses. Most studies have reported an increase in heart rate and/or electrodermal activity (measured as an increase in evoked skin conductance responses, nonspecific skin conductance responses, and skin conductance level), suggesting a more general activation response. However, studies that have simultaneously assessed combinations of multiple cardiovascular and/or cardiorespiratory parameters have yielded a more complete description of the pattern of fear-related physiological responses. These studies have reported an increase in vasoconstriction (measured as a decrease in finger temperature, finger pulse amplitude, and/or reduced pulse transit time) in conjunction with increases in heart rate. Associated increases in blood pressure (systolic, diastolic, and mean arterial pressure) have also been frequently reported (Kreibig et al., 2007). In contrast, studies measuring peripheral vascular resistance typically demonstrate a decrease in this measure (Stemmler et al., 2001).

Where measured, fear-associated increases in heart rate co-occur with increases in myocardial contractility (e.g., an increase in ejection speed, shortened pre-ejection period, and/or decreased left ventricular ejection time; Kreibig et al., 2007; Stemmler et al., 2001). These changes in cardiac contractility have also been associated with consequent changes in cardiac pump function; however, the effect of these changes on stroke volume and/or cardiac output is less clear. Increased sympathetic cardiac control is also indicated by increases in P-wave and decreases in T-wave amplitude (Stemmler et al., 2001).

Evidence of fear-associated vagal withdrawal has come from a number of studies showing a reduction in heart rate variability using a range of measures; for example, mean difference between successive RR intervals, root mean square of successive RR interval differences, and spectral respiratory sinus arrhythmia (Gilissen, Bakermans-Kranenburg, van Ijzendoorn, & van der Veer, 2008). Studies measuring both cardiovascular and respiratory measures have reported increases in both heart rate and respiratory activity to fear stimuli (Levenson, Heider, Ekman, & Friesen, 1992; Rainville et al., 2006), in particular, a reduction in

expiration time (Etzel et al., 2006; Kreibig et al., 2007). Supporting these findings, volumetric measures have shown an increase in minute ventilation (Kreibig et al., 2007), and gas exchange analyses have found a reduction in pCO_2 (Kreibig et al., 2007), both of which are consistent with an increase in ventilation rate. Increased variability of respiratory parameters, such as respiratory amplitude, inspiratory flow rate, and pCO_2 levels, has also been described (Rainville et al., 2006).

In animal behavioral studies the concept of a "predatory imminence continuum" is frequently used to investigate responses to threatening or fear-inducing stimuli. The imminence of fearful stimuli has been proposed to modulate consequent fight, flight, or freeze behaviors (Blanchard & Blanchard, 1990). It is interesting therefore to explore the context in which fear was elicited in those human studies that reported a fear-associated decrease rather than an increase in heart rate. In several of those studies, "real-life" fear-induction paradigms (e.g., a sudden and unexpected light outage) were used, whereas another study used a film clip eliciting fear of falling as the fear-eliciting stimulus (Fredrickson & Levenson, 1998; Stemmler & Fahrenberg, 1989). It is therefore possible that participants in these studies were further along the fear imminence continuum, and their responses were characterized more by an immobilization than an active coping response associated with sympathetic inhibition. The importance of considering threat imminence in studying fear responses is further supported by a recent human neuroimaging study that investigated the neural structures sensitive to threat imminence in humans (Mobbs et al., 2007). This study demonstrated a shift from the vmPFC to PAG activity that may mediate the activation of inhibitory circuits on sympathetic outflow with increasing threat imminence.

Anger

Studies investigating the pattern of physiological responses to anger have used a wide variety of emotion-elicitation paradigms, including real-life induction of anger through harassment or a stressful interview, pictures, film clips, directed facial action, and personalized recall. It should, however, be noted that, unlike for many of the other emotions, such as fear or happiness, use of pictures or film clips as emotional-induction stimuli may be associated with either a mirroring anger response or, alternately, a reciprocating fear response. The implications for this response on the interpretation of patterns of physiological activity to anger are discussed later.

Anger elicited in the context of harassment or personalized recall is associated with a general increase in sympathetic activity, a reduction in parasympathetic cardiac influences, and an increase in respiratory rate. The observed sympathetic activation includes both α- and β-adrenergically mediated cardiovascular effects (e.g., an increase in heart rate, systolic and diastolic blood pressure, and, unlike fear, total peripheral resistance) and cholinergically mediated effects at the eccrine sweat glands (measured as an increase in specific and nonspecific skin conductance responses and skin conductance level). Anger induced in this context is also typically associated with an increase in cardiac output (Prkachin, Mills, Zwaal, & Husted, 2001), although reported effects on stroke volume are more variable. Similar broad sympathetically mediated cardiovascular effects (but without changes on peripheral resistance) have been reported in personalized recall of anger (Sinha, Lovallo, & Parsons, 1992) and, without the associated increase in heart rate, in anger induced during a stressful interview (Adsett, Schottstaedt, & Wolf, 1962).

Additional measures, such as a shortening of the pre-ejection period, reduced left ventricular ejection time, and lower T-wave amplitude, further characterize this anger-associated response as both an α- and β-adrenergically mediated response (Kreibig, 2010). Findings of a reduction in finger temperature, pulse amplitude, and pulse transit time point to vasoconstrictive effects in the periphery, whereas findings of an increase in

forehead temperature suggest an associated increase in facial circulation (Stemmler et al., 2001). In this regard, it is interesting to note that increases in facial blood flow and temperature have also been noted with the elicitation of anger and other negative emotions in rhesus monkeys (Nakayama, Goto, Kuraoka, & Nakamura, 2005). Based on heart rate variability measures, the majority of studies have reported an anger-associated inhibition of cardiac parasympathetic activity (Christie & Friedman, 2004). With regard to respiration, the majority of studies indicate an increase in respiratory activity, particularly an increase in respiratory rate (Ax, 1953; Levenson et al., 1992; Rainville et al., 2006).

As discussed in the introduction to this section, responses to pictures of angry facial expressions differ from those induced through the use of harassing material. Specifically, physiological responses to angry facial expressions include heart rate decreases instead of increases, skin conductance level decreases instead of increases, and heart rate variability increases instead of decreases (Dimberg & Thunberg, 2007; Jonsson & Sonnby-Borgstrom, 2003). This pattern of physiological responses is suggestive of a fear, rather than an anger, response and is likely the result of the inherently threatening anger expressions inducing reciprocal fear, rather than mirroring anger. Thus, it seems that effects of anger expressions are less contagious than, for example, those of fear and happiness, but rather elicit a reciprocal response.

A number of differences in physiological patterning have also been reported in relation to motivational direction in anger. For example, approach-oriented anger has been characterized by unchanged heart rate; withdrawal-oriented anger by a reduction in heart rate (Stemmler, Aue, & Wacker, 2007); and anger directed toward the self by an increase in heart rate, stroke volume, and cardiac output; unchanged systolic and diastolic blood pressure; and decreased total peripheral resistance (Adsett et al., 1962). Together, these findings suggest that motivational direction may influence the heart rate and α-adrenergic responses in anger and that various subtypes of anger may exist, which are differentiated by motivational direction.

Disgust

Influenced by the pioneering work of Paul Rozin on the variety of different forms of disgust (Rozin, Lowery, & Ebert, 1994), most studies of autonomic responding to disgust have used stimuli that elicit either core/contamination–related/ingestive or extended/body-boundary-violation forms of disgust. Examples of core disgust- inducing stimuli include pictures or videos of unpalatable food, maggots on food, foul smells, facial expressions of expelling food, and pictures of dirty toilets or cockroaches. Body-boundary-violation disgust-inducing stimuli, by contrast, include images of injections, mutilation scenes, bloody injuries and surgical videos. These broad classes of disgust-inducing stimuli have also been associated with characteristic facial expressions. For example, whereas core disgust is characterized by nose wrinkle, mouth gape, and tongue protrusion, body-boundary-violation disgust is instead associated with upper lip retraction (Rozin et al., 1994). The following discussion differentiates physiological responses associated with each of these discrete disgust forms.

Broadly, autonomic responses to core disgust-inducing stimuli are characterized by increases in both sympathetic and parasympathetic indices. Core disgust is associated with either increased or unchanged heart rate, increased heart rate variability, and decreased stroke volume (Kreibig, 2010; Prkachin, Williams-Avery, Zwaal, & Mills, 1999). Total peripheral resistance is also raised. Effects on breathing include an increase in respiration rate secondary to a reduction in inspiration time and in respiratory volume (e.g., decreased tidal and minute volumes; Kreibig, 2010). This finding is noteworthy because it is at variance with the marked increase in inspiration time typically seen before vomiting. Of note, unchanged or sometimes decreased skin conductance responses have been reported to static pictures of core disgust and no change in nonspecific skin conductance responses to core disgust-related film clips (Kreibig, 2010).

In contrast, autonomic responses to body-boundary-violation disgust-inducing stimuli are characterized by reduced sympathetic cardiac activation (reduced heart rate), increased electrodermal activity, faster breathing (and reduced tidal volume), and unchanged stroke volume and total peripheral resistance (Rohrmann & Hopp, 2008). Increased T-wave amplitude has also been described. Several studies have additionally described an unusual temporal pattern of heart rate responses, including one that showed a triphasic heart rate response with early and late decelerations separated by a brief acceleration period (Winton, Clark, & Edelmann, 1995). Together, these findings suggest decreased cardiac and increased electrodermal sympathetic activity together with unchanged or decreased cardiac vagal activity (Harrison, Gray, Gianaros, & Critchley, 2010). Increased skin conductance response for body-boundary-violation versus core/contamination disgust has also been reported (Bradley, Codispoti, Cuthbert, & Lang, 2001).

Interestingly, the reduction in cardiac output seen across disgust forms distinguishes it from the other negative emotions, which are typically associated with an increase in cardiac output. Furthermore, core disgust, unlike the other negative emotions, is associated with an increase in heart rate variability. Reports of disgust-associated changes in other cardiovascular measures (e.g., systolic, diastolic, and mean blood pressure; pre-ejection period; left ventricular ejection time; and pulse transit time), however, appear more variable, with no discernible pattern emerging (Kreibig, 2010).

Across emotion-induction paradigms (e.g., picture viewing, film clips, directed facial action, and personalized recall), and regardless of disgust form, increased electrodermal activity (increased skin conductance response and nonspecific skin conductance responses) is consistently reported (Lang et al., 1993). However, there is some suggestion that the character of these electrodermal changes may vary according to the induction paradigm used. For example, disgusting odors may be associated with longer duration skin conductance responses than observation of facial expressions of disgust (Kreibig, 2010).

Given the lay association between feelings of disgust and gastrointestinal responses, it is surprising that few studies to date have investigated changes in gastric contractility or electrical activity associated with elicitors of disgust. In the few studies that have done so (using electrogastrographic recordings), core disgust appears to be related either to a decrease in normogastric (normal frequency of stomach electrical activity of three cycles per minute; Jokerst, Levine, Stern, & Koch, 1997; Stern, Jokerst, Levine, & Koch, 2001) or an increase in tachygastric responses (an increase in the rate of stomach electrical activity in the stomach to more than four cycles per minute; Harrison et al., 2010). In the one study comparing gastric responses to both core and body-boundary-violation disgust, tachygastric responses appeared to be greater to core than to body-boundary-violation disgust (Harrison et al., 2010). Relevant to this field are a small number of studies that have suggested an association between tachygastric responses in the stomach and feelings of nausea associated with motion sickness (Levine, 2005), suggesting a potential association between mechanisms underlying the experience of nausea and core disgust. A recent study has also shown an increase in salivary inflammatory cytokines in response to visual disgust stimuli (Stevenson, Hodgson, Oaten, Barouei, & Case, 2011).

Sadness

Broadly, autonomic responses to sadness demonstrate a heterogeneous pattern of sympathetic and parasympathetic coactivation. This pattern may be further defined by subclassifying the sadness induced into crying or noncrying forms (Kreibig, 2010). Those few studies that have considered crying status in this way show uncoupled sympathetic activation in crying-associated sadness and sympathetic and parasympathetic withdrawal associated with noncrying sadness (Gross, Frederickson, & Levenson, 1994). Interestingly, those studies in which the presence or absence of crying has not been reported also suggest the existence of two broad patterns of sadness-associated physiological activity (Kreibig, 2010). The first, an activating response, partially overlaps with physiological responses to crying-associated sadness and is characterized by an increase in sympathetic cardiovascular control and unchanged respiratory activity. The second, a deactivating response, partially overlaps with physiological responses to noncrying sadness and is characterized by sympathetic withdrawal. A further characteristic of deactivating/noncrying sadness compared to all other negative emotions is a decrease in electrodermal activity (Christie & Friedman, 2004; Gross & Levenson, 1997).

Physiological responses to crying-associated sadness include a ubiquitously reported increase in heart rate (Gross et al., 1994) and in skin conductance level and/or nonspecific skin conductance responses (Gross et al., 1994). Increased vasoconstriction (reduction in finger pulse amplitude and temperature) and respiratory rate have also been reported (Gross et al., 1994). Similarly, activating sadness elicited by film clips, personalized recall, or directed facial action is typically associated with an increase in heart rate, skin conductance level, and measures of vasoconstriction and respiratory rate (Ekman, Levenson, & Friesen, 1983). Studies using personalized recall to induce sadness have also reported an increase in systolic and diastolic blood pressure and total peripheral resistance (Prkachin et al., 1999). Cardiac output, stroke volume, and finger temperature (a measure of vasoconstriction) are reported to decrease or remain unchanged (Prkachin et al., 1999) with no discernible pattern of effects on heart rate variability. Effects on respiration include an increase in respiration period and respiration period variability (Rainville et al., 2006).

In contrast, noncrying sadness has been associated with a reduction in heart rate, reduced electrodermal activity (measured as a reduction in skin conductance level and smaller nonspecific skin reaction responses), reduced heart rate variability, and an increase in respiratory rate (Gross et al., 1994; Rottenberg, Wilhelm, Gross, & Gotlib, 2003). Interestingly, the majority of studies using film clips, music, or standardized imagery to induce sadness report a deactivating sadness response. Film-clip-induced sadness is characterized by a reduction in cardiac activation and decreased electrodermal activity; in particular, a reduction in heart rate, increased or unchanged heart rate variability, decreased or unchanged diastolic and mean arterial blood pressure, and reduction in measures of vasoconstriction (Kreibig, 2010). Some also report a reduction in respiratory activity, indicated by a reduction in respiratory rate and consequent increase in pCO_2 (Kreibig et al., 2007). Similarly, reports of sadness induced by music or standardized imagery find a reduction in heart rate and respiratory rate (Etzel et al., 2006).

In addition to these studies reporting patterns of cardiovascular and electrodermal responses to the observation or experience of sadness, a recent study has also identified the role of a visual physiological response, pupil size, in the perception of facial expressions of sadness. In this study, Harrison and colleagues suggested that, in the context of expressions of sadness, smaller observed pupils are interpreted as signaling a greater intensity of experienced sadness (Harrison, Singer, Rotshtein, Dolan, & Critchley, 2006; Harrison, Wilson, & Critchley, 2007). Pupillary constriction can be indicative of increased parasympathetic and/or decreased sympathetic influences. This study implied that a reduction in pupil size may contribute to the pattern of physiological responses associated with sadness. This position has recently been strengthened by a single report of a woman who despite having a light-unresponsive pupil (due to Holmes Adie syndrome) showed a marked reduction in pupil size during crying-associated sadness (del Valle & Garcia Ruiz, 2009).

To summarize, the published literature suggests two broad patterns of sadness-associated physiological responses – an activating and a deactivating response – that substantially overlap with the patterns of physiological responses observed for crying and noncrying sadness. It is therefore interesting to consider the contexts of sadness induction that result in either an activating or a deactivating sadness response. In her recent review of this literature, Kreibig (2010) noted a potential dissociation on the basis of the imminence of the sadness-associated loss. For example, the activating pattern typically occurs in response to film clips that depict scenes related to impending loss (e.g., a man talking to his dying sister). In contrast, the deactivating pattern typically occurs in response to clips that depict scenes related to a loss that has already occurred (e.g., a young boy crying over his father's death). It is possible that anticipatory sadness as opposed to the sadness experienced after a loss or during grieving, together with the crying status, may play a role in differentiating physiological responses in sadness (Kreibig, 2010).

Happiness

Happiness has been induced with a wide variety of emotion-elicitation paradigms, including directed facial action, personalized recall, standardized imagery, film clips, music, and pictures. The pattern of physiological response in happiness can be characterized by an increase in cardiac activity secondary to vagal withdrawal, vasodilation, and increased electrodermal and respiratory activity. This pattern suggests a differentiated sympathetic response characterized by a decrease in α- and β-adrenergic and increase in cholinergically mediated effects. Similar to many of the negative emotions, happiness is associated with cardiac activation secondary to vagal withdrawal. However, in contrast to many of the negative emotions, it is associated with peripheral vasodilation.

More specifically, cardiovascular responses reported in happiness typically include an increase in heart rate and decreased or unchanged heart rate variability. Studies recording blood pressure responses also typically indicate an increase in systolic, diastolic, and/or mean arterial pressure (Prkachin et al., 1999). Vasodilation – inferred from an increase in finger temperature, increased finger pulse amplitude, and finger and ear pulse transit time – has also been described in a number of studies (Levenson et al., 1992; Stemmler & Fahrenberg, 1989). Increased electrodermal activity (skin conductance level and nonspecific skin conductance response rate) is also sometimes seen, though not uniformly reported. Increased respiratory activity is evidenced by an increase in respiratory rate associated with a reduction in both inspiratory and expiratory time and in postexpiratory pause time (Kreibig, 2010).

Whereas we consider here only one positive emotion, it appears important to carefully define and distinguish among positive emotions (e.g., amusement, contentment, joy, pride, relief) when studying and characterizing physiological responses (Kreibig, Gendolla, & Scherer, 2010). It has also been recently suggested that happiness may not be the only positive "basic emotion" and that pride may also be universally expressed and recognized (Tracy & Robins, 2004).

Summary of Findings

Table 3.1 summarizes these modal changes in physiological responses in the heart, lungs, stomach, skin, peripheral blood vessels, pupil, and immune systems across these five primary emotions. This table shows that use of a single or a limited number of physiological measures will often fail to reveal emotion-specific patterns of physiological responses, which are identified only when a broader set of measures are recorded. It also illustrates the importance of the context in which individual emotions are elicited for the patterns of associated physiological responses (e.g., elicitors of core or body-boundary-violation disgust and activating or deactivating sadness).

Afferent Effects of Autonomic Nervous System Activity in Emotion

Taking the alternative causal direction of the influence of physiology on emotion, specifically the experiential aspect of emotional feelings, let us now consider the anatomy and physiology of visceral afferent neurons and their potential role in the generation of feelings.

Visceral Afferent Neurons

Both physiological outflow, as discussed earlier, and physiological inflow have been proposed to play a role in emotion. Although the physiological feedback hypothesis of emotional feelings has received less attention than physiological (efferent) effects of emotion, the underlying physiological architecture warrants discussion. In addition to the tissue-specific efferent control of the internal organs via the ANS, the brain also receives continuous afferent feedback from the viscera through pathways using neuronal, hormonal, chemical, and physical mediators (Janig, 2006). This continuous afferent feedback provides information about the state of homeostatic parameters, such as levels of blood oxygen, bicarbonate, and glucose, as well as the size of fat stores. It signals the filling state of the internal organs, systemic arterial blood pressure, activity of endocrine glands, and the state of the immune system. This section focuses on neural feedback mechanisms, although hormonal, chemical, and physical feedback mechanisms may also operate through interactions with central components of this neural pathway. For example, effects of circulating feeding-related peptides, such as glucagon-like peptide 1 and pancreatic polypeptide, on gastric motility, acid secretion, or feelings of satiety are likely to be mediated via direct actions on the area postrema (Travagli & Rogers, 2001). This brain region has a weak blood-brain barrier that is neurally connected both to the vagal afferent nucleus (nucleus tractus solitarius) and the vagal efferent dorsal motor nucleus (Rogers, McTigue, & Hermann, 1995).

Visceral organs in the thoracic, abdominal, and pelvic cavities are innervated by vagal and spinal visceral afferent neurons that convey physical and chemical events in the visceral organs to the brainstem and spinal cord (Janig, 2006). These afferent feedback signals connect to all levels of the

Table 3.1. Summary of Physiological Responses Associated with Each Emotion

Organ	Fear	Anger	Disgust	Sadness	Happiness
Heart	↑HR ↑contractility ↓HRV ↑blood pressure	↑HR ↑contractility ↓HRV ↑ boold pressure	c↑b↓HR c↓stroke volume cb↓cardiac output c↑b↔HRV ↑ blood pressure	a↑d↓HR a↓stroke volume a↑cardiac output a↓d↑HRV a↑d↓ blood pressure	↑HR ↓HRV ↑blood pressure
Lungs	↑respiratory rate ↓CO$_2$ ↓expiration time	↑respiratory rate	cb↑respiratory rate c↑expiration time c↓inspiration time	ad↑respiratory rate d↑CO$_2$	↑respiratory rate ↓ expiration time ↓inspiration time
Stomach			↑ tachygastria ↓normogastria		
Sweat glands	↑EDA	↑EDA	↑EDR	a↑d↓EDA	↑EDA
Peripheral blood vessels	↓finger temp ↓pulse transit time ↓total periph resistance	↓ finger temp ↓pulse transit time ↑total periph resistance	c↑b↔total periph resist	d↓ finger temp d↑ pulse transit time a↑ total peripheral resist	↑ finger temp ↑pulse transit time
Pupil				↓pupil size	
Immune System			↑TNF saliva ↓ IgA saliva		

Notes: HR – heart rate, HRV – high-frequency components of heart rate variability (an index of parasympathetic influences on the heart), EDA – electrodermal activity, TNF – tumor necrosis factor. Disgust: c – core disgust, b – body-boundary-violation disgust. Sadness: a – activated sadness, d – deactivated sadness.

autonomic motor hierarchy, including cortical centers such as the insula, that are believed to be responsible for conscious sensations (Craig, Chen, Bandy, & Reiman, 2000) and to regions regulating behavioral states (Swanson, 2000). Afferents traveling in the vagus nerve represent about 80–85% of all vagus nerve fibers and are subdivided into several functional types. With a few exceptions, they are not involved in visceral pain, but they are involved in other visceral sensations, such as hunger, satiety, thirst, nausea, and respiratory sensations (Morley, Levine, Kneip, & Grace, 1982). Subgroups of vagal afferents are activated by inflammatory processes and by pro-inflammatory cytokines, such as tumor necrosis factor (TNF-alpha) and interleukin 1beta (IL-1beta; Goehler

et al., 1997). Their activation generates "sickness behaviors" (Bluthe et al., 1994; Harrison et al., 2009) – the collection of cognitive, emotional, behavioral, and motivational change associated with infection or inflammation.

Vagal afferents project viscerotopically to the medullary nucleus tractus solitarius (NTS). Sensations generated by the activation of vagal afferents are represented in the middle part of the dorsal insula (Craig & Blomqvist, 2002). In primates, the sensations elicited by vagal afferent neurons are mediated by a viscerotopically organized pathway, projecting from the NTS either directly or indirectly via the external medial nucleus of the parabrachial nucleus to the basal part of the ventromedial nucleus (VMb) of the thalamus and from there to the dorsal insula (Craig, 2002). Taste is represented rostrally with the gastrointestinal tract, and respiratory and cardiovascular systems are represented more caudally.

In addition to vagal afferent fibers, the viscera are also innervated by spinal visceral afferent neurons. Spinal afferent fibers project to lamina I, lamina V, and deeper lamina of the spinal gray matter (Craig & Blomqvist, 2002) and are involved in visceral pain and nonpainful visceral sensations. Sensations associated with spinal visceral afferent neurons (e.g., thermal sensations and pain) probably originate in neurons ascending in lamina I, which is composed of functionally distinct neural channels that are activated by afferent neurons innervating skin, deep somatic tissues, and viscera. In primates, lamina I neurons project directly to the posterior part of the ventromedial nucleus of the thalamus (VMpo). The VMpo, which is caudal to VMb, projects topographically to the dorsal insula and caudally to the projection field of the VMb (Craig, 2002).

The dorsal insula is the primary sensory cortex of interoception and represents sensations related to the states of the tissues of the body, including the visceral organs (Craig et al., 2000). It has been proposed that re-representation and integration of the physiological state of all bodily tissues with other contextual information within the anterior insula provide a substrate for conscious awareness of changes in one's internal physiological state (interoception) and emotional feelings (Craig, 2002; Critchley et al., 2004; see Figure 3.3). These structures might provide a physiological basis for proposed autonomic feedback mechanisms that could support a role of autonomic sensations in emotion generation and the mental representation of emotional feelings.

Role of Peripheral-Physiological Responses in Emotional Feelings

Do we run from a bear because we are afraid or are we afraid because we run? William

James posed this question more than a century ago (what is an emotion) (James, 1894), yet the notion that afferent visceral signals are essential for the unique experiences of distinct emotions has remained a key unresolved question at the heart of affective neuroscience (Cacioppo et al., 2000; Rainville et al., 2006). Cannon then later Hess' early challenges to the James-Lange position, that emotional feelings result from central representations of changes in body physiology, argued that autonomic outflow was both too slow and also too poorly differentiated to enable emotion-specific response patterns (Cannon, 1931).

Each of these criticisms to the James-Lange theory has received focused attention in the intervening years. For example, Damasio (1999) has argued for the existence of an "as if loop," conceptually similar to notions of efference copy in motor theory. It would allow for a real-time central representation of centrally generated physiological motor commands and further provide a temporally sensitive system to detect peripherally generated changes in physiological activity. Similarly, with regard to differentiation of autonomic activity, the demonstration that both the sympathetic (Morrison, 2001) and the parasympathetic (Porges, 2007) nervous systems possess exquisite organ-specific regulation has powerfully countered this argument and contributed to a revival of somatic theories (Damasio, 1994).

As detailed in the section, "Patterned Autonomic Responses to Distinct Emotions," emotion-specific patterns of peripheral autonomic activity have been reported to many of the basic emotions. Similarly, emotion-specific patterns of neural activity have also been demonstrated in association with discrete feeling states (Damasio et al., 2000). Recently, using a combination of fMRI and simultaneous recording of cardiac and gastric activity during the experience of core and body-boundary-violation disgust, two of the authors addressed the question of whether central neural representations of emotion-specific peripheral-physiological patterning also contribute to reported subjective feeling states (Harrison et al.,

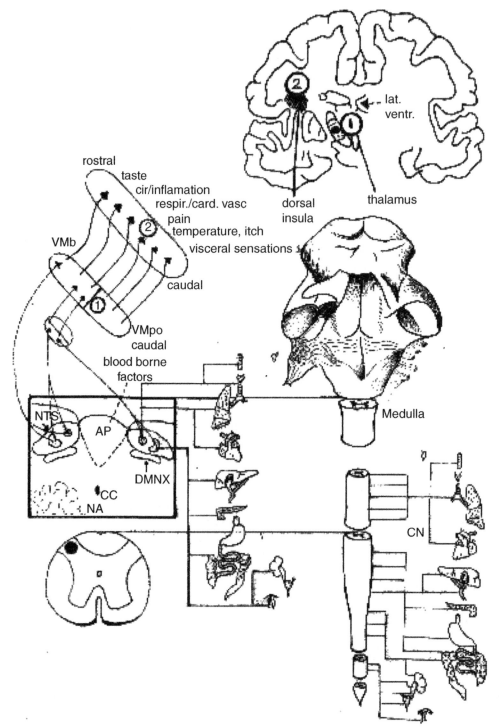

Figure 3.3. Schematic representation of visceral afferent pathways. Spinal visceral afferents project to lamina I of the spinal cord and afferents traveling with the facial, glossopharangeal, and vagus nerves project to the nucleus tractus solitarius (NTS). Blood-borne mediators (e.g., ghrelin, angiotensin) act via the adjacent area postrema (AP). The transverse section at the level of the medullary obex demonstrates the close anatomical relationship and connectivity of the afferent NTS and AP and efferent vagus dorsal motor nucleus (DMNX) and nucleus ambiguus (NA). Visceral afferent fibers from lamina I and NTS then project viscerotopically either directly or via the external medial nucleus of the parabrachial nucleus to the basal and posterior parts, respectively, of the thalamic ventromedial nucleus (VMb VMpo). Fibers then project to the dorsal posterior/mid-insula while maintaining their viscerotopic organization. *Courtesy:* We are grateful to Dr. Sarah Garfinkel for producing this figure.

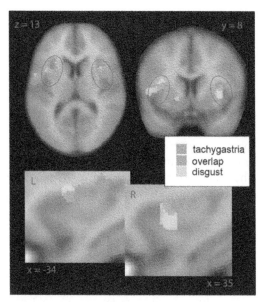

Figure 3.4. Co-localization of insula activations to subjective feelings of disgust and associated increase in tachygastric responses. The figure shows brain regions activated to the experience of disgust (both core and body-boundary-violation) in yellow and the associated tachygastric response in blue. Commonly activated regions illustrated in green show that insula regions underpinning subjective feelings of disgust also provide a representation of peripheral gastric responses. Activations illustrated at $p < 0.005$. Reproduced with permission from Harrison et al., *Journal of Neuroscience* (2010), 30(38):12878–84. See color plate 3.4.

2010). In this study, we showed that experience of core or body-boundary-violation disgust was associated with differential cardiac and gastric responses. Further, central representation of these changes in peripheral-physiology in the anterior insula co-localized with insula regions that correlated with the experience of core or body-boundary-violation disgust (see Figure 3.4). Together, these findings demonstrated that mid/anterior insula regions provide both a representation of emotion-related peripheral-physiological change and the associated subjective emotional experience, suggesting a potential neural substrate through which changes in peripheral physiology may contribute to emotional feeling states.

Practical Implications, Future Challenges, and Outstanding Questions

In this final section, we consider practical implications of these research findings for studying the physiology of emotion responses. In particular, we address issues regarding the number of physiological channels to measure and the psychological and physiological measurement context.

How Many Channels of Physiological Activity Should Be Measured?

The preceding sections have demonstrated the broad range of functionally distinct channels that together make up the ANS and regulate all aspects of human visceral functioning. The functional specificity of many of these channels and their independent regulation by central neural control mechanisms have been demonstrated by microneurography studies of individual sympathetic or parasympathetic fibers (as illustrated in Figure 3.1). To date, however, even the most sophisticated studies investigating physiological responses to distinct emotions (Stemmler et al., 2001) have measured only a dozen or so peripheral indices of autonomic activity, suggesting a massive subsampling of all of the available channels. Most published studies have also focused predominantly on changes within the cardiovascular, respiratory, and electrodermal systems. However, it is unlikely that emotion-specific patterning of physiological responses is restricted to these organs. Indeed, where measured, physiological responses in other organs – in pupils to sadness (Harrison et al., 2007), the stomach to disgust (Harrison et al., 2010; Jokerst et al., 1997), and even the peripheral immune system (which has both visceral afferent and autonomic efferent innervation) to happiness (Matsunaga et al., 2008) and disgust (Stevenson et al., 2011) – have been observed.

Furthermore, *direct* sampling of multiple individual functional subunits using microneurography is not feasible in most psychophysiological studies. Instead, indirect measures, such as frequency domain analyses of cardiac interbeat intervals, are used in their place. Although many of these indices (e.g., heart rate) have the advantage of being relatively easy to measure, their value in discriminating activity within individual functional subunits or even in distinguishing sympathetic from parasympathetic influences on individual organs is more equivocal. Similarly, the use of individual convenience measures, such as skin conductance responses, as a summary measure of sympathetic arousal, is, at best, naive and, at worst, may lead to false conclusions about emotion-associated changes in patterned sympathetic activity. Consequently, future studies aiming to discriminate emotion-specific physiological responses will benefit from a careful selection of multiple physiological indices sensitive to functionally distinct autonomic pathways, both within and between individual organ systems. Thus, until we arrive at a clear understanding of which response channels are most indicative of a particular emotion and most discriminative between certain emotion contrasts, a comprehensive sampling will be necessary.

Of note, a recent study found that as few as five measures – pre-ejection period, skin conductance response rate, end-tidal pCO_2, and the two facial muscles corrugator supercilii and zygomatic major – may be adequate to distinguish between two emotional states (fear and sadness), if they are selected such that they are maximally discriminant (Kolodyazhniy, Kreibig, Gross, Roth, & Wilhelm, 2011). However, to identify such maximally discriminant response measures, a broad assessment of ANS functioning is necessary, because response measures that might be discriminative of one emotion contrast (e.g., fear and sadness) need not to be discriminating of another emotion contrast (e.g., fear and anger; Kolodyazhniy et al., 2011; Stemmler, 2004).

What Are the Roles of Physical and Psychological Context?

Throughout the earlier discussion on emotion-specific physiological patterning, it was repeatedly noted that the context of emotion induction influences the pattern of observed autonomic responses. It has previously been argued that the effects of physical and psychological contextual factors, such as physical activity and body posture, attention, and mental effort, on patterns of physiological activation may cause the low consistency found in meta-analyses of physiological patterning observed to individual emotions (Stemmler et al., 2001). Because physical and nonemotional psychological contexts vary widely across studies of emotion, a low degree of consistency of emotion-specific physiological configurations may be expected.

Concepts of context-deviation specificity view emotion specificity as a conditional concept, in which an emotional stimulus modifies a context-bound physiological pattern. Thus, emotion and contextual influences on patterns of observed physiological responses are usually confounded. It has been argued that emotion specificity can therefore only be demonstrated once this confound has been pulled apart. Emotion specificity therefore may only be found when there are systematic and specific deviations of the emotion-plus-context pattern of physiological reactivity from the context-alone pattern. Currently, relatively few studies have systematically investigated either context–emotion confounds or the validity of context-deviation specificity (Kreibig, Wilhelm, Gross, & Roth, 2005; Stemmler et al., 2001). This will need to be considered in future studies.

What Is the Role of Physiological Context?

In addition to psychological context, the processing of environmental stimuli is also influenced by the organism's visceral state at the time of stimulus presentation. As discussed in the section on visceral afferents, the brain receives continuous afferent information about internal bodily functions. Cardiovascular homeostasis depends on such feedback, notably phasic signals from aortic arch and carotid sinus baroreceptors activated by blood-volume distension during cardiac systole. Baroreceptor firing during cardiac systole is known to modulate efferent autonomic responses in an organ-specific manner; for example, inhibiting muscle sympathetic nerves while leaving skin sympathetic outflow unaltered (Wallin & Fagius, 1988). Interestingly, the central processing of painful stimuli and consequently the perception of pain are also influenced by physiological state, including resting blood pressure and time during the cardiac cycle (i.e., systole or diastole; Gray, Minati, Paoletti, & Critchley, 2010) and experimentally increasing aortic baroreceptor firing by applying pressure to the neck at specific phases of the cardiac cycle.

Similarly, presentation of unexpected somatosensory stimuli early in cardiac systole also inhibits muscle sympathetic nerve activity, whereas presenting stimuli before cardiac systole does not. Intriguingly, this pattern is exaggerated in patients with blood phobia and syncope, suggesting that feedback mechanisms supporting cardiac homeostasis shape an individual's affective style. Recent data from our laboratory (Gray et al., 2012) suggest that the presentation of brief visual emotional stimuli at different points in the cardiac cycle may also influence the pattern of subsequent physiological responses and associated subjective experience. Together these data suggest that physiological context (e.g., timing in the cardiac cycle or even blood pressure more broadly) influences both the processing of motivationally significant nociceptive stimuli applied directly to the body and also visually presented emotional stimuli. Whether physiological context, such as resting blood pressure, or timing of stimuli presentation relative to recurrent autonomic events, such as cardiac and respiratory cycles, influences physiological and subjective responses to emotional stimuli more broadly remains an open empirical question and will need to be addressed in future studies.

Conclusion

In this chapter, we have considered the physiology of emotion responses from two perspectives: from the perspective of efferent pathways, through which central emotional processes may organize autonomic responding, and, vice versa, from the perspective of afferent pathways through which changes in peripheral visceral state may feed back and contribute to the experience of emotional feelings. The review of the anatomy and central control of the ANS illustrated a system consisting of multiple functionally distinct units, controlled by a hierarchy of direct and indirect central synaptic connections known as the central autonomic network that together provide the hardware for emotion-specific autonomic responding. Consistent with this anatomical perspective our review of patterned autonomic physiological responses to distinct emotions identified separable response patterns for fear, anger, disgust, sadness, and happiness.

The existence of such differentiated autonomic patterning in emotion leads to the related question of whether and if so to what extent visceral afferent information contributes to subjectively experienced emotional feelings. Various neural feedback mechanisms exist that allow for the transmission of information on homeostatic parameters. Re-representation and integration of the physiological state of all bodily tissues with other contextual information within the anterior insula may provide a substrate for conscious awareness of changes in physiological state and emotional feelings. However, the exact nature and role of peripheral physiological responses to emotional feelings remain to be determined.

Based on our review of the literature, we considered practical implications and future challenges, highlighting the need for a comprehensive sampling of physiological response measures at least until we develop a better understanding of which channels are most indicative of a particular emotion and most discriminative between distinct emotions. Furthermore, we noted the potential influences of physical, psychological, and physiological context variables on physiological responses on emotion. Taken together, we hope that this chapter inspires new and innovative research on the contribution of efferent outflows and afferent inputs of autonomic activity to patterned emotional responding and the experience of emotional feelings.

Outstanding Questions and Future Directions

- What are the most appropriate channels of physiological activity to differentiate individual emotional states?
- Emotion-specific physiological responses are typically confounded by contextual influences on patterns of physiological response. Will studies controlling for contextual confounds reveal more conclusive evidence for emotional specificity of physiological responses?
- How does physiological context (e.g., blood pressure, inflammatory status, or phase of the cardiac cycle) influence the perception of emotional stimuli?
- How does this physiological context influence emotional experience and the associated patterning of physiological responses?

References

Adsett, C. A., Schottstaedt, W. W., & Wolf, S. G. (1962). Changes in coronary blood flow and other hemodynamic indicators induced by stressful interviews. *Psychosomatic Medicine*, 24, 331–36.

Asahina, M., Suzuki, A., Mori, M., Kanesaka, T., & Hattori, T. (2003). Emotional sweating response in a patient with bilateral amygdala damage. *International Journal of Psychophysiology*, 47(1), 87–93.

Ax, A. F. (1953). The physiological differentiation between fear and anger in humans. *Psychosomatic Medicine*, 15(5), 433–42.

Bartness, T. J., Shrestha, Y. B., Vaughan, C. H., Schwartz, G. J., & Song, C. K. (2010). Sensory and sympathetic nervous system control of white adipose tissue lipolysis. *Molecular and Cellular Endocrinology*, 318(1–2), 34–43.

Blanchard, R. J., & Blanchard, D. C. (1990). Antipredator defense as models of animal fear and anxiety. In P. F. Brain, S. Parmigiani, R. J. Blanchard & D. Mainardi (Eds.), *Fear and*

defense (pp. 89–108). Amsterdam: Harwood Academic Publishers.

Blessing, W. M. (1997). *The lower brainstem and bodily homeostasis*. Oxford: Oxford University Press.

Bloom, S. R., & Edwards, A. V. (1975). The release of pancreatic glucagon and inhibition of insulin in response to stimulation of the sympathetic innervation. *Journal of Physiology*, 253(1), 157–73.

Blumberg, H., Janig, W., Rieckmann, C., & Szulczyk, P. (1980). Baroreceptor and chemoreceptor reflexes in postganglionic neurones supplying skeletal muscle and hairy skin. *Journal of the Autonomic Nervous System*, 2(3), 223–40.

Bluthe, R. M., Walter, V., Parnet, P., Laye, S., Lestage, J., Verrier, D. et al. (1994). Lipopolysaccharide induces sickness behavior in rats by a vagal mediated mechanism. *Comptes Rendus de l Academie des Sciences Serie Iii-Sciences de la Vie-Life Sciences*, 317(6), 499–503.

Bradley, M. M., Codispoti, M., Cuthbert, B. N., & Lang, P. J. (2001). Emotion and motivation I: Defensive and appetitive reactions in picture processing. *Emotion*, 1(3), 276–98.

Cacioppo, J. T., Berntson, G. G., & Larsen, J. T. (2000). The psychophysiology of emotion. In M. Lewis & J. M. Haviland-Jones (Eds.), *The handbook of emotion* (2nd ed., pp. 173–91). New York: Guilford Press.

Cacioppo, J. T., & Tassinary, L. G. (1990). Inferring psychological significance from physiological signals. *American Psychologist*, 45, 16–28.

Cannon, W. B. (1931). Again the James-Lange and the thalamic theories of emotion. *Psychological Review*, 38, 281–95.

Christie, I. C., & Friedman, B. H. (2004). Autonomic specificity of discrete emotion and dimensions of affective space: A multivariate approach. *International Journal of Psychophysiology*, 51(2), 143–53.

Craig, A. D. (2002). How do you feel? Interoception: The sense of the physiological condition of the body. *Nature Reviews Neuroscience*, 3, 655–67.

Craig, A. D., & Blomqvist, A. (2002). Is there a specific lamina I spinothalamocortical pathway for pain and temperature sensations in primates? *Journal of Pain*, 3(2), 95–101.

Craig, A. D., Chen, K., Bandy, D., & Reiman, E. M. (2000). Thermosensory activation of insular cortex. *Nature Neuroscience*, 3(2), 184–90.

Critchley, H. D. (2009). Psychophysiology of neural, cognitive and affective integration: fMRI and autonomic indicants. *International Journal of Psychophysiology*, 73(2), 88–94.

Critchley, H. D., Corfield, D. R., Chandler, M. P., Mathias, C. J., & Dolan, R. J. (2000). Cerebral correlates of autonomic cardiovascular arousal: A functional neuroimaging investigation in humans. *Journal of Physiology*, 523 (Pt. 1), 259–70.

Critchley, H. D., Elliott, R., Mathias, C. J., & Dolan, R. J. (2000). Neural activity relating to generation and representation of galvanic skin conductance responses: A functional magnetic resonance imaging study. *Journal of Neuroscience*, 20(8), 3033–40.

Critchley, H. D., Wiens, S., Rotshtein, P., Ohman, A., & Dolan, R. J. (2004). Neural systems supporting interoceptive awareness. *Nature Neuroscience*, 7(2), 189–95.

Damasio, A. R. (1994). *Descartes' error: Emotion, reason and the human brain*. New York: Grosset/Putnam.

Damasio, A. R. (1999). *The feeling of what happens: Body and emotion in the making of consciousness*. New York: Harcourt Brace.

Damasio, A. R., Grabowski, T. J., Bechara, A., Damasio, H., Ponto, L. L. B., Parvizi, J., et al. (2000). Subcortical and cortical brain activity during the feeling of self-generated emotions. *Nature Neuroscience*, 3(10), 1049–56.

del Valle, L. M., & Garcia Ruiz, P. J. (2009). A new clinical sign in Holmes-Adie syndrome. *Journal of Neurology*, 256(1), 127–28.

Dimberg, U., & Thunberg, M. (2007). Speech anxiety and rapid emotional reactions to angry and happy facial expressions. *Scandinavian Journal of Psychology*, 48(4), 321–28.

Ekman, P., Levenson, R. W., & Friesen, W. V. (1983). Autonomic nervous-system activity distinguishes among emotions. *Science*, 221(4616), 1208–10.

Etzel, J. A., Johnsen, E. L., Dickerson, J., Tranel, D., & Adolphs, R. (2006). Cardiovascular and respiratory responses during musical mood induction. *International Journal of Psychophysiology*, 61(1), 57–69.

Feldman-Barrett, L. (2006). Are emotions natural kinds? *Perspectives on Psychological Science*, 1, 28–58.

Fredrickson, B. L., & Levenson, R. W. (1998). Positive emotions speed recovery from the cardiovascular sequelae of negative emotions. *Cognition and Emotion*, 12(2), 191–220.

Furness, J. B., Morris, J. L., Gibbins, I. L., & Costa, M. (1989). Chemical coding of neurons and plurichemical transmission. *Annual Review of Pharmacology and Toxicology*, 29, 289–306.

Gianaros, P. J., Derbyshire, S. W., May, J. C., Siegle, G. J., Gamalo, M. A., & Jennings, J. R. (2005). Anterior cingulate activity correlates with blood pressure during stress. *Psychophysiology*, 42(6), 627–35.

Gibbins, I. L. (1995). Chemical neuroanatomy of sympathetic ganglia. In E. M. McLachlan (Ed.), *Autonomic ganglia* (pp. 73–122(. Luxemburg: Harwood Academic Publishers.

Gilissen, R., Bakermans-Kranenburg, M. J., van Ijzendoorn, M. H., & van der Veer, V. (2008). Parent-child relationship, temperament, and physiological reactions to fear-inducing film clips: Further evidence for differential susceptibility. *Journal of Experimental Child Psychology*, 99(3), 182–95.

Goehler, L. E., Relton, J. K., Dripps, D., Kiechle, R., Tartaglia, N., Maier, S. F., et al. (1997). Vagal paraganglia bind biotinylated interleukin-1 receptor antagonist: A possible mechanism for immune-to-brain communication. *Brain Research Bulletin*, 43(3), 357–64.

Gray, M. A., Beacher, F. D., Minati, L., Nagai, Y., Kemp, A. H., Harrison, N. A., et al. (2012). Emotional appraisal is influenced by cardiac afferent information. *Emotion* 12(1), 180–91.

Gray, M. A., Minati, L., Paoletti, G., & Critchley, H. D. (2010). Baroreceptor activation attenuates attentional effects on pain-evoked potentials. *Pain*, 151(3), 853–61.

Gross, J. J., Frederickson, B. L., & Levenson, R. W. (1994). The psychophysiology of crying. *Psychophysiology*, 31(5), 460–68.

Gross, J. J., & Levenson, R. W. (1997). Hiding feelings: The acute effects of inhibiting negative and positive emotion. *Journal of Abnormal Psychology*, 106(1), 95–103.

Harrison, N. A., Brydon, L., Walker, C., Gray, M. A., Steptoe, A., Dolan, R. J., et al. (2009). Neural origins of human sickness in interoceptive responses to inflammation. *Biological Psychiatry*, 66(5), 415–22.

Harrison, N. A., Gray, M. A., Gianaros, P. J., & Critchley, H. D. (2010). The embodiment of emotional feelings in the brain. *Journal of Neuroscience*, 30(38), 12878–84.

Harrison, N. A., Singer, T., Rotshtein, P., Dolan, R. J., & Critchley, H. D. (2006). Pupillary contagion: Central mechanisms engaged in sadness processing. *Social Cognitive and Affective Neuroscience*, 1(1), 5–17.

Harrison, N. A., Wilson, C. E., & Critchley, H. D. (2007). Processing of pupil size modulates perception of sadness and predicts empathy. *Emotion*, 7(4), 724–29.

Hilton, S. M. (1975). Ways of viewing the central nervous control of the circulation – old and new. *Brain Research*, 87, 213–19.

Izard, C. E. (2007). Basic emotions, natural kinds, emotion schemas, and a new paradigm. *Perspectives on Psychological Science*, 2(3), 260–80.

James, W. (1894). Physical basis of emotion. *Psychological Review*, 1, 516–29.

Janig, W. (2006). *The integrative action of the autonomic nervous system: Neurobiology of homeostasis*. Cambridge: Cambridge University Press.

Janig, W., Sundlof, G., & Wallin, B. G. (1983). Discharge patterns of sympathetic neurons supplying skeletal muscle and skin in man and cat. *Journal of the Autonomic Nervous System*, 7(3–4), 239–56.

Jokerst, M. D., Levine, M., Stern, R. M., & Koch, K. L. (1997). Modified sham feeding with pleasant and disgusting foods: Cephalic-vagal influences on gastric myoelectric activity. *Gastroenterology*, 112(4), A755.

Jonsson, P., & Sonnby-Borgstrom, M. (2003). The effects of pictures of emotional faces on tonic and phasic autonomic cardiac control in women and men. *Biological Psychology*, 62(2), 157–73.

Kaada, B. R. (1951). Somato-motor, autonomic and electrocorticographic responses to electrical stimulation of rhinencephalic and other structures in primates, cat, and dog; a study of responses from the limbic, subcallosal, orbito-insular, piriform and temporal cortex, hippocampus-fornix and amygdala. *Acta Physiological Scandinavia Supplement*, 24(83), 1–262.

Kolodyazhniy, V., Kreibig, S. D., Gross, J. J., Roth, W. T., & Wilhelm, F. H. (2011). An affective computing approach to physiological emotion specificity: Toward subject-independent and stimulus-independent classification of film-induced emotions. *Psychophysiology*, 48(7), 908–22.

Kreibig, S. D. (2010). Autonomic nervous system activity in emotion: A review. *Biological Psychology*, 84(3), 394–421.

Kreibig, S. D., Gendolla, G. H., & Scherer, K. R. (2010). Psychophysiological effects of emotional responding to goal attainment. *Biological Psychology*, 84(3), 474–87.

Kreibig, S. D., Wilhelm, F. H., Gross, J. J., & Roth, W. T. (2005). Specific emotional responses as deviations from the experimental context. *Psychophysiology*, 42(s1), s77.

Kreibig, S. D., Wilhelm, F. H., Roth, W. T., & Gross, J. J. (2007). Cardiovascular, electrodermal, and respiratory response patterns to fear- and sadness-inducing films. *Psychophysiology*, 44(5), 787–806.

Lang, P. J., Bradley, M. M., & Cuthbert, B. N. (1993). Emotion, arousal, valence, and the startle reflex. In N. Birbaumer & A. Ohman (Eds.), *The structure of emotion: Psychophysiological, cognitive and clinical aspects* (pp. 243–51). Seattle: Hogrefe & Huber.

Langley, J. N. (1900). The sympathetic and other related systems of nerves. In *Textbook of Physiology*. London: Young J. Pentland.

Levenson, R. W. (1988). Emotion and the autonomic nervous system: A prospectus for research on autonomic specificity. In H. L. Wagner (Ed.), *Handbook of affective sciences* (pp. 212–24). Chichester: Wiley.

Levenson, R. W., Heider, K., Ekman, P., & Friesen, W. V. (1992). Emotion and autonomic nervous-system activity in the Minangkabau of West Sumatra. *Journal of Personality and Social Psychology*, 62(6), 972–88.

Levine, M. E. (2005). Sickness and satiety: Physiological mechanisms underlying perceptions of nausea and stomach fullness. *Current Gastroenterology Reports*, 7(4), 280–88.

Mangina, C. A., & Beuzeron-Mangina, J. H. (1996). Direct electrical stimulation of specific human brain structures and bilateral electrodermal activity. *International Journal of Psychophysiology*, 22(1–2), 1–8.

Matsunaga, M., Isowa, T., Kimura, K., Miyakoshi, M., Kanayama, N., Murakami, H., et al. (2008). Associations among central nervous, endocrine, and immune activities when positive emotions are elicited by looking at a favorite person. *Brain, Behavior, and Immunity*, 22(3), 408–17.

Mauss, I. B., & Robinson, M. D. (2009). Measures of emotion: A review. *Cognition and Emotion*, 23(2), 209–37.

Mobbs, D., Petrovic, P., Marchant, J. L., Hassabis, D., Weiskopf, N., Seymour, B., et al. (2007). When fear is near: Threat imminence elicits prefrontal-periaqueductal gray shifts in humans. *Science*, 317(5841), 1079–83.

Morley, J. E., Levine, A. S., Kneip, J., & Grace, M. (1982). The effect of vagotomy on the satiety effects of neuropeptides and naloxone. *Life Sciences*, 30(22), 1943–47.

Morrison, S. F. (2001). Differential control of sympathetic outflow. *American Journal of Physiology-Regulatory Integrative and Comparative Physiology*, 281(3), R683–R698.

Morrison, S. F., & Cao, W. H. (2000). Different adrenal sympathetic preganglionic neurons regulate epinephrine and norepinephrine secretion. *American Journal of Physiology-Regulatory Integrative and Comparative Physiology*, 279(5), R1763–R1775.

Nagai, Y., Critchley, H. D., Featherstone, E., Trimble, M. R., & Dolan, R. J. (2004). Activity in ventromedial prefrontal cortex covaries with sympathetic skin conductance level: A physiological account of a "default mode" of brain function. *Neuroimage*, 22(1), 243–51.

Nakayama, K., Goto, S., Kuraoka, K., & Nakamura, K. (2005). Decrease in nasal temperature of rhesus monkeys (Macaca mulatta) in negative emotional state. *Physiology & Behavior*, 84, 783–90.

Pick, J. (1970). *The autonomic nervous system*. Philadelphia: Lippincott.

Porges, S. W. (2007). The polyvagal perspective. *Biological Psychology*, 74(2), 116–43.

Prkachin, K. M., Mills, D. E., Zwaal, C., & Husted, J. (2001). Comparison of hemodynamic responses to social and nonsocial stress: Evaluation of an anger interview. *Psychophysiology*, 38(6), 879–85.

Prkachin, K. M., Williams-Avery, R. M., Zwaal, C., & Mills, D. E. (1999). Cardiovascular changes during induced emotion: An application of Lang's theory of emotional imagery. *Journal of Psychosomatic Research*, 47(3), 255–67.

Rainville, P., Bechara, A., Naqvi, N., & Damasio, A. R. (2006). Basic emotions are associated with distinct patterns of cardiorespiratory activity. *International Journal of Psychophysiology*, 61, 5–18.

Rogers, R. C., McTigue, D. M., & Hermann, G. E. (1995). Vagovagal reflex control of digestion: Afferent modulation by neural and "endoneurocrine" factors. *American Journal of Physiology*, 268(1 Pt. 1), G1–10.

Rohrmann, S., & Hopp, H. (2008). Cardiovascular indicators of disgust. *International Journal of Psychophysiology*, 68(3), 201–8.

Rottenberg, J., Wilhelm, F. H., Gross, J. J., & Gotlib, I. H. (2003). Vagal rebound during resolution of tearful crying among depressed and nondepressed individuals. *Psychophysiology*, 40(1), 1–6.

Rozin, P., Lowery, L., & Ebert, R. (1994). Varieties of disgust faces and the structure of disgust. *Journal of Personality and Social Psychology*, 66(5), 870–81.

Saper, C. B. (2002). The central autonomic nervous system: Conscious visceral perception and autonomic pattern generation. *Annual Review of Neuroscience*, 25, 433–69. Retrieved from PM:12052916

Scherer, K. R. (2004). Feelings integrate the central representation of appraisal-driven response organisation in emotion. In A.S.R. Manstead, N. H. Frijda, & A. H. Fischer (Eds.), *Feelings and emotions: The Amsterdam Symposium* (pp. 136–57). Cambridge: Cambridge University Press.

Scherer, K. R. (2005). What are emotions? And how can they be measured? *Social Science Information*, 44(4), 693–727.

Scherer, K. R. (2009). The dynamic architecture of emotion: Evidence for the component process model. *Cognition & Emotion*, 23(7), 1307–51.

Shimazu, T., & Fukuda, A. (1965). Increased activities of glycogenolytic enzymes in liver after splanchnic-nerve stimulation. *Science*, 150(703), 1607–8.

Sinha, R., Lovallo, W. R., & Parsons, O. A. (1992). Cardiovascular differentiation of emotions. *Psychosomatic Medicine*, 54(4), 422–35.

Stemmler, G. (2004). Physiological processes during emotion. In P. Philippot & R. S. Feldman (Eds.), *The regulation of emotion*. Mahwah, NJ: Erlbaum.

Stemmler, G., Aue, T., & Wacker, J. (2007). Anger and fear: Separable effects of emotion and motivational direction on somatovisceral responses. *International Journal of Psychophysiology*, 66(2), 141–53.

Stemmler, G., & Fahrenberg, J. (1989). Psychophysiological assessment: Conceptual, psychometric, and statistical issues. In G. Turpin (Ed.), *Handbook of clinical psychophysiology* (pp. 71–104). Chichester,: Wiley.

Stemmler, G., Heldmann, M., Pauls, C. A., & Scherer, T. (2001). Constraints for emotion specificity in fear and anger: The context counts. *Psychophysiology*, 38(2), 275–91.

Stern, R. M., Jokerst, M. D., Levine, M. E., & Koch, K. L. (2001). The stomach's response to unappetizing food: Cephalic-vagal effects on gastric myoelectric activity. *Neurogastroenterology and Motility*, 13(2), 151–54.

Stevenson, R. J., Hodgson, D., Oaten, M. J., Barouei, J., & Case, T. I. (2011). The effect of disgust on oral immune function. *Psychophysiology*, 48(7), 900–7.

Svensson, T. H. (1987). Peripheral, autonomic regulation of locus coeruleus noradrenergic neurons in brain: Putative implications for psychiatry and psychopharmacology. *Psychopharmacology (Berl)*, 92(1), 1–7.

Swanson, L. W. (2000). Cerebral hemisphere regulation of motivated behavior. *Brain Research*, 886(1–2), 113–64.

Tracey, K. J. (2002). The inflammatory reflex. *Nature*, 420(6917), 853–59.

Tracy, J. L., & Robins, R. W. (2004). Show your pride: Evidence for a discrete emotion expression. *Psychological Science*, 15(3), 194–97.

Travagli, R. A., & Rogers, R. C. (2001). Receptors and transmission in the brain-gut axis: Potential for novel therapies. V. Fast and slow extrinsic modulation of dorsal vagal complex circuits. *American Journal of Physiology and Gastrointestinal Liver Physiology*, 281(3), G595–G601.

Vollmer, R. R. (1996). Selective neural regulation of epinephrine and norepinephrine cells in the adrenal medulla – cardiovascular implications. *Clinical and Experimental Hypertension*, 18(6), 731–51.

Wager, T. D., Waugh, C. E., Lindquist, M., Noll, D. C., Fredrickson, B. L., & Taylor, S. F. (2009). Brain mediators of cardiovascular responses to social threat: part I: Reciprocal dorsal and ventral sub-regions of the medial prefrontal cortex and heart-rate reactivity. *Neuroimage*, 47(3), 821–35.

Wallin, B. G., & Fagius, J. (1988). Peripheral sympathetic neural activity in conscious humans. *Annual Review of Physiology*, 50, 565–76.

Winton, E. C., Clark, D. M., & Edelmann, R. J. (1995). Social anxiety, fear of negative evaluation and the detection of negative emotion in others. *Behaviour Research and Therapy*, 33(2), 193–96.

CHAPTER 4

Electro- and Magneto-Encephalography in the Study of Emotion

Andreas Keil

The conscious stream has fuzzy water in it, as well as driftwood, swimming fish, floating leaves and grass, and of course, careful scientific thinking.

– William James, Principles of Psychology

Affective neuroscience studies using electro-encephalography (EEG) or magneto-encephalography (MEG) frequently highlight these methods' exquisite temporal resolution for capturing the electrophysiology[1] of emotion. Although this is already a desirable property, electrophysiological measurements have additional advantages: They are more affordable than hemodynamic imaging techniques, are widely available, and impose little if any discomfort on research participants. As a consequence, electrophysiological methods have found wide application in the cognitive and affective neurosciences. Recent years have seen exciting developments in virtually every aspect of EEG/MEG research of emotion, ranging from innovation in data-recording tech-

niques to novel experimental paradigms and sophisticated analysis techniques. It is now possible to record from high-density sensor arrays at hundreds of extracranial locations, providing impressive spatial sampling along with high temporal accuracy. Combination of electrophysiological methods with other imaging modalities has been particularly fruitful. Modeling studies of meso- and macroscopic brain activity (i.e., activity in small and large groups of neurons) have provided a constantly improving conceptual framework for interpreting the measured signals.

Because of this rich potential for addressing pertinent questions in the affective neurosciences, human electrophysiology has been a popular avenue for studying emotion. Over the last decade, this field has seen high productivity, with increasing numbers of published research reports, now accounting for hundreds of papers per year. In fact, electrophysiological measures have been used to address questions centered on human emotional experience and behavior since their inception in the late 1920s. It is thus helpful to begin by reviewing a few key events that have shaped the present state of the field.

A (Very) Short History of EEG and MEG in Affective Neuroscience

Hans Berger conducted the first series of human EEG recordings using scalp electrodes in the city of Jena, Germany, during the years 1910 to 1929 (see Berger, 1969, for an English version of his first report on these experiments). He initially used silver-chloride needle electrodes placed in the scalp tissue together with a delicate galvanometer apparatus to record the voltage oscillations reflective of electrocortical processes. These efforts were characterized by setbacks, doubts, and very small samples of subjects, mostly consisting of Berger's laboratory assistant, Fräulein Von Bülow (whom he married in 1911), his son Klaus, and Berger himself, who also attempted the first neurofeedback procedure, trying to monitor his own EEG using a mirror system. From the beginning, the focus of the work of Berger and other early EEG researchers was on characterizing the frequency content of EEG in response to a task or event. Most prominently, Berger identified "first-order waves" oscillating at a rate of 10 cycles/second (10 Hz, later referred to as *alpha waves*) and faster "second-order waves," oscillating at about 20 to 30 Hz (i.e., *beta waves*). The protocols of the recording sessions during those years were scripted by Berger in great detail and contain precise instructions for the presentation of events to the subject; for example, "count to ten (watch clock!), then gently touch Fräulein Von Bülow's cheek with the glass probe [underline by Berger], simultaneously pressing trigger key for the wave recorder. N.B. No physical contact is to be made with Fräulein Von Bülow, or the reclining chair."

In the context of this chapter, it is of interest that this choreography regularly included the elements of startle and distress. For instance, on the first of November 1927, Berger noted in his diary "affective arousal, particularly startle, causes pronounced heightening and slowing of the 90 σ [waves with a duration of approximately 90 ms, i.e, alpha waves around 10 Hz; AK] waves." Later, he revised this view to suggest that "I tend to the conclusion that during arousal, distress, and mental work, the bigger 90 σ waves . . . fade, and the smaller 35 σ waves [that is, waves at roughly 20–30 Hz; presently referred to as upper beta, AK] get more abundant" (Borck, 2005).

For the next 30 years, most researchers agreed that the spectral composition of ongoing EEG during emotion was best interpreted along the lines proposed by Berger. For instance, in 1950, Donald Lindsley, a pioneer of EEG research in the United States, summarized the state of the art as follows:

Two principal kinds of changes are reflected in the EEG under conditions of emotional arousal, like apprehension, unexpected sensory stimulation, and anxiety states: reduction or suppression of alpha rhythm and increase in amount of beta-like fast activity. EEG studies now provide data on cortical diencephalic relationships and thus may resolve the problem of central and autonomic factors in relation to emotion. (Lindsley, 1950)

We see later that the use of alpha as a measure of cortical/behavioral idling and low arousal is still an important concept in contemporary affective neuroscience, although more recent work has demonstrated that certain tasks and stimuli heighten, rather than reduce, alpha power in the EEG (Klimesch, Sauseng, & Hanslmayr, 2006). Early recordings with intracranial electrodes indicated that oscillatory brain activity is relevant for behavior, for instance when epilepsy patients showed heightened beta and gamma oscillations in the amygdala during fear conditioning (Lesse, 1957).

With the advent of computer technology, extracting representative waveforms from the EEG by averaging across many similar events became possible. This procedure yields event-related brain potentials (ERPs) that reflect the typical response to a given, repeated event – sensory, behavioral, or cognitive. Although initial attempts focused on the registration of sensory cortical responses to simple external stimuli, ERPs were soon studied in relationship to affectively arousing events as well. The contingent negative variation (CNV) was among the first of these "cognitive" ERP waveforms (Walter, 1967). It is typically elicited in response to warning stimuli predicting a subsequent behavioral or sensory event and is heightened in cases where the warning stimulus predicts arousing events such as a painful shock (Knott & Irwin, 1968). A host of paradigms for analyzing averaged waveforms followed this discovery, currently making ERP research the most active subdiscipline of affective electrophysiology.

The history of MEG in the affective neurosciences begins a half-century later, when MEG is developed as an accessible and practical research tool for recording the incredibly small fluctuations in the magnetic field that accompany electrocortical processes (Cohen, 1968, 1972). Because of the high sensitivity of MEG to activity in cortical sulci (Melcher & Cohen, 1988), MEG studies of auditory and somatosensory perception were initially popular and remain so today. It is thus not surprising that one very productive use of the MEG technique to addressing issues of emotional reactivity has focused on brain responses to somatosensory pain stimuli (Flor, Braun, Elbert, & Birbaumer, 1997). Recent decades have seen a dramatic increase in MEG applications to a variety of research questions in affective neuroscience, which are addressed in the "Applications" section; see also Chapter 13 for linguistic stimuli and Chapter 7 for facial material.

A major advantage of electrophysiological time series is that they directly reflect neuroelectric processes rather than blood flow (such as functional magnetic resonance imaging, fMRI) or metabolic processes (such as positron emission tomography, PET), which makes them unique indices of neuronal activity. In the next section, let us consider what is known about the specific properties of the neural population activity that underlies EEG/MEG recordings.

The Neurophysiological Underpinnings of EEG and MEG

Most neurophysiological studies concur that a condition for the ongoing EEG and MEG to be visible outside the brain is the synchronized activity of significant numbers of cortical pyramidal cells. Estimates of this number range from thousands to millions of neurons and vary between EEG and MEG, with MEG generally considered more sensitive to smaller neuronal populations. In terms of neuronal events, researchers also agree that the majority of electromagnetic events measured outside the skull are due to synaptic activity at dendrites, the tree-like structures at which neurons receive inhibitory or excitatory input (Olejniczak, 2006). In particular, apical dendrites, emerging at the top (apex) of the pyramidal neuron, tend to be aligned in parallel to each other and perpendicular to the cortical surface, which enables them to collectively generate electromagnetic fields. Pyramidal cells account for 80–90% of all cortical neurons, with some variance between cortical regions, thus representing a major portion of the neuronal population. This is good news for EEG/MEG researchers: Although electromagnetic field changes of a single pyramidal neuron cannot be detected through the layers of cerebrospinal fluid, skin, and scalp that separate the neural tissue from the sensors, it is easily possible to measure the synchronous activity evoked by millions of favorably oriented pyramidal neurons (Nunez et al., 1997). Specifically, the relatively slow and dipolar voltage changes induced by postsynaptic activity at the apical dendrites are reliably measurable outside the brain. This implies that the scalp-recorded electrophysiology reflects a very specific subset of cortical information processing in large areas of tissue; namely, postsynaptic signals targeting apical dendrites of cortical pyramidal cells. Other contributions to the generation of scalp-recorded electrophysiological signals have been noted, such as current gradients in glia cells and spike (action potential) activity in neurons; however, authors agree that these processes are to be neglected for all practical purposes (Olejniczak, 2006), although specific oscillatory events contained in the EEG/MEG may be reflective of nonsynaptic events when properly recorded and extracted from the raw signal (Whittingstall & Logothetis, 2009).

Pronounced differences between EEG and MEG emerge in terms of their sensitivity to these intracranial events: To arrive at EEG scalp electrodes, currents generated by the cortical processes outlined earlier need to travel through the tissue of the human body. Thus, relatively strong currents originating close to a given sensor electrode are spatially well represented in the human EEG (Nunez & Srinivasan, 2006). However, currents are conducted through the body and brain and may be measured at remote electrodes, impeding spatial specificity. Thus, the fact that the original extracellular voltage gradient is reduced and distorted in the process of volume conduction favors registration of EEG from near-surface cortex oriented parallel to the scalp, over that from deep brain regions with less favorable orientation. Moreover, because the different types of tissue that the current passes through (e.g., brain, cerebrospinal fluid, skull, skin) each have different electric properties, the original electric field is not veridically represented. Volume conduction effects may also vary across the recording period, thus affecting the EEG as a function of time. Overall, the scalp-recorded EEG represents the true underlying voltage gradients as they are altered by properties of the tissues between the electrical source and the recording electrode on the scalp, conductive properties of the electrode itself, and the orientation of the cortical generator to the recording electrode. Excellent overviews of the methods and physiology of the EEG are given by Nunez and Srinivasan (2006) and in the textbook by Regan (1989), which are highly recommended reading.

In contrast, MEG is directly sensitive to the original cellular events not mediated by volume conduction; this property eliminates the problem of spatial distortion of the neural signal (Cohen & Cuffin, 1987). There is also no need to select a reference and interpret the data in the light of that particular reference. Thus, a major advantage of MEG over EEG recordings is their greater spatial specificity. Further differences exist with regard to the orientation of the generating tissue: Because a magnetic field is oriented orthogonal to the generating electric field, and because the brain has a near-spherical shape, sources oriented radially (i.e., perpendicular) to the scalp surface generate only very weak magnetic field gradients outside the skull. Thus, MEG studies tend to contain a strong bias toward activity in the cortical sulci, which results in sources that are oriented tangentially to the scalp surface. Many authors have emphasized that MEG might not be as sensitive to activity in deep brain regions, given that the magnetic field strength declines with the square of the distance to the source (Wennberg, Valiante, & Cheyne, 2011).

To summarize, scalp-recorded human electrophysiology reflects neural mass activity in near-surface gray matter. Specifically, it is highly sensitive to the integrated synaptic afferent processes at dendritic trees of pyramidal neurons to the extent that they are synchronously active, thus generating sufficiently strong electromagnetic fields. The orientation of these fields differentially affects EEG and MEG, with MEG being more sensitive to tangential generators and EEG more sensitive to radial generators. Some of these properties vary as a function of the recording parameters and recording apparatus employed, and I review these aspects next.

The Recording Process

EEG and MEG are safe and noninvasive procedures that are associated with minimum discomfort to the participant. Over the last two decades, the application of sensors to the scalp has become even more comfortable with technical innovations such as all-in-one EEG electrode caps, which can hold hundreds of sensors. MEG systems likewise have grown to contain dense arrays of sensors in an expensive and intricate piece of engineering: A large vacuum flask

(Dewar) shaped as a helmet-like structure contains superconducting quantum interference devices (SQUIDs) immersed in liquid helium, at a temperature of 4° Kelvin. When cooled to the temperature of liquid helium, superconducting elements carry electricity without resistance. This lack of resistance allows a SQUID to measure the magnetic interference induced at detection coils also embedded in the MEG helmet, close to the participant's head. In contemporary EEG recordings, electrodes are placed over many different scalp locations. The most frequently used sensors involve a silver-silver chloride contact that is filled with conductive paste, but other technologies are now available that provide excellent electric contact between the scalp and the amplifier. For instance, electrode contacts can be placed in a sponge, which conducts current when it is bathed in a saline solution prior to recording (Ferree, Luu, Russell, & Tucker, 2001). Active and shielded electrodes are also available now, further improving the quality of the recorded signal and reducing the impact of extracranial noise.

Because voltage is a relative measure – that is, a difference in electrical potential between two sites – EEG voltage at any specific sensor is measured with respect to a reference site. Clinical EEG studies often use bipolar recordings in which a voltage gradient is measured between paired electrodes. Most frequently used today is the common reference, in which all of the recording electrodes measure the voltage gradient at their location against the same metric, derived from one or more reference electrodes. The location of the common reference electrode(s) is critical to the interpretation of the resulting scalp distribution of the measured voltage. Ideally one would place the reference at a site that is electrically silent, allowing an estimate of the neural activity at each of the recorded sensor locations. Thus, distant and presumably electrically "quiet" regions have been used as reference sites, such as a sensor mounted on the tip of the nose, the front of the forehead, or on the earlobes. Nonetheless, both cranial currents and extracranial sources (e.g., muscle activity) can affect current flow at those sites and distort the measured voltage. For instance, it has been proposed that use of a nose reference may enhance sensitivity of the EEG to certain noncerebral (ocular) signals, which then may be represented at frontal electrodes and misinterpreted as oscillatory brain activity (Yuval-Greenberg, Tomer, Keren, Nelken, & Deouell, 2008). Alternatively, the EEG may be recorded using any one of the sensors on the scalp itself (for instance, the vertex electrode at the top of the head) as the reference site during recording, and the so-called average reference is computed offline as the mean difference across all electrodes. Use of this average reference avoids biases due to the specific reference location, but requires extensive coverage over the entire head for accurate estimates. Simulation studies are available to guide the choice of the reference for a given electrode montage (Junghöfer, Elbert, Tucker, & Braun, 1999).

In this context, one major advantage of MEG technology becomes clear: There is no need to define or use a reference sensor, because both magnetometer-based (measuring the strength of the magnetic field) and gradiometer-based (measuring the local gradient; i.e., the difference in magnetic flux) MEG systems measure the magnetic field (or the gradient, respectively) at a given location, with no external reference needed. MEG recordings, however, pose stronger requirements than EEG with respect to the shielding of the recording environment. Whereas in EEG research a Faraday cage is considered state-of-the-art shielding against stray electric currents, MEG requires a magnetically shielded participant room. Such a room excludes almost all of the fluctuating external fields, which are several orders of magnitude greater than the neuromagnetic fields (Cohen, 1972). The degree of shielding tends to increase with the number of wall layers, made of non-ferromagnetic metals such as aluminum.

In the majority of cases, electrophysiological signals are continuously recorded and digitized at an even rate – the sampling frequency. For many applications in affective neuroscience, sampling frequencies of 250 Hz allow accurate reconstruction of

brain activity over time. By contrast, studying high-frequency oscillatory activity and
very brief transient responses requires higher
sampling rates (e.g., 1,000 Hz or higher),
which afford sufficient temporal resolution for monitoring very fast neural events.
Knowing the fundamental physics of sampling and digital filtering is certainly beneficial to affective neuroscientists interested in
using electrophysiology, but is outside the
scope of this chapter. Readers are referred
to the excellent overviews and tutorials in
Cook and Miller (1992) and in Nitschke,
Miller, & Cook (1998).

After the electrophysiological time series
are recorded, several sources of noise may
still be present in the signal. Extracranial
electrical activity that leads to artifacts in the
measured EEG include eyeblinks, eye movements, muscular activity, external electromagnetic noise, sweating, and heart rate
potentials. Such artifacts are often identified in a process of visual inspection and
then discarded or corrected by appropriate
algorithms. In traditional approaches to artifact correction, EEG segments (or sensors)
containing artifacts or contaminated sensors
are completely removed from the data, leading to data attrition. More recent methods
try to retain as much of the recorded data
as possible by mathematically modeling certain types of artifacts (e.g., eyeblinks), and
then correcting (i.e., recalculating) a version
of the original EEG/MEG that estimates
the true signal without the targeted artifact (Ille, Berg, & Scherg, 2002; Junghofer,
Elbert, Tucker, & Rockstroh, 2000). Independent component analysis (Makeig, Jung,
Bell, Ghahremani, & Sejnowski, 1997; discussed later in this chapter) is increasingly
used for this purpose and has shown the
capability to identify, isolate, and remove
unwanted signals from the data.

The Measures: What to Record and
What to Look for in Studies of Emotion

Spectral Analyses of Ongoing Activity

As evident from the historic overview,
changes in the spectral properties of the

ongoing raw waveforms during task performance are prima facie properties of EEG
and MEG – they are obvious when visually inspecting the ongoing electrophysiological time series. Because communication
within and between coupled neuronal populations of neurons involves excitatory as
well as inhibitory connections, the overall
activity of the network in time is likely to
be oscillatory in nature. Oscillatory activity represents a general feature of other biological large-scale systems as well, such as
motor or cardiovascular systems (Haken,
1983). Given its salience even with basic
recording setups, the oscillatory character of
EEG and the relationship between different
types of oscillations and mental processes
were the focus of pioneering work in EEG
(Berger, 1969) and MEG research (Cohen,
1972). In the affective neurosciences, spectral analyses of extended periods of resting
and task-related EEG have been particularly
fruitful, leading to the establishment of an
entire research field concerned with lateralized alpha band power as a predictor of
affective states or traits (Davidson, 1995).
Open-source software packages that include
sophisticated ways of calculating and quantifying frequency-domain aspects of electrophysiological time series include the
fieldtrip toolbox (http://fieldtrip.fcdonders.
nl/start), EEGLAB (http://sccn.ucsd.edu/
eeglab/), and EMEGS (http://www.emegs.
org/), all written in Matlab code and available to researchers for download at no
cost.

The frequency spectrum of a sufficiently
long data segment can be obtained with a
host of different methods, but traditional
Fourier-based methods represent the most
popular and most prevalent approach. These
methods are applied to time-domain data
(where data points along the x-axis represent a temporal sequence) and transform
them into a spectral representation (where
data points represent different frequencies),
called the frequency domain. In principle, the discrete Fourier transform (DFT,
often implemented as the fast Fourier transform, FFT, in commercial analysis packages)
can be illustrated by a simple sequence of

steps: First, sine and cosine waves at the frequencies of interest are multiplied to the measured digitized signal, and the resulting values are summed over time. This leads to greater weighting of aspects of the time series that follow the shape of a given sine or cosine wave, and the resulting sums (one for the sine, one for the cosine) are thus a measure of how much variance there is in the original signal for each frequency. The information contained in the sine and cosine parts of the signal can be used to estimate the spectral *power*, by calculating the modulus (here, the square root of the sum of the squares) of the sine and cosine parts. In addition, the *phase* of the measured signal can be derived from the relationship between the sine and cosine parts, using the arctangent function. Often, the phase is considered a measure of latency or temporal displacement of the oscillation relative to the sine function, again at a specific frequency. Alternative approaches use different basis functions other than sine and cosine waves and therefore have different weighting rules, but rely on the same principle of modeling the desired oscillation by analytic time series resembling the oscillation of interest. Although widely used, not all of the problems relevant for estimating spectral properties of EEG and MEG by means of Fourier transform are known to affective neuroscientists or reported in research reports. Let us consider a few interesting issues that inform but also constrain the use of frequency-domain techniques in affective neuroscience research.

STATIONARITY OF THE TIME SERIES
One important premise underlying all Fourier-based procedures is the assumption that the signal is stationary. The concept of temporal stationarity implies that a series of values has a stable mean and variance over time, which on the level of physiology may mean that the underlying neural process does not change qualitatively during the epoch of interest. In the formulation of Fourier analysis, sine and cosine waves – which are of infinite length – are used to describe the signal. This has an important

consequence: The data epoch that is submitted to DFT is regarded as a segment of an infinite-length time series with stable periodic properties over time. Hence, DFT will result in a summary spectrum of the entire signal that can be regarded as an average over all the periodic and nonperiodic processes in the time segment of interest that match the sine and cosine templates employed. Information as to whether any nonstationary change in the original time series contributed to the resulting frequency spectrum will be lost, as illustrated in Figure 4.1. Electrophysiological time series from affective neuroscience studies are often not stationary. For instance, the presentation of an emotional stimulus may result in a transient, nonperiodic change in the signal, which does not meet the stationarity assumption when submitted to DFT. Interpretation of frequency spectra recorded during emotional engagement (e.g., when listening to music or viewing film clips) should take this limitation into account. Methods – experimental and computational – are available to avoid nonstationarity. They include the selection of stationary segments as evident by formal statistical testing. For instance, the augmented Dickey-Fuller test (see e.g., Elliott, Rothenberg, & Stock, 1996) has been established as a means to examine electrocortical time series for (non)stationarity. In addition, de-trending methods such as the subtraction of a linear regression line across sample points are often used to remove slow aspects of nonstationary change (e.g., slow drifting signals) from a time series. Experimental approaches for obtaining stationary neurophysiological time series include steady-state stimulation (see "Applications") and prolonged stimulus exposure.

SPECTRAL LEAKING AND THE
UNCERTAINTY PRINCIPLE
Because of the properties outlined earlier, the quality of the Fourier-based frequency spectrum of EEG and MEG depends on the periodicity and duration of the signal submitted to the DFT. As an important constraint, the frequency resolution of the spectrum is inversely related to the time

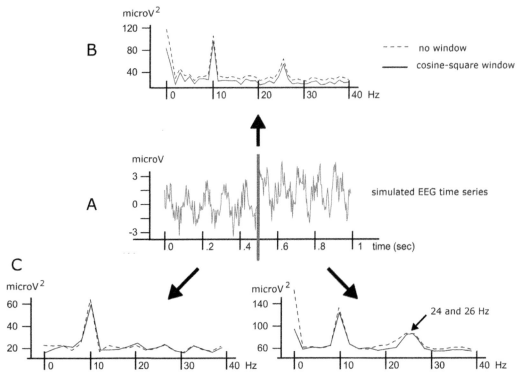

Figure 4.1. Fourier analysis of electrophysiological time series. **Middle Panel (A)**: A noisy time domain signal was constructed to resemble an EEG/MEG with strong alpha contribution. To this end, a 10-Hz sine wave was superimposed with real MEG noise, filtered between 12 and 50 Hz. The first 500 ms of the signal contain the 10-Hz oscillation plus noise; the second 500 ms contain an offset of .5 microV and an additional 25-Hz oscillation (sine wave) having half the amplitude of the 10-Hz signal. Note that this second oscillation is not visible to the unaided eye at the noise level present in the data. This time series looks quite regular, but significantly fails to be stationary (Augmented Dickey-Fuller Test). The cosine-square function used for windowing is shown overlaid to the nonwindowed signal (thick gray lines). **Top Panel (B)**: Discrete Fourier transform (dashed line) of the entire time series (1,000-ms duration) yields 1-Hz frequency resolution (see text). The addition of a cosine-square taper window function reduces the amount of noise in the signal (solid line) as it attenuates on- and offset artifacts. This analysis fails to detect that the 25-Hz oscillation is present only in the second half of the time domain signal. **Bottom Panels (C)**: Discrete Fourier transforms of the first and second half of the time domain signal. This analysis yields a frequency resolution of 2 Hz (each epoch is 500 ms in duration). Thus, the 25-Hz oscillation in the second part of the signal is detected, but is shown at 24 and 26 Hz (leakage into neighboring frequency bins), due to the absence of a 25-Hz bin. Also shown with the shorter data segments in panel C: Windowing reduces leaking and the offset at 0 Hz (i.e., the so-called DC component).

resolution. Submitting short epochs of EEG/MEG to DFT (high time resolution) leads to large steps in the frequency-domain representation of the signal (poor frequency resolution), whereas submitting longer time epochs allows for precise identification of a given frequency at the cost of temporal resolution. Thus, this problem can be regarded a variant of the Heisenberg (or Fourier) uncer-

tainty principle, which states that time localization trades off against frequency localization. For instance, submitting a time segment of 500 ms to DFT results in a frequency resolution of 2 Hz, with the maximum frequency meaningfully represented being the Nyquist frequency (i.e., 50% of the sampling rate). Formally, the spectral resolution, measured as the size of the available frequency steps Δf, is a simple function of the signal duration: Δf (in Hz) $= 1,000$/duration (ms). In practice, this means that to achieve a given resolution in the frequency domain, researchers should aim to use stationary time segments of sufficient length. For instance, time segments with a 500-ms duration will not enable one to make distinctions between the 25-Hz and 26-Hz activity in a signal, because only frequency steps at 0, 2, 4, 6 Hz, and so forth, will be available, given the frequency resolution of $1,000/500 = 2$ Hz. As shown in Figure 4.1, true oscillatory activity at a frequency not represented in the spectrum (e.g., 25 Hz in the previous example) shows at the neighboring frequencies in the spectrum (24 and 26 Hz), thus smearing the appearance of the signal in the frequency domain. If a researcher is interested in a given *a priori* frequency, particular care should be taken when selecting the duration of the to-be-analyzed signal to ensure that it is covered accurately with the resulting frequency spectrum.

WINDOWS AND OVERLAPPING SEGMENTS
Method sections of affective neuroscience manuscripts on spectral properties of EEG/MEG often refer to windowed FFTs, tapers, and zero-padding, but the reasons for selecting these parameters in a particular manner are often opaque. In fact, when using convenient interactive analysis tools, novice users often face difficulties when they are asked by a pop-down menu to decide whether they would like to use "Hamming," "Hanning," "Welch," or other types of windows/procedures. Although a complete discussion of these issues is outside the scope of this chapter, let us consider a few basic issues that affect the looks and the interpretation of spectral domain data in the affective neuroscience. For a more comprehensive description, readers are referred to Nitschke et al. (1998). Because Fourier analysis is designed to assume infinite repetitions of the signal, any short segment of data that is cut out of the ongoing signal and submitted to DFT is represented as repetitive; that is, the segment within the measured time repeats for all time. In practice, most real signals have discontinuities at the ends of the measured time. When the FFT assumes that the signal repeats, it will therefore introduce discontinuities at the edges, which are not really present in the signal (see Figure 4.1). Because sharp discontinuities have broad frequency spectra, they cause the signal's frequency spectrum to spread, resulting in increased leakage and/or misrepresentation of frequencies.

This problem is addressed by so-called window functions that attenuate the signal of interest at the edges. "Windowing" a signal thus means multiplication of the signal with a weighting function that has low values at the beginning and end. Most window functions provide greater weight to events at the center of the signal, with decreasing sensitivity to events at the edges. Thus, they tend to have a symmetrical, tapered shape. In Figure 4.1, we used a simple cosine-square function (illustrated as thick gray lines in the middle panel) to address this issue, leading to reduction of noise overall (solid lines). Other window functions, such as Hanning, Hamming, Kaiser, and so forth, differ in shape and have specific applications in digital signal processing, but they serve the same purpose of providing desired weighting functions along a time series. Hence, windowing can be harnessed to enhance temporal localization when many adjacent Fourier transforms are computed for one time series, leading to a spectrogram – the representation of spectral power as it changes over time in several frequency bands. Often, windows are shifted along the signal with an overlap of 50% to ensure sensitivity to each spectral event in the data and avoid exclusion of processes around the edges of the shifted windows. A similar approach is used in the so-called Welch periodogram method, in which overlapping windows are moved over the signal and the resulting spectra are averaged to increase the signal-to-noise ratio and further attenuate effects of noise and edges. An excellent overview of window functions and frequency-domain issues in EEG/MEG research is given by Nitschke and colleagues (1998).

Event-Related Potentials and Event-Related Fields

Event-related potentials/event-related magnetic fields (ERPs and ERFs) are derived from the ongoing electrophysiological activity by means of time-domain averaging of artifact-free epochs related to a particular event. As a consequence, they specifically measure the part of the neural activity that is temporally related to this specific event (e.g., a word, picture, sound, or any other stimulus or behavior). Neural activity that is not systematically modulated at the same time, with the same phase (e.g., with a positive or negative peak), is suppressed. By averaging neural mass activity over many trials, a representative temporal waveform of brain voltage changes is obtained, which characterizes the event of interest. Trial averaging is essential both because ongoing EEGs and MEGs are noisy and because the amplitude of changes to specific events is on the scale of several microvolts (μV) or femtotesla (fT), whereas the raw recordings involve spontaneous voltage and field fluctuations that can be several orders of magnitude higher. Along with extracranial noise and spontaneous brain activity, many types of stimulus-related neural mass activity exist that are not precisely phase-locked and/or time-locked to the respective event. They are also "averaged out" when time-domain averaging is applied. For an overview of the ERP and ERF techniques, the reader is directed to recent textbooks covering the topic such as the excellent volume by Luck (2005). An upcoming volume has a chapter devoted to the use of ERP in emotion research, which is also recommended (Hajcak, Weinberg, MacNamara, & Foti, 2011).

Depending on the magnitude of the event-related neural activity of interest, recommendations for trial numbers necessary to obtain meaningful ERP/ERF waveforms range between 15–20 trials (e.g., for extracting large responses to salient visual target stimuli) and thousands of trials (e.g., for extracting the brainstem's response to specific sounds). After averaging, the ERP represents the part of the signal in each trial that is time-locked and phase-locked to the event, which means that the peaks and troughs of the waveform in each trial must occur at the same time, with the same voltage direction (positive or negative). Averaged ERP waveforms thus consist of a sequence of positive and negative voltage deflections, which vary in their magnitude (amplitude) and topographical distribution across the scalp at a given point in time. ERF data are likewise characterized by characteristic changes in the magnetic field strength, or the field gradient, over time. The averaged waveform is a rich source of information with very typical time courses for different experimental designs and at different sensor locations. This information is best thought of as a matrix with $n \times t$ elements, where n represents sensors and t represents sample points. Given the availability of dense sensor arrays and high sampling rates, these matrices can be large, and finding a meaningful dependent variable of interest may require specific a priori knowledge or specific statistical methods. In addition, many different types of parameters can be extracted from such an ERP matrix and can be categorized into measures of amplitude, latency, and topography.

ERP/ERF AMPLITUDE MEASURES

ERP/ERF amplitudes (just like latencies and topographies) are meaningful only within the context of the experimental paradigm in which they were recorded. They are generally taken as indices of neural activation, with more amplitude suggesting stronger neural activity at the time point selected. The simplest and most common approach to determining the amplitude of an ERP or ERF has been to pick a time point at a given sensor and use the voltage amplitude value at this time point and sensor as the variable of interest. However, this approach is limited because it reduces the sensor x samples matrix to one element. A popular alternative has been to select time ranges and sensor groups for which a representative value is found, using an appropriate function such as the arithmetic mean or the maximum value.

Paralleling fMRI research, difference waveforms between two experimental conditions are sometimes used to highlight a neural difference between situations and events that were kept identical, except for one aspect of interest that was manipulated by the experimenter.

Related to this approach, researchers have conducted statistical tests for each sensor (and possibly time point) available, comparing experimental conditions or groups. The resulting parameters are then displayed in a color-coded fashion as a scalp map or projected to a brain volume. This mapping approach does not reduce the information contained in the ERP/ERF matrix because it can be conducted for each sensor-sample pair in the $n \times t$ matrix, but it is associated with alpha error accumulation. Thus, false-positive tests must be expected with large matrices, and means for adjusting the alpha level are needed. Recent advances in the field of statistics have led to novel applications such as permutation tests for scalp topographies and time points (Blair & Karniski, 1993), in which a test statistic is evaluated against an empirical distribution resulting from large numbers of tests conducted over the same data, but with shuffled (permutated) conditions. Two recent reviews (Groppe, 2011; Maris, 2012) give an overview of the current thinking in ERP/ERF statistical testing and are recommended for the interested reader.

In addition to neurophysiological reasoning and mass testing of all information available, multivariate statistical approaches such as principal component analysis (PCA) or independent component analysis (ICA; see Makeig, Debener, Onton, & Delorme, 2004) have been used to extract time points and scalp regions that are sensitive to the experimental manipulation (Foti, Hajcak, & Dien, 2009). Both PCA and ICA are families of procedures that aim to statistically de-correlate or factorize the spatiotemporal EEG (or MEG) data and then extract temporal and spatial features that are unique and specific, so they may be attributed to a given brain process or artifact. Dien (2010) has explicitly compared different compo-nent analysis techniques with real and simulated data and has provided specific recommendations along with a tutorial description and open source code allowing their application. Likewise, the EEGLab toolbox (Delorme & Makeig, 2004) contains useful applications to conduct ICA and combine it with time-frequency analysis, single-trial visualization, and source estimation.

LATENCY MEASURES

In addition to amplitude measures, the *latency* at which specific ERP components occur may be relevant to hypotheses in affective neuroscience research. Component latency is often defined as the point in time at which the peak of the deflection occurs or as the time at which a certain criterion is reached (e.g., 50% of the maximum amplitude). More elaborate approaches involve use of lagged cross-correlations, which estimate the relative displacement of an entire waveform with respect to a standard waveform by calculating the cross-correlation function at different lags. Accurate estimates of latency are highly dependent on the signal-to-noise ratio of the individual ERP, and thus several methods have been proposed to obtain information regarding statistical significance of a given latency difference. In many situations researchers may consider use of the jackknife approach (Miller, Patterson, & Ulrich, 1998) to examine latency differences between experimental conditions or groups. Jackknifing is often preferred over individual peak-picking methods because it has been shown to be more sensitive to real latency differences than single-subject-based scoring methods while at the same time being less affected by noise. This feature is achieved by using averages rather than individual participant data as the observation variable: Jackknife-based statistics involve recomputation of the desired test statistic, leaving out one observation at a time from the sample set. New averaged waveforms are formed to replace each of the participants' individual waveforms or time-varying spectra, or other event, for each experimental condition. Each of these waveforms then represents a grand mean across all participants but one. The latency of each event of interest can be scored as the point in time when a criterion is reached. Jackknifed statistics are then calculated and appropriate corrections are applied to account for the averaging (Miller et al., 1998).

TOPOGRAPHY

With the advent of dense-array EEG/ERP recordings, the interest in localization of the generators underlying the scalp-recorded EEG has dramatically increased. Although the spatial sensitivity of ERPs is poor compared to hemodynamic imaging techniques such as fMRI or PET, the spatial information inherent in multichannel ERP recordings can be harnessed, using appropriate algorithms, to guide careful estimates as to their cerebral origin. I address the topic of source estimation later in more detail. An alternative use of the topographical information from multichannel ERPs is to inform so-called microstate analysis (Pascual-Marqui, Michel, & Lehmann, 1995). Microstates are hypothetical constructs extracted from the ERP $n \times t$ matrix that reflect periods of time in which the topographical distribution is stable, thus potentially reflecting a specific state of the central nervous system. These states can be variable in duration, but are conceptualized to be non-overlapping in time. Thus, microstate analysis results in a temporal sequence of topographies characteristic of each state. In affective neuroscience, microstate analysis has been used to demonstrate the temporal and spatial locus of ERP activity related to hedonic valence and the emotional intensity of affective pictures (Gianotti et al., 2008). Other work has used this approach to segment the ERP time course of face processing as a function of expression and observers' affective traits into meaningful temporal regions (i.e., the microstates), which were then submitted to source estimation (Pizzagalli, Lehmann, Koenig, Regard, & Pascual-Marqui, 2000). In support of the microstate concept, the previously mentioned visual ERP work showed that the sequence of microstates converged with early processing stages as suggested by ERP source estimation and animal models of vision.

STEADY-STATE EVOKED POTENTIALS/FIELDS

A special case of ERPs are steady-state potentials, elicited by oscillating stimuli – visual, auditory, or somatosensory. In the visual domain, steady-state visual evoked potentials (ssVEPs) can be used as a continuous measure of visual cortical engagement when processing a visual stimulus (Müller, Teder-Salejarvi, & Hillyard, 1998). They represent responses to stimuli modulated in luminance (i.e., flickered), in which the frequency of the electrocortical response recorded from the scalp equals that of the driving stimulus. Of significant advantage, the oscillatory cortical response has a known frequency and can thus be reliably separated from noise and quantified in the frequency domain. Another advantage of this paradigm is that multiple stimuli flickering at different frequencies can be presented simultaneously to the visual system, but their electrocortical signature can be separated (a technique referred to as "frequency tagging"). With respect to emotional stimulus features, it has been demonstrated that highly arousing affective stimuli generate greater ssVEPs than neutral stimuli in visual and frontoparietal networks (Keil, Gruber, et al., 2003), pointing to facilitation of attention and perception when processing visual objects that bear high motivational relevance (Moratti, Keil, & Stolarova, 2004).

Time-Frequency Analyses

We discussed earlier that EEG/MEG recordings mirror the activity at hundreds of thousands of cortical neurons, which are engaged in an interdependent and oscillatory fashion. This activity may change its frequency composition over time, as a function of subjective state or external demands. Spectral analyses as shown earlier cannot fully address the issue of overlapping and rapidly changing neural oscillations during emotional processing. To fill this gap, time-frequency analyses have been developed (see Tallon-Baudry & Bertrand, 1999, for a review). They allow researchers to study the changes of the signal spectrum over time, taking into account the power (or amplitude) of the signal at a given frequency, as well as changes in the phase (latency). Such a comprehensive analysis of neural population activity is helpful given that not all meaningful neural activity is exactly time- and phase-locked to an event. For instance, based on recordings in experimental animals, Galambos (1992) proposed to distinguish among (1) spontaneous rhythms, which are not related to external stimuli; (2) evoked responses, which are elicited by and precisely time-locked to the onset of an external stimulus; (3) emitted oscillations, which are time-locked to a stimulus that has been omitted; and (4) induced oscillations that are initiated by but not time- and phase-locked to the onset of a stimulus.

As we saw earlier, the most widely used electrocortical parameters in the affective neurosciences, the ERP and the ERF, are based on time-domain averaging across stimulus events. In Galambos' terms, the ERP thus measures time- and phase-locked processes (i.e., evoked activity). In contrast, measures involving frequency-domain averaging across events are sensitive to induced, in addition to evoked neuronal activity, because the single trials are first transformed into the time-frequency plane and then averaged. This procedure prevents attenuation of neural activity that is not aligned with the affective event in the time domain. Further advantages of time-frequency approaches to the study of oscillatory activity lie in their more immediate relationship with neurophysiological processes and their ability to retain single-trial information. For instance, time-frequency representations of EEG/MEG signals have allowed a description of temporal dynamics that overlap in the time domain, but are located in different frequency ranges (Kranczioch, Debener, Maye, & Engel, 2007). They have enabled researchers to characterize the effects of prestimulus and ongoing activity on evoked activity, which is difficult with time-domain approaches alone

(Moratti, Clementz, Ortiz, & Keil, 2007). Importantly, they also allow follow-up analyses using algorithms that are defined best in the frequency domain, such as phase-locking across single trials or phase-locking across recording sites – indices that are sensitive to the connectivity and coherence underlying the electrophysiological data recorded. The spectral range of time-frequency techniques is only constrained by the sampling rate. As opposed to band-pass filtering as used in earlier studies, most time-frequency transforms do not require that a frequency range of interest is known a priori, thus yielding a rich and unconstrained database.

How are time-frequency analyses implemented? The uncertainty principle dictates that time and frequency cannot be measured both at arbitrary accuracy, but that there is a tradeoff between the two domains. Wavelet transform represents a group of methods that allow the researcher to use variable temporal (and thus frequency) resolution across different frequencies (Tallon-Baudry & Bertrand, 1999). Appropriate compromises between time and frequency resolution can be defined for different frequencies, resulting in a near-optimum representation of the signal. A popular wavelet in human electrophysiology has been the continuous Morlet wavelet, first suggested for use in geophysics and introduced into neuroscience by Olivier Bertrand in the mid 1990s (Bertrand, Bohorquez, & Pernier, 1994). The Morlet wavelet is a sine wave segment multiplied by a Gaussian window function that is dilated and extended to be sensitive to different frequencies, also resulting in shorter/longer duration of the wavelet, depending on the dilation/extension. As a consequence, the width of the wavelets in the frequency domain changes as a function of the analysis frequency, while having a constant ratio between the frequency resolution and the time resolution. With standard parameters, time resolution for high frequencies is superior compared to low-frequency ranges, where frequency resolution is high, but time resolution is coarse. Conversely, spectral resolution in higher frequency ranges is low, as is the time resolution in the lower bands. Importantly, these properties are consistent with the behavior of oscillatory activity as observed in the mammalian cortex: Bursts of high-frequency oscillatory activity tend to appear reliably after a given stimulus, but may vary in terms of center frequency, phase, and exact latency (Singer et al., 1997). Thus, the high temporal resolution at the cost of frequency smearing at high frequencies – as afforded by wavelet analysis – matches the physiological properties of cortical networks. The high temporal sensitivity of Morlet wavelets in the upper spectral range helps identify brief epochs of high-frequency oscillations (above 20 Hz), which are assumed to occur during formation of percepts or memories, activation of learned associations, and preparation and execution of actions. These high-frequency phenomena have often been referred to as gamma-band activity. Gamma-band and other oscillations are a potentially useful tool for examining the network aspects of emotional processing in the brain (see, e.g., Keil, Stolarova, Moratti & Ray, 2007). Parameters of lower frequency electrocortical dynamics are often seen as necessary to complete this picture, and of course they provide important information on their own. For instance, modern views of alpha oscillations (8–12 Hz) relate these rhythms not only to "idling" states of the brain but also to diverse functions comprising affective, motor, and memory processes (Klimesch et al., 2006).

As mentioned earlier, wavelet analysis of single trials allows researchers to quantify the amount of phase-locking over many stimulus repetitions. In addition to time-varying spectral power, it is possible to quantify the intertrial phase-locking of the neural oscillations measured with the wavelet family. To this end, the normalized, complex representations of the time-frequency matrices are averaged according to the algorithm described (e.g., in Tallon-Baudry & Bertrand, 1999). This procedure results in a measure of phase stability across trials, for each time point and frequency, which is referred to as the phase-locking index (PLI; see e.g., Keil, Stolarova, Moratti, &

Ray, 2007). The PLI is bounded between 0 and 1; 0 indicating random distribution of phase across trials and 1 indicating perfect identity of the phase across trials, at a given time and frequency. In the domain of visual perception, time-frequency analysis of signals collected at occipital sensors has converged to show an early, evoked, lower frequency burst around 80 ms that is followed by a late, induced, higher frequency oscillation. Figure 4.2 illustrates this for the oscillatory activity in response to a conditioned stimulus (here: a gray-and-white grating stimulus) predicting a loud noise. Both the early evoked and the late induced gamma response have been related to emotional processing; for instance, during classical conditioning of brief visual stimuli (Keil, Stolarova, et al., 2007).

Source Analysis

As noted previously, knowing the topography of a specific ERP component does not provide specific information regarding the original brain generators (i.e., the sources) of the electrical activity that have been measured over the scalp. Nonetheless, since the advent of dense array EEG/MEG recordings, there have been computational efforts to estimate the location of brain electric sources. It helps to be familiar with a few conceptual issues that affect the use of source analyses techniques in affective neuroscience.

The inverse problem. EEG and MEG in principle can be regarded as two-dimensional projections of a three-dimensional reality to a surface (the scalp or the MEG helmet), and it has long been known that *an infinite number of three-dimensional source configurations exists that will produce a given two-dimensional projection.* This is referred to as the inverse problem: It is not possible to unambiguously infer the three-dimensional origin of a two-dimensional representation, a fact that is often illustrated by the shadow cast by an object on a screen. A given rectangular shadow can be the result of someone holding up a teacup or a pocket calculator.

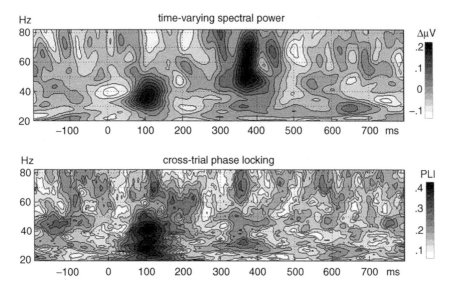

Figure 4.2. Time-frequency analysis. **Top panel**: Grand mean (n = 16) baseline-corrected time by frequency plots obtained at a posterior EEG electrode when participants viewed a visual cue (the CS+) predicting an unpleasant noise (the US) during a classical conditioning paradigm. Values were obtained by wavelet analyses of the single-trial source waveforms. The plots show time running from left to right and frequency from bottom to top. The amount of spectral amplitude change at a given time and frequency is coded by gray scale, with increase over the baseline level coded in increasingly dark shades. A pre-stimulus segment was used as the baseline, and amplitude values indicate relative change after subtracting the baseline mean. Note the two oscillatory responses to the visual cue: an early low-frequency response and a late higher-frequency response **Bottom panel**: Grand mean time by frequency representation of the phase-locking index for the same experiment. Phase-locking indices reflect the amount of phase stability across trials for a given time and frequency. Again, the amount of spectral phase-locking across trials is coded by grayscale. High phase-locking is evident for the first low-frequency oscillatory response and is lacking for the late, high-frequency response.

In practice, this means that there is no mathematically unambiguous way to calculate the neural sources of an ERP/ERF field distribution. Nonetheless, several methods have been developed that use additional knowledge to constrain the infinite solution space or to infer gross source configurations by means of simple data transformations.

Mapping techniques. The extent of the spatial sampling of scalp voltages affects the ability of researchers to use topographical information of scalp distributions to infer sources. By taking into account the physics of current flow in a conducting volume together with sufficient spatial sampling, transformations of the topographical map are available that highlight the current flow on the scalp and allow one to infer possible sources of brain-electric activity. Among the most widely used techniques is the current

source density (CSD) mapping approach that is mathematically based on the Laplace operator (Tenke & Kayser, 2005). The Laplacian can be conceived of as the second spatial derivative of the voltage map, thus showing the change of the voltage gradient across the scalp. Assuming that there are no sources in the scalp itself, the CSD map will be proportional to the radial current flow in or out of the skull at a given site. Because it is reasonable to assume that most generators of the ERP/ERF are located in near-surface cortex, this type of data transformation allows a first approximation of the underlying electrocortical sources.

Source estimation techniques. More elaborate source analysis techniques harness the spatial and temporal information inherent in multichannel recordings using different algorithms to guide estimates as to their cerebral origin. One of the first techniques used was to fit the surface potential distribution by a single equivalent current dipole (Scherg & Von Cramon, 1986). In this procedure, the assumption is that the voltage map at the scalp reflects the activity of a single neural source with a positive and negative pole. Knowledge about the possible distortion of this signal is used together with other neuroanatomical information to systematically fit a source dipole that is most similar to the measured voltage distribution. To this end, a forward calculation is performed many times, which computes various voltage distributions based on many different dipole locations and orientations, and the dipolar source with the location, strength, and orientation that lead to the distribution most similar to the measured signal is identified. Generally, MEG has been shown to have slightly better spatial sensitivity than EEG (Cohen & Cuffin, 1991), although putative differences in the depth sensitivity are still subject to empirical testing (Cohen et al., 1990).

So-called distributed source modeling procedures have been proposed as a means for enhancing the resolution of electrophysiological data without constraining the inferred electric activity to point sources or single dipoles. In these procedures, hundreds of potential dipoles at various locations in a three-dimensional volume are included in the inverse modeling process, and a unique solution is achieved by adopting certain border conditions, such as favoring the solution with minimum power of the source currents (Hämäläinen & Ilmoniemi, 1984). In EEG-based affective neuroscience research, LORETA (Pascual-Marqui, Michel, & Lehmann, 1994), has been popular; it is a distributed source estimation approach that maximizes smoothness and minimizes localization error under ideal conditions. Such approaches have been employed to identify the sequence of cortical activation during perception of an aversive conditioned stimulus (Pizzagalli, Greischar, & Davidson, 2003) or to test whether the orienting of attention to emotional face stimuli is accompanied by

early visual cortex engagement (Pourtois, Grandjean, Sander, & Vuilleumier, 2004). The development of distributed source approaches to address the inverse problem is ongoing (Ding & He, 2008), and current discussions include methods for including neurophysiological rather than physical constraints to guide selection from the infinite solution space (Grave de Peralta, Hauk, & Gonzalez, 2009).

In addition to the methods outlined earlier, spatial filtering techniques such as beamforming have been implemented in MEG, and increasingly in EEG research, typically in conjunction with realistic models of a participant's head and brain as obtained from magnet resonance images. These head models are then filled with a grid of voxels at meaningful locations, used as reference points for the source estimation. Beamforming does not attempt to model the entire scalp field or minimize residual variance. By contrast, a beamformer is a collection of spatial filters, each being optimally tuned to a voxel in the source volume. Raw MEG (and EEG) data can be projected through these spatial filters to obtain an estimate of electrical activity at each voxel. Correlated electrocortical activity at two different locations is suppressed by this technique, further illustrating that the choice of any source estimation technique must follow consideration of its suitability for a given type of data and experimental design.

As evident in this volume, work in the animal model as well as studies with hemodynamic imaging have highlighted the importance of deep brain structures such as the amygaloid bodies, insulae, nucleus accumbens, the bed nucleus of the stria terminalis, and others for affective behavior and experience. An ongoing debate in EEG/MEG research on emotions in humans concerns the extent to which electrophysiological methods can specifically identify and quantify neural activity in those deep structures. A number of authors have reported for instance that recording activity from the amygdala during emotional engagement is possible with MEG (see, e.g., Bayle, Henaff, & Krolak-Salmon, 2009; Luo et al., 2009) and even EEG (Homma, Nakajima, Toma, Ito, & Shibata, 1998), but others have doubted these claims. Because of the nature of the inverse problem, validation of deep source findings is difficult without a reference data set from another measurement modality. Such data sets are often given in studies of epileptic spike activity, in which findings obtained with MEG/EEG-based source estimation can be cross-validated against intracranial recordings, neuroimaging, and the surgical findings. Although a systematic large-scale validation study capitalizing on this methodology has not yet been conducted, this work strongly suggests a cautious approach to deep source localization with noninvasive electrophysiology: Although epileptic spikes are stronger electric signals than those evoked during emotional processing, numerous reports have failed to correctly identify known epileptic foci located in the medial temporal regions, based on extracranial MEG/EEG (e.g., Wennberg et al., 2011).

Psychometric Properties of EEG and MEG Parameters

The reliability and validity of electrophysiological measures are not routinely reported or discussed in human neuroscience studies. As an exception, the affective neurosciences have seen some discussions of the topic; for instance, as it relates to the reliability of affective trait measures extracted from resting EEG (Tomarken, Davidson, Wheeler, & Kinney, 1992). Although not tested for many variables, the *reliability* of electrophysiological indices of affect is a topic of increasing importance, particularly in the context of potential clinical applications. As Simons and Miles point out in their comprehensive review of reliability issues in ERP research (Simons & Miles, 1990), indices of psychometric quality can be easily obtained when considering the consistency of a given brain measure from trial to trial or from block to block. Reliability is said to be high if the rank ordering of subjects remains stable across trials (e.g., participants with larger amplitudes on one trial also have larger amplitudes on subsequent trials, compared to other participants) or other repetitions of the task (i.e., blocks or conditions). It can easily be assessed using Cronbach's coefficient alpha. Coefficients may be calculated for each sensor and/or brain location, resulting in topographical maps that reflect the reliability of the measure under consideration in a topographic fashion. Such efforts exist for oscillatory activity in the gamma range (Frund, Schadow, Busch, Korner, & Herrmann, 2007; Keil, Stolarova, Heim, Gruber, & Muller, 2003), the steady-state visual evoked potential (Keil et al., 2008), and the P300 component of the ERP (Ravden & Polich, 1999) – all pointing to surprisingly high stability and consistency of electrophysiological measures. The potential of these properties is yet to be fully employed.

The *validity* of electrophysiological parameters – their ability to index the intended brain process – is typically studied using cross-correlation with external validation variables, whether continuous or discrete. In the affective neurosciences, such validation has shown that the emotional modulation of late positive ERP potentials in response to affective pictures covaries with widespread cortical activation as measured by fMRI (Sabatinelli, Lang, Keil, & Bradley, 2007). Other examples include establishing correlations between electrophysiology and clinical or trait measures (Davidson, Pizzagalli, Nitschke, & Putnam, 2002). A substantial body of work has adopted this strategy and has converged to suggest that brain-electric and neuromagnetic parameters can be used as valid indicators of emotional engagement (Cahn & Polich, 2006).

Similar to the question of reliability and validity, the *sensitivity and specificity* of EEG/MEG derived measures for addressing issues in affective neurosciences have not been widely studied empirically. It is important to emphasize that an ERP component does not exist independently of the specific experimental context in which it is measured. Thus sensitivity of an electrophysiological index to an affective process of interest is dependent on the way it was measured. If an electrophysiological index with similar timing and topography is found in different experimental contexts, careful experimentation is needed to conclude that the same latent process is responsible. Such experimentation will involve systematic comparisons of the contexts prompting that ERP component within the same participants. For instance, if a study finds that the amplitude of a visual P1 component (which is often sensitive to spatial attention) is enhanced with lateralized fear faces, this finding cannot be taken to indicate that spatial attention was paid to the fear face stimuli. Rather, P1 amplitude can be affected by whether the stimulus is brighter, closer, and more salient in another context; has greater spatial contrast; or has other properties that may lead to the observed change.

Applications: Typical Paradigms for MEG and EEG in the Affective Neurosciences

As outlined earlier, the versatility of electrophysiological measures allows researchers to address a host of experimental questions in affective neuroscience, ranging from studies of perception to attention to social cognition paradigms addressing high-level constructs such as ethnic biases or empathy. Accordingly, the measures extracted from electrophysiological time series are diverse and are used for different purposes in the experimental process: They may provide timing information, complementing a behavioral or physiological measure. They may index the amount of electrocortical activation during different tasks or in different situations, and they can help generate hypotheses about neuroanatomical localization. To avoid fishing for significant results in the wealth of multidimensional result matrices containing sensors, time points, and/or frequencies, researchers should select theoretically meaningful dependent variables in an a priori fashion. The following section describes some of the most widely used paradigms, addressing the use of particular EEG/MEG

methods in the context of different research questions.

Event-Related Potentials/Fields When Processing Transient Emotional Stimuli

A host of electrophysiological studies have capitalized on the ERP or ERF elicited by the onset of an emotional stimulus, whether visual or auditory. Typically, researchers compare ERP/ERF waveforms obtained by separate time-domain averaging for different contents (e.g., pleasant, neutral, unpleasant). They then draw conclusions regarding the amount of discrimination among contents, its timing, and its locus in the brain. In the visual domain, early ERP work (Johnston & Wang, 1991; Radilova, 1982) has suggested that late positive potentials (LPPs), appearing at around 300 ms after stimulus onset, are enhanced when participants view emotionally arousing visual stimuli, compared to neutral exemplars. In the last decades, pictures taken from the International Affective Picture System (IAPS; Lang, Bradley, & Cuthbert, 2005) have frequently been used in ERP studies of visual emotion processing. The IAPS is a collection of more than 1,000 pictures and provides normative ratings regarding emotional arousal and hedonic valence associated with each picture. Affectively arousing IAPS pictures, pleasant and unpleasant, have been shown to engage motivational reflex physiology reflective of appetitive or aversive/defensive response tendencies (Lang, 1994). Electrophysiological work has established that passive viewing of affectively arousing, compared to nonarousing IAPS pictures, is associated with amplification (enhancement) of the LPP (Cuthbert, Schupp, Bradley, Birbaumer, & Lang, 2000). This centroparietal ERP effect has been related to heightened activity in occipital cortex (Keil et al., 2002) and has also been observed in MEG recordings (Peyk, Schupp, Elbert, & Junghofer, 2008). The modulation of the LPP closely correlates with other physiological measures of affective processing, such as skin conductance;

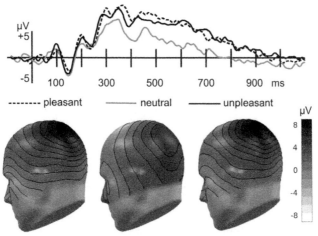

Figure 4.3. The late positive potential. **Top panel**: Grand mean (averaged across n =11 participants) event-related potential at electrode site Pz (centro-parietal), evoked by presentation of pleasant (dashed), neutral (gray), and unpleasant (black) pictures from the IAPS. *Note:* positive is up. **Bottom panel**: Grand mean topography of the mean scalp voltage during the LPP window (400–800 ms after stimulus onset). Note the voltage difference between the neutral and arousing (pleasant, unpleasant) contents. Redrawn from data published in Keil et al. (2002).

it also has a strong positive linear relationship with the emotional arousal as indicated in self-report questionnaire data (Cuthbert, Schupp, Bradley, Birbaumer, & Lang, 2000). Figure 4.3 shows the typical scalp topography and time course of the posterior LPP that is enhanced for emotionally engaging, compared to neutral pictures.

Other ERP/ERF components continue to be explored regarding their systematic relationship with the emotional content of a given stimulus. For instance, several studies have reported that an early difference between ERPs to emotional (pleasant and unpleasant) and neutral IAPS pictures develops around 120–150 ms after stimulus onset and extends up to 300 ms (Junghöfer, Bradley, Elbert, & Lang, 2001; Schupp, Junghofer, Weike, & Hamm, 2003). Picture complexity and potentially other physical properties of the stimulus contribute to this modulation, raising the question of validity (Bradley, Hamby, Low, & Lang, 2007). This early differential ERP response has been taken to reflect a processing advantage of

affective stimuli already at initial stages of perception and has been reported for other stimulus types as well, including faces and words. For references, the reader may want to read Chapter 13 where this response is extensively discussed.

A large body of work has examined processing of emotional facial expressions with ERP/ERF methods (see Chapter 7). Overall, these results have been mixed, but robust patterns of findings have emerged when studying participants high and low in social phobia (Bar-Haim, Lamy, Pergamin, Bakermans-Kranenburg, & van Ijzendoorn, 2007). For instance, several studies suggest that social anxiety is associated with enhanced visual occipitotemporal P1 components to faces in general, regardless of expression, and with heightened right temporoparietal N170 components to angry and happy faces (Kolassa, Kolassa, Musial, & Miltner, 2007; Kolassa & Miltner, 2006; Wieser, Pauli, Reicherts, & Muhlberger, 2010). Such findings are consistent with the notion that the fear relevance of a given stimulus is associated with facilitation in the cortices specialized to process the features of that stimulus (Keil, Stolarova, et al. 2007).

Paradigms with Probe Stimuli

The abrupt presentation of a brief, intense acoustic stimulus (e.g., a burst of white noise) elicits a reflexive startle response that is modulated by emotion. One component of the startle response – the reflexive eyeblink – is modulated by hedonic valence, with larger eyeblinks elicited when processing unpleasant stimuli and smaller blinks when processing pleasant content. In contrast, the electrocortical response to the same startling probe varies with emotional arousal, rather than hedonic valence: The amplitude of the P3 component of the ERP is smaller when viewing either pleasant or unpleasant, compared to neutral, pictures (Cuthbert et al., 1998; Schupp, Cuthbert, Bradley, Birbaumer, & Lang, 1997; Schupp et al., 2004). The P3 is a positive component, which is prompted by task-relevant stimuli, and is also present in response to novel or infrequent stimuli (Linden, 2005). Using dense-array EEG recordings and a source estimation procedure, Keil, Bradley, et al. (2007) observed that P3 amplitude was indeed smaller when startle probes were presented during emotional, compared to neutral, stimuli for both sound and picture foregrounds. Source modeling indicated a common frontocentral maximum of P3 modulation by affect. These data support the notion that emotionally arousing stimuli transmodally attract resources, leading to optimized processing of the affective stimulus at the cost of processing concurrent information.

Sharing of limited resources between an emotional stimulus and a concurrent probe within a modality and even between spatially overlapping stimuli can also be assessed by means of frequency-tagged ssVEPs. This approach allows researchers to continuously measure the time course of competition for processing resources arising from emotionally salient but task-irrelevant stimuli while performing a foreground target detection task. In a study by Müller and co-workers (2008), ssVEPs were recorded to rapidly flickering squares (here used as a probe stimulus) superimposed on neutral and emotionally highly arousing pictures, and variations in ssVEP amplitude over time were calculated. As reflected in ssVEP amplitude and target detection rates, arousing emotional background pictures withdrew processing resources from the detection task compared to neutral exemplars for several hundred milliseconds after stimulus onset. The amplitude was found to bear a close temporal relationship with accurate target detection as a function of time after stimulus onset.

The ssVEP approach also allows examining the competition between two emotional and/or neutral stimuli, each of which can then serve as a probe or as a target stimulus, if tagged with different frequencies. This technique was adopted in a study examining competition between two spatially separated facial expressions in high and low socially anxious individuals (Wieser, McTeague, & Keil, 2011). Two facial expressions were flickered at different frequencies (14 and 17.5 Hz) to separate the electrocortical signals evoked by the competing stimuli ("frequency-tagging"). Angry faces compared to happy and neutral expressions were linked to greater electrocortical facilitation over visual areas in the high but not the low socially anxious individuals. Using the time information inherent in the ssVEP, it was found that heightened electrocortical engagement in socially anxious participants was present after 200 ms and was sustained for the entire presentation period. These results, based on a continuous measure of attentional resource allocation, support the view that stimuli of high personal significance are associated with early and sustained prioritized sensory processing.

Classical Conditioning

Learning the contingencies between threat signals and the potential dangers that they predict is considered a ubiquitous adaptive behavior across species (LeDoux, 1993). Pavlovian fear conditioning is probably the best studied laboratory model for this type of learning. During fear conditioning, a neutral stimulus becomes an effective trigger (i.e., the conditioned stimulus, CS+) of a conditioned fear response after having been paired with an aversive event (i.e., the unconditioned stimulus, US), compared with a stimulus that signals safety (CS-). It has been consistently shown that the activation of primary sensory cortices related to the modality of the CS+ increases after successful learning of the CS-US relationship (Büchel, Coull, & Friston, 1999; Moratti, Keil, & Miller, 2006).

The ERP technique was used in numerous studies to study deep cortical (Pizzagalli et al., 2003) or sensory cortical (Stolarova, Keil, & Moratti, 2006) processes associated with acquisition of the conditioned response. This work has demonstrated enhancement of the very early C1 visual event-related component for threat-related stimuli, compared to neutral stimuli, and that this selective amplitude difference increases as learning progresses. In terms of early oscillatory activity during classical conditioning, a similar gradual increase in amplitude and synchrony was seen specifically for the CS+ across conditioning sessions in the visual (Keil, Stolarova, et al. 2007) and auditory modalities (Heim & Keil, 2006). Converging evidence was found when examining driven oscillatory activity in the auditory system elicited by amplitude-modulated acoustic CSs (Weisz, Kostadinov, Dohrmann, Hartmann, & Schlee, 2007), where sensory enhancement was observed for the CS+, particularly in participants with a greater fear response. This parallels findings obtained with steady-state evoked magnetic fields recorded using MEG: Analysis of the heart rate response during classical conditioning separated subjects into those who showed either acceleration or deceleration when presented with the flickering CS+. Heart rate accelerators showed increased ssVEF amplitude in visual and parietal cortex during CS+ presentation when awareness of the CS-US contingencies was not controlled (Moratti & Keil, 2005) as well as when fully aware (Moratti et al., 2006). Manipulating both the number of learning trials and the expectation

regarding US delivery in a given trial, subsequent work (Moratti & Keil, 2009) has suggested that the cortical facilitation of fear cue processing is determined by associative strength and previous exposure to learning contingencies, rather than by cognitive processes such as the anticipation of the US.

Conclusion

Large-scale brain electric activity can be measured using EEG/MEG and is a useful index of specific processes related to emotional engagement, when considered in a meaningful experimental context. Electrophysiological work converges with animal studies, suggesting a central role of dynamic cortical networks in establishing widespread connectivity during affective processing. These widespread networks may rely on oscillatory activity to provide short-term links between sensory and motor systems and to induce long-term changes in neuronal architecture. Multimodal recordings and computational models of human electrophysiology suggest that deep structures such as the amygdala and insula form rapid and flexible links with neocortical areas during emotional engagement. Differences in emotional behavior and experience may ultimately be determined by which structures link to particular areas in the neocortex, as well as by the spatiotemporal dynamics of cortical activation and integration. Dramatic technological and conceptual advances have taken the field to a point where the physiology underlying the modulation of extracranial fields is increasingly understood. Thus, electrophysiological studies of emotion may move beyond a descriptive analysis of waveforms to consider the data as measures of in-vivo neurophysiology.

Outstanding Issues and Future Directions

- To better exploit the rich information in electrophysiological data, *multidisciplinary research* is needed that brings together research areas as diverse as physics, experimental psychology, computational modeling, psychophysiology, and bioengineering, among others. Training of the next generation of affective neuroscientists may aim to provide a solid basis for exchange with those disciplines.

- Explicit and formal testing of the *reliability and validity* of electrophysiological indices of affect will be increasingly important in their application, particularly in the clinical research arena.
- There is an increasing need for robust methods that allow researchers to identify and quantify electrophysiological responses on the level of *single events* (i.e., single trials), to avoid the information loss associated with averaging across different brain responses.
- Multivariate and mass univariate *statistical analysis techniques* of electrophysiological data are being developed to fit the rich spatiotemporal information in EEG/MEG. These methods will increasingly replace traditional statistical approaches that are less appropriate for the data structure of human electrophysiology studies.
- Imaging modalities are increasingly combined, and the availability of *multimodal imaging facilities* has expanded to allow simultaneous recordings of, for instance, EEG and fMRI. Such data will be crucial to develop neurophysiological models of emotional processing.
- Assessing *specific neural circuit function* during appetitive versus aversive engagement is a necessary step toward more objective measurements of affective psychopathology, as well as for the development of new treatment modalities that target emotional processes in the central nervous system.
- The development of robust measures of *connectivity, dependency, and directionality* of neural communication will play an important role.
- Finding reliable and valid quantitative neural parameters of appetitive and aversive processing, potentially in real time, has the potential of establishing elec-

trophysiological *neurofeedback regimes* whose aim is to change the relevant circuitry. Because electrophysiological methods are widely available and relatively cheap, the potential applications in diagnostic assessment and intervention are manifold and can have a strong impact on mental health care.

Acknowledgments

The author would like to thank Sabine Heim, Andreas Meinel, E. Menton McGinnis, Lisa M. McTeague, Vincent D. Costa, and Margaret M. Bradley for comments on earlier drafts of this chapter. The ongoing financial support from the National Institutes of Health and the National Science Foundation is gratefully acknowledged.

Notes

1   For the purpose of clarity and to avoid cumbersome lists of measures, this chapter refers to different methods and measures derived from EEG and MEG as "human electrophysiology." As we see later, similar neuronal events underlie both the EEG and MEG signal, which allows us this simplification.

References

Bar-Haim, Y., Lamy, D., Pergamin, L., Bakermans-Kranenburg, M. J., & van, Ijzendoorn, M. H. (2007). Threat-related attentional bias in anxious and nonanxious individuals: A meta-analytic study. *Psychological Bulletin*, 133(1), 1–24.

Bayle, D. J., Henaff, M. A., & Krolak-Salmon, P. (2009). Unconsciously perceived fear in peripheral vision alerts the limbic system: A MEG study. *PLoS One*, 4(12), e8207.

Berger, H. (1969). On the electroencephalogram of man. *Electroencephalography and Clinical Neurophysiology*, 28[Suppl.], 37.

Bertrand, O., Bohorquez, J., & Pernier, J. (1994). Time-frequency digital filtering based on an invertible wavelet transform: An application to evoked potentials. *IEEE Transactions of Biomedical Engineering*, 41(1), 77–88.

Blair, R. C., & Karniski, W. (1993). An alternative method for significance testing of waveform difference potentials. *Psychophysiology*, 30(5), 518–24.

Borck, C. (2005). *Hirnströme – Eine Kulturgeschichte der Elektroenzephalographie*. Göttingen: Wallstein.

Bradley, M. M., Hamby, S., Low, A., & Lang, P. J. (2007). Brain potentials in perception: Picture complexity and emotional arousal. *Psychophysiology*, 44(3), 364–73.

Büchel, C., Coull, J. T., & Friston, K. J. (1999). The predictive value of changes in effective connectivity for human learning. *Science*, 283(5407), 1538–41.

Cahn, B. R., & Polich, J. (2006). Meditation states and traits: EEG, ERP, and neuroimaging studies. *Psychology Bulletin*, 132(2), 180–211.

Cohen, D. (1968). Magnetoencephalography: Evidence of magnetic fields produced by alpha-rhythm currents. *Science*, 161(843), 784–86.

Cohen, D. (1972). Magnetoencephalography: Detection of the brain's electrical activity with a superconducting magnetometer. *Science*, 175(22), 664–66.

Cohen, D., & Cuffin, B. N. (1987). A method for combining MEG and EEG to determine the sources. *Physics in Medicine and Biology*, 32(1), 85–89.

Cohen, D., & Cuffin, B. N. (1991). EEG versus MEG localization accuracy: Theory and experiment. *Brain Topography*, 4(2), 95–103.

Cohen, D., Cuffin, B. N., Yunokuchi, K., Maniewski, R., Purcell, C., Cosgrove, G. R., et al. (1990). MEG versus EEG localization test using implanted sources in the human brain. *Annals of Neurology*, 28(6), 811–17.

Cook, E. W., III, & Miller, G. A. (1992). Digital filtering: Background and tutorial for psychophysiologists. *Psychophysiology*, 29(3), 350–67.

Cuthbert, B. N., Schupp, H. T., Bradley, M. M., Birbaumer, N., & Lang, P. J. (2000). Brain potentials in affective picture processing: Covariation with autonomic arousal and affective report. *Biological Psychology*, 52(2), 95–111.

Cuthbert, B. N., Schupp, H. T., Bradley, M., McManis, M., & Lang, P. J. (1998). Probing affective pictures: Attended startle and tone probes. *Psychophysiology*, 35(3), 344–47.

Davidson, R. J. (1995). Cerebral asymmetry, emotion, and affective style. In R. J. Davidson & K. Hugdahl (Eds.), *Brain asymmetry* (pp. 361–87). Cambridge, MA: MIT Press.

Davidson, R. J., Pizzagalli, D., Nitschke, J. B., & Putnam, K. (2002). Depression: Perspectives from affective neuroscience. *Annual Review of Psychology*, 53, 545–74.

Delorme, A., & Makeig, S. (2004). EEGLAB: An open source toolbox for analysis of single-trial EEG dynamics including independent component analysis. *Journal of Neuroscience Methods*, 134(1), 9–21.

Dien, J. (2010). Evaluating two-step PCA of ERP data with Geomin, Infomax, Oblimin, Promax, and Varimax rotations. *Psychophysiology*, 47(1), 170–83.

Ding, L., & He, B. (2008). Sparse source imaging in electroencephalography with accurate field modeling. *Human Brain Mapping*, 29(9), 1053–67.

Elliott, G., Rothenberg, T. J., & Stock, J. (1996). Efficient tests for an autoregressive unit root. *Econometrica*, 64(4), 813–36.

Ferree, T. C., Luu, P., Russell, G. S., & Tucker, D. M. (2001). Scalp electrode impedance, infection risk, and EEG data quality. *Clinical Neurophysiology*, 112(3), 536–44.

Flor, H., Braun, C., Elbert, T., & Birbaumer, N. (1997). Extensive reorganization of primary somatosensory cortex in chronic back pain patients. *Neuroscience Letters*, 224(1), 5–8.

Foti, D., Hajcak, G., & Dien, J. (2009) Differentiating neural responses to emotional pictures: evidence from temporal-spatial PCA. *Psychophysiology*, 46, 521–30.

Frund, I., Schadow, J., Busch, N. A., Korner, U., & Herrmann, C. S. (2007). Evoked gamma oscillations in human scalp EEG are test-retest reliable. *Clinical Neurophysiology*, 118(1), 221–27.

Galambos, R. (1992). A comparison of certain gamma-band (40 Hz) brain rhythms in cat and man. In E. Basar & T. Bullock (Eds.), *Induced rhythms in the brain* (pp. 103–22). Berlin: Springer.

Gianotti, L. R., Faber, P. L., Schuler, M., Pascual-Marqui, R. D., Kochi, K., & Lehmann, D. (2008). First valence, then arousal: The temporal dynamics of brain electric activity evoked by emotional stimuli. *Brain Topography*, 20(3), 143–56.

Grave de Peralta, R., Hauk, O., & Gonzalez, S. L. (2009). The neuroelectromagnetic inverse problem and the zero dipole localization error. *Computational Intelligence and Neuroscience*, 659247. doi:10.1155/2009/659247

Groppe, D. (2011). Mass univariate analysis of event-related brain potentials/fields I: A critical tutorial review. *Psychophysiology*, 48(12),1726–37.

Hajcak, G., Weinberg, A., MacNamara, A., & Foti, D. (2011). ERPs and the study of emotion. In S. J. Luck & E. Kappenman (Eds.), *Oxford handbook of event-related potential components* (pp. 441–74). New York: Oxford University Press.

Haken, H. (1983). *Synergetics: An introduction.* Berlin: Springer.

Hämäläinen, M., & Ilmoniemi, R. (1984). *Interpreting measured magnetic fields of the brain: Estimates of current distributions.* (Technical Report No. TKK-F-A559). Helsinki: Helsinki University of Technology.

Heim, S., & Keil, A. (2006). Effects of classical conditioning on identification and cortical processing of speech syllables. *Experimental Brain Research*, 175, 411–24.

Homma, S., Nakajima, Y., Toma, S., Ito, T., & Shibata, T. (1998). Intracerebral source localization of mental process-related potentials elicited prior to mental sweating response in humans. *Neuroscience Letters*, 247(1), 25–28.

Ille, N., Berg, P., & Scherg, M. (2002). Artifact correction of the ongoing EEG using spatial filters based on artifact and brain signal topographies. *Journal of Clinical Neurophysiology*, 19(2), 113–24.

Johnston, V. S., & Wang, X. T. (1991). The relationship between menstrual phase and the P3 component of ERPs. *Psychophysiology*, 28(4), 400–9.

Junghöfer, M., Bradley, M. M., Elbert, T. R., & Lang, P. J. (2001). Fleeting images: A new look at early emotion discrimination. *Psychophysiology*, 38(2), 175–78.

Junghöfer, M., Elbert, T., Tucker, D. M., & Braun, C. (1999). The polar average reference effect: A bias in estimating the head surface integral in EEG recording. *Clinical Neurophysiology*, 110(6), 1149–55.

Junghofer, M., Elbert, T., Tucker, D. M., & Rockstroh, B. (2000). Statistical control of artifacts in dense array EEG/MEG studies. *Psychophysiology*, 37(4), 523–32.

Keil, A., Bradley, M. M., Hauk, O., Rockstroh, B., Elbert, T., & Lang, P. J. (2002). Large-scale neural correlates of affective picture processing. *Psychophysiology*, 39(5), 641–49.

Keil, A., Bradley, M. M., Junghoefer, M., Russmann, T., Lowenthal, W., & Lang, P. J. (2007). Cross-modal attention capture by affective stimuli: Evidence from event-related potentials. *Cognitive, Affective, & Behavioral Neuroscience*, 7(1), 18–24.

Keil, A., Gruber, T., Muller, M. M., Moratti, S., Stolarova, M., Bradley, M. M., et al. (2003). Early modulation of visual perception by emotional arousal: Evidence from steady-state visual evoked brain potentials. *Cognitive, Affective, & Behavioral Neuroscience*, 3(3), 195–206.

Keil, A., Smith, J. C., Wangelin, B., Sabatinelli, D., Bradley, M. M., & Lang, P. J. (2008). Electrocortical and electrodermal responses co-vary as a function of emotional arousal: A single-trial analysis. *Psychophysiology*, 45(4), 511–15.

Keil, A., Stolarova, M., Heim, S., Gruber, T., & Muller, M. M. (2003). Temporal stability of high-frequency brain oscillations in the human EEG. *Brain Topography*, 16(2), 101–10.

Keil, A., Stolarova, M., Moratti, S., & Ray, W. J. (2007). Adaptation in visual cortex as a mechanism for rapid discrimination of aversive stimuli. *Neuroimage*, 36, 472–79.

Klimesch, W., Sauseng, P., & Hanslmayr, S. (2007). EEG alpha oscillations: The inhibition-timing hypothesis. *Brain Research Reviews*, 53(1), 63–88.

Knott, J. R., & Irwin, D. A. (1968). Anxiety, stress and contingent negative variation (CNV). *Electroencephalography and Clinical Neurophysiology*, 24(3), 286–87.

Kolassa, I., Kolassa, S., Musial, F., & Miltner, W. H. (2007). Event-related potentials to schematic faces in social phobia. *Cognition and Emotion*, 21(8), 1721–44.

Kolassa, I. T., & Miltner, W. H. (2006). Psychophysiological correlates of face processing in social phobia. *Brain Research*, 1118(1), 130–41.

Kranczioch, C., Debener, S., Maye, A., & Engel, A. K. (2007). Temporal dynamics of access to consciousness in the attentional blink. *Neuroimage*, 37(3), 947–55.

Lang, P. J. (1994). The motivational organization of emotion: Affect-reflex connections. In S. H. M. Van Goozen, N. E. Van de Poll, & J. E. Sergeant (Eds.), *Emotions: Essays on emotion theory* (pp. 61–93). Hillsdale, NJ: Erlbaum.

Lang, P. J., Bradley, M. M., & Cuthbert, B. N. (2005). *International Affective Picture System: Technical manual and affective ratings.* Gainesville, FL: NIMH Center for the Study of Emotion and Attention.

LeDoux, J. E. (1993). Emotional networks in the brain. In J. M. H. Lewis (Ed.), *Handbook of emotions.* (pp. 109–18). New York: Guilford Press.

Lesse, H. (1957). *Amygdoloid electrical activity during a conditioned response.* Paper presented at the International Congress of Electroencephalography and Clinical Neurophysiology, Brussels.

Linden, D. E. (2005). The p300: Where in the brain is it produced and what does it tell us? *Neuroscientist,* 11(6), 563–76.

Lindsley, D. B. (1950). Emotions and the electroencephalogram. In M. Reymert (Ed.), *Feelings and emotions; The Mooseheart Symposium* (pp. 238–46). New York: McGraw-Hill.

Luck, S. J. (2005). *An introduction to the event-related potential technique.* Cambridge, MA: MIT Press.

Luo, Q., Mitchell, D., Cheng, X., Mondillo, K., McCaffrey, D., Holroyd, T., et al. (2009). Visual awareness, emotion, and gamma band synchronization. *Cerebral Cortex,* 19(8), 1896–1904.

Makeig, S., Debener, S., Onton, J., & Delorme, A. (2004). Mining event-related brain dynamics. *Trends in Cognitive Sciences,* 8(5), 204–10.

Makeig, S., Jung, T. P., Bell, A. J., Ghahremani, D., & Sejnowski, T. J. (1997). Blind separation of auditory event-related brain responses into independent components. *Proceedings of the National Academy of Sciences,* 94, 10979–84.

Maris, E. (2012). Statistical testing in electrophysiological studies. *Psychophysiology,* 9(4), 549–65.

Melcher, J. R., & Cohen, D. (1988). Dependence of the MEG on dipole orientation in the rabbit head. *Electroencephalography and Clinical Neurophysiology,* 70(5), 460–72.

Miller, J., Patterson, T., & Ulrich, R. (1998). Jackknife-based method for measuring LRP onset latency differences. *Psychophysiology,* 35(1), 99–115.

Moratti, S., Clementz, B., Ortiz, T., & Keil, A. (2007). Neural mechanisms of evoked oscillations: Stability and interaction with transient events. *Human Brain Mapping,* 28(12), 1318–33.

Moratti, S., & Keil, A. (2005). Cortical activation during Pavlovian fear conditioning depends on heart rate response patterns: An MEG study. *Brain Research: Cognitive Brain Research,* 25(2), 459–71.

Moratti, S., & Keil, A. (2009). Not what you expect: Experience but not expectancy predicts conditioned responses in human visual and supplementary cortex. *Cerebral Cortex,* 19(12), 2803–9.

Moratti, S., Keil, A., & Miller, G. A. (2006). Fear but not awareness predicts enhanced sensory processing in fear conditioning. *Psychophysiology,* 43(2), 216–26.

Moratti, S., Keil, A., & Stolarova, M. (2004). Motivated attention in emotional picture processing is reflected by activity modulation in cortical attention networks. *Neuroimage,* 21(3), 954–64.

Müller, M. M., Andersen, S., & Keil, A. (2008). Time course of competition for visual processing resources between emotional pictures and a foreground task. *Cerebral Cortex,* 18, 1892–99.

Müller, M. M., Teder-Salejarvi, W., & Hillyard, S. A. (1998). The time course of cortical facilitation during cued shifts of spatial attention. *Nature Neuroscience,* 1(7), 631–34

Nitschke, J. B., Miller, G. A., & Cook, E. W. (1998). Digital filtering in EEG/ERP analysis: Some technical and empirical comparisons. *Behavior Research Methods Instruments & Computers,* 30(1), 54–67.

Nunez, P. L., & Srinivasan, R. (2006). *Electric fields of the brain* (2nd ed.). New York: Oxford University Press.

Nunez, P. L., Srinivasan, R., Westdorp, A. F., Wijesinghe, R. S., Tucker, D. M., Silberstein, R. B., et al. (1997). EEG coherency. I: Statistics, reference electrode, volume conduction, Laplacians, cortical imaging, and interpretation at multiple scales. *Electroencephalography and Clinical Neurophysiology,* 103(5), 499–515.

Olejniczak, P. (2006). Neurophysiologic basis of EEG. *Journal of Clinical Neurophysiology,* 23(3), 186–89.

Pascual-Marqui, R. D., Michel, C. M., & Lehmann, D. (1994). Low resolution electromagnetic tomography: A new method for localizing electrical activity in the brain. *International Journal of Psychophysiology,* 18(1), 49–65.

Pascual-Marqui, R. D., Michel, C. M., & Lehmann, D. (1995). Segmentation of brain electrical activity into microstates: Model estimation and validation. *IEEE Transactions of Biomedical Engineering,* 42(7), 658–65.

Peyk, P., Schupp, H. T., Elbert, T., & Junghofer, M. (2008). Emotion processing in the visual brain: A MEG analysis. *Brain Topography,* 20(4), 205–215.

Pizzagalli, D. A., Greischar, L. L., & Davidson, R. J. (2003). Spatio-temporal dynamics of brain mechanisms in aversive classical conditioning: High-density event-related potential and brain electrical tomography analyses. *Neuropsychologia*, 41(2), 184–94.

Pizzagalli, D., Lehmann, D., Koenig, T., Regard, M., & Pascual-Marqui, R. D. (2000). Face-elicited ERPs and affective attitude: Brain electric microstate and tomography analyses. *Clinical Neurophysiology*, 111(3), 521–31.

Pourtois, G., Grandjean, D., Sander, D., & Vuilleumier, P. (2004). Electrophysiological correlates of rapid spatial orienting towards fearful faces. *Cerebral Cortex*, 14(6), 619–33.

Radilova, J. (1982). The late positive component of visual evoked response sensitive to emotional factors. *Act Nerv Super (Praha)*, 3(Suppl., Pt. 2), 334–37.

Ravden, D., & Polich, J. (1999). On P300 measurement stability: Habituation, intra-trial block variation, and ultradian rhythms. *Biological Psychology*, 51(1), 59–76.

Regan, D. (1989). *Human brain electrophysiology: Evoked potentials and evoked magnetic fields in science and medicine.* New York: Elsevier.

Sabatinelli, D., Lang, P. J., Keil, A., & Bradley, M. M. (2007). Emotional perception: Correlation of functional MRI and event related potentials. *Cerebral Cortex*, 17, 1066–73.

Scherg, M., & Von Cramon, D. (1986). Evoked dipole source potentials of the human auditory cortex. *Electroencephalography and Clinical Neurophysiology*, 65(5), 344–60.

Schupp, H. T., Cuthbert, B. N., Bradley, M. M., Birbaumer, N., & Lang, P. J. (1997). Probe P3 and blinks: Two measures of affective startle modulation. *Psychophysiology*, 34(1), 1–6.

Schupp, H. T., Cuthbert, B. N., Bradley, M. M., Hillman, C. H., Hamm, A. O., & Lang, P. J. (2004). Brain processes in emotional perception: Motivated attention. *Cognition and Emotion*, 18(5), 593–611.

Schupp, H. T., Junghofer, M., Weike, A. I., & Hamm, A. O. (2003). Emotional facilitation of sensory processing in the visual cortex. *Psychological Science*, 14(1), 7–13.

Simons, R. F., & Miles, M. A. (1990). Nonfamilial strategies for the identification of subjects at risk for severe psychopathology: Issues of reliability in the assessment of event-related potentials (ERP). In J. W. Rohrbaugh, R. Parasuraman, & R. J. Johnson (Eds.), *Event-related brain potentials: Basic issues and applications* (pp. 343–63). Amsterdam: Elsevier.

Singer, W., Engel, A. K., Kreiter, A. K., Munk, M. H. J., Neuenschwander, S., & Roelfsema, P. R. (1997) Neuronal assemblies: Necessity, signature and detectability. *Trends in Cognitive Sciences*, 1, 252–61.

Stolarova, M., Keil, A., & Moratti, S. (2006). Modulation of the C1 visual event-related component by conditioned stimuli: Evidence for sensory plasticity in early affective perception. *Cerebral Cortex*, 16(6), 876–87.

Tallon-Baudry, C., & Bertrand, O. (1999). Oscillatory gamma activity in humans and its role in object representation. *Trends in Cognitive Sciences*, 3(4), 151–62.

Tenke, C. E., & Kayser, J. (2005). Reference-free quantification of EEG spectra: Combining current source density (CSD) and frequency principal components analysis (fPCA). *Clinical Neurophysiology*, 116(12), 2826–46.

Tomarken, A. J., Davidson, R. J., Wheeler, R. E., & Kinney, L. (1992). Psychometric properties of resting anterior EEG asymmetry: Temporal stability and internal consistency. *Psychophysiology*, 29(5), 576–92.

Walter, W. G. (1967). The analysis, synthesis and identification of evoked responses and contingent negative variation (CNV). *Electroencephalography and Clinical Neurophysiology*, 23(5), 489.

Weisz, N., Kostadinov, B., Dohrmann, K., Hartmann, T., & Schlee, W. (2007). Tracking short-term auditory cortical plasticity during classical conditioning using frequency-tagged stimuli. *Cerebral Cortex*, 17(8), 1867–76.

Wennberg, R., Valiante, T., & Cheyne, D. (2011). EEG and MEG in mesial temporal lobe epilepsy: Where do the spikes really come from? *Clinical Neurophysiology*, 122(7), 1295–1313.

Whittingstall, K., & Logothetis, N. K. (2009). Frequency-band coupling in surface EEG reflects spiking activity in monkey visual cortex. *Neuron*, 64(2), 281–89.

Wieser, M. J., McTeague, L. M., & Keil, A. (2011). Sustained preferential processing of social threat cues: Bias without competition? *Journal of Cognitive Neuroscience*, 23(8), 1973–86.

Wieser, M. J., Pauli, P., Reicherts, P., & Muhlberger, A. (2010). Don't look at me in anger! Enhanced processing of angry faces in anticipation of public speaking. *Psychophysiology*, 47(2), 271–80.

Yuval-Greenberg, S., Tomer, O., Keren, A. S., Nelken, I., & Deouell, L. Y. (2008). Transient induced gamma-band response in EEG as a manifestation of miniature saccades. *Neuron*, 58(3), 429–41.

CHAPTER 5

PET and fMRI

Basic Principles and Applications in Affective Neuroscience Research

Jorge Armony & Jung Eun Han

It is generally accepted that neurons are the basic elements in the brain that perform the computations necessary to generate the wide range of mental processes that can be observed in humans and other animals. Specifically, neurons communicate with each other through electrochemical processes: They (1) receive information from other cells mainly through the docking of neurotransmitters in their specialized receptors; (2) open ion channels that change their electric potential (voltage) to transmit the signal from the receiving terminals, the dendrites, to the transmitter end, the axon; and (3) release neurochemicals to pass the information to other neurons. Naturally, this process requires energy, which is mainly obtained from glucose and oxygen carried by the blood. It is therefore reasonable to assume that an increase in neural activity in a given region would be associated with an increase in blood flow or volume in that part of the brain.

The existence of a close relation between brain activity and blood flow already received strong experimental support in the late 19th century, with the work of the Italian physiologist Angelo Mosso. He conducted a series of studies in individuals with head lesions, most famously Michele Bertino, a 37-year-old worker who, as a result of an accident, had a piece of skull missing in his forehead, leaving the brain exposed. Mosso used an apparatus to record Bertino's brain pulsations and noticed that they increased when he received sensory stimulation or when he was asked to perform mental calculations or remember events (Mosso, 1881). In contrast, blood flow and volume in the forearm were not affected, suggesting that the effects were specific to the brain and not a result of peripheral changes in circulation. The findings of Mosso and others were refined and extended by Roy and Sherrington (1890), who performed seminal studies in animals examining the effects of various manipulations, including sensory nerve stimulation and muscle movement, on cerebral blood circulation. Their observations led them to conclude that "the brain possesses an intrinsic mechanism by which its vascular supply can be varied locally in correspondence with local variations of functional activity" (p. 105).

Mosso also constructed what is arguably the first apparatus to record hemodynamic-based brain activity in healthy humans. He built a wooden bed mounted on a fulcrum so it behaved as a scale: Any change of weight on either side would cause it to tip in that direction. This "scientific cradle," as Mosso called it, was big enough for a person to comfortably lie on it and stay in equilibrium (and even fall asleep). The balance was "so sensitive that it oscillated according to the rhythm of respiration" (Mosso, 1896; p. 97). Critically, Mosso observed that "if one speaks to the person while he's lying horizontally on the balance, in equilibrium and perfectly quiet, it inclines immediately towards the head. The legs become lighter and the head heavier" (p. 97). This was also the case when the subject was asked to perform mental calculations or when he became upset (for example, by being told that he would not get paid for participating in the experiment). Based on these results, Mosso concluded, "It was proved by my balance that, at the slightest emotion, the blood rushes to the head" (p. 98). Whether such an experiment was actually performed remains controversial, because it is unlikely that changes in blood volume caused by neural activity would be large enough to result in appreciable changes in the weight of the brain (Buxton, 2002). Furthermore, although Mosso's cradle could arguably measure with a reasonable temporal resolution the hemodynamic changes caused by brain activity, it provided no way of determining in which part of the brain such activity had occurred. It took almost a century and several discoveries in the seemingly unrelated field of quantum physics to allow researchers to be able to use changes in blood flow and volume to identify areas of neural activity. The two most widely used techniques to do so – positron emission tomography (PET) and functional magnetic resonance imaging (fMRI) – are described next. It is important to point out that other hemodynamic-based neuroimaging modalities are employed in neuroscience and have contributed to the field of affective neuroscience, notably single-photon emission computed tomography (SPECT; Abraham & Feng, 2011).

Positron Emission Tomography

Physical Basis of PET

Matter is made up of atoms, which are comprised of electrons and a nucleus containing protons and (in most cases) neutrons. Protons and neutrons are made up of fundamental particles known as quarks; the proton consists of one *down* and two *up* quarks, whereas the neutron has one *up* and two *down* quarks. In certain unstable isotopes one of the protons is converted into a neutron by having one of its *up* quarks change into a *down* one. Because of the conservation of charge, this process is accompanied by the emission of a positron (together with a neutrino due to the conservation of energy). The positron is the antimatter counterpart of electrons; its existence was originally postulated by Paul Dirac (1928) and later demonstrated by Andersen (1932). Soon after its release, the positron loses most of its kinetic energy through interactions with nearby particles until it collides with an electron, causing the annihilation of both particles. The conservation of energy dictates, through Einstein's famous equation $E = mc^2$, that the electron-positron annihilation will result in the release of two photons (gamma rays) with an energy of 511 keV each, traveling in nearly opposite directions (the actual degree of separation depends on the momentum of the particles at the time of collision, with 180 degrees corresponding to both being at rest). Thus, if gamma ray detectors are placed around the object containing isotopes that are experiencing beta decay (as the process originally described by Enrico Fermi [1934] is also known), they can be used to detect the byproducts of the positron emission and to localize its origin. Namely, if two photons are detected nearly simultaneously, this suggests that they were originated by a beta decay that took place somewhere along the line connecting the two detection points. By recording several of these photon pairs, one can trace the location of the decays and thus build a quantitative image of the distribution of the radionucleides at a given time (interval). Such a procedure constitutes the basis of PET.

For this technique to be useful for cognitive neuroscience research, the isotopes employed need to have a half-life (the time that it takes for 50% of the nuclei in a sample to decay) long enough to allow them to reach the target area, in this case the brain, and short enough to generate a sufficient number of decays for an accurate image reconstruction and identification of the source of activity associated with an experimental condition, typically over the course of a few minutes. In addition, they have to be able to be introduced easily into the body and incorporated into substances that are involved in the process of interest (e.g., metabolism, blood flow, neuroreceptor pharmacology). Fortunately, several isotopes fulfill these criteria; the most widely used are oxygen-15 (t$\frac{1}{2}$: 2 min), fluorine-18 (t$\frac{1}{2}$: 110 min), nitrogen-13 (t$\frac{1}{2}$: 10 min), and carbon-11 (t$\frac{1}{2}$: 20 min). However, because of the short half-life of these radionucleides, the cyclotron that produces them needs to be located close to the PET scanner.

Importantly, there are several issues that limit the spatial resolution that can be achieved with PET. First, positrons are capable of traveling a non-negligible distance before their collision with an electron. This mean free path, which depends on the energy of the particle and the medium in which is traveling, can be up to 5 mm long and thus lead to an inaccurate localization of the original beta decay. In addition, the emitted photons can interact with electrons in the medium, losing energy and changing their path. These collisions, known as Compton scattering, also introduce errors in the image reconstruction, because the true location of the decay will no longer be on the line connecting the two detected photons.

Cerebral Blood Flow PET

PET has proven particularly appropriate for measuring regional cerebral blood flow (rCBF) that, as mentioned earlier, can be used as a marker of neural activity. The majority of rCBF PET studies employ oxygen15-labeled water molecules ($[^{15}O]H_2O$) as the radiotracer. This technique was instrumental, particularly during the 1980s and 1990s, in advancing our understanding of the neural correlates of a variety of mental processes in healthy humans, including emotional processing, such as perception of emotional faces (Morris et al., 1996) or pictures (Kosslyn et al., 1996), and mood induction (George et al., 1995). In addition, PET has been used to identify functional abnormalities associated with neurological and psychiatric disorders by, for example, comparing resting-state rCBF between individuals suffering from panic disorder and healthy controls (Reiman, Raichle, Butler, Herscovitch, & Robins, 1984). However, this technique's temporal resolution presents an important limitation, because the different experimental conditions need to be presented in a so-called block design to allow for a sufficient number of photon pairs to be detected. Block designs typically involve the repeated presentation of trials of the same experimental category (e.g., fearful faces) in one block lasting a minute or so, alternating with a second condition, usually the control one (e.g., neutral faces). In such a design, any temporal information about the hemodynamic (and therefore neural) response is limited to the duration of the block.

[^{18}F]deoxyglucose PET

Another index of brain activity, namely local changes in cerebral glucose metabolism, can be assessed with the PET tracer [^{18}F]deoxyglucose (FDG). When administered, FDG is distributed to active brain regions in need of glucose, where it is phosphorylated to FDG-6-phosphate, which gets trapped in those brain areas. The quantity of radioactivity of trapped FDG-6-phosphate reflects regional glucose uptake and metabolism. FDG PET is less suitable for imaging ongoing neuronal activity, because of its low time resolution: One scan image represents the average brain glucose metabolic activity of about 40 minutes. Regional cerebral metabolic rate of glucose ($rCMR_{GLU}$) during the resting state is most frequently explored in the FDG PET literature. Most often, this "baseline" glucose metabolism measure is used to differentiate clinical populations (e.g., depressed) from healthy controls (Baxter et al., 1989) or to examine treatment-related changes (Goldapple et al., 2004). The use of FDG PET can contribute to our knowledge of emotion in the healthy brain as well, by localizing glucose utilization at rest in relation to personality traits (Volkow et al., 2011). Finally, resting $rCMR_{GLU}$ PET can test the intraindividual stability of the baseline neuronal activity in different brain areas across time, which is an underlying assumption of typical fMRI and PET activation studies that require repeated measurements (Schaefer et al., 2000).

Ligand PET

In addition to measuring task-induced changes in CBF or cerebral metabolism, PET imaging can be used to directly and selectively assess the action of different neurotransmitters in the human brain in vivo. The basic principles of ligand-based PET involve competition for occupancy of the receptor sites between the endogenous neurotransmitter and the injected PET ligand, both of which target the same receptors in the brain. Ligand PET can be used to quantify baseline receptor density (e.g., at rest), which can be then correlated with other measures (e.g., neuropsychological measures, hormone levels, etc.), as well as task-induced changes in the levels of endogenous neurotransmitter. In the latter case, comparison of the regional radioactivity concentrations (either increases or decreases) during control and experimental conditions provides spatial and temporal information about the task-induced neurotransmission.

Most often, the outcome parameter is the binding potential (BP) of specific tracer binding, determined by the receptor concentration available for binding and the radioligand affinity constant, ultimately representing receptor density. To account for the specificity of binding, the model requires the use of a reference region devoid of, or low in, the binding sites of investigation (e.g., generally the cerebellum for dopamine and serotonin, the occipital cortex for opioids). Differences in the BPs between the control and experimental conditions are assumed to be caused by the task-induced change in the levels of endogenous neurotransmitter. When the BP cannot be determined, a related measure, the distribution volume (DV), is used, which is the ratio of the radioligand concentration in the region of interest to its plasma concentration at equilibrium.

One of the most crucial and difficult aspects in performing neurotransmission studies with PET is the synthesis of an appropriate radiotracer for the neurotransmitter system of interest. PET tracers need to fulfill several criteria for reliable and accurate neurotransmission mapping. Ideal radioligands are manufactured to (1) yield highly specific radioactivity and to have (2) good permeability through the blood-brain barrier (e.g., having appropriate lipophilicity), (3) sufficient affinity and high selectivity for the target receptor system, (4) low nonspecific binding, and (5) minimal binding of their metabolites in the brain. Despite continuous effort to develop PET ligands, only a subset of molecules can be investigated today. A description and some examples of the use in emotion research of two of the most studied neurotransmitters with this technique, dopamine and serotonin, are presented next.

DOPAMINERGIC SYSTEM

Dopamine is by far the most extensively studied neuromodulator of emotion in the molecular PET literature, particularly in reward and addiction research. The striatum is the brain region known to have the highest density of dopamine receptors (see Chapter 19) and is therefore the region typically targeted in dopamine PET studies, usually with [11C]raclopride as the tracer. With relatively low affinity, injected

[^{11}C]raclopride binds to dopamine D2/D3 receptors in high-receptor density areas such as the striatum within a few minutes and reliably detects changes in endogenous levels of striatal dopamine. A [^{11}C] raclopride PET study (Pruessner, Champagne, Meaney, & Dagher, 2004) used a stress task to examine the stress-induced release of endogenous dopamine (i.e., reduced [^{11}C]raclopride BP) in the ventral striatum in healthy individuals, which was also significantly correlated with cortisol levels.

Emotion processing also engages brain regions other than the striatum where dopamine may play a significant role. However, the low affinity of [^{11}C]raclopride makes it unsuitable for regions with low dopamine receptor density. The dopaminergic system in the extrastriatal regions can be better explored using the tracer [^{18}F]fallypride. Shortly after injection, this high-affinity ligand binds to available dopamine receptors (D2/D3) in brain areas with low dopamine receptor density, whereas binding of this tracer in the striatum takes hours. Using [18F]fallypride PET, Badgaiyan and colleagues (2009) observed increase in dopaminergic activity in the amygdala, medial temporal lobe, and inferior frontal gyrus when subjects were presented with emotional, compared to neutral, words. Although [^{11}C]raclopride and [^{18}F]fallypride bind to both D2 and D3 receptors, because the ratio of D2 to D3 receptors is high in most brain regions, D2 is assumed to be the target of these tracers.

In addition, a relatively small number of PET ligands are currently available for in vivo imaging of D1 receptors. The two most commonly used ligands are [^{11}C]SCH23390 and [^{11}C]NNC112, both of which have high affinity for D1 receptors and are appropriate tracers to target the striatum, where the highest concentration of D1 receptor is found, although they can be used for other regions as well. For instance, Takahashi and colleagues (2010) used [11C]SCH23390 PET, in combination with fMRI (in a separate session), to show that amygdala activation to fearful faces was significantly related to D1 receptor availability. In contrast, no relation

was observed with D2 receptor availability, measured with [11C]FLB457.

These postsynaptic dopamine receptors are not the only system probed by ligand-based PET. Available PET ligands for dopamine synthesis and dopamine transporter (DAT) have also enabled the investigation of presynaptic dopamine function. Despite complicated analysis and interpretation because of its peripheral metabolism and labeled metabolites, [^{18}F]fluorodopa ([^{18}F]FDOPA), a radiolabeled dopamine precursor, is still widely used to explore dopamine synthesis capacity. Because the [^{18}F]FDOPA PET signal extracted from extrastriatal regions is not likely to be specific to the dopaminergic system (Brown et al., 1999), [^{18}F]FDOPA is typically used to target the striatum. The uptake of this ligand reflects the decarboxylation of fluorodopa to fluorodopamine, which is stored in synaptic vesicles. Laakso and colleagues (2003) used [18F]FDOPA PET to assess the relationship between presynaptic dopamine synthesis and various personality traits. They observed that high scores on somatic anxiety, muscular tension, and irritability were associated with low [(18)F]fluorodopa uptake in the caudate. Using the DAT ligand [18F]CFT ([18F]WIN 35,428), the group also found a negative correlation between DAT binding in the putamen and detachment personality scores.

SEROTONINERGIC (5-HT) SYSTEM

Despite the prominent role that the serotonergic system plays in affective disorders such as mood disorders, aggression, and anxiety, little attention has been given to the study of serotonin and emotion in healthy individuals in the neuroreceptor PET literature. Moreover, among numerous subtypes of serotonergic receptors and their PET tracers available today, emotion research has so far focused mainly on 5-HT$_{1A}$ and 5-HT$_{2A}$ receptors, serotonin uptake transporter (SERT), and 5-HT synthesis in healthy subjects.

5-HT$_{1A}$ receptors are distributed in high densities in the amygdala, hippocampus, hypothalamus, septum, and neocortex.

With selectivity and high affinity, [carbonyl-^{11}C]WAY-100635 is the tracer of choice for 5-HT$_{1A}$ receptors. For instance, Tauscher and colleagues (2001) were able to explore, using this tracer, the significant negative association between baseline 5-HT$_{1A}$ receptor availability in the dorsolateral prefrontal, occipital and parietal cortices and anxiety.

5-HT$_{2A}$ receptors are found in high density in the neocortex and are virtually absent in the cerebellum. Previous studies in healthy individuals have explored these receptors with respect to emotion processing using [^{18}F]setoperone and [^{18}F]altanserin, both of which show good reproducibility. [^{18}F]setoperone binds to both striatal dopamine D$_2$ receptors and cortical 5-HT$_{2A}$ receptors. Although less lipophilic than the parent compound, this tracer also produces radiometabolites. By comparing [^{18}F]setoperone binding in the low receptor density area (cerebellum) to that in the rich receptor density areas (orbitofrontal cortex [OFC] and anterior cingulate cortex [ACC]), and correlating the receptor availability to several questionnaire scores, Gerretsen and colleagues (2010) were able to provide evidence for the potential modulatory role of the serotonergic system in OFC and ACC on the desire for social relationships. Today, [^{18}F]altanserin is the most widely used 5-HT$_{2A}$ PET ligand, despite the lipophilic radiometabolites that the tracer produces, which necessitates the use of complex kinetic modeling or a 2-hour bolus-infusion paradigm. [^{18}F]altanserin contains longer lived ^{18}F label and is more selective than [^{18}F]setoperone.

As the target of a number of antidepressant medications (e.g., selective serotonin reuptake inhibitors; SSRIs), SERT has been investigated extensively in the literature of depression, bipolar disorder, and social phobia, among many other psychiatric conditions, using various methods including ligand-based PET imaging. Although distributed widely throughout the brain, the highest concentrations of SERT are found in the amygdala, hippocampus, striatum, thalamus, and midbrain. Among a few successful PET tracers, [^{11}C]DASB is used most widely, and it is the only one documented in previous studies on emotion in healthy populations. [^{11}C]DASB is known to have high selectivity and affinity, be highly reproducible and reliable, and require simple quantification. One [^{11}C]DASB study (Kupers et al., 2011) explored the relationship between baseline SERT binding in several brain regions and pain tolerance ratings to noxious heat stimuli, further corroborating the role of the serotonergic system in pain processing and modulation.

In summary, ligand PET constitutes a powerful tool to examine neurotransmitter function during emotional processing, especially when combined with complementary techniques. For instance, a recent study Salimpoor and colleagues (2011) investigated reward responses to pleasurable music using [^{11}C]raclopride PET and blood-oxygen-level-dependent (BOLD) fMRI measures, in separate scans but using the same stimuli. In the PET experiment, they observed a significant release of dopamine in the striatum associated with emotional arousal while listening to highly pleasant music. Then, using fMRI, the authors explored the time course of the response and found that the caudate and the nucleus accumbens were more active during the anticipation and experience, respectively, of peak emotional responses to music.

Functional MRI

Although early neuroimaging studies of emotion mostly used PET, over the last decade the field has experienced a shift in methodology, and currently most emotion-related experiments employ functional magnetic resonance imaging. Advances in acquisition techniques and methodological approaches, together with the dramatic increase in MR scanner availability, have made this technique ubiquitous in cognitive and affective neuroscience research. Functional MRI has several advantages over PET, such as increased temporal and spatial resolution, described later, as well as the important fact that it does not involve ionizing radiation.

Physical Basis of MRI

MRI is based on nuclear magnetic resonance (NMR). As its name suggests, this phenomenon is related to the interaction, through resonance, between atomic nuclei and magnetic fields. Simple NMR behavior can be discussed using classical physics, whereas a more complete and accurate view requires quantum physics. We present next a very brief and simplified description of the principles of NMR. For a more thorough account of the physical basis of MRI, the interested reader is referred to the numerous excellent reviews and textbooks on the topic (e.g., Bernstein, King, & Zhou, 2004; Haacke, Brown, Thompson, & Venkatesan, 1999; Huettel, Song, & McCarthy, 2009).

In addition to mass and charge, atomic nuclei can have intrinsic angular momentum, or spin. Although spin is a quantum mechanical property of particles, which cannot be explained by classical physics, it may be helpful to think of it as representing a physical rotation of the nucleus around its axis, like a top. Nuclei with an odd number of protons or neutrons have nonzero spin. In particular, the nucleus of hydrogen – the most abundant element in the universe and, critically, in the human body (mostly in the form of water) – is composed of a single proton and thus has a nonzero (1/2) spin. A key property of nuclei with nonzero spin is that they possess a magnetic moment, related to the nuclear spin through a nucleus-specific multiplicative constant known as the gyromagnetic ratio γ. The nuclear magnetic moment is a vector, and hence it has, in addition to a magnitude, a defined direction in space. In the absence of an external magnetic field, there is no preferred orientation for a magnetic moment so that different spins will be pointing in different, random directions. This means that the vector sum of the individual magnetic moments of a collection of nuclear spins (e.g., those constituting an object) will be zero and there will be no net macroscopic magnetic moment.

In contrast, when the object is placed in a strong magnetic field Bo, spins will assume one of a few specific energy levels. In the case of the spin $\frac{1}{2}$ hydrogen nuclei, spins will be either in a low-energy spin-up (parallel) state or a high-energy spin-down (antiparallel) state. Because the parallel state has lower energy than the antiparallel one, there will be slightly more spins in the parallel state (about 3 per million protons, for an external field of 1 Tesla at room temperature). It is this excess of protons pointing "up," resulting in a net macroscopic magnetization of the object being studied, which underlies the generation of the MRI signal.

Given the appropriate amount of energy, spins in the lower energy state (spin-up) can jump to the higher energy level. The amount of energy required for this transition is equal to the difference in energy between levels and can be delivered by an electromagnetic field that oscillates with a frequency that is tuned to the required energy value (the energy of an electromagnetic wave is proportional to its frequency). This *resonant frequency*, known as the Larmor frequency, is equal to the product of the gyromagnetic ratio γ – a property of the spinning nucleus (approximately 42 MHz per Tesla for hydrogen nuclei) – and the external field Bo. If this electromagnetic field is left on for a sufficient time, enough spins will jump to the higher energy level so that the number of parallel and antiparallel spins becomes equal, and therefore there is no longer a net magnetization along the direction of the Bo field. In the classical view, the electromagnetic field, applied in a direction perpendicular to the static main magnetic field, tips the spins 90 degrees so that they are now lying on the orthogonal plane. After the *radiofrequency (RF) pulse* is turned off, spins go back to the original equilibrium state, with an excess of spin-up protons, so that the bulk magnetization along the axis of Bo is recovered. This process, in which the energy acquired through the radiofrequency pulse is released (and captured by the receiver coil), is known as *longitudinal relaxation* or recovery and is governed by a time constant T_1 that depends on the medium in which the protons are embedded. Differences in T_1 values between gray matter, white matter, and cerebrospinal fluid provide the basis for the identification of these tissue types in standard anatomical, T_1-weighted MR images.

Individual spins do not completely align in the direction of the external magnetic field. Instead, they "precess" around this axis at the Larmor frequency. In the classical view, this motion is similar to the wobbling of a top around the direction of gravity. This precession means that, in addition to a longitudinal component parallel to the external magnetic field, each spin's magnetic moment has a rotating transverse component. Because the direction of this component at any given time is different for the different spins (they are out of phase), the net bulk magnetic moment in the transverse plane is zero. However, the RF pulse that tips the spins also causes them to start precessing in phase, creating a net macroscopic magnetization in the plane perpendicular to the static magnetic field. Once the RF pulse is turned off, spins begin to lose coherence due to their interaction and gradually become out of phase and the net transverse magnetization disappears. This *transverse relaxation* or decay process also depends on the medium in which the protons precess, as does the longitudinal relaxation, but it has a different time constant, known as T_2. MR images based on transverse relaxation (T_2-weighted) also provide important information about brain structure and are particularly useful for clinical applications (e.g., detection of tumors).

Importantly, local magnetic inhomogeneities will cause spins in different spatial locations to experience slightly different magnetic fields. This in turn will result in spins precessing at different frequencies (because of different Larmor frequencies; see the earlier discussion), leading to a more rapid decay of transverse relaxation than that predicted by the spin-spin interactions process just described. The combined effects of spin-spin interactions and local magnetic inhomogeneities on transverse magnetization decay are characterized by a T_2^* time

constant. As explained later, the most common type of functional MRI relies on T_2^*-weighted images.

A large proportion of current MRI protocols for T_1-, T_2-, or T_2^*-weighted images consist of the sequential acquisition of a series of two-dimensional images, or slices. The thickness of the slices, typically on the order of 2–5 mm, is normally a selectable parameter of the acquisition. Each slice, in turn, is divided into a grid of pixels (e.g., 64x64, 192x192), which, together with the field of view (FOV, region of space being imaged), determine the in-plane resolution, much like a digital camera. Thus, the final reconstructed 3D image is composed of three-dimensional pixels, or voxels, which constitute the resolution elements of the image. The chosen voxel size usually represents a tradeoff between spatial resolution, signal-to-noise ratio, and scan duration.

BOLD fMRI: Principles and First Studies

Materials can have magnetic properties; that is, they can behave in specific ways when placed in a magnetic field. The most well-known type of interaction is *ferromagnetism*, through which compounds such as iron become strongly attracted to magnets and can even become magnetic themselves. Most materials, however, do not show any noticeable behavior when exposed to an external magnetic field. Yet, the British physicist Michael Faraday observed, in 1845, that a large variety of common "nonmagnetic" compounds, from glass to wood to beef, were slightly repelled by magnets (Faraday, 1846). He termed this small but measurable effect *diamagnetism*. Interestingly, Faraday also tested blood and found it to be diamagnetic.

About 80 years later, Linus Pauling and Charles Coryell (Pauling & Coryell, 1936) reexamined the magnetic properties of blood and made a startling discovery that would have profound implications for the development of fMRI a half-century later. They found that, whereas oxy-hemoglobin (oxygenated blood) is mildly diamagnetic, as originally reported by Faraday, deoxy-hemoglobin (i.e., hemoglobin without oxygen, dHb) is *paramagnetic*; that is, it possesses a positive magnetic susceptibility and therefore is attracted by magnetic fields.[1] Thus, the magnetic properties of blood are drastically different depending on whether oxygen is attached to the hemoglobin molecules. The relevance of this finding for fMRI becomes apparent when we put it together with what was described in the previous sections: (1) Increased neural activity in a given brain region is associated with an increase in (oxygenated) blood flow in that area, (2) oxy- and deoxy-hemoglobin have different magnetic properties, and (3) T_2^* values depend on the local magnetic properties of the region where the hydrogen spins reside. Thus, areas in which there is a change in neural activity – for instance when comparing an "active" versus "rest" condition – will be associated with a change in the oxy- and deoxy-hemoglobin concentrations, which will alter the local magnetic properties of the medium and thus result in differences in signal intensity in T_2^*-weighted images.

The hypothesis that differences in the relative concentration of oxygen in blood could be quantitatively measured through T_2^* values in MRI was confirmed by Thulborn and colleagues in 1982. They observed a quadratic relation between $1/T_2$ values and the fraction of deoxygenated hemoglobin in blood samples, so that T_2 values were smaller for larger concentrations of dHb, consistent with the paramagnetic properties of this molecule and its effects on the local magnetic field. They also reported that the $1/T_2$ values, and hence the sensitivity to detect relative differences in dHB concentrations, increased quadratically with the strength of the static magnetic field.

A few years later, Ogawa and colleagues showed that this technique could be used to view the brain vasculature *in vivo* in rodents (Ogawa, Lee, Nayak, & Glynn, 1990). They termed this effect *blood-oxygenation-level-dependent* (BOLD) contrast (Ogawa, Lee, Kay, & Tank, 1990). They suggested that it could be used to produce real-time brain

activity functional maps and could therefore become an alternative to other hemodynamic techniques, notably PET, with the key advantage that it did not require the injection of an external tracer or contrast agent. Indeed, very soon thereafter, three groups published, in the same year, studies using BOLD fMRI to track neural-related activity in humans while viewing visual stimuli (Kwong et al., 1992; Ogawa et al., 1992) or performing a motor task (Bandettini, Wong, Hinks, Tikofsky, & Hyde, 1992).

Although the first fMRI studies mostly focused on relatively simple visual and motor responses, researchers quickly realized the potential of this new technique to explore a variety of cognitive processes, including language (Rao et al., 1992), memory (Stern et al., 1996), and mental imagery (Le Bihan et al., 1993). Emotion was certainly not left out: A study by Breiter and colleagues on symptom provocation in patients suffering from obsessive-compulsive disorder was presented at an international conference in 1993 (Breiter et al., 1993) and published about three years later (Breiter et al., 1996; Breiter & Rauch, 1996).[2] In 1995, Grodd and colleagues published a study in *Der Radiologe* reporting significant left amygdala activation (i.e., signal intensity differences) during sad, but not happy, mood induction, compared to baseline (Grodd, Schneider, Klose, & Nagele, 1995). These studies were followed by many more, using more sophisticated acquisition techniques, analysis methods, and experimental paradigms to explore an impressive variety of mental processes – so much so that fMRI has arguably become the most popular technique in cognitive neuroscience in general and in affective neuroscience in particular, as exemplified in most chapters in the present volume.

The BOLD Response

The change in the BOLD signal triggered by a brief neural event is known as the hemodynamic response (HDR). Neural activity causes an initial increase in dHb concentration due to local oxygen consumption, which results in a rapid and brief decrease in the BOLD signal (an increase in the relative concentration of paramagnetic dHb increases local magnetic inhomogeneities, resulting in faster de-phasing of transversal spin precession and hence a loss of signal). This "initial dip" has been reported by some research groups (Ernst & Hennig, 1994; Hu, Le, & Ugurbil, 1997; Yacoub & Hu, 1999), but its existence remains controversial (Lindauer et al., 2002; Logothetis, 2000; Vanzetta & Grinvald, 2001). This dip is followed by an increase in the BOLD signal, the main component of the hemodynamic response, which is caused by a gradual increase in oxygenated blood flow to the active region; this increase is more than is necessary to replenish the depleted oxygen consumed by the active neurons. Because of the slow temporal dynamics of this process, this phase of the HDR becomes visible only 2–3 seconds after the onset of neuronal activity, and it takes another 2 to 3 seconds to reach its peak. Once neural activation has ceased, the HDR slowly returns to baseline, often exhibiting an undershoot that brings it to below baseline levels for a few seconds. Thus, fMRI has a temporal resolution of the order of seconds, much lower than that of EEG and MEG, which is at, or below, the millisecond level (see Chapter 4), but significantly better than that of PET (see the earlier discussion).

Although in most cases the qualitative behavior of the HDR is as just described, it is important to emphasize that its precise shape – in terms of delay, time-to-peak, duration, undershoot magnitude and duration, and so on – depends on the underlying neural event that triggered it, the region of the brain where it takes place, and the individual to which the brain belongs (Aguirre, Zarahn, & D'Esposito, 1998; Huettel & McCarthy, 2001). It is therefore important to be careful when comparing HDRs from different brain regions or individuals. This caution is particularly relevant when attempting to infer neuronal causality through connectivity analyses (S. M. Smith et al., 2011).

fMRI Data Analysis

During the past decade, there has been an impressive development of sophisticated statistical approaches to analyze fMRI data, including multivariate approaches. Still, to date, the vast majority of fMRI experiments are analyzed in a so-called massively univariate approach using the general linear model (GLM). Basically, this means that each voxel is analyzed independently of the others, and the expected response for each event is modeled (for instance, by assuming a typical hemodynamic response shape as described earlier) and entered in a regression analysis. The weight, or parameter estimate, associated with each event type, for each subject, is obtained through ordinary least-squares estimation and taken to a second-level analysis, typically a t-test or ANOVA comparing the conditions of interest. Those voxels in which the test reaches statistical significance are assigned a color (representing the degree of significance), whereas those that do not are ignored. The resulting statistical parametric map (SPM) can be overlaid onto a structural image to relate the significant voxels to a specific anatomical region. Because a separate test is performed for each voxel (up to 100,000 of them), it is important to minimize Type I errors (false-significant activations) by correcting the threshold of significance to account for these multiple tests. Several multiple comparisons corrections have been proposed, including those based on Bonferroni (Logan & Rowe, 2004), Gaussian random field theory (Worsley et al., 1996), and the false discovery rate (Genovese, Lazar, & Nichols, 2002), either at a voxel or cluster (island of contiguous activated voxels) level. For more details about the analysis of fMRI data with the GLM, including assumptions, limitations, extensions, and generalizations, the reader is referred to the many articles and books published on the topic (e.g., Huettel, Song, & McCarthy, 2009; Jezzard, Matthews, & Smith, 2001; Penny, Friston, Ashburner, Kiebel, & Nichols, 2007).

Neural Correlates of BOLD

Whereas intracranial electrodes are typically used to record action potentials from one or multiple neurons, EEG is most sensitive to local field potentials (LFPs), which mainly represent extracellular currents associated with synaptic activity (see Chapter 4 for more details). Therefore, to properly interpret the results from experiments using BOLD fMRI and to compare them to those from other techniques, it is critical to understand which aspect of brain (neuronal) response is measured by this technique.

Early studies reported a correlation between hemodynamic and spike (action potential) activity (Shmuel & Grinvald, 1996; A. J. Smith et al., 2002). Direct comparison between BOLD signal and multi-unit spiking activity (MUA), either separately in different human subjects (Mukamel et al., 2005) or simultaneously in rhesus monkeys (Logotehtis, Pauls, Augath, Trinath, & Oeltermann, 2001), revealed that both MUA and LFP predicted the fMRI response. This observation should not be surprising, because in general LFPs and MUA are highly correlated. However, when LFPs and MUA are dissociated, it is only the local field potentials that predict the corresponding BOLD response (Logothetis et al., 2001). This tighter relation between LFPs and hemodynamic activity has been confirmed in several studies using a variety of species and techniques (Lauritzen, 2005; Viswanathan & Freeman, 2007). Thus, there is now strong evidence that the BOLD signal measured in fMRI experiments reflects mainly input-related activity and local processing, rather than output signals (for more comprehensive reviews, see Logothetis & Wandell, 2004; Shmuel, 2010).

These findings are consistent with calculations of the energy consumption associated with different aspects of neuronal communication. Extrapolating from measurements conducted in rodents (Attwell & Laughlin, 2001), it has been estimated that up to 75% of the energy budget in primates is spent on reversing the ionic currents through the postsynaptic membrane; in contrast, only about 10% of the total energy is spent on action potentials (Attwell & Iadecola, 2002).

Finally, it is important to mention that, although it is generally accepted that BOLD fMRI reflects some aspect(s) of neuronal activity, there is growing evidence highlighting a possible role of astrocytes in the regulation of blood flow and hence on the generation of the fMRI signal; however, many of the details remain poorly understood (Takano et al., 2006). Astrocytes play a key role in the uptake and recycling of neurotransmitters released by the adjacent presynaptic neuron terminals into the synaptic cleft. One theory is that this energy-consuming process results in the increased release of lactate, through glycolisis, which acts as a vasodilator and hence increases blood flow to that region (for a review, see Figley & Stroman, 2011).

Negative BOLD

In most studies, we are typically interested in increases in the BOLD signal as a result of an experimental manipulation; that is, we look for "activations." However, in certain situations, the BOLD response associated with the experimental condition is smaller than that of the control or baseline. In such cases, we speak of a task- or stimulus-induced "deactivation," which is often interpreted as reflecting inhibitory processes taking place in that region. However, there are several possible alternative interpretations for these deactivations that do not assume the presence of inhibitory neural responses (see Gusnard & Raichle, 2001). Perhaps the most common situation is that of a reverse subtraction effect, which is described in the next section. A second, physiological, explanation relates to the vascular-steal phenomenon; in this case, an increase in local blood flow in an active area will be associated with a similar decrease in a remote area (Harel, Lee, Nagaoka, Kim, & Kim, 2002; Kannurpatti & Biswal 2004), due to the overall conservation of blood volume (think of the experiment by Mosso described earlier). Importantly, according to this model, decreases in blood flow and in the BOLD signal can be observed even if there is an underlying increase in neuronal response in that region.

Still, there is now compelling evidence suggesting that, in some cases, negative BOLD responses do indeed reflect actual decreases in neural responses. For instance, using simultaneous electrophysiological recordings and fMRI in anesthetized macaque monkeys, Shmuel and colleagues (2006) showed that negative BOLD responses in the visual cortex were directly associated with decreases in neural activity to levels below their spontaneous rate. Furthermore, Devor et al. (2007) confirmed, in experiments of rat forepaw stimulation, that whereas increased blood oxygenation and volume were mainly associated with neuronal excitation and arteriolar vasodilation, decreases in blood oxygenation were observed in areas of neuronal inhibition and arterioral vasoconstriction.

Some Issues Related to fMRI Acquisition, Design, and Analysis

When designing, running, or analyzing an fMRI experiment, there are a number of choices that need to be made and potential pitfalls to be avoided. Although most of these considerations apply to any study in cognitive neuroscience, they are particularly relevant to emotion-related research. In this section we present a few of the more important issues in our view.

Susceptibility Artifacts

As described in the "Physical Basis" section, T_2^* contrast is sensitive to local inhomogeneities in magnetic susceptibility, such as those induced by the presence of deoxyhemoglobin. However, macroscopic field inhomogeneities, like those that arise in tissue-air interfaces (which have different magnetic susceptibilities), also affect the signal and introduce important artifacts, usually in the form of image distortion and signal loss in the voxels near air-filled cavities. Unfortunately for affective neuroscience

research, two of the most important areas in emotional processing, the amygdala and ventromedial PFC, are particularly affected by these susceptibility artifacts. Indeed, it was not uncommon in the early days of fMRI to question any reported amygdala activation because of this issue (Merboldt, Fransson, Bruhn, & Frahm, 2001). Fortunately, several modifications to reduce susceptibility artifacts and improve image quality have been developed over the years, both for the amygdala (Chen, Dickey, Yoo, Guttman, & Panych, 2003; Morawetz et al., 2008; Rick et al., 2010) and ventromedial PFC (Preston, Thomason, Ochsner, Cooper, & Glover, 2004; Truong & Song, 2008). Nonetheless, these artifacts remain an issue that deserves careful attention, and it is therefore wise to routinely examine the raw functional images to ensure that adequate signal is obtained in these regions.

Categorical versus Parametric Designs

Because the absolute magnitude of the BOLD signal is arbitrary (i.e., has no direct physical or physiological meaning), an fMRI experiment typically requires the comparison of one (or more) experimental conditions against a control one. Researchers usually spend most of their time and effort designing the perfect experimental trials so that they engage the mental process of interest; for example, perception of fearful faces, empathic responses, or remembered emotional events. Selection of an appropriate control condition, however, is also critical if one is to draw the appropriate conclusions from the observed activation, because this approach relies on the notion of cognitive subtraction and the principle of pure insertion (Donders, 1969). That is, it is assumed that the only difference between the experimental and control trials is the factor of interest (e.g., emotionality) and that the mathematical subtraction of the responses it generates will isolate those, and only those, areas specifically involved in that process. As an illustration of this issue, we observed in a recent meta-analysis of brain responses to visual emotional stimuli

(Sergerie, Chochol, & Armony, 2008) that effect sizes of amygdala activation are larger when comparing an emotional visual stimulus with a low-level condition, such as a fixation cross or a scrambled stimulus, than when using a neutral version of the same stimulus (e.g., fearful vs. neutral faces). Although this finding suggests that the use of a simpler control is preferable in terms of statistical power, because it increases sensitivity, this is done at the expense of specificity. In other words, an activation obtained in the contrast fearful faces versus fixation cross may reflect an involvement of that region in emotional (fear) processing, in the processing of faces, or more generally in the processing of complex visual stimuli, with little or no relation to their emotional value.

Another important issue that deserves attention when contrasting two trial types is that of apparent deactivations. Specifically, if the control condition elicits a stronger response than the experimental one, the standard comparison will yield negative values, which could be interpreted as deactivations (representing neural inhibition) associated with the condition of interest. Although this result will typically not arise in the case of a simple, low-level baseline (such as a fixation cross), it is quite common when the comparison involves two similarly complex or demanding conditions. For instance, a deactivation associated with the contrast of fearful minus happy faces could represent a true decrease in the BOLD signal for the fearful faces or a stronger response for the happy ones. Introducing a third condition (e.g., neutral faces or a low-level baseline condition) may sometimes help in distinguishing between these different possibilities.

An alternative approach to the subtraction method, which does not require an explicit control condition, is the use of a parametric design. In this case, the factor of interest (e.g., emotional valence or intensity) is varied along a given scale, and a regression analysis is then performed, instead of a categorical comparison (e.g., t-test between experimental and control conditions). For instance, using this type of design, Anderson and colleagues (2003) reported that amygdala activation correlated with subjects' ratings of emotional intensity, but not valence, of olfactory stimuli, whereas the orbitofrontal cortex exhibited the opposite pattern; that is, a correlation with valence but not intensity. This approach, however, assumes that the subjects and their brains do process the factor of interest in a parametric fashion, which may not always be the case (e.g., a morphed face with 20% of fear may be perceived as neutral, whereas one with 30% may be considered to be fearful). Indeed, a recent study by Zaretsky, Mendelsohn, Mintz, and Hendler (2010) showed significant amygdala activation associated with the perceived level of threat from dynamic facial expressions of various levels of fear (obtained through morphing different percentages of neutral and fear expressions of the same individual), but not with the actual degree of fear present in the stimuli.

Block versus Event-Related Designs

Early fMRI studies employed a block design, similar to those used in PET. However, as acquisition and analysis techniques improved, it became possible to present stimuli in any given order and model individual events within the framework of the GLM. These event-related designs, named after ERP studies in electroencephalography (see Chapter 4), are very flexible and allow for the study of a variety of phenomena in a way that is not possible (or at least far from optimal) with block designs; these phenomena include learning, oddball, and priming effects, as well as paradigms requiring an *a posteriori* assignment of stimuli to a particular category based on the subject's response, such as those exploring the subsequent memory effect (Dolcos, LaBar, & Cabeza, 2004; Sergerie, Lepage, & Armony, 2006) or the effects of stimulus awareness (Pessoa, Japee, Sturman, & Ungerleider, 2006; Vuilleumier et al., 2002). In addition, event-related designs are less susceptible to habituation, an issue of particular relevance in the case of the amygdala, where neurons rapidly decrease their response to repeated stimuli (Bordi & LeDoux, 1992; Wilson & Rolls, 1993). Indeed, several fMRI studies have shown rapid amygdala habituation to repeated presentations of emotional stimuli (Breiter et al., 1996; Fischer et al., 2003), an effect that appears to be more pronounced in the right hemisphere (Sergerie et al., 2008). Nonetheless, it should be noted that amygdala activation has been reported with block designs in both PET and fMRI studies, even when using blocks of 17.5 minutes in an FDG PET experiment (Fernandez-Egea et al., 2009). However, block designs do have the advantages of being easier to analyze and not requiring an accurate model of the elicited hemodynamic response (see the later discussion). In addition, they have much higher statistical power than event-related or any other type of designs, even in the case of the amygdala (Sergerie et al., 2008).

Modeling the HDR

There are several underlying assumptions in the GLM approach, two of which are important enough to have made it into its name. As mentioned earlier, the expected response for each event needs to be modeled; that is, an assumption of its shape is required. The particular model used can be very specific, such as when a "synthetic" hemodynamic response function (HRF) is used. This has the advantages that only one parameter needs to be estimated and its value is easy to interpret: It directly represents the magnitude of the HDR for that particular event type. Its disadvantage, however, is that this model will only capture HDRs that behave like those of the model and will fail to capture responses that have a different behavior (e.g., longer latencies, shorter duration, and so on). This disadvantage is important given that, as previously mentioned, the exact shape of the HDR is likely to vary as a function of regions, individuals, and stimuli or tasks. To account for this potential variability in the HDR, one can use a general set of basis functions, such as Fourier, gamma, or boxcar ("finite impulse response") functions.

In this case, each event is characterized by a set of parameters (one for each function used in the model), and the resulting HDR is built by the linear combination of the basis functions, each multiplied by its parameter estimate. The obvious advantage of such an approach is that it can capture a wide range of HDRs with this flexible model. In contrast, its drawback is that in this case each parameter estimate is difficult to interpret on its own, and perhaps more importantly, some of the results may correspond to "non-physiological" HDRs (i.e., their shapes are unlikely to correspond to a real response, for example, by failing to follow the known hemodynamic slow temporal course).

An often used compromise between these two extreme options is to use the standard or canonical HRF together with its temporal derivative. Functions that, like the HRF, go to zero at plus and minus infinity, have the property of being orthogonal to their temporal derivatives. Thus, these two basis functions explain different, non-overlapping components of the variance of the data (see the section, "Independence of Explanatory Variables"). In addition, the shape of the temporal derivative is such that, when linearly combined with the HRF, it produces HDRs with different delays, depending on the relative weight of each function. Thus, such combinations can be used to examine differences in the latency of the response as a function of the stimulus type. Reinders et al. (2006) employed this approach to show that responses in the amygdala-hippocampus junction occurred earlier for fearful than for neutral faces. The authors interpreted this finding as providing support for a preconscious, subcortically mediated amygdala response to threat-related stimuli.

Linearity of the HDR

A second assumption of the GLM is that of the linearity of the responses, in accordance with the superposition principle. That is, if a stimulus elicits a specific HDR, presenting the same (type of) stimulus twice within a short time interval should result in an overall response that is simply the sum of the individual responses that each stimulus would elicit independently of the other. Although this seems to be the case for intertrial intervals (ITI) longer than a couple of seconds (the specific cutoff time depends on various factors), the linearity assumption no longer holds for very short ITIs (Birn & Bandettini, 2005; de Zwart et al., 2009). The nonlinear effect usually manifests as a reduced amplitude of the HDR for the second stimulus and therefore can, if not taken into account, lead to an under-estimation of the true response to the stimulus. Interestingly, this limitation can be turned into an advantage in studying the stimulus specificity of neural responses in a particular region, as evidenced by the growing use of the so-called fMRI adaptation technique (for a description and review of this approach, see Krekelberg, Boynton, & van Wezel, 2006). Rotshtein and colleagues (2001) employed an fMRI adaptation paradigm to explore amygdala and cortical responses to unpleasant faces obtained by an "expressional transfiguration" (ET) effect (inverting eyes and mouth). They observed that the lateral occipital complex was not affected by valence, but exhibited differential patterns of adaptation depending on the stimulus value. In contrast, the amygdala responded differently to ET and normal faces, but its adaptation was not affected. One interpretation provided by the authors is that the emotional valence of the stimuli prevented neurons in the visual cortex from adapting to repeated presentations of the ET stimuli.

Independence of Explanatory Variables

In addition to the basis functions representing the hemodynamic response (e.g., canonical HRF and its the temporal derivative), it is possible to include in the model or design matrix other variables that can explain some of the variance in the data. These can be entered at the level of each scan (e.g., physiological measures; see Chapter 3), trial (e.g., reaction times or valence ratings), or subject

(e.g., age or anxiety scores; see Chapter 24). One can then identify brain regions whose activity is modulated by that explanatory variable. In addition, one can enter variables of no interest, included simply to remove variance that has no experimental interest but that can explain some of the variability in the data. Introducing these confounding variables has two main objectives: to reduce the residuals ("error") of the model and hence increase statistical power, and to account for some of the noise in the data that otherwise could be assigned to the experimental conditions.

Typical examples of these variables are the movement parameters obtained in the realignment preprocessing step, which capture the signal changes associated with the subject's movement during the scan; these parameters can be nonspecific (e.g., slowly adjusting the position of the head to improve comfort), or they can be related to the task, such as when they are caused by button pressing, speech, startle caused by loud auditory stimuli or sudden changes in luminosity of the visual stimulus, and so on. At the level of the subject, typical examples are age, overall performance in the task, or some other factor that can influence brain responses.

One could be tempted to include as many potential confounding variables as one can think of. However, it is important to keep in mind that the GLM is essentially a multiple regression model, and the parameter estimates represent the values of the semipartial correlation of the data and each covariate, after the variance explained by all the other regressors in the model has been removed. Therefore, if two covariates are correlated (i.e., they explain some of the same variance in the data), the contribution of each of them will be reduced. As an illustration, if one were to enter the exact same regressor twice, the parameter estimate for each instance of that regressor would be half of the original value. One alternative to avoid this issue is to sequentially orthogonalize each new covariate that is entered in the model with respect to the others, although in this case the interpretation of their corresponding parameter estimates becomes more difficult. Sometimes it is desirable to enter an additional covariate *because* it is correlated with the one of interest, to show that the results obtained are not due to this other (usually uninteresting) factor. For instance, Dickie, Bruner, Akerib, and Armony (2008) reported a correlation between amygdala and ventromedial PFC activations for successful memory encoding of fearful faces and symptom severity in individuals suffering from posttraumatic stress disorder (PTSD). Because depression is often a comorbid condition in PTSD and is likely to influence emotional processing, it was important to rule out the possibility that the results were due to depression rather than PTSD symptomatology. By entering both variables in the analysis, the researchers showed that, although the strength of the correlation with PTSD symptom severity was reduced, as expected because both variables are typically highly correlated, the results were still statistically significant. In contrast, the correlations with depression scores did not reach the threshold of statistical significance and therefore could not explain the observed activations.

Conclusion

In summary, functional neuroimaging techniques, particularly fMRI, have allowed researchers to make great advances in affective neuroscience research. Although earlier studies largely confirmed findings previously obtained in experimental animals and with neurological patients, more recently researchers have begun using sophisticated and innovative paradigms and analysis techniques to advance our understanding of the neural basis of emotional processing in the healthy brain and to shed light on the dysfunction of the emotional brain in a variety of psychiatric disorders. The integration of these techniques with EEG, transcranial magnetic stimulation (TMS), and other approaches should pave the way for even further advances in this exciting field. Nonetheless, it is important to keep in mind that, as is the case with any experimental method, there are limitations and potential pitfalls that one needs to consider when designing, analyzing, or interpreting experiments using PET or fMRI.

Outstanding Questions

- The amygdala is composed of several subnuclei with unique cytoarchitectonic and physiological properties. Yet, to date, the spatial resolution of most fMRI systems does not allow for an unambiguous localization of the observed activations to specific regions within this structure. Will high-field (e.g., 7T) fMRI hold the key to solve this problem?
- Functional neuroimaging techniques are inherently correlational and thus do not speak to causality. Will further developments in analysis techniques (e.g., connectivity), as well as the combination of neuroimaging with other methods (e.g., lesions, electrical or magnetic stimulation), help better understand the role of the different brain regions in emotional processing?
- Most reported findings from neuroimaging studies are based on group averages. Whereas results from single-subject data are fairly robust and easy to interpret for simple sensory or motor tasks, that is not the case for most of the emotional paradigms used in the literature. Could further advances in acquisition and analysis methods solve this problem and eventually pave the way for the use of fMRI as a diagnostic tool in psychiatry?

Acknowledgments

We are grateful to Bruce Pike for comments on an earlier version of this chapter. JLA was supported by the Canada Research Chairs Program.

Notes

1   On a historical note, Pauling and Coryell began their seminal article by quoting Faraday as mentioning that he had examined the

magnetic properties of dried blood and that he needed to (but never did) try "recent fluid blood." However, it seems that Faraday did try fluid blood and still found it to be diamagnetic. In fact, he argued that "if a man could be suspended... and placed in the magnetic field, he would point equatorially [perpendicular to the magnetic field lines]; for all the substances of which he is formed, including the blood, possess this property [of diamagnetism]."

2 The authors mention that the study actually begun before the publication of the first fMRI articles in 1992 and was submitted for publication in May 1994, but that it took more than two years for it to finally appear in press (Breiter & Rauch, 1996).

References

Abraham, T., & Feng, J. (2011). Evolution of brain imaging instrumentation. *Seminars in Nuclear Medicine*, 41(3), 202–19.

Aguirre, G. K., Zarahn, E., & D'Esposito, M. (1998). The variability of human, BOLD hemodynamic responses. *Neuroimage*, 8(4), 360–69.

Anderson, A. K., Christoff, K., Stappen, I., Panitz, D., Ghahremani, D. G., Glover, G.,... Sobel, N. (2003). Dissociated neural representations of intensity and valence in human olfaction. *Nature Neuroscience*, 6(2), 196–202.

Anderson, C. D. (1932). The apparent existence of easily deflectable positives. *Science*, 76(1967), 238–39.

Attwell, D., & Iadecola, C. (2002). The neural basis of functional brain imaging signals. *Trends in Neurosciences*, 25(12), 621–25.

Attwell, D., & Laughlin, S. B. (2001). An energy budget for signaling in the grey matter of the brain. *Journal of Cerebral Blood Flow & Metabolism*, 21(10), 1133–45.

Badgaiyan, R. D., Fischman, A. J., & Alpert, N. M. (2009). Dopamine release during human emotional processing. *Neuroimage*, 47(4), 2041–45.

Bandettini, P. A., Wong, E. C., Hinks, R. S., Tikofsky, R. S., & Hyde, J. S. (1992). Time course EPI of human brain function during task activation. *Magnetic Resonance in Medicine*, 25(2), 390–97.

Baxter, L. R., Jr., Schwartz, J. M., Phelps, M. E., Mazziotta, J. C., Guze, B. H., Selin, C. E.,... Sumida, R. M. (1989). Reduction of pre-

frontal cortex glucose metabolism common to three types of depression. *Archives of General Psychiatry*, 46(3), 243–50.

Bernstein, M. A., King, K. F., & Zhou, Z. J. (2004). *Handbook of MRI pulse sequences*. Amsterdam: Elsevier Academic Press.

Birn, R. M., & Bandettini, P. A. (2005). The effect of stimulus duty cycle and "off" duration on BOLD response linearity. *Neuroimage*, 27(1), 70–82.

Bordi, F., & LeDoux, J. (1992). Sensory tuning beyond the sensory system: An initial analysis of auditory response properties of neurons in the lateral amygdaloid nucleus and overlying areas of the striatum. *Journal of Neuroscience*, 12(7), 2493–2503.

Breiter, H. C., Etcoff, N. L., Whalen, P. J., Kennedy, W. A., Rauch, S. L., Buckner, R.... Rosen, B. R. (1996). Response and habituation of the human amygdala during visual processing of facial expression. *Neuron*, 17(5), 875–87.

Breiter, H. C., Kwong, K. K., Baker, J. R., Stern, J. W., Belliveau, J. W., Davis, T. L.,... Rosen, B. R. (1993). *Functional magnetic resonance imaging of symptom provocation in patients with obsessive-compulsive disorder versus controls*. Paper presented at the International Society for Magnetic Resonance in Medicine.

Breiter, H. C., & Rauch, S. L. (1996). Functional MRI and the study of OCD: From symptom provocation to cognitive-behavioral probes of cortico-striatal systems and the amygdala. *Neuroimage*, 4(3 Pt. 3), S127–38.

Breiter, H. C., Rauch, S. L., Kwong, K. K., Baker, J. R., Weisskoff, R. M., Kennedy, D. N.,... Rosen, B. R. (1996). Functional magnetic resonance imaging of symptom provocation in obsessive-compulsive disorder. *Archives of General Psychiatry*, 53(7), 595–606.

Brown, W. D., Taylor, M. D., Roberts, A. D., Oakes, T. R., Schueller, M. J., Holden, J. E.,... Nickles, R. J. (1999). FluoroDOPA PET shows the nondopaminergic as well as dopaminergic destinations of levodopa. *Neurology*, 53(6), 1212–18.

Buxton, R. B. (2002). *Introduction to functional magnetic resonance imaging: Principles and techniques*. Cambridge: Cambridge University Press.

Chen, N. K., Dickey, C. C., Yoo, S. S., Guttmann, C. R., & Panych, L. P. (2003). Selection of voxel size and slice orientation for fMRI in the presence of susceptibility field gradients: Application to imaging of the amygdala. *Neuroimage*, 19(3), 817–25.

de Zwart, J. A., van Gelderen, P., Jansma, J. M., Fukunaga, M., Bianciardi, M., & Duyn, J. H. (2009). Hemodynamic nonlinearities affect BOLD fMRI response timing and amplitude. *Neuroimage*, 47(4), 1649–58.

Devor, A., Tian, P., Nishimura, N., Teng, I. C., Hillman, E. M., Narayanan, S. N., . . . Dale, A. M. (2007). Suppressed neuronal activity and concurrent arteriolar vasoconstriction may explain negative blood oxygenation level-dependent signal. *Journal of Neuroscience*, 27(16), 4452–59.

Dickie, E. W., Brunet, A., Akerib, V., & Armony, J. L. (2008). An fMRI investigation of memory encoding in PTSD: Influence of symptom severity. *Neuropsychologia*, 46(5), 1522–31.

Dirac, P. A. M. (1928). The quantum theory of the electron. *Proceedings of the Royal Society of London A*, 117, 15.

Dolcos, F., LaBar, K. S., & Cabeza, R. (2004). Dissociable effects of arousal and valence on prefrontal activity indexing emotional evaluation and subsequent memory: An event-related fMRI study. *Neuroimage*, 23(1), 64–74.

Donders, F. C. (1969). Over de snelheid van psychische processen [On the speed of psychological processes]. In W. G. Koster & Instituut voor Perceptie Onderzoek (Eindhoven Netherlands) (Eds.), *Attention and performance II: Proceedings of the Donders Centenary Symposium on Reaction Time, held in Eindhoven, July 29-August 2, 1968*. Amsterdam: North-Holland Publishing.

Ernst, T., & Hennig, J. (1994). Observation of a fast response in functional MR. *Magnetic Resonance in Medicine*, 32(1), 146–49.

Faraday, M. (1846). Experimental researches in electricity. Nineteenth series. On the magnetization of light and the illumination of magnetic lines of force. *Philosophical Transactions of the Royal Society of London*, 136, 1–20.

Fermi, E. (1934). Versuch einer Theorie der β-Strahlen [Towards the Theory of β-Rays]. *Z. Phys.*, 88, 17.

Fernandez-Egea, E., Parellada, E., Lomena, F., Falcon, C., Pavia, J., Mane, A., . . . Bernardo, M. (2009). A continuous emotional task activates the left amygdala in healthy volunteers: (18)FDG PET study. *Psychiatry Research*, 171(3), 199–206.

Figley, C. R., & Stroman, P. W. (2011). The role(s) of astrocytes and astrocyte activity in neurometabolism, neurovascular coupling, and the production of functional neuroimag-

ing signals. *European Journal of Neuroscience*, 33(4), 577–88.

Fischer, H., Wright, C. I., Whalen, P. J., McInerney, S. C., Shin, L. M., & Rauch, S. L. (2003). Brain habituation during repeated exposure to fearful and neutral faces: A functional MRI study. *Brain Research Bulletin*, 59(5), 387–92.

Genovese, C. R., Lazar, N. A., & Nichols, T. (2002). Thresholding of statistical maps in functional neuroimaging using the false discovery rate. *Neuroimage*, 15(4), 870–78.

George, M. S., Ketter, T. A., Parekh, P. I., Horwitz, B., Herscovitch, P., & Post, R. M. (1995). Brain activity during transient sadness and happiness in healthy women. *American Journal of Psychiatry*, 152(3), 341–51.

Gerretsen, P., Graff-Guerrero, A., Menon, M., Pollock, B. G., Kapur, S., Vasdev, N., Houle, S., & Mamo, D. (2010). Is desire for social relationships mediated by the serotonergic system in the prefrontal cortex? An [(18)F]setoperone PET study. *Social Neuroscience*, 5(4), 375–83.

Goldapple, K., Segal, Z., Garson, C., Lau, M., Bieling, P., Kennedy, S., & Mayberg, H. (2004). Modulation of cortical-limbic pathways in major depression: Treatment-specific effects of cognitive behavior therapy. *Archives of General Psychiatry*, 61(1), 34–41.

Grodd, W., Schneider, F., Klose, U., & Nagele, T. (1995). [Functional magnetic resonance tomography of psychological functions exemplified by experimentally induced emotions. *Radiologe*, 35(4), 283–89.

Gusnard, D. A., & Raichle, M. E. (2001). Searching for a baseline: Functional imaging and the resting human brain. *Nature Reviews Neuroscience*, 2(10), 685–94.

Haacke, E. M., Brown, R. W., Thompson, M. R., & Venkatesan, R. (1999). *Magnetic resonance imaging: Physical principles and sequence design*. New York: Wiley-Liss.

Harel, N., Lee, S. P., Nagaoka, T., Kim, D. S., & Kim, S. G. (2002). Origin of negative blood oxygenation level-dependent fMRI signals. *Journal of Cerebral Blood Flow & Metabolism*, 22(8), 908–17.

Hu, X., Le, T. H., & Ugurbil, K. (1997). Evaluation of the early response in fMRI in individual subjects using short stimulus duration. *Magnetic Resonance in Medicine*, 37(6), 877–84.

Huettel, S. A., & McCarthy, G. (2001). Regional differences in the refractory period of the hemodynamic response: An event-related fMRI study. *Neuroimage*, 14(5), 967–76.

Huettel, S. A., Song, A. W., & McCarthy, G. (2009). *Functional magnetic resonance imaging* (2nd ed.). Sunderland, MA: Sinauer Associates.

Jezzard, P., Matthews, P. M., & Smith, S. M. (2001). *Functional MRI: An introduction to methods.* Oxford: Oxford University Press.

Kannurpatti, S. S., & Biswal, B. B. (2004). Negative functional response to sensory stimulation and its origins. *Journal of Cerebral Blood Flow & Metabolism*, 24(6), 703–12.

Kosslyn, S. M., Shin, L. M., Thompson, W. L., McNally, R. J., Rauch, S. L., Pitman, R. K., & Alpert, N. M. (1996). Neural effects of visualizing and perceiving aversive stimuli: A PET investigation. *Neuroreport*, 7(10), 1569–76.

Krekelberg, B., Boynton, G. M., & van Wezel, R. J. (2006). Adaptation: From single cells to BOLD signals. *Trends in Neurosciences*, 29(5), 250–56.

Kupers, R., Frokjaer, V. G., Erritzoe, D., Naert, A., Budtz-Joergensen, E., Nielsen, F. A., . . . Knudsen, G. M. (2011). Serotonin transporter binding in the hypothalamus correlates negatively with tonic heat pain ratings in healthy subjects: A [11C]DASB PET study. *Neuroimage*, 54(2), 1336–43.

Kwong, K. K., Belliveau, J. W., Chesler, D. A., Goldberg, I. E., Weisskoff, R. M., Poncelet, B. P., . . . Rosen, B. R. (1992). Dynamic magnetic resonance imaging of human brain activity during primary sensory stimulation. *Proceedings of the National Academy of Sciences*, 89(12), 5675–79.

Laakso, A., Wallius, E., Kajander, J., Bergman, J., Eskola, O., Solin, O., . . . Hietala, J. (2003). Personality traits and striatal dopamine synthesis capacity in healthy subjects. *American Journal of Psychiatry*, 160(5), 904–910.

Lauritzen, M. (2005). Reading vascular changes in brain imaging: Is dendritic calcium the key? *Nature Reviews Neuroscience*, 6(1), 77–85.

Le Bihan, D., Turner, R., Zeffiro, T. A., Cuenod, C. A., Jezzard, P., & Bonnerot, V. (1993). Activation of human primary visual cortex during visual recall: A magnetic resonance imaging study. *Proceedings of the National Academy of Sciences*, 90(24), 11802–5.

Lindauer, U., Royl, G., Leithner, C., Kühl, M., Gethmann, J., Kohl-Bareis, . . . Dirnagl, U. (2002). Neural activation induced changes in microcirculatory haemoglobin oxygenation: To dip or not to dip. In M. Tomita, I. Kanno, & E. Hamel (Eds.), *Brain activation and CBF control* (Vol. 1235, pp. 137–44). Amsterdam: Elsevier.

Logan, B. R., & Rowe, D. B. (2004). An evaluation of thresholding techniques in fMRI analysis. *Neuroimage*, 22(1), 95–108.

Logothetis, N. (2000). Can current fMRI techniques reveal the micro-architecture of cortex? *Nature Neuroscience*, 3(5), 413–14.

Logothetis, N. K., Pauls, J., Augath, M., Trinath, T., & Oeltermann, A. (2001). Neurophysiological investigation of the basis of the fMRI signal. *Nature*, 412(6843), 150–57.

Logothetis, N. K., & Wandell, B. A. (2004). Interpreting the BOLD signal. *Annual Review of Physiology*, 66, 735–69.

Merboldt, K. D., Fransson, P., Bruhn, H., & Frahm, J. (2001). Functional MRI of the human amygdala? *Neuroimage*, 14(2), 253–57.

Morawetz, C., Holz, P., Lange, C., Baudewig, J., Weniger, G., Irle, E., & Dechent, P. (2008). Improved functional mapping of the human amygdala using a standard functional magnetic resonance imaging sequence with simple modifications. *Magnetic Resonance Imaging*, 26(1), 45–53.

Morris, J. S., Frith, C. D., Perrett, D. I., Rowland, D., Young, A. W., Calder, A. J., & Dolan, R. J. (1996). A differential neural response in the human amygdala to fearful and happy facial expressions. *Nature*, 383(6603), 812–15.

Mosso, A. (1881). *Uber den Kreislauf des Blutes im menschlichen Gehirn.* Leipzig: Veit.

Mosso, A. (1896). *Fear.* London: Longmans, Green.

Mukamel, R., Gelbard, H., Arieli, A., Hasson, U., Fried, I., & Malach, R. (2005). Coupling between neuronal firing, field potentials, and FMRI in human auditory cortex. *Science*, 309(5736), 951–54.

Ogawa, S., Lee, T. M., Kay, A. R., & Tank, D. W. (1990). Brain magnetic resonance imaging with contrast dependent on blood oxygenation. *Proceedings of the National Academy of Sciences*, 87(24), 9868–72.

Ogawa, S., Lee, T. M., Nayak, A. S., & Glynn, P. (1990). Oxygenation-sensitive contrast in magnetic resonance image of rodent brain at high magnetic fields. *Magnetic Resonance in Medicine*, 14(1), 68–78.

Ogawa, S., Tank, D. W., Menon, R., Ellermann, J. M., Kim, S. G., Merkle, H., & Ugurbil, K. (1992). Intrinsic signal changes accompanying sensory stimulation: Functional brain mapping with magnetic resonance imaging.

Proceedings of the National Academy of Sciences, 89(13), 5951–55.

Pauling, L., & Coryell, C. D. (1936). The magnetic properties and structure of hemoglobin, oxyhemoglobin and carbonmonoxyhemoglobin. *Proceedings of the National Academy of, 22*(4), 210–16.

Penny, W. D., Friston, K. J., Ashburner, J. T., Kiebel, S. J., & Nichols, T. E. (2007). *Statistical parametric mapping: The analysis of functional brain images.* Amsterdam: Elsevier.

Pessoa, L., Japee, S., Sturman, D., & Ungerleider, L. G. (2006). Target visibility and visual awareness modulate amygdala responses to fearful faces. *Cerebral Cortex, 16*(3), 366–75.

Preston, A. R., Thomason, M. E., Ochsner, K. N., Cooper, J. C., & Glover, G. H. (2004). Comparison of spiral-in/out and spiral-out BOLD fMRI at 1.5 and 3 T. *Neuroimage, 21*(1), 291–301.

Pruessner, J. C., Champagne, F., Meaney, M. J., & Dagher, A. (2004). Dopamine release in response to a psychological stress in humans and its relationship to early life maternal care: A positron emission tomography study using [11C]raclopride. *Journal of Neuroscience, 24*(11), 2825–31.

Rao, S., Bandettini, P. A., Wong, E. C., Yetkin, F. Z., Hammeke, T. A., Mueller, W. M., . . . Hyde, J. S. (1992). *Gradient echo EPI demonstrates bilateral superior temporal gyrus activation during passive word presentation.* Paper presented at the 11th Annual Meeting of the Society of Magnetic Resonance in Medicine, Berlin.

Reiman, E. M., Raichle, M. E., Butler, F. K., Herscovitch, P., & Robins, E. (1984). A focal brain abnormality in panic disorder, a severe form of anxiety. *Nature, 310*(5979), 683–85.

Reinders, A. A., Glascher, J., de Jong, J. R., Willemsen, A. T., den Boer, J. A., & Buchel, C. (2006). Detecting fearful and neutral faces: BOLD latency differences in amygdala-hippocampal junction. *Neuroimage, 33*(2), 805–14.

Rotshtein, P., Malach, R., Hadar, U., Graif, M., & Hendler, T. (2001). Feeling or features: Different sensitivity to emotion in high-order visual cortex and amygdala. *Neuron, 32*(4), 747–57.

Roy, C. S., & Sherrington, C. S. (1890). On the regulation of the blood-supply of the brain. *Journal of Physiology, 11*(1–2), 85–158.

Salimpoor, V. N., Benovoy, M., Larcher, K., Dagher, A., & Zatorre, R. J. (2011). Anatomically distinct dopamine release during antic-

ipation and experience of peak emotion to music. *Nature Neuroscience, 14*(2), 257–62.

Schaefer, S. M., Abercrombie, H. C., Lindgren, K. A., Larson, C. L., Ward, R. T., Oakes, T. R., . . . Davidson, R. J. (2000). Six-month test-retest reliability of MRI-defined PET measures of regional cerebral glucose metabolic rate in selected subcortical structures. *Human Brain Mapping, 10*(1), 1–9.

Sergerie, K., Chochol, C., & Armony, J. L. (2008). The role of the amygdala in emotional processing: A quantitative meta-analysis of functional neuroimaging studies. *Neuroscience & Biobehavioral Reviews, 32*(4), 811–30.

Sergerie, K., Lepage, M., & Armony, J. L. (2006). A process-specific functional dissociation of the amygdala in emotional memory. *Journal of Cognitive Neuroscience, 18*(8), 1359–87.

Shmuel, A. (2010). Locally measured neuronal correlates of functional MRI signals. In C. Mulert & L. Lemieux (Eds.), *EEG-fMRI: Physiological basis, technique, and applications* (pp. 63–82). Heidelberg: Springer.

Shmuel, A., Augath, M., Oeltermann, A., & Logothetis, N. K. (2006). Negative functional MRI response correlates with decreases in neuronal activity in monkey visual area V1. *Nature Neuroscience, 9*(4), 569–77.

Shmuel, A., & Grinvald, A. (1996). Functional organization for direction of motion and its relationship to orientation maps in cat area 18. *Journal of Neuroscience, 16*(21), 6945–6964.

Smith, A. J., Blumenfeld, H., Behar, K. L., Rothman, D. L., Shulman, R. G., & Hyder, F. (2002). Cerebral energetics and spiking frequency: The neurophysiological basis of fMRI. *Proceedings of the National Academy of Sciences, 99*(16), 10765–70.

Smith, S. M., Miller, K. L., Salimi-Khorshidi, G., Webster, M., Beckmann, C. F., Nichols, T. E., . . . Woolrich, M. W. (2011). Network modelling methods for FMRI. *Neuroimage, 54*(2), 875–91.

Stern, C. E., Corkin, S., Gonzalez, R. G., Guimaraes, A. R., Baker, J. R., Jennings, P. J., . . . Rosen, B. R. (1996). The hippocampal formation participates in novel picture encoding: Evidence from functional magnetic resonance imaging. *Proceedings of the National Academy of Sciences, 93*(16), 8660–65.

Takahashi, H., Takano, H., Kodaka, F., Arakawa, R., Yamada, M., Otsuka, T., . . . Suhara, T. (2010). Contribution of dopamine D1 and D2 receptors to amygdala activity in human. *Journal of Neuroscience, 30*(8), 3043–47.

Takano, T., Tian, G. F., Peng, W., Lou, N., Libionka, W., Han, X., & Nedergaard, M. (2006). Astrocyte-mediated control of cerebral blood flow. *Nature Neuroscience*, 9(2), 260–67.

Tauscher, J., Bagby, R. M., Javanmard, M., Christensen, B. K., Kasper, S., & Kapur, S. (2001). Inverse relationship between serotonin 5-HT(1A) receptor binding and anxiety: A [(11)C]WAY-100635 PET investigation in healthy volunteers. *American Journal of Psychiatry*, 158(8), 1326–28.

Thulborn, K. R., Waterton, J. C., Matthews, P. M., & Radda, G. K. (1982). Oxygenation dependence of the transverse relaxation time of water protons in whole blood at high field. *Biochimica et Biophysica Acta*, 714(2), 265–70.

Truong, T. K., & Song, A. W. (2008). Single-shot dual-z-shimmed sensitivity-encoded spiral-in/out imaging for functional MRI with reduced susceptibility artifacts. *Magnetic Resonance in Medicine*, 59(1), 221–27.

Vanzetta, I., & Grinvald, A. (2001). Evidence and lack of evidence for the initial dip in the anesthetized rat: Implications for human functional brain imaging. *Neuroimage*, 13(6 Pt. 1), 959–67.

Viswanathan, A., & Freeman, R. D. (2007). Neurometabolic coupling in cerebral cortex reflects synaptic more than spiking activity. *Nature Neuroscience*, 10(10), 1308–12.

Volkow, N. D., Tomasi, D., Wang, G. J., Fowler, J. S., Telang, F., Goldstein, R. Z., . . . Alexoff, D. (2011). Positive emotionality is associated with baseline metabolism in orbitofrontal cortex and in regions of the default network. *Molecular Psychiatry*, 16(8), 818–25.

Vuilleumier, P., Armony, J. L., Clarke, K., Husain, M., Driver, J., & Dolan, R. J. (2002). Neural response to emotional faces with and without awareness: Event-related fMRI in a parietal patient with visual extinction and spatial neglect. *Neuropsychologia*, 40(12), 2156–66.

Wilson, F. A., & Rolls, E. T. (1993). The effects of stimulus novelty and familiarity on neuronal activity in the amygdala of monkeys performing recognition memory tasks. *Experimental Brain Research*, 93(3), 367–82.

Worsley, K. J., Marrett, S., Neelin, P., Vandal, A. C., Friston, K. J., & Evans, A. C. (1996). A unified statistical approach for determining significant signals in images of cerebral activation. *Human Brain Mapping*, 4(1), 58–73.

Yacoub, E., & Hu, X. (1999). Detection of the early negative response in fMRI at 1.5 Tesla. *Magnetic Resonance in Medicine*, 41(6), 1088–92.

Zaretsky, M., Mendelsohn, A., Mintz, M., & Hendler, T. (2010). In the eye of the beholder: Internally driven uncertainty of danger recruits the amygdala and dorsomedial prefrontal cortex. *Journal of Cognitive Neuroscience*, 22(10), 2263–75.

CHAPTER 6

Lesion Studies in Affective Neuroscience

Lesley K. Fellows

Why Lesion Studies?

Some of the earliest evidence relating neurobiology to human behavior came from clinical observations of the effects of brain injury. Anecdotal descriptions stretching back to ancient Greece have helped convince a sometimes doubting public that the brain, and not the heart, is the seat of both intellect and emotion (Crivellato & Ribatti, 2007; Gross, 1995). Indeed, observations in individual patients continue to be a source of inspiration for neurologists, neuropsychologists, and cognitive neuroscientists (Chatterjee, 2005; Eslinger & Damasio, 1985).

The melding of modern neurology and experimental psychology in the early part of the 20th century led to a more systematic, experimental approach to understanding how brain injury can affect behavior (Macmillan, 2000). Experimental neuropsychology was a key source of evidence about brain-behavior relationships for much of the last century, providing a foundation for the fields of cognitive and affective neuroscience. However, the advent of neuroimaging methods allowing the study of the healthy brain has dramatically altered the landscape of this field in the last two decades (Fellows et al., 2005). The 21st-century affective neuroscientist now has an array of methods to choose from: functional magnetic resonance imaging (fMRI), positron emission tomography, electoencephalography, magnetoencephalography, and transcranial magnetic stimulation. fMRI, in particular, has taken the field by storm, serving as the main technique for studying human brain-behavior relationships. With this panoply of new methods, it seems appropriate to ask critically whether human lesion studies are still useful. Arguing that the answer to this question is a resounding "yes!," this chapter defines the main experimental designs possible with lesion methods and discusses both the strengths and weaknesses of these techniques. Although these arguments hold for cognitive neuroscience generally, their specific relevance for the study of emotional and social processes is highlighted here.

Lesion studies remain a crucial part of the experimental toolbox in this field because of the nature of evidence that can be obtained with this method. In principle, such studies allow testing of necessity claims: that is, they can provide evidence to support the hypothesis that a particular brain region is necessary for a given process or component of behavior (Fellows et al., 2005; Rorden & Karnath, 2004). Such loss-of-function evidence is an important complement to the activation studies common with fMRI or EEG methods. The latter two approaches instead relate measures of regional brain activation to aspects of behavior. Thus, fMRI or EEG studies can identify brain regions that participate in a given cognitive or affective process, but cannot establish that these regions are critical for the process.

This point may be particularly important in affective and social neuroscience, a newer area of study that aims to understand complex processes that may be particularly challenging to dissect. For example, recognizing an emotional facial expression may also invoke the experience of a similar emotion in the subject, with attendant autonomic changes. All of these processes may be correlated with emotion recognition performance, although only some are critical to recognition itself. It can be very challenging to disentangle the processes of interest from epiphenomena as they relate to fMRI activation patterns (Fusar-Poli et al., 2009).

Converging lesion evidence can be very helpful in this regard. We might choose a candidate region of the brain from an fMRI study of emotion recognition, such as the ventromedial prefrontal cortex, for example, and ask whether damage to that region disrupts emotion recognition. Finding that this is the case reassures us that this region participates in the process of interest, rather than in some correlated additional process (Heberlein, Padon, Gillihan, Farah, & Fellows, 2008; Hornak et al., 2003).

A second, related application of lesion methods is in testing the dissociability of (putative) processes. Closely linked aspects of behavior may rely on distinct neuroanatomical circuits: Work in patients with focal damage can demonstrate this involvement in ways that correlative methods such as fMRI cannot. A classic example comes from observations stretching back to Broca

and Wernicke about how language is disrupted after brain injury. The clinical observations that language production could be impaired, and comprehension spared (and vice versa), first made more than a century ago, ground our understanding of how language is organized in the brain still today (Caplan, 2003).

Lesion studies thus offer particular inferential strengths, complementing other approaches (Chatterjee, 2005; Fellows et al., 2005; Rorden & Karnath, 2004). As with any method, the quality of the evidence provided depends on thoughtful and careful experimental design. Advances in anatomical neuroimaging, systematic patient recruitment, and analytic methods "borrowed" from fMRI all provide new opportunities to ensure that modern experimental neuropsychology can be effectively brought to bear to inform our understanding of human brain functions.

Experimental Design

General Considerations

Human lesion studies are at best quasi-experimental. For obvious reasons, the lesions are not under experimental control, which means that the extent of brain injury is at the whim of nature, as is the "selection" of the individuals who suffer those injuries. The researcher using these methods is carrying out an observational study, akin to a case-control study in epidemiology. The fundamentally observational nature of this work means that the experimenter can choose whether to consider the brain (i.e., the lesion location) or the behavior as the independent variable. Thus, studies can enroll subjects with a particular behavioral deficit – for example, patients with depression after stroke – and then ask whether they have common locations of damage (the tentative answer, it turns out, is "no"; Carson et al., 2000). Alternatively, one can ask about the behavioral effects of damage to a particular region: for example, selecting patients with amygdala damage and ascertaining their behavioral deficits (Adolphs et al., 2005; Adolphs & Spezio, 2006; Adolphs & Tranel, 2003; Heberlein & Adolphs, 2004). Finally, some studies are concerned not with structure-function relationships, but with understanding the relationship between psychological processes. If two abilities rely on identical underlying psychological (and neural) processes, then it should not be possible to disrupt one ability and not the other. Thus, studies in clinical populations can test whether processes are shared or dissociable, with or without considering their neurobiological substrates (Johnsen, Tranel, Lutgendorf, & Adolphs, 2009; Robinson & Sahakian, 2009).

Patient Recruitment and Selection

Although a study may be behavior driven or lesion driven, it certainly should not be both. Selecting patients on the basis of both a clinical deficit and a particular lesion will introduce a strong bias toward finding a (possibly spurious) structure-function relationship, a kind of "cherry-picking" that undermines any conclusions (Rorden, Fridriksson, & Karnath, 2009). Other forms of selection bias may be less obvious, but still need consideration in interpreting lesion studies. In principle, one should study every patient with either the lesion or behavior of interest. In practice, there are nonrandom limitations to this goal: At the least patients must consent to be studied and be willing and able to participate in the experiments. This form of selection bias may be a particular issue for affective neuroscience. Patients suffering from loss of motivation, depression, impairments in empathy, or social deficits may be less likely to volunteer for studies, meaning that those who do participate might have less of the behavior of interest, biasing the results toward the null. On similar grounds, lesions that lead to very difficult behavioral changes – impulsivity, social inappropriateness, or aggression – will similarly be underrepresented in most studies. Even if such patients consent, the researcher may find it impossible to carry out the experiments. Finally, certain personality or demographic characteristics may be risk factors for suffering the lesion to begin with and so will be over-represented in the lesion group compared to a healthy control group. A classic example is risk-taking, which might plausibly predispose to head injury rather than being its consequence.

There may be other reasons for the behavioral deficit not to be caused by the focal brain injury itself. Common contributors to poor performance include nonspecific additional injury that may or may not be identifiable on brain imaging. Examples of such coincident injury include diffuse axonal injury in traumatic brain injury, hydrocephalus complicating cerebral hemorrhage, or periventricular ischemic changes in patients with a large-vessel stroke. Other important and common clinical confounds include psychoactive medication use, depression, or past or present drug or alcohol abuse. There are two main approaches to controlling for these issues: One is to exclude participants for these reasons, and the other is to ensure that these factors are also present in the reference group. A third approach is to include one or more of these variables as a covariate in the analyses. The covariate approach can be useful, but often is not, because the small sample sizes of most lesion studies bias toward failing to detect (statistically) the effects of confounding clinical variables even when they exist.

Lesion chronicity also needs consideration. The acute effects of stroke clearly differ from the chronic effects, examined weeks or months later (see, e.g., Ochfeld et al., 2011). For feasibility reasons, most lesion studies are carried out when patients are "stable," typically at least several months (and often many years) after the brain injury. Hyperacute studies can be done in the right setting (see, e.g., Marsh & Hillis, 2008; Newhart, Ken, Kleinman, Heidler-Gary, & Hillis, 2007). It is obviously important to consider why there are differences between acute and chronic lesion effects. Some of the reasons are definitely relevant to interpreting structure-function claims: Chronic injury likely leads to compensation, whether through plastic changes in the brain, strategic adjustments in behavior, or both. It has been proposed that behavioral deficits present in patients with chronic damage should be considered evidence that the damaged region is necessary for *recovery* of the function in question, rather than necessary for that function in the strictest sense. However, there may be other reasons for impairment in the acute setting than the brain injury as visualized on imaging: dysfunction of marginally perfused brain tissue or acute nonspecific changes in attention or other abilities related either to brain dysfunction or to the experience of a serious acute illness, for example. In any case, acute studies have practical limitations that make it unlikely they will be widely applied, perhaps particularly in studying affective or social processes that may not be easily tested in the usually brief time window available for that kind of work. Further, although there are differences between acute and chronic effects of focal injury, they are typically in extent, rather than dramatic differences in kind, of behavioral dysfunction. Although this chapter discusses lesion studies in relation to their contribution to basic affective neuroscience, the findings from such studies are obviously of clinical relevance as well. A better understanding of the mechanisms and trajectories of recovery after brain injury is an important clinical issue and will also ensure that the evidence acquired through lesion studies that address basic questions is interpreted appropriately.

These subtleties aside, perhaps the major concern in patient selection is having access to an even vaguely suitable patient population at all. Recruitment has always been the rate-limiting step in such research, but as the field of cognitive neuroscience moves further from the clinic, this is becoming ever more the case. One solution is to develop patient registries or databases specifically to support lesion research. If the calls for converging methods that populate any introductory textbook of cognitive neuroscience are to be properly met, then patient registries should be seen as a required core facility, funded by user fees or common sources, just as neuroimaging facilities are

(although costing substantially less!). Registries provide crucial information about the feasibility of a planned study, can permit efficient recruitment of the appropriate control groups, can serve an important role in ensuring the ethical conduct of recruitment, and, when working well, allow group studies to be carried out within a reasonable time. The advantages and practical details of establishing such registries are discussed in more detail elsewhere (Fellows, Stark, Berg, & Chatterjee, 2008).

Reference Groups

Most studies in affective neuroscience make use of novel behavioral measures and so usually require a reference group made up of healthy subjects demographically similar to the target patient population to help interpret the performance of the patient group. However, the appropriate reference population for the experiment may not be healthy subjects. Depending on the hypothesis, patients with brain injury may provide more relevant comparison data. The simplest lesion control group would involve patients with injury sparing the brain region affected in the single case or lesion group being studied (Fellows & Farah, 2003). Such a contrast helps control for nonspecific effects of illness or brain injury. Where possible, an even more focused design may be desirable: comparing two groups with lesions affecting two specific brain regions, thus both controlling for nonspecific brain injury effects and testing a more specific structure-function hypothesis; see, for example, Johnsen et al., 2009).

Single Cases

Careful study of a single patient can be very informative. Broca's patient, known as "Tan" because it was the only word he could reliably produce after his brain injury, launched the study of aphasia (Broca, 1861). The study of the effects of bilateral medial temporal lobe resection in the patient H. M. contributed immeasurably to our understanding of human memory (Corkin,

2002). Case studies have been important in affective neuroscience as well: As examples, a detailed case report describing the social and decision-making deficits following ventromedial frontal lobe damage in patient E. V. R. set the scene for much of the work on the functions of this region in the last 20 years (Eslinger & Damasio, 1985), and a set of interesting studies on emotion recognition has been carried out in a unique patient with bilateral amygdala injury (Adolphs et al., 2005; Adolphs, Tranel, Damasio, & Damasio, 1994; Adolphs, Tranel, Damasio, & Damasio, 1995; Heberlein & Adolphs, 2004).

Although single cases have been a rich source of inspiration in the history of neuropsychology, in principle they are weak evidence taken alone: It is impossible to generalize any finding with confidence. Observed deficits in a single patient may be due to premorbid differences in function, so that normal individual differences may thus be misattributed to the lesion. This attribution, however, may be implausible for some deficits: Common sense dictates that major hemiparesis or visual field defects are outside the range of "normal" variation and can generally be safely linked to the brain injury. Yet other aspects of behavior, particularly in emotional or social domains, may differ substantially across healthy individuals, making it more likely that such a difference will be found by chance in a brain-injured patient. Idiosyncrasies in brain organization, structure-function mapping, or recovery from brain injury can also contribute to "exceptional" performance in a single case. Finally, observations in a single case may be confounded by lesion-related factors other than the site of damage, such as lesion etiology, comorbidities, or medication use.

The critical reader of a single case study should consider the following issues: How well defined is the lesion? How precisely characterized is the behavior being studied? Are there clinical or demographic features that might be confounding factors? Were control tasks administered to rule out alternative explanations for an observed deficit? Careful attention should also be paid to the

reference group: It should be large enough to definitively establish that the deficit in the patient is not within the range of normal, and it should be appropriately matched on relevant variables, whether clinical or demographic. Statistical tests that address the common issues that arise when comparing individual performance to small reference groups should be applied as relevant (for a review of these important statistical analysis issues, see Crawford & Garthwaite, 2012). Even if the experiment passes these standards with flying colors, the result can be considered interesting or provocative, but not definitive in isolation.

Group Studies

Many of the drawbacks of single case studies can be addressed with group designs. At their most basic, such experiments can be seen simply as a series of single cases. If each individual patient with a similar lesion shows a similar behavioral deficit, then the generality of the structure-function claim is obviously much stronger: Individual differences, whether premorbid or lesion related, become less and less likely explanations for the observed effects.

Group studies can do better than this, however, by providing opportunities to further refine lesion analysis. Lesions are often more extensive, or less precisely located, than is ideal for testing a given structure-function hypothesis. If the function is disrupted but the lesion is large, the conclusions cannot be very specific. If a group of patients with lesions varying in extent, but overlapping in some smaller area, are found to have a common impairment in function, one can tentatively infer that the function relies on the region of overlap that is common across patients. Recent methods have built on this logic to allow statistical tests of structure-function relations at the voxel cluster level, and they are discussed in more detail later. Thus, lesion extent can limit structure-function mapping in single case studies, but can at least be addressed and maybe turned to an advantage in group studies.

Lesion Characterization

Most experimental designs require defining the location and extent of each participant's brain injury. The first step in characterizing lesions is to acquire either MRI or computed tomography (CT) images of each patient's brain. MRI is preferred because it offers better resolution and in many cases better sensitivity than CT, and it avoids exposing the participant to ionizing radiation. However, MRI may be contraindicated in patients with pacemakers or surgical clips, for example, or may not be tolerated because of claustrophobia. Ideally, high-resolution imaging should be acquired in the whole patient sample using standard parameters and equipment, as close to the time of behavioral testing as possible. However, relying on the available clinical imaging may be more practical, and such imaging often provides lesion data that are of more than adequate quality for testing a given hypothesis.

The simplest way of representing lesion data is to present the imaging for each patient. This works well for single cases, but becomes awkward for group studies. Indeed, there is little point in presenting individual scans unless the behavioral data are also presented for each individual (i.e., in a case series format). If behavioral data are presented as group means, imaging data also need to be presented in a form that allows insights into what is common in the group. This can be achieved very simply; for example, by tabulating the number of subjects with damage to particular Brodmann areas (Stuss, Murphy, Binns, & Alexander, 2003). However, modern imaging data are acquired in digital form, permitting group lesion data to be presented as brain images that are more visually accessible and also more easily related to fMRI studies (Damasio & Damasio, 1989; Rorden & Brett, 2000).

The most common aggregate representation of lesions is the "overlap" image, generated by representing the arithmetic sum of damage in each voxel, across the group. These images show the degree to which damage affects common brain structures for a given group of patients (Frank, Damasio, & Grabowski, 1997; Makale et al., 2002; Rorden & Brett, 2000). Such images can also demonstrate the absence of common damage in two groups that are meant to be anatomically distinct. Digitized lesion data that are represented in a common space also can be submitted to more complex statistical analyses of structure-function relationships (see the later discussion).

Any group lesion analysis first requires representing individual lesions in a common space. This can be achieved in two main ways: either by manually tracing the lesion onto some common template (Damasio & Damasio, 1989; Kimberg, Coslett, & Schwartz, 2007) or by manually or automatically defining the lesion on the individual patient's anatomical scan and then warping the brain (and the lesion) onto a standard template. The first method is labor intensive and requires substantial expertise. The second method relies on the same algorithms used to warp individual scans into common space for fMRI analysis in healthy subjects and can be more automatized. However, the anatomical distortions caused by the presence of a lesion lead to particular technical issues that need to be addressed thoughtfully if this second approach is taken (Nachev, Coulthard, Jager, Kennard, & Husain, 2008; Rorden & Brett, 2000). Either way, defining the boundaries of lesions always involves some judgment and so is a potential source of error. This error may vary with lesion etiology: The boundary between normal and injured brain may be much clearer for stroke than for brain tumors, for example.

Behavioral Measures

Capturing the brain function of interest is nearly always the most challenging aspect of lesion study design, particularly in the relatively virgin territory of social and affective neuroscience. As with any method, testing well-specified hypotheses based on clear theory is always a good way to begin. As in experimental psychology more generally, tasks must have robust dependent measures, whether reaction times, errors, or other (eye movements, autonomic measures, and so on). It is important to ask whether these behavioral measures will be influenced by nonspecific or correlated disabilities in the patient group. For example, insula damage is often accompanied by damage to adjacent motor pathways, so patients may have slower reaction times because of simple motor dysfunction. Autonomic measures have been used to interesting effect in lesion studies in affective neuroscience (see, e.g., Bechara, Damasio, Tranel, & Damasio, 1997). Some patients may be more likely to take medications (for hypertension, for example) that might affect such measures, requiring extra care in reference group selection and interpretation of the results.

In general, ideal behavioral measures will have good psychometric properties: no ceiling or floor performance, good test-retest reliability, and with minimal influence of demographic or educational factors (Laws, 2005). Measurement variation (i.e., the extent to which task performance will vary if the same subject is tested repeatedly) is a source of noise that, in principle, is under the experimenter's control. It may have important influences on the analysis and should be minimized to the extent possible (Bates, Appelbaum, Salcedo, Saygin, & Pizzamiglio, 2003). When developing novel tasks, consider that patients tend to be older and less educated, on average, than the samples of undergraduate students often conveniently available for piloting. Pilot work in healthy older subjects is usually an excellent investment during task development, although such subjects may be at least as hard to find as subjects with brain injury.

Control Tasks

Brain injury rarely affects only a single process, so control tasks are important in supporting almost any claim. At the least, patients should generally undergo a thorough neuropsychological screening assessment to reassure researcher and readers alike that difficulties with obviously crucial abilities, such as language comprehension or vigilance, are not the explanation for deficits on the experimental tasks of interest. It is better still to develop specific control tasks that closely mimic the demands of the experimental tasks without requiring the particular process of interest. An example might be judging age as a control task for judging trustworthiness from faces, using the same stimulus set for both tasks.

Lesion-Symptom Mapping

With the brain lesions characterized and the behavior of interest precisely measured, we are in position to test brain structure-function relationships. There are three common approaches that are considered in turn.

Behavior-Driven Approaches

A major challenge in cognitive neuroscience is to define the architecture of behavior; that is, to parse complex behavior into analyzable constituents, whether conceptualized as modules, processes, or interacting networks (Dunn & Kirsner, 2003). The challenge is to identify the appropriate constituent parts and then to understand how they interact from both a psychological and a neural point of view. This enterprise obviously requires data gathered with a variety of methods. Studies in patients with brain injury can provide important insights into the biologically relevant lines of cleavage for a given (complex) behavior by helping identify associations and dissociations between putative component processes.

When behavior is treated as the independent variable, patients are selected based on the presence of some behavioral manifestation – either a clinical syndrome or performance on a particular task. Additional behavioral measures aiming to isolate putative component processes are then administered to determine whether these processes are, in fact, distinct (i.e., dissociable). A single dissociation refers to a situation in which subjects are impaired on a task that presumably assesses a particular ability, but are unimpaired on another task that assesses a separate ability. Single dissociations are evidence in favor of the hypothesis that the tasks measure distinct component processes (Damasio & Damasio, 1989; Shallice, 1988). However, there are practical issues that make alternative explanations for such patterns quite likely: As one example, dissociations assume that the tasks being used are approximately equally difficult. An easy task and a hard task tapping the same component process would show apparent dissociation, because at least some patients would fail the hard task but pass the easy task (Shallice, 1988).

This potential explanation is less likely if a double dissociation can be demonstrated: Here, one set of patients fails task A but does well on task B, whereas another set shows the opposite pattern. The explanatory power and experimental elegance of double dissociation have been recognized since the early days of experimental neuropsychology (Teuber, 1955). Nonetheless, dissociations are not always straightforward to establish (for a more detailed analysis of these challenges, see Dunn & Kirsner, 2003). How intact must a group be in task A? How impaired in task B? What is the likelihood of apparent dissociations occurring by chance, in a given population and for any given pair of tasks? Although a common approach is to test for a crossover interaction in the performance of two tasks, across two groups, other patterns may be as or more important, depending on the relations between the tasks and between a given cognitive process and performance on the task meant to measure it (Bates, Appelbaum, et al., 2003; Dunn & Kirsner, 2003; Shallice, 1988).

As discussed earlier, dissociations can be important findings even without determining their relationship to specific lesions. However, showing dissociable patterns of performance related to damage to particular brain regions both bolsters confidence that the dissociation is not spurious and adds important evidence about structure-function relationships (Robertson, Knight, Rafal, & Shimamura, 1993).

Region-of-Interest Approaches

Perhaps the most common hypothesis tested with group studies is that a particular brain region is critically involved in a particular process. A region-of-interest (ROI) design addresses such questions directly: Patients with damage affecting (or, even better, restricted to) the ROI are compared either to a demographically similar reference group or to patients with damage sparing the ROI on some set of tasks aiming to measure the process of interest. The major advantages of this approach are its hypothesis-driven design and the resulting statistical power. This power means that relatively small sample sizes may be adequate, particularly because effect sizes in lesion studies are often quite large. Such designs may have directional hypotheses, making one-tailed statistical tests appropriate.

When the data are considered as group means, the same statistical approaches used for comparing groups in any study are appropriate. ROI designs commonly have limited sample size and may involve skewed behavioral data (i.e., because of ceiling effects in the control group or floor effects in the patients). These issues obviously need to be taken into account when planning the analysis, if they cannot be avoided in the design. As mentioned earlier, sometimes group studies are better analyzed as a series of single cases. This approach may be suitable when the group of patients varies widely on relevant demographic or other variables or, indeed, in task performance. Sometimes this approach is taken post hoc, in which case the results should be considered with particular caution, given the ease with which confounds other than lesion location may explain variability.

ROI studies often involve both a healthy reference group and a brain-damaged control group. It is worth remembering that showing that the performance of the patient group of interest is significantly different from that of a healthy reference sample, but that the brain-damaged control group performance does not differ from controls, is not the same as directly testing whether the

ROI-damaged group differs from the brain-damaged control group, which provides much stronger support for the existence of a specific structure-function relationship (Nieuwenhuis, Forstmann, & Wagenmakers, 2011).

It is important to consider what an ROI design does not do, because it imposes an anatomical boundary that may or may not be optimal. Obviously, nothing will be learned about the potential contributions of brain regions outside that boundary. Perhaps less obviously, there can be a risk of not detecting effects that are, in fact, related to damage within the boundary. This can happen if the defined ROI is much larger than the actually critical brain area; effects due to damage in the smaller area are diluted by normal performance in those with damage affecting the larger, but not critical, area. The group as a whole will have variable performance, and the statistical analyses may fail to detect effects. Even effects that are detected with a given ROI may nevertheless have been better captured by a different anatomical boundary.

Voxel-Based Methods

Regions of interest can, in principle, be any size. In practice, there is a lower limit of resolution imposed by the volume of brain tissue that is injured in individual subjects, the extent to which those volumes overlap in a given sample, or the resolution of the imaging methods that are used to characterize the injury. Lesion volume, rather than imaging resolution, is typically the limiting factor in the MRI era. The upper limit of resolution is determined by conceptual issues; determining that some function is related to the integrity of the whole brain, for example, is likely to be of limited interest. That said, many core concepts in neuropsychology began with regions of interest encompassing entire cerebral hemispheres, and defining such broad structure-function relations may still be important as cognitive neuroscience tackles new areas of study, such as in social or affective domains.

Converging evidence argues that structure-function relations are considerably more discrete than is captured by examining hemispheric, or even lobar, effects, but there are practical limits to the regional specificity that can be attained with ROI designs. If the study is restricted to patients with damage to some very specific and small brain area, an adequate sample is unlikely to be recruited in a reasonable time. An alternative is to enroll patients with variable damage to a relatively broad region – even one hemisphere or the whole brain – and then undertake analyses to establish which subregion contributes to the observed deficits in function.

There are three main approaches to analyzing data from patients who have variable damage in a large brain region. The one with the longest history involves a secondary analysis in a standard ROI study. Having established that some anatomically defined group is impaired, and observing the usual variability in that impairment, one may ask whether there is an anatomical basis to that variability; that is, whether damage to a specific subregion is a main determinant of task performance. This question can be addressed qualitatively by examining the pattern of lesions in the impaired and unimpaired subgroups, essentially carrying out a behavior-driven analysis nested in the original ROI study. Lesion overlap methods are often used to this end: The lesion overlap image for impaired and unimpaired subgroups can be examined visually, or lesion extent can be subtracted across these groups in an effort to identify the potentially critical subregion. Alternative but analogous methods include tabulating the presence or absence of injury to Brodmann areas and comparing the outcome in patients with and without behavioral impairment.

There are drawbacks to pursuing subgroup analyses in ROI studies. First, it is important to realize that these analyses are usually undertaken post hoc, and any finding needs confirmation in a new experiment that is designed to test the specific ROI a priori. Selection bias and confounding factors can easily influence the results. Such analyses usually involve very small sample sizes, and it can be impossible to properly account for other contributors to observed effects, such as demographic variables. Results from such analyses should be treated with particular caution when the a priori, ROI-based analysis did not establish significant differences between groups. A "multiple ROI" approach can be applied a priori, of course. Several studies have taken this tack (Picton et al., 2007; Stuss et al., 2003). The main difficulty, in addition to the perennial limitation of sample size, is determining how to appropriately correct for multiple comparisons.

Recently, statistical methods that were developed for fMRI have been adapted for examining structure-dysfunction relationships at a voxel-by-voxel level. This is a natural extension of multi-ROI designs, with the advantage of principled control of multiple comparisons. Once lesions volumes are registered to a common template, univariate statistics can be applied to test whether the performance of patients with damage to a given voxel differs from performance of patients with damage that spares that voxel. This results in a statistical map showing the strength of association between damage and dysfunction in anatomical space.

This approach, commonly referred to as voxel-based lesion-symptom mapping (VLSM), does not require imposing potentially arbitrary ROI boundaries and allows task performance to be considered either as a dichotomous (intact/impaired) or continuous variable. The use of continuous behavioral measures avoids having to impose a second potentially arbitrary boundary on the data. VLSM also has the potential to map networks (i.e., to identify several regions that may contribute to task performance within a single experiment). Several variations of this method, using different statistical approaches, have been developed (Bates et al., 2003; Chen, Hillis, Pawlak, & Herskovits, 2008; Kinkingnehun et al., 2007; Rorden et al., 2009; Rorden & Karnath, 2004; Rorden, Karnath, & Bonilha, 2007; Solomon, Raymont, Braun, Butman, & Grafman, 2007).

These advantages come with tradeoffs. As with fMRI analysis, this massively univariate analysis requires very conservative correction for multiple comparisons, which in turn demands a substantial sample size. The number of subjects is not the only consideration; lesion overlap and distribution are also important determinants of a study's power. Methods exist to estimate the anatomical extent of adequate power in a given sample, and their use is important for interpreting VLSM analyses (Kimberg et al., 2007; Rudrauf et al., 2008).

White Matter Damage and Disconnection Effects

With the exception of certain neurosurgical resections, lesions are rarely confined to a single structure and often disrupt the white matter leading into or away from a given gray matter region, or fibers of passage (i.e., adjacent tracts that may have nothing to do with the damaged gray matter beyond physical proximity). This damage can pose challenges in interpreting lesion studies. Observed behavioral effects might be due to the white matter damage, which would be particularly misleading if it involves fibers of passage. Modern neuroimaging can assess the extent of white matter injury, either with standard structural scans, or by using tract-specific imaging such as diffusion tensor imaging. Further, white matter atlases are becoming increasingly sophisticated. Thus, methods exist to address possible white matter contributions and are beginning to be applied to structure-function mapping (Catani, Jones, & ffytche, 2005; Karnath, Rorden, & Ticini, 2009; Philippi, Mehta, Grabowski, Adolphs, & Rudrauf, 2009; Rudrauf, Mehta, & Grabowski, 2008; Thiebaut de Schotten et al., 2008; Urbanski et al., 2008).

Developments in image analysis to study network properties of the brain, whether captured by structural or functional measures, may prove useful as adjuncts to the lesion approaches discussed so far (Dosenbach, Fair, Cohen, Schlaggar, & Petersen,

2008; He, Dagher, et al., 2009; He, Wang, et al., 2009). At the least, these techniques draw attention to network-oriented conceptual frameworks and are likely to be important in providing a more complete description of the brain basis of complex behaviors.

Clinical Conditions with Diffuse Damage

Brain-behavior relations can also be studied in clinical conditions that produce multifocal or diffuse damage. Traumatic brain injury, multiple sclerosis, and degenerative conditions such as frontotemporal dementia are examples. Imaging methods can quantify regional cortical and white matter changes, even when they are subtle or diffuse, and such changes can be correlated with behavior. Most of the pitfalls that have been discussed already also apply to such studies. There are additional challenges in interpreting both anatomical data, when multiple areas are dysfunctional in more or less correlated (and more or less detectable) ways, and behavioral data, when multiple cognitive functions that may be necessary for a given task are also degraded in more or less correlated ways.

Critically Reading Group Studies

In summary, group lesion studies provide stronger support for the generalizability of a given brain-structure function claim than do single cases. The critical reader of such a study should first consider the appropriateness of the behavioral measures and whether the reference group is suitable for testing the stated hypothesis. Are alternative explanations for group differences, such as demographic, clinical, or task-related factors, ruled out? How focal is the brain injury, and how consistent is the damage (in terms of extent, etiology, and chronicity) across subjects? What selection biases might have been introduced by the patient recruitment method? Is the sample size ade-

quate? Null findings (especially null findings meant to reassure the reader about potential confounders) should be considered critically whenever sample size is limited. With these basic questions in mind, the alert reader should be well prepared to integrate lesion findings with other forms of evidence and is encouraged to do so to move the field of affective neuroscience forward with all the rigor that can be mustered.

Conclusion

Lesion studies can provide strong tests of the necessary relationship between a brain structure and a psychological process, as well as providing a means to test whether processes are dissociable. This chapter has reviewed the common experimental designs, highlighting their strengths and weaknesses, and provided some practical insights into the challenges and opportunities afforded by this method. Lesion studies have made many interesting contributions to affective neuroscience and are especially important in building a converging evidence base for the brain basis of complex processes.

Outstanding Questions and Future Directions

- How can advances in neuroimaging best be combined with behavioral measures to understand how focal lesions disrupt the functions of brain networks?
- What are the mechanisms underlying improvement after an acute focal brain injury, and how should these changes be accommodated in the inferences about causal structure-function relationships that are drawn from lesion studies?
- What is the best research platform to ensure that nonclinicians have access to suitable, well-characterized patients so that lesion studies can continue to inform cognitive and affective neuroscience theories?

References

Adolphs, R., Gosselin, F., Buchanan, T. W., Tranel, D., Schyns, P., & Damasio, A. R. (2005). A mechanism for impaired fear recognition after amygdala damage. *Nature*, 433(7021), 68–72.

Adolphs, R., & Spezio, M. (2006). Role of the amygdala in processing visual social stimuli. *Progress in Brain Research*, 156, 363–78.

Adolphs, R., & Tranel, D. (2003). Amygdala damage impairs emotion recognition from scenes only when they contain facial expressions. *Neuropsychologia*, 41(10), 1281–89.

Adolphs, R., Tranel, D., Damasio, H., & Damasio, A. (1994). Impaired recognition of emotion in facial expressions following bilateral damage to the human amygdala. *Nature*, 372(6507), 669–72.

Adolphs, R., Tranel, D., Damasio, H., & Damasio, A. R. (1995). Fear and the human amygdala. *Journal of Neuroscience*, 15(9), 5879–91.

Bates, E., Appelbaum, M., Salcedo, J., Saygin, A. P., & Pizzamiglio, L. (2003). Quantifying dissociations in neuropsychological research. *Journal of Clinical and Experimental Neuropsychology*, 25(8), 1128–53.

Bates, E., Wilson, S. M., Saygin, A. P., Dick, F., Sereno, M. I., Knight, R. T., & Dronkers, N.F. (2003). Voxel-based lesion-symptom mapping. *Nature and Neuroscience*, 6(5), 448–50.

Bechara, A., Damasio, H., Tranel, D., & Damasio, A. R. (1997). Deciding advantageously before knowing the advantageous strategy. *Science*, 275(5304), 1293–95.

Broca, P. (1861). Remarques sure la siège de la faculté de langage articulé, suivies d'une observation d'aphémie (perte de la parole). *Bulletin et Mémoires de la Société Anatomique de Paris* 36, 330–57.

Caplan, D. (2003). Aphasic syndromes. In K. M. Heilman & E. Valenstein (Eds.), *Clinical neuropsychology* (pp. 14–34). Oxford: Oxford University Press.

Carson, A. J., MacHale, S., Allen, K., Lawrie, S. M., Dennis, M., House, A., & Sharp M. (2000). Depression after stroke and lesion location: A systematic review. *Lancet*, 356(9224), 122–26.

Catani, M., Jones, D. K., & ffytche, D. H. (2005). Perisylvian language networks of the human brain. *Annals of Neurology*, 57(1), 8–16.

Chatterjee, A. (2005). A madness to the methods in cognitive neuroscience? *Journal of Cognitive Neuroscience*, 17(6), 847–49.

Chen, R., Hillis, A. E., Pawlak, M., & Herskovits, E. H. (2008). Voxelwise Bayesian lesion-deficit analysis. *Neuroimage*, 40(4), 1633–42.

Corkin, S. (2002). What's new with the amnesic patient H.M.? *Nature Reviews Neuroscience*, 3(2), 153–60.

Crawford, J. R., & Garthwaite, P. H. (2012). Single-case research in neuropsychology: A comparison of five forms of t-test for comparing a case to controls. *Cortex*, 48(8), 1009–16.

Crivellato, E., & Ribatti, D. (2007). Soul, mind, brain: Greek philosophy and the birth of neuroscience. *Brain Research Bulletin*, 71(4), 327–36.

Damasio, H., & Damasio, A. R. (1989). *Lesion analysis in neuropsychology*. New York: Oxford University Press.

Dosenbach, N. U., Fair, D. A., Cohen, A. L., Schlaggar, B. L., & Petersen, S. E. (2008). A dual-networks architecture of top-down control. *Trends in Cognitive Sciences*, 12(3), 99–105.

Dunn, J. C., & Kirsner, K. (2003). What can we infer from double dissociations? *Cortex*, 39(1), 1–7.

Eslinger, P. J., & Damasio, A. R. (1985). Severe disturbance of higher cognition after bilateral frontal lobe ablation: Patient EVR. *Neurology*, 35(12), 1731–41.

Fellows, L. K., & Farah, M. J. (2003). Ventromedial frontal cortex mediates affective shifting in humans: evidence from a reversal learning paradigm. *Brain*, 126(8), 1830–37.

Fellows, L. K., Heberlein, A. S., Morales, D. A., Shivde, G., Waller, S., & Wu, D. H. (2005). Method matters: An empirical study of impact in cognitive neuroscience. *Journal of Cognitive Neuroscience*, 17(6), 850–58.

Fellows, L. K., Stark, M., Berg, A., & Chatterjee, A. (2008). Establishing patient registries for cognitive neuroscience research: Advantages, challenges, and practical advice based on the experience at two centers. *Journal of Cognitive Neuroscience*, 20(6), 1107–13.

Frank, R. J., Damasio, H., & Grabowski, T. J. (1997). Brainvox: An interactive, multimodal visualization and analysis system for neuroanatomical imaging. *Neuroimage*, 5(1), 13–30.

Fusar-Poli, P., Placentino, A., Carletti, F., Landi, P., Allen, P., Surguladze, S., et al. (2009). Functional atlas of emotional faces processing: A voxel-based meta-analysis of 105 functional magnetic resonance imaging studies. *Journal of Psychiatry and Neuroscience*, 34(6), 418–32.

Gross, C. G. (1995). Aristotle on the brain. *Neuroscientist*, 1, 245.

He, Y., Dagher, A., Chen, Z., Charil, A., Zijdenbos, A., Worsley, K., & Evans, A. (2009). Impaired small-world efficiency in structural cortical networks in multiple sclerosis associated with white matter lesion load. *Brain*, 132(Pt. 12), 3366–79.

He, Y., Wang, J., Wang, L., Chen, Z. J., Yan, C., Yang, H., . . . Evans, A.C. (2009). Uncovering intrinsic modular organization of spontaneous brain activity in humans. *PLoS One*, 4(4), e5226.

Heberlein, A. S., & Adolphs, R. (2004). Impaired spontaneous anthropomorphizing despite intact perception and social knowledge. *Proceedings of the National Academy of Sciences*, 101(19), 7487–91.

Heberlein, A. S., Padon, A. A., Gillihan, S. J., Farah, M. J., & Fellows, L. K. (2008). Ventromedial frontal lobe plays a critical role in facial emotion recognition. *Journal of Cognitive Neuroscience*, 20(4), 721–33.

Hornak, J., Bramham, J., Rolls, E. T., Morris, R. G., O'Doherty, J., Bullock, P. R., & Polkey, C.E. (2003). Changes in emotion after circumscribed surgical lesions of the orbitofrontal and cingulate cortices. *Brain*, 126(Pt. 7), 1691–1712.

Johnsen, E. L., Tranel, D., Lutgendorf, S., & Adolphs, R. (2009). A neuroanatomical dissociation for emotion induced by music. *International Journal of Psychophysiology*, 72(1), 24–33.

Karnath, H. O., Rorden, C., & Ticini, L. F. (2009). Damage to white matter fiber tracts in acute spatial neglect. *Cerebral Cortex*, 19(10), 2331–37.

Kimberg, D. Y., Coslett, H. B., & Schwartz, M. F. (2007). Power in Voxel-based lesion-symptom mapping. *Journal of Cognitive Neuroscience*, 19(7), 1067–80.

Kinkingnehun, S., Volle, E., Pelegrini-Issac, M., Golmard, J. L., Lehericy, S., du Boisgueheneuc, F., . . . Dubois, B. (2007). A novel approach to clinical-radiological correlations: Anatomo-Clinical Overlapping Maps (AnaCOM): method and validation. *Neuroimage*, 37(4), 1237–49.

Laws, K. R. (2005). "Illusions of normality": A methodological critique of category-specific naming. *Cortex*, 41(6), 842–51; discussion 852–43.

Macmillan, M. (2000). *An odd kind of fame.* Cambridge, MA: MIT Press.

Makale, M., Solomon, J., Patronas, N. J., Danek, A., Butman, J. A., & Grafman, J. (2002). Quantification of brain lesions using interactive automated software. *Behavioral Research Methods, Instruments, & Computers*, 34(1), 6–18.

Marsh, E. B., & Hillis, A. E. (2008). Dissociation between egocentric and allocentric visuospatial and tactile neglect in acute stroke. *Cortex*, 44(9), 1215–20.

Nachev, P., Coulthard, E., Jager, H. R., Kennard, C., & Husain, M. (2008). Enantiomorphic normalization of focally lesioned brains. *Neuroimage*, 39(3), 1215–26.

Newhart, M., Ken, L., Kleinman, J. T., Heidler-Gary, J., & Hillis, A. E. (2007). Neural networks essential for naming and word comprehension. *Cognitive and Behavioral Neurology*, 20(1), 25–30.

Nieuwenhuis, S., Forstmann, B. U., & Wagenmakers, E. J. (2011). Erroneous analyses of interactions in neuroscience: a problem of significance. *Nature Neuroscience*, 14(9), 1105–7.

Ochfeld, E., Newhart, M., Molitoris, J., Leigh, R., Cloutman, L., Davis, C., . . . Hillis, A. E. (2011). Ischemia in Broca area is associated with Broca aphasia more reliably in acute than in chronic stroke. *Stroke*, 41(2), 325–30.

Philippi, C. L., Mehta, S., Grabowski, T., Adolphs, R., & Rudrauf, D. (2009). Damage to association fiber tracts impairs recognition of the facial expression of emotion. *Journal of Neuroscience*, 29(48), 15089–99.

Picton, T. W., Stuss, D. T., Alexander, M. P., Shallice, T., Binns, M. A., & Gillingham, S. (2007). Effects of focal frontal lesions on response inhibition. *Cerebral Cortex*, 17(4), 826–38.

Robertson, L. C., Knight, R. T., Rafal, R., & Shimamura, A. P. (1993). Cognitive neuropsychology is more than single-case studies. *Journal of Experimental Psychology, Learning, Memory, and Cognition*, 19(3), 710–17; discussion 718–34.

Robinson, O. J., & Sahakian, B. J. (2009). A double dissociation in the roles of serotonin and mood in healthy subjects. *Biological Psychiatry*, 65(1), 89–92.

Rorden, C., & Brett, M. (2000). Stereotaxic display of brain lesions. *Behavioral Neurology*, 12, 191–200.

Rorden, C., Fridriksson, J., & Karnath, H. O. (2009). An evaluation of traditional and novel tools for lesion behavior mapping. *Neuroimage*, 44(4), 1355–62.

Rorden, C., & Karnath, H. O. (2004). Using human brain lesions to infer function: A relic from a past era in the fMRI age? *Nature Reviews Neuroscience*, 5(10), 813–19.

Rorden, C., Karnath, H. O., & Bonilha, L. (2007). Improving lesion-symptom mapping. *Journal of Cognitive Neuroscience*, 19(7), 1081–88.

Rudrauf, D., Mehta, S., Bruss, J., Tranel, D., Damasio, H., & Grabowski, T. J. (2008). Thresholding lesion overlap difference maps: Application to category-related naming and recognition deficits. *Neuroimage*, 41(3), 970–84.

Rudrauf, D., Mehta, S., & Grabowski, T. J. (2008). Disconnection's renaissance takes shape: Formal incorporation in group-level lesion studies. *Cortex*, 44(8), 1084–96.

Shallice, T. (1988). *From neuropsychology to mental structure*. New York: Cambridge University Press.

Solomon, J., Raymont, V., Braun, A., Butman, J. A., & Grafman, J. (2007). User-friendly software for the analysis of brain lesions (ABLe). *Computer Methods and Programs in Biomedicine*, 86(3), 245–54.

Stuss, D. T., Murphy, K. J., Binns, M. A., & Alexander, M. P. (2003). Staying on the job: The frontal lobes control individual performance variability. *Brain*, 126(Pt. 11), 2363–80.

Teuber, H. L. (1955). Physiological psychology. *Annual Review of Psychology*, 6, 267–96.

Thiebaut de Schotten, M., Kinkingnehun, S., Delmaire, C., Lehericy, S., Duffau, H., Thivard, L., et al. (2008). Visualization of disconnection syndromes in humans. *Cortex*, 44(8), 1097–1103.

Urbanski, M., Thiebaut de Schotten, M., Rodrigo, S., Catani, M., Oppenheim, C., Touze, E., et al. (2008). Brain networks of spatial awareness: Evidence from diffusion tensor imaging tractography. *Journal of Neurology, Neurosurgery, & Psychiatry*, 79(5), 598–601.

Section III

EMOTION PERCEPTION AND ELICITATION

CHAPTER 7

The Facial Expression of Emotions

Nathalie George

With its fine musculature and its (mostly) hairless nature, the human face has evolved as a major signaling and communication channel for emotions, through facial expressions. This evolution took place in parallel with the acquisition of bipedalism, which placed the face in a fully exposed-to-the-view position and favored the development of vision as a prominent sensory modality to gather information on the environment – including conspecifics. The facial expressions of emotions form an important part of nonverbal communication. Signaling and communication are among the basic functions of emotion expressiveness in general: Emotional reactions – as adaptive reactions to eliciting events (see Chapter 1), which may include facial expressions as well as body movements (see Chapter 8), and vocal demonstrations (see Chapter 11) – inform others about one's needs or intention of action, such as the intents of fleeing, fighting, or friendly approaching. Furthermore, the emotional reactions of others give indications about surrounding events; for instance, fear expression indi-

cates impeding danger. These communication functions seem to be at their acme with the facial expressions of emotions in humans.

In this chapter, we review how the facial expressions of emotions are produced and which physical features of the face convey emotional expressions. We then turn to the neural substrates of the perception of emotion from faces, addressing the brain regions involved and the temporal dynamics of their responses. Finally, we discuss other aspects of faces that are related to emotion perception and elicitation.

The Production of Emotional Facial Expressions

The Movements of Facial Muscles Produce the Facial Expressions of Emotions

The scientific approach to the facial expressions of emotion goes back to the 19th century with the research about the muscular command of the facial expressions of emotion conducted by Duchenne de Boulogne in 1862 and the study of emotional expressions in humans and animals published by Charles Darwin in 1872.

Facial expressions are the result of the combined and coordinated action of facial muscles. For example, a typical happy expression involves the zygomaticus muscles that go from cheekbones to mouth corners and pull lip corners up in a smile, together with the orbicularis oculi that are involved in the squinting of the eyes and the raising of the cheeks, which accompany the "true" smiles of happiness.

These muscles are under the command of the VIIth cranial nerve, which emerges from the basis of the brain between the pons and the medulla oblongata and divides into different branches that innervate the numerous facial muscles. It is interesting to note that the central nervous system command of facial muscles involves two parallel routes. One originates in the motor cortex and comprises direct and indirect fibers to the facial nucleus from which the facial nerve arises (pyramidal pathway); it is responsible for the voluntary command of facial muscles. The other route originates from accessory motor areas such as cingulate areas and from subcortical structures particularly in the ventral forebrain, including the basal ganglia and hypothalamus. This extrapyramidal pathway comprises multisynaptic projections through the reticular formation and red nucleus to the facial nucleus. It is involved in the involuntary command of facial expressions. Thus, the voluntary and involuntary components of the face muscular control are partly dissociable. Accordingly, some patients with subcortical lesions or lesions in the extrapyramidal pathway may be able to produce a smile on command while not showing spontaneous or so-called Duchenne smiles in association with positive feeling. Reciprocally, other patients with cortical lesions or lesions affecting the pyramidal motor pathway may show a spontaneous smile while being unable to produce a voluntary or fake smile.

The Facial Displays of Basic Emotions: Are There Universals in Emotional Facial Expressions?

Charles Darwin underlined that the patterns of muscular actions forming the facial expressions of different emotions have developed through the course of animal evolution. He emphasized the similarities across species in the facial expressions of emotions, giving rise to the idea of the universality of emotion expression in humans. This idea fostered research that demonstrated the existence of constants across cultures and geographical groups in some typical patterns of facial expressions that correspond to the so-called basic emotions (e.g. Ekman, Sorenson, & Friesen, 1969). Researchers then developed systems for coding facial expressions, such as the Facial Action Coding System developed by Ekman's group. This system relies on the analysis of elementary facial movements – or action units – produced by facial muscles, and it codes the facial expressions in terms of the combination of the action units involved. The coded facial expressions can then be associated with felt or fake emotions, although this association remains quite empirical.

The pan-cultural elements of at least some emotional facial expressions suggest that there may be a set of discrete emotions with corresponding prototypical patterns of facial displays. In this framework, six categories of basic emotions have been proposed: disgust, anger, fear, sadness, happiness, and surprise (although the latter is sometimes difficult to distinguish from fear; see Figure 7.1a). Contempt (which shares some properties with disgust), shame, and interest have sometimes been added to this list, but with much less consistency, as detailed in Chapter 1.

The facial movements corresponding to these basic emotions may have partly evolved under selection pressure related to the regulation of sensory receptivity associated with specific face configurations (Susskind et al., 2008; see also Chapter 2). For example, the typical fearful expression

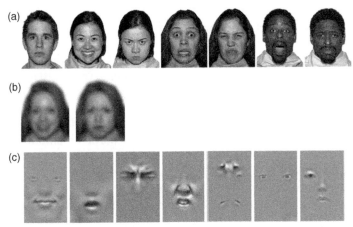

Figure 7.1. **The facial expression of emotions**. (a) Example faces displaying a neutral expression and the six basic emotions (from left to right: neutral, happy, angry, fearful, disgusted, surprised, and sad). These faces are taken from the NimStim face stimulus set, available freely for research purposes only at http://www.macbrain.org/resources.htm. (b) Low-pass filtered faces with happy (on the left) and angry (on the right) expression. The low spatial frequencies convey important information for emotion categorization. (c) Distinct face parts as well as different frequency bands convey diagnostic information for different emotions. These faces represent the combination of the diagnostic information in different frequency bands used by subjects to categorize the face as – from left to right – happy, surprised, angry, disgusted, sad, fearful, or neutral; adapted from Smith and Schyns (2009).

includes wide eye opening, which may favor the acquisition of visual information necessary for finding a way out of danger. In contrast, a disgusted expression would correspond to a reduction of sensory exposure. These prototypical patterns of emotional facial expressions seem to appear across early child development, probably in parallel with the differentiation and enrichment of infant emotional life, as well as with the maturation of neuromuscular systems.

Of course, basic emotions form only a primary set of the emotions that the human face can express. Facial expressions can convey a large (possibly infinite?) number of subtler and/or mixed emotions whose meaning is dependent on culture (Russell, 1991). Other emotions, including guilt, shame, envy, gratefulness, pride, vanity, and so forth, may involve more complex social cognition processes as well as moral cognition processes, as presented in the section on social emotions. The study of moral emotions in particular, as detailed in Chapter 21, constitutes a distinct area of research, largely

independent from that on the perception of facial expressions, because such emotions do not correspond to well-identified patterns of facial movements.

In addition, although bearing some universality, the facial expressions of (even basic) emotions show both interindividual variability and context dependency, and their display is contingent on cultural codes. Thus, there seems to be better recognition of emotions expressed by members of a common social – geographical, ethnical, or national – group (e.g., Jack, Blais, Scheepers, Schyns, & Caldara, 2009). The interpretation of facial expressions of emotions has also been shown to be dependent on the situational and perceptual context in which they arise (for a recent review, see Aviezer, Hassin, Bentin, & Trope, 2008). Overall, these influences underline the social dimension of emotional expressions as communication signals. However, although long debated, the idea of universals in the facial expressions of emotions and of a corresponding set of basic emotions has proven very influential in the field of research on the neuropsychological mechanisms of emotional facial expression perception.

Models of Emotional Facial Expressions

Two main types of models have been proposed to classify the facial expressions of emotions. These models are detailed in Chapter 1 and are here reviewed only briefly. The categorical models derive directly from the theory of universals in emotional expressions. Indeed, these models concern the basic emotions that have been shown to be associated with specific and highly recognizable facial displays. They propose that the facial displays of basic emotions are perceived and recognized as discrete categories. This proposal has received empirical support following the development of morphing methods[1]: The use of faces morphed across emotions has indicated that the six basic emotions are perceived and recognized in a categorical manner (Young et al., 1997).

There are, however, opposing models that argue for low-dimensional accounts of the perception of facial emotional expressions. These models put into question the existence of prototypical patterns of emotional facial expression. They argue that emotions vary continuously along a few underlying dimensions and that facial expressions vary accordingly and can be systematically located or differentiated in the low-dimensional space engendered (for a review, see Young et al., 1997). Two main dimensions of emotions are usually considered: one that is related to valence, with pleasant and unpleasant emotions at both ends, and the other one that is related to intensity or arousal with low and high values at both ends. Rolls (2005) also proposed a model focused on the delivery versus nondelivery of expected reward and punishment. According to this model, anger and relief would be located on the two sides of an axis opposing the nondelivery of an expected reward ver-

sus the nondelivery of an expected punishment; fear and enjoyment would be on the two sides of a second, orthogonal axis opposing the delivery of the expected punishment versus that of the expected reward. The dimension of approach versus withdrawal is another important dimension in motivated behavior along which the facial displays of emotions can be classified. Under this latter framework, anger and happiness are considered as negatively and positively valenced approach-related emotions, respectively, whereas fear and disgust are both negative withdrawal-related emotions.

Mixed models have also been proposed: They postulate discrete boundaries between a few basic or primary emotions together with a continuous, orthogonal dimension of intensity or arousal level along which these emotions can vary, giving rise to the variety of human emotional feelings and their displays. Overall, the multiplicity of these models reveals the wealth of human emotions and of their facial expressions.

Which Visual Information from the Face Conveys Emotions?

Emotional Expressions Are Encoded Separately from Other Facial Information such as Identity

Which physical features of the face convey emotions? One piece of knowledge in this domain is that the facial information relative to emotional expression is processed largely independently from the facial information relative to the person's identity. This is illustrated by the facts that you may rather easily recognize someone's identity under different emotions and reciprocally have no problem recognizing similar emotions on the faces of different individuals. However, it is interesting to go beyond this trivial evidence to examine what experimental psychology has learned in this domain.

It was initially thought that the facial signs of emotion and identity might be related because both identity and emotion recognition are markedly affected by face inversion. However, this phenomenon instead reflects that inversion disrupts the processing of configural information (constituted by the fine spatial arrangement of features) from the faces and that an important amount of information about both individual identity and emotional expression is contained in this information. Furthermore, inversion also disrupts the orientation of facial features, which is crucial for certain emotions (see, for example, the raised-up corners of a happy mouth). However, the information essential for emotion and that for identity recognition are different and processed independently from each other. Evidence for this dissociation comes in particular from neuropsychological studies: some brain-lesioned patients show selective deficits in the perception and recognition of emotional expressions, with spared processing of other aspects of the face (e.g., Young, Newcombe, de Haan, Small, & Hay, 1993); other patients show a reverse clinical pattern with impaired identity recognition but preserved emotion perception from faces (e.g., Tranel, Damasio, & Damasio, 1988). Another stream of evidence comes from cell recordings that have revealed the existence of "face neurons" in different temporal areas of the macaque brain. Face neurons respond selectively to faces in comparison with a multitude of other objects whether biologically relevant or not or meaningful or meaningless. Some of these neurons respond selectively to only one aspect of faces, such as facial expression, identity, or gaze direction (for a review, see Rolls, 2007).

Functional Models of Face Processing

In line with these findings, the most influential model of face perception and recognition has proposed that the processing of facial emotional expressions and that of other attributes of faces, including identity, rely on distinct functional routes (Bruce & Young, 1986). Interestingly, this model

was recently put in question (Calder & Young, 2005; Pourtois, Spinelli, Seeck, & Vuilleumier, 2010a; Tsuchiya, Kawasaki, Oya, Howard, & Adolphs, 2008). Calder and Young proposed a principal-component-analysis framework in which a single multidimensional coding system can analyze both identity and expression, thus challenging the view of the independent perceptual analysis of these facial attributes. This model accounts for the interference between emotion and identity recognition that has been reported in some studies. It also fits with the finding that single neurons of the macaque temporal cortex can code for different facial attributes (such as global configural information, facial identity, and emotional expression) in different time intervals of their response (for a review, see Calder & Young, 2005); this finding was recently extended to humans through the use of intracerebral recordings[2] (Pourtois et al., 2010a; Tsuchiya et al., 2008). Importantly, however, although Calder and Young (2005) argue that there may be a common perceptual representation stage for both facial identity and expression, they emphasize that this common representation would entail different facial information coding for facial identity and expression. In other words, their model emphasizes that the cues about emotional expressions and identity seem to be conveyed by different visual information. Furthermore, there would be different optimal facial cues as well as distinct neural systems for perceiving different emotional expressions.

Neuroanatomical versions of Bruce and Young's model have been proposed. Gobbini and Haxby (2007) postulate a core system for the perceptual analysis of faces, comprising the inferior occipital gyrus, the lateral fusiform gyrus, and the superior temporal sulcus (STS; Figure 7.2). We come back later to the involvement of these regions in emotional processing. What is interesting to mention here is that this model postulates distinct neural routes for the perceptual analysis of invariant attributes of faces – such as identity – and

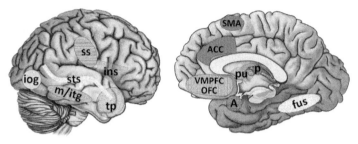

Figure 7.2. The brain network involved in the processing of emotional faces. The core system for the perceptual analysis of faces comprises the inferior occipital (iog) and fusiform (fus) gyri, which would be selectively involved in the perceptual analysis of the invariant attributes of faces (such as identity), and the superior temporal sulcus (sts), which would be selectively involved in the perception of changeable aspects or dynamic features of faces (including emotional expressions). The other regions illustrated belong to the emotional brain per se. The amygdala (A) and the insula (ins; located in the fundus of the sylvian fissure) have been specifically associated with the perception of fearful and disgusted faces, respectively, but they play a general role in the perception of emotional faces. Other regions include the pulvinar (P), the putamen (pu) (both of which are nuclei located in the depth of the hemispheres), the ventromedial prefrontal and orbitofrontal cortices (VMPFC, OFC), the anterior cingulate cortex (ACC), the supplementary motor area (SMA), the somatosensory cortex (ss), the middle and inferior temporal gyri (m/itg), and the temporal pole (tp).

for that of dynamic features – such as emotional expression (see Figure 7.2). Thus, it underlines that movement is an essential component of emotional facial expressions. In agreement with this idea, dynamic facial emotions have been shown to be perceived as somewhat more intense and emotionally arousing than their static versions (e.g., Sato, Kochiyama, Uono, & Yoshikawa, 2010). Furthermore, the perception of dynamic (relative to static) facial emotions seems to recruit an extended neural network and induce greater level of activation in the facial emotion perception network (e.g., Pitcher, Dilks, Saxe, Triantafyllou, & Kanwisher, 2011; Trautmann, Fehr, & Herrmann, 2009). However, to date, only a few studies have focused on moving faces, and future studies will have to characterize precisely the dynamics of emotion expression and the contribution of motion to emotional face perception.

Different Spatial Frequency Bands Convey Different Facial Emotions

Which visual information conveys cues about emotional expressions? Configural information – an important compound of facial emotional expressions – is in particular conveyed by the low spatial frequency content of the face. Accordingly, Schyns and Oliva (1999) have shown that the recognition of emotional expressions may rely selectively on low spatial frequencies. More precisely, the detection and the categorization of emotional expressions may involve distinct processes. Whereas the detection of expressive versus nonexpressive faces would rely more on high than low spatial frequencies, the categorization of facial expressions as angry, happy, or neutral appears to be based on the low spatial frequency content of the faces (Schyns & Oliva, 1999; see Figure 7.1b). This is in agreement with the findings that the brain regions responsive to the emotional facial expressions are selectively sensitive to the low spatial frequencies of the face (e.g., Vuilleumier, Armony, Driver, & Dolan, 2003) and that early brain responses to faces are enhanced for fearful relative to neutral faces containing low spatial frequencies only (Vlamings, Goffaux, & Kemner, 2009).

Moreover, different emotions and different tasks may be supported by different spatial frequency bands (Smith & Schyns, 2009). For example, the explicit identification of happy emotional expressions seems to rely on broad-band information from the face encompassing both high and low spatial frequencies (comprised between 7.5 and 120 cycles per face). By contrast, fear appears to be conveyed by high spatial frequencies (more than 30 cycles per face), and lower bands may convey diagnostic information for anger and surprise. The origin and the functional role of such differences in the optimal frequency bands for recognizing basic emotions are unclear. Because the range of spatial frequencies perceived gets confined to lower frequencies with increasing viewing distance, spatial frequency may in particular influence the range of distances over which the facial expression of a given emotion constitutes an effective communication signal (Smith & Schyns, 2009).

Distinct Face Parts Are Important for Different Emotions

In addition to spatial frequencies conveying different visual information, distinct parts of the face may be important for different emotional expressions. This issue was investigated by Schyns' group using spatial filtering techniques combined with the "bubbles" method[3] (e.g., Smith & Schyns, 2009). These authors demonstrated that fear lies selectively in the eyes. Accordingly, differences in gaze fixation onto the eyes of seen faces have been shown to account for some gender differences in fear recognition from faces (Halla, Huttona, & Morgana, 2010). By contrast, the identification of disgust seems to

rely on the region of the face bridging the lower part of the nose and the mouth; the diagnostic region for both happiness and surprise is the mouth but with a distinct physical structure of that feature for these two expressions (open mouth for surprise, smile for happiness). In addition, faces seem to be categorized as neutral on the basis of distributed information over the eyes, nose, and mouth, with a bias toward the right eye (Figure 7.1c). In agreement with this behavioral evidence, Schyns' group has also shown with EEG (see Chapter 4) that the temporal dynamics of early brain responses correlate with the dynamics of face feature integration during emotional face perception.

In conclusion, these data support the idea of distinct categories of emotions relying on discrete information from the face, which is distinct from the information conveying the person's identity. Whereas the discrimination of emotional expressions may rely preferentially on low spatial frequencies, the diagnostic features of the facial expressions of different emotions seem to lie in different frequency bands and to involve distinct face parts.

The Neural Network of the Perception of Emotional Facial Expressions

Faces, and particularly emotional faces, are among the most frequently used stimuli in the field of social and affective neuroscience. This has enabled substantial insight to be gained into the neural system involved in the perception of emotional facial expressions. The research in this domain has been markedly influenced by two streams of data. First the finding of universals in facial expressions and the definition of basic emotions have led to a focus on the neural substrates of the perception of these basic emotions, mostly adopting a categorical approach. Second, the long tradition of animal studies that have concentrated on fear-related emotional reactions has led to a focus on the perception of fearful faces in humans. It is mostly for this emotion, as well as for disgust, that specific neural substrates have been described and discussed. This emphasis has led to a major focus on the amygdala (in relation to fear) and secondarily on the anterior insula and basal ganglia (in relation to disgust). We thus first review the evidence regarding the involvement of these regions in emotional face perception. The neural network involved in the perception of emotion facial expressions is, however, extended (for a recent review, see Fusar-Poli et al., 2009), and the other regions involved are then described.

The Amygdala

The amygdala is a structure of the medial temporal lobe situated just in front of the hippocampus, within the so-called limbic system (Figure 7.2). It has attracted a great deal of attention in the field of emotion study in general and of emotional face perception in particular. A now classic study in this domain examined a patient with a selective, bilateral lesion of the amygdala (Adolphs, Damasio, & Damasio, 1994). This patient, SM, was strikingly impaired in her ability to recognize the facial expression of fear. However, she had not lost the concept of fear as such (although she did not appear to experience fear in a normal way); neither did she have some visuoperceptual deficit that could have accounted for her impairment. In particular, she was able to describe situations likely to elicit fear in people and how this feeling of fear would manifest in terms of bodily reaction and behavior. She was also unimpaired in recognizing the persons she knew from their faces as well as in learning new faces and discriminating among unfamiliar faces. Thus, she seemed selectively impaired in fearful face recognition. Other patients with an amygdala lesion and a similar pattern of deficits have been examined since then. Moreover, the development of functional brain imaging techniques has complemented these data with the finding of greater amygdala activation in response to fearful than neutral and/or happy faces in normal subjects (Breiter et al., 1996; Morris et al., 1996).

These early findings about amygdala involvement in emotional face perception were consistent with the knowledge accumulated on amygdala function from animal studies, particularly its well-established role in the processing of emotional – especially fear-related – and social stimuli (for a recent review, see Adolphs, 2010). However, the focus on fearful faces raised the question of the specificity of amygdala involvement in fear perception, as discussed in detail in Chapter 1. In this regard, several points of the seminal and later studies may be emphasized. First, although the deficit of patient SM seemed to be particularly marked for fearful faces, she was also impaired in decoding mixed emotions from possibly less prototypical yet customary facial expressions (Adolphs et al., 1994). Other patients with partial or total amygdalectomy showed some global impairment in the recognition of emotional facial expressions or at least deficits in the recognition of negative emotions such as anger, disgust, and sadness, as well as impaired perception of gaze direction. Moreover, brain imaging studies have found involvement of the amygdala not only during fearful face perception but also during the perception of angry, disgusted, sad, surprised, and happy faces, as compared to neutral faces (e.g., Breiter et al., 1996; Derntl et al., 2009). Some authors even found no difference between the levels of amygdala activation for different emotional expressions including positive ones (e.g., Winston, O'Doherty, & Dolan, 2003). Thus, the role of the amygdala is not limited to the perception of fearful expression or of negative emotion expressions.

In addition, the role of the amygdala extends to the perception of emotion from other cues than faces, as discussed in detail in the other chapters in this book section. Indeed, although inconsistently observed, it seems that the loss of fear recognition following amygdala damage can extend to vocal expressions. With fMRI, the amygdala has been shown to be involved in the perception of facial, vocal, and bodily expressions of fear, as well as in the cross-modal integration between facial and vocal signals of fear. One study, however, showed a differential impairment of the recognition of anger-related scenes when the facial expressions of the scene's protagonists were visible as opposed to concealed, suggesting a special role of the amydgala in the perception of some emotions from facial expression (Adolphs & Tranel, 2003). This notwithstanding, the amygdala clearly receives multisensory inputs, and it is involved in emotion perception from multiple sensory channels. Its dense and reciprocal connections with the visual system, which is a prevailing sensory modality in the human primates, may explain why it has been particularly implicated in the perception of facial displays of emotions.

As detailed in Chapters 14 and 15, amygdala involvement in emotional, particularly fear-related, perception has been found in conditions where the processing of facial expression was implicit as well as when the faces were unattended or not consciously perceived. In contrast, some studies reported that amygdala involvement was dependent on attention, task relevance, and/or awareness. It is thus likely that the amygdala is involved in multiple emotion-related processes, some of which are automatic and largely unconscious and others that depend on attention and/or awareness (for reviews, see Adolphs, 2010, and Chapters 14–15).

Moreover, there seems to be important interindividual variability in amygdala involvement for the perception of different emotions. For example, amygdala responsiveness to happy faces has been reported to depend on the personality trait of extraversion (Canli, Sivers, Whitfield, Gotlib, & Gabrieli, 2002). Gender and anxiety are other sources of interindividual differences that may modulate amygdala reactivity to different types of emotional expressions, including fear, as detailed in Chapters 24 and 26. In addition, culture and the familiarity with the social group of an individual whose fearful face is perceived can also modulate the amygdala response to that face (e.g., Chiao et al., 2008). These modulatory variables could at least partly account for the inconsistent findings on amygdala activation to different facial emotional expressions. Interestingly, they could also contribute to the important variability of the results regarding the type and the selectivity of the deficits associated with amygdala lesions, although etiology, disease history (particularly onset age), precise delineation of the lesion, and compensatory mechanisms are bound to be essential factors in this case.

Overall, this overview of the findings on amygdala involvement in emotional processing raises two important questions: First, what exactly is the role of this key structure in emotional face perception? Second, to which facial cues is the amygdala sensitive?

A general view has emerged over recent years that allows accommodation of the various results regarding amygdala involvement in face and person perception under a unifying theory. The amygdala is a structure that is at the crossroad of (1) the perceptual analysis of incoming stimuli, (2) the evaluation of stimuli and events in relation to (innate and acquired) endogenous knowledge, and (3) emotional reactions. It plays a key role in the interaction between emotion and memory: It is involved in the binding of events to an affective value and in the representation and memorization of this link, as detailed in the section on emotional learning and memory (for recent reviews, see Morrison & Salzman, 2010; Murty, Ritchey, Adcock, & LaBar, 2010). The amygdala is thus ideally placed to play a pivotal role in the appraisal of stimuli and in the processing of behaviorally relevant and salient stimuli: It evaluates and combines information from incoming stimuli with information related to prior experiences as well as to current goals of the perceiver, allowing adaptive responses to the stimuli. As discussed in Chapter 1, the amygdala may thus be viewed as a relevance detector or, in other words, as a key structure for the appraisal of events that are relevant to the organism.

This view of the amygdala allows us to understand its notable involvement in the perception of emotional faces and its more general role in social cognition (for a recent review, see Adolphs, 2010). Social stimuli have become among the most relevant stimuli through human evolution, and faces may form the most relevant class of social stimuli. This holds true from birth, because faces convey information about others' identity, emotions, and intentions, and the decoding and integration of facial signals guide our interpersonal behavior. Among the information conveyed by faces, emotional expressions are particularly salient and relevant because they often signal an intention of action (such as in anger or happiness, which are both approach related but convey very different intents) and/or the presence of a danger in the environment (such as in fear). Furthermore, the meaning of emotional expressions depends both on the sender and on the perceiver, as well as on the context of emotion elicitation. Thus, the specific role of the amygdala in the perception of emotional faces, the variability of its involvement across subjects and studies, and its more general role in social cognition may be understood in the light of its general role in the appraisal of stimulus relevance. This role may also account for its implication in various pathologies characterized by impairments in social interactions, such as autism, schizophrenia, or social phobia, where impairments in emotional face perception and/or in amygdala responses have been described (for review, see Schumann, Bauman, & Amaral, 2011). In addition, appraisal processes are multistage processes, including automatic and nonconscious mechanisms as well as more controlled and awareness-dependent processes, which fits with the view of the multistage involvement of the amygdala in emotion perception.

The amygdala has also been proposed to be involved in processing stimulus ambiguity, particularly for threat-related stimuli and in relation with decision making (Adams, Gordon, Baird, Ambady, & Kleck, 2003; Hsu, Bhatt, Adolphs, Tranel, & Camerer, 2005). Such a proposal is, however, not in contradiction with the role of amygdala in relevance appraisal, because ambiguous stimuli call for deepened evaluation to decipher their meaning and relevance.

The second important question raised earlier asked to which visual information from the face is the amygdala sensitive. Two types of findings appear of particular interest. First, the amygdala seems to be particularly sensitive to the low spatial frequency content of threat-related faces (e.g., Vuilleumier et al., 2003). This is consistent with the finding that low spatial frequencies contribute preferentially to the categorization of emotional facial expressions (Schyns & Oliva, 1999). Yet, it is contradictory to the earlier described finding of Smith and Schyns (2009) about the selective contribution of high spatial frequencies to fearful face recognition. These effects might, however, depend on the task, and further fMRI studies will be necessary to clarify these discrepant findings.

Second, the amygdala seems to be particularly sensitive to the information conveyed by the eyes. It has been shown to be particularly responsive to fearful eyes, even when they are perceived unconsciously. This may in fact explain the finding of selective amygdala responses to fearful expression, because, as mentioned earlier, fear lies especially in the eyes, and the widening of the eyes typical of fearful expression makes the eye region very salient. In agreement with this idea, it was recently shown that the patient SM of Adolphs and colleagues' (1994) study scanned faces abnormally, neglecting the eye region, which is the first and most frequently fixated region of the face in normal subjects. Her impairment in recognizing the facial expression of fear was in fact nonexistent when she was explicitly instructed to fixate on the eyes (Adolphs et al., 2005). In the same vein, it has been reported that the level of amygdala activation to faces correlated with the amount of gaze fixation onto the eye region of seen faces in autistic patients, who have core deficits in social interactions (Dalton et al., 2005). Amygdala activation was also found to predict fixation onto the eyes of fearful faces in healthy subjects (Gamer & Buchel, 2009).

In conclusion, the amygdala appears to be a key structure in the perception and recognition of facial expressions of emotions. Its primary responsiveness to fearful faces may have been somewhat overestimated, and this responsiveness may be in particular attributed to the sensitivity of amygdala to the eye region. The amygdala may also be particularly sensitive to the low spatial frequency content of faces. It bears a general role in the processes of relevance appraisal. Thus, the amygdala may be particularly involved in the processing of emotions from faces because emotional faces are highly relevant stimuli, which human beings may be tuned to detect and evaluate automatically.

Disgust and the Anterior Insula and Putamen

In addition to fear, disgust is the other emotion that has been most reliably associated with some specific neutral substrate. In a seminal study, Sprengelmeyer et al. (1996) showed that patients with Huntington's disease have a profound and selective deficit in the perception of disgust from both facial and vocal expressions, together with somewhat milder problems in recognizing anger and fear. These patients were also impaired in matching unfamiliar faces and showed borderline deficits in perceiving gaze direction. More recently, the recognition of disgust was found to be selectively impaired in preclinical carriers of the Huntington's disease dominant gene. By contrast, the recognition of vocal emotions and the experience of emotions seemed unimpaired at this preclinical stage, suggesting that the defect in the recognition of the facial expression of disgust may be an early phenotypic correlate of carrying the gene for Huntington's disease. This defect was associated with a lack of activation in the anterior insula and putamen (a striatal region of the basal ganglia; Figure 7.2), whereas control subjects activated these regions selectively when viewing disgusted faces as compared to neutral or surprised faces (Hennenlotter et al., 2004). Moreover, other neuropsychological

studies have reported impairments in the recognition of disgust in patients with insula lesions, eventually extending into the putamen, as well as in patients with Parkinson's disease in whom basal ganglia dysfunction is involved. Disrupted perception of disgust from facial expressions and scenes was also demonstrated in patients with obsessive-compulsive disorder, in association with abnormal insula functioning.

These findings have been corroborated by fMRI studies in healthy subjects, which showed that the anterior insula is activated not only by the perception of disgusted faces but also by that of disgusting scenes and by the experience of disgust (e.g., Wicker, Keysers et al., 2003). Thus, the involvement of the anterior insula is not limited to the processing of disgust from facial expressions. What remains unclear, however, is whether the insula and striatal regions are involved equally in both hemispheres, because inconsistent results have been found depending on the lateralization of insula-putamen lesions and of the activations in response to disgusted faces. Furthermore, similarly to the role of the amygdala with fear, the anterior insula does not seem to be involved only in disgust-related processing. In particular, it has been found to be activated during the perception of facial expressions of anger, fear, pain, and even happiness. Thus, considering its role in the representation of the self's bodily state, visceral sensation, and pain, the anterior insula, particularly in the right hemisphere, may be involved more generally in the empathic processes triggered by the perception of others' emotions, in the conscious experience of emotions and understanding of others' emotions, or perhaps even in more general functions related to the predictive significance of corresponding events (for recent reviews, see Craig, 2011; Lamm & Singer, 2010). It would play this role in close interaction with the striatal region of the basal ganglia with which it is highly interconnected.

As for the striatum, it has been suggested that the ventral part of this region, centered on the ventral putamen, would in fact play a prominent and selective role in the percep tion of the facial expression of anger (e.g., Calder, Keane, Lawrence, & Manes, 2004). Future studies will thus have to determine whether the processing of anger and disgust may actually be segregated within different regions of the striatum. It is also possible that disgust processing implicates disproportionately the anterior insula, whereas anger processing selectively recruits some part of the ventral striatal system. In addition, these findings will have to be articulated with those implicating the ventral striatum in reward and positive emotions.

Other Brain Regions

The network of brain regions involved in the perception of the facial expressions of emotions is in fact quite extended (Figure 7.2). This is likely related to the fact that the perception of facial expressions triggers multiple elementary processes related to emotion processing (such as detection, attention orienting, appraisal, emotion recognition processes), as well as to person perception (such as inference of the other's mental state and intention, personality trait attribution, empathy). This section, which reviews the role of the main regions involved in the perception of emotions from faces, is organized into three parts. I first discuss the pulvinar, which in close interaction with the amygdala may play an important role in several routes of emotion processing. Second, I describe the involvement of the regions classically associated with the perceptual analysis of faces. Finally, I briefly mention other cortical regions that have general roles in emotion.

THE PULVINAR

The pulvinar is a thalamic nucleus that has been proposed to play a special role in the processing of fear-related expressions, particularly when they are unconsciously perceived. This role may involve several pathways. First, there is a route from the superior colliculus to the pulvinar that, in turn, projects to the amygdala. Evidence for this route came initially from functional imaging studies that showed functional cou-

pling between these brain regions during the processing of unconsciously perceived threat-related faces (for a review, see Tamietto & de Gelder, 2010). This was recently complemented by effective and anatomical connectivity studies (Garrido, Barnes, Sahani, & Dolan, 2012; Tamietto, Pullens, de Gelder, Weiskrantz, & Goebel, 2012). This route would rely on the magnocellular pathway of the visual system that is sensitive to low spatial frequencies and has the property of conveying coarse visual information but with fast response dynamics. It would thus subtend the amygdala responsiveness to the low spatial frequency content of fearful faces, and it would subserve the rapid and automatic detection of fear-related facial expressions and the subsequent enhanced perceptual processing of these stimuli (e.g., Vuilleumier et al., 2003). However, the involvement of this subcortical route in the perception of emotional faces remains debated, and an alternative route, also involving the pulvinar, may play a central role (for a recent review, see Pessoa & Adolphs, 2010).

The pulvinar is densely and reciprocally connected to other regions involved in emotions, such as the anterior cingulate and the orbitofrontal and insular cortices; hence, it also reaches the amygdala indirectly. Its projections further include the superior temporal sulcal and gyral regions, which are involved in the perception of emotional expressions, as detailed later. Finally, the pulvinar has also connections with the posterior parietal regions and, together with the superior colliculus, pertains to the attention-orienting system of the human brain; it may thus play a role in rapid orienting toward emotionally relevant stimuli.

In sum, the pulvinar has rich and reciprocal connections with many cortical areas subtending the multiple processes involved in the detection and recognition of the facial expressions of emotion, and it may play a general role in cortical integration, as well as be a point of convergence of the cortical and subcortical routes involved in emotion processing. Thus, it may be a key structure of emotional face processing, as discussed by

Pessoa and Adolphs (2010). The extended cortical-pulvinar connectivity may account for the selective disruption of fear recognition from faces following damage to the medial part of the pulvinar, and it may also explain why evidence for intact fearful face detection was recently found in the patient SM, despite the bilateral lesion of her amygdala. It is, however, unclear why such a functional pathway would be restricted to fearful face perception. There is some evidence of pulvinar involvement in the perception of other emotions expressed by faces or bodies. Future research will have to determine the precise extent of the functional involvement of the pulvinar in emotional face processing.

THE CORE SYSTEM INVOLVED IN THE
PERCEPTUAL ANALYSIS OF FACES
According to Gobbini and Haxby's (2007) model of face processing, the core system for the perceptual analysis of faces comprises two sets of regions: (1) the fusiform and inferior occipital regions involved in the processing of the invariant features of faces that is necessary for identity recognition and (2) the posterior region of the superior temporal sulcus (STS) that subtends the processing of the dynamic features of faces including emotional expressions (Figure 7.2). The activity throughout the visual pathway has been shown to be modulated by the emotions conveyed by faces, but the modulation of fusiform and STS responses has been scrutinized most extensively.

It is well established that the activity of the fusiform regions selectively responsive to faces is influenced by the emotion conveyed by the faces (for a review, see Vuilleumier & Pourtois, 2007). The emotional enhancement of face-selective fusiform responses has been most commonly obtained for fearful faces compared to neutral faces. However, it was also reported for the facial display of other emotions. In addition, the emotional enhancement of stimulus-selective perceptual processes does not seem limited to faces and extends to bodies as well as scenes. These modulations seem to be tightly linked to the anatomo-functional coupling between

extrastriate visual cortex and the amygdala. Indeed, the enhancement of face-selective fusiform responses to fearful relative to neutral faces has been shown to be driven by the low spatial frequency content of the faces, which also drives the amygdala responses to those faces (Vuilleumier et al., 2003). Furthermore, an amygdala lesion abolishes the increase in fusiform responses to fearful relative to neutral faces (Vuilleumier, Richardson, Armony, Driver, & Dolan, 2004). Moreover, the pattern of relative attention independency of the response to emotional faces seems very similar for both the fusiform gyrus and amygdala, although the activity of visual regions may be overall more liable to the influence of attention and/or awareness, as discussed in Chapters 14–15. Thus, the dominant view is that coarse visual information first reaches the amygdala via either the subcortical colliculo-pulvinar pathway or a rapid visual cortical route and that the amygdala then exerts top-down influence onto the network of cortical areas involved in emotion processing, including the visual regions responsible for the perceptual analysis of faces. This process would be constitutive of a mechanism of emotional attention allowing attentional capture by and enhanced processing of highly behaviorally relevant stimuli such as emotional faces (see Chapter 14). The precise temporal dynamics of the interplay among amygdala, subcortical, and cortical responses to different facial expressions of emotions remain, however, to be established.

The modulation of STS activity by the facial expressions of emotions is usually interpreted quite differently from that of the fusiform activity. STS involvement in the processing of facial expressions was first shown with intracerebral recording in macaque monkeys (for a review, see Rolls, 2007). According to Gobbini and Haxby's (2007) model of face recognition, the posterior STS would be primarily involved in the encoding of changeable facial features; hence, of emotional facial expressions. This would be related to the more general role of the STS in the perception of biological motion (for a recent review, see Beauchamp, 2011).

Surprisingly, however, the evidence for the involvement of the STS (and adjacent superior temporal gyrus regions) in the perception of the facial expression of emotion in humans is somewhat more limited than the evidence regarding the emotional modulation of ventral occipitotemporal responses (for a review, see Calder & Young, 2005). This may be related to the fact that most studies have focused on static stimuli. Indeed, it seems that the STS responses to emotional faces are enhanced for dynamic relative to static displays of facial expressions (e.g., Pitcher et al., 2011; Trautmann et al., 2009).

STS responses to facial expressions do not seem to be specific to a particular emotion. Furthermore, these responses have been observed under conditions where the faces were not consciously perceived, although the responses seem to be enhanced under conditions of explicit processing of the emotional expression. Importantly, STS responses may not be specific to the facial signals of emotion, because they have also been observed for vocal expressions of emotions, as detailed in Chapter 11. In addition, the STS is known to be involved in the processing of other facial attributes, such as gaze, and it seems to play a role in the integration of gaze and facial expression cues, as well as in the integration of facial and vocal emotion (for a review, see Beauchamp, 2011). It is also involved in the processing of motion from various face and body cues.

Altogether, these findings have led to the proposal that the role of the STS in the perception of the facial expression of emotion may be related to its sensitivity to multisensory inputs. Indeed, emotional signals in real-life situations are essentially multidimensional: They combine multiple channels of information such as vocal and facial expression, for example, or gaze and facial expression cues (the signification of a fearful face will certainly not be the same if that face is looking at you rather than at something behind you; Calder & Young, 2005). Thus, some regions of the STS would

have evolved as an ideal substrate for the decoding of emotional facial expressions, and even when facial expressions are presented in isolation, their multidimensional aspect may be implied. Furthermore, the STS may have a general role in the analysis of others' intentions from the combination of their emotional expression, gaze, and action (e.g., Wyk, Hudac, Carter, Sobel, & Pelphrey, 2009).

OTHER CORTICAL REGIONS

Two frontal regions have been consistently reported as activated during the perception of emotional faces: the orbitofrontal and ventromedial prefrontal cortices (OFC/vmPFC), which have been particularly involved in the processing of angry faces and of positively valenced emotional faces, and the anterior cingulate cortex (ACC), which has been shown to be responsive to various emotions from faces including happiness, anger, sadness, disgust, and fear (for a review, see Fusar-Poli et al., 2009). Both regions appear to play a general role in emotion processing. The OFC/vmPFC is quite generally involved in emotion identification from multiple sensory channels as well as in emotion experience, as revealed by the classical clinical description of Phineas Gage's symptoms, an early case of an accidental ventromedial prefrontal lesion. It would play a role in linking a stimulus with its affective or emotional value and adapting this link as a function of the changes in incoming events. It may also be involved in the top-down control and regulation of behavior, as well as in decision making on the basis of the affective values of stimuli and of the predicted outcomes of actions or events (for a recent review, see Roy, Shohamy, & Wager, 2012). The ACC is also implicated in the perception of different types of emotional stimuli and in the subjective experience of emotion. It is a region of integration of emotional, attentional, cognitive, autonomic, and visceral information, which is involved in conflict monitoring and the regulation of motivated behavior, as well as in the conscious experience of emotion. Thus, the ACC, particularly in its ventral part, would play a general role in emotion (for a review, see Rushworth, Behrens, Rudebeck, & Walton, 2007). Both the OFC/vmPFC and ACC regions have strong anatomical connections with the amygdala and show functional coupling with it during the perception of emotional faces.

Moreover, premotor regions of the frontal lobe have been reported to be activated during the perception of emotional faces. A discrete region of the pre- supplementary motor area (pre-SMA) showed selective response to the perception of happy faces during intracerebral recording in an epileptic patient. The contact of the electrode that showed this selective response elicited laughter and merriment when electrically stimulated (Krolak-Salmon, Henaff, Vighetto, et al., 2006). This finding adds to the body of evidence that the perception of others' emotions involves the same regions as those implicated in one's own experience of emotions. This is indeed the case for the amygdala and anterior insula, which are involved in the experience and in the perception of fear and disgust, respectively; it seems to be also the case for the ventral striatum and dopaminergic system, which are involved in the feeling and in the perception of anger. This network of regions could participate in an "emotional mirror neuron system," which assumes that the recognition of the emotion expressed by a conspecific is subtended by an activation of the structures that mediate the feeling of that emotion in ourselves. The available evidence for involvement of the right somatosensory cortices in the recognition of seen facial expressions is also in line with this view (e.g., Adolphs, Damasio, Tranel, Cooper, & Damasio, 2000; Winston et al., 2003).

In addition, several neocortical regions of the temporal lobe have been reported to be activated during the perception of emotional faces, although somewhat more anecdotally (for a review, see Fusar-Poli et al., 2009). For example, the temporal pole was found to be activated during angry and sad face perception. Although the exact role of this region is unclear, it may be implicated in biographical knowledge, particularly affect-laden autobiographical memory, as well as in various aspects of semantic memory including conceptual knowledge of social behavior. Activations in discrete parts of the inferior, middle, and superior temporal gyri have also been found during sad, disgusted, and happy face perception, respectively. These activations may reflect some aspects of perceptual learning and/or perceptual analysis of emotional expressions.

CONCLUSION

A large network of cortical and subcortical regions is involved in the perception of the facial expressions of emotions, among which the amygdala seems to play a central role. Although it is likely that the perception of different emotions engages preferentially distinct parts of this network, it seems also clear that there are common regions engaged by different emotions and that the regions involved depend on task, context, and individual variables. Moreover, part of this network is engaged in the perception of emotions from face as well as from nonface stimuli.

The Temporal Dynamics of the Brain Responses to Emotional Faces

How quickly are the facial expressions of emotions encoded by the human brain, and which stages of face processing are affected by emotion? The importance of the perception and recognition of others' emotional facial expressions for adaptive behavior, particularly when they signal danger, has led to the classical hypothesis that there should be very rapid brain responses to emotional faces, at least to threat-related ones, in the course of face processing. The best illustration of this view is provided by an early model of the unfolding in time of emotional face processing (Adolphs, 2002). According to this model, a coarse representation of the emotion expressed, conveyed by the low spatial frequency content of the face, would be extracted either through the subcortical colliculo-pulvinar pathway to the amygdala or through a fast feedforward cortical sweep of information from visual areas to the OFC and amygdala. Thus, such coarse information would be extracted by about 100 ms and fed back to the visual regions responsible for the perceptual analysis of faces, resulting in enhanced processing of the seen emotional face around 150 ms poststimulus onset. Then the distributed cortical stage of emotional face processing would allow extracting the meaning of and conceptual knowledge about the emotion expressed, from about 300 ms after stimulus onset.

However, the experimental evidence for such a model is largely indirect, particularly concerning its first part, which draws mainly on fMRI and lesion studies of conscious and nonconscious emotional face perception (e.g., Vuilleumier et al., 2004). Such studies lack the temporal resolution necessary for assessing the time course of face processing. However, time-resolved brain responses can be recorded with human electrophysiological methods, including electroencephalography (EEG) and magnetoencephalography (MEG) techniques in healthy subjects, as well as intracerebral EEG recordings in epileptic patients, as detailed in Chapter 4. These methods have uncovered some aspects of the temporal dynamics of the neural responses to emotional faces (for a review, see Vuilleumier & Pourtois, 2007).

Brain Responses to Emotional Facial Expressions Have Often Been Found in a Late Time Range

A large number of event-related potential (ERP) studies have reported late, sustained effects of the emotion conveyed by faces (Figure 7.3a,b). These effects are typically observed after the face stimulus onset in the form of enhanced late positive components, with greater P300 or late positive potentials (LPPs) in response to emotional than neutral faces (e.g., Krolak-Salmon, Fischer, Vighetto, & Mauguiere, 2001; Schupp et al., 2004). These late positive effects start between 250 and 400 ms poststimulus and

may last up to 500 ms. They are sometimes preceded by a posterior N2 (a negative component peaking between about 200 and 300 ms) that is enhanced to the emotional faces (e.g., Schupp et al., 2004).

These late effects, particularly the P300/LPP effects, seem to be most clearly seen when the task involves an explicit processing of the emotional facial expression (e.g., Krolak-Salmon et al., 2001). In agreement with this idea, intracerebral recordings in epileptic patients have shown a selective response to disgusted faces (as compared to fearful, happy, surprised, and neutral faces) in the anterior insula, which began 300 ms postface onset and was dependent on the explicit processing of emotion. Furthermore, selective amygdala responses to fearful faces dependent on the explicit nature of the task with regard to the seen emotions were reported between 200 and 800 ms (for a review, see Krolak-Salmon, Henaff, Bertrand, Vighetto, & Mauguiere, 2006). A late amygdala response (starting from 700 ms) selective to fearful relative to neutral faces has also been reported to be dependent on visuospatial attention in another recent intracerebral EEG study (Pourtois, Spinelli, Seeck, & Vuilleumier, 2010b). Finally, emotional expression has been shown to modulate the electrical responses specific to faces from 200 to 1,000 ms in the fusiform region (Pourtois et al., 2010a). Thus the late effects recorded at the scalp surface may reflect late stages of emotional face processing in a distributed network of regions, including amygdala, insula, and extrastriate regions selective for faces. This is also supported by source localization of MEG and EEG responses, which has shown that these effects implicate the extended network of temporal and frontal cortical regions known to be involved in emotional face processing (e.g., Esslen, Pascual-Marqui, Hell, Kochi, & Lehmann, 2004).

Emotion influence on late brain responses to faces has been reported for different types of emotions, including positive (e.g., happy) and negative (e.g., fearful, threatening, or disgusted) facial expressions. Thus, although sometimes debated, these late

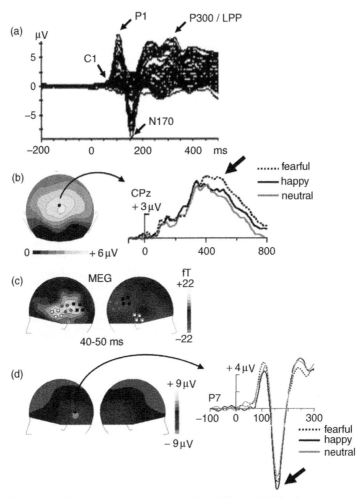

Figure 7.3. The dynamics of brain responses to emotional faces. (a) The brain responses to emotional faces as reflected in evoked potentials or magnetic fields comprise a succession of components, including the C1, P1, N170, and P300 or LPP (following the EEG nomenclature). These components are here illustrated on an overlay of the time course of evoked potentials recorded on 64 electrodes distributed over the scalp (with potentials in ordinate, in μV, and time in abscissa, in ms). Note that the C1 is best recorded with stimuli displayed peripherally (see Rauss et al., 2011, for a recent review). Here, faces were presented foveally, thus eliciting a very small C1. Data from Morel et al. (2009). (b) Effects of emotion have typically been found in the late time range. On the left: grand mean topographical map of the P300 averaged between 300 and 600 ms for fearful, happy, and neutral faces, shown on a back view of the head. On the right: time course of the evoked potential on CPz, the centro-parietal electrode site where the P300 culminated, showing enhanced P300 for fearful relative to neutral and happy faces between 300 and 600 ms. Data from Morel et al. (2009). (c) There is growing evidence for early to very early influence of emotion on brain responses to faces, including in the time range of the C1. Here, MEG data are presented. There was a differentiated repetition effect (difference in the brain responses for the second relative to the first presentation of stimuli) for emotional versus neutral faces, between 40 and 50 ms. A grand mean topographical map of the repetition effect averaged between 40 and 50 ms is shown on the left and right side views of the head, highlighting the sensors where the repetition effect peaked for the fearful (black squares), the happy (gray circles), and the neutral faces (white squares). Data from Morel et al. (2009). (d) Modulation of the face-specific N170 by emotional expressions. On the left: a grand mean topographical map of the N170 in response to emotional and neutral faces is shown at the latency of its peak (160 ms), on left and right side views of the head. On the right: time course of the evoked potential on a left temporal electrode, P7; on the first presentation of fearful, happy, and neutral faces, the amplitude of the N170 was found to be greater for the emotional than the neutral faces. Data from Morel et al. (2009).

effects do not seem to reflect a processing stage selective for a particular emotion. It is, however, possible that the precise network of regions subtending such generally widespread effects varies as a function of the seen emotion, which may explain why selective or differentiated effects have sometimes been reported (for a review, see Vuilleumier & Pourtois, 2007). Overall, the late effects have been proposed to reflect post-perceptual stages of processing related to the decoding of the meaning of emotions, global activation processes elicited by the appraisal of the seen emotional faces, and/or cortical integration mechanisms associated with emotional processing. They are not specific to the perception of emotions from faces, because they have been reported for other types of emotional stimuli such as scenes and words.

Accumulating Evidence for Early to Very Early Effects of Emotions

Are the early stages of the perceptual analysis of faces really immune to the influence of the emotion displayed by the face? The studies that addressed this question have concentrated on two types of emotional influences on brain responses to faces: (1) the emotional modulations that may occur at the earliest stages of visual processing, which take place within about the first 100 ms and are not specific to faces, and (2) the emotional influences on the early brain responses selective to faces, that is, on $N170$ (in EEG) and $M170$ (in MEG; Figure 7.3a,c,d).

An increasing number of studies have shown that emotional modulation of the brain responses to seen faces could occur within the first 100 ms of face processing (for reviews, see George, Morel, & Conty, 2008; Vuilleumier & Pourtois, 2007). Such modulations have been reported in the time range of the $C1$ (or $N70m$ in the MEG vocabulary), which is the earliest ERP component in response to visual stimuli, peaking between 50 and 90 ms. The $C1$ was found to be greater in response to fearful than happy faces that were presented laterally and were incidental to a main tar-

get discrimination task (Pourtois, Grandjean, Sander, & Vuilleumier, 2004). This effect does not seem to be specific to emotional faces, because it has also been shown that the $C1$ in response to laterally presented gratings can be modulated when these gratings acquire an affective value through conditioning (Stolarova, Keil, & Moratti, 2006). In addition, in a study combining EEG and MEG, the emotional expression of centrally viewed faces has been shown to modulate the repetition effects elicited by those faces between 40 and 50 ms, over posterior occipitotemporal regions (Morel, Ponz, Mercier, Vuilleumier, & George, 2009; Figure 7.3c). In a follow-up study, the prior association of neutral faces with an emotional auditory-verbal context was found to modulate the brain responses to these faces in a similar time range (Morel, Beaucousin, Perrin, & George, 2012). Altogether, these findings provide evidence for very early differentiated processing of emotional stimuli, which could reflect not only coarse categorization mechanisms of low-level visual features predictive of emotions (such as local contrast variations produced by the widened eyes of fearful faces), but also the influence of acquired salience or emotional significance on the earliest stages of visual processing.

The neural origin of these very early effects is unclear. Although long held to originate mainly from the primary visual cortex, the $C1$ is now known to reflect neural activity from the striate and extrastriate cortices (for a review, see Rauss, Schwartz, & Pourtois, 2011). It might also be influenced by some neural activity from a subcortical origin. Indeed, intracerebral recordings in the pulvinar and in mutiple visual cortical areas in the cat have shown that the initial processing of information in the visual system is parallel, with response latencies in the pulvinar comprised between 50 and 85 ms for simple stimuli. More surprisingly, thalamic sources of activity have been localized with MEG as early as 10 to 20 ms after the onset of the display of fearful faces (Luo, Holroyd, Jones, Hendler, & Blair, 2007). In addition, in this study, selective responses to fearful faces were shown to originate in the amygdala from 20 to 30 ms, earlier than the first neural sources of MEG signals in the visual cortex (between 40 and 50 ms). A recent MEG study has also shown activities differentiating the perception of fearful, happy, and neutral faces in the STS, medial prefrontal cortex, and amygdala between 35 and 96 ms (Liu & Ioannides, 2010; see also, Garrido et al., 2012 and Morel et al., 2012), and an EEG study indicated differentiated responses to emotional and neutral faces from 70 ms in the superior temporal polysensory area in a patient with bilateral destruction of the primary visual cortex (Andino, Menendez, Khateb, Landis, & Pegna, 2009). Although these results need further confirmation, they raise the interesting possibility that (1) the subcortical colliculo-pulvinar route to the amygdala may effectively be involved in the perception of emotional faces, in parallel with or with a small temporal precedence over the feedforward visual cortical route, and (2) this route may involve much faster information flow than previously thought. It is, however, also possible that the very early effects of emotional face perception reflect purely a tuning of the responses of neuronal assemblies to relevant categories of stimuli (defined either by overlearned visual cues or by associative – including emotional – learning, for example), or that they might be associated with predictive coding mechanisms (Rauss et al., 2011).

Moreover, several studies have shown that the emotional expression of seen faces can modulate the P1 component that follows the C1 and peaks typically between 80 and 130 ms (for a review, see Vuilleumier & Pourtois, 2007). The P1 shows some general face sensitivity; however, it is not considered to be a face-specific component. P1 modulation by facial expression has been observed for the different basic emotions (compared to neutral condition), as well as for faces yielding positive versus negative affective judgment or whose emotional value was reinforced by aversive conditioning. Thus, it seems to reflect a global emotional effect. Furthermore, the emotional effects on the P1 are not spe-

cific to faces, because they have also been observed in response to nonhumanoid emotional robots, emotional pictures, and gratings predictive of painful shocks, as well as in association with the integration of emotions from faces and bodies or from faces and scenes (e.g., Dubal, Foucher, Jouvent, & Nadel, 2011; Righart & de Gelder, 2008).

The emotional effects on the P1 may in particular be conveyed by the low spatial frequency content of the face stimuli (e.g., Vlamings et al., 2009). They could reflect attentional modulation of stimulus processing induced by emotion (or so-called emotional attention processes, discussed in Chapter 14). Indeed, P1 amplitude modulations have often been associated with selective attention processes, and the emotional modulation over frontocentral recording sites described by Eimer and colleagues in the time range of the P1 was dependent on the presentation of the faces at the attended location, being abolished for ignored faces. However, some of the emotional effects on the P1 were obtained in conditions where the faces were presented centrally and the processing of emotional expressions was incidental to the task at hand (e.g., Bayle & Taylor, 2010; for reviews, see Eimer & Holmes, 2007; Vuilleumier & Pourtois, 2007). The attentional processes associated with emotional face processing thus seem to encompass an automatic component related to attentional capture by emotional faces.

These emotional modulations of the P1 may be mainly of extrastriate visual origin, reflecting gain control and amplification mechanisms induced by emotional attention. However, the contribution of other brain regions cannot be excluded. Indeed, with intracerebral recordings, early responses to aversive visual stimuli have been reported as early as from 120 ms poststimulus onset in the OFC (Kawasaki et al., 2001). Differentiated amygdala responses to fearful versus neutral faces have also recently been reported from about 140 ms, a time range compatible with some P1 effect (Pourtois et al., 2010b). The top-down influence of these regions may be responsible for the processes of emotional attention reflected in P1 modulations. Furthermore, the localization of the brain sources of EEG/MEG signal has confirmed the involvement of a distributed cortical network in the emotional modulation of the P1, including insular, amygdalar, orbitofrontal, lateral frontal, and somatosensory cortex regions (e.g., Esslen et al., 2004; Hung et al., 2010). This involvement is consistent with the early establishment of a large-scale network during emotional processing.

Another type of early emotional influence concerns the N170 in response to faces. This component follows the P1, and it peaks typically around 150–170 ms. The N170 (or M170 for its MEG counterpart) was historically characterized as associated with an early stage of face-selective perceptual analysis (e.g., George, Evans, Fiori, Davidoff, & Renault, 1996). Following Bruce and Young's (1986) model, this stage was initially considered to be immune to the influences of emotional and/or cognitive factors. Accordingly, a number of studies manipulating the emotional expressions of faces did not find any impact of this manipulation on the N170 (e.g., Krolak-Salmon et al., 2001). However, more and more studies have put this view into question, reporting an influence of the facial expression of emotion on the N170 or on its magnetic counterpart, the M170, in response to faces (e.g., Morel et al., 2009; Figure 7.3d). This N/M170 modulation does not seem to be specific either to a given emotion or to emotion valence, but it may vary with the intensity of the emotion expressed (Sprengelmeyer & Jentzsch, 2006). It is unclear whether it is conveyed by some particular spatial frequencies of the face because inconsistent results have been obtained in this regard (e.g., Pourtois, Dan, Grandjean, Sander, & Vuilleumier, 2005; Vlamings et al., 2009). In any case, it seems to reflect an automatic influence of emotion, because the processing of emotional expressions was incidental in many studies and one study reported an N170 modulation for masked fearful versus nonfearful faces (Pegna, Landis, & Khateb, 2008). The

influence of facial expression of emotions on the N170 and M170 could reflect differences in configural information for distinct emotional expressions, which may be extracted from a perceptual representation stage common with that of face identity, even if the configural cues relative to emotional expression and identity differ, as mentioned earlier. It is also possible that the emotional modulation of N170 and M170 reflects emotional attention processes driven by the amygdala, similarly to the emotional modulation of the face-selective fusiform responses observed with fMRI.

This raises the question of the neural origin of the N170 and M170 modulations by emotional expression. Note first that these EEG and MEG components may reflect at least partly different neural activity. The N170 has been proposed to reflect STS activity (e.g., Henson et al., 2003), whereas the M170 would reflect activity in the inferior occipital and fusiform regions (e.g., Itier, Herdman, George, Cheyne, & Taylor, 2006). It seems, however, more plausible that both components reflect brain responses within a distributed and partially overlapping network of ventral and lateral occipitotemporal regions. Overall, the localization of the brain sources of EEG and MEG signals has revealed that the emotional modulation of the N170 and M170 reflected activity of extrastriate regions, including the fusiform gyrus region (e.g., Pegna et al., 2008). Moreover, nonvisual regions could contribute to N170 and M170 emotional modulations, because intracerebral recordings in epileptic patients have shown that an extended network of regions is activated in response to faces by 150 ms, including medial temporal structures such as the amygdala and extending into parietal and frontal – including premotor – regions (e.g., Barbeau, et al., 2008; Krolak-Salmon, Henaff, Vighetto, et al., 2006; Pourtois et al., 2010b). Accordingly, a recent study with EEG source localization found an extended set of regions showing differentiated responses to distinct facial emotional expressions in the time range of the N170. These regions included the STS, the inferior frontal gyrus, the OFC, the ACC, and the right amygdala (Andino et al., 2009). Furthermore, several studies concentrated on the localization of amygdala activity from MEG signals, and they found amygdala responses sensitive to emotional expressions in the time range of the M170 (for a review, see Dumas, Attal, Dubal, Jouvent, & George, 2011). Thus, it is likely that the modulation of the N170 and M170 responses to faces by emotional expressions reflects distributed and possibly recurrent activity in a network of interconnected regions involved in emotional face processing.

Finally, it is interesting to underline that the emotional modulations of the C1, P1, and N170 have sometimes been found independently of each other (for a review, see Vuilleumier & Pourtois, 2007). This finding emphasizes that some information about the emotional value of a face may be extracted before the brain "knows" it is a face (that is, before face-selective mechanisms are triggered). Moreover, it suggests that these effects reflect different types of emotional influences. In brief, some coarse aspects of emotional expressions, possibly conveyed by low spatial frequencies, may be processed very early, independently of the face-selective perceptual analysis. It is possible that this very early processing engages a fast subcortical route to the amygdala, or that it reflects a rapid feedforward flow of information through cortical areas whose neurons are tuned to diagnostic features of emotional expressions. It is unclear whether a first sweep of the top-down influence from anterior regions (such as the amygdala and/or OFC) onto posterior visual regions may also take place as early as by ~50 ms. Furthermore, more detailed, possibly configural, information about emotional expression would be extracted at a face-selective perceptual representation stage that may be common to identity processing, although relying on a different type of information. At this stage, the functional interaction and coupling between amygdala and perceptual regions, as well as among a wider set of regions, are clearly taking place. It is important to mention

that these early stages may not be associated with any conscious access, explicit appraisal, or conceptual knowledge related to the perceived emotional expression. These processes may rather be reflected by later ERP components, starting from about 200 ms.

Beyond the Facial Expression of Emotion: The Many Faces of Emotions

Neutral Faces Can Elicit Emotion-Related Processes

Facial expressions of emotions constitute the main aspect of emotion perception and elicitation obtained from face information. However, even when not displaying any particular emotion, faces may trigger emotion-related processes. In particular, it has been shown that several processes associated with social perception and social cognition are rooted in emotion-related processing. For example, the evaluation of some personality traits of neutral faces, such as trustworthiness, seems to be tightly linked to general processes of valence appraisal; it involves overgeneralization of emotion-related facial features, based on similarity to expressions that signal approach or avoidance behavior. Such processes seem to take place automatically, because evidence for amygdala involvement has been found in a paradigm of implicit evaluation of face trustworthiness (for a review, see Todorov, 2008).

In the same vein, the emotional value of contextual information concomitant with a face encounter seems to be very easily attached to that face, influencing both the affective judgment and the neural representation of the face, and also biasing the evaluation of new faces having some likeness to the previously encountered one (e.g., Morel et al., 2012; Verosky & Todorov, 2010). In other words, even neutral faces may have or easily acquire an intrinsic affective value. This may be why the mere perception of neutral faces activates a distributed network of regions, including the amygdala (e.g., Ishai, Schmidt, & Boesiger, 2005).

Emotion Perception and Elicitation Associated with Gaze Perception

Gaze – particularly eye contact or mutual gaze – may bear a special, intrinsic emotional value (for a review, see George & Conty, 2008). Eye contact is a salient stimulus that is often the preliminary to interindividual interaction. Accordingly, the perception of eye contact has been shown to trigger enhanced emotional arousal, as reflected by enhanced skin conductance response during the perception of direct relative to averted gaze or closed eyes (Conty et al., 2010). Moreover, the perception of direct as compared to averted gaze activates the amygdala and results in increased amygdala coupling with face-responsive fusiform regions, which may subserve deeper encoding of the faces displaying direct gaze (George, Driver, & Dolan, 2001). Altogether, these findings may reflect a mechanism of social attention partly rooted in that of emotional attention (for a review, see Senju & Johnson, 2009).

Gaze also contributes directly to emotion elicitation obtained from faces insofar as gaze direction modulates the meaning of expressed emotions. Approach-related emotions (such as anger or happiness) are perceived as more intense when combined with direct gaze, whereas conversely, the perceived intensity of the facial expressions of withdrawal-related emotions (such as fear) is increased when the face displays an averted gaze (e.g., N'Diaye, Sander, & Vuilleumier, 2009). Accordingly, gaze direction modulates the neural responses to emotional expressions, particularly in the STS and amygdala regions (Adams et al., 2003; N'Diaye et al., 2009; Wicker, Perrett, Baron-Cohen, & Decety, 2003).

Finally, the perceived direction of gaze may modify the hedonic value of faces as well as that of surrounding objects. Observers judged as more likable faces shifting their gaze toward them than faces shifting their gaze away from them (Mason, Tatkow, & Macrae, 2005). In the same vein, attractive faces have been found to elicit enhanced activation of the ventral striatum – a region pertaining to the reward system of the brain – under direct relative to averted gaze (Kampe, Frith, Dolan, & Frith, 2001). Perceived gaze can also modify the hedonic value of surrounding objects. Consider the situation where a participant sees the face of a conspecific either looking at concomitantly displayed objects or looking away from these objects. It has been shown that the looked-at objects acquire a positive affective value for the participant in comparison with the non-looked-at objects. In addition, objects looked at by a happy face are liked more than objects looked at by a disgusted face (for a review, see Frischen, Bayliss, & Tipper, 2007). This affective transfer is dependent on gaze because the objects presented side by side with an emotional face but not looked at do not acquire such a differentiated hedonic value.

Conclusion

Faces are privileged stimuli for studying multiple aspects of emotion perception in relation with social cognition. Emotion perception from faces is essential for adaptive behavior, and it recruits an extended network of regions central to emotion and person perception. This has led to an increasing interest in the investigation of emotional face perception skills in various neurological and psychiatric pathologies: Emotion perception from faces is a highly sensitive skill whose dysfunction can be observed at the behavioral and neural levels in numerous pathologies (including autism, schizophrenia, bipolar disorder, posttraumatic stress disorder, obsessive-compulsive disorder, and Alzheimer's disease), and reveals abnormal functioning of the neural system of emotion. Furthermore, the impairment of emotion recognition from faces could constitute a phenotypic marker of the vulnerability to some pathology. Future studies will thus have to further elucidate the precise impact of face emotion perception skills in normal and in abnormal sociocognitive functioning. In the meanwhile, emotional faces, with directed or averted gaze, will remain among the most powerful stimuli for research in human affective neuroscience.

Outstanding Questions and Future Directions

- Emotions are dynamic in nature, but most of the knowledge accumulated so far on the perception of emotional faces has been obtained with static images. What are the neural pathways and the time course of the perception of dynamic emotional expressions?
- The positive side of emotion is likely to be particularly important in regard with social stimuli such as faces, but it has been somewhat neglected so far. Is the same spatially and temporally distributed network of activity involved in the processing of the facial displays of positive affects?
- Numerous studies in social psychology have shown the impact of the physical presence of others on human perceptual and cognitive processes. How can emotion perception and elicitation from faces be studied in a real-life setup? Would such study lead to the uncovering of different mechanisms for the perception of emotion in the context of live social interactions?
- Emotion perception from faces and social perception are tightly interrelated. What are the relative weights of nature, culture, and individual differences on the neural network and temporal dynamics of emotional face perception?
- What exactly is the role of the pulvinar in the different stages of emotional face perception? And to what extent is a fast subcortical colliculo-pulvinar-amygdalar route actually involved in the perception of emotional faces?

Notes

1 Morphing allows computing the smooth and continuous transformation that turns a stimulus into another stimulus. For example, it allows the transformation of a happy expression of a face into an angry expression of that same face, and intermediate images showing varying degrees of emotion on the continuum between enjoyment and anger can then be extracted.

2 Intracerebral electrodes are implanted for presurgical diagnostic purposes in pharmacologically intractable epilepsy.

3 This method allows applying various masks over faces, with each mask being generated as random holes or "bubbles" in an otherwise black screen. The bubbles through which the stimulus can be seen have different sizes according to the different frequency bands explored. This technique allows the generation of numerous incomplete stimuli that can then be used in various detection, discrimination, recognition, or categorization tasks. The diagnostic visual cues used by the subjects to perform the task can then be computed by averaging the stimuli as a function of the task responses.

References

Adams, R. B., Jr., Gordon, H. L., Baird, A. A., Ambady, N., & Kleck, R. E. (2003). Effects of gaze on amygdala sensitivity to anger and fear faces. *Science*, 300(5625), 1536.

Adolphs, R. (2002). Neural systems for recognizing emotion. *Current Opinions in Neurobiology*, 12(2), 169–177.

Adolphs, R. (2010). What does the amygdala contribute to social cognition? *Annals of the New York Academy of Sciences*, 1191, 42–61.

Adolphs, R., Damasio, H., & Damasio, A. R. (1994). Impaired recognition of emotion in facial expressions following bilateral damage to the human amygdala. *Nature*, 372, 669–72.

Adolphs, R., Damasio, H., Tranel, D., Cooper, G., & Damasio, A. R. (2000). A role for somatosensory cortices in the visual recognition of emotion as revealed by three-dimensional lesion mapping. *Journal of Neuroscience*, 20(7), 2683–90.

Adolphs, R., Gosselin, F., Buchanan, T. W., Tranel, D., Schyns, P., & Damasio, A. R. (2005). A mechanism for impaired fear recognition after amygdala damage. *Nature*, 433(7021), 68–72.

Adolphs, R., & Tranel, D. (2003). Amygdala damage impairs emotion recognition from scenes only when they contain facial expressions. *Neuropsychologia*, 41(10), 1281–89.

Andino, S. L., Menendez, R. G., Khateb, A., Landis, T., & Pegna, A. J. (2009). Electrophysiological correlates of affective blindsight. *Neuroimage*, 44(2), 581–89.

Aviezer, H., Hassin, R. R., Bentin, S., & Trope, Y. (2008). Putting facial expressions back in context. In N. Ambady & J. J. Skowronski (Eds.), *First impressions* (pp. 255–86). New York: Guilford Press.

Barbeau, E. J., Taylor, M. J., Regis, J., Marquis, P., Chauvel, P., & Liegeois-Chauvel, C. (2008). Spatiotemporal dynamics of face recognition. *Cerebral Cortex*, 18(5), 997–1009.

Bayle, D. J., & Taylor, M. J. (2010). Attention inhibition of early cortical activation to fearful faces. *Brain Research*, 1313, 113–23.

Beauchamp, M. S. (2011). Biological motion and multisensory integration: The role of the superior temporal sulcus. In R. B. Adams, N. Ambady, K. Nakayama, & S. Shimojo (Eds.), *The science of social vision* (pp. 409–20). New York: Oxford University Press.

Breiter, H. C., Etcoff, N. L., Whalen, P. J., Kennedy, W. A., Rauch, S. L., Buckner, R. L., et al. (1996). Response and habituation of the human amygdala during visual processing of facial expression. *Neuron*, 17(5), 875–87.

Bruce, V., & Young, A. (1986). Understanding face recognition. *British Journal of Psychology*, 77, 305–27.

Calder, A. J., Keane, J., Lawrence, A. D., & Manes, F. (2004). Impaired recognition of anger following damage to the ventral striatum. *Brain*, 127(Pt. 9), 1958–69.

Calder, A. J., & Young, A. W. (2005). Understanding the recognition of facial identity and facial expression. *Nature Reviews Neuroscience*, 6(8), 641–51.

Canli, T., Sivers, H., Whitfield, S. L., Gotlib, I. H., & Gabrieli, J. D. (2002). Amygdala response to happy faces as a function of extraversion. *Science*, 296(5576), 2191.

Chiao, J. Y., Iidaka, T., Gordon, H. L., Nogawa, J., Bar, M., Aminoff, E., et al. (2008). Cultural specificity in amygdala response to fear faces. *Journal of Cognitive Neuroscience*, 20(12), 2167–174.

Conty, L., Russo, M., Loehr, V., Hugueville, L., Barbu, S., Huguet, P., et al. (2010). The mere perception of eye contact increases arousal during a word-spelling task. *Social Neuroscience*, 5(2), 171–86.

Craig, A. D. (2011). Significance of the insula for the evolution of human awareness of feelings from the body. *Annals of the New York Academy of Sciences*, 1225, 72–82.

Dalton, K. M., Nacewicz, B. M., Johnstone, T., Schaefer, H. S., Gernsbacher, M. A., Goldsmith, H. H., et al. (2005). Gaze fixation and the neural circuitry of face processing in autism. *Nature Neuroscience*, 8(4), 519–26.

Derntl, B., Habel, U., Windischberger, C., Robinson, S., Kryspin-Exner, I., Gur, R. C., et al. (2009). General and specific responsiveness of the amygdala during explicit emotion recognition in females and males. *BMC Neuroscience*, 10, 91.

Dubal, S., Foucher, A., Jouvent, R., & Nadel, J. (2011). Human brain spots emotion in non humanoid robots. *Social, Cognitive, and Affective Neuroscience*, 6(1), 90–97.

Dumas, T., Attal, Y., Dubal, S., Jouvent, R., & George, N. (2011). Detection of activity from the amygdala with magnetoencephalography. *IRBM*, 32(1), 42–47.

Eimer, M., & Holmes, A. (2007). Event-related brain potential correlates of emotional face processing. *Neuropsychologia*, 45(1), 15–31.

Ekman, P., Sorenson, E. R., & Friesen, W. V. (1969). Pan-cultural elements in facial displays of emotion. *Science*, 164(3875), 86–88.

Esslen, M., Pascual-Marqui, R. D., Hell, D., Kochi, K., & Lehmann, D. (2004). Brain areas and time course of emotional processing. *Neuroimage*, 21(4), 1189–1203.

Frischen, A., Bayliss, A. P., & Tipper, S. P. (2007). Gaze cueing of attention: visual attention, social cognition, and individual differences. *Psychology Bulletin*, 133(4), 694–724.

Fusar-Poli, P., Placentino, A., Carletti, F., Landi, P., Allen, P., Surguladze, S., et al. (2009). Functional atlas of emotional faces processing: A voxel-based meta-analysis of 105 functional magnetic resonance imaging studies. *Journal of Psychiatry and Neuroscience*, 34(6), 418–32.

Gamer, M., & Buchel, C. (2009). Amygdala activation predicts gaze toward fearful eyes. *Journal of Neuroscience*, 29(28), 9123–26.

Garrido, M.I., Barnes, G.R., Sahani, M., & Dolan, R.J. (2012). Functional evidence for a dual route to amygdala. *Current Biology*, 22, 129–134.

George, N., & Conty, L. (2008). Facing the gaze of others. *Neurophysiologie Clinique/Clinical Neurophysiology*, 38(3), 197–207.

George, N., Driver, J., & Dolan, R. J. (2001). Seen gaze-direction modulates fusiform activity and its coupling with other brain areas during face processing. *Neuroimage*, 13(6 Pt. 1), 1102–12.

George, N., Evans, J., Fiori, N., Davidoff, J., & Renault, B. (1996). Brain events related to normal and moderately scrambled faces. *Brain Research: Cognitive Brain Research*, 4(2), 65–76.

George, N., Morel, S., & Conty, L. (2008). Visages et electrophysiologie. In E. Barbeau, S. Joubert, & O. Felician (Eds.), *Traitement et reconnaissance des visages: du percept à la personne* (pp. 113–42). Marseille: Solal (collection Neuropsychologie).

Gobbini, M. I., & Haxby, J. V. (2007). Neural systems for recognition of familiar faces. *Neuropsychologia*, 45(1), 32–41.

Halla, J. K., Huttona, S. B., & Morgana, M. J. (2010). Sex differences in scanning faces: Does attention to the eyes explain female superiority in facial expression recognition? *Cognition and Emotion*, 24(4), 629–37.

Hennenlotter, A., Schroeder, U., Erhard, P., Haslinger, B., Stahl, R., Weindl, A., et al. (2004). Neural correlates associated with impaired disgust processing in pre-symptomatic Huntington's disease. *Brain*, 127(Pt. 6), 1446–53.

Henson, R. N., Goshen-Gottstein, Y., Ganel, T., Otten, L. J., Quayle, A., & Rugg, M. D. (2003). Electrophysiological and haemodynamic correlates of face perception, recognition and priming. *Cerebral Cortex*, 13(7), 793–805.

Hsu, M., Bhatt, M., Adolphs, R., Tranel, D., & Camerer, C. F. (2005). Neural systems responding to degrees of uncertainty in human decision-making. *Science*, 310(5754), 1680–83.

Hung, Y., Smith, M. L., Bayle, D. J., Mills, T., Cheyne, D., & Taylor, M. J. (2010). Unattended emotional faces elicit early lateralized amygdala-frontal and fusiform activations. *Neuroimage*, 50(2), 727–33.

Ishai, A., Schmidt, C. F., & Boesiger, P. (2005). Face perception is mediated by a distributed cortical network. *Brain Research Bulletin*, 67(1–2), 87–93.

Itier, R. J., Herdman, A. T., George, N., Cheyne, D., & Taylor, M. J. (2006). Inversion and contrast-reversal effects on face processing assessed by MEG. *Brain Research*, 1115(1), 108–20.

Jack, R. E., Blais, C., Scheepers, C., Schyns, P. G., & Caldara, R. (2009). Cultural confusions show that facial expressions are not universal. *Current Biology*, 19(18), 1543–48.

Kampe, K. K., Frith, C. D., Dolan, R. J., & Frith, U. (2001). Reward value of attractiveness and gaze. *Nature*, 413(6856), 589.

Kawasaki, H., Kaufman, O., Damasio, H., Damasio, A. R., Granner, M., Bakken, H., et al. (2001). Single-neuron responses to emotional visual stimuli recorded in human ventral prefrontal cortex. *Nature Neuroscience*, 4(1), 15–16.

Krolak-Salmon, P., Fischer, C., Vighetto, A., & Mauguiere, F. (2001). Processing of facial emotional expression: spatio-temporal data as assessed by scalp event-related potentials. *European Journal of Neuroscience*, 13(5), 987–94.

Krolak-Salmon, P., Henaff, M. A., Bertrand, O., Vighetto, A., & Mauguiere, F. (2006). Part II: Recognising facial expressions. *Revue Neurologique (Paris)*, 162(11), 1047–58.

Krolak-Salmon, P., Henaff, M. A., Vighetto, A., Bauchet, F., Bertrand, O., Mauguiere, F., et al. (2006). Experiencing and detecting happiness in humans: The role of the supplementary motor area. *Annals of Neurology*, 59(1), 196–99.

Lamm, C., & Singer, T. (2010). The role of anterior insular cortex in social emotions. *Brain Structure and Function*, 214(5–6), 579–91.

Liu, L., & Ioannides, A. A. (2010). Emotion separation is completed early and it depends on visual field presentation. *PLoS One*, 5(3), e9790.

Luo, Q., Holroyd, T., Jones, M., Hendler, T., & Blair, J. (2007). Neural dynamics for facial threat processing as revealed by gamma band synchronization using MEG. *Neuroimage*, 34(2), 839–47.

Mason, M. F., Tatkow, E. P., & Macrae, C. N. (2005). The look of love: Gaze shifts and person perception. *Psychological Science*, 16(3), 236–39.

Morel, S., Beaucousin, V., Perrin, M., & George, N. (2012). Very early modulation of brain responses to neutral faces by a single prior association with an emotional context: Evidence from MEG. *Neuroimage*, 61, 1461–70.

Morel, S., Ponz, A., Mercier, M., Vuilleumier, P., & George, N. (2009). EEG-MEG evidence for early differential repetition effects for fearful, happy and neutral faces. *Brain Research*, 1254, 84–98.

Morris, J. S., Frith, C. D., Perrett, D. I., Rowland, D., Young, A. W., Calder, A. J., et al. (1996). A differential neural response in the human amygdala to fearful and happy facial expressions. *Nature*, 383(6603), 812–15.

Morrison, S. E., & Salzman, C. D. (2010). Re-valuing the amygdala. *Current Opinions in Neurobiology*, 20(2), 221–30.

Murty, V. P., Ritchey, M., Adcock, R. A., & LaBar, K. S. (2010). fMRI studies of successful emotional memory encoding: A quantitative meta-analysis. *Neuropsychologia*, 48(12), 3459–69.

N'Diaye, K., Sander, D., & Vuilleumier, P. (2009). Self-relevance processing in the human amygdala: Gaze direction, facial expression, and emotion intensity. *Emotion*, 9(6), 798–806.

Pegna, A. J., Landis, T., & Khateb, A. (2008). Electrophysiological evidence for early non-conscious processing of fearful facial expressions. *International Journal of Psychophysiology*, 70(2), 127–36.

Pessoa, L., & Adolphs, R. (2010). Emotion processing and the amygdala: From a 'low road' to 'many roads' of evaluating biological significance. *Nature Reviews Neuroscience*, 11(11), 773–83.

Pitcher, D., Dilks, D. D., Saxe, R. R., Triantafyllou, C., & Kanwisher, N. (2011). Differential selectivity for dynamic versus static information in face-selective cortical regions. *Neuroimage*, 56(4), 2356–63.

Pourtois, G., Dan, E. S., Grandjean, D., Sander, D., & Vuilleumier, P. (2005). Enhanced extrastriate visual response to bandpass spatial frequency filtered fearful faces: Time course and topographic evoked-potentials mapping. *Human Brain Mapping*, 26(1), 65–79.

Pourtois, G., Grandjean, D., Sander, D., & Vuilleumier, P. (2004). Electrophysiological correlates of rapid spatial orienting towards fearful faces. *Cerebral Cortex*, 14(6), 619–33.

Pourtois, G., Spinelli, L., Seeck, M., & Vuilleumier, P. (2010a). Modulation of face processing by emotional expression and gaze direction during intracranial recordings in right fusiform cortex. *Journal of Cognitive Neuroscience*, 22(9), 2086–2107.

Pourtois, G., Spinelli, L., Seeck, M., & Vuilleumier, P. (2010b). Temporal precedence of emotion over attention modulations in the lateral amygdala: Intracranial ERP evidence from a patient with temporal lobe epilepsy. *Cognitive Affective and Behavioral Neuroscience*, 10(1), 83–93.

Rauss, K., Schwartz, S., & Pourtois, G. (2011). Top-down effects on early visual processing in humans: A predictive coding framework. *Neuroscience and Biobehavioral Reviews*, 35(5), 1237–53.

Righart, R., & de Gelder, B. (2008). Rapid influence of emotional scenes on encoding of facial expressions: An ERP study. *Social, Cognitive, and Affective Neuroscience*, 3(3), 270–78.

Rolls, E. T. (2005). *Emotion explained*. Oxford: Oxford University Press.

Rolls, E. T. (2007). The representation of information about faces in the temporal and frontal lobes. *Neuropsychologia*, 45(1), 124–43.

Roy, M., Shohamy, D., & Wager, T.D. (2012). Ventromedial prefrontal-subcortical systems and the generation of affective meaning. *Trends in Cognitive Sciences*, 16, 147–156.

Rushworth, M. F. S., Behrens, T. E. J., Rudebeck, P. H., & Walton, M. E. (2007). Contrasting roles for cingulate and orbitofrontal cortex in decisions and social behaviour. *Trends in Cognitive Sciences*, 11(4), 168–76.

Russell, J. A. (1991). Culture and the categorization of emotions. *Psychological Bulletin*, 110(3), 426–50.

Sato, W., Kochiyama, T., Uono, S., & Yoshikawa, S. (2010). Amygdala integrates emotional expression and gaze direction in response to dynamic facial expressions. *Neuroimage*, 50(4), 1658–65.

Schumann, C. M., Bauman, M. D., & Amaral, D. G. (2011). Abnormal structure or function of the amygdala is a common component of neurodevelopmental disorders. *Neuropsychologia*, 49(4), 745–59.

Schupp, H. T., Ohman, A., Junghofer, M., Weike, A. I., Stockburger, J., & Hamm, A. O. (2004). The facilitated processing of threatening faces: An ERP analysis. *Emotion*, 4(2), 189–200.

Schyns, P. G., & Oliva, A. (1999). Dr. Angry and Mr. Smile: When categorization flexibly modifies the perception of faces in rapid visual presentations. *Cognition*, 69(3), 243–65.

Senju, A., & Johnson, M. H. (2009). The eye contact effect: Mechanisms and development. *Trends in Cognitive Sciences*, 13(3), 127–34.

Smith, F. W., & Schyns, P. G. (2009). Smile through your fear and sadness: transmitting and identifying facial expression signals over a range of viewing distances. *Psychological Science*, 20(10), 1202–8.

Sprengelmeyer, R., & Jentzsch, I. (2006). Event related potentials and the perception of intensity in facial expressions. *Neuropsychologia*, 44(14), 2899–2906.

Sprengelmeyer, R., Young, A. W., Calder, A. J., Karnat, A., Lange, H., Homberg, V., et al. (1996). Loss of disgust. Perception of faces and emotions in Huntington's disease. *Brain*, 119(Pt.5), 1647–65.

Stolarova, M., Keil, A., & Moratti, S. (2006). Modulation of the C1 visual event-related component by conditioned stimuli: Evidence for sensory plasticity in early affective perception. *Cerebral Cortex*, 16(6), 876–87.

Susskind, J. M., Lee, D. H., Cusi, A., Feiman, R., Grabski, W., & Anderson, A. K. (2008). Expressing fear enhances sensory acquisition. *Nature Neuroscience*, 11(7), 843–50.

Tamietto, M., & de Gelder, B. (2010). Neural bases of the non-conscious perception of emotional signals. *Nature Reviews Neuroscience* 11, 697–709.

Tamietto, M., Pullens, P., de Gelder, B., Weiskrantz, L., & Goebel, R. (2012). Subcortical connections to human amygdala and changes following destruction of the visual cortex. *Current Biology*, 22, 1449–55.

Todorov, A. (2008). Evaluating faces on trustworthiness: an extension of systems for recognition of emotions signaling approach/avoidance behaviors. *Annals of the New York Academy of Sciences*, 1124, 208–24.

Tranel, D., Damasio, A. R., & Damasio, H. (1988). Intact recognition of facial expression, gender, and age in patients with impaired recognition of face identity. *Neurology*, 38, 690–96.

Trautmann, S. A., Fehr, T., & Herrmann, M. (2009). Emotions in motion: Dynamic compared to static facial expressions of disgust and happiness reveal more widespread emotion-specific activations. *Brain Research*, 1284, 100–15.

Tsuchiya, N., Kawasaki, H., Oya, H., Howard, M. A., III, & Adolphs, R. (2008). Decoding face information in time, frequency and space from direct intracranial recordings of the human brain. *PLoS One*, 3(12), e3892.

Verosky, S. C., & Todorov, A. (2010). Generalization of affective learning about faces to perceptually similar faces. *Psychological Science*, 21(6), 779–85.

Vlamings, P. H., Goffaux, V., & Kemner, C. (2009). Is the early modulation of brain activity by fearful facial expressions primarily mediated by coarse low spatial frequency information? *Journal of Vision*, 9(5), 12.1–13.

Vuilleumier, P., Armony, J. L., Driver, J., & Dolan, R. J. (2003). Distinct spatial frequency sensitivities for processing faces and emotional expressions. *Nature Neuroscience*, 6(6), 624–31.

Vuilleumier, P., & Pourtois, G. (2007). Distributed and interactive brain mechanisms during emotion face perception: Evidence from functional neuroimaging. *Neuropsychologia*, 45(1), 174–94.

Vuilleumier, P., Richardson, M. P., Armony, J. L., Driver, J., & Dolan, R. J. (2004). Distant influences of amygdala lesion on visual cortical activation during emotional face processing. *Nature Neuroscience*, 7(11), 1271–78.

Wicker, B., Keysers, C., Plailly, J., Royet, J. P., Gallese, V., & Rizzolatti, G. (2003). Both of us disgusted in My insula: The common neural basis of seeing and feeling disgust. *Neuron*, 40(3), 655–64.

Wicker, B., Perrett, D. I., Baron-Cohen, S., & Decety, J. (2003). Being the target of another's emotion: A PET study. *Neuropsychologia*, 41(2), 139–46.

Winston, J. S., O'Doherty, J., & Dolan, R. J. (2003). Common and distinct neural responses during direct and incidental processing of multiple facial emotions. *Neuroimage*, 20(1), 84–97.

Wyk, B. C., Hudac, C. M., Carter, E. J., Sobel, D. M., & Pelphrey, K. A. (2009). Action understanding in the superior temporal sulcus region. *Psychological Science*, 20(6), 771–77.

Young, A. W., Newcombe, F., de Haan, E. H. F., Small, M., & Hay, D. C. (1993). Face perception after brain injury: Selective impairments affecting identity and expression. *Brain*, 116, 941–59.

Young, A. W., Rowland, D., Calder, A. J., Etcoff, N. L., Seth, A., & Perrett, D. I. (1997). Facial expression megamix: Tests of dimensional and category accounts of emotion recognition. *Cognition*, 63(3), 271–313.

CHAPTER 8

Bodily Expressions of Emotion

Visual Cues and Neural Mechanisms

Anthony P. Atkinson

Emotions are often expressed or signaled via postures and movements of the whole body or its parts. Although faces are body parts, the face and the rest of the body are distinct means for expressing, or channels for signaling, emotions. There is a large corpus of research on facial expressions and their perception, surveyed elsewhere in this book (see Chapter 7). A central aim of this chapter is to survey the smaller but nevertheless important corpus of research devoted to investigating the perception of bodily expressed emotions and its neural substrate. Its particular focus is on the visual cues underlying body and bodily emotion perception.

The chapter begins with a consideration of what constitutes a bodily expression or signal of emotion, highlighting a difference between actions that directly convey an emotion and actions that do not but are nevertheless performed in an emotional way. This is followed by a brief summary of studies that have demonstrated the ability of human observers to distinguish between and identify a range of emotions from body posture and movement stimuli. The subsequent two sections, consider the different visual cues that humans use to perceive bodies per se and emotional bodies in particular. I then survey the current state of knowledge about how the brain processes visual information relating to other people's bodies and bodily expressions of emotion. In these latter two sections we see that viewing other people's bodies and bodily expressions engages not only neural mechanisms with primarily visual functions but also neural mechanisms involved in planning and executing actions and in eliciting emotional responses and representing the changes in body state that are important and probably essential components of emotions (see Chapter 1). In the last section, we see that some of this evidence points to simulation or "shared substrates" hypotheses of emotion recognition, according to which recognizing another's emotional expression recruits neural mechanisms in the perceiver responsible for generating his or her own emotional experience and behavior.

What Constitutes a Bodily Expression or Signal of Emotion?

I begin with a note on terminology. It is important to distinguish between "expressions" and "signals" (or "displays") of emotion. The former term captures the idea that what are primarily internal changes in bodily states and feelings nevertheless often have external manifestations visible to the naked eye (or audible to the naked ear); one's emotional state is expressed or revealed to the world via one's body, face, and voice. This is what some authors have called the "readout" hypothesis (e.g., Buck, 1994). By contrast, calling something an emotion signal signifies its intentionally communicative nature, whether the signaler is experiencing the displayed emotion or not. Fridlund (1991), for example, argued that displays of emotion are specific to the intentions of the displayer and the social context of the display and rarely, if ever, directly reflect underlying emotional or motivational states. For present purposes I am simply going to note my agreement with Buck (1994) – and, I suspect, many other emotion researchers and affective neuroscientists – that people sometimes unintentionally express emotions and sometimes intentionally signal emotions even when they are not experiencing them, but in many instances emotions involve mixtures of both unintentional expression and intentional signal. I will also ride roughshod over the distinction I have just drawn by henceforth using "expression" as shorthand to refer both to unintentionally expressed and intentionally signaled emotions. Nonetheless, the distinction will rear its head again shortly when we consider symbolic gestures.

In Darwin's (1872/1998) seminal work, emotional expressions were characterized in terms of three principles: those of "serviceable habits," "antithesis," and "direct action of the nervous system." Serviceable habits are actions with direct or indirect adaptive significance that are reliably associated with "certain states of the mind, in order to relieve or gratify certain sensations, desires, etc." (Darwin, 1872/1998,

p. 34). Such actions, being habitual, can become reliable predictors of a person's subsequent actions and clues to his or her state of mind. Furthermore, Darwin suggested that the attempt to exert voluntary control over such habitual actions nevertheless often leaves behind or may itself directly result in still visible expressive movements. The principle of antithesis expresses the idea that some actions that are not themselves serviceable (i.e., do not or did not serve an adaptive function) are nevertheless performed because they are opposite in nature to actions that are serviceable. For example, shrugging of the shoulders, Darwin suggested, is the antithetical action of a confident or aggressive stance. The principle of direct action of the nervous system is essentially the idea that emotions involve some direct and usually automatic activity of certain parts of the nervous system, reflected in movements and physiological changes characteristic of particular emotions that are independent of the will and are largely habitual. Examples include physiological changes evident in the skin or internal organs, the trembling associated with fear or rage, and apparently purposeless movements such as clapping hands and jumping in joy.

With respect to the visual perception of bodily expressed emotions, more recent research has focused on bodily postures and movements, leaving aside other visible bodily changes, such as color of the skin and sweating. An examination of contemporary research on emotion perception reveals a distinction, often implicit, between two ways in which emotions can be expressed via bodily postures and movements, which cuts across Darwin's three principles. On the one hand, there are what we can call expressive actions – actions that are direct manifestations of internal emotional states, such as fleeing or freezing in fear, retching in disgust, or standing erect with expanded chest and clenched fists in anger. On the other hand, there are everyday actions that are performed in an emotional way. In such cases, the emotion in some sense "leaks out" of one's action. For example, one might perform a transitive action, such as picking up an object or knocking on or closing a door, with a sharp, aggressive movement that could readily be interpreted as an expression of anger, whether or not one intended it to be so. Or one's slow, slumped walk might suggest a sad, depressed state.

Both expressive actions and nonemotional actions performed in an emotional way can be and often have been adopted or adapted as conventional gestures with symbolic meaning. In many cultures, for example, raised fists are symbolic of anger, and a bowed head with the face buried in one's hands or the miming of sniffing and wiping away tears can signal sadness. There are also bodily gestures whose origin may not lie either with expressive actions or nonemotional actions; namely, arbitrary signals with culture-specific meanings. There are many examples of such gestures, particularly involving the hands, in sign languages (e.g., Poizner, 1981). Following Ekman and Friesen (1969) and other emotion researchers (e.g., Buck, 1984; Fridlund, 1991), I refer to the general class of symbolic gestures, whether they are arbitrary or originate from expressive or everyday nonemotional actions, as *emblems*. The class of bodily emblems consisting of arbitrary gestures has been studied little, if at all, by affective neuroscientists, perhaps because of the cultural specificity of such gestures and of how few of them signal specific emotional states, particularly when unaccompanied by facial gestures. Nonetheless, it is worth bearing in mind that specific examplars of nonemotional actions and particularly of expressive actions used by affective neuroscientists can vary in how symbolic or conventional they are.

The Visual Perception of Bodily Expressed Emotions

For theoretical and practical reasons, research on emotion perception and recognition has focused predominantly on the ability of people to discriminate or identify "basic" emotions (e.g., Ekman, 1992),

such as anger, fear, happiness, and disgust, which are distinguished from more complex social and moral emotions, such as jealousy, guilt, and embarrassment. One such reason is that basic emotions are in part defined by characteristic facial expressions, consisting in distinct sets of facial muscle actions (see Chapter 1 for further discussion). It is less clear whether these basic emotions can be defined by distinct sets of bodily as well as facial actions (an issue that is ripe for further investigation). In any case, considerable research has shown that human observers are readily able to distinguish or identify at least a limited set of emotions – particularly basic emotions – from bodily expressions in the absence of facial and vocal cues. Evidence comes from several different types of tasks, but most commonly from forced-choice emotion-labeling tasks, in which observers typically show significantly above-chance performance when asked to select from a limited list the single word that best describes the viewed bodily expression. Accurate forced-choice emotion classification has been demonstrated with static images depicting people intentionally portraying emotions with static body postures (e.g., Atkinson, Heberlein, & Adolphs, 2007), computer-generated mannequins manipulated to reflect descriptions of emotional postures (Coulson, 2004), and single frames extracted from movie clips of people intentionally portraying emotions (e.g., Atkinson, Dittrich, Gemmell, & Young, 2004; Atkinson, Heberlein, et al., 2007; Hadjikhani & de Gelder, 2003). Examples of such images are shown in Figure 8.1.

Accurate forced-choice emotion classification has also been demonstrated with moving images of whole-body expressions in the form of expressive actions (Atkinson et al., 2004; Atkinson, Heberlein, et al., 2007; Atkinson, Tunstall, & Dittrich, 2007), dance movements intended to portray specific emotions (e.g., Dittrich, Troscianko, Lea, & Morgan, 1996; Hejmadi, Davidson, & Rozin, 2000), combinations of specific body movements that were not deliberate expressions of particular emotions (de Meijer, 1989), and walking movements either intended to

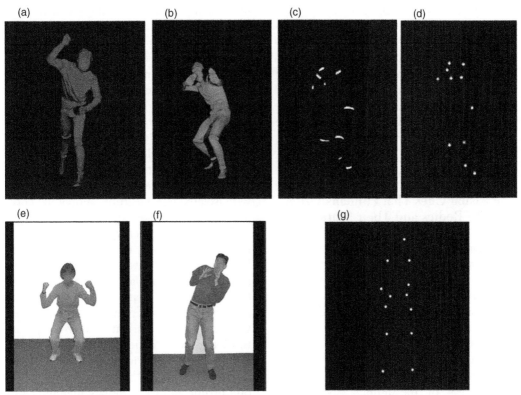

Figure 8.1. a–d. Still images extracted from short movie clips of body movements intended to express anger (a) and fear (b–d). Images a and b were extracted from full-light or fully illuminated displays, in which the whole body is visible (with the face covered). Images c and d are stills from, respectively, patch-light and point-light displays of the same movement sequence and time point as for image b. For details of how these stimuli were constructed, see Atkinson et al. (2004) and Atkinson et al. (2012). e–f: Photographs of emotional postures intended to express anger (e) and fear (f), drawn from a set used by Atkinson, Heberlein, and Adolphs (2007) (created by A. S. Heberlein). g: A still frame from a point-light display of a human walking (with no intention to express any emotion). Point-light and patch-light stimuli are useful for studies of movement-based emotion perception because both face and morphological cues are absent or minimal, but kinematic cues are preserved.

portray specific emotions (e.g., Heberlein, Adolphs, Tranel, & Damasio, 2004; Montepare, Goldstein, & Clausen, 1987) or that reflected self-induced emotional states (Roether, Omlor, Christensen, & Giese, 2009; Roether, Omlor, & Giese, 2008). Drinking and knocking arm movements alone, performed with the intention of expressing specific emotional states, are sufficient for observers to distinguish among those emotions (Pollick, Paterson, Bruderlin, & Sanford, 2001). Forced-choice classification accuracy is greater for moving whole-body expressive actions than from single static frames extracted from the same video footage (Atkinson et al., 2004),

suggesting that observers make use of the motion or multiple form cues (or both) available in the moving images to help them identify the emotions. Observers also use motion information to aid their judgments of the emotional intensity of whole-body expressive actions (Atkinson et al., 2004).

Accurate classification of emotions in whole-body movements has also been demonstrated using emotion-rating tasks, in which observers are required to rate either how compatible the viewed movements are with the emotion that the actor intended to portray (Sawada, Suda, & Ishii, 2003) or how much of each particular emotion is in each display (i.e., its intensity) without being told what emotion the actor was intending to portray (Atkinson, Heberlein, et al., 2007). Even when asked simply to describe what they see, observers are able to identify intended expressions of some emotions at greater than chance levels in individual displays of whole-body dance movements (Hejmadi et al., 2000) and in expressive action portrayals (Hubert et al., 2007; Moore, Hobson, & Lee, 1997).

The Visual Cues That Humans Use to Perceive Bodies and Their Motion

What form and motion information does the human visual system extract from others' body postures and movements that might be used as a basis for judging their emotional states? In this section, I consider what form and motion information our visual systems extract from bodies per se. In a later section this discussion is extended to emotional bodies.

The *form* of the human body could be represented in several different ways, demarcating points on a configural-processing continuum from part-based to holistic processing. Thus, bodies could be represented in terms of individual body parts or features, the relative positions of those parts (i.e., first-order spatial relations), the structural hierarchy of body parts (i.e., first-order configuration plus information about the relative position of features with respect to the whole body), or whole-body posture templates (Reed, Stone, Grubb, & McGoldrick, 2006). Unlike faces, the relative positions of body parts change as people move, which suggests the need for a relatively fine-grained structural description of the spatial relationships among body parts.

A series of experiments by Reed and colleagues (Reed et al., 2006) suggests that the recognition of (nonemotional) body postures depends on the processing of the structural hierarchy of body parts. This study drew on the well-known inversion effect in face recognition: that turning faces upside down impairs the ability to recognize their identity more than inverting nonface objects

impairs the recognition of their identity. It is generally considered that face inversion disrupts configural processing, specifically the coding of second-order relational information; that is, the metric distances amongst features (e.g., Diamond & Carey, 1986). In Reed et al.'s (2006) study, participants were impaired in discriminating pairs of inverted compared to upright whole-body postures but not houses. However, the matching of isolated body parts (arms, legs, heads) was unaffected by inversion, indicating that, as with isolated facial features, individual body parts do not evoke configural processing. Disrupting first-order spatial relations, by rearranging the body parts around the trunk (by, for example, putting the arms in the leg and head positions), abolished the inversion effect, indicating that such first-order configural cues do not contribute to body posture recognition. Presenting half-body postures that were divided along the vertical midline (i.e., left or right halves), which preserves the structural hierarchy of body parts but disrupts holistic template matching, did not abolish the body inversion effect. In contrast, presenting half-body postures that were divided along the horizontal midline (the waist), which preserves salient parts (e.g., both arms) but disrupts structural hierarchy information, did not produce an inversion effect. Thus, the particular form of configural processing critical to body posture recognition, as indexed by the presence of an inversion effect, appears to be the structural hierarchy of body parts; that is, the positions of body parts relative to themselves and to the whole body. Nonetheless, there is no body inversion effect for headless bodies (Minnebusch, Suchan, & Daum, 2009; Yovel, Pelc, & Lubetzky, 2010), implying that configural information about the head is critical to body posture processing.

There are three main classes of information pertaining to the *movements* of human bodies: the changes of structural or form information over time (including motion-mediated structural information), kinematics (e.g., velocity, acceleration, displacement) and dynamics (motion specified in terms of mass and force). Considerable attention has been given to the role of kine- matics in specifying cues for action and person perception (e.g., Westhoff & Troje, 2007). Typically, these studies employ point- light or patch-light displays of human or other biological motion (see Figure 8.1), in which static form information is minimal or absent but motion information (kinematics and dynamics) and motion-mediated struc- tural information are preserved (Johansson, 1973). Point-light displays of body move- ments provide a sufficient basis for observers to discriminate biological motion from other types of motion and to make accurate judg- ments about the people making the move- ments, including sex from gait, identity from gait or actions, and complex individ- ual or social actions from whole-body move- ments (reviewed by Blake & Shiffrar, 2007). Some of this evidence shows equivalent or near equivalent performance with point- light compared to full-light (or solid-body) displays, in which the whole body is visi- ble (e.g., Runeson & Frykholm, 1981), which suggests that static form cues are less impor- tant than motion cues and may often be unnecessary for successful judgments about people and their actions based on their visi- ble behavior.

Evidence for the relative importance of kinematic cues comes from studies that measure the effects on recognition of changes in certain kinematic or structural dimensions of point-light stimuli. For ex- ample, accuracy in judging the sex of point-light walkers was influenced more by "body sway" than by the ratio of shoulder to hip width in Mather and Murdoch's (1994) study, and it was greater when point-light walkers were normalized with respect to their size (thus providing only motion information) than when they were normalized with respect to their motion information (thus providing only size cues) in Troje's (2002) study.

It has been argued that the ability to dis- criminate at least simple biological move- ments in point-light displays may be based on relatively low-level or mid-level visual processing that does not involve the recon- struction of the form of body parts or of the whole body, either from static form or motion-mediated structural cues (e.g., Casile & Giese, 2005; Mather, Radford, & West, 1992). Nevertheless, neuropsychologi- cal and neurophysiological evidence demon- strates that form information can indeed subserve biological motion perception from point-light displays (e.g., McLeod, Dittrich, Driver, Perrett, & Zihl, 1996; Vaina, Cowey, LeMay, Bienfang, & Kikinis, 2002). The pro- cessing of changes in the form of the body over time may be particularly important (e.g., Beintema & Lappe, 2002), especially in the context of more sophisticated tasks, such as recognizing emotional states or com- plex actions (Giese & Poggio, 2003).

This conclusion gains some support from inversion effects in biological motion per- ception. The spontaneous identification of point-light motion displays as biological motion is impaired when they are shown upside down (e.g., Bertenthal & Pinto, 1994; Shipley, 2003). Moreover, neural activation characteristic of upright biological motion displays is attenuated or absent when such displays are inverted (Grossman & Blake, 2001; Pavlova, Lutzenberger, Sokolov, & Birbaumer, 2004). Inversion of point-light displays also disrupts the ability to distin- guish the identity of the actors from their actions (Loula, Prasad, Harber, & Shiffrar, 2005), and sex judgments based on gait tend to be reversed (Barclay, Cutting, & Kozlowski, 1978). Although it is likely that inversion of biological motion disrupts the processing of dynamic cues related to move- ment within the earth's gravitational field (e.g., Barclay et al., 1978), there is also some evidence to suggest that inversion of whole-body movements impairs the pro- cessing of configural information (e.g., Pinto & Shiffrar, 1999).

Finally, recent research provides evidence that the relative contributions of form and motion cues to biological motion perception depend on the body parts in question and the stimulus duration (Thurman, Giese & Grossman, 2010): Observers relied on form information in the upper body (head and shoulder posture) and on dynamic informa- tion in the lower body (the relative motion of the feet particularly) when discriminating the walking direction of point-light or stick figures; moreover, the reliance on form cues was greater for shorter stimulus durations.

The Visual Cues That Humans Use to Perceive Bodily Expressions of Emotion

What specific features or properties of body postures and movements do people use to distinguish between and identify expressed or portrayed emotions? Actors, directors, and dramatists have long recognized and exploited the fact that particular body movements and postures indicate specific emotional states (e.g., Laban & Ullmann, 1988; Stanislavski, 1936); early psychologists did too (Darwin, 1872/1998; James, 1932). More recent work in both the sciences and arts has developed more detailed descriptions and analyses of specific postures and movements associated with different emotional states. One common method has been to have untrained or occasionally trained observers rate body movements and postures on scales that describe certain pre-specified characteristics chosen on the basis of previous research or systematic analyses of gait, dance, or acted scenarios (de Meijer, 1989; Montepare et al., 1987; Wallbott, 1998). For example, Wallbott (1998) found that various emotions portrayed in video clips of fully illuminated whole-body movements can be differentiated from each other according to a combination of specific patterns of movements and the vigor or quality of those movements. He found that bodily expressions of both disgust and sadness, for instance, involve passive, low-activity movements with low energy or power and that they both often involve forward movements of the shoulders and downward movements of the head. To take another example, terror and "hot" anger involve high movement activity, whereas "cold" anger and fear are typically characterized by moderate movement activity.

Another method for characterizing the motion cues that people use to distinguish between and identify bodily expressed emotions is to use computerized image-processing techniques to measure specific kinematic parameters and then to relate those parameters to observer performance. For example, Sawada et al. (2003) reported that arm movements during dance sequences intended to express joy, sadness, or anger varied in their velocity, acceleration, and displacement and that differences in these factors predicted the ability of observers to distinguish among the three types of emotional expression. In another study, Pollick et al. (2001) had participants classify emotions in point-light displays of knocking and drinking arm movements. Multidimensional scaling of the classification data revealed that the emotion categories clustered within a psychological space defined by two dimensions: "activation" and "pleasantness." The activation dimension correlated with the velocity, acceleration, and jerkiness of the arm movements, such that fast and jerky movements tended to be judged as emotions with high activation (e.g., anger, happiness), whereas slow and smooth movements were more likely to be judged as emotions with low activation (e.g., sadness). The pleasantness dimension, in contrast (which distinguishes between, for example, anger and happiness), was more closely correlated with the phase relations between the limb segments.

The work highlighted in the previous two paragraphs provided initial but nevertheless compelling evidence that the kinematics of body and body-part movements are at least sufficient, and may often be important, in furnishing cues for the perception of emotional expressions. (The latest advances in this area are discussed at the end of this section.) Yet there is also evidence that form-related cues in moving bodies, in addition to kinematics, contribute to emotion perception. It was noted earlier that equivalent or near equivalent behavioral performance with point-light compared to full-light displays indicates little or no contribution from static form cues to judgments about people and their actions based on their visible behavior. Research on emotion judgments, however, indicates a role for static form cues for both face and body stimuli. Bassili (1978) reported greater emotion classification accuracy for full-light compared to point-light facial movements (except for happy expressions), and Dittrich (1991) reported equivalent emotion recognition performance for point-light face stimuli in which the dots demarcated key facial structures (e.g., eyes, mouth) and those in which the dots were positioned randomly on the face. This latter result contrasts with Hill, Jinno, and Johnston's (2003) finding that sex judgments from facial movements were more accurate with spatially normalized than pseudo-random dot placement and thus highlights the relationship between form and motion information in specifying cues for emotion perception. For bodily expressed emotions, emotion recognition accuracy tends to be lower with point-light (Dittrich et al., 1996) and patch-light (Atkinson et al., 2004) compared to full-light displays of body movements.

Building on this earlier work, my colleagues and I have demonstrated robust effects of stimulus inversion and motion reversal on the classification of basic emotions from patch-light and full-light movie clips of bodily expressions (Atkinson, Tunstall, et al., 2007). Spatially inverting the 3-second-long movies significantly impaired emotion recognition accuracy, but did so more in the patch-light than in the full-light displays, indicating that spatial inversion disrupts the processing of form cues more than it does the processing of kinematic and dynamic cues. Playing the movies backward also significantly impaired emotion recognition accuracy, but this effect was only marginally greater for the patch-light than for the full-light displays, providing qualified support for the importance of the sequencing of changes in form to judgments of emotions from body gestures. Although we cannot be certain that our stimulus manipulations completely eliminated all cues other than kinematics, even when in combination, the substantial reduction in emotion classification performance – especially for the spatially inverted, reversed patch-light displays

– attests to the importance of form cues in emotion perception; conversely, the fact that emotion classification performance was still substantially above chance, even in the spatially inverted, reversed patch-light displays, attests to the importance of kinematics in providing cues for emotion perception. Although it is likely that spatial inversion of biological motion disrupts the processing of dynamic cues related to movement within the earth's gravitational field, if that were *all* that spatial inversion impaired, then we should not have seen a greater effect of orientation for the patch-light compared to full-light stimuli.

What specific form-related cues are used in emotion perception from body expressions? One suggestion is that the overall shape of particular body postures, such as their angularity or roundedness, informs emotion judgments (Aronoff, Woike, & Hyman, 1992). The spatial inversion effects that we found (Atkinson, Tunstall, et al., 2007) highlight the importance of relational or configural cues, adding weight to previous claims that configural information plays an important role in subserving emotion perception from bodily expressions (Dittrich et al., 1996; Stekelenburg & de Gelder, 2004). In contrast, the effects of motion reversal tentatively suggest a possible role for spatiotemporal cues (changes in form over time) in emotion recognition. Given the conventional and sometimes symbolic (Buck, 1984) nature of our actors' movements (see Atkinson et al., 2004, for details), we speculate that configurations of static form and their changes over time are more closely associated with representations of *what* people do with their bodies than with how they move them, the latter being specified mostly by kinematics (see also Giese & Poggio, 2003).

A recent and comprehensive attempt to extract critical motion and posture features for the perception of bodily expressed emotions is the work of Giese, Roether, and colleagues (Roether et al., 2008, 2009). First, these researchers used motion-capture technology to record the movements of 25 individuals as they walked across the recording space after having self-induced one of four emotional states (anger, fear, happiness, and sadness) by recalling a past situation in which they had experienced that emotion. Emotionally neutral walks were also recorded before the emotion-induction procedure. Then, using machine-learning techniques, Roether and colleagues extracted the average flexion angles of the joints (shoulders, elbows, hips, and knees) and the joint-angle trajectories that best distinguished among gaits of the different emotions (Roether et al., 2009). (This approach is reminiscent of work done with facial expressions of emotion; see Chapter 2 and Susskind, Littlewort, Bartlett, Movellan, & Anderson, 2007.) Subsequent experiments with human observers who classified and rated computer avatars animated with the same motion-capture information confirmed a close match between the features used by these observers and the machine-learning algorithm or "ideal observer" (Roether et al., 2009). For example, leg-movement changes and postural cues defined in terms of limb flexion were found to be important for the perception of anger and fear, whereas head inclination was particularly important for the perception of sadness.

Speed of gait was another important cue that human observers used to distinguish among the different emotions. Moreover, comparison of the motion parameters between emotionally expressive gaits and velocity-matched neutral gaits showed that quantitative aspects of movement activity varied independently of gait velocities (Roether et al., 2009). For emotions associated with higher gait velocities there was more movement activity relative to velocity-matched neutral gaits, particularly in the arms, whereas for emotions associated with lower gait velocities there was less movement activity. Emotion-specific body postures were found to vary largely independently of gait velocity. Finally, for expressions of anger, happiness, and sadness, the left side of the body was found to contain significantly greater maximum joint-angle amplitudes and movement energy (defined in terms of change in joint angles over time) and consequently was judged as more emotionally expressive than the right side (Roether et al., 2008).

The Neural Processing of Bodily Form and Motion

The form of the human (or primate) body is a category of visual object for which there appears to be both selectivity and functional specialization in higher level visual cortices. By selectivity, I mean the extent to which a mechanism is activated by or operates over a particular stimulus class, such as faces or bodies, as compared to other stimulus classes. By functional specialization (or function for short), I mean a mechanism's specificity for performing a particular process. Evidence for body-selective visual mechanisms comes from studies of both humans and nonhuman primates (reviewed by Peelen & Downing, 2007). In humans, the evidence points to two distinct regions, dubbed the extrastriate body area (EBA), located in the lateral occipitotemporal cortex (Downing, Jiang, Shuman, & Kanwisher, 2001), and the fusiform body area (FBA), located in the fusiform gyrus (Peelen & Downing, 2005; Schwarzlose, Baker, & Kanwisher, 2005). The EBA and FBA respond selectively to human bodies and body parts compared with objects, faces, and other control stimuli, despite considerable anatomical overlap between the FBA and the face-selective fusiform face area (FFA; Peelen & Downing, 2005; Schwarzlose et al., 2005) and between the EBA, motion-processing area V5/MT, and object-form-selective lateral occipital complex (Downing, Wiggett, & Peelen, 2007). These functional imaging findings are complemented by intracranial recordings in humans (McCarthy, Puce, Belger, & Allison, 1999; Pourtois, Peelen, Spinelli, Seeck, & Vuilleumier, 2007) and single-cell recordings in monkeys (e.g., Desimone, Albright, Gross, & Bruce, 1984) showing responses specific to bodies or body parts compared to faces, other objects, or complex shapes.

With respect to functional specialization, the EBA represents the static structure of viewed bodies (Downing, Peelen, Wiggett, & Tew, 2006; Peelen, Wiggett, & Downing, 2006), although these representations appear to be at the level of individual body parts rather than at the level of the whole-body configuration (Taylor, Wiggett, & Downing, 2007; Urgesi, Calvo-Merino, Haggard, & Aglioti, 2007). As discussed earlier, configural cues in body perception include the relative positions of body parts and the positions of those parts with respect to the whole body (Reed et al., 2006), and there is evidence indicating that the processing of one or other or both of these configural cues is more a function of the FBA than of the EBA (Taylor et al., 2007). More recent work suggests that both the EBA and FBA also process body motion cues. Initial reports showed selectivity to whole-body point-light motion in the posterior inferior temporal sulcus/middle temporal gyrus (e.g., Grossman & Blake, 2002; Saygin, Wilson, Hagler, Bates, & Sereno, 2004), which reflected activation of body-selective populations of neurons constituting the EBA rather than of motion-selective neuronal populations in the overlapping V5/MT (Peelen et al., 2006). There are also reports of selectivity to whole-body movements in the fusiform cortex (e.g., Grossman & Blake, 2002; Jastorff & Orban, 2009), which reflects activation of body-selective rather than face-selective neuronal populations (Peelen et al., 2006). It has been suggested that these findings reflect the extraction by the EBA and FBA of "snapshots" that represent the various static postures comprising a movement sequence (Giese & Poggio, 2003; Peelen et al., 2006). However, the findings of a more recent study suggest instead that both the EBA and FBA integrate form and motion (kinematic) information (Jastorff & Orban, 2009). Nonetheless, that study also indicated that the EBA has a relatively greater role in processing kinematics, whereas the FBA's role is more in processing body configuration (Jastorff & Orban, 2009). Recent behavioral evidence implicates regions responsive to both the form and motion of human bod-

ies – perhaps the EBA and FBA – in representing the three-dimensional orientation of those bodies (Jackson & Blake, 2010).

A recent study by my colleagues and me (Atkinson, Vuong, & Smithson, 2012) provides evidence that body-selective EBA and FBA and face-selective FFA are sensitive to specific motion-related cues – particularly form-from-motion cues – characteristic of their proprietary stimulus categories, rather than to human motion per se (i.e., to motion regardless of whether it is from the face or body). Using fMRI, we directly contrasted responses to point-light face and body movements, which provides a stronger test of selectivity than contrasts against some baseline stimulus condition such as scrambled point-light displays, as performed in previous studies (e.g., Grossman & Blake, 2002; Peelen et al., 2006). By statistically controlling for differences in perceived emotional intensity based on kinematics, we focused particularly on the contribution of form-from-motion information.

Standard region-of-interest (ROI) analyses revealed that point-light body movements activated body-selective regions in the lateral occipitotemporal cortex (right and left EBA) and fusiform gyrus (right but not left FBA), regardless of whether participants were judging the expressed emotion or the color change of the stimulus dots (Atkinson et al., 2012). Point-light face movements activated face-selective FFA bilaterally, although this greater activation to point-light faces than to point-light bodies was evident in the right hemisphere only when participants were explicitly judging the expressed emotion. Voxelwise correlation analyses revealed that, even in bilateral regions of fusiform cortex containing overlapping populations of body-selective and face-selective neurons, the patterns of activity elicited by point-light bodies were positively correlated with voxelwise selectivity for static bodies but not for static faces (which was also the case in right and left EBA), whereas activity elicited by point-light faces was positively correlated with voxelwise selectivity for static faces but not for static bodies. We further demonstrated enhanced activation of several body- and face-selective regions for happy or angry relative to emotionally neutral movements, in some regions depending on the task set (Atkinson et al., 2012).

The EBA appears to constitute a critical early stage in the perception of other people (Chan, Peelen, & Downing, 2004), rather than a later processing stage via, for example, top-down effects related to imaginary gestures and movement (de Gelder, 2006). Evidence in support of this claim comes from recent studies using either intracranial recordings or transcranial magnetic stimulation (TMS). Pourtois et al. (2007) recorded highly body-selective visual evoked potentials over the EBA of a patient that started approximately 190 ms and peaked 260 ms after stimulus onset. Consistent with this finding are reports of selectively impaired perception of body form following application of TMS over the EBA at 150–250 ms (Urgesi, Berlucchi, & Aglioti, 2004; Urgesi, Calvo-Merino, et al., 2007) and at 150–350 ms (Urgesi, Candidi, Ionta, & Aglioti, 2007) poststimulus onset. Despite this evidence, however, it is entirely possible that, in addition to its role in the early visual processing of body form and motion, the EBA also plays a role in later processing stages of person perception. Little is yet known about the timing of the FBA and ventral premotor cortex involvement in body and person perception, although given that they preferentially represent configural over body-part cues it is likely that their initial involvement occurs subsequent to that of the EBA. Nonetheless, as Taylor et al. (2007) comment, a strictly serial model is probably too simplistic, given the widespread bidirectional connectivity in the visual cortex.

Human lesion, electrophyshiological, and neuroimaging studies confirm an important role for the superior temporal cortex, particularly its posterior aspects, in the perception of body and facial movement compared to static images of the same body parts and to nonbiological motion. Neuroimaging studies in humans have also revealed distinct regions of the superior temporal sulcus (STS) selective for the movements of dif-

ferent body parts (for reviews, see Blake & Shiffrar, 2007; Puce & Perrett, 2003). Disruption of the activity of the right posterior STS using TMS has confirmed a critical role for this region in perceiving body movement (Grossman, Battelli, & Pascual-Leone, 2005). More recently, a lesion-overlap study with 60 brain-damaged subjects showed that impairments in the ability to discriminate whole-body from nonbiological motion in point-light displays were most reliably associated with lesions in the posterior temporal and ventral premotor cortices, which corresponded with the regions whose activity in neurologically intact subjects was selective for the same point-light whole-body movements (Saygin, 2007). The critical involvement of the ventral premotor cortex in this study confirms earlier studies showing selectivity in this region for point-light whole-body movements (e.g., Saygin et al., 2004).

The distribution of responses in the STS and surrounding cortex to the motion of different body parts suggests a functional organization in which distinct but overlapping patches of the cortex extract body-part specific representations of biological motion, with a posterior region of the STS, especially in the right hemisphere, thereby encoding a higher level representation of biological motion that is not dependent on the particular body part generating that motion. There is considerable evidence for an important role for areas of the STS in the integration of motion and form (as well as auditory) information (e.g., Beauchamp, 2005), especially that related to social perception (Puce & Perrett, 2003). Thus, as Jastorff and Orban (2009) suggest, the contribution of the posterior STS is probably particularly important when movement complexity or task demands require a detailed analysis of the action for which the more basic processing in the EBA and FBA of articulated human movement per se is insufficient.

There is some debate over whether the posterior STS analyzes local image motion and higher level optic flow (e.g., Giese & Poggio, 2003) or some more global motion of the whole figure (e.g., Lange & Lappe,

2006). Nonetheless, it is possible that the posterior STS both analyzes local image motion and (probably at a later stage) the more global motion information related to changes in body and body-part configurations over time. Furthermore, it has recently been shown that the STS as well as regions in the inferior parietal lobe and in inferior frontal gyrus respond to human movements, regardless of whether those movements comply with or violate normal kinematic laws of motion. Only regions of the dorsal premotor and dorsolateral prefrontal cortex in the left hemisphere and a region of the ventromedial prefrontal cortex showed greater activity to movement complying with kinematic laws of human movement (Casile et al., 2010).

So far I have emphasized the use of structural form and motion information in the perception and identification of bodies, body postures, and movements. There is also likely to be a role for processes that rely on visual semantics about body postures and movements related to emotion categories as stored in long-term memory (Dittrich, 1991), especially for symbolic gestures or emblems. Yet is such an image-processing account, or an extension of it, sufficient for explaining our ability to perceive and understand bodily *actions*? The majority of human postures and movements are not aimless, but are directed toward some purpose or goal and thus reflect the person's intentions and may also or instead reflect his or her emotional and other internal states. Moreover, humans are not passive observers but, like the people whose postures and movements they are observing, have intentions and emotions and act in a purposive, goal-directed manner.

Research and theory over the past decade or so suggest that one (and perhaps the main) route to understanding others' actions depends on the observer's own action capabilities. Neuroimaging studies, for example, have shown that ventral premotor and intraparietal cortices respond with differential selectivity to the motion of different body parts, in a somatotopic manner (e.g., Buccino et al., 2001). In addition, the ventral premotor cortex, particularly in the left hemisphere, is known for its role in both the planning of motor actions (Johnson & Grafton, 2003) and in the visual discrimination of such actions (e.g., Urgesi, Candidi, et al., 2007) and has a critical role in processing configural body cues (Urgesi, Calvo-Merino, et al., 2007). Such evidence has helped spawn a variety of simulation accounts of action understanding, according to which observing another perform an action triggers in the observer an offline simulation of the viewed action (e.g., Blakemore & Decety, 2001; Gallese, Keysers, & Rizzolatti, 2004).

Work on motor control indicates ways in which such simulations may be computationally instantiated, in the form of forward models, inverse models, or both (Grush, 2004; Wolpert, Doya, & Kawato, 2003). Forward models use copies of the motor commands to map the current sensory states and motor commands to the future sensory and motor states that will result once the current motor commands have been executed. Inverse models perform the opposite transformations, by mapping sensory representations associated with the intended action to the motor commands to execute the action. One suggestion, for example, is that proposed by Wolpert et al. (2003): When observing another's action, the observer's brain generates a set of motor commands that would be produced given the observed movements and the current state of the observed person. Rather than driving the observer's own motor behavior, these motor commands are used to predict the sensory and motor consequences of the observed action, which are then compared with the observed new state of the actor.

The Neural Processing of Emotional Bodies

The neural substrates of bodily emotion perception have only recently begun to be revealed. This section briefly summarizes that work.

A consistent finding from functional imaging studies of body and face perception is enhanced activation of occipital and temporal regions in response to body and face stimuli expressing emotions relative to emotionally neutral versions of these same stimuli (for a review, see Vuilleumier & Driver, 2007). Such emotional modulation is thought to prioritize visual processing of emotionally salient events (Vuilleumier, 2005) via feedback from the amygdala (Vuilleumier, Richardson, Armony, Driver, & Dolan, 2004; see also Chapter 14).

This emotional modulation of lateral occipitotemporal and fusiform cortices by facial and bodily expressions includes the EBA and FBA, as well as the face-selective fusiform face area (FFA). Indeed, studies using functional ROI analyses have confirmed that FFA activity is increased by emotional compared to emotionally neutral faces (e.g., Pessoa, McKenna, Gutierrez, & Ungerleider, 2002) and that the activity of both the EBA and FBA is increased by emotional compared to emotionally neutral body movements (Peelen, Atkinson, Andersson, & Vuilleumier, 2007). Figure 8.2 provides an illustrative example of emotional modulation of cortical activity, including that of the EBA and fusiform, produced by viewing body stimuli.

Given the roles of the EBA and FBA in extracting and integrating kinematic and static form cues (as discussed in the previous section), these findings suggest that something about emotional as compared to emotionally neutral bodily postures and movements instigates enhanced processing of those kinematic and form cues. For example, to the extent that the amygdala is the source of the emotional modulation of the EBA and FBA, this might reflect an initial, basic appraisal of the emotional valence or significance of the viewed body by the amygdala and a consequent increased allocation of attentional or processing "resources" to those regions involved in extracting kinematic and form cues. Of course, such an account assumes that some initial visual processing has already taken place that is sufficient for distinguishing the emotional valence or significance of the viewed bodies. Further research is required to elucidate these processes.

That viewed emotional bodies and faces modulate body- and face-selective regions raises the intriguing possibility that emotion signals from the body or face might modulate precisely those populations of neurons that code for the viewed stimulus category (see Sugase, Yamane, Ueno, & Kawano, 1999), instead of reflecting "synergies" between the perception of facial and bodily expressions (de Gelder, Snyder, Greve, Gerard, & Hadjikhani, 2004) or a global boost to all visual processing in extrastriate visual cortex. However, body-selective FBA partially overlaps face-selective FFA, although these regions can be dissociated when using high spatial resolution (Schwarzlose et al., 2005) or multivoxel pattern analysis (Downing et al., 2007; Peelen & Downing, 2005). Thus, it might be that both face- and body-selective neurons in the fusiform are modulated by emotional body expressions. Alternatively, bodily expressed emotion could enhance processing only in body-selective neuronal populations, with significant modulation in FFA being observed due to the strong overlap of this region with FBA. Peelen et al. (2007) reported evidence in favor of the latter possibility. Voxelwise correlation analyses (a form of multivoxel pattern analysis) showed that the strength of emotional modulation by viewed dynamic body stimuli in the fusiform and EBA was related to the degree of body selectivity, whereas there was no relation with the degree of selectivity for faces.

This evidence from Peelen et al. (2007) is, however, only one part of what ought to be a two-part argument. The situation is analogous to the distinction between single and double dissociations in neuropsychology. A finding that a group of patients is impaired on one task but not another does not constitute strong evidence for the claim that distinct or independent processes subserve the two tasks, because such single dissociations do not preclude the possibility that performance on one task is merely more

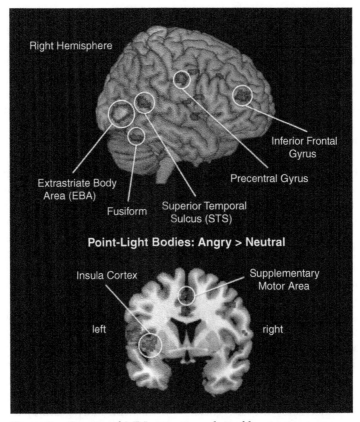

Figure 8.2. Functional MRI activations elicited by viewing angry relative to emotionally neutral whole-body movements presented in point-light displays. Clusters of significant activation ($p < .001$, uncorrected, at the voxel level) are overlaid on a right hemisphere saggital view (top image) and a coronal slice (bottom image) of a standard human brain; they lie within or incorporate the labeled regions. Angry as well as other emotional body movements typically activate the labeled regions, as discussed in the text (see the section, "The Neural Processing of Emotional Bodies"). These data are taken from Atkinson et al. (2012).

sensitive to damage than is performance on the other task (e.g., Shallice, 1988). In a similar vein, Peelen et al.'s (2007) finding that dynamic emotional body stimuli increased the activity of body-selective but not face-selective regions of cortex might reflect a greater sensitivity of body-selective than face-selective cortical regions to emotional modulation per se, rather than category-specific emotional modulation. Evidence of truly category-specific emotional modulation would be provided by modulation both of body-selective (but not face-selective) areas by bodies and of face-selective (but

not body-selective) areas by faces. However, this is not what my colleagues and I found in a recent study (Atkinson et al., 2012) – not for point-light displays of emotional face and body movements, at any rate. We found only a limited degree of stimulus category-selective emotional modulation. Specifically, emotional body movements enhanced right and left EBA activity, but emotional face movements did not. In both these ROIs, voxels that were more strongly body selective were also more strongly modulated by the emotional expressions displayed by body but not face movements, regardless of task. Yet, although emotional face and particularly body movements modulated activity in the fusiform gyrus and emotional body movements modulated activity in the right posterior STS, there was no evidence that emotional modulation in these regions occurred in a stimulus category-selective manner. Thus, our findings (Atkinson et al., 2012) suggest an asymmetry in emotional modulation of neural responses by body and face motion in body- and face-selective regions. This asymmetry constrains the claim that expressive movements modulate neuronal populations that code for the viewed stimulus category (Peelen et al., 2007). Further research is required to test whether these findings extend to emotional expressions other than of anger and happiness and to fully illuminated displays of faces and bodies, in which static form is visible.

So far we have seen imaging evidence for a role for the amygdala in processing bodily expressions of emotion. Although more work is required to uncover the exact nature of that and any other roles the amygdala might play in bodily emotion perception, evidence from lesion studies is not consistent with the amygdala being *necessary* for emotional body perception. Sprengelmeyer et al. (1999) found impaired fearful posture recognition in a subject with bilateral amygdala damage, consistent with this individual's impaired recognition of fear from faces and vocal expressions. However, this subject's lesion was not entirely restricted to the amygdala, notably including some damage to the left thalamus, nor did the lesion encompass the entire extent of both amygdalae, the damage to the left amygdala being incomplete and smaller than that to the right amygdala. Thus, it is possible that the impaired recognition of fear from body postures in this subject was not entirely a consequence of amygdala damage.

Two other studies have demonstrated normal emotion recognition from several differing whole-body stimulus sets in another subject with bilateral amygdala damage, SM, whose brain damage encompassed all of the amygdala bilaterally and

who was previously demonstrated to have impairments recognizing fearful faces (for this latter evidence, see, e.g., Adolphs, Tranel, Damasio, & Damasio, 1994). In one of these studies, photographs of dramatic, emotionally charged movie scenes were altered so that the facial expressions were not visible. Although this alteration significantly reduced normal subjects' ability to recognize all emotions, including fear, from the characters, SM recognized fear normally in a forced-choice paradigm – in fact, her performance was *better* for these stimuli than for the intact photographs (Adolphs & Tranel, 2003). (Note that three other participants with bilateral damage that included the amygdala as well as other medial temporal lobe structures were similarly normal on both the masked and intact photographs.) In the second study (Atkinson, Heberlein, et al., 2007), SM was tested with four different whole-body stimulus sets: a set of emotional body posture photographs with the faces blurred; dynamic stimuli in which the actors faced forward and expressed emotion with a full-body gesture; the same stimuli edited to be patch-light (similar to point-light: Atkinson et al., 2004); and a set of emotional point-light walkers in which the actors were filmed walking, creeping, dancing, or otherwise locomoting across the field of view (Heberlein et al., 2004; Heberlein & Saxe, 2005). Another bilaterally amygdala-damaged subject, AP, was tested on two of these sets (the posture photographs and the point-light walkers). Both participants recognized fear normally, in forced-choice tasks, in all the stimulus sets that they judged (Atkinson, Heberlein et al., 2007). These two findings make it impossible to claim that the amygdala is necessary for normal recognition of emotional body movements.

Consistent with the data of de Gelder and colleagues (e.g., de Gelder et al., 2004), it may be the case that in intact brains the amygdala serves to associate perceived bodily expressions of fear with relevant motor plans. By this view, SM – although she is able to know that the perceived individual is afraid – would not prepare escape behavior in response to seeing another person's fearful bodily expression. Potential future experiments examining the role of the amygdala in responding to whole-body expressions might include an examination of evoked motor responses or motor-related activity in patients with bilateral amygdala damage as well as further studies of amygdala responses to dynamic and static whole-body emotional expressions, ideally with the inclusion of individual differences measures.

So far, I have been emphasizing the roles of configural form cues and kinematics in the recognition of emotions from body movements. Yet, as with action understanding in general, purely image-processing accounts may not be sufficient for emotional expression understanding or at any rate may not detail the only means by which we can understand others' emotional expressions. One way in which we might be able to recognize the emotional state of another is via our perception of an emotional response within ourselves (e.g., Adolphs, 2002; Gallese et al., 2004; Heberlein & Atkinson, 2009). One version of this idea is that a visual representation of another's expression leads us to experience what that person is feeling (i.e., emotional contagion), which allows us then to infer that person's emotional state. That is, the grounds for inferring the viewed person's emotional state is knowledge from the "inside;" experiencing the emotion for oneself (even in an attenuated or unconscious form) is an important, perhaps necessary step to making accurate judgments about the other's emotion. A different but conceivably compatible idea is that coming to know what another is feeling involves simulating the viewed emotional state via the generation of a somatosensory image of the associated body state (Adolphs, 2002) or simulating the motor programs for producing the viewed expression (e.g., Gallese et al., 2004; Leslie, Johnson-Frey, & Grafton, 2004).

An important source of evidence for simulation accounts of emotion recognition is research showing somatosensory cortex involvement in the explicit judgment of emotional expressions. Using lesion overlap analyses with large groups of brain-damaged subjects, three separate studies found that impaired recognition of a range of emotions in static faces (Adolphs, Damasio, Tranel, Cooper, & Damasio, 2000), prosody (Adolphs, Damasio, & Tranel, 2002), and body movements represented in point-light stimuli (Heberlein et al., 2004) correlated best with lesions in the right somatosensory cortex. The region of maximal lesion overlap among impaired patients in these studies was in the right posterior postcentral gyrus, bordering on the supramarginal gyrus, thus including not just primary but also more posterior secondary somatosensory regions. Impaired emotion recognition performance was also associated with damage to the insula and left frontal operculum. Given that the lesion method can reveal critical roles for structures only when lesions are confined to those structures, it is significant that in two of these studies (Adolphs et al., 2002; Heberlein et al., 2004) a small number of people had lesions restricted to the right somatosensory cortex and were impaired at recognizing emotions, whereas people with lesions that spared the right somatosensory cortex – including damage to nearby motor regions in the postcentral gyrus – tended not to have impaired emotion recognition. Several studies using functional neuroimaging have corroborated these lesion-based findings, of which I mention two. (Figure 8.3 provides an illustrative example of regions activated when observers judge the emotions expressed in body and face stimuli.)

Winston, O'Doherty, and Dolan (2003) found that the activity of the right somatosensory cortices, as well as the ventromedial prefrontal cortex (which also represents somatic states), was enhanced when participants were judging the emotion as compared to the masculinity of faces. Heberlein and Saxe (2005) found that a region at the border of the right postcentral and supramarginal gyri was more active when subjects made emotion judgments about point-light walkers (given one of a known set of emotion words, rating how well it fit the stimulus) than when they made personality trait judgments (a comparable task with trait words) based on the same

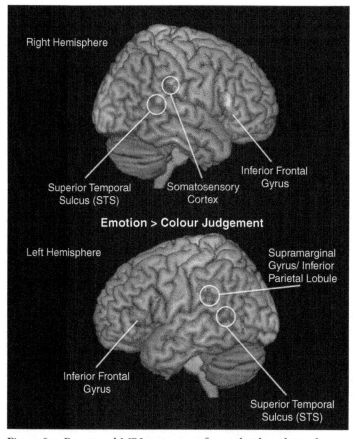

Figure 8.3. Functional MRI activations for explicitly judging the emotions expressed in point-light displays of body and face movements, as compared to judging the color change of the dots in those same stimuli. Clusters of significant activation ($p < .001$, uncorrected, at the voxel level) are overlaid on right- and left-hemisphere saggital views of a standard human brain; they lie within or incorporate the labeled regions. As discussed in the text (see the section, "The Neural Processing of Emotional Bodies"), other fMRI studies have also shown activation in somatosensory cortices, including the supramarginal gyrus, when observers judge the emotions expressed in body, face, or voice stimuli; moreover, lesion and TMS evidence shows that somatosensory regions are critically involved in emotion recognition. These data are from a study conducted by Atkinson et al. (2012), although these particular results were not reported in that article.

stimuli. Further, a region of interest based on the maximal lesion overlap reported in Heberlein et al. (2004) – that is, the posterior right somatosensory cortex – was significantly more active for emotion judgments as compared to personality trait judgments. A separate region, in the left inferior frontal gyrus, was associated with personality trait judgments in both the lesion and fMRI studies (Heberlein & Saxe, 2005).

In addition, three studies using TMS have confirmed the critical role of the right somatosensory cortex in emotion recognition from faces (Pitcher, Garrido, Walsh, & Duchaine, 2008; Pourtois et al., 2004) and voices (van Rijn et al., 2005) in the healthy brain. The important contribution of Pitcher et al.'s (2008) study was its demonstration of different critical periods for the involvement of the right somatosensory cortex and right occipital face area (OFA) in emotion discrimination: The right OFA's involvement was pinpointed to a window of 60–100 ms from stimulus onset, whereas the involvement of the right somatosensory cortex was pinpointed to a later processing stage, 100–170 ms from stimulus onset. TMS has not yet been used to confirm whether the involvement of the right somatosensory cortex is critical for neurologically intact individuals to recognize bodily expressed emotions. Further studies using TMS on the right and left somatosensory regions will help establish the role of somatosensory cortices in emotion recognition based on facial or bodily expressions.

Adolphs and Spezio (2006) have proposed a role also for the amygdala in simulation accounts of emotion recognition. They suggest that the amygdala modulates somatosensory and insula cortices, in an analogous fashion to its modulation of higher level visual cortices. The amygdala's action might thus increase the sensitivity of somatosensory cortex and insula to signals received from the observer's own body, enhance the selectivity of these regions to particular types of input, or reactivate previously learnt associations between stimuli and bodily responses. Although this proposal is supported by direct and indirect anatomical connections from the amygdala to somatosensory cortices and insula in the monkey (reviewed by Adolphs & Spezio, 2006), further evidence is required from neuroimaging and single-cell recording studies that examine functional connectivity between these regions when human observers are required to judge the emotions expressed in bodies, faces, and voices.

Finally, neural regions known to be involved in motor planning and execution have also been implicated in the processing of bodily expressions of emotion. For example, de Gelder et al. (2004) reported that fearful but not happy static body postures activated cortical regions involved in motor planning and action representation, relative to emotionally neutral postures, including the supplementary motor area and inferior frontal and precentral gyri bilaterally. They proposed that this enhancement of action representation regions by fearful, but not happy or neutral, static bodies reflected direct engagement of fear-related motor plans in the observer, as if the motion implied in such images were initiating preparations for flight. Yet although Grèzes, Pichon, and de Gelder (2007) found that fearful compared to neutral bodies, regardless of dynamic or static information, activated a small number of action representation regions, the only such region preferentially activated by fearful vs. neutral body movements was the right premotor cortex. Grèzes et al. concluded that it remains unclear whether this increased fear-related response in the premotor cortex reflects the engagement of motor simulation routines as a means of action and emotion understanding, rather than the preparation of fearful motor responses. A more recent study by the same group showed that viewing threat-related (fearful or angry) compared to neutral whole-body actions activated a network of action-related regions, including the premotor cortex, regardless of task set or "attentional control" – specifically, whether participants were naming the emotion portrayed by the action or the color of a dot that appeared briefly during the video clip (Pichon, de Gelder, & Grèzes, 2011; for more on the interactions between emotion and top-down attention, see Chapter 14).

Conclusion

This chapter has surveyed the burgeoning body of research devoted to investigating the perception of bodily expressed emotions and its neural substrate. This review has been necessarily brief; complementary reviews of the visual and neural processing of bodily expressed emotions are provided by de Gelder (2006, 2009) and de

Gelder et al. (2010) and of bodies per se by Peelen and Downing (2007) and de Gelder et al. (2010). In this chapter, we have seen that the ability to discriminate or identify different bodily expressed emotions relies on a variety of visual cues: bodily kinematics, the sequencing of changes in body form over time, and static form and particularly configural form cues. Cortical regions that extract bodily form and motion information show enhanced activity to emotional bodies and thus play roles in emotion perception, although exactly what those roles are is still being investigated. This emotional modulation of visual regions is facilitated at least in part by feedback from the amygdala, yet the amygdala itself is not necessary for successful identification of bodily expressed emotions. The perception of emotional bodies is not solely a visual capacity, however. Viewing emotional bodies also sometimes engages regions involved in planning and executing motor actions, suggesting preparation for an appropriate action by the observer or simulation of the observed action to allow it to be understood (or perhaps both). Furthermore, explicitly judging expressed emotions engages regions involved in representing somatic changes associated with the viewed emotional states, suggesting that coming to know what another is feeling involves simulating the viewed emotional state via the generation of a somatosensory image of the associated body state.

Given that in everyday life we do not rely solely on one source of cues to other people's emotional states, it is important also to consider the perception of multimodal emotion signals (i.e., as expressed in two or more of the body, face, and voice). On this matter the interested reader might like to begin with Van den Stock, Righart, and de Gelder (2007). Furthermore, it is important to consider that we are able to evaluate how someone feels despite the disparate sensory nature of emotions signaled by the body, face, and voice. Those disparate sensory cues – movements and postures of body parts; changes in the size, shape, and relations between facial features; and acoustic changes in voices – are all typically interpreted to mean the same thing, that someone is fearful or happy for example. Thus when evaluating how someone feels, our representation of another person's emotional state must be abstracted away from the specific sensory input. A recent study provides evidence that two high-level brain areas previously implicated in affective processing, mental state attribution, and "theory of mind" – the medial prefrontal cortex (MPFC) and left superior temporal sulcus (STS) – represent perceived emotions at an abstract level, independent of the modality (body, face, voice) of the expressed emotion (Peelen, Atkinson, & Vuilleumier, 2010). In this fMRI study, participants evaluated the intensity of emotions perceived from fully illuminated body movements, face movements, or vocal intonations. Using multivoxel pattern analysis, Peelen and colleagues found stimulus modality-independent but emotion category-specific activity patterns in the MPFC and left STS. Multivoxel patterns in these regions contained information about the category of the perceived emotions (anger, disgust, fear, happiness, sadness) across all modality comparisons (face–body, face–voice, body–voice) and independently of the perceived intensity of the emotions. These results suggest that the MPFC and left STS play key roles in the understanding and categorization of others' emotional mental states. Future research will need to investigate such issues as whether supramodal emotion-specific representations exist for emotions other than those tested by Peelen and colleagues and when observers are not explicitly evaluating the emotional content of, or attending to, the stimuli. Another interesting avenue for future research will be to investigate whether the MPFC and left STS are similarly activated by perceived and self-experienced emotions, particularly given other evidence that the MPFC is involved in both the perception and experience of emotions (Kober et al., 2008; Lee & Siegle, 2009). The MPFC might be involved in evaluating others' emotions in virtue of its role in the generation of the perceiver's own emotional responses.

Outstanding Questions and Future Directions

- How does the brain process the specific kinematic and configural form and motion cues that behavioral research has shown observers use to discriminate and identify bodily expressed emotions?
- What specific aspects of visual processing are enhanced when one views emotional as compared to emotionally neutral bodies? Does this emotional modulation of visual cortical regions reflect enhanced processing of cues specific to bodies or of more general visual cues, at least some of which are contained in body stimuli?
- What specific aspects of motor planning and action preparation are engaged when one views emotional as compared to emotionally neutral bodies? Do all bodily expressed emotions engage neural regions involved in motor planning and action preparation or just certain specific emotions? Does such activity reflect preparation for action appropriate to the viewed emotion (e.g., freezing or fleeing in fear when one sees another being fearful or angry) or some offline simulation of the viewed action, perhaps to aid understanding of the emotion or action?
- Does the critical involvement of somatosensory cortex and insula in emotion judgments from bodies (and faces) reflect interoception – specifically, a simulation of changes in internal body state associated with the viewed emotion – or proprioception, specifically a simulation of the viewed bodily movements and postures?
- What are the functional relationships among the various regions implicated in processing bodies per se and emotional bodies in particular, including the body-selective EBA and FBA, STS, amygdala, somatosensory cortex, insula, and regions of frontal cortex? For example, does the amygdala function to associate perceived bodily expressions of emotions such as fear with relevant motor plans, in order to facilitate action preparation or action/emotion understanding? Or does the amygdala modulate the activity of the somatosensory cortex and insula and thus increase the sensitivity of these regions to signals received from the observer's own body, enhance the selectivity of these regions to particular types of input, or reactivate previously learned associations between stimuli and bodily responses?
- Problems in identifying bodily expressed emotions in autism are associated with impairments in perceiving global coherent motion (Atkinson, 2009). Individuals with autism also show deficient activity in and abnormal functional connections between brain regions involved in the visual processing of bodies and in the generation and understanding of bodily actions (e.g., Grèzes, Wicker, Berthoz, & de Gelder, 2009; Hadjikhani et al., 2009). What are the relationships between visual and attentional impairments in autism and impaired emotion recognition? How are these deficits related to individual differences in autism symptomatology and comorbid conditions such as attention deficits and low IQ? How are these deficits explained by compromised functioning of and connectivity between particular brain regions? What training techniques or other interventions might be able to ameliorate the effects of such deficits on everyday social functioning?

References

Adolphs, R. (2002). Recognizing emotion from facial expressions: Psychological and neurological mechanisms. *Behavioral and Cognitive Neuroscience Reviews*, 1, 21–62.

Adolphs, R., Damasio, H., & Tranel, D. (2002). Neural systems for recognition of emotional prosody: A 3-D lesion study. *Emotion*, 2, 23–51.

Adolphs, R., Damasio, H., Tranel, D., Cooper, G., & Damasio, A. R. (2000). A role for somatosensory cortices in the visual recognition of emotion as revealed by three-dimensional lesion mapping. *Journal of Neuroscience*, 20, 2683–90.

Adolphs, R., & Spezio, M. (2006). Role of the amygdala in processing visual social stimuli. *Progress in Brain Research*, 156, 363–78.

Adolphs, R., & Tranel, D. (2003). Amygdala damage impairs emotion recognition from scenes only when they contain facial expressions. *Neuropsychologia, 41*, 1281–89.

Adolphs, R., Tranel, D., Damasio, H., & Damasio, A. (1994). Impaired recognition of emotion in facial expressions following bilateral damage to the human amygdala. *Nature, 372*, 669–72.

Aronoff, J., Woike, B. A., & Hyman, L. M. (1992). Which are the stimuli in facial displays of anger and happiness? Configurational bases of emotion recognition. *Journal of Personality and Social Psychology, 62*, 1050–66.

Atkinson, A. P. (2009). Impaired recognition of emotions from body movements is associated with elevated motion coherence thresholds in autism spectrum disorders. *Neuropsychologia, 47*, 3023–29.

Atkinson, A. P., Dittrich, W. H., Gemmell, A. J., & Young, A. W. (2004). Emotion perception from dynamic and static body expressions in point-light and full-light displays. *Perception, 33*, 717–46.

Atkinson, A. P., Heberlein, A. S., & Adolphs, R. (2007). Spared ability to recognise fear from static and moving whole-body cues following bilateral amygdala damage. *Neuropsychologia, 45*, 2772–82.

Atkinson, A. P., Tunstall, M. L., & Dittrich, W. H. (2007). Evidence for distinct contributions of form and motion information to the recognition of emotions from body gestures. *Cognition, 104*, 59–72.

Atkinson, A. P., Vuong, Q. C., & Smithson, H. E. (2012). Modulation of the face- and body-selective visual regions by the motion and emotion of point-light face and body stimuli. *Neuroimage, 59*, 1700–12.

Barclay, C. D., Cutting, J. E., & Kozlowski, L. T. (1978). Temporal and spatial factors in gait perception that influence gender recognition. *Perception and Psychophysics, 23*, 145–52.

Bassili, J. N. (1978). Facial motion in the perception of faces and of emotional expression. *Journal of Experimental Psychology: Human Perception and Performance, 4*, 373–79.

Beauchamp, M. S. (2005). See me, hear me, touch me: Multisensory integration in lateral occipital-temporal cortex. *Current Opinion in Neurobiology, 15*, 145–53.

Beintema, J. A., & Lappe, M. (2002). Perception of biological motion without local image motion. *Proceedings of the National Academy of Sciences, 99*, 5661–63.

Bertenthal, B. I., & Pinto, J. (1994). Global processing of biological motions. *Psychological Science, 5*, 221–25.

Blake, R., & Shiffrar, M. (2007). Perception of human motion. *Annual Review of Psychology, 58*, 47–73.

Blakemore, S. J., & Decety, J. (2001). From the perception of action to the understanding of intention. *Nature Reviews Neuroscience, 2*, 561–67.

Buccino, G., Binkofski, F., Fink, G. R., Fadiga, L., Fogassi, L., Gallese, V., et al. (2001). Action observation activates premotor and parietal areas in a somatotopic manner: An fMRI study. *European Journal of Neuroscience, 13*, 400–4.

Buck, R. (1984). *The communication of emotion.* New York: Guilford Press.

Buck, R. (1994). Social and emotional functions in facial expression and communication: The readout hypothesis. *Biological Psychology, 38*, 95–115.

Casile, A., Dayan, E., Caggiano, V., Hendler, T., Flash, T., & Giese, M. A. (2010). Neuronal encoding of human kinematic invariants during action observation. *Cerebral Cortex, 20*, 1647–55.

Casile, A., & Giese, M. A. (2005). Critical features for the recognition of biological motion. *Journal of Vision, 5*, 348–60.

Chan, A. W., Peelen, M. V., & Downing, P. E. (2004). The effect of viewpoint on body representation in the extrastriate body area. *Neuroreport, 15*, 2407–10.

Coulson, M. (2004). Attributing emotion to static body postures: Recognition accuracy, confusions, and viewpoint dependence. *Journal of Nonverbal Behavior, 28*, 117–39.

Darwin, C. (1998). *The expression of the emotions in man and animals* (3rd ed.). London: Harper Collins. (Original work published in 1872)

de Gelder, B. (2006). Towards the neurobiology of emotional body language. *Nature Reviews Neuroscience, 7*, 242–49.

de Gelder, B. (2009). Why bodies? Twelve reasons for including bodily expressions in affective neuroscience. *Philosophical Transactions of the Royal Society B: Biological Sciences, 364*, 3475–84.

de Gelder, B., Snyder, J., Greve, D., Gerard, G., & Hadjikhani, N. (2004). Fear fosters flight: A mechanism for fear contagion when perceiving emotion expressed by a whole body. *Proceedings of the National Academy of Sciences, 101*, 16701–6.

de Gelder, B., Van den Stock, J., Meeren, H. K. M., Sinke, C. B. A., Kret, M. E., & Tamietto, M. (2010). Standing up for the body: Recent progress in uncovering the networks involved in the perception of bodies and bodily expressions. *Neuroscience & Biobehavioral Reviews*, 34, 513–27.

de Meijer, M. (1989). The contribution of general features of body movement to the attribution of emotions. *Journal of Nonverbal Behavior*, 13, 247–68.

Desimone, R., Albright, T. D., Gross, C. G., & Bruce, C. (1984). Stimulus-selective properties of inferior temporal neurons in the macaque. *Journal of Neuroscience*, 4, 2051–62.

Diamond, R., & Carey, S. (1986). Why faces are and are not special: An effect of expertise. *Journal of Experimental Psychology: General*, 115, 107–17.

Dittrich, W. H. (1991). Das Erkennen von Emotionen aus Ausdrucksbewegungen des Gesichts. *Psychologische Beitrage*, 33, 366–77.

Dittrich, W. H., Troscianko, T., Lea, S., & Morgan, D. (1996). Perception of emotion from dynamic point-light displays represented in dance. *Perception*, 25, 727–38.

Downing, P. E., Jiang, Y., Shuman, M., & Kanwisher, N. (2001). A cortical area selective for visual processing of the human body. *Science*, 293, 2470–73.

Downing, P. E., Peelen, M. V., Wiggett, A. J., & Tew, B. D. (2006). The role of the extrastriate body area in action perception. *Social Neuroscience*, 1, 52–62.

Downing, P. E., Wiggett, A. J., & Peelen, M. V. (2007). Functional magnetic resonance imaging investigation of overlapping lateral occipitotemporal activations using multi-voxel pattern analysis. *Journal of Neuroscience*, 27, 226–33.

Ekman, P. (1992). An argument for basic emotions. *Cognition & Emotion*, 6, 169–200.

Ekman, P., & Friesen, W. (1969). The repertoire of nonverbal behavior: Categories, origins, usage, and coding. *Semiotica*, 1, 49–98.

Fridlund, A. J. (1991). Evolution and facial action in reflex, social motive, and paralanguage. *Biological Psychology*, 32, 3–100.

Gallese, V., Keysers, C., & Rizzolatti, G. (2004). A unifying view of the basis of social cognition. *Trends in Cognitive Sciences*, 8, 396–403.

Giese, M. A., & Poggio, T. (2003). Neural mechanisms for the recognition of biological movements. *Nature Reviews Neuroscience*, 4, 179–92.

Grèzes, J., Pichon, S., & de Gelder, B. (2007). Perceiving fear in dynamic body expressions. *Neuroimage*, 35, 959–67.

Grèzes, J., Wicker, B., Berthoz, S., & de Gelder, B. (2009). A failure to grasp the affective meaning of actions in autism spectrum disorder subjects. *Neuropsychologia*, 47, 1816–25.

Grossman, E. D., Battelli, L., & Pascual-Leone, A. (2005). Repetitive TMS over posterior STS disrupts perception of biological motion. *Vision Research*, 45, 2847–53.

Grossman, E. D., & Blake, R. (2001). Brain activity evoked by inverted and imagined biological motion. *Vision Research*, 41, 1475–82.

Grossman, E. D., & Blake, R. (2002). Brain areas active during visual perception of biological motion. *Neuron*, 35, 1167–75.

Grush, R. (2004). The emulation theory of representation: motor control, imagery, and perception. *Behavioral and Brain Sciences*, 27, 377–96; discussion 396–442.

Hadjikhani, N., & de Gelder, B. (2003). Seeing fearful body expressions activates the fusiform cortex and amygdala. *Current Biology*, 13, 2201–5.

Hadjikhani, N., Joseph, R. M., Manoach, D. S., Naik, P., Snyder, J., Dominick, K., et al. (2009). Body expressions of emotion do not trigger fear contagion in autism spectrum disorder. *Social Cognitive and Affective Neuroscience*, 4, 70–78.

Heberlein, A. S., Adolphs, R., Tranel, D., & Damasio, H. (2004). Cortical regions for judgments of emotions and personality traits from point-light walkers. *Journal of Cognitive Neuroscience*, 16, 1143–58.

Heberlein, A. S., & Atkinson, A. P. (2009). Neuroscientific evidence for simulation and shared substrates in emotion recognition: Beyond faces. *Emotion Review*, 1, 162–77.

Heberlein, A. S., & Saxe, R. R. (2005). Dissociation between emotion and personality judgments: Convergent evidence from functional neuroimaging. *Neuroimage*, 28, 770–77.

Hejmadi, A., Davidson, R. J., & Rozin, P. (2000). Exploring Hindu Indian emotion expressions: Evidence for accurate recognition by Americans and Indians. *Psychological Science*, 11, 183–87.

Hill, H., Jinno, Y., & Johnston, A. (2003). Comparing solid-body with point-light animations. *Perception*, 32, 561–66.

Hubert, B., Wicker, B., Moore, D. G., Monfardini, E., Duverger, H., Da Fonseca, D., et al. (2007). Recognition of emotional and non-emotional biological motion in individuals with autistic spectrum disorders. *Journal of Autism and Developmental Disorders*, 37, 1386–92.

Jackson, S., & Blake, R. (2010). Neural integration of information specifying human structure from form, motion, and depth. *Journal of Neuroscience*, 30, 838–48.

James, W. (1932). A study of the expression of bodily posture. *Journal of General Psychology*, 7, 405–36.

Jastorff, J., & Orban, G. A. (2009). Human functional magnetic resonance imaging reveals separation and integration of shape and motion cues in biological motion processing. *Journal of Neuroscience*, 29, 7315–29.

Johansson, G. (1973). Visual perception of biological motion and a model for its analysis. *Perception and Psychophysics*, 14, 201–11.

Johnson, S. H., & Grafton, S. T. (2003). From 'acting on' to 'acting with': The functional anatomy of object-oriented action schemata. *Progress in Brain Research*, 142, 127–39.

Kober, H., Barrett, L. F., Joseph, J., Bliss-Moreau, E., Lindquist, K., & Wager, T. D. (2008). Functional grouping and cortical-subcortical interactions in emotion: A meta-analysis of neuroimaging studies. *Neuroimage*, 42, 998–1031.

Laban, R., & Ullmann, L. (1988). *The mastery of movement* (4th ed.). Plymouth, England: Northcote House.

Lange, J., & Lappe, M. (2006). A model of biological motion perception from configural form cues. *Journal of Neuroscience*, 26, 2894–2906.

Lee, K. H., & Siegle, G. J. (2009). Common and distinct brain networks underlying explicit emotional evaluation: A meta-analytic study. *Social Cognitive and Affective Neuroscience*. doi: 10.1093/scan/nsp001

Leslie, K. R., Johnson-Frey, S. H., & Grafton, S. T. (2004). Functional imaging of face and hand imitation: Towards a motor theory of empathy. *Neuroimage*, 21, 601–7.

Loula, F., Prasad, S., Harber, K., & Shiffrar, M. (2005). Recognizing people from their movement. *Journal of Experimental Psychology: Human Perception and Performance*, 31, 210–20.

Mather, G., & Murdoch, L. (1994). Gender discrimination in biological motion displays based on dynamic cues. *Proceedings of the Royal Society of London, Series B: Biological Sciences*, 258, 273–79.

Mather, G., Radford, K., & West, S. (1992). Low-level visual processing of biological motion. *Proceedings of the Royal Society of London Series B: Biological Sciences*, 249, 149–55.

McCarthy, G., Puce, A., Belger, A., & Allison, T. (1999). Electrophysiological studies of human face perception. II: Response properties of face-specific potentials generated in occipitotemporal cortex. *Cerebral Cortex*, 9, 431–44.

McLeod, P., Dittrich, W., Driver, J., Perrett, D., & Zihl, J. (1996). Preserved and impaired detection of structure from motion by a "motion-blind" patient. *Visual Cognition*, 3, 363–91.

Minnebusch, D. A., Suchan, B., & Daum, I. (2009). Losing your head: Behavioral and electrophysiological effects of body inversion. *Journal of Cognitive Neuroscience*, 21, 865.

Montepare, J., Goldstein, S. B., & Clausen, A. (1987). The identification of emotions from gait information. *Journal of Nonverbal Behavior*, 11, 33–42.

Moore, D. G., Hobson, R. P., & Lee, A. (1997). Components of person perception: An investigation with autistic, non-autistic retarded and typically developing children and adolescents. *British Journal of Developmental Psychology*, 15, 401–23.

Pavlova, M., Lutzenberger, W., Sokolov, A., & Birbaumer, N. (2004). Dissociable cortical processing of recognizable and non-recognizable biological movement: Analysing gamma MEG activity. *Cerebral Cortex*, 14, 181–88.

Peelen, M. V., Atkinson, A. P., Andersson, F., & Vuilleumier, P. (2007). Emotional modulation of body-selective visual areas. *Social Cognitive and Affective Neuroscience*, 2, 274–83.

Peelen, M. V., Atkinson, A. P., & Vuilleumier, P. (2010). Supramodal representations of perceived emotions in the human brain. *Journal of Neuroscience*, 30, 10127–34.

Peelen, M. V., & Downing, P. E. (2005). Selectivity for the human body in the fusiform gyrus. *Journal of Neurophysiology*, 93, 603–8.

Peelen, M. V., & Downing, P. E. (2007). The neural basis of visual body perception. *Nature Reviews Neuroscience*, 8, 636–48.

Peelen, M. V., Wiggett, A. J., & Downing, P. E. (2006). Patterns of fMRI activity dissociate overlapping functional brain areas that respond to biological motion. *Neuron*, 49, 815–22.

Pessoa, L., McKenna, M., Gutierrez, E., & Ungerleider, L. G. (2002). Neural processing of emotional faces requires attention. *Proceedings of the National Academy of Sciences*, 99, 11458–63.

Pichon, S., de Gelder, B., & Grèzes, J. (2011). Threat prompts defensive brain responses independently of attentional control. *Cerebral Cortex*. doi: 10.1093/cercor/bhr060

Pinto, J., & Shiffrar, M. (1999). Subconfigurations of the human form in the perception of biological motion displays. *Acta Psychologica*, 102, 293–318.

Pitcher, D., Garrido, L., Walsh, V., & Duchaine, B. (2008). TMS disrupts the perception and embodiment of facial expressions. *Journal of Vision*, 8, 700.

Poizner, H. (1981). Visual and "phonetic" coding of movement: Evidence from American Sign Language. *Science*, 212, 691–93.

Pollick, F. E., Paterson, H. M., Bruderlin, A., & Sanford, A. J. (2001). Perceiving affect from arm movement. *Cognition*, 82, B51–61.

Pourtois, G., Peelen, M. V., Spinelli, L., Seeck, M., & Vuilleumier, P. (2007). Direct intracranial recording of body-selective responses in human extrastriate visual cortex. *Neuropsychologia*, 45, 2621–25.

Pourtois, G., Sander, D., Andres, M., Grandjean, D., Reveret, L., Olivier, E., et al. (2004). Dissociable roles of the human somatosensory and superior temporal cortices for processing social face signals. *European Journal of Neuroscience*, 20, 3507–15.

Puce, A., & Perrett, D. (2003). Electrophysiology and brain imaging of biological motion. *Philosophical Transactions of the Royal Society of London, Series B: Biological Sciences*, 358, 435–45.

Reed, C. L., Stone, V. E., Grubb, J. D., & McGoldrick, J. E. (2006). Turning configural processing upside down: Part and whole body postures. *Journal of Experimental Psychology: Human Perception and Performance*, 32, 73–87.

Roether, C. L., Omlor, L., Christensen, A., & Giese, M. A. (2009). Critical features for the perception of emotion from gait. *Journal of Vision*, 9, 1–32.

Roether, C. L., Omlor, L., & Giese, M. A. (2008). Lateral asymmetry of bodily emotion expression. *Current Biology*, 18, R329–R330.

Runeson, S., & Frykholm, G. (1981). Visual perception of lifted weight. *Journal of Experimental Psychology: Human Perception and Performance*, 7, 733–40.

Sawada, M., Suda, K., & Ishii, M. (2003). Expression of emotions in dance: Relation between arm movement characteristics and emotion. *Perceptual and Motor Skills*, 97, 697–708.

Saygin, A. P. (2007). Superior temporal and premotor brain areas necessary for biological motion perception. *Brain*, 130, 2452–61.

Saygin, A. P., Wilson, S. M., Hagler, D. J., Bates, E., & Sereno, M. I. (2004). Point-light biological motion perception activates human premotor cortex. *Journal of Neuroscience*, 24, 6181–88.

Schwarzlose, R. F., Baker, C. I., & Kanwisher, N. (2005). Separate face and body selectivity on the fusiform gyrus. *Journal of Neuroscience*, 25, 11055–59.

Shallice, T. (1988). *From neuropsychology to mental structure*. Cambridge: Cambridge University Press.

Shipley, T. F. (2003). The effect of object and event orientation on perception of biological motion. *Psychological Science*, 14, 377–80.

Sprengelmeyer, R., Young, A. W., Schroeder, U., Grossenbacher, P. G., Federlein, J., Buttner, T., et al. (1999). Knowing no fear. *Proceedings of the Royal Society of London. Series B: Biological Sciences*, 266, 2451–56.

Stanislavski, K. (1936). *An actor prepares* (E. R. Hopgood, Trans.). New York: Theatre Arts Books.

Stekelenburg, J. J., & de Gelder, B. (2004). The neural correlates of perceiving human bodies: An ERP study on the body-inversion effect. *Neuroreport*, 15, 777–80.

Sugase, Y., Yamane, S., Ueno, S., & Kawano, K. (1999). Global and fine information coded by single neurons in the temporal visual cortex. *Nature*, 400, 869–73.

Susskind, J. M., Littlewort, G., Bartlett, M. S., Movellan, J., & Anderson, A. K. (2007). Human and computer recognition of facial expressions of emotion. *Neuropsychologia*, 45, 152–62.

Taylor, J. C., Wiggett, A. J., & Downing, P. E. (2007). Functional MRI analysis of body and body part representations in the extrastriate and fusiform body areas. *Journal of Neurophysiology*, 98, 1626–33.

Thurman, S. M., Giese, M. A., & Grossman, E. D. (2010). Perceptual and computational analysis of critical features for biological motion. *Journal of Vision*, 10(12):15, 1–14. doi: 10.1167/10.12.15

Troje, N. F. (2002). Decomposing biological motion: A framework for analysis and synthesis of human gait patterns. *Journal of Vision*, 2, 371–87.

Urgesi, C., Berlucchi, G., & Aglioti, S. M. (2004). Magnetic stimulation of extrastriate body area impairs visual processing of nonfacial body parts. *Current Biology*, 14, 2130–34.

Urgesi, C., Calvo-Merino, B., Haggard, P., & Aglioti, S. M. (2007). Transcranial magnetic stimulation reveals two cortical pathways for visual body processing. *Journal of Neuroscience*, 27, 8023–30.

Urgesi, C., Candidi, M., Ionta, S., & Aglioti, S. M. (2007). Representation of body identity and body actions in extrastriate body area and ventral premotor cortex. *Nature Neuroscience*, 10, 30–1.

Vaina, L. M., Cowey, A., LeMay, M., Bienfang, D. C., & Kikinis, R. (2002). Visual deficits in a patient with 'kaleidoscopic disintegration of the visual world'. *European Journal of Neurology*, 9, 463–77.

Van den Stock, J., Righart, R., & de Gelder, B. (2007). Body expressions influence recognition of emotions in the face and voice. *Emotion*, 7, 487–94.

van Rijn, S., Aleman, A., van Diessen, E., Berckmoes, C., Vingerhoets, G., & Kahn, R. S. (2005). What is said or how it is said makes a difference: Role of the right fronto-parietal operculum in emotional prosody as revealed by repetitive TMS. *European Journal of Neuroscience*, 21, 3195–3200.

Vuilleumier, P. (2005). How brains beware: Neural mechanisms of emotional attention. *Trends in Cognitive Sciences*, 9, 585–94.

Vuilleumier, P., & Driver, J. (2007). Modulation of visual processing by attention and emotion: Windows on causal interactions between human brain regions. *Philosophical Transactions of the Royal Society B: Biological Sciences*, 362, 837–55.

Vuilleumier, P., Richardson, M. P., Armony, J. L., Driver, J., & Dolan, R. J. (2004). Distant influences of amygdala lesion on visual cortical activation during emotional face processing. *Nature Neuroscience*, 7, 1271–78.

Wallbott, H. G. (1998). Bodily expression of emotion. *European Journal of Social Psychology*, 28, 879–96.

Westhoff, C., & Troje, N. F. (2007). Kinematic cues for person identification from biological motion. *Perception & Psychophysics*, 69, 241–53.

Winston, J. S., O'Doherty, J., & Dolan, R. J. (2003). Common and distinct neural responses during direct and incidental processing of multiple facial emotions. *Neuroimage*, 20, 84–97.

Wolpert, D. M., Doya, K., & Kawato, M. (2003). A unifying computational framework for motor control and social interaction. *Philosophical Transactions of the Royal Society B: Biological Sciences*, 358, 593–602.

Yovel, G., Pelc, T., & Lubetzky, I. (2010). It's all in your head: Why is the body inversion effect abolished for headless bodies? *Journal of Experimental Psychology: Human Perception and Performance*, 36, 759–67.

CHAPTER 9

Pain and the Emotional Responses to Noxious Stimuli

Pierre Rainville

The somatosensory system is at the heart of emotion. First and foremost, this sensory system provides the most immediate and direct information to the central nervous system (CNS) about potential shifts toward or away from biophysiological stability (homeostasis/allostasis); it thereby constitutes the fundamental monitoring component essential for the integrated neural regulation of basic physiological functions (e.g., Craig, 2003). This integrated regulation is especially critical when local physiological processes are insufficient to respond adequately to threatening conditions that require the mobilization of additional resources involving coordinated emotional systems ranging from low-level motor and autonomic responses to higher order brain processes. Furthermore, from psychological and experiential perspectives, whereas signals originating from other sensory modalities are normally perceived as properties of external objects, signals processed in the somatosensory system provide information about the body itself, a core component of self-representation in influential theories of emotion and consciousness (e.g., Craig, 2002, 2009; Damasio, 1999; Metzinger, 2000).

Although the somatosensory system provides the most basic form of emotional inducers, somatosensory inputs are not distinctly perceived as pertaining to the self, because some can also be considered exteroceptive signals. Interoceptive perception refers to somatosensory experiences attributed to the state or function of the body itself and constitutes a fundamental component of self-representation. According to this general conception, interoception may include not only visceral sensation but also all sensory signals conveying information about the state of the body, including the skin, the musculoskeletal system, and humoral state. In contrast, exteroceptive somatosensory perception refers to experiences attributed to external objects that are in direct contact with the body. In the somatosensory system, exteroceptive information is typically conveyed by components of the skin senses (e.g., low-threshold mechanoreceptors), as well as other subsystems (e.g., proprioceptive) involved in body representation (i.e., the position of the fingers inform about the shape of an object held in one's hand). Although they are most proximal to the body, these external objects do not have intrinsic properties sufficient to be considered primordial emotional inducers because their emotional impact is dependent on the interpretation of their potential effects on the body-self.

Although there is no strict separation between interoceptive and exteroceptive pathways in the somatosensory system, exteroceptive information is generally associated with lemniscal function, whereas the multiple extra-lemniscal pathways contribute primarily, but not exclusively, to interoceptive function (for a major exception involving visceral input from the lower abdomen transmitted through the dorsal column, see Willis, Al-Chaer, Quast, & Westlund, 1999). In this respect, acute cutaneous pain is particularly interesting because the sensory signals convey information about both the state of the body (i.e., actual or potential tissue damage) and the properties of the nociceptive stimulus. Experientially, this information translates into experiences of states of the self ("I" am in pain) and perceived properties of external objects ("this burner" is hot).

In addition to emotional induction, the somatosensory system also provides key information about the emotional responses elicited in the body. Somatovisceral and skeletomotor activation are fundamental constituents of emotional responses, and sensory feedback from the body is central to classical theories of emotions (Damasio, 1994, 1996; James, 1994; see Chapter 1). Somatosensory feedback may also contribute to self-perception of emotional states and provides meaningful psychophysiological information relevant to cognitive processes, particularly decision making (Bechara, 2004; Bechara, Damasio, Tranel, & Damasio, 1997).

Nociception and Pain

The International Association for the Study of Pain (IASP) defines pain as a "an unpleas-

ant sensory and emotional experience associated with actual or potential tissue damage, or described in terms of such damage" (Merskey & Spear, 1967). Price (1999, pp. 1–2) has proposed a slightly different definition in which pain is "a somatic perception containing (1) a bodily sensation with qualities like those reported during tissue damaging stimulation, (2) an experienced threat associated with this sensation, and (3) a feeling of unpleasantness or other negative emotions based on this experienced threat." In both definitions, negative emotions, at least in their most basic expression, are a constituent of the pain experience. Importantly, this definition distinguishes pain from nociception, with the latter notion referring to the biological processes associated with tissue damage. Of course, pain may result from nociception (i.e., nociceptive pain), but in several conditions, pain may be experienced without evidence of tissue damage and nociception may be observed without resulting in a pain experience.

Price (1999) has further described stages of pain processing that distinguish between primary pain affect and secondary emotions. The primary affective stage refers to the immediate unpleasantness that is integral to the pain experience and is intimately related to the sense of immediate threat. The second stage is characterized by emotions related to the broader meaning of pain and the evaluation of the future consequences of pain. Although the sensory experience and the first stage of pain affect are necessary and sufficient for an experience to be characterized as painful, the emotions associated with the secondary stage of pain complement the experience in relation to its broader significance and future implications.

Is Pain an Emotion?

There are several features that characterize emotions and are given different weights in theories of emotions (see Chapter 1). Emotions are triggered by objects or events that are immediately present or evoked mentally ("emotion inducer"). The immediate, anticipated, or simulated impact of the inducer on the organism/self is evaluated consciously and/or unconsciously to establish its biological/affective relevance. Emotions include some motor-behavioral and expressive components along with a variety of responses affecting the physiological state of the body (e.g., autonomic and hormonal). Finally, most theories recognize that distinctive subjective experiences generally accompany different emotions.

These multiple aspects covered by emotion theories clearly relate to pain processes in many ways. The main difference between pain and emotion may be that pain *requires* the presence of "a bodily sensation with qualities like those reported during tissue damaging stimulation" (Price, 1999, p. 1). In this respect, pain sensations may be considered a specific inducer of a primordial emotional response, consistent with the widely accepted view that emotion systems are intimately related to adaptive biological processes (e.g., Izard, 1993; Plutchik, 1980). Prototypical facial expressions of pain have also been documented that can be clearly differentiated from the basic emotions of fear, anger, and sadness (Craig, Prkachin, & Grunau, 2001; Simon, Craig, Gosselin, Belin, & Rainville, 2008; see an evolutionary theoretical perspective in Williams, 2002). Patterns of autonomic responses to nociceptive stimuli are well documented, mainly in animals (Sato, Sato, & Schmidt, 1997) and may contribute to pain-related emotional responses, as well as subjective feelings of unpleasantness (e.g., Fillingim, Maixner, Bunting, & Silva, 1998; Rainville, Carrier, Hofbauer, Bushnell, & Duncan, 1999). It is also noteworthy that the model of pain discussed earlier includes primary and secondary affective stages (Price 1999): The first stage corresponds to the basic experience of a threat, or the fear of tissue damage, and may include self-perception of autonomic and motor responses triggered automatically, and the second stage reflects secondary evaluative processes consistent with modern views on the role of cognitive evaluative processes in emotions. This is also consistent with an experiential model in which emotional experiences are related to goals, desires, and expectations (Price & Barrell, 1984). This experiential model of emotions has been shown to predict variations in pain unpleasantness, but not pain intensity (Price, Barrell, & Gracely, 1980), consistent with the view that pain-related affective processes may be considered somatosensory emotions. Consistent with this theory, the nociceptive system is closely related to the emotional systems in the brain.

Ascending Nociceptive Pathways

Functional imaging of pain in humans is based firmly on the fundamental knowledge acquired in animal studies on the transmission and integration of noxious information at multiple levels of the CNS. Thus, the examination and the interpretation of cerebral activations are first directed toward the areas that are known to receive the information from the dorsal horn of the spinal cord, the first site of central integration of the noxious messages. Several reviews have provided detailed descriptions of the ascending pathways (e.g., Dostrovsky & Craig, 2006; Willis, & Westlund, 1997). These pathways include projections from the superficial and deep layers of the dorsal horn toward a number of targets in the medulla (e.g., subnucleus reticularis dorsalis), the pons and the mesencephalon (e.g., nucleus parabrachial and periacqueductal gray area [PAG]), and of course to several thalamic nuclei. Several relays of the brainstem also send ascending projections toward the diencephalon (medial and intralaminar nuclei of the thalamus, hypothalamus, and amygdala; e.g., see Bernard, Bester, & Besson, 1996, and Figure 9.1. Lastly, these diencephalic structures maintain close reciprocal relations with specific cortical territories (for example, projections between the amygdala and the orbitofrontal prefrontal cortex).

Recent research in nonhuman primates has examined the precise ascending projections of the dorsal horn using a technique of transsynaptic anterograde tracing (Dum, Levinthal, & Strick, 2009), as summarized in

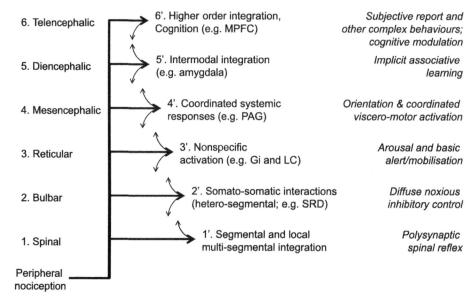

Figure 9.1. Hierarchical organization of the nociceptive system. The stimulation of peripheral nociceptors activates spinal neurons and ascending pathways that transmit the nociceptive signal to multiple targets at the bulbar, reticular, mesencephalic, diencephalic, and telencephalic level. At each of those levels (1 to 6), new integration processes (1′ to 6′) are possible that can be indexed by output measures and/or modulatory effects (right column). In addition to the ascending pathways, interactions between levels are possible through ascending and descending connections between levels (curved arrows).

Figure 9.2. This study shows very clearly that the spinothalamocortical ascending system targets the primary (SI) and secondary (SII) somatosensory areas, the insular cortex, and the anterior cingulate cortex (ACC). Importantly, this study further demonstrates that the primary target territory in the ACC corresponds to the caudal part of the supracallosal ACC, also associated with motor control. In contrast, the insular cortex has been associated with autonomic and homeostatic regulation (Augustine, 1996; Craig, 2003). Although all cortical targets receive information about the intensity of the noxious input, the somatosensory areas, including part of the insula, have been associated more specifically, although perhaps not exclusively, with the conscious perception

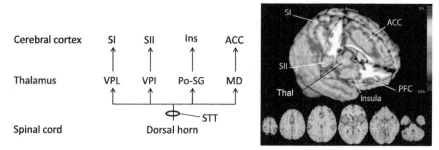

Figure 9.2. Spinothalamocortical pathways (left) convey the nociceptive signal from the dorsal horn of the spinal cord to four thalamic nuclei and four target cortical areas (Dum et al., 2009). Thalamocortical activation is consistently observed during acute pain as demonstrated by the activation likelihood estimation (ALE) map (right) showing highly significant responses found across 117 brain imaging studies in healthy individuals published before 2008 (Duerden et al., 2008).

and memory of the sensory properties of pain (spatiotemporal and intensity) and with sensory-discriminative functions (e.g., Albanese, Duerden, Rainville, & Duncan, 2007; Hofbauer, Rainville, Duncan, & 2001; Ploner, Freund, & Schnitzler, 1999).

In addition to those more classical pain pathways, the prefrontal cortex is also a target of ascending projections activated via additional relay nuclei (thalamus, nucleus parabrachial, and amygdala; e.g., Bernard & Villanueva, 2009; Bourgeais, Monconduit, Villanueva, & Bernard, 2001; Monconduit, Bourgeais, Bernard, Le Bars, & Villanueva, 1999). Important anatomical connections are also present between the amygdala, the insula (Augustine, 1996), and the prefrontal cortices (Sah, Faber, Lopez de, & Power, 2003) that could play an important part in the regulation of pain responses (e.g., Ji et al., 2010). In summary, the nociceptive transmission channels involve disynaptic spinothalamocortical pathways that are generally associated with the perception of pain sensation and pain affective responses, as well as several multisynaptic pathways that include additional sites of integration at the bulbar, reticular, mesencephalic, and diencephalic levels, before reaching various cortical territories.

Functional Brain Imaging of Acute Pain

The results of human functional neuroimaging studies have been compiled by Apkarian in an important review article (Apkarian, Bushnell, Treede, & Zubieta, 2005). This article describes the activations induced by the application of acute noxious stimulations (e.g. thermal, mechanical, and so on) in each cortical area targeted by the spinothalamic pathways, including SI, SII, the insula, and the ACC. Activations were also noted in the prefrontal cortex, the motor and premotor areas (including the supplementary motor areas, near the caudal ACC), and the posterior parietal cortex. Subcortical activation was also reported in some studies in the thalamus and the basal ganglia and, more rarely, in the amygdala, cerebel-

lum, hypothalamus, and brainstem, including the region of the mesencephalic PAG. The relation between the activity in these various areas and the level of pain felt by the participants was also examined using various experimental approaches. These observations generally supported the notion of a "pain (neuro)matrix," a distributed cerebral network in which activity is *associated* with pain. However, this idea, fundamental to the pioneer theorization of Melzack (1990), raised important questions about the relation of identity between pain and the activity in this cerebral network. It recently nourished an animated debate on the specificity of pain-related brain activation.

Sensitivity and Specificity of Pain-Related Brain Activity

The sensitivity of a test corresponds to its capacity to detect the presence of a given condition, as determined by a universally recognized criterion (i.e., the *gold standard*). In the context of pain neuroimagery, this measurement of reference generally corresponds to subjective reports of pain, consistent with the experiential emphasis put on pain phenomena by the IASP. A coordinate-based meta-analysis carried out on the results of 117 pain imaging studies published from 1991 to 2008 confirmed the reliable activation of the thalamus, as well as the SI, SII, insula, and ACC (Duerden, Fu, Rainville, & Duncan, 2008; see Figure 9.2). Other sites where the probability of observing[1] an activation exceeded chance were several prefrontal and subcortical sites, particularly in the putamen and the cerebellum. This coordinate-based meta-analysis confirmed that activation sites in separate studies were likely superimposed spatially on the target structures. Results also confirmed the greatest sensitivity of the insula and the ACC to the presence of acute pain. However, the observation of high sensitivity to the presence of pain is insufficient to conclude that there is a "relation of identity" between these activations and pain experiences.

Although the unique nature of painful experiences is generally recognized, as compared to other sensory or emotional experiences, it is not completely clear that it results in a unique and distinctive pattern of brain activation in functional brain imaging studies. Brain areas activated by painful stimuli receive spinothalamocortical inputs (Dum et al., 2009) and contain nociceptive neurons (e.g., Kenshalo, Iwata, Sholas, & Thomas, 2000; Shyu, Sikes, Vogt, & Vogt, 2010; Treede, Kenshalo, Gracely, & Jones, 1999; Vogt, 2005); however, in some conditions, innocuous (and nonpainful) stimulation may also produce robust activation in somatosensory areas as well as in the insula and ACC (Legrain, Iannetti, Plaghki, & Mouraux, 2011). The ACC and the insula are considered multisensory areas associated with cognitive and emotional processes (Augustine, 1996; Shackman et al., 2011; Vogt, 2005). These areas are also activated by salient but nonpainful stimuli in the auditory, visual, and somatosentory modalities (Baliki, Geha, & Apkarian, 2009; Downar, Crawley, Mikulis, & Davis, 2000; Legrain et al., 2011). Some studies relying on cortical evoked potential measurements have arrived at similar conclusions, stressing that the pain responses can be explained by a somatosensory activation evoked by a very salient stimulation (Legrain et al., 2011). High saliency being an intrinsic property of painful stimuli, one may therefore interpret the strongest activation found to painful versus nonpainful stimulation in functional brain imaging studies as reflecting somatosensory processing of highly salient stimuli (Legrain et al., 2011).[2]

The factors that contribute to saliency include stimulus intensity, contrast, novelty, and intrinsic or extrinsic affective value, and each of these influences may reflect at least partly different neural mechanisms. According to this perspective, pain is inherently salient based on its strong sensory intensity and intrinsic aversive valence, two basic properties that translate into experiential dimensions of pain intensity and unpleasantness. These observations suggest that the pattern of brain activation associated with pain reflects the activation of a functional network involved in the detection and the evaluation of biologically or psychologically relevant sensory information. Activation of this network may further reflect the spontaneous mobilization of higher order resources to respond adaptively to biologically and psychologically relevant inputs (Shackman et al., 2011). Thus, the notion of a pain matrix should refer to functional systems reliably involved in pain (i.e., high sensitivity) but not necessarily specific to pain. The relative neurofunctional specificity of pain processes may be found at the level of the neural networks (Shyu et al., 2010) within each area that are activated by painful stimuli and reflect the underlying factors that make pain highly salient based on its strong intensity and inherent affective valence.

Beyond the Stimulus Model of Pain-Related Activation

The functional analysis of the cerebral networks implied in pain extends beyond the simple examination of brain activations evoked by noxious stimuli. Indeed, functional brain imaging studies generally try to relate these activations to some aspect of the participants' experience or responses. In the vast majority of studies, the self-report of pain intensity on a visual or numerical scale constitutes the principal behavioral measure. This choice is justified by the crucial importance of this measurement in clinical studies of pain, consistent with the experiential definition of pain, as discussed earlier. Because this subjective experience of pain is generally considered to reflect the activation of the spinothalamocortical pathway(s), the primary focus is largely on the activations observed within the cortical targets of this system. These self-report measurements are the result of the multiple stages of integration of the noxious signal at the various levels of the CNS, and not simply the passive spinal and thalamic transmission of nociceptive signals.

At each level of integration of the noxious signal in the CNS, a variety of additional output responses can be initiated (Figure 9.1). The integration of nociceptive signals from the primary afferents in the dorsal horn of the spinal cord activates not only the ascending nociceptive pathways but also the spinal networks involved in the production of spinal reflexes that can be measured by the activation of the target peripheral effectors. At the level of the brainstem, bulbar integration is essential for the regulation of the hetero-segmental somato-somatic interactions (e.g., noxious counterstimulation analgesia), whereas reticular sites are critical for the production of nonspecific systemic responses, such as systemic autonomic activation and general arousal (see reviews by Bandler & Shipley, 1994; Villanueva & Bourgeais, 2009; Villanueva & Fields, 2004). Mesencephalic and diencephalic nuclei provide yet another stage of integration, allowing for the production of coordinated systemic activation involving complex musculoskeletal, visceral, and hormonal responses. Lastly, the diencephalon and the telencephalon allow for the intermodal integration of nociceptive information, a process essential to various forms of associative learning (e.g., the amygdala, the thalamus, and the ACC in aversive conditioning; Gabriel, 1993; LeDoux, 2007); they provide the additional mechanisms for the psychological regulation of the experience and the communication of pain. Importantly, these higher order sites of integration also exert regulatory influences on the lower order levels.

Stimulus Intensity and Self-Reports of Pain

The simplest and most direct manipulation of the magnitude of the pain experience is generally based on a precise and controlled modification of the intensity of the stimulus to verify if the cerebral responses are indeed proportional to the stimulus and the pain reported by the participants (Coghill, Sang, Maisog, & Iadarola, 1999; Derbyshire et al., 1997; Porro, Cettolo, Francescato, & Baraldi, 1998). Although these studies do not generally allow for a separation between processes involved in the coding of stimulus intensity and those involved more specifically in perceived intensity, this research confirms that self-reports of pain are generally proportional to the stimulus-driven increase in the cortical responses within the areas SI and SII, the insula, and the ACC (and adjacent SMA). These results thereby demonstrate a robust correspondence between the level of activation of the spinothalamocortical pathways by the stimulus and the subjective experience of pain. However, some subareas present monotonic increases to increasing stimulus intensity that do not necessarily code specifically or linearly for the perceived intensity of pain. For example, whereas the ACC generally presents a response proportional to pain, some sectors show a gradual increase to both nonpainful and painful stimulations (consistent with the coding of stimulus intensity not specific to pain). Other subsectors of the ACC display an increase mainly at the level of the pain threshold, with no additional increases to suprathreshold intensities (Büchel et al., 2002; see a similar stimulus-response function analysis of other pain-activated areas in Bornhövd et al., 2002). Thus, some subareas could be primarily sensitive to the occurrence of pain (threshold), whereas others may code more generally for the intensity of the stimulus or more specifically for the intensity of pain.

This relation between cerebral activity and pain experiences is also critical to the understanding of interindividual differences commonly observed in self-reports and the variations observed spontaneously or induced by various experimental manipulations in intraindividual paradigms using constant stimuli. Coghill and his collaborators have clearly shown that individuals reporting greater painful sensitivity (i.e., a higher pain rating) during the application of stimulations of constant intensity also display stronger activation in cortical targets of the spinothalamocortical pathway (e.g., SI and the ACC; Coghill, McHaffie, & Yen, 2003). These results are extremely important because they indicate that the interindividual differences in the subjective reports of pain are not simply a consequence of response biases, but rather imply that these differences reflect, at least in part, individual differences in the neurophysiological processing of the nociceptive input in cerebral areas and/or at earlier stages of nociceptive processes in the spinothalamocortical pathways.

The multiple experimental studies investigating the psychological modulation of pain also support these conclusions on the role of various cerebral areas in the subjective experience of pain. Indeed, modulation of the pain by hypnosis, attention, expectations (e.g., placebo), and emotions generally produces changes in cerebral activation in one or more target sectors of the noxious ascending pathways, in particular in the territories receiving the spinothalamocortical input (see table 3 in Apkarian et al., 2005). These studies also suggest that various psychological manipulations can act on various sectors of this network (e.g., Hofbauer et al., 2001; Rainville, Duncan, Price, Carrier, & Bushnell, 1997) that are thought to be involved more specifically, although not necessarily exclusively, in the sensory (e.g., SI) or affective (e.g., ACC) dimensions of pain.

In addition to the modulation of the noxious responses, the studies interested in the psychological modulation of pain also examine the areas potentially implicated in the production of analgesic/hyperalgesic effects. These analyses have revealed prefrontal activation during hypnotic modulation (e.g., Faymonville et al., 2003; Rainville et al., 1999), distraction (e.g., Frankenstein, Richter, McIntyre, & Remy, 2001; Valet et al., 2004), or placebo (e.g., Bingel, Lorenz, Schoell, Weiller, & Buchel, 2006; Wager et al., 2004; Watson et al., 2009). Moreover, several of these studies also show mesencephalic activation during analgesia. These brainstem responses are generally thought to reflect the activation of descending pain control mechanisms (Tracey & Mantyh, 2007). This interpretation is certainly plausible, but the cerebral imaging results are insufficient to determine whether these activations indeed reflect the activation of the cerebrospinal systems affecting noxious activity in the dorsal horn, as postulated by Melzack, Wall, and Casey more than 40 years ago (Melzack & Casey, 1968; Melzack & Wall, 1965).

Spinal Nociceptive Responses and Brain Activity

The integration of noxious information at the spinal level can trigger a reflex withdrawal response simultaneous with the activation of the ascending nociceptive pathways that will in turn activate the higher order brain centers. Experimentally, sensorimotor spinal activation can be induced by a brief electric stimulation to the skin or to a cutaneous nerve (e.g., the sural nerve), which will induce a fast activation of the flexor muscle of the corresponding limb measured in the EMG (e.g., the biceps femoris). The latency of this nociceptive flexion reflex (RIII reflex) is 80–90 ms, and its duration is 60–90 ms. Over the last 35 years, this experimental model has been used to study spinal nociception and has been applied to various clinical and experimental contexts to assess the involvement of descending regulatory systems (Sandrini et al., 2005). Including this additional measure of nociception in fMRI studies recently allowed us to further explore the relation between spinal and cerebral responses.

The earlier discussion of interindividual differences in cerebral activation emphasized the interindividual differences in the subjective experience of pain as reflected in pain reports and brain activity. Some of these cerebral differences may also reflect, more or less directly, some differences in the integration of noxious signals at lower levels of the neuraxis, including the spinal cord. Indeed, when examining the cerebral responses to the acute painful electrical stimulations used to elicit the RIII reflex, one finds that the amplitude of the response in some areas is proportional to the gain in the spinal responses, as measured by the amplitude of the RIII, whereas other areas appear to correlate more specifically

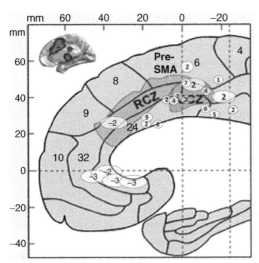

Figure 9.3. Acute pain-evoked activity in the anterior cingulate cortex (ACC) in relation to various output responses. Activation within the posterior subsector of the ACC correlates positively with between- (1) and within-subjects (2) variability in spontaneous facial expression, RIII-reflex gain (4 – between-subjects, and 5 – within-subjects variability), and SCR (6 – between-subjects, and 7 – within-subjects variability). In contrast, responses in the more rostral parts of the supracallosal ACC correlate with facial expression (2, within-subject analysis), pain intensity ratings (8, between-subject analysis), and pain unpleasantness ratings (9, within-subject analysis). Interestingly, additional rostral and perigenual areas correlate negatively with facial responses (-2 and -3), consistent with a role in the suppression of pain/emotional facial expression. Results taken from Kunz et al. (2011), Piché et al. (2010), and Rainville et al. (1997) are overlaid on a representation of the caudal (CCZ) and rostral (RCZ) cingulate motor areas, as described by the group of Strick (e.g., see Dum et al., 2009), and illustrated by Ridderinkhof, Ullsperger, Crone, and Nieuwenhuiss (2004). Numbers on the anatomical image refer to Brodmann areas, and the upper left inset shows ACC activity in a meta-analysis of brain responses to acute pain stimuli, as described in Duerden et al. (2008).

to the subjective evaluation of pain (Piché, Arsenault, & Rainville, 2010). The response of the ACC is particularly interesting in this respect (Figure 9.3).

The ACC receives the nociceptive signals from the spinothalamocortical pathway, as

described earlier, and its level of activation – in particular in its supracallosal sector about halfway on the anteroposterior axis between the posterior ACC and the most anterior (perigenual) part of the ACC – is generally associated with the subjective experience of pain (e.g., Büchel et al., 2002; Rainville et al., 1997). In contrast, individual differences in spinal sensorimotor processes, as measured by the RIII, relate more specifically to activation within the more posterior sector of the ACC, which is within the cortical territory implicated in the regulation of simple motor responses (Dum et al., 2009). Obviously, the spinal reflex response is very fast and does not depend directly on the activation of the ACC. However, this caudal ACC activation proportional to the spinal response could reflect the cortical representation of lower levels of sensorimotor integration, consistent with the classical descriptions of the hierarchical organization of the CNS. This pattern of response is quite consistent with the general role of the ACC in "adaptive control" (Shackman et al., 2011) and further suggests a caudo-rostral continuum underlying the representation and regulation of low- to high-level output systems.

In addition to allowing a more refined functional analysis of activation within the cortical targets of the spinothalamocortical pathways, reflex measurements also help reveal modulatory effects that are not necessarily detected by changes in subjective evaluations. In two recent studies, we examined the modulation of the pain and RIII reflex. In the first study, a series of electric stimulations were applied to the ankle to evoke an acute pain and an RIII reflex. Then, a constant painful cold stimulation was applied to the contralateral foot to produce the well-known phenomenon of counter-irritation analgesia. In these conditions, participants reported a robust reduction in shock pain, and some also displayed a significant reduction in the amplitude of the RIII, consistent with the activation of descending inhibitory controls (diffuse noxious inhibitory control, DNIC; see Villaneuva & Bourgeais, 2009; Villanueva & Fields, 2004). The analysis of changes in shock-evoked activation during the counter-irritation stimulus confirmed the expected decrease of activity consistent with the analgesic effect reported. However, the more detailed examination of the modifications associated with analgesia (self-reports) or changes in the amplitude of the RIII showed at least a partial segregation between the cerebral network more specifically associated with analgesia and that associated with spinal inhibition. Indeed, the reduction in self-reports of shock pain was predicted by the sustained activation of the orbitofrontal cortex to the tonic cold pain stimulus and by the corresponding reduction in the phasic responses to painful shocks in the SI, ACC, right prefrontal cortex, and amygdala. In contrast, reductions in the RIII reflex were predicted by the sustained activation induced by cold pain stimulus in the SMA, SI, the posterior cingulate cortex, and the rostro-dorsal mesencephalon (possibly PAG), as well as by a reduction in the phasic response to the noxious shocks in the SMA, insula, and prefrontal cortex. These differences suggest that the modulation of pain by counter-irritation does not reflect simply an activation of the descending regulatory systems affecting spinal responses, resulting in a suppression of nociceptive transmission at the earliest stage of the spinothalamo-cortical pathways. These separable effects observed in the RIII and pain reports also likely reflect the coactivation of several regulatory mechanisms, some of which affect spinal responses, whereas others contribute more specifically to the modulation of pain experiences through supraspinal mechanisms affecting later stages of nociceptive processing. Some of these processes may involve the establishment of priorities based on the relative affective impact of competing noxious stimuli. Interestingly, in the counter-irritation paradigm the co-occurrence of two aversive stimuli lead to a competition, resulting in the relative inhibition of acute pain responses by the tonic noxious stimulus, whereas studies on the interaction between pain and emotions instead demonstrate an exacerbation of acute pain by sustained negative emotions.

The Modulation of Pain and Spinal Responses by Emotions

The investigation of the effects of emotions on pain has demonstrated reliable hyperalgesic effects of negative emotions and a less robust analgesic effect of positive emotions (e.g., Rainville, Bao, & Chretien, 2005; Villemure, Slotnick, & Bushnell, 2003; reviewed in Duquette, Roy, Lepore, Peretz, & Rainville, 2007, and Rainville, 2004). In a recent study we examined the effect of the modulation of pain and the RIII responses by emotions induced by pleasant and unpleasant images (Roy, Piche, Chen, Peretz, & Rainville, 2009). In agreement with previous studies showing a modulation of spinal nociceptive responses by emotions (e.g., Rhudy, Williams, McCabe, Nguyen, & Rambo, 2005), pictures taken from the International Affective Picture System and evoking negative emotions produced an increase in both pain and in the amplitude of the RIII, compared to neutral and positive stimuli. Consistent with the conclusion of the earlier study examining the effects of counter-irritation, the cerebral networks associated with the modulation of pain or the RIII responses were at least partially distinct. Indeed, the modulation of pain was correlated with changes in the activation of the right anterior insula, as predicted by the theoretical model of Craig that proposed a dominant role of this area in the integration of the somatic signals to the emotional context (Craig, 2002, 2009). In contrast, the modulation of the RIII responses was correlated with SI and prefrontal responses, as well as with several other subcortical nuclei including the medial thalamus, amygdala, brainstem, and cerebellum. These results imply again that the modulation of pain by emotions does not simply reflect the descending modulation of spinal nociceptive responses secondarily and passively transmitted through the ascending nociceptive pathways. These data indicate that various measurements of nociception and pain reflect the activation of circuits that are at least partially dissociable. These observations further demonstrate the need for incorporating multiple pain-related responses in our experimental paradigms to better appreciate the potential interactions among multiple regulating mechanisms acting at the various levels of the CNS. Much remains to be done in this multidimensional exploration to better account for the complexity of pain modulation reflected in various pain responses.

Brain Correlates of the Autonomic Responses to Pain

In addition to the spinal reflex responses, acute pain is generally accompanied by a robust autonomic activation. Contrary to the RIII reflect, however, this autonomic activation does not reflect specifically a nociceptive response, because it can be produced under various non-nociceptive physiological conditions (e.g., cardiorespiratory arrhythmia regulated by the baroreflex system) or by an intense or unexpected innocuous stimulation in any sensory modality (cf. the saliency effect as discussed earlier). In spite of their poor specificity, these autonomic responses are generally very sensitive to the occurrence of acute pain and likely reflect the nonspecific alerting induced through the activation of various brainstem nuclei. Given these properties, autonomic measures are certainly not the tools of choice to evaluate pain. Nevertheless, they provide highly relevant means to improve our understanding of the mechanisms involved in the integration and the regulation of nociceptive responses, some of which are obviously based on networks that play functional roles nonspecific to pain.

The relation between cerebral activity and autonomic activity evoked by acute pain stimuli has been examined in two recent studies combining fMRI and skin conductance responses (SCRs). In the first, the interindividual differences in cerebral responses were assessed in relation to interindividual differences in the amplitude of the SCR evoked by painful and nonpainful thermal stimuli (Dube et al., 2009). Several areas targeted by the thermal and

nociceptive ascending pathways (e.g., SI, SII, insula, ACC, and medulla) presented activity levels proportional to the sympathetic reactivity of the participants. However, the activation of SI and the insula correlated better with the brain responses in the nonpainful condition (warm). This finding was suggested to reflect a role of these structures in the monitoring and possibly the top-down regulation of autonomic activity that was masked in the pain condition when the predominant ascending noxious signals overshadowed the less important effects associated with sympathetic reactivity. In contrast, a more robust relation with the SCR was observed in the painful condition compared to the notpainful condition in the ACC, amygdala, thalamus, and hypothalamus (and to a lesser extent in SII and the medulla). Thus, the SCR could reflect the spinothalamocortical activity during innocuous thermal stimulations, as well as the activation of brainstem responses including the spinoparabrachial pathway activating the hypothalamus and amygdala in the painful condition. This interpretation is compatible with the role of this pathway in the regulation of arousal and emotional responses evoked by nociceptive inputs and is highly consistent with the central role of the amygdala in aversive leaning involving noxious unconditioned stimuli.

In a separate study, the cerebral responses produced by noxious electrical stimulations evoking an RIII reflex were examined in relation with the SCR. In this case, the analysis aimed at exploring individual differences in activation specifically associated with the SCR, after having controlled for (by covariance) effects explained by the variations in the RIII and in the self-reports of pain. Intraindividual fluctuations in the SCR were correlated with the activation of the insula and the ACC, consistent with a central role of these structures in autonomic monitoring and regulation (see Chapter 3). However, the examination of the interindividual differences in the SCR revealed a very intriguing pattern of cerebral activation. Indeed, the response evoked by the electric stimuli in the orbitofrontal cortex (among others) was slightly negative; more importantly, it was negatively correlated with the interindividual differences in the amplitude of the SCR (i.e., stronger SCRs in subjects showing larger decreases in OFC), while being positively correlated with the interindividual differences in the amplitude of RIII response (i.e., stronger RIII in subjects showing smaller decreases or some increase in OFC). A multiple regression model further demonstrated that the combination of interindividual differences in the motor (RIII) and autonomic (SCR) responses predicted the orbitofrontal activation to the stimulus with a very high level of precision ($R^2 = 0.93$). This unexpected relation certainly deserves a thorough examination in future studies.

These effects may be relevant to the pattern of nociceptive responses observed in mild cognitive impairment and dementia, where an increase in motor reflex responses (RIII) is associated with a reduction in autonomic activation (Kunz, Mylius, Scharmann, Schepelman, & Lautenbacher, 2009; Kunz, Mylius, Schepelmann, & Lautenbacher, 2009). These clinical physiological signs could be explained by prefrontal damage involving orbitofrontal sectors and leading to a motor disinhibition, combined with reduced sympathetic reactivity. These studies clearly illustrate the advantage of considering multiple physiological responses evoked during pain to better detect and interpret the functional role of the various areas activated by noxious stimulations. These responses may be complemented by the assessment of complex behavioral responses.

The Nonverbal Expression of Pain

At a higher level in the hierarchy of noxious and pain-related responses are mechanisms involved in the regulation of the behavioral expression of pain. Among these responses, facial expression constitutes one of the privileged output channels for the communication of pain experiences (Craig et al., 2001; Hadjistavropoulos & Craig, 2002; Williams,

2002). However, this important expressive channel is often neglected in pain research because it is subject to contextual, social, and cultural rules that complicate its interpretation.

We recently examined the spontaneous facial expression of pain in an fMRI study involving acute thermal stimulation. In this study, the intensity of the stimuli was adjusted individually to control for differences in pain sensitivity as reported in the subjective evaluations of the participants, thus enabling us to examine more specifically the cerebral correlates of the facial expression of pain (Kunz, Chen, Lautenbacher, Vachon-Presseau, & Rainville, 2011). In addition to foreseeable activations in the region of the face in the primary motor cortex two important effects were observed.

First, the intraindividual analysis comparison of trials with versus without spontaneous facial responses showed that the occurrence of such an expression reflects a more important activation in several cerebral sites such as the thalamus, SI, SII, insula, and the ACC (see Figure 9.3). A response proportional to the expression of pain was also observed across individuals in SI and the insula (i.e., stronger responses in more expressive participant). Again, these effects were observed even though the subjective reports of pain did not show significant differences between trials with and without expression, or across subjects displaying weak/no or strong facial responses. These observations indicate that the facial expression of pain conveys unique information that is at least partially independent from the subjective report and that these two output response channels of communication reflect at least in part the activation of the cortical targets of the spinothalamic pathways. This finding contributes to the validation of the facial expression for the evaluation of pain (at least in within-subject conditions). However, the absence of facial expression should not be interpreted simply as a reduced sensitivity to pain.

The second important finding in this study relates to the stronger cerebral activations to the painful thermal stimulations in the absence of spontaneous facial expression. Such enhanced brain responses were observed mainly in the prefrontal cortices (including the perigenual ACC) of the less expressive individuals and in the trials without facial expression in the more expressive participants (see Figure 9.3). Moreover, this enhanced prefrontal response was significantly decreased when nonexpressive participants were asked to voluntarily communicate their painful experience by their facial expression. Consistent with classical studies showing lower thresholds for "wincing" and withdrawal responses to acute heat pain stimuli in prefrontal lobotomy patients (Chapman, Rose, & Solomon, 1950), these results suggest that "stoicism" during pain reflects the active suppression of the facial expression by prefrontal cortices.

From a clinical perspective, these results are important because they imply that the spontaneous presence and the magnitude of pain facial expression signal the activation and magnitude of the neurophysiological responses within brain systems involved in the experience of pain. However, the absence of expression in a patient who nevertheless reports an intense pain experience on self-report pain scales likely reflects the inhibition of the facial expressive channel. Reciprocally, the spontaneous and intense facial expression of pain in a patient who is unable to use self-report scales could signal intense pain that is not adequately communicated voluntarily. This is particularly important in populations presenting some limitations in verbal communication and for whom nonverbal expression is obviously an alternative way to assess pain (Hadjistavropoulos, von Baeyer, & Craig, 2001). Recent research further demonstrates that, for comparable levels of self-reports of pain, patients presenting with symptoms of dementia or even mild cognitive impairments may more adequately communicate pain by their facial expression (Hadjistavropoulos, Voyer, Sharpe, Verreault, & Aubin, 2008; Kunz, Scharmann, Hemmeter, Schepelmann, & Lautenbacher, 2007; Kunz et al., 2009). Their facial expressions may reflect a reduced ability to take into account the sociocontextual factors typically leading to the suppression of pain expression. The nonverbal behavioral expression, being free of inhibitory influences, may constitute more direct measurement of activity within the nociceptive-responsive brain systems and thereby constitute a more valid method of pain assessment in these populations.

Conclusion

Understanding the functional roles of the higher order centers of the brain in pain relies primarily on the anatomical and physiological knowledge gained from animal studies on the nociceptive and homeostatic regulatory systems. Research in functional neuroimaging further provides indispensable information about areas implicated in the perception and the modulation of pain in humans. This analysis relates cerebral activation to subjective responses reported by participants on pain-rating scales. This approach is certainly essential to understand the mechanisms underlying pain processes, but it does not provide a comprehensive account of the complexity of nociceptive processes. The analysis of neurophysiological activity underlying nociception and pain must also consider the multiple responses that accompany painful experiences and are not necessarily encoded adequately in subjective responses.

Noxious neurophysiological activation is expressed in various ways at each level of integration of the central nervous system. In this brief review, I highlighted the cerebral activations associated with spinal withdrawal reflexes, the SCR, and the facial expression. Each of these response channels provides information that complements the subjective evaluation of pain and is more strongly associated with the activation of partly distinct subsectors of pain-responsive brain networks. This approach to pain research may contribute to the advancement of emotion research to the extent that pain-related responses can be conceived as emotional responses to direct threats to the integrity of the body. This multivariate approach could also contribute to a better understanding of the interindividual differences in emotion responses and help refine the physiopathological analysis of abnormal pain states and emotional responses across various clinical populations.

Outstanding Questions

- Pain reflects potential injury to the body (i.e., interoceptive signal) and, at least in some circumstances, properties of nociceptive stimuli (i.e., exteroceptive signal). What are the brain mechanisms involved in the interoceptive versus exteroceptive functions associated with pain?
- The brain activation associated with acute pain is very similar to that produced by other salient sensory experiences. Is there a pattern of brain activity specifically associated with pain experiences? What are the distinctive features of pain-related brain responses that make pain experiences unique?
- Although pain is not typically considered an emotion, it does share almost all of its defining features with emotions (with the exception of being necessarily triggered by a somatic inducer with specific sensory qualities). Shared features include behavioral and autonomic responses as well as affective experiential dimensions. How much convergence is there between brain systems involved in pain and emotions?
- Human affective neuroscience in general and neuroimaging studies in particular have largely focused on the conditions that lead to pain and emotion induction. However, pain and emotion are also defined by patterns of responses that reflect the engagement of several neurological subsystems involved in behavioral, autonomic, and hormonal regulation. How does the pattern of brain activity observed during pain and emotion, including the diencephalic and telecephalic components, reflect the complex pattern of responses in these separate output systems?
- Individuals vary greatly in the pattern of responses (e.g., facial expression, self-report, autonomic) they exhibit during pain and emotion. How does this variability reflect differences in brain activity, and how are those differences related to biopsychosocial factors ranging from genetic predispositions to cultural context?

Acknowledgments

This research is funded mainly by the "Fonds de la recherche en santé du Québec," the Canadian Institutes of Health Research (CIHR), and the Natural Science and Engineering Council of Canada (NSERC).

Notes

1   Note that coordinate-based meta-analyses are vulnerable to report biases where a priori hypotheses (including valid ones) often guide the search and report of activation peaks using lower statistical threshold. This increases the probability of reporting an activation peak and leads to higher activation likelihood estimates in target areas. This is not to say that these estimates do not reflect true activation but simply emphasizes that areas outside these target sites are less likely to be reported, given the weakest a priori hypotheses for these additional areas and the corresponding more stringent activation threshold used to detect these responses.
2   Note nevertheless that this is not incompatible with a neuro-functional specificity of pain processes at the level of the neural networks within each area, as acknowledged by Legrain et al. (2011).

References

Albanese, M. C., Duerden, E. G., Rainville, P., & Duncan, G. H. (2007). Memory traces of pain in human cortex. *Journal of Neuroscience*, 27, 4612–20.

Apkarian, A. V., Bushnell, M. C., Treede, R. D., & Zubieta, J. K. (2005). Human brain mechanisms of pain perception and regulation in health and disease. *European Journal of Pain*, 9, 463–84.

Augustine, J. R. (1996). Circuitry and functional aspects of the insular lobe in primates including humans. *Brain Research: Brain Research Reviews*, 22, 229–44.

Baliki, M. N., Geha, P. Y., & Apkarian, A. V. (2009). Parsing pain perception between nociceptive representation and magnitude estimation. *Journal of Neurophysiology*, 101, 875–87.

Bandler, R., & Shipley, M. T. (1994). Columnar organization in the midbrain periaqueductal gray: Modules for emotional expression? *Trends in Neuroscience*, 17, 379–89.

Bechara, A. (2004). The role of emotion in decision-making: Evidence from neurological patients with orbitofrontal damage. *Brain and Cognition*, 55, 30–40.

Bechara, A., Damasio, H., Tranel, D., & Damasio, A. R. (1997). Deciding advantageously before knowing the advantageous strategy. *Science*, 275, 1293–95.

Bernard, J. F., Bester, H., & Besson, J. M. (1996). Involvement of the spinoparabrachio amygdaloid and hypothalamic pathways in the autonomic and affective emotional aspects of pain. *Progress in Brain Research*, 107, 243–55.

Bernard, J. F. & Villanueva, L. (2009). Architecture fonctionnelle des systèmes nociceptifs. In D. Bouhassira & B. Calvino (Eds.), *Douleurs: Physiologie, physiopathologie et pharmacologie* (pp. 1–29). Paris: Arnette.

Bingel, U., Lorenz, J., Schoell, E., Weiller, C., & Buchel, C. (2006). Mechanisms of placebo analgesia: rACC recruitment of a subcortical antinociceptive network. *Pain*, 120, 8–15.

Bornhövd, K., Quante, M., Glauche, V., Bromm, B., Weiller, C., & Büchel, C. (2002). Painful stimuli evoke different stimulus-response functions in the amygdala, prefrontal, insula and somatosensory cortex: A single-trial fMRI study. *Brain*, 125, 1326–36.

Bourgeais, L., Monconduit, L., Villanueva, L., & Bernard, J. F. (2001). Parabrachial internal lateral neurons convey nociceptive messages from the deep laminas of the dorsal horn to the intralaminar thalamus. *Journal of Neuroscience*, 21, 2159–65.

Büchel, C., Bornhovd, K., Quante, M., Glauche, V., Bromm, B., & Weiller, C. (2002). Dissociable neural responses related to pain intensity, stimulus intensity, and stimulus awareness within the anterior cingulate cortex: A parametric single-trial laser functional magnetic resonance imaging study. *Journal of Neuroscience*, 22, 970–76.

Chapman, W. P., Rose, A. S., & Solomon, H. C. (1950). A follow-up study of motor withdrawal reaction to heat discomfort in patients before and after frontal lobotomy. *American Journal of Psychiatry*, 107, 221–24.

Coghill, R. C., McHaffie, J. G., & Yen, Y. F. (2003). Neural correlates of interindividual differences in the subjective experience of pain. *Proceedings of the National Academy of Sciences*, 100, 8538–42.

Coghill, R. C., Sang, C. N., Maisog, J. M., & Iadarola, M. J. (1999). Pain intensity processing within the human brain: A bilateral, distributed mechanism. *Journal of Neurophysiology*, 82, 1934–43.

Craig, A. D. (2002). How do you feel? Interoception: The sense of the physiological condition of the body. *Nature Reviews Neuroscience*, 3, 655–66.

Craig, A. D. (2003). A new view of pain as a homeostatic emotion. *Trends in Neuroscience*, 26, 303–7.

Craig, A. D. (2009). How do you feel – now? The anterior insula and human awareness. *Nature Reviews Neuroscience*, 10, 59–70.

Craig, K. D., Prkachin, K. M., & Grunau, R. V. E. (2001). The facial expression of pain. In D. C. Turk & R. Melzack (Eds.), *Handbook of pain assessment* (2nd ed., pp. 153–69). New York: Guilford Press.

Damasio, A. R. (1994). *Descartes' error: Emotion, reason and the human brain*. New York: Avon Books.

Damasio, A. R. (1996). The somatic marker hypothesis and the possible functions of the prefrontal cortex. *Philosophical Transactions of the Royal Society of London Series B: Biological Sciences*, 351, 1413–20.

Damasio, A. R. (1999). *The feeling of what happens: Body and emotion in the making of consciousness*. New York: Hartcourt Brace.

Derbyshire, S. W., Jones, A. K., Gyulai, F., Clark, S., Townsend, D., & Firestone, L. L. (1997). Pain processing during three levels of noxious stimulation produces differential patterns of central activity. *Pain*, 73, 431–45.

Dostrovsky, J. O., & Craig, A. D. (2006). Ascending projection systems. In S. B. McMahon &

M. Koltzenburg (Eds.), *Textbook of pain of Wall and Melzack* (5th ed., pp. 187–203). London: Elsevier Science.

Downar, J., Crawley, A. P., Mikulis, D. J., & Davis, K. D. (2000). A multimodal cortical network for the detection of changes in the sensory environment. *Nature Neuroscience, 3,* 277–83.

Dube, A. A., Duquette, M., Roy, M., Lepore, F., Duncan, G., & Rainville, P. (2009). Brain activity associated with the electrodermal reactivity to acute heat pain. *Neuroimage, 45,* 169–80.

Duerden, E. G., Fu, J. M., Rainville, P., & Duncan, G. H. (2008). *Activation likelihood estimation map of pain-evoked functional brain imaging data in healthy subjects: A meta-analysis.* Paper presented at the 12th International Association for the Study of Pain (IASP) World Congress, Glasgow.

Dum, R. P., Levinthal, D. J., & Strick, P. L. (2009). The spinothalamic system targets motor and sensory areas in the cerebral cortex of monkeys. *Journal of Neuroscience, 29,* 14223–35.

Duquette, M., Roy, M., Lepore, F., Peretz, I., & Rainville, P. (2007). [Cerebral mechanisms involved in the interaction between pain and emotion]. *Revue Neurologique (Paris), 163,* 169–79.

Faymonville, M. E., Roediger, L., Del Fiore, G., Delgueldre, C., Phillips, C., Lamy, M., et al. (2003). Increased cerebral functional connectivity underlying the antinociceptive effects of hypnosis. *Brain Research: Cognitive Brain Research, 17,* 255–62.

Fillingim, R. B., Maixner, W., Bunting, S., & Silva, S. (1998). Resting blood pressure and thermal pain responses among females: Effects on pain unpleasantness but not pain intensity. *International Journal of Psychophysiology, 30,* 313–18.

Frankenstein, U. N., Richter, W., McIntyre, M. C., & Remy, F. (2001). Distraction modulates anterior cingulate gyrus activations during the cold pressor test. *Neuroimage., 14,* 827–36.

Gabriel, M. (1993). Discriminative avoidance learning: A model system. In B. A. Vogt & M. Gabriel (Eds.), *Neurobiology of cingulate cortex and limbic thalamus: A comprehensive handbook* (pp. 479–523). Boston: Birkhäuser.

Hadjistavropoulos, T., & Craig, K. D. (2002). A theoretical framework for understanding self-report and observational measures of pain: A communications model. *Behaviour Research and Therapy, 40,* 551–70.

Hadjistavropoulos, T., von Baeyer, C., & Craig, K. D. (2001). Pain assessment in persons with limited ability to communicate. In D. C. Turk & R. Melzack (Eds.), *Handbook of pain assessment* (2nd ed., pp. 134–49). New York: Guilford.

Hadjistavropoulos, T., Voyer, P., Sharpe, D., Verreault, R., & Aubin, M. (2008). Assessing pain in dementia patients with comorbid delirium and depression. *Pain Management in Nursing, 9,* 48–54.

Hofbauer, R. K., Rainville, P., Duncan, G. H., & Bushnell, M. C. (2001). Cortical representation of the sensory dimension of pain. *Journal of Neurophysiology, 86,* 402–11.

Izard, C. E. (1993). Four systems for emotion activation: Cognitive and noncognitive processes. *Psychological Review, 100,* 68–90.

James, W. (1994). The physical bases of emotion: 1894. *Psychological Review, 101,* 205–10.

Ji, G., Sun, H., Fu, Y., Li, Z., Pais-Vieira, M., Galhardo, V., et al. (2010). Cognitive impairment in pain through amygdala-driven prefrontal cortical deactivation. *Journal of Neuroscience, 30,* 5451–64.

Kenshalo, D. R., Iwata, K., Sholas, M., & Thomas, D. A. (2000). Response properties and organization of nociceptive neurons in area 1 of monkey primary somatosensory cortex. *Journal of Neurophysiology, 84,* 719–29.

Kunz, M., Chen, J. I., Lautenbacher, S., Vachon-Presseau, E., & Rainville, P. (2011). Cerebral regulation of facial expressions of pain. *Journal of Neuroscience, 31,* 8730–38.

Kunz, M., Mylius, V., Scharmann, S., Schepelman, K., & Lautenbacher, S. (2009). Influence of dementia on multiple components of pain. *European Journal of Pain, 13,* 317–25.

Kunz, M., Mylius, V., Schepelmann, K., & Lautenbacher, S. (2009). Effects of age and mild cognitive impairment on the pain response system. *Gerontology, 55*(6), 674–82.

Kunz, M., Scharmann, S., Hemmeter, U., Schepelmann, K., & Lautenbacher, S. (2007). The facial expression of pain in patients with dementia. *Pain, 133,* 221–28.

LeDoux, J. (2007). The amygdala. *Current Biology, 17,* R868–R874.

Legrain, V., Iannetti, G. D., Plaghki, L., & Mouraux, A. (2011). The pain matrix reloaded: A salience detection system for the body. *Progress in Neurobiology, 93,* 111–24.

Melzack, R. (1990). Phantom limbs and the concept of a neuromatrix. *Trends in Neurosciences, 13,* 88–92.

Melzack, R., & Casey, K. L. (1968). Sensory, motivational, and central control determinants of pain: A new conceptual model. In D. Kenshalo (Ed.), *The skin senses* (pp. 423–443). Springfield, IL: Thomas.

Melzack, R., & Wall, P. D. (1965). Pain mechanisms: A new theory. *Science, 150,* 971–78.

Merskey, H., & Spear, F. G. (1967). The concept of pain. *Journal of Psychosomatic Research, 11,* 59–67.

Metzinger, T. (2000). The subjectivity of subjective experience: A representationalist analysis of the first-person perspective. In T. Metzinger (Ed.), *Neural correlates of consciousness: Empirical and conceptual questions* (pp. 285–306). Cambridge, MA: MIT Press.

Monconduit, L., Bourgeais, L., Bernard, J. F., Le Bars, D., & Villanueva, L. (1999). Ventromedial thalamic neurons convey nociceptive signals from the whole body surface to the dorsolateral neocortex. *Journal of Neuroscience, 19,* 9063–72.

Piché, M., Arsenault, M., & Rainville, P. (2010). Dissection of perceptual, motor and autonomic components of brain activity evoked by noxious stimulation. *Pain, 149,* 453–62.

Ploner, M., Freund, H. J., & Schnitzler, A. (1999). Pain affect without pain sensation in a patient with a postcentral lesion. *Pain, 81,* 211–14.

Plutchik, R. (1980). A general psychoevolutionary theory of emotion. In R. Plutchik & H. Kellerman (Eds.), *Emotion: Theory, research, and experience: Vol. 1. Theories of emotion* (pp. 3–33). New York: Academic Press.

Porro, C. A., Cettolo, V., Francescato, M. P., & Baraldi, P. (1998). Temporal and intensity coding of pain in human cortex. *Journal of Neurophysiology, 80,* 3312–20.

Price, D. D. (1999). *Psychological mechanisms of pain and analgesia.* Seattle, WA: IASP Press.

Price, D. D., & Barrell, J. J. (1984). Some general laws of human emotion: Interrelationships between intensities of desire, expectation, and emotional feeling. *Journal of Personality, 52,* 389–409.

Price, D. D., Barrell, J. J., & Gracely, R. H. (1980). A psychophysical analysis of experimental factors that selectively influence the affective dimension of pain. *Pain, 8,* 137–49.

Rainville, P. (2004). Pain and emotions. In D. D. Price & M. C. Bushnell (Eds.), *Psychological methods of pain control: Basic science and clinical perspectives* (pp. 117–41). Seattle WA: IASP Press.

Rainville, P., Bao, Q. V., & Chretien, P. (2005). Pain-related emotions modulate experimental pain perception and autonomic responses. *Pain, 118,* 306–18.

Rainville, P., Carrier, B., Hofbauer, R. K., Bushnell, M. C., & Duncan, G. H. (1999). Dissociation of pain sensory and affective dimensions using hypnotic modulation. *Pain, 82,* 159–71.

Rainville, P., Duncan, G. H., Price, D. D., Carrier, B., & Bushnell, M. C. (1997). Pain affect encoded in human anterior cingulate but not somatosensory cortex. *Science, 277,* 968–71.

Rainville, P., Hofbauer, R. K., Paus, T., Duncan, G. H., Bushnell, M. C., & Price, D. D. (1999). Cerebral mechanisms of hypnotic induction and suggestion. *Journal of Cognitive Neuroscience, 11,* 110–25.

Rhudy, J. L., Williams, A. E., McCabe, K. M., Nguyen, M. A., & Rambo, P. (2005). Affective modulation of nociception at spinal and supraspinal levels. *Psychophysiology, 42,* 579–87.

Ridderinkhof, K. R., Ullsperger, M., Crone, E. A., & Nieuwenhuiss, S. (2004). The role of the medial frontal cortex in cognitive control. *Science, 306,* 443–47.

Roy, M., Piche, M., Chen, J. I., Peretz, I., & Rainville, P. (2009). Cerebral and spinal modulation of pain by emotions. *Proceedings of the National Academy of Sciences, 106*(49), 20900–5.

Sah, P., Faber, E. S., Lopez de, A. M., & Power, J. (2003). The amygdaloid complex: Anatomy and physiology. *Physiology Review, 83,* 803–34.

Sandrini, G., Serrao, M., Rossi, P., Romaniello, A., Cruccu, G., & Willer, J. C. (2005). The lower limb flexion reflex in humans. *Progress in Neurobiology, 77,* 353–95.

Sato, A., Sato, Y., & Schmidt, R. F. (1997). The impact of somatosensoty input on autonomic functions. In M. P. Blaustein, H. Grunicke, D. P. Konstanz, G. Schultz, & M. Schweiger (Eds.), *Reviews of physiology biochemistry and pharmacology* (pp. 1–310). Berlin: Springer-Verlag.

Shackman, A. J., Salomons, T. V., Slagter, H. A., Fox, A. S., Winter, J. J., & Davidson, R. J. (2011). The integration of negative affect, pain and cognitive control in the cingulate cortex. *Nature Reviews Neuroscience, 12,* 154–67.

Shyu, B. C., Sikes, R. W., Vogt, L. J., & Vogt, B. A. (2010). Nociceptive processing by anterior cingulate pyramidal neurons. *Journal of Neurophysiology, 103,* 3287–3301.

Simon, D., Craig, K. D., Gosselin, F., Belin, P., & Rainville, P. (2008). Recognition and discrimination of prototypical dynamic expressions of pain and emotions. *Pain, 135,* 55–64.

Tracey, I., & Mantyh, P. W. (2007). The cerebral signature for pain perception and its modulation. *Neuron, 55,* 377–91.

Treede, R. D., Kenshalo, D. R., Gracely, R. H., & Jones, A. K. P. (1999). The cortical representation of pain. *Pain, 79,* 105–11.

Valet, M., Sprenger, T., Boecker, H., Willoch, F., Rummeny, E., Conrad, B., et al. (2004). Distraction modulates connectivity of the cingulo-frontal cortex and the midbrain during pain–an fMRI analysis. *Pain, 109,* 399–408.

Villanueva, L., & Bourgeais, L. (2009). Systèmes de modulation de la douleur. In D. Bouhassira & B. Calvino (Eds.), *Douleurs: Physiologie, physiopathologie et pharmacologie* (pp. 30–45). Paris: Arnette.

Villanueva, L., & Fields, H. L. (2004). Endogenous central mechanisms of pain modulation. In L. Villanueva, A. Dickenson, & H. Ollat (Eds.), *The pain system in normal and pathological states: A primer for clinicians.* Vol. 31: *Progress in pain research and management* Seattle: IASP Press.

Villemure, C., Slotnick, B. M., & Bushnell, M. C. (2003). Effects of odors on pain perception: Deciphering the roles of emotion and attention. *Pain, 106,* 101–8.

Vogt, B. A. (2005). Pain and emotion interactions in subregions of the cingulate gyrus. *Nature Reviews Neuroscience, 6,* 533–44.

Wager, T. D., Rilling, J. K., Smith, E. E., Sokolik, A., Casey, K. L., Davidson, R. J., et al. (2004). Placebo-induced changes in FMRI in the anticipation and experience of pain. *Science, 303,* 1162–67.

Watson, A., El-Deredy, W., Iannetti, G. D., Lloyd, D., Tracey, I., Vogt, B. A., et al. (2009). Placebo conditioning and placebo analgesia modulate a common brain network during pain anticipation and perception. *Pain, 145,* 24–30.

Williams, A. C. (2002). Facial expression of pain: An evolutionary account. *Behavioral Brain Science, 25,* 439–55.

Willis, W. D., Al-Chaer, E. D., Quast, M. J., & Westlund, K. N. (1999). A visceral pain pathway in the dorsal column of the spinal cord. *Proceedings of the National Academy of Sciences, 96,* 7675–79.

Willis, W. D., & Westlund, K. N. (1997). Neuroanatomy of the pain system and of the pathways that modulate pain. [Review] *Journal of Clinical Neurophysiology, 14,* 2–31.

CHAPTER 10

Examining Emotion Perception and Elicitation via Olfaction

Aprajita Mohanty & Jay A. Gottfried

*Madhavika parimala lalite naba malati
jati sugandhau
Munimanasampi mohanakarini taruna
karana bandhau*

The strong scent of the flowers *Madhavi,
Malati and Jati*
pervade the air, enchanting, even the
meditating
hermits (*Munis*), who feel again the
passion of intimate
bonds of youth, which they had
abandoned
–from Gitagovinda, 12th-century
Sanskrit poetry by Jayadeva

Historically, odors have been recognized for their power to evoke strong emotional reactions. This view is well substantiated in the scientific literature, showing that odor perception is commonly associated both with emotional reactions measured at the verbal (Berglund, Berglund, Engen, & Ekman, 1973; Schiffman, 1974), behavioral (Bensafi et al., 2003), and physiological levels (Bensafi et al., 2002a) and with more long-lasting changes in mood (Schiffman & Miller, 1995). In contrast to vision, audition, and somesthesia, which involve early cortical processing in sensory unimodal brain areas, chemosensory processing initially occurs in limbic and paralimbic heteromodal regions that are heavily implicated in emotional processing (Carmichael, Clugnet, & Price, 1994; Gottfried, 2006). Indeed, many of these centers function as a key hub linking smells, tastes, emotions, and behavior. Nonetheless, despite the demonstration of strong perceptual and anatomical links between emotion and olfaction, the visuo-centric perspective of human sensory experience has long dominated the field of affective psychology and neuroscience – as evidenced by the overwhelming reliance on visual stimuli such as the International Affective Picture System (Lang, Bradley, & Cuthbert, 2008) and the Ekman and Friesen series of Pictures of Facial Affect (Ekman & Friesen, 1976) – with the general effect of crowding out olfactory-based models of emotional processing.

One bias that may have contributed to the under-utilization of olfactory stimuli in affective neuroscience research is that humans are assumed to have a bad sense of smell. Genetic evidence showing a decline in the number of functional olfactory receptor genes in the course of evolution from mice to humans certainly supports this viewpoint (Shepherd, 2004). Yet, contradictory behavioral evidence suggests that humans have a surprisingly good sense of smell despite their reduced receptor gene repertoire. For example, ethyl mercaptan, an odorant that is often added to alert the presence of odorless propane gas, can be detected at concentrations as low as 0.2 parts per billion (Yeshurun & Sobel, 2010). A series of studies by Laska and colleagues show that not only can humans detect minuscule quantities of odor but they can also tell apart one odorant from another, based on molecular identity or concentration. Humans can discriminate aliphatic odorants equal in number of carbons but differing in functional group, odorants differing in chain length by one carbon, and odors of enantiomer (mirror-image) molecules like (+) and (−) carvone (Laska & Seibt, 2002). Furthermore, humans can detect certain odorants with better acuity than can rats (Laska & Seibt, 2002) and have the ability to track scents and roughly mimic the tracking patterns of dogs (Porter et al., 2007). In fact, contrary to popular opinion, human olfactory discrimination ability is in the same range as vision and audition (Mueller, 1951). Hence, by virtue of its acuity in humans, its ability to evoke strong emotional reactions, and its intrinsic overlap with the limbic emotional system, the olfactory modality provides a unique window into emotional processing.

In recent years, the development of sophisticated imaging technologies has significantly advanced our understanding of both human olfactory perception and affective neuroscience. This chapter focuses on olfactory hedonic perception and through this focus highlights mechanisms of basic emotional processing as well as more complex aspects such as emotion-cognition interactions. It describes how an examination of limbic brain areas involved in odor perception has resulted in considerable progress in delineating the neural mech-

anisms that support different aspects of emotion coding and emotion-related learning in the amygdala, orbitofrontal cortex, and olfactory cortices. Another important emphasis of the chapter is on the malleability of olfactory hedonic perception. By highlighting this aspect of olfactory perception, we can delineate the psychological and neural mechanisms of contextual modulation and plasticity of emotional processing. Finally, we discuss odor memory as an example of how olfactory research has brought new insights into mechanisms of emotion-cognition interactions. This chapter begins with a discussion of basic properties of olfactory perception to illustrate how the anatomy and function of olfaction and emotion are closely intertwined.

What Constitutes an Olfactory Stimulus?

Brains have evolved to perceive sensory events that hold behavioral relevance. The sensory events that are relevant to one species may entirely differ from those relevant to another species, but for each and every creature its sensory perceptual repertoire is constrained by the natural real-world form of the sensory stimulus. This holds for all sensory systems. In the case of an odor stimulus, a defining characteristic is its multimolecular complexity. For example, the odor of chocolate contains many hundreds of volatile organic compounds, yet the olfactory system seamlessly integrates these disparate elements into a perceptual whole, resulting in configural, rather than elemental odor perception (Gottfried, 2006). This stimulus composite of different odorous molecules comprises an odor object. Thus, just as humans perceive the visual object "chocolate," a synthetic percept fabricated out of many component features, they also perceive the odor object "chocolate" (Gottfried, 2010).

Odor objects possess many of the same properties described for visual objects (Gottfried, 2010). For example, when walking into a bakery, our olfactory system is capable of filtering out the irrelevant (background) smells so that the chocolate odor stands out as an object. This property, known as figure–ground segmentation, is evident in visual and auditory object perception, and its principles equally apply to odor object perception (Linster, Henry, Kadohisa, & Wilson, 2007). Moreover, although the aroma of freshly baked chocolate brownies is different from the scent of chocolate liqueur, we are able to retain the "objectness" of chocolate, a perceptual property referred to as object constancy. Extraction of perceptual sameness across different stimuli, or object categorization, is an important aspect of object constancy and is balanced by the ability to discriminate among individual objects (for example, white versus dark chocolate). Both odor categorization and odor discrimination are well-established properties of olfactory perception in the human brain (Howard, Plailly, Grueschow, Haynes, & Gottfried, 2009; Li, Luxenberg, Parrish, & Gottfried, 2006). In summary, although the visual and olfactory systems have evolved under different ecological constraints, the basic principles underlying visual object perception are also applicable to olfactory object perception. Like the visual or auditory system, the olfactory system is optimized to detect and encode behaviorally salient events (objects) that are encountered in the real world. However, compared to visual or auditory objects, an overwhelming majority of odor objects tend to be salient by virtue of their association to appetitive or aversive consequences.

Anatomy of Olfaction: A Direct Pathway to Emotion

Olfaction in mammals starts with a sniff. This simple motor action primes the olfactory system for the arrival of odors (Sobel et al., 1998) and physically transports odorant molecules to the nose. Binding of an odorant to the receptors of olfactory sensory neurons in the nasal epithelium initiates the process of signal transduction. Neural information is relayed through the axons of the olfactory sensory neurons (i.e., olfac-

tory nerve) that synapse onto the dendritic endings of mitral and tufted cells within spheroid units called glomeruli located in the olfactory bulb. Each olfactory sensory neuron innervates just one or two glomeruli, and each glomerulus is innervated by sensory neurons expressing the same type of receptor (Firestein, 2001). Thus, this processing stage facilitates a powerful convergence of input from same-type receptors. Patterns of activity within the olfactory bulb grossly reflect discrimination of one odorant from another, although a finer scale chemotypic organization has not been well established (Gottfried, 2010). Olfactory information is then conveyed via axonal projections from the mitral and tufted cells that form the lateral olfactory tract, terminating in several areas in the basal frontal and medial temporal lobes, including the anterior olfactory nucleus, olfactory tubercle, anterior and posterior piriform cortices, medial and cortical nuclei of the amygdala, and rostral entorhinal cortex (Figure 10.1). These areas are sometimes collectively referred to as the "primary olfactory cortex." It is assumed that here olfactory categorical information is represented in the form of odor objects (Gottfried, 2010). Higher order projections arising from these olfactory structures relay to the orbitofrontal cortex, agranular insula, other amygdala subnuclei, thalamus, hypothalamus, basal ganglia, and hippocampus (Carmichael et al., 1994). This complex network of connections provides the basis for odor-guided modulation of behavior, feeding, emotion, autonomic states, and memory. In addition, each region of the primary olfactory cortex (apart from the olfactory tubercle) sends dense feedback projections to the olfactory bulb (Gottfried, 2006) through which central or "top-down" modulation of olfactory information processing can occur as early as the second-order neurons.

Piriform Cortex

The piriform cortex, named for its pear-shaped structure, is a three-layer paleocortex that lies at the medial junction of the

(a)

(b)

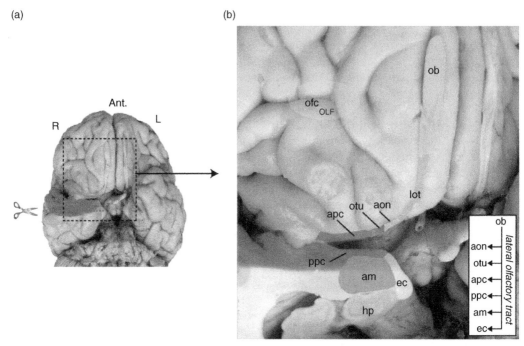

Figure 10.1. Anatomy of the human olfactory brain. (a) A ventral view of the human brain in which the right anterior temporal lobe has been resected in the coronal plane to expose the limbic olfactory areas depicted in panel (b). Afferent output from the olfactory bulb (OB) passes through the lateral olfactory tract (LOT) and projects monosynaptically to numerous regions, including the anterior olfactory nucleus (AON), olfactory tubercle (OTUB), anterior piriform cortex (APC), posterior piriform cortex (PPC), amygdala (AM), and entorhinal cortex (EC). Downstream relays include the hippocampus (HP) and the putative olfactory projection site in the human orbitofrontal cortex (OFColf). As noted in the inset, information is not transferred serially through this circuit. Monosynaptic projections from the lateral olfactory tract reach numerous downstream regions in parallel, and these regions are then reciprocally interconnected (not shown). Adapted from Gottfried (2010). See color plate 10.1.

frontal and temporal lobes. It is the largest recipient of projections from the olfactory bulb. In contrast to the coarse chemotypic modular spatial architecture in the olfactory bulb, the piriform cortex shows a more distributed pattern of connectivity (Stettler & Axel, 2009). It is reciprocally and extensively connected with several high-order areas of the cerebral cortex, including the prefrontal, amygdaloid, perirhinal, and entorhinal cortices (Carmichael et al., 1994; Gottfried, 2006). Some piriform neurons project to more than one of these areas, and neighboring piriform cells can have highly dissimilar projection targets. This widely distributed pattern of connectivity, with direct links to brain regions that mediate cognition, emotion, memory, and behavior, suggests

that the piriform cortex functions as a sensory association cortex where representations of individual components are assembled into holistic odor objects (Gottfried, 2010; Howard et al., 2009).

Amygdala

Projections from the olfactory bulb terminate in several discrete subnuclei situated in the dorsomedial margin of the amygdala, including the periamygdaloid region, anterior and posterior cortical nuclei, the nucleus of the lateral olfactory tract, and the medial nucleus (Carmichael et al., 1994). The olfactory amygdala is continuous rostrally with the piriform cortex, and in addition to sending projections back to the bulb, it provides direct input to other portions of the amygdala, including lateral, basolateral, and central amygdaloid nuclei (Pitkänen, 2000), as well as to the basal ganglia, thalamus, hypothalamus, and prefrontal cortex. In fact, olfaction is the only sensory modality possessing direct bidirectional projections between the amygdala and primary sensory cortex. Not surprisingly, during inhalation of odorants, the medial amygdala shows increased firing rates measured electrophysiologically in conscious monkeys and humans, and odor stimulation induces both evoked potentials and oscillatory activity in the human amygdala (Gottfried, 2006).

Orbitofrontal Cortex

The orbitofrontal cortex (OFC) is the main neocortical projection of the olfactory cortex. The OFC is located along the basal surface of the caudal frontal lobes. It receives direct afferent input (without thalamic relay) from the primary olfactory areas, including the piriform cortex, amygdala, and entorhinal cortex. In turn, the OFC provides direct feedback projections to each of these regions. Physiological (Tanabe, Iino, & Takagi, 1975) and anatomical (Carmichael et al., 1994) data in monkeys suggest that, within the OFC, it is the posterior orbital cortex in areas Iam, Iapm, and 13a that receives maximum input from the olfactory areas. However, a meta-analysis of human neuroimaging studies indicates that the secondary olfactory areas in OFC appear to be located more rostral (near area 11l) than the corresponding sites in monkeys (Gottfried & Zald, 2005). Finally, it is important to note that adjacent, non-overlapping regions of the OFC receive sensory input from gustatory and visual centers, as well as information about visceral states, providing a neural substrate for associative learning and cross-modal integration (Rolls, 2004) that supports feeding and odor-related behaviors.

Unique Features

The central organization of the olfactory system has several unique anatomical features that distinguish it from other sensory modalities. In contrast to the visual and olfactory modalities, odor processing remains ipsilateral from the nasal periphery all the way to the primary olfactory cortex. Also unlike visual and auditory modalities, transmission of olfactory information to central brain regions, including the primary olfactory cortex and neocortical (prefrontal) areas, is achieved without thalamic modulation. For example, monosynaptic projections from the piriform cortex to the OFC (Carmichael et al., 1994) ensure that odor information has access to the neocortex without first passing through the thalamus. The absence of a thalamic node in the processing hierarchy may help preserve the fidelity of the original olfactory percept in the context of unpredictable shifts in stimulus concentration, background smells, and respiratory patterns. Finally, as noted earlier, there is substantial anatomical overlap between the structures involved in olfactory processing and those devoted more generally to emotional processing. The manifestation of this anatomical overlap is evident in the role odorous stimuli play in motivating almost every aspect of animal behavior, including maternal bonding, kinship recognition, food search, mate selection, predator avoidance, and territorial marking.

Does Olfaction Function via Emotion?

Based on a review of the human olfaction literature, Stevenson has classified olfactory functions into three major categories relating to (1) ingestive behavior, (2) avoidance of environmental hazards, and (3) social communication (Stevenson, 2010). All three functions are inextricably linked with emotional evaluation, emphasizing the strong link between olfaction and emotion.

With regard to ingestive behavior, smell plays a very important role in the perception of flavor and the formation of cognitive and emotional responses to foods. Olfaction is described as having a unique "dual nature" (Rozin, 1982), because it involves sensing externally (orthonasal) and internally (retronasal) originating signals. Orthonasal stimulation involves sniffing odors in the outside environment through the external nares of the nose and is useful in identifying a food's suitability for ingestion. Retronasal stimulation occurs during food ingestion, when volatile odorous molecules released from the food in the mouth are channeled from the back of the oral cavity up through the nasopharynx to the olfactory epithelium. This retronasal food molecule-laden air is what imparts "flavor" to the food (Shepherd, 2006). Retronasal stimulation is important in regulating food intake via changes in hedonic responsiveness to flavors in a state-specific manner. An example of these regulatory effects in the Stevenson (2010) review includes the "appetizer effect," when brief exposure to a palatable food makes participants hungrier, resulting in greater subsequent consumption of the food. Another regulatory effect that involves a strong affective component is that of sensory-specific satiety. Hedonic ratings of the odor of a food eaten to satiety, relative to a control (uneaten) food odor, show significant negative shifts changing from like at the start to dislike at the end of a meal (Rolls & Rolls, 1997), and human imaging studies have consistently revealed parallel changes in the magnitude of activation in the orbitofrontal cortex (Gottfried, O'Doherty, & Dolan, 2003).

Detection of olfactory signals that indicate danger is very well developed in humans. This is evidenced by their impressive ability to detect minute amounts of volatile agents that signal the presence of odorless airborne hazards or by their ability to detect and avoid sources that emit chemicals resulting from the biological decay process (Stevenson, 2010). Stevenson divided chemical hazard signals into two functional categories, each associated with a different emotion – nonmicrobial hazards (e.g., predators, fire, degraded air, and poisons), which are typically associated with a fear response, and microbial threats (e.g., feces, vomit, bodily odors and organic decay), which are associated with disgust. Microbial threats signal the presence of pathogens, and exposure to disgust-eliciting odors may help in priming the immune system for a potential microbial attack. In animals and humans, odors have been shown to function as conditioned cues that stimulate or suppress immune responses (see Stevenson, 2010, for a review). The facial-motor response elicited by disgusting odors, including drawing in the nostrils, constricting the nostril airway diameter, and pinching together the lips, all serve to minimize any further entry of potential toxins into the oronasal cavity (Susskind & Anderson, 2008). The insula appears to play an important role in processing disgust as evidenced by increased insular activation after inhaling disgust-eliciting odors (Royet, Plailly, Delon-Martin, Kareken, & Segebarth, 2003; Zald & Pardo, 1997).

In Salman Rushdie's novel *Midnight's Children* (Rushdie, 1981), the main protagonist Saleem inherits an acute sense of smell that enables him to detect other people's emotions such as "the acrid stench of his mother's embarrassment" (p. 20), "the whiff of things concealed mingling with the odours of burgeoning romance and the sharp stink of my grandmother's curiosity and strength" (p. 52), and "the heady but quick-fading perfume of new love, and also the deeper, longer lasting pungency of hate" (p. 298). In contrast to this fictional account, the scientific evidence for the social communication function of odors in humans remains debatable. The role of pheromones as a means of interspecies communication in invertebrates is well established; however, the existence of pheromonal communication among mammals, especially human mammals, is not well substantiated in the scientific literature (Doty, 2010). The emotional and behavioral effects of androstadienone and estratetraenol, putative human pheromones found in sweat and saliva, are well studied. Administration of these steroids has been shown to result in greater distraction from emotional information on attention tasks and increased sympathetic arousal and reports of positive mood in women and decreased positive mood in men (Hummer & McClintock, 2009; Jacob,

Hayreh, & McClintock, 2001). Functional imaging findings have shown that the physiological effects of androstadienone, such as increased hypothalamic activation, tended to differ not only by biological sex but also by sexual orientation (Berglund, Lindstrom, & Savic, 2006). In addition to being sex-dependent, the steroid effects on emotions were found to be context-dependent, occurring only in women in the presence of a male experimenter (Jacob et al., 2001). Overall, however, the findings from these putative human pheromone studies have been somewhat unreliable. A general tentative conclusion that can be inferred from these data is that the putative human pheromones function as "chemosignals" that *modulate* rather than trigger or release stereotyped behaviors and emotions (Jacob et al., 2001).

Chen and colleagues have examined these "chemosignals" in several studies investigating whether human body odors can signal information indicative of the emotional state of the source and whether this information can then influence the emotional or cognitive state of the receiver. In one study, underarm sweat samples were collected from volunteers viewing excerpts of a funny or frightening movie, and then presented to another group of participants, along with a control (no sweat) condition (Chen & Haviland-Jones, 2000). Results showed that women were able to identify the emotion-related body odors more accurately than men. Furthermore, it has been argued that these emotion-related chemosignals transmitted via body odors of donors act on behavior and cognition of receivers in a manner that is consistent with their inherent emotional content. For example, fear or anxiety-related chemosignals augmented the startle reflex, decreased the bias in judging neutral emotional faces as being happy, and increased cautiousness – resulting in women performing more accurately on a word-association task and reacting more slowly to ambiguous word pairs; these chemosignals also biased women toward interpreting ambiguous expressions as more fearful (Zhou & Chen, 2009) and elicited greater amygdala activation during

fear-odor compared to neutral-odor conditions (Mujica-Parodi et al., 2009).

In summary, olfactory stimuli are unique in that three of their key behavioral functions involve some sort of emotional response followed by either approach or avoidance of the stimulus. Keeping in mind the function of emotions – to alter physiological, behavioral, and cognitive states that prepare us to deal with environmental events by either directing us toward or away from them (Levenson 1994) – olfactory stimuli provide an excellent tool for examining emotional processing and the neural mechanisms that implement it.

Neural Correlates of Olfactory Hedonic Processing

As discussed earlier, odor valence is a prominent component of olfactory perception. It follows that there is substantial overlap in the brain regions implementing olfactory and emotional processes. Hence, the anatomical and behavioral characteristics of *olfactory* processing make it an ideal candidate for examining *emotional* processing in the brain. In fact, examination of limbic brain areas involved in odor perception has resulted in considerable progress in delineating the neural mechanisms that support different aspects of emotion coding and emotion-related learning.

Piriform Cortex

The piriform cortex functions as a sensory-associative region that incorporates cognitive, experiential, and emotional factors into the assembly of odor object percepts. This region plays a critical role in almost every aspect of odor object perception, including the ability to integrate odor components into perceptual wholes (odorant feature synthesis), filter out irrelevant background smells (odor-background segmentation), retain the "objectness" of an odor object across different variations (odor constancy), extract perceptual sameness across different stimuli (odor categorization), and discriminate individual odor objects (for a review, see Gottfried, 2010).

There appears to be a functional heterogeneity with regard to representation of valence in the anterior and posterior subdivisions of the piriform cortex. fMRI studies have shown that the anterior segment of the piriform cortex (which also incorporates the frontal piriform cortex) is sensitive to valence, showing increased activity for unpleasant and pleasant odors compared to neutral odors (Gottfried, Deichmann, Winston, & Dolan, 2002), as well as increased activity for unpleasant versus pleasant odorants during odor imagery (Bensafi, Sobel, & Khan, 2007) and odor perception (Zelano, Montag, Johnson, Khan, & Sobel, 2007). Coding of odor valence at such an early stage of processing is consistent with behavioral findings showing that humans react faster to aversive and dangerous odors than to appetitive odors (Bensafi et al., 2003), which may reflect the survival value in deciding very quickly whether the environmental stimulus is noxious or dangerous. It is likely that this early coding of valence is mediated by strong reciprocal connections between anterior piriform cortex and orbitofrontal structures (Gottfried, Deichmann, et al., 2002).

The receptiveness of the anterior piriform cortex to the hedonic quality of odors stands in contrast to the insensitivity of the posterior piriform cortex (PPC) to valence; the PPC seems to be broadly tuned to different odors irrespective of valence (Gottfried, Deichmann, et al., 2002). Although the PPC does not seem to be involved in coding emotional aspects of odors, by virtue of its extensive connectivity with other limbic regions, it serves as an important substrate for encoding emotional learning and memory-related changes in odor object coding. Its participation in emotional learning has been demonstrated in animals and humans (Li, Howard, Parrish, & Gottfried, 2008; Sacco & Sacchetti, 2010). For example, in an olfactory fMRI study of aversive learning, subjects smelled two odor enantiomers, or mirror-image molecules, before and after an aversive conditioning session in which one of the two enantiomers (the conditioned stimulus,

CS) was repeatedly paired with a mild electric shock (the unconditioned stimulus; Li et al., 2008; Sacco & Sacchetti, 2010). After conditioning, subjects were better able to discriminate between the previously indistinguishable enantiomers (CS+), but this was not the case for a control pair of odor enantiomers (CS–; Figure 10.2). Olfactory aversive learning was associated with a reorganization of fMRI ensemble activity patterns in the PPC, specifically for the enantiomer pair that was used during conditioning.

This spatial reorganization of sensory coding in the piriform cortex may reflect changes in olfactory receptive-field tuning, leading to improved perception of odor cues, such that piriform representations "tagged" with salience might gain privileged access to networks mediating behaviorally relevant actions. In fact, a recent study in rats reported that excitotoxic lesions of the PPC impaired remote, but not recent, fear memories (Sacco & Sacchetti, 2010). Although similar results were found for secondary auditory and visual cortices, the memory impairment was modality specific and was not due to an interference with sensory or emotional processes. Furthermore, lesions of the same areas left intact the memory of sensory stimuli *not* associated with fear. This study further highlights the role of the piriform cortex (and secondary associative cortices in other modalities) in memory storage and retrieval of sensory stimuli that have acquired behavioral salience as a consequence of experience.

Amygdala

A dominant model in emotion research posits that emotion is best represented on a circumplex, or two orthogonal axes (Russell, 1980). The first axis, referred to as the valence axis, represents the pleasantness/unpleasantness of emotion, whereas the second axis represents the degree of arousal associated with the emotion. These two dimensions are hypothesized to map onto two independent neurophysiological systems, and every affective experience is

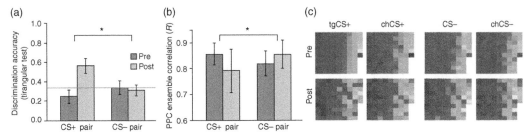

Figure 10.2. Role of olfactory cortical areas in aversive learning. In an fMRI version of olfactory fear learning, subjects smelled pairs of odor enantiomers that were perceptually indistinguishable. One of these enantiomers, designated the target CS+ (tgCS+), was subsequently paired with mild footshock. Neither its chiral counterpart (chCS+) nor a control pair (CS- and chCS-) was paired with shock. From preconditioning to postconditioning, perceptual discrimination between tgCS+ and chCS+ selectively increased (a), in parallel with fMRI ensemble decorrelation (less pattern overlap) in PPC (b). Ensemble activation maps across PPC voxels in one subject (c) show increasing pattern divergence between tgCS+ and chCS+ after learning. Adapted from Li et al. (2008). See color plate 10.2.

the consequence of a linear combination of these two independent systems. Although valence and arousal are believed to be orthogonal and to independently contribute to emotional experience, real-world experience shows that these dimensions tend to be correlated. Negative stimuli are deemed more intense (e.g., a mutilated body) than positive stimuli (e.g., a cute puppy). Furthermore, intensity can amplify valence or even shift it. For example, the smell of a rose may increase in pleasantness with increasing intensity, but at extremely high intensity it may become unpleasant. Because odor intensity and valence are so highly correlated, one researcher has proposed that odor hedonics may be evaluated along a single dimension (Henion, 1971). In the case of olfaction, subjective reports of odor intensity (how strong or weak an odor is) have been used as a proxy for subjective reports of emotional arousal (Anderson et al., 2003) because they are highly intercorrelated (Bensafi et al., 2002a; Henion, 1971), although this assumption is open to debate.

Because there is considerable evidence implicating the amygdala in emotional processing (LeDoux, 2000), it has been hypothesized that neural representations of odor valence (pleasantness) are maintained in the amygdala. Zald and Pardo (1997) first tested this hypothesis and showed bilateral amygdala activation in response to highly aversive (compared to minimally aversive) smells. However, because the unpleasant stimuli were very intense, it is possible that the amygdala activity in the Zald and Pardo study partially indexes intensity rather than valence-related differences. Follow-up experiments have yielded contradictory findings in various ways. Studies have found greater amygdala activity for unpleasant than pleasant odors, matched for intensity, suggesting a valence-specific effect (Hudry, Perrin, Ryvlin, Mauguiere, & Royet, 2003; Royet et al., 2003). Another study suggested the amygdala is insensitive to valence, being similarly activated by pleasant, neutral, and unpleasant odors (Gottfried, Deichmann, et al., 2002), whereas a third group demonstrated correlations between perceived intensity and neural activity in temporal structures adjacent to the amygdala (Rolls, Kringelbach, & de Araujo, 2003).

In an effort to resolve these inconsistencies, odor intensity and valence were dissociated within a single experiment, by presenting one pleasant odor (citral: lemon smell) and one unpleasant odor (valeric acid: sweaty sock smell), each at low and high intensity (Anderson et al., 2003). This study found that the amygdala was significantly activated by intensity (high versus low), but not valence (unpleasant versus pleasant, or vice versa), suggesting that it codes for odor intensity. In another study, valence

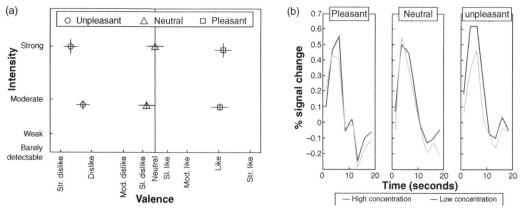

Figure 10.3. Amygdala codes an interaction of valence and intensity. Experimental design and behavioral data (A) show that that valence (three levels: pleasant, neutral, or unpleasant) and intensity (two levels: high or low) were independently manipulated in a 3 × 2 factorial design. Behavioral ratings are depicted in the plot of psychophysical odor space: valence on the abscissa, intensity on the ordinate. Sl., Slightly; Mod., moderately; Str., strongly. Dark symbols, high concentration odors; light symbols, low-concentration odors. Error bars show SEM; vertical bars represent error in intensity dimension; horizontal bars represent error in valence ratings. (B) fMRI findings show differential effects of odor valence on intensity coding in the amygdala. Response time courses of amygdala activation for each level of odor concentration and odor type show the selective effects of intensity on amygdala activity only at the extremes of odor valence. Adapted from Winston et al. (2005).

and intensity were similarly dissociated, but a neutrally valenced odor was added to the pleasant and unpleasant odor conditions (Winston, Gottfried, Kilner, & Dolan, 2005). Hence, high- and low-intensity versions of pleasant, neutral, and unpleasant odors were delivered to subjects (Figure 10.3). The study then examined whether the amygdala coded intensity regardless of valence (greater activation for high versus low intensity for all three odor types) or a combination of valence and intensity (greater activation for high versus low intensity for pleasant and unpleasant odors, but not for neutral odor). The study findings were consistent with the latter hypothesis, suggesting that the amygdala codes an interaction between intensity and valence, caring mainly about the overall behavioral salience of an odor.

The problem with the Anderson et al. study (and the Winston et al. study) is that they are not a reflection of real-world valence-arousal relationships. To dissociate valence and intensity, Anderson et al. selected odors in a narrow valence and intensity range (bordering on neutral). Further-

more, it is debatable whether odor intensity is the same as odor-elicited arousal. For example, peppermint odor was associated with increases in self-rated alertness whereas ylang-ylang was associated with decreases in alertness and increases in self-rated calmness, despite the odors being equated for intensity (Moss, Hewitt, Moss, & Wesnes, 2008). In another study, lemon oil administration resulted in elevated norepinephrine levels compared to water or lavender (Kiecolt-Glaser et al., 2008) indicating that odor-elicited arousal may not be equivalent to odor intensity. Furthermore, the relationship between stimulus-related arousal and intensity may differ in the chemosensory modality where arousal is linked more closely to the physical characteristics of the stimulus (Bensafi et al., 2002a), as opposed to the auditory and visual domain where the two are not as closely related (Junghofer, Bradley, Elbert, & Lang, 2001). For example, judgments of the calming or arousing nature of visual scenes do not depend greatly on the contrast, luminance, or hue of the scenes. Given the close anatomical connections between the amygdala and olfactory cortices, increased amygdala activation related to physical stimulus intensity across differently valenced stimuli or specifically for unpleasant or pleasant stimuli (Anderson et al., 2003; Winston et al., 2005) accords well with increased neural activity in response to physically intense visual or auditory stimuli in primary and secondary sensory areas (e.g., Mohamed, Pinus, Faro, Patel, & Tracy, 2002).

Orbitofrontal Cortex

The OFC receives inputs from several modalities, including taste, smell, somatosensory, and visual modalities, and is believed to play a critical role in representing the identity and reward value of tastes and odors. This places the OFC in the unique position of integrating information, some of which is rewarding or punishing, from different sensory modalities – a process that is critical for associative learning and emotional and motivational behavior. The OFC has been implicated in olfactory processing in both monkey electrophysiological (Critchley & Rolls, 1996b; Tanabe et al., 1975) and human lesion and imaging (Li et al, 2010; Zatorre, Jones-Gotman, Evans, & Meyer, 1992) studies. Single-cell recording during olfactory information encoding in the OFC of monkeys showed that, among odor-responsive neurons, representation of the olfactory stimulus depended on its association with taste in 35% of neurons, whereas in the remaining 65%, the representation of the odor stimulus identity was not influenced by the associated taste (Critchley & Rolls, 1996b). Furthermore, OFC neurons decreased their responses to the odor of the food with which the monkey was fed to satiety (Critchley & Rolls, 1996a), indicating that not only do OFC neurons represent the rewarding stimuli but also that the reward value of each stimulus is continually updated, albeit in a sensory-specific manner.

The OFC has also been implicated in classical (Pavlovian) conditioning in which odors are used as unconditioned stimuli (UCS; Gottfried & Dolan, 2004; Gottfried, O'Doherty, & Dolan, 2002, 2003). For example, after a neutral face (conditioned stimulus, CS) was repetitively paired with either a pleasant or unpleasant odor UCS, presentation of the conditioned face by itself elicited dissociable activations in human OFC according to whether the learning mode was appetitive or aversive, indicating that this region is involved in the valence-specific establishment of picture-odor contingencies (Gottfried, O'Doherty, et al., 2002). Related studies have shown that the OFC encodes olfactory predictive value. In an fMRI version of a reinforcer inflation paradigm, subjects were conditioned to associate two neutral faces with two different aversive odors (Gottfried & Dolan, 2004). Subsequently, the aversive value of one of the two odors was enhanced or "inflated" by presenting it at increased intensity after conditioning. A final scanning session was conducted during extinction, with the presentation of faces in the absence of any odor. Imaging data from the extinction session revealed greater activation in the lateral OFC in response to the face associated with the inflated odor value, compared to the control face, suggesting that representations of the original conditioned value persist even as extinction ensues. Finally, in a selective satiety fMRI study, two arbitrary visual stimuli were presented with different pleasant food smells, both before and after an olfactory devaluation procedure in which subjects ate a food corresponding to one of the odors until satiation. Amygdala and orbitofrontal cortex responses evoked by a predictive target stimulus were decreased after devaluation, whereas responses to the nondevalued stimulus were maintained (Gottfried et al., 2003), indicating that these regions encode the current predictive value of reward representations.

In summary, by showing that the OFC is involved in representing odors and their reward value, as well as in learning and modulating associations between visual and odor stimuli, olfactory learning studies have helped delineate its role in controlling and adjusting emotional and motivational behavior.

Is an Odor Object Equivalent to the Emotion It Elicits?

That the olfactory system is intimately related to emotional processing at the anatomical, psychological, and functional levels raises an interesting question: Do odor objects constitute emotional "primitives"? It has been recognized for some time that odorant pleasantness is the primary aspect of odors spontaneously used by subjects in olfactory discrimination tasks (Schiffman, 1974) and in odor categorization (Berglund et al., 1973). When using large numbers of verbal descriptors to describe odorants, pleasantness repeatedly emerges as the primary dimension in a principal components analysis (PCA) of the resultant descriptor space (Khan et al., 2007). Further support for this view is drawn from studies showing differential behavioral and autonomic responses (Bensafi et al., 2002a, 2002b, 2003) and neuroanatomical substrates (Anderson et al., 2003; Gottfried, Deichmann, et al., 2002; Rolls et al., 2003; Royet et al., 2003; Zald & Pardo, 1997) for pleasant and unpleasant odorants. Finally, the principal axis that best explains the variance in the molecular structure of more than 1,500 odorants was found to correlate significantly with ratings of odorant pleasantness, indicating that pleasantness may be an inherent property encoded in the molecular structure of odors (Khan et al., 2007). This principal axis was also found to be the odorant metric that best explained the variance in neural activity across a wide range of species (Yeshurun & Sobel, 2010). Taken to an extreme, it has been suggested that olfactory perception is based on a unidimensional representation of valence, whereby the pleasantness of an odor object is the odor object itself, and discrimination of odor objects essentially amounts to a discrimination of their pleasantness (Yeshurun & Sobel, 2010).

Although these lines of evidence highlight valence as a principal axis in olfactory perception, characterizing olfactory perception as a unidimensional valence-based phenomenon is highly debatable. First, the presence of separate psychological and physiological substrates for pleasant and unpleasant odors does not necessarily indicate that pleasantness-unpleasantness is the primary dimension of olfaction. For example, pleasant and unpleasant pictures may evoke differential autonomic or neuroimaging responses, but one would not quickly conclude that valence is the primary dimension of vision. Second, although there is no gold standard for determining unidimensionality in the context of PCA (Hattie, 1985), one rule of thumb is based on the notion that, when data are unidimensional, the primary component in a PCA should account for a large portion of the variance (30–50% in terms of an absolute value and have an eigenvalue about three times higher than the second factor), and the remaining components should each account for about the same amount of the remaining variance. In olfactory perception, although the first principal component relates to valence, the variance accounted for by the other components is not negligible. In many of the PCA studies in which valence was the primary dimension, edibility emerged as a potential second dimension accounting for an important portion of the variance (Khan et al., 2007). This finding suggests that, in addition to valence, odors can also be classified according to their edibility. Furthermore, in a recent study the utility of a unidimensional valence-related scale in capturing not only the overall olfactory perceptual experience but also a more limited olfactory hedonic experience did not hold up (Chrea et al., 2009). Using PCA to examine the nature of the verbal labels that best describe subjective emotional experience elicited by odors, these authors found that the structure of odor-elicited affective responses differed from the bidimensional (valence and arousal) models of emotional experience. Rather, the structure consisted of five dimensions that reflect the role of olfaction in well-being, social interaction, danger prevention, arousal or relaxation sensations, and conscious recollection of emotional memories.

If odor objects cannot be reduced to the emotions that they elicit, then it is reasonable to ask why emotional valence consistently emerges as the dominant psychophysical dimension of olfactory perception. In considering this question, it is important to examine how quirks in the sensory testing methodology can account for disparate findings regarding olfactory perceptual dimensions. In the context of olfactory perception, the inclusion of particular variables or descriptors in the testing set can bias results toward yielding more valence-based dimensions in factor analytic studies. This is more colorfully conceptualized as the "garbage in garbage out" phenomenon, in which inclusion of a large proportion of variables that measure the same thing will yield a dimension that relates to those variables. Hence, it is important that the descriptors are randomly sampled from a population of possible indicators. This may be harder to achieve in the case of odors, where a large proportion of the descriptors tap hedonic aspects of the odor.

One theory to explain how variables or descriptors on a rating scale can affect sensory testing is "halo dumping." If forced to rate a multi-attribute sensory object on a single attribute scale, perceivers tend to overcompensate for the missing attributes by giving a higher score to the set of attributes that they are rating (Abdi, 2002). In other words, subjects "dump" the other attributes onto the only available scale, a phenomenon that is also referred to as "halo-attribute dumping" (Clark & Lawless, 1994). For example, if subjects were asked to compare a strawberry odor and a minty odor using perceptual ratings, halo dumping would occur if subjects were provided with only a pleasantness scale to rate a mixture of attributes (pleasantness, edibility, intensity, berriness, mintyness), forcing them to "dump"' the other attributes onto the only available pleasantness scale. Most of the studies that have conducted PCA and found that valence was the primary dimension used the Dravnieks atlas of odor character profiles, which consists of 146 verbal descriptors each applied to 144 different odorants (Dravnieks, 1982). It would be important to confirm that the descriptors in this atlas are randomly sampled from

a possible population of descriptors and to sample a wide variety of odor attributes.

Another way that results of factor analyses can be biased toward a valence-based solution is by using stimuli that are sampled from the extremes of the valence dimension or are of a nature that compel the use of valence-related descriptors. This potential confound can be illustrated in a follow-up analysis of our recent published research on odor-quality coding (Howard et al., 2009). In this study, subjects were presented with a set of relatively familiar odors, including minty, woody, and citrus smells. Naïve subjects (who were not given prior information about the odorants) were asked to rate each odor stimulus using the Dravnieks 146-item questionnaire. Subsequently, the descriptor ratings for each odorant were averaged across specific odor-quality categories and across each of the odorants belonging to a given category (Figure 10.4). The results showed that participants differentiated odorants more effectively along their perceptual characteristics than along their perceived pleasantness. For example, the minty odors (white bars) and citrusy odors (dark-gray bars) were easily discriminated with regard to their minty and citrus ratings, but were indistinguishable in terms of their unpleasant and pleasant ratings. This example directly illustrates how the dimensional "potency" of hedonics loses explanatory power when subjects are given a more familiar set of odorants with limited hedonic variability.

Odor Hedonics: Innate or Learned?

If odor hedonics is encoded in the physicochemical structure of the odorant molecules (Khan et al., 2007), as is suggested by the unidimensional theory of odor coding, then odor-hedonic responses should be innate. The innateness of odor hedonics has some corroboration in the animal literature where there is evidence for pheromonal communication (Doty, 2010); however, claims of innate odor-hedonic responses in humans are not well substantiated. There is limited evidence indicating consistency

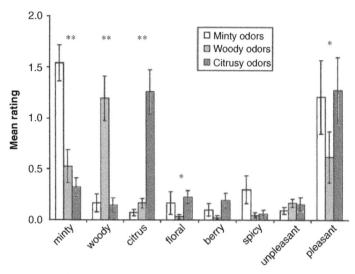

Figure 10.4. Familiar odorants are differentiated along their perceptual characteristics rather than their perceived pleasantness. Ratings of odorants using the Dravnieks 146-item questionnaire were averaged across specific odor-quality categories and across each of the odorants belonging to a given category. Minty odors (white bars) and citrusy odors (dark-gray bars) were easily discriminated with regard to their minty and citrus ratings, but were indistinguishable in terms of their unpleasant and pleasant ratings.

of differential responses to pleasant and unpleasant odors across age groups and species. As reviewed in Yeshurun and Sobel (2010), neonate facial expressions (e.g., wrinkling nose, raising upper lip) discriminate between a pleasant vanillin odor and unpleasant butyric acid, and there is some agreement in adult and child ratings of various pure odorants and personal odors. Furthermore, odorants that are rated pleasant by humans are also the ones that mice investigate longer and human subjects sniff longer, and odor pleasantness ratings in humans and investigation time in mice are both correlated with the physicochemical properties of the molecules. However, a preponderance of the behavioral and neural data, as reviewed next, indicates that odor hedonics are highly plastic and depend on learning, sensory context, and past experience (Rouby, Pouliot, & Bensafi, 2009; Stevenson & Wilson, 2007).

Olfactory Hedonic Plasticity

Although there is evidence of physicochemically driven, hard-wired olfactory hedo-

nic responses that are under evolutionary control (e.g., pheromones and predator or host odors) in animals, a large portion of these responses are acquired via experience and learning. For example, the odorant eugenol (the "clove" odor used in dental cement) was evaluated negatively and elicited autonomic fear responses in patients who were fearful of dental procedures, but not in patients who were not fearful (Robin, Alaoui-Ismaili, Dittmar, & Vernet-Maury, 1998). A novel ambient odor associated with a negative emotional state had a detrimental impact on behavior when presented at a later time, suggesting that the hedonic evaluation of a novel odor changed in accordance with the emotional experience with which it had been associated (Herz, 2005). An unfamiliar pleasant odor paired with a negative emotional experience was subsequently perceived as less pleasant, whereas an unfamiliar unpleasant odor paired with a positive emotional experience became more acceptable – again demonstrating the effect of associative learning on odor-hedonic perception (Herz, 2005).

There is evidence from the animal and human literature indicating that neural representations of odors can be modified through associative learning with appetitive or aversive stimuli. For example, in honeybees learning to discriminate an odor associated with reward (sucrose) from an unrewarded odor, associative learning transformed the odor representations, such that activity for only the rewarded odor increased in the antennal lobe (olfactory bulb equivalent in insects), and there was a decorrelation in the activity patterns for the rewarded and unrewarded odor, making them less similar (Faber, Joerges, & Menzel, 1999). As discussed earlier, following olfactory aversive learning (odor-footshock conditioning) human subjects were able to discriminate odors that had been originally perceived as identical. These behavioral changes were associated with changes in ensemble patterns for the shocked and unshocked odors in the posterior piriform cortex (cf. Figure 10.2), suggesting that associative learning has a direct influence on how perceptual information about an odor stimulus is represented in sensory-specific cortex (Li et al., 2008).

Context also has an important modulatory effect on olfactory hedonic perception. According to Rouby et al. (2009), odor-hedonic judgments are influenced by nonhedonic characteristics of the odor (e.g., odor intensity and familiarity), characteristics of the perceiver (e.g., sex, hormonal status, age, emotional state, physiological state), and context of the stimulus or perceiver (e.g., stimulation of other modalities, accompanying verbal information, experimental task or instructions, semantic knowledge, and cultural background). The concept of an odor stimulus being endowed with intrinsic emotional value becomes more difficult to reconcile given the influences of stimulus, perceiver, and context on odor affect.

Stimulus Characteristics

Hedonic evaluations of odorants are strongly influenced by other characteristics of the odorants such as prior exposure, familiarity, and intensity. Pleasantness and familiarity are usually highly correlated. As reviewed in Herz (2005), studies show that infants of mothers who consumed distinctive smelling substances (e.g., garlic, alcohol, cigarette smoke) during pregnancy or lactation showed preferences for these odors compared to infants who had not been exposed. An odorant, methyl salicylate (wintergreen), was rated less pleasant in the United Kingdom, where it is commonly associated with medication. By contrast, it was rated more pleasant in United States where it was associated with a candy mint smell. Generally, familiar odors are rated as more pleasant than unfamiliar odors, and pleasant odors are perceived as being more familiar (Ayabe-Kanamura, Saito, Distel, Martinez-Gomez, & Hudson, 1998; Moskowitz, Dravnieks, & Klarman, 1976).

The relation between familiarity and pleasantness has been attributed to the exposure effect, which involves an enhancement of one's attitude toward a stimulus after its repeated exposure (Zajonc, 1968). However, researchers have argued that simple exposure is not enough to increase liking. When different odors were exposed equally but some as designated targets and others as nontargets in an attentional task, only target odors were liked more after exposure (Prescott, Kim, & Kim, 2008). Furthermore, the relationship between pleasantness and familiarity may not be as clear-cut and can vary based on the pleasantness of the odors. For example, one study found that after 30 minutes of exposure, a pleasant lemon odor was rated less pleasant, whereas an unpleasant rancid odor was rated as less unpleasant (Cain & Johnson, 1978). Delplanque and colleagues showed that the positive correlation between pleasantness and familiarity was found to be specific for pleasant, but not unpleasant odors. Furthermore, appraisal processes of novelty/familiarity and pleasantness appear to proceed in a sequential manner, in which an odor is detected as novel or familiar before it is evaluated as pleasant or unpleasant (Delplanque et al., 2009). Finally, another way of examining familiarity and exposure-related effects is by examining how cultural context affects odor hedonics. Ayabe-Kanamura et al. (1998) found differences between German and Japanese populations in pleasantness ratings for the same set of odorants, as well as a positive relationship between pleasantness and edibility ratings, suggesting that culture-specific experiences regarding foods may significantly influence odor perception.

Hedonic judgment and intensity also bear a complex relationship, with odorants showing a positive correlation, negative correlation, inverted U-shaped function, or no relationship at all between pleasantness and intensity (Bensafi et al., 2002a; Distel et al., 1999; Doty, 1975; Henion, 1971; Moskowitz, et al., 1976). Thus, how intense an odor is and how pleasant it is judged to be are dependent on the particular odor (Figure 10.5). For example, methyl salicylate is neutral at low intensity, but becomes pleasant with increasing intensity (positive correlation); furfural is neutral at low intensity and becomes unpleasant with increasing intensity (negative correlation); weak benzaldehyde is neutral at low intensity, pleasant at medium intensity, and unpleasant at strong intensity (inverted U-shaped function); and geraniol is pleasant throughout most of its intensity range (no correlation; Doty, 1975).

Perceiver Characteristics

Odor-hedonic judgment is influenced by the characteristics not only of the stimulus but also of the perceiver. For example, hormonal status influences the pleasantness of androstenone odor such that women rate this odor as less unpleasant during their ovulatory phase but as unpleasant during the other phases (Hummel, Gollisch, Wildt, & Kobal, 1991). When different moods were induced via films, androstadienone and estratetraenol (putative human sex pheromones) increased sexual arousal after a sexually arousing film, but no effect was observed after a neutral film (Bensafi, Brown, Khan, Levenson, & Sobel, 2004). In another study, different moods were

induced via film clips followed by administration of different kinds of odors (Chen & Dalton, 2005). The study found that, regardless of emotional state or personality, women responded to the emotionally valenced (i.e., pleasant) odorants faster than the neutral ones. Personality modulated reaction time and perceived intensity, such that neurotic and anxious individuals were more responsive to both pleasant and unpleasant odorants. Odor hedonics is also modulated by the physiological state of the perceiver; for example, when a food is eaten to satiety (as discussed earlier in this chapter), the reward value of its odor decreases, an effect that does not generalize to other foods (O'Doherty et al., 2000; Rolls & Rolls, 1997).

Contextual Characteristics

Odor perception is strongly influenced by accompanying visual and verbal cues. In an example of visual cues affecting olfactory perception, a strawberry-smelling solution was rated as smelling stronger when colored (e.g., red) than when colorless (Zellner & Kautz, 1990). White wine artificially colored red with an odorless dye was described as possessing olfactory properties of red wine (Morrot, Brochet, & Dubourdieu, 2001). Gottfried and colleagues used functional imaging to examine the neural mechanisms involved in the visual modulation of olfactory perception (Gottfried & Dolan, 2003). Behaviorally, they found that olfactory detection was faster and more accurate when odors appeared in the context of semantically congruent visual cues. This behavioral advantage was associated with greater neural activity in the anterior hippocampus and rostromedial orbitofrontal cortex, implicating these regions in the cross-modal integration of visual and olfactory information.

Verbal information also affects hedonic judgments of the odor. For example, pleasantness, familiarity, and intensity of common odors were rated higher when names were provided compared with when the same odors were evaluated without names

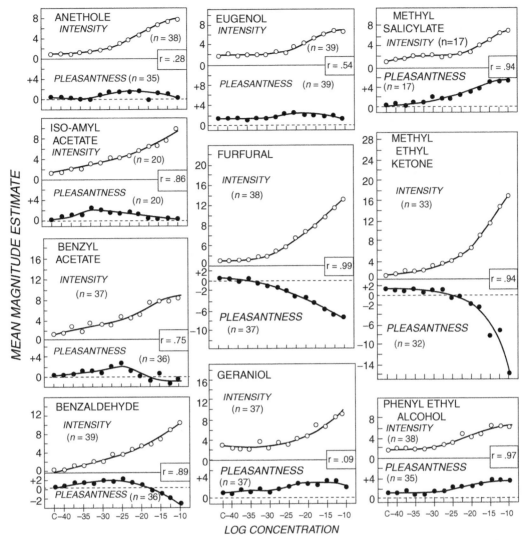

Figure 10.5. Relationship between pleasantness and intensity of odorants. Mean pleasantness and intensity magnitude ratings (on the ordinate) and log-volume concentration in propylene glycol diluent (on the abscissa) are depicted for 10 odorants. Pearson product-moment correlations between pleasantness and intensity estimates across data points differ across odorants. All correlations are significant beyond the $p < .01$ level except those for anethole ($p > 0.20$), eugenol ($p < 0.06$), and geraniol ($p > 0.20$). Adapted from Doty (1975).

(Ayabe-Kanamura et al., 1998; Distel et al., 1999). Unfamiliar odors were rated as more pleasant when they were given positive names (Ayabe-Kanamura, Kikuchi, & Saito, 1997). When verbal information regarding odors was provided to subjects, hedonic evaluations of odors were in agreement with the connotation of the label regardless of whether an odorant was present. However, when odorants were presented without verbal labels, olfactory evaluations were based on sensation and experiential familiarity (Herz, 2003). The same odor was perceived as more pleasant (e.g., "parmesan cheese") or unpleasant (e.g., "vomit") depending on the associated verbal label (Herz & von Clef, 2001). These behavioral findings are substantiated by imaging results. Compared to control air, a test odor (iso-valeric acid, with a cheesy, sweaty type of odor) was rated as more pleasant when labeled "cheddar cheese" and more unpleasant when labeled "body odor." Functional imaging results showed that the rostral anterior cingulate cortex, medial orbitofrontal cortex, and amygdala were more activated by the test odor when labeled "cheddar cheese" than when labeled "body odor," and the activations were correlated with the pleasantness ratings (de Araujo, Rolls, Velazco, Margot, & Cayeux, 2005).

The hedonic value of an odor has been found to change when it is presented in the context of more pleasant or unpleasant odors. For example, in a preliminary investigation, Mohanty and colleagues found that a nominally neutral odor is rated as relatively unpleasant when presented with a pleasant odor and as relatively pleasant when presented with an unpleasant odor (Mohanty et al., 2010). Using fMRI, Grabenhorst and Rolls investigated how the subjective pleasantness of an odor is influenced by whether the odor is presented in the context of a relatively more pleasant or less pleasant odor (Grabenhorst & Rolls, 2009). Participants smelled two of a set of four odors and rated the pleasantness of the second odor. Results showed that, although anterior insula activity correlated with the absolute pleasantness rating of the second odor, activations in the anterolateral orbitofrontal cortex correlated with the difference in pleasantness of the second from the first odor; that is, with relative pleasantness. Thus, it is likely that the brain maintains representations of both absolute and relative reward value of odors.

Taken together, findings from the behavioral and physiological literature indicate that an individual's olfactory hedonic perception is profoundly shaped – if not generated – by higher order operations and is likely to be mediated via central olfactory processes. In addition to highlighting top-down influences on olfactory hedonic perception, these studies shed light on the plasticity in the central circuitry of emotion, including the profound impact of context in modulating emotional response and its neural circuitry.

Odor Memory: An Instance of Emotion-Cognition Interaction

The powerful nature of odor-evoked memories is famously described in Marcel Proust's novel *Swann's Way* (Proust, 1919), in which the smell of a Madeleine biscuit dipped in linden tea triggers intense memories of the author's childhood. This experience, now referred to as the "Proust phenomenon," is considered an example of the emotional potency of odor-evoked memories. These anecdotal reports have been supported by experimental findings showing that odors have an unusual capacity to evoke highly vivid and emotional autobiographical memories, much more so than other mnemonic sensory triggers (Herz & Engen, 1996). In a review of the literature on odor-evoked memories, Herz and Engen summarized that (1) odor-evoked memories appear to be more emotionally potent compared to memories elicited by other sensory stimuli, (2) the power of odors to elicit memories is related to the hedonic properties of odors, and (3) contextual odors cues serve as especially good retrieval cues, an influence possibly mediated by affect.

The robust relationship between emotion and odor-evoked memory is also supported by the strong anatomical connectivity between olfactory cortices and the amygdala-hippocampal complex. A functional imaging investigation of the neural mechanisms that implement odor-evoked memory showed significantly greater activation in the amygdala and hippocampal regions during recall of personally meaningful odors (perfumes) than any other cue (Herz, Eliassen, Beland, & Souza, 2004). These findings were supplemented by behavioral evidence confirming that emotional responses were greatest to these same odors. In addition to hippocampus and amygdala, the sensory cortices play an important role in odor-evoked memory. For example, Gottfried et al. presented visual images with odors during memory encoding (Gottfried, Smith, Rugg, & Dolan, 2004). They then examined the effect of odor context on neural responses at retrieval when these same images were presented alone. Greater activation of the piriform cortex and anterior hippocampus during retrieval of old (compared to new) objects indicates the importance of the olfactory cortices in preserving the sensory features of the original engram. Overall, olfactory stimuli have a distinctive capacity to evoke highly vivid and emotional autobiographical memories, and studies of odor-evoked memory offer new insights into the affective organization of memory.

Conclusions

In recent years, studies of olfactory perception have contributed greatly to the field of affective neuroscience. These studies have delineated the neural mechanisms that are involved in emotion coding and emotion-related learning in the amygdala, orbitofrontal cortex, and sensory cortices.

For example, by independently manipulating valence and arousal of olfactory stimuli, studies have shown that the amygdala codes an interaction between intensity and valence, representing the overall behavioral salience of an odor. The OFC plays an important role in representing odors and their reward value and is intimately involved in cross-modal associative learning between olfactory and nonolfactory stimuli. Finally, olfactory studies have shed light on the psychological and neural mechanisms of contextual modulation and plasticity of emotional processing in the olfactory sensory cortices including the piriform cortex, illustrating for example that conditioning between an odor CS+ and a salient US (electric shock) updates perceptual representations of the CS+ itself. Although olfactory research has contributed significantly to the understanding of emotional function, there is vast untapped potential in this area of research that can help elucidate the neural mechanisms that implement emotional function and its interaction with cognitive processes.

Outstanding Questions

Visual stimuli used to probe emotional processing tend to elicit fear, whereas olfactory stimuli generally elicit disgust (rotten eggs, sour sweat, etc.). Disgust and fear tend to be negative-valence/high-arousal emotions but are also considered as being categorically different (Ekman, 1992), suggesting that emotional stimuli used in vision and olfactory research may involve different psychological and neural mechanisms.

1. Emotional arousal is typically assessed either via self-reports of how calming/arousing the visual stimulus is or by physiological measures like skin conductance. Is odor stimulus intensity, as a proxy for emotional arousal, really an appropriate arousal index in olfactory research? Does the relationship between stimulus intensity and stimulus arousal differ in the olfactory and visual domain?

2. Humans possess an impressive ability to detect and discriminate odors, but are surprisingly poor at naming even common odors. Because emotion emerges as a primary dimension of olfactory perception, it is important to examine if the poor ability to identify odors results in the emphasis on using hedonic descriptors; that is, because odors are harder to identify with verbal semantic labels, people use emotional labels to categorize them instead.

3. The neurobiological mechanisms underlying the emotional and mnemonic potency of odors is still unknown. Are odors emotional because they are intrinsically so (cf. Yeshurun and Sobel, 2010)? Are olfactory stimuli really more emotionally provocative than the other senses, or are odors simply thought to be provocative because they are hard to name?

4. We have reviewed a considerable amount of evidence showing that olfactory hedonic perception is profoundly modulated by several factors including

prior learning and context. Are olfactory stimuli more susceptible to such higher order modulation than visual and auditory stimuli, and if so, what are the neural mechanisms that implement this heightened plasticity?

Acknowledgments

We would like to acknowledge NIH grant support from the National Institute on Deafness and Other Communications Disorders (5R01DC010014 and 5K08DC007653–05 to J.A.G.), as well as supplemental NIH funding through the American Recovery and Reinvestment Act of 2009 (ARRA) (3R01DC010014–01S1).

References

Abdi, H. (2002). What can cognitive psychology and sensory evaluation learn from each other? *Food Quality and Preference*, 13, 445–51.

Anderson, A. K., Christoff, K., Stappen, I., Panitz, D., Ghahremani, D. G., Glover, G., ... Sobel, N. (2003). Dissociated neural representations of intensity and valence in human olfaction. *Nature Neuroscience*, 6(2), 196–202. doi: 10.1038/nn1001nn1001

Ayabe-Kanamura, S., Kikuchi, T., & Saito, S. (1997). Effect of verbal cues on recognition memory and pleasantness evaluation of unfamiliar odors. [Empirical Study]. *Perceptual and Motor Skills*, 85(1), 275–85. doi: 10.2466/pms.85.5.275-285

Ayabe-Kanamura, S., Saito, S., Distel, H., Martinez-Gomez, M., & Hudson, R. (1998). Differences and similarities in the perception of everyday odors – A Japanese-German cross-cultural study. *Olfaction and Taste XII*, 855, 694–700.

Bensafi, M., Brown, W. M., Khan, R., Levenson, B., & Sobel, N. (2004). Sniffing human sex-steroid derived compounds modulates mood, memory and autonomic nervous system function in specific behavioral contexts. *Behavioural Brain Research*, 152(1), 11–22. doi: DOI 10.1016/j.bbr.2003.09.009

Bensafi, M., Rouby, C., Farget, V., Bertrand, B., Vigouroux, M., & Holley, A. (2002a). Autonomic nervous system responses to odours: The role of pleasantness and arousal. *Chemical Senses*, 27(8), 703–9.

Bensafi, M., Rouby, C., Farget, V., Bertrand, B., Vigouroux, M., & Holley, A. (2002b). Influence of affective and cognitive judgments on autonomic parameters during inhalation of pleasant and unpleasant odors in humans. *Neuroscience Letters*, 319(3), 162–66. doi: Pii S0304-3940(01)02572–1

Bensafi, M., Rouby, C., Farget, V., Bertrand, B., Vigouroux, M., & Holley, A. (2003). Perceptual, affective, and cognitive judgments of odors: Pleasantness and handedness effects. *Brain and Cognition*, 51(3), 270–75. doi: 10.1016/S0278-2626(03)00019–8

Bensafi, M., Sobel, N., & Khan, R. M. (2007). Hedonic-specific activity in piriform cortex during odor imagery mimics that during odor perception. *Journal of Neurophysiology*, 98(6), 3254–62. doi: 00349.2007 [pii]10.1152/jn.00349.2007

Berglund, B., Berglund, U., Engen, T., & Ekman, G. (1973). Multidimensional analysis of 21 odors. *Scandinavian Journal of Psychology*, 14(2), 131–37.

Berglund, H., Lindstrom, P., & Savic, I. (2006). Brain response to putative pheromones in lesbian women. *Proceedings of the National Academy of Sciences* 103(21), 8269–74. doi: 0600331103 [pii]10.1073/pnas.0600331103

Cain, W. S., & Johnson, F. (1978). Lability of odor pleasantness – Influence of mere exposure. *Perception*, 7(4), 459–65.

Carmichael, S. T., Clugnet, M. C., & Price, J. L. (1994). Central olfactory connections in the macaque monkey. *Journal of Comparative Neurology*, 346(3), 403–34.

Chen, D., & Dalton, P. (2005). The effect of emotion and personality on olfactory perception. *Chemical Senses*, 30(4), 345–51. doi: 10.1093/chemse/bji029

Chen, D., & Haviland-Jones, J. (2000). Human olfactory communication of emotion. *Perceptual and Motor Skills*, 91(3), 771–81.

Chrea, C., Grandjean, D., Delplanque, S., Cayeux, I., Le Calve, B., Aymard, L., & Scherer, K. R. (2009). Mapping the semantic space for the subjective experience of emotional responses to odors. *Chemical Senses*, 34(1), 49–62. doi: 10.1093/chemse/bjn052

Clark, C. C., & Lawless, H. T. (1994). Limiting response alternatives in time-intensity scaling: An examination of the halo-dumping effect. *Chemical Senses*, 19(6), 583–94.

Critchley, H. D., & Rolls, E. T. (1996a). Hunger and satiety modify the responses of olfactory and visual neurons in the primate orbitofrontal cortex. *Journal of Neurophysiology*, 75(4), 1673–86.

Critchley, H. D., & Rolls, E. T. (1996b). Olfactory neuronal responses in the primate orbitofrontal cortex: Analysis in an olfactory discrimination task. *Journal of Neurophysiology*, 75(4), 1659–72.

de Araujo, I. E., Rolls, E. T., Velazco, M. I., Margot, C., & Cayeux, I. (2005). Cognitive modulation of olfactory processing. *Neuron*, 46(4), 671–79. doi: S0896–6273(05)00357–0 [pii]10.1016/j.neuron.2005.04.021

Delplanque, S., Grandjean, D., Chrea, C., Coppin, G., Aymard, L., Cayeux, I., . . . Scherer, K. R. (2009). Sequential unfolding of novelty and pleasantness appraisals of odors: Evidence from facial electromyography and autonomic reactions. *Emotion*, 9(3), 316–28. doi: 10.1037/A0015369

Distel, H., Ayabe-Kanamura, S., Martinez-Gomez, M., Schicker, I., Kobayakawa, T., Saito, S., & Hudson, R. (1999). Perception of everyday odors – Correlation between intensity, familiarity and strength of hedonic judgement. *Chemical Senses*, 24(2), 191–99.

Doty, R. L. (1975). Examination of relationships between pleasantness, intensity, and concentration of 10 odorous stimuli. *Perception & Psychophysics*, 17(5), 492–96.

Doty, R. L. (2010). *The great pheromone myth*. Baltimore: Johns Hopkins University Press.

Dravnieks, A. (1982). Odor quality: Semantically generated multidimensional profiles are stable. *Science*, 218(4574), 799–801.

Ekman, P. (1992). An argument for basic emotions. *Cognition and Emotion*, 6(3/4), 169–200.

Ekman, P., & Friesen, W. (1976). *Pictures of facial affect*. Palo Alto, CA Consulting Psychologists Press.

Faber, T., Joerges, J., & Menzel, R. (1999). Associative learning modifies neural representations of odors in the insect brain. *Nature Neuroscience*, 2(1), 74–78. doi: 10.1038/4576

Firestein, S. (2001). How the olfactory system makes sense of scents. *Nature*, 413(6852), 211–18.

Gottfried, J. A. (2006). Smell: Central nervous processing. *Advances in Otorhinolaryngology*, 63, 44–69. doi: 10.1159/000093750 [pii]10.1159/000093750

Gottfried, J. A. (2010). Central mechanisms of odour object perception. *Nature Reviews Neuroscience*, 11(9), 628–41. doi: nrn2883 [pii]10.1038/nrn2883

Gottfried, J. A., Deichmann, R., Winston, J. S., & Dolan, R. J. (2002). Functional heterogeneity in human olfactory cortex: An event-related functional magnetic resonance imaging study. *Journal of Neuroscience*, 22(24), 10819–28.

Gottfried, J. A., & Dolan, R. J. (2003). The nose smells what the eye sees: Crossmodal visual facilitation of human olfactory perception. *Neuron*, 39(2), 375–86. doi: S0896627303003921 [pii]

Gottfried, J. A., & Dolan, R. J. (2004). Human orbitofrontal cortex mediates extinction learning while accessing conditioned representations of value. *Nature Neuroscience*, 7(10), 1144–52. doi: 10.1038/nn1314nn1314 [pii]

Gottfried, J. A., O'Doherty, J., & Dolan, R. J. (2002). Appetitive and aversive olfactory learning in humans studied using event-related functional magnetic resonance imaging. *Journal of Neuroscience*, 22(24), 10829–37.

Gottfried, J. A., O'Doherty, J., & Dolan, R. J. (2003). Encoding predictive reward value in human amygdala and orbitofrontal cortex. *Science*, 301(5636), 1104–7. doi: 10.1126/science.1087919301/5636/1104 [pii]

Gottfried, J. A., Smith, A. P., Rugg, M. D., & Dolan, R. J. (2004). Remembrance of odors past: Human olfactory cortex in cross-modal recognition memory. *Neuron*, 42(4), 687–95. doi: S0896627304002703 [pii]

Gottfried, J. A., & Zald, D. H. (2005). On the scent of human olfactory orbitofrontal cortex: Meta-analysis and comparison to non-human primates. *Brain Research: Brain Research Reviews*, 50(2), 287–304. doi: S0165–0173(05)00118–9 [pii]10.1016/j.brainresrev.2005.08.004

Grabenhorst, F., & Rolls, E. T. (2009). Different representations of relative and absolute subjective value in the human brain. *Neuroimage*, 48(1), 258–68. doi: DOI 10.1016/j.neuroimage.2009.06.045

Hattie. J. A. (1985). Methodology review: Assessing unidimensionality of tests and items. [Literature Review]. *Applied Psychological Measurement*, 9(2), 139–64. doi: 10.1177/01466216-8500900204

Henion, K. E. (1971). Odor pleasantness and intensity: A single dimension? *Journal of Experimental Psychology*, 90(2), 275–79.

Herz, R. S. (2003). The effect of verbal context on olfactory perception. *Journal of*

Experimental Psychology-General, 132(4), 595–606. doi: 10.1037/0096-3445.132.4.595

Herz, R. S. (2005). Odor-associative learning and emotion: Effects on perception and behavior. *Chemical Senses*, 30, I250–I251. doi: 10.1093/chemse/bjh209

Herz, R. S., Eliassen, J., Beland, S., & Souza, T. (2004). Neuroimaging evidence for the emotional potency of odor-evoked memory. *Neuropsychologia*, 42(3), 371–78. doi: 10.1016/j.neuropsychologia.2003.08.009

Herz, R. S., & Engen, T. (1996). Odor memory: Review and analysis. *Psychonomic Bulletin & Review*, 3(3), 300–13.

Herz, R. S., & von Clef, J. (2001). The influence of verbal labeling on the perception of odors: Evidence for olfactory illusions? [Empirical Study]. *Perception*, 30(3), 381–91. doi: 10.1068/p3179

Howard, J. D., Plailly, J., Grueschow, M., Haynes, J. D., & Gottfried, J. A. (2009). Odor quality coding and categorization in human posterior piriform cortex. *Nature Neuroscience*, 12(7), 932–38. doi: nn.2324 [pii] 10.1038/nn.2324

Hudry, J., Perrin, F., Ryvlin, P., Mauguiere, F., & Royet, J. P. (2003). Olfactory short-term memory and related amygdala recordings in patients with temporal lobe epilepsy. *Brain*, 126(Pt. 8), 1851–63. doi: 10.1093/brain/awg192awg192 [pii]

Hummel, T., Gollisch, R., Wildt, G., & Kobal, G. (1991). Changes in olfactory perception during the menstrual cycle. *Experientia*, 47(7), 712–15.

Hummer, T. A., & McClintock, M. K. (2009). Putative human pheromone androstadienone attunes the mind specifically to emotional information. *Hormones and Behavior*, 55(4), 548–59. doi: 10.1016/j.yhbeh.2009.01.002

Jacob, S., Hayreh, D. J., & McClintock, M. K. (2001). Context-dependent effects of steroid chemosignals on human physiology and mood. *Physiology & Behavior*, 74(1-2), 15–27. doi: S0031-9384(01)00537-6 [pii]

Junghofer, M., Bradley, M. M., Elbert, T. R., & Lang, P. J. (2001). Fleeting images: A new look at early emotion discrimination. [Empirical Study]. *Psychophysiology*, 38(2), 175–178. doi: 10.1017/s0048577201000762

Khan, R. M., Luk, C. H., Flinker, A., Aggarwal, A., Lapid, H., Haddad, R., & Sobel, N. (2007). Predicting odor pleasantness from odorant structure: pleasantness as a reflection of the physical world. *Journal of Neu-*

roscience, 27(37), 10015–23. doi: 27/37/10015 [pii]10.1523/JNEUROSCI.1158–07.2007

Kiecolt-Glaser, J. K., Graham, J. E., Malarkey, W. B., Porter, K., Lemeshow, S., & Glaser, R. (2008). Olfactory influences on mood and autonomic, endocrine, and immune function. *Psychoneuroendocrinology*, 33(3), 328–39. doi: S0306-4530(07)00264-8 [pii]10.1016/j.psyneuen.2007.11.015

Lang, P. J., Bradley, M. M., & Cuthbert, B. N. (2008). *International affective picture system (IAPS): Affective ratings of pictures and instruction manual*. Technical Report A-8. Gainesville, FL: University of Florida.

Laska, M., & Seibt, A. (2002). Olfactory sensitivity for aliphatic esters in squirrel monkeys and pigtail macaques. *Behavioural Brain Research*, 134(1-2), 165–74. doi: Pii S0166-4328(01)00464-8

LeDoux, J. E. (2000). Emotion circuits in the brain. *Annual Review of Neuroscience*, 23, 155–84. doi: 10.1146/annurev.neuro.23.1.155

Levenson, R. W. (1994). Human emotion: A functional view. In P. Ekman & R. J. D. Davidson (Eds.), *The nature of emotion: Fundamental questions* (pp. 123–26). New York: Oxford University Press.

Li, W., Howard, J. D., Parrish, T. B., & Gottfried, J. A. (2008). Aversive learning enhances perceptual and cortical discrimination of indiscriminable odor cues. *Science*, 319(5871), 1842–45. doi: 319/5871/1842 [pii]10.1126/science.1152837

Li, W., Lopez, L., Osher, J., Howard, J. D., Parrish, T. B., & Gottfried, J. A. (2010). Right orbitofrontal cortex mediates conscious olfactory perception. *Psychological Science*, 21(10), 1454–63.

Li, W., Luxenberg, E., Parrish, T., & Gottfried, J. A. (2006). Learning to smell the roses: Experience-dependent neural plasticity in human piriform and orbitofrontal cortices. *Neuron*, 52(6), 1097–1108. doi: S0896-6273(06)00825-7 [pii]10.1016/j.neuron.2006.10.026

Linster, C., Henry, L., Kadohisa, M., & Wilson, D. A. (2007). Synaptic adaptation and odor-background segmentation. *Neurobiology of Learning and Memory*, 87(3), 352–60. doi: S1074-7427(06)00141-9 [pii]10.1016/j.nlm.2006.09.011

Mohamed, F. B., Pinus, A. B., Faro, S. H., Patel, D., & Tracy, J. I. (2002). BOLD fMRI of the visual cortex: Quantitative responses measured with a graded stimulus at 1.5 Tesla.

Journal of Magnetic Resonance Imaging, 16(2), 128–36. doi: 10.1002/jmri.10155

Mohanty, A., Howard, J. D., Phillips, K. M., Wu, K. N., Zelano, C., & Gottfried, J. A. (2010). *Contextual modulation of odor valence coding.* Paper presented at the Association for Chemoreception Sciences, St. Pete Beach, FL.

Morrot, G., Brochet, F., & Dubourdieu, D. (2001). The color of odors. *Brain and Language, 79*(2), 309–20.

Moskowitz, H. R., Dravnieks, A., & Klarman, L. A. (1976). Odor intensity and pleasantness for a diverse set of odorants. *Perception & Psychophysics, 19*(2), 122–28.

Moss, M., Hewitt, S., Moss, L., & Wesnes, K. (2008). Modulation of cognitive performance and mood by aromas of peppermint and ylang-ylang. *International Journal of Neuroscience, 118*(1), 59–77. doi: 787459816 [pii]10.1080/00207450601042094

Mueller, C. G. (1951). Frequency of seeing functions for intensity discrimination at various levels of adapting intensity. *Journal of General Physiology, 34,* 463–74. doi: 10.1085/jgp.34.4.463

Mujica-Parodi, L. R., Strey, H. H., Frederick, B., Savoy, R., Cox, D., Botanov, Y., . . . Weber, J. (2009). Chemosensory cues to conspecific emotional stress activate amygdala in humans. *PloS One, 4*(7). doi: Artn E6415oi 10.1371/Journal.Pone.0006415

Pitkänen, A. (2000). Connectivity of the rat amygdaloid complex. In J. P. Aggleton (Ed.), *The amygdala: A functional analysis* (2nd ed., pp. 31–116). Oxford: Oxford University Press.

Porter, J., Craven, B., Khan, R. M., Chang, S. J., Kang, I., Judkewicz, B., . . . Sobel, N. (2007). Mechanisms of scent-tracking in humans. *Nature Neuroscience, 10*(1), 27–29. doi: 10.1038/Nn1819

Prescott, J., Kim, H., & Kim, K. O. (2008). Cognitive mediation of hedonic changes to odors following exposure. *Chemosensory Perception, 1*(1), 2–8. doi: 10.1007/s12078-007-9004-y

Proust, M. (1919). *Du cote de chez Swann* (3rd ed.). Paris: Gallimard, Editions de la Nouvelle Revue Francaise.

Robin, O., Alaoui-Ismaili, O., Dittmar, A., & Vernet-Maury, E. (1998). Emotional responses evoked by dental odors: An evaluation from autonomic parameters. *Journal of Dental Research, 77*(8), 1638–46.

Rolls, E. T. (2004). Convergence of sensory systems in the orbitofrontal cortex in primates and brain design for emotion. *Anatomical Record: Part A. Discoveries in Mollecular, Cel-*

lular, and Evolutionary Biology, 281(1), 1212–25. doi: 10.1002/ar.a.20126

Rolls, E. T., Kringelbach, M. L., & de Araujo, I. E. T. (2003). Different representations of pleasant and unpleasant odours in the human brain. *European Journal of Neuroscience, 18*(3), 695–703. doi: 10.1046/j.1460-9568.2003.02779.x

Rolls, E. T., & Rolls, J. H. (1997). Olfactory sensory-specific satiety in humans. *Physiology & Behavior, 61*(3), 461–73.

Rouby, C., Pouliot, S., & Bensafi, M. (2009). Odor hedonics and their modulators. *Food Quality and Preference, 20*(8), 545–49. doi: 10.1016/j.foodqual.2009.05.004

Royet, J. P., Plailly, J., Delon-Martin, C., Kareken, D. A., & Segebarth, C. (2003). fMRI of emotional responses to odors: Influence of hedonic valence and judgment, handedness, and gender. *Neuroimage, 20*(2), 713–28. doi: 10.1016/S1053-8119(03)00388-4

Rozin, P. (1982). Taste-smell confusions and the duality of the olfactory sense. *Perception & Psychophysics, 31*(4), 397–401.

Rushdie, S. (1981). *Midnight's children [a novel]* (1st American ed.). New York: Knopf.

Russell, J. A. (1980). A circumplex model of affect. *Journal of Personality and Social Psychology, 39*(6), 1161–78. doi: 10.1037/h0077714

Sacco, T., & Sacchetti, B. (2010). Role of secondary sensory cortices in emotional memory storage and retrieval in rats. *Science, 329*(5992), 649–56. doi: 329/5992/649 [pii]10.1126/science.1183165

Schiffman, S. S. (1974). Physicochemical correlates of olfactory quality. *Science, 185*(4146), 112–17.

Schiffman, S. S., & Miller, E. A. S. (1995). The effect of environmental odors emanating from commercial swine operations on the mood of nearby residents. [Empirical Study]. *Brain Research Bulletin, 37*(4), 369–75. doi: 10.1016/0361-9230(95)00015-1

Shepherd, G. M. (2004). The human sense of smell: Are we better than we think? *PLoS Biol, 2*(5), E146. doi: 10.1371/journal.pbio.0020146

Shepherd, G. M. (2006). Smell images and the flavour system in the human brain. *Nature, 444*(7117), 316–21. doi: 10.1038/Nature05405

Sobel, N., Prabhakaran, V., Desmond, J. E., Glover, G. H., Goode, R. L., Sullivan, E. V., & Gabrieli, J. D. (1998). Sniffing and smelling: Separate subsystems in the human olfactory cortex. *Nature, 392*(6673), 282–86. doi: 10.1038/32654

Stettler, D. D., & Axel, R. (2009). Representations of odor in the piriform cortex. *Neuron*, 63(6), 854–64. doi: S0896-6273(09)00684-9 [pii]10.1016/j.neuron.2009.09.005

Stevenson, R. J. (2010). An initial evaluation of the functions of human olfaction. *Chemical Senses*, 35(1), 3–20. doi: 10.1093/chemse/bjp083

Stevenson, R. J., & Wilson, D. A. (2007). Odour perception: An object-recognition approach. *Perception*, 36(12), 1821–33. doi: 10.1068/P5563

Susskind, J. M., & Anderson, A. K. (2008). Facial expression form and function. *Communicative and Integrative Biology*, 1(2), 148–149.

Tanabe, T., Iino, M., & Takagi, S. F. (1975). Discrimination of odors in olfactory bulb, pyriform-amygdaloid areas, and orbitofrontal cortex of the monkey. *Journal of Neurophysiology*, 38(5), 1284–96.

Winston, J. S., Gottfried, J. A., Kilner, J. M., & Dolan, R. J. (2005). Integrated neural representations of odor intensity and affective valence in human amygdala. *Journal of Neuroscience*, 25(39), 8903–7. doi: 10.1523/Jneurosci.1569-05.2005

Yarita, H., Iino, M., Tanabe, T., Kogure, S., & Takagi, S. F. (1980). A transthalamic olfactory pathway to orbitofrontal cortex in the monkey. *Journal of Neurophysiology*, 43(1), 69–85.

Yeshurun, Y., & Sobel, N. (2010). An odor is not worth a thousand words: From multidimensional odors to unidimensional odor objects. *Annual Review of Psychology*, 61, 219–241, C211–15. doi: 10.1146/annurev.psych.60.110707.163639

Zajonc, R. B. (1968). Attitudinal effects of mere exposure. *Journal of Personality and Social Psychology*, 9(2 Pt. 2), 1–27.

Zald, D. H., & Pardo, J. V. (1997). Emotion, olfaction, and the human amygdala: Amygdala activation during aversive olfactory stimulation. *Proceedings of the National Academy of Sciences*, 94(8), 4119–24.

Zatorre, R. J., Jones-Gotman, M., Evans, A. C., & Meyer, E. (1992). Functional localization and lateralization of human olfactory cortex. *Nature*, 360(6402), 339–40.

Zelano, C., Montag, J., Johnson, B., Khan, R., & Sobel, N. (2007). Dissociated representations of irritation and valence in human primary olfactory cortex. *Journal of Neurophysiology*, 97(3), 1969–76. doi: 01122.2006 [pii]10.1152/jn.01122.2006

Zellner, D. A., & Kautz, M. A. (1990). Color affects perceived odor intensity. *Journal of Experimental Psychology-Human Perception and Performance*, 16(2), 391–97.

Zhou, W., & Chen, D. (2009). Fear-related chemosignals modulate recognition of fear in ambiguous facial expressions. *Psychological Science*, 20(2), 177–83. doi: DOI 10.1111/j.1467-9280.2009.02263.

CHAPTER 11

Emotional Voices

The Tone of (True) Feelings

Carolin Brück, Benjamin Kreifelts, Thomas Ethofer,
& Dirk Wildgruber

Although frequently associated with speech and language, the human voice provides a wealth of information beyond spoken words. Whether in talking or singing, screaming or laughing, the sheer sound of a voice may not only divulge information about a person's age, gender or origin but may also reveal a person's current affective state to listeners (Belin, Fecteau, & Bedard, 2004). Voice-based cues such as the tone of voice while speaking (i.e., prosody) or laughter, for instance, offer powerful means to express and decipher emotional meaning alongside spoken language. In our day-to-day experiences, it is often such *nonverbal* emotional information carried by the human voice that "speaks volumes." Just picture the following situation: You have asked two colleagues to review a book chapter that you have written. One concludes his review with the sentence, "Your chapter is really great," spoken in a praising tone of voice. The other, however, passes his judgment using the same sentence spoken in a scornful, taunting tone of voice. Although both colleagues used the exact same words, most listeners will probably derive a totally differ-

ent message from both sentences based on the vocal cues that accompanied the verbal content.

Yet how do human beings infer emotional meaning from vocal signals? To address this question, this chapter reviews research on cerebral processes that contribute to the decoding of emotions from vocal cues such as speech prosody or nonverbal vocalizations like laughter.

Neurobiological Correlates of Prosody Processing

In speech communication, information transfer does not solely depend on the meaning of words we use. In fact, often the manner in which we say something is much more revealing than what is actually said. In particular, information about a speaker's current affective state may predominantly be conveyed by the sound of the speaker's voice rather than vocabulary (Mehrabian & Ferris, 1967; Mehrabian & Wiener, 1967). Here is a simple example: Even when we cannot understand the semantic content of a verbal message presented to us, because the speaker is using a foreign language or dialect, we are still adept in inferring the emotional state of our interaction partner just by listening to the tone of his or her voice (Pell, Monetta, Paulmann, & Kotz, 2009).

Whether happy or sad, enraged or surprised, each emotional state expresses itself in a characteristic *prosody of speech* – a typical way of speaking mediated by distinctive modulations of vocal parameters such as voice pitch, voice quality, loudness, or speech rhythm (Banse & Scherer, 1996). When happy, for instance, our voices tend to rise in pitch; we are inclined to speak louder and perhaps even faster. When sad, however, we speak quietly in a low-pitch voice at a slowed pace (Banse & Scherer, 1996; Juslin & Scherer, 2005). Prosodic markers of a speaking voice not only "support words but give them life" (Krapf, 2007, p. 33). They are not "some postscript added on to the verbal message" (Krapf, 2007, p. 58), but rather in themselves a rich source of information.

Listeners in turn are able to perceive and use prosodic acoustic cues with remarkable ease and accuracy when inferring the emotional state of a speaker. Current meta-analytical reviews (Juslin & Laukka, 2003) have noted accuracy rates of decoding well above chance level for various emotions, with the highest decoding accuracies observed for prosodic expressions of anger and sadness, followed by fear and happiness, and the lowest scores obtained for vocal expressions of love and tenderness.

But which brain processes contribute to the decoding of prosodic signals? Early neuroanatomical models (Ross, 1981) identify prosody processing as a function dominant to the right cerebral hemisphere whose organization in the brain closely mirrors the left-lateralized cerebral representation of language production and comprehension. These early models assumed that prosody production was mediated by a region within the right inferior frontal cortex corresponding in location to Broca's area while prosody comprehension relied on right superior temporal structures homologous to Wernicke's area. However,

decades of research since have shifted concepts away from the idea of a single processing center toward models regarding a more widespread cerebral network as the neurobiological basis of prosody comprehension (Ackermann, Hertrich, Grodd, & Wildgruber, 2004; Schirmer & Kotz, 2006; Wildgruber, Ackermann, Kreifelts, & Ethofer, 2006; Wildgruber, Ethofer, Grandjean, & Kreifelts, 2009). Several brain structures have been suggested as constituents of a "prosody network": Superior temporal as well inferior frontal and subcortical structures such as the amygdala have consistently been related to prosody processing (Ackermann et al., 2004; Schirmer & Kotz, 2006; Wildgruber et al., 2006, 2009).

Beyond the mere identification of a "prosody network," neuroscientific studies have helped characterize the specific functional properties of several brain regions implicated in prosody perception. *Task-dependent* as well as *stimulus-driven* response profiles have been described for different structures associated with prosody processing, and building on the respective characterizations, hypotheses regarding the functional roles of these structures have been developed in the literature (e.g., reviewed in Wildgruber et al., 2009).

Stimulus-Driven Activation Associated with the Processing of Affective Prosody

With the advent of modern brain imaging techniques, research has achieved substantial progress in delineating the neurobiological bases of (emotional) voice perception. In particular, functional magnetic resonance imaging (fMRI) has contributed greatly to our understanding of how the brain processes emotional information in human voices. Over the years numerous studies pertaining to the field of emotional voice perception have been published. In reviewing this body of research, one consistent pattern of results appears to emerge: Across studies, findings suggest a contribution of the mid-superior temporal cortex (m-STC) to the decoding of emotional

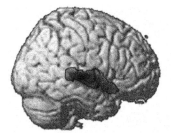
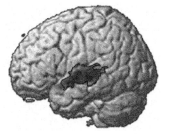

Figure 11.1. Voice-sensitive aspects of the superior temporal cortex defined using a functional localizer (Belin et al., 2000; stimulus material as well as further information available at http://vnl.psy.gla.ac.uk). Voice-sensitive activations are averaged across 24 healthy volunteers.

speech cues (Figure 11.1). Empirical evidence to support this claim can be derived from a variety of imaging studies indicating enhanced responding of the m-STC to emotional voices (e.g., Ethofer, Kreifelts, et al., 2009; Ethofer et al., 2007; Grandjean et al., 2005; Wiethoff et al., 2008), with increases in m-STC activation further linked to increases in the emotional intensity of a speaker's voice (Ethofer, Anders, Wiethoff, et al., 2006) and the behavioral relevance of a given prosodic signal (Ethofer et al., 2007). Activation maxima have been pinpointed to aspects of the m-STC frequently suggested to play a crucial role in the processing of human voices regardless of emotional connotation (Ethofer et al., 2012): Studies contrasting activation patterns associated with the perception of human vocal sounds (e.g., speech, laughter, coughs, cries) to brain responses induced by other natural sound structures, such as animal cries or musical or machine sounds, consistently indicate a heightened sensitivity to voices for cortical regions located along the middle parts of the right and left superior temporal cortex (e.g., Belin & Zatorre, 2003; Belin, Zatorre, & Ahad, 2002; Belin, Zatorre, Lafaille, Ahad, & Pike, 2000; Figure 11.1).

Analogous to the fusiform face area, a specialized region for human face perception (Kanwisher, McDermott, & Chun, 1997), regions of heightened voice-sensitivity – or *temporal voice areas* (Belin & Grosbras, 2010) – may represent a processing module that subserves the anal-

ysis of voices relevant to a rich set of perceptual abilities in a variety of different contexts or settings (Belin et al., 2000; Campanella & Belin, 2007). Indeed, the involvement of temporal voice areas has been suggested for several voice perception skills, such as speaker's identification (von Kriegstein, Kleinschmidt, Sterzer, & Giraud, 2005), voice imagery (Linden et al., 2010), or the extraction of emotional information from laughter or speech prosody (Ethofer, Van De Ville, Scherer, & Vuilleumier, 2009; Grandjean et al., 2005; Szameitat et al., 2010).

In addition to a modulation of response amplitudes, different prosodic emotional categories have been linked to distinctive spatial activation patterns within the voice-sensitive m-STC. Emotions such as anger, sadness, joy, or relief each elicit a specific response that permits a differentiation of emotional categories based on activation data of temporal voice areas (Ethofer et al., 2009). Neuroimaging studies further underline that responses within the m-STC occur irrespective of task demands (Ethofer, Anders, Wiethoff, et al., 2006) or spatial attention focus (Grandjean et al., 2005). Ethofer and colleagues (Ethofer, Anders, Wiethoff, et al., 2006), for instance, demonstrate that the presentation of happy or angry speech prosody enhances m-STC activation, regardless of whether the subject's attention was directed away or toward prosodic cues. Aiming to delineate cerebral responses of the associative auditory cortex, Ethofer et al. recorded brain activations of

24 healthy young volunteers while processing digital recordings of single adjectives spoken either in a happy, neutral, or angry tone of voice. After each stimulus presentation, participants were asked either to judge the emotional states conveyed by the tone of a speaker's voice or classify each stimulus according to its word content (positive, negative, or neutral meaning of the word). Data analysis indicated that, both during the evaluation of speech prosody and during word content judgment, stimuli spoken with an angry or happy tone of voice elicited stronger responses of the m-STC as compared to neutrally spoken stimuli. In other words, regardless of whether a participant's attention was focused on the decoding of speech prosody or word content, the perception of stimuli spoken with an emotional tone of voice was associated with an enhanced activation of temporal voice areas relative to activation patterns obtained for neutrally spoken stimuli.

Findings of task independence, in turn, suggest that activation of the m-STC might not be mediated by specific cognitive demands or attention focus, but rather be stimulus-driven in nature and linked to basic acoustic features that define prosodic markers irrespective of context. Indeed, strong correlations between hemodynamic responses within the right m-STC and several acoustic features, such as mean intensity, mean fundamental frequency, or stimulus duration, have been reported in the literature (Wiethoff et al., 2008). However, when analyzed for their individual contribution, neither stimulus intensity, fundamental frequency, nor duration alone sufficed to explain the observed activation patterns. Rather only by modeling the combined effect of all acoustic parameters could increases in m-STC activation during the processing of affective prosody be predicted sufficiently (Wiethoff et al., 2008).

Such findings suggesting that m-STC responses are driven by acoustic parameters that index emotions at a signal level, in turn, have led to the assumption that the activation of the voice-sensitive m-STC to

a broad range of prosodic emotional cues might reflect processing stages related to the perceptual analysis of acoustic voice properties (e.g., Ethofer, Kreifelts, et al., 2009; Wildgruber et al., 2009). Moreover, based on the observation that m-STC responses could only be explained by a combination of several acoustic features, a contribution of this structure to the analysis of complex acoustic patterns related to speech prosody has been assumed (Wiethoff et al., 2008).

Task-Dependent Activation Associated with the Processing of Affective Prosody

Whereas m-STC activation to emotional prosody proved to be independent of task demands or attention focus, response patterns of several other structures implicated in prosody processing have been reported to be task related and linked to task instructions requiring participants to focus attention on naming or labeling vocally expressed emotions. Task-dependent response characteristics, for instance, have been described for several activation clusters observed within the frontal and temporal cortex (Ethofer, Anders, Erb, Herbert, et al., 2006; Ethofer, Kreifelts, et al., 2009; - Mitchell, Elliott, Barry, Cruttenden, & Woodruff, 2003; Quadflieg, Mohr, Mentzel, Miltner, & Straube, 2008; Wildgruber et al., 2004). For example, Wildgruber and colleagues (2005) found task-related increases in activation for brain structures located within the right posterior superior temporal cortex (p-STC) as well as the right inferior frontal cortex (IFC). Using fMRI, Wildgruber et al. obtained brain activation patterns of healthy young adults while processing emotional speech stimuli. Stimulus material comprised short German sentences spoken either in a happy, sad, disgusted, fearful, or an angry tone of voice. Participants were asked to perform two different tasks: One task required participants to label the emotion expressed by the speakers' tone of voice (identification task), whereas the other asked them to name the first vowel following the first /a/ in each presented sentence (control task). Systematic comparisons computed between brain activation patterns associated with both experimental conditions allowed the delineation of cerebral structures implicated in the respective tasks. Results revealed that, relative to vowel identification, the explicit evaluation of prosodic emotional cues was associated with enhanced activation of the right posterior temporal cortex and the right inferior frontal cortex.

Building on the observation that similar prefrontal areas have consistently been suggested to subserve working memory (Chein, Ravizza, & Fiez, 2003; D'Esposito et al., 1998), prosody processing related responses within the frontal cortex might be assumed to reflect an engagement of working memory processes relevant to the decoding of affective speech cues (Mitchell, 2007).

Considering the contribution of the p-STC, reports of involvement of this structure in the audiovisual integration of nonverbal emotional signals (see the section, "Emotional Voices in Context: Audiovisual Integration of Emotional Signals"), have led to the assumption that p-STC activation reflects stages of multimodal binding, which in turn may aid the identification of emotional information (Wildgruber et al., 2009). But how might multimodal integration relate to the evaluation of (unimodal) prosodic cues? One may assume that, even in situations where no sensory input from other channels of communication is available, additional cues might be retrieved from memory on the basis of established multimodal associations, and through recalling and integrating those retrieved cues with presented prosodic signals, additional information becomes available on which to base emotional inferences. In other words, hearing emotional voices during, for instance, a phone conversation might cue memories of matching facial expressions that one has encountered before in a similar context. Listening to a happy voice might thus, for example, almost automatically evoke mental images of smiling faces, because those particular facial and vocal signals have often been closely linked in the past. At the cerebral level, this process of retrieving and integrating matching facial cues might not only be mediated by the p-STC itself but might also rely on modality- specific processing modules, such as the fusiform face area (FFA; Kanwisher et al., 1997), which in addition to being implicated in perceptual processes, has also been associated with the mental imagery of faces (O'Craven & Kanwisher, 2000). Proceeding from this observation, one might assume that "images" triggered by listening to emotional voices are supported by activation of the FFA, and via a complex interplay between this modality-specific processing module and integration sites within the p-STC, mental images are combined with perceived voice cues, thus maximizing the information available. However, at this point of time this notion remains hypothetical in nature, and future research is needed to evaluate the claims.

Task-Dependent Deactivation: Implicit vs. Explicit Processing

In addition to increases in activation, task instructions requiring participants to focus attention on the evaluation of prosodic speech cues might also be linked to a *de*activation of specific brain areas. Particularly, response patterns observed for subcortical limbic regions such as the amygdala provide the empirical foundation for claims of task-related decreases in hemodynamic responding: Considering the contribution of the amygdala to prosody decoding, seemingly contradictory empirical evidence has been presented in the literature: Reports of the amydala's increased (Wiethoff et al., 2009), decreased (Morris, Scott, & Dolan, 1999), or no "critical" (Adolphs & Tranel, 1999) involvement during the processing of vocally expressed emotions leave its exact role in emotional voice decoding an issue of debate. However, across studies a pattern of results has begun to emerge that might allow the resolution of some inconsistencies in the literature: Enhanced activation of the amygdala often appears to be associated with task conditions requiring a more pre-attentive or implicit[1] processing of prosodic signals (Bach et al., 2008; Ethofer, Anders, Erb, Droll, et al., 2006; Wiethoff et al., 2009), whereas studies focusing on the explicit[2] evaluation of vocally expressed emotions rarely report increases in amygdala activation, but rather indicate strong frontal responses (Ethofer, Anders, Erb, Herbert, et al., 2006; Wildgruber et al., 2004, 2005). Based on these observations one might conclude that, whereas processing prosodic signals outside of attention focus may result in an increased response from limbic areas, explicit attentional processing might, in comparison, lead to a deactivation of limbic structures. The latter assumption is corroborated by findings suggesting that frontal brain structures inhibit limbic responses during the performance of demanding cognitive tasks (Blair et al., 2007; Mitchell et al., 2007).

However, research on the implicit processing of prosodic signals (needed to substantiate the aforementioned hypothesis) struggles with methodological difficulties that limit the interpretation of obtained results. The most important methodological challenge associated with this line of research may be summarized in a simple question: How can one operationalize implicit processing in experiments in a way that allows delineating cerebral brain structures selectively responsive to this mode of processing?

One approach to the problem is suggested by experimental designs that employ identical sets of prosodic stimuli under differing task conditions: one (explicit) task requiring the classification of prosodically expressed emotions, and another (implicit) control task used to distract attention away from emotional cues, for instance, by asking the participant to determine a speaker's gender based on the presented speech samples. Brain activity associated with the processing of emotional prosody then can be compared between tasks to delineate activation patterns specific to each processing conditions. However, do cerebral responses during the chosen control condition solely relate to the implicit processing of emotional prosody, or might obtained activation pat-

terns also reflect cognitive processes associated with the task used to distract attention away from prosodic speech cues?

A second approach to study implicit processing that circumvents the issue of competing task effects might be provided by passive listening designs that present prosodic cues without any instructions but to listen to each speech sample. Given that attention is not directed toward the decoding of emotional signals, passive listening might be considered to "model" implicit processing conditions. However, the lack of a behavioral control to ascertain the exact focus of the listener's attention prevents a straightforward interpretation of results. Even in the absence of specific instructions subjects might focus their attention on emotional signals presented by the stimuli. Moreover, if subjects realize that modulations of emotional valence and intensity mark a prominent feature of the employed stimulus material, they might even start to create an explicit emotional discrimination task by themselves.

With respect to the outlined difficulties associated with both experimental designs, the most convincing approach, when aiming to identify neurobiological correlates of implicit processing, might be to evaluate the convergence of results obtained during both "distracter tasks" and passive listening paradigms.

Despite the methodological limitations, however, empirical evidence and hypotheses reviewed in this section suggest the idea of two distinct modes of speech prosody processing, each implemented differently in the human brain:

1. Explicit processing associated with focusing attention on the evaluation of emotional information presented by means of speech prosody
2. Implicit processing during which speech prosody is decoded without deliberately directing attention toward prosodic signals and often even without conscious awareness

In sum, as far as the cerebral correlates of both modes of processing are concerned, experimental data indicate a predominant role of inferior frontal as well as posterior superior temporal regions during the explicit decoding of emotional signals, whereas implicit modes of processing have been described to rely on limbic pathways (Critchley et al., 2000; Hariri, Mattay, Tessitore, Fera, & Weinberger, 2003; Tamietto & de Gelder, 2010), including the amygdala as well as aspects of the anterior rostral mediofrontal cortex (arMFC; Bach et al., 2008; Ethofer, Anders, Erb, Droll, et al., 2006; Sander et al., 2005; Szameitat et al., 2010; Wiethoff et al., 2009).

Ideas of a "limbic" processing path, on the one hand, and a "cortical" pathway, on the other hand, are in accordance with a classic model of emotional information processing proposed by Joseph LeDoux (1998): LeDoux argues that, after basic stages of sensory analysis within the thalamus, emotion processing relies on two distinct neural circuits: (1) the "low road," a pathway connecting the thalamus directly with the amydgala, and (2) the "high road" relaying information from the thalamus to the cortex, which in turn projects back to the amygdala. The low road is described as representing a "safety system" bypassing conscious awareness that, in a quick and efficient way, triggers emotional responses that alert and prepare the body to act. In contrast, the second loop – the so-called high road – relates to a slower, yet conscious and much more elaborate way of processing that creates a more precise representation of the environment and a more thorough appraisal of the situation at hand. Moreover, via projections to the amygdala this pathway allows the control and finetuning of emotional responses triggered by the "low road" to fit the needs of a given environment.

Applying LeDoux's ideas to prosody processing, the following hypotheses can be derived: Whereas limbic activation tied to implicit modes of prosody processing may reflect the automatic induction of emotional responses, cortical activation patterns observed during the explicit processing condition, in contrast, may be linked to cognitive control and appraisal processes that help regulate limbic responses and above all allow a thorough evaluation of the prosodic cues sent by our partners of interaction.

Summary: A Cerebral Network Model of Prosody Comprehension

When the individual pieces of empirical evidence provided in this section are put together, prosody comprehension emerges as a complex function tied to several cortical and subcortical brain structures. Research has established a contribution of temporal regions such as the p-STC and m-STC, frontal structures including the IFC, and limbic regions such as the amygdala or aspects of the arMFC. Each of these brain structures, in turn, has been suggested to be associated with distinct aspects of prosody decoding from the basic stages of acoustic analysis to higher order evaluative processes.

The localization of cerebral correlates, in addition, is complemented by empirical evidence that further details the complex interplay of brain structures implicated in prosody decoding. Investigations modeling interactions among different nodes of the prosody network point to a strong coupling between the activation of frontal and temporal sites and suggest a flow of information from the right STC to the right and left IFC during the processing of emotional speech prosody (Ethofer, Anders, Erb, Herbert, et al., 2006).

In sum, current research findings propose the idea that prosody comprehension is mediated by a sequential multistep process unfolding from the basic stages of acoustic voice analysis (bound to temporal brain areas) and proceeding to higher level stages of categorization and recognition (associated with frontal aspects of the brain). After the processing of auditory information within the ear, brainstem, thalamus, and primary acoustic cortex (A1), three successive steps of prosody decoding can be identified:

Step 1: Extraction of acoustic features of prosodic cues

Step 2: Identification of vocally expressed emotion by means of multimodal integration

Step 3: Explicit evaluation and cognitive elaboration of vocally expressed emotions

Each of these steps, in turn, appears to be differentially represented in the human brain. Whereas the extraction of acoustic features have been linked to voice-sensitive structures of the m-STC, more posterior aspects of the right STC have been recognized for their contribution to the identification and integration of emotional signals expressed by means of speech prosody (please refer to the subsections, "Stimulus-Driven Activation Associated with the Processing of Affective Prosody" and "Task-Dependent Activation Associated with the Processing of Affective Prosody"). In contrast, subprocesses concerned with the evaluation and cognitive elaboration of vocally expressed emotions have been linked to inferior frontal structures of both cerebral hemispheres. Within the prosody network, information transfer from primary acoustic regions (A1) to the m-STC has been characterized as primarily stimulus driven in nature, whereas projection to the p-STC and IFC has been described as depending on focusing attention on the explicit evaluation of expressed emotions (please refer to the subsections, "Stimulus-Driven Activation Associated with the Processing of Affective Prosody" and "Task-Dependent Activation Associated with the Processing of Affective Prosody").

The sequential nature of the proposed processing steps is further corroborated by electrophysiological studies that allow discerning the time course of various aspects of prosody decoding. Recordings of event-related potentials (ERPs), for example, link the acoustic analysis of a given speech cue to changes in brain activation occurring within the first 100 ms after stimulus onset, whereas processes related to the evaluation of emotional meaning appear to be reflected in variations of brain responses with higher latencies: Research findings, for instance, indicate that modulations of acoustic properties such as frequency and intensity affect ERP components (i.e., N1) that peak as early as approximately 60–80 ms (Woods, 1995) after the onset of an auditory event (see ERP evidence reviewed in Schirmer & Kotz, 2006), thus underlining the assertions that the analysis of the auditory input signal occurs early in the process of speech prosody decoding. However, experimental conditions requiring participants to focus attention on identifying emotions based on prosodic markers of a speaker's voice have been shown to modulate ERP signals around 360 ms post stimulus onset (Wambacq, Shea-Miller, & Abubakr, 2004), suggesting processing steps concerned with the explicit evaluation of emotional information follow stages of acoustic analysis in time.

In addition to the explicit decoding tied to the three processing steps detailed earlier, a second implicit mode of prosody processing has been assumed. In contrast to the explicit evaluation, implicit processing is believed to occur without intentionally devoting attention to the interpretation of prosodic signals. Considering cerebral correlates associated with this mode of processing, studies suggest that a network including the amygdala and arMFC subserves the implicit analysis of prosodic speech cues (please refer to the subsection, "Task-Dependent Deactivation: Implicit vs. Explicit Processing").

Recent neuroimaging studies indicate a complex interaction between the structures of the implicit and explicit processing routes: Findings support the idea that frontal cortical areas implicated in the explicit analysis of prosodic cues might also contribute to the inhibition of limbic activation when individuals actively attend to emotional signals. Suppression of limbic activation, in turn, has been assumed to reflect a recruitment of emotion regulation processes that attenuate the automatic induction of emotional reactions associated with limbic activation in order to avoid emotional interference in goal-directed behavior (Blair et al., 2007).

Questions, however, remain as to how complete is this proposed model of prosody

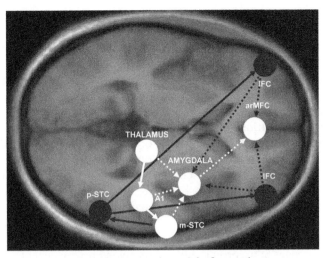

Figure 11.2. A cerebral network model of prosody processing: Illustrated are cerebral structures contributing to explicit as well as implicit modes of prosody processing. A1= primary acoustic cortex, m-STC = middle aspects of the superior temporal cortex, p-STC = posterior aspects of the superior temporal cortex, IFC = inferior frontal cortex, arMFC = anterior rostral medial frontal cortex. Flow of information during implicit processing is indicated by dotted lines. Stimulus-driven modulations of brain responses are illustrated by white arrows. Task-dependent modulations of brain responses are marked with black arrows (solid black arrow = activation; dashed black arrow= deactivation). Note that depicted connections do not necessarily imply direct neuronal connections between different regions; rather the flow of information might be mediated through additional neuronal structures.

processing. At this point, the current account can only provide a framework to understand the contributions of frontotemporal and subcortical brain structures most consistently implicated in the process of prosody decoding. Yet several reports published in the literature suggest an involvement of other brain regions as well: An increasing amount of clinical data, for instance, indicate marked impairments in prosody decoding after traumatic or degenerative lesions of the basal ganglia (Breitenstein, Van Lancker, Daum, & Waters, 2001; Cancelliere & Kertesz, 1990; Pell & Leonard, 2003). Such clinical observations are further supported by imaging studies reporting a recruitment of the basal ganglia during the decoding of prosodic cues (Bach et al., 2008; Kotz et al., 2003). Similarly, both lesion (Hornak et al., 2003) and fMRI data (Ethofer, Kreifelts, et al., 2009; Quadflieg et al., 2008; Wildgruber et al., 2004) also point to an involvement of the orbitofrontal cortex (OFC) in the processing of vocal prosodic markers. However, despite the growing body of evidence, the exact role of the basal ganglia and OFC in prosody processing remains elusive. Initial evidence links both structures to the later cognitive-evaluative stage of prosody processing (Paulmann, Ott, & Kotz, 2011; Schirmer & Kotz, 2006), yet further specifications appear to be needed.

Nonverbal Vocalizations

Even though speech and language no doubt constitutes humankind's most sophisticated means of information transfer, the vocal communication of emotions extends well beyond speech-related phenomena. In fact, human beings quite frequently rely on a variety of nonverbal vocalizations,[3] such as sighs, sobs, screams, groans, moans, or laughter, to express how they feel. And although nonverbal vocalizations in a sense may resemble animal calls (Scott, Sauter, & McGettigan, 2009) rather than more elaborate human vocal behaviors such as speech, nonverbal tokens nonetheless prove to be effective carries of emotional information. Not only are listeners able to decode nonverbal vocalization with remarkably high accuracy (Schröder, 2003; 81% correct classifications on average across 10 different emotions) but research findings also suggest that in vocal communication some emotions might typically be expressed by short vocalizations rather than by speech-related cues (Schröder, 2003). Disgust, for example, serves as a prime example to illustrate the latter idea: Although recognition rates tend to be comparatively low when expressed by means of speech prosody (Banse & Scherer, 1996), vocalizations of disgust (e.g. Yuck!, Eww!) rank among the most reliably decoded types of "affective bursts" (Schröder, 2003; average decoding accuracy: 93 %).

Despite differences in recognizability, however, similarities emerge at the level of acoustic characteristics: A recent study conducted by Sauter and colleagues (2010), for instance, found that different emotions expressed by means of nonverbal vocalizations map onto distinctive acoustic profiles that resemble to a certain degree acoustic patterns obtained for vocal-prosodic markers of the respective emotional state (for more details see Banse & Scherer, 1996; Juslin & Laukka, 2003; Sauter, Eisner, Calder, & Scott, 2010).

Commonalities further translate to cerebral correlates associated with the processing of nonverbal vocalizations and prosodic vocal emotional cues: Similar to speech prosody, contributions of the superior temporal cortex (Meyer, Baumann, Wildgruber, & Alter, 2007; Meyer, Zysset, Von Cramon, & Alter, 2005; Sander & Scheich, 2005; Scott et al., 2009) and of subcortical structures such as the amygdala (Fecteau, Belin, Joanette, & Armony, 2007) or basal ganglia (Morris et al., 1999) have been suggested for the processing of nonverbal emotional vocalization.

However, compared to the sizable body of research on the decoding of emotional prosody, knowledge concerning the processing of nonverbal vocalizations remains limited. Nonetheless, in recent years, particularly vocalizations of laughter – or more precisely the (cerebral) processes that allow us to perceive laughter signals – have received growing attention.

The Neurobiological Basis of Laughter Perception

Asked for a simple definition of the word "laughter," most people would probably resort to descriptions characterizing it as a vocal expression of joy and happiness. However, challenged to recall different situations in which we have experienced laughter, we most certainly will arrive at the conclusion that, in addition to joy and happiness, laughter may encode various other emotional states and may serve as a valuable communicational signal in a variety of social situations and emotional contexts.

Different emotions appear to be associated with the characteristic sound of laughter defined by distinctive modulations of voice pitch, loudness, or duration of laughter segments (Szameitat et al., 2009; Szameitat, Darwin, Szameitat, Wildgruber, & Alter, 2011). Just picture the nervous giggles of a speaker who has lost his train of thought or the sound of laughter meant to taunt and ridicule its addressee. Thus, whether a person, for instance, feels joy or comtempt towards his or her communication partner might be discerned based solely on the acoustic signals that constitute human laughter. Indeed, even if no information but the sheer sound of laughter is available, human beings are still able to infer and classify the emotional states of their partners of interaction with good accuracy, as illustrated by a study conducted by Szameitat, Alter, Szameitat, and Darwin (2009).

To evaluate the role of laughter as a communicative signal, Szameitat and colleagues investigated whether healthy adults would be able to determine a person's current emotional state based on the sound of his or her laughter. In preparation for this experiment, the authors recorded portrayals of different types of "emotional laughter" from eight professional actors. To aid their acting performance, actors were instructed to imagine or recall one of four mental states or situations: (1) being tickled, (2) being happy, (3) taunting somebody, or (4) enjoying the misfortune of another person. As soon as they "felt the mood" of the given situation, actors were encouraged to produce laughter sounds typical of their current state of mind. Each uttered laugh was digitally recorded, which resulted in a set of laughter sequences comprising multiple examples of four basic types of laughter: (1) tickling and (2) taunting laughter, as well as laughter conveying (3) joy, and (4) schadenfreude. The authors then asked a group of 72 healthy volunteers to classify recorded laughter sequences according to the emotions conveyed by each sound bit. Despite the fact that no further information was provided, listeners were able to infer the expressed emotional state on the basis of presented acoustic laughter signals with accuracy rates of decoding well above chance level (25% correct identifications) for each laughter type (joy: 44%, tickling: 45%, taunting: 50%, schadenfreude: 37%).

Considering the neurobiological underpinnings of laughter perception, an involvement of temporal brain structures, particularly the superior temporal cortex as well as frontal and limbic regions, has been described in the literature (Meyer et al., 2005, 2007; Sander & Scheich, 2001, 2005; Szameitat et al., 2010). Moreover, different types of laughter have been associated with distinct cerebral activation patterns: Whereas joyous and taunting forms of laughter (i.e., emotional laughter), for instance, have been shown to elicit particularly strong responses of the arMFC, laughter induced by tickling has been related to a more pronounced recruitment of voice-sensitive structures of the right m-STC (Szameitat et al., 2010). Differences in m-STC activation have been assumed to reflect variations in acoustic complexity among different types of emotional laughter, whereas differential activation of the arMFC has been suggested to relate to differences in social meaning (Szameitat et al., 2010). Unlike different types of "emotional" laughter that may carry different messages in various social contexts (e.g., laughter meant to taunt or reject somebody, joyous laughter inviting bystanders to join in), laughter induced by tickling can be considered a more unequivocal cue related to playful interactions that promote social bonding (Szameitat et al., 2010). Considering the aforementioned differences in social meaning, one may assume that the processing of emotional laughter may pose a greater challenge to social cognition – a set of processes supporting social functioning (see Amodio & Frith, 2006) – and thus more strongly activate cerebral structures implicated in social-cognitive processing such as the arMFC (reviewed in Amodio & Frith, 2006).

In sum, however, empirical evidence to date can only provide a glimpse into the cerebral bases of laughter perception, as well as encouragement for future research to broaden our insights into how the brain "understands" emotional vocalizations such as laughter.

Emotional Voices in Context: Audiovisual Integration of Emotional Signals

Although single pieces of "emotional evidence," such as vocal signals, may on their own already provide valuable cues, inferences about the mental states of our partners of interaction most often are based on a variety of information derived from different channels of communication.

Vocal signals, for instance, are often complemented by facial expressions that provide further information as to what others might think or feel. Combining or *integrating* such visual and acoustic emotional signals, on the one hand, may facilitate emotion judgments; as for example, behavioral data (Dolan, Morris, & de Gelder, 2001; de Gelder & Vroomen, 2000; Kreifelts, Ethofer, Grodd, Erb, & Wildgruber, 2007; Massaro & Egan, 1996), indicating shortened response latencies and higher classification accuracy for stimuli providing matching facial and vocal information (e.g., a happy facial expression paired with a happy tone of voice while speaking) evidences. On the other hand, information gathered from one channel of communication may also modulate or alter the interpretation of emotional signals conveyed by the other. Pictures of facial expressions, for instance, may be evaluated rather differently when paired with vocal cues of different emotional connotation (de Gelder & Vroomen, 2000; Ethofer, Anders, Erb, Droll, et al., 2006; Massaro & Egan, 1996; Müller et al., 2010). Neutral faces, for example, are regarded as more fearful when combined with a fearful voice – even when participants are asked to ignore co-occurring vocal information (de Gelder & Vroomen, 2000).

In sum, seeing an affective facial expression while at the same time hearing an emotional voice appears to trigger an involuntary process of audiovisual binding (Pourtois, de Gelder, Vroomen, Rossion, & Crommelinck, 2000) that shapes affective judgments. In recent years, an increasing number of neuroscientific studies have aimed at defining the cerebral mechanisms that contribute to the integration of audio and visual affective information. Groundbreaking insights into how the brain processes multisensory stimulation have been gathered from anatomical and electrophysiological studies both in humans and animals (reviewed in Campanella & Belin, 2007; Ethofer, Pourtois, & Wildgruber, 2006). Building on the results obtained in these studies, numerous brain regions have been related to multisensory processing: "Sensory-specific" brain areas such as the auditory cortex (Kayser, Petkov, & Logo-

thetis, 2009), as well as "convergence zones" (Damasio, 1989) – brain areas that receive afferent input from several senses, such as the superior temporal (Seltzer & Pandya, 1978) and orbitofrontal cortex (Chavis & Pandya, 1976), the insula (Mesulam & Mufson, 1982), the superior colliculi (Fries, 1984), the claustrum (Pearson, Brodal, Gatter, & Powell, 1982), thalamus (Mufson & Mesulam, 1984), or amygdala (McDonald, 1998) – have been suggested as potential sites of audiovisual integration.

Knowledge derived from anatomical and electrophysiological studies is further complemented by a growing body of fMRI research. Even though approaches taken to explore audiovisual integration tend to differ considerably among studies, a pattern has begun to emerge that suggests a crucial role of the superior temporal cortex in the integration of facial and vocal emotional cues. Compelling evidence for an involvement of the STC is presented, for instance, in a series of fMRI experiments conducted by Kreifelts and collaborators (Kreifelts et al., 2007; Kreifelts, Ethofer, Huberle, Grodd, & Wildgruber, 2010; Kreifelts, Ethofer, Shiozawa, Grodd, & Wildgruber, 2009). Aiming to delineate audiovisual integration sites in the human brain, Kreifelts and colleagues chose to contrast brain activation to audiovisual emotional stimulation with brain responses evoked by unimodal (visual or auditory) stimuli. Participants were asked to classify a range of audiovisual (video clips), visual (mute videos), and auditory (sound clips) stimuli according to the conveyed emotions. Each video or sound clip depicted men and women expressing different emotional states by means of verbal, vocal, and facial signals, and each participant was instructed to label the type of emotion based on the nonverbal cues (facial expressions, tone of voice) presented. Contrasts between the audiovisual and unimodal processing conditions computed on behavioral data (i.e., reaction times, accuracy of decoding) and brain activation data allowed detailing effects of audiovisual integration both at the behavioral and cerebral level. Compared to unimodal processing conditions, the audiovisual presentation of nonverbal emotional signals was associated with a significant perceptual gain that resulted in markedly higher accuracy rates. At the cerebral level, observed increases in decoding accuracy were associated with increasing activation of the right and left p-STC during the processing of audiovisual nonverbal cues – suggesting the p-STC as a site of audiovisual integration (Kreifelts et al., 2007). Considerations of connectivity further support this idea: Not only do projections from both primary auditory and visual cortices converge within the p-STC but rather analyses employed to estimate the functional coupling of different brain regions also reveal an enhanced synchronization of activation within the bilateral p-STC and temporal voice areas within the m-STC, as well as face-sensitive aspects of the fusiform gyrus during the processing of audiovisual nonverbal signals (Kreifelts et al., 2007). Building on the observed enhanced functional coupling between unimodal associative cortices and the p-STC associated with audiovisual emotional stimulation, audiovisual integration has been proposed to be a process during which information from spatially distinct modality-specific processing sites (e.g., the fusiform face area; Kanwisher et al., 1997; and temporal voice areas; Belin et al., 2000) is transmitted to integration areas within the p-STC where the information is bound into a single percept (Kreifelts et al., 2007). In sum, current empirical evidence suggests that the integration of vocal emotional information with co-occurring facial signals might rely on a common "supramodal" processing step tied to brain structures implicated in audiovisual integration in general (e.g., the p-STC), as well as modality-specific processing steps associated with the recruitment of "unimodal" cortices (Campanella & Belin, 2007).

In uniting this idea with current data regarding the processing of emotional facial expressions and of emotional vocal cues, a working model of affective face-voice integration can be conceived. It builds on similarities between the processing of emotions

in both sensory modalities such as the following:

a. The reliance on modality-specific "processing modules" (i.e., FFA; Kanwisher, et al., 1997, and temporal voice areas; Belin, et al., 2000) related to basic stages of perceptual analysis
b. An involvement of orbito- as well as inferior frontal brain structures during the explicit evaluation of both visually and vocally expressed emotions (evidence reviewed in Posamentier & Abdi, 2003; Wildgruber et al., 2009)
c. Two routs of processing: explicit "cortical" and implicit "limbic" processing (evidence reviewed in Posamentier & Abdi, 2003; Wildgruber et al., 2009) reported for both emotional face processing and emotional voice processing

One might then propose three (general) processing steps associated with the perception of audiovisual nonverbal emotional signals (Wildgruber et al., 2009):

1. Extraction of visual and vocal communicative signals within the respective modality-specific primary cortices and specialized processing modules
2. Integration of audio and visual information into a single percept within the posterior superior temporal cortex
3. Cognitive elaboration and explicit evaluation of emotional information related to the activation of inferior and orbitofrontal brain structures

Moreover, in analogy to concepts reviewed for speech prosody processing (see the earlier discussion) and in accordance with the published literature on the decoding of emotional facial expression (reviewed elsewhere, e.g., Posamentier & Abdi, 2003), our working model assumes that the processing of audiovisual emotional information can occur in two ways, each of which is tied to different neural circuits and functional meaning: Audiovisual emotional signals may, on the one hand, be decoded in an explicit, cognitive controlled way represented by the three

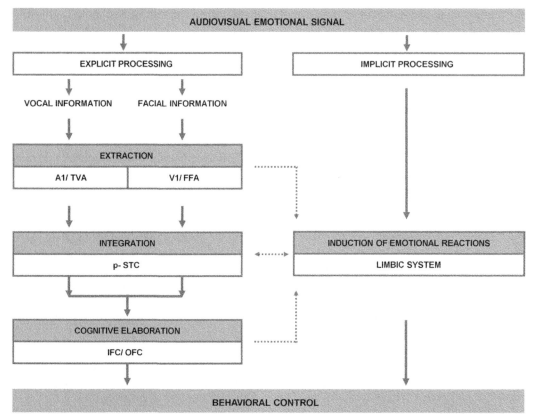

Figure 11.3. A working model of the integration and perception of *audiovisual* emotional signals: Processing steps and corresponding neural substrates are depicted for explicit and implicit modes of processing. Hypothetical interactions between cerebral structures are marked with dashed arrows. A1 = primary auditory cortex; TVA = temporal voice areas, V1 = primary visual cortex; FFA = fusiform face area, p-STS = posterior aspects of the superior temporal cortex, IFC = inferior frontal cortex; OFC = orbitofrontal cortex.

steps described earlier. On the other hand, nonverbal emotional cues may be processed in a rather implicit or un-intentional manner implemented mainly via limbic pathways (see Figure 11.3).

Overall Summary: Current Knowledge and Future Research

Similar to visual emotional signals such as facial expressions or gestures, vocal sounds provide a powerful means of affective communication. Each and every day of our lives, we are surrounded by emotional voices and we use voice-based acoustic cues such as laughter or speech prosody to infer and decipher the emotional messages sent by our partners of interaction.

At the cerebral level, the human ability to derive emotional meaning from vocal signals draws on the complex interplay of several cortical regions located in the middle and posterior superior temporal lobe and frontal lobe, as well as subcortical structures such as the amygdala or thalamus. Each contributing structure, in turn, has been tied to distinct aspects of decoding emotional voices from the basic stages of acoustic analysis to higher order evaluative processes: Superior temporal regions have been suggested to subserve stages of acoustic analysis and multimodal binding, whereas frontal structures implicated in emotional voice perception have been related to subprocesses including the explicit evaluation of vocally expressed emotions or social cognition in general.

Although research of the past decades has greatly broadened our insight into the neurobiology of emotional voice perception, current evidence and models mark only the beginning, not the end, of the endeavor to understand how the brain processes emotional vocal cues. Rather than providing an exhaustive and coherent picture, current knowledge forms a solid ground on which to base future research. In fact, despite the wealth of data available on the topic, numerous questions remain as of yet unanswered. Here are just a few examples:

• Can we further specify and extend models of emotional voice processing?

Various brain structures have been identified as contributing to the processing of emotional voice, yet the functional role of some structures implicated in the process warrants further elaboration. Approaches that could lead the way to a better understanding of how the brain deciphers vocal markers of emotions may be guided by the following subset of questions: What are the similarities and differences in the cerebral processes mediating the decoding of affective prosody or vocalizations such as laughter? Can we delineate differences among various emotional categories? For instance, are happy voices processed in a different way than fearful ones? How does the brain respond to vocal patterns of "mixed" emotions, which we might frequently encounter in everyday life (e.g., leaving a job to take a new position at another firm may render an individual excited about the new challenge while at the same time sad to leave old friends and colleagues)?

• How do potential determinants of interindividual differences such as age, gender, past experience, or personality affect the cerebral processing of emotional voice cues?

Although in some respects each and every member of the human races shares fundamental mechanisms of information processing with his or her fellow human beings, the ways in which human beings perceive and process their emotional environment nonetheless often appear to differ tremendously among individuals. Considering the cerebral processing of emotional signals, individual differences have been shown to modulate emotional brain responses to facial expressions or emotional pictures (see Chapters 24 and 25; Hamann & Canli, 2004).

With respect to individual differences in the processing of emotional voices, however, empirical evidence remains sparse. Nontheless, particularly sex differences have been discussed in the literature (see Chapter 26). Neuroimaging studies, for instance, indicate sex-related modulations of brain responses associated with the decoding of emotional voices (Schirmer, Zysset, Kotz, & Yves von Cramon, 2004), as well as differences in the time course of emotional voice processing between men and women (Schirmer, Kotz, & Friederici, 2002). Beyond sex differences, research evidence also suggests a strong influence of personality on brain activation related to the processing of vocal emotional cues (Brück, Kreifelts, Kaza, Lotze, & Wildgruber, 2011). To date, however, research regarding the impact of interindividual differences appears to focus almost exclusively on sex or personality. Thus, future studies should aim not only to reevaluate current findings but also to investigate effects of neglected parameters such as age or personal experience on the cerebral processing of emotional voice cues.

• Can we distinguish persons skilled in the decoding of vocally expressed emotions from those individuals with difficulties in interpreting such social signals based on typical patterns of brain activation?

Although most individuals would probably consider the decoding of vocal emotional signals a task easily solved, difficulties in emotional voice processing have been reported for several patient groups, including individuals diagnosed with schizophrenia (Hoekert, Kahn, Pijnenborg, & Aleman, 2007), depression (Kan, Mimura, Kamijima, & Kawamura, 2004; Uekermann,

Abdel-Hamid, Lehmkamper, Vollmoeller, & Daum, 2008), and autism (Chevallier, Noveck, Happe, & Wilson, 2011; Van Lancker, Cornelius, & Kreiman, 1989). Recent evidence, moreover, suggests differences in the cerebral processing of vocal emotional signals associated with those diseases (Bach et al., 2009; Gervais et al., 2004; Leitman et al., 2007). Based on the aforementioned observations, one might ask, Can brain activation patterns be used to classify normal and dysfunctional voice perception? Or can we differentiate specific psychopathologies on the basis of brain responses elicited by vocal emotional cues?

- How does the processing context influence the neurobiological basis of emotional voice decoding?

In addition to person-specific variables such as personality, age, or gender, contextual factors need to be regarded as another source of influence that might modulate the cerebral processing of emotional voices. Are there differences in how the brain responds to vocal social cues directed to oneself as compared to signals addressed to an unknown third person or a group of persons? Are there differences in how we process familiar as compared to unfamiliar emotional voices or voice cues sent by several individuals simultaneously? How does the brain handle conflict that may arise from contradictory emotional information accompanying vocal cues (e.g., conflicting facial expressions)?

- Does the processing of spontaneous, naturally occurring vocal expressions differ from the processing of actors' portrayals?

Finally, with respect to study design and stimulus selection, particularly one question needs to be addressed in the future: Do naturally occurring vocal expressions of emotions differ from actors' portrayals of the respective emotional state? A majority of studies in the field of emotional voice perception to date have relied on acted emotional portrayals. The reasons are not far to seek: Acted portrayals are relatively easy to

collect for a large variety of different types of emotions, and they can be recorded with great quality in a highly controlled acoustic environment. However, do actors' displays really mirror emotional expressions we encounter in everyday life, or are they merely masks reflecting exaggerated stereotypes of ways to express ourselves? Research aiming to extrapolate results to the "real world" and not just any laboratory environment, of course, would greatly benefit from the use of natural, spontaneously occurring displays of emotion. But how can we gather a large set of stimuli that are highly ecologically valid and controlled or matched with respect to basic perceptual features (to meet the current standards of brain research)? What further complicates the use of naturalistic stimulus material are difficulties in determining a label for emotions conveyed in spontaneously occurring expressions, because we can never be sure about a sender's true emotional state or intentions. One way of tackling or at least ameliorating this problem is to use long-term behavioral observations during day-to-day social interaction and to focus on context cues to decipher underlining emotional states. Of course this is easier said than done, particularly because those real-life events would need to be recorded to become usable stimulus material. However, a potential source from which to derive such material could be reality television – a genre of television that (supposedly) documents real-life situations and broadcasts them with high picture and sound quality (see also Juslin & Scherer, 2005, on the issue of obtaining voice samples).

The questions listed here are only a few examples of a myriad of research topics that await further elaboration. Of course, many more questions ensue, each holding the potential to advance our understanding of how the brain processes vocal cues of emotions.

Acknowledgments

Parts of this chapter have been taken from a review article originally prepared by the authors for *Physics of Life Reviews*, 8(4), 383–403.

Abbreviations

arMFC	anterior rostral medial frontal cortex
ERPs	event-related potentials
fMRI	functional magnetic resonance imaging
FFA	fusiform face area
IFC	inferior frontal cortex
OFC	orbitofrontal cortex
m-STC	middle aspects of the superior temporal cortex
p-STC	posterior aspects of the superior temporal cortex

Notes

1 The term "implicit" is uses to described conditions during which the processing of prosodic signals is task- irrelevant and occurs rather incidentally or unintentionally (Tamietto & de Gelder, 2010).

2 "Explicit" refers to processing conditions during which the evaluation of prosodic signals is task-relevant and attention is devoted to interpreting emotions expressed by speech prosody.

3 In some publications nonverbal vocalizations are also referred to as vocal „affective bursts" (Scherer, 1994).

References

Ackermann, H., Hertrich, I., Grodd, W., & Wildgruber, D. (2004). Das Hören von Gefühlen: Funktionell-neuroanatomische Grundlage der Verarbeitung affektiver Prosodie. *Aktuelle Neurologie*, 31, 449–60.

Adolphs, R., & Tranel, D. (1999). Intact recognition of emotional prosody following amygdala damage. *Neuropsychologia*, 37(11), 1285–92.

Amodio, D. M., & Frith, C. D. (2006). Meeting of minds: the medial frontal cortex and social cognition. *Nature Reviews Neuroscience*, 7(4), 268–77.

Bach, D. R., Grandjean, D., Sander, D., Herdener, M., Strik, W. K., & Seifritz, E. (2008). The effect of appraisal level on processing of emotional prosody in meaningless speech. *Neuroimage*, 42(2), 919–27.

Bach, D. R., Herdener, M., Grandjean, D., Sander, D., Seifritz, E., & Strik, W. K. (2009). Altered lateralisation of emotional prosody processing in schizophrenia. *Schizophrenia Research*, 110(1–3), 180–87.

Banse, R., & Scherer, K. R. (1996). Acoustic profiles in vocal emotion expression. *Journal of Personality and Social Psychology*, 70(3), 614–36.

Belin, P., Fecteau, S., & Bedard, C. (2004). Thinking the voice: Neural correlates of voice perception. *Trends in Cognitive Science*, 8(3), 129–35.

Belin, P., & Grosbras, M. H. (2010). Before speech: Cerebral voice processing in infants. *Neuron*, 65(6), 733–35.

Belin, P., & Zatorre, R. J. (2003). Adaptation to speaker's voice in right anterior temporal lobe. *Neuroreport*, 14(16), 2105–9.

Belin, P., Zatorre, R. J., & Ahad, P. (2002). Human temporal-lobe response to vocal sounds. *Brain Research: Cognitive Brain Research*, 13(1), 17–26.

Belin, P., Zatorre, R. J., Lafaille, P., Ahad, P., & Pike, B. (2000). Voice-selective areas in human auditory cortex. *Nature*, 403(6767), 309–12.

Blair, K. S., Smith, B. W., Mitchell, D. G., Morton, J., Vythilingam, M., Pessoa, L., et al. (2007). Modulation of emotion by cognition and cognition by emotion. *Neuroimage*, 35(1), 430–40.

Breitenstein, C., Van Lancker, D., Daum, I., & Waters, C. H. (2001). Impaired perception of vocal emotions in Parkinson's disease: Influence of speech time processing and executive functioning. *Brain Cognition*, 45(2), 277–314.

Brück, C., Kreifelts, B., Kaza, E., Lotze, M., & Wildgruber, D. (2011). Impact of personality on the cerebral processing of emotional prosody. *Neuroimage*, 58(1), 259–68.

Campanella, S., & Belin, P. (2007). Integrating face and voice in person perception. *Trends in Cognitive Science*, 11(12), 535–43.

Cancelliere, A. E., & Kertesz, A. (1990). Lesion localization in acquired deficits of emotional expression and comprehension. *Brain Cognition*, 13(2), 133–47.

Chavis, D. A., & Pandya, D. N. (1976). Further observations on corticofrontal connections in the rhesus monkey. *Brain Research*, 117(3), 369–86.

Chein, J. M., Ravizza, S. M., & Fiez, J. A. (2003). Using neuroimaging to evaluate models of working memory and their implications for language processing. *Journal of Neurolinguistics*, 16, 315–39.

Chevallier, C., Noveck, I., Happe, F., & Wilson, D. (2011). What's in a voice? Prosody as a test case for the Theory of Mind account of autism. *Neuropsychologia*, 49(3), 507–17.

Critchley, H., Daly, E., Phillips, M., Brammer, M., Bullmore, E., Williams, S., et al. (2000). Explicit and implicit neural mechanisms for processing of social information from facial expressions: A functional magnetic resonance imaging study. *Hum Brain Mapping*, 9(2), 93–105.

D'Esposito, M., Aguirre, G. K., Zarahn, E., Ballard, D., Shin, R. K., & Lease, J. (1998). Functional MRI studies of spatial and nonspatial working memory. *Brain Research: Cognitive Brain Research*, 7(1), 1–13.

Damasio, A. R. (1989). Time-locked multiregional retroactivation: A systems-level proposal for the neural substrates of recall and recognition. *Cognition*, 33(1–2), 25–62.

de Gelder, B., & Vroomen, J. (2000). The perception of emotions by ear and by eye. *Cognition and Emotion*, 14(3), 289–311.

Dolan, R. J., Morris, J. S. & de Gelder, B. (2001). Crossmodal binding of fear in voice and face. *Proceedings of the National Academy of Sciences of the United States of America*, 98(17), 10006–10010.

Ethofer, T., Anders, S., Erb, M., Droll, C., Royen, L., Saur, R., et al. (2006). Impact of voice on emotional judgment of faces: An event-related fMRI study. *Human Brain Mapping*, 27(9), 707–14.

Ethofer, T., Anders, S., Erb, M., Herbert, C., Wiethoff, S., Kissler, J., et al. (2006). Cerebral pathways in processing of affective prosody: A dynamic causal modeling study. *Neuroimage*, 30(2), 580–87.

Ethofer, T., Anders, S., Wiethoff, S., Erb, M., Herbert, C., Saur, R., et al. (2006). Effects of prosodic emotional intensity on activation of associative auditory cortex. *Neuroreport*, 17(3), 249–53.

Ethofer, T., Bretscher, J., Gschwind, M., Kreifelts, B., Wildgruber, D., & Vuilleumier, P. (2012). Emotional voice areas: Anatomic location, functional properties, and structural connections revealed by combined fMRI/DTI. *Cerebral Cortex*, 22(1), 191–200.

Ethofer, T., Kreifelts, B., Wiethoff, S., Wolf, J., Grodd, W., Vuilleumier, P., et al. (2009). Differential influences of emotion, task, and novelty on brain regions underlying the processing of speech melody. *Journal of Cognitive Neuroscience*, 21(7), 1255–68.

Ethofer, T., Pourtois, G., & Wildgruber, D. (2006). Investigating audiovisual integration of emotional signals in the human brain. *Progress in Brain Research*, 156, 345–61.

Ethofer, T., Van De Ville, D., Scherer, K., & Vuilleumier, P. (2009). Decoding of emotional information in voice-sensitive cortices. *Current Biology*, 19(12), 1028–33.

Ethofer, T., Wiethoff, S., Anders, S., Kreifelts, B., Grodd, W., & Wildgruber, D. (2007). The voices of seduction: Cross-gender effects in processing of erotic prosody. *Social Cognition and Affective Neuroscience*, 2(4), 334–37.

Fecteau, S., Belin, P., Joanette, Y., & Armony, J. L. (2007). Amygdala responses to nonlinguistic emotional vocalizations. *Neuroimage*, 36(2), 480–87.

Fries, W. (1984). Cortical projections to the superior colliculus in the macaque monkey: A retrograde study using horseradish peroxidase. *Journal of Comparative Neurology*, 230(1), 55–76.

Gervais, H., Belin, P., Boddaert, N., Leboyer, M., Coez, A., Sfaello, I., et al. (2004). Abnormal cortical voice processing in autism. *Nature Neuroscience*, 7(8), 801–2.

Grandjean, D., Sander, D., Pourtois, G., Schwartz, S., Seghier, M. L., Scherer, K. R., et al. (2005). The voices of wrath: Brain responses to angry prosody in meaningless speech. *Nature Neuroscience*, 8(2), 145–46.

Hamann, S., & Canli, T. (2004). Individual differences in emotion processing. *Current Opinion in Neurobiology*, 14(2), 233–38.

Hariri, A. R., Mattay, V. S., Tessitore, A., Fera, F., & Weinberger, D. R. (2003). Neocortical modulation of the amygdala response to fearful stimuli. *Biological Psychiatry*, 53(6), 494–501.

Hoekert, M., Kahn, R. S., Pijnenborg, M., & Aleman, A. (2007). Impaired recognition and expression of emotional prosody in schizophrenia: Review and meta-analysis. *Schizophrenia Research*, 96(1–3), 135–45.

Hornak, J., Bramham, J., Rolls, E. T., Morris, R. G., O'Doherty, J., Bullock, P. R., et al. (2003). Changes in emotion after circumscribed surgical lesions of the orbitofrontal and cingulate cortices. *Brain*, 126(Pt. 7), 1691–1712.

Juslin, P. N., & Laukka, P. (2003). Emotional expression in speech and music: evidence of cross-modal similarities. *Annals of the New York Academy of Sciences*, 1000, 279–82.

Juslin, P. N., & Scherer, K. R. (2005). Vocal expression of affect. In J. Harrigan, R. Rosenthal, & K. R. Scherer (Eds.), *The new handbook of methods in nonverbal behavior research* (pp. 65–135). Oxford: Oxford University Press.

Kan, Y., Mimura, M., Kamijima, K., & Kawamura, M. (2004). Recognition of emotion from moving facial and prosodic stimuli in depressed patients. *Journal of Neurology, Neurosurgery and Psychiatry*, 75, 1667–71.

Kanwisher, N., McDermott, J., & Chun, M. M. (1997). The fusiform face area: A module in human extrastriate cortex specialized for face perception. *Journal of Neuroscience*, 17(11), 4302–11.

Kayser, C., Petkov, C. I., & Logothetis, N. K. (2009). Multisensory interactions in primate auditory cortex: fMRI and electrophysiology. *Hearing Research*, 258(1–2), 80–88.

Kotz, S. A., Meyer, M., Alter, K., Besson, M., von Cramon, D. Y., & Friederici, A. D. (2003). On the lateralization of emotional prosody: An event-related functional MR investigation. *Brain and Language*, 86(3), 366–76.

Krapf, A. (2007). *The human voice: The story of a remarkable talent*. London: Bloomsbury.

Kreifelts, B., Ethofer, T., Grodd, W., Erb, M., & Wildgruber, D. (2007). Audiovisual integration of emotional signals in voice and face: An event-related fMRI study. *Neuroimage*, 37(4), 1445–56.

Kreifelts, B., Ethofer, T., Huberle, E., Grodd, W., & Wildgruber, D. (2010). Association of trait emotional intelligence and individual fMRI-activation patterns during the perception of social signals from voice and face. *Human Brain Mapping*, 31(7), 979–91.

Kreifelts, B., Ethofer, T., Shiozawa, T., Grodd, W., & Wildgruber, D. (2009). Cerebral representation of non-verbal emotional perception: fMRI reveals audiovisual integration area between voice- and face-sensitive regions in the superior temporal sulcus. *Neuropsychologia*, 47(14), 3059–66.

LeDoux, J. (1998). *The emotional brain: The mysterious underpinnings of emotional life*. London: Phoenix.

Leitman, D. I., Hoptman, M. J., Foxe, J. J., Saccente, E., Wylie, G. R., Nierenberg, J., et al. (2007). The neural substrates of impaired prosodic detection in schizophrenia and its sensorial antecedents. *American Journal of Psychiatry*, 164(3), 474–82.

Linden, D. E., Thornton, K., Kuswanto, C. N., Johnston, S. J., van de Ven, V., & Jackson, M. C. (2010). The brain's voices: Comparing non-clinical auditory hallucinations and imagery. *Cerebral Cortex*, 21(2), 330–37.

Massaro, D. W., & Egan, P. B. (1996). Perceiving affect from the voice and the face. *Psychonomic Bulletin & Review*, 3(2), 215–21.

McDonald, A. J. (1998). Cortical pathways to the mammalian amygdala. *Progress in Neurobiology*, 55(3), 257–332.

Mehrabian, A., & Ferris, S. R. (1967). Inference of attitudes from nonverbal communication in two channels. *Journal of Consulting Psychology*, 31(3), 248–52.

Mehrabian, A., & Wiener, M. (1967). Decoding of inconsistent communications. *Journal of Personality and Social Psychology*, 6(1), 109–14.

Mesulam, M. M., & Mufson, E. J. (1982). Insula of the old world monkey. III: Efferent cortical output and comments on function. *Journal of Comparative Neurology*, 212(1), 38–52.

Meyer, M., Baumann, S., Wildgruber, D., & Alter, K. (2007). How the brain laughs. Comparative evidence from behavioral, electrophysiological and neuroimaging studies in human and monkey. *Behavioural Brain Research*, 182(2), 245–60.

Meyer, M., Zysset, S., Von Cramon, D. Y., & Alter, K. (2005). Distinct fMRI responses to laughter, speech, and sounds along the human peri-sylvian cortex. *Cognitive Brain Research*, 24(2), 291–306.

Mitchell, D. G., Nakic, M., Fridberg, D., Kamel, N., Pine, D. S., & Blair, R. J. (2007). The impact of processing load on emotion. *Neuroimage*, 34(3), 1299–1309.

Mitchell, R. L. (2007). fMRI delineation of working memory for emotional prosody in the brain: Commonalities with the lexico-semantic emotion network. *Neuroimage*, 36(3), 1015–25.

Mitchell, R. L., Elliott, R., Barry, M., Cruttenden, A., & Woodruff, P. W. (2003). The neural response to emotional prosody, as revealed by functional magnetic resonance imaging. *Neuropsychologia*, 41(10), 1410–21.

Morris, J. S., Scott, S. K., & Dolan, R. J. (1999). Saying it with feeling: Neural responses to emotional vocalizations. *Neuropsychologia*, 37(10), 1155–63.

Mufson, E. J., & Mesulam, M. M. (1984). Thalamic connections of the insula in the rhesus monkey and comments on the paralimbic connectivity of the medial pulvinar nucleus.

Journal of Comparative Neurology, 227(1), 109–20.

Müller, V. I., Habel, U., Derntl, B., Schneider, F., Zilles, K., Turetsky, B. I., et al. (2010). Incongruence effects in crossmodal emotional integration. *Neuroimage*, 4(3), 2257–66.

O'Craven, K. M., & Kanwisher, N. (2000). Mental imagery of faces and places activates corresponding stiimulus-specific brain regions. *Journal of Cognitive Neuroscience*, 12(6), 1013–23.

Paulmann, S., Ott, D. V. M., & Kotz, S. A. (2011). Emotional speech perception unfolding in time: The role of the basal ganglia. *PLoS One*, 6(3), e17694.

Pearson, R. C., Brodal, P., Gatter, K. C., & Powell, T. P. (1982). The organization of the connections between the cortex and the claustrum in the monkey. *Brain Research*, 234(2), 435–41.

Pell, M. D., & Leonard, C. L. (2003). Processing emotional tone from speech in Parkinson's disease: A role for the basal ganglia. *Cognitive, Affective & Behavioral Neuroscience*, 3(4), 275–88.

Pell, M. D., Monetta, L., Paulmann, S., & Kotz, S. A. (2009). Recognizing emotions in a foreign language. *Journal of Nonverbal Behavior*, 33(2), 107–20

Posamentier, M. T., & Abdi, H. (2003). Processing faces and facial expressions. *Neuropsychology Reviews*, 13(3), 113–43.

Pourtois, G., de Gelder, B., Vroomen, J., Rossion, B., & Crommelinck, M. (2000). The time-course of intermodal binding between seeing and hearing affective information. *Neuroreport*, 11(6), 1329–33.

Quadflieg, S., Mohr, A., Mentzel, H. J., Miltner, W. H., & Straube, T. (2008). Modulation of the neural network involved in the processing of anger prosody: The role of task-relevance and social phobia. *Biological Psychology*, 78(2), 129–37.

Ross, E. D. (1981). The aprosodiasL Functional-anatomic organization of the affective components of language in the right hemisphere. *Archives of Neurology*, 38(9), 561–69.

Sander, D., Grandjean, D., Pourtois, G., Schwartz, S., Seghier, M. L., Scherer, K. R., et al. (2005). Emotion and attention interactions in social cognition: Brain regions involved in processing anger prosody. *Neuroimage*, 28(4), 848–58.

Sander, K., & Scheich, H. (2001). Auditory perception of laughing and crying activates human amygdala regardless of attentional state. *Cognitive Brain Research*, 12, 181–198.

Sander, K., & Scheich, H. (2005). Left auditory cortex and amygdala, but right insula dominance for human laughing and crying. *Journal of Cognitive Neuroscience*, 17, 1519–31.

Sauter, D. A., Eisner, F., Calder, A. J., & Scott, S. K. (2010). Perceptual cues in nonverbal vocal expressions of emotion. *Quarterly Journal of Experimental Psychology (Colchester)*, 63(11), 2251–72.

Scherer, K. R. (Ed.). (1994). *Affect bursts*. Hillsdale, NJ: Erlbaum.

Schirmer, A., & Kotz, S. A. (2006). Beyond the right hemisphere: Brain mechanisms mediating vocal emotional processing. *Trends in Cognitive Science*, 10(1), 24–30.

Schirmer, A., Kotz, S. A., & Friederici, A. D. (2002). Sex differentiates the role of emotional prosody during word processing. *Brain Research: Cognitive Brain Research*, 14(2), 228–33.

Schirmer, A., Zysset, S., Kotz, S. A., & von Cramon, Y. D. (2004). Gender differences in the activation of inferior frontal cortex during emotional speech perception. *Neuroimage*, 21(3), 1114–23.

Schröder, M. (2003). Experimental study of affect bursts. *Speech Communication*, 40(1–2), 99–116.

Scott, S. K., Sauter, D. A., & McGettigan, C. (2009). Brain mechanisms for processing perceived emotional vocalizations in humans. In S. M. Brudzynski (Ed.), *Handbook of mammalian vocalization: An integrative neuroscience approach* (pp. 187–98). Oxford: Academic Press.

Seltzer, B., & Pandya, D. N. (1978). Afferent cortical connections and architectonics of the superior temporal sulcus and surrounding cortex in the rhesus monkey. *Brain Research*, 149(1), 1–24.

Szameitat, D. P., Alter, K., Szameitat, A. J., Wildgruber, D., Sterr, A., & Darwin, C. J. (2009). Acoustic profiles of distinct emotional expressions in laughter. *Journal of Acoustic Society of America*, 126(1), 354–66.

Szameitat, D. P., Darwin, C. J., Szameitat, A. J., Wildgruber, D., & Alter, K. (2011). Formant characteristics of human laughter. *Journal of Voice*, 25(1), 32–37.

Szameitat, D. P., Kreifelts, B., Alter, K., Szameitat, A. J., Sterr, A., Grodd, W., et al. (2010). It is not always tickling: Distinct cerebral responses during perception of different laughter types. *Neuroimage*, 53(4), 1264–71.

Tamietto, M., & de Gelder, B. (2010). Neural bases of the non-conscious perception of emotional signals. *Nature Reviews Neuroscience*, 11(10), 697–709.

Uekermann, J., Abdel-Hamid, M., Lehmkamper, C., Vollmoeller, W., & Daum, I. (2008). Perception of affective prosody in major depression: A link to executive functions? *Journal of the International Neuropsychology Society*, 14(4), 552–61.

Van Lancker, D., Cornelius, C., & Kreiman, J. (1989). Recognition of emotional-prosodic meaning in speech by autistic, schizophrenic, and normal children. *Developmental Neuropsycholgy*, 5(2), 207–26.

von Kriegstein, K., Kleinschmidt, A., Sterzer, P., & Giraud, A. L. (2005). Interaction of face and voice areas during speaker recognition. *Journal of Cognitive Neuroscience*, 17(3), 367–76.

Wambacq, I. J., Shea-Miller, K. J., & Abubakr, A. (2004). Non-voluntary and voluntary processing of emotional prosody: An event-related potentials study. *Neuroreport*, 15(3), 555–59.

Wiethoff, S., Wildgruber, D., Grodd, W., & Ethofer, T. (2009). Response and habituation of the amygdala during processing of emotional prosody. *Neuroreport*, 20(15), 1356–60.

Wiethoff, S., Wildgruber, D., Kreifelts, B., Becker, H., Herbert, C., Grodd, W., et al. (2008). Cerebral processing of emotional prosody – influence of acoustic parameters and arousal. *Neuroimage*, 39(2), 885–93.

Wildgruber, D., Ackermann, H., Kreifelts, B., & Ethofer, T. (2006). Cerebral processing of linguistic and emotional prosody: fMRI studies. *Progress in Brain Research*, 156, 249–68.

Wildgruber, D., Ethofer, T., Grandjean, D., & Kreifelts, B. (2009). A cerebral network model of speech prosody comprehension. *International Journal of Speech-Language Pathology*, 11(4), 277–81.

Wildgruber, D., Hertrich, I., Riecker, A., Erb, M., Anders, S., Grodd, W., et al. (2004). Distinct frontal regions subserve evaluation of linguistic and emotional aspects of speech intonation. *Cerebral Cortex*, 14(12), 1384–89.

Wildgruber, D., Riecker, A., Hertrich, I., Erb, M., Grodd, W., Ethofer, T., et al. (2005). Identification of emotional intonation evaluated by fMRI. *Neuroimage*, 24(4), 1233–41.

Woods, D. L. (1995). The component structure of the N1 wave of the human auditory evoked potential. *Electroencephalography and Clinical Neurophysiology. Supplement*, 44, 102–9.

CHAPTER 12

Emotion and Music

Stefan Koelsch

Music as a Tool of Affective Neuroscience

Music belongs to what makes us human. The oldest musical instruments discovered so far – flutes made out of vulture bones – date back about 35,000 calendar years (Conard, Malina, & Münzel, 2009). However, it is conceivable that humans made music since they originated about 100,000 to 200,000 years ago. In every known culture, humans make (or made) music together in groups. It appears that infant-directed singing of lullabies and playsongs is very similar across cultures (Papousek, 1996; Trehub, Unyk, & Trainor, 1993), presumably because of a number of the universal emotional effects of music. It has been shown that the expression of emotion in music can be recognized across cultures (Fritz et al., 2009) and that humans have an inborn neural architecture that is sensitive to music at birth (e.g., newborns are already sensitive to changes in tonal key and to differences in consonance and dissonance; Perani et al., 2010). The importance of music for humans, as well as the capability of music to strongly affect emotion and

mood in most humans, makes music an extremely interesting experimental stimulus for affective neuroscientists. In fact, because music belongs to what makes us human, the understanding of human emotions remains incomplete unless we have a thorough knowledge about music-evoked emotions and their neural correlates.

Using music to investigate the neural correlates of emotion has several benefits:

(a) Music is a powerful tool to evoke emotions (usually more powerful than, for example, static faces).

(b) Music can evoke a wide variety of emotions (Zentner, Grandjean, & Scherer, 2008); for example, with regard to positive emotions, music can evoke joy, amusement, amazement, extremely pleasurable experiences such as musical frissons (physical sensations involving goose bumps or shivers down the spine), feelings of vitalization, soothing, spirituality, calmness, and triumph.

(c) Both listening to music and making music can evoke emotions, enabling investigators to study interactions between emotion and action.

(d) With regard to human evolution, music is originally a social activity. Therefore, music is well suited to study interactions between emotion and social factors.

(e) Music can be used to study the time course of emotional processes: both short-term emotional phenomena (in the range of seconds) and longer term emotional phenomena (in the range of minutes).

(f) Music can be used to investigate mixed emotions such as "pleasant sadness."

(g) Studying the neural correlates of emotions with music also has direct relevance for music-therapeutic applications.

It is for such reasons that functional neuroimaging studies with music can extend our views on the neural correlates of emotion in general.

However, using music in the study of emotion also bears several difficulties:

(a) Musical preferences often differ substantially between individuals (a death-metal enthusiast can utterly despise thrash metal), and the necessary control over the stimulus material might result in quite different emotional responses in different subjects.

(b) Participants have to be equally familiar with different musical pieces, or styles, used in different experimental conditions (so that differences in neural activity between different emotion conditions are not simply due to differences in familiarity).

(c) It is often quite difficult to control for the musical and acoustical parameters that differ between pieces used for different experimental conditions. For example, when comparing the effects of happy and sad music, differences between conditions observed in functional neuroimaging data might simply be caused by differences in the tempo of the pieces, which might result in different cardiovascular responses, which probably interact with activity in some limbic/paralimbic brain structures.

(d) Some emotions are better investigated with other stimuli than music. For example, although individuals might feel disgusted by certain music, disgust is likely to be investigated more appropriately by odors and images. Moreover, music is presumably not optimal to investigate emotional phenomena that involve a high load of cognitive processing and cognitive appraisal such as jealousy, shame, and regret; however, it is nevertheless likely that music can evoke the affective turmoil of such emotions.

Notably, it is a common misconception that music-evoked emotions only involve aesthetic experiences, lacking motivational components and goal relevance (for a detailed discussion see Juslin & Västfjäll, 2008; Koelsch, Siebel, & Fritz, 2010). That view implies that music is not capable of evoking "everyday emotions" and is therefore not well suited to investigate the neural basis of "real emotions." The following points speak against that view.

Simply listening to music can evoke changes in the major reaction components of an emotion: It elicits changes in (a) physiological arousal (i.e., in autonomic and endocrine activity); (b) subjective feeling (e.g., when music evokes feelings of pleasure, happiness, sadness, and so on); (c) motor expression (e.g., smiling, crying); (d) action tendencies (dancing, foot tapping, clapping, or even just premotor activity); and (e) possibly (but not necessarily) cognitive appraisal. In addition, as reviewed later, music is capable of modulating activity in all limbic/paralimbic brain structures, rendering it unlikely that music cannot evoke real emotions.

With regard to the so-called basic emotions, many individuals experience the evocation of joy through listening to music (for many individuals, this is actually a frequent motivation for listening to music; Sloboda, 1992). Music can evoke sadness (Zentner et al., 2008) and surprise (Koelsch, Kilches, et al., 2008; Meyer, 1956), and some subjects in an earlier study (Koelsch, Fritz, Cramon, Müller, & Friederici, 2006) reported that the permanently, highly dissonant stimuli used in that study evoked feelings of disgust and vertigo. Most people get quite angry when they have to listen to music that they utterly dislike, and music is sometimes even used to stimulate anger and aggression in listeners (e.g., the "hate music" of neo-Nazis, and partly also military music).

Some people seek negative emotions in music, for example sadness (for the rewarding effects of sad music see Levinson, 1990, and Chapter 10). However, one mechanism (among many others; Levinson, 1990) accounting for this phenomenon is that music evokes *real* sadness (which is indistinguishable from "everyday" sadness with regard to its underlying neural activity) and that the psychological realization that in fact nothing bad happened leads to reward-related feelings of pleasure. Obviously, there might be different patterns of motor expression, cognition, and neurophysiology while listening to sad music compared with when being sad because of a loss. Importantly, that difference between the subjective experience of sadness during music listening and the subjective experience of "day-to-day" sadness by no means rules out that neural correlates of sadness are active in both cases. Instead it argues for the notion that sadness can in fact be evoked by listening to music. Likewise, even if music does not evoke a basic emotion in an individual with the same intensity as a particular real-life situation, the underlying brain circuits are nevertheless presumably the same (whether I am strongly or moderately happy – the emotion is still happiness).

In addition, social functions of music such as communication, action coordination, cooperation, and group cohesion (summarized in Koelsch, Offermanns, & Franzke, 2010), are functions that were critical for the survival of the human species and that are vital for the well-being of an individual. Therefore, the pleasure in practicing these social functions is indeed related to survival functions.

Finally, regenerative effects of music (e.g., beneficial hormonal and immunological effects; see Koelsch & Siebel, 2005) *are* material effects for the individual (a polypeptide, for example, consists of matter), thus serving the criterion of a "utilitarian emotion" (as opposed to an "aesthetic emotion;" see Scherer, 2004, for this distinction).

Mechanisms through which Music Evokes Emotions

Many emotion theorists are puzzled by the fact that music is capable of evoking emotions, because music is not a stimulus that would obviously interfere with, or support, the survival of an individual or the species. How is it then that music can nevertheless "hale souls out of men's bodies" (W. Shakespeare, *Much Ado about Nothing*, Act II, Scene 3)? Juslin and Västfjäll (2008) suggested several mechanisms underlying the evocation of emotions with music. These mechanisms include brainstem reflexes (due to basic acoustic properties of music such as timbre, attack time, intensity, and consonance/dissonance); evaluative conditioning (the process of evoking emotion with music that has been paired repeatedly with other positive or negative stimuli); emotional contagion (where a listener perceives an emotionally relevant feature or expression of the music and then copies this feature or expression internally; see also Juslin & Laukka, 2003); visual imagery (where music evokes images with emotional qualities); episodic memory (where music evokes a memory of a particular event, also referred to as the "Darling, they are playing our tune" phenomenon; Davies, 1978), and musical expectancy (where a specific musical feature violates, delays, or confirms the expectations of listeners, leading to feelings of tension and suspense).

Additional factors suggested by other researchers include the repeated mere exposure that can also contribute to, and modify the liking of music (Moors & Kuppens, 2008); semantic associations with emotional valence (Fritz & Koelsch, 2008); movement (movement elicited by music, even when it is not directly expressive of emotion, can modify emotional states, such as the impetus to move in a depressed individual; Bharucha & Curtis, 2008); and engagement in social activities (summarized in Koelsch et al., 2010). However, the mechanisms through which music can evoke emotions are still debated, and only few functional imaging studies have so far investigated the neural correlates of different mechanisms underlying the evocation of emotion with music (Ball et al., 2007; Koelsch et al., 2006; Koelsch, Fritz, & Schlaug, 2008). The next sections provide a review of functional neuroimaging studies on music and emotion to illustrate the potential of this field for the advancement of our understanding of human emotion; they relate the findings where possible to the emotion-evoking mechanisms described earlier.

Limbic and Paralimbic Correlates of Music-Evoked Emotions

Although not well defined, "limbic" and "paralimbic" structures are considered as core structures of emotional processing, because their lesion or dysfunction is associated with emotional impairment (for an overview see, e.g., Dalgleish, 2004). How limbic/paralimbic structures interact and which functional networks they form are still not well understood.

A central structure within the limbic/paralimbic neural circuitry is the amygdala, which has been implicated in the initiation, generation, detection, maintenance, and termination of emotions that are assumed to be important for the survival of the individual and the species (Price, 2005). A number of functional neuroimaging (Ball et al., 2007; Baumgartner, Lutz, Schmidt, & Jäncke, 2006; Blood & Zatorre, 2001; Eldar, Ganor, Admon, Bleich, & Hendler, 2007; Koelsch et al., 2006; Koelsch et al., 2008; Lerner, Papo, Zhdanov, Belozersky, & Hendler, 2009) and lesion studies (Dellacherie, Ehrlé, & Samson, 2008; Gosselin et al., 2005; Gosselin, Peretz, Johnsen, & Adolphs, 2007) have shown involvement of the amygdala in emotional responses to music (see Figure 12.1 for illustration). The first neuroimaging study showing activity changes in the amygdala was a positron emission topography (PET) study by Blood and Zatorre (2001), in which changes in regional cerebral blood flow (rCBF) were measured during "chills" (i.e., extensive emotional experiences involving sensations

such as goose bumps or shivers down the spine). The participants listened to a piece of their own favorite music to which they usually had a chill experience. Increasing chill intensity correlated with rCBF decrease in the amygdala and in the anterior hippocampal formation. An increase in rCBF correlating with increasing chill intensity was observed in the ventral striatum, midbrain, anterior insula, anterior cingulate cortex, and orbitofrontal cortex (for patient studies on music-evoked pleasure see Griffiths, Warren, Dean, & Howard, 2004; Matthews et al., 2009; Stewart, von Kriegstein, Warren, & Griffiths, 2006).

Even if individuals do not have intense "chill" experiences, music can evoke activity changes in the amygdala, ventral striatum, and hippocampus. Investigating the emotional valence dimension with music, Koelsch et al. (2006) compared brain responses to joyful instrumental tunes (played by professional musicians) to those evoked by electronically manipulated, permanently dissonant counterparts of these tunes (for other studies using consonant and dissonant music see Ball et al., 2007; Blood, Zatorre, Bermudez, & Evans, 1999; Gosselin et al., 2006; Khalfa et al., 2008; Sammler, Grigutsch, Fritz, & Koelsch, 2007; Mueller et al., 2011). During the presentation of pleasant music, increases in blood-oxygen-level dependent (BOLD) signals were observed in the ventral striatum (presumably the nucleus accumbens; NAc) and the anterior insula (among other structures). Dissonant music, in contrast, elicited increases in BOLD signals in the amygdala, hippocampus, parahippocampal gyrus, and temporal poles (and decreases of BOLD signals were observed in these structures in response to the pleasant music). Notably, patients with unilateral resection of the medial temporal lobe including the parahippocampal cortex show diminished emotional sensitivity to dissonant music (Gosselin et al., 2006; Khalfa et al., 2008), consistent with activity changes within the parahippocampal gyrus observed in functional neuroimaging studies using stimuli with varying degrees of dissonance (Blood et al., 1999; Koelsch et al.,

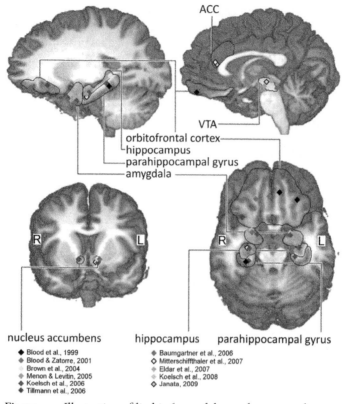

Figure 12.1. Illustration of limbic (amygdala, nucleus accumbens, anterior cingulate cortex [AAC], and hippocampus) and paralimbic structures (orbitofrontal cortex, parahippocampal gyrus). The diamonds represent music-evoked activity changes in these structures (see figure legend for references and the main text for details). Note the repeatedly reported activations of amygdala, nucleus accumbens, and hippocampus, reflecting that music is capable of modulating activity in core structures of emotion (see the text for details). Top left: view of the right hemisphere; top right: medial view; bottom left: anterior view; bottom right: bottom view. See color plate 12.1.

2006). The results of these studies (Blood et al., 1999; Gosselin et al., 2006; Khalfa et al., 2008; Koelsch et al., 2006) suggest a specific role of the mid-portion of the parahippocampal gyrus for the processing of acoustic roughness, which is perhaps also relevant for decoding the affective content of vocal signals.

In an attempt to investigate the neural correlates of sadness, fear, and joy, Baumgartner, Lutz, et al. (2006) observed that auditory information interacts with visual information in several limbic- and paralimbic structures, including the amygdala and the hippocampus (for other studies using

joyful and sad music, see Gosselin et al., 2006; Khalfa et al., 2008; Mitterschiffthaler, Fu, Dalton, Andrew, & Williams, 2007): Activity changes in these structures were stronger during the combined presentation of fearful or sad photographs with fearful or sad music, compared to when only visual information was presented. The combined presentation of music and photographs also elicited stronger activation in the parahippocampal gyrus and temporal poles. Activity changes in the amygdala, hippocampal formation, parahippocampal gyrus, and temporal poles was also found in another fMRI study (Koelsch et al., 2006), suggesting that these structures form a network that plays a prominent role in emotional processing (see also Koelsch, 2010).

The findings from Baumgartner, Lutz, et al. (2006) received support from a study by Eldar et al. (2007), which showed that when either positive (joyful) or negative (fearful) music was played simultaneously with an emotionally neutral film clip, it evoked stronger signal changes in the amygdala and in areas of the ventrolateral frontal cortex, compared to when only music or only film clips were presented. Moreover, the combination of negative (but not positive) music and neutral film clips evoked stronger signal changes in the anterior hippocampal formation compared to when only music or only film clips were presented. Subjective ratings showed that the music plus film conditions were not perceived as significantly more positive or negative than when music was presented alone. Therefore, the functional significance of the increase in signal change (in the amygdala and hippocampal formation) remains to be specified. However, the findings that the visual system modulates signal changes in the amygdala are corroborated by data showing that simply closing the eyes during listening to fearful music also leads to increased amygdalar activity (Lerner et al., 2009).

Another important finding of the study by Eldar et al. (2007) was that activity changes in the amygdala were observed in response to both positive and negative stimulus combinations. This supports the view that the amygdala is involved not only in negative but also in positive emotions (e.g., Murray, 2007), clearly challenging the rather simplistic view that the amygdala is primarily a "fear center" in the human brain. Notably, the amygdala is not an anatomical unity: It comprises several distinct nuclei (the lateral, basal, accessory basal, central, medial, and cortical nuclei), and although the amygdala has become one of the most heavily studied brain structures, the functional significance of these nuclei, as well as their interaction with other structures, is not well understood (LeDoux, 2007).

A music study by Ball et al. (2007) provided the first insight into different functional properties of subregions of the human amygdala in response to auditory stimulation. That study used original (mainly consonant) piano pieces as pleasant stimuli, and permanently dissonant versions of these stimuli as unpleasant stimuli (similar to other studies investigating the valence dimension with music; Blood et al., 1999; Koelsch et al., 2006; Sammler et al., 2007). The authors investigated signal changes in the amygdala in response to both consonant and dissonant music. An increase of BOLD signal was observed in the basolateral amygdala (to both types of music) and signal decrease in superficial and centromedial amygdala (again, to both types of music).

Also using consonant and dissonant music, Fritz and Koelsch (2005) reported BOLD signal decreases with increasing emotional valence in a central aspect of the amygdala (presumably lateral and/or basal nuclei), whereas BOLD signals increased with increasing valence in a superior aspect of the amygdala (superficial amygdala, extending into the substantia innominata). Importantly, the central aspect of the amygdala was found to be functionally connected to the temporal pole, hippocampus, and parahippocampal gyrus, whereas the superior aspect of the amygdala (presumably the superficial amygdala) was functionally connected with the ventral striatum and orbitofrontal cortex. This suggests that different nuclei of the amygdala are involved in modulating activity of different emotion networks.

As mentioned earlier, the amygdala and related limbic structures play a critical role for emotions that some assume to have survival value for the individual and for the species (Dalgleish, 2004). The studies mentioned in this section provide evidence that music can evoke activity changes in these brain structures, suggesting that at least some music-evoked emotions involve the very core of evolutionarily adaptive neuroaffective mechanisms. This evidence supports the view that music can evoke "real emotions," a view that is further supported in the next section, which reviews studies investigating neural correlates of music-evoked pleasure.

Music Affects Dopaminergic Neural Activity

Several studies have shown that listening to pleasant music activates brain structures implicated in reward and experiences of pleasure. Blood and Zatorre (2001) reported that the ventral striatum (presumably the NAc; see Figure 12.1 for an illustration) is involved in intensely pleasurable "chill" responses to music. Similarly, another PET study by Brown, Martinez, and Parsons (2004) reported activation of the ventral striatum (in addition to the subcallosal cingulate cortex, anterior insula, and posterior part of the hippocampus) during listening to two unfamiliar, pleasant pieces contrasted with a resting condition. Activation of the ventral striatum in response to pleasant music was also observed in three studies using fMRI: One investigated the valence dimension (Koelsch et al., 2006), another one examined differences in pleasantness due to the predictability of music (Menon & Levitin, 2005), and the third investigated music-evoked memories Janata (2009). The study by Menon & Levitin, 2005 reported that activation of the ventral striatum was connected to activity in the ventral tegmental area (VTA) and the hypothalamus. This finding suggests that the hemodynamic changes observed in the ventral striatum reflect dopaminergic activity: The NAc is innervated in part by dopaminergic brainstem neurons (located mainly in the VTA as well as in the substantia nigra), and is part of the so-called reward circuit (e.g., Berridge, Robinson, & Aldridge, 2009). This circuit includes projections from the lateral hypothalamus via the medial forebrain bundle to the mesolimbic dopamine pathway involving the VTA with projections to the NAc (Björklund & Dunnett, 2007). Further support for the assumption that the hemodynamic changes in the ventral striatum reported earlier (Blood & Zatorre, 2001;

Brown et al., 2004; Janata, 2009; Koelsch et al., 2006; Menon & Levitin, 2005) involved dopaminergic neural activity stems from a recent PET study by Salimpoor, Benovoy, Larcher, Dagher, and Zatorre (2011) showing that strong music-evoked pleasure (including "musical frissons") is associated with increased dopamine binding in the NAc.

Importantly, activity in the NAc (as well as activity in the ventral pallidum; Berridge et al., 2009) correlates with motivation- and reward-related experiences of pleasure; for instance during the process of obtaining a goal, when encountering an unexpected but reachable incentive, or when presented with a reward cue (reviewed in Berridge et al., 2009; Nicola, 2007). In humans, NAc activity has been reported; for example, during sexual activity, intake of drugs, eating of chocolate, and drinking water when dehydrated (Berridge et al., 2009; Nicola, 2007). It has, therefore, previously been suggested that NAc activity correlates with the subjective experience of *fun* (Koelsch, Siebel, & Fritz, 2010), but more detailed information about its functional significance is needed to determine the role that the NAc possibly plays for other emotions as well.

The NAc also appears to play a role in invigorating, and perhaps even selecting and directing, behavior in response to stimuli with incentive value, as well as in motivating and rewarding such behavior (Nicola, 2007). The NAc is considered to be a "limbic motor interface" (Nieuwenhuys, Voogd, & Huijzen, 2008), because (1) it receives input from limbic structures such as amygdala and hippocampus, (2) injecting dopamine in the NAc causes an increase in locomotion, and (3) the NAc projects to other compartments of the basal ganglia, which play an important role in the learning, selection, and execution of actions. This motor-related function of the NAc puts it in a key position for the generation of a drive to move to, join in, and dance to pleasant music, although the neural basis for this drive needs to be specified.

It is important to note that in three of the earlier mentioned studies (Brown et al., 2004; Koelsch et al., 2006; Menon & Levitin, 2005) participants did not report "chill" responses during music listening, suggesting that dopaminergic pathways including the NAc can be activated by music as soon as it is perceived as pleasant (i.e., even in the absence of extreme emotional experiences involving chills). Results from the reviewed studies indicate that music can easily evoke experiences of pleasure or fun, associated with the activity of a reward pathway involving the hypothalamus, the VTA, and the NAc. This emotional power of music needs to be explored further to provide more systematic knowledge that could be used in support of the therapy of affective disorders that are related to dysfunctions involving the mesolimbic reward pathway (such as depressive disorders or Parkinson's disease; see also Koelsch, 2010). It has previously been argued that music can evoke not only subjective experiences of fun (involving the NAc) but also experiences of joy and happiness (Koelsch, Siebel, & Fritz, 2010). The next section puts forward the hypothesis that experiences of joy involve different neural systems than those involved in experiences of fun.

Music and the Hippocampus

Compared to studies investigating emotion with stimuli such as emotional faces, affective pictures, pain stimuli, or reward stimuli, the review of functional neuroimaging studies on music and emotion reveals a particularly noticeable feature: The proportion of studies reporting activity changes within the (anterior) hippocampal formation in response to music is remarkably high (such activity changes have been reported in Baumgartner, Lutz, et al., 2006; Blood & Zatorre, 2001; Brown et al., 2004; Eldar et al., 2007; Fritz & Koelsch, 2005; Koelsch et al., 2006, 2007; Mitterschiffthaler et al., 2007; see also Figure 12.1). It is well established that the hippocampus plays an important role for learning and memory, spatial orientation, novelty, and expectedness (for reviews see, e.g., Moscovitch, Nadel, Winocur, Gilboa, & Rosenbaum, 2006; Nadel, 2008). However, at least in some of the functional neuroimag-

ing studies that used music to investigate emotion, it is unlikely that the hippocampal activations were simply due to such processes. With regard to memory, for example, participants were probably comparably familiar with neutral and sad pieces in the study by Mitterschiffthaler et al. (2007), in which sad (as compared to neutral) music elicited changes in the anterior hippocampal formation (e.g., sad stimuli included pieces such as the "Concerto de Aranjuez" by Rodrigo and a suite for violin and orchestra by Sinding; neutral pieces featured "L'oiseau prophete: by Schumann or the second violin romance by Beethoven). Similarly, participants were presumably equally unfamiliar with the happy and fearful musical pieces used in the study by Eldar et al. (2007). Even more importantly, in the study by Blood and Zatorre (2001), rCBF changes in the anterior hippocampal formation were observed even when analyzing responses only to stimuli that participants brought themselves into the experiment (supporting Figure 5 of Blood & Zatorre, 2001); thus every subject was highly familiar with the music included in that analysis.

Therefore, studies on music and emotion remind us of the view of James Papez (1937) and Paul MacLean (1990) that the hippocampus also plays an important role in emotional processes. It has dense reciprocal connections with structures involved in the regulation of behaviors essential for survival (such as ingestive, reproductive, and defensive behaviors) and with those involved in the regulation of autonomic, hormonal, and immune system activity (Nieuwenhuys et al., 2008). Such structures include the amygdala, hypothalamus, thalamic nuclei, septal-diagonal band complex, cingulate gyrus, insula, and autonomic brainstem nuclei. Efferent connections project to the NAc, other parts of the striatum, and to numerous other limbic, paralimbic, and nonlimbic structures (Nieuwenhuys et al., 2008). The functional significance of these connections places the hippocampus (along with the amygdala and the orbitofrontal cortex) in a pivotal position for emotional processing. Thus, it has previously been noted that the key to understanding the function of the hippocampus lies in the fact that it has major projections not only to cortical association areas but also to subcortical limbic structures (Nieuwenhuys et al., 2008).

The notion that the hippocampus is involved in emotional processes (in addition to more cognitive functions such as memory and spatial representation) is supported by a wealth of empirical evidence. First, lesion of the hippocampus leads to impairment of maternal behavior in rats (Kimble, Rogers, & Hendrickson, 1967), as indexed by less frequent and less efficient nursing, poorer nest building, increased maternal cannibalism, poorer retrieving, and fewer pups surviving to weaning. Second, individuals with depression show both structural and functional abnormalities of the hippocampus (reviewed in Videbech & Ravnkilde, 2004; Warner-Schmidt & Duman, 2006). Third, the hippocampus is unique in its vulnerability to chronic emotional stressors: In animals, chronic stress related to helplessness and despair leads to death of hippocampal neurons and related hippocampal atrophy (Warner-Schmidt & Duman, 2006), consistent with studies on humans that show reduced hippocampal volume in individuals suffering from childhood sexual abuse (Stein, Koverola, Hanna, Torchia, & McClarty,1997) and posttraumatic stress disorder (PTSD; Bremner, 1999). The loss of hippocampal volume during and after emotional traumatization or during depression is assumed to be due to both a downregulation of neurogenesis in the hippocampal formation and the death of hippocampal neurons (Warner-Schmidt & Duman, 2006). Fourth, activity changes in the anterior hippocampal formation (as well as in the amygdala) in response to pleasant and unpleasant music are reduced in individuals with a reduced capability of producing tender positive feelings (i.e., feelings that can be described as soft, loving, warm, and happy) compared to individuals in a normal control group (Koelsch et al., 2007). Although only little specific information about the involvement of the hippocampus in the processing of emotions is yet available, the results

of the studies mentioned here motivate the hypothesis that the hippocampus is a critical structure for the generation of joy and happiness, and therefore for emotions that play a particular role in social attachments.

We (Koelsch et al., 2007) have referred to such emotions as *tender emotions*, a term derived from Charles Darwin's *The Expression of Emotions in Man and Animals* (Darwin, 1872/1998), in which Darwin wrote that "tender feelings...seem to be compounded of affection, joy, and especially of sympathy" (p. 247; note that Darwin means sympathy in the sense with which the word "empathy" is often used today; that is, either pity for the grief of someone else or feeling the other's happiness or good fortune). These feelings are "of a pleasurable nature" (p. 247), and it is interesting to note that in this chapter about love, joy, and devotion Darwin also writes about "the wonderful power of music" (p. 250), an idea that he elaborated on in *The Descent of Man*. The experience of social attachments is related to positive tender emotions (such as joy and happiness), whereas social loss is related to negative tender emotions (such as sadness). Attachment-related behavior includes licking, grooming, nest building, and pup retrieval, and, particularly in humans, hugging, kissing, caressing, stroking, softly touching, and softly vocalizing. At least in humans, an important attachment-related emotion is love. According to our experience from experiments using music as stimuli to evoke emotions, hippocampal activity appears to be related to emotional experiences described by the participants as "being moved."

Negative feelings such as anxiety and depression appear to be related to the inhibition of hippocampal activity. Notably, because of its particular sensitivity to emotional stressors, inhibition of neural pathways projecting to the hippocampus during the perception of unpleasant stimuli might represent a sensitive neural mechanism that serves to prevent potential damage of hippocampal neurons. Therefore, it is important that researchers are more cautious in attributing activity changes observed in the amygdala and the hippocampus during the presentation of unpleasant (or threatening) stimuli simply to the generation of fear (or other unpleasant emotions); instead they should also consider the possibility that these activity changes reflect inhibitory processes activated automatically to prevent the hippocampus (a particularly sensitive brain structure) from traumatization during the exposure to potentially harmful stimuli.

It is also important to differentiate the feelings related to the activation of the reward circuit (including the lateral hypothalamus, as well as the mesolimbic dopamine pathway involving the VTA with projections to the NAc; see the earlier discussion) from the tender positive emotions that involve activity of the hippocampus (although both are not mutually exclusive). We (Koelsch, Siebel, & Fritz, 2010) have previously noted that feelings arising from activity of the former circuit (involving the NAc) might perhaps best be referred to as *fun*, whereas attachment-related (tender positive) emotions such as *joy*, *love*, and *happiness* appear to involve hippocampal activity (see also Siebel, 2009) Another important difference between reward-related and attachment-related emotions is that the former ones satiate: Once an organism has satisfied bodily needs and achieved homeostasis, it is satiated, and stimuli that served as incentives before can become even aversive (because too much of a chemical compound, for example, can be harmful for an organism). In contrast, the hippocampus-centered emotions do not become satiated. Note that a brain system for attachment-related affect that does not satiate is evolutionary adaptive, because, for example, feeling attached to a child, loving a child, and feeling the joy of being together with the child are emotions that serve the continuous protection and nurturing of the offspring. Similarly, the need to belong to a social group and the feeling of social inclusion (both of which do not appear to satiate) serve the formation and maintenance of social bonds, thus strengthening social cohesion. It has previously been argued that music can promote social cohesion (for a review see Koelsch, 2010),

providing an interesting link between emotion, social cohesion, and the evolutionarily adaptive value of music.

Whether the present conception of the quality of hippocampus-centered emotions is already sufficient or needs to be expanded, it is important to recognize the importance of the hippocampus for emotional processing in affective neuroscience. Future neuroimaging studies on emotion should carefully control for familiarity, novelty, and memory processes elicited by different stimulus categories to rule out the possibility that hippocampal activations are caused by such factors. Notably, because of the capability of music to evoke activity changes in the hippocampus, it is conceivable that music therapy with depressed patients and with PTSD patients has positive effects on the upregulation of neurogenesis in the hippocampus, but this is still an open question.

Effects of Music on Insular and Anterior Cingulate Cortex Activity

Current theories of emotion emphasize the association between emotion and changes in physiological arousal (mainly involving changes in autonomic and endocrine activity). Changes in autonomic activity have been reported to be associated with activity changes in the anterior cingulate cortex (ACC) and the insular cortex (Craig, 2009; Critchley, 2005; Critchley, Corfield, Chandler, Mathias, & Dolan, 2000), and music studies using PET or fMRI have observed activity changes in both of these structures during music-evoked chills (Blood & Zatorre, 2001), as well as during experiences of fear and sadness (Baumgartner, Lutz, et al., 2006). Note, however, that activity changes in the ACC or insular cortex are not necessarily related to emotional processing. For example, the ACC is also involved in performance monitoring, movement-related functions, and the perception of speech and music (e.g., Cole, Yeong, Freiwalkd, & Botvinick, 2009; Koelsch, Siebel, & Fritz, 2010; Mutschler et al., 2007). It has recently been suggested

(Koelsch, Siebel, & Fritz, 2010) that the ACC is involved in the *synchronization of biological subsystems* (a term coined by Scherer, 2000). These "subsystems" comprise physiological arousal, motor expression, motivational processes, monitoring processes, and cognitive appraisal. The synchronization of activity of these subsystems is likely to occur as an effect of every emotional instance, and it may even be indispensable for subjective emotional experiences (usually referred to as *feelings*). The ACC is in a unique position to accomplish such synchronization because of its involvement in cognition, autonomic nervous system activity, motor activity, motivation, and monitoring. Emotions are usually accompanied not only by autonomic but also by endocrine effects, which, in turn, have effects on immune system function (Dantzer, O'Connor, Freund, Johnson, & Kelley, 2008; Koelsch & Siebel, 2005). With regard to music, such effects are particularly relevant when they are related to a reduction of stress or an amelioration of depression and anxiety (Koelsch, 2009; Koelsch et al., 2011). This relevance also encourages efforts to gather more systematic empirical evidence supporting the use of music therapy in the treatment of diseases related to endocrine, autonomic, or immune system dysfunction (such as autoimmune-diseases).

Musical Expectancies and Emotional Responses

The studies reviewed so far used experimental paradigms employing "pleasant," "unpleasant," "scary," "happy," or "peaceful" tunes. However, as mentioned in the beginning of this chapter, an important mechanism capable of evoking emotional responses is musical expectancy. Leonard Meyer, one of the most influential music psychologists of the last century, proposed a theory of musical emotions on the basis of fulfilled or suspended musical expectancies (Meyer, 1956). He proposed that the confirmation or violation of such musical expectancies produces emotions in the

listener. In accordance with this proposal, Sloboda (1991) found that specific musical structures were associated with specific psychophysiological reactions (shivers, for example, were often evoked by new or unexpected harmonies).

A study by Steinbeis, Koelsch, and Sloboda (2006) tested the hypothesis that emotional responses can be evoked by unexpected chord functions. In that study, physiological measures including EEG, electrodermal activity (EDA), and heart rate were recorded while subjects listened to three versions of Bach chorales. One version was the original version composed by Bach with a harmonic sequence that ended on an unexpected chord function (also referred to as "deceptive cadence"). The same chord was also rendered as expected (using a tonic chord) and as very unexpected (a Neapolitan sixth chord). The EDA to these three different chord types showed clear differences between the expected and the unexpected (as well as between expected and very unexpected) chords. Because the EDA reflects activity of the sympathetic nervous system and because this system is intimately linked to emotional experiences, these data corroborate the assumption that unexpected harmonies elicit emotional responses. The findings from this study were later replicated in another study (Koelsch, Kilches, et al., 2008) that also obtained behavioral data showing that irregular chords were perceived by listeners as more surprising, more arousing, and less pleasant than regular chords.

Functional neuroimaging experiments using chord sequences with unexpected harmonies supported these findings, showing activations of the amygdala (Koelsch, Fritz, & Schlaug, 2008), orbitofrontal cortex (Tillmann et al., 2006), and orbito-lateral cortex (Koelsch, Fritz, Schulze, Alsop, & Schlaug, 2005) in response to unexpected chord functions. The combined findings show that unexpected musical events elicit responses not only related to the processing of the structure (e.g., the syntax) of the music but also emotional responses; notably, this presumably also holds for unexpected words in sentences and for any other stimulus that is perceived as more or less expected.

Major-Minor and Happy-Sad Music

Several functional neuroimaging studies have used major and minor music to investigate "happiness and sadness" (Khalfa, Schon, Anton, & Liégeois-Chauvel, 2005; Mitterschiffthaler et al., 2007), "musical beauty" (Suzuki et al., 2008), or "liking" (Green et al., 2008). However, these studies have not yet yielded a consistent picture, except perhaps activation of the anterior frontomedian cortex (BA 10 m/9 m) for minor contrasted to major music in two studies (Green et al., 2008; Khalfa et al., 2005). Problems in comparing these studies include (1) different participant populations; for example, only males in one study (Suzuki et al., 2008) compared to eight males and five females in another (Khalfa et al., 2005); (2) interpretation of unsystematic effects (such as an rCBF decrease in a striatal region during "beautiful major," an increase during "beautiful minor," an increase during "ugly major," and a decrease during "ugly minor" musicl Suzuki et al., 2008); (3) the use of "true performances" (Khalfa et al., 2005; Mitterschiffthaler et al., 2007) on the one hand, and the use of melodies (Green et al., 2008) or chords (Mizuno & Sugishita, 2007; Suzuki et al., 2008) played without musical expression on the other; and (4) the use of different tasks: Participants were asked "how well they liked it" (Green et al., 2008), to "rate the beauty of the chord sequence" (Suzuki et al., 2008), to rate "their moodstate . . . from sad . . . to happy" (Mitterschiffthaler et al., 2007), or to "judge the emotion represented in the music . . . from sad to happy" (Khalfa et al., 2005).

Moreover, whereas some studies aimed to match major and minor stimuli in tempo and timbre (Green et al., 2008; Mizuno & Sugishita, 2007; Suzuki et al., 2008), happy and sad stimuli differed considerably in their acoustic and musical properties in other studies (e.g., "happy" excerpts having a faster tempo than "sad" excerpts; Khalfa

et al., 2005; Mitterschiffthaler et al., 2007). Thus, future studies are needed to provide more information about the neural correlates of happiness and sadness, how major and minor tonal features might contribute to emotional effects related to happiness and sadness, and how such effects are related to musical preference and cultural experience.

Electrophysiological Effects of Music-Evoked Emotions

This section briefly reviews electrophysiological studies on music and emotion. Only a few EEG studies (Altenmüller, Schürmann, Lim & Parlitz, 2002; Baumgartner, Esslen, & Jäncke, 2006; Sammler et al., 2007; Schmidt & Trainor, 2001) have so far investigated this issue (and up to now, there is a lack of studies on music and emotion using magnetoencephalography). All of these studies investigated the valence dimension: contrasting the effects of pleasant music with the effects of unpleasant music. Schmidt and Trainor (2001) and Altenmüller et al. (2002) reported more pronounced neural activity in the left compared to the right frontal lobes in response to music with positive valence (and the opposite hemispheric weighting for music with negative valence). One of these studies (Altenmüller et al., 2002) measured direct current EEG, whereas the other one (Schmidt & Trainor, 2001) measured oscillatory neural activity in the alpha band.

However, this effect was not observed in the studies by Baumgartner, Esslen, and Jäncke (2006) and Sammler et al. (2007). Instead, the study by Baumgartner and colleagues (2006) reported a bilateral increase of alpha power for happy music (combined with happy pictures) compared to sad and scary music (combined with sad and scary pictures), and the study by Sammler et al. (2007) did not find any differences in the alpha band (or in sub-bands of the alpha frequency range) between pleasant and unpleasant music. However, the latter study (Sammler et al., 2007) reported an increase in fronto-midline theta power in response to pleasant music. This increased oscillatory activity supposedly reflected emotional processing interlinked with attentional functions and presumably originated from the dorsal anterior cingulate cortex. Further research is needed to gain more insights into electrophysiological correlates of music-evoked emotions; the most promising approach to this topic appears to involve the analysis of oscillatory activity in different frequency bands.

Music in the Investigation of the Time Course of Emotion

Another interesting property of music is that it allows us to investigate the time course of emotional processing and the underlying neural mechanisms – an issue that has received only little attention in scientific research. Intuitively, it seems plausible that aversive sounds elicit quick emotional responses (although long durations of such sounds might even increase the degree of unpleasantness) and that especially tender emotions might take a while to emerge.

One of the few psychophysiological studies that have investigated the time course of emotion was conducted by Krumhansl (1997). In that study, several physiological measures (including cardiac, vascular, electrodermal, and respiratory functions) were recorded while listeners heard musical excerpts (each about 3 minutes long) chosen to represent sadness, fear, or happiness. Significant correlations were found between most of the recorded physiological responses and time (measured in one-second intervals from the beginning of the presentation of each musical excerpt). The strongest physiological effects for each emotion type tended to increase over time, suggesting that the intensity of an emotional experience is likely to increase over time during the perception of a musical excerpt. In studies measuring changes in heart rate and breathing rate to music, we found that these two physiological parameters mainly change within the first 20 seconds of a musical excerpt and then remain relatively stable (Orini et al., 2010; see also Lundqvist, Carlsson, Hilmersson, & Juslin, 2009). Recent studies have also shown physiological changes related to emotional valence and arousal as elicited by music over time (Grewe, Nagel, Kopiez, & Altenmüller, 2007a,b).

Activity changes over time due to emotional processing were also observed in a previous fMRI study (Koelsch et al., 2006). In that study, pleasant and unpleasant musical excerpts had a duration of about one minute, and data were modeled not only for the entire excerpt but also separately for the first 30 sec, and for the remaining 30 sec to investigate possible differences in brain activity over time. When looking at activation differences between the first 30 sec and the remaining 30 sec, activations of the amygdala, parahippocampal gyrus, temporal poles, insula, and ventral striatum were stronger during the second block of the musical excerpts, presumably because the intensity of listeners' emotional experiences increased during the perception of both the pleasant and the unpleasant musical excerpts. These findings support the notion of a canonical activation and deactivation of the different neural correlates of emotional processing.

Using both fMRI and PET, Salimpoor et al. (2011) showed dopaminergic activity in the dorsal striatum during the anticipation of a musical frisson, and in the ventral striatum during the experience of the frisson. The activation of the dorsal striatum corresponds with an activation of this structure in response to unexpected (music-syntactically irregular) chord functions (Koelsch, Fritz, & Schlaug, 2008), probably reflecting that irregular chords evoke the anticipation for a resolution (which perhaps then evokes activity in the ventral striatum).

Information about the temporal order in which neural structures of emotional processing become active, or inactive, remains to be specified. Note that music is an ideal stimulus to investigate this time course, because it always unfolds over time (see also the study by Blood & Zatorre, 2001, in which musical stimuli selected to evoke chills had durations of about 90 sec). To learn more about this effect, studies of emotional processing with music should conduct investigations of the activity of the structures involved in emotional processing over time (e.g., by doing split-half analyses of the data). Information about activity changes over time of the structures implicated in emotion (such as information about how activity in one structure affects activity in another) would provide important insight into the functional significance of these structures.

Concluding Remarks

Despite active research in the area of affective neuroscience, the different roles of various brain regions involved in emotions are still not well understood. This review illustrated that music is an important, perhaps even indispensable, tool to gain such knowledge. Future work with music can contribute to the investigation of the neural networks underlying different emotions, with the particular advantages that music can be used to study a range of positive and negative emotions, as well as mixed emotions, and to investigate the time course of emotion. As yet only little is known about the neural correlates of different psychological mechanisms underlying the evocation of emotion with music, such as emotional contagion, musical expectancy, or musical memories. Specific knowledge can be gained by systematically manipulating such processes to identify their neural correlates. Finally, future work needs to further fathom the therapeutic potential of music by determining which types of music (taking into account individual experiences and preferences) are best suited to stimulate activity in specific limbic and paralimbic brain structures (e.g., the hippocampus in depressive patients or dopaminergic system activity in patients with Parkinson's disease). Such insights into the neural basis of music-evoked emotions can thus also lead to a more systematic use of music in the therapy of disorders.

Outstanding Questions and Future Directions

- What are the neural correlates of the different mechanisms underlying the

evocation of emotions by music? This chapter has outlined several mechanisms underlying the evocation of emotions by music, but the neural correlates of these mechanisms are largely unknown.
- What are the neural correlates of mixed emotions? Because of its potential to evoke "pleasant sadness," "fascinating fear," and other mixed emotions, music is an interesting tool to investigate such emotions.
- What role does the ACC play in the synchronization of biological subsystems? Functional neuroimaging studies combined with peripheral-physiological measures could try to answer whether the ACC is involved in synchronizing peripheral-physiological arousal, motor expression, and perhaps action tendencies.
- What is the nature of the emotions generated by hippocampal activity? It has been proposed in this chapter that emotional activity of the hippocampus is related to attachment-related emotions and to feelings of joy, love, and happiness. This hypothesis, however, needs direct empirical testing.
- How can the emotion-evoking power of music be used in the therapy of affective disorders related to anhedonia, such as depressive disorders, or of Parkinson's disease? So far, the empirical evidence for beneficial effects of music therapy in the treatment of depressive disorders is quite weak, and neural correlates of such possible effects are not known. Research in this area could provide an empirical basis for the application of music therapy. One way to investigate the use of music could be to study hippocampal activity and hippocampal volume in depressed patients or patients with PTSD undergoing music therapy.

References

Altenmüller, E., Schürmann, K., Lim, V., & Parlitz, D. (2002). Hits to the left, flops to the right: Different emotions during listening to music are reflected in cortical lateralisation patterns. *Neuropsychologia*, 40(13), 2242–56.

Ball, T., Rahm, B., Eickhoff, S., Schulze-Bonhage, A., Speck, O., & Mutschler, I. (2007). Response properties of human amygdala subregions: Evidence based on functional MRI combined with probabilistic anatomical maps. *PLoS One*, 2(3).

Baumgartner, T., Esslen, M., & Jäncke, L. (2006). From emotion perception to emotion experience: Emotions evoked by pictures and classical music. *International Journal of Psychophysiology*, 60(1), 34–43.

Baumgartner, T., Lutz, K., Schmidt, C., & Jäncke, L. (2006). The emotional power of music: How music enhances the feeling of affective pictures. *Brain Research*, 1075(1), 151–164.

Berridge, K., Robinson, T., & Aldridge, J. (2009). Dissecting components of reward: Liking, wanting, and learning. *Current Opinions in Pharmacology*, 9(1), 65–73.

Bharucha, J., & Curtis, M. (2008). Affective spectra, synchronization, and motion: Aspects of the emotional response to music. *Behavioral & Brain Sciences*, 31, 579.

Björklund, A., & Dunnett, S. (2007). Dopamine neuron systems in the brain: an update. *Trends in Neurosciences*, 30(5), 194–202.

Blood, A., & Zatorre, R. (2001). Intensely pleasurable responses to music correlate with activity in brain regions implicated in reward and emotion. *Proceedings of the National Academy of Sciences*, 98(20), 11818.

Blood, A. J., Zatorre, R., Bermudez, P., & Evans, A. C. (1999). Emotional responses to pleasant and unpleasant music correlate with activity in paralimbic brain regions. *Nature Neuroscience*, 2(4), 382–87.

Bremner, J. (1999). Does stress damage the brain? *Biological Psychiatry*, 45(7), 797–805.

Brown, S., Martinez, M., & Parsons, L. (2004). Passive music listening spontaneously engages limbic and paralimbic systems. *NeuroReport*, 15(13), 2033–37.

Cole, M., Yeung, N., Freiwald, W., & Botvinick, M. (2009). Cingulate cortex: Diverging data from humans and monkeys. *Trends in Neurosciences*, 32(11), 566–74.

Conard, N., Malina, M., & Münzel, S. (2009). New flutes document the earliest musical tradition in southwestern Germany. *Nature*, 460(7256), 737–40.

Craig, A. (2009). How do you feel – now? The anterior insula and human awareness. *Nature Reviews Neuroscience*, 10, 59–70.

Critchley, H. (2005). Neural mechanisms of autonomic, affective, and cognitive integration. *Journal of Comparative Neurology*, 493(1), 154–66.

Critchley, H., Corfield, D., Chandler, M., Mathias, C., & Dolan, R. (2000). Cerebral correlates of autonomic cardiovascular arousal: A functional neuroimaging investigation in humans. *Journal of Physiology*, 523(1), 259–70.

Dalgleish, T. (2004). The emotional brain. *Nature Reviews Neuroscience*, 5(7), 583–89.

Dantzer, R., O'Connor, J., Freund, G., Johnson, R., & Kelley, K. (2008). From inflammation to sickness and depression: When the immune system subjugates the brain. *Nature Reviews Neuroscience*, 9(1), 46–56.

Darwin, C. (1998). *The expression of emotion in man and animals.* London: Murray. (Original work published 1872)

Davies, J. (1978). *The psychology of music.* Stanford: Stanford University Press.

Dellacherie, D., Ehrlé, N., & Samson, S. (2008). Is the neutral condition relevant to study musical emotion in patients? *Music Perception*, 25(4), 285–94.

Eldar, E., Ganor, O., Admon, R., Bleich, A., & Hendler, T. (2007). Feeling the real world: Limbic response to music depends on related content. *Cerebral Cortex*, 7(12), 2828–40.

Fritz, T., Jentschke, S., Gosselin, N., Sammler, D., Peretz, I., Turner, R., et al. (2009). Universal recognition of three basic emotions in music. *Current Biology*, 19(7), 573–76.

Fritz, T., & Koelsch, S. (2005). Initial response to pleasant and unpleasant music: An fMRI study. *Neuroimage*, 26.

Fritz, T., & Koelsch, S. (2008). The role of semantic association and emotional contagion for the induction of emotion with music. *Behavioral & Brain Sciences*, 31, 579–80.

Gosselin, N., Peretz, I., Johnsen, E., & Adolphs, R. (2007). Amygdala damage impairs emotion recognition from music. *Neuropsychologia*, 45(2), 236–44.

Gosselin, N., Peretz, I., Noulhiane, M., Hasboun, D., Beckett, C., Baulac, M., et al. (2005). Impaired recognition of scary music following unilateral temporal lobe excision. *Brain*, 128(3), 628–40.

Gosselin, N., Samson, S., Adolphs, R., Noulhiane, M., Roy, M., Hasboun, D., et al. (2006). Emotional responses to unpleasant music correlates with damage to the parahippocampal cortex. *Brain*, 129(10), 2585.

Green, A., Bærentsen, K., Stødkilde-Jørgensen, H., Wallentin, M., Roepstorff, A., & Vuust, P.

(2008). Music in minor activates limbic structures: A relationship with dissonance? *Neuroreport*, 19(7), 711–15.

Grewe, O., Nagel, F., Kopiez, R., & Altenmüller, E. (2007a). Emotions over time: Synchronicity and development of subjective, physiological, and facial affective reactions of music. *Emotion*, 7(4), 774–88.

Grewe, O., Nagel, F., Kopiez, R., & Altenmüller, E. (2007b). Listening to music as a re-creative process: Physiological, psychological, and psychoacoustical correlates of chills and strong emotions. *Music Perception*, 24(3),297–314.

Griffiths, T., Warren, J., Dean, J., & Howard, D. (2004). "When the feeling's gone": A selective loss of musical emotion. *British Medical Journal*, 75(2), 344.

Janata, P. (2009). The neural architecture of music-evoked autobiographical memories. *Cerebral Cortex*, 19(11), 2579.

Juslin, P., & Laukka, P. (2003). Communication of emotions in vocal expression and music performance: Different channels, same code? *Psychological Bulletin*, 129(5), 770–814.

Juslin, P., & Västfjäll, D. (2008). Emotional responses to music: The need to consider underlying mechanisms. *Behavioral and Brain Sciences*, 31(05), 559–75.

Khalfa, S., Guye, M., Peretz, I., Chapon, F., Girard, N., Chauvel, P., et al. (2008). Evidence of lateralized anteromedial temporal structures involvement in musical emotion processing. *Neuropsychologia*, 46(10), 2485–93.

Khalfa, S., Schon, D., Anton, J., & Liégeois-Chauvel, C. (2005). Brain regions involved in the recognition of happiness and sadness in music. *Neuroreport*, 16(18), 1981–84.

Kimble, D., Rogers, L., & Hendrickson, C. (1967). Hippocampal lesions disrupt maternal, not sexual, behavior in the albino rat. *Journal of Comparative and Physiological Psychology*, 63(3), 401–7.

Koelsch, S. (2009). A neuroscientific perspective on music therapy. *Annals of the New York Academy of Sciences*, 1169 (The Neurosciences and Music III Disorders and Plasticity), 374–84.

Koelsch, S. (2010). Towards a neural basis of music-evoked emotions. *Trends in Cognitive Sciences*, 14(3), 131–37.

Koelsch, S., Fritz, T., Cramon, D., Müller, K., & Friederici, A. (2006). Investigating emotion with music: An fMRI study. *Human Brain Mapping*, 27(3), 239–50.

Koelsch, S., Fritz, T., & Schlaug, G. (2008). Amygdala activity can be modulated by unex-

pected chord functions during music listening. *Neuroreport*, 19(18), 1815–19.

Koelsch, S., Fritz, T., Schulze, K., Alsop, D., & Schlaug, G. (2005). Adults and children processing music: An fMRI study. *Neuroimage*, 25(4), 1068–76.

Koelsch, S., Fuermetz, J., Sack, U., Bauer, K., Hohenadel, M., Wiegel, M., et al. (2011). Effects of music listening on cortisol levels and propofol consumption during spinal anesthesia. *Frontiers in Psychology*, 2, 210.

Koelsch, S., Kilches, S., Steinbeis, N., & Schelinski, S. (2008). Effects of unexpected chords and of performer's expression on brain responses and electrodermal activity. *PLoS One*, 3(7).

Koelsch, S., Offermanns, K., & Franzke, P. (2010). Music in the treatment of affective disorders: An exploratory investigation of a new method for music-therapeutic research. *Music Perception*, 27(4), 307–16.

Koelsch, S., Remppis, A., Sammler, D., Jentschke, S., Mietchen, D., Fritz, T., et al. (2007). A cardiac signature of emotionality. *European Journal of Neuroscience*, 26(11), 3328–38.

Koelsch, S., & Siebel, W. (2005). Towards a neural basis of music perception. *Trends in Cognitive Sciences*, 9(12), 578–84.

Koelsch, S., Siebel, W. A., & Fritz, T. (2010). Functional neuroimaging. In P. Juslin & J. Sloboda (Eds.), *Handbook of music and emotion: Theory, research, applications* (2nd ed., pp. 313–46). Oxford: Oxford University Press Oxford.

Krumhansl, C. (1997). An exploratory study of musical emotions and psychophysiology. *Canadian Journal of Experimental Psychology*, 51(4), 336–53.

LeDoux, J. (2007). The amygdala. *Current Biology*, 17(20), R868.

Lerner, Y., Papo, D., Zhdanov, A., Belozersky, L., & Hendler, T. (2009). Eyes wide shut: Amygdala mediates eyes-closed effect on emotional experience with music. *PLoS One*, 4(7), e6230.

Levinson, J. (1990). *Music and negative emotion*. Ithaca, NY: Cornell University Press.

Lundqvist, L., Carlsson, F., Hilmersson, P., & Juslin, P. (2009). Emotional responses to music: Experience, expression, and physiology. *Psychology of Music*, 37(1), 61.

MacLean, P. (1990). *The triune brain in evolution: Role in paleocerebral functions*. New York: Plenum Press.

Matthews, B., Chang, C., De May, M., Engstrom, J., & Miller, B. (2009). Pleasurable emotional response to music: A case of neurodegenerative generalized auditory agnosia. *Neurocase*, 15(3), 248–59.

Menon, V., & Levitin, D. (2005). The rewards of music listening: Response and physiological connectivity of the mesolimbic system. *Neuroimage*, 28(1), 175–84.

Meyer, L. (1956). *Emotion and meaning in music.* Chicago: University of Chicago Press.

Mitterschiffthaler, M. T., Fu, C. H., Dalton, J. A., Andrew, C. M., & Williams, S. C. (2007). A functional MRI study of happy and sad affective states evoked by classical music. *Human Brain Mapping*, 28, 1150–62.

Mizuno, T., & Sugishita, M. (2007). Neural correlates underlying perception of tonality-related emotional contents. *Neuroreport*, 18(16), 1651–55.

Moors, A., & Kuppens, P. (2008). Distinguishing between two types of musical emotions and reconsidering the role of appraisal. *Behavioral & Brain Sciences*, 31, 588–89.

Moscovitch, M., Nadel, L., Winocur, G., Gilboa, A., & Rosenbaum, R. (2006). The cognitive neuroscience of remote episodic, semantic and spatial memory. *Current Opinions in Neurobiology*, 16(2), 179–90.

Mueller, K., Mildner, T., Fritz, T., Lepsien, J., Schwarzbauer, C., Schroeter, M., & Möller, H. (2011). Investigating brain response to music: A comparison of different fmri acquisition schemes. *Neuroimage*, 54, 337–43.

Murray, E. (2007). The amygdala, reward and emotion. *Trends in Cognitive Sciences*, 11(11), 489–97.

Mutschler, I., Schulze-Bonhage, A., Glauche, V., Demandt, E., Speck, O., & Ball, T. (2007). A rapid sound-action association effect in human insular cortex. *PLoS One*, 2(2), e259.

Nadel, L. (2008). Hippocampus and context revisited. In S. Mizumori (Ed.), *Hippocampal place fields: Relevance to learning and memory* (pp. 3–15). New York: Oxford University Press.

Nicola, S. (2007). The nucleus accumbens as part of a basal ganglia action selection circuit. *Psychopharmacology*, 191(3), 521–50.

Nieuwenhuys, R., Voogd, J., & Huijzen, C. V. (2008). *The human central nervous system.* Berlin: Springer.

Orini, M., Bailón, R., Enk, R., Koelsch, S., Mainardi, L., & Laguna, P. (2010). A method for continuously assessing the autonomic response to music-induced emotions through HRV analysis. *Medical and Biological Engineering and Computing*, 48(5), 423–33.

Papez, J. (1937). A proposed mechanism of emotion. *Archives of Neurology and Psychiatry*, 38(4), 725–43.

Papousek, M. (1996). Intuitive parenting: A hidden source of musical stimulation in infancy. *Musical Beginnings: Origins and Development of Musical Competence*, 88–112.

Perani, D., Saccuman, M., Scifo, P., Spada, D., Andreolli, G., Rovelli, R., et al. (2010). Functional specializations for music processing in the human newborn brain. *Proceedings of the National Academy of Sciences*, 107(10), 4758.

Price, J. (2005). Free will versus survival: Brain systems that underlie intrinsic constraints on behavior. *Journal of Comparative Neurology*, 493(1), 132–39.

Salimpoor, V., Benovoy, M., Larcher, K., Dagher, A., & Zatorre, R. (2011). Anatomically distinct dopamine release during anticipation and experience of peak emotion to music. *Nature Neuroscience*, 14(2), 257–62.

Sammler, D., Grigutsch, M., Fritz, T., & Koelsch, S. (2007). Music and emotion: Electrophysiological correlates of the processing of pleasant and unpleasant music. *Psychophysiology*, 44(2), 293–304.

Scherer, K. R. (2000). Emotions as episodes of subsystem synchronization driven by nonlinear appraisal processes. In M. Lewis & I. Granic (Eds.), *Emotion, development, and self-organization: Dynamic systems approaches to emotional development* (pp. 70–99). Cambridge: Cambridge University Press.

Scherer, K. (2004). Which emotions can be induced by music? What are the underlying mechanisms? and how can we measure them? *Journal of New Music Research*, 33(3), 239–51.

Schmidt, L., & Trainor, L. (2001). Frontal brain electrical activity (EEG) distinguishes valence and intensity of musical emotions. *Cognition & Emotion*, 15(4), 487–500.

Siebel, W. A. (2009). Thalamic balance can be misunderstood as happiness. *Journal for Interdisciplinary Research*, 3, 48–50.

Sloboda, J. A. (1991). Music structure and emotional response: Some empirical findings. *Psychology of Music*, 19, 110–20.

Sloboda, J. A. (1992). Empirical studies of emotional response to music. In M. Jones & S. Holleran (Eds.), *Cognitive bases of musical communication* (pp. 33–46). Washington: American Psychological Association.

Stein, M., Koverola, C., Hanna, C., Torchia, M., & McClarty, B. (1997). Hippocampal volume in women victimized by childhood sexual abuse. *Psychological Medicine*, 27(4), 951–59.

Steinbeis, N., Koelsch, S., & Sloboda, J. (2006). The role of harmonic expectancy violations in musical emotions: Evidence from subjective, physiological, and neural responses. *Journal of Cognitive Neuroscience*, 18(8), 1380–93.

Stewart, L., Von Kriegstein, K., Warren, J., & Griffiths, T. (2006). Music and the brain: Disorders of musical listening. *Brain*, 129(10), 2533–53.

Suzuki, M., Okamura, N., Kawachi, Y., Tashiro, M., Arao, H., Hoshishiba, T., et al. (2008). Discrete cortical regions associated with the musical beauty of major and minor chords. *Cognitive, Affective & Behavioral Neuroscience*, 8(2), 126–31.

Tillmann, B., Koelsch, S., Escoffier, N., Bigand, E., Lalitte, P., Friederici, A., et al. (2006). Cognitive priming in sung and instrumental music: Activation of inferior frontal cortex. *Neuroimage*, 31(4), 1771–82.

Trehub, S., Unyk, A., & Trainor, L. (1993). Adults identify infant-directed music across cultures. *Infant Behavior and Development*, 16(2), 193–211.

Videbech, P., & Ravnkilde, B. (2004). Hippocampal volume and depression: A meta-analysis of MRI studies. *American Journal of Psychiatry*, 161(11), 1957.

Warner-Schmidt, J., & Duman, R. (2006). Hippocampal neurogenesis: Opposing effects of stress and antidepressant treatment. *Hippocampus*, 16(3), 239–49.

Zentner, M., Grandjean, D., & Scherer, K. (2008). Emotions evoked by the sound of music: Characterization, classification, and measurement. *Emotion*, 8(4), 494–521.

CHAPTER 13

Love Letters and Hate Mail

Cerebral Processing of Emotional Language Content

Johanna Kissler

Language As a Symbol System for Emotions

Humans are a symbolic species. They use language to communicate in a way that is apparently not available to any other species. Although we share much of our nonlinguistic communicatory repertoire with other animals, and evolutionary continua can be laid out, human languages in their generative and referential properties seem to be unique. Human language is about the world, but unlike the pictorial renderings in photography and the visual arts, the mapping between the linguistic symbol and the denoted referent is arbitrary. There is no clear physical relationship between the symbol and its meaning, perhaps with the exception of onomatopoeia in spoken language – the formation of words whose sound is imitative of the noise or the sound of the action designated, such as *hiss*, *buzz*, and *bang*, or *plink*. Onomatopoeic processing therefore may be related to prosodic processing. With this notable exception, in human language the mapping between symbol and

meaning is arbitrary, and any symbol or set of letters may represent any object, action, or descriptor. As such, both the lexical meaning and the emotional meaning of words and sentences are entirely acquired through learning. This characteristic has been used as an argument that language is less biologically prepared than other signals of emotion and that, in the absence of a clear referential context (as is often the case in laboratory experiments), emotional language may be a less evocative stimulus class than other means of emotion elicitation and communication.

Nevertheless, human language provides an amazingly versatile and potent means to induce emotions in real life. Affective neuroscience has only recently begun to systematically explore the processing of emotional content in language, although neurological case reports indicating a special status for emotional content in language date back to the 19th century (Hughlings Jackson, 1866). This chapter reviews current empirical evidence on the processing of emotional content in human language, provides an integrative summary of the extant findings, and identifies new perspectives for future research.

Emotions are commonly viewed as culturally universal, largely innate, evolutionary "old" signaling and activation systems residing in the "old," subcortical parts of the brain. They are phylogenetically designed to promote survival in critical situations (i.e., to signal and activate fight, flight, or feeding, attachment, and sexual behavior). In contrast, language, in general, and reading and writing, in particular, represent comparatively recent developments in the history of humankind, and in individual development they appear later than basic emotional expressions that appear within weeks after birth (Meltzoff & Moore, 1983; see also Chapter 27 for a review of emotional development). Language and emotion share a communicative function, but linguistic communicative functions are obviously not restricted to the communication of affect.

Still language is rich in affective content, and influential approaches to the study of emotion (Russell, 2003; see Chapter 1 for an overview) have derived their basic dimensions from analyses of written language. Osgood and collaborators, using the "semantic differential" technique, were the first to demonstrate empirically that affective connotations of words are determined by three principal dimensions: evaluation or valence (positive – negative), activation or arousal (calm – active/aroused), and potency (weak – strong). The semantic differential technique determines a word's evaluative connotation by ratings on a multitude of seven-point scales, spanned by pairs of antonyms such as hot-cold, soft-hard, happy-sad, and so forth. Factor analyses of the judgments of many words on such scales, given by large subject samples, reveal a three-dimensional evaluative space, the structure of which has been replicated many times and across different cultures (Osgood, Miron, & May, 1975). Osgood's principal dimensions are at the core of circumplex theories of affect (Russell, 2003) that, however, often refer to only two principal dimensions – namely, arousal and valence – as accounting for most of the variance

(Bradley & Lang, 1994) and drop the dominance dimension. This approach has generated a large body of research in affective neuroscience, part of which is reviewed later.

A more recent investigation into the dimensionality of emotional language identified four basic dimensions of emotion: valence, potency, arousal, and predictability (Fontaine, Scherer, Roesch, & Ellsworth, 2007). Neural correlates of these four dimensions, however, have not yet been explored. Likewise, the otherwise popular categorical emotion theories have not yet inspired much language-related research, although emerging experimental evidence is compatible with the view that language pertaining to discrete emotion categories elicits distinct brain activities (see the later discussion).

The study of hemispheric asymmetries in emotional processing has a long tradition in neuropsychology. Studies of brain-damaged patients, in particular, often have been conducted to test two competing theories regarding hemispheric lateralization of emotional processing. The "right brain" hypothesis posits that the right hemisphere is dominant in processing emotional stimuli (Borod et al., 1998). Alternatively, the "valence" hypothesis suggests hemispheric specialization, with the left hemisphere (particularly frontal regions) subserving the processing of positive stimuli and the right hemisphere (again putatively frontal regions) predominantly engaging in the processing of negative stimuli (Davidson & Irwin, 1999). Emotional language may be a particularly interesting test case of these hemispheric lateralization theories, because in right-handed people core language regions are predominantly located in the left hemisphere. Lateralization of emotional language processing has been investigated in some detail for the case of affective prosody (see also Chapter 11), with a considerable body of evidence implying that the right hemisphere predominantly extracts the suprasegmental, low-frequency aspects of spoken language that code for its affective modulation. Regarding emotional semantics, the question of whether the right hemisphere plays a special role is of considerable theoretical interest because of its implications for the organization of the semantic system in general. To what extent is the semantic system organized in a distributed manner, perhaps encompassing right-hemisphere areas that specifically code for emotional semantics? To what extent does emotion exert a primarily modulatory role, altering the accessibility of items in the left-hemispheric semantic system?

These theoretical questions are discussed within the framework of empirical contributions generated via different methodological approaches. Theoretical considerations obviously influence stimulus-selection strategies, which in turn affect experimental outcomes, rendering generalizations across studies difficult. For instance, emotional language is sometimes compared with neutral language without further valence distinctions when testing the right-hemisphere hypothesis. At other times only valence-negative stimuli are compared with neutral ones without reference to other dimensions such as arousal, or valence-negative and valence-positive language are contrasted, disregarding stimulus intensity (arousal). Also, when emotional factors are contrasted, other nonemotional variables, such as word length, frequency, or concreteness, should be kept constant, which has not always been the case in extant studies (see Kissler, Assadollahi, & Herbert, 2006, for a detailed review of stimulus-selection effects in affective language processing).

How do emotional and linguistic brain networks interact in the processing of emotional language? Several theories posit that linguistic expressions are stored within semantic networks that encompass links to all aspects of their linguistic and pragmatic usage and emotional connotations. The word "bomb," for example, not only represents the object itself but also includes links to its linguistic properties, real-world uses, purposes, and their consequences, as well as their emotional evaluation (Lang, 1979). This view is shared by scientists in neurolinguistics (Pulvermüller, 1999) and cognitive semantics (Barsalou, 2008): All information related to a word is assumed to be stored in a dynamic network. Figure 13.1 depicts such a dynamic network of an emotional episode, showing how stimulus perception interacts with the semantic code representing this stimulus and the associated responses.

Figure 13.2 illustrates a model of the neural implementation of the linguistic and semantic codes of emotion and their interaction. Although the core units of linguistic networks are centered around the left hemisphere's Sylvian fissure, where the primary language-processing regions of the brain reside, subnetworks representing different aspects of a word can be separately activated. A popular view maintains that the semantic system is represented in the brain in a modal manner, meaning that neural organization reflects the organization of input and output modalities and attributes. For instance, functional divisions of the semantic system mirroring functional divisions in the organization of the cortex have repeatedly been shown for verbs relating to visual perception and different types of actions. Investigating verbs pertaining to limb (or bodily) movements, Pulvermüller and colleagues (for a review see Pulvermüller & Fadiga, 2010) demonstrated that the referential meaning of action words has a correlate in the somatotopic activation of motor and premotor cortex. These patterns of coactivations presumably reflect individual learning history, where the symbolic representation of meaning has been acquired by repeated coactivation of the body movement and the descriptive speech pattern. For instance, a child would jump and simultaneously hear a caregiver say the word. In the acquisition of written language, this phonological code is later mapped onto the visual word form (Perfetti & Sandak, 2000).

Similarly, for emotional concepts, Lang, Greenwald, Bradley, and Hamm (1993) assume that not only associated semantic and motor correlates but also emotion-specific physiological response information are coactivated in such associative networks (see Figure 13.1). Thus, activation of core language processing regions in concert with the circuitry processing the associated emotion should represent the emotional

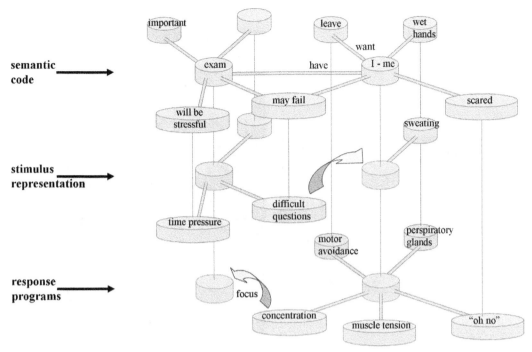

Figure 13.1. A multilayer associative network representation of a complex emotional scene (exam situation) illustrates how, in dynamic emotional processing, perceptual, semantic, and response systems are interactively linked. Activation on any level of this system can spread to other subsystems. Reprinted from Kissler et al. (2006).

significance of language (see also Cato-Jackson & Crosson, 2006, for a related suggestion). Specifically limbic and frontal brain structures that together encompass the "emotional brain" would be expected to be involved. The involvement of these regions should become apparent using functional neuroimaging studies, and lesion of those regions should result in specific deficits. If the limbic system is activated during the processing of emotional language, one question would regard the status of such activations: Are they an integral part of the meaning of an expression, or are they due to secondary processes – "coactivations" rather than activations?

A similar discussion surrounds the theoretical status of motor cortex activations during the processing of action words (e.g., Hauk, Davis, Kerif, & Pulvermuller, 2008) and can be traced to the dual-coding (Paivio, 1991) and embodiment (Barsalou, 2008) debates. Dual-coding theory proposes that humans have the capacity to store and access

information both symbolically and perceptually. In terms of the symbolic language system it is debated to what extent perceptual information associated with a concept is an integral part of a concept, is supplementary imagination, or even interferes with the concept itself. In this regard, hemispheric asymmetries have been proposed. The left hemisphere is traditionally seen as the home of the symbolic processing system and the right hemisphere as housing the perceptual processing system. In favor of dual coding, highly imaginable words have sometimes been found to activate the right hemisphere more than abstract words (Gazzaniga & Hillyard, 1971; Holcomb, Kounios, Anderson, & West, 1999). Similarly, "embodiment" or "grounded cognition" theories propose that abstract linguistic concepts are grounded in embodied and situated knowledge. People possess extensive knowledge about their bodies and experience bodily physiological changes during both movement and emotion, and abstract linguistic

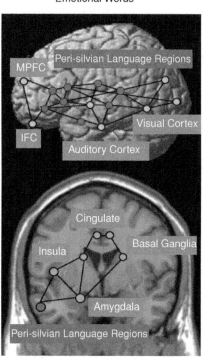

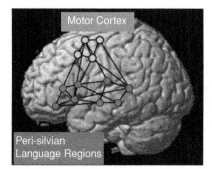

Figure 13.2. The distributed representation of language meaning in neural networks. Processing a word's meaning activates both left-hemispheric peri-sylvian language areas and associated perceptual and motor systems in a modal fashion. On the left, the idea is illustrated for the neural representation of movement-related words (after Pulvermüller, 1999, and Pulvermüller and Fadiga, 2010). On the right, this concept is extended to the processing of emotion-related language that has been shown to activate secondary sensory cortices, prefrontal areas, and, notably, limbic brain structures in addition to classic language regions. Dark nodes indicate classic language regions and light nodes the modality-dependent extensions of this network that code for specific aspects of movement- (left) or emotion-related (right) language (see also text for more details).

concepts are supposed to immediately draw on this experience, such that processing movement-related language would activate movement-related areas in the brain and processing emotional language would activate emotion-related brain structures. Figure 13.2 schematically illustrates this idea, comparing the hypothetical representation of movement-related language (left) with an analogous suggestion for the processing of emotional language (right). Evidence on involved brain regions is detailed in the lesion and functional imaging sections of this chapter.

For emotional semantics, as for concrete and highly imaginable language, a specific contribution of the right hemisphere is often discussed. Is there evidence that right-hemisphere areas contribute to the understanding of a word's or a sentence's emotional significance (independent of prosody)? If the right hemisphere plays a special role in decoding the emotional meaning of language, then what exactly is its function? Is right-hemisphere functioning crucial for understanding emotional language in the sense that lesions abolish the ability to understand emotional aspects of language, or does the right hemisphere rather exhibit a relative propensity that may be a consequence of dual coding (Paivio, 1991), perhaps secondary to emotional imagery?

Of considerable theoretical interest from a psycholinguistic point of view is the temporal integration of lexico-semantic and emotional information in the processing stream. Is a word's or an utterance's emotional "connotation" activated only after full lexico-semantic analysis, with emotional significance being subordinate to other lexical attributes? Is emotional meaning processed concurrently with other lexico-semantic attributes, with emotional meaning being one particular aspect of semantics? Or does the response to emotional aspects of a language interact with or sometimes even precede the analysis of other linguistic features? Such questions regarding the timing of neural events can best be answered using electromagnetic measures of brain activity that offer temporal resolution on a millisecond level (see Chapter 4).

The following is a summary of the empirical evidence on neural mechanisms of emotional language processing, against this brief theoretical background and with reference to the questions posed earlier. It integrates current knowledge on the anatomical and functional cerebral correlates, as well as on the temporal dynamics of emotion language processing. Contributions from different neuroscience methods such as lesion studies, functional magnetic resonance imaging (fMRI), and electro- and magneto-encephalography (EEG/MEG) are distinguished, and the theoretical implications of the results are highlighted. Finally, I identify outstanding questions in need of future research.

Lesion Studies on the Processing of Emotional Language

Studies of brain-damaged patients reveal the brain regions critically involved in affective or cognitive functions, particularly when lesions interfere with or abolish a certain function. However, this evidence does not indicate that those same regions are the only ones or even the ones typically involved in normal functioning. Moreover, lesions often vary in size, precluding a close structure–function mapping. Nevertheless, lesion studies are helpful in delineating, on a large scale, areas of the brain that are critical for a particular function and are, of course,

clinically valuable in mapping out the range of deficits to be expected after a certain type of brain damage.

Historically, in affective neuropsychology, one popular approach focused on the relative effects of left- and right-hemispheric lesions on processing different types of emotional stimuli, mostly aiming to test the right-hemisphere hypothesis against the valence hypothesis. As early as the 1860s, John Hughlings Jackson observed that emotional (swear) words could be selectively spared in patients with severe global aphasia with large left-hemisphere lesions (Hughlings Jackson, 1866). This observation was later confirmed in a case of left hemispherectomy (Smith, 1966). As in Hughlings Jackson's report, the patient's first successful speech attempts after the operation consisted of curses and emotional utterances. Conversely, Bloom and colleagues (1992) found right-hemisphere brain-damaged patients to be impaired in producing emotional content (Bloom, Borod, Obler, & Gerstman, 1992).

Investigating aphasic patients with left-sided lesions, Landis, Graves, and Goodglass (1982) also found improved performance when patients had to read aloud or write to dictation emotional rather than neutral words. Using hemifield presentation in healthy controls, Graves, Landis, and Goodglass (1981) confirmed a greater benefit for emotional words presented to the right hemisphere (left visual field), and this pattern held in aphasics (Graves et al., 1981; Landis et al., 1982). Although in healthy people the best performance in absolute terms is for emotional words presented to the left hemisphere (right visual field), the data indicate a specific role of the right hemisphere in processing emotional language: Across studies, the relative advantage for emotional words is often largest in the right hemisphere.

Comparing the extent of left- versus right-hemisphere involvement, J. C. Borod and colleagues conducted several studies on unilaterally brain-damaged patients' auditory identification and discrimination, as well as oral production of emotional language. Together, these studies confirm a greater relative decrement following right- than left-hemispheric lesions in the perception and production of emotional language, both on a single word and sentence level and regardless of valence (e.g., Borod, Bloom, Brickman, Nakhutina, & Curko, 2002). Again, after left-hemisphere lesions, the impairment is about the same for emotional and nonemotional semantics; in contrast, after right-hemispheric lesions the decrement is disproportionately larger for emotional content, implying that processing of emotional semantics is one of the right hemisphere's specific language functions.

Thus, the right hemisphere may not be generally superior for processing emotional language. Rather, it seems specialized in the sense that it retains language capacities for emotional language and is disproportionately poor at processing nonemotional language. Moreover, its processing capacities even for emotional language may be restricted to concrete and relatively short words (Eviatar & Zaidel, 1991), perhaps suggesting that some of the right hemisphere's emotion advantage in language processing capitalizes on imagery and dual coding.

Blonder et al. (1991) suggest a further thematic specificity in right- hemisphere patients' impairment for emotional content, in that patients were most impaired for verbal descriptions of emotional prosody or facial expressions. Prosody and facial affect are stimuli for which right-hemisphere-damaged patients have primary processing deficits (Kucharska-Pietura, Phillips, Gernand, & David, 2003). Thus, this observation could have interesting implications for the general organization of semantic processing and would be in line with other recent observations for domain-specific language deficits outside the classic language areas (Neininger & Pulvermuller, 2003). More fine-grained analyses or inferences are, however, complicated by the small number of patients generally included in the lesion studies (typically 10 per group) and the heterogeneity of the lesions.

Thus, the laterality studies preclude inference on the role of specific brain regions of either hemisphere for the processing of emotional semantics. On theoretical grounds, one would expect frontal and limbic lesions to have pronounced effects on the processing of emotional language, and on the basis of the earlier evidence, lateralization effects might be suspected. Indeed, Adolphs and colleagues (2000), in a large lesion mapping study (N = 108) of different subcomponents of facial emotion recognition, reported that specific emotion-naming impairments, involving the retrieval of appropriate lexical labels for facial expressions, rather than their perceptual discrimination, were associated with bilateral lesions in the frontal operculum or the supramarginal gyrus, and with right temporal lesions. Right temporal lobe involvement in the ability to name facial expressions – that is, to successfully retrieve their lexical labels – in the absence of a perceptual deficit had previously been reported in two case studies (Rapcsak, Comer, & Rubens, 1993), although in these reports there was the possibility of atypical language lateralization.

An exceptionally large number of studies document amygdala involvement in emotion perception. Patients with unilateral temporal lobectomy, including the amygdala fail to exhibit an otherwise observed identification advantage for emotional words presented in the attentional blink (Anderson & Phelps, 2001) – interestingly, left lateralized lesions drive this effect. The left amygdala also appears to play a specific role in enhanced memory for emotional words, but not scenes (Buchanan, Denburg, Tranel, & Adolphs, 2001). A particular role of the left amygdala in the perception of emotional language is also supported by functional neuroimaging studies and intracranial recordings (see the later discussion).

Amygdala activation has been shown to be modulated by dopamine input (Takahashi et al., 2010); this neurotransmitter is also otherwise implicated in the processing of affect and language. In particular, patients with Parkinson's disease characterized by dopamine depletion in the basal ganglia show "blunted" ratings of valence and arousal of emotional words (Hillier,

Beversdorf, Raymer, Williamson, & Heilman, 2007). Reduced accuracy of emotion recognition in Parkinson's disease has been documented across different input channels, including lexico-semantics (Paulmann & Pell, 2010). The basal ganglia are generally involved in integrating dynamic perceptual input, with a specific role in syntactic (Kotz, Frisch, von Cramon, & Friederici, 2003), semantic (Lieberman, 2001), and prosodic (Van Lancker Sidtis, Pachana, Cummings, & Sidtis, 2006) language processes. Testing basal ganglia involvement in emotional speech processing, Paulmann and colleagues (Paulmann, Pell, & Kotz, 2009) found patients with a left-sided basal ganglia lesion impaired in integrating semantic and prosodic emotional information, in particular relating to disgust and fear. Although these data leave open the question whether these results are specific to dynamic displays of emotion as provided by the auditory channel or by video clips, they clearly point to the possibility that selective lesions may result in categorical impairments in recognizing and understanding emotional semantics. Along these lines, one may, for instance, suspect that individuals with lesions to the insula, which processes proprioceptive bodily signals and appears particularly involved in the emotional experience of disgust (Phillips et al., 1997), could be selectively impaired in the processing of disgust-related words. Indeed individual differences in disgust sensitivity affect lexical decision reaction times to disgust related words (Silva, Montant, Ponz, & Ziegler, 2012).

In sum, lesion studies indicate a considerable capacity of the right hemisphere to process specifically emotional semantics. This capacity may not represent an absolute advantage in comparison to the left hemisphere, but rather a relative propensity on which patients with left-hemispheric lesions may capitalize. Extant studies therefore are partly in line with the right-hemisphere dominance theory of emotion, but do not provide tangible evidence for a valence asymmetry. Studies of individuals with lesions indicate amygdala involvement at least in the visual processing of emotional language, and here evidence suggests a particular importance of the left amygdala. Furthermore, dopamine availability affects the processing of emotional language, and basal ganglia lesions and dopamine depletion appear to impair particularly negative emotions, perhaps disgust and fear specifically, although these effects might be modality dependent and restricted to the auditory channel. Future studies with larger samples of patients differentiated according to more circumscribed lesions may reveal more fine-grained, perhaps even categorical subdivisions in the semantic organization of emotional language both within and across hemispheres.

Functional neuroimaging studies complement and extend lesion studies and have made tremendous contributions to our knowledge of the functional anatomy of emotion and language in the brain. I turn to these studies next.

Hemodynamic Studies of Emotional Language Processing

Functional neuroimaging can provide much more detailed insights into the organization of cerebral structures involved in the processing of emotional language than lesion studies, with the additional advantage of imaging healthy brain function. In recent years, functional magnetic resonance imaging (fMRI) has been used most widely and has surpassed positron emission tomography (PET) in popularity. For details on these methods, see Chapter 5). Only one study on emotional language has used PET (Beauregard et al., 1997).

Unlike lesion studies, functional neuroimaging studies generally do not indicate a pronounced role of the right hemisphere in the processing of emotional semantics. Although some right-hemispheric activity is found, a consistent observation across studies is a preponderance of left-hemispheric activity. The comparison of emotional with content-neutral language shows that activity enhancement for emotional language is generally found in lateral temporal and frontal brain regions, portions of the cingulate cortex, and sometimes in the amygdala. Regions most likely involved in perceptual and linguistic stimulus processing are occipitotemporal structures such as the fusiform gyrus or the occipital gyri (visual stimuli) or extended auditory cortices (acoustic stimuli). Regions more likely to be implicated in semantic processing itself include the angular gyrus, the mid and inferior temporal gyri, as well as the medial prefrontal cortex and the inferior frontal gyri. These regions do not show modality-dependent activity modulation. The more posterior areas are hypothesized to store the brain's semantic knowledge, whereas the frontal ones are hypothesized to be involved in semantic retrieval and lexical selection (for a review, see Binder, Desai, Graves, & Conant, 2009). Together, regions implicated in the perceptual and semantic analysis of language often show enhanced activity in response to emotional language input.

Retrosplenial posterior cingulate cortex also has been found active during the processing of emotional language (Cato et al., 2004), as well as in semantic processing in general (see Binder et al., 2009). However, its genuine role across these studies is probably to act as an interface between semantic and episodic systems and to aid episodic encoding of the stimuli in the scanning session. Its enhanced activity during the processing of emotional language has therefore been linked to better subsequent recall of words with emotional content (Maddock, Garrett, & Buonocore, 2003).

Brain structures devoted to the processing of emotional stimuli, including emotional language, are the orbitofrontal and medial frontal regions, anterior and subgenual parts of the cingulate cortex, the insula, and the amygdala. Thus, an extended network of frontal, temporal, and mesial structures is active in concert during the processing of emotional compared to neutral language.

One important issue regarding the organization of emotional semantics in the brain is to what extent the activations seen in

neuroimaging studies represent distinct activations in a separate semantic subsystem for emotion or rather the transient modulatory influence of distant emotion-processing centers of the brain on a unitary semantic store. Allison Cato-Jackson and Bruce Crosson (2006) interpreted the outcome of their three imaging studies of emotion word processing as indicative of a separate retrieval mechanism, a distinct "output lexicon" for emotional semantics that consistently activates the predominantly left superior frontal cortex. Conceptually some of the earlier described lesion studies on emotion naming deficits support this view.

In contrast, enhanced activity in extrastriate visual areas elicited by emotional words, in parallel or correlated with enhanced amygdala activity, has been taken to indicate amygdala-mediated amplification processes, so-called reentrant processing (Herbert et al., 2009; Isenberg et al., 1999). Extrastriate regions located in the ventral and lateral parts of the inferior temporal and occipital lobes are sensitive to a word's lexical and semantic aspects (Cohen et al., 2002). Therefore, these brain areas could represent target sites for amygdala-driven reentrant processing. Figure 13.3 illustrates correlative evidence for this process from a recent study from our group (Herbert et al., 2009). The finding is consistent with bidirectional modulatory connections between the amygdala and extrastriate cortex in non-human primates and supported by human lesion data on the processing of emotional words (Anderson & Phelps, 2001) and faces (Vuilleumier, Richardson, Armony, Driver, & Dolan, 2004). Many authors have favored reentrant processing as a model to explain facilitated sensory processing of faces and pictures in the visual cortex (see Chapter 14 for an in-depth review and discussion), and evidence suggests that it applies also to visual processing of emotional language. Facilitated visual processing thus occurs for content with evolutionary prepared as well as learned emotional significance. Although reentrant processing in emotional perception has been associated most widely with the amygdala, regional

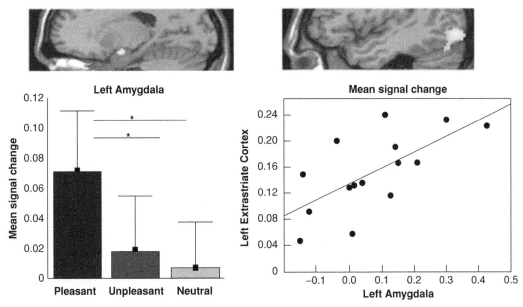

Figure 13.3. Activation of the left amygdala (top left) and extrastriate visual cortex (top right) during reading of pleasant emotional words as revealed by fMRI. Activity in the amygdala and visual cortex was found to be correlated, supporting the idea that the amygdala, via back-projections, can amplify visual processing of a wide range of stimuli, including symbolic language representations of emotion. Reproduced from Herbert et al. (2009).

interactions modulating amplification are likely to operate more widely in the brain. For instance, for emotional picture processing reentrant amplification mechanisms have been recently demonstrated in parieto-occipital networks (Keil et al., 2009).

Both transient amplification mechanisms and temporally stable distinct semantic organization may contribute to some aspects of the differential processing of emotional language in the brain. Naturally, the experimental task plays an important role in determining the mechanism and may account for some activation differences across studies.

Studies that require the active retrieval of emotional words or their explicit evaluation find, particularly left frontal activations, often in orbital and rostral frontal regions (for an overview see Cato-Jackson & Crosson, 2006). A similar pattern is also reported by Kuchinke et al. (2005) who found lexical decisions on emotional words to elicit specific activities in orbitofrontal and inferior frontal gyri. Orbitofrontal activities are supposed to primarily indicate stimulus evaluation, whereas inferior frontal

gyri are active primarily during semantic retrieval. Additionally, many of these studies also report posterior cingulate activation, which is supposed to mediate emotion-related episodic memory enhancement (Maddock et al., 2003).

Several neuroimaging studies on emotional word processing report enhanced activation in dorsolateral and medial prefrontal and middle temporal brain regions during processing of emotional in contrast to neutral words, but fail to find amygdala activation (e.g., Kuchinke et al., 2005). In these studies "active tasks" have often been used in which subjects were explicitly asked to categorize or retrieve words according to emotional, lexical, or semantic aspects. Although attention often facilitates emotional perception, cognitively demanding experimental tasks involving higher order controlled processing can mitigate stimulus-driven perceptual processing, attenuating amygdala activation (Pessoa, McKenna, Gutierrez, & Ungerleider, 2002). Task demands and emotional stimulus content recently have been found to interact when subjects performed either gender discriminations on fearful or neutral faces or judgments on words overlaid on these faces. Although during gender discrimination the task-irrelevant fearful expression led to enhanced amygdala activation, it was greatly attenuated when subjects performed the linguistic task. At the same time medial prefrontal and sensory cortex activity decreased and dorsolateral prefrontal and parietal cortex activity increased with task difficulty (Mitchell et al., 2007). This study provides evidence for an impact of a task-irrelevant emotional stimulus property on cognitive processes and for cognitive load modulating brain responses to an emotional stimulus.

Again, the existence of valence-specific activations or activations reflecting even more fine-grained, possibly categorical subdivisions of emotional space is debated. Several studies have specifically investigated valence versus arousal-related brain activation during processing of emotional words: Kensinger and Schacter using nonevaluative tasks, found the left amygdala, dorsomedial prefrontal cortex, and ventromedial prefrontal cortex to respond to stimulus arousal (Kensinger & Schacter, 2006). In the frontal cortex, valence-specific effects were also identified, with left ventrolateral (inferior frontal) prefrontal cortex responding to negative stimuli in particular. Other arousal effects in this study were identified near the temporal pole and the temporoparietal junction. Further valence effects were found in the superior temporal gyrus, with more activity for negative than positive words, whereas the middle temporal gyrus and fusiform gyrus were activated more strongly by positive words. The inferior parietal cortex exhibited a preference for positive words. Examining the mnemonic consequences of emotional word content in an abstract-concrete decision task, Kensinger and Corkin (2004) also found valence-specific effects in left inferior and dorso-lateral prefrontal cortex, whereas the amygdala responded to both arousing and strongly valent words, the stimuli having been divided into arousing and

nonarousing positive and negative stimuli of equally high valence (see Chapter 20 for an in-depth discussion of emotion effects in episodic memory). Lewis et al. investigated the separate and combined effects of word valence and arousal on brain activity (Lewis, Critchley, Rotshtein, & Dolan, 2007). They had participants decide on a word's self-reference and reported valence sensitivity in lateral orbitofrontal cortex. Additional valence-specific effects were identified in the insula and the anterior cingulate. Unlike in the studies of Kensinger and Schacter (2006) or Kuchinke et al. (2005), these valence effects were predominantly right lateralized, however, without apparent positive-negative asymmetries. Arousal-induced activities were identified in the left amygdala, insula, and basal ganglia, with the distribution of activity within these structures differing somewhat depending on whether arousal increased in positive or negative words.

Thus, as a rule of thumb regarding valence- or arousal-specific activity, dorsal and orbitofrontal structures tend to respond to a word's valence, whereas the amygdala, insula, and basal ganglia are more sensitive to arousal. In functional imaging studies, more left than right hemispheric activity is found during word processing in general. However, this simple rendering is complicated by the fact that, within these structures, hitherto not clearly delineated subregions may code for different dimensions. For instance, the amygdala has been shown to sometimes respond to valence regardless of arousal (Kensinger & Corkin, 2004), possibly because dorsal regions of the amygdala respond to arousal whereas ventral ones might respond to valence (Kim, Somerville, Johnstone, Alexander, & Whalen, 2003). Similarly, although the evidence reviewed earlier implicates the basal ganglia in arousal and/or negative affect, the dopaminergic nucleus accumbens of the basal ganglia is consistently found active during rewarding and pleasurable stimulation (Sabatinelli, Versace, Costa, Bradley, & Lang, 2006). Similarly, Lewis et al. (2007) identified the insula as particularly responsive to arousal in words, although anterior parts coded for arousal in positive words, whereas posterior parts responded to arousal in negative words. At the same time, the insula has also been specifically implicated in the experience of disgust and the processing of nonverbal disgusting stimuli (Wicker et al., 2003).

In this regard, it is important to keep in mind that the emotion word categories used in most experiments are very broad, possibly obscuring more fine-grained differences, as suggested, for instance, by studies on movement- versus vision-related verbs (Hauk et al., 2008). Indeed, a recent study identified specific brain activities during processing of pain-related compared with arousal- and valence-matched negative words in general (Richter, Eck, Straube, Miltner, & Weiss, 2010). Interestingly, this study also showed huge regional differences depending on whether the words were explicitly evaluated or implicitly processed. Notably, frontal activities were considerably attenuated during implicit processing. This is somewhat reminiscent of findings of emotion word studies that used "passive" tasks such as reading and reported mainly effects of arousal-driven perceptual amplification, but little evidence of valence-based evaluation.

Across studies, there is also some ambiguity regarding the relative impact of negative versus positive words on brain activity. Many studies found relatively symmetric activation for both valences when arousal is controlled for, but some studies reported a greater impact of negative and others of positive information. Such asymmetries have been explained in terms of general (Fredrickson, 2001), self-referential (Fossati et al., 2003), or mood-congruent (Herbert et al., 2009) processing biases or differences in the internal structure of positive versus negative material in the semantic network (Ashby, Isen, & Turken, 1999; Kuchinke et al., 2005). Alternatively, appraisal theory suggests a dynamic tuning of emotional networks (Sander, Grandjean, & Scherer, 2005; see also Chapter 1). According to this view, emotional processing depends on a cascade of stimulus-evaluation checks: Situational and individual relevance checks are proposed to determine whether stimuli will elicit emotional responses and what kind of response will result. In the absence of more specific evidence, this approach is able to account for the empirical variability in responses to emotional stimuli that is becoming increasingly evident in the literature.

In sum, functional neuroimaging studies of emotion word processing delineate a network of activations in visual and auditory perceptual regions, perisylvian language regions, and limbic and frontal brain structures. Activities are predominantly left lateralized, although some right-hemispheric activity is found. The activities partly reflect emotion-related processing enhancement, some of which appears to be driven by the amygdala. Valence-dependent activations are mostly found in prefrontal structures, but have also been observed in the insula and the cingulate. Regarding the processing of emotional language, there is so far practically no functional neuroimaging evidence for the "valence hypothesis" in the sense of valence-dependent hemispheric asymmetries. As yet, there are virtually no examinations of category-specific activations during emotion word processing, although this would appear to provide a promising direction for future research.

Identifying category-specific activations in emotion word processing may be somewhat complicated by the spatial resolution of fMRI or PET. Although much more precise than lesion studies, these methods are still extremely coarse compared to cellular neuroscience methods. Moreover, the measured activities are integrated over several seconds, possibly obscuring more transient or weaker local activations. Finally, neither lesion nor functional imaging studies give information as to the temporal dynamics of emotional language processing, and indeed, different processes may take place at distinct temporal processing stages. The temporal dynamics of emotional language processing is discussed in the next section.

Temporal Dynamics in Emotional Language Processing – EEG/MEG Studies

Electro- and magneto-encephalographic techniques (EEG and MEG) are best suited to determine the temporal evolution of cerebral activity underlying emotional and cognitive processes (see Chapter 4). Moreover, with sufficiently dense electrode coverage on the scalp, the sources of the measured activity can be estimated in the brain, although these reconstructions are never entirely unambiguous. Regarding the processing of emotional language, event-related potentials (ERPs) have been the predominant methodological approach. Both ERPs and steady-state visual evoked potentials (ssVEPs) measure the cortical activity evoked by the presentation of a stimulus. Time-frequency analysis of stimulus induced activity have occasionally been used in ssVEP studies of emotion language processing, but are still underused.

Electrophysiological studies of emotional semantics generally focus on the temporal stages at which emotional-neutral differences occur, trying to relate them to known functional stages of cognitive, and in particular, language processing.

Some studies have also examined laterality by evaluating whether activity evoked by emotional compared to neutral language showed distinct topographies, indicative of separate generator sources. Two ERP studies used hemifield paradigms to address the lateralization of emotion word processing. Ortigue and colleagues (2004) found the best performance for emotion words presented in the right visual field. However, in line with the earlier mentioned behavioral studies, the relative advantage for emotional over neutral words was most pronounced for left hemifield presentation. Electrophysiologically, emotional words elicited larger posterior activation already between 100 and 140 ms after stimulus presentation, and source analysis revealed bilateral but predominantly right visual cortex as generating the effect.

These data are compatible with at least a relative right-hemisphere advan-tage for emotion word processing. However, Kanske and Kotz (2007), although confirming behavioral and neurophysiological facilitation for emotional words, reported no evidence for a specific right-hemisphere involvement. Likewise, two other studies that used EEG source localization techniques to estimate the sources of cortical emotion-neutral differences (Hofmann, Kuchinke, Tamm, Vo, & Jacobs, 2009; Kissler, Herbert, Peyk, & Junghofer, 2007) found mainly left occipitotemporal generators, although these two studies did not use hemifield presentation.

Many ERP studies in the field have tried to determine the speed of emotional modulation in language processing. Even in the early days of event-related potential (ERP) research, emotional words were used as a potent class of stimuli expected to affect the visually evoked potential. In the earliest study, Lifshitz based on visual inspection failed to find an impressive ERP differentiation between emotional and neutral words (Lifshitz, 1966). However, in probably the first quantitative study on the effects of emotional content on the visual ERP, Begleiter and Platz reported differences between negative "taboo words" and neutral words within the first 200 ms after word presentation (Begleiter & Platz, 1969). To date, there is ample evidence for effects of emotional content on visual ERPs during word processing. These effects fall into two main categories: early effects (i.e., within the first 300 ms after stimulus onset), and late effects (i.e., after 300 ms). Early effects are often reflected in an early posterior negativity (EPN), occurring around 200 ms (Kissler et al., 2007; Schacht & Sommer, 2009; Scott, O'Donnell, Leuthold, & Sereno, 2009). This early negativity over posterior cortex for emotional versus neutral stimuli (Junghofer, Bradley, Elbert, & Lang, 2001) has been identified for a variety of stimuli, including faces, scenes, hand gestures, and even consumer goods (for a review, see Schupp, Flaisch, Stockburger, & Junghofer, 2006). Combined results indicate a domain-general amplification mechanism for the visual processing of evolutionary prepared emotionally significant stimuli, as well as for those

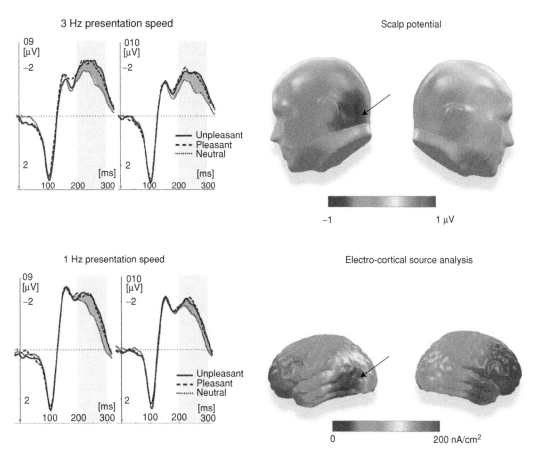

Figure 13.4. Left panel: During the reading of emotionally arousing nouns, event-related cortical potentials are found to be amplified in comparison to neutral words. This amplification can be found for a variety of stimulation rates (top left, 3 Hz; bottom left, 1 Hz) and takes the form of an early posterior negativity (EPN) occurring around 250 ms after word onset. It shows a broad occipitotemporal scalp distribution with a left-hemisphere preponderance (see arrow, top right). The sources of this activity are localized in predominantly left posterior-temporal cortical regions (see arrow, bottom right). Adapted from Kissler et al. (2007). See color plate 13.4.

stimuli whose emotional significance has been acquired by learning (see also Chapter 14 for a related account on emotional face processing). Figure 13.4 illustrates this effect in a silent reading task.

ERP modulations driven by emotional content and arising before 300 ms after stimulus onset are confirmed by many studies and have also been found on the P2 and sometimes even N1 or P1 components. They have been observed in both healthy subjects (Begleiter & Platz, 1969; Herbert, Junghofer, & Kissler, 2008; Ortigue et al., 2004) and clinical groups (Pauli, Amrhein, Muhlberger, Dengler, & Wiedemann, 2005). Such early responses are unlikely to reflect

conscious stimulus evaluation, which has been linked to ERPs occurring later than 300 ms after stimulus onset (Del Cul, Baillet, & Dehaene, 2007). However, enhanced ERPs to emotional words around 200 ms after onset are consistent with the view that emotion can enhance early lexico-semantic analysis during word processing (Kissler et al., 2006), because early effects of semantics in the ERP have been reported around 250 ms (Hinojosa, Martin-Loeches, Munoz, Casado, & Pozo, 2004). A recent study directly compared early perceptual enhancements as evident in steady-state potentials (SSVEPs) with lexico-semantic processing effects reflected in the EPN/P2

effect and found emotional words to modulate the later, but not the former, supporting a lexico-semantic locus of such effects
(Trauer, Andersen, Kotz, & Müller, 2012).

Still, a number of studies report emotion-
dependent ERP differences in word processing even before 150 ms (Hofmann et al.,
2009; Scott et al., 2009; Skrandies, 1998). This
suggests that the processing of emotional
content sometimes can precede or bypass
full semantic analysis. Some data also suggest very early ERP effects of "unseen" emotional words, which were presented subliminally (Bernat, Bunce, & Shevrin, 2001).
Other results indicate increased skin conductance to unseen unpleasant words (Silvert, Delplanque, Bouwalerh, Verpoort, &
Sequeira, 2004). Naccache and colleagues
(2005) add further evidence for the subcortical processing of invisible emotional
words by showing that subliminally presented threat words evoked stronger field
potentials in the amygdala than neutral
words, although in a later time window
(around 800 ms after word onset). Also
supporting subliminal effects of emotional
content on word processing, although not
addressing their neural origin, are results of
lowered detection thresholds for emotional
than for neutral words following their subliminal presentation (Gaillard et al., 2006).

ERP effects of emotional content within
the first 150 ms after word onset have
been reported most frequently, although not
exclusively, in patient populations (Pauli et
al., 2005) who are thought to have an attentional bias toward disorder-related stimuli.
These earliest responses to disorder-relevant
material may, at least partly, reflect conditioned responses to these stimuli. Effects
of aversive conditioning on word processing have been observed at the N100 component (Montoya, Larbig, Pulvermuller, Flor,
& Birbaumer, 1996), and aversive conditioning of simple geometric patterns can
affect even the C1 ERP, the earliest primary
visual cortex response (Stolarova, Keil, &
Moratti, 2006). Recent data support a role
of conditioning processes in the acquisition
of early emotion word ERPs, but not specificity to negative associations. Schacht et al.
(2012) demonstrate that associating Chinese

words with monetary gain in an operant
conditioning procedure induced an emotion
effect around 150 ms in non-Chinese readers.
Regardless of the underlying mechanism, a
number of ERP studies demonstrate that
even very early brain potentials, indicative of
preconscious and sometimes also prelexical
processing, can distinguish between affective
and neutral words across several different experimental designs, tasks and subject groups.

A considerable number of studies have
found effects of emotional content on electrophysiological cortical activity later than
300 ms after word onset. For these, as for the
early effects, task dependence and covariation with arousal or valence of the presented stimuli are not quite clear. Still,
in contrast to the very early effects, they
occur in a time range where the modulation of cortical responses by word meaning is not unusual in itself. By 300–400 ms
after stimulus onset, ERP tracings reflect
conscious processing stages and clearly vary
with semantic expectancy (Kutas & Federmeier, 2000), task relevance (Sutton, Tueting, Zubin, & John, 1967), or depth of mental engagement (Dien, Spencer, & Donchin,
2004). Thus, it is not surprising that ERPs in
this time range can reflect processing differences between words of different emotional
content. Considering emotional content as
a semantic aspect of words would suggest
that N400 might represent a likely "classical" ERP candidate component to assess for
emotion effects. Indeed, some studies have
found modulations of the N400 response
to emotion words, usually with smaller
N400 activation to emotional than to neutral
words, indicating facilitated semantic integration (Herbert et al., 2008; Kiehl, Hare,
McDonald, & Brink, 1999).

Still, there is a comparative paucity of
reports on N400 modulation by emotional
words, which may partly reflect a surprising
investigator bias, considering that the N400
is often regarded as "the" electrophysiological indicator of semantic processes in the
brain. However, the N400 response does not
index lexical access or semantic processing
per se, but reflects semantic integration
within a larger context, either created
by expectations on sentence content or

other contextual constraints within experiments (Kutas & Federmeier, 2000). Thus, single-word studies may only result in N400 modulations if strong expectations of emotional word content are established. Priming studies or experiments establishing an emotional expectation within a sentence context therefore may provide a better testing ground for N400 modulations by emotional language content than single-word studies. Some studies found N400 modulations to targets semantically (mis-)matching the prosody of the preceding sentence (Schirmer, Kotz, & Friederici, 2002; for a review, see Chapter 26) or distinct effects of semantic and prosodic (mis-)match within a sentence (Paulmann & Kotz, 2008). Mood may also mediate N400 effects and influence the ease of semantic integration, as well as the subjective expectation of mood-congruent versus incongruent information. Federmeier, Kirson, Moreno, and Kutas (2001) found that when participants were in a mildly positive mood, their semantic processing was facilitated, as reflected by a smaller N400 potential to more distant members of given categories. Similar mood effects were recently observed by Chwilla and colleagues (2011). Interestingly, a study from our group reported an N400 reduction specifically to positive words in a silent reading task. This finding suggests that the positive words were easier to semantically integrate than neutral or negative words (Herbert et al., 2008), perhaps because healthy students tend to be mostly in mildly positive moods (Diener & Diener, 1996). Thus, although not very abundant, a number of studies suggest that both a word's emotional content and a participant's emotional state may affect the N400 ERP.

Many studies of the impact of emotional content on language processing have focused on centroparietal late positive potentials (LPPs), arising around 500 ms after stimulus onset. These late parietal positivities are indicative of later stages of attention allocation and evaluation and have been shown to predict subsequent episodic recall (Dolcos & Cabeza, 2002), implying a functional role in encoding. During the processing of emotional words, enhanced LPPs have

been reported repeatedly, but not invariably (see, for instance, Vanderploeg, Brown, & Marsh, 1987). Fischler and Bradley (2006), in a series of studies, found the LPP to be sensitive to the arousal and not to the valence dimension of words, being larger for both pleasant and unpleasant compared to neutral words. Moreover, a larger LPP to emotional content arose only when the task required semantic processing. An attenuation or even absence of emotional-neutral differences on the LPP during structural processing of the stimuli was confirmed by Schacht and Sommer (2009).

As in many sub-areas of affective neuroscience, the extent to which emotion effects in word processing are resource and task dependent or occur (relatively) automatically is debated (see Chapters 14 and 15 for in-depth discussions). Several studies have found larger ERPs to emotional compared to neutral words in the absence of overt instructions or even to subliminally presented stimuli, supporting a "spontaneous" processing enhancement. Still, this finding alone does not speak in favor of strictly automatic processing and complete non-interference of competing tasks. A minimum of lexico-semantic processing seems required for EPN and LPP emotion effects to occur, because none are found when a task can be performed on the basis of discrimination of low-level perceptual features rather than word reading (Hinojosa, Mendez-Bertolo, & Pozo, 2010; Rellecke, Palazova, Sommer, & Schacht, 2011). In recent lexical decision studies that, by definition, require lexical access, emotion effects have been found quite consistently in the EPN/P2 time range (from 200 ms onwards), with emotion effects either coinciding or following lexicality effects (Palazova, Mantwill, Sommer, & Schacht, 2011; Scott et al., 2009). Indeed, very recent data suggest that the EPN effect arises as a consequence of faster lexical access to emotional than to neutral words (Kissler & Herbert, 2012).

Regarding the automaticity of emotion effects in word processing, a grammatical decision task does not interfere with the emotion EPN effect (Kissler, Herbert,

Winkler, & Junghofer, 2009), indicating considerable robustness even in the face of a competing task, provided a minimum of lexical processing occurs. Where exactly this minimum lies is open to future research. Also, non-interference of one particular competing task may not generalize across other tasks, providing further challenges for future studies.

Enhanced LPPs to emotional words are seen most clearly during semantic stimulus processing and in particular during emotion evaluation. Emotional-neutral differences were attenuated or even absent during structural processing of the stimuli and were attenuated for lexical compared with evaluative decisions (Fischler & Bradley, 2006; Schacht & Sommer, 2009). A recent grammatical decision task found no significant interference between the primary task and emotion processing on the LPP (Kissler et al., 2009), but the emotion effect was considerably smaller than the task effect. During silent reading, the LPP response pattern diverges from that of the preceding EPN, and the effect is also smaller (Herbert et al., 2008), indicating a dissociation of underlying mechanisms. So far, results suggest a higher degree of automaticity in the processes that drive the EPN response to emotional words (Schacht & Sommer, 2009). This is also supported in two recent studies on emotional picture processing: Codispoti and colleagues found habituation of the LPP, but not the EPN response to emotional content (Codispoti, Mazzetti, & Bradley, 2009), and Schupp and colleagues reported that the LPP both benefits more from directed attention to emotional content and suffers more from interference from a primary feature-based attention task (Schupp et al., 2006).

Although recent studies have investigated the extent to which directed attention can interfere with different stages of emotional face (Eimer & Holmes, 2007; see also Chapter 14), picture (Schupp et al., 2006), and to some extent word processing (Kissler et al., 2009), there is little work on other contextual factors, such as mood, self-reference, or personality variables. However, manip-

ulating the participants' mood affects their responses to syntactic violations as reflected in the amplitude of the P600 brain potential (Vissers et al., 2010) and findings of rapid and pronounced responses to disorder-related words in patient groups support an importance of contextual factors and individual differences. In healthy people a larger LPP response to pleasant adjectives may be an accidental finding. Yet, adjectives with emotional connotation often describing emotional states or traits, such as "happy" or "fearful," may induce more self-referential processing, engaging more resources over a longer period of time. Depending on personality factors such self-referential processing may favor positive or negative stimuli, and perhaps in healthy young students it may induce a bias toward positive stimuli.

As mentioned earlier, not all studies of emotion language processing have separately assessed or reported stimulus arousal and valence, let alone other potential dimensions or categories of emotion. Even from those that have, it is not easy to discern a clear pattern of arousal or valence effects on ERPs. Whereas Fischler and Bradley (2006) reported all of their effects to be driven by arousal, other studies present more variable patterns. In fact, behavioral and neural processing advantages appear to be reported more frequently for positive language (Herbert, Kissler, Junghofer, Peyk, & Rockstroh, 2006; Hofmann et al., 2009; Schapkin, Gusev, & Kuhl, 2000). Schapkin and colleagues (2000) reported enhanced LPPs to pleasant compared to both neutral and unpleasant words during evaluative decision tasks (Schapkin et al., 2000). Also using an evaluation task, Herbert and colleagues (2006) found that earlier positivities (P2, P3a) responded to the arousal dimension of the words, whereas the later LPP was selectively enhanced during the processing of pleasant adjectives (Herbert et al., 2006). This effect is shown in Figure 13.5.

A similar pattern of responses driven initially by arousal and later by "pleasure" was also found when subjects read emotional adjectives without receiving an explicit processing instruction (Herbert et al.,

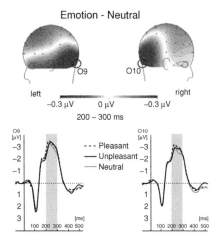

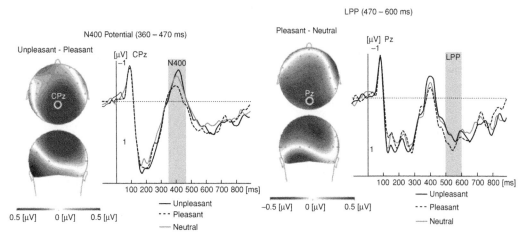

Figure 13.5. Event-related brain potential responses in different time windows during the evaluation of emotional and neutral adjectives, indicating enhanced initial attention to emotionally arousing words. The P2 around 230 ms after word onset and the P3 between 300 and 400 ms respond to emotionally arousing words, regardless of valence (top: scalp topography of the difference waveforms and ERP tracings from electrode Pz). By contrast, the late positive component (LPC) of the brain is larger for positive than for neutral or negative words, suggesting more pronounced elaborative processing of positive material (bottom left: scalp topography of the difference waveforms and ERP tracing from one parietal electrode). Data indicate that emotional words are preferentially processed at different stages, although following the initial attention capture by both positive and negative arousing words the pattern can differ, selectively favoring one valence. Adapted from Herbert et al. (2006).

2008). This sequence underscores the earlier suggested functional differentiation between early and late ERPs in affective processing. Several studies from my group indicate that early ERPs like the EPN respond to the arousal dimension of stimuli, being enhanced for both pleasantly and unpleasantly arousing words. By contrast, later potentials such as the N400 or LPP in healthy students mostly show an enhanced response to positively arousing over neutral stimuli, with negative stimuli not differing from neutral. Figure 13.5 illustrates this sequence of early arousal-driven and late valence-driven responses. Because this pattern is seen most clearly when adjectives, which often describe states or traits, are used as stimuli (Herbert et al., 2006, 2008), the degree of self-referential processing induced by the words may determine processing in the LPP window. At least for student subjects, this latter thesis is supported by recent rating data (Herbert, et al., 2008, 2009).

Variation of the linguistic reference (e.g., "your success" or "my success" versus "your fear" or "my fear") has been found to modulate early and late emotion-related ERPs during reading (Herbert, Herbert, Ethofer, & Pauli, 2011). It also provides an important step toward more linguistically and socially complex designs. Furthermore, the internal semantic structure of positive versus negative language may also contribute to valence-specific processing biases (Hofmann et al., 2009; Kuchinke et al., 2005). Positive information may be better integrated within associative networks and be represented in a more cohesive manner than negative information, thereby facilitating the processing of positive words.

Taken together, extant studies demonstrate reliable amplification of visual ERPs in response to emotional compared to neutral words from about 200 ms after word presentation. Although enhanced responses are frequently found for both positively and negatively arousing words alike, particularly for the later processing stages a larger impact of pleasant content is often reported. Clarification of the relative role of valence and arousal on ERPs elicited by emotional language at different temporal processing stages awaits further research. Similarly, ERP findings are somewhat inconclusive regarding the dominance of either hemisphere in the processing of emotional language. However, current findings are in line with the view that emotional content amplifies lexico-semantic word processing after initial stimulus identification. This enhancement may occur by means of amplificatory reentrant processing via bidirectional connections between extrastriate visual cortex and the amygdala. However, given that even earlier, pre-lexical responses to emotional words have been identified, other mechanisms may also play a role. Such pre-semantic response enhance-

ments may, for instance, reflect fast conditioned responses to a few highly individually relevant words. Indeed, evidence for a role of operant conditioning in generating very early emotion effects in words. As in many areas of affective neuroscience the amygdala has been shown to be active in emotion word processing, and given its established prominent role in affective conditioning and in emotional vision in general it is likely that it will contribute to some of these ERP enhancements. However, its precise role in the processing of emotional language is much less well understood than its role in the processing of emotional faces. Several of the previously described effects may therefore not rely on online amygdala activity (or the online activity of any other back-projecting structure), but result from established properties of an individual's mental lexicon. Conceivably, structures like the amygdala are involved only during the acquisition of a word's or phrase's emotional significance, permanently enhancing an item's accessibility. Thus, studying the processes by which linguistic symbols acquire emotional significance will be highly relevant to the functional characterization of ERP enhancements to emotional words at different processing stages.

Summary and Outlook

From the perspective of different methodological approaches, this chapter outlined how the processing of emotional language content differs from the processing of semantically neutral language. Emotional language is unique in that it can be partly preserved in otherwise aphasic patients with left-hemisphere strokes. Data from the damaged brain indicate a special capacity of the right hemisphere for processing emotional language, but functional neuroimaging data from healthy people indicate that such processing normally occurs predominantly in the left hemisphere. Regions more strongly activated by emotional than by content-neutral language include the secondary visual and auditory cortices and mid-temporal and inferior frontal regions, which are typically activated during semantic processing; medial and orbitofrontal regions that are commonly involved in emotional evaluation; and the amygdala, insula, and basal ganglia. Regarding the temporal evolution of emotion effects in word processing, effects have been found from the earliest stages (N100, EPN), apparently rapidly alerting the individual to a word's or phrase's emotional significance, but also affecting contextual integration (N400), evaluation, and memory encoding (LPP) at later processing stages. Together, the current findings indicate activity of a widespread network of brain regions, including, but also exceeding, regions traditionally viewed as part of the semantic processing system. Thus, from a neurolinguistic viewpoint, the data appear to support the view of a distributed, "modal" semantic system and outline the elements of a processing system for emotional semantics.

Nevertheless, our knowledge on how the brain processes emotional language content is incomplete in many respects: Although lesion and imaging studies have succeeded in identifying the elements of a processing system for emotional semantics, the interaction between these elements and its temporal course are virtually unknown. Moreover, we do not yet know how the brain differentiates between emotional subcategories. So far, most data reveal differences between "the emotional" and "the mundane," but it is not even quite clear how the brain differentiates between the meaning of "good" and "bad" (i.e., differentiates between positive and negative language), even though a difference would appear salient. Clearly, our linguistic capabilities go far beyond differentiating the meanings of good, neutral, and bad, and obviously so should those of our brains. Furthermore, most research has been on the processing of single words or very short phrases. Yet, linguistic discourse is normally much more complex, and neuroscience should begin to capture this complexity without losing its ambition to strive for experimental control. Finally, language is fundamentally about communicating with other people. Although the emotional significance of language often arises from its significance in communicatory context, practically no research has been conducted using more realistic communicatory settings, establishing clear sender–receiver relationships. Thus, as in much of cognitive and affective neuroscience, a knowledge base has been built, but many of the interesting issues are still unresolved.

Outstanding Questions

- Spatiotemporal dynamics of emotional language processing: How and when do different brain regions interact to decode the emotional meaning of language?
- Cerebral differentiation between emotional subcategories: How does the brain differentiate between emotional categories and subtle emotional nuances that a listener or reader can interpret?
- Processing of complex emotional language: How does the brain integrate the significance of emotional language beyond individual words and very simple phrases, laying the groundwork for the emotional experience of poetry and literature?
- Emotional language in realistic communicatory settings: How are communicatory context and social sender–receiver relationships integrated in the processing of emotional language?

References

Adolphs, R., Damasio, H., Tranel, D., Cooper, G., & Damasio, A. R. (2000). A role for somatosensory cortices in the visual recognition of emotion as revealed by three-dimensional lesion mapping. *Journal of Neuroscience, 20*(7), 2683–90.

Anderson, A. K., & Phelps, E. A. (2001). Lesions of the human amygdala impair enhanced perception of emotionally salient events. *Nature, 411*(6835), 305–9.

Ashby, F. G., Isen, A. M., & Turken, A. U. (1999). A neuropsychological theory of positive affect and its influence on cognition. *Psychology Review, 106*(3), 529–50.

Barsalou, L. W. (2008). Grounded cognition. *Annual Review of Psychology, 59*, 617–45.

Beauregard, M., Chertkow, H., Bub, D., Murtha, S., Dixon, R., & Evans, A. (1997). The neural substrate for concrete, abstract, and emotional word lexica: A positron emission tomography study. *Journal of Cognitive Neuroscience*, 9(4), 20.

Begleiter, H., & Platz, A. (1969). Cortical evoked potentials to semantic stimuli. *Psychophysiology*, 6(1), 91–100.

Bernat, E., Bunce, S., & Shevrin, H. (2001). Event-related brain potentials differentiate positive and negative mood adjectives during both supraliminal and subliminal visual processing. *International Journal of Psychophysiology*, 42(1), 11–34.

Binder, J. R., Desai, R. H., Graves, W. W., & Conant, L. L. (2009). Where is the semantic system? A critical review and meta-analysis of 120 functional neuroimaging studies. *Cerebral Cortex*, 19(12), 2767–96.

Blonder L. X., Bowers D., & Heilman K. M. (1991). The role of the right hemisphere in emotional communication. *Brain*, 114(3), 1115–27.

Bloom, R. L., Borod, J. C., Obler, R. K., & Gerstman, L. J. (1992). Impact of emotional content on discourse production in patients with unilateral brain damage. *Brain and Language*, 42(2), 153–64.

Borod, J. C., Bloom, R. L., Brickman, A. M., Nakhutina, L., & Curko, E. A. (2002). Emotional processing deficits in individuals with unilateral brain damage. *Applied Neuropsychology*, 9(1), 23–36.

Borod, J. C., Cicero, B. A., Obler, L. K., Welkowitz, J., Erhan, H. M., Santschi, C., et al. (1998). Right hemisphere emotional perception: Evidence across multiple channels. *Neuropsychology*, 12(3), 446–58.

Bradley, M. M., & Lang, P. J. (1994). Measuring emotion: The self-assessment manikin and the semantic differential. *Journal of Behavioral Therapy and Experimental Psychiatry*, 25(1), 49–59.

Buchanan, T. W., Denburg, N. L., Tranel, D., & Adolphs, R. (2001). Verbal and nonverbal emotional memory following unilateral amygdala damage. *Learning and Memory*, 8(6), 326–35.

Cato, M. A., Crosson, B., Gokcay, D., Soltysik, D., Wierenga, C., Gopinath, K., et al. (2004). Processing words with emotional connotation: an FMRI study of time course and laterality in rostral frontal and retrosplenial cortices. *Journal of Cognitive Neuroscience*, 16(2), 167–77.

Cato-Jackson, M. A., & Crosson, B. (2006). Emotional connotation of words: Role of emotion in distributed semantic systems. *Progress in Brain Research*, 156, 205–16.

Chwilla, D.J., Virgillito, D., Vissers, C. T. (2011). The relationship of language and emotion: N400 support for an embodied view of language comprehension. *Journal of Cognitive Neuroscience*, 23(9), 2400–14.

Codispoti, M., Mazzetti, M., & Bradley, M. M. (2009). Unmasking emotion: Exposure duration and emotional engagement. *Psychophysiology*, 46(4), 731–38.

Cohen, L., Lehericy, S., Chochon, F., Lemer, C., Rivaud, S., & Dehaene, S. (2002). Language-specific tuning of visual cortex? Functional properties of the Visual Word Form Area. *Brain*, 125(Pt. 5), 1054–69.

Davidson, R. J., & Irwin, W. (1999). The functional neuroanatomy of emotion and affective style. *Trends in Cognitive Sciences*, 3(1), 11–21.

Del Cul, A., Baillet, S., & Dehaene, S. (2007). Brain dynamics underlying the nonlinear threshold for access to consciousness. *PLoS Biol*, 5(10), e260.

Dien, J., Spencer, K. M., & Donchin, E. (2004). Parsing the late positive complex: Mental chronometry and the ERP components that inhabit the neighborhood of the P300. *Psychophysiology*, 41(5), 665–78.

Diener, E., & Diener, C. (1996). Most people are happy. *Psychological Science*, 7(3), 181–85.

Dolcos, F., & Cabeza, R. (2002). Event-related potentials of emotional memory: Encoding pleasant, unpleasant, and neutral pictures. *Cognitive, Affective & Behavioral Neuroscience*, 2(3), 252–63.

Eimer, M., & Holmes, A. (2007). Event-related brain potential correlates of emotional face processing. *Neuropsychologia*, 45(1), 15–31.

Eviatar, Z., & Zaidel, E. (1991). The effects of word length and emotionality on hemispheric contribution to lexical decision. *Neuropsychologia*, 29(5), 415–28.

Federmeier, K. D., Kirson, D. A., Moreno, E. M., & Kutas, M. (2001). Effects of transient, mild mood states on semantic memory organization and use: An event-related potential investigation in humans. *Neuroscience Letters*, 305(3), 149–52.

Fischler, I., & Bradley, M. (2006). Event-related potential studies of language and emotion: words, phrases, and task effects. *Progress in Brain Research*, 156, 185–203.

Fontaine, J. R., Scherer, K. R., Roesch, E. B., & Ellsworth, P. C. (2007). The world of emotions is not two-dimensional. *Psychological Science*, 18(12), 1050–57.

Fossati, P., Hevenor, S. J., Graham, S. J., Grady, C., Keightley, M. L., Craik, F., et al. (2003). In search of the emotional self: An fMRI study using positive and negative emotional words. *American Journal of Psychiatry*, 160(11), 1938–45.

Fredrickson, B. L. (2001). The role of positive emotions in positive psychology. The broaden-and-build theory of positive emotions. *American Psychologist*, 56(3), 218–26.

Gaillard, R., Del Cul, A., Naccache, L., Vinckier, F., Cohen, L., & Dehaene, S. (2006). Nonconscious semantic processing of emotional words modulates conscious access. *Proceedings of the National Academy of Sciences*, 103(19), 7524–29.

Gazzaniga, M. S., & Hillyard, S. A. (1971). Language and speech capacity of the right hemisphere. *Neuropsychologia*, 9(3), 273–80.

Graves, R., Landis, T., & Goodglass, H. (1981). Laterality and sex differences for visual recognition of emotional and non-emotional words. *Neuropsychologia*, 19(1), 95–102.

Hauk, O., Davis, M. H., Kherif, F., & Pulvermuller, F. (2008). Imagery or meaning? Evidence for a semantic origin of category-specific brain activity in metabolic imaging. *European Journal of Neuroscience*, 27(7), 1856–66.

Herbert, C., Ethofer, T., Anders, S., Junghofer, M., Wildgruber, D., Grodd, W., et al. (2009). Amygdala activation during reading of emotional adjectives – an advantage for pleasant content. *Social Cognition and Affective Neuroscience*, 4(1), 35–49.

Herbert, C., Herbert, B. M., Ethofer, T., & Pauli, P. (2011). His or mine? The time course of self-other discrimination in emotion processing. *Social Neuroscience*, 6(3), 277–88.

Herbert, C., Junghofer, M., & Kissler, J. (2008). Event related potentials to emotional adjectives during reading. *Psychophysiology*, 45(3), 487–98.

Herbert, C., Kissler, J., Junghofer, M., Peyk, P., & Rockstroh, B. (2006). Processing of emotional adjectives: Evidence from startle EMG and ERPs. *Psychophysiology*, 43(2), 197–206.

Hillier, A., Beversdorf, D. Q., Raymer, A. M., Williamson, D. J., & Heilman, K. M. (2007). Abnormal emotional word ratings in Parkinson"s disease. *Neurocase*, 13(2), 81–85.

Hinojosa, J. A., Martin-Loeches, M., Munoz, F., Casado, P., & Pozo, M. A. (2004). Electrophysiological evidence of automatic early semantic processing. *Brain and Language*, 88(1), 39–46.

Hinojosa, J. A., Mendez-Bertolo, C., & Pozo, M. A. (2010). Looking at emotional words is not the same as reading emotional words: Behavioral and neural correlates. *Psychophysiology*, 47(4), 748–57.

Hofmann, M. J., Kuchinke, L., Tamm, S., Vo, M. L., & Jacobs, A. M. (2009). Affective processing within 1/10th of a second: High arousal is necessary for early facilitative processing of negative but not positive words. *Cognitive, Affective & Behavioral Neuroscience*, 9(4), 389–97.

Holcomb, P. J., Kounios, J., Anderson, J. E., & West, W. C. (1999). Dual-coding, context-availability, and concreteness effects in sentence comprehension: an electrophysiological investigation. *Journal of Experimental Psychology: Learning, Memory & Cognition*, 25(3), 721–42.

Hughlings Jackson, J (1866). Clinical remarks on emotional and intellectual language in some cases of disease of the nervous system. *Lancet*, i, 5.

Isenberg, N., Silbersweig, D., Engelien, A., Emmerich, S., Malavade, K., Beattie, B., et al. (1999). Linguistic threat activates the human amygdala. *Proceedings of the National Academy of Sciences*, 96(18), 10456–59.

Junghofer, M., Bradley, M. M., Elbert, T. R., & Lang, P. J. (2001). Fleeting images: A new look at early emotion discrimination. *Psychophysiology*, 38(2), 175–78.

Kanske, P., & Kotz, S. A. (2007). Concreteness in emotional words: ERP evidence from a hemifield study. *Brain Research*, 1148, 138–48.

Keil, A., Sabatinelli, D., Ding, M., Lang, P. J., Ihssen, N., & Heim, S. (2009). Re-entrant projections modulate visual cortex in affective perception: Evidence from Granger causality analysis. *Human Brain Mapping*, 30(2), 532–40.

Kensinger, E. A., & Corkin, S. (2004). Two routes to emotional memory: Distinct neural processes for valence and arousal. *Proceedings of the National Academy of Sciences*,, 101(9), 3310–15.

Kensinger, E. A., & Schacter, D. L. (2006). Processing emotional pictures and words: Effects of valence and arousal. *Cognitive, Affective & Behavioral Neuroscience*, 6(2), 110–26.

Kiehl, K. A., Hare, R. D., McDonald, J. J., & Brink, J. (1999). Semantic and affective processing in psychopaths: An event-related potential (ERP) study. *Psychophysiology*, 36(6), 765–74.

Kim, H., Somerville, L. H., Johnstone, T., Alexander, A. L., & Whalen, P. J. (2003). Inverse amygdala and medial prefrontal cortex responses to surprised faces. *Neuroreport*, 14(18), 2317–22.

Kissler, J., Assadollahi, R., & Herbert, C. (2006). Emotional and semantic networks in visual word processing: Insights from ERP studies. *Progress in Brain Research*, 156, 147–83.

Kissler, J., Herbert, C., Peyk, P., & Junghofer, M. (2007). Buzzwords: Early cortical responses to emotional words during reading. *Psychological Science*, 18(6), 475–80.

Kissler, J., Herbert, C., Winkler, I., & Junghofer, M. (2009). Emotion and attention in visual word processing: An ERP study. *Biological Psychology*, 80(1), 75–83.

Kissler, J. & Herbert, C. (2012). Emotion, Emntooi, Emitoon? Faster lexical access to emotional words during reading. Manuscript accepted for publication in *Biological Psychology*. doi:pii: S0301-0511(12)00195-0. 10.1016/j.biopsycho.2012.09.004. [Epub ahead of print] PMID:23059636 [PubMed – as supplied by publisher].

Kotz, S. A., Frisch, S., von Cramon, D. Y., & Friederici, A. D. (2003). Syntactic language processing: ERP lesion data on the role of the basal ganglia. *Journal of the International Neuropsychology Society*, 9(7), 1053–60.

Kucharska-Pietura, K., Phillips, M. L., Gernand, W., & David, A. S. (2003). Perception of emotions from faces and voices following unilateral brain damage. *Neuropsychologia*, 41(8), 1082–90.

Kuchinke, L., Jacobs, A. M., Grubich, C., Vo, M. L., Conrad, M., & Herrmann, M. (2005). Incidental effects of emotional valence in single word processing: An fMRI study. *Neuroimage*, 28(4), 1022–32.

Kutas, M., & Federmeier, K. D. (2000). Electrophysiology reveals semantic memory use in language comprehension. *Trends in Cognitive Science*, 4(12), 463–70.

Landis, T., Graves, R., & Goodglass, H. (1982). Aphasic reading and writing: Possible evidence for right hemisphere participation. *Cortex*, 18(1), 105–12.

Lang, P. J. (1979). Presidential address, 1978: A bio-informational theory of emotional imagery. *Psychophysiology*, 16(6), 495–512.

Lang, P. J,, Greenwald, M.K., Bradley M.M., Hamm, A.O. (1993). Looking at pictures: affective, facial, visceral, and behavioral reactions. *Psychophysiology*, 30(3), 261–73.

Lewis, P. A., Critchley, H. D., Rotshtein, P., & Dolan, R. J. (2007). Neural correlates of processing valence and arousal in affective words. *Cerebral Cortex*, 17(3), 742–48.

Lieberman, P. (2001). Human language and our reptilian brain. The subcortical bases of speech, syntax, and thought. *Perspectives in Biological Medicine*, 44(1), 32–51.

Lifshitz, K. (1966). The averaged evoked cortical response to complex visual stimuli. *Psychophysiology*, 3(1), 55–68.

Maddock, R. J., Garrett, A. S., & Buonocore, M. H. (2003). Posterior cingulate cortex activation by emotional words: fMRI evidence from a valence decision task. *Human Brain Mapping*, 18(1), 30–41.

Meltzoff, A. N., & Moore, M. K. (1983). Newborn infants imitate adult facial gestures. *Child Development*, 54(3), 702–9.

Mitchell, D. G., Nakic, M., Fridberg, D., Kamel, N., Pine, D. S., & Blair, R. J. (2007). The impact of processing load on emotion. *Neuroimage*, 34(3), 1299–1309.

Montoya, P., Larbig, W., Pulvermuller, F., Flor, H., & Birbaumer, N. (1996). Cortical correlates of semantic classical conditioning. *Psychophysiology*, 33(6), 644–49.

Naccache, L., Gaillard, R., Adam, C., Hasboun, D., Clémenceau, S., Baulac, M., Dehaene, S., & Cohen, L. (2005). A direct intracranial record of emotions evoked by subliminal words. *Proceedings of the National Academy of Sciences*, 102(21), 7713–17.

Neininger, B., & Pulvermuller, F. (2003). Word-category specific deficits after lesions in the right hemisphere. *Neuropsychologia*, 41(1), 53–70.

Ortigue, S., Michel, C. M., Murray, M. M., Mohr, C., Carbonnel, S., & Landis, T. (2004). Electrical neuroimaging reveals early generator modulation to emotional words. *Neuroimage*, 21(4), 1242–51.

Osgood, C. E., Miron, M. S., & May, W. H. (1975). *Cross-cultural universals of affective meaning*. Urbana: University of Illinois Press.

Paivio, A. (1991). Dual coding theory – retrospect and current status. *Canadian Journal of Psychology-Revue Canadienne De Psychologie*, 45(3), 255–87.

Palazova, M., Mantwill, K., Sommer, W., & Schacht, A. (2011). Are effects of emotion in single words non-lexical? Evidence from event-related brain potentials. *Neuropsychologia*, 49(9), 2766–75.

Pauli, P., Amrhein, C., Muhlberger, A., Dengler, W., & Wiedemann, G. (2005). Electrocortical evidence for an early abnormal processing of panic-related words in panic disorder patients. *International Journal of Psychophysiology*, 57(1), 33–41.

Paulmann, S., & Kotz, S. A. (2008). An ERP investigation on the temporal dynamics of emotional prosody and emotional semantics in pseudo- and lexical-sentence context. *Brain and Language*, 105(1), 59–69.

Paulmann, S., & Pell, M. D. (2010). Dynamic emotion processing in Parkinson's disease as a function of channel availability. *Journal of Clinical and Experimental Neuropsychology*, 1–14.

Paulmann, S., Pell, M. D., & Kotz, S. A. (2009). Comparative processing of emotional prosody and semantics following basal ganglia infarcts: ERP evidence of selective impairments for disgust and fear. *Brain Research*, 1295, 159–69.

Perfetti, C. A., & Sandak, R. (2000). Reading optimally builds on spoken language: implications for deaf readers. *Journal of Deaf Studies and Deaf Education*, 5(1), 32–50.

Pessoa, L., McKenna, M., Gutierrez, E., & Ungerleider, L. G. (2002). Neural processing of emotional faces requires attention. *Proceedings of the National Academy of Sciences*, 99(17), 11458–63.

Phillips, M. L., Young, A. W., Senior, C., Brammer, M., Andrew, C., Calder, A. J., et al. (1997). A specific neural substrate for perceiving facial expressions of disgust. *Nature*, 389(6650), 495–98.

Pulvermüller, F. (1999). Words in the brain's language. *Behavioral Brain Science*, 22(2), 253–79; discussion 280–336.

Pulvermuller, F., & Fadiga, L. (2010). Active perception: Sensorimotor circuits as a cortical basis for language. *Nature Reviews Neuroscience*, 11(5), 351–60.

Rapcsak, S. Z., Comer, J. F., & Rubens, A. B. (1993). Anomia for facial expressions: Neuropsychological mechanisms and anatomical correlates. *Brain and Language*, 45(2), 233–52.

Rellecke, J., Palazova, M., Sommer, W., & Schacht, A. (2011). On the automaticity of emotion processing in words and faces: Event-related brain potentials evidence from a superficial task. *Brain Cognition*.

Richter, M., Eck, J., Straube, T., Miltner, W. H., & Weiss, T. (2010). Do words hurt? Brain activation during the processing of pain-related words. *Pain*, 148(2), 198–205.

Russell, J. A. (2003). Core affect and the psychological construction of emotion. *Psychological Review*, 110(1), 145–72.

Sabatinelli, D., Versace, F., Costa, V. D., Bradley, M. M., & Lang, P. J. (2006). Selective nucleus accumbens and medial frontal cortex activation in appetitive picture processing. *Psychophysiology*, 43, S84.

Sander, D., Grandjean, D., & Scherer, K. R. (2005). A systems approach to appraisal mechanisms in emotion. *Neural Networks*, 18(4), 317–52.

Schacht, A., & Sommer, W. (2009). Time course and task dependence of emotion effects in word processing. *Cognitive, Affectove & Behavioral Neuroscience*, 9(1), 28–43.

Schacht, A, Adler, N, & Chen, P, Guo, T, Sommer, W. (2012). Association with positive outcome induces early effects in event-related brain potentials. *Biological Psychology*, 89(1), 130–6.

Schapkin, S. A., Gusev, A. N., & Kuhl, J. (2000). Categorization of unilaterally presented emotional words: an ERP analysis. *Acta Neurobiologiae Experimentalis (Warsaw)*, 60(1), 17–28.

Schirmer, A., Kotz, S. A., & Friederici, A. D. (2002). Sex differentiates the role of emotional prosody during word processing. *Brain Research: Cognitive Brain Research*, 14(2), 228–33.

Schupp, H. T., Flaisch, T., Stockburger, J., & Junghofer, M. (2006). Emotion and attention: Event-related brain potential studies. *Progress in Brain Research*, 156, 31–51.

Scott, G. G., O'Donnell, P. J., Leuthold, H., & Sereno, S. C. (2009). Early emotion word processing: Evidence from event-related potentials. *Biological Psychology*, 80(1), 95–104.

Silva C., Montant M., Ponz A., & Ziegler J.C. (2012). Emotions in reading: Disgust, empathy and the contextual learning hypothesis. *Cognition*. 2012 Aug 9. [Epub ahead of print] PMID: 22884243.

Silvert, L., Delplanque, S., Bouwalerh, H., Verpoort, C., & Sequeira, H. (2004). Autonomic responding to aversive words without conscious valence discrimination.

International Journal of Psychophysiology, 53(2), 135–45.

Skrandies, W. (1998). Evoked potential correlates of semantic meaning – A brain mapping study. *Brain Research: Cognitive Brain Research*, 6(3), 173–83.

Smith, A. (1966). Speech and other functions after left (dominant) hemispherectomy. *Journal of Neurology, Neurosurgery and Psychiatry*, 29(5), 467–71.

Stolarova, M., Keil, A., & Moratti, S. (2006). Modulation of the C1 visual event-related component by conditioned stimuli: Evidence for sensory plasticity in early affective perception. *Cerebral Cortex*, 16(6), 876–87.

Sutton, S., Tueting, P., Zubin, J., & John, E. R. (1967). Information delivery and the sensory evoked potential. *Science*, 155(768), 1436–39.

Takahashi, H., Takano, H., Kodaka, F., Arakawa, R., Yamada, M., Otsuka, T., et al. (2010). Contribution of dopamine D1 and D2 receptors to amygdala activity in human. *Journal of Neuroscience*, 30(8), 3043–47.

Trauer, S.M., Andersen, S.K., Kotz, S.A., & Müller, M.M. (2012). Capture of lexical but not visual resources by task-irrelevant emotional words: a combined ERP and steady-state visual evoked potential study. *Neuroimage*, 60(1),130–8.

Van Lancker Sidtis, D., Pachana, N., Cummings, J. L., & Sidtis, J. J. (2006). Dysprosodic speech following basal ganglia insult: toward a conceptual framework for the study of the cerebral representation of prosody. *Brain and Language*, 97(2), 135–53.

Vanderploeg, R. D., Brown, W. S., & Marsh, J. T. (1987). Judgments of emotion in words and faces – ERP correlates. *International Journal of Psychophysiology*, 5(3), 193–205.

Vissers, C.T., Virgillito, D., Fitzgerald, D.A, Speckens, A.E, Tendolkar, I., van Oostrom, I., & Chwilla, D.J. (2010). The influence of mood on the processing of syntactic anomalies: evidence from P600. *Neuropsychologia*, 48(12), 3521–31.

Vuilleumier, P., Richardson, M. P., Armony, J. L., Driver, J., & Dolan, R. J. (2004). Distant influences of amygdala lesion on visual cortical activation during emotional face processing. *Nature Neuroscience*, 7(11), 1271–78.

Wicker, B., Keysers, C., Plailly, J., Royet, J. P., Gallese, V., & Rizzolatti, G. (2003). Both of us disgusted in My insula: The common neural basis of seeing and feeling disgust. *Neuron*, 40(3), 655–64.

Section IV

COGNITIVE-EMOTION INTERACTIONS

CHAPTER 14

Affective Biases in Attention and Perception

Judith Domínguez-Borràs & Patrik Vuilleumier

In real life, sensory behaviorally relevant stimuli must compete for conscious representation among distracters to elicit appropriate responses. Selective attention refers to various brain processes that serve to resolve this competition by controlling the allocation of processing resources as a function of the salience of external events, as well as the internal goals of the observer. Affective processes interact closely with these attentional mechanisms. Just like attention, emotion may guide perception and behavior based on the biological or motivational significance of sensory information, as well as on internal states (Pourtois, Schettino, & Vuilleumier, 2012; Vuilleumier, 2005). In this chapter we present a general overview of these effects and of current knowledge about their neural mechanisms. We focus on the impact of emotion on attention, whereas the reverse interactions are reviewed by Pessoa and colleagues in Chapter 15.

Emotion is crucial for orchestrating a wide range of physiological reactions that allow the organism to adjust to the environment. A modulation of action tendencies and of the current focus of thoughts is a defining component of many, if not most, emotions (Scherer & Peper, 2001). Among these effects, compelling evidence indicates that some emotions may act to facilitate attention to significant stimuli, thereby regulating sensory processing. Such emotional biases in perception and attention may favor adaptive behavior and survival in some conditions, but also may potentially contribute to pathological situations, such as in anxiety or phobia (see Chapter 24). The exact mechanisms involved in these effects, as well as their specificities and commonalities with respect to other attentional processes, are incompletely known. However, recent research has provided many novel insights by using a variety of experimental techniques, including behavioral measures, functional neuroimaging in humans, and single-unit recordings in animals. A large part of this research focuses on *negative emotional events* (i.e., threat) and often on the visual modality only, but attention-biasing effects of emotion extend to other domains than fear, as indicated by a growing number of studies on a range of affective dimensions, including positive (happiness, erotica, food) or nonthreatening negative cues, such as sadness or disgust. Nevertheless, there are also some reasons to think that fear may represent a particular kind of affect that has, by essence, a stronger impact on attention focus. In addition, many studies on the neural substrates of emotional biases in attention have focused on the role of the amygdala (Vuilleumier, 2005); however, it is likely that other brain regions make important contributions too, particularly the (so-called limbic) prefrontal areas (e.g., orbitofrontal cortex [OFC] and anterior cingulate cortex [ACC]) and subcortical regions in the basal ganglia, thalamus, and brainstem. However, their exact role still remains to be determined.

In this chapter we review behavioral and neuroimaging data illustrating the impact of threat and other emotional signals on attention and perception. We present both current models and remaining issues concerning the brain mechanisms subserving these effects.

Behavioral Evidence for Emotional Biases in Attention

A great deal of research indicates that, when concurrent stimuli compete for processing resources and awareness, information with emotionally relevant meaning is often detected more readily than neutral information or is more likely to interfere with another concomitant task. Classic examples come from visual search experiments showing that the detection of a visual target among an array of distracters is quicker for emotional than for neutral targets. This effect is often reported for negative or threat-related stimuli, such as faces with angry and fearful expressions among neutral faces, or pictures of snakes and spiders among fruits or plants (see Figure 14.1a,b; Flykt & Caldara, 2006; Gerritsen, Frischen, Blake, Smilek, & Eastwood, 2008); but it also occurs for positive stimuli (Cunningham & Brosch, 2012). Alternatively, when emotional stimuli are distracters embedded in search or selective attention tasks,

they may slow down target detection (e.g., Fenske & Eastwood, 2003), suggesting that some degree of involuntary emotional processing may operate even when it is irrelevant (or counterproductive) to the task performance.

However, enhanced detection of emotional targets (or interference by emotional distracters) does not necessarily imply that emotional stimuli are unaffected by current attention focus or that they simply *pop out* from a scene (e.g., as a red target does among blue shapes). Thus, the search for emotional stimuli is still serial and its facilitation only relative, reflecting a preferential guidance of attention to their location, rather than an obligatory breaking through into attention. In visual search tasks with targets differing in low-level features, detection latencies do not increase substantially with an increasing number of distracters, whereas latencies for emotional targets increase with the number of distracters but with a shallower slope than neutral targets (Gerritsen et al., 2008; Lucas & Vuilleumier, 2008). This indicates that emotional processing may bias and speed up detection, but does not constitute a shortcut to conscious perception. However, this emotional advantage is observed only when all items are presented together on the array, but disappears when items are revealed one by one at locations that participants consecutively explore with a mouse pointer (Smilek, Frischen, Reynolds, Gerritsen, & Eastwood, 2007). These findings suggest that the facilitation of detection depends on a coarse perceptual analysis operating outside or before attentive fixation, rather than on later processes, such as quicker recognition or quicker response selection, after attention has been focused. Furthermore, this preattentive analysis might be limited to certain regions in the visual field or certain stimulus characteristics, because involuntary capture by task-irrelevant emotional faces is stronger when they are presented at locations where targets are also expected, but weaker for distracters presented at other locations (Huang, Chang, & Chen, 2011; see also Notebaert, Crombez, Van Damme, De Houwer, & Theeuwes, 2010). Likewise,

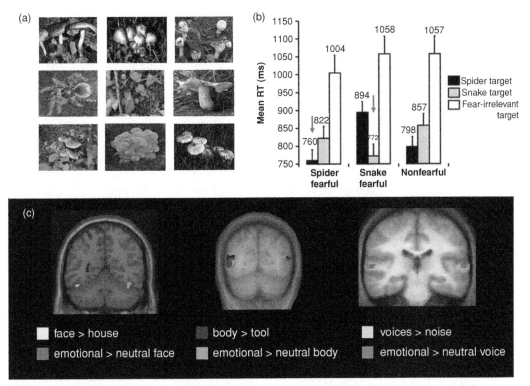

Figure 14.1. Effects of the emotional meaning of stimuli on attention and brain responses. **(A)** Example of a visual search task where an emotional target (spider or snake) must be detected (present/absent) among neutral images (mushrooms). **(B)** Search performance (response time, RT) of spider fearful, snake fearful, and nonfearful participants. Fearful participants were faster at detecting their feared targets, compared to both nonfeared (but still fear-relevant) and nonemotional targets. Adapted from Flykt & Caldara (2006). **(C)** Blood-oxygenation-level-dependent (BOLD) response observed with fMRI shows a precise overlap between emotional modulation effects and category-selective areas for face (fusiform face area; FFA), body (extrastriate body area; EBA), and voice processing, demonstrating that the emotional modulation is category specific. Adapted from Vuilleumier et al. (2001), Grandjean et al., (2005) and Peelen et al. (2007). See color plate 14.1.

preferential attention to threatening (e.g., angry) than neutral faces is observed when searching for any discrepant facial expression among an homogeneous crowd of faces, but not when specifically searching for another specific (e.g., happy) expression (Hahn & Gronlund, 2007); this finding suggests that current top-down goals can modulate the impact of more involuntary biases guiding attention to emotionally salient stimuli. Taken together, these findings indicate that emotional influences on visual search and perception may be unintentional and preattentive but not fully automatic, partly depending on the attentional goals, resources, or internal states of the observer.

Other attentional tasks are also influenced by emotional cues. Whereas visual search highlights competition for processing resources between concurrent stimuli close in space, a different type of competition between stimuli appearing close in time occurs during the *attentional blink* phenomenon. When different items are shown one after the other at fixation in a rapid serial visual presentation stream (RSVP), the detection of a given target is typically impaired when it occurs shortly (200–500 ms) after another target, as if attention capacity transiently *blinked*. However, this impairment is reduced when the second target is emotional, rather than neutral

(Anderson and Phelps, 2001; De Martino, Kalisch, Rees, & Dolan, 2009; Schwabe et al., 2011). This effect has also been observed with words, with either negative or positive meaning (Anderson & Phelps, 2001). Conversely, attentional blink for the second target may increase when it is neutral but is preceded by a first emotional target (Schwabe et al., 2011). These emotional effects are observed in tasks requiring dual-target detection, where access to processing resources is taxed, but not in conditions with single targets where no competition occurs (Anderson & Phelps, 2001). Again, this finding suggests that emotional processes operate at perceptual stages in which processing resources are limited, thereby controlling access to awareness, rather than stimulus recognition per se. Interestingly, in attentional blink conditions, a better detection of emotional words, relative to neutral, may occur only when semantic processing is required and not during a purely perceptual or phonological task (Huang, Baddeley, & Young, 2008). Task goals and expectations may thus also interact with involuntary emotional biases in these conditions.

An emotional advantage is also observed in change blindness paradigms where a stimulus in a scene is unexpectedly changed into another one (Peelen, Lucas, Mayer, & Vuilleumier, 2009). Other examples come from studies using binocular rivalry (in which each eye is presented with a different stimulus; Alpers & Gerdes, 2007) or continuous flash suppression (where a stimulus presented to one eye is rendered invisible by dynamic noise presented to the other eye; Yang, Zald, & Blake, 2007). In these conditions, fearful faces emerge into awareness more frequently and more quickly than neutral faces, whereas disgust or happy faces may not show the same advantage (Amting, Greening, & Mitchell, 2010).

Finally, in the dot-probe task, a neutral target (e.g., dot) is preceded by a nonpredictive cue with emotional meaning (e.g., a face or picture; see Figure 14.2a) that is briefly presented at the same or at a different location (Armony & Dolan, 2002; Pourtois, Grandjean, Sander, & Vuilleumier, 2004).

Target detection is typically faster when the emotional cue is shown at the same location (valid), but slower when it is presented at a different location (invalid), suggesting that attention is initially oriented to the emotional stimulus and facilitates responding to the subsequent target. This facilitation involves reflexive (exogenous) orienting mechanisms, because it occurs after short time intervals between the cue and target (< 300 ms) and even when the cue is masked (Mogg & Bradley, 2002). Likewise, a brief emotional stimulus (e.g., a fearful face presented for 75 ms) can enhance contrast sensitivity and potentiate the effect of spatial attention on detection accuracy for a subsequent visual target (gabor pattern), suggesting a modulation of early perceptual processing in the primary visual cortex (Phelps, Ling, & Carrasco, 2006). In keeping with reflexive orienting, eye movement studies also show faster saccades and earlier fixation on emotional than neutral faces, but with some differences across expression categories (Nummenmaa, Hyona, & Calvo, 2009).

Taken together, these behavioral findings converge to indicate that affective biases may guide attention and enhance perception for emotionally significant stimuli across various conditions. These biases are generally unintentional, independent of explicit relevance, and triggered without overt attention, although they may be modulated by expectations, task characteristics, and available resources for covert attention. It remains to be seen, however, whether all emotional biases in attention observed with this large variety of stimuli, emotions, and paradigms are subserved by similar or partly distinct brain mechanisms.

Nature of Emotionally Salient Cues

A major question that still remains unresolved is *what* makes an emotional stimulus attention capturing. It is generally assumed that the emotional meaning per se is crucial, but it is also possible that part of these effects are driven by physical features,

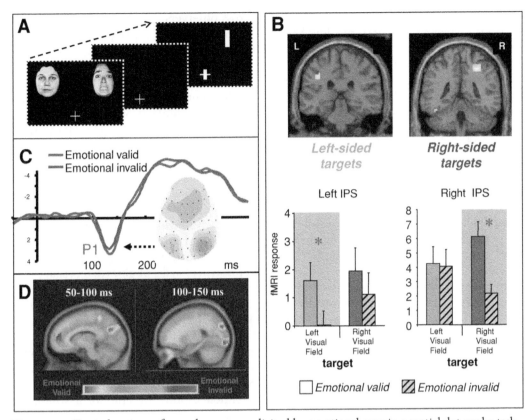

Figure 14.2. Typical pattern of neural responses elicited by emotional cues in a spatial dot-probe task. (A) In this task, targets (vertical or horizontal bars) are always preceded by pairs of faces, one neutral and one emotional, which do not predict the side of target presentation. To avoid eye movements, participants are instructed to press a response button when the orientation of the bar presented in the left or right upper visual field matches that of the thicker segment in the fixation cross. Adapted from Pourtois, Grandjean, Sander, & Vuilleumier (2004). (B) Targets preceded by neutral cues at the same location (i.e., with fearful cues presented contralaterally; that is, *emotional invalid* cues) lead to reduced fMRI responses in the intraparietal sulcus (IPS) ipsilateral to the target, relative to when targets are preceded by emotional cues on the same side (*emotional valid*). This suggests a capture of attention by the contralateral emotional cue and a reduced ability to reorient to the target. Adapted from Pourtois, Schwartz, Seghier, Lazeyras, & Vuilleumier (2006). (C) During EEG recording, targets preceded by emotional cues (*emotional valid*) elicit a larger visual P1 component, relative to those preceded by neutral cues (*emotional invalid*). This is consistent with enhanced visual processing of targets when cued by emotion. Adapted from Pourtois et al. (2004). (D) Neural source estimation for EEG modulations at different latencies after *target* onset. When the target is preceded by an emotional valid cue, activity to the target is first increased in parietal areas (50–100 ms), presumably reflecting top-down attentional signals induced by the emotional cue and responsible for faster spatial orienting to the target location and enhanced processing in extrastriate visual cortex at the P1 latency (100–150 ms). When targets are preceded by an invalid neutral cue, increased activity is observed in the anterior cingulate cortex instead, reflecting some interference and conflict in attentional orienting due to initial capture by the fearful face on the opposite side. Adapted from Pourtois, Thut, Grave de Peralta, Michel, & Vuilleumier (2005). See color plate 14.2.

such as contrast and spatial frequency for the visual modality, loudness and spectral frequency for audition, or perceptual distinctiveness more generally. In fact, attention capture by schematic emotional faces during visual search also occurs when using stimuli made of oblique lines, physically comparable to negative (frown) and positive (smile) expressions, with no residual resemblance to a face, suggesting that some low-level features are sufficient (Coelho, Cloete, & Wallis, 2010). Experiments using real face photographs have yielded conflicting results. Some studies reported that attention capture may be caused by systematic differences in the shape or contrast of facial features associated with emotional expression (e.g., Coelho et al., 2010), whereas other studies demonstrated that veridical pictures of angry faces are detected better even amid heterogeneous crowds of both neutral and emotional distracters, where low-level differences also exist between the distracters (Pinkham, Griffin, Baron, Sasson, & Gur, 2010).

In contrast, when faces are inverted or replaced by a single distinctive feature (a line resembling the curve of a mouth that distinguishes among different expressions), the emotional advantage of negative expressions (relative to neutral or positive) disappears, supporting an important role of holistic face perception in triggering emotional biases (Gerritsen et al., 2008). Similar results were observed for happy facial expressions (see Cunningham & Brosch, 2012). Likewise, patients with spatial neglect, who have difficulties in directing attention toward the left side because of right parietal damage, show better detection in the left visual field for drawings of spiders, relative to drawings of flowers made of the same elements arranged in different configurations (see Domínguez-Borràs, Saj, Armony, & Vuilleumier, 2012). Nevertheless, in some studies, a role for holistic face processing is unclear or absent for certain emotion categories, because some expressions (surprise, disgust, happiness) continue to elicit a facilitation of visual search when inverted (Calvo & Nummenmaa, 2008).

However, an important role for emotional meaning in attentional biases is supported by several findings. First, some effects can be elicited by stimuli exposed to aversive conditioning while their physical features are unchanged. In one study (Gerritsen et al., 2008) different emotional meanings were paired with identical faces across observers, eliminating any confound between physical characteristics and emotional valence. In this case, search was still facilitated for negative versus positive conditioned faces. Similar effects of aversive conditioning were obtained during visual search with simple color targets (Notebaert, Crombez, Van Damme, De Houwer, & Theeuwes, 2011) or for spatial orienting in the dot-probe task (Armony & Dolan, 2002; Stolarova, Keil, & Moratti, 2006).

Second, there is evidence that emotional biases in various tasks are exaggerated in people with high anxiety (Mogg & Bradley, 2002), specific phobias (Flykt & Caldara, 2006), or mood disorders (Leppanen, 2006). For instance, snake phobics detect snake pictures faster than spider pictures in search tasks, whereas the opposite occurs in spider phobics (Flykt & Caldara, 2006; see Figure 14.1b). This dissociation cannot be explained by visual features only, because all participants saw the same snake and spider pictures. Nonetheless, the degree of attention capture by emotional stimuli in search does not necessarily correlate with the strength of negative evaluation. Thus, people who are experts in snakes and spiders do not associate these stimuli with unpleasant meaning, even in implicit priming tests, but show a similar attentional capture as control subjects (Purkis & Lipp, 2007). This finding suggests that distinct mechanisms may underlie affective appraisal and reflexive attentional orienting or that personal experience and emotion regulation exert stronger influences on appraisal than on orienting.

A third point supporting a role for emotional rather than just perceptual processing in the emotional bias of attention is the finding that a faster detection of emotional targets in visual search may be accompanied by specific physiological responses, such as subtle heart rate changes, which are not observed during the detection of physical pop-out targets (Flykt, 2005).

Finally, another approach to test for the role of meaning is to use verbal material, such as words, although this material may require more elaborate processing and be more sensitive to cognitive factors than *simpler* (and more *natural*) stimulus categories. For example, emotional words are better detected than neutral words when presented in rapid succession in the attentional blink paradigm (Anderson & Phelps, 2001). Masked negative words are also better detected than masked positive words (Nasrallah, Carmel, & Lavie, 2009), whereas a reduction of attentional blink has been reported for both negative and positive words (Anderson & Phelps, 2001; Keil & Ihssen, 2004). These effects are not explained by differences in visual appearance between word categories, persist when controlling for lexical frequency or verbal distinctiveness, and, as noted earlier, increase when participants must process word meaning rather than just phonology (Huang et al., 2008). Altogether, these findings imply that written words may still undergo semantic processing under conditions where attentional resources are limited (Naccache et al., 2005), and that their semantic meaning may lower their threshold to access consciousness (Anderson & Phelps, 2001; Huang et al., 2008). Yet, these results do not eliminate the possibility that emotion and semantic processing may be reduced when attentional resources are further depleted (see Chapter 13 and 15). In addition, Stroop interference effects are also observed when emotional words are presented during a nonemotional judgment task (e.g., counting words) or during an emotional judgment task involving another stimulus dimension (e.g., categorizing the expressions of superimposed faces). These data indicate that emotional word meaning can produce involuntary effects on selective attention, even when semantic processing is not required. Likewise, facial expressions slow down face color judgments, and nonwords associated to emotion through conditioning interfere with word-recognition performance.

In sum, there is converging evidence that emotional biases in attention and perception are at least partly mediated by emotional processing, rather than just by a discrimination of distinctive perceptual features.

However, the exact nature of the effective emotional signals remains largely unknown. On the one hand, many results show that the arousal value of stimuli, rather than their valence, may play a crucial role. On the other hand, stronger biasing effects are sometimes observed with negative, threatening stimuli (i.e., fear or anger) relative to positive stimuli despite equal arousal. Stronger impact of negative cues on attention may reflect a preferential tuning of the human brain to threat signals acquired by experience or shaped through evolution. Young infants, for instance, already turn more quickly to images of snakes than flowers or other animals (Blue, 2010). Yet, different kinds of negative emotion might affect attention and perception performance differently. For example, compared to fear, disgust expression appears to slow down rather than speed up the visual search for faces (Krusemark & Li, 2011), and attentional blink for a second target is reduced after disgusted faces but increased after fearful faces (Vermeulen, Godefroid, & Mermillod, 2009). These differences accord with the view that disgust cues may lead to sensory inhibition rather than facilitation (see Chapter 2). Finally, positive or appetitive stimuli, such as pictures of happy faces, babies, food, or, erotic scenes, can also influence attention (see Cunningham & Brosch, 2012). Some attentional effects may also be evoked by nonemotional information when it is personally relevant to the observer, such as food items for people with eating disorders or even pictures from familiar TV programs (see Cunningham & Brosch, 2012). These findings give support to appraisal theories suggesting that a central mechanism of emotional processing and its impact on attention orienting might reflect an evaluation of stimulus relevance for the goals, needs, and well-being of the individual, regardless of valence (see Chapter 1).

Therefore, more research is needed to clarify the affective dimensions responsible for the emotional attention bias, as well as their interaction with individual differences, such as anxiety and personality traits (see also Chapter 24). Furthermore, a distinction between perceptually driven and emotionally driven effects might not be as sharp as it seems. In fact, rudimentary perceptual cues might be sufficient to evoke emotion-specific effects through associative mechanisms, as found for simple silhouettes from animals (Forbes, Purkis, & Lipp, 2011), wide-open eyes from fearful faces (Whalen et al., 2004), or even spiky shapes (Bar & Neta, 2007). A greater sensitivity of perceptual systems to detect specific sensory features could contribute to enhance attention to emotionally meaningful information, but this remains to be explored more systematically.

Neural Bases of Emotional Biases in Perceptual Processing

Neuroimaging and electrophysiological investigation in humans suggest that emotional signals can bias attention and influence awareness both by direct effects on sensory processing and by indirect effects via modulation of the attentional systems themselves. Thus, the facilitated detection of emotional stimuli observed in behavioral studies (see the earlier discussion) is generally paralleled by greater neural responses in sensory areas, relative to the processing of neutral information. This enhancement has been observed in early sensory cortices, including the primary visual area in the occipital lobe (V1; Lang et al., 1998; Pessoa, McKenna, Gutierrez, & Ungerleider, 2002; Pourtois et al., 2004), or primary auditory cortex in the temporal lobe (Ethofer et al., 2012; Grandjean et al., 2005), as well as in higher level cortical regions associated with object recognition (Keil et al., 2011; Morris et al., 1998; Sabatinelli, Bradley, Fitzsimmons, & Lang, 2005). Moreover, these increased responses are often specific to the corresponding stimulus (Figure 14.1c). For instance, viewing scenes with emotional content, such as mutilated bodies or threatening animals, produces stronger activations in the lateral occipital cortex (LOC), as compared to neutral scenes (Lang et al., 1998). Faces with emotional

expressions, such as fear, produce selective increases in the fusiform face area (FFA), relative to neutral faces (Morris et al., 1998; Vuilleumier, Armony, Driver, & Dolan, 2001). In turn, emotional body expressions modulate both the fusiform and extrastriate body areas (FBA and EBA; Peelen, Atkinson, Andersson, & Vuilleumier, 2007), whereas emotional written words elicit increased activity in bilateral visual cortex as compared with nonemotional items (see Chapter 13). In a similar vein, sounds of emotional vocalizations and prosody, such as of anger, fear, joy, or sexual pleasure, as well as nonverbal sounds such as animal cries or gunshots, evoke stronger neural responses, as compared with neutral sounds, in auditory cortical areas (Grandjean et al., 2005; see Chapter 11), particularly in regions of the superior temporal gyrus (STG) that are specialized for voice processing and sound recognition (Ethofer et al., 2011).

These findings indicate that the emotional meaning of stimuli does not elicit a general boosting of visual or auditory processing, but rather modulates cortical areas that are selectively responsive to the stimulus type. This is similar to the effects typically produced by endogenous or exogenous attention mechanisms mediated by frontoparietal systems (Driver, 2001), leading to more robust neural representation and stronger competitive weight of these stimuli for capturing attention. This also accords with a meta-analysis of fMRI studies (Sabatinelli et al., 2011) indicating that the main effects of emotional face expression overlap with face-selective regions in the FFA and temporal lobe, whereas emotional scenes specifically affect the LOC, even after subtracting basic visual effects (Sabatinelli et al., 2011). Furthermore, a study comparing fMRI responses to face and body expressions (fearful, angry, disgusted, sad, and happy) demonstrated with a multivoxel pattern analysis that, although emotion in both stimulus categories increased activation in the fusiform cortex, body expression effects correlated with the degree of category-selective response to bodies (versus tools) at the voxel-by-voxel level, but not with the degree of response to faces (versus tools), and vice versa (Peelen et al., 2007). Some modulatory effects might also involve more global increases, perhaps via indirect modulations from frontoparietal attentional systems or other neuromodulatory mechanisms.

As observed in behavioral tasks, emotional effects in category-selective areas are often determined by the arousal value of stimuli, rather than by valence (e.g., Peelen et al., 2007). However, some studies did find stronger responses in the FFA to fearful than to happy faces, even though both were equally arousing (e.g., Morris et al., 1998). Emotional enhancement of cortical processing is also observed when neutral stimuli become associated with an aversive value through classical conditioning (Armony & Dolan, 2002), again demonstrating a key role for the emotional significance rather than the physical features of the stimuli. It remains possible that arousal and valence produce interactive effects depending on task demands or concomitant endogenous attention (Monroe et al., 2011), two factors that have not systematically been manipulated.

Studies using time-resolved techniques such as event-related brain potentials (ERPs) and magneto-encephalography (MEG) in humans also support the idea that an emotional modulation of perception may take place at early stages of stimulus processing (see Chapter 4). Early components associated with visual attention ~100–200 ms after stimulus onset show increased amplitudes to emotional faces, emotional scenes, or fear-conditioned stimuli (Dolan, Heinze, Hurlemann, & Hinrichs, 2006; Pourtois et al., 2004). These effects overlap with the P1 and N1 exogenous waveforms generated in early extrastriate cortex, which are also typically enhanced by top-down and bottom-up attention. Similar effects occur for emotional words (see Chapter 13). Less frequent modulations are reported for components associated with object-categorization processes, such as the occipitotemporal N170, which may

code for face features or configuration more than emotion information (see Chapter 7). Accordingly, direct intracranial recordings of fusiform responses to faces have shown an emotional enhancement starting only after the N170 peak (Pourtois, Spinelli, Seeck, & Vuilleumier, 2010a; Figure 14.3a). In some cases, even earlier increases may occur for the C1 (a component arising ~80–90 ms poststimulus and presumably generated in the primary visual cortex) when fearful or threat-conditioned faces are presented in the peripheral visual field (Pourtois et al., 2004; Stolarova et al., 2006). In the auditory domain, fearful vocalizations or sounds conditioned with pleasant and unpleasant scenes may also elicit larger ERPs relative to neutral stimuli already ~150 ms after onset (see Chapter 11). It should be noted, however, that some emotional effects may not always reflect prioritized processing, but instead emerge due to reduced habituation over time for emotionally laden stimuli (see Chapter 11).

In addition to these modulations of early perceptual responses, emotional stimuli also produce distinctive ERPs at longer latencies (i.e., 300–400 ms), characterized by modulations of the P3, or sustained late positive potentials (LPPs; see Chapter 4). These effects might be related to more elaborate affective and cognitive evaluations, as well as memory (see Chapter 4). Source localization analyses suggest that these LPPs are generated by a widespread cortical network including prefrontal, cingulate and parietal, associated with voluntary attentional control and emotion regulation. One study combining EEG and fMRI in the same participants found, however, that the amplitude of LPPs was also correlated with increased hemodynamic responses in occipitotemporal areas (Sabatinelli, Lang, Keil, & Bradley, 2007). Moreover, the face-responsive fusiform cortex may show sustained activation to fearful expressions (> 700–800 s), clearly outlasting stimulus duration itself (Pourtois et al., 2010a).

As with fMRI, emotional enhancement of sensory responses in EEG occurs for

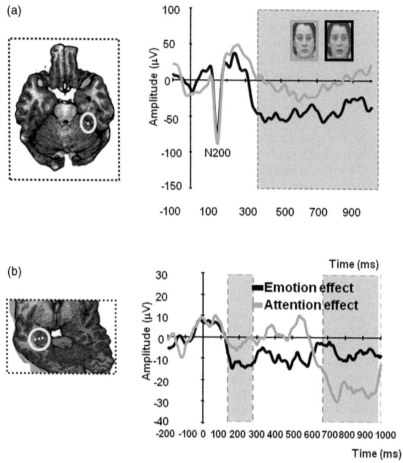

Figure 14.3. Intracranial recordings of emotion and attention effects during face processing in patients prior to epilepsy surgery. **(A)** Average local-field potentials recorded from an electrode over the right fusiform gyrus, showing the average response to neutral and fearful faces during a one-back repetition task. An increased cortical response to fearful faces, compared to neutral, arose after the face-specific N200 (the intracranial counterpart of the N170), in the form of a sustained negative component lasting more than 500 ms. Adapted from Pourtois, Spinelli, Seeck, & Vuilleumier (2010a). **(B)** Average local-field potentials recorded in the amygdala during the face-house attention task illustrated in figure 14.4A, showing the main effect of emotion (subtraction between neutral and fearful faces; dark line) and the main effect of attention (subtraction between task-irrelevant and task-relevant faces; light line). The emotional modulation started around 130–140 ms, whereas the attentional modulation appeared later, around 600–700 ms poststimulus onset. Adapted from Pourtois, Spinelli, Seeck, & Vuilleumier (2010b).

both negative and positive stimuli. Thus, although abundant research has focused on fearful and angry faces, more pleasant and arousing stimuli elicit very similar increases (at both early and late latencies), relative to neutral images, including images of babies (see Cunningham & Brosch, 2012). Nonetheless, these effects are sometimes stronger or even earlier for threatening than positive stimuli (Weymar, Low, Öhman, & Hamm, 2011). Again, however, different types of negative emotion might produce different effects. For instance, although disgust represents a bodily threat and speeds up target detection in behavioral studies (Bayle, Schoendorff, Henaff, & Krolak-Salmon, 2011), it was found to elicit weaker sensory responses in EEG in some studies, possibly akin to mechanisms of sensory rejection (Krusemark & Li, 2011; see Chapter 2). Moreover, at the peripheral level, disgust is mainly parasympathetically mediated, whereas fear implicates the sympathetic system (see also Chapter 3). However, these effects might depend on other factors related to complex semantic processing and scene integration mechanisms, rather than more basic and reflexive stimulus appraisal processes associated with emotional attention. Furthermore, they might be difficult to disentangle from top-down attention effects without manipulating attention and emotion separately.

In any case, taken together, data from functional imaging and electrophysiology converge to show that emotion signals may boost perceptual processing in early sensory cortices for different sensory modalities and different stimulus categories. Such boosting may consist of stimulus-specific and non-specific increases in perceptual processing, leading to a more robust representation of affectively relevant events. Such increases may also serve to enhance cortical plasticity and learning in response to emotional information, particularly when associated with later and prolonged cortical enhancements (e.g., Pourtois et al., 2010a). Remarkably, many aspects of the early sensory modulations by emotion are comparable to those produced by endogenous (top-down) or exogenous (bottom-up) attention mechanisms, which also gate perceptual analysis in the P1 or N1 time windows. Hence, emotional brain systems may provide an additional source of modulation on sensory processing, biasing competition for conscious awareness at similar perceptual stages.

Yet, emotional and attentional mechanisms seem relatively independent, involving partly distinct neural circuits and being additive to each other (Amting et al., 2010; Brosch, Pourtois, Sander, & Vuilleumier, 2011; Keil, Moratti, Sabatinelli, Bradley, & Lang, 2005; Lucas & Vuilleumier, 2008). Moreover, emotional biases cannot be simply designated as top-down or bottom-up, because they share components with both attentional systems (Figures 14.2 and 14.5B).

These biases might rather be understood as reflecting specialized neural mechanisms for *emotional attention* (Vuilleumier, 2005) or *motivated attention* (Lang et al., 1998), contributing to select sensory information in parallel with other top-down and bottom-up attentional mechanisms. It remains to be clarified, however, which of these emotional effects are truly shared (in terms of neural sites and latencies) with other attentional enhancements, which are more specific to emotion, and which are distinct between different emotion categories or different emotion dimensions (such as valence and arousal). It seems unlikely that all emotional cues have similar relevance and impact on perceptual processing. Furthermore, more research is also needed to relate more precisely the observed increases in brain responses to the behavioral benefits in attentional tasks. Few studies have directly investigated the correlations between enhanced sensory responses and improved detection of emotional stimuli in search or blink experiments (e.g., De Martino, Kalisch, Rees, & Dolan, 2009; Krusemark & Li, 2011).

Finally, it must be noted that, in addition to enhancing responses in sensory regions, emotion signals may also increase activity in brain regions associated with attention control, including the posterior parietal cortex (Vuilleumier, 2005). This might in turn influence top-down attentional signals on sensory pathways. In particular, such effects have been observed in dot-probe tasks with fear-conditioned images (Armony & Dolan, 2002), threatening faces (Pourtois, Thut, Grave de Peralta, Michel, & Vuilleumier, 2005), or even positive affective stimuli (e.g., baby faces; see Cunningham & Brosch, 2012). Presentation of a peripheral threat-related cue in these tasks typically produces an increased activation in frontoparietal networks, presumably reflecting a shift of attention to the location of the emotional cue (Armony & Dolan, 2002). Moreover, when a neutral target (dot) is preceded by a pair of face cues (one neutral and one emotional), those targets preceded by neutral cues, as compared to by emotional ones, elicited reduced BOLD responses in intraparietal sulcus (IPS) ipsilateral to the targets, consistent with a capture of attention by the emotional cue on the contralateral side and a reduced ability to reorient to the target on the ipsilateral side (Pourtois, Schwartz, Seghier, Lazeyras, & Vuilleumier, 2006; see Figure 14.2b). In addition, targets appearing after an emotional cue produce stronger BOLD responses in the lateral occipital cortex (Pourtois et al., 2006) and a larger P1 component in EEG recordings (Pourtois et al., 2004; Figure 14.2c), consistent with improved visual processing and better target detection (Phelps et al., 2006). A detailed analysis of the time course of these effects with EEG (Pourtois et al., 2005) suggests that the modulation of parietal areas in this paradigm may be triggered by an initial response to the emotional cue, and subsequently induce top-down spatial attentional signals responsible for enhanced processing of the target, but only when the target appears at the same location as the emotional cue (Figure 14.2d). Further research is needed, however, to clarify how emotion inputs reach parietal areas and to what extent the spatial cueing effects depend on expectations about possible target locations (e.g., Huang et al., 2011; Notebaert et al., 2010).

Role of the Amygdala in Emotional Bias Signals

What brain circuits are responsible for boosting sensorineural responses to emotional stimuli, and are they different from attentional mechanisms driven by frontoparietal areas? Converging evidence from anatomy, imaging, and neuropsychology suggests that the amygdala might be a crucial source for affective biases on perception and attention, in keeping with its key role in orchestrating emotional responses (see also Chapters 1 and 5).

First, the strength of emotional modulation of cortical sensory areas is often correlated with the magnitude of amygdala activation (Morris et al., 1998; Peelen et al., 2007; Pessoa et al., 2002; Sabatinelli et al.,

2005). Conditions associated with selective increases in amygdala, such as exaggerated responses to pictures of snakes in individuals with snake phobia, relative to nonphobics, are associated with similar exaggerated increases in visual areas (e.g., Sabatinelli et al., 2005), in parallel with enhanced behavioral detection (Flykt & Caldara, 2006). Second, the profile of amygdala reactivity is generally compatible with biases observed in behavioral performance or in sensory regions. Indeed, the amygdala seems to primarily activate in response to the arousal or relevance value of sensory events, rather than to negative valence only, although arousal-valence interactions and stronger responses to threat are frequently observed (see Chapter 1).

Second, the amygdaloid complex is well designed to exert modulations on cortical pathways involved in perception and attention, because it entertains bidirectional connections with all sensory systems. In the visual modality, tracing studies in the macaque show that projections to visual cortices are highly organized, so that rostral regions of the amygdala project to rostral (i.e., higher level) visual areas, whereas caudal regions of the amygdala project to caudal (i.e., lower level) visual areas (Freese & Amaral, 2006). At the microscopic level, there is evidence that projections from the amygdala reach pyramidal neurons in early visual areas with synaptic patterns suggestive of excitatory feedback (Freese & Amaral, 2006). Similar feedback projections have been observed for the auditory and somatosensory modalities. In humans, MRI studies using diffusion tensor imaging (DTI) have also identified topographically organized fibers in the inferior longitudinal fasciculus, which directly connect the amygdala with early visual areas and might contain such back-projections (Gschwind, Pourtois, Schwartz, Van De Ville, & Vuilleumier, 2012).

More direct evidence for a causal role of amygdala feedback has been obtained by lesion studies. In particular, fMRI experiments revealed that patients with medial temporal lobe sclerosis, which selectively

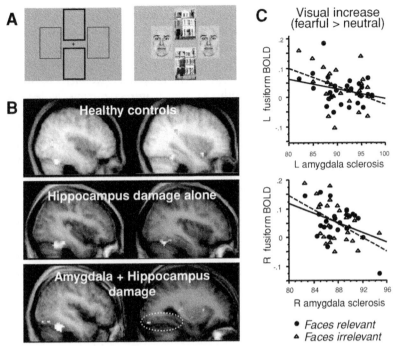

Figure 14.4. Deficit in emotional attention after amygdala damage in patients with medial temporal lobe sclerosis. **(A)** Visual matching task used to test for brain responses to fearful expressions when face stimuli are task relevant (*faces attended*) or task irrelevant (*faces ignored*). Two faces and two houses appear on each trial, orthogonally aligned to each other (right). Participants are instructed to respond either to the horizontal or to the vertical pair, according to a preceding cue (left). **(B)** Contrast between fearful vs. neutral faces regardless of task relevance. Healthy controls and patients with damage to the hippocampus (sparing the amygdala) show intact modulation of fusiform gyrus to fearful faces, relative to neutral faces. However, patients with both amygdala and hippocampus damage show no emotional enhancement. **(C)** This loss of modulation in visual areas correlates with the degree of sclerosis measured in the amygdala ipsilateral to the face-responsive fusiform area, suggesting that each amygdala predominantly projects to the ipsilateral visual cortex, and causally mediates the emotional enhancement observed in visual cortex (L: left; R: right). Adapted from Vuilleumier, Richardson, Armony, Driver, & Dolan (2004).

destroys the amygdala and hippocampus, do not show a modulation of the fusiform gyrus when visualizing fearful faces, relative to neutral, unlike the increase typically observed in healthy controls (Vuilleumier, Richardson, Armony, Driver, & Dolan, 2004; Figure 14.4). A normal modulation, however, was observed in patients with temporal lobe sclerosis affecting only the hippocampus but sparing the amygdala. Furthermore, the loss of modulation in visual areas was correlated with the degree of sclerosis in ipsilateral amygdala. That is, more severe sclerosis in the right amygdala predicted a greater loss of emotional

effects in the right fusiform, whereas left amygdala sclerosis predicted a loss of effects in the left fusiform. These findings imply that each amygdala predominantly projects to the ipsilateral hemisphere, in keeping with anatomical tracing data from monkeys (Freese & Amaral, 2006). A similar loss of emotional enhancement of visual areas in response to faces was observed in another group of patients with right medial temporal lobe epilepsy, an effect that correlated with disease duration (Benuzzi et al., 2004).

Importantly, patients with amygdala sclerosis still showed an enhancement of fusiform activity when directing attention to faces, as compared to directing attention to other stimuli (houses) in the same visual display (Vuilleumier et al., 2004), showing that other top-down attentional influences under voluntary control were intact. These results point not only to a direct causal role for the amygdala in the affective modulation of face processing in visual cortex, beyond its well-established involvement in affective appraisal and learning, but also reveal a dissociation between involuntary *emotional* and voluntary *top-down attention* mechanisms. In addition, both in healthy subjects (Vuilleumier et al., 2001) and in patients with intact amygdala (Vuilleumier et al., 2004), fusiform activity was also higher when a fearful face was presented outside the current focus of attention (relative to a neutral face), even though inattention reduced overall fusiform activity. This finding indicates that modulatory influences from the amygdala on visual cortex may persist, at least to some extent, even when endogenous attention is not focused on emotional stimuli, consistent with a separate effect on visual processing prior to overt attention.

EEG results in patients with medial temporal lobe sclerosis have also shown anomalies in cortical responses to fearful faces (Rotshtein et al., 2010). Amygdala damage leads to a selective loss of emotional effects in the early P1 (around 100–150 ms) and late P3 (around 500–600 ms) time range, which are still present in epilepsy patients with spared amygdala. These changes are consistent with a disruption of perceptual processing and subsequent attentional or memory encoding stages, respectively. By contrast, there was no effect of amygdala lesions on a distinct emotional modulation at intermediate latencies (150–250 ms), corresponding to the N1-N2 components and presumably related to structural visual processing of faces and expressions. These data converge with previous work in rodents (Armony, Quirk, & LeDoux, 1998) showing that amygdala lesions can abolish a late (500–1500 ms) modulation of auditory cortex response to fear-conditioned tones, with no effect on the initial bottom-up short-latency (0–50 ms) response.

Behavioral studies in patients with amygdala damage have also reported impaired performance in visual and attentional tasks with emotional stimuli. For example, in patient PS who has selective destruction of the amygdala (Kennedy & Adolphs, 2010), a deficit in recognizing the fearful expression in faces was found to be primarily caused by a lack of attention to the eye region (which contains the most distinctive information), suggesting that amygdala damage did not abolish an internal representation of fear expression but rather disrupted oculomotor exploration of facial features. Furthermore, in an attentional blink task with a rapid succession of written words, no emotional advantage was observed in patients suffering from left amygdala damage after temporal lobectomy (Anderson & Phelps, 2001), even though these patients could still recognize the affective semantic meaning of words. Consistent with this finding, an fMRI study on attentional blink with words (Schwabe et al., 2011) reported that left amygdala activation to emotional T2 targets was associated with an increased detection rate. In addition, the prolonged attentional blink following an emotional T1 target, relative to neutral T1, was correlated with greater activation in the ACC and OFC, possibly reflecting deeper emotion appraisal and/or stronger interaction with cortical attention networks. However, another fMRI study (De Martino et al., 2009) found that ACC response correlated with improved emotional T2 detection, with no differential effect in the amygdala. Other results during binocular rivalry showed that increased detection of emotional stimuli correlated with stronger functional connectivity between the amygdala and ventral visual areas, as compared with visual suppression (Amting et al., 2010). Altogether, these data agree with the idea that the amygdala may play an important role in enhancing cortical processing of emotional stimuli and thus facilitating their access to awareness.

By contrast, a few recent studies in patients with unilateral or bilateral amygdala lesions have reported a preserved advantage for emotional stimuli during attentional blink tasks, both when shown as distracters

(T1; Piech et al., 2011) and targets (T2; Bach, Talmi, Hurlemann, Patin, & Dolan, 2011), or during visual search tasks (Piech et al., 2010; Tsuchiya, Moradi, Felsen, Yamazaki, & Adolphs, 2009). Enhanced detection in these conditions could still operate based on distinctive features that have been over-learned and might be processed in other brain regions, including the ACC and OFC, because activity in these regions also cor-relates with attention capture by emotion (De Martino et al., 2009; Lucas & Vuilleu-mier, 2008; Schwabe et al., 2011). Thus, the neural sources of emotional biases in per-ception and attention might not rely exclu-sively on the amygdala, but might also impli-cate alternative structures when the former is dysfunctional. Likewise, it has been pro-posed that the pulvinar nucleus of the thala-mus might contribute, in concert or in par-allel with the amygdala, to integrate sensory information coded in different cortical areas and amplify sensory processing in order to guide attention to stimuli of potential rele-vance (Pessoa & Adolphs, 2010). This would be in agreement with an important role of this subcortical structure in other atten-tional processes and frequent coactivation of pulvinar and amygdala (Tamietto & de Gelder, 2010; Vuilleumier, Armony, Driver, & Dolan, 2003). A better understanding of the role of these different circuits for pro-cessing stimulus saliency and of their speci-ficity for emotional information relative to other characteristics (such as novelty, deviance, and ambiguity) is clearly needed.

Distinct Sources for Emotional and Attentional Biases

A key issue in the framework described here is that perception can be modulated by multiple sources simultaneously, including not only endogenous, exogenous, or object-based attention but also emotional feedback signals from the amygdala, together with other emotion-processing regions (Pourtois et al., 2012). As mentioned earlier, processing biases due to different sources may operate relatively independently and additively to each other, interacting under certain condi-tions and combining their influence to mod-ulate perceptual pathways. Thus, just like exogenous and object-based attention are known to interact with endogenous mecha-nisms (Driver, 2001), emotion-based biasing systems may operate in parallel, but be con-strained (Pessoa et al., 2002) or facilitated (Phelps et al., 2006) by other concomitant attentional influences.

Evidence for independent and additive effects of emotion and endogenous atten-tion comes from various studies where both factors were manipulated or measured sep-arately. For instance, in an fMRI experi-ment described earlier, pictures of faces and houses were presented at different locations, while participants had to focus on either the faces or the houses (see an example in Figure 14.4a). In addition, faces could be fearful or neutral. Selectively attending to faces rather than houses enhanced the fusiform cortex, but fearful faces produced an additional increase in the same area whether faces were attended or ignored. This pattern was replicated in several studies using the same paradigm on different participants (Bent-ley, Vuilleumier, Thiel, Driver, & Dolan, 2003; Vuilleumier et al., 2001, 2004), which suggests that emotional signals can still act when attention is directed to other stimuli (i.e., houses). In parallel, the amygdala was also activated by fearful faces, both when attended and when ignored, consistent with its presumed role in modulating fusiform activity. In another study using steady-state EEG (Keil et al., 2005), emotional or neutral scenes were flashed to the right or left visual field, while attention was directed to one or the other side in different trials. Again, visual responses in contralateral visual areas were enhanced both for attended pictures and for emotional pictures irrespective of atten-tion. By contrast, in a different paradigm with emotional faces presented centrally and peripheral bar targets presented in the upper peripheral field (Pessoa et al., 2002), fusiform responses were totally abolished (despite the presence of central faces), and no emo-tional modulation was found when partici-pants attended to the bar. These results sug-gest that emotion processing and subsequent feedback cannot arise when task demands are harder and lead to a total suppression of cortical processing for unattended stimuli (see Chapter 15). However, the blocked design of the attentional conditions and the absence of fusiform activity in the fMRI data could have prevented a reliable measure of emotion effects for the unattended stimuli.

Similar dissociations between attention and emotion effects are observed in behavioral studies. As noted earlier, facilitated detection of emotional targets in visual search is accompanied by a general slowing when increasing the number of distractors (Gerritsen et al., 2008). Likewise, patients with left spatial neglect or extinction after a right parietal lesion often show better detection of emotional than neutral stimuli in contralesional space, although they fail to voluntarily orient attention to this contralesional side and miss more emotional stimuli on the contralesional than the ipsilesional side (see Domínguez-Borràs et al., 2012). Again, this pattern indicates that emotional biases can still operate and boost attention (or partly counteract attentional deficits) in these patients, despite damage to frontoparietal networks controlling endogenous and/or exogenous spatial attention. Interestingly, in two studies investigating left neglect for faces (Lucas & Vuilleumier, 2008) and voices (Grandjean, Sander, Lucas, Scherer, & Vuilleumier, 2008), a parametric anatomical lesion analysis demonstrated that the relative advantage for emotional stimuli was stronger in patients with larger damage in parietal areas, whereas emotional effects were reduced in patients with damage extending to the orbitofrontal cortex and subcortical basal ganglia circuits. These findings add further support to the idea of independent neural substrates mediating emotional and spatial biases in perception, and they also accord with the possibility that the orbitofrontal cortex might provide an important interface between emotion processing and attention control (see the earlier discussion).

Moreover, fMRI studies in patients with left neglect have shown preserved emotional effects in visual cortex, with increased responses in the fusiform cortex for fearful faces (Vuilleumier et al., 2002) and in the parahippocampal cortex for negative scenes (Grabowska et al., 2011), relative to neutral stimuli. These effects arose even for stimuli presented in the left visual field, despite losses in top-down attention due to parietal damage, and may explain the relative improvement of detection for emotional stimuli in neglected space. Furthermore, in a single case study of a parietal patient with left neglect (Domínguez-Borràs et al., 2012), a brief session of aversive conditioning through frequent pairing of red shapes with a loud unpleasant noise led to a selective reduction in left visual misses for shapes with red but not other colors, which was accompanied by a marked increase in visual cortex responses to these stimuli, as well as significant amygdala activation. These findings converge with results in healthy subjects showing that affective conditioning of simple visual stimuli can boost their representation in early visual cortex and improve detection (Stolarova et al., 2006). More generally, these findings are consistent with distinct sources for emotional and attentional effects on visual perception.

Finally, one study systematically manipulated three types of attentional biases within a single task using the dot-probe paradigm (Brosch et al., 2011) and showed additive effects of bottom-up (exogenous), top-down (endogenous), and emotional cues on spatial orienting. Targets (small rectangles) were presented on either side of the screen, while attention could be manipulated in advance by an instruction arrow (engaging endogenous attention), by a bright flash (exogenous), or by fearful faces. Each of these cues could be valid or invalid, orthogonally to each other. Behavioral results demonstrated that the facilitation of target detection latencies added up in a linear fashion with the combined validity of different cues (such that a valid fearful face or exogenous flash preceding a target speeded up reaction times even when attention was endogenously oriented to the other side, but less than when all cues directed attention to the correct side). A subsequent EEG experiment used a similar approach to contrast the two involuntary effects triggered by exogenous and emotional cues (Brosch et al., 2011) and revealed that these two factors operated during two distinct time windows: ERPs time-locked to the exogenous cue showed a specific enhancement of the N2pc component, consistent with a rapid shift in attention to the cued side, whereas the emotional cue enhanced the P1 time-locked to the target, consistent with enhanced visual perception. Thus, ERPs clearly differentiated between processes mediating attentional biases induced by emotional meaning or by exogenous physical properties of the stimuli.

Nevertheless, despite this evidence for independent sources of emotional biases, some data also point to interactive effects in some conditions. For instance, both fMRI (Pessoa et al., 2002; Vuilleumier et al., 2001) and psychophysiological findings (Phelps et al., 2006) suggest that emotion cues might potentiate activity in early visual cortex (e.g., V1) for attended but not for unattended stimuli. It remains to be seen whether this may reflect a crucial role of V1 in integrating different top-down signals to build a visual saliency map (Li, 2002), which serves, in turn, to guide attention or to promote conscious vision. By contrast, emotion effects on other regions (such as the FFA) seem more often additive to attention and sometimes unrelated to conscious perception of the stimuli (Vuilleumier et al., 2001, 2002).

Preattentive and Unconscious Processing of Emotional Cues

Another important aspect of emotional biases in perception is that they should take place even in parallel or prior to full attention to the relevant stimuli. Although there is considerable controversy around this question (see Chapter 15; Pourtois et al., 2012), the amygdala may activate to stimuli without explicit attention or awareness in many (though not all) situations (Tamietto & de Gelder, 2010; Whalen et al., 2004).

However, amygdala responses and its projections to sensory areas can be regulated by signals from distinct brain areas, such as the prefrontal cortex (see Figure 14.5a), producing different biasing effects according to the context (Vuilleumier, 2008). Thus, amygdala reactivity might be modulated by task-related demands, including voluntary attention or cognitive load (see Chapter 15), as well as by current emotional states and personality dispositions (see Chapter 24). Thus, acute stress can not only increase amygdala responses and counteract the effect of task load but also diminish threat selectivity (van Marle, Hermans, Qin, & Fernandez, 2009).

The neural pathways allowing preattentive stimulus processing still remain unknown. In the visual modality, one hypothesis suggests that rudimentary visual signals might be extracted through subcortical visual (perhaps magnocellular) pathways including the superior colliculus, and pulvinar nucleus of the thalamus, then projecting directly to the amygdala (Tamietto & de Gelder, 2010). This subcortical route (see Figure 14.5a) was postulated based on residual emotional processing in patients with *blindsight* after destruction of the occipital cortex (Tamietto & de Gelder, 2010) and on preserved fear conditioning in animals without the sensory cortex (Romanski & LeDoux, 1992). Direct connections between visual pulvinar and amygdala remain questionable in humans (Pessoa & Adolphs, 2010), but exist in lower primates (Day-Brown, Wei, Chomsung, Petry, & Bickford, 2010). Other subcortical visual pathways from the brainstem to the amygdala were also reported in rodents (although unknown in humans; Usunoff, Itzev, Rolfs, Schmitt, & Wree, 2006). Alternatively, blindsight may depend on direct inputs from the lateral geniculate nucleus to extrastriate temporal cortex (Schmid et al., 2010) or from the pulvinar to fusiform in humans (Clarke, Riahi-Arya, Tardif, Eskenasy, & Probst, 1999), providing another subcortical route bypassing early occipital cortex and potentially projecting to the amygdala (and other brain areas) prior to awareness. However, unconscious or preattentive emotional processing

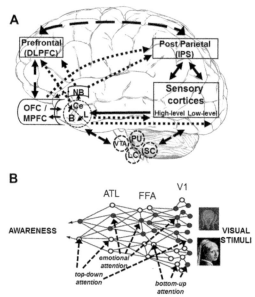

Figure 14.5. Schematic diagram of reciprocal pathways between emotional and attentional control. **(A)** Bottom-up sensory inputs mainly project to the lateral (L) nucleus of the amygdala, whereas feedback projections mainly originate from the lateral and basal (B) nuclei and can amplify neural representations of emotionally relevant information at different stages along sensory pathways (e.g., in lower versus higher visual cortical areas for the basal and lateral nucleus, respectively). Amygdala outputs via the central nucleus (Ce) can also activate cholinergic projections from the nucleus basalis (NB) in the forebrain, which in turn can influence neuronal activity in parietal and frontal cortices. Cholinergic effects in frontal and parietal areas may promote alerting reactions and shifts of attention. Projections to other systems in brainstem (LC: locus coeruleus; VTA: ventral tegmental area; PU: pulvinar; SC: superior colliculus) also exist, but are not shown here. Top-down interactions between parietal cortex and sensory areas may focus attentional resources on task-relevant information or instead on emotional stimuli tagged at preattentive stages via amygdala response and modulatory feedback signals to sensory areas. Although feedback loops are reflexive and involuntary, their gain can be modulated by direct influences from orbitofrontal cortex (OFC) and other areas in medial prefrontal cortex (MPFC), as well as indirectly through interconnections with anterior cingulate (ACC) and dorsolateral prefrontal cortex (DLPFC). Adapted from Vuilleumier (2008).

in healthy subjects may not necessarily be achieved through a *special* subcortical route. Some visual input could spread through cortico-cortical pathways, shared with conscious and attentive processing, yet with different latencies, oscillatory frequencies, or amplitudes (Pourtois et al., 2012; Vuilleumier, 2005). Likewise, subliminal stimuli can evoke unconscious semantic processing without requiring a special subcortical pathway (Dehaene, Changeux, Naccache, Sackur, & Sergent, 2006).

The latency of amygdala responses to emotional cues also remains poorly known. Differential amygdala activations to emotional faces occur around 40–140 ms poststimulus onset in humans with MEG (Luo et al., 2010), but around 140 ms (Pourtois et al., 2010b) or 200 ms poststimulus onset with intracranial recordings (e.g., Krolak-Salmon, Henaff, Vighetto, Bertrand, & Mauguiere, 2004). These effects may thus arise just before, or in parallel with, the neural signature of stimulus identification in the cortex. Early activations in the orbitofrontal cortex have also been reported around 120 ms after onset, using intracranial (Kawasaki et al., 2001) and scalp recordings (Pourtois, Dan, Grandjean, Sander, & Vuilleumier, 2005; Pourtois, et al., 2004; see Chapter 7). These findings support the idea that the OFC might be critically implicated in the modulation of attention by emotion (Grandjean et al., 2008; Lucas & Vuilleumier, 2008; see Chapter 6 and Figure 14.5a). Furthermore, intracranial recordings revealed similar amygdala responses up to 140 ms after onset when fearful faces are

Figure 14.5. **(B)** Both attention and emotion mechanisms may bias stimulus processing in a similar gain control manner at partly overlapping perceptual stages, but with independent and potentially additive sources of influences. Emotional biases cannot be simply designated as top-down or bottom-up, because they share some components with both attentional systems. Abbreviations are: anterior temporal lobe (ATL), fusiform face area (FFA) and primary visual cortex (V1). Adapted from Serences & Yantis (2006).

presented at attended or unattended locations (see the task in Figure 14.4a), but a later and prolonged response after 600 ms that is enhanced by overt attention to faces (Figure 14.3b). Scalp recordings using the same task also found an early emotional effect around 100 ms over frontal sites, but at top-down attentional effects starting around 200 ms (Holmes, Vuilleumier, & Eimer, 2003).

Therefore, it is plausible that both the amygdala and other limbic regions involved in affective appraisal, such as the OFC, might activate at early latencies through an initial volley of feedforward inputs (Vuilleumier, 2005), before or in parallel with the recruitment of exogenous or endogenous attentional systems. A rapid emotional categorization in the amygdala might operate on coarse perceptual features associated with emotional meaning, such as low spatial frequencies conveyed by visual magnocellular channels (e.g., Alorda, Serrano-Pedraza, Campos-Bueno, Sierra-Vázquez, & Montoya, 2007; Pourtois, Dan, et al., 2005; Vuilleumier et al., 2003; but see Morawetz, Baudewig, Treue, & Dechent, 2011), or other simple shape attributes such as sharp contours (Bar & Neta, 2007). This idea would accord with the counterintuitive finding that facial expressions of fear and disgust in faces are better detected when presented at higher eccentricities in the visual field, even though visual resolution decreases (Bayle et al., 2011). This early activation of the amygdala (or other area such as the OFC or ACC) would then modulate sensory cortices via direct feedback (Amaral et al., 2003; Vuilleumier, 2005) or indirect projections to the dorsal attention system in prefrontal and parietal areas (Vuilleumier, 2005; see Figure 14.5a). Clearly, more work is needed to clarify the exact timing of emotion and attention effects in different brain regions and to test the causality of interactions between them.

Neuromodulation by Cholinergic and Adrenergic Pathways

Another pathway for emotional attention involves indirect influences of amygdala on cortical areas through the activation of modulatory neurotransmitters in the cholinergic and adrenergic systems. Cholinergic nuclei in the basal forebrain receive dense inputs from the amygdala and modulate vigilance through projections to frontal, parietal, and sensory areas (Holland & Gallagher, 2004). Relative to placebo, the pro-cholinergic drug physostigmine does not modify the emotional enhancement of the fusiform cortex to fearful faces (Bentley et al., 2003). However, when fearful faces are unattended, physostigmine leads to greater responses in the lateral OFC and ACC, but reduced responses in the intraparietal sulcus. These findings suggest that acetylcholine is not responsible for enhanced activation of sensory areas, but might promote "distraction" by unattended emotional information through frontoparietal interactions (Bentley et al., 2003).

The central amygdala also has strong outputs to the sympathetic pathways and locus coeruleus in the brainstem. The locus coeruleus sends noradrenaline inputs to widespread regions throughout the brain, which regulate arousal and autonomic functions. These projections operate in a phasic or tonic manner promoting endogenous attention or flexibility, respectively, and modulate the receptive field of sensory neurons (e.g., Aston-Jones, Rajkowski, & Cohen, 1999). Moreover, the locus coeruleus responds to fearful faces despite a lack of conscious awareness (Liddell et al., 2005). These effects are likely to contribute to emotional attention, but have not been systematically investigated in humans in relation to this specific function.

Reward and Positive Emotions

Most results and models concerning the neural mechanisms of emotional enhancement in perception and attention refer to stimuli with negative affective load. However, similar patterns of brain activation have been observed for positive stimuli, particularly when they are highly arousing. Thus, appetitive visual scenes, erotica, smiling faces, joyful voices, and even humor may activate the amygdala (Sabatinelli et al., 2005; see Chapter 11) and sometimes produce attentional biases similar to threat (see the earlier discussion). In contrast, positive stimuli or positive mood has also been reported to produce distinct effects, opposite to negative emotion. For instance, the size of the attentional span in spatial orienting or flanker filtering tasks is larger when associated with positive events, but smaller with negative events (Fenske & Eastwood, 2003). Positive emotions may also enlarge the breadth of attention, increasing, for instance, cortical visual response to peripheral distracters (Schmitz, De Rosa, & Anderson, 2009). More research is needed to better disentangle these different influences of valence on attention – in particular to clarify the critical affective dimensions that are responsible for such effects and to identify which mechanisms are common or distinct across different emotion categories or tasks.

A special case of positive or appetitive cues might concern reward. In addition to the amygdala, reward signals activate dopaminergic projections from the ventral tegmental area to the striatum and prefrontal cortex. Dopamine might also play a role in the enhanced processing and detection of emotionally significant events. For example, mesolimbic and striatal dopaminergic neurons seem to respond to salient changes in environmental conditions, both appetitive and aversive (see Chapter 19). Furthermore, several studies found that visual search is facilitated for targets or features previously paired with rewards (Hickey, Chelazzi, & Theeuwes, 2010), suggesting an involuntary capture of attention by stimuli of high value. These effects are stronger in participants with reward-seeking personalities (Hickey et al., 2010).

In keeping with these behavioral effects, neurophysiology data in animals show that neuronal activity is enhanced by reward in numerous brain regions controlling attention and/or eye movements, such as the intraparietal cortex, frontal eye field, or superior colliculus (see Vuilleumier, 2005), overlapping with networks involved in top-down attention. Reward associations may also enhance cortical representation of valued stimuli in sensory areas, including the primary visual cortex, at notably early latencies (Shuler & Bear, 2006). As observed for threat-related effects with other stimuli, such effects seem to arise without attention and without voluntary control. Neuropsychological findings show that they still arise in patients with parietal lesions and spatial neglect, improving attention to the neglected side, suggesting mechanisms partly independent from frontoparietal attentional systems (see Domínguez-Borràs et al., 2012). However, the exact mechanisms subserving these reward biases and their relation to the dopaminergic signaling are not clear. The possible resemblance or difference in neural circuits with respect to those associated with amygdala function remains to be fully explored.

Conclusions

In accord with the view that emotions involve adaptive responses of the organism to potential challenges in the environment, both behavioral and neuroimaging data demonstrate tight links between emotional and attentional processes that jointly act to bias perception and awareness. Several aspects of emotion appear to be shared with functions classically associated with attentional mechanisms, as both may influence the selection of sensory inputs (and perhaps other representations, such as actions and memories) through feedback modulatory signals (Figure 14.5b). There is considerable evidence from numerous tasks, ranging from simple detection and orienting to search and binocular rivalry, that attention is preferentially guided to targets or captured by distracters with emotional significance. Although threat cues have often been investigated and found to produce the strongest effects, other emotions, including pleasant cues or reward, might also trigger similar advantages in attention performance. Nonetheless, some differences between negative and positive affect are likely to exist.

From a phenomenological point of view, fear might be more specifically linked to changes in attention focus, compared to other emotions. It is also possible that distinct types pf aversive emotional stimuli produce different effects, such as when threat or disgust cues attract or divert attention, respectively. However, more research is needed to support this idea.

At the neural level, there is also considerable evidence that emotional influences on perception and attention are mediated both by direct enhancement of stimulus representations in sensory cortices and, more indirectly, by modulations of frontoparietal attentional systems. The amygdala seems to play a key role in triggering these modulations through direct feedback projections to sensory areas and indirect projections to frontoparietal areas (possibly via the OFC and ACC), as well as through cholinergic and noradrenergic subcortical systems. It is likely that other systems than the amygdala also contribute to bias sensory processing based on affective meaning, notably in relation to reward values where mesolimbic dopaminergic pathways might be implicated, or in patients with amygdala damage who still show residual affective biases in some attention tasks. We still need to better understand the neural substrates recruited by different emotions, their role in different tasks, and their reactivity to different categories of stimuli.

Finally, there is evidence that modulatory effects exerted by affective systems might be partly independent and complementary (additive or competitive) to those controlled by voluntary attentional mechanisms. However, although these effects may be reflexive or even unconscious in many situations, their efficacy might be amplified or minimized by various factors, just as other reflex loops in the nervous system. Such factors might include task demands, but also expectations, situational context, past experience, or internal states such as anxiety or stress. Overall, this neural architecture suggests a *"multiple attention gain control"* model of perceptual processing (Pourtois et al., 2012), in which different sources of neural biases

might act together to guide the selection of relevant information among competing stimuli, yet through partly distinct pathways and partly distinct time courses. Hence, attention selection works not only by modulating the gain of neuronal responses based on spatial location and feature cues but also based on the potential affective value of sensory events.

In sum, just as attention can be influenced by feature- or object-based effects, reflecting the *readiness* of our perceptual systems to preferentially encode certain aspects of sensory, it is also influenced by emotion-based or value-based representations. These effects may reflect the existence of specific brain circuits for *emotional attention* or *motivated attention*, which complement the dynamic interplay between bottom-up and top-down processes underlying conscious perception.

Outstanding Questions and Future Directions

- Are mechanisms of emotion-based attention partly dependent on other neural circuits than the amygdala, and if so which ones? What is the role of these different systems? Are they differently recruited in different conditions?
- What are the common and specific effects of *emotional attention* observed for different emotional cues, particularly when related to negative (e.g., threat) or positive (e.g., reward) information? Which are the critical emotional dimensions to produce these effects?
- Are emotion-based attention effects similar for different stimuli categories (faces, scenes, sounds, voices) and for different tasks? What is the exact role of specific physical features, as opposed to affective meaning of the stimuli, in triggering these effects?
- What are the conditions (or stimuli) allowing emotional influences on perception to be induced without overt attention or without conscious awareness?
- What is the role of contextual or individual factors in modulating emotion-based

attention effects; for instance, in relation to current affect states or moods, expectations, prior experience, habituation, or task goals?

- Can direct neuronal recordings in humans (e.g., intracranial EEG) or animal models with causal interventions (e.g., microstimulation, optogenetics) help determine the functional interactions and time course of activity in different brain regions during emotional and attentional processing?

References

Alorda, C., Serrano-Pedraza, I., Campos-Bueno, J. J., Sierra-Vazquez, V., & Montoya, P. (2007). Low spatial frequency filtering modulates early brain processing of affective complex pictures. *Neuropsychologia*, 45(14), 3223–33.

Alpers, G. W., & Gerdes, A. B. (2007). Here is looking at you: Emotional faces predominate in binocular rivalry. *Emotion*, 7(3), 495–506.

Amaral, D. G., Bauman, M. D., Capitanio, J. P., Lavenex, P., Mason, W. A., Mauldin-Jourdain, M. L., & Mendoza, S. P. (2003). The amygdala: is it an essential component of the neural network for social cognition? *Neuropsychologia*, 41(4), 517–22.

Amting, J. M., Greening, S. G., & Mitchell, D. G. (2010). Multiple mechanisms of consciousness: The neural correlates of emotional awareness. *Journal of Neuroscience*, 30(30), 10039–47.

Anderson, A. K., & Phelps, E. A. (2001). Lesions of the human amygdala impair enhanced perception of emotionally salient events. *Nature*, 411(6835), 305–9

Armony, J. L., & Dolan, R. J. (2002). Modulation of spatial attention by fear-conditioned stimuli: an event-related fMRI study. *Neuropsychologia*, 40(7), 817–26.

Armony, J. L., Quirk, G. J., & LeDoux, J. E. (1998). Differential effects of amygdala lesions on early and late plastic components of auditory cortex spike trains during fear conditioning. *Journal of Neuroscience*, 18(7), 2592–2601.

Aston-Jones, G., Rajkowski, J., & Cohen, J. (1999). Role of locus coeruleus in attention and behavioral flexibility. *Biological Psychiatry*, 46(9), 1309–20.

Bach, D. R., Talmi, D., Hurlemann, R., Patin, A., & Dolan, R. J. (2011). Automatic relevance detection in the absence of a functional amygdala. *Neuropsychologia*, 49(5), 1302–5.

Bar, M., & Neta, M. (2007). Visual elements of subjective preference modulate amygdala activation. *Neuropsychologia*, 45(10), 2191–2200.

Bayle, D. J., Schoendorff, B., Henaff, M. A., & Krolak-Salmon, P. (2011). Emotional facial expression detection in the peripheral visual field. *PLoS ONE*, 6(6), e21584.

Bentley, P., Vuilleumier, P., Thiel, C. M., Driver, J., & Dolan, R. J. (2003). Cholinergic enhancement modulates neural correlates of selective attention and emotional processing. *Neuroimage*, 20(1), 58–70.

Benuzzi, F., Meletti, S., Zamboni, G., Calandra-Buonaura, G., Serafini, M., Lui, F., Nichelli, P. (2004). Impaired fear processing in right mesial temporal sclerosis: A fMRI study. *Brain Research Bulletin*, 63(4), 269–81.

Blue, V. L. (2010). And along came a spider: An attentional bias for the detection of spiders in young children and adults. *Journal of Experimental Child Psychology*, 107, 8.

Brosch, T., Pourtois, G., Sander, D., & Vuilleumier, P. (2011). Additive effects of emotional, endogenous, and exogenous attention: Behavioral and electrophysiological evidence. *Neuropsychologia*, 49(7), 1779–87.

Calvo, M. G., & Nummenmaa, L. (2008). Detection of emotional faces: Salient physical features guide effective visual search. *Journal of Experimental Psychology: General*, 137(3), 471–94.

Clarke, S., Riahi-Arya, S., Tardif, E., Eskenasy, A. C., & Probst, A. (1999). Thalamic projections of the fusiform gyrus in man. *European Journal of Neuroscience*, 11(5), 1835–38.

Coelho, C. M., Cloete, S., & Wallis, G. (2010). The face-in-the-crowd effect: When angry faces are just cross(es). *Journal of Vision*, 10(1), 7, 1–14.

Cunningham, W. A., Brosch, T. (2012). Motivational salience: Amygdala tuning from traits, needs, values, and goals. *Current Directions in Psychological Science*, 21(1), 54–59.

Day-Brown, J. D., Wei, H., Chomsung, R. D., Petry, H. M., & Bickford, M. E. (2010). Pulvinar projections to the striatum and amygdala in the tree shrew. *Frontiers in Neuroanatomy*, 4, 143.

De Martino, B., Kalisch, R., Rees, G., & Dolan, R. J. (2009). Enhanced processing of threat stimuli under limited attentional resources. *Cerebral Cortex*, 19(1), 127–33.

Dehaene, S., Changeux, J. P., Naccache, L., Sackur, J., & Sergent, C. (2006). Conscious, preconscious, and subliminal processing: A testable taxonomy. *Trends in Cognitive Science*, 10(5), 204–11.

Dolan, R. J., Heinze, H. J., Hurlemann, R., & Hinrichs, H. (2006). Magnetoencephalography (MEG) determined temporal modulation of visual and auditory sensory processing in the context of classical conditioning to faces. *Neuroimage*, 32(2), 778–89.

Domínguez-Borràs, J., Saj, A., Armony, J. L., & Vuilleumier, P. (2012). Emotional processing and its impact on unilateral neglect and extinction. *Neuropsychologia*, 50(6), 1054–71.

Driver, J. (2001). A selective review of selective attention research from the past century. *British Journal of Psychology*, 92, 53–78.

Ethofer, T., Bretscher, J., Gschwind, M., Kreifelts, B., Wildgruber, D., & Vuilleumier, P. (2012). Emotional voice areas: Anatomic location, functional properties, and structural connections revealed by combined fMRI/DTI. *Cerebral Cortex*, 22(1), 191–200

Fenske, M. J., & Eastwood, J. D. (2003). Modulation of focused attention by faces expressing emotion: Evidence from flanker tasks. *Emotion*, 3(4), 327–43.

Flykt, A. (2005). Visual search with biological threat stimuli: Accuracy, reaction times, and heart rate changes. *Emotion*, 5(3), 349–53.

Flykt, A., & Caldara, R. (2006). Tracking fear in snake and spider fearful participants during visual search: A multi-response domain study. *Cognition and Emotion*, 20(8), 16.

Forbes, S. J., Purkis, H. M., & Lipp, O. V. (2011). Better safe than sorry: Simplistic fear-relevant stimuli capture attention. *Cognition and Emotion*, 25(5), 794–804.

Freese, J. L., & Amaral, D. G. (2006). Synaptic organization of projections from the amygdala to visual cortical areas TE and V1 in the macaque monkey. *Journal of Comparative Neurology*, 496(5), 655–67.

Gerritsen, C., Frischen, A., Blake, A., Smilek, D., & Eastwood, J. D. (2008). Visual search is not blind to emotion. *Perception and Psychophysics*, 70(6), 1047–59

Grabowska, A., Marchewka, A., Seniow, J., Polanowska, K., Jednorog, K., Krolicki, L., Kossut, M., Czlonkowska, A. (2011). Emotionally negative stimuli can overcome attentional deficits in patients with visuo-spatial hemineglect. *Neuropsychologia*, 49(12), 3327–37.

Grandjean, D., Sander, D., Lucas, N., Scherer, K. R., & Vuilleumier, P. (2008). Effects of emotional prosody on auditory extinction for voices in patients with spatial neglect. *Neuropsychologia*, 46(2), 487–96.

Grandjean, D., Sander, D., Pourtois, G., Schwartz, S., Seghier, M. L., Scherer, K. R., & Vuilleumier, P. (2005). The voices of wrath: Brain responses to angry prosody in meaningless speech. *Nature Neuroscience*, 8(2), 145–46.

Gschwind, M., Pourtois, G., Schwartz, S., Van De Ville, D., & Vuilleumier, P. (2012). White-matter connectivity between face-responsive regions in the human brain. *Cerebral Cortex*, 22(7), 1564–76.

Hahn, S., & Gronlund, S. D. (2007). Top-down guidance in visual search for facial expressions. *Psychonomic Bulletin and Review*, 14(1), 159–65.

Hickey, C., Chelazzi, L., & Theeuwes, J. (2010). Reward guides vision when it's your thing: Trait reward-seeking in reward-mediated visual priming. *PLoS ONE*, 5(11), e14087.

Holland, P. C., & Gallagher, M. (2004). Amygdala-frontal interactions and reward expectancy *Current Opinion in Neurobiology*, 14(2), 148–55.

Holmes, A., Vuilleumier, P., & Eimer, M. (2003). The processing of emotional facial expression is gated by spatial attention: Evidence from event-related brain potentials. *Brain Research: Cognitive Brain Research*, 16(2), 174–84.

Huang, S. L., Chang, Y. C., & Chen, Y. J. (2011). Task-irrelevant angry faces capture attention in visual search while modulated by resources. *Emotion*, 11(3), 544–52.

Huang, Y. M., Baddeley, A., & Young, A. W. (2008). Attentional capture by emotional stimuli is modulated by semantic processing. *Journal of Experimental Psychology: Human Perception Performance*, 4(2), 328–39.

Kawasaki, H., Kaufman, O., Damasio, H., Damasio, A. R., Granner, M., Bakken, H., ... Adolphs, R. (2001). Single-neuron responses to emotional visual stimuli recorded in human ventral prefrontal cortex. *Nature Neuroscience*, 4(1), 15–16.

Keil, A., Costa, V., Smith, J. C., Sabatinelli, D., McGinnis, E. M., Bradley, M. M., & Lang, P. J. (2011). Tagging cortical networks in emotion: A topographical analysis. *Human Brain Mapping*. doi: 10.1002/hbm.21413

Kiel, A., & Ihssen, N. (2004). Identification facilitation for emotionally arousing verbs during the attentional blink. *Emotion*, 4(1), 23–35.

Keil, A., Moratti, S., Sabatinelli, D., Bradley, M. M., & Lang, P. J. (2005). Additive effects of emotional content and spatial selective attention on electrocortical facilitation. *Cerebral Cortex*, 15(8), 1187–97.

Kennedy, D. P., & Adolphs, R. (2010). Impaired fixation to eyes following amygdala damage arises from abnormal bottom-up attention. *Neuropsychologia*, 48(12), 3392–98.

Krolak-Salmon, P., Henaff, M. A., Vighetto, A., Bertrand, O., & Mauguiere, F. (2004). Early amygdala reaction to fear spreading in occipital, temporal, and frontal cortex: A depth electrode ERP study in human. *Neuron*, 42(4), 665–76.

Krusemark, E. A., & Li, W. (2011). Do all threats work the same way? Divergent effects of fear and disgust on sensory perception and attention. *Journal of Neuroscience*, 31(9), 3429–34.

Lang, P. J., Bradley, M. M., Fitzsimmons, J. R., Cuthbert, B. N., Scott, J. D., Moulder, B., & Nangia, V. (1998). Emotional arousal and activation of the visual cortex: An fMRI analysis. *Psychophysiology*, 35(2), 199–210.

Leppanen, J. M. (2006). Emotional information processing in mood disorders: A review of behavioral and neuroimaging findings. *Current Opinion in Psychiatry*, 19(1), 34–39.

Li, Z. (2002). A saliency map in primary visual cortex. *Trends in Cognitive Science*, 6(1), 9–16.

Liddell, B. J., Brown, K. J., Kemp, A. H., Barton, M. J., Das, P., Peduto, A., Williams, L. M. (2005). A direct brainstem-amygdala-cortical "alarm" system for subliminal signals of fear. *Neuroimage*, 24(1), 235–43.

Lucas, N., & Vuilleumier, P. (2008). Effects of emotional and non-emotional cues on visual search in neglect patients: Evidence for distinct sources of attentional guidance. *Neuropsychologia*, 46(5), 1401–14.

Luo, Q., Holroyd, T., Majestic, C., Cheng, X., Schechter, J., & Blair, R. J. (2010). Emotional automaticity is a matter of timing. *Journal of Neuroscience*, 30(17), 5825–29.

Mogg, K., & Bradley, B. P. (2002). Selective orienting of attention to masked threat faces in social anxiety. *Behavior Research and Therapy*, 40(12), 1403–14.

Monroe, J. F., Griffin, M., Pinkham, A., Loughead, J., Gur, R. C., Roberts, T. P., & Edgar, J. (2011). The fusiform response to faces: Explicit versus implicit processing of emotion. *Human Brain Mapping*. doi: 10.1002/hbm.21406

Morawetz, C., Baudewig, J., Treue, S., & Dechent, P. (2011). Effects of spatial frequency and location of fearful faces on human amygdala activity. *Brain Research*, 1371, 87–99.

Morris, J. S., Friston, K. J., Buchel, C., Frith, C. D., Young, A. W., Calder, A. J., & Dolan, R. J. (1998). A neuromodulatory role for the human amygdala in processing emotional facial expressions. *Brain*, 121(Pt. 1), 47–57.

Naccache, L., Gaillard, R., Adam, C., Hasboun, D., Clemenceau, S., Baulac, M., Cohen, L. (2005). A direct intracranial record of emotions evoked by subliminal words. *Proceedings of the National Academy of Sciences*, 102(21), 7713–17.

Nasrallah, M., Carmel, D., & Lavie, N. (2009). Murder, she wrote: Enhanced sensitivity to negative word valence. *Emotion*, 9(5), 609–18.

Notebaert, L., Crombez, G., Van Damme, S., De Houwer, J., & Theeuwes, J. (2010). Looking out for danger: An attentional bias towards spatially predictable threatening stimuli. *Behavior Research and Therapy*, 48(11), 1150–54.

Notebaert, L., Crombez, G., Van Damme, S., De Houwer, J., & Theeuwes, J. (2011). Signals of threat do not capture, but prioritize, attention: A conditioning approach. *Emotion*, 11(1), 81–89.

Nummenmaa, L., Hyona, J., & Calvo, M. G. (2009). Emotional scene content drives the saccade generation system reflexively. *Journal of Experimental Psychology: Human Perception and Performance*, 35(2), 305–23.

Peelen, M. V., Atkinson, A. P., Andersson, F., & Vuilleumier, P. (2007). Emotional modulation of body-selective visual areas. *SCAN – Social Cognitive and Affective Neuroscience*, 2, 274–83.

Peelen, M. V., Lucas, N., Mayer, E., & Vuilleumier, P. (2009). Emotional attention in acquired prosopagnosia. *Social Cognitive and Affective Neuroscience*, 4(3), 268–77.

Pessoa, L., & Adolphs, R. (2010). Emotion processing and the amygdala: From a "low road" to "many roads" of evaluating biological significance. *Nature Reviews. Neuroscience*, 11(11), 773–83.

Pessoa, L., McKenna, M., Gutierrez, E., & Ungerleider, L. G. (2002). Neural processing of emotional faces requires attention. *Proceedings of the National Academy of Sciences*, 99(17), 11458–63.

Phelps, E. A., Ling, S., & Carrasco, M. (2006). Emotion facilitates perception and potentiates the perceptual benefits of attention. *Psychological Science*, 17(4), 292–99.

Piech, R. M., McHugo, M., Smith, S. D., Dukic, M. S., Van Der Meer, J., Abou-Khalil, B., Zald, D. H. (2011). Attentional capture by emotional stimuli is preserved in patients with amygdala lesions. *Neuropsychologia*, 49(12), 3314–19.

Piech, R. M., McHugo, M., Smith, S. D., Dukic, M. S., Van Der Meer, J., Abou-Khalil, B., & Zald, D. H. (2010). Fear-enhanced visual search persists after amygdala lesions. *Neuropsychologia*, 48(12), 3430–35.

Pinkham, A. E., Griffin, M., Baron, R., Sasson, N. J., & Gur, R. C. (2010). The face in the crowd effect: Anger superiority when using real faces and multiple identities. *Emotion*, 10(1), 141–46.

Pourtois, G., Dan, E. S., Grandjean, D., Sander, D., & Vuilleumier, P. (2005). Enhanced extrastriate visual response to bandpass spatial frequency filtered fearful faces: Time course and topographic evoked-potentials mapping. *Human Brain Mapping*, 26(1), 65–79.

Pourtois, G., Grandjean, D., Sander, D., & Vuilleumier, P. (2004). Electrophysiological correlates of rapid spatial orienting towards fearful faces. *Cerebral Cortex*, 14(6), 619–33.

Pourtois, G., Schettino, & Vuilleumier, P. (2012). Brain mechanisms for emotional influences on perception and attention: what is magic and what is not. *Biological Psychology*. doi:10.1016/j.biopsycho.2012.02.007

Pourtois, G., Schwartz, S., Seghier, M. L., Lazeyras, F., & Vuilleumier, P. (2006). Neural systems for orienting attention to the location of threat signals: An event-related fMRI study. *Neuroimage*, 31(2), 920–33.

Pourtois, G., Spinelli, L., Seeck, M., & Vuilleumier, P. (2010a). Modulation of face processing by emotional expression and gaze direction during intracranial recordings in right fusiform cortex. *Journal of Cognitive Neuroscience*, 22(9), 2086–2107.

Pourtois, G., Spinelli, L., Seeck, M., & Vuilleumier, P. (2010b). Temporal precedence of emotion over attention modulations in the lateral amygdala: Intracranial ERP evidence from a patient with temporal lobe epilepsy. *Cognitive, Affective & Behavioral Neuroscience*, 10(1), 83–93.

Pourtois, G., Thut, G., Grave de Peralta, R., Michel, C., & Vuilleumier, P. (2005). Two electrophysiological stages of spatial orienting towards fearful faces: Early temporo-parietal activation preceding gain control in extrastriate visual cortex. *Neuroimage*, 26(1), 149–63.

Purkis, H. M., & Lipp, O. V. (2007). Automatic attention does not equal automatic fear: Preferential attention without implicit valence. *Emotion*, 7(2), 314–23.

Romanski, L. M., & LeDoux, J. E. (1992). Equipotentiality of thalamo-amygdala and thalamo-cortico-amygdala circuits in auditory fear conditioning. *Journal of Neuroscience*, 12(11), 4501–9.

Rotshtein, P., Richardson, M. P., Winston, J. S., Kiebel, S. J., Vuilleumier, P., Eimer, M., Dolan, R. J. (2010). Amygdala damage affects event-related potentials for fearful faces at specific time windows. *Human Brain Mapping*, 31(7), 1089–1105.

Sabatinelli, D., Bradley, M. M., Fitzsimmons, J. R., & Lang, P. J. (2005). Parallel amygdala and inferotemporal activation reflect emotional intensity and fear relevance. *Neuroimage*, 24(4), 1265–70.

Sabatinelli, D., Fortune, E. E., Li, Q., Siddiqui, A., Krafft, C., Oliver, W. T., Jeffries, J. (2011). Emotional perception: Meta-analyses of face and natural scene processing. *Neuroimage*, 54(3), 2524–33.

Sabatinelli, D., Lang, P. J., Keil, A., & Bradley, M. M. (2007). Emotional perception: Correlation of functional MRI and event-related potentials. *Cerebral Cortex*, 17(5), 1085–91

Scherer, K. R., & Peper, M. (2001). Psychological theories of emotion and neuropsychological research. In G. Gainotti (Ed.), *Handbook of neuropsychology*. Vol. 5: *Emotional behavior and its disorders* (pp. 17–48). New York: Elsevier.

Schmid, M. C., Mrowka, S. W., Turchi, J., Saunders, R. C., Wilke, M., Peters, A. J., . . . Leopold, D. A. (2010). Blindsight depends on the lateral geniculate nucleus. *Nature*, 466(7304), 373–77.

Schmitz, T. W., De Rosa, E., & Anderson, A. K. (2009). Opposing influences of affective state valence on visual cortical encoding. *Journal of Neuroscience*, 29(22), 7199–7207.

Schwabe, L., Merz, C. J., Walter, B., Vaitl, D., Wolf, O. T., & Stark, R. (2011). Emotional modulation of the attentional blink: The neural structures involved in capturing and holding attention. *Neuropsychologia*, 49(3), 416–25.

Serences, J. T., & Yantis, S. (2006). Selective visual attention and perceptual coherence. *Trends in Cognitive Science*, 10(1), 38–45.

Shuler, M. G., & Bear, M. F. (2006). Reward timing in the primary visual cortex. *Science*, 311(5767), 1606–9.

Smilek, D., Frischen, A., Reynolds, M. G., Gerritsen, C., & Eastwood, J. D. (2007). What influences visual search efficiency? Disentangling contributions of preattentive and postattentive processes. *Perception and Psychophysics*, 69(7), 1105–16.

Stolarova, M., Keil, A., & Moratti, S. (2006). Modulation of the C1 visual event-related component by conditioned stimuli: Evidence for sensory plasticity in early affective perception. *Cerebral Cortex*, 16(6), 876–87.

Tamietto, M., & de Gelder, B. (2010). Neural bases of the non-conscious perception of emotional signals. *Nature Reviews. Neuroscience*, 11(10), 697–709.

Tsuchiya, N., Moradi, F., Felsen, C., Yamazaki, M., & Adolphs, R. (2009). Intact rapid detection of fearful faces in the absence of the amygdala. *Nature Neuroscience*, 12(10), 1224–25.

Usunoff, K. G., Itzev, D. E., Rolfs, A., Schmitt, O., & Wree, A. (2006). Brain stem afferent connections of the amygdala in the rat with special references to a projection from the parabigeminal nucleus: A fluorescent retrograde tracing study. *Anatomy and Embryology*, 211(5), 475–96.

van Marle, H. J., Hermans, E. J., Qin, S., & Fernandez, G. (2009). From specificity to sensitivity: How acute stress affects amygdala processing of biologically salient stimuli. *Biological Psychiatry*, 66(7), 649–55.

Vermeulen, N., Godefroid, J., & Mermillod, M. (2009). Emotional modulation of attention: Fear increases but disgust reduces the attentional blink. *PLoS ONE*, 4(11), e7924.

Vuilleumier, P. (2005). How brains beware: Neural mechanisms of emotional attention. *Trends in Cognitive Science*, 9(12), 585–94.

Vuilleumier, P. (2008). The role of human amygdala in perception and attention. In P. J. Whalen & E. A. Phelps (Eds.), *The human amygdala* (pp. 220–49). New York: Guilford Press.

Vuilleumier, P., Armony, J. L., Clarke, K., Husain, M., Driver, J., & Dolan, R. J. (2002). Neural response to emotional faces with and without awareness: Event-related fMRI in a parietal patient with visual extinction and spatial neglect. *Neuropsychologia*, 40(12), 2156–66.

Vuilleumier, P., Armony, J. L., Driver, J., & Dolan, R. J. (2001). Effects of attention and emotion on face processing in the human brain: An event-related fMRI study. *Neuron*, 30(3), 829–41.

Vuilleumier, P., Armony, J. L., Driver, J., & Dolan, R. J. (2003). Distinct spatial frequency sensitivities for processing faces and emotional expressions. *Nature Neuroscience*, 6(6), 624–31.

Vuilleumier, P., Richardson, M. P., Armony, J. L., Driver, J., & Dolan, R. J. (2004). Distant influences of amygdala lesion on visual cortical activation during emotional face processing. *Nature Neuroscience*, 7(11), 1271–78.

Weymar, M., Low, A., Ohman, A., & Hamm, A. O. (2011). The face is more than its parts – Brain dynamics of enhanced spatial attention to schematic threat. *Neuroimage*, 58(3), 946–54.

Whalen, P. J., Kagan, J., Cook, R. G., Davis, F. C., Kim, H., Polis, S., Johnstone, T. (2004). Human amygdala responsivity to masked fearful eye whites. *Science*, 306(5704), 2061.

Yang, E., Zald, D. H., & Blake, R. (2007). Fearful expressions gain preferential access to awareness during continuous flash suppression. *Emotion*, 7(4), 882–86.

CHAPTER 15

Top-Down Attention and the Processing of Emotional Stimuli

Luiz Pessoa, Leticia Oliveira, & Mirtes Pereira

Prioritization

Emotion helps shape information gathering, such that motivationally relevant items receive heightened attention (Lang & Davis, 2006). But how does emotion depend on attention? Here, we consider this problem from a cognitive/affective neuroscience perspective as informed by experimental paradigms that have investigated this question by manipulating attention during the processing of (mostly) emotion-laden visual items. For related reviews, please consult (Adolphs, 2008) and (Vuilleumier, 2005); for the roles of attention and awareness, please see (Pessoa, 2005).

The processing of emotion-laden visual stimuli is often proposed to take place in an "automatic" fashion. More generally, although "automaticity" is a concept that is operationalized in quite different ways across studies in cognitive and social psychology, it can be characterized as involving processing occurring independently of the availability of processing resources, not affected by intentions and strategies, and not necessarily tied to conscious

processing (Jonides, 1981; Posner & Snyder, 1975).

A host of experimental paradigms have documented the many ways in which the processing of emotion-laden visual stimuli is prioritized (see Chapter 14). These include detection, search, interference, masking, and the attentional blink. For instance, during the attentional blink paradigm, subjects are asked to report both a first (T1) and a second (T2) visual target within a stream of distracter items (Raymond, Shapiro, & Arnell, 1992). Detecting a second target is believed to be hampered by the initial T1 processing (because of limited processing resources). Interestingly, an emotional T2 item is better detected than a corresponding neutral one, demonstrating that the affective dimension of the item counteracts the "blink" (Anderson, 2005; Anderson & Phelps, 2001). Emotional stimuli also elicit attentional blinks themselves, suggesting that their processing is prioritized (and that this processing leaves fewer resources for other stimuli). For instance, negative arousing pictures capture and hold attention, impairing participants' ability to perform a simple task on a subsequent target stimulus in a rapid stream of visual items (Most, Chun, Widders, & Zald, 2005).

The mechanisms underlying affective prioritization continue to be the target of much research, but are generally believed to be related to increased sensory processing to affective stimuli (Pessoa, 2010a, 2010b; see Chapter 14). Indeed, relative to neutral stimuli, emotional stimuli evoke increased fMRI responses across all of the ventral occipitotemporal cortex, including early, intermediate, and late visual areas. For instance, Bradley and colleagues reported more extensive visual cortex activity when participants viewed emotional, compared to neutral, pictures (Bradley et al., 2003). More recently, Padmala and Pessoa showed a close link between improvements in behavioral performance and trial-by-trial responses in early visual cortex (including primary visual cortex) during the processing of affectively significant visual items (Padmala & Pessoa, 2008). Increased cortical responses in visual cortex to affective stimuli may be due to modulatory signals from the amygdala, consistent with the existence of efferent projections from this structure that reach many levels of the visual cortex (Amaral, Behniea, & Kelly, 2003; Freese & Amaral, 2005). Indeed, patients with amygdala lesions failed to exhibit differential responses in the visual cortex when viewing emotional faces (Vuilleumier, Richardson, Armony, Driver, & Dolan, 2004). It is also of relevance that, in some cases, individuals with lesions in the left amygdala do not exhibit a reduced attentional blink for T2 emotional words (Anderson & Phelps, 2001) – but new findings challenge a causal role for the amygdala (Bach, Talmi, Hurlemann, Patin, & Dolan, 2011; Piech et al., 2011).

As outlined earlier, the processing of emotional stimuli is known to be rapid and to occur under a variety of "challenging conditions." These conditions may involve brief durations, crowded displays, masking, as well as situations in which a stimulus is task irrelevant or its consequences are unintended. Accordingly, emotional processing is frequently characterized as preattentive,

automatic, or unaware. It is important, therefore, to briefly review what is meant by these terms.

"Early vision" was frequently conceptualized in terms of two sequential processing stages (Treisman & Gelade, 1980). In the first, *preattentive* stage, processing was suggested to be rapid and to occur in parallel across the entire visual field. In contrast, in the second, *attentive* stage, processing was viewed as limited in capacity and thus serial. The nature of a preattentive stage was suggested by psychophysical data and also by the existence of "built-in analyzers" that are capable of determining several basic stimulus attributes (e.g., orientation). This information gathered at the preattentive stage was then suggested to be made available to the subsequent attentive stage, which was responsible for assembling the basic features into meaningful objects (Treisman & Gelade, 1980). Let us now turn to automaticity. Early usage identified processes as automatic when they were effortless, unconscious, or involuntary (see Tzelgov, 1997). As pointed out by Tzelgov, this definition was useful because it allowed diverse phenomena, involving different psychological mechanisms, to be viewed under a single theoretical umbrella. These phenomena included preattentive processing, well-practiced cognitive or perceptual-motor skills, and even social information processing. Finally, unaware processing refers to those conditions in which a participant does not appear to have access to (representations of) the items being processed. For instance, words can be presented in a manner so that subjects appear not to be aware of them, yet a Stroop effect may be observed (Marcel, 1983).

Although it is beyond the scope of this chapter to provide an in-depth evaluation of these three concepts – preattentive, automatic, and unaware – a brief discussion of their limitations is in order. First, the notion that a *separate* preattentive stage feeds into a capacity-limited, attentive stage encounters several problems (Di Lollo, Kawahara, Zuvic, & Visser, 2001; Nakayama & Joseph, 1998). Second, the problem with automaticity is not only in terms of counter evidence, but with the term itself, which has been used in a variety of contexts (Logan, 1988). Third, in the context of awareness, historically, several authors have suggested that unaware effects are automatic. However, the relationship between automaticity and unawareness is far from simple, as both conceptual and experimental work have recently suggested (Koch & Tsuchiya, 2007; Lamme, 2003; Most, Scholl, Clifford, & Simons, 2005). Thus, terms such as preattentive, automatic, and unaware, which are routinely used when describing the effects of emotional information, have many unintended meanings and relationships. Whereas in some cases they should be simply avoided, as in the case of preattentive, in others, for progress to be made, the use of automatic and unaware should be made as precise as possible. In the subsequent sections, we review some of the specific evidence against and for the idea that attention is required for emotional processing.

Attention Is Not Required for Emotional Perception

Emotional stimuli effectively divert processing resources and interfere with performance even when they are task irrelevant (Pessoa & Ungerleider, 2004; Vuilleumier, 2005). For instance, reaction times when subjects performed auditory tasks (e.g., word discrimination) were slower when they viewed distracter pictures that were unpleasant relative to neutral ones (Bradley, Cuthbert, & Lang, 1996; Buodo, Sarlo, & Palomba, 2002). Strikingly, such type of interference has been observed even when the primary task is very basic, such as the detection of a simple visual stimulus (Pereira et al., 2006). Interference effects are not only evident in terms of behavioral performance but are also manifested physiologically. For example, specific event-related potential (ERP) components activated by picture viewing were modulated by emotional content even when the main task involved simply detecting a checkerboard stimulus that was interspersed with picture presentation (Schupp, Junghofer, Weike, & Hamm, 2003). Together, these studies are often interpreted as supporting the notion that the processing of emotional stimuli is obligatory and that increased processing resources are allocated toward their processing even when they are irrelevant to the task at hand.

A stronger argument can be advanced that emotional processing is obligatory based on studies in which the spatial focus of attention is explicitly manipulated – note that in the experiments described the previous paragraph, emotional stimuli, although task irrelevant, were fully attended. In a well-known study (Vuilleumier, Armony, Driver, & Dolan, 2001), the attentional focus was manipulated by having subjects maintain central fixation while they were asked to compare either two faces or two houses presented eccentrically. On each trial, subjects either compared the faces to each other or the houses to each other (Figure 15.1a). Thus, the focus of attention was varied by having subjects attend to the left and the right of fixation (while ignoring top/bottom stimuli) or above and below fixation (while ignoring left/right stimuli). In each case, participants indicated whether the attended stimuli were the same or not. When conditions involving fearful faces were contrasted to those involving neutral ones, differential responses in the amygdala – which are often considered as a "signature" of emotional processing – were not modulated by the focus of attention, consistent with the view that the processing of emotional items does not require attention (Figure 15.1b). Related findings were observed when manipulating object-based attention while maintaining constant the spatial locus of attention (Anderson, Christoff, Panitz, De Rosa E., & Gabrieli, 2003). Amygdala responses evoked by fearful faces were equivalent whether or not the faces were attended. Interestingly, however, during unattended conditions, responses evoked by fear and disgust faces were comparable to each other, consistent with the idea that attention is needed to discriminate emotional content

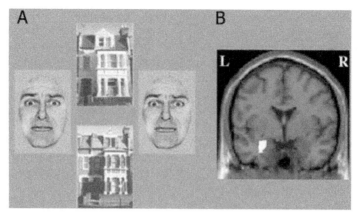

Figure 15.1. Attention and the processing of emotional stimuli. (A) Paradigm employed to manipulate the spatial focus of attention during the presentation of emotional faces. (B) Activation in the left amygdala to fearful versus neutral faces regardless of the focus of attention. Adapted from Vuilleumier et al. (2001) with permission.

(both expressions evoked greater responses than neutral faces). We now turn to reviewing evidence that suggests that emotional perception requires attention.

Attention Is Required for Emotional Perception

Based on the findings summarized in the previous section, emotional stimuli comprise a privileged stimulus category that is not only prioritized but whose processing also takes place in an obligatory fashion that is independent of attention. However, it is also known that, in general, visual processing capacity is limited. Because of this finite capacity, competition among visual items is proposed to "select" the most important information at any given time (Desimone & Duncan, 1995; Grossberg, 1980). When resources are not fully consumed, it has been suggested that spare processing capacity is used to process unattended items (Lavie, 1995). This line of reasoning, which has been successfully applied to regular, nonemotional stimuli, suggests that the automaticity of affective processing can be tested by attentional manipulations that more fully consume processing resources. Thus, a critical variable in understanding the extent of unattended processing is the

attentional demand of a task – namely, the extent to which it uses up resources.

Several fMRI studies have attempted to follow the strategy just outlined. For example, they evaluated the responses evoked by centrally presented emotional faces when a very demanding peripheral task was performed. Under these conditions, differential responses to fearful vs. neutral faces were eliminated in both the amygdala and visual cortex (Pessoa, McKenna, Gutierrez, & Ungerleider, 2002). Consistent with the notion that task demand was important in determining the extent of processing of the face stimuli, when the difficulty of the peripheral task was parametrically manipulated, a valence effect (i.e., fearful > neutral) was observed during low task demand conditions, but not during medium or high-demand conditions (Pessoa, Padmala, & Morland, 2005). The dependence of emotional perception on attention was also observed in studies that used centrally presented, overlapping competing stimuli (i.e., paradigms that manipulate object-based attention; Mitchell et al., 2007), including emotional stimuli of higher affective significance that were paired with shock (Lim, Padmala, & Pessoa, 2008) – or by using highly aversive, mutilation pictures (Erthal et al., 2005). Posner-type manipulations of attention also indicate that amygdala activation depends on the focus of attention (Brassen, Gamer, Rose, & Buchel, 2010). Furthermore, attentional modulation of the emotional valence effect has also been observed for peripherally presented faces (Silvert et al., 2007).

ERP studies, which unlike fMRI studies offer temporal information on the order of milliseconds (see Chapters 4 and 5), have also investigated how emotional perception depends on attentional factors. In one study (Schupp et al., 2007), the processing of emotional pictures from the International Affective Picture System (IAPS) was strongly attenuated (as measured by an ERP component labeled the "early posterior negativity") when participants performed demanding attention tasks. On the contrary, passively viewing the same emotional images generated increased responses relative to those evoked by neutral stimuli. Likewise, differential ERP responses to peripheral, emotional IAPS pictures also relied on the availability of processing resources (De Cesarei, Codispoti, & Schupp, 2009). Emotional pictures in the near periphery modulated brain activity only when they were attended (though passively viewed), but not when participants were engaged in a distracter task (determining whether a rectangular outline contained a gap or not).

Attention Is Not Required for Emotional Perception, Again

The results suggesting that emotional perception is automatic or that it depends on attention can be reconciled by making use of the concept of attentional demand (Lavie, 1995). When demand is low, "spillover" capacity is available for the processing of task-irrelevant emotional stimuli. As demand is increased, however, fewer resources will be available, and in the limit, emotional perception will be eliminated. Whereas this framework can be used to explain a broad set of results, some findings appear to resist this explanation (and for recent twists concerning the notion of "load," see Tsal & Benoni, 2010;

Wilson, Muroi, & MacLeod, 2011). In one study, subjects performed a difficult target-detection task while task-irrelevant though emotionally arousing pictures were shown in the background (Muller, Andersen, & Keil, 2008). Despite the difficulty of the task, emotional pictures interfered behaviorally with the main task. Parallel findings were registered in steady-state visual evoked potentials, which were reduced during the presentation of emotional relative to neutral background images (such reduction was suggested to reflect the withdrawal of processing resources from the main task by the emotional distracters).

Another recent MEG study provided evidence for mandatory processing of fearful faces (Fenker et al., 2010). Both low- and high-demand conditions were investigated in separate experiments. During the high-demand condition, the target was defined by a conjunction of features, such as a red-green (vs. blue-yellow) vertical bar. In the low-demand condition, subjects determined the orientation of an oriented bar (vertical versus horizontal) presented in a given color (indicated at the beginning of the block). During the low-demand condition, task-irrelevant fearful faces slowed down reaction time when they were presented in the same visual field as the bar target (relative to when faces were presented in the opposite visual field). To investigate the neural impact of the task-irrelevant faces, the authors probed the so-called N2pc component, which is believed to reflect attentional focusing in visual search. They observed that lateralized fearful faces elicited an N2pc approximately 240–400 ms in the contralateral visual cortex. Importantly, the N2pc was observed during conditions of high demand, although no behavioral effects were detected.

Interim Summary

Taken together, results from behavioral and neuroimaging methods suggest that although emotional processing is prioritized, in many contexts it depends on processing resources. These findings come from diverse paradigms, including those using peripheral emotional stimuli and those in which affective and neutral stimuli are spatially separated. In general, the discrepancy between studies suggesting that emotional perception is automatic, and those illustrating the dependence on attention, is accounted for by the concepts of capacity limitation and competition. Thus, to reveal that emotional perception is not immune to the effects of attention, processing resources need to be largely consumed – otherwise, performance will appear to be relatively automatic. Yet, as outlined in the previous section, this account may not explain all cases, and there may be circumstances in which more true automaticity is observed. At present, the reasons for this discrepancy are unclear, suggesting that it would be profitable for future studies to tackle this issue more directly. One possibility is that individual differences are important predictors of sensitivity to emotional stimuli and help explain the impact of emotional stimuli. For instance, studies from the literature on anxiety have revealed that anxious participants exhibit greater interference from threat-related stimuli (MacLeod, Mathews, & Tata, 1986). More recent studies have investigated the extent to which amygdala responses to threat-related distracters depend on individual anxiety levels (Bishop, Duncan, & Lawrence, 2004; Dickie & Armony, 2008; Chapter 24). Whereas low-anxious individuals only showed increased amygdala responses to attended fearful faces, high-anxious individuals showed increased amygdala responses to both attended and unattended threat-related stimuli. These findings suggest that the threat value of a stimulus varies as a function of a participant's anxiety level, although attention is important even for high-anxious individuals (Bishop, Jenkins, & Lawrence, 2007; Fox, Russo, & Georgiou, 2005).

Temporal Paradigms and Mechanisms of Prioritization

A particularly rich paradigm to study capacity limitations is the attentional blink, a manipulation that is especially interesting given its temporal dimension – as opposed to the spatial nature of several of the manipulations discussed in the preceding sections. As noted, the strength of the attentional blink is influenced by the emotional content of the stimuli involved, such that participants are better at detecting the second target when it is emotionally laden. However, until recently, the neural mechanisms by which emotional content influences perceptual processing remained unclear (see also Chapter 15).

In a recent study (Lim, Padmala, & Pessoa, 2009), we investigated how affective significance shapes visual perception during an attentional blink paradigm combined with aversive conditioning (Figure 15.2a). Behaviorally, following aversive learning, affectively significant T2 scenes (CS+) were better detected than neutral (CS-) ones (72% versus 62%, respectively). In terms of mean brain responses, both amygdala and visual cortical responses were stronger during CS+ relative to CS- trials. Increased responses in these regions were associated with improved behavioral performance across participants and followed a mediation-like pattern (Figure 15.2b). Specifically, although amygdala responses were predictive of behavioral performance, once responses in visual cortex were taken into account, the initial relationship was no longer statistically significant, consistent with the idea that the influence of the amygdala was mediated via visual cortex.

We hypothesized that if fluctuations in evoked responses in the brain determine the accuracy of the detection of the second target, *trial-by-trial* variability in response amplitude should predict behavioral reports. In addition, because T2 performance was better during the CS+ than in the CS- condition, this relationship should be stronger for the former. To evaluate these predictions, we performed logistic regression analysis and modeled the probability of a hit trial (i.e., correctly reporting "house" or "building") as a function of single-trial amplitude. In visual cortex, the mean logistic regression slopes, which represented the strength of the predictive effect, were

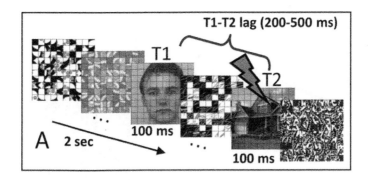

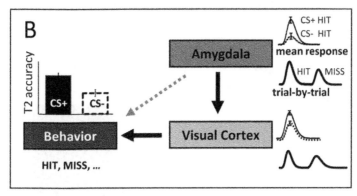

Figure 15.2. Attentional blink paradigm. (A) Participants were asked to report on the face stimulus (T1) and on whether the stream contained a house, a building, or no scene (T2). Houses or buildings were paired with mild electrical stimulation during an initial learning phase (counterbalanced across subjects). (B) The link between responses evoked in the amygdala and behavior (i.e., detection of T2) was mediated via specific regions of visual cortex – in this case, the parahippocampal gyrus given its involvement in the processing of scenes and spatial layouts. This relationship was observed in terms of mean responses (across participants; shown schematically in red and blue) and in terms of moment-to-moment fluctuations in evoked brain responses and behavior (shown in purple). Adapted from Lim et al. (2009) with permission.

significant for both CS+ and CS- trials, indicating that trial-by-trial fluctuations in fMRI signals reliably predicted perceptual T2 decisions (Figure 15.3a,b). Importantly, a direct comparison of the CS+ and CS- conditions revealed that the predictive power of the logistic regression fit was stronger during CS+ relative to CS- scenes. An analogous trial-by-trial analysis was performed for the amygdala (Figure 15.3c,d). The mean logistic regression slope was significant for CS+ trials, but not for CS- trials, indicating that variability in fMRI signals in the amygdala contributed to perceptual T2 decisions more robustly when these stimuli were affectively

significant (a direct paired comparison was also significant).

Taken together with other findings, our results suggest that affective significance potentially determines the fate of a visual item during competitive interactions by enhancing sensory processing. By helping establish affective significance, the amygdala helps separate the significant from the mundane. One way to interpret these results is in terms of an attentional function of the amygdala (Pessoa, 2010b). For example, in studies of attention and visual cortical function, fluctuation of responses in the visual cortex is often conceptualized as dependent

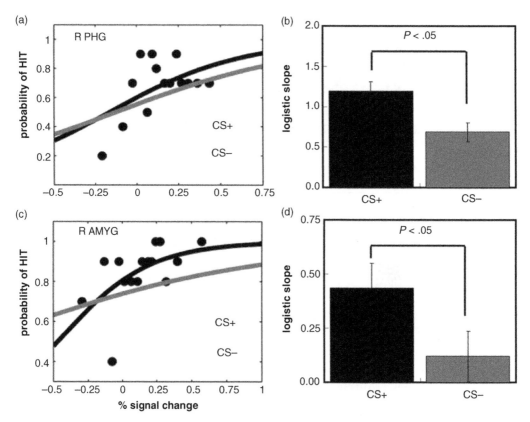

Figure 15.3. Trial-by-trial analysis. (A) Logistic regression analysis of evoked responses in the right parahippocampal gyrus (PHG) as a function of affective significance (CS+ and CS-) for a sample individual (dichotomous variable: hits vs. misses). The slope of the logistic fit indicates the strength of the predictive effect. For clarity, only binned data for the CS+ condition are shown (red dots). (B) Mean logistic slopes across individuals for the parahippocampal gyrus. (C) The same analysis as in (A) but for the right amygdala (AMYG). (D) Mean logistic slopes across individuals for the amygdala. Adapted from Lim et al. (2009) with permission.

on "source" regions in parietal and frontal cortices (Corbetta & Shulman, 2002; Kastner & Ungerleider, 2000), and these mechanisms are typically viewed as linked to how the processing of attended objects is prioritized. In our study of the attentional blink, something quite similar was observed insofar as fluctuations in the amygdala were predictive of the strength of the link between visual cortex and behavior. In this case, the amygdala was found to behave much like an "attentional device" would be expected to – namely, it helped prioritize the processing of certain stimuli over others (Pessoa, 2010b; see also Vuilleumier, 2005 and Chapter 14). For closely related findings suggesting a role of the pulvinar in prioritizing the processing

of affectively significant stimuli, see Padmala et al., (2010) and Pessoa and Adolphs, (2010).

In the context of this chapter, an especially important finding of the study was that the contrast of affectively significant and neutral Miss trials did not reveal significant differential responses in the amygdala. In contrast, the comparison of affectively significant and neutral Hit trials exhibited differential responses. In other words, differential responses were not produced unless a T2 scene was detected. More generally, this finding suggests that affective perception is indeed under the control of attentional mechanisms during temporal "bottleneck" conditions, in addition to during spatial competition conditions. These findings are

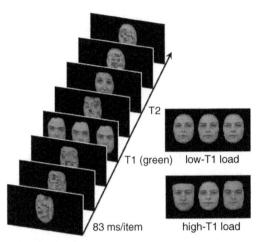

Figure 15.4. Attentional blink paradigm by Stein et al. (2010). The demand of the attentional blink was manipulated by the type of flanker stimuli during the T1-containing stimulus. During the low-demand condition, the central face was flanked by identical copies. During the high-demand condition, the central face was flanked by random faces, making the task considerably more demanding. Reproduced from Stein et al. (2010) with permission.

of particular interest because they involve stimuli that were particularly potent (given the history of pairing with shock). A previous study also reported that fear-conditioned faces (via pairing with a loud tone) were also subject to an attentional blink (Milders, Sahraie, Logan, & Donnellon, 2006).

A recent attentional blink study introduced a clever manipulation in an attempt to influence the demand associated with processing the first target (Stein, Peelen, Funk, & Seidl, 2010). Specifically, perceptual demand of the blink-inducing target was manipulated by varying flanker interference (Figure 15.4). During the low-demand condition, the center face was flanked by identical copies of that face. During the high-demand condition, the center face was flanked by randomly sampled faces. For the first (T1) task, observers were instructed to report the sex of the central face. For the second (T2) task, observers were asked to detect (present vs. absent) faces presented during the attentional blink period that could depict either a fearful or a happy expres-

sion. For the low-demand condition, fearful faces were detected more often than happy faces, replicating previous reports. Importantly, this advantage for fearful faces disappeared for the high-demand condition, during which fearful and happy faces were detected equally often. These results suggest that the privileged access of fearful faces to awareness does not occur mandatorily, but instead depends on attentional resources. It is important to note, furthermore, that in all conditions a blink was observed – a property that appears to be shared by all affective emotional blink experiments. It was only the advantage for fearful faces that was eliminated during the high-demand condition. In other words, capacity limitations for the processing of emotional faces were obtained for both demand levels. At the relatively more moderate T1 demand, even though fearful faces blinked, they counteracted the blink to a greater extent than happy faces. At the more stringent T1 demand, this advantage disappeared. For similar effects in neuropsychological disturbances of attention, see Chapter 14.

In summary, the results from attentional blink experiments suggest that emotion-laden stimuli are also subject to the blink, which goes counter to the notion of strong automaticity. In line with the notion that emotional items receive privileged processing, affective items show a greater degree of blink sparing (i.e., reduced attentional blink), an effect that involves interactions between the amygdala and visual cortex, as discussed earlier (Lim et al., 2009). However, as in the case of spatial paradigms, some have interpreted results of the emotional attentional blink in terms of automaticity (Anderson, 2005).

Timing of Emotion and Attention Effects

Techniques that provide fast temporal information in humans, notably EEG and MEG, have been used to probe the timing of affective processing. Two recent studies are particularly noteworthy because they explicitly manipulated attention and emotion while brain signals were measured with MEG or intracranial recordings in an attempt to evaluate responses evoked in the amygdala. These studies are also important because a possible concern with fMRI studies, which have investigated this question in some depth, is that the technique may be relatively blind to fast effects. In other words, rapid effects of emotional items that are independent of attention may have been missed by fMRI, which only provides a low-pass version of the associated neural events.

In the first study, MEG was employed to investigate responses in the amygdala while participants viewed task-irrelevant fearful and neutral faces (Luo et al., 2010). Although the amygdala is a deep structure in the brain and, accordingly, one that is challenging to probe with techniques such as EEG and MEG, it has been suggested that advanced source analysis techniques are capable of measuring signals from this structure (Ioannides et al., 1995; Streit et al., 2003) – although this contention is controversial. On each trial, the observer's task was to discriminate the orientation of peripherally located bars (same or different?). As in previous studies, attention was manipulated by varying task difficulty. During the low-demand condition, the bar orientation difference was high (90 degrees), making the task very easy. During the high-demand condition, the bar orientation difference was low (15 degrees), making the task relatively hard.

MEG responses revealed a significant main effect of facial expression in the left amygdala. Specifically, increased gamma-band activity was observed in response to fearful relative to neutral expressions very soon after stimulus onset (30 to 60 ms). Consistent with the notion of automaticity, no main effect of attentional demand or demand-by-expression interaction was detected during this early time window. Such an interaction was observed in the right amygdala, however, at a later time (280 to 340 ms). Importantly, under high-demand conditions, emotional expression had no effect on amygdala responses during this later time window. In contrast, under the low-demand condition, increased gamma-band activity was observed for fearful relative to neutral expressions. The authors suggest that "emotional automaticity is a matter of timing" and that fMRI may simply miss the fast, first pass of emotional information, which would be automatic.

Localizing sources with EEG and/or MEG data is a complex problem, and it is not entirely clear that signals from deep structures in the brain, such as the amygdala, can be localized with certainty at this point in time. An approach that bypasses this problem is to record directly from the amygdala in humans (e.g., during presurgical preparation). That was the strategy adopted by Pourtois and colleagues (Pourtois, Spinelli, Seeck, & Vuilleumier, 2010), who used the same paradigm employed in an earlier fMRI study (Vuilleumier et al., 2001), in which two houses (e.g., to the left and right of fixation) and two faces (e.g., below and above fixation) were employed (Figure 15.1a). The subject's task was to determine if the horizontal or vertical stimulus pair was identical. Recordings from face-sensitive sites in the lateral amygdala showed an early and systematic differential neural response between fearful and neutral faces, regardless of attention. Differences were observed from 140 to 290 ms. Furthermore, comparing trials with task-relevant versus task-irrelevant faces (regardless of emotion expression) revealed a sustained attentional effect in the left amygdala, but starting only at 710 ms poststimulus onset.

These two studies provide important advances in our attempt to understand the interactions between emotion and attention. By employing techniques that offer millisecond temporal resolution, the studies attempted to determine the temporal evolution of affective processing and how it is influenced by attention. However, the two studies also pose some important questions.

Let us consider the MEG study first. It was suggested that responses in the amygdala are modulated by affective content within 30–40 ms, possibly via a fast pathway. Yet, the timing is puzzling in light of known response latencies in the visual system. For instance, the earliest responses in the LGN, which receives direct retinal input, are observed at approximately 30 ms, and on average they occur around 33 ms (for the magno system) and 50 ms (for the parvo system; Lamme & Roelfsema, 2000). When considering neuronal response latencies, other issues are also important. In addition to the latency itself, one needs to consider "computation time." It has been estimated (Tovee & Rolls, 1995) that most of the information encoded by visual neurons may be available in segments of activity 100 ms long, and that a fair amount of information is available in 50-ms segments, and even some is found in 20- to 30-ms segments (note that these segments take into account response latency; namely, they consider neuronal spikes after a certain delay). Although these figures demonstrate the remarkable speed of neuronal computation (at least under some conditions), they add precious milliseconds to the time required to, for instance, discriminate between stimuli (e.g., hypothetical differential responses in the LGN itself would be expected no earlier than 60 ms poststimulus onset). An additional consideration is that responses in humans are possibly slower than in monkeys, further adding time. For instance, in one human study (Yoshor, Bosking, Ghose, & Maunsell, 2007), the fastest recording sites had latencies just under 60 ms and were probably located in V1 (or possibly V2). In monkey, the fastest responses in V1 can be observed under 40 ms (Lamme & Roelfsema, 2000).

What are the response latencies of neurons in the amygdala? In the monkey, amygdala responses typically range from 100 to 200 ms (Gothard, Battaglia, Erickson, Spitler, & Amaral, 2007; Kuraoka & Nakamura, 2007; Leonard, Rolls, Wilson, & Baylis, 1985; Nakamura, Mikami, & Kubota, 1992) – although shorter response latencies to unspecific stimuli (e.g., fixation spots) have at times been reported (Gothard et al., 2007). Differences in evoked responses between threat and neutral or appeasing facial expressions in the monkey amygdala have been reported in the range of 120–250 ms (Gothard et al., 2007).

Intracranial studies in humans generally find the earliest single-unit responses around 200 ms (Mormann et al., 2008; Oya, Kawasaki, Howard, & Adolphs, 2002). In addition, in a lesion case study, affective modulation of amygdala responses was also observed starting at 200 ms (Krolak-Salmon, Henaff, Vighetto, Bertrand, & Mauguiere, 2004); see also (Oya et al., 2002). For more extensive discussion, see Pessoa and Adolphs (2010).

Recently, we have advocated that bypass systems involving the cortex may rapidly convey affective information throughout the brain (Pessoa & Adolphs, 2010) – see the related notion of a two-stage mechanism underlying emotion and attention prioritization (Rudrauf et al., 2008; Vuilleumier, 2005). This "parallel processing" architecture would allow fast affective responses, certainly around 100–150 ms poststimulus onset. Interestingly, this potential time course matches the one observed in the intracranial study by Pourtois and colleagues, in which affective influences were observed starting at 140 ms. A potential concern with that study, however, is that the task employed was not challenging. Specifically, the patient was correct 95% of the time during face trials, and 97% of the time during house trials. Whereas this made for balanced task performance for faces and houses (and was probably determined by the testing of a patient in the context of neurosurgery), in all likelihood, the task was not sufficiently demanding. As discussed, processing resources "spill over" when the central task is not taxing (Lavie, 1995), and therefore effects of valence under these conditions are not entirely surprising. And although the effect of valence can be referred to as "automatic" in the sense of implicit processing of task-irrelevant information, the task does not allow for a stricter test of automaticity in terms of obligatory processing.

In light of these remarks on capacity limitations, it is worth considering that, even in the MEG study, the attentional manipulation may not have been sufficiently strong. Observers performed at 83% correct in the high-demand condition. In contrast, in a similar bar-orientation task,

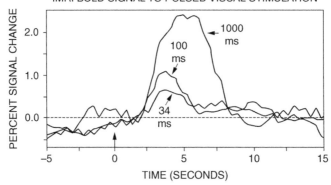

Figure 15.5. fMRI responses to brief stimuli. Original results by Savoy and colleagues, illustrating the fact that a clear signal change is observed for very brief events. Data from Savoy et al. (1995). Reproduced from Rosen, Buckner, and Dale (1998) with permission.

performance was at 64% correct during the most demanding condition (Pessoa et al., 2002); notably, in another bar-orientation study, we did observe valence effects on reaction time when performance was at 79% correct, but they disappeared when performance was at approximately 60% correct (Erthal et al., 2005). In general, attentional manipulations that more completely exhaust processing capacity must be sought, as in similar questions of the need for attention during scene perception in which a clearer demonstration of the impact of the attentional manipulation has been provided (Li, VanRullen, Koch, & Perona, 2002).

A second important issue with the intracranial study refers to the timing of the attention effect, which was reported to start at around 700 ms. As noted by the authors, this timing is considerably later than effects of attention on sensory processing, which can be observed as early as 60–100 ms (Luck, Woodman, & Vogel, 2000). As the authors suggested, this late effect may be due to other task-related differences associated with processing the emotional significance of the faces. In any case, the effect would seem to have a different origin than the modulation of visual processing by attentional mechanisms.

A final issue merits discussion. A common objection to fMRI is that it might not be sensitive to brief events. Whereas this is a possible concern given the low-pass characteristics of the BOLD signal, several examples show that this concern does not necessarily hold. Perhaps surprisingly at first, the BOLD signal is indeed sensitive to transient events, as originally demonstrated by Savoy and colleagues (1995; Figure 15.5). Furthermore, fMRI responses have been consistently reported for stimuli that are presented very briefly (~30 ms) and even masked (Morris, Ohman, & Dolan, 1998; Whalen et al., 1998), a result replicated many times with affective stimuli, for instance. Thus, whereas it is clearly desirable to obtain millisecond-level data, such as provided by techniques like MEG, fMRI is certainly not blind to brief, transient events, as illustrated in Figure 15.6. Indeed, even sub-millisecond stimulation has been shown to evoke detectable hemodynamic responses (Hirano, Stefanovic, & Silva, 2011).

In summary, both studies described here provide important insights about the temporal unfolding of affective responses in the brain. Both argued that the effects of emotional content temporally precede those of attention and that prior discrepancies in the literature may stem from the temporal characteristics of the fMRI signal. The points raised earlier suggest, however, that it may not be yet time to accept those conclusions:

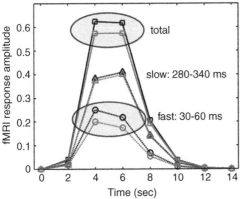

Figure 15.6. Simulated fMRI responses and timing. During the hard condition in the study by Luo et al. (2010), fast responses varied as a function of valence, whereas later responses did not – that is, attention affected the latter, but not the former. However, fast responses are not inherently invisible to fMRI, and are expected to generate differential fMRI responses, as suggested by the simulation labeled "fast" (bottom two lines). The "slow" component was also simulated, and no differential responses would be expected (middle two lines; the slight displacement was used for display only). A typical fMRI study would pick up the "total" signal containing the contributions of both fast and slow components (upper two lines) and, in theory, should be sensitive to the differences that were present in the first time window (see also Figure 15.5). For these simulations, it was assumed that fMRI signals were sampled every 2 s. Black lines: negative stimuli; gray lines: neutral stimuli; solid lines: total response; dotted lines: responses to the fast component (bottom two lines) and to the slow component (middle two lines). Adapted from Pessoa (2010c) with permission.

Emotion and attention may be linked more closely than suggested in the two studies discussed in this section.

Conclusions

An impasse can be discerned: Although a great deal has been learned about the extent and limits of affective visual processing, the two camps (*unlimited* vs. limited processing) seem to have somewhat entrenched views. This is not too surprising. After all

emotional stimuli are sufficiently potent that they exhibit a host of properties that are not readily observed with neutral items. At the same time, affective processing is subject to processing limitations, as revealed by several experimental manipulations.

Can the impasse go away? One the one hand, advocates of limited processing can often claim that processing resources have not been sufficiently consumed – if only the manipulation were stronger, the impact of affective items would go away. On the other hand, showing that the emotional effect has disappeared is always subject to the "null problem;" namely, claiming the absence of an effect, which is fraught with possibly insurmountable difficulties. For instance, whereas a clear statistical interaction was detected in the study by Pessoa et al. (2002), one could argue that the pattern of results for the left amygdala (but possibly not for the right amygdala) was consistent with automatic processing (see Fig. 2B of Pessoa et al. 2002). In other words, the pattern of evoked responses to unattended faces was in the "correct direction," with a less negative deflection for fearful being apparent in the plot. Thus, even though statistical differences were not detected between unattended fearful and neutral faces, an argument could be made that the difference would have been significant had the experiment had more statistical power (with a sufficiently large N, any difference is potentially significant). Curiously, statistical power also comes into play when providing evidence for *unlimited* processing. For instance, when attention-by-emotion interactions are not detected, results may be interpreted in favor of automaticity (Luo et al., 2010); here, it is noteworthy that attaining adequate statistical power to assess interactions is more challenging than in the case of other simple or main effects (Murphy & Myors, 2004).

In this chapter, we reviewed the role of attention in the processing of emotion-laden visual information and discussed both evidence for and against automaticity. In addition to presenting empirical data, we noted that three concepts frequently used to describe affective processing – preattentive, automatic, and unaware – are saturated with both intended and unintended connotations. It would thus appear that progress in the ongoing "automaticity debate" will require developments both along the empirical and conceptual fronts.

Outstanding Questions and Future Directions

- Studies that evaluate the contributions of both attention and emotion with millisecond temporal resolution are needed to advance our understanding of the exact role of attention. Ideally, diverse behavioral paradigms should be examined.
- How should attentional demand be operationalized? Whereas task difficulty in terms of percent correct is a reasonable measure, more sophisticated approaches are needed. For instance, a task may be difficult due to sensory limitations and less so to capacity limitations (Lavie & de Fockert, 2003). This means that a task that is associated with low accuracy does not necessarily consume processing resources to a great extent. Thus, careful consideration of the multiple factors that contribute to task performance is needed. Notably, recent work on "dilution" effects has challenged operationalizations of "load" in terms of set size, for instance, by demonstrating "reverse load" effects (Tsal & Benoni, 2010; Wilson et al., 2011).
- Although visual awareness was not discussed at length here, it is clearly an important variable when attempting to characterize the potency of affective processing. Now that both conceptual work and empirical studies are describing important ways in which attention and awareness differ from each other, it would be valuable to investigate affective processing in light of these advances.
- What is the role of individual differences in the processing of affective stimuli in general, and the role of attention in particular? Whereas some studies have

investigated this issue, further research could further clarify the role of individual differences as important predictors of sensitivity to emotional stimuli and the role of attention.
- The role of attention in affective processing has been investigated largely in the visual domain. How does this research generalize to other types of information, including auditory, somatosensory, and olfactory? Evidence for capacity limitation in the case of auditory processing has been recently reported (Mothes-Lasch, Mentzel, Miltner, & Straube, 2011).

Acknowledgments

We thank Jorge Armony and Patrik Vuilleumier for feedback on this chapter and the National Institute of Mental Health for support (MH071589).

References

Adolphs, R. (2008). Fear, faces, and the human amygdala. *Current Opinions in Neurobiology*, 18(2), 166–72.

Amaral, D. G., Behniea, H., & Kelly, J. L. (2003). Topographic organization of projections from the amygdala to the visual cortex in the macaque monkey. *Neuroscience*, 118(4), 1099–1120.

Anderson, A. K. (2005). Affective influences on the attentional dynamics supporting awareness. *Journal of Experimental Psychology: General*, 134(2), 258–81.

Anderson, A. K., Christoff, K., Panitz, D., De Rosa E., & Gabrieli, J. D. (2003). Neural correlates of the automatic processing of threat facial signals. *Journal of Neuroscience*, 23(13), 5627–33.

Anderson, A. K., & Phelps, E. A. (2001). Lesions of the human amygdala impair enhanced perception of emotionally salient events. *Nature*, 411(6835), 305–9.

Bach, D. R., Talmi, D., Hurlemann, R., Patin, A., & Dolan, R. J. (2011). Automatic relevance detection in the absence of a functional amygdala. *Neuropsychologia*, 49(5), 1302–5.

Bishop, S. J., Duncan, J., & Lawrence, A. D. (2004). State anxiety modulation of the amygdala response to unattended threat-related stimuli. *Journal of Neuroscience*, 24(46), 10364–68.

Bishop, S. J., Jenkins, R., & Lawrence, A. D. (2007). Neural processing of fearful faces: effects of anxiety are gated by perceptual capacity limitations. *Cerebral Cortex*, 17(7), 1595–1603.

Bradley, M. M., Cuthbert, B. N., & Lang, P. J. (1996). Picture media and emotion: Effects of a sustained affective context. *Psychophysiology*, 33(6), 662–70.

Bradley, M. M., Sabatinelli, D., Lang, P. J., Fitzsimmons, J. R., King, W., & Desai, P. (2003). Activation of the visual cortex in motivated attention. *Behavioral Neuroscience*, 117(2), 369–80.

Brassen, S., Gamer, M., Rose, M., & Buchel, C. (2010). The influence of directed covert attention on emotional face processing. *Neuroimage*, 50(2), 545–51.

Buodo, G., Sarlo, M., & Palomba, D. (2002). Attentional resources measured by reaction times highlight differences within pleasant and unpleasant, high arousing stimuli. *Motivation and Emotion*, 26, 123–38.

Corbetta, M., & Shulman, G. L. (2002). Control of goal-directed and stimulus-driven attention in the brain. *Nature Reviews Neuroscience*, 3(3), 201–15.

De Cesarei, A., Codispoti, M., & Schupp, H. T. (2009). Peripheral vision and preferential emotion processing. *Neuroreport*, 20(16), 1439–43.

Desimone, R., & Duncan, J. (1995). Neural mechanisms of selective attention. *Annual Review of Neuroscience*, 18, 193–222.

Di Lollo, V., Kawahara, J., Zuvic, S. M., & Visser, T. A. (2001). The preattentive emperor has no clothes: A dynamic redressing. *Journal of Experimental Psychology: General*, 130(3), 479–92.

Dickie, E. W., & Armony, J. L. (2008). Amygdala responses to unattended fearful faces: Interaction between sex and trait anxiety. *Psychiatry Research*, 162(1), 51–57.

Erthal, F. S., de Oliveira, L., Mocaiber, I., Pereira, M. G., Machado-Pinheiro, W., Volchan, E., & Pessoa, L. (2005). Load-dependent modulation of affective picture processing. *Cognitive, Affective, & Behavioral Neuroscience*, 5(4), 388–95.

Fenker, D. B., Heipertz, D., Boehler, C. N., Schoenfeld, M. A., Noesselt, T., Heinze, H. J., . . . Hopf, J. M. (2010). Mandatory processing of irrelevant fearful face features in

visual search. *Journal of Cognitive Neuroscience*, 22(12), 2926–38.

Fox, E., Russo, R., & Georgiou, G. A. (2005). Anxiety modulates the degree of attentive resources required to process emotional faces. *Cognitive, Affective, & Behavioral Neuroscience*, 5(4), 396–404.

Freese, J. L., & Amaral, D. G. (2005). The organization of projections from the amygdala to visual cortical areas TE and V1 in the macaque monkey. *Journal of Comparative Neurology*, 486(4), 295–317.

Gothard, K. M., Battaglia, F. P., Erickson, C. A., Spitler, K. M., & Amaral, D. G. (2007). Neural responses to facial expression and face identity in the monkey amygdala. *Journal of Neurophysiology*, 97(2), 1671–83.

Grossberg, S. (1980). How does a brain build a cognitive code? *Psychological Review*, 87(1), 1–51.

Hirano, Y., Stefanovic, B., & Silva, A. C. (2011). Spatiotemporal evolution of the functional magnetic resonance imaging response to ultrashort stimuli. *Journal of Neuroscience*, 31(4), 1440–47.

Ioannides, A. A., Liu, M. J., Liu, L. C., Bamidis, P. D., Hellstrand, E., & Stephan, K. M. (1995). Magnetic field tomography of cortical and deep processes: Examples of "real-time mapping" of averaged and single trial MEG signals. *International Journal of Psychophysiology*, 20(3), 161–75.

Jonides, J. (1981). Voluntary vs. automatic control over the mind's eye's movement. In J. B. Long & A.D. Baddeley (Eds.), *Attention and performance XI* (pp. 187–203). Hillsdale, NJ: Erlbaum.

Jonides, J., & Yantis, S. (1988). Uniqueness of abrupt visual onset in capturing attention. *Attention, Perception, & Psychophysics*, 43(4), 346–54.

Kastner, S., & Ungerleider, L. G. (2000). Mechanisms of visual attention in the human cortex. *Annual Review of Neuroscience*, 23, 315–41.

Koch, C., & Tsuchiya, N. (2007). Attention and consciousness: Two distinct brain processes. *Trends in Cognitive Sciences*, 11(1), 16–22.

Krolak-Salmon, P., Henaff, M. A., Vighetto, A., Bertrand, O., & Mauguiere, F. (2004). Early amygdala reaction to fear spreading in occipital, temporal, and frontal cortex: A depth electrode ERP study in human. *Neuron*, 42(4), 665–76.

Kuraoka, K., & Nakamura, K. (2007). Responses of single neurons in monkey amygdala to facial and vocal emotions. *Journal of Neurophysiology*, 97(2), 1379–87.

Lamme, V. A. (2003). Why visual attention and awareness are different. *Trends in Cognitive Sciences*, 7(1), 12–18.

Lamme, V. A., & Roelfsema, P. R. (2000). The distinct modes of vision offered by feedforward and recurrent processing. *Trends in Neurosciences*, 23(11), 571–79.

Lang, P. J., & Davis, M. (2006). Emotion, motivation, and the brain: Reflex foundations in animal and human research. *Progress in Brain Research*, 156, 3–29.

Lavie, N. (1995). Perceptual load as a necessary condition for selective attention. *Journal of Experimental Psychology: Human Perception and Performance*, 21(3), 451–68.

Lavie, N., & de Fockert, J. W. (2003). Contrasting effects of sensory limits and capacity limits in visual selective attention. *Attention, Perception, & Psychophysics*, 65(2), 202–12.

Leonard, C. M., Rolls, E. T., Wilson, F. A., & Baylis, G. C. (1985). Neurons in the amygdala of the monkey with responses selective for faces. *Behavioural Brain Research*, 15(2), 159–76.

Li, F. F., VanRullen, R., Koch, C., & Perona, P. (2002). Rapid natural scene categorization in the near absence of attention. *Procedings of the National Academy of Sciences*, 99(14), 9596–9601.

Lim, S. L., Padmala, S., & Pessoa, L. (2008). Affective learning modulates spatial competition during low-load attentional conditions. *Neuropsychologia*, 46(5), 1267–78.

Lim, S. L., Padmala, S., & Pessoa, L. (2009). Segregating the significant from the mundane on a moment-to-moment basis via direct and indirect amygdala contributions. *Proceedings of the National Academy of Sciences*, 106(39), 16841–46.

Logan, G. D. (1988). Automaticity, resources, and memory: Theoretical controversies and practical implications. *Human Factors*, 30(5), 583–98.

Luck, S. J., Woodman, G. F., & Vogel, E. K. (2000). Event-related potential studies of attention. *Trends in Cognitive Sciences*, 4, 432–40.

Luo, Q., Holroyd, T., Majestic, C., Cheng, X., Schechter, J., & Blair, R. J. (2010). Emotional automaticity is a matter of timing. *Journal of Neuroscience*, 30(17), 5825–29.

MacLeod, C., Mathews, A., & Tata, P. (1986). Attentional bias in emotional disorders. *Journal of Abnormal Psychology*, 95(1), 15–20.

Marcel, A. J. (1983). Conscious and unconscious perception: Experiments on visual masking and word recognition. *Cognitive Psychology*, 15(2), 197–237.

Milders, M., Sahraie, A., Logan, S., & Donnellon, N. (2006). Awareness of faces is modulated by their emotional meaning. *Emotion*, 6(1), 10–17.

Mitchell, D. G., Nakic, M., Fridberg, D., Kamel, N., Pine, D. S., & Blair, R. J. (2007). The impact of processing load on emotion. *Neuroimage*, 34(3), 1299–1309.

Mormann, F., Kornblith, S., Quiroga, R. Q., Kraskov, A., Cerf, M., Fried, I., & Koch, C. (2008). Latency and selectivity of single neurons indicate hierarchical processing in the human medial temporal lobe. *Journal of Neuroscience*, 28(36), 8865–72.

Morris, J. S., Ohman, A., & Dolan, R. J. (1998). Conscious and unconscious emotional learning in the human amygdala. *Nature*, 393(6684), 467–470.

Most, S. B., Chun, M. M., Widders, D. M., & Zald, D. H. (2005). Attentional rubbernecking: Cognitive control and personality in emotion-induced blindness. *Psychonomic Bulletin & Review*, 12(4), 654–61.

Most, S. B., Scholl, B. J., Clifford, E. R., & Simons, D. J. (2005). What you see is what you set: Sustained inattentional blindness and the capture of awareness. *Psychological Review*, 112(1), 217–42.

Mothes-Lasch, M., Mentzel, H. J., Miltner, W. H., & Straube, T. (2011). Visual attention modulates brain activation to angry voices. *Journal of Neuroscience*, 31(26), 9594–98.

Muller, M. M., Andersen, S. K., & Keil, A. (2008). Time course of competition for visual processing resources between emotional pictures and foreground task. *Cerebral Cortex*, 18(8), 1892–99.

Murphy, K. R., & Myors, B. (2004). *Statistical power analysis: A simple and general model for traditional and modern hypothesis tests* (2nd ed.). Mahwah, NJ: Erlbaum.

Nakamura, K., Mikami, A., & Kubota, K. (1992). Activity of single neurons in the monkey amygdala during performance of a visual discrimination task. *Journal of Neurophysiology*, 67(6), 1447–63.

Nakayama, K., & Joseph, J. S. (1998). Attention, pattern recognition, and pop-out in visual search. In R. Parasuraman (Ed.), *The attentive brain* (pp. 279–98). Cambridge: MIT Press.

Oya, H., Kawasaki, H., Howard, M. A., III, & Adolphs, R. (2002). Electrophysiological responses in the human amygdala discriminate emotion categories of complex visual stimuli. *Journal of Neuroscience, 22*(21), 9502–12.

Padmala, S., Lim, S.-L., & Pessoa, L. (2010). Pulvinar and affective significance: Responses track moment-to-moment visibility. *Frontiers in Human Neuroscience, 4*, 1–9.

Padmala, S., & Pessoa, L. (2008). Affective learning enhances visual detection and responses in primary visual cortex. *Journal of Neuroscience, 28*(24), 6202–10.

Pereira, M. G., Volchan, E., de Souza, G. G., Oliveira, L., Campagnoli, R. R., Pinheiro, W. M., & Pessoa, L. (2006). Sustained and transient modulation of performance induced by emotional picture viewing. *Emotion, 6*(4), 622–634.

Pessoa, L. (2005). To what extent are emotional visual stimuli processed without attention and awareness? *Current Opinions in Neurobiology, 15*(2), 188–96.

Pessoa, L. (2010a). Emergent processes in cognitive-emotional interactions. *Dialogues in Clinical Neuroscience, 12*(4), 433–48.

Pessoa, L. (2010b). Emotion and cognition and the amygdala: From "what is it?" to "what's to be done?" *Neuropsychologia, 48*(12), 3416–29.

Pessoa L. (2010c). Emotion and attention effects: is it all a matter of timing? Not yet. *Frontiers in Human Neuroscience, 4*, 172.

Pessoa, L., & Adolphs, R. (2010). Emotion processing and the amygdala: From a 'low road' to 'many roads' of evaluating biological significance. *Nature Reviews Neuroscience, 11*(11), 773–83.

Pessoa, L., McKenna, M., Gutierrez, E., & Ungerleider, L. G. (2002). Neural processing of emotional faces requires attention. *Proceedings of the National Academy of Sciences, 99*(17), 11458–63.

Pessoa, L., Padmala, S., & Morland, T. (2005). Fate of unattended fearful faces in the amygdala is determined by both attentional resources and cognitive modulation. *NeuroImage, 28*(1), 249–55.

Pessoa, L., & Ungerleider, L. G. (2004). Neuroimaging studies of attention and the processing of emotion-laden stimuli. *Progress in Brain Research, 144*, 171–82.

Piech, R. M., McHugo, M., Smith, S. D., Dukic, M. S., van der Meer, E., Abou-Khali, B., . . . Zald, D. H. (2011). Attentional capture by emotional stimuli is preserved in patients with amygdala lesions. *Neuropsychologia, 49*(12), 3314–19.

Posner, M. I., & Snyder, C. R. R. (1975). Attention and cognitive control. In R. L. Solso (Ed.), *Information processing and cognition: The Loyola symposium* (pp. 55–85). Hillsdale, NJ: Erlbaum.

Pourtois, G., Spinelli, L., Seeck, M., & Vuilleumier, P. (2010). Temporal precedence of emotion over attention modulations in the lateral amygdala: Intracranial ERP evidence from a patient with temporal lobe epilepsy. *Cognitive, Affective, & Behavioral Neuroscience, 10*(1), 83–93.

Raymond, J. E., Shapiro, K. L., & Arnell, K. M. (1992). Temporary suppression of visual processing in an RSVP task: An attentional blink? *Journal of Experimental Psychology: Human Perception and Performance, 18*(3), 849–60.

Rosen, B. R., Buckner, R. L., & Dale, A. M. (1998). Event-related functional MRI: Past, present, and future. *Proceedings of the National Academy of Sciences, 95*(3), 773–80.

Rudrauf, D., David, O., Lachaux, J. P., Kovach, C. K., Martinerie, J., Renault, B., & Damasio, A. (2008). Rapid interactions between the ventral visual stream and emotion-related structures rely on a two-pathway architecture. *Journal of Neuroscience, 28*(11), 2793–2803.

Savoy, R. L., Bandettini, P. A., O'Craven, K. M., Kwong, K. K., Davis, T. L., Baker, J. R., . . . Rosen, B. R. (1995). Pushing the temporal resolution of fMRI: Studies of very brief visual stimuli, onset variability and asynchrony, and stimulus-correlated changes in noise. Presented at the Annual Meeting of the Society of Magnetic Resonance in Nice, France, August.

Schupp, H. T., Junghofer, M., Weike, A. I., & Hamm, A. O. (2003). Attention and emotion: an ERP analysis of facilitated emotional stimulus processing. *Neuroreport, 14*(8), 1107–10.

Schupp, H. T., Stockburger, J., Bublatzky, F., Junghofer, M., Weike, A. I., & Hamm, A. O. (2007). Explicit attention interferes with selective emotion processing in human extrastriate cortex. *BMC Neuroscience, 8*, 16.

Silvert, L., Lepsien, J., Fragopanagos, N., Goolsby, B., Kiss, M., Taylor, J. G., . . . Nobre, A. C. (2007). Influence of attentional demands on the processing of emotional facial expressions in the amygdala. *Neuroimage*, 38(2), 357–66.

Stein, T., Peelen, M. V., Funk, J., & Seidl, K. N. (2010). The fearful-face advantage is modulated by task demands: Evidence from the attentional blink. *Emotion*, 10(1), 136–40.

Streit, M., Dammers, J., Simsek-Kraues, S., Brinkmeyer, J., Wolwer, W., & Ioannides, A. (2003). Time course of regional brain activations during facial emotion recognition in humans. *Neuroscience Letters*, 342(1–2), 101–4.

Tovee, M. J., & Rolls, E. T. (1995). Information encoding in short firing rate epochs by single neurons in the primate temporal visual cortex. *Visual Cognition*, 2(1), 35–58.

Treisman, A. M., & Gelade, G. (1980). A feature-integration theory of attention. *Cognitive Psychology*, 12(1), 97–136.

Tsal, Y., & Benoni, H. (2010). Diluting the burden of load: Perceptual load effects are simply dilution effects. [Research Support, Non-U.S. Gov't]. *Journal of Experimental Psychology: Human Perception and Performance*, 36(6), 1645–56.

Tzelgov, J. (1997). Specifying the relations between automaticity and consciousness: A theoretical note. *Consciousness and Cognition*, 6(2–3), 441–51.

Vuilleumier, P. (2005). How brains beware: Neural mechanisms of emotional attention. *Trends in Cognitive Sciences*, 9(12), 585–94.

Vuilleumier, P., Armony, J. L., Driver, J., & Dolan, R. J. (2001). Effects of attention and emotion on face processing in the human brain: An event-related fMRI study. *Neuron*, 30(3), 829–41.

Vuilleumier, P., Richardson, M. P., Armony, J. L., Driver, J., & Dolan, R. J. (2004). Distant influences of amygdala lesion on visual cortical activation during emotional face processing. *Nature Neuroscience*, 7(11), 1271–78.

Whalen, P. J., Rauch, S. L., Etcoff, N. L., McInerney, S. C., Lee, M. B., & Jenike, M. A. (1998). Masked presentations of emotional facial expressions modulate amygdala activity without explicit knowledge. *Journal of Neuroscience*, 18(1), 411–18.

Wilson, D. E., Muroi, M., & MacLeod, C. M. (2011). Dilution, not load, affects distractor processing. [Research Support, Non-U.S. Gov't]. *Journal of Experimental Psychology: Human Perception and Performance* 37(2), 319–35.

Yoshor, D., Bosking, W. H., Ghose, G. M., & Maunsell, J. H. (2007). Receptive fields in human visual cortex mapped with surface electrodes. *Cerebral Cortex*, 17(10), 2293–2302.

CHAPTER 16

Emotion Regulation

K. Luan Phan & Chandra Sekhar Sripada

Emotions are ever present in our day-to-day lives. We experience emotions when we watch horror movies, listen to amusing stories, witness the birth of our child, ruminate over the death of a loved one, and experience perceived disrespect. Indeed it is hard to imagine a person going through these events without experiencing profound emotions, illustrating the importance of emotions in imbuing structure and meaning to life events. Emotions attach salience to goal-relevant aspects of the environment and, once triggered, bias cognition and action in characteristic ways that have proven to be adaptive across evolutionary time. Emotions are thus often helpful and indeed essential for survival. However, emotions are not always useful or adaptive; they can be problematic when they are exaggerated in intensity, persist for long periods, emerge unpredictably, or are evoked out of context. When emotional reactions are inappropriate, humans are uniquely able to deploy an array of strategies to flexibly modify the experience of emotion. Humans can alter the onset, duration, content, and quality of an emotion experience based on the current situational context in order to respond more effectively to situations and pursue their long-term goals (Gross, 1999).

The past two decades have seen a flood of interest in affective neuroscience in investigating the psychological, social, and biological basis of the production and experience of emotions. Mostly in parallel, the field of cognitive neuroscience has been clarifying the brain basis of higher order cognitive processes such as attention, reasoning, memory, and problem solving. The study of emotion regulation invites a synthesis of theories and findings from these two perspectives. In the study of the cognitive regulation of emotions, "hot" emotional processes (e.g., fear, pleasure, anger) and "cold" cognitive processes (e.g., decision making, memory, attention) are inextricably linked (also see Chapters 14, 15, and 17). This chapter draws on existing frameworks for understanding emotion regulation to critically review a large and growing body of work in affective and cognitive neuroscience on the cognitive regulation of emotion. It focuses on studies employing neuroimaging, which is one powerful and widely used method to delineate the neural mechanisms underlying the capacity to flexibly alter and refine the experience of emotions in humans.

What Is Emotion Regulation?

To understand emotion regulation, it is critical to gain a clearer understanding of emotion. According to current integrative models (Levenson, 1994), emotions consist of transient, valenced responses that are elicited by prototypical environmental situations (see Chapter 1). Once triggered, they produce a coordinated suite of changes across multiple cognitive and physiological systems, and they generate specific tendencies to act. Additionally, they are typically accompanied by distinctive subjective feelings and facial expressions. It is useful to divide the unfolding of an emotion into a perception/appraisal stage and response phase, though doing so does not imply that the stages are temporally non-overlapping or that the causal links between the stages are unidirectional. In the perception/appraisal stage, the individual confronts a situation and allocates attention to its key perceptual features. Additionally, the person engages in cognitive appraisals, which can be fast and automatic or slower, deliberate evaluations of how the situation relates to his or her goals (Ortony, Clore, & Collins, 1990). These goals can be momentary or enduring; they can be held consciously with volitional intent or reflexively without awareness (Gross & Thompson, 2007). Specific emotions are then triggered depending on how the situation is appraised relative to the person's goals (e.g., fear is triggered if a core survival-related goal is threatened, anger is triggered if a goal is frustrated, and so on) (Ortony et al., 1990).

Turning now to the response stage, emotions are expressed across multiple response systems including (1) cognitive systems (attention, memory; see Chapters 15 and 20); (2) physiological systems (parasympathetic/sympathetic tone, peripheral vasculature; see Chapter 3); and (3) motivation/action systems (see Chapter 19). These coordi-

nated effects across response systems can be seen as evolutionary-conserved "response profiles" that have proven to be effective in recurrent adaptive challenges (Nesse, 1990). For example, the emotion of fear arising from an impromptu encounter with a snake promotes a coordinated sequence of adaptive responses including enhanced sympathetic arousal, freezing, recoil, and withdrawal.

Although emotions specify certain prototypical ways of appraising and responding to recurrent situations in the environment, many aspects of the unfolding of an emotion are nonetheless importantly subject to modification. For example, whereas some appraisals are often thought to be fast, automatic, and largely outside conscious awareness (Ortony et al., 1990), others may be subsequently modified thorough conscious, volitional strategies. Additionally, autonomic responses and action tendencies associated with an emotion can be modulated or suppressed (Gross, 1998; Gross & Thompson, 2007). Indeed, the foregoing description of emotions raises the possibility that there are multiple points during the unfolding of an emotion where a person can intervene to modulate or alter the emotion in fundamental respects, and in the third section we discuss specific strategies for emotion regulation that have been developed and elaborated by Gross (Gross, 1998, 1999, 2002; Gross & Thompson, 2007).

Two terminological caveats are in order. First, it can be argued that emotion regulation could also encompass the processes by which emotions *regulate* thoughts and actions (i.e., regulation *by* emotions; Campos, Frankel, & Camras, 2004). Indeed, a parallel literature has emerged regarding the processes by which emotions can affect sensory perception and cognitive functions such as attention, working memory, and decision making and their associated brain substrates; a detailed discussion of this literature can be found in Chapters 14 and 16. For example, emotional information can facilitate or interfere with cognitive processes such as threat-mediated avoidance and appetitive-mediated approach, which are known to facilitate behavioral responding and activation in the amgydala and ventral striatum, respectively (see Chapter 19). However, Gross has noted that if "emotion regulation" also refers to ways by which emotions coordinate and regulate subsequent responding (and cognition) then the term itself is redundant with that of "emotion" – as such, all situations that involve emotion would also involve emotion regulation (Gross, 1999, 2002), suggesting that using the term "emotion regulation" to refer to the cognitive regulation of emotion rather than vice versa has certain advantages.

Second, the concept of emotion could be interpreted broadly to encompass several other related psychological states – affect, mood, feeling, motivation. In the literature, these terms are at times used interchangeably, and in human imaging neuroscience research they are all often studied using identical or closely related paradigms. It has been argued that emotion differs from mood in that the former involves a discrete mental state change and is associated with a specified duration and/or with an identifiable trigger. Nonetheless, it is not yet clear whether the difference between emotion and mood is critical for emotion regulation research or whether, for the purposes of studying regulation, we could subsume emotion, mood, and related concepts such as stress response and motivational impulse under the broader concept of "affect" (Gross & Thompson, 2007). In what follows, we focus on the regulation of "emotion" and allow that future work may demonstrate that a broader concept of affect regulation may be more justified or meaningful.

In sum, emotion regulation is defined here as the processes by which emotional responses are interrupted and/or altered such that the experience and expression of emotional states are different from the case in which they are left unregulated. Regulation can potentially alter features along multiple dimensions of the emotion episode, including latency (when it starts), time to peak (how fast it emerges), magnitude (how intensely it manifests), duration (how long it lasts), and pace of offset (how slowly it

dissipates). This chapter focuses on the neural mechanisms that underlie emotion regulation: What is the brain basis by which people regulate their experience of emotions?

Why Is Emotion Regulation Important?

The importance of emotion regulation can be appreciated by recognizing its roots in a number of influential psychological traditions, including work on psychological defenses against impulses and inhibition of anxious states (Freud, 1946), coping under stress (Lazarus, 1966), parent-child attachment (Bowlby, 1969), cognitive-behavioral strategies to treat depression (Beck, 1963), and emotional growth and development (Thompson, 1994). Moreover, dysregulated emotion is a prominent part of the clinical phenotype in more than half of the classified mental disorders, and contemporary process models of psychopathology centrally implicate faulty, insufficient, or absent emotion regulation. Even in psychiatric illnesses that are not conceptualized as disorders of emotion, emotion regulation may nonetheless be important. For example, in substance use disorders, difficulty with coping with day-to-day stress is linked to worsened control of drug-directed impulses, undermining attempts at abstinence and treatment success, and increasing vulnerability to relapse back to addiction (Fox, Hong, & Sinha, 2008). Moreover, the benefits of an effective capacity to regulate emotion extends beyond "psychiatric" illness to a broader sense of well-being; for example, greater use of emotion regulation strategies by hemodialysis patients improves subjective well-being and self-management of their kidney disease (Gillanders, Wild, Deighan, & Gillanders, 2008), and interventions aimed at improving emotion regulation lead to physical and psychosocial improvement for patients with medical or psychiatric illness (Smyth & Arigo, 2009). In short, emotion regulation has a far-reaching impact on multiple aspects of health, disease, and interpersonal functioning and is now recognized as a critical

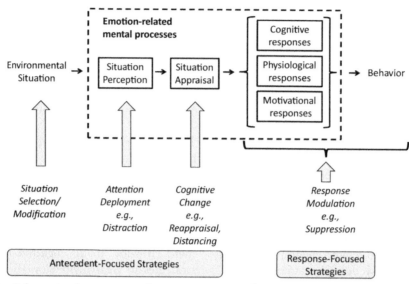

Figure 16.1. Schematic of emotion regulation strategies in which each strategy targets a specific phase during an unfolding process model of emotion.

area of study in psychology, psychiatry, and neuroscience.

What Strategies Are Deployed during Emotion Regulation?

Earlier, we described a model of emotions dividing the unfolding of emotions into a perception/appraisal stage and a response stage. The schematic illustrated in Figure 16.1 provides the backdrop for the studies discussed in this chapter and is derived from the contemporary and influential model of emotion regulation developed by Gross and colleagues, who propose a number of strategies that intervene during the unfolding emotional episode at relatively specific places (Gross, 1998, 1999, 2002; Gross & Thompson, 2007). First, at least two *antecedent-focused* (or prior to behavioral responding) strategies occur at the stage of perception/appraisal before the emotional response is evoked: (1) "situation selection" or taking actions to change the likelihood that the situation will lead to the un/desired emotional outcome and (2) "situation modification" or changing the situation to alter its emotional impact. Second, during the appraisal phase, two additional antecedent-focused strate-

gies can be deployed: (1) "attentional deployment" or directing attention toward/away from the inciting stimulus within the situation to change its emotional impression and (2) "cognitive change" or modifying the evaluation of the situation to change its meaning or emotional significance. Lastly, "response modulation" refers to changing the reaction after the emotional/behavioral response has been generated and represents a *response-focused* emotion regulation strategy; here, response modulation is conceptualized as an alteration that can occur in the internal (e.g., heart rate change) or external (e.g., facial expression change) milieu.

As with all frameworks used to describe a relatively new, rapidly growing, and changing domain of research, the model conceptualized by Gross and colleagues does not encompass all elements that may be involved, as they note and acknowledge (see, for example, Gross & Thompson, 2007). First, emotion is a dynamic process, and the path from stimulus/situation to response may not always proceed in a stepwise sequential fashion, continuous feedback and feedforward could occur at each step, and steps could be skipped as an emotion unfolds. Second, emotion regulation is an interactive process, by which one strategy can influence the emergence or impact of another strategy. Third, attempts to regulate emotion are iterative, additive, and/or synergistic. We humans likely use trial and error to test which among many candidates is the best strategy to use at the moment given the situation; we likely adopt and try more than one strategy at any given time; and we are likely to order and reorder strategies based on their immediate success at modifying the emotional response according to our goals. Despite these observations, the model proposed by Gross is nonetheless a straightforward and highly useful heuristic based on a synthesis of convergent ideas over the past decades about how we generate and regulate emotions (Gross, 1999). A number of human neuroscience studies using functional brain imaging techniques (mostly functional magnetic resonance imaging [fMRI], but also positron emission tomography [PET] and event-related potential electroencephalography [ERP EEG]) have experimentally probed these component processes and their neural correlates. The following section reviews, organizes, and critically evaluates these findings.

As a prelude, it is worth noting that contemporary research in human imaging neuroscience has focused primarily on volitional, effortful, cognitive strategies – attentional deployment and cognitive change – and less on those that involve antecedent attempts to select and modify the external environment/situation or on those that occur automatically or without conscious awareness. This focus is partly driven by the limiting confines of the functional brain imaging environment, which make it more difficult to approximate real-life scenarios and behaviors, and by the lack of validated techniques to objectively measure and ascribe brain-function interpretations of unconscious phenomena. Nonetheless, the growing literature on the functional neuroanatomy of the cognitive control of emotion has richly informed us about the brain mechanisms by which cognitive strategies can modify subjective and neural correlates of emotions, and it is producing convergent findings across studies and laboratories.

Successes of the existing literature thus prompt extending our investigation to hitherto less tractable processes related to how we regulate our emotions.

As with all studies that couple functional brain imaging methods and experimental tasks and that make brain-behavior inferences from observations of changes in maps of brain "activation," it is worthwhile to inquire about additional evidence (other than patterns of *differences* in brain activation) that supports the interpretation that regulation was successful and change in emotion has indeed occurred. Such corroborating data should come from more than just the brain readout of emotions. First, an index of "regulation success" can be derived from subjective awareness of change in the intensity of affect or arousal, as measured by asking subjects to rate their emotional state during the course of the imaging experiment. Second, changes in peripheral physiology can also mark the change as measured by skin conductance, startle reflexes, and/or cardiac-respiratory reactivity. Third, emotion modification can also be indexed by changes in central brain responses. There are rich, growing, and converging data from animal and human lesion studies and human functional imaging studies that implicate a set of brain regions during the appraisal, processing, and generation of emotions; see Chapters 6–13 as well as previous reviews and meta-analyses (Adolphs, 2002; Fusar-Poli et al., 2009; Phan et al., 2003).

Chief among these brain regions is the amygdala, thought of as the gateway to emotional expression and perception (Adolphs, 2002). Most relevant to the topic of emotion regulation in humans, several studies have observed that the extent to which amygdala reacts is in part dependent on (1) the amount of perceived threat, (2) the magnitude of subjective and physiological arousal, and/or (3) the salience of the stimulus/environmental change (Adolphs, 2002; Phan et al., 2003). In addition, a set of paralimbic structures are increasingly recognized as part of an emotion sensing and generating circuit in humans including, though not limited to, the insula (Craig, 2009), ventral

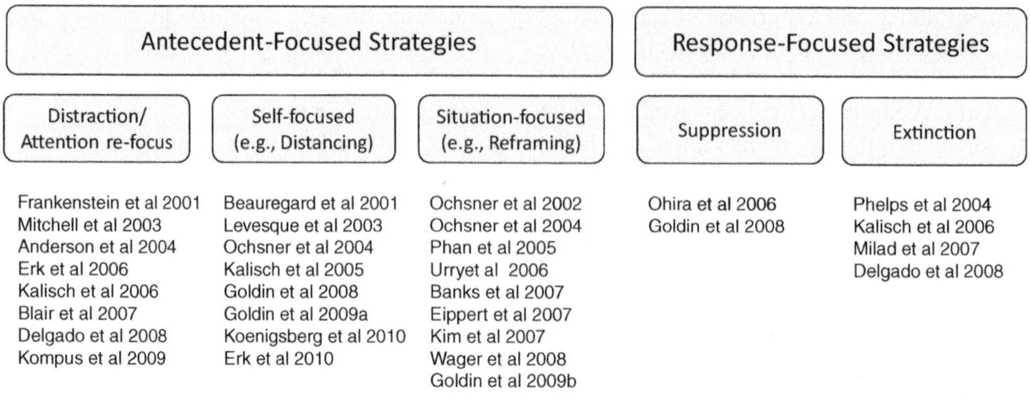

Antecedent-Focused Strategies			Response-Focused Strategies	
Distraction/ Attention re-focus	Self-focused (e.g., Distancing)	Situation-focused (e.g., Reframing)	Suppression	Extinction
Frankenstein et al 2001	Beauregard et al 2001	Ochsner et al 2002	Ohira et al 2006	Phelps et al 2004
Mitchell et al 2003	Levesque et al 2003	Ochsner et al 2004	Goldin et al 2008	Kalisch et al 2006
Anderson et al 2004	Ochsner et al 2004	Phan et al 2005		Milad et al 2007
Erk et al 2006	Kalisch et al 2005	Urryet al 2006		Delgado et al 2008
Kalisch et al 2006	Goldin et al 2008	Banks et al 2007		
Blair et al 2007	Goldin et al 2009a	Eippert et al 2007		
Delgado et al 2008	Koenigsberg et al 2010	Kim et al 2007		
Kompus et al 2009	Erk et al 2010	Wager et al 2008		
		Goldin et al 2009b		

Figure 16.2. Representative citations of functional neuroimaging studies investigating brain correlates of the various emotion regulation strategies.

striatum including the nucleus accumbens, and orbitofrontal cortex (OFC; Rolls, 2000). Moreover, negative emotional experience and attempts to *maintain* negative affect are also associated with increases in amygdala and insula activity. Compared against a control condition involving passive viewing of negatively valenced pictures, actively maintaining a negative emotional state leads to greater self-reported negative affect and greater amygdala reactivity (Schaefer et al., 2002). Moreover, volitional self-induced sadness has been shown to lead to greater negative affect, which was correlated with increased amygdala activation (Posse et al., 2003). Interestingly, greater self-reported regular/day-to-day use of reappraisal is associated with decreased amygdala activity and increased PFC and parietal engagement when processing negative information during fMRI scanning (Drabant, McRae, Manuck, Hariri, & Gross, 2009). Thus, a number of functional neuroimaging studies of emotion regulation (summarized in Figure 16.2 and discussed later) have focused on these structures broadly, and on the amygdala in particular, as neural markers for the efficacy of regulation in altering emotion. Here, the neural representations of emotion regulation, classified as cognitive control over emotion, can be subsumed under a broader construct of bidirectional emotion-cognition interactions, as noted in Figure 16.3 and earlier reviews (Ochsner & Gross, 2005, 2007). To date, regions of interest represent the current conceptualization that different brain regions are segregated in function or modules. However, as our understanding of brain function increases and we advance more sophisticated analyses of brain activity, we will likely deepen our understanding that an integrated (rather than segregated) neural network subserves the multiple strategies for regulation of emotion.

What Are the Functional Brain Mechanisms that Implement Emotion Regulation?

Perception Change: Attentional Control and Distraction

Perception change refers to the emotion regulatory process by which we can alter what we perceive or become aware of directly through our senses, especially vision. It includes how we control our attentional stance (i.e., "attentional deployment") by looking toward or away from emotionally salient (aversive or pleasant) cues in the environment. For example, to down-regulate affect, we can use distraction to refocus our attention to a different aspect of the stimulus to lessen its emotional impact; we may direct our gaze from the eyes to the nose when looking at someone who expresses anger, or we can focus our attention on how wide the nose is rather than how angry that person is. Similarly, we can

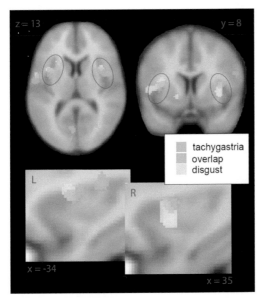

Figure 3.4. Co-localization of insula activations to subjective feelings of disgust and associated increase in tachygastric responses. The figure shows brain regions activated to the experience of disgust (both core and body-boundary-violation) in yellow and the associated tachygastric response in blue. Commonly activated regions illustrated in green show that insula regions underpinning subjective feelings of disgust also provide a representation of peripheral gastric responses. Activations illustrated at $p < 0.005$. Reproduced with permission from Harrison et al., *Journal of Neuroscience* (2010), 30(38):12878–84.

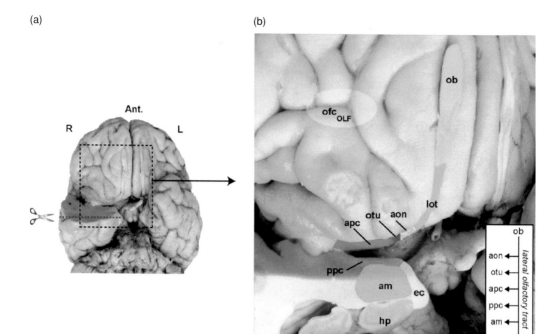

Figure 10.1. **Anatomy of the human olfactory brain. (a)** A ventral view of the human brain in which the right anterior temporal lobe has been resected in the coronal plane to expose the limbic olfactory areas depicted in panel **(b)**. Afferent output from the olfactory bulb (OB) passes through the lateral olfactory tract (LOT) and projects monosynaptically to numerous regions, including the anterior olfactory nucleus (AON), olfactory tubercle (OTUB), anterior piriform cortex (APC), posterior piriform cortex (PPC), amygdala (AM), and entorhinal cortex (EC). Downstream relays include the hippocampus (HP) and the putative olfactory projection site in the human orbitofrontal cortex (OFColf). As noted in the inset, information is not transferred serially through this circuit. Monosynaptic projections from the lateral olfactory tract reach numerous downstream regions in parallel, and these regions are then reciprocally interconnected (not shown). Adapted from Gottfried (2010).

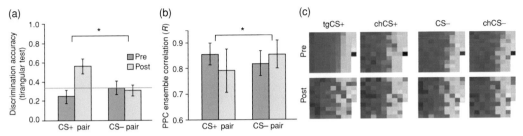

Figure 10.2. Role of olfactory cortical areas in aversive learning. In an fMRI version of olfactory fear learning, subjects smelled pairs of odor enantiomers that were perceptually indistinguishable. One of these enantiomers, designated the target CS+ (tgCS+), was subsequently paired with mild footshock. Neither its chiral counterpart (chCS+) nor a control pair (CS- and chCS-) was paired with shock. From preconditioning to postconditioning, perceptual discrimination between tgCS+ and chCS+ selectively increased (a), in parallel with fMRI ensemble decorrelation (less pattern overlap) in PPC (b). Ensemble activation maps across PPC voxels in one subject (c) show increasing pattern divergence between tgCS+ and chCS+ after learning. Adapted from Li et al. (2008).

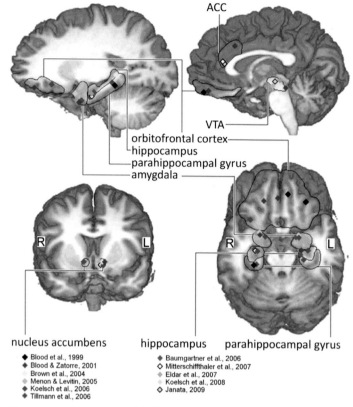

ACC

VTA

orbitofrontal cortex
hippocampus
parahippocampal gyrus
amygdala

R   L   R   L

nucleus accumbens   hippocampus   parahippocampal gyrus

◆ Blood et al., 1999   ◆ Baumgartner et al., 2006
◆ Blood & Zatorre, 2001   ◇ Mitterschiffthaler et al., 2007
   Brown et al., 2004   ◆ Eldar et al., 2007
◆ Menon & Levitin, 2005   Koelsch et al., 2008
◆ Koelsch et al., 2006   ◇ Janata, 2009
◆ Tillmann et al., 2006

Figure 12.1. Illustration of limbic (amygdala, nucleus accumbens, anterior cingulate cortex [AAC], and hippocampus) and paralimbic structures (orbitofrontal cortex, parahippocampal gyrus). The diamonds represent music-evoked activity changes in these structures (see figure legend for references and the main text for details). Note the repeatedly reported activations of amygdala, nucleus accumbens, and hippocampus, reflecting that music is capable of modulating activity in core structures of emotion (see the text for details). Top left: view of the right hemisphere; top right: medial view; bottom left: anterior view; bottom right: bottom view.

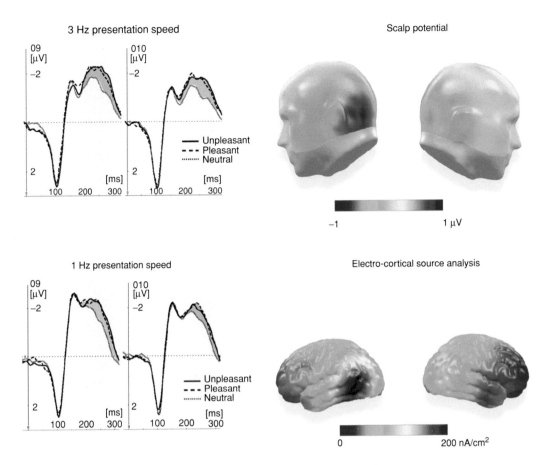

Figure 13.4. Left panel: During the reading of emotionally arousing nouns, event-related cortical potentials are found to be amplified in comparison to neutral words. This amplification can be found for a variety of stimulation rates (top left, 3 Hz; bottom left, 1 Hz) and takes the form of an early posterior negativity (EPN) occurring around 250 ms after word onset. It shows a broad occipitotemporal scalp distribution with a left-hemisphere preponderance. The sources of this activity are localized in predominantly left posterior-temporal cortical regions. Adapted from Kissler et al. (2007).

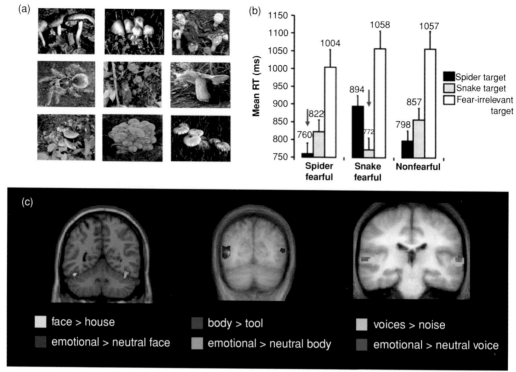

Figure 14.1. Effects of the emotional meaning of stimuli on attention and brain responses. **(A)** Example of a visual search task where an emotional target (spider or snake) must be detected (present/absent) among neutral images (mushrooms). **(B)** Search performance (response time, RT) of spider fearful, snake fearful, and nonfearful participants. Fearful participants were faster at detecting their feared targets, compared to both nonfeared (but still fear-relevant) and nonemotional targets. Adapted from Flykt & Caldara (2006). **(C)** Blood-oxygenation-level-dependent (BOLD) response observed with fMRI shows a precise overlap between emotional modulation effects and category-selective areas for face (fusiform face area; FFA), body (extrastriate body area; EBA), and voice processing, demonstrating that the emotional modulation is category specific. Adapted from Vuilleumier et al. (2001), Grandjean et al., (2005) and Peelen et al. (2007).

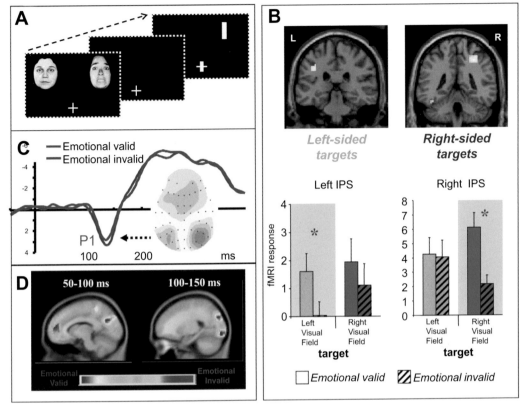

Figure 14.2. Typical pattern of neural responses elicited by emotional cues in a spatial dot-probe task. **(A)** In this task, targets (vertical or horizontal bars) are always preceded by pairs of faces, one neutral and one emotional, which do not predict the side of target presentation. To avoid eye movements, participants are instructed to press a response button when the orientation of the bar presented in the left or right upper visual field matches that of the thicker segment in the fixation cross. Adapted from Pourtois, Grandjean, Sander, & Vuilleumier (2004). **(B)** Targets preceded by neutral cues at the same location (i.e., with fearful cues presented contralaterally; that is, *emotional invalid* cues) lead to reduced fMRI responses in the intraparietal sulcus (IPS) ipsilateral to the target, relative to when targets are preceded by emotional cues on the same side (*emotional valid*). This suggests a capture of attention by the contralateral emotional cue and a reduced ability to reorient to the target. Adapted from Pourtois, Schwartz, Seghier, Lazeyras, & Vuilleumier (2006). **(C)** During EEG recording, targets preceded by emotional cues (*emotional valid*) elicit a larger visual P1 component, relative to those preceded by neutral cues (*emotional invalid*). This is consistent with enhanced visual processing of targets when cued by emotion. Adapted from Pourtois et al. (2004). **(D)** Neural source estimation for EEG modulations at different latencies after *target* onset. When the target is preceded by an emotional valid cue, activity to the target is first increased in parietal areas (50–100 ms), presumably reflecting top-down attentional signals induced by the emotional cue and responsible for faster spatial orienting to the target location and enhanced processing in extrastriate visual cortex at the P1 latency (100–150 ms). When targets are preceded by an invalid neutral cue, increased activity is observed in the anterior cingulate cortex instead, reflecting some interference and conflict in attentional orienting due to initial capture by the fearful face on the opposite side. Adapted from Pourtois, Thut, Grave de Peralta, Michel, & Vuilleumier (2005).

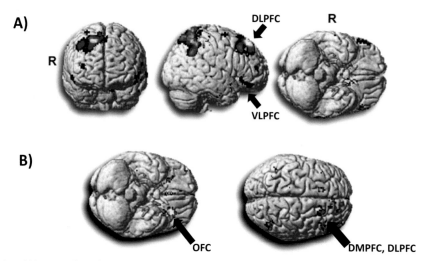

Figure 16.4. (A) Lateral prefrontal cortex engagement during reappraisal. Greater activation of right DLPFC, bilateral VLPFC, and right superior parietal cortex during reappraise (vs. maintain/look) negative images; concurrent activations in OFC, dmPFC, and dorsal ACC not shown. Data from Phan et al. (2005). (B) Task-dependent amygdala-frontal connectivity during reappraisal. Greater coupling of bilateral OFC, bilateral DLPFC, dmPFC, and parietal cortex during reappraise (vs. maintain/look) negative images; amygdala-subgengual ACC not shown. Data from Banks et al. (2008).

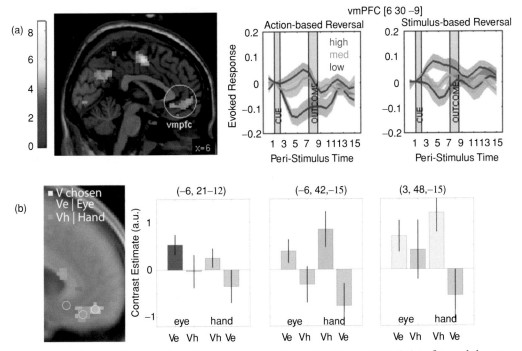

Figure 17.2. Chosen value signals tied to actions as well as stimuli in vmPFC. (A) Left panel depicts vmPFC area showing common correlations with chosen values in both an action-based choice task and a stimulus-based choice task. Right panel shows evoked responses in this region as a function of different levels of chosen value (low, medium, high). Data from Glascher et al., (2009). (B) Left panel shows areas of vmPFC exhibiting correlations with chosen values that depend on the specific action implemented on that choice. Areas correlating with chosen values for eye movements only are shown in red, areas correlating with chosen values for hand movements are shown in green, whereas areas correlating with chosen values regardless of the effector modality of the action involved are shown in yellow. The right panel shows the parameter estimates for the value signals for each movement separately from each region, as depicting by the color code (Vh = action value of hand movement; Ve = action value of eye movement). For example, the plot with the red bar indicates significant responses to the value of an eye movement only if that movement is chosen (but not otherwise). Data from Wunderlich et al., (2009).

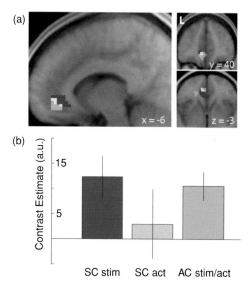

Figure 17.3. Evidence for pure stimulus-based chosen value signals in vmPFC. (A) Area exhibiting significant correlations with the value of a stimulus that is ultimately chosen is shown in red. This signal is from trials where the stimuli are presented before the actions needed to select those stimuli are made available. The area in green is also a chosen value signal, but from trials where both stimuli and actions are presented simultaneously. The area in yellow shows overlap between the two signals. (B) Plots of parameter estimates corresponding to chosen value signals from these regions (red and green color code as in A; SC stim = chosen value at time of stimulus from condition where stimuli are presented before actions are made available; SC action = chosen value at time of action selection (once actions are revealed) from stimulus condition; AC stim/act = chosen value signals from condition when both stimuli and actions are revealed simultaneously).

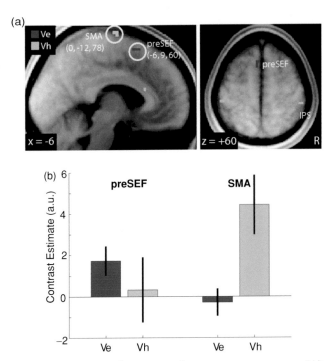

Figure 17.4. Action values in supplementary motor cortex. (A) Region of supplementary motor area and pre-supplementary eye fields correlating with action values for hand movements (green; Vh), and eye movements (red, Ve), respectively. (B) Plot of parameter estimates depicting correlations with action values for eye and hand movements in these areas.

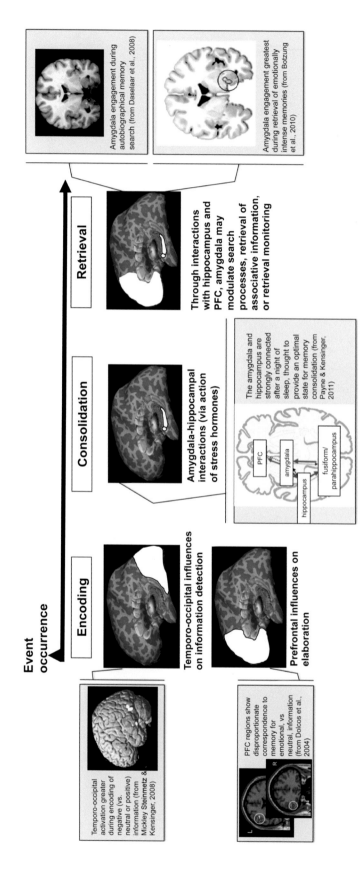

Figure 20.1. The basic mechanisms through which the emotional content of an experience can influence the way in which it is remembered.

Pride x Positive Self-Agency

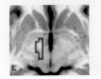

Temporal lobe activity common across all conditions

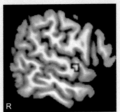

Gratitude x Positive Other-Agency

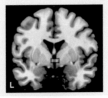

Guilt x Negative Self-Agency

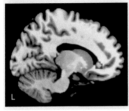

Indignation/Anger x Negative Other-Agency

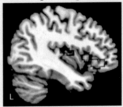

Figure 21.2. Using fMRI in healthy participants this study investigated the neuroanatomical basis of abstract moral and social values (figure adapted from Zahn, Moll, Paiva. et al., 2009). Participants had to imagine actions in accordance with or counter to a value described by a written sentence and to decide whether they would feel pleasantly or unpleasantly about the action. After the scan they rated the unpleasantness/pleasantness on a scale and chose labels that best described their feelings (the analysis compares each moral sentiment versus visual fixation and versus two other moral sentiments; only selective effects were reported). There were four experimental conditions: (1) positive self-agency: "Tom (first name of participant) acts generously toward Sam (first name of best friend)"– pride in this condition was associated with ventral tegmental, septal, and ventral medial FPC activation (not depicted); 2) positive other-agency: "Sam acts generously toward Tom" – gratitude in this condition was associated with hypothalamic activation; (3) negative self-agency: "Tom acts stingily toward Sam" – guilt in this condition was associated with subgenual cingulate cortex as well as ventral medial FPC activation (not depicted and only when modeling individual frequency of guilt trials); and (4) negative other-agency: "Sam acts stingily toward Tom" – indignation/anger in this condition was associated with lateral orbitofrontal/insular activation. In the center, one can see the right superior aTL region showing equally strong activation during all moral sentiment and agency contexts; this region showed increased activity with increasing richness of conceptual details describing social behavior and is identical to the activation found in a semantic judgment task (Zahn et al., 2007). These results confirmed the right superior anterior temporal lobe as a context-independent store of social conceptual knowledge that allows us to understand the core meaning of social and moral values regardless of what exact feelings or actions we tie to the value.

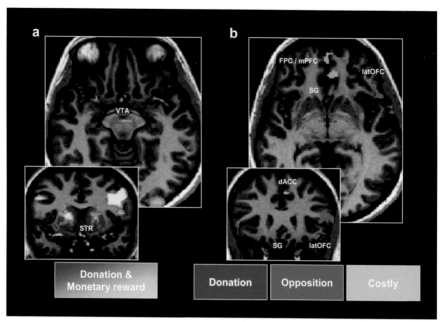

Figure 21.3. Brain regions activated when participants donated or were opposed to donate to charitable organizations during fMRI (Moll et al., 2006); figure adapted from Moll & Schulkin (2009). (a) Both pure monetary rewards and decisions to donate (with or without personal financial costs) activated the mesolimbic reward system, including the ventral tegmental area (VTA) and the ventral and dorsal striatum. (b) The septal-subgenual region (SG), however, was selectively activated by decisions to donate, as compared with pure monetary rewards (both by costly and noncostly decisions, conjunction analysis). The lateral orbitofrontal cortex (latOFC) was activated by decisions to oppose charities. This activation extended to the anterior insula and to the inferior dorsolateral PFC and was present both for costly and noncostly decisions (conjunction analysis). The FPC and ventral medial PFC (mPFC) were activated for costly decisions (when voluntarily sacrificing one's own money either to donate to a charity or to oppose it (conjunction analysis).

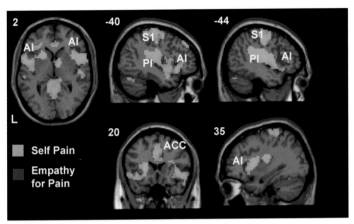

Figure 23.2. Shared and distinct neural networks for
self-experienced pain and empathy for pain. Depicted functional
neural activations are the result of a meta-analysis based on nine
fMRI studies investigating empathy for pain (Lamm et al., 2011).
Activations related to self-experienced pain (green) encompass a
large portion of the insula, including the middle and posterior
insular cortex, whereas activations related to empathy for pain (red)
are restricted to the most anterior parts of AI, where they overlap
with activations related to self-experienced pain. Functional
activation maps are overlaid on a high-resolution structural MRI
scan in standard stereotactic space (MNI space). White labels
indicate slice number in stereotactic space, L = left hemisphere, AI
= anterior insula, ACC = anterior cingulated cortex, PI = posterior
insula, S1 = primary somatosensory cortex. With permission from
Springer Science+Business Media: Brain Structure and Function,
The role of anterior insular cortex in social emotions, 214, 2010,
p. 581, Lamm, C., & Singer, T., Figure 1.

a) Condition by Group interaction in ventromedial PFC for Affective ToM relative to Physical Causality

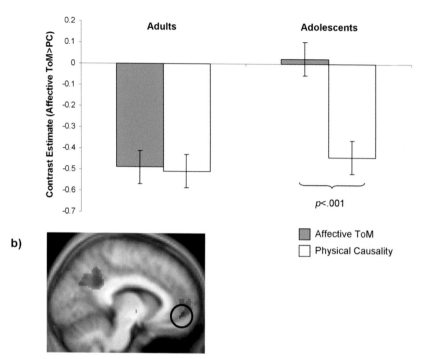

b)

Figure 27.1. Recent studies suggest that development of the functional neural bases of complex affective processing continues between adolescence and adulthood. This figure shows a region of the ventromedial prefrontal cortex (peak voxel: −10 46 8) that responded to a greater extent in adolescent males (mean age 14.1 years; n = 15) than in matched adult controls during the presentation of cartoon scenarios requiring affective Theory of Mind (understanding emotions in a social context) relative to those requiring cause-and-effect reasoning (physical causality). Group differences in this region were not seen in response to scenarios requiring cognitive Theory of Mind (mentalizing), suggesting that integrating affective and social cognition may represent a unique challenge for the developing adolescent brain. Figure adapted from Sebastian et al. (2011).

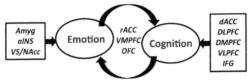

Figure 16.3. A brain-process model of cognition-emotion interactions in the context of emotion regulation. *Abbreviations*: Amyg, amygdala; aINS, anterior insula; VS, ventral striatum; NAcc, nucleus accumbens; rACC, rostral anterior cingulate cortex; VMPFC, ventral medial prefrontal cortex; OFC, orbitofrontal cortex; dACC, dorsal anterior cingulate cortex; DLPFC, dorsolateral prefrontal cortex; DMPFC, dorsal medial prefrontal cortex; VLPFC, ventrolateral prefrontal cortex; IFG, inferior frontal gyrus.

alter perception by evoking thoughts that are completely unrelated to the stimulus (i.e., thought distraction) or by engaging in tasks that command a shift of attention away from the stimulus (e.g., cognitive distraction). To up-regulate affect, the opposing strategy would be to focus directly and persistently on the most evocative aspects of the salient cue (i.e., concentration, rumination), thereby evoking more emotional responding. Of course, unless there is an explicit effortful attempt to knowingly direct attention by an individual, many forms of perception change are automatic, proceed below the threshold of conscious awareness, and thus are less amenable to functional neuroimaging investigation.

Here we start with studies that experimentally manipulate the direction of attention by instructing subjects to pay attention to the nonemotional/nonperceptual aspects of an evocative stimulus (versus to the emotional aspects). It is hypothesized that allocating attention to or away from emotionally provocative stimuli should modulate the extent of activation of brain systems responsible for emotional appraisal/generation/responding (e.g., the amygdala, ventral striatum including nucleus accumbens, insula, and ventral PFC including OFC). For example, Gur and colleagues showed that focusing on the age of an emotional face (versus

on the emotional expression) is associated with less amygdala reactivity (Gur et al., 2002); because the former task is associated with greater effort (e.g., slowed reaction time), it is inferred that task difficulty diverted focus away from the emotional features (i.e., less attention, less emotional engagement). The notion that amygdala responses are dependent on attention allocation and are linked with top-down mechanisms is supported by a number of studies by Pessoa et al. on emotional face processing (see Chapter 15 for a review). Although several prefrontal brain areas including the anterior cingulate cortex (ACC) and dorsolateral prefrontal cortex (DLPFC) are thought to implement attentional control (Carter, Botvinick, & Cohen, 1999), few of the earlier noted studies assessed or reported whether these or other prefrontal brain areas are specifically recruited during the allocation of attention away from emotional aspects of stimuli. Interestingly, Kompus and colleagues showed that directing attention away from the negative emotion displayed on faces (from labeling the angry, fearful, or neutral expression toward rating attractiveness of the person) was associated with greater activation of anterior/ventral medial prefrontal cortex (MPFC) and superior parietal gyrus and decreased amygdala reactivity (Kompus, Hugdahl, Ohman, Marklund, & Nyberg, 2009).

Another type of manipulation of attention allocation comes from studies that redistribute attentional resources *away* from the emotion task. For example, a study by Erk et al. showed that graded cognitive distraction (using a working memory load manipulation) engages the DLPFC, ventrolateral PFC (VLPFC), ACC, and inferior parietal cortex during the anticipation of emotional stimuli (i.e., negative words) and down-regulates anterior MPFC and amygdala activation (Erk, Abler, & Walter, 2006). Blair and colleagues specifically identified the VLPFC as engaged during goal-directed, load-driven processing of incongruent distracters, while attenuating amygdala reactivity to both negative and positively valenced images (Blair et al., 2007). Moreover, the authors observed negative connectivity between the VLPFC and amygdala, and positive connectivity between VLPFC and dorsal ACC and superior frontal gyrus, including DLPFC, consistent with current models of emotion regulation circuitry (Ochsner, 2004, Ochsner & Gross, 2005).

However, two points should be noted. First, the observation that directing attention away from emotional inputs can effectively dampen amygdala reactivity is in contrast to the prevailing view that amygdalar emotional processing, particularly fear processing, is carried out in an automatic manner, with little dependence on attentional resources (Anderson, Christoff, Panitz, De Rosa, & Gabrieli, 2003; Whalen et al., 1998). Second, the findings that attention modification is an effective regulator of emotional reactivity in the brain have been inconsistent. For example, several studies have observed that amygdala responses *increase* when participants attend to perceptual (rather than emotional) features (e.g., Critchley, et al., 2000; Hariri, Bookheimer, & Mazziotta, 2000). A recent meta-analysis did confirm this variability in findings but reported that, on the whole across studies, implicit processing of emotional faces (e.g., attention directed to nonemotional features) is associated with *less* amygdala reactivity compared to explicit processing of emotional faces (e.g., attention to emotional expressions; Fusar-Poli et al., 2009),

As an alternative strategy to modify attentional allocation, some studies have investigated the neurocircuitry subserving *thought distraction*, whereby subjects are instructed to use an alternative focus of attention (e.g., self-generated focus or focus on incidental external/internal stimuli) rather than the emotional content of the stimulus. Kalisch and colleagues asked participants to self-distract away from anticipatory anxiety for pain ("suppress any thought or feeling of anxiety or about the shock"). Thought distraction was inconclusively associated with reduction of behavioral measures of anxiety and was associated only with tonic activation of left LPFC (nearby DLPFC), suggesting that self-distraction by this method may

be less effective than other cognitive change strategies to regulate anxiety and emotional reactivity (Kalisch, Wiech, Herrmann, & Dolan, 2006). This finding is in contrast with another study that employed a distracting verbal attention task in the context of cold pressor pain induction; it found rostral ACC, not LPFC, activation during cognitive distraction from pain (Frankenstein, Richter, McIntyre, & Remy, 2001).

Self-generation of autobiographical memories, particularly those that are incongruent with the current evoked or to-be-evoked negative emotional state, may be another way to direct attention away from the current situation. For example, Cooney and colleagues instructed participants to retrieve positive memories while watching sadness-inducing film clips; during mood-incongruent recall, they observed activation of the VLPFC and OFC, but not activation of more dorsal PFC networks (Cooney, Joormann, Atlas, Eugene, & Gotlib, 2007). The authors speculated that interruption of a negative affective state with positive memories may occur via a more ventral regulatory circuit, unlike other strategies such as reappraisal and/or distancing (discussed later).

Physical pain can be thought of as an emotion-like state, which is highly arousing, is negatively valenced (and thus affectively colored), and tends to activate regions associated with emotional responding (see Chapter 9 for a review). Active distraction strategies that limit attention to a pain stimulus, such as engaging in a parallel verbal fluency task (Frankenstein et al., 2001) or a Stroop task (Bantick et al., 2002) or simply thinking of something else (Tracey et al., 2002), are associated with reduced pain-related responding in mid-cingulate cortex, insula, and periacqueductal gray; enhanced activation of orbitofrontal cortex (OFC), ACC, DLPFC, VLPFC; and lowered subjective perception of pain intensity. Unlike other emotion evocation paradigms using low-intensity stimuli (faces, pictures), studies using physical elicitation of pain have produced more consistent and direct evidence of prefrontal engagement during cognitive distraction away from the emotionally evocative stimulus, showing that prefrontal engagement robustly reduces the affective significance of the stimulus. However, "distraction" from pain may not be driven by increases in cognitive load per se. Using high-cognitive load on a concurrent working memory task as a proxy for a regulation strategy for anticipatory anxiety (impending pain), Kalisch and colleagues showed that high load was associated with a *decrease* (not increase) in dorsal ACC, DMPFC, DLPFC, and VLPFC activity (Kalisch, Wiech, Critchley, & Dolan, 2006).

In sum, studies examining attention allocation away from emotional content and cognitive labeling (even if it is the emotional content that is labeled) have yielded discrepant findings. Shifting attention may limit the brain's emotional production systems (amgydala, insula), but whether these effects constitute emotion regulation and, if so whether regulation occurs via recruitment of prefrontal cortex, is not clear. Existing studies have certain limitations and leave some questions unanswered. First, emotional stimuli such as faces are thought of as emotional *perception* probes, and in the absence of social context, they typically are not associated with the evocation of emotional experience and are devoid of their emotional significance. Second, it is not clear whether some of the tasks used genuinely work by attentional modulation, rather than by imposing a higher cognitive load, each of which might limit the extent to which the emotional elements are processed, though presumably in importantly different ways. Third, the "control" condition employed across studies varies substantially, making it more difficult to interpret findings (we return to this topic when we discuss affect labeling as an emotion regulation strategy in greater detail). Finally, most of these studies have focused almost entirely on brain activation patterns as the index of emotion change. It would be preferable to collect other indices of emotion change, including subjective, behavioral, or peripheral-physiological measures.

Interpretation Change: Reappraisal and Distancing

As noted earlier (Figure 16.1), cognitive change is an antecedent-focused emotion regulation strategy that involves modifying the evaluation of the situation to change its meaning or significance and, thus, the subsequent emotional response. Cognitive change is thus a volitional, effortful, conscious process by which one reframes the emotional content of an emotionally evocative situation. Cognitive change strategies have been extensively studied in neuroimaging (indeed, significantly more so than other strategies). In these studies, subjects are typically taught to use reappraisal to change their interpretation of the emotional content (typically negative in valence) of stimuli or situations in a way that the content no longer elicits the affective response had the subjects experienced the content passively without any regulation. One way to implement reappraisal is to reframe the meaning of an aversive situation from a negative interpretation to a more positive one (e.g., an image of women crying outside of a church is initially perceived as conveying the sadness of the women at some somber event, but can be reframed as conveying "tears of joy" during a wedding celebration). In an alternative reappraisal-related strategy, subjects are taught to use distancing to take the perspective of a detached and distant observer while processing emotional content. Much of what we know about the neural circuitry involved in emotion regulation comes from studies using reappraisal-based strategies.

In the first study of cognitive change via reappraisal, Ochsner and colleagues instructed subjects to reappraise highly negative, arousing images to alter their emotional response; they showed that, relative to the unregulated, passive experience, reappraisal reduced subjective negative affect and increased activation in the DLPFC, VLPFC, and dmPFC while decreasing emotion appraisal/generation areas (amygdala, OFC). Moreover, the extent of reappraisal-mediated change in the dorsal ACC predicted the extent of attenuation of negative affect (Ochsner, Bunge, Gross, & Gabrieli, 2002). The authors followed up these initial findings with another study to further dissect the neural mechanisms underlying different component processes of cognitive change (Ochsner et al., 2004). First, subjects were taught to use reappraisal strategies using a self-focused (i.e., distancing, decreasing self-relevance of the situation) or a situation-focused (i.e., positive reframing of the situation) approach to decrease negative emotion. Second, they were instructed to down- *and* up-regulate their negative emotion. The authors found that both self- and situation-focused strategies similarly reduced subjective negative affect, attenuated amygdala responses, and engaged overlapping regions in prefrontal and cingulate cortices. When down-regulating (but not up-regulating) emotion, distancing recruited greater rostral MPFC and ACC activity, areas involved in self-referential processing (Kelley et al., 2002), whereas situation-based reinterpretation engaged more lateral PFC areas associated with maintenance and manipulation of alternative meanings of a given event based on current and past experience. Similarly, both up- and down- regulation evoked activity in the lateral PFC thought to relate to the maintenance of these strategies in the context of immediate goals, as well as dorsal ACC activity that may involve performance monitoring of the task at hand (Botvinick, Braver, Barch, Carter, & Cohen, 2001), while modifying amygdala activity and negative affect in concert with the regulatory goal (up-regulation was associated with greater amygdala reactivity and greater negative affect, whereas down-regulation was associated with less amygdala reactivity and less negative affect); in general, up- and down-regulation goals engaged very similar, overlapping areas of the prefrontal cortex thought to reflect the common processes shared by both strategies. More engagement of the left rostral MPFC was related to up-regulation, interpreted by the authors as relating to the retrieval of emotional knowledge, and greater activation of right lateral PFC and OFC was associated with down-

regulation, thought to represent behavioral inhibition, interference resolution, and/or reversal learning. The authors also noted that down-regulation was associated with more widespread activation across both left and right PFC, whereas up-regulation localized primarily in the left PFC.

A number of studies have confirmed and elaborated on these initial findings on the neural bases of reappraisal (see also Harenski & Hamann, 2006; van Reekum et al., 2007). Phan and colleagues compared volitional attempts at reappraisal to maintaining a negative emotional state (e.g., responding naturally) evoked by highly arousing, aversive images (similar to those used by Ochsner and colleagues) and observed greater activity in the dmPFC, DLPFC, lateral OFC, right VLPFC, and dorsal ACC and less activity in the extended amygdala, nucleus accumbens, and lateral PFC during reappraisal (Phan et al., 2005; Figure 16.4a). Moreover, the authors reported that greater activations of the dorsal ACC and anterior insula were associated with decreasing negative affect, whereas greater activation of the amygdala and visual association occipital cortex was correlated with increasing negative affect. These findings were followed up with a functional connectivity analysis that showed (1) activity in the DLPFC, dmPFC, ACC, OFC, and inferior parietal cortex (IPC) covaried with activity in the amygdala in a task-dependent manner (that is, coupling was greater in the reappraisal task than the maintenance task; Figure 16.4); and (2) the strength of amygdala-OFC and amygdala-dmPFC connectivity predicted the extent of attenuation of negative affect following reappraisal (Banks, Eddy, Angstadt, Nathan, & Phan, 2007).

Using several sources of emotional readouts as indices of effective emotion regulation, Eippert and colleagues used fMRI along with peripheral psychophysiological recordings (startle eyeblink responses [SERs] and skin conductance responses [SCRs]) while subjects reappraised threat-related images in order to down- and up-regulate their emotional responses. Down-regulation was associated with dampened amygdala response,

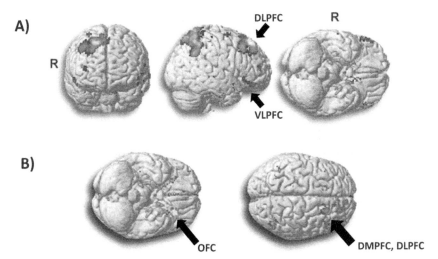

Figure 16.4. (A) Lateral prefrontal cortex engagement during reappraisal. Greater activation of right DLPFC, bilateral VLPFC, and right superior parietal cortex during reappraise (versus maintain/look) negative images; concurrent activations in OFC, dmPFC, and dorsal ACC not shown. Data from Phan et al. (2005). (B) Task-dependent amygdala-frontal connectivity during reappraisal. Greater coupling of bilateral OFC, bilateral DLPFC, dmPFC, and parietal cortex during reappraise (versus maintain/look) negative images; amygdala-subgengual ACC not shown. Data from Banks et al. (2008). See color plate 16.4.

along with greater ACC, DLPFC, and OFC activation, whereas up-regulation was associated with greater SER, SCR, and amygdala reactivity along with widespread PFC activation; the authors noted a significant overlap in activation of the PFC associated with both strategies (Eippert et al., 2007). Along with new evidence on effects of appraisal on peripheral physiology, this report also showed that trial-by-trial indices of reappraisal success (subjective ratings of affect) correlated with amygdala reactivity during up-regulation and with OFC activity during down-regulation.

Until recently, it was unknown whether the same neural circuitry as that used to regulate negative emotions would be engaged in reappraising positive emotions. To answer this question, Kim and Hamann exposed participants to images of negative, positive, and neutral valence and instructed them to increase or decrease this evoked affect using reappraisal, or to just watch (Kim & Hamann, 2007). Consistent with the findings of Ochsner and colleagues (2004), this study observed broadly shared activations in prefrontal and cingulate cortices

(dmPFC, left LPFC, ACC, left OFC) and attenuated amygdala reactivity when engaging in both up- and down-regulation of emotional responding of both negative and positive pictures. This result further supports the notion that, during reappraisal, a core set of cognitive processes (working memory, action monitoring, response inhibition, reversal learning, and so on) are engaged, regardless of the regulatory goal (i.e., up- or down-regulation) or the valence of the reappraisal target (negative or positive). Yet in addition to these common core processes, the authors also point out some salient differences in brain activations based on emotion and task. For negative emotions, although brain activation in the PFC recruited for up-regulation was not greater than that recruited for down-regulation (negative, up > down), the reverse contrast engaged greater bilateral OFC and other right PFC and right parietal areas (negative, down > up). In contrast, for positive emotions, activity for down-regulation was not greater than that for up-regulation (positive, down > up). However, up-regulation selectively engaged the ventral medial (orbitofrontal) PFC, additional medial PFC, and left frontal thalamus, and caudate (positive, up > down).

These findings were partly replicated in a subsequent study by Mak, Hu, Zhang, Xiao, and Lee, (2009) using a design with negative and positive pictures, in which subjects were allowed to use a regulation strategy of their own choosing (see Delgado, Gillis, & Phelps, 2008; Staudinger, Erk, Abler, & Walter, 2009; Staudinger, Erk, & Walter, 2011 for studies of regulation of positive stimuli consisting of monetary rewards). Down-regulation of negative and positive emotions was associated with increased activation of the DLPFC and dmPFC/ACC, and the OFC was selectively recruited to regulate negative affect. Finally, online (collected while scanning) ratings of arousal were correlated with insula and ventral and dorsal MPFC activity specifically during negative emotion regulation, and OFC activity tracked both positive and negative emotion regulation. As observed previously, amgydala reactivity to emotional stimuli was modulated in accord with the regulatory goal. Interestingly, because the study also employed positive images, the authors were able to demonstrate that regulation of positive emotion was related to changes in ventral striatal responses, a region associated with reward and pleasure (see Chapter 19).

Despite the convergence of evidence supporting an apparent reciprocal relationship between emotion reappraisal systems (dmPFC, DLPFC, ACC, OFC, VLPC) and emotion appraisal/generation regions (amygdala, extended amygdala, ventral striatum), little is known about how these systems might interact and how these circuits might mediate the observed changes in subjective emotional experience (e.g., negative affect). It had been shown that amygdala-OFC and amygdala-dmPFC reappraisal-dependent coupling predicts the extent of attenuation of negative affect (Banks, et al., 2007). Using a novel mediation effect parametric mapping (MEPM) analysis, Wager and colleagues formally tested two competing hypotheses: (1) a mediation hypothesis that interactions

between the PFC and subcortical/limbic regions underlie the mechanism for regulation, such that the PFC reduces negative emotion by influencing the reactivity of these emotional appraisal/responding systems, and (2) a direct path hypothesis that success in negative affect reduction is directly due to PFC activation with little influence on appraisal/responding systems (Wager, Davidson, Hughes, Lindquist, & Ochsner, 2008). First, consistent with prior studies, greater activation of the cognitive change network, including bilateral DLPFC, VLPFC (encompassing inferior frontal gyrus), MPFC, anterior PFC, and dorsal ACC, and inferior parietal lobe (IPL), was observed during reappraisal. Success of the reappraisal strategy (drop in negative affect) was associated with activation of the bilateral VLPFC, dmPFC, and IPL. Selecting the right VLPFC region as the predictor region and reappraisal success as the outcome, the authors observed that reappraisal-induced activation in this region was associated with activation of two emotion appraising and/or generating regions: the amygdala and ventral striatum/nucleus accumbens. Moreover, these regions mediated the link between VLPFC activation and negative affect reduction, although in opposite directions – VLPFC increased nucleus accumbens activation, which led to increased reappraisal success, whereas the VLPFC increased amygdala activation, which led to reduced reappraisal success. The two paths via the nucleus accumbens (less negative emotion) and via the amygdala (more negative emotion) explained as much as 50% of the variance in subjective negative affect.

In a subsequent analysis in which the authors specified the amygdala and nucleus accumbens as mediators and performed a whole-brain search for predictors, it was noted that the amygdala and nucleus accumbens also mediate the relationship between other PFC regions and reappraisal success. In particular, the amygdala also mediated the OFC, whereas the nucleus accumbens mediated rostral MPFC, anterior PFC, DLPFC, and dmPFC. This study, using a novel path analytic method, suggests that there are two pathways (via the nucleus accumbens and via the amygdala) by which prefrontal activation influences emotion during reappraisal.

It should be noted that not all studies on the reappraisal of negative images have produced the expected pattern of robust PFC activation and amygdala attenuation. For example, Urry and colleagues showed that older (62- to 64-year old) volunteers using reappraisal strategies engaged the VLPFC, DLPFC, dmPFC and amygdala when asked to enhance (vs. attend) negative affect evoked by unpleasant images, consistent with previous observations (Ochsner et al., 2004). However, the authors observed few prefrontal or amygdala activation differences in comparing decrease versus attend conditions (Urry et al., 2006). Instead, they showed that individuals who exhibited greater attenuation of the amygdala by reappraisal (attend > decrease) showed greater vmPFC/medial OFC activation and a "steeper, more normative" diurnal decline in the stress hormone cortisol. Interestingly, this pattern was selective for downregulation attempts and not observed during enhancement of negative emotion. The study also showed a similar reciprocal relationship between the amygydala and dmPFC during reappraisal and that vmPFC mediated this dmPFC-amygdala relationship.

Additional corroborating evidence of emotion regulation comes from measurements of pupil reactivity, such that both increasing and decreasing negative emotion evoked greater proportional change in pupillary diameter. Using this index, the authors observed a positive relationship between the VLPFC/inferior frontal gyrus and pupil diameter, whereas its relationship with the amygdala was negative, during attempts to decrease negative emotion. Collectively, these findings support the notion that downregulation of negative affect is associated with meaningful interindividual differences in brain activity, particularly that between the vmPFC and amygdala, and corresponding change in diurnal variation in cortisol and pupillary reactivity.

Most studies of reappraisal using fMRI and PET have used emotionally evocative images, typically from the validated stimulus set, the International Affective Picture System (IAPS; Lang, Bradley, & Cuthbert, 1997); relatively few laboratories have employed other affective probes. One such study comes from Goldin and colleagues who instructed participants to reappraise the emotional interpretation of "harsh" (angry, contemptuous) faces (using linguistic-cognitive self-talk such as "This does not involve me," "This does not influence me," or "This does not impact me"), in the context of comparing healthy controls (HC) and patients with social anxiety disorder (SAD), also known as social phobia (Goldin, Manber, Hakimi, Canli, & Gross, 2009). Although not the primary focus of the study, the authors did report subjective ratings and brain activation data from within-group analyses of the healthy participants. Looking at harsh faces produced higher levels of subjective negative emotion and activation of the bilateral dorsal amygdala, relative to looking at neutral scenes. When viewing harsh faces, compared to the unregulated "look" condition, the reappraise task resulted in reduced negative affect and greater activation of the bilateral VLPFC/inferior frontal gyrus and dmPFC and less activation of the bilateral insula. A separate study (Goldin, Manber-Ball, Werner, Heimberg, & Gross, 2009) of SAD vs. HC by the same group used linguistic probes of negative self-beliefs (NSBs; e.g., "No one likes me," "Others think I'm a fool", "I am weird"). Participants were trained to reframe these NSBs in a way that reinterprets and thus diminishes their negative content, using linguistic-cognitive self-talk thoughts (e.g., "That is not always true"). In the HC group alone, relative to the unregulated "react" condition, reappraisals of NSBs produced less negative emotion, attenuated amygdala reactivity, and recruited activation of the dmFC, DLPFC, and VLPFC. Moreover, follow-up analyses of functional connectivity during the reappraisal task using the amygdala as the seed region showed the amygdala has an inverse/reciprocal relationship with the DLPFC and VLPFC, but lacks positive connectivity with any regions in the PFC. Findings from these two studies complement those using aversive pictures as emotion probes and extend the evidence for VLPFC and dmPFC engagement during reappraisal of aversive social signals.

Very few studies have directly compared reappraisal against another emotion regulation strategy to investigate shared and nonshared neural substrates. One study by McRae and colleagues contrasted reappraisal and distraction (McRae et al., 2010), and another by Goldin and colleagues (discussed later) compared reappraisal and suppression (Goldin, McRae, Ramel, & Gross, 2008). Relative to looking at aversive images, reappraisal and cognitive distraction (using a working memory distracter) similarly reduced negative affect and amygdala reactivity and similarly increased activation in the middle and inferior LPFC, dmPFC, dorsal ACC. Interestingly, distraction was shown to be more effective than reappraisal in reducing amygdala response and selectively engaged LPFC, inferolateral PFC, and superior parietal cortex, whereas reappraisal engaged dmPFC, DLPFC, and VLPFC. Reductions in negative affect were associated with activation of dmPFC and DLPFC via reappraisal-based strategies but only with activation of the superior parietal cortex for distraction-based strategies. These findings preliminarily suggest that these two approaches taken to regulate emotions recruit different brain areas and/or recruit the same PFC areas to different extents, which is likely explained by the different cognitive processes (i.e., attention deployment in distraction and reframing or interpretation change in reappraisal) underlying the strategies.

As noted earlier, a distinct and alternative reappraisal-related strategy involves *distancing*, a process of taking the perspective of a detached and distant observer while processing emotional content. Beauregard and colleagues were among the first to study conscious, effortful, voluntary emotion regulation with functional neuroimaging (Beauregard, Levesque, & Bourgouin, 2001). Using erotic films, they evoked in participants sexual arousal, arguably a transient emotional state. Subjects were instructed to "distance themselves from these stimuli, that is, to become a detached observer" in order to voluntarily decrease the intensity of the sexual arousal felt in reaction to the erotic films (of note, the authors refer to this emotion regulatory strategy as "suppression," but it would be classified as a form of reappraisal according to the typology adopted in this chapter). As intended, the participants experienced less subjective sexual arousal during the inhibition task (versus passive view/ "react normally" task). When allowing sexual arousal to emerge, greater responses were observed in the amygdala, temporal pole, and hypothalamus, whereas the distancing task reduced amygdala (as well as that in the temporal pole and hypothalamus) responses and engaged activation of the right anterior MPFC (superior frontal gyrus) and right ACC, as well as left VLPFC (inferior frontal gyrus) and bilateral superior parietal lobule. A follow-up study from this laboratory also involved distancing, this time in response to sad film clips, which were confirmed to selectively evoke sadness and emotion-related activation of VLPFC, amygdala, insula, and temporal pole (Levesque, et al., 2003). Along with reductions in subjective sadness, distancing was associated with activation of right-sided OFC, DLPFC, and to a lesser extent, VLPFC. Positive correlations between self-report ratings of sadness and OFC and DLPFC activation were also observed, which the authors interpret in terms of the hypothesis that residual sadness that remained during the reappraisal task led to greater activation/work in OFC and DLPFC regulatory circuits. Together, these findings are in agreement with those reported by Ochsner and colleagues (2004) and suggest that the same neural machinery employed during distancing is used to down-regulate general negative affect evoked by aversive pictures and more specific emotional states (e.g., sexual arousal, sadness) evoked by films.

Kalisch and colleagues also trained subjects on a distancing strategy, but in this case to suppress state anxiety evoked during anticipation of receiving painful shock stimuli (Kalisch, Wiech, Herrmann, & Dolan, 2006). The authors instructed the subjects to distance by imagining themselves to be in a "Special Place" of their choosing, and in particular to think to themselves "I am here in my ["Special Place"], feeling safe and comfortable. Those emotions out there cannot reach me here. Nothing bothers me." In the control condition, subjects were told to imagine themselves in the actual laboratory surroundings at Queens Square while thinking "I am now in this experiment at Queens Square. I can clearly feel my emotions. They affect my body and my mind." In a behavioral study, the authors confirmed that the distancing task reduced subjective anxiety, heart rate, and SCRs. In a follow-up fMRI experiment, subjects who engaged in distancing during pain anticipation also reported reduced anxiety, reduced pain-related heart rate acceleration response and pain anticipation-related MPFC/ACC activation, and displayed enhanced activation in anterolateral PFC (located at the junction between DLPFC and VLPFC). This study extended prior findings by demonstrating that detachment produced an anxiolytic effect using subjective, physiological, and neural indices of pain, and also identified a discrete source in anterior lateral PFC that is associated with these effects.

In another study, Koenigsberg and colleagues were particularly interested in the neural correlates of distancing from negative emotion elicited by pictures with social content (e.g., pictures of situations involving loss or grief, abuse, or physical threat) rather than nonsocial content (e.g., fearsome animals, weapons; Koenigsberg, et al., 2010). Here, subjects were trained to distance themselves from the emotional material by relating to the emotionally aversive images as though they themselves were not personally connected in any way to the pictured individuals in the depicted unpleasant situation. As expected, relative to neutral images, socially aversive pictures elicited activation in the amygdala, dmPFC, and sensory cortices responding to the visual salience (e.g., fusiform gyrus, thalamus). Compared to looking, regulation by distancing from negative (>neutral) images was associated with less negative emotion scores, greater activity in dorsal ACC/dmPFC, VLPFC including inferior frontal gyrus, anterior vmPFC, and superior temporal gyrus, as well as less activity in the amygdala. These findings corroborate those previously observed by Ochsner and colleagues (2004), who also trained subjects to use distancing to regulate negative affect evoked by *both* social and nonsocial content; the findings also suggest that distancing from aversive social cues engages a sociocognitive network of regions associated with social perception, perspective-taking, and attentional control.

In sum, distancing appears to engage a PFC network (ACC, dmPFC, VLPFC, DLPFC, OFC) similar to that recruited by situation-focused reinterpretation (e.g., reframing negative content to neutral or positive terms). Recently, Erk and colleagues showed that distancing has long-term effects on episodic memory and subsequent brain activation patterns when tested one year later (Erk, von Kalckreuth, & Walter, 2010). Here the authors showed that successful recognition of negative images that were previously subjected to distancing was positively associated with DLPFC activation, whereas the opposite relationship was observed with the amygdala – greater activation of amygdala during distancing-mediated down-regulation of negative affect was associated with less memory for these items.

Turning now to a strategy that is closely related to distancing and reinterpretation, Kross and colleagues first evoked negative affect by asking participants to recall a series of highly arousing negative autobiographical memories (Kross, Davidson, Weber, & Ochsner, 2009); they then trained subjects to engage in emotion regulatory strategies such as *accept* ("to recognize that the feelings they experienced during recollection were passing mental events that were psychologically distant from the self and did not control them") and *analyze* ("to objectively analyze the causes and reasons underlying their feelings"). The authors did not observe that these strategies activated PFC areas more so than the control condition of *feel* ("to focus on the specific feelings that naturally flowed through their mind as they thought about their recalled experiences"). Instead, the feel condition, previously associated with pathological rumination and dysfunctional coping, was associated with the greatest activity in the rostral, anterior MPFC, VLPFC, and subgenual ACC, and activity in this "rumination" network was positively correlated with the participants' self-reported negative affect. Here, unlike many of the other studies of cognitive strategies, the analyze condition may have been less effective in reducing negative affect, as indicated by greater engagement of regions in the "rumination" network in the analyze condition compared to the accept condition. These findings provide a neural model for understanding the maladaptive recall of negative memories and are thus potentially highly relevant to understanding certain psychopathologies (e.g., major depression, generalized anxiety). However, the model has not yet been formally tested in clinical populations.

A relatively unique antecedent-focused strategy was investigated by Herwig and colleagues. They instructed subjects to perform "reality checking" while anticipating images of negative valence in order to reduce their negative affect; subjects were told to repeatedly reconsider the context of their actual situation by, e.g., thinking: "I am lying in a scanner," "They will show me a picture, this is part of the study" (Herwig, et al., 2007). Compared to a control group of subjects who did not engage in this reality-checking strategy, subjects who took on a realistic stance to the experimental context showed higher MPFC and DLPFC activation while attenuating activity in extended amygdala and sensory areas (e.g., fusiform gyrus). Moreover, the extent to which the amygdala activated during reality checking was correlated negatively with reappraisal

scores from the emotion regulation questionnaire (ERQ; Gross & John, 2003).

The preceding studies of antecedent-focused emotion regulation differed widely in the duration of regulation that subjects engaged in during each regulation trial, with the duration ranging 5 to 25 seconds. Using activation likelihood estimation (ALE) meta-analytic methods, Rafael Kalisch investigated the role of duration of regulation in explaining variability in brain activations in studies of regulation of negative stimuli (Kalisch, 2009). He found that, as the duration of regulation increased, frontal cortical activation reliably shifted both from left to right and from posterior to anterior. Kalisch proposed that this shift reflects two dissociable stages of emotion regulation, an early implementation stage during which the specific regulation strategy is selected, and a later maintenance phase during which the selected strategy is continued and monitored for success. Kalisch's quantitative review sheds important light on the temporal dynamics of emotion regulation and underscores the need for further investigation into this understudied topic.

Response Change: Suppression and Extinction

Suppression is a "response modulation" strategy, and thus it takes place after the perception and appraisal stages are completed and the emotional response has already begun to unfold (Figure 16,1; Gross, 1998; Gross & Levenson, 1993; Gross & Thompson, 2007). Suppression involves fairly direct attempts to influence cognitive, physiological, or behavioral manifestations of emotion responses; for example, attempts to inhibit the facial expressions and other physical displays associated with emotions. Unlike cognitive reappraisal, suppression results in little or no change in subjective negative emotion, and it is associated with increased sympathetic activation and reduced emotional memory (Gross, 1998, 2002; Gross & Levenson, 1997). In addition to suppression, extinction is another process that reduces the expression of negative emotional responses, but it specifically applies to responses that have previously been acquired through stimulus-reinforced/conditioned associations. Although extinction is not directly considered in contemporary models of "response modulation" as proposed by Gross (Gross, 2002; Gross & Thompson, 2007), because extinction is increasingly recognized as involving active learning and inhibitory processing (Milad, Rauch, Pitman, & Quirk, 2006), it is potentially usefully thought of as a more automatic, less effortful kind of emotion regulation strategy (Ochsner & Gross, 2005).

SUPPRESSION

Ohira and colleagues examined the neural correlates of suppression using PET – instructing participants "to voluntarily suppress any emotional responses" during viewing of emotionally negative, positive, and neutral images; it should be noted that the authors did not expand on this instruction (suppress expression *or* experience), nor did they provide specifics about which strategies were used by subjects to implement suppression, except that all subjects denied using cognitive distraction or verbal processing of stimuli (Ohira et al., 2006). Emotion suppression, regardless of the valence of the emotional response, did not result in a change in negative affect, heart rate, or the stress-related adrenocorticotropic hormone (ACTH), but did increase SCRs and activity in bilateral OFC, rostral-ventral ACC, superior parietal gyrus, and lateral PFC. Moreover, activation in the medial OFC was positively correlated with SCR amplitude during suppression. The unregulated "attend" condition, in contrast, elicited greater amygdala activity.

In addition to the study by McRae et al. discussed earlier, only one other study has directly compared two emotion regulation strategies. Goldin and colleagues examined commonalities and differences in the use of reappraisal and suppression (subjects were instructed to "keep their face still" [expression suppression]) to regulate emotional responses to negative/aversive film clips (Goldin, et al., 2008). As pre-dicted from prior studies, reappraisal attenuated reactivity in the insula and amygdala and engaged MPFC, DLPFC, VLPFC, lateral OFC, and inferior frontal gyrus. Interestingly, analyses of the temporal dynamics of these PFC regions showed that their activation emerged early (within 5 s of the film clip starting). Suppression did not modify amygdala reactivity, but in fact, increased insula reactivity. It also increased activity in VLPFC, dmPFC, and DLPFC, but in a later phase of emotional responding (last 5 s of the film clip). Although both strategies reduced subjective negative affect and extent of facial disgust expressions, reappraisal was more effective in reducing negative affect, whereas suppression was more effective in reducing facial expressions. At the brain level, reappraisal was more effective than suppression in reducing amygdala and insula responses to negative emotion, perhaps because reappraisal engaged PFC at an earlier phase of responding than suppression. Resonant with prior findings on subjective and autonomic psychophysiological change associated with suppression (Gross, 1998), these results demonstrate that different strategies for regulation, reappraisal vs. suppression, are differentially effective in their ability to affect emotional experience, expressive behavior, and brain responses. Moreover, the different temporal patterns of prefrontal engagement associated with suppression versus reappraisal (i.e., significantly later engagement with suppression), provide a potential brain-based mechanism for the reduced efficacy of suppression.

FEAR LEARNING AND EXTINCTION

We now turn to the emerging imaging neuroscience of fear learning and extinction (see Chapter 18). Negative emotions, particularly fear, can be acquired by Pavlovian learning, in which a previously neutral stimulus such as a tone (the conditioned stimulus, CS) acquires emotional importance when paired with an aversive stimulus (Quirk, Garcia, & Gonzalez-Lima, 2006) such as a footshock (the unconditioned stimulus, US). After a few such pairings, the presentation of the CS alone is capable of eliciting the conditioned fear response (CR). In extinction, the CR degrades over time when the CS is presented repeatedly without being paired with the US. The success of extinction learning can be later tested and confirmed (typically the next day) by once again presenting the CS and observing a diminished conditioned response.

Current models propose that during extinction, the original CS-US association is not erased or overwritten. Rather, extinction involves active learning of a new CS-US relationship, along with inhibition of the old CS-US relationship that remains encoded, but its manifestation is suppressed (Bouton, 2004). Extinction can thus usefully be conceptualized as a form of emotion regulation in that conditioned fear responses are suppressed with this newly acquired learning. Of the various emotion strategies deployed by animals (e.g., active coping, reconsolidation), extinction learning has been most often translated to human studies.

In a elegant study that examines interconnections between traditional strategies for cognitive emotion regulation and fear extinction, Delgado and colleagues used a partial reinforcement procedure to instill conditioned fear in subjects (Delgado, Nearing, Ledoux, & Phelps, 2008). Subjects then used volitional emotion regulation techniques (relaxation and distraction ["try to think of something calming in nature"]) in response to fear-conditioned stimuli, and results were compared with this group's prior neuroimaging study of fear extinction. Cognitive regulation of fear responses engaged lateral PFC regions, which modulated amygdala activity via vmPFC. Activations in vmPFC and the amygdala associated with volitional regulation exhibited substantial overlap with similar regions identified in their prior study of extinction learning and retrieval. The authors propose that volitional regulation strategies involve lateral PFC regions that interact with and harness a phylogenetically older emotion regulation circuit linking vmPFC and amygdala (see also Schiller & Delgado, 2010). Given the paucity of data in this area, more studies are needed to directly compare and contrast

the neural mechanisms by which we volitionally and cognitively regulate and more effortlessly inhibit fear.

Other Strategies: Mental State Change, Meditation

A number of other strategies exist that may not easily fit into the emotion regulation classification scheme (perception change, interpretation change, response change) developed in this chapter. These strategies may span multiple phases of emotion (perception, experience, and response) across self- versus situation-focused stances. Alternatively, they may be difficult to define or relate to a particular cognitive construct (e.g., attention, appraisal, and so on).

One prime example is the family of strategies that evoke enhanced self-awareness: so-called mindfulness or other meditation strategies. To understand how mindfulness might work as an emotion regulation strategy, its useful to revisit previous neuroimaging research that showed that the seemingly simple act of labeling the emotional impact of visually salient stimuli changes their effects on subjective and brain (e.g., amygdala and paralimbic) responses. For example, when looking at an aversive stimulus, we can view, process, and experience the unpleasantness of its content *passively*, or we can direct our attention toward linguistically labeling our subjective emotional response by asking "how unpleasant does this picture make *me* feel?" This procedure of cognitive labeling of evocative stimuli and shifting attention to one's own mental state (self-awareness) represents a mental process (mixed with cognitive, experiential, linguistic components) that could allow subjects to regulate their experience of the emotionally salient stimuli. It is noteworthy that rating the intensity of an anxiety-producing situation is a mainstay of behavioral therapy that permits patients to gain a feeling of control over their anxiety (Marks, 1985).

In one of the first imaging studies of this phenomenon, Taylor and colleagues showed that switching from passively viewing aversive pictures to rating their unpleasantness reduces subjective sadness and amygdala and insula activity, and engages dmFPC and paracingulate gyrus, including the ACC (Taylor, Phan, Decker, & Liberzon, 2003). The rating task itself required several mental operations: comparing the experience of the image with other emotional images, recalling appropriate anchors from the scale, and assigning a value to the picture. One or more of these processes may have reduced the subjective experience of the negative emotion (e.g., sadness) and the associated limbic responses to negatively valenced content. Moreover, affect labeling (putting emotions into words) has been shown to decrease amygdala reactivity and increase activity in the right VLPFC when viewing negative images; interestingly, VLPFC and amygdala activity during affect labeling have been shown to be inversely correlated, a relationship that was mediated by activity in medial prefrontal cortex (MPFC; Lieberman, et al., 2007). Other studies have also demonstrated an inverse, reciprocal relationship between prefrontal and amygdala reactivity during the affect labeling task (Hariri et al., 2000; Taylor et al., 2003).

In contrast, Hutcherson and colleagues found that rating one's own emotional state while viewing emotionally (amusing or sad) engaging film clips did *not* decrease either subjective affect or emotion-related activations in the amygdala and paralimbic regions; however, it did increase, relative to passive viewing, activation of the ACC, insula, dorsal PFC/middle frontal gyrus, and inferior parietal lobule (Hutcherson et al., 2005), suggesting that reporting one's emotional state during a temporally extended film clip may engage different processes than rating one's affective response to a static stimulus.

More recent studies have offered additional insights on the connections between self-related awareness and emotion regulation. For example, "cognitive" self-reflection and emotion-introspection (awareness of one's own actual emotions and feelings) may engage different brain areas and affect

emotion-related responding in the amygdala in different ways. Herwig and colleagues instructed participants to engage in three mental tasks: (1) the "think" condition: "think about yourself, reflect who you are, about your goals, etc." (2) the "feel" condition: "feel yourself, be aware about your current emotions and bodily feelings;" and (3) the "neutral" condition: "do nothing specific, just await the neutral picture" (Herwig, Kaffenberger, Jancke, & Bruhl, 2010). The authors reported that the emotion introspection " feel" condition was associated with the lowest amgydala activation and in greater posterior MPFC regions, whereas cognitive self-reflection was associated with higher activation in anterior MPFC regions. Moreover, thinking about oneself was associated with activation in the left VLPFC adjacent to inferior frontal regions, and emotion introspection activated more posterior bilateral inferior frontal/premotor regions and also small regions of middle insula. They conclude that the mental state of being aware of emotional state changes is capable of down-regulating emotional arousal, as indexed by reduced amygdala reactivity, although there was no emotional confrontation or evocation in the paradigm per se.

As noted earlier, Lieberman and colleagues have shown that the basic act of labeling affect (vs. gender) activates VLPFC and deactivates amygdala (Lieberman, et al., 2007). In a follow-up analysis, the authors showed that greater levels of trait mindfulness (as measured by the Mindful Attention Awareness Scale [MAAS]) predict greater activity in bilateral VLPFC, vmPFC, MPFC, DLPFC, and the left insula, and reduced bilateral amygdala activation (Creswell, Way, Eisenberger, & Lieberman, 2007). These findings are in contrast to those reported in the study by Herwig et al. described earlier, in which the authors reported that another measure of dispositional mindfulness, the Freiburg Mindfulness Inventory, but not the MAAS, was *inversely* correlated with several PFC areas, including those that activated during cognitive self-reflection (rostral ACC, dmPFC) and during emotion introspection (posterior

MPFC, mid cingulate cortex; Herwig, et al., 2010).

Most recently, Modinos and colleagues directly examined the relationship between dispositional mindfulness and brain activation during the reappraisal of negative emotion. As with prior studies on reappraisal, the authors observed that reinterpretation (versus viewing) negative images engaged DLPFC, dmPFC, IFG including the VLPFC, and dorsal ACC and attenuated amygdala reactivity; moreover they reported that activation of bilateral dorsal PFC, particularly the dmPFC, predicted reappraisal success (Modinos, Ormel, & Aleman, 2010). Correlation analyses of several PFC regions of interest (ROIs) showed that dmPFC activity during reappraisal was positively correlated with individual differences in mindfulness traits as measured by the Kentucky Inventory of Mindfulness Skills (KIMS) and negatively correlated with amygdala response to negative emotion. In support, Farb and colleagues showed that individuals with moderate levels of depression and anxiety who underwent 8 weeks of mindfulness training using mindfulness-based stress reduction had reduced symptoms posttraining and exhibited more activation of insula, lateral PFC, and subgenual ACC while watching sadness-inducing film clips (Farb et al., 2010). These findings lend support to the prior findings from this group on the neural effects of mindfulness meditation training (Farb et al., 2007).

How does meditation training work? One possibility is that meditation training enhances control over focused and sustained attention, enhancing the individual's ability to engage frontal networks to reduce distraction and better focus (Lutz et al., 2009). Compared to untrained individuals or novices, expert meditation practitioners appear to have a greater ability to detect emotional sounds and, in doing so, are able to tap into neural circuitry involved in empathy and theory of mind (Lutz, Brefczynski-Lewis, Johnstone, & Davidson, 2008). That said, the exact psychological mechanisms by which mindfullness exerts its emotion regulatory effects on negative affect and on brain activation require further study. Together

the existing studies add to a growing literature regarding the role of enhancing self-awareness, meditation, and mindfulness as a distinct form of emotion regulation from interpretation change (e.g., cognitive reappraisal), although whether they recruit differential specialized brain circuitry remains an unanswered question.

Problems and Future Directions

Temporal Dynamics – Use of ERP/EEG

Although emotion and its regulation are thought of as processes that unfold dynamically over time, most measures of central physiology such as functional MRI are limited by their temporal resolution (over several seconds) and thus have low sensitivity to detect neural processes that occur within a 2- to 3-second window (see Chapter 5). Methodologies such as event-related potentials (ERPs) using electroencephalography (EEG) have much better temporal resolution (on the order of milliseconds; see Chapter 4). Using these methods, researchers have identified several components related to the automatic and controlled processing of emotional information (e.g., positive potential at 300 ms [P300], and late positive potential [LPP] between 300–1500 ms) that could be used to provide more detailed information on the temporal dynamics of emotion regulation (Hajcak, MacNamara, & Olvet, 2010). However, there are no published reports that link ERP and fMRI data in the same subjects or that combine simultaneous acquisition of ERP and fMRI data during emotion regulation.

Emotion Regulation in Psychopathologies

The dysregulation of emotion is a hallmark of psychiatric disorders, including mood disorders (e.g., major depression and bipolar disorder), anxiety disorders, and personality disorders (e.g., borderline personality disorder), suggesting that deficits in emotion regulation play a prominent role in the pathophysiology of these disorders (Aldao,

Nolen-Hoeksema, & Schweizer, 2010). Neuroimaging studies are increasingly uncovering the brain basis of abnormalities in emotion regulation in psychiatric conditions. Major depression has been studied most extensively in relation to emotion regulation. In an early study, Beauregard and colleagues showed that depressed individuals (compared to controls) report greater subjective difficulty distancing themselves from sad films, and the degree of reported difficulty correlated with activation in a medial PFC region that this group had previously linked to the regulation of emotion (Beauregard, Paquette, & Levesque, 2006). Using pupillary dilation as an index of effort, Johnstone and colleagues confirmed that depressed individuals expend more effort in regulating emotion. They also showed that a regulation circuit present in control subjects that links VLPFC and vmPFC in the suppression of amygdala activity is not present in depressed patients, who instead show a positive relationship between the amygdala and vmPFC (Johnstone, van Reekum, Urry, Kalin, & Davidson, 2007). A very similar pattern of hyperactivation in emotion generation regions (e.g., amygdala, insula), and hypoactivation in emotion regulation regions (DLPFC, dACC, dmPFC) has been reported in other psychiatric disorders, including social anxiety disorder (Goldin, Manber, et al., 2009; Goldin, Manber-Ball, et al., 2009), borderline personality disorder (Koenigsberg et al., 2009; Schulze et al., 2011), and posttraumatic stress disorder (New et al., 2009). Further work is required to clarify whether this pattern of results across disorders represents a unitary deficit in emotion regulation that spans multiple disorders or whether there are more subtle emotion regulation deficits that are relatively specific to each of these disorders that await further clarification.

Conclusion

Emotion regulation is a distinctively human capacity that is increasingly recognized as critical to understanding psychological health and well-being, interpersonal functioning, and psychiatric disease. Research over the last decade has elucidated the functional neuroanatomy of the regulation of emotions, focusing on cognitive strategies aimed at attention modification and interpretation change. It has implicated a broad network involving the prefrontal cortex (including DLPFC, VLPFC, dmPFC, ACC, OFC) in the successful regulation of emotions. Moreover, recent studies have started to inform us about complex interrelationships among emotion regulation, personality, genetics, and psychopathology. Much has been learned, but many more questions remained unanswered. Moreover, existing research has yet to be connected with translational approaches that link evolving theory and findings with fMRI-to-bedside strategies to identify individuals vulnerable to psychopathology and to refine existing and innovate new clinical interventions. Ongoing and new approaches taken by the human affective neuroscience of emotion regulation promise to be one of the most interesting and impactful avenues of inquiry in basic and translational neuroscience for many years to come.

Outstanding Questions

- A growing number of studies point to a broad prefrontal regulatory circuit that is engaged across emotion regulation strategies, though very few have directly examined overlapping and discrete activations between different strategies head to head (Goldin et al., 2008; McRae, et al., 2010; Ochsner, et al., 2004). Do these findings imply that a common brain mechanism is shared among the various emotion regulation strategies, or might there be more subtle differences that distinguish one from strategy from another at the neural level?
- Growing evidence suggests that pharmacological strategies, particularly those using empirically validated anxiolytic, antidepressant, and/or mood-altering compounds, can regulate amygdala reactivity to negative emotional stimuli (e.g., Paulus, Feinstein, Castillo, Simmons, &

Stein, 2005; Phan et al., 2008), much like cognitive strategies. Do pharmacological and cognitive strategies for emotion regulation share common prefrontal circuitry?

- Emotion regulation is a core aspect of empirically validated cognitive and behavioral therapies for psychiatric disorders. Moreover, neuroimaging is being used to study brain mechanisms of the effects and response to treatments for psychiatric disorders, including psychosocial interventions. However, no study to date has directly examined emotion regulation strategies in the context of psychotherapy clinical trials using functional brain imaging. Does cognitive-behavioral therapy directly modify the neural substrates subserving emotion regulation? Can we use what we know about the brain mechanisms that underlie different cognitive (attention modification, reappraisal) and behavioral (suppression) strategies to refine interventions and improve the likelihood of their success?

- Exciting methodological advances in fMRI have allowed for the opportunity to measure brain activation in real time (e.g., Phan et al., 2004; Posse, et al., 2003), which opens the possibility that brain signals can be used as a source of "neurofeedback" to guide the training or retraining of emotion regulation circuits. Given evidence of substantial individual differences in emotion regulation, especially in relation to maladaptive personality styles and psychiatric disease, fMRI-based real-time neurofeedback provides a promising avenue for helping people change their characteristic styles of emotion regulation. Can real-time fMRI reveal the dynamic mechanisms by which we *regulate* emotion regulation?

Abbreviations

ACC: anterior cingulate cortex
DLPFC: dorsolateral prefrontal cortex
dmPFC: dorsomedial prefrontal cortex
VLPFC: ventrolateral prefrontal cortex
OFC: orbitofrontal cortex
R: Right

References

Adolphs, R. (2002). Neural systems for recognizing emotion. *Current Opinions in Neurobiology*, 12(2), 169–77.

Aldao, A., Nolen-Hoeksema, S., & Schweizer, S. (2010). Emotion-regulation strategies across psychopathology: A meta-analytic review. *Clinical Psychology Review*, 30(2), 217–37.

Anderson, A. K., Christoff, K., Panitz, D., De Rosa, E., & Gabrieli, J. D. (2003). Neural correlates of the automatic processing of threat facial signals. *Journal of Neuroscience*, 23(13), 5627–33.

Banks, S. J., Eddy, K. T., Angstadt, M., Nathan, P. J., & Phan, K. L. (2007). Amygdala–frontal connectivity during emotion regulation. *Social, Cognitive, & Affective Neuroscience*, 2, 303–12.

Bantick, S. J., Wise, R. G., Ploghaus, A., Clare, S., Smith, S. M., & Tracey, I. (2002). Imaging how attention modulates pain in humans using functional MRI. *Brain*, 125(Pt. 2), 310–19.

Beauregard, M., Levesque, J., & Bourgouin, P. (2001). Neural correlates of conscious self-regulation of emotion. *Journal of Neuroscience*, 21(18), RC165.

Beauregard, M., Paquette, V., & Levesque, J. (2006). Dysfunction in the neural circuitry of emotional self-regulation in major depressive disorder. *Neuroreport*, 17(8), 843–46.

Beck, A. T. (1963). Thinking and depression. I. Idiosyncratic content and cognitive distortions. *Archives of General Psychiatry*, 9, 324–33.

Blair, K. S., Smith, B. W., Mitchell, D. G., Morton, J., Vythilingam, M., Pessoa, L., et al. (2007). Modulation of emotion by cognition and cognition by emotion. *Neuroimage*, 35(1), 430–40.

Botvinick, M. M., Braver, T. S., Barch, D. M., Carter, C. S., & Cohen, J. D. (2001). Conflict monitoring and cognitive control. *Psychological Review*, 108(3), 624–52.

Bouton, M. E. (2004). Context and behavioral processes in extinction. *Learning & Memory*, 11(5), 485–494.

Bowlby, J. (1969). *Attachment and loss: Attachment*. New York: Basic Books.

Campos, J. J., Frankel, C. B., & Camras, L. (2004). On the nature of emotion regulation. *Child Development*, 75(2), 377–94.

Carter, C. S., Botvinick, M. M., & Cohen, J. D. (1999). The contribution of the anterior cingulate cortex to executive processes in cognition. *Reviews in the Neurosciences*, 10(1), 49–57.

Cooney, R. E., Joormann, J., Atlas, L. Y., Eugene, F., & Gotlib, I. H. (2007). Remembering the good times: Neural correlates of affect regulation. *Neuroreport*, 18(17), 1771–74.

Craig, A. D. (2009). How do you feel – now? The anterior insula and human awareness. *Nature Reviews Neuroscience*, 10(1), 59–70.

Creswell, J. D., Way, B. M., Eisenberger, N. I., & Lieberman, M. D. (2007). Neural correlates of dispositional mindfulness during affect labeling. *Psychosomatic Medicine*, 69(6), 560–65.

Critchley, H., Daly, E., Phillips, M., Brammer, M., Bullmore, E., Williams, S., et al. (2000). Explicit and implicit neural mechanisms for processing of social information from facial expressions: A functional magnetic resonance imaging study. *Human Brain Mapping*, 9(2), 93–105.

Delgado, M. R., Gillis, M. M., & Phelps, E. A. (2008). Regulating the expectation of reward via cognitive strategies. *Nature Neuroscience*, 11(8), 880–81.

Delgado, M. R., Nearing, K. I., Ledoux, J. E., & Phelps, E. A. (2008). Neural circuitry underlying the regulation of conditioned fear and its relation to extinction. *Neuron*, 59(5), 829–38.

Drabant, E. M., McRae, K., Manuck, S. B., Hariri, A. R., & Gross, J. J. (2009). Individual differences in typical reappraisal use predict amygdala and prefrontal responses. *Biological Psychiatry*, 65(5), 367–73.

Eippert, F., Veit, R., Weiskopf, N., Erb, M., Birbaumer, N., & Anders, S. (2007). Regulation of emotional responses elicited by threat-related stimuli. *Human Brain Mapping*, 28(5), 409–23.

Erk, S., Abler, B., & Walter, H. (2006). Cognitive modulation of emotion anticipation. *European Journal of Neuroscience*, 24(4), 1227–36.

Erk, S., von Kalckreuth, A., & Walter, H. (2010). Neural long-term effects of emotion regulation on episodic memory processes. *Neuropsychologia*, 48(4), 989–96.

Farb, N. A., Anderson, A. K., Mayberg, H., Bean, J., McKeon, D., & Segal, Z. V. (2010). Minding one's emotions: Mindfulness training alters the neural expression of sadness. *Emotion*, 10(1), 25–33.

Farb, N. A., Segal, Z. V., Mayberg, H., Bean, J., McKeon, D., Fatima, Z., et al. (2007). Attending to the present: mindfulness meditation reveals distinct neural modes of self-reference. *Social, Cognitive, & Affective Neuroscience*, 2(4), 313–22.

Fox, H. C., Hong, K. A., & Sinha, R. (2008). Difficulties in emotion regulation and impulse control in recently abstinent alcoholics compared with social drinkers. *Addictive Behaviors*, 33(2), 388–94.

Frankenstein, U. N., Richter, W., McIntyre, M. C., & Remy, F. (2001). Distraction modulates anterior cingulate gyrus activations during the cold pressor test. *Neuroimage*, 14(4), 827–36.

Freud, S. (1946). *The ego and the mechanisms of defense*. New York: International Universities Press.

Fusar-Poli, P., Placentino, A., Carletti, F., Landi, P., Allen, P., Surguladze, S., et al. (2009). Functional atlas of emotional faces processing: A voxel-based meta-analysis of 105 functional magnetic resonance imaging studies. *Journal of Psychiatry and Neuroscience*, 34(6), 418–32.

Gillanders, S., Wild, M., Deighan, C., & Gillanders, D. (2008). Emotion regulation, affect, psychosocial functioning, and well-being in hemodialysis patients. *American Journal of Kidney Disease*, 51(4), 651–62.

Goldin, P. R., Manber, T., Hakimi, S., Canli, T., & Gross, J. J. (2009). Neural bases of social anxiety disorder: Emotional reactivity and cognitive regulation during social and physical threat. *Archives of General Psychiatry*, 66(2), 170–80.

Goldin, P. R., Manber-Ball, T., Werner, K., Heimberg, R., & Gross, J. J. (2009). Neural mechanisms of cognitive reappraisal of negative self-beliefs in social anxiety disorder. *Biological Psychiatry*, 66(12), 1091–99.

Goldin, P. R., McRae, K., Ramel, W., & Gross, J. J. (2008). The neural bases of emotion regulation: Reappraisal and suppression of negative emotion. *Biological Psychiatry*, 63(6), 577–86.

Gross, J. J. (1998). Antecedent- and response-focused emotion regulation: Divergent consequences for experience, expression, and physiology. *Journal of Personality and Social Psychology*, 74(1), 224–37.

Gross, J. J. (1999). Emotion regulation: Past, present, future. *Cognition and Emotion*, 13(5), 551–73.

Gross, J. J. (2002). Emotion regulation: Affective, cognitive, and social consequences. *Psychophysiology*, 39(3), 281–91.

Gross, J. J., & John, O. P. (2003). Individual differences in two emotion regulation processes: Implications for affect, relationships, and well-being *Journal of Personality and Social Psychology*, 85(2), 348–62.

Gross, J. J., & Levenson, R. W. (1993). Emotional suppression: Physiology, self-report, and expressive behavior. *Journal of Personality and Social Psychology*, 64(6), 970–86.

Gross, J. J., & Levenson, R. W. (1997). Hiding feelings: The acute effects of inhibiting negative and positive emotion. *Journal of Abnormal Psychology*, 106(1), 95–103.

Gross, J.J., & Thompson, R. A. (2007). Emotion regulation: Conceptual foundations. In J. J. Gross (Ed.), *Handbook of emotion regulation* (pp. 3–24). New York: Guilford Press.

Gur, R. C., Schroeder, L., Turner, T., McGrath, C., Chan, R. M., Turetsky, B. I., et al. (2002). Brain activation during facial emotion processing. *Neuroimage*, 16(3 Pt. 1), 651–62.

Hajcak, G., MacNamara, A., & Olvet, D. M. (2010). Event-related potentials, emotion, and emotion regulation: An integrative review. *Developmental Neuropsychology*, 35(2), 129–55.

Harenski, C. L., & Hamann, S. (2006). Neural correlates of regulating negative emotions related to moral violations. *Neuroimage*, 30(1), 313–24.

Hariri, A. R., Bookheimer, S. Y., & Mazziotta, J. C. (2000). Modulating emotional responses: Effects of a neocortical network on the limbic system. *Neuroreport*, 11(1), 43–48.

Herwig, U., Baumgartner, T., Kaffenberger, T., Bruhl, A., Kottlow, M., Schreiter-Gasser, U., et al. (2007). Modulation of anticipatory emotion and perception processing by cognitive control. *Neuroimage*, 37(2), 652–62.

Herwig, U., Kaffenberger, T., Jancke, L., & Bruhl, A. B. (2010). Self-related awareness and emotion regulation. *Neuroimage*, 50(2), 734–41.

Hutcherson, C. A., Goldin, P. R., Ochsner, K. N., Gabrieli, J. D., Barrett, L. F., & Gross, J. J. (2005). Attention and emotion: Does rating emotion alter neural responses to amusing and sad films? *Neuroimage*, 27(3), 656–68.

Johnstone, T., van Reekum, C. M., Urry, H. L., Kalin, N. H., & Davidson, R. J. (2007). Failure to regulate: Counterproductive recruitment of top-down prefrontal-subcortical circuitry in major depression. *Journal of Neuroscience*, 27(33), 8877–84.

Kalisch, R. (2009). The functional neuroanatomy of reappraisal: Time matters. *Neuroscience and Biobehavioral Review*, 33(8), 1215–26.

Kalisch, R., Wiech, K., Critchley, H. D., & Dolan, R. J. (2006). Levels of appraisal: A medial prefrontal role in high-level appraisal of emotional material. *Neuroimage*, 30(4), 1458–66.

Kalisch, R., Wiech, K., Herrmann, K., & Dolan, R. J. (2006). Neural correlates of self-distraction from anxiety and a process model of cognitive emotion regulation. *Journal of Cognitive Neuroscience*, 18(8), 1266–76.

Kelley, W. M., Macrae, C. N., Wyland, C. L., Caglar, S., Inati, S., & Heatherton, T. F. (2002). Finding the self? An event-related fMRI study. *Journal of Cognitive Neuroscience*, 14(5), 785–94.

Kim, S. H., & Hamann, S. (2007). Neural correlates of positive and negative emotion regulation. *Journal of Cognitive Neuroscience*, 19(5), 776–98.

Koenigsberg, H. W., Fan, J., Ochsner, K. N., Liu, X., Guise, K., Pizzarello, S., et al. (2010). Neural correlates of using distancing to regulate emotional responses to social situations. *Neuropsychologia*, 48(6), 1813–22.

Koenigsberg, H. W., Fan, J., Ochsner, K. N., Liu, X., Guise, K. G., Pizzarello, S., et al. (2009). Neural correlates of the use of psychological distancing to regulate responses to negative social cues: A study of patients with borderline personality disorder. *Biological Psychiatry*, 66(9), 854–63.

Kompus, K., Hugdahl, K., Ohman, A., Marklund, P., & Nyberg, L. (2009). Distinct control networks for cognition and emotion in the prefrontal cortex. *Neuroscience Letters*, 467(2), 76–80.

Kross, E., Davidson, M., Weber, J., & Ochsner, K. (2009). Coping with emotions past: The neural bases of regulating affect associated with negative autobiographical memories. *Biological Psychiatry*, 65(5), 361–66.

Lang, P. J., Bradley, M. M., & Cuthbert, B. N. (1997). *International Affective Picture System (IAPS): Technical manual and affective ratings*. Gainesville, FL: NIMH Center for the Study of Emotion and Attention, University of Florida.

Lazarus, R. S. (1966). *Psychological stress and the coping process*. New York: McGraw Hill.

Levenson, R. W. (1994). Human emotions: A functional view. In P. Ekman & R. J. Davidson (Eds.), *The nature of emotion.* (pp. 123–126). New York: Oxford University Press.

Levesque, J., Eugene, F., Joanette, Y., Paquette, V., Mensour, B., Beaudoin, G., et al. (2003). Neural circuitry underlying voluntary suppression of sadness. *Biological Psychiatry*, 53(6), 502–10.

Lieberman, M. D., Eisenberger, N. I., Crockett, M. J., Tom, S. M., Pfeifer, J. H., & Way, B. M. (2007). Putting feelings into words: Affect labeling disrupts amygdala activity in response to affective stimuli. *Psychological Science*, 18(5), 421–28.

Lutz, A., Brefczynski-Lewis, J., Johnstone, T., & Davidson, R. J. (2008). Regulation of the neural circuitry of emotion by compassion meditation: Effects of meditative expertise. *PLoS One*, 3(3), e1897.

Lutz, A., Slagter, H. A., Rawlings, N. B., Francis, A. D., Greischar, L. L., & Davidson, R. J. (2009). Mental training enhances attentional stability: Neural and behavioral evidence. *Journal of Neuroscience*, 29(42), 13418–27.

Mak, A. K., Hu, Z. G., Zhang, J. X., Xiao, Z. W., & Lee, T. M. (2009). Neural correlates of regulation of positive and negative emotions: an fmri study. *Neuroscience Letters*, 457(2), 101–6.

Marks, I. (1985). Behavioral psychotherapy for anxiety disorders. *Psychiatric Clinics of North America*, 8(1), 25–35.

McRae, K., Hughes, B., Chopra, S., Gabrieli, J. D., Gross, J. J., & Ochsner, K. N. (2010). The neural bases of distraction and reappraisal. *Journal of Cognitive Neuroscience*, 22(2), 248–62.

Milad, M. R., Rauch, S. L., Pitman, R. K., & Quirk, G. J. (2006). Fear extinction in rats: Implications for human brain imaging and anxiety disorders. *Biological Psychology*, 73(1), 61–71.

Modinos, G., Ormel, J., & Aleman, A. (2010). Individual differences in dispositional mindfulness and brain activity involved in reappraisal of emotion. *Social, Cognitive, & Affective Neuroscience*, 5(4), 369–77.

Nesse, R. (1990). Evolutionary explanations of emotions. *Human Nature*, 1(3), 261–89.

New, A. S., Fan, J., Murrough, J. W., Liu, X., Liebman, R. E., Guise, K. G., et al. (2009). A functional magnetic resonance imaging study of deliberate emotion regulation in resilience and posttraumatic stress disorder. *Biological Psychiatry*, 66(7), 656–64.

Ochsner, K. N. (2004). Current directions in social cognitive neuroscience. *Current Opinions in Neurobiology*, 14(2), 254–58.

Ochsner, K. N., Bunge, S. A., Gross, J. J., & Gabrieli, J. D. (2002). Rethinking feelings: An FMRI study of the cognitive regulation of emotion. *Journal of Cognitive Neuroscience*, 14(8), 1215–29.

Ochsner, K. N., & Gross, J. J. (2005). The cognitive control of emotion. *Trends in Cognitive Sciences*, 9(5), 242–49.

Ochsner, K. N., & Gross, J. J. (2007). The neural architecture of emotion regulation. In J. J. Gross (Ed.), *Handbook of emotion regulation* (pp. 87–109). New York: Guilford Press.

Ochsner, K. N., Ray, R. D., Cooper, J. C., Robertson, E. R., Chopra, S., Gabrieli, J. D., et al. (2004). For better or for worse: Neural systems supporting the cognitive down- and up-regulation of negative emotion. *Neuroimage*, 23(2), 483–99.

Ohira, H., Nomura, M., Ichikawa, N., Isowa, T., Iidaka, T., Sato, A., et al. (2006). Association of neural and physiological responses during voluntary emotion suppression. *Neuroimage*, 29(3), 721–33.

Ortony, A., Clore, G., & Collins, A. (1990). *The cognitive structure of emotions*. Cambridge: Cambridge University Press.

Paulus, M. P., Feinstein, J. S., Castillo, G., Simmons, A. N., & Stein, M. B. (2005). Dose-dependent decrease of activation in bilateral amygdala and insula by lorazepam during emotion processing. *Archives of General Psychiatry*, 62(3), 282–88.

Phan, K. L., Angstadt, M., Golden, J., Onyewuenui, I., Povpovska, A., & de Wit, H. (2008). Cannabinoid modulation of amygdala reactivity to social signals of threat in humans. *Journal of Neuroscience*, 28(9).

Phan, K. L., Fitzgerald, D. A., Gao, K., Moore, G. J., Tancer, M. E., & Posse, S. (2004). Real-time fMRI of cortico-limbic brain activity during emotional processing. *Neuroreport*, 15(3), 527–32.

Phan, K. L., Fitzgerald, D. A., Nathan, P. J., Moore, G. J., Uhde, T. W., & Tancer, M. E. (2005). Neural substrates for voluntary suppression of negative affect: A functional magnetic resonance imaging study. *Biological Psychiatry*, 57(3), 210–19.

Phan, K. L., Taylor, S. F., Welsh, R. C., Decker, L. R., Noll, D. C., Nichols, T. E., et al. (2003). Activation of the medial prefrontal cortex and extended amygdala by individual ratings of emotional arousal: A functional magnetic resonance imaging study. *Biological Psychiatry*, 53, 211–15.

Posse, S., Fitzgerald, D., Gao, K., Habel, U., Rosenberg, D., Moore, G. J., et al. (2003).

Real-time fMRI of temporolimbic regions detects amygdala activation during single-trial self-induced sadness. *Neuroimage*, 18(3), 760–68.

Quirk, G. J., Garcia, R., & Gonzalez-Lima, F. (2006). Prefrontal mechanisms in extinction of conditioned fear. *Biological Psychiatry*, 60(4), 337–43.

Rolls, E. T. (2000). Precis of *The brain and emotion. Behavioral Brain Sciences*, 23(2), 177–91; discussion 192–233.

Schaefer, S. M., Jackson, D. C., Davidson, R. J., Aguirre, G. K., Kimberg, D. Y., & Thompson-Schill, S. L. (2002). Modulation of amygdalar activity by the conscious regulation of negative emotion. *Journal of Cognitive Neuroscience*, 14(6), 913–21.

Schiller, D., & Delgado, M. R. (2010). Overlapping neural systems mediating extinction, reversal and regulation of fear. *Trends in Cognitive Sciences*, 14(6), 268–76.

Schulze, L., Domes, G., Kruger, A., Berger, C., Fleischer, M., Prehn, K., et al. (2011). Neuronal correlates of cognitive reappraisal in borderline patients with affective instability. *Biological Psychiatry*, 69(6), 564–73.

Smyth, J. M., & Arigo, D. (2009). Recent evidence supports emotion-regulation interventions for improving health in at-risk and clinical populations. *Current Opinion in Psychiatry*, 22(2), 205–10.

Staudinger, M. R., Erk, S., Abler, B., & Walter, H. (2009). Cognitive reappraisal modulates expected value and prediction error encoding in the ventral striatum. *Neuroimage*, 47(2), 713–21.

Staudinger, M. R., Erk, S., & Walter, H. (2011). Dorsolateral prefrontal cortex modulates striatal reward encoding during reappraisal of reward anticipation. *Cerebral Cortex*, 21(11), 2578–88.

Taylor, S. F., Phan, K. L., Decker, L. R., & Liberzon, I. (2003). Subjective rating of emotionally salient stimuli modulates neural activity. *Neuroimage*, 18(3), 650–59.

Thompson, R. A. (1994). Emotion regulation: a theme in search of definition. *Monographs of the Society for Research in Child Development*, 59(2–3), 25–52.

Tracey, I., Ploghaus, A., Gati, J. S., Clare, S., Smith, S., Menon, R. S., et al. (2002). Imaging attentional modulation of pain in the periaqueductal gray in humans. *Journal of Neuroscience*, 22(7), 2748–2752.

Urry, H. L., van Reekum, C. M., Johnstone, T., Kalin, N. H., Thurow, M. E., Schaefer, H. S., et al. (2006). Amygdala and ventromedial prefrontal cortex are inversely coupled during regulation of negative affect and predict the diurnal pattern of cortisol secretion among older adults. *Journal of Neuroscience*, 26(16), 4415–25.

van Reekum, C. M., Johnstone, T., Urry, H. L., Thurow, M. E., Schaefer, H. S., Alexander, A. L., et al. (2007). Gaze fixations predict brain activation during the voluntary regulation of picture-induced negative affect. *Neuroimage*, 36(3), 1041–55.

Wager, T. D., Davidson, M. L., Hughes, B. L., Lindquist, M. A., & Ochsner, K. N. (2008). Prefrontal-subcortical pathways mediating successful emotion regulation. *Neuron*, 59(6), 1037–50.

Whalen, P. J., Rauch, S. L., Etcoff, N. L., McInerney, S. C., Lee, M. B., & Jenike, M. A. (1998). Masked presentations of emotional facial expressions modulate amygdala activity without explicit knowledge. *Journal of Neuroscience*, 18(1), 411–18.

CHAPTER 17

Neural Mechanisms Underlying Value-Based Decision Making

John P. O'Doherty

Value-based decision making can be defined as the process of selecting actions from among several alternatives to maximize future possible rewards and minimize future possible punishers. Underlying this capacity are a number of distinct neural signals. The first signal is the "experienced utility" or outcome value. It is essentially a neural representation of the subjective affective response engendered by a stimulus as it is consumed or experienced by an individual. Another key signal is the chosen value, which codes for the expected utility of a particular decision option after that option has been chosen. Another key signal is the decision value and/or action value – the value assigned to particular decision options or possible paths of action based on the expected utility that would occur if and only if those decision options are selected. Such decision value signals are used as inputs into the decision process. Finally, these decision value signals need to be compared to yield a decision about which option ultimately should be chosen.

In this chapter, I consider each of these signals in turn and evaluate evidence about

the contribution of specific neural circuits to these functions. I focus on the situation where the relevant information to make decisions must be learned through trial-and-error experience, in the presence of considerable uncertainty about the underlying decision variables, rather than the situation where complete information about all the decision variables is provided using explicit description. The former scenario is perhaps the most realistic framework for studying decision making in the real world where all the relevant information about particular decision options must be inferred on the basis of prior experience, as opposed to being provided up front. Knowledge about decision-making mechanisms and reward outcome processing has major implications for several domains beyond neuroscience, including the economy, addiction, and social behavior (see Chapter 19).

Outcome Values

Outcome values correspond to the overall subjective utility or benefit that a given stimulus outcome conveys to an organism. They are computed in real time as that outcome is experienced and are modulated by intrinsic motivational states such as hunger or thirst. Empirical studies on the neural representation of outcome values has provided evidence that these signals appear to be represented in at least one key brain region: the orbitofrontal cortex (OFC). Early neurophysiologal investigations in nonhuman primates reported neurons in the OFC that responded to the receipt of olfactory and gustatory stimuli (Critchley & Rolls, 1996; Rolls, Sienkiewicz, & Yaxley, 1989; Thorpe, Rolls, & Maddison, 1983). Furthermore these neurons were found to be modulated by changes in the motivational state of the animal so that if it was satiated on a particular food, the firing rate of neurons responsive to the particular taste or odor of the food decreased (Critchley & Rolls, 1996; Rolls et al., 1989). Similar findings were observed in human functional neuroimaging studies: Regions of the OFC were identified as responding to the presentation of gustatory and olfactory stimuli, and these responses were subsequently modulated if the value of those specific stimuli were changed by feeding volunteers to satiety (de Araujo, Kringelbach, Rolls, & McGlone, 2003; O'Doherty et al., 2000; Small, Zatorre, Dagher, Evans, & Jones-Gotman, 2001). The orbitofrontal cortex has been found to be responsive not only to food-related stimuli but also to the experienced value of visual stimuli such as attractive faces (Cloutier, Heatherton, Whalen, & Kelley, 2008; Kranz & Ishai, 2006; O'Doherty, Winston, et al., 2003) and the subjective beauty of visual art (Kawabata & Zeki, 2004; Kirk, Skov, Hulme, Christensen, & Zeki, 2009), as well as to the experienced value of auditory stimuli such as a musical sequence (Blood, Zatorre, Bermudez, & Evans, 1999). Further, it has been shown to be responsive to the experienced value of abstract reinforcers not tied to a specific sensory modality, such as winning or losing money (O'Doherty, Kringelbach, Rolls, Hornak, & Andrews, 2001) or receiving social praise or feedback (Elliott, Frith, & Dolan, 1997; Vrticka, Andersson,

Grandjean, Sander, & Vuilleumier, 2008). It is important to emphasize that outcome value representations in the OFC are not invariant. Not only can such representations be modulated as a function of changes in internal motivational state as mentioned earlier but activity in this region can also be influenced by cognitive factors such as the provision of price information (Plassmann, O'Doherty, Shiv, & Rangel, 2008) or merely the use of semantic labels (de Araujo, Rolls, Velazco, Margot, & Cayeux, 2005). Thus, the online computation of outcome value in the OFC is highly flexible and can be directly influenced by a variety of internal and external factors.

Functional Segregation of Outcome Values in the Orbitofrontal Cortex

A major focus in the literature has been to determine whether distinct regions of the OFC can be segregated as a function of variation in the type or modality of outcome value signals, such as whether an outcome value is positively or negatively valenced. One claim has been that there may be a medial versus lateral gradient within the OFC in the representation of rewarding versus punishing stimuli (Kringelbach & Rolls, 2004). An extremely robust finding in the literature is that the medial OFC is especially responsive to the receipt of rewarding compared to punishing stimuli and that its activity is positively correlated with the subjective pleasantness reported for those stimuli (O'Doherty et al., 2001; O'Doherty, Winston, et al., 2003; Plassmann et al., 2008; Small et al., 2001). Activity appears to increase in this region the more rewarding an outcome is, and activity decreases relative to baseline the more aversive an outcome is. In the lateral OFC, a number of studies have reported the opposite profile: Aversive or punishing reinforcers, such as pain, unattractive or angry faces, and losing money, often recruit this area, and activity in this region is reported as being correlated with the degree of aversiveness experienced in response to an outcome (Blair, Morris, Frith, Perrett, & Dolan, 1999; Cloutier et al., 2008; Kirk et al., 2009; O'Doherty et al., 2001; O'Doherty, Winston, et al., 2003; Ursu & Carter, 2005). However, several studies have also reported activity in the lateral OFC in response to reward outcomes (Breiter, Aharon, Kahneman, Dale, & Shizgal, 2001; Elliott, Newman, Longe, & Deakin, 2003; O'Doherty, Critchley, Deichmann, & Dolan, 2003), and this region has also been implicated in possible functions other than outcome values, such as inhibiting previously learned responses following a change in contingencies (Cools, Clark, Owen, & Robbins, 2002), encoding aversive prediction errors (Seymour et al., 2005), and detecting changes in contingency (O'Doherty, Critchley, et al., 2003).

Because aversive outcome values are often confounded with these other variables, ascertaining the precise role of human OFC in encoding aversive outcomes is still an ongoing issue in the literature. Nevertheless, it is known that at the single-neuron level, spatially intermingled populations of neurons in lateral and central parts of the OFC encode both rewarding and punishing outcomes (Morrison & Salzman, 2009). It is possible therefore that at the resolution available for fMRI measurements, a standard univariate contrast between appetitive and aversive outcome values would fail to identify some regions encoding outcome values, even if neurons at the single-neuron level are coding for both types of outcome signal. The deployment of multivariate pattern analysis approaches may help provide new insight into this question (Kahnt, Heinzle, Park, & Haynes, 2010) and clarify the contribution of the medial and lateral OFC in encoding positive and negative outcome value signals.

It has also been proposed that outcome values within the OFC can be differentiated with respect to the "complexity" of the reinforcer. A meta-analysis revealed a trend for abstract reinforcers such as monetary gain or loss to be represented more anteriorly, whereas more basic reinforcers such as odor and taste were represented more posteriorly (Kringelbach & Rolls, 2004). To date little direct evidence beyond the meta-analysis has been forthcoming to support

these claims, although a recent study did report that activity in response to monetary outcomes was located more anteriorly within the OFC than activity in response to sexual rewards (Sescousse, Redoute, & Dreher, 2010).

Chosen Values

Another key signal present during the decision process is the chosen value, which corresponds to the anticipatory value for the expected outcome associated with the decision option that is ultimately selected. Like outcome values, chosen values are a post-decision signal, in that they are a consequence as opposed to a precursor or input into the decision process. A number of studies have revealed chosen value signals to be present in the medial OFC extending dorsally up the medial wall of the prefrontal cortex. For example, Hampton, Bossaerts, and O'Doherty (2006) scanned volunteers while they participated in a probabilistic choice task in which they could choose between pairs of stimuli yielding rewarding or punishing outcomes with varying frequencies. Furthermore, the outcome probabilities assigned to the different stimuli switched or reversed over time. Hampton et al. used a computational model that took into account the pattern of each subjects' choices and the outcomes obtained in the past for selecting those options to derive trial-by-trial estimates about the expected value of particular decision options as subjects proceeded through the experiment. Those model-based predictions were then correlated against the fMRI data in a procedure that has come to be known as "model-based fMRI" (Glascher, Daw, Dayan, & O'Doherty, 2010). Using this approach, Hampton and colleagues looked for brain areas exhibiting activity at the time of choice but before the outcome was received, which correlated with the value of the chosen stimulus. This analysis revealed activity in the medial OFC and adjacent medial prefrontal cortex (Figure 17.1A), implicating these areas in encoding the expected value of the chosen

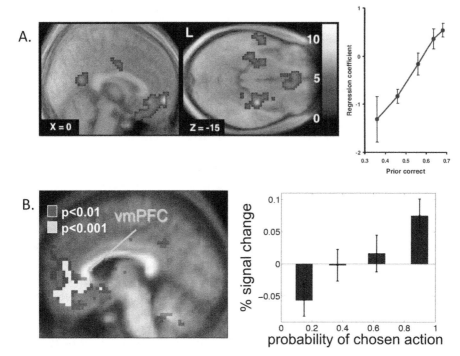

Figure 17.1. **Chosen value signals in vmPFC.** (A) Left panel shows areas of vmPFC exhibiting significant correlations with the expected value of the chosen action at the time of choice while human volunteers are performing a simple reward-based choice task (data from Hampton et al., 2006). Right panel shows the BOLD activity in this region plotted against a measure of expected reward (prior correct) generated by the computational model. (B) Similar findings from a study by Daw et al., (2006).

option. The more reward that was expected for the option that was chosen, the greater the activity in this area; in contrast, if the volunteer chose an option that was predicted by the model to lead to less reward, activity was decreased.

Similarly, Daw, O'Doherty, Dayan, Seymour, and Dolan (2006) presented subjects with a four-armed bandit task in which on each trial they were invited to choose one of four different colored slot machines. The magnitude of reward available on each slot machine drifted over time, although volunteers were not made aware of the specific underlying reward contingencies, but rather had to infer the value of each machine at different points in the course of the experiment through sampling. Daw et al. also used a computational model to derive trial-by-trial estimates for the expected value associated with each of the available slots. Once again,

when activity at the time of choice was correlated against the model-estimated predictions about the expected value corresponding to the option that was ultimately chosen, significant effects were found in the medial OFC and adjacent medial prefrontal cortex (Figure 17.1B). In a recording study from a region of the central OFC in nonhuman primates, Padoa-Schioppa and Assad (2006) also found single neurons that coded for the value of the chosen option. When taken together these studies indicate that chosen value signals are encoded within the ventromedial prefrontal cortex (vmPFC) during decision making.

Chosen Values: Associated with Actions or Stimuli?

The finding of chosen value signals in the vmPFC raises the question as to the nature of the underlying associations underpinning such representations. To make a choice, an individual typically performs a particular motor response in order to select the specific stimulus that denotes the decision option. For instance, in the study by Daw et al. described earlier, the slot machines were denoted by different colors (different stimuli), and to select one of those stimuli, the subject had to make one of four button presses corresponding to the location of the stimulus on the screen. Thus, neural activity relating to the chosen value could be driven by an association established between the stimulus and the corresponding outcome or else an association between the specific motor action and the same outcome. To determine which of these associations underpins the encoding of chosen values, Glascher, Hampton, and O'Doherty (2009) scanned subjects with fMRI while they participated in two different types of decision tasks. In one "stimulus-based" task, in all practical respects identical to that used by Hampton et al. (2006), subjects observed two fractal stimuli that were presented randomly on either side of a fixation cross. Subjects had to select one of these using either a left or right button press, and after a delay they received an outcome (either a monetary gain or loss). In this type of task, subjects are most likely to learn to associate a particular fractal stimulus with the associated outcomes engendered by that stimulus and then to use this learned association to drive value expectancies following choice, or alternatively to deploy a more complex conditional stimulus-response–outcome association. As in Hampton et al., (2006), significant chosen value signals were found at the time of choice using a model-based fMRI analysis.

The second "action-based" task used by Gläscher et al. (2009) was similar to the first, except instead of two fractals being presented on the screen, only one was presented and the subject was required to choose between one of two physical actions: pressing a button versus operating a tracker ball. The point here is that in this design there was no visual stimulus to signal which of the two physical actions needed to be selected, so subjects instead had to learn to associate different physical actions with their corresponding outcomes and choose on the basis of those learned associations. Gläscher et al. used the same model-based procedure to identify chosen value signals in the action-based task, reporting significant correlations with chosen values in the same area of the vmPFC that was found to be activated in the stimulus-based task (Figure 17.2A). The finding that chosen-value signals were present in the vmPFC, even during the action-based task in which no discriminative stimuli were available to drive choice, suggests that the chosen value signal can be encoded via action-outcome-based associations and not merely through stimulus-outcome-based associations.

Further evidence that chosen value representations pertain to specific chosen actions has come from Wunderlich, Rangel, and O'Doherty (2009). In this study, Wunderlich et al. also used an action-based choice task, except in each trial subjects needed to choose between two physical action modalities: making an eye movement (a saccade from a central fixation point to a target in the right of the visual field) versus making a hand movement (using a right-handed button press). The probability of winning on each action varied over time using a random walk, and subjects had to keep sampling the two movements to work out which movement was generating the greatest probability of reward, so that they could then exploit this movement until such time as the contingencies changed again. Once again Wunderlich et al. found signals correlating with the value of the chosen action in the vmPFC, consistent with the suggestion that these signals could be driven by action-outcome relationships as opposed to purely being stimulus bound. However, even more critically, Wunderlich et al. observed a topographical arrangement of choice values within the vmPFC with regard to the specific action modality that was chosen: Whereas an anterior region of the vmPFC was correlated with choice values regardless of whether

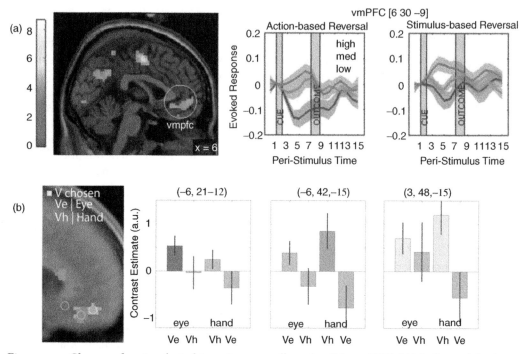

Figure 17.2. Chosen value signals tied to actions as well as stimuli in vmPFC. (A) Left panel depicts vmPFC area showing common correlations with chosen values in both an action-based choice task and a stimulus-based choice task. Right panel shows evoked responses in this region as a function of different levels of chosen value (low, medium, high). Data from Glascher et al., (2009). (B) Left panel shows areas of vmPFC exhibiting correlations with chosen values that depend on the specific action implemented on that choice. Areas correlating with chosen values for eye movements only are shown in red, areas correlating with chosen values for hand movements are shown in green, whereas areas correlating with chosen values regardless of the effector modality of the action involved are shown in yellow. The right panel shows the parameter estimates for the value signals for each movement separately from each region, as depicting by the color code (Vh = action value of hand movement; Ve = action value of eye movement). For example, the plot with the red bar indicates significant responses to the value of an eye movement only if that movement is chosen (but not otherwise). Data from Wunderlich et al., (2009). See color plate 17.2.

the action chosen was an eye or a hand movement, a mid-region of the vmPFC was correlated with choice values only when a hand movement was selected; a more posterior region again correlated only with choice values only when an eye movement was selected (Figure 17.2B). Such modality-specific signals could not easily be explained in a stimulus-based account and likely reflect encoding of action-specific chosen value signals in this region.

These findings raise the question of whether the vmPFC encodes only action-based chosen values or whether this region is involved in encoding both stimulus-

based and action-based chosen values. To address this question, Wunderlich, Rangel, and O'Doherty (2010) used a task in which the presentation of stimuli depicting the available decision options was temporally separated from the time at which specific actions could be selected to make a choice. At the beginning of a trial, the subject was presented with a choice between two of three possible stimuli, each of which was associated with distinct drifting probabilities of obtaining reward. After a delay, subjects were subsequently presented with additional symbols informing them whether a given stimulus could be selected by

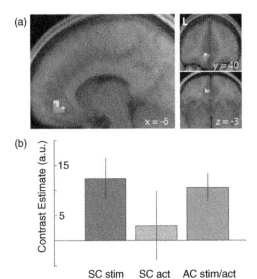

(a)

(b)

Figure 17.3. Evidence for pure stimulus-based chosen value signals in vmPFC. (A) Area exhibiting significant correlations with the value of a stimulus that is ultimately chosen is shown in red. This signal is from trials where the stimuli are presented before the actions needed to select those stimuli are made available. The area in green is also a chosen value signal, but from trials where both stimuli and actions are presented simultaneously. The area in yellow shows overlap between the two signals. (B) Plots of parameter estimates corresponding to chosen value signals from these regions (red and green color code as in A; SC stim = chosen value at time of stimulus from condition where stimuli are presented before actions are made available; SC action = chosen value at time of action selection (once actions are revealed) from stimulus condition; AC stim/act = chosen value signals from condition when both stimuli and actions are revealed simultaneously). See color plate 17.2.

performing an eye movement or a hand movement. Critically, subjects were not informed at the time when the choice stimuli were presented what particular action was needed to select a particular stimulus; the stimulus-action mappings were only made available subsequently. Thus, subjects could potentially make a choice of stimuli before they could select particular actions to implement that choice. Once again, Wunderlich et al. used a computational model to derive trial-by-trial predictions for the

chosen value signal and tested for the presence of this signal at two different time points in the trial: first, when the choice stimuli were initially presented, and second, once the actions required to implement the choice were made available immediately before an action was performed. Remarkably, at the time of stimulus presentation, a robust chosen value signal was observed, whereas at the time that the actions were made available, no such signal was found (Figure 17.3). These findings demonstrate (perhaps unsurprisingly) that at least in some circumstances choices of stimuli can be made even before knowing the specific actions needed to implement that choice. More importantly for the present discussion, the findings also show that chosen value signals can be computed even in the absence of specific actions, suggesting that chosen value signals in the vmPFC need not necessarily be tied to actions, but can be elicited by stimuli as well.

Pre-Choice Value Signals: Action Values and Decision Values

The value signals we have considered so far are all post-decision signals: They are contingent on a decision that has already been made and are thus unlikely to contribute directly to the decision process, but rather reflect a consequence of that process. To achieve a mechanistic understanding of decision making, it is also important to consider the type of value signals that would be required to be used as an input into the decision process as opposed to being a consequence of that process. To make a decision between different options, it is necessary to represent the value of each possible option, so that ultimately those values can be compared. This representation of value could be done in two ways: Values could be assigned to the individual actions available for implementing a particular choice, or else values could be tied to stimuli that symbolize the different decision options and rendered over the different outcomes associated with this stimuli.

Let us first consider values assigned to individual actions. These are referred to as "action values" in the computational reinforcement learning literature. Consider an action a that is available in a state of the world s; then the action value $Q(s,a)$, corresponds to the average future reward that would be expected to be obtained if action a were selected. Assuming actions b and c are also available to be selected in the same state, then it follows that a value signal will exist for each of these other actions as well: $Q(s,b)$ and $Q(s,c)$. At its simplest, a decision-making strategy for the course of action to pursue in state s could involve opting to choose the action associated with the highest action value. For such a decision to be rendered in the brain, it is necessary to encode separately the value of each action simultaneously: $Q(s,a)$, $Q(s,b)$, and $Q(s,c)$. Importantly these signals should not be modulated by or dependent on choice in the way that chosen values are, but instead should remain the same regardless of the choice made on a given trial (at least before the outcome is experienced).

Relatively few studies have looked for or provided direct evidence for pure action value signals in humans. In monkeys, (Samejima, Ueda, Doya, and Kimura (2005), recorded from the striatum while monkeys performed a simple choice task in which they could choose between one of four possible actions associated with different amounts of reinforcement in different stimulus conditions. By correlating neural signals against action values generated from a reinforcement learning model, the researchers reported that some neurons appeared to uniquely code for the value of individual actions (as opposed to the value of the action ultimately chosen). Lau and Glimcher (2007) also reported action value signals in the striatum using a similar monkey choice paradigm. Many other neurophysiology studies have reported action-dependent value signals in striatum and in areas of the cortex such as the lateral-intraparietal sulcus or supplementary motor cortex (Lee, Conroy, McGreevy, & Barraclough, 2004; Platt

& Glimcher, 1999; Sohn & Lee, 2007; Sugrue, Corrado, & Newsome, 2004). However, with respect to the LIP, these signals appear not to be pure action value signals, because they are ultimately modulated as a function of what action is ultimately chosen. In the supplementary motor cortex, although the value signals reported may be action values, the monkey experimental paradigms to date have not generally permitted action values to be fully disambiguated from other kinds of value signal (such as action-dependent chosen values).

In humans, the Wunderlich et al. (2009) study referred to earlier attempted to identify the existence of action values in the brain above and beyond chosen values. Recall that the paradigm required subjects to make a choice between an eye movement and a hand movement, whereby the probability of obtaining a reward following the choice of these actions changed over the course of the experiment. That experiment required choices to be made between effector modalities rather than between individual motor movements within a modality because, although it might be expected that neurons coding for action values within a modality would be located within the same overlapping area of the cortex and/or striatum and thus would be difficult to separate with fMRI, action values for choices made between modality effectors might be expected to be represented in spatially distinct brain areas, thus enabling their identification with fMRI. To identify action values for eye movements, the researchers looked for areas correlating with the reinforcement-learning-derived value for an eye movement, with the proviso that such value signals are invariant regardless of whether the eye movement was chosen or is not chosen. Similarly, to identify action values for hand movements, it was possible to look for areas showing correlations with the value of hand movement regardless of whether that movement was chosen on a given trial. Activity in a region of the presupplementary eye fields in the medial frontal cortex was found to be correlated with action values for eye

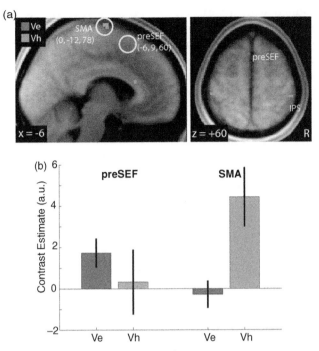

Figure 17.4. Action values in supplementary motor cortex.
(A) Region of supplementary motor area and
pre-supplementary eye fields correlating with action values
for hand movements (green; Vh), and eye movements (red,
Ve), respectively. (B) Plot of parameter estimates depicting
correlations with action values for eye and hand movements
in these areas. See color plate 17.2.

movements, whereas a nearby region of supplementary motor cortex was found to be
correlated with action values for hand movements (Figure 17.4). These findings suggest
that it is indeed possible to detect pre-choice
action value signals in the human brain and
that these signals can be found in supplementary motor areas. Given the single-unit
neurophysiology findings described earlier,
it is also likely that such signals are present
elsewhere in the human brain, such as the
dorsal striatum; however, if such signals in
those other areas are intermixed at the neuronal population level, conventional univariate fMRI analyses may not permit their identification.

Moving on from action values, another
type of pre-decision signal corresponds to
the values of particular decision options
regardless of the action needed to select
them, which are often called decision val-

ues. Such value signals are tied not to specific actions, but instead to particular stimuli
that denote particular available options. Evidence that such signals likely exist in monkey orbitofrontal cortex came from Padoa-
Schioppa and Assad (2006), who recorded
from the OFC while monkeys made choices
between stimuli denoting different amounts
of one of two types of liquid juices. Single
neurons were found that correlated with the
subjective value of the particular magnitude
of juice denoted by each stimulus, with separate neurons coding for the value of each
juice type, independently of the particular
action the monkey needed to perform to
obtain it. Padoa-Schioppa and Assad (2006)
proposed that these signals corresponded to
the value of "goods" and that these were
deployed as inputs into the decision process.

In a human fMRI study (Plassmann,
O'Doherty, & Rangel, 2007), hungry human

subjects were presented with a variety of food stuffs while eliciting their "willingness to pay" for each of the food items (from an initial endowment of $4), yielding a trial-by-trial representation of their underlying subjective value for each item. After the experiment was over, one of the trials was selected at random, and if the reported willingness to pay exceeded a random draw from a lottery then subjects were provided with the food item and invited to consume it (and their endowment was drawn on); otherwise they kept the endowment and did not receive the good. This procedure is designed to ensure that subjects give their true underlying valuation for each item. Activity in a region of the vmPFC was found to be correlated with trial-by-trial variations in the willingness to pay, suggesting a role for this region in encoding the value of potential outcomes. This signal was suggested to correspond to a representation of "decision values" that were used as an input to the decision process, which in this case corresponded to how much money to pay for a given item.

Decision Values versus Action Values: Which Are Necessary for Choice?

Action values and decision values are not only distinct types of pre-choice value signals but are also the core signals underlying what seem at first glance to be two very different ways to compute choices. In the action value case, decisions are made in "action space" by considering each of the possible actions available for a given choice, attaching values to those actions, and then implementing those actions yielding the highest expected reward. Alternatively, in the decision value case, decisions are computed in "goods space," and they constitute a more abstract decision whether to select a particular "good" or "goal," independent of the actions needed to implement that selection, which are argued to occur at a later time. There is an ongoing debate in the decision neuroscience literature as to which of these mechanisms accounts for how choices are computed: Some argue strongly in favor of the action-based account

(Glimcher, Dorris, & Bayer, 2005; Shadlen, Britten, Newsome, & Movshon, 1996), whereas others argue in favor of the goods-based framework (Padoa-Schioppa, 2007; Padoa-Schioppa & Assad, 2006).

Although this remains an area of active research, one possible "hybrid" proposal on the basis of the findings from the Glaescher et al. and Wunderlich et al. studies described earlier is that both mechanisms might exist for computing choice at the same time, and the extent to which a particular mechanism is engaged for a particular decision problem (whether an action-based or a goods-based mechanism) may depend substantively on how the decision problem is framed, such as the extent to which relevant outcomes and relevant actions are made salient (Wunderlich et al., 2010). It appears that the vmPFC likely contributes to both kinds of decision making, and one possibility is that, in both types, decisions are ultimately rendered by retrieving goal values by virtue of their association with either individual actions or with individual stimulus cues. This proposal is also compatible with another set of findings that implicate the vmPFC in goal-directed learning (involving learning derived from stimuli, actions and the current incentive value of outcomes; Valentin, Dickinson, & O'Doherty, 2007).

Comparing Decision Values or Action Values: Locating the Comparator Process

To actually generate a choice, it is necessary to compare the different values assigned to particular decision options to establish which option yields the highest utility. This is the case regardless of whether decisions are computed over actions or over stimuli linked to outcomes, although the input signals into a comparator and the neural system implementing the comparison process might potentially differ depending on whether decisions are taken over actions or stimuli. Putting aside the action versus goods debate, what would such a comparison process look like on a computational level?

The simplest possible comparator might consist of distinct pools of neurons each "voting" for a particular decision option. Assume that the neurons in each pool are recruited in direct proportion to the action values associated with each of the decision options. Through a mechanism of stochastic competitive inhibition, one of these neuronal pools might end up being the winner, such that by the end of the process some neurons from one of the pools are left standing while all the other neurons from the other pools have been switched off through inhibition. Most of the time the winning pool would happen to correspond to the most valuable decision option (by virtue of the scaling in the neural populations as a function of value), but other times because the competitive process is stochastic, less favorable options are selected – fulfilling the occasional need for an organism to explore decision options other than the most valuable one for informational purposes, the so-called exploration/exploitation tradeoff (Daw et al., 2006).

What would such a process look like in terms of brain signals? If such a process were being implemented in the brain, a region doing such a comparison process would first correlate with the sum of the values of the available decision options (representing all the pools being turned on). Through the process of competitive interaction, after the decision process was complete, the signal would end up (in the simple case of binary choice) resembling the value of the chosen option minus the value of the unchosen option (for an elaboration of this simple model and a more detailed explanation of the putative neural signals, see Wunderlich et al., 2009).

Wunderlich et al., (2009) reported just such a signal in the brain in a region of the dorsomedial prefrontal cortex (Figure 17.5), with the caveat that rather than correlating with Vchosen-Vunchosen (as would be predicted by the model), the signal in the dmPFC was correlated with the opposite: Vunchosen-Vchosen. One possible interpretation of this finding is that the Vunchosen-Vchosen signal reflects an inhibitory mechanism to suppress activation corresponding to the action that is not chosen, compared to the action that is ultimately selected. Wunderlich et al. did not find any regions correlating with Vchosen-Vunchosen. However, in another fMRI study (Boorman, Behrens, Woolrich, & Rushworth, 2009), activity was reported as correlating with Vchosen-Vunchosen in a part of the vmPFC. Note that both Vchosen-Vunchosen and its converse correspond to the endpoint or output of a putative decision comparator. Therefore, although finding evidence for such signals in parts of the brain is intriguing, it is still unknown where precisely the decision process itself (i.e., the competition between action or decision values) is implemented or even if the decision process can be localized to a specific brain region as opposed to being computed in a distributed fashion across multiple brain areas.

Given that simple value-based decisions can typically be rendered in less than a second after the initial presentation of the decision options, limits in temporal resolution using only hemodynamic imaging techniques will mitigate against the likelihood of detecting rapidly changing neural signals underpinning the competition process itself. However, the increased temporal resolution offered by electrodynamic imaging tools such as EEG or MEG might, when integrated with fMRI, provide further insights into where and how the decision process is implemented. It should also be noted that the very simple decision model suggested here is a poor cousin of more sophisticated computational models such as accumulator and diffusion models that generally perform well in capturing rich behavioral features of human choice data, such as variation in reaction times (Busemeyer & Townsend, 1993; Ratcliff & McKoon, 2008; Smith & Ratcliff, 2004). A fruitful and ongoing avenue of research involves generating specific predictions about the neural implementation of different kinds of comparator processes and using functional imaging and neurophysiology data to compare and contrast different putative comparator mechanisms.

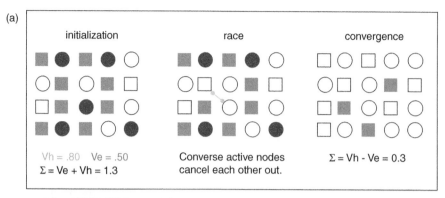

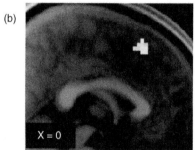

Figure 17.5. Decision comparator signals in dmPFC. (A) Illustration of a simple model of a putative decision process. Processing units for eye (circle) and hand movements (square) are activated in proportion to the magnitude of the predicted value for the corresponding actions. The average activity corresponds to the sum of the constituent action values. These activated populations compete with each other through mutual inhibition. Ultimately only some units remain, and the average activity remaining corresponds to the value of the action chosen compared to the action not chosen. (B) Area of dmPFC corresponding to the difference between the action not chosen and the action chosen (the inverse of the outcome of the decision signal described earlier). Data from Wunderlich et al., (2009).

Functional Relevance of Post-Decision Value Signals in the Choice Process

Now that we have considered value signals that serve as inputs into the choice process, as well as briefly reviewed evidence for the existence of comparison signals that resemble the outcome of such a decision process, we can return to the post-decision value signals we described earlier in this chapter. To recapitulate, these signals are outcome values, corresponding to the hedonic evaluation of an experienced outcome, and chosen values, corresponding to the expected reward at the time of choice for the decision option that is ultimately chosen. Given that chosen value and outcome value signals are post-decision signals and are therefore a consequence rather than a precursor of the decision process, this raises the question

of what function these signals might serve. One very plausible idea is that these post-decision signals play a key role in updating or learning about the pre-decision value signals, whether they be action values or decision values. A now pervasive notion in the domain of reward learning is that value signals (whether tied to stimuli or actions) are acquired by means of a prediction error signal that codes the difference between what is expected (one's current value prediction) and the value of the outcome that is ultimately received.

There is a wealth of evidence implicating the phasic activity of dopamine neurons in the midbrain in encoding just such a reward prediction error signal (Hollerman & Schultz, 1998; Schultz, 1998) and implicating parts of the midbrain and striatum in processing such a prediction error during human reward learning (McClure, Berns, & Montague, 2003; O'Doherty, Dayan, Friston, Critchley, & Dolan, 2003; O'Doherty et al., 2004). As it happens, chosen values and outcome values are precisely the kinds of value signal that could be provided as input into the generation of a prediction error signal that could be used to update the pre-choice value signals. The prediction error signal would correspond to the difference between outcome values (the value of what is experienced) and chosen values (the value of what is predicted to occur given a choice made). Thus, a very plausible functional interpretation of these post-decision signals is that they serve as an input for generating prediction error signals that are then subsequently used to update the value signals needed to compute future choice.

Conclusions

In the present chapter we have reviewed several types of value signals that are likely to play an important role in the decision-making process, either as an input into or a consequence of that process. Action values and decision values enable decisions to be computed in the first place, because they are the signals that need to be compared and contrasted to generate a decision. We have reviewed evidence to suggest that decision and action values may be located in distinct parts of the cortex. Whereas decision values are present in the ventromedial prefrontal cortex, action values are present in the supplementary motor cortex and are likely (as shown in monkey neurophysiology studies but not fMRI) in parts of the human striatum. The role that such signals play in the decision process may depend on whether decisions are computed over stimuli that elicit outcomes or over actions. We also considered evidence for the existence of signals that may reflect the output of the decision-making process, most prominently the difference between the value of the option that is ultimately chosen and the option that is not chosen and its converse; these signals were found in the ventromedial prefrontal

cortex and the dorsomedial prefrontal cortex, respectively. Furthermore, other post-decision signals such as chosen values and outcome values appear to be located in the ventromedial prefrontal cortex. These post-decision signals are likely to serve a key role in facilitating updating of action and/or decision values through trial-and-error learning. Taken together, these findings appear to implicate two key brain areas in value-based decision making: the ventromedial prefrontal cortex, and the dorsomedial prefrontal cortex and adjacent supplementary motor cortex. Although the vmPFC appears to participate in the decision process regardless of whether decisions are computed over stimuli or actions, dorsomedial frontal areas may be involved more selectively in decisions over actions, as opposed to stimuli.

Understanding the neural mechanisms underlying value-based decision making is still in its early stages. Many open questions remain. Perhaps the most fundamental of these questions concerns the nature of the mechanism by which the values assigned to different options are compared in the brain. As yet we do not know where this comparison process takes place, nor do we know how this comparison is implemented on a computational level. Another major issue alluded to here is that, although mechanisms exist to enable decisions to be computed over stimuli as well as actions, it is unclear what factors influence or control which of these mechanisms is to be deployed for a given decision. Although it is possible to set up experimental paradigms in which the nature of the task is such as to make actions more salient than stimuli and vice versa, and thus differentially bias individuals toward action-based and stimulus-based decision making, the role that these different decision mechanisms might play in more complex everyday choices is unclear. The role of individual differences related to gender (see Chapter 26) and genetics (see Chapter 25) needs also to be clarified. Furthermore, it is likely that decisions emerge as a function of the interaction among a number of distinct brain regions – not only the two areas focused on in this chapter but also additional regions such as the amygdala, striatum, and intra-parietal cortex. A complete understanding of the neural computations underlying value-based decision making is likely to be achievable only if the nature of the causal interactions among distinct brain regions during this process is fully elucidated. Finally, significant progress in the neurobiology of human decision making is unlikely to be achieved through the pursuit of hemodynamic imaging methods alone. To answer some of the key questions raised here, it will be necessary to combine hemodynamic and electrodynamic methods to obtain sufficient temporal resolution to characterize the type of rapid dynamic changes underlying the value comparison process itself.

Outstanding Questions and Future Directions

- How is the value comparison implemented on a computational level, and where in the brain does this process happen?
- Do neural systems involved in assigning value to actions and those involved in assigning value to stimuli interact, compete, or cooperate to facilitate value-based decision making, and how is this implemented?
- What properties of the decision-making network give rise to individual differences in decision-making behavior, and what role do genetic factors play in this process?
- What is the nature of the causal interactions among different brain regions during value-based decision making?
- What are the temporal dynamics underpinning the contribution of different regions to the decision-making process?

References

Blair, R. J., Morris, J. S., Frith, C. D., Perrett, D. I., & Dolan, R. J. (1999). Dissociable neural responses to facial expressions of sadness and anger. *Brain*, 122(Pt. 5), 883–93.

Blood, A. J., Zatorre, R. J., Bermudez, P., & Evans, A. C. (1999). Emotional responses to pleasant and unpleasant music correlate with activity in paralimbic brain regions. *Nature Neuroscience*, 2(4), 382–87.

Boorman, E. D., Behrens, T. E., Woolrich, M. W., & Rushworth, M. F. (2009). How green is the grass on the other side? Frontopolar cortex and the evidence in favor of alternative courses of action. *Neuron*, 62(5), 733–43.

Breiter, H. C., Aharon, I., Kahneman, D., Dale, A., & Shizgal, P. (2001). Functional imaging of neural responses to expectancy and experience of monetary gains and losses. *Neuron*, 30(2), 619–39.

Busemeyer, J. R., & Townsend, J. T. (1993). Decision field theory: A dynamic-cognitive approach to decision making in an uncertain environment. *Psychological Review*, 100(3), 432–59.

Cloutier, J., Heatherton, T. F., Whalen, P. J., & Kelley, W. M. (2008). Are attractive people rewarding? Sex differences in the neural substrates of facial attractiveness. *Journal of Cognitive Neuroscience*, 20(6), 941–51.

Cools, R., Clark, L., Owen, A. M., & Robbins, T. W. (2002). Defining the neural mechanisms of probabilistic reversal learning using event-related functional magnetic resonance imaging. *Journal of Neuroscience*, 22(11), 4563–67.

Critchley, H. D., & Rolls, E. T. (1996). Hunger and satiety modify the responses of olfactory and visual neurons in the primate orbitofrontal cortex. *Journal of Neurophysiology*, 75(4), 1673–86.

Daw, N. D., O'Doherty, J. P., Dayan, P., Seymour, B., & Dolan, R. J. (2006). Cortical substrates for exploratory decisions in humans. *Nature*, 441(7095), 876–79.

de Araujo, I. E., Kringelbach, M. L., Rolls, E. T., & McGlone, F. (2003). Human cortical responses to water in the mouth, and the effects of thirst. *Journal of Neurophysiology*, 90(3), 1865–76.

de Araujo, I. E., Rolls, E. T., Velazco, M. I., Margot, C., & Cayeux, I. (2005). Cognitive modulation of olfactory processing. *Neuron*, 46(4), 671–79.

Elliott, R., Frith, C. D., & Dolan, R. J. (1997). Differential neural response to positive and negative feedback in planning and guessing tasks. *Neuropsychologia*, 35(10), 1395–1404.

Elliott, R., Newman, J. L., Longe, O. A., & Deakin, J. F. (2003). Differential response patterns in the striatum and orbitofrontal cortex to financial reward in humans: A parametric functional magnetic resonance imaging study. *Journal of Neuroscience*, 23(1), 303–7.

Glascher, J., Daw, N., Dayan, P., & O'Doherty, J. P. (2010). States versus rewards: Dissociable neural prediction error signals underlying model-based and model-free reinforcement learning. *Neuron*, 66(4), 585–95.

Glascher, J., Hampton, A. N., & O'Doherty, J. P. (2009). Determining a role for ventromedial prefrontal cortex in encoding action-based value signals during reward-related decision making. *Cerebral Cortex*, 19(2), 483–95.

Glimcher, P. W., Dorris, M. C., & Bayer, H. M. (2005). Physiological utility theory and the neuroeconomics of choice. *Games and Economic Behavior*, 52(2), 213–56.

Hampton, A. N., Bossaerts, P., & O'Doherty, J. P. (2006). The role of the ventromedial prefrontal cortex in abstract state-based inference during decision making in humans. *Journal of Neuroscience*, 26(32), 8360–67.

Hollerman, J. R., & Schultz, W. (1998). Dopamine neurons report an error in the temporal prediction of reward during learning. *Nature Neuroscience*, 1(4), 304–9.

Kahnt, T., Heinzle, J., Park, S. Q., & Haynes, J. D. (2010). The neural code of reward anticipation in human orbitofrontal cortex. *Proceedings of the National Academy of Sciences*, 107(13), 6010–15.

Kawabata, H., & Zeki, S. (2004). Neural correlates of beauty. *Journal of Neurophysiology*, 91(4), 1699–1705.

Kirk, U., Skov, M., Hulme, O., Christensen, M. S., & Zeki, S. (2009). Modulation of aesthetic value by semantic context: an fMRI study. *Neuroimage*, 44(3), 1125–32.

Kranz, F., & Ishai, A. (2006). Face perception is modulated by sexual preference. *Current Biology*, 16(1), 63–68.

Kringelbach, M. L., & Rolls, E. T. (2004). The functional neuroanatomy of the human orbitofrontal cortex: Evidence from neuroimaging and neuropsychology. *Progress in Neurobiology*, 72(5), 341–72.

Lau, B., & Glimcher, P. W. (2007). Action and outcome encoding in the primate caudate nucleus. *Journal of Neuroscience*, 27(52), 14502–14.

Lee, D., Conroy, M. L., McGreevy, B. P., & Barraclough, D. J. (2004). Reinforcement learning and decision making in monkeys during a competitive game. *Brain Research: Cognitive Brain Research*, 22(1), 45–58.

McClure, S. M., Berns, G. S., & Montague, P. R. (2003). Temporal prediction errors in a passive learning task activate human striatum. *Neuron*, 38(2), 339–46.

Morrison, S. E., & Salzman, C. D. (2009). The convergence of information about rewarding and aversive stimuli in single neurons. *Journal of Neuroscience*, 29(37), 11471–83.

O'Doherty, J., Critchley, H., Deichmann, R., & Dolan, R. J. (2003). Dissociating valence of outcome from behavioral control in human orbital and ventral prefrontal cortices. *Journal of Neuroscience*, 23(21), 7931–39.

O'Doherty, J., Dayan, P., Friston, K., Critchley, H., & Dolan, R. J. (2003). Temporal difference models and reward-related learning in the human brain. *Neuron*, 38(2), 329–37.

O'Doherty, J., Dayan, P., Schultz, J., Deichmann, R., Friston, K., & Dolan, R. J. (2004). Dissociable roles of ventral and dorsal striatum in instrumental conditioning. *Science*, 304(5669), 452–54.

O'Doherty, J., Kringelbach, M. L., Rolls, E. T., Hornak, J., & Andrews, C. (2001). Abstract reward and punishment representations in the human orbitofrontal cortex. *Nature Neuroscience*, 4(1), 95–102.

O'Doherty, J., Rolls, E. T., Francis, S., Bowtell, R., McGlone, F., Kobal, G., et al. (2000). Sensory-specific satiety-related olfactory activation of the human orbitofrontal cortex. *Neuroreport*, 11(4), 893–97.

O'Doherty, J., Winston, J., Critchley, H., Perrett, D., Burt, D. M., & Dolan, R. J. (2003). Beauty in a smile: The role of medial orbitofrontal cortex in facial attractiveness. *Neuropsychologia*, 41(2), 147–55.

Padoa-Schioppa, C. (2007). Orbitofrontal cortex and the computation of economic value. *Annals of the New York Academy of Sciences*, 1121, 232–53.

Padoa-Schioppa, C., & Assad, J. A. (2006). Neurons in the orbitofrontal cortex encode economic value. *Nature*, 441(7090), 223–26.

Plassmann, H., O'Doherty, J., & Rangel, A. (2007). Orbitofrontal cortex encodes willingness to pay in everyday economic transactions. *Journal of Neuroscience*, 27(37), 9984–88.

Plassmann, H., O'Doherty, J., Shiv, B., & Rangel, A. (2008). Marketing actions can modulate neural representations of experienced pleasantness. *Proceedings of the National Academy of Sciences*, 105(3), 1050–54.

Platt, M. L., & Glimcher, P. W. (1999). Neural correlates of decision variables in parietal cortex. *Nature*, 400(6741), 233–38.

Ratcliff, R., & McKoon, G. (2008). The diffusion decision model: Theory and data for two-choice decision tasks. *Neural Computation*, 20(4), 873–922.

Rolls, E. T., Sienkiewicz, Z. J., & Yaxley, S. (1989). Hunger modulates the responses to gustatory stimuli of single neurons in the caudolateral orbitofrontal cortex of the macaque monkey. *European Journal of Neuroscience*, 1(1), 53–60.

Samejima, K., Ueda, Y., Doya, K., & Kimura, M. (2005). Representation of action-specific reward values in the striatum. *Science*, 310(5752), 1337–40.

Schultz, W. (1998). Predictive reward signal of dopamine neurons. *Journal of Neurophysiology*, 80(1), 1–27.

Sescousse, G., Redoute, J., & Dreher, J. C. (2010). The architecture of reward value coding in the human orbitofrontal cortex. *Journal of Neuroscience*, 30(39), 13095–13104.

Seymour, B., O'Doherty J, P., Koltzenburg, M., Wiech, K., Frackowiak, R., Friston, K., et al. (2005). Opponent appetitive-aversive neural processes underlie predictive learning of pain relief. *Nature Neuroscience*, 8(9), 1234–40.

Shadlen, M. N., Britten, K. H., Newsome, W. T., & Movshon, J. A. (1996). A computational analysis of the relationship between neuronal and behavioral responses to visual motion. *Journal of Neuroscience*, 16(4), 1486–1510.

Small, D. M., Zatorre, R. J., Dagher, A., Evans, A. C., & Jones-Gotman, M. (2001). Changes in brain activity related to eating chocolate: From pleasure to aversion. *Brain*, 124(Pt. 9), 1720–33.

Smith, P. L., & Ratcliff, R. (2004). Psychology and neurobiology of simple decisions. *Trends in Neurosciences*, 27(3), 161–68.

Sohn, J. W., & Lee, D. (2007). Order-dependent modulation of directional signals in the supplementary and presupplementary motor areas. *Journal of Neuroscience*, 27(50), 13655–66.

Sugrue, L. P., Corrado, G. S., & Newsome, W. T. (2004). Matching behavior and the representation of value in the parietal cortex. *Science*, 304(5678), 1782–87.

Thorpe, S. J., Rolls, E. T., & Maddison, S. (1983). The orbitofrontal cortex: Neuronal activity in the behaving monkey. *Experimental Brain Research*, 49(1), 93–115.

Ursu, S., & Carter, C. S. (2005). Outcome representations, counterfactual comparisons and the human orbitofrontal cortex: Implications for neuroimaging studies of decision-making. *Brain Research: Cognitive Brain Research*, 23(1), 51–60.

Valentin, V. V., Dickinson, A., & O'Doherty, J. P. (2007). Determining the neural substrates of goal-directed learning in the human brain. *Journal of Neuroscience*, 27(15), 4019–26.

Vrticka, P., Andersson, F., Grandjean, D., Sander, D., & Vuilleumier, P. (2008). Individual attachment style modulates human amygdala and striatum activation during social appraisal. *PloS One*, 3(8), e2868.

Wunderlich, K., Rangel, A., & O'Doherty, J. P. (2009). Neural computations underlying action-based decision making in the human brain. *Proceedings of the National Academy of Sciences*, 106(40), 17199–17204.

Wunderlich, K., Rangel, A., & O'Doherty, J. P. (2010). Economic choices can be made using only stimulus values. *Proceedings of the National Academy of Sciences*, 107(34), 15005–10.

Section V

EMOTIONAL LEARNING
AND MEMORY

CHAPTER 18

Neural Basis of Human Fear Learning

Joseph E. Dunsmoor & Kevin S. LaBar

An important goal for the study of emotions is to design research experiments for the laboratory that can help shed light on real-life behaviors. Fear provides a model emotional response that transitions well from the laboratory to the real world. The range of behaviors associated with fear can be evoked without much difficulty in a laboratory setting, where these behaviors can be systematically observed and measured. In addition, many of the biological mechanisms involved in fear learning and expression are shared across species, which makes it a model emotion for comparative research. In fact, because a number of different species are predisposed to rapidly learn and retain fear memories, several branches of neuroscience without a direct interest in human emotions use fear learning as a useful instrument.

Yet, despite the basic nature of fear behaviors, it is not a simple emotion. For instance, although fearful reactions to imminent threats are more or less hard-wired responses, organisms must learn to adapt these behaviors to predict and avoid a diversity of potential threats from the environment. And although evolution has favored a behavioral system that reacts quickly (but not always appropriately) to signals of danger, how these signals are perceived and interpreted involves a host of other systems. Understanding how fear integrates with other emotional and cognitive systems can be particularly complex when trying to understand disorders of fear.

Fear Pathways in the Brain

Much of what we know about the cognitive neuroscience of human fear learning has been informed by neurophysiological studies in nonhuman animals. Decades of animal research has delineated the neural circuitry important for processing and responding to both acquired and innate fears. Although an in-depth review of the neurophysiology of animal fear learning is beyond the scope of this chapter, an overview of the essential findings from this line of research is important to fully appreciate investigations into human fear learning.

To investigate how organisms learn about and respond to threats, researchers often use classical, or Pavlovian, fear-conditioning paradigms. In this procedure, an emotionally neutral stimulus (conditioned stimulus, CS), such as a tone or light, predicts a naturally aversive or threatening stimulus (unconditioned stimulus, US), such as an electric shock. Just as Pavlov's experimental dogs would salivate to a tone that had been paired with food, animals that undergo fear conditioning will begin to express a number of autonomic emotional responses (e.g., a change in heart rate, perspiration, or respiration rate) to the presentation of the previously neutral CS. These fear-conditioned responses (CR) reflect the well-known fight-or-flight-or-freezing behaviors and indicate that an association has been formed between the CS and US.

Studies of fear conditioning, predominantly in rodents, have traced the neural pathways involved in forming the CS-US association and in producing the CR. Neurophysiological studies have shown that sensory information concerning the CS and US converges in the amygdala (see Pape & Pare, 2010, for a review; Figure 18.1). The amygdala is a structure within the anterior portion of the medial temporal lobe (MTL) that receives extensive afferent projections from a number of brain systems, including all sensory systems and higher order association cortex. A widespread distribution of efferent projections from the amygdala is important for modulating information processing broadly across the brain. For instance, projections from the amygdala to the ventral visual stream may be important for modulating the representation of sensory stimuli following emotional experiences (Vuilleumier, 2005). Importantly, the amygdala is not a homogeneous structure, but is instead a collection of interconnected subnuclei. The nuclei most often implicated in fear conditioning include the basal (B), accessory basal (AB), lateral (LA), and central (CE) nuclei. The L, AB, and B nuclei are often referred to collectively as the basolateral complex (BLA), and the subnuclei within this complex can be further reduced into anatomically distinct regions. Interposed between

the BLA and CE are clusters of intercalated cell masses that may serve a role in gating activity between these subnuclei of the amygdala. In the classic anatomical model of fear conditioning, the BLA is the principal site for receiving sensory information and is important for forming the association between the CS and US. This region may also be involved in the consolidation and storage of conditioned fear memories (Schafe, Nader, Blair, & LeDoux, 2001). The CE receives projections from the BLA and is principally involved in initiating the conditioned fear response through output projections to the hypothalamus and brainstem structures.

Notably, anatomically constrained models of fear conditioning are continually evolving. For instance, the roles of the BLA and CE in forming the CS-US association and producing the CR, respectively, may not be entirely dissociable, and some evidence suggests that the CE may in some cases be involved in forming the CS-US association and consolidating fear memories (Wilensky, Schafe, Kristensen, & LeDoux, 2006). In addition, other regions closely associated with the amygdala may play distinct roles in fear-related behaviors. The bed nucleus of the stria terminalis (BNST) in particular may contribute to behaviors associated with sustained tonic fear states indicative of anxiety, rather than phasic fear responses (Davis, Walker, Miles, & Grillon, 2010).

A key feature of amygdala neurocircuitry is that sensory information reaches the amygdala from two partially separated neural pathways: (1) a relatively slow cortical pathway that flows from the thalamus to primary sensory cortex and then to higher level association cortex before reaching the amygdala and (2) a more rapid subcortical pathway that sends projections directly from the thalamus. Whereas the cortical route supplies detailed information concerning a sensory stimulus, the subcortical route quickly detects potentially threatening objects and generates immediate fear responses. These dual processing routes to the amygdala may have implications for understanding

Simplified fear conditioning circuit centered on the amygdala

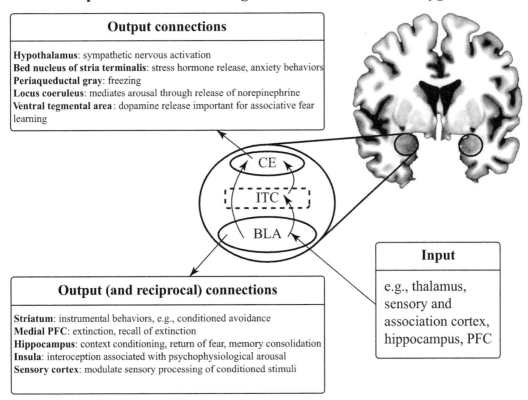

Output connections

Hypothalamus: sympathetic nervous activation
Bed nucleus of stria terminalis: stress hormone release, anxiety behaviors
Periaqueductal gray: freezing
Locus coeruleus: mediates arousal through release of norepinephrine
Ventral tegmental area: dopamine release important for associative fear learning

CE
ITC
BLA

Input

e.g., thalamus, sensory and association cortex, hippocampus, PFC

Output (and reciprocal) connections

Striatum: instrumental behaviors, e.g., conditioned avoidance
Medial PFC: extinction, recall of extinction
Hippocampus: context conditioning, return of fear, memory consolidation
Insula: interoception associated with psychophysiological arousal
Sensory cortex: modulate sensory processing of conditioned stimuli

Figure 18.1. Simplified fear-conditioning circuit depicting the inputs and outputs to the amygdala, as well as the role of the output regions in fear conditioning. The diagram simplifies the layout of the amygdala subnuclei, combining several distinct nuclei that constitute the basolateral complex. The intrinsic connections between the amygdala subnuclei and the ITC are not detailed here. BLA = basolateral complex; CE = central nucleus; ITC = intercalated cells.

complex fear behaviors (LeDoux, 1996). For instance, because the thalamo-amygdala pathway contains fewer synapses, information about potential threats is sped to the amygdala before the cortex has had time to process the stimulus thoroughly. Therefore, an organism might react rapidly to a potential threat (e.g., initiating a freezing response), only to realize a split second later that the threat has passed or was nonexistent. Once a CR is initiated, however, it is difficult to quickly shut it off, because the physiological response systems engaged have a relatively slow time course compared to the neural response.

Although discoveries of the neurophysiological substrates of fear conditioning have been made predominantly in rodents using invasive procedures, the role of particular brain regions in fear conditioning is now being explored in humans using noninvasive functional brain imaging techniques. In the following sections we highlight findings from human patients with brain damage and from functional magnetic resonance imaging (fMRI) studies, which have revealed a crucial role for the amygdala and other regions in the acquisition, expression, and control of fear. Although positron emission tomography (PET) studies on fear processes have also been conducted, the blocked designs inherent to the PET technique constrain interpretations. Specifically, because PET signals are integrated over many seconds, brain activity uniquely associated with CS and US presentations cannot be readily distinguished, and different trial types cannot be intermixed in the experimental design (see Chapter 5). Pre- versus post-conditioning comparisons can be made with PET (e.g., Morris, Öhman, & Dolan, 1998), but event-related fMRI designs have proved optimal for examining the neural systems involved in fear conditioning not only because of these design issues but also because of improved spatial resolution (e.g., for distinguishing activation in the amygdala and adjacent hippocampus).

Acquiring Fear

From Historical to Contemporary Views of Conditioned Fear Learning

The earliest behavioral studies of fear conditioning in humans demonstrated that laboratory-based fear conditioning might be a useful analog to investigate psychophysiological reactions to emotional experiences. Early behaviorist researchers, such as James B. Watson, used these conditioning principles as a basis to refute theories of anxiety grounded in Freudian psychology, which placed the origin of neuroses in various complexes and developmental issues while minimizing the role of direct stimulus learning.

Perhaps the most infamous early study of human fear conditioning was the "Little Albert" experiment conducted by Watson and Raynor (1920). In this study, an 11-month-old infant was conditioned to fear a white rat that was not feared prior to conditioning. The experimenters fear-conditioned Little Albert by presenting a white rat (CS) with the loud noise of a hammer knocking a steel bar (US). After several rat-noise pairings, Albert began to cry when the rat appeared and would attempt to avoid it by crawling away (CR). This fear of the rat then generalized to other neutral but perceptually related stimuli, such as a white rabbit or white beard. Because these responses resembled those observed in phobias, early Pavlovian fear conditioning research supported the notion that anxiety was a reflection of stimulus-response (S-R) learning. The process of S-R learning

was widely cast as the explanatory mechanism behind the acquisition of pathological behaviors (Pavlov, 1927; Watson & Rayner, 1920).

Theories of how mental illness arises through S-R learning fell out of favor in the mid- to late 20th century, due in part to the shift away from behaviorism toward cognitive models of learning and behavior. One of the chief criticisms leveled at behaviorism was that it was too simplistic to explain the etiology of fear and anxiety disorders. For instance, behaviorism made little account for differences between humans and other animals in their ability to condition, and it considered all classes of conditioned stimuli more or less equally (the equipotentiality fallacy; Seligman, 1970). Moreover, S-R models could not readily account for why some individuals are more susceptible to acquire a fear disorder following a conditioning experience than others. The direct correspondence between presentations of a CS and the production of the behavioral response, characterized by S-R theory, was not sufficient to explain how the CS can evoke variable displays of behavior. Finally, individuals frequently develop fears to stimuli or situations to which they have never been directly exposed, seemingly circumventing S-R learning altogether.

Models of classical conditioning that evolved in the 20th century led to new insights into fear learning. One of the monumental shifts away from behaviorism toward cognitive models was the conception that conditioned learning involves forming mental representations of conditioned and unconditioned stimuli (S-S learning). In contrast to the black-box approach of S-R theories, these more cognitively oriented learning models described how contingencies surrounding CS-US pairing influence the acquisition of learned behaviors. For instance, conditioning will only occur to stimuli that provide predictive value for the US, and learning is a result of experiencing the difference between what a CS predicts and what actually occurs (e.g., Rescorla & Wagner, 1972). Importantly, because conditioning can involve representations of

CSs and USs, learning can occur even in the absence of direct CS-US pairing. For instance, increasing or decreasing the aversive intensity of the US after conditioning leads to an increase or decrease in fear to the CS when it is later encountered – an effect known as US deflation and inflation, respectively (Davey, 1992). Advances in cognitive models of associative learning have had beneficial applications to understanding fear disorders from the perspective of behavior theory (Mineka & Zinbarg, 2006).

An important development in theories of fear acquisition concerns the qualitative nature of the CS. Animal research has shown that learning occurs best to particular classes of stimuli that, in many cases, are species-specific. For instance, a rat can readily learn to associate a taste (CS) with illness (US), or a noise (CS) with shock (US), but cannot easily form the crossed associations (taste with shock, or noise with illness; Garcia & Koelling, 1966). Seligman (1971) proposed that humans are also predisposed to form associations between particular types of CSs and USs. As evidence for the selectiveness of stimuli to which people readily condition, Seligman noted that phobias generally fall under a select number of "fear-relevant" objects or situations that have served as evolutionarily significant stimuli throughout mammalian development. These include certain animals (e.g., snakes and spiders), environmental phenomenon (e.g., thunder and lightning), physical locations (e.g., being in an enclosed space or high off the ground), and social interactions (e.g., emotionally charged exchanges or evaluations). Fear learning between conditional stimuli from these prepared classes of stimuli and an aversive US may occur more readily than between stimuli that are not related through fear relevance.

In support of Seligman's theory, fear-relevant stimuli (e.g., images of snakes and spiders) sometimes lead to superior conditioning and they delay extinction learning relative to fear-irrelevant environmental stimuli (e.g., images of flowers and mushrooms), suggesting a strong selective association between fear-relevant stimuli and aversive USs (for a review see Öhman & Mineka, 2001). Öhman and Mineka (2001) have incorporated the idea of selective associations into an encompassing "fear module," which supports rapid and automatic fear learning between fear-relevant and biologically significant stimuli. The putative anatomical substrate of this fear module is the amygdala, which they regard as operating independently of conscious control during fear learning and expression. However, as discussed later, neuroimaging studies have shown that the amygdala's response is modulated by regulatory processes during fear learning. The amygdala's emotional response profile is not exclusively concerned with fear, and it contributes to other functions, such as social cognition and motivation (see Chapter 19).

Human Lesion Studies of Fear Acquisition

Early nonhuman primate studies revealed that large lesions of the medial temporal lobe (MTL) led to a marked loss of fear responses and abnormal social behavior (Kluver & Bucy, 1939). Although initial accounts attributed these results to the hippocampal damage sustained in the animals, the behavioral effects were later replicated when lesions were restricted to the amygdala alone (Weiskrantz, 1956). Experiments in human patients with MTL damage due to epilepsy, viral encephalitis, or a congenital disease known as Urbach-Wiethe syndrome demonstrated a necessary link between the integrity of the MTL and fear learning. In these studies, fear conditioning was assessed by measuring changes in the skin conductance response (SCR), which measures the change in electrodermal conductance on the palmar surface of the hands due to sympathetic arousal (see Chapter 3). Patients with MTL damage, including the amygdala, are impaired at acquiring and expressing conditioned SCRs, but are similar to controls in responding to the aversive US. This pattern of results suggests that the amygdala and surrounding cortex are crucial for learning

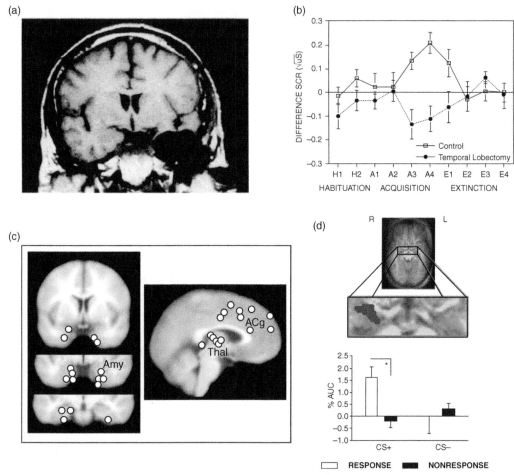

Figure 18.2. (A, B) Patients with unilateral amygdala lesions show impaired fear conditioning, as assessed by the skin conductance response (SCR). (C) Neuroimaging studies of healthy adults shows that several areas, including the amygdala, thalamus, and prefrontal cortex, respond to a fear-conditioned stimulus. (D) Activity in the amygdala tracks conditioned fear responses to a fear-conditioned stimulus (CS+), whereas fear responses evoked by an unpaired control stimulus (CS−) are not correlated with amygdala activations. Panels A and B reproduced with permission from LaBar et al. (1995). Panel C from LaBar & Cabeza (2006). Panel D from Cheng et al. (2006).

and initiating conditioned responses (Figure 18.2A,B; LaBar, LeDoux, Spencer, & Phelps, 1995). Importantly, amygdala damage does not interfere with declarative knowledge of the fear-learning episode – non-amnesic patients with amygdala lesions are able to explicitly state that the CS was paired with the US (contingency awareness). In contrast, patients with damage to the hippocampus, but not the amygdala, retain the capacity to fear condition, but lack declarative knowledge of the stimulus contingencies

(Bechara et al., 1995; LaBar & Phelps, 2005). This double dissociation between the physiological expression of learning and explicit awareness suggests that fear conditioning can operate at an implicit level of processing.

In another study, individuals with amygdala damage were shown to have impaired fear-potentiated startle responses (Weike et al., 2005), another measure of conditioned fear that relies extensively on the amygdala (Davis, 1992). The startle response, which is often measured using electromyography on facial muscles, is a reflexive response to a sudden stimulus (e.g., a 50-ms burst of 100-dB white noise). During a state of fear, the startle amplitude is increased relative to a quiescent state. Unilateral temporal lobectomy patients were impaired at expressing fear-potentiated startle responses compared to control subjects. Interestingly, in contrast to earlier findings, patients who could successfully report knowledge of the CS-US relationship in a post-experimental report did show conditioned SCRs. However, only a small number of patients could correctly report the CS-US association, which may indicate that damage extended further into the MTL.

Coppens, Spruyt, Vandenbulcke, Van Paessohen, and Vansteenwegen (2009) also found that amygdala-lesioned patients could demonstrate intact conditioned SCRs when awareness was assessed throughout the experimental session. Using a variable rating of US expectancy throughout the session, patients with unilateral amygdala lesions performed similarly to a control group in terms of declarative knowledge of the CS-US relationship and the magnitude of the conditioned SCR. The apparent discrepancy between this and previous findings (Bechara et al., 1995; LaBar et al., 1995) may be attributed to the use of online measures of awareness throughout fear conditioning, as opposed to assessing declarative knowledge at the end of the experimental session. For instance, concurrent ratings of expectancy may draw attention to the stimulus contingencies during learning, making fear conditioning a more explicit task that relies less on the amygdala.

Overall, although studies of lesion patients were critical for demonstrating the role of the amygdala in human fear learning, focal bilateral lesions of the amygdala are rare, and the precise role of the amygdala in fear learning is difficult to assess in individuals with additional damage to neighboring cortical and subcortical structures. Also, patients with unilateral damage to the amygdala may in some cases receive compensation from the intact amygdala, which may

be sufficient to support fear conditioning in some individuals.

Human Neuroimaging Studies of Pavlovian Fear Conditioning

Advances in noninvasive functional brain imaging have allowed researchers to probe the brain systems involved during the course of fear learning in healthy adults and clinical populations. Early fMRI studies of fear conditioning revealed the role of the human amygdala in forming the CS-US association. These studies showed that a predictive CS+ evoked greater activity in the amygdala than an explicitly unpaired CS- (Buchel, Morris, Dolan, & Friston, 1998; LaBar, Gatenby, Gore, LeDoux, & Phelps, 1998). A network of other brain regions has been consistently implicated in human fear conditioning, including the sensory cortex, anterior cingulate cortex, hippocampus, insula, thalamus, and prefrontal cortex (Figure 18.2C; LaBar & Cabeza, 2006; Sehlmeyer et al., 2009).

Brain imaging studies have shown a positive relationship between the magnitude of the SCR and amygdala activity either on a trial-by-trial basis or as an individual difference measure (Cheng, Knight, Smith, Stein, & Helmstetter, 2003; LaBar et al., 1998), suggesting that the amygdala has a prominent role in expressing conditioned learning in humans. The amygdala mediates the expression of fear responses through anatomical connections with areas controlling bodily reflexes and autonomic nervous system activity, such as the brainstem and hypothalamus (Davis, 1992). Consistent with the amygdala-lesioned patient data, amygdala activity is selective to the production of conditioned SCRs, but not during the production of spontaneous, orienting, or unconditioned SCRs (Knight, Nguyen, & Bandettini, 2005). Cheng and colleagues (Cheng, Knight, Smith, & Helmstetter, 2006) compared amygdala activity on CS+ trials in which subjects either produced or did not produce an SCR and found that the amygdala was only engaged in trials in which subjects produced a conditioned SCR (Figure 18.2D). In combination, these results suggest that the amygdala may be particularly involved during the behavioral expression of learned fear, although it is challenging in human studies to tease apart learning and performance effects, because the index of emotional learning is a change in physiological response.

Although the focus of fear conditioning is mostly on the learned response to the CS, learning-related changes can also be observed in the unconditioned response (UR) to the US. Even though the UR has typically been considered innate (e.g., salivating to the appearance of food), these responses can reflect a significant amount of information related to stimulus learning, such as whether or not the US was predicted (Domjan, 2005). For example, using eyeblink conditioning Kimble and Ost (1961) showed that the unconditioned eyeblink response evoked by an airpuff to the eye was reduced when preceded by a conditioned stimulus. This reduction in the UR following a signaled US is sometimes referred to as *unconditioned response diminution* (Domjan, 2005) and may be related to preparation for an imminent threat as a means to lessen its impact (Domjan, 2005). Neuroimaging data also support the hypothesis that a predicted US can lead to a decrease in the UR. Dunsmoor and colleagues (2008) conducted a neuroimaging study in which an aversive 100-dB white-noise US followed one tone in 100% of the trials, but followed another tone in only 50% of the trials. Behaviorally, the US evoked a smaller unconditioned SCR when it followed a CS that reliably predicted its delivery. A reduction in the fMRI signal was also observed following a predicted US in areas typically observed during fear learning, including the amygdala, thalamus, and auditory cortex. Moreover, activity in the dorsolateral prefrontal cortex and anterior cingulate cortex showed an inverse relationship with subjective expectancy for receiving the US, such that unconditioned fMRI activity in these regions decreased when the US was highly expected. Interestingly, enhanced activity in response to an unex-

pected US is similar in many respects to a prediction error signal, which is important for controlling learning based on the difference between expected and actual outcomes (Rescorla & Wagner, 1972). In fact, many of the brain regions showing enhanced activity in response to an unexpected versus expected US in Dunsmoor et al. (2008) have been reported to show prediction-error-related activity in rodents and humans (McNally, Johansen, & Blair, 2011).

Indirect Fear Learning

It is not uncommon for fears to develop toward objects or situations that have never been directly experienced in the presence of a biologically aversive US. Because the first encounter with a dangerous stimulus such as a predator might also be the last encounter, it is adaptive for organisms to learn about the signals for a threat without ever directly encountering the threat itself. Rachman (1977) proposed that there are three primary pathways by which individuals acquire fear (Figure 18.3). The first is the well-described "direct" pathway, whereby individuals experience the CS and US together. The second is a vicarious pathway, whereby individuals can learn by observing others endure a fear-inducing or painful outcome in association with a CS. The third pathway consists of communicating information about the CS-US relationships without witnessing these cues directly. Because the latter two processes do not involve direct encounters with the CS and US, they are considered indirect fear-learning pathways.

Research on vicarious or observational fear learning conducted on nonhuman primates has revealed that fears can be transmitted through observing conspecifics undergo an aversive experience with a CS. For example, laboratory-reared monkeys can rapidly acquire a fear of snakes after they observe a video of another monkey reacting fearfully to either a toy snake or a real snake (Mineka, Davidson, Cook, & Keir, 1984). Interestingly, this type of fear learning appears specific to fear-relevant stimuli and does not extend to observing a model engage

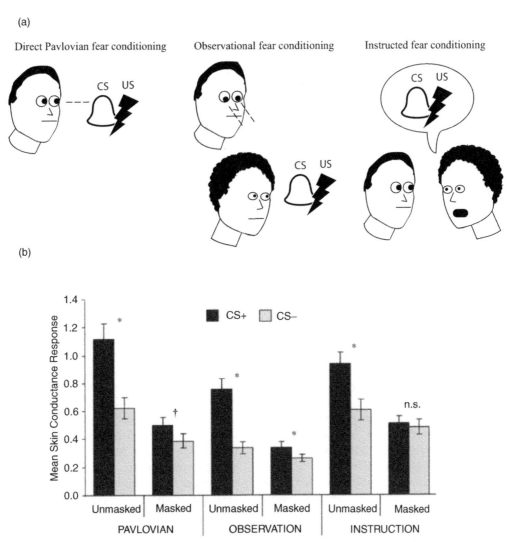

Figure 18.3. Direct and indirect fear-learning paradigms. (A) In standard Pavlovian fear conditioning, the individual encounters the CS and US directly. In observational fear conditioning, the individual acquires fear of the CS vicariously by watching another individual undergo Pavlovian conditioning. In instructed fear conditioning, the individual acquires fear of the CS without ever experiencing the CS and US together, often through language. (B) Results from a behavioral study that directly compared these three forms of fear conditioning across individuals using both supraliminal (unmasked) and subliminal (masked) presentations of the fear-conditioned stimulus (CS+) and an unpaired control stimulus (CS−). Although fear was acquired to the CS+ using all three procedures, a masked CS+ only evoked a fear response if fear was acquired through Pavlovian or observational fear conditioning. CS = conditioned stimulus. Panel B reprinted with permission from Olsson & Phelps (2004).

fearfully with stimuli that are affectively neutral (Cook & Mineka, 1989). Observational fear learning has also been reported in mice, and the effect of vicarious fear learning was more pronounced when the observer mouse was a sibling or a long-term mate of the mouse receiving electric shocks (Jeon, 2010). Inactivation of the medial pain system, including the anterior cingulate cortex, reduced observational fear learning in the observer mouse, suggesting that this form of fear learning necessitates an intact pain pathway to vicariously acquire a learned fear response.

Olsson and Phelps (2004) showed that human observers acquire fear of a CS after watching someone else react as if they themselves had received a shock paired with a CS. Observationally acquired CRs were also elicited when the CS was later presented subliminally. Neuroimaging studies have revealed that the amygdala, a region implicated in direct fear learning, is activated during observational fear learning as well. For instance, when subjects watch a video of an individual undergo fear conditioning, exposure to the observationally conditioned CS during fMRI evokes activity in the amygdala (Olsson & Phelps, 2007).

Another indirect fear-learning pathway involves the verbal communication of threat. Several animal species communicate threat through vocalizations. For instance, rats produce an ultrasonic vocalization when they are in aversive situations, and this may send an alarm to conspecifics about nearby threats (Blanchard, Blanchard, Agullana, & Weiss, 1991). The ability to communicate through symbolic language has greatly facilitated this ability in humans. In laboratory studies of instructed fear conditioning, subjects are merely told that a CS will be paired with a US, but they never actually receive the US in combination with the CS. Nonetheless, the CS can still evoke a CR when presented alone, suggesting that similar fear-conditioning circuits operate under conditions of direct and instructed fear learning (Olsson & Phelps, 2007). Unlike an observationally fear-conditioned stimulus, an instructed CS does not evoke a CR when it is presented subliminally, suggesting that conscious awareness is necessary to detect a threat learned through language (Figure 18.3; Olsson & Phelps, 2004). The left amygdala is active in response to a CS that subjects have been told will be followed by a US, even when no direct pairing occurs (Phelps et al., 2001).

Involvement of Stress Hormones in Human Fear Learning

Stress hormones that are released during fearful situations have widespread effects across brain systems involved in learning and memory (for a review see Rodrigues, LeDoux, & Sapolsky, 2009). For instance, during avoidance learning the amygdala is involved in initiating the peripheral release of glucocorticoids from the adrenal cortex. Stress hormones released from the periphery can then circulate to the brain, where they bind to the amygdala and hippocampus (among other areas) and modulate activity in these regions (McGaugh, Cahill, & Roozendaal, 1996). In humans, there are gender differences in the effects of stress hormones on fear learning (Jackson, Payne, Nadel, & Jacobs, 2006). For instance, introducing a psychosocial stressor (giving a public speech) prior to fear conditioning enhances fear acquisition in males, but diminishes fear acquisition in females (Jackson et al., 2006). Similarly, endogenous cortisol levels measured after fear acquisition correlate positively with CRs in males but not females (Zorawski, Cook, Kuhn, & LaBar, 2005). These sex differences are hypothesized to relate to a neuroprotective effect of estrogen on the stress response in females. Subjects with high endogenous cortisol levels during fear learning also have a higher magnitude of conditioned SCRs expressed in a 24-hour retrieval test, suggesting that stress hormones released during conditioning strengthen consolidation of the fear memory (Zorawski, Blanding, Kuhn, & LaBar, 2006).

Learning to Fear the Context Surrounding an Aversive Event

The discrete sensory cues present during fear learning rarely occur in isolation, but rather exist among a wide set of environmental stimuli. These background features provide the context for a fear-learning event. In context conditioning the organism learns that the CS is not the only predictor for the US, but instead the context itself should be regarded as threatening. Importantly, a context can be made up of numerous sensory, spatial, and temporal features, and thus the features that constitute a context can differ markedly from a more easily defined sensory

CS. Because contextual cues remain relatively constant in the environment, an organism may be in a prolonged state of fear in a context that has been associated with fearful experiences, even though cued fears are only expressed in the presence of the CS (Davis, Walker, Miles, & Grillon, 2009). Learning to fear a context and learning to fear a cue may therefore involve partially distinct neural systems and cognitive processes.

Animal models of context conditioning have focused on the role of the hippocampus in encoding and representing the feared environment. The hippocampus is thought to provide a substrate for binding the numerous features of the context into a unitary representation; it may be specialized for calling to mind a full representation of a feared context from partial information through the process of pattern completion (O'Reilly & Rudy, 2001). For instance, animals that undergo cued fear conditioning in a particular environment will later express fear to that context, but damage to the dorsal hippocampus following conditioning reduces that fear (e.g., Anagnostaras, Maren, & Fanselow, 1999). Although portions of the amygdala are required for both cued and context conditioning, the dorsal hippocampus is primarily involved in context conditioning (Phillips & LeDoux, 1992).

The vast majority of context conditioning investigations have been conducted in animals, because manipulating the context for animals often only requires a change from one testing cage to another one with distinctive features. Manipulating the context in human studies is more difficult, because humans might not construe a subtle change in a traditional laboratory room as an altogether new context. One approach to conducting human behavioral studies with a context manipulation has been to conduct different phases of the experiment in entirely different rooms with distinct environmental features (LaBar & Phelps, 2005). This approach has the advantage of being multimodal and immersive, although the number of rooms and kinds of manipulations are limited in most research settings

and the manipulations are not readily transferrable to neuroimaging applications. A second approach has been to simply change background environments on a computer screen on which the CS is presented. This approach has the advantages of portability and a wide selection of background images, but is limited to unimodal context shifts. Using this latter approach during fMRI, Alvarez, Biggs, Chen, Pine, and Grillon (2008) showed that activity in the hippocampus and amygdala was elevated when participants were presented with a background visual context associated with an unpredictable aversive US relative to another one in which the US was never presented. In this study, however, no explicit CS was presented, so the neural substrates differentiating cued and contextual fear could not be ascertained.

Is Fear Conditioning a Purely Implicit Form of Learning?

In Squire's taxonomy of memory (Squire, 1986), simple conditioning is described as a nondeclarative form of learning. In support of this view, MTL damage, including the hippocampus, impairs declarative memory while leaving cued fear conditioning intact (Bechara et al., 1995; LaBar & Phelps, 2005). Interestingly, some patients can express an intact CR to an explicit CS physiologically, but fail to declaratively state that the CS predicts the reinforcer. Yet, the extent to which conscious awareness plays a role in Pavlovian conditioning is a long-standing issue that is not easily resolved (LaBar & Disterhoft, 1998; Lovibond & Shanks, 2002).

Some behavioral studies have shown that conscious awareness in healthy participants may be necessary for fear conditioning. For instance, Hamm and Vaitl (1996) showed that subjects who cannot accurately report the CS-US association fail to show conditioned SCRs. Lovibond and Shanks (2002) have argued that organisms produce a CR in preparation for the US, and therefore awareness of the CS-US relationship is essential to the expression of learned fear. They argue that studies that show conditioning without awareness use imprecise measures of awareness; for instance, making retrospective ratings of awareness using post-experimental questionnaires. The issue of when awareness is assessed might be particularly important for assessing contingency awareness in patients with MTL damage, because these individuals would likely have trouble recalling any details from the event after a delay. Moreover, making retrospective ratings of awareness activates long-term memory processes, and this system is likely different from that involved during initial fear acquisition. Some studies have therefore opted to use online measures of awareness (i.e., making a rating for US expectancy on every trial) to resolve issues related to retrospective reports. However, these procedures alter task demands and draw attention to the stimulus contingences (LaBar & Disterhoft, 1998), putting more emphasis on declarative systems during fear learning.

Numerous studies have endeavored to resolve the relationship between awareness and conditioning. For the most part, these studies have relied on the notion that separate memory systems are used during fear learning (LeDoux, 1996). On the one hand, the declarative memory system is important for the conscious aspects of a fear-learning experience. This system might be important for processing the contextual details of the fear-learning episode and relating it to previous experiences or acquired knowledge. For example, an individual who regularly travels on airplanes might disregard turbulence based on past experiences that turbulence is common. On the other hand, the nondeclarative system is concerned with the automatic processes involved in acquiring and producing learned behavioral responses (Squire & Zola, 1996). This system may be less concerned with interpreting a potential threat with regard to its prior history and more concerned with reacting in the moment. For example, an abrupt change in altitude might jolt even the most regular plane traveler, despite the fact that he or she is consciously aware that turbulence is usually not dangerous. LeDoux (1996, 2000) proposed that the neural over-lap between these systems is in the amygdala, a region that receives extensive projections from both higher order cortical and lower level subcortical regions. In this way, the amygdala is uniquely situated to rapidly detect and respond to low-level sensory information that may initially bypass the higher level sensory systems in the cortex. More detailed information concerning the stimulus (e.g., sensory information and related memories) is then supplied to the amygdala via sensory and association cortex, which helps inform the individual about the threat relevance of the stimulus and modify emotional reactions.

Behavioral studies manipulating conscious awareness of CS-US contingencies in healthy adults often employ backward masking procedures, wherein the CS is rapidly presented (on the order of 10 to 30 ms) and then quickly "masked" by another stimulus. In this case, the subject is made unaware of the presentation of the CS, but might still produce a CR when the CS is later presented supraliminally (Esteves, Parra, Dimberg, & Öhman, 1994). A potential issue with backward masking procedures, however, is that some subjects may be able to consciously perceive the CS or to perceptually discriminate a masked CS+ and CS−, but are just unable to precisely describe the details of the masked stimulus (Lovibond & Shanks, 2002). Avoiding this problem of backward masking, Knight, Waters, and Bandettini (2009) used a novel approach to investigate subjective levels of awareness of fear conditioning by manipulating the threshold of auditory CSs on a trial-by-trial basis. During fMRI, subjects pressed a button to indicate that they heard one of two auditory CSs, one of which (the CS+) was paired with the US. Unbeknownst to the subjects, the volume for the CS was lowered by 5 dB on the next trial if they reported hearing the tone, or raised by 5 dB if they did not press a button to indicate hearing the tone. Ratings of US expectancy were measured continuously throughout the experiment, and these ratings confirmed that subjects only expected the US on CS+ trials that were perceived, and not when the CS+ was unperceived. Activity in the hippocampus increased during perceived, relative to unperceived, CS+ trials as well, which suggests that contingency awareness evoked differential activity in this region. In contrast, conditioned SCRs and amygdala activity were observed on CS+ trials that were both perceived and unperceived. This finding demonstrates that individuals can acquire conditioned fears to stimuli that are presented below the threshold of awareness and that this learning is likely mediated by the amygdala. One issue with measuring awareness in conditioning is the conflation of CS awareness with CS-US contingency awareness (Lovibond & Shanks, 2002), highlighting the complexities of how awareness as a construct is defined (see Chapter 15).

Another way to test the role of awareness in conditioning is by using trace conditioning procedures. In trace conditioning, a temporal gap is introduced between the offset of the CS and the onset of the US, during which time organisms must maintain a representation of the CS to successfully learn the CS-US relationship. This form of associative learning involves the hippocampus and may entail a higher degree of conscious awareness than standard delay conditioning, in which the CS co-terminates with the US. For instance, it has been shown that taxing working memory processes during the course of acquisition differentially impairs trace conditioning relative to delay conditioning (Carter, Hofstotter, Tsuchiya, & Koch, 2003). Trace conditioning has also been conducted in individuals with minimal conscious awareness (i.e., vegetative states; Bekinschtein et al., 2009). Using a trace eyeblink conditioning task with an aversive airpuff to the eye as the US, individuals with minimal consciousness were capable of producing a conditioned eyeblink response to a tone that predicted the delivery of the US. Performance in the trace eyeblink conditioning task was positively related to patient recovery. In contrast, subjects under general anesthesia (i.e., near total loss of awareness) did not show a conditioned eyeblink response.

In sum, evidence from behavioral and fMRI experiments supports the view that conditioning is in some ways an automatic form of implicit learning that can occur outside a high degree of cognitive awareness. Of course, the distinct role of deliberative and automatic systems in mediating conditioning begs the question of whether there are in fact dissociable fear-learning systems (Shanks, 2010). It may be the case that different systems interact and overlap in the course of learning about affective stimuli and that these systems may not be as easily dissociated as suggested by Squire's taxonomy.

Learning to Avoid a Feared Stimulus

Once an organism has learned through classical conditioning that the CS portends delivery of an aversive US, it can begin to take measures to avoid the US altogether. The latter process involves instrumental behaviors, in which the organism learns that a particular course of action (i.e., response) will result in a particular outcome. In the case of active avoidance, the desired outcome is to steer clear of the US. This outcome can be achieved in some cases by learning to escape to another location or performing an action that terminates the CS.

Extensive research by McGaugh and colleagues has shown that the amygdala plays a critical role in acquiring and expressing avoidance learning (reviewed in McGaugh, 2004). The basal nucleus of the amygdala provides the output connections to the striatum that may be important for initiating the motor movements associated with escape behaviors, or "active coping" (LeDoux & Gorman, 2001). This pathway between the amygdala and striatum may compete with the pathway between the CE and the brainstem for behavioral expression. For instance, projections from the CE to the brainstem lead to freezing behaviors that would inhibit motor movements needed to avoid the impending US. If the CE is blocked, however, then the animal can express avoidance behaviors, such as fleeing to another chamber to avoid a footshock

(Choi, Cain, & LeDoux, 2010). Human neuroscience research on active avoidance is sparse, but one fMRI study found that active avoidance of the US (achieved by pressing a particular button during CS+ trials) resulted in increased activity in the striatum that was positively correlated with amygdala activity (Delgado, Nearing, LeDoux, & Phelps, 2008).

Controlling Fear

Although acquiring and expressing learned fear are evolutionarily adaptive abilities, it is also important to control fears when they no longer serve an adaptive purpose. For instance, once a stimulus no longer predicts a threat, reacting as if it was still a reliable danger signal would be a waste of time and energy resources. In humans and other species, the ability to control fear responses relies extensively on the prefrontal cortex.

Extinction

Through conditioned learning, an organism forms the association between the CS and aversive US and learns to produce a CR. If the CS is repeatedly presented without the US, then the acquired CR will begin to decrease over time. The process that leads to a reduction in CR expression (by eliminating the predictive relationship between the CS and US) is called *extinction* and represents an important form of learning originally identified in Pavlov's laboratory. Repeated exposure to a feared stimulus forms the basis for several cognitive behavioral therapies aimed to treat clinical anxiety disorders, such as phobias and obsessive-compulsive disorder. Exposure therapies based on the principles of Pavlovian conditioning have proved to be highly effective treatments for certain anxiety disorders (e.g., Foa et al., 2005).

Fear extinction implies that the organism no longer conceives of the CS as threatening. The question arises whether the organism has simply forgotten that the CS was once threatening or, alternatively, has formed a new memory for the CS as safe while simultaneously maintaining the previous memory of the CS as a danger signal. The latter view is supported by the fact that extinguished fear responses can return. For instance, numerous human and animal studies have shown that an extinguished CR can return and be expressed when some amount of time has passed since extinction training (*spontaneous recovery*), when the CS is encountered in a different context from where it was originally extinguished (*fear renewal*), or when the US is presented alone (*reinstatement*; for a review see Bouton, Westbrook, Corcoran, & Maren, 2006). These phenomena (collectively referred to as *the return of fear*) indicate that the old CS-US association is far from forgotten and may compete with the new memory of the CS formed after extinction (Bouton, 2004).

The neural substrates of fear extinction have been explored in depth using animal models. Neurophysiological research has established a critical role of the medial PFC for extinction learning. In particular, the ventromedial PFC (vmPFC) appears to be important for exerting inhibitory control over the amygdala in order to reduce fear expression (Milad & Quirk, 2002). The vmPFC may be important for consolidating memories of extinction learning for later recall, because lesions to this region prior to fear extinction do not delay extinction over the course of training, but impair extinction when tested at a later date (Quirk, Russo, Barron, & Lebron, 2000). The amygdala is also critical for extinction learning; blocking activity in the basolateral amygdala has been shown to block extinction (Kim et al., 2007). The hippocampus also serves a role in the context specificity of extinction learning (Bouton et al., 2006). For instance, presentation of the US or a reminder of it can reinstate fear responses to a CS that has previously been extinguished. This effect is context dependent, such that reinstatement only leads to a return of fear if the CS is encountered in the same context as the US reminder. Amnesic patients with hippocampal damage do not show context-dependent reinstatement, however, indicating that the hippocampus is important for regulating

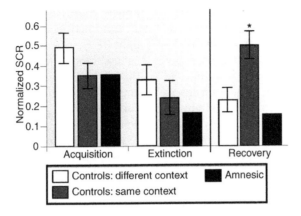

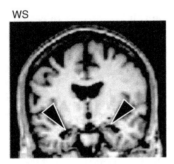

WS

Figure 18.4. The recall of fear extinction is mediated in large part by the context in which an extinguished CS is later encountered. For instance, a US presented alone following extinction learning often reinstates an extinguished fear response. Reinstatement is dependent on the context, such that a CS encountered in a novel context does not undergo reinstatement. Contextual reinstatement is also dependent on the hippocampus, because amnesic patients with damage to the hippocampus do not show contextual reinstatement when they encounter the CS in the same context. Data from LaBar & Phelps (2005).

the expression of fear following extinction learning (LaBar & Phelps, 2005; Figure 18.4). Together, the medial PFC, amygdala, and hippocampus provide an important neural circuit for fear extinction, although their relative contributions and interactions remain to be specified.

Findings from animal studies of extinction have been extended to humans using fMRI. In the first demonstration of extinction in humans using fMRI, LaBar et al. (1998) showed that responses in the amygdala initially increased in early extinction trials and then decreased over the course of extinction. In a 2-day fMRI study of fear

extinction, Phelps et al. (2004) showed that the recall of extinction over a 24-hour delay involved activity in the vmPFC, replicating findings from animal research (Milad & Quirk, 2002). Using a context manipulation in extinction learning, Milad et al. (2009) found that the recall of extinction memory in an extinguished context involves activity in the hippocampus and vmPFC, replicating findings from nonhuman animal studies (Milad & Quirk, 2002).

Widespread clinical observations that fears can return following extinction suggest that extinction memory may be weaker in kind than the competing fear memory.

An emerging approach to bolster extinction memories has been through the use of pharmacological aides that act as N-methyl-D-aspartate (NMDA) receptor agonists and putatively enhance learning and memory processes during extinction learning (Ledgerwood, Richardson, & Cranney, 2003). Animal research has shown that blocking NMDA receptors in the amygdala during extinction impairs extinction learning, suggesting that amygdala activity at the time of extinction learning is critical for learning (Falls, Miserendino, & Davis, 1992). Conversely, administration of an NMDA agonist known as D-cycloserine (DCS) into the amygdala has been shown to have the reverse effect of enhancing fear extinction (Walker, Ressler, Lu, & Davis, 2002). Human studies have shown that the use of DCS during exposure therapy successfully reduces the fear of heights (Ressler et al., 2004) and social phobia (Hofmann et al., 2006), but controlled laboratory studies have yet to show the effectiveness of DCS in reducing conditioned fears in healthy volunteers (Grillon, 2009). Grillon (2009) has proposed that DCS may operate on fears acquired through low-order conditioning processes that, for instance, use fear-relevant stimuli and an intense US.

Other Forms of Emotion Regulation

Humans possess a remarkable ability to strategize emotional responses in aversive situations. For instance, while watching a scary movie some people will cover their eyes, cling to a friend, or distract themselves with more pleasant thoughts. These responses often seem uniquely human, but the behavioral consequence is the same as during extinction learning – a reduction in emotional responses. Human neuroimaging research on emotion regulation has used paradigms designed to assess how voluntary regulation strategies reduce responses in emotional processing areas, such as the amygdala, relative to focusing on the negative qualities of affective material (Ochsner & Gross, 2008). For instance, subjects might be instructed to cognitively reappraise an image that is potentially negative (e.g., a wounded soldier) in a less negative light (e.g., the solider will receive medical assistance and survive). Emotion regulation strategies such as cognitive reappraisal engage the cingulate gyrus, parietal cortex, and lateral PFC, including both dorsal and ventral regions, which may in turn lead to reductions in amygdala activity (Ochsner & Gross, 2008). For a more detailed discussion of emotion regulation, see Chapter 16.

Although emotion regulation strategies like reappraisal involve cognitive processes that may be unique to humans, reappraisal may share an underlying final common pathway with more automatic forms of emotional control such as extinction. In a study by Delgado et al. (2008), subjects were trained to use emotion regulation strategies in a fear-conditioning experiment using simple colored shapes as CSs. Subjects were told to either attend to the CS or to reappraise the CS as less fear arousing by, for instance, using the color of the CS to imagine a calming field of flowers. Similar to previous studies of extinction (e.g., Phelps, Delgado, Nearing, and LeDoux, 2004), reduction of fear resulted in a decrease in amygdala activity. In addition, active regulation of conditioned fear resulted in an increase in dorsolateral PFC activity, in line with studies of emotion regulation without an associative fear-learning component. This neural circuitry engaged during voluntary regulation of emotion was found to be related to activity in the vmPFC as well, a region implicated in fear extinction, suggesting that higher order cognitive regulation is related to systems involved in fear extinction (Delgado et al., 2008).

Reconsolidation of Fear Memories

An emerging frontier in the neuroscience of emotion involves modifying existing memories of fearful experiences (Nader & Hardt, 2009). In the standard model of memory, the short-term memory trace is consolidated and stored into long-term memory, where it is activated on retrieval. An alternate hypothesis proposes that reactivating a

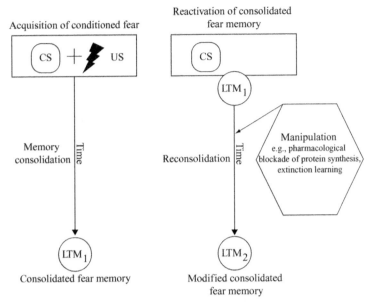

Acquisition of conditioned fear

Reactivation of consolidated
fear memory

CS + US

CS

LTM₁

Memory
consolidation | Time

Reconsolidation | Time

Manipulation
e.g., pharmacological
blockade of protein synthesis,
extinction learning

LTM₁

LTM₂

Consolidated fear memory

Modified consolidated
fear memory

Figure 18.5. Reconsolidation of conditioned fear memories. After fear learning, the memory of the CS is consolidated and stored in long-term memory (LTM₁). According to the hypothesis of reconsolidation, reactivation of the fear memory returns the memory to a labile state. During this time, the memory can be modified through manipulations to reduce, or possibly terminate, the fearful memory associated with the CS. Thus, the individual now retains a new memory of the CS (LTM₂) in which the CS is no longer affectively salient.

stable long-term memory requires the memory to be *reconsolidated.* Reconsolidation temporarily makes the long-term memory labile before it once again returns to a stable state. Relevant to emotional memories, the reconsolidation hypothesis suggests that a labile memory can be modified such that new information can alter an existing memory before it once again becomes stable (Figure 18.5; Nader & Hardt, 2009).

The notion that existing fear memories can be altered via reconsolidation processes has received some empirical support in both human and animal experiments. For example, Nader, Schafe, and LeDoux (2000) fear-conditioned rodents to a tone paired with an aversive US. Later, the tone was replayed without the US to reactive the memory. Soon after the memory was reactivated, the protein synthesis inhibitor anisomycin was injected into the amygdala. Blocking protein synthesis during the reconsolidation time window led to a decrease in fear responses to the CS, suggesting that the fearful memory was modified. These find-

ings have been extended to humans using the nonselective beta-blocker propranolol. For instance, Kindt and colleagues (Kindt, Soeter, & Vervliet, 2009) showed that reactivation of a fear memory led to a significant decrease in the expression of fear 24 hours later – but only if the individual had been administered propranolol prior to reactivation. A group-administered placebo prior to reactivation did not show the same effect in the test of fear expression 24 hours later. Importantly, the subjects' declarative knowledge of the CS-US contingencies was unaffected by propranolol, suggesting that pharmacological blockade of the beta-adrenergic system differentially affects the expression of fear while leaving the explicit memory intact. The impact of reactivating fear memories under the effect of propranolol has been shown to extend to a one-month follow-up of fear expression (Kindt & Soeter, 2010).

The ability to behaviorally modify fear memories without the use of protein blocking drugs or pharmacological agents has also been shown both in rodents and humans (Monfils, Cowansage, Klann, & LeDoux, 2009; Schiller et al., 2010). These studies take advantage of the reactivation window provided by reconsolidation to introduce new information regarding the feared CS. In a human behavioral study, a decrease of fear expression was observed when extinction learning was conducted within the reconsolidation time window (10 minutes after reactivation), and this effect persisted up to a year after fear conditioning (Schiller et al., 2010). Conversely, a group that received extinction learning outside the reconsolidation time window (6 hours after reactivation) did show recovery of fear 24 hours after reactivation. These results indicate that new learning that occurs during a period of memory reconsolidation can control the expression of fear. The clinical implications for this procedure are particularly relevant for treating anxiety disorders, especially given that fear memories are often persistent and return over time. One caution about reconsolidation, however, is that subtle changes in the experimental parameters can greatly affect the outcome and, consequently, the interpretation of the behavioral data (Soeter & Kindt, 2011). Therefore, further investigations using both pharmacological and nonpharmacological interventions will be needed to better understand reconsolidation effects in humans and assess how well these controlled laboratory studies generalize to the treatment of anxiety disorders (Schiller & Phelps, 2011).

Future Issues

Cellular and systems neuroscience research that is based on animal models has steadily advanced for several decades since Pavlov's original discoveries. The cognitive neuroscience of human fear learning has advanced more recently, facilitated by functional brain imaging techniques. Many important challenges still exist in extending findings from animal research to human populations, especially for developing novel clinical treatments. In addition, there are still many questions concerning the biobehavioral systems involved in different aspects of human fear learning.

Generalization of Learned Fears

An important question that has received sparse attention in human fear-learning research concerns how fears acquired to a particular conditioned stimulus generalize to other stimuli that have never directly predicted an aversive outcome. The phenomenon of stimulus generalization was uncovered in early classical conditioning experiments in Pavlov's laboratory (Pavlov, 1927) where he found that animals conditioned to salivate to a specific stimulus (e.g., a tone of 1,000 Hz) would salivate to other stimuli that were perceptually similar to the CS (e.g., tones above and below 1,000 Hz). Remarkably, the amount of salivation was in proportion to the similarity between the nonconditioned stimulus and the CS. Because tones do not naturally cause an animal to salivate, Pavlov deduced that learning acquired to one stimulus transferred to other, perceptually similar stimuli. Other studies of stimulus generalization, using instrumental conditioning procedures, showed that generalization gradients could be quantified on the basis of individual subjects' response patterns (Guttman & Kalish, 1956). These generalization gradients were found to track similarity along the sensory dimension itself and were not influenced by the organism's ability to perceptually discriminate between the CS and another stimulus. This finding formed the basis for the contemporary view that stimulus generalization is in large measure a cognitive process, not simply a failure to discriminate between conditioned and nonconditioned stimuli (Shepard, 1987).

Fear generalization occurs when the fear-related CR is evoked by stimuli other than the CS. In humans, fear generalization is perhaps best demonstrated in anxiety disorders characterized by excessive fear responses to innocuous cues, such as in post-traumatic stress disorder (PTSD). In PTSD, a number of stimuli can act as reminders of a traumatic event and can lead to a state of fear similar to that experienced during the initial trauma. Behavioral studies have reported generalization gradients of the CR following fear conditioning when participants are presented with stimuli that resemble the CS to varying degrees (Dunsmoor, Mitroff, & LaBar, 2009; Lissek et al., 2008). Generalization gradients are broader in patients with panic disorder, indicating that fears are readily elicited to a wider range of stimuli in this population (Lissek et al., 2010).

Dunsmoor et al. (2009) demonstrated a unique form of fear generalization in humans that was found to be influenced by the amount of fear intensity in non-conditioned stimuli (Figure 18.6). During fear conditioning, subjects received pairings of a face expressing a moderate amount of fear intensity (CS+) with an electrical shock US. A control stimulus (CS−) was also presented during fear conditioning and was alternated between groups as either the most intense or least intense fear face. Before fear conditioning, stimuli evoked undifferentiated SCRs; after fear conditioning, however, a gradient was observed that peaked at stimuli of greater intensity than the CS+. Interestingly, this gradient was reduced for the group that received discriminative fear conditioning between the same CS+ and a CS− that expressed the most fear, suggesting that associative learning processes acting against a natural gradient of fear intensity can influence the extent to which individuals generalize conditioned fear. These behavioral findings were extended to fMRI, wherein brain activity related to fear generalization was observed in areas involved in initial fear learning, including the striatum, insula, thalamus, and periaqueductal gray (Dunsmoor, Prince, Murty, Kragel, & LaBar, 2011). Moreover, the behavioral expression of fear generalization (i.e., SCRs) was correlated with activity in the amygdala and insula, and functional connectivity between the amygdala and fusiform gyrus during fear generalization was cor-

related with individual differences in trait anxiety.

The limited number of human behavioral and neuroimaging studies examining fear generalization show that stimuli that never enter into direct association with a US, but are perceptually similar to a CS, evoke a generalized CR. However, there are still many questions regarding the biobehavioral mechanisms governing generalization in humans and their role in anxiety disorders.

Genetics of Human Fear Learning

The genetic basis of fear conditioning has received increasing interest in human behavioral and imaging research. One advantage to using this model system is that the effects of pharmacological agents and neurotransmitters are well documented from analogous studies in nonhuman animals, so the putative actions of the genetic markers can be inferred more readily. Early findings have demonstrated a link between the expression of conditioned fear in humans and genes involved in emotional reactivity (i.e., serotonin transporter gene, 5-HTTLPR polymorphism) and neuroplasticity (i.e., brain-derived neurotrophic factor, BDNF; Garpenstrand, Annas, Ekblom, Oreland, & Fredrikson, 2001; Mahan & Ressler, 2012). For example, Garpenstrand et al. (2001) found that strong fear conditioning, as assessed by the SCR, was related to the short serotonin transporter promoter allele, whereas delayed extinction (that is, sustained fear responses over the course of extinction trials) was related to a long dopamine D4 receptor allele. Findings related to the genetic basis of fear conditioning, in combination with evidence on the role of specific brain regions, are helping inform comprehensive models of fear learning that may be important for profiling certain anxiety disorders. However, it is important to note that there are only a limited number of genetic studies of human fear learning at this time, and further research is needed in this area, especially when extrapolating results

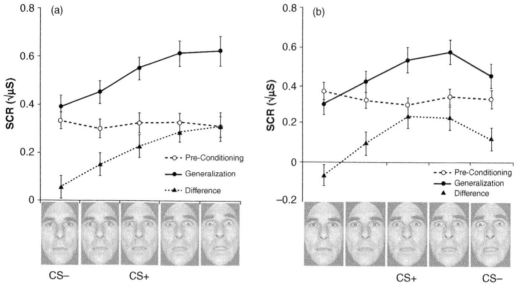

Figure 18.6. Results from a fear-generalization study by Dunsmoor et al. (2009), in which subjects were exposed to morphed faces of the same identity before (Pre-conditioning) and after (Generalization) discriminative fear conditioning. During fear conditioning, the intermediate morph value (CS+) was paired with an aversive electrical shock while a control face (CS−) was explicitly unpaired. (A) Skin conductance responses (SCR) were undifferentiated before fear conditioning, but showed an increasing gradient of response magnitude after fear conditioning. (B) Subjects who received discriminative fear conditioning between the CS+ and the most intense faces as the CS− also showed a gradient of SCRs, but the gradient was sharper and SCRs were reduced to the most intense face in this group. These findings suggest that fear generalization is influenced by the intensity value of nonconditioned stimuli, but that discriminative fear-learning processes may lead to stimulus control.

to understand the molecular basis of anxiety disorders.

Laboratory and Real-World Fear Learning Using Virtual Reality

The study of human fear conditioning has typically involved laboratory or neuroimaging examinations that make use of two-dimensional objects as CSs presented to the subject over a computer monitor. Although these studies have provided a model of real-world encounters with feared stimuli, they do not approximate some aspects of complex fearful experiences in the real world. For instance, environmental CSs are often encountered during a dynamic exchange rather than passively presented, and real-world contexts are far richer than a typical laboratory setting. A frontier in the study of fear learning that has direct implications for understanding and treating anxiety disor-

ders involves the use of virtual reality environments. The advantage of this technology is that it simulates real-world settings, including immersive 3-D applications that can be tailored to the fearful stimuli or contexts experienced by a particular patient or groups of patients. This technology is being employed not only to simulate outcomes of extinction-based therapies in anxiety disorders but also as a basic research tool to investigate context specificity of conditioned fears (Huff et al., 2011). As reviewed earlier, previous animal research has shown that extinction learning is specific to the context in which it was acquired (Bouton, 2004). This effect has proved problematic for the treatment of anxiety disorders, because anxieties often relapse outside the confines of the therapist's office. Human research on the context specificity of extinction learning is limited by the ability to manipulate the environment in a behavioral testing room. Immersive virtual reality, however, promises to shed light on how fears return when CSs are encountered in a variety of lifelike contexts, which allows for an in-depth examination of different parameters that mediate the contextual recall of extinction memories.

Concluding Remarks

In this chapter, we highlighted behavioral and neuroimaging research on human fear learning that has been informed and supported by advancements in nonhuman animal research. The human brain mechanisms involved in the acquisition, expression, and extinction of fear are becoming increasingly well delineated. This knowledge is being used to develop advanced neurobehavioral models of anxiety disorders that have led to innovative treatments, including the use of pharmacological agents that putatively enhance learning systems to strengthen the effect of exposure therapy. Nevertheless, future research will be needed to answer many remaining questions in the realm of human and nonhuman fear learning.

Outstanding Questions and Future Directions

- Under what circumstances do humans generalize fear from a single learning episode? Is fear generalization influenced solely by the perceptual similarity between the CS and a nonconditioned stimulus, or is generalization also influenced by the conceptual or categorical relationship between stimuli or situations? What neural systems mediate the generalization of learned fear, and what procedures (e.g., extinction, cognitively based emotion regulation) best limit fear generalization?
- What is the genetic basis of fear learning? Are some individuals genetically predisposed to form associations between stimuli and aversive outcomes, and are some individuals better equipped to inhibit

fear responses? What environmental influences mitigate against genetic risk factors?
- Can fear memories be selectively erased using knowledge of the neuroscience of memory? Can these practices be successfully modified for use as therapeutic treatment of clinical anxiety disorders? What ethical issues arise when applying fear-erasure techniques to treat anxiety disorders?

Acknowledgments

This work was supported in part by NSF grant 0745919 and NIH grants 2 P01 NS041328 and R01 DA027802. J. E. D. was supported by National Research Service Award no. F31MH090682,

References

Alvarez, R. P., Biggs, A., Chen, G., Pine, D. S., & Grillon, C. (2008). Contextual fear conditioning in humans: Cortical-hippocampal and amygdala contributions. *Journal of Neuroscience*, 28(24), 6211–19.

Anagnostaras, S. G., Maren, S., & Fanselow, M. S. (1999). Temporally graded retrograde amnesia of contextual fear after hippocampal damage in rats: Within-subjects examination. *Journal of Neuroscience*, 19(3), 1106–14.

Bechara, A., Tranel, D., Damasio, H., Adolphs, R., Rockland, C., & Damasio, A. R. (1995). Double dissociation of conditioning and declarative knowledge relative to the amygdala and hippocampus in humans. *Science*, 269(5227), 1115–18.

Bekinschtein, T. A., Shalom, D. E., Forcato, C., Herrera, M., Coleman, M. R., Manes, F. F., & Sigman, M. (2009). Classical conditioning in the vegetative and minimally conscious state. *Nature Neuroscience*, 12(10), 1343–49.

Blanchard, R. J., Blanchard, D. C., Agullana, R., & Weiss, S. M. (1991). 22 khz alarm cries to presentation of a predator, by laboratory rats living in visible burrow systems. *Physiology & Behavior*, 50(5), 967–72.

Bouton, M. E. (2004). Context and behavioral processes in extinction. *Learning & Memory*, 11(5), 485–94.

Bouton, M. E., Westbrook, R. F., Corcoran, K. A., & Maren, S. (2006). Contextual and temporal modulation of extinction: Behavioral and biological mechanisms. *Biological Psychiatry*, 60(4), 352–60.

Buchel, C., Morris, J., Dolan, R. J., & Friston, K. J. (1998). Brain systems mediating aversive conditioning: An event-related fMRI study. *Neuron*, 20(5), 947–57.

Carter, R. M., Hofstotter, C., Tsuchiya, N., & Koch, C. (2003). Working memory and fear conditioning. *Proceedings of the National Academy of Sciences*, 100(3), 1399–1404.

Cheng, D. T., Knight, D. C., Smith, C. N., & Helmstetter, F. J. (2006). Human amygdala activity during the expression of fear responses. *Behavioral Neuroscience*, 120(6), 1187–95.

Cheng, D. T., Knight, D. C., Smith, C. N., Stein, E. A., & Helmstetter, F. J. (2003). Functional MRI of human amygdala activity during Pavlovian fear conditioning: Stimulus processing versus response expression. *Behavioral Neuroscience*, 117(1), 3–10.

Choi, J. S., Cain, C. K., & LeDoux, J. E. (2010). The role of amygdala nuclei in the expression of auditory signaled two-way active avoidance in rats. *Learning & Memory*, 17(3), 139–47.

Cook, M., & Mineka, S. (1989). Observational conditioning of fear to fear-relevant versus fear-irrelevant stimuli in rhesus-monkeys. *Journal of Abnormal Psychology*, 98(4), 448–59.

Coppens, E., Spruyt, A., Vandenbulcke, M., Van Paesschen, W., & Vansteenwegen, D. (2009). Classically conditioned fear responses are preserved following unilateral temporal lobectomy in humans when concurrent US-expectancy ratings are used. *Neuropsychologia*, 47(12), 2496–2503.

Davey, G. C. L. (1992). Classical-conditioning and the acquisition of human fears and phobias – A review and synthesis of the literatures. *Advances in Behaviour Research and Therapy*, 14(1), 29–66.

Davis, M. (1992). The role of the amygdala in fear and anxiety. *Annual Review of Neuroscience*, 15, 353–75.

Davis, M., Walker, D. L., Miles, L., & Grillon, C. (2009). Phasic vs. sustained fear in rats and humans: Role of the extended amygdala in fear vs. anxiety. *Neuropsychopharmacology*, 1–31.

Davis, M., Walker, D. L., Miles, L., & Grillon, C. (2010). Phasic vs. sustained fear in rats and humans: Role of the extended amygdala

in fear vs anxiety. *Neuropsychopharmacology*, 35(1), 105–35.

Delgado, M. R., Nearing, K. I., LeDoux, J. E., & Phelps, E. A. (2008). Neural circuitry underlying the regulation of conditioned fear and its relation to extinction. *Neuron*, 59(5), 829–38.

Domjan, M. (2005). Pavlovian conditioning: A functional perspective. *Annual Review of Psychology*, 56, 179–206.

Dunsmoor, J. E., Bandettini, P. A., & Knight, D. C. (2008). Neural correlates of unconditioned response diminution during Pavlovian conditioning. *Neuroimage*, 40(2), 811–17.

Dunsmoor, J. E., Mitroff, S. R., & LaBar, K. S. (2009). Generalization of conditioned fear along a dimension of increasing fear intensity. *Learning & Memory*, 16(7), 460–69.

Dunsmoor, J. E., Prince, S. E., Murty, V. P., Kragel, P. A., & LaBar, K. S. (2011). Neurobehavioral mechanisms of human fear generalization. *Neuroimage*, 55(4), 1878–88.

Esteves, F., Parra, C., Dimberg, U., & Öhman, A. (1994). Nonconscious associative learning – Pavlovian conditioning of skin-conductance responses to masked fear-relevant facial stimuli. *Psychophysiology*, 31(4), 375–85.

Falls, W. A., Miserendino, M. J. D., & Davis, M. (1992). Extinction of fear-potentiated startle – blockade by infusion of an NMDA antagonist into the amygdala. *Journal of Neuroscience*, 12(3), 854–63.

Foa, E. B., Hembree, E. A., Cahill, S. P., Rauch, S. A. M., Riggs, D. S., Feeny, N. C., & Yadin, E. (2005). Randomized trial of prolonged exposure for posttraumatic stress disorder with and without cognitive restructuring: Outcome at academic and community clinics. *Journal of Consulting and Clinical Psychology*, 73(5), 953–64.

Garcia, J., & Koelling, R. A. (1966). Relation of cue to consequence in avoidance learning. *Psychonomic Science*, 4, 123–24.

Garpenstrand, H., Annas, P., Ekblom, J., Oreland, L., & Fredrikson, M. (2001). Human fear conditioning is related to dopaminergic and serotonergic biological markers. *Behavioral Neuroscience*, 115(2), 358–64.

Grillon, C. (2009). D-cycloserine facilitation of fear extinction and exposure-based therapy might rely on lower-level, automatic mechanisms. *Biological Psychiatry*, 66(7), 636–41.

Guttman, N., & Kalish, H. I. (1956). Discriminability and stimulus-generalization *Journal of Experimental Psychology*, 51(1), 79–88.

Hamm, A. O., & Vaitl, D. (1996). Affective learning: Awareness and aversion. *Psychophysiology*, 33(6), 698–710.

Hofmann, S. G., Meuret, A. E., Smits, J. A. J., Simon, N. M., Pollack, M. H., Eisenmenger, K., . . . Otto, M. W. (2006). Augmentation of exposure therapy with D-cycloserine for social anxiety disorder. *Archives of General Psychiatry*, 63(3), 298–304.

Huff, N. C., Hernandez, J. A., Fecteau, M. E., Zielinski, D. J., Brady, R., & Labar, K. S. (2011). Revealing context-specific conditioned fear memories with full immersion virtual reality. *Frontiers in Behavioral Neuroscience*, 5, 75.

Jackson, E. D., Payne, J. D., Nadel, L., & Jacobs, W. J. (2006). Stress differentially modulates fear conditioning in healthy men and women. *Biological Psychiatry*, 59(6), 516–22.

Jeon, D. E. A. (2010). Observational fear learning involves affective pain system and Cav1.2 Ca2 +channels in ACC. *Nature Neuroscience*, 13(4), 482–88.

Kim, J., Lee, S., Park, H., Song, B., Hong, I., Geum, D., . . . Choi, S. (2007). Blockade of amygdala metabotropic glutamate receptor subtype 1 impairs fear extinction. *Biochemical and Biophysical Research Communications*, 355(1), 188–93.

Kimble, G. A., & Ost, J. W. P. (1961). Conditioned inhibitory process in eyelid conditioning. *Journal of Experimental Psychology*, 61(2), 150–56.

Kindt, M., & Soeter, M. (2010). Dissociating response systems: Erasing fear from memory. *Neurobiology of Learning and Memory*, 94(1), 30–41.

Kindt, M., Soeter, M., & Vervliet, B. (2009). Beyond extinction: Erasing human fear responses and preventing the return of fear. *Nature Neuroscience*, 12(3), 256–58.

Kluver, H., & Bucy, P. C. (1939). Preliminary analysis of functions of the temporal lobes in monkeys. *Archives of Neurology and Psychiatry*, 42(6), 979–1000.

Knight, D. C., Nguyen, H. T., & Bandettini, P. A. (2005). The role of the human amygdala in the production of conditioned fear responses. *Neuroimage*, 26(4), 1193–1200.

Knight, D. C., Waters, N. S., & Bandettini, P. A. (2009). Neural substrates of explicit and implicit fear memory. *Neuroimage*, 45(1), 208–14.

LaBar, K. S., & Cabeza, R. (2006). Cognitive neuroscience of emotional memory. *Nature Reviews Neuroscience*, 7(1), 54–64.

LaBar, K. S., & Disterhoft, J. F. (1998). Conditioning, awareness, and the hippocampus. *Hippocampus*, 8(6), 620–26.

LaBar, K. S., Gatenby, J. C., Gore, J. C., LeDoux, J. E., & Phelps, E. A. (1998). Human amygdala activation during conditioned fear acquisition and extinction: A mixed-trial fMRI study. *Neuron*, 20(5), 937–45.

LaBar, K. S., LeDoux, J. E., Spencer, D. D., & Phelps, E. A. (1995). Impaired fear conditioning following unilateral temporal lobectomy in humans. *Journal of Neuroscience*, 15(10), 6846–55.

LaBar, K. S., & Phelps, E. A. (2005). Reinstatement of conditioned fear in humans is context dependent and impaired in amnesia. *Behavioral Neuroscience*, 119(3), 677–86.

Ledgerwood, L., Richardson, R., & Cranney, J. (2003). Effects of D-cycloserine on extinction of conditioned freezing. *Behavioral Neuroscience*, 117(2), 341–49.

LeDoux, J. E. (1996). *The emotional brain*. New York: Simon and Schuster.

LeDoux, J. E. (2000). Emotion circuits in the brain. *Annual Review of Neuroscience*, 23, 155–84.

LeDoux, J. E., & Gorman, J. M. (2001). A call to action: Overcoming anxiety through active coping. *American Journal of Psychiatry*, 158(12), 1953–55.

Lissek, S., Biggs, A. L., Rabin, S. J., Cornwell, B. R., Alvarez, R. P., Pine, D. S., & Grillon, C. (2008). Generalization of conditioned fear-potentiated startle in humans: Experimental validation and clinical relevance. *Behaviour Research and Therapy*, 46(5), 678–87.

Lissek, S., Rabin, S., Heller, R. E., Lukenbaugh, D., Geraci, M., Pine, D. S., & Grillon, C. (2010). Overgeneralization of conditioned fear as a pathogenic marker of panic disorder. *American Journal of Psychiatry*, 167(1), 47–55.

Lovibond, P. F., & Shanks, D. R. (2002). The role of awareness in Pavlovian conditioning: Empirical evidence and theoretical implications. *Journal of Experimental Psychology – Animal Behavior Processes*, 28(1), 3–26.

Mahan, A. L., & Ressler, K. J. (2012). Fear conditioning, synaptic plasticity and the amygdala: Implications for posttraumatic stress disorder. *Trends in Neurosciences*, 35(1), 24–35.

McGaugh, J. L. (2004). The amygdala modulates the consolidation of memories of emotionally arousing experiences. *Annual Review of Neuroscience*, 27, 1–28.

McGaugh, J. L., Cahill, L., & Roozendaal, B. (1996). Involvement of the amygdala in memory storage: Interaction with other brain systems. *Proceedings of the National Academy of Sciences*, 93(24), 13508–14.

McNally, G. P., Johansen, J. P., & Blair, H. T. (2011). Placing prediction into the fear circuit. *Trends in Neurosciences*, 34(6), 283–92.

Milad, M. R., Pitman, R. K., Ellis, C. B., Gold, A. L., Shin, L. M., Lasko, N. B., . . . Rauch, S. L. (2009). Neurobiological basis of failure to recall extinction memory in posttraumatic stress disorder. *Biological Psychiatry*, 66(12), 1075–82.

Milad, M. R., & Quirk, G. J. (2002). Neurons in medial prefrontal cortex signal memory for fear extinction. *Nature*, 420(6911), 70–74.

Mineka, S., Davidson, M., Cook, M., & Keir, R. (1984). Observational conditioning of snake fear in rhesus-monkeys. *Journal of Abnormal Psychology*, 93(4), 355–72.

Mineka, S., & Zinbarg, R. (2006). A contemporary learning theory perspective on the etiology of anxiety disorders – It's not what you thought it was. *American Psychologist*, 61(1), 10–26.

Monfils, M. H., Cowansage, K. K., Klann, E., & LeDoux, J. E. (2009). Extinction-reconsolidation boundaries: Key to persistent attenuation of fear memories. *Science*, 324(5929), 951–55.

Morris, J. S., Öhman, A., & Dolan, R. J. (1998). Conscious and unconscious emotional learning in the human amygdala. *Nature*, 393(6684), 467–70.

Nader, K., & Hardt, O. (2009). A single standard for memory: The case for reconsolidation. *Nature Reviews Neuroscience*, 10(3), 224–34.

Nader, K., Schafe, G. E., & Le Doux, J. E. (2000). Fear memories require protein synthesis in the amygdala for reconsolidation after retrieval. *Nature*, 406(6797), 722–26.

Ochsner, K. N., & Gross, J. J. (2008). Cognitive emotion regulation: Insights from social cognitive and affective neuroscience. *Current Directions in Psychological Science*, 17(2), 153–58.

Öhman, A., & Mineka, S. (2001). Fears, phobias, and preparedness: Toward an evolved module of fear and fear learning. *Psychological Review*, 108(3), 483–522.

Olsson, A., & Phelps, E. A. (2004). Learned fear of "unseen" faces after Pavlovian, observational, and instructed fear. *Psychological Science*, 15(12), 822–28.

Olsson, A., & Phelps, E. A. (2007). Social learning of fear. *Nature Neuroscience*, 10(9), 1095–1102.

O'Reilly, R. C., & Rudy, J. W. (2001). Conjunctive representations in learning and memory: Principles of cortical and hippocampal function. *Psychological Review*, 108(2), 311–45.

Pape, H. C., & Pare, D. (2010). Plastic synaptic networks of the amygdala for the acquisition, expression, and extinction of conditioned fear. *Physiological Reviews*, 90(2), 419–63.

Pavlov, I. P. (1927). *Conditioned reflexes*. London: Oxford University Press.

Phelps, E. A., Delgado, M. R., Nearing, K. I., & LeDoux, J. E. (2004). Extinction learning in humans: Role of the amygdala and vmPFC. *Neuron*, 43(6), 897–905.

Phelps, E. A., O'Connor, K. J., Gatenby, J. C., Gore, J. C., Grillon, C., & Davis, M. (2001). Activation of the left amygdala to a cognitive representation of fear. *Nature Neuroscience*, 4(4), 437–41.

Phillips, R. G., & LeDoux, J. E. (1992). Differential contribution of amygdala and hippocampus to cued and contextual fear conditioning. *Behavioral Neuroscience*, 106(2), 274–85.

Quirk, G. J., Russo, G. K., Barron, J. L., & Lebron, K. (2000). The role of ventromedial prefrontal cortex in the recovery of extinguished fear. *Journal of Neuroscience*, 20(16), 6225–31.

Rachman, S. (1977). Conditioning theory of fear-acquisition – critical-examination. *Behaviour Research and Therapy*, 15(5), 375–87.

Rescorla, R. A., & Wagner, A. R. (1972). *A theory of Pavlovian conditioning: Variations in the effectiveness of reinforcement and nonreinforcement*. New York: Appleton-Century-Crofts.

Ressler, K. J., Rothbaum, B. O., Tannenbaum, L., Anderson, P., Graap, K., Zimand, E., . . . Davis, M. (2004). Cognitive enhancers as adjuncts to psychotherapy – Use of D-cycloserine in phobic individuals to facilitate extinction of fear. *Archives of General Psychiatry*, 61(11), 1136–44.

Rodrigues, S. M., LeDoux, J. E., & Sapolsky, R. M. (2009). The Influence of stress hormones on fear circuitry. *Annual Review of Neuroscience*, 32, 289–313.

Schafe, G. E., Nader, K., Blair, H. T., & LeDoux, J. E. (2001). Memory consolidation of Pavlovian fear conditioning: A cellular and molecular perspective. *Trends in Neurosciences*, 24(9), 540–46.

Schiller, D., Monfils, M. H., Raio, C. M., Johnson, D. C., LeDoux, J. E., & Phelps, E.

A. (2010). Preventing the return of fear in humans using reconsolidation update mechanisms. *Nature*, 463(7277), 49–51.

Schiller, D., & Phelps, E. A. (2011). Does reconsolidation occur in humans? *Frontiers in Behavioral Neuroscience*, 5, 24.

Sehlmeyer, C., Schoning, S., Zwitserlood, P., Pfleiderer, B., Kircher, T., Arolt, V., & Konrad, C. (2009). Human fear conditioning and extinction in neuroimaging: A systematic review. *PloS One*, 4(6), 16.

Seligman, M. E. (1970). On the generality of the laws of learning. *Psychological Review*, 77(5), 406–18.

Seligman, M. E. (1971). Phobia and preparedeness. *Behavior Therapy*, 2(3), 307–20.

Shanks, D. R. (2010). Learning: From association to cognition. *Annual Review of Psychology*, 61, 273–301.

Shepard, R. N. (1987). Toward a universal law of generalization for psychological science. *Science*, 237(4820), 1317–23.

Soeter, M., & Kindt, M. (2011). Disrupting reconsolidation: Pharmacological and behavioral manipulations. *Learning & Memory*, 18(6), 357–66.

Squire, L. R. (1986). Mechanisms of memory. *Science*, 232(4758), 1612–19.

Squire, L. R., & Zola, S. M. (1996). Structure and function of declarative and nondeclarative memory systems. *Proceedings of the National Academy of Sciences*, 93(24), 13515–22.

Vuilleumier, P. (2005). How brains beware: Neural mechanisms of emotional attention. *Trends in Cognitive Sciences*, 9(12), 585–94.

Walker, D. L., Ressler, K. J., Lu, K. T., & Davis, M. (2002). Facilitation of conditioned fear extinction by systemic administration or intra-amygdala infusions of D-cycloserine as assessed with fear-potentiated startle in rats. *Journal of Neuroscience*, 22(6), 2343–51.

Watson, J. B., & Rayner, R. (1920). Conditioned emotional reactions. *Journal of Experimental Psychology*, 3, 1–14.

Weike, A. I., Hamm, A. O., Schupp, H. T., Runge, U., Schroeder, H. W. S., & Kessler, C. (2005). Fear conditioning following unilateral temporal lobectomy: Dissociation of conditioned startle potentiation and autonomic learning. *Journal of Neuroscience*, 25(48), 11117–24.

Weiskrantz, L. (1956). Behavioral changes associated with ablation of the amygdaloid complex in monkeys. *Journal of Comparative and Physiological Psychology*, 49(4), 381–91.

Wilensky, A. E., Schafe, G. E., Kristensen, M. P., & LeDoux, J. E. (2006). Rethinking the fear circuit: The central nucleus of the amygdala is required for the acquisition, consolidation, and expression of Pavlovian fear conditioning. *Journal of Neuroscience*, 26(48), 12387–96.

Zorawski, M., Blanding, N. Q., Kuhn, C. M., & LaBar, K. S. (2006). Effects of stress and sex on acquisition and consolidation of human fear conditioning. *Learning & Memory*, 13(4), 441–50.

Zorawski, M., Cook, C. A., Kuhn, C. M., & LaBar, K. S. (2005). Sex, stress, and fear: Individual differences in conditioned learning. *Cognitive Affective & Behavioral Neuroscience*, 5(2), 191–201.

CHAPTER 19

Reward Learning

Contributions of Corticobasal Ganglia Circuits to Reward Value Signals

Dominic S. Fareri & Mauricio R. Delgado

Throughout our lives, we learn to value behaviors and stimuli in our environment that are likely to bring satisfaction or achievement. We might learn to value certain foods, for example, because they are healthier or satisfy our hunger more so than others, or we may learn to value something such as a school bell in the middle of the day that signals that it is time to eat. As humans, we also come to value more secondary, less immediate reinforcers such as money and the actions that allow the accumulation of wealth (e.g., working overtime for bonus pay). Research across species has implicated a specific neural circuitry subserving these goal-directed behaviors, centering largely on corticobasal ganglia circuits. Valued social outcomes and considerations play additional motivating roles in our environment, as we often strive for social approval or praise and are motivated during social interactions by preferences for valued actions, such as reciprocity and fairness. These social values aid in learning about others and inform our social behavior. Recent investigations have begun to examine whether social rewards are valued and experienced similarly to pri-mary rewards, whether they rely on a common neural reward circuitry, and whether learning socially relevant information occurs via similar reward-learning mechanisms.

The goal of this chapter is to provide an overview of neural mechanisms involved in reward learning, concentrating largely on corticobasal ganglia circuits. Detailing findings primarily from human neuroimaging research, a specific focus is on how these neural circuits contribute to computing value signals for both natural and more abstract social rewards and how these value signals contribute to learning.

The Neuroanatomy of Reward Processing

A large body of nonhuman animal research has sought to delineate neural correlates underlying reward processing at both the cellular and more circuit-based level. A common finding across many of these investigations is the involvement of corticobasal ganglia loops as a key component of a re-ward-processing circuit (Haber & Knutson,

2010; Sesack & Grace, 2010). These functional loops are formed based on both communication between structures within the basal ganglia and prefrontal cortex and on modulatory influence by dopaminergic neurons in midbrain regions; for example, the substantia nigra (SN) and ventral tegmental area (VTA). The integrity of connections and of interactions between these areas subserves both motor and cognitive behavior (for a review see Middleton & Strick, 2000). Given its heterogeneity in terms of connectivity and functionality, the basal ganglia and associated projections are a key component of a putative reward circuit and are the focus of the research described in this chapter.

The basal ganglia comprise several subregions including the striatum, globus pallidus (internal [GPi] and external [GPe] components), and subthalamic nucleus (for a review see Middleton & Strick, 2000), with the striatum receiving vital projections from both prefrontal and midbrain dopaminergic regions. The striatum serves as the input unit of the basal ganglia, in turn playing an integral role in processing and integrating reward-related information (Haber & Knutson, 2010). The striatum can be further subdivided into dorsal and ventral components (Figure 19.1), each with important afferent and efferent connections (Haber & Knutson, 2010). The caudate nucleus and putamen comprise the dorsal striatum and share connections with higher cognitive, motor, and sensory regions. The dorsal striatum receives afferents from the dorsolateral prefrontal cortex (DLPFC; Haber & Knutson, 2010), frontal eyefields, and motor cortex (Alexander, Crutcher, & DeLong, 1990; Middleton & Strick, 2000), connections that may facilitate reward processing. Projections from the anterior medial prefrontal cortex to medial portions of the dorsal striatum, for instance, have been postulated to be important for learning reward-related actions (e.g., Ostlund & Balleine, 2005), whereas projections from the sensorimotor cortex to the lateral portions of dorsal striatum are important for habit learning (e.g., Barnes, Kubota, Hu, Jin, & Graybiel, 2005). Both of these pathways project back to regions of cortex from which they

originate via the SN/GPi and mediodorsal and posterior nuclei of the thalamus (for a review see Sesack & Grace, 2010).

The ventral striatum shares connections with ventral cortical and subcortical regions. It comprises ventral portions of the caudate nucleus and putamen, as well as the nucleus accumbens (NAcc), which can be divided into core (medial) and shell (lateral) subcomponents (for a review see Sesack & Grace, 2010). Findings from nonhuman primates indicate that the ventral caudate and ventral putamen receive afferents from the orbitofrontal cortex (OFC) and dorsal anterior cingulate cortex (dACC; Haber & Knutson, 2010). The NAcc, in contrast, receives excitatory afferents from the prefrontal cortex (e.g., ventromedial prefrontal cortex, vmPFC) and subcortical structures including the midline and intralaminar nuclei of the thalamus, basolateral amygdala, and ventral subiculum of the hippocampus (Haber & Knutson, 2010; Sesack & Grace, 2010). The ventral striatum, particularly the NAcc, has been shown to be integral for both appetitive and consummatory aspects of reward processing, as well for learning associations between stimuli and rewards (Belin, Jonkman, Dickinson, Robbins, & Everitt, 2009). Further, the structures connecting with the ventral striatum have been implicated in different aspects of affective learning and reward evaluation and representation (for reviews, see Haber & Knutson, 2010; Kringelbach, 2005; Sesack & Grace, 2010). The NAcc also has reciprocal inhibitory connections with the VTA, from which dopamine modulates NAcc activity (Sesack & Grace, 2010). These dopaminergic projections from the VTA have been suggested to be critical for the learning of reward-related information (Niv, 2009).

Other functional and structural neural models exist that complement and extend the current knowledge of reward processing gained from the ideas of corticobasal ganglia functional loops and the dorsal-ventral divide of the striatum. One such model focuses on information processing and integration within striatal subregions, proposing a striato-nigral-striatal loop that facilitates communication within the striatum via

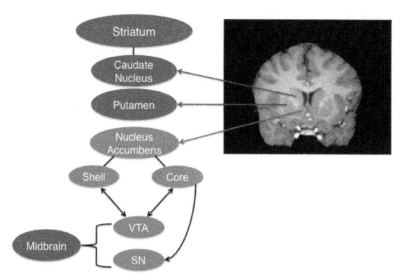

Figure 19.1. Striatum subdivisions. Dorsal striatum includes the caudate nucleus and putamen. Ventral striatum includes the nucleus accumbens (NAcc), which is subdivided into core and shell components, as well as ventral portions of the caudate nucleus and putamen. The NAcc is critically connected with the dopaminergic midbrain, particularly the substantia nigra (SN) and ventral tegmental area (VTA); the NAcc shell projects to the substantia nigra pars compacta (SNc), whereas the NAcc core sends projections to the SNc and substantia nigra pars reticulata (SNr). Both subdivisions of the NAcc share reciprocal connections with the VTA.

connections with midbrain dopaminergic cells in the substantia nigra in an ascending spiral-like fashion – providing a mechanism for integration of affective, cognitive, and motor information (for a review, see Haber & Knutson, 2010). Another model argues for alternative ways of dividing the striatum with respect to anatomical and functional considerations. Specifically, it proposes that striatum subdivisions lie along a dorsolateral to ventromedial continuum that allows for better segregation of striatal subregions (e.g., NAcc core/shell) than does the typical dorsal-ventral divide (for details, see Voorn, Vanderschuren, Groenewegen, Robbins, & Pennartz, 2004). Thus, research suggests that anatomical and functional considerations of the striatum are a focal point for a reward-processing circuit.

Neural Processing of Reward-Related Information

The Role of Dopamine during Reward Processing

One of the primary modulatory inputs into the striatum comes from midbrain

dopaminergic neurons. Extensive research in both rodents and nonhuman primates has examined the role of dopamine neurons in response to primary rewards and cues that predict them (for a review, see Wise, 2004), inspiring several theories regarding the functional significance of dopamine during reward processing. A prominent theory follows from the idea that there are two separable components to the processing of rewards and reward-predicting cues – that is, between wanting and liking. Reward wanting refers to the desire for a given reward, whereas reward liking refers to the actual hedonic experience of consumption (see Wise, 2004, for a review). Dopamine is thought to be involved specifically in reward wanting; for example, Wyvell and Berridge (2000) showed that injections of amphetamine (a dopamine agonist) into the NAcc of rats increased instrumental responding to a reward-predicting cue, but did not increase behaviors associated with hedonic reactions to reward consumption. In contrast, other evidence suggests that dopamine may be involved in the hedonic experience of reward: Rats treated with a neuroleptic drug (which blocks dopamine receptors) showed decreased responding for food over time in comparison to controls, advocating a role for dopamine in the reinforcing effects of rewarding stimuli (e.g., food; for a review, see Wise, 2004). This theory has been revised over the years to propose that dopamine is important for motivation (e.g., lever pressing for food) and that elevated levels aid in reinforcing action-outcome associations (Wise, 2004). A third hypothesis is that midbrain dopamine signals aid in the learning or reinforcement of novel actions (see Redgrave & Gurney, 2006). This hypothesis operates on the premise that dopaminergic signaling actually responds to preattentive sensory processing, because the time course of phasic dopamine signals does not allow (i.e., they occur too quickly) coding for the value of unexpected rewards.

A functional model of dopaminergic function that has been highly influential comes from elegant electrophysiological recordings from midbrain dopamine neurons in nonhuman primates (Schultz, Dayan, & Montague, 1997). In these recordings, it was observed that dopamine neurons responded to the delivery of unexpected rewards (i.e., when unaware of contingencies leading to juice delivery) and the earliest predictor of a reward (i.e., a conditioned cue that signaled an expected reward). These neurons further showed a depressed firing rate when an expected reward was omitted. Taken together, these findings suggest that dopamine neurons code a learning signal known as a prediction error (e.g., the difference between the expected and received reward; Niv & Schoenbaum, 2008). This theory continues to be developed and linked to other specific processes, such as temporal prediction learning signals (for a review see Niv, 2009) while being quantified even further by suggestions that the error signal is computed by comparing the average previous reward history and current experienced reward, with a specificity for positive prediction errors (i.e., unexpected rewards; Bayer & Glimcher, 2005). In sum, reward-related midbrain dopaminergic activity serves to inform animals of the value of actions and stimuli in their environment that will best allow the achievement of positive outcomes. This notion is related to computational ideas put forth by reinforcement learning theory, which holds that agents attempt to learn which actions to take when navigating an environment to achieve optimal reward (for a review, see Niv, 2009).

Evidence of this learning signal in nonhuman primates spurred the search for similarities within the human brain. However, much of this work has been indirect, employing neuroimaging techniques such as positron emission tomography (PET) and functional magnetic resonance imaging (fMRI). Taking advantage of the ability of radioactive tracers (e.g., raclopride) to bind to dopamine receptors in the striatum, PET allows for the measurement of changes in striatal dopaminergic release; decreased tracer binding potential is thought to indicate dopamine release into the striatum. Because cocaine functions by blocking the reuptake of striatal dopamine, PET studies have revealed impaired dopaminergic function in cocaine addicts as compared to control subjects: Addicts show decreased striatal binding potential for raclopride both when given methylphenidate (similar effects to cocaine) and a placebo (Volkow et al., 1997).

Measuring the blood-oxygen-level-dependent (BOLD) response, fMRI provides an alternative, indirect measure of neural activity that is thought to reflect synaptic input to a region (Logothetis, Pauls, Augath, Trinath, & Oeltermann, 2001; see Chapter 5). High-resolution fMRI scanning demonstrates that increases in VTA BOLD activation correspond to a positive reward prediction error signal to unexpected primary (liquid) and secondary (money) rewards (D'Ardenne, McClure, Nystrom, & Cohen, 2008). Thus, although there is some evidence of reward-related dopamine function in humans, most neuroimaging investigations of the human brain have focused primarily on the targets of midbrain dopaminergic regions, such as the striatum and prefrontal cortex.

Valuation in the Human Striatum: Affective Learning and Decision Making

Because the striatum is a major target of midbrain dopamine neurons, a rich animal literature has also investigated its role during the processing of reward-related information, and particularly the functional significance of dopaminergic input into the striatum (for a review see Belin et al., 2009). For instance, dopaminergic projections to the NAcc have been suggested to be critical to processing the reinforcing effects of drugs such as cocaine, because depletion of NAcc dopamine via lesioning midbrain dopaminergic projections disrupts cocaine self-administration (for a review, see Belin et al., 2009). Additionally, dopaminergic projections into the dorsal striatum have been associated with reward-related processing (Haber & Knutson, 2010), especially when learning the associations between actions and outcomes, processing the value associated with different goal-directed actions, and encoding well-learned motor sequences (for a review, see Delgado, 2007). The striatum is thus involved in a variety of reward-related processes, contributing to the formation of different valuation signals that code the expectation and delivery of a reward and aid learning and decision making. These animal findings have laid the groundwork for similar inquiries focusing on the human striatum using neuroimaging techniques – a focus of this chapter – which have reported a great deal of evidence corroborating the animal literature.

Value Signals in the Striatum during Reward Expectation and Outcome

Early studies of reward processing in humans paralleled animal studies, suggesting that activity in the striatum correlated with value signals during reward processing. Initial neuroimaging experiments investigated the appetitive and hedonic effects of substances such as cocaine to parse out some of the different value-related components of reward processes. A benefit of studying these processes in humans as compared to animals is that humans can provide explicit reports of what they are feeling at different times. Cocaine addicts demonstrate differential neural activation patterns corresponding to different aspects of drug seeking/consumption (Risinger et al., 2005). In one early study, increases in BOLD signals in the NAcc were associated with reported feelings of drug craving (e.g., expectation of/desire for upcoming drug), whereas activity in the VTA, caudate, and putamen was associated with feelings of rush (e.g., a high in response to drug consumption; Breiter et al., 1997).

Subsequent research has turned to more commonly experienced primary reinforcers, such as food and juice. Reward-expectation-related neural activity for these types of reinforcers is modulated by both affective properties of the stimuli and the individual's own internal states. The expectation of predictable pleasant, as compared to unpleasant, taste rewards has been associated with increased BOLD signals in a subset of regions including the striatum, VTA, OFC, and amygdala (O'Doherty, Deichmann, Critchley, & Dolan, 2002), and the expectation of potential food stimuli in hungry subjects leads to increases in dopamine release in the dorsal striatum as measured by PET (Volkow et al., 2002). Similar types of expectation responses are also seen for secondary rewards, such as money, that can be put toward the attainment of other goals. Both the dorsal (caudate nucleus) and ventral (NAcc) striatum are sensitive to the expectation of impending monetary rewards during a gambling task, with NAcc activity showing a particular sensitivity to high-magnitude rewards (Knutson, Fong, Bennett, Adams, & Hommer, 2003; see also Figure 19.2). Corroborating PET and fMRI findings (Schott et al., 2008) found increases in activation to cues predicting monetary reward (as compared to neutral feedback) in the dorsal and ventral striatum and in midbrain regions (SN and VTA), as well as increased dopaminergic release in the ventral striatum during reward conditions.

a   b

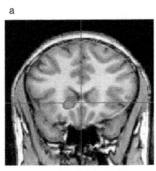
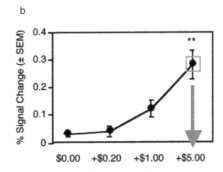

Figure 19.2. Expectation of high-magnitude monetary rewards elicits significant increases in ventral striatum (NAcc) BOLD activity. Adapted from "Anticipation of monetary reward selectively recruits nucleus accumbens," by B. Knutson, C.M. Adams, G.W. Fong, and D. Hommer, 2001, *Journal of Neuroscience*, 21, RC159. Adapted with permission.

Recent work also has shown that the striatal BOLD response nonlinearly increases with expected reward probability during choices between risky options (Hsu, Krajbich, Zhao, & Camerer, 2009), supporting a potential role for the striatum in coding subjective value – which can be thought of as a series of considerations based on one's perception of the objective properties of available choices and outcomes (for extensive review of valuation and decision making, see Doya, 2008).

Reward value signals are also generated on the receipt or consumption of potentially rewarding outcomes, which can facilitate subsequent behavior and formation of expectations. Initial fMRI experiments used monetary reinforcers to demonstrate the involvement of cortical regions such as the OFC (O'Doherty, Kringelbach, Rolls, Hornak, & Andrews, 2001) and medial prefrontal cortex (Knutson et al., 2003) in the affective valuation of rewards at the time of outcome. The role of the dorsal and ventral striatum in outcome processing was suggested to involve differentiating between positive (gains) and negative (losses) outcomes (Delgado, Nystrom, Fissell, Noll, & Fiez, 2000). The dorsal striatal response to outcome-related reward value signals is particularly interesting, given that it is modulated by magnitude (Nieuwenhuis et al., 2005), probability (Haruno et al., 2004), and motivational properties of the outcome (Delgado, Stenger, & Fiez, 2004), suggesting

a sensitivity to the specific context in which value is represented (De Martino, Kumaran, Holt, & Dolan, 2009).

Advancing this idea, reward-outcome-related activity in the striatum has been shown to be modulated by the manner in which a reward is obtained. For example, increases in both dorsal and ventral striatum activity (caudate nucleus and NAcc) have been reported when reward delivery was contingent on a successful button press (Zink, Pagnoni, Martin-Skurski, Chappelow, & Berns, 2004), although in that study, the authors interpreted the activity as due to the salience of the condition. An alternative interpretation is that the dorsal striatum, specifically the caudate nucleus, is critical for establishing action-outcome contingencies. Evidence indicates that the caudate nucleus comes online when an action is required during the presentation of a reward-predicting cue, and specifically when participants believed the valence of the outcome (e.g., monetary reward/punishment) was contingent on this response (Tricomi, Delgado, & Fiez, 2004). This finding is not limited to the use of monetary reinforcers. Outcomes reflecting performance and goal achievement on declarative memory tasks elicit caudate nucleus activity similarly to monetary reinforcers (Tricomi & Fiez, 2008); this activity may also be modulated specifically by one's goals and motivations (Han, Huettel, Raposo, Adcock, & Dobbins, 2010). These studies suggest that the human striatum value signal at the time of reward outcome may not be coding a reward per se, but instead a reinforcement value signal that facilitates learning (O'Doherty et al., 2004; Tricomi et al., 2004).

Affective Learning and the Human Striatum

The notion that expected reward value signals and reward-outcome value signals might contribute to an overall neural learning mechanism corresponds with associative learning models such as that proposed by Rescorla and Wagner (1972). This model suggests that learning the value of stimuli occurs most effectively when there is a mismatch between one's expectations and experience, because it allows for an updating of one's environmental model. Although the Rescorla-Wagner model was initially conceived for Pavlovian learning situations, its basic principles have since been extended to develop learning models that can explain behavior in more varied (e.g., instrumental) and complex situations. A shared underlying tenet across these more detailed models is that learning occurs when there is an error between predicted and experienced outcomes (Niv & Schoenbaum, 2008).

Because these models of value learning appear to conform to the functioning of the dopamine reward prediction error model put forth by Schultz and colleagues (1997), recent efforts have examined whether mechanisms of human reward learning might function in a similar way. Initial human work searching for confirmations of a prediction error learning signal focused on responses of midbrain dopaminergic targets, primarily the striatum, to predicted and unpredicted rewards. The human ventral striatum and the medial OFC region were found to be particularly sensitive to passively delivered unpredicted rewards (Berns, McClure, Pagnoni, & Montague, 2001), with the striatum also being sensitive to the temporal delay of expected rewards (Pagnoni, Zink, Montague, & Berns, 2002); these findings echo evidence from nonhuman primates suggesting that dopamine neurons code a temporal prediction error (see Niv, 2009, for a review).

After these first attempts, an explosion of modeling-based fMRI studies has come about that aimed to fit reinforcement-learning models to the BOLD response during reward-learning paradigms. One influential model is a temporal difference (TD) learning model (for a review, see Niv, 2009) that, as alluded to, attempts to predict the outcomes of future events based on incorporating information regarding the temporal relationship between stimuli and rewards that may occur at any time point (see Niv & Schoenbaum, 2008 for a review). Increases in BOLD signals in the ventral striatum have been observed in response to reward-predicting cues and to both positive and negative temporal prediction errors in Pavlovian learning tasks (O'Doherty, Dayan, Friston, Critchley, & Dolan, 2003). Furthermore, activity in the left ventral putamen shifts from outcome to cue over time, suggesting a neural representation for learning (O'Doherty, Dayan, et al., 2003).

Differential contributions of striatal subregions during instrumental and Pavlovian reward-learning tasks have also been proposed (O'Doherty et al., 2004) akin to a model of reinforcement learning known as the actor-critic model (for a review, see Niv, 2009). Briefly, this model suggests that a critic uses a TD learning signal to generally evaluate situations, whereas an actor keeps track of past outcome history in order to choose an effective plan of action (see Niv & Schoenbaum, 2008, for a review). Prediction-error-related activations were seen in the ventral striatum, particularly in the ventral putamen and NAcc in both Pavlovian and instrumental learning conditions, supporting a role for the ventral striatum as critic (O'Doherty et al., 2004). Interestingly, prediction error activity was also observed in the caudate nucleus, but only during instrumental learning, which is congruent with the notion of the dorsal striatum as the actor that puts into action the evaluative information coded by the critic (O'Doherty et al., 2004; Tricomi et al., 2004);

this finding correlates with improved behavioral learning indices (Haruno et al., 2004). Prediction error learning signals have since been reported in the striatum in multiple investigations (Daw, Gershman, Seymour, Dayan, & Dolan, 2011; Hare, O'Doherty, Camerer, Schultz, & Rangel, 2008), as well as in the midbrain (D'Ardenne et al., 2008); recent findings suggest that these signals play a role not just in trial-and-error learning situations but also during other forms of learning (Burke, Tobler, Baddeley, & Schultz, 2010) and can be modulated by explicit knowledge about a situation (Li, Delgado, & Phelps, 2011).

Findings of prediction error signals in humans thus enable a more detailed characterization of the striatum's role in reward learning and allow for parallels to be made to electrophysiological studies of reward learning and prediction error in nonhuman primates. Finally, the combination of pharmacological agents and neuroimaging (e.g., Pessiglione, Seymour, Flandin, Dolan, & Frith, 2006) as well as investigations of learning models in populations with deficient dopaminergic systems such as Parkinson's disease (e.g., Rutledge et al., 2009) have helped strengthen the hypothesis that dopaminergic learning signals influence striatal function during reward-related processing.

Prefrontal Cortex and Reward Valuation

Prefrontal cortical regions are another key component of corticobasal ganglia circuits that aid in the computation of reward value signals that mediate goal-directed behavior. The most commonly identified regions in the prefrontal cortex involved in reward valuation include the ventral portions of PFC, medial PFC, dorsolateral PFC, and anterior cingulate. Although the specific contributions of these regions to reward processing are reviewed elsewhere (e.g., Doya, 2008), the role of the orbitofrontal cortex (OFC) in reward valuation has been a subject of widespread investigation and is worth noting here. Electrophysiological recordings

in nonhuman primates have long suggested that the OFC is involved in reward representation and affective learning, demonstrating diverse functionality among neuronal populations within this region (Kringelbach, 2005; Ostlund & Balleine, 2007). Lesions to the OFC lead to deficits in learning the reward value of a stimulus and adapting to changing reward contingencies (Clarke, Robbins, & Roberts, 2008). Other groups of OFC neurons code for relative preference or value when choosing among outcome predictive cues, and OFC neurons track changing reward expectations and preferences over time (e.g., before and after learning action-outcome contingencies; for a review, see Ostlund & Balleine, 2007).

Neuroimaging investigations show similar functional dissociations within human OFC; it is involved in the hedonic response to rewards – monitoring reward value and coding positive and negative outcomes (for review see Kringelbach, 2005). The medial OFC (mOFC), for example, is more sensitive to rewards than punishments, with BOLD activity there scaling with increasing magnitude, whereas the lateral OFC and ventral PFC are more sensitive to punishments (O'Doherty et al., 2001). Human mOFC is also implicated in more complex representation processes, showing similar BOLD activation when representing experienced and imagined rewards (Bray, Shimojo, & O'Doherty, 2010), as well as contributing to complex subjective value signals, such as how much one is willing to pay for an item – a goal value (Hare et al., 2008). Such goal value representations in the mOFC can be susceptible to top-down control from more cognitive dorsal regions (e.g., DLPFC) when control over behavior is exerted (e.g., when choosing healthy over unhealthy, but favored, food items; Hare, Camerer, & Rangel, 2009).

Prefrontal cortical regions also serve important integrative functions that aid in guiding behavior. Caudal portions of the OFC are important for tracking outcome history, thereby facilitating subsequent behavioral choices (O'Doherty,

Critchley, Deichmann, & Dolan, 2003). Evidence from recordings in nonhuman primates suggests that a proscribed region of the ACC (ACC sulcus) act in a similar manner (Kennerley, Walton, Behrens, Buckley, & Rushworth, 2006), and parallel neuroimaging work in humans points to a specific region in the ACC as critical for relying on an overall reward history, particularly under rapidly changing (volatile) circumstances (Behrens, Woolrich, Walton, & Rushworth, 2007). Prefrontal regions are thus critical for representing and computing various reward-related value signals that guide understanding of one's environment and behavior.

Additional Regions Involved in Reward Processing

Learning about rewards in a dynamic environment is critically dependent on the integrity of corticobasal ganglia circuitry. It is worth noting, however, that other regions that generally support affective processing and learning also play direct or indirect functions in the computation of reward value signals. Although the amygdala is typically thought of as involved in aversive processing and fear learning – associating stimuli with aversive outcomes such as electric shock (for review, see Phelps & LeDoux, 2005) – it has also been implicated in reward processing and generating reward value signals. Recordings from amygdala neurons in nonhuman primates during an affective reversal learning task (Paton, Belova, Morrison, & Salzman, 2006) show that some amygdala neurons respond after the presentation of predictive cues, whereas other populations respond to stimuli predicting both positive and negative outcomes. Interestingly, amygdala neuronal response patterns change with changing contingencies. A related study focused on an anticipatory period before presentation of reward- or punishment-predicting cues (Belova, Paton, & Salzman, 2008), revealing that populations of amygdala neurons demonstrate differential response patterns. Reward-preferring neurons showed increased response rates during the anticipatory period, whereas punishment-preferring neurons showed decreased response rates, lending credence to a role for the amygdala in encoding or representing an organism's state values.

Neuroimaging investigations have corroborated these animal findings, showing decreased BOLD activity in the amygdala after devaluation of a food item after satiation (Gottfried, O'Doherty, & Dolan, 2003). Patients with bilateral amygdala lesions also showed impairments in the use of positive feedback to guide subsequent behavioral choices in comparison to control participants (Hampton, Adolphs, Tyszka, & O'Doherty, 2007). In that study, amygdala-lesioned patients also exhibited irregular expected reward-related BOLD activity in the mPFC: BOLD activity increased linearly with increases in expected reward only in control participants, indicating that connectivity between the amygdala and prefrontal regions contributes to the appropriate appraisal of reward values.

In addition to the amygdala, the insular cortex has been linked with reward processing at various stages. Although many studies implicate this region in the general affective processing and experience of pain (for a review, see Hein & Singer, 2008), functional activity in the insula has also been linked to predictive learning. Reports implicate the insula in coding a temporal difference learning signal in aversive learning studies of pain (Seymour et al., 2004). Further, BOLD activity in the insula has been reported to correlate with an aversive prediction error signal in an instrumental learning task for cues predicting losses only (Pessiglione et al., 2006). Finally, the insula has been linked with risky behaviors and coding for a risk prediction error (e.g., Preuschoff, Quartz, & Bossaerts, 2008). These results highlight the fact that, although reward-related processing and learning are highly dependent on corticobasal ganglia loops, particularly the striatum and prefrontal cortex, other regions can also play key roles in the evaluation of potential choices and outcomes.

Summary

Processing of reward-related information is highly dependent on components of corticobasal ganglia circuits such as the striatum, OFC, and ACC, along with modulation by dopaminergic input. Communication between these regions is essential for computing reward expectation and outcome-related value signals for primary and secondary reinforcers, such as juice or monetary rewards. Integration of information from these various value signals facilitates learning and modification of subsequent behavior and choice.

Reward-Related Processing and Social Values

As humans, we have the ability to focus our efforts not only toward specific reinforcers necessary for survival (e.g., water) but also toward more abstract goals and ideas. Valuation of more social rewards, such as feedback from peers or praise from a superior, for example, has been postulated to have similar influences on goal-directed behavior as primary reinforcers (for review see Rilling & Sanfey, 2011). Other social considerations might also affect value signals, such as whether altruistic actions (e.g., giving to those less fortunate) might be held in higher regard than pursuing one's own personal gain (for review, see Rilling & Sanfey, 2011). Moreover, in our daily lives, we frequently interact with others in a variety of situations to achieve common goals, and in doing so we must rely on socially relevant information (e.g., is this person trustworthy? Is this person making a fair offer?) to form social expectations and guide behavior (for review, see Fehr & Camerer, 2007). A logical question, then, is whether such social value considerations might be computed via neural reward circuitry.

Social Rewards and Preferences

One of the most basic and common social experiences we strive for and value is social approval. On meeting a new person, we might be interested to know how we are perceived and whether this perception matches self-expectations. Evidence suggests that social expectancy violations (e.g., thinking someone will like you and then finding out that he or she does not) depend in part on processing in the ventral striatum (ventral putamen) and dorsal ACC, whereas differentiating positive and negative social feedback (e.g., being accepted or rejected by someone) recruits the ventral ACC (Somerville, Heatherton, & Kelley, 2006). These dissociable patterns of ACC activation are consistent with previous research implicating this region in processes such as cognitive conflict and emotional arousal (for a review, see Amodio & Frith, 2006). Corroborating findings demonstrate that the receipt of both monetary and social rewards (e.g., what another thinks of you) elicit overlapping striatal BOLD response patterns (Izuma, Saito, & Sadato, 2008) and that learning from social (emotional faces) and monetary rewards recruits similar corticobasal ganglia mechanisms (Lin, Adolphs, & Rangel, 2012). Basic social rewards, then, appear to be processed in overlapping corticobasal ganglia circuits observed in studies of primary and secondary reinforcers.

We might also value and derive pleasure from another's success. Viewing someone deemed as socially similar winning on a game show, for example, engenders positive feelings and recruits activity in corticobasal ganglia circuitry such as the ventral striatum, vmPFC, and vACC (Mobbs et al., 2009), whereas activity in the ventral striatum is further modulated when individuals share a monetary reward with a close friend rather than with someone with whom they lack a relationship (Fareri, Niznikiewicz, Lee, & Delgado, 2012). More complex social acts regarding others' success or gains (e.g., charitable giving) may hold value similar to one's personal gain. Forced transfers of monetary endowments to charity elicit increases in striatal BOLD activity overlapping with those seen during mandatory transfers of money to a participant; however, activity in the dorsal and ventral striatum is more sensitive to the act of giving to charity than to a forced transfer to charity (Harbaugh, Mayr, & Burghart, 2007). Higher tendencies to donate to charities (as opposed to keeping money for oneself) and associated ventral striatal responses are modulated by the presence of others and expectations of social (dis)approval based on one's decision (Izuma, Saito, & Sadato, 2010). These studies suggest that attitudes toward others may play a significant role in goal-directed behaviors and modulating the processing of social outcomes.

In a similar vein, certain competitive behaviors or attitudes may bring about satisfaction or pleasure, particularly in the context of social comparisons. Outcome-related responses in the ventral striatum are modulated by relative social comparison, showing increases when participants earn more monetary reward than a partner for the same correct performance, but decreases in the reverse situation (Fliessbach et al., 2007). Similarly, receiving information that misfortune has come to envied others recruits the OFC and dorsal and ventral striatum (Takahashi et al., 2009), suggesting that this information may be valued as a positive outcome. A potential motivating explanation for responses observed during social comparisons is a dislike for social inequity (Fehr & Camerer, 2007; Tricomi, Rangel, Camerer, & O'Doherty, 2010). When monetary inequity is established between two people, the one with a higher initial endowment exhibits both blunted subjective feelings of pleasure and responses in the ventral striatum and vmPFC when receiving subsequent positive financial outcomes in comparison to his or her partner, whereas the opposite pattern is observed for those with a lower initial endowment (Tricomi et al., 2010). Results from these studies thus provide evidence that social considerations and preferences play important modulatory roles in the computation of reward value signals.

Social Interactions

Our daily experiences are frequently marked by social interactions from which we can acquire social value signals to facilitate learning and decision making. Employing economic game paradigms aimed to study interactive behavior, recent studies in the burgeoning field of neuroeconomics have begun to explore the neural underpinnings of how social information may modulate neural reward circuitry during social interactions. Economic theory generally holds that typical human behavior should be self-interested; that is, one should always aim to maximize one's outcome no matter the circumstances (Camerer & Fehr, 2006). However, behavior in social interactions may be informed by other-regarding preferences (e.g., empathic concerns), perhaps because these preferences confer future benefits or are viewed as inherently rewarding (Fehr & Camerer, 2007). Two-person interactive economic games have been instrumental in showing that social preferences such as cooperation, reciprocity, trust, and fairness motivate behavior during interactions with others, perhaps in part because these considerations may be evolutionarily adaptive (Axelrod & Hamilton, 1970).

One cooperative economic game known as the prisoner's dilemma game (Rapoport & Chammah, 1965), for instance, allows two participants to choose to either cooperate or defect for monetary outcomes or some kind of "good." Mutual decisions to cooperate result in slightly lower than maximal payouts for both participants. This is the most commonly occurring outcome, even though unilateral defection results in the maximum possible amount for one person at the complete expense of the other, who is left with nothing (see Fehr & Camerer, 2007, for a review).

In another interactive economic paradigm known as the trust game, which has been used to examine reciprocity and cooperation, one participant (investor) is endowed with a sum of money, any amount of which can be sent to a partner (trustee). Whatever amount is sent to the trustee is multiplied, typically by a factor of three or four, and the trustee can then choose how much to return. Although standard self-interested behavior suggests that the optimal decision would be for the investor to send no money, so as to ensure an optimal outcome, participants often send nonzero amounts, likely motivated by concern for their reputation and the hope of reciprocity (Berg, Dickhaut, & McCabe, 1995). Finally, in a bargaining paradigm (ultimatum game), one participant (proposer) proposes a manner of splitting a sum of money with another (responder), who can accept the offer or reject it so both participants get nothing. Responders typically reject offers they perceive as unfair, although any nonzero offer should be accepted according to economic theory (Güth, Schmittberger, & Schwarze, 1982).

Neuroimaging investigations have built on the groundwork laid by behavioral economics to investigate how these social preferences that influence behavior during interactions may influence reward expectations and neural reward circuitry. Early work began looking at cooperative behavior in social interactions, using the trust and prisoner's dilemma paradigms. During a trust game when participants were awaiting a response after having cooperated with a human opponent (McCabe, Houser, Ryan, Smith, & Trouard, 2001), regions of the medial PFC demonstrated increased BOLD activity as compared to when playing with a computer, suggesting that the social component of an interaction creates a heightened sense of expectation. The medial PFC has additionally been implicated in processing social information about self and others (see Amodio & Frith, 2006, for review) and reward expectation in certain social contexts (Hampton, Bossaerts, & O'Doherty, 2008). Confirming findings from behavioral economic studies, mutual cooperation was the behavior of choice when participants played a prisoner's dilemma game with real freely acting human partners (Rilling et al., 2002), again demonstrating a general preference against self-interested behavior that is not observed when playing with human confederates or computer partners. Further, on viewing outcomes from mutual cooperation, the ventral striatum, vmPFC/OFC, and the subgenual ACC (sgACC) exhibited increases in BOLD activity, and decisions to cooperate following reciprocation elicited caudate nucleus and ACC activity. Dissociable patterns of outcome-related BOLD activity in the ventral striatum and sgACC also occur when contrasting mutual cooperation (BOLD increases) and unreciprocated cooperation (e.g., unilateral defection; BOLD decreases; Rilling, Sanfey, Aronson, Nystrom, & Cohen, 2004). This latter result might be explained by a social prediction error signal, whereby social expectations may modulate reward-related circuitry (Rilling et al., 2004).

In certain social interactions, agents do not always act in a trustworthy or fair manner (e.g., cooperation may not be reciprocated). Such occurrences may be viewed as a violation of social norms, which evidence suggests is processed in the anterior insula (for a review, see Rilling & Sanfey, 2011). Opportunities may arise in interactions in which we may be able to respond to perceived norm violations, but at costs to ourselves. An interesting PET study examined decisions to punish defections by an opponent in a trust game (de Quervain et al., 2004). Punishments could be costly to the punishers (e.g., they would lose some of their earnings), free (e.g., it would not cost them anything to punish), or symbolic (e.g., they could send a message of punishment, but with no monetary penalty). Caudate nucleus activity was strongest preceding all decisions to punish intentional norm violations, whereas the vmPFC and OFC showed increased sensitivity preceding a costly decision to punish, as compared to a free punishment. Although these authors suggest that altruistic punishment (e.g., punishing despite a cost to oneself) is valued and rewarding, their results might also be explained by inequity aversion (Fehr & Camerer, 2007; Tricomi et al., 2010). Behavior in social interactions is therefore motivated by considerations for others, along with values acting to confer social success that are coded in neural structures that also code for primary and secondary reward value.

Learning in Social Interactions

Many early neuroeconomic studies (see Rilling & Sanfey, 2011, for a review) focused on one-shot games, and although they demonstrated that social preferences modulate both behavior and activity in neural reward circuitry, those studies did not address how learning about another person over time might be modulated by social value considerations. We are often presented with multiple opportunities to inform our opinions of others (e.g., colleagues at work, people within our social network), allowing us to learn about them (e.g., should I trust this person?) and discern whether to pursue further interactions or establish a relationship. One fMRI study employed an iterated trust game (e.g., repeated interactions) to examine how both behavior and neural activity might change over continued interactions with the same partner (King-Casas et al., 2005). It found that reciprocity (e.g., repayment for previous behavior) was an important predictor of participant behavior: Trustee responses were best predicted by deviations from neutral reciprocity (e.g., exact repayment for past actions) by the investor. Generous investor repayments in response to trustee defections elicited increased BOLD activation in the caudate nucleus of trustees. Further, correlations between activity in the cingulate cortex and caudate showed temporal sensitivity, driven by peak caudate activation: During early rounds of the trust game, maximal BOLD activity in the caudate of trustees was observed on revelation of the investor's response, but by the late rounds, this activity peaked before revelation of the decision. This pattern of BOLD activity suggests that the striatum may process a social learning signal, similar to the dopaminergic reward prediction error signal reported by Schultz et al. (1997), but one informed by learning socially valued information (e.g., will this person reciprocate my trust?).

Reciprocity is an important modulator of neural activity during a trust game (van den Bos, van Dijk, Westenberg, Rombouts, & Crone, 2009), such that making decisions incongruent to one's disposition (e.g., a prosocial person chooses to defect) elicits increased BOLD activation in the anterior cingulate, anterior insula, right temporoparietal junction, and the precuneus. Specific portions of the cingulate cortex are noted to underlie processing information specifically related to agency in two-person trust interactions: The middle cingulate shows sensitivity to actions involving the self, whereas anterior and posterior cingulate regions are more sensitive to processing information about the actions of others (Tomlin et al., 2006). Further, ventral striatal BOLD activity is sensitive to partner reciprocity patterns in a trust game, demonstrating increased responses when partners cooperate as compared to defect, particularly during interactions with those who have demonstrated a reputation for reciprocal behavior (Phan, Sripada, Angstadt, & McCabe, 2010).

There may be other times in which previously acquired social information can inform our behavior in an interaction. For example, a friend might instruct us to be wary of interacting much with someone in particular, and this might guide our future decisions and our ability to incorporate outcomes from any interactions we might undertake. Prior information from something as simple as a fictional bio about another's moral character can indeed influence perceptions of trustworthiness and behavior in a trust game (Delgado, Frank, & Phelps, 2005). Here, participants played a modified, iterated trust game with three fictional characters whose moral characters were manipulated in short vignettes that participants read before playing the game. Importantly, all characters were preprogrammed to reinforce (e.g., share money back with participants) at a 50% rate. Even though all characters reinforced at the same rate and participants showed some explicit knowledge of this on postsession subjective reports, they invested most often with partners deemed as having praiseworthy moral character, as compared to those of neutral or morally questionable character. Neural

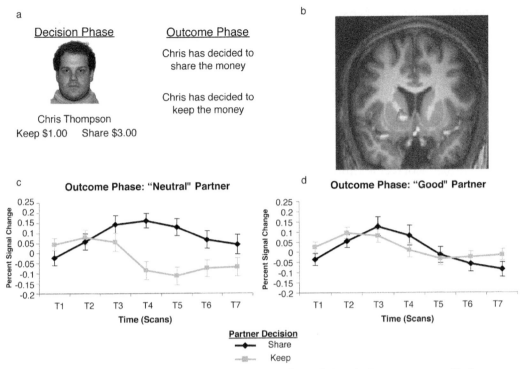

Figure 19.3. a) Depiction of trust game task from Delgado et al. (2005). Participants would choose whether to keep or share money with one of three fictional characters on any given trial. If participants chose to share, they would receive either positive (partner shared) or negative (partner did not share) feedback. If participants chose to keep the money for themselves, they would receive feedback saying "You have decided to keep the money." b) Increases in caudate nucleus BOLD activity were observed for positive versus negative outcomes. c) Time course of caudate nucleus region-of-interest (ROI) activation during the outcome phase with the neutral partner shows differential responses to positive (share) and negative (keep) outcomes. d) Time course of caudate nucleus ROI activation during the outcome phase with the good partner reveals no significant differences in responses to positive and negative outcomes. Adapted from "Perceptions of moral character modulate the neural systems of reward during the trust game," by M.R. Delgado, R.H. Frank, and E.A. Phelps, 2005, *Nature Neuroscience*, 8 (11), 1611–1618. Adapted with permission.

signals in the striatum differentiated positive and negative outcomes (e.g., partner sharing /defecting) most strongly for the neutral character, consistent with previous findings of differential signals with monetary rewards (see Delgado, 2007, for a review) and suggestive of a learning signal within the striatum (Haruno et al., 2004; O'Doherty et al., 2004; Tricomi et al., 2004). However, no differential responses between positive and negative outcomes were observed when interacting with the good partner, suggesting that the previously acquired social information modulated the ability of the caudate to effectively respond to and learn from feedback (Figure 19.3). Similarly, memory of social

expectation violations elicits increased activity in portions of corticobasal ganglia circuitry including the dorsal and ventral striatum and anterior cingulate, corroborating the idea that previous social value considerations can modulate reward learning (Chang & Sanfey, 2009).

Neuroendocrine influences may underlie the propensity to exhibit other-regarding behavior in goal-directed situations. The hormone oxytocin is implicated in affiliative social behavior in animals (for a review, see Insel & Young, 2001); administering oxytocin to investors in a trust game led to significantly more generous amounts sent to trustees as compared to a placebo group of participants, lending credence to oxytocin's role in affiliative behavior (Kosfeld, Heinrichs, Zak, Fischbacher, & Fehr, 2005). A recent neuroimaging study (Baumgartner, Heinrichs, Vonlanthen, Fischbacher, & Fehr, 2008) used a similar trust game paradigm with an added learning component: After investors made a certain number of offers to anonymous partners, feedback was presented indicating how many of those offers were met with reciprocation or defection. Importantly, this feedback was fixed at approximately 50% reciprocation across participants. After receiving feedback, participants who received oxytocin did not change their rate of investment, but the placebo group exhibited a significant decrease in the average amount sent. Further, the oxytocin group exhibited diminished BOLD responses in the caudate nucleus and the amygdala, which is dense in oxytocin receptors (Insel & Young, 2001) suggesting that trust behavior might be modulated by oxytocin via a decreased fear of betrayal (e.g., defection).

Modeling Acquisition of Social Values

Evidence indicating that learning in social interactions recruits corticobasal ganglia circuitry leads to the obvious question of whether this learning relies on similar associative mechanisms as those involved in associating stimuli with food, juice, and money. Investigations of both cooperative and competitive social interactions have thus begun to employ reinforcement-learning models in attempts to further characterize how the acquisition of social information influences behavior.

As noted earlier, an important social phenomenon that has been the basis of numerous investigations is trust. Discerning whether someone is trustworthy can guide actions in social interactions by indicating when we might wish to follow someone's advice, for instance. Recent work suggests that learning when to trust someone in order to guide future actions might be acquired via reinforcement- learning mechanisms simi-

lar to those that characterize associative learning of primary reward value (Behrens, Hunt, Woolrich, & Rushworth, 2008). Using a social probabilistic learning task in which a human confederate provided correct or incorrect advice regarding which choices to make (requiring learning of both changing reward contingencies and confederate trustworthiness), participants tracked and integrated social and reward-related information by following a Bayesian learning rule (see Behrens et al., 2007). Dissociable neural activity was observed for both social (dmPFC, medial temporal gyrus, and superior temporal sulcus [STS]/TPJ) and reward (ventral striatum, vmPFC, and ACC sulcus [ACCs]) prediction error signals, as well as volatility signals (e.g., stability of contingencies) in the ACC – ACCs: reward history volatility; ACC gyrus (ACCg): social history volatility. Further, vmPFC activity during decisions was best predicted by the strength of ACCg or ACCs activity at the time of outcome, supporting a role for the vmPFC in integrating information. Thus, tracking reward-related and social information to guide decision making and learning in social contexts demonstrates both dissociation and integration of neural function.

Appraising and learning whether someone is trustworthy might require more than taking advice into account. We can make appraisals of trustworthiness very quickly just by looking at someone's face, taking into account specific facial characteristics in doing so; this work has implicated the amygdala as important for such social judgments (for review see Said, Haxby, & Todorov, 2011). When interacting with someone, we might make an initial judgment and then continually update it based on subsequent experience, thus making trustworthiness judgments malleable (Fareri, Chang & Delgado, 2012). Support for this malleability comes from a model-based study using an iterated trust game (Chang, Doll, van't Wout, Frank, & Sanfey, 2010), in which participants as investors were presented with photos of high and low trustworthy partners. Application of a number of reinforcement-learning models to participant behavior supports the notion of trustworthiness being dynamic: A model that incorporated both initial appraisals (e.g., based on facial evaluations) and outcomes from interactions as continually influencing trustworthiness perceptions best accounted for participant investment behavior. Such a model provided a better fit than other models based solely on either initial appraisals or outcomes, suggesting that learning of complex social information to guide behavior requires more than just simple associative learning mechanisms.

Although determining trustworthiness can aid in determining whether to cooperate with someone in the hope of achieving an optimal outcome, other situations call for more competitive or strategic behavior, which can influence decision making (Delgado, Schotter, Ozbay, & Phelps, 2008). For instance, an individual might attempt to anticipate an opponent's next move in a game or an opposing counsel's strategy during litigation. Doing so might require incorporating not only experienced reward-related information but also an opponent's past behavior or considering how one's own behavior influences the opponent. In a two-person strategic game during which participants' maximal outcomes were dependent on diametrically opposed behaviors (Hampton et al., 2008), participants indeed accounted for both their opponent's past behaviors and how their own behavior influenced their opponent's. Simple reward prediction errors were found in the ventral striatum. However, a learning model that incorporated the more social considerations mentioned earlier characterized behavior and BOLD activity in the mPFC while making choices and calculating reward expectations in this competitive task better than a simple reinforcement model (e.g., prediction error) or a model that accounted only for opponent behavior. Further, correlates of social updating signals were observed in both the mPFC and the STS, noted earlier to be important for representing self/other and in mentalizing (Amodio &

Frith, 2006); activity in the mPFC correlated most strongly with a combination of signals from the STS and ventral striatum rather than with either region alone. These findings highlight the importance of integrating many types of information during competitive interactions.

Thus, when modeling the acquisition of social information during cooperative and competitive social interactions, although certain components seem to be dependent on corticobasal ganglia circuitry, other regions are necessary to support the coding of social expectations. The further characterization of interactions among these areas is vital for advancing our understanding of reward-related learning during complex social situations.

Summary

Social factors are important modulators of corticobasal ganglia reward-related activity. Social rewards such as approval from others or sharing success with a friend recruit similar prefrontal and striatal mechanisms to the ones involved in the representation of value of typical primary reinforcers such as food. Behavior in cooperative and competitive social interactions is also influenced by valued social considerations that inform learning about others via integrative associative learning mechanisms.

Outstanding Questions and Future Directions

- Recent studies have also highlighted a potential role for the striatum in aversive processing, a domain typically associated with amygdala function (Delgado, Li, Schiller, & Phelps, 2008). What are the specific contributions of the striatum during aversive processing, and how does it interact with structures such as the amygdala to allow for active coping within aversive contexts?
- Adolescents at times exhibit increased risk-taking behavior, poor decision making, and sensitivity to peer influence.

One potential explanation for these behavioral patterns is that prefrontal cortical gray matter development is protracted and continues into early adulthood in comparison to subcortical gray matter (Somerville & Casey, 2010). What are the implications for these developmental patterns in reward-related learning and decision making in a social context? That is, do adolescents place differential value on social as compared to nonsocial rewards, and how might this affect decision making?

- How can we apply our understanding of social and nonsocial reward values to a clinical setting? For instance, there is evidence to suggest that dissociable portions of the cingulate cortex are sensitive to processing social information, particularly within the context of social interactions with others (Tomlin et al., 2006). Interestingly, individuals with autism spectrum disorders demonstrate a decreased ability to effectively recruit this region during social interactions. Considering that the neural mechanisms facilitating the learning of social information have begun to be delineated, do individuals with autism spectrum disorders demonstrate abnormal social learning patterns that underlie their social deficits?

Acknowledgments

This work was supported by a National Institute of Mental Health grant (MH084081).

References

Alexander, G. E., Crutcher, M. D., & DeLong, M. R. (1990). Basal ganglia-thalamocortical circuits: Parallel substrates for motor, oculomotor, "prefrontal" and "limbic" functions. *Progress in Brain Research*, 85, 119–46.

Amodio, D. M., & Frith, C. D. (2006). Meeting of minds: The medial frontal cortex and social cognition. *Nature Reviews Neuroscience*, 7(4), 268–77.

Axelrod, R., & Hamilton, W. (1970). The evolution of cooperation. *Science*, 211, 1390–96.

Barnes, T. D., Kubota, Y., Hu, D., Jin, D. Z., & Graybiel, A. M. (2005). Activity of striatal neurons reflects dynamic encoding and recoding of procedural memories. *Nature*, 437(7062), 1158–61.

Baumgartner, T., Heinrichs, M., Vonlanthen, A., Fischbacher, U., & Fehr, E. (2008). Oxytocin shapes the neural circuitry of trust and trust adaptation in humans. *Neuron*, 58(4), 639–50.

Bayer, H. M., & Glimcher, P. W. (2005). Midbrain dopamine neurons encode a quantitative reward prediction error signal. *Neuron*, 47(1), 129–41.

Behrens, T. E., Hunt, L. T., Woolrich, M. W., & Rushworth, M. F. (2008). Associative learning of social value. *Nature*, 456(7219), 245–49.

Behrens, T. E., Woolrich, M. W., Walton, M. E., & Rushworth, M. F. (2007). Learning the value of information in an uncertain world. *Nature Neuroscience*, 10(9), 1214–21.

Belin, D., Jonkman, S., Dickinson, A., Robbins, T. W., & Everitt, B. J. (2009). Parallel and interactive learning processes within the basal ganglia: Relevance for the understanding of addiction. *Behavioral Brain Research*, 199(1), 89–102.

Belova, M. A., Paton, J. J., & Salzman, C. D. (2008). Moment-to-moment tracking of state value in the amygdala. *Journal of Neuroscience*, 28(40), 10023–30.

Berg, J., Dickhaut, J., & McCabe, K. (1995). Trust, reciprocity, and social history. *Games and Economic Behavior*, 10, 122–42.

Berns, G. S., McClure, S. M., Pagnoni, G., & Montague, P. R. (2001). Predictability modulates human brain response to reward. *Journal of Neuroscience*, 21(8), 2793–98.

Bray, S., Shimojo, S., & O'Doherty, J. P. (2010). Human medial orbitofrontal cortex is recruited during experience of imagined and real rewards. *Journal of Neurophysiology*, 103(5), 2506–12.

Breiter, H. C., Gollub, R. L., Weisskoff, R. M., Kennedy, D. N., Makris, N., Berke, J. D.,…Hyman, S. E. (1997). Acute effects of cocaine on human brain activity and emotion. *Neuron*, 19(3), 591–611.

Burke, C. J., Tobler, P. N., Baddeley, M., & Schultz, W. (2010). Neural mechanisms of observational learning. *Proceedings of the National Academy of Sciences*, 107(32), 14431–36.

Camerer, C. F., & Fehr, E. (2006). When does "economic man" dominate social behavior? *Science*, 311(5757), 47–52.

Chang, L. J., Doll, B. B., van 't Wout, M., Frank, M. J., & Sanfey, A. G. (2010). Seeing is believing: Trustworthiness as a dynamic belief. *Cognitive Psychology*, 61(2), 87–105.

Chang, L. J., & Sanfey, A. G. (2009). Unforgettable ultimatums? Expectation violations promote enhanced social memory following economic bargaining. *Frontiers in Behavioral Neuroscience*, 3, 36.

Clarke, H. F., Robbins, T. W., & Roberts, A. C. (2008). Lesions of the medial striatum in monkeys produce perseverative impairments during reversal learning similar to those produced by lesions of the orbitofrontal cortex. *Journal of Neuroscience*, 28(43), 10972–82.

D'Ardenne, K., McClure, S. M., Nystrom, L. E., & Cohen, J. D. (2008). BOLD responses reflecting dopaminergic signals in the human ventral tegmental area. *Science*, 319(5867), 1264–67.

Daw, N. D., Gershman, S. J., Seymour, B., Dayan, P., & Dolan, R. J. (2011). Model-based influences on humans' choices and striatal prediction errors. *Neuron*, 69(6), 1204–15.

Delgado, M. R. (2007). Reward-related responses in the human striatum. *Annals of the New York Academy of Sciences*, 1104, 70–88.

Delgado, M. R., Frank, R. H., & Phelps, E. A. (2005). Perceptions of moral character modulate the neural systems of reward during the trust game. *Nature Neuroscience*, 8, 1611–18.

Delgado, M. R., Li, J., Schiller, D., & Phelps, E. A. (2008). The role of the striatum in aversive learning and aversive prediction errors. *Philosophical Transactions of the Royal Society of London. Series B: Biological Sciences*, 363(1511), 3787–00.

Delgado, M. R., Nystrom, L. E., Fissell, C., Noll, D. C., & Fiez, J. A. (2000). Tracking the hemodynamic responses to reward and punishment in the striatum. *Journal of Neurophysiology*, 84(6), 3072–77.

Delgado, M. R., Schotter, A., Ozbay, E. Y., & Phelps, E. A. (2008). Understanding overbidding: Using the neural circuitry of reward to design economic auctions. *Science*, 321(5897), 1849–52.

Delgado, M. R., Stenger, V. A., & Fiez, J. A. (2004). Motivation-dependent responses in the human caudate nucleus. *Cerebral Cortex*, 14(9), 1022–30.

De Martino, B., Kumaran, D., Holt, B., & Dolan, R. J. (2009). The neurobiology of reference-dependent value computation. *Journal of Neuroscience*, 29(12), 3833–42.

de Quervain, D. J., Fischbacher, U., Treyer, V., Schellhammer, M., Schnyder, U., Buck, A., & Fehr, E. (2004). The neural basis of altruistic punishment. *Science*, 305(5688), 1254–58.

Doya, K. (2008). Modulators of decision making. *Nature Neuroscience*, 11(4), 410–16.

Fareri, D. S., Chang, L. J., & Delgado, M. R. (2012). Effects of direct social experience on trust decisions and neural reward circuitry. *Frontiers in Decision Neuroscience*, 6(148).

Fareri, D. S., Niznikiewicz, M. A., Lee, V. K. & Delgado, M. R. (2012). Social network modulation of reward-related signals. *Journal of Neuroscience*, 32(26), 9045–52.

Fehr, E., & Camerer, C. F. (2007). Social neuroeconomics: The neural circuitry of social preferences. *Trends in Cognitive Sciences*, 11(10), 419–27.

Fliessbach, K., Weber, B., Trautner, P., Dohmen, T., Sunde, U., Elger, C. E., & Falk, A. (2007). Social comparison affects reward-related brain activity in the human ventral striatum. *Science*, 318(5854), 1305–8.

Gottfried, J. A., O'Doherty, J., & Dolan, R. J. (2003). Encoding predictive reward value in human amygdala and orbitofrontal cortex. *Science*, 301(5636), 1104–7.

Güth, W., Schmittberger, R., & Schwarze, B. (1982). An experimental analysis of ultimatum bargaining. *Journal of Economic Behavior & Organization*, 3, 367–88.

Haber, S. N., & Knutson, B. (2010). The reward circuit: Linking primate anatomy and human imaging. *Neuropsychopharmacology*, 35(1), 4–26.

Hampton, A. N., Adolphs, R., Tyszka, M. J., & O'Doherty, J. P. (2007). Contributions of the amygdala to reward expectancy and choice signals in human prefrontal cortex. *Neuron*, 55(4), 545–55.

Hampton, A. N., Bossaerts, P., & O'Doherty, J. P. (2008). Neural correlates of mentalizing-related computations during strategic interactions in humans. *Proceedings of the National Academy of Sciences*, 105(18), 6741–46.

Han, S., Huettel, S. A., Raposo, A., Adcock, R. A., & Dobbins, I. G. (2010). Functional significance of striatal responses during episodic decisions: Recovery or goal attainment? *Journal of Neuroscience*, 30(13), 4767–75.

Harbaugh, W. T., Mayr, U., & Burghart, D. R. (2007). Neural responses to taxation and voluntary giving reveal motives for charitable donations. *Science*, 316(5831), 1622–25.

Hare, T. A., Camerer, C. F., & Rangel, A. (2009). Self-control in decision-making involves modulation of the vmPFC valuation system. *Science*, 324(5927), 646–48.

Hare, T. A., O'Doherty, J., Camerer, C. F., Schultz, W., & Rangel, A. (2008). Dissociating the role of the orbitofrontal cortex and the striatum in the computation of goal values and prediction errors. *Journal of Neuroscience*, 28(22), 5623–30.

Haruno, M., Kuroda, T., Doya, K., Toyama, K., Kimura, M., Samejima, K., . . . Kawato, M. (2004). A neural correlate of reward-based behavioral learning in caudate nucleus: A functional magnetic resonance imaging study of a stochastic decision task. *Journal of Neuroscience*, 24(7), 1660–5.

Hein, G., & Singer, T. (2008). I feel how you feel but not always: The empathic brain and its modulation. *Current Opinion in Neurobiology*, 18(2), 153–58.

Hsu, M., Krajbich, I., Zhao, C., & Camerer, C. F. (2009). Neural response to reward anticipation under risk is nonlinear in probabilities. *Journal of Neuroscience*, 29(7), 2231–37.

Insel, T. R., & Young, L. J. (2001). The neurobiology of attachment. *Nature Reviews Neuroscience*, 2(2), 129–36.

Izuma, K., Saito, D. N., & Sadato, N. (2008). Processing social and monetary rewards in the human striatum. *Neuron*, 58(2), 284–294.

Izuma, K., Saito, D. N., & Sadato, N. (2010). Processing of the incentive for social approval in the ventral striatum during charitable donation. *Journal of Cognitive Neuroscience*, 22(4), 621–31.

Kennerley, S. W., Walton, M. E., Behrens, T. E., Buckley, M. J., & Rushworth, M. F. (2006). Optimal decision making and the anterior cingulate cortex. *Nature Neuroscience*, 9(7), 940–47.

King-Casas, B., Tomlin, D., Anen, C., Camerer, C. F., Quartz, S. R., & Montague, P. R. (2005). Getting to know you: Reputation and trust in a two-person economic exchange. *Science*, 308(5718), 78–83.

Knutson, B., Fong, G. W., Bennett, S. M., Adams, C. M., & Hommer, D. (2003). A region of mesial prefrontal cortex tracks monetarily rewarding outcomes: Characterization with rapid event-related fMRI. *Neuroimage*, 18(2), 263–72.

Kosfeld, M., Heinrichs, M., Zak, P. J., Fischbacher, U., & Fehr, E. (2005). Oxytocin increases trust in humans. *Nature*, 435(7042), 673–76.

Kringelbach, M. L. (2005). The human orbitofrontal cortex: Linking reward to hedonic experience. *Nature Reviews Neuroscience*, 6(9), 691–702.

Li, J., Delgado, M. R., & Phelps, E. A. (2011). How instructed knowledge modulates the neural systems of reward learning. *Proceedings of the National Academy of Sciences*, 108(1), 55–60.

Lin, A., Adolphs, R., & Rangel, A. (2012). Social and monetary reward learning engage overlapping neural substrates. *Social Cognitive & Affective Neuroscience*, 7(3), 274–81.

Logothetis, N. K., Pauls, J., Augath, M., Trinath, T., & Oeltermann, A. (2001). Neurophysiological investigation of the basis of the fMRI signal. *Nature*, 412(6843), 150–57.

McCabe, K., Houser, D., Ryan, L., Smith, V., & Trouard, T. (2001). A functional imaging study of cooperation in two-person reciprocal exchange. *Proceedings of the National Academy of Sciences*, 98(20), 11832–35.

Middleton, F. A., & Strick, P. L. (2000). Basal ganglia and cerebellar loops: Motor and cognitive circuits. *Brain Research Review*, 31(2–3), 236–50.

Mobbs, D., Yu, R., Meyer, M., Passamonti, L., Seymour, B., Calder, A. J., . . . Dalgleish, T. (2009). A key role for similarity in vicarious reward. *Science*, 324(5929), 900.

Nieuwenhuis, S., Heslenfeld, D. J., von Geusau, N. J., Mars, R. B., Holroyd, C. B., & Yeung, N. (2005). Activity in human reward-sensitive brain areas is strongly context dependent. *Neuroimage*, 25(4), 1302–9.

Niv, Y. (2009). Reinforcement learning in the brain. *Journal of Mathematical Psychology*, 53(3), 139–54.

Niv, Y., & Schoenbaum, G. (2008). Dialogues on prediction errors. *Trends in Cognitive Sciences*, 12(7), 265–72.

O'Doherty, J., Critchley, H., Deichmann, R., & Dolan, R. J. (2003). Dissociating valence of outcome from behavioral control in human orbital and ventral prefrontal cortices. *Journal of Neuroscience*, 23(21), 7931–39.

O'Doherty, J. P., Dayan, P., Friston, K., Critchley, H., & Dolan, R. J. (2003). Temporal difference models and reward-related learning in the human brain. *Neuron*, 38(2), 329–37.

O'Doherty, J., Dayan, P., Schultz, J., Deich-mann, R., Friston, K., & Dolan, R. J. (2004). Dissociable roles of ventral and dorsal striatum in instrumental conditioning. *Science*, 304(5669), 452–54.

O'Doherty, J. P., Deichmann, R., Critchley, H. D., & Dolan, R. J. (2002). Neural responses during anticipation of a primary taste reward. *Neuron*, 33(5), 815–26.

O'Doherty, J., Kringelbach, M. L., Rolls, E. T., Hornak, J., & Andrews, C. (2001). Abstract reward and punishment representations in the human orbitofrontal cortex. *Nature Neuroscience*, 4(1), 95–102.

Ostlund, S. B., & Balleine, B. W. (2005). Lesions of medial prefrontal cortex disrupt the acquisition but not the expression of goal-directed learning. *Journal of Neuroscience*, 25(34), 7763–70.

Ostlund, S. B., & Balleine, B. W. (2007). The contribution of orbitofrontal cortex to action selection. *Annals of the New York Academy of Sciences*, 1121, 174–92.

Pagnoni, G., Zink, C. F., Montague, P. R., & Berns, G. S. (2002). Activity in human ventral striatum locked to errors of reward prediction. *Nature Neuroscience*, 5(2), 97–98.

Paton, J. J., Belova, M. A., Morrison, S. E., & Salzman, C. D. (2006). The primate amygdala represents the positive and negative value of visual stimuli during learning. *Nature*, 439(7078), 865–70.

Pessiglione, M., Seymour, B., Flandin, G., Dolan, R. J., & Frith, C. D. (2006). Dopamine-dependent prediction errors underpin reward-seeking behaviour in humans. *Nature*, 442(7106), 1042–45.

Phan, K. L., Sripada, C. S., Angstadt, M., & McCabe, K. (2010). Reputation for reciprocity engages the brain reward center. *Proceedings of the National Academy of Sciences*, 107(29), 13099–13104.

Phelps, E. A., & LeDoux, J. E. (2005). Contributions of the amygdala to emotion processing: from animal models to human behavior. *Neuron*, 48(2), 175–87.

Preuschoff, K., Quartz, S. R., & Bossaerts, P. (2008). Human insula activation reflects risk prediction errors as well as risk. *Journal of Neuroscience*, 28(11), 2745–52.

Rapoport, A., & Chammah, A. M. (1965). *Prisoner's dilemma*. Ann Arbor: University of Michigan Press.

Redgrave, P., & Gurney, K. (2006). The short-latency dopamine signal: a role in discovering novel actions? *Nature Reviews Neuroscience*, 7(12), 967–75.

Rescorla, R. A., & Wagner, A. R. (1972). A theory of Pavolovian conditioning: Variations in the effectiveness of reinforcement and nonreinforcement. In A. H. Black & W. F. Prokasy (Eds.), *Classical conditioning II* (pp. 64–99). New York: Appleton-Century-Crofts.

Rilling, J., Gutman, D., Zeh, T., Pagnoni, G., Berns, G., & Kilts, C. (2002). A neural basis for social cooperation. *Neuron*, 35(2), 395–405.

Rilling, J. K., & Sanfey, A. G. (2011). The neuroscience of social decision-making. *Annual Review of Psychology*, 62, 23–48.

Rilling, J. K., Sanfey, A. G., Aronson, J. A., Nystrom, L. E., & Cohen, J. D. (2004). Opposing BOLD responses to reciprocated and unreciprocated altruism in putative reward pathways. *Neuroreport*, 15(16), 2539–43.

Risinger, R. C., Salmeron, B. J., Ross, T. J., Amen, S. L., Sanfilipo, M., Hoffmann, R. G., . . . Stein, E. A. (2005). Neural correlates of high and craving during cocaine self-administration using BOLD fMRI. *Neuroimage*, 26(4), 1097–1108.

Rutledge, R. B., Lazzaro, S. C., Lau, B., Myers, C. E., Gluck, M. A., & Glimcher, P. W. (2009). Dopaminergic drugs modulate learning rates and perseveration in Parkinson's patients in a dynamic foraging task. *Journal of Neuroscience*, 29(48), 15104–14.

Said, C. P., Haxby, J. V., & Todorov, A. (2011). Brain systems for assessing the affective value of faces. *Philosophical Transactions of the Royal Society of London. Series B: Biological Sciences*, 366(1571), 1660–70.

Schott, B. H., Minuzzi, L., Krebs, R. M., Elmenhorst, D., Lang, M., Winz, O. H., . . . Bauer, A. (2008). Mesolimbic functional magnetic resonance imaging activations during reward anticipation correlate with reward-related ventral striatal dopamine release. *Journal of Neuroscience*, 28(52), 14311–19.

Schultz, W., Dayan, P., & Montague, P. R. (1997). A neural substrate of prediction and reward. *Science*, 275(5306), 1593–99.

Sesack, S. R., & Grace, A. A. (2010). Cortico-basal ganglia reward network: Microcircuitry. *Neuropsychopharmacology*, 35(1), 27–47.

Seymour, B., O'Doherty, J. P., Dayan, P., Koltzenburg, M., Jones, A. K., Dolan, R. J., . . . Frackowiak, R. S. (2004). Temporal difference models describe higher-order learning in humans. *Nature*, 429(6992), 664–67.

Somerville, L. H., & Casey, B. J. (2010). Developmental neurobiology of cognitive control and motivational systems. *Current Opinions in Neurobiology*, 20(2), 236–41.

Somerville, L. H., Heatherton, T. F., & Kelley, W. M. (2006). Anterior cingulate cortex responds differentially to expectancy violation and social rejection. *Nature Neuroscience*, 9(8), 1007–8.

Takahashi, H., Kato, M., Matsuura, M., Mobbs, D., Suhara, T., & Okubo, Y. (2009). When your gain is my pain and your pain is my gain: Neural correlates of envy and schadenfreude. *Science*, 323(5916), 937–39.

Tomlin, D., Kayali, M. A., King-Casas, B., Anen, C., Camerer, C. F., Quartz, S. R., & Montague, P. R. (2006). Agent-specific responses in the cingulate cortex during economic exchanges. *Science*, 312(5776), 1047–50.

Tricomi, E. M., Delgado, M. R., & Fiez, J. A. (2004). Modulation of caudate activity by action contingency. *Neuron*, 41(2), 281–92.

Tricomi, E., & Fiez, J. A. (2008). Feedback signals in the caudate reflect goal achievement on a declarative memory task. *Neuroimage*, 41(3), 1154–67.

Tricomi, E., Rangel, A., Camerer, C. F., & O'Doherty, J. P. (2010). Neural evidence for inequality-averse social preferences. *Nature*, 463(7284), 1089–91.

van den Bos, W., van Dijk, E., Westenberg, M., Rombouts, S. A., & Crone, E. A. (2009). What motivates repayment? Neural correlates of reciprocity in the Trust Game. *Social, Cognitive, & Affective Neuroscience*, 4(3), 294–304.

Volkow, N. D., Wang, G. J., Fowler, J. S., Logan, J., Gatley, S. J., Hitzemann, R., . . . Pappas, N. (1997). Decreased striatal dopaminergic responsiveness in detoxified cocaine-dependent subjects. *Nature*, 386(6627), 830–33.

Volkow, N. D., Wang, G. J., Fowler, J. S., Logan, J., Jayne, M., Franceschi, D., . . . Pappas, N. (2002). "Nonhedonic" food motivation in humans involves dopamine in the dorsal striatum and methylphenidate amplifies this effect. *Synapse*, 44(3), 175–80.

Voorn, P., Vanderschuren, L. J., Groenewegen, H. J., Robbins, T. W., & Pennartz, C. M. (2004). Putting a spin on the dorsal-ventral divide of the striatum. *Trends in Neurosciences*, 27(8), 468–74.

Wise, R. A. (2004). Dopamine, learning and motivation. *Nature Reviews Neuroscience*, 5(6), 483–94.

Wyvell, C. L., & Berridge, K. C. (2000). Intra-accumbens amphetamine increases the conditioned incentive salience of sucrose reward: Enhancement of reward "wanting" without enhanced "liking" or response reinforcement. *Journal of Neuroscience*, 20(21), 8122–30.

Zink, C. F., Pagnoni, G., Martin-Skurski, M. E., Chappelow, J. C., & Berns, G. S. (2004). Human striatal responses to monetary reward depend on saliency. *Neuron*, 42(3), 509–17.

CHAPTER 20

Emotion in Episodic Memory

The Effects of Emotional Content, Emotional State, and Motivational Goals

Alisha C. Holland & Elizabeth A. Kensinger

Memory can take many forms. It can reflect the conscious access of factual knowledge or past experiences (explicit or declarative memory), or it can be revealed as a change in our behavior that results from the influence of past experiences (implicit or non-declarative memory). This chapter focuses on *episodic memory*, a form of consciously accessible memory (see Chapter 18 for a discussion of the effects of emotion on implicit learning). More specifically, episodic memory refers to memory for a unique event. Episodic memories generally include the content of the event itself, as well as information on the spatial and temporal context in which the event occurred (Tulving, 1972).

For an event to be remembered in an episodic fashion, three phases of processing must occur. First, the information from the initial experience must be *encoded* into a format that can be stored in memory. Second, that information must be *consolidated* or stabilized into a lasting representation. Third, that representation must be *retrieved* and consciously ascribed to our own personal past. Not all experiences progress through these phases to become a part of our

episodic memory stores. We may be able to remember most of yesterday's events, but it is likely that we remember only a minority of the events from one month ago. Although many factors influence the likelihood that an experience becomes part of our memory stores, one important factor is the experience of emotion. Many of our episodic memories pertain to experiences that elicited an emotional reaction; we experienced altered physiological or somatic reactions, or changes in our subjective feelings, as the event unfolded (see Chapter 1 for discussion of the best way to define emotion). The term "emotional memory" refers to our ability to remember these episodic events.

Extensive research on emotional memory demonstrates that emotion can interact with episodic memory processes in a number of ways that influence each of the encoding, consolidation, and retrieval phases of processing. When an event elicits an emotion, it can influence which event details we initially encode and how cognitive demanding it is for us to encode them. The emotion experienced during or shortly after an event can also influence the likelihood that the encoded information becomes consolidated in memory. The emotional content of the event we are retrieving can influence how subjectively rich our memories for the experience seem, or how easily the details of the experience come to mind when we are presented with a retrieval cue. Not only can the emotion experienced during the initial event affect memory processes, so too can the emotions experienced during later memory phases. For instance, the emotions we experience while retrieving an event can influence which events come to mind most easily and can also influence the way in which different aspects of a past experience are reconstructed. This chapter discusses the ways in which emotion interacts with encoding, consolidation, and retrieval processes, focusing on how both the *emotional content* of an event and the *emotional state* of the individual can influence memory.

The Encoding of Emotional Experiences

Encoding refers to the set of processes that transform an initial experience into a format that can be stored in memory. Just as the signals from the keys we press on a computer must be transformed into a format that can be recognized and stored within a document, so must the sights, sounds, and other details of an event be converted into a format that can be stored in memory. The way we initially process an event can therefore have large implications for the types of information that become stored in memory. If our attention is captured by some part of the event or if we contemplate a particular feature of an experience, then those aspects are more likely to become encoded. In fact, encoding may be best thought of as a byproduct of the way that we initially process an experience (Paller & Wagner, 2002).

In a broad sense, the factors that influence the encoding of emotional events can be broken down into those that involve relatively automatic influences and those that arise via the engagement of more controlled

processes (see Figure 20.1). Relatively automatic influences can include the capture of attention by emotion-relevant information, the preattentive or prioritized processing of such stimuli, and the enhanced fluidity of processing of such stimuli (see Chapters 14 and 15; see also Whittlesea, 1993). Controlled processes encompass the enhanced elaboration and rehearsal given to emotional information, as well as the sustained attention focused on it (Talmi, Luk, McGarry, & Moscovitch, 2007).

A few lines of evidence suggest that the distribution of automatic and controlled processes may differ for emotional information with different affective characteristics. Emotions are often described in a two-dimensional space consisting of valence (pleasantness or unpleasantness) and arousal (level of excitation; Russell, 1980). As we describe next, where an emotional reaction falls along each of these axes seems to influence the types of processing that contribute most readily to the information's encoding.

The Effects of High-Arousal Emotion on Encoding Processes

For information that is highly arousing, many of the effects of emotion on encoding processes may occur relatively automatically. Information that is high in arousal is noticed more quickly and more often than lower arousal information, and attention is directed selectively toward that information (e.g., Leclerc & Kensinger, 2008). High-arousal information may also require fewer attentional resources to process than low-arousal information (see Chapter 14; see also Matthews & Margetts, 1991), and it may be prioritized for processing such that it will beat out the competition when attentional resources are taxed (see Chapter 15).

These alterations in processing for high-arousal information can have downstream effects on the likelihood that people can remember the information. For example, people show enhanced detection of high-arousal stimuli on the emotional Stroop task, and they also are more likely to remember the high-arousal items (e.g., MacKay

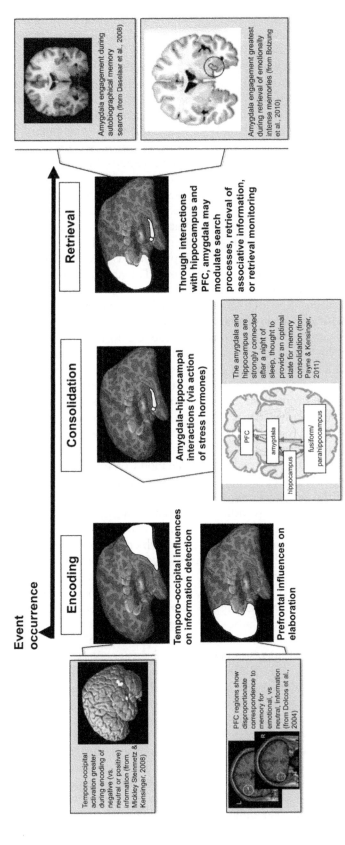

Figure 20.1. The basic mechanisms through which the emotional content of an experience can influence the way in which it is remembered. See color plate 20.1.

et al., 2004). Similarly, when people's attention is divided across two tasks as they attempt to encode information (e.g., when they are asked to encode words while simultaneously monitoring sound patterns), they appear better able to process the high-arousal information as compared to the low-arousal information, and their memory suffers less for the high-arousal information (Kensinger & Corkin, 2004; Kern, Libkuman, Otani, & Holmes, 2005). These findings are consistent with the proposal that high-arousal information is privy to automatic processing advantages, which enhance the likelihood that the information will be encoded into memory.

At a neural level, many of these relatively automatic influences seem to stem from amygdala activation. Research conducted in patients with amygdala damage has revealed the necessity of this region for enhanced detection of high-arousal information: Individuals with amygdala damage do not show the same automatic detection and rapid processing of high-arousal information as do those with intact amygdalae (e.g., LaBar & Phelps, 1998). More recent neuroimaging studies have confirmed that the activation patterns of the amygdala make it a likely candidate for such automatic influences. In particular, the amygdala shows increases in activity when salient stimuli – such as a fearful face or a snake – are presented, even when those stimuli are afforded only minimal attention (e.g., Whalen et al., 2004). There has been debate over whether the amygdala can become activated in the absence of attention (see Chapters 14 and 15), raising doubt as to whether high-arousal stimuli could be encoded without the exertion of *any* cognitively demanding resources (see also Pottage & Schaefer, 2012). But evidence does suggest that the amygdala can process even those high-arousal stimuli that have not been afforded extensive attention, suggesting that high-arousal stimuli can be encoded using *fewer* of these cognitively demanding resources than are required for the encoding of lower arousing stimuli.

Although the amygdala seems to play a critical role in the rapid encoding of salient information, it does not exert these influences on its own. In fact, it seems that some of the largest contributions that the amygdala makes to successful encoding reflect its modulation of other sensory and mnemonic processes. Once active, the amygdala sends efferent connections to many regions of the brain (e.g., Amaral, Price, Pitkanen, & Carmichael, 1992), innervating regions important for sensory and mnemonic processing. Neuroimaging analyses have suggested that the amygdala has strong functional connections with the fusiform gyrus and extrastriate visual cortex (e.g., Tabert et al., 2001), as well as with the hippocampus (reviewed by LaBar & Cabeza, 2006). The amygdala may also evoke activity in a broader affective-attentional network (see meta-analysis by Murty, Ritchey, Adcock, & LaBar, 2010), including regions of the orbitofrontal cortex, anterior cingulate gyrus, and caudate nucleus (discussed in Kensinger, 2009). This broader network of regions is brought online when a task requires attention to affective stimuli (e.g., Robbins & Everitt, 1996), and it may help focus attention selectively on the high-arousing information, increasing the likelihood of remembering it (discussed in Kensinger, 2009).

It seems, therefore, that the successful encoding of high-arousal items results from a combination of domain-general factors, which could enhance the encoding of any type of information, and of domain-specific factors that are uniquely associated with the encoding of emotional information. The engagement of sensory cortices (e.g., Talmi, Anderson, Riggs, Caplan, & Moscovitch, 2008) or of medial temporal lobe regions (e.g., Dolcos, LaBar, & Cabeza, 2004) can be considered domain general, because although activity in these regions is increased when stimuli are high in arousal, their activity also occurs for nonarousing information and their engagement enables the encoding of both neutral information and emotional information. In fact, in some circumstances these regions may be activated independently of the amygdala (e.g., Talmi et al., 2008), suggesting that the encoding of emotional information can sometimes be explained by domain-general processes. However, in the majority of studies to date, the modulation of this sensory and mnemonic activation seems to be enhanced by activation of the amygdala and of other affective-processing regions such as the orbitofrontal cortex. These regions are not brought online unless information is interpreted to have particular saliency (e.g., Sander, Grafman, & Zalla, 2003; Chapter 1), and therefore their engagement can be considered to be domain specific. Thus, although the end result may be domain-general activity, the route through which that activity becomes enhanced often appears to be specific to the processing of emotionally salient information. In other words, engagement of emotion-specific processes can influence memory by modulating domain-general sensory and mnemonic processes.

The Effects of Low-Arousal Emotion on Encoding Processes

For emotional items that are lower in arousal, automatic processes seem to play less of a role in guiding encoding. Low-arousal items are less likely to be detected than high-arousal items (see Chapters 14 and 15), and their encoding is impeded by the presence of a secondary task (Kensinger & Corkin, 2004). In contrast to encoding of high-arousal items, encoding of items that are low in arousal seems to benefit from more controlled processes. As we discuss in this section, some of the key processes that may affect the encoding of low-arousal items are the elaboration it evokes and the semantic clustering and organization from which it benefits.

Elaboration refers to the processes by which new information becomes linked to previously stored information. This linkage can occur by extracting meaning from new information, by forming associations with other semantic knowledge or episodic experiences, or by integrating the information into a person's self-view. It is well known that these elaborations enhance the suc-

cess of encoding (reviewed by Symons & Johnson, 1997), and a few lines of evidence suggest that these types of processes may be particularly important for enhancing the encoding of low-arousal information. For one, neuroimaging studies have confirmed that regions implicated in elaborative processing, such as the lateral prefrontal cortex, are disproportionately recruited during the successful encoding of emotional information (e.g., Dolcos et al., 2004), particularly if that emotional information is low in arousal (e.g., Kensinger & Corkin, 2004). Second, when participants' attention is divided as they encode information, memory for low-arousal items is disproportionately impaired. Because elaboration is an attention-demanding process, divided attention tasks disrupt the ability to engage those processes; the fact that the encoding of low-arousal information is most affected by this disruption suggests that memory for those items was particularly reliant on elaboration (e.g., Kensinger & Corkin, 2004; Kern et al., 2005).

Emotion can also benefit memory by providing semantic coherence and an organizing principle (e.g., Talmi et al., 2007). "Emotion" can be thought of as a category, and so stimuli that elicit any emotion (or particular emotions) may be clustered together in memory. It is well known that this type of organization assists in the encoding of information and can later be used as a powerful retrieval cue, and so the ability for emotional information to be clustered together may affect the way it is retained in memory. Evidence to support this view has come from studies that have revealed elevated false recognition of emotional information (e.g., Brainerd, Stein, Silveira, Rohenkohl, & Reyna, 2008). These data have been interpreted as suggesting that individuals use the thematic coherence of emotional information to encode the "gist" or general theme of the associated information and then endorse any information that is consistent with that encoded theme. Interestingly, many of the studies that have revealed these effects of emotion on false memory have used words and other stimuli that are fairly low in arousal (e.g., Brainerd et al., 2008; Kapucu, Rotello, Ready, &Seidl, 2009). Although the effects of emotion on false memory are not limited to low-arousal stimuli (e.g., Gallo, Foster, & Johnson, 2009), and more research is needed to clarify whether high-arousal stimuli are less prone to false memory effects than low-arousal stimuli, it is possible that the tendency to encode gist-based information is greater when information is low arousal than when it is high arousal because the reliance on semantic clustering is greater for low-arousal items (see discussion by Kapucu et al., 2009). It is also possible that high- and low-arousal stimuli are equally likely to be encoded in a way that takes advantage of semantic clustering, but that because high-arousal stimuli benefit from additional, automatic processes, it is easier for people to encode item-specific information, as well as gist-based, categorical information, about high-arousal items. This item-specific information may be used to combat category-consistent false memories in some instances.

In summary, there has been extensive evidence to suggest that memory for high-arousal items may benefit from automatic processes, whereas memory for low-arousal items is more likely to be enhanced because of controlled processes. This dissociation does not require that controlled processing is unique to low-arousal information; it is likely that high-arousal items also are elaborated on and semantically organized. However, because memory for the high-arousal information is so strongly influenced by relatively automatic processes, these more controlled processes are less likely to exert an impact. By contrast, because low-arousal information does not seem to be privy to the same automatic processing advantages as high-arousal information, the encoding of low-arousing information is dominated by the changes in these controlled processes.

The Effects of Valence on Encoding

Although so far we have discussed the effects of *arousal* on automatic and controlled processes, it is also possible that the *valence* of information influences the engagement of these processes. In other words, even if positive and negative experiences elicit an equal amount of arousal, the two types of information may be encoded differently because of their valence. There is not a large body of research that has explored this topic, but two lines of evidence suggest that negative valence may enhance the automatic processing of emotional information. First, manipulations of divided attention seem to have less of an impact on memory for negative information than positive information (Kern et al., 2005; Talmi et al., 2007), suggesting that negative information may be encoded more automatically than positive information. Second, neuroimaging studies have revealed that the successful encoding of negative high-arousal information is more likely to be tied to sensory activity than is the successful encoding of positive information (e.g., Mickley Steinmetz & Kensinger, 2009). Positive high-arousal information, by contrast, may be more associated with thematic or gist-based processing, such that its encoding is more likely to be disrupted by divided attention (Kern et al., 2005; Talmi et al., 2007) and to be associated with activity in lateral prefrontal regions associated with elaborative encoding and semantic organization (e.g., Mickley Steinmetz & Kensinger, 2009).

The Effects of Emotional State and Emotional Goals on Encoding

So far, we have discussed how the emotions elicited by the content of an event can influence the way that event is encoded. But the way we process an event is also shaped by our current affective state and by our goals. Our emotional states can modulate the type of event details we attend to and therefore encode (see Figure 20.2). Generally, we are more likely to attend to information that is congruent in valence to our current emotional state; for example, being in a negative mood (either transiently or chronically, as in depression) enhances our attention to negative information and makes it more likely that this negative information

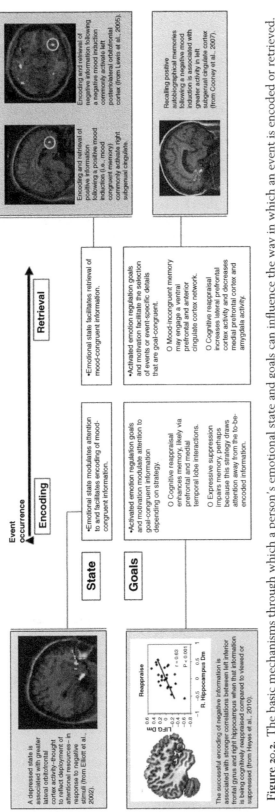

Event occurrence

State

Encoding

•Emotional state modulates attention to and facilitates encoding of mood-congruent information.

Goals

•Activated emotion regulation goals and motivation modulate attention to goal-congruent information depending on strategy.

O Cognitive reappraisal enhances memory, likely via prefrontal and medial temporal lobe interactions.

O Expressive suppression impairs memory, perhaps because this strategy draws attention away from the to-be-encoded information.

Retrieval

•Emotional state facilitates retrieval of mood-congruent information.

•Activated emotion regulation goals and motivation facilitate the selection of events or event-specific details that are goal-congruent.

O Mood-incongruent memory may engage a ventral prefrontal and anterior cingulate cortex network.

O Cognitive reappraisal increases lateral prefrontal cortex activity and decreases medial prefrontal cortex and amygdala activity.

A depressed state is associated with greater lateral orbitofrontal cortex activity–thought to reflect deployment of attentional resources–in response to negative stimuli (from Elliott et al., 2002).

The successful encoding of negative information is associated with stronger correlations between left inferior frontal gyrus and right hippocampus when that information is being cognitively reappraised compared to viewed or suppressed (from Hayes et al., 2010).

Encoding and retrieval of positive information following a positive mood induction (i.e., mood congruent memory) commonly activate right subgenual cingulate.

Encoding and retrieval of negative information following a negative mood induction commonly activate left posteriolateral orbitofrontal cortex (from Lewis et al., 2005).

Recalling positive autobiographical memories following a negative mood induction is associated with greater activity in left subgenual cingulate cortex (from Cooney et al., 2007).

Figure 20.2. The basic mechanisms through which a person's emotional state and goals can influence the way in which an event is encoded or retrieved.

becomes part of our memory stores (e.g., Mathews & MacLeod, 2005).

Motivational goals also can affect encoding in a comparable way to mood. For instance, approach motivation during a task leads to an overestimation of the remembered happiness during that task, whereas avoidance motivation during encoding leads to an overestimation of remembered anxiety (Lench & Levine, 2010). Our emotional goals – in other words, how we want to feel – can similarly affect the information that we encode. Perhaps one of the clearest demonstrations of the influence of emotion goals on memory is age-related changes in the types of experiences that are remembered. As adults progress from middle age into older adulthood, they appear to place additional emphasis on emotional fulfillment and to have emotion regulation goals chronically activated; this shift has been proposed to occur because older adults perceive their time as limited and want to maximize their emotional well-being (reviewed by Mather, 2006). In line with these emotion goals, older adults are more likely than young adults to sustain their attention on, and therefore to encode, positive information (Mather, 2006).

The changes in emotion goals may yield a positivity bias by affecting the controlled processing of emotional information (Mather, 2006): Older adults may be more likely than young adults to process positive information in a controlled fashion. Consistent with this interpretation, older adults are most likely to show a positivity bias if they have good cognitive control ability and can deploy their full resources toward task performance (Mather, 2006) and if they are encoding low-arousal items that, as noted earlier, may be a type of information whose retention is particularly dependent on controlled processing. The conclusion that emotion goals affect controlled processing of emotional information is further supported by neuroimaging evidence. Aging does not seem to have a large effect on amygdala activity, but instead seems to increase prefrontal cortex activity (particularly medial) during encoding (see Chapter 28). The

increased prefrontal activity might reflect increased emotion regulation and/or an increase in self-referential processing in response to positive information (see Chapter 28; Kensinger & Leclerc, 2009).

Although these studies of age-related changes in emotional memory provide one window into exploring the effects of emotional goals on memory, there is a need for further clarification of the ways in which affect-relevant goals influence the memories of younger adults. Studies in young adults will be important because it is currently difficult to disentangle the age-related changes due specifically to alterations in goal states from those that are due to more general age-related changes in cognition or in brain function (see discussion by Nashiro, Sakaki, & Mather, 2012).

Most of the research examining the effects of emotion goals on young adults' memory has focused on distinguishing the influences of different types of strategies that can be used to regulate emotions. Many studies concerning emotion regulation contrast two dissociable emotion regulation strategies. One is cognitive reappraisal, a specific type of emotion regulation strategy that involves changing the way that one reacts to or thinks about an emotional stimulus (Gross, 1998). The second type of strategy involves suppressing one's outward emotional reaction to a stimulus (Gross, 1998; see also Chapter 16).

The type of strategy employed at encoding can have important implications for what is later remembered. Several studies have demonstrated that reappraising negative emotions associated with information improves free recall of that information after a short delay, but that emotion-expressive suppression impairs recall (e.g., Dillon, Ritchey, Johnson, & LaBar, 2007; Richards & Gross, 1999). As with the age-related changes in emotional memory, the different mnemonic implications of these emotion regulation strategies may have to do with the way in which controlled processes are engaged during the encoding of an experience. Cognitive reappraisal engages cognitive control regions in the prefrontal cortex that seem to dampen amygdala activity as emotional stimuli are being attended to; thus, reappraisal results in increased prefrontal engagement but reduced amygdala activity (e.g., Ochsner. Bunge, Gross, & Gabrieli, 2002). By contrast, suppression is associated with a rebound in amygdala activity (Goldin, McRae, Ramel, & Gross, 2008). The fact that cognitive reappraisal leads to maximal encoding suggests that the mnemonic benefit stems from the engagement of the controlled processes implemented by the prefrontal cortex, rather than from the engagement of the amygdala.

It is also possible that it is the interactions between the more controlled (prefrontal) and more automatic (amygdala) processes that lead to such a robust memory trace. Indeed, the successful encoding of negative images during cognitive reappraisal (versus suppression and passive viewing) more strongly coactivates the left inferior frontal gyrus, hippocampus, and amygdala (Hayes et al., 2010). Further, a separate study revealed that the fronto-amygdalar neural circuitry involved with reappraisal (versus passive viewing) of emotional pictures during encoding was reactivated up to a year later during retrieval (Erk, von Kalckreuth, & Walter, 2010), suggesting that there may be a permanent change in the connectivity within these regions that helps solidify memory. It will be important for future research to clarify why the neural activity recruited for cognitive reappraisal leads to such strong memories and to examine why emotion suppression may have different long-term neural effects with regard to the permanency of a memory.

The Consolidation and Retention of Emotional Experiences

As the previous section has emphasized, emotion exerts large influences on the way we initially attend and encode information. If emotion only affected encoding processes, then its effects should be consistent regardless of whether memory was tested after a short or after a long delay: There should be a comparable effect of emotion across all possible delay intervals. In actuality, however, the effects of emotion often become exaggerated after a long delay. If we think back to this morning, we probably can remember the mundane moments (what we ate for breakfast, what traffic was like on our morning commute), but if we think back to last week, we are unlikely to remember these types of details unless they were particularly emotional (we might remember if the milk had spoiled or we hit a traffic jam, but we probably will not remember those parts of our day if they proceeded in a usual fashion). Indeed, although emotion conveys a benefit to memory even after a short delay (e.g., Talmi et al., 2007), this benefit tends to become exaggerated across longer intervals (e.g., Sharot & Yonelinas, 2008). This pattern cannot easily be explained by the effects of emotion on encoding processes alone. Rather, this pattern suggests that emotion exerts its influence not only during encoding but also during the subsequent consolidation phase of episodic memory.

Consolidation refers to the set of processes that stabilize a memory trace, making it less prone to disruption (see McGaugh, 2004). It is generally agreed that the hippocampus is required for consolidation to occur, although there are debates over the time course of hippocampal involvement (see Nadel & Moscovitch, 1997; Squire & Zola, 1998). As noted earlier, the amygdala is well connected with a number of regions, including the hippocampus, and amygdala activation is believed to modulate hippocampal function, increasing the likelihood that an emotional experience is consolidated. Indeed, patients with damage to the amygdala show normal enhancements in emotional memory over short delays, but do not retain those enhancements over long delays (e.g., LaBar & Phelps, 1998), consistent with the proposal that the amygdala exerts many of its effects via its influences on hippocampal consolidation.

Many neuroimaging studies have confirmed that the amygdala and hippocampus interact to create durable episodic memories (reviewed by LaBar & Cabeza, 2006).

Furthermore, the effects of emotion on long-term episodic memory are mediated by the influence of stress hormones. The administration of cortisol enhances the long-term recall of emotional information, whereas the administration of beta-blockers eliminates the enhancement (reviewed by McGaugh, 2004). Thus, these neuroimaging and neuropharmacological findings are consistent with a role for arousal-dependent amygdalar modulation of consolidation.

Another way that researchers have tried to isolate the effects of emotion on consolidation processes is by keeping the encoding phase constant but manipulating whether participants are then allowed to sleep after encoding. Because sleep is thought to create ideal circumstances for episodic memory consolidation (reviewed by Walker & Stickgold, 2006), participants who sleep after encoding would be expected to benefit from consolidation processes to a greater degree than those who remained awake after encoding.

To date, the studies that have compared the effects of sleep on memory for emotional and nonemotional information have found that sleep conveys particular benefits for emotional memory. Most of these studies have compared subsequent memory performance in participants who sleep soon after encoding to performance in those who remained awake after encoding. As compared to participants who have remained awake, participants who have slept remembered more emotional words or images, whereas there was a lesser sleep advantage for neutral information (e.g., Wagner. Hallschmid, Rasch, & Born, 2006). The circumscribed effects of sleep on emotional (but not neutral) memory can be long lasting. For instance, participants who studied emotional and neutral narratives and then took a nap were more likely to remember the emotional narratives 3 years later when compared to those participants who had not taken a nap after reading the narratives. Yet sleep provided no benefit in memory to the neutral narratives (Wagner et al., 2006).

Neuroimaging evidence supports the notion that emotion can influence the consolidation of memories, yielding memory traces that can be retrieved with activity within a fairly narrow network of regions, including the amygdala, hippocampus, and ventromedial or orbitofrontal cortex (see Figure 20.3 for a depiction of these regions). After a delay of as little as 12 sleep-filled hours, this refined network was revealed to support the retrieval of emotional memories (Payne & Kensinger, 2011), and this network appears to be recruited after much longer delays as well (Dolcos, LaBar, & Cabeza, 2005; Sterpenich et al., 2009). These results suggest that the retrieval process for emotional memories may be more efficient after time for consolidation, such as occurs over a night of sleep.

Although the evidence discussed so far suggests that emotion facilitates memory consolidation, it is important to note that emotion may not facilitate consolidation of all aspects of the event. Rather, emotion may lead some aspects of an event to be consolidated and other aspects of the event to fade away. For instance, when participants slept after encoding scenes that contained an emotional item (such as a snake) presented within a nonemotional context (such as a forest), they showed preserved memory for the emotional item but not for the corresponding context (Payne, Swanberg, Stickgold, & Kensinger, 2008). These results suggest that consolidation processes may act not on the whole representation of an emotional experience; rather the interaction between emotion and memory consolidation may be more sophisticated, acting only on select elements of an experience and enabling only those elements to be available for later retrieval (see Payne & Kensinger, 2011, for more discussion).

The Retrieval of Emotional Experiences

Given the mnemonic benefits that emotion confers at the stages of encoding and consolidation, it is perhaps not surprising that emotion also affects the output stage of memory. Memory retrieval involves accessing internal representations of past experiences and

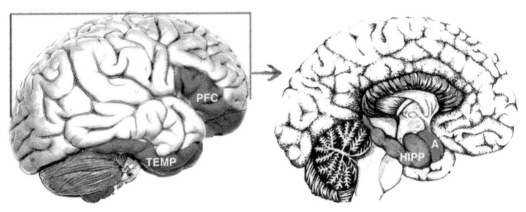

Figure 20.3. The key regions involved in emotion's modulation of memory encoding and consolidation. PFC = prefrontal cortex (shaded portions highlight the ventrolateral and orbitofrontal regions that are most often implicated in studies of emotional memory), TEMP = inferior temporal lobe, HIPP = hippocampus, A = amygdala.

requires the reconstruction – rather than reproduction – of the details from those past events (see Bartlett, 1932; Conway & Pleydell-Pearce, 2000). The reconstructive nature of episodic memory is evident from a behavioral standpoint in the existence of various types of memory errors that occur at retrieval and from a neural standpoint in the widely distributed network of brain regions recruited during retrieval (Schacter & Addis, 2008). Autobiographical memory retrieval in particular recruits a network of regions, including medial and lateral prefrontal cortex, medial temporal lobe, and medial and lateral parietal lobe (see Cabeza & St. Jacques, 2007; Svoboda, McKinnon, & Levine, 2006, for reviews).

The hippocampal complex, located in the medial temporal lobe (see Figure 20.3), is perhaps the most critical area necessary for the process of memory construction. By acting as a "pointer system" to cortical areas that store the separate details of an episode (Nadel & Moscovitch, 1997), the hippocampal complex orchestrates the binding of details together into a coherent recollection. Critically, this hippocampal activity can be modulated by activity in the amygdala, which may enhance memory search and retrieval processes, as well as phenomenological characteristics associated with emotional memory, as discussed later.

Emotional autobiographical memories are recalled more vividly (e.g., Rubin & Kozin, 1984) and more confidently (e.g., Talarico & Rubin, 2003) than neutral or fictitious memories. The enhanced sensory detail with which emotional information is recalled leads to a greater sense of recollection or reliving (Rubin, Schrauf, & Greenberg, 2003). Emotion is also sometimes associated with retrieval of more accurate details from an event, at least for the information that is focal to the emotional aspect of the episode (Kensinger, 2009; but see Sharot, Delgado, & Phelps, 2004).

Although a good deal of neuroimaging work has focused on the activity present during encoding that is predictive of subsequent memory, much less work has examined emotional memory retrieval. This is partly due to the difficulty in teasing apart neural activation supporting retrieval versus that supporting the processing of emotional cues or the reexperiencing of emotion. Two types of clever study designs avoid these problems. First, laboratory memory tasks can test memory for neutral information presented within an emotional context (e.g., recognition of a neutral word that appeared in an emotional sentence). By presenting only neutral information as memory cues, these designs avoid the issue of cue-induced emotion processing (reviewed by LaBar & Cabeza, 2006). The second type of design examines autobiographical memories to discriminate among the neural processes engaged over the course of this type of memory's protracted retrieval time (e.g., Daselaar et al., 2008; Greenberg et al., 2005).

Evidence from laboratory and autobiographical memory studies implicates an overlap in the neural network engaged during both the encoding and retrieval of emotional information (Dolcos et al., 2005; Maratos, Dolan, Morris, Henson, & Rugg, 2001). In particular, the amygdala, the hippocampus, and regions of the prefrontal cortex are engaged not only during the encoding of an experience but also when emotional information is recalled. Thus, to some extent, retrieval of emotional experiences may involve the recapitulation of activity that was present during the instantiation of emotion during the initial experience. As is true during encoding, it appears that emotional memory retrieval engages many of the same regions as neutral memory retrieval – with the prefrontal cortex guiding memory selection and monitoring and the hippocampus implicated in the reconstruction of past event features – but that the activity in these regions is modulated by limbic areas key for emotional processing (Kensinger & Schacter, 2007; see Figure 20.3). Functional connectivity analyses have revealed reciprocal connections between the amygdala and hippocampus as well as between the prefrontal cortex and these medial temporal lobe regions during the retrieval of information encoded in an emotional context (Smith, Stephan, Rugg, & Dolan, 2006). These results suggest that the retrieval of emotional information might be orchestrated by top-down processing originating in the prefrontal cortex, which then influences activity in regions known to be critical for emotion (the amygdala) and episodic recollection (the hippocampus; Buchanan, 2007; Greenberg et al., 2005). It is possible that the amygdala's role in modulating retrieval may be to index the past behavioral significance of an event (Dolan, Lane, Chua, & Fletcher, 2000); if the amygdala is a "salience detector" during encoding (Sander et al., 2003), then

its activation during retrieval may enable the recall of the event's importance.

Interestingly, despite this overlap in the neural structures implicated in the encoding and retrieval of emotional information, there may also be laterality differences between these two phases of emotional memory. For instance, Sergerie, LePage, and Armony (2006) found that right amygdala activity predicted successful encoding of emotional information, whereas left amygdala activity predicted successful retrieval. Although other studies have found the opposite laterality effects (see Cabeza & St. Jacques, 2007), the extant data do not provide strong evidence for engagement of the identical regions within the amygdala during both encoding and retrieval.

Although the connectivity between the amygdala and hippocampus during emotional memory retrieval is fairly well established, one remaining question is how this connectivity leads to the qualitative and quantitative differences between emotional and neutral memory retrieval. One possibility is that emotion facilitates the memory search process. It has been proposed that early activation of the amygdala and medial prefrontal cortex, through some partial cue of an emotional event, produces an affective state. In turn, the presence of an affective state serves as a further retrieval cue for emotional information; the engagement of prefrontal regions and of the amygdala subsequently enhances the hippocampally mediated retrieval of event details (Buchanan, 2007). The retrieval of additional affective details by the hippocampus leads to a recapitulation of the regions active during the initial perception of those details (Buchanan, 2007). Evidence from studies using event-related potentials (ERPs), which provide excellent temporal resolution, suggests that the retrieval of emotional information recruits additional early and late processing relative to the retrieval of neutral information, possibly reflecting the early facilitation of emotional memory search and the later recapitulation of emotion during recollection (reviewed by Buchanan, 2007). Recent research using fMRI has further suggested that emotional retrieval cues may trigger stronger retrieval-related activity in early sensory areas than in areas associated with higher-level cognition (Hofstetter, Achaibou, & Vuilleumier, 2012), suggesting that emotion may enhance sensory recapitulation during retrieval.

The findings of another fMRI study lend further evidence to the hypothesis that emotion might facilitate the search for memory representations during retrieval. The authors took advantage of the relatively lengthy process required for autobiographical memory retrieval and of the emotional nature of most autobiographical memories to examine the time course over which emotion modulated memory retrieval (Daselaar et al., 2008). They measured neural activity during both the initial construction phase of autobiographical memories and the later elaboration and maintenance phase of those memories. Analyses revealed that regions critical for memory retrieval, including the hippocampus, retrosplenial cortex, and prefrontal cortex, were active in the early, initial access phase of the retrieval. Critically, participants' ratings of emotional intensity were related to the amount of amygdala and hippocampal activity during this initial period, but not during the later elaboration period. The early activation of the amygdala – before the memories were even fully constructed – supports the hypotheses that emotion can act as an early "warning" that a personally significant event is being retrieved and that amygdala activity may help guide the memory search process (Daselaar et al., 2008). Amygdala activity was not increased during the elaboration phase, suggesting that the amygdala is not simply responding to the emotional appraisal of an event after it is already retrieved (Daselaar et al., 2008).

The amygdala and hippocampal activity that seems to be critical for the retrieval of emotional memories might also be related to the phenomenological characteristics of emotional memory mentioned at the beginning of this section. For example, activity of both the hippocampus and amygdala is associated with the reported emotional intensity of a retrieved autobiographical memory

(Daselaar et al., 2008). Increased amygdala activity is also positively correlated with a sense of recollection (Sharot et al., 2004). There has been debate as to whether amygdala engagement during retrieval corresponds with the accuracy or amount of detail recovered about an experience or whether amygdala activity during retrieval serves only to inflate the subjective vividness or the confidence associated with a memory (Sharot et al., 2004). We return to this point later, when we discuss the effects of emotion on memory confidence.

Mood-Congruent Memory

Evidence reviewed to this point in the chapter demonstrates that the emotions we experience when an event is occurring can influence the way we encode, consolidate, and retrieve that event. It is also the case, however, that our emotional experience at the time of memory retrieval can affect memory. Our emotional state during retrieval can influence both which events are most accessible for recall and which details from those events are most likely to be remembered.

A robust example of mood's influence on memory is mood-congruent recall, or the tendency to recall events that are congruent in valence to one's current mood (e.g., to recall negative information when in a negative mood; see Rusting, 1988, for review). In addition to influencing *which* memories are recalled, the mood-congruency effect can also affect the speed with which memories are recalled and how positively or negatively memories are rated. Mood-congruent memory appears to occur under both induced and naturally occurring moods like depression and is evident on both laboratory and autobiographical memory tasks (see Rusting, 1998, for review). This effect is most often explained in terms of Bower's (1981) network theory of affect, which purports that information associated with particular emotion "nodes" becomes activated when those nodes are engaged, as in the case of a mood state (see Rusting, 1998, for a review of alternative views). Thus, being in a negative mood would activate the negative node and the information associated with that node, facilitating the retrieval of memories congruent with a negative mood.

Neuroimaging work conducted in the past several years has begun to examine the underlying neural correlates of mood-congruent memory (Lewis & Critchley, 2003). Perhaps unsurprisingly, some of the same limbic and paralimbic regions that have been implicated in the experience of emotional states and in the encoding of emotional experiences are implicated in remembering mood-congruent information (see Buchanan, 2007, for a review). For example, the subgenual cingulate gyrus is active during both the successful encoding and retrieval of positive information following a happy mood induction, whereas the posteriolateral orbitofrontal cortex is linked to the successful encoding and retrieval of negative information during a sad mood induction (Lewis, Critchley, Smith, & Dolan, 2005). The overlap of the regions recruited during the encoding and mood-congruent retrieval of negative versus positive information may provide support for Bower's (1981) network theory, with the subgenual cingulate gyrus serving as the positive emotion "node" and the posteriolateral orbitofrontal cortex serving as the negative emotion "node" (Lewis et al., 2005).

The amygdala may also play a role in mood-congruent memory: Increased amygdala activity in formerly depressed patients at high risk for relapse is associated with mood-congruent retrieval of negative self-referential information following a sad mood induction (Ramel et al., 2007). Although the reason for this association is not known, one possibility is that the amygdala guides mood-congruent retrieval because, as discussed earlier, it facilitates the search for a personally significant memory (Daselaar et al., 2008) and activates to salient information (Sander et al., 2003). It is likely that individuals at highest risk for relapse are those for whom negative memories are perceived to be most self-relevant and salient.

Although mood congruency is often discussed as a *retrieval* effect, as noted earlier, mood can also influence the types of infor-

mation that are attended and encoded. Indeed, neuroimaging evidence suggests that mood-congruency effects occur during both the encoding phase and the retrieval phase. Encoding emotional information that is mood congruent appears to be less effortful in terms of semantic processing, with mood-congruent information leading to a lesser neural signature of semantic processing (the N400) than mood-incongruent information (Kiefer, Schuch, Schenck, & Fiedler, 2007). ERP and fMRI investigations also have demonstrated that depressed individuals allocate a greater proportion of working memory (associated with increased dorsolateral prefrontal cortex activity) and attentional (associated with lateral orbitofrontal activity) resources to negative information (e.g., Elliott, Rubinsztein, Sahakian, & Dolan, 2002). If mood-congruent information is privy to easier processing and a greater share of cognitive resources, then this might help explain the later mnemonic benefit evident for the retrieval of mood-congruent information.

Episodic Memory and Emotion Regulation

Although mood congruency has been an often replicated effect, mood is sometimes associated with just the opposite effect: Mood-*incongruent* memory occurs when memories opposite in valence to mood are retrieved under induced (e.g., Josephson, Singer, & Salovey, 1996) or natural mood conditions (Parrott & Sabini, 1990). Mood-incongruent memory sometimes occurs after an initial period of mood congruency (e.g., Josephson et al., 1996) and therefore is often ascribed the function of mood regulation or repair (e.g., Isen, 1984). Indeed, emotion or mood regulation is a reported function of autobiographical remembering in everyday life (Bluck, Ale, Habermas, & Rubin, 2005). Such goals can influence episodic retrieval by at least two routes. First, emotion regulation goals can influence which memories are most likely to be recalled in a given context. For example, when individuals in one study were told that they would be playing a game in which aggressive behavior would be rewarded, they preferred to recall angry memories prior to playing that game (Tamir, Mitchell, & Gross, 2008). There is also some evidence to suggest that regulation goals can influence which specific emotional details we remember about particular events (Holland, Tamir, & Kensinger, 2010).

The second way in which emotion regulation goals can influence memory retrieval is by modulating the level of specificity with which a memory is recalled. The construction of autobiographical memories can occur at either a temporally and contextually specific level (e.g., my first day of classes in college) or at a general level that incorporates similar, repeated events (e.g., every time I attended class on Tuesdays; reviewed by Conway & Pleydell-Pearce, 2000). A large body of literature has demonstrated that individuals with a range of affective disorders are more likely to recall these latter general autobiographical events that are repeated over time than those that are specific in time and place (reviewed by Williams et al., 2007). One possible explanation for this so-called overgeneral memory phenomenon is affect regulation (see Williams et al., 2007, for a review). Williams and colleagues (2007) have proposed that overgeneral recall allows for the functional avoidance of specific, negative event-related details (though note that this avoidance may actually be dysfunctional; Phillipot, Baeyens, Douilliez, & Francart, 2004).

Several studies examining the neural correlates of emotion regulation in response to emotional images have established that the down-regulation of negative emotion engages dorsolateral prefrontal, orbitofrontal, and cingulate cortices, which appear to suppress ventral and limbic regions associated with emotional responding, including the amygdala and insula (see Ochsner & Gross, 2008, for a review; see Chapter 16 for discussion of the key regions implicated in emotion regulation). As we discussed earlier, a small amount of work has focused on the effects of regulation on memory encoding. There has also been a limited amount of work examining the relationship between regulation and emotional autobiographical memory retrieval at a neural level. One study found that, in contrast to the more dorsal regions implicated in top-down emotion regulation, being instructed to recall a positive memory following induction into a negative mood (i.e., mood-incongruent recall) led to engagement of ventral regions including ventromedial prefrontal and orbitofrontal cortices, as well as the subgenual cingulate gyrus (Cooney, Joormann, Atlas, Eugène, & Gotlib, 2007).

In contrast to mood-incongruent recall, regulating the emotions associated with a specific past experience by changing the way that event is interpreted is presumably a more effortful task and perhaps as such engages different neural circuitry. Kross, Davidson, Weber, and Ochsner (2009) found that subjective emotion ratings and neural activity depended on the type of regulation strategy employed during the recall of negative autobiographical memories. Both emotion ratings and activity in subgenual anterior cingulate gyrus and medial prefrontal cortex activity were greatest when participants focused on their negative feelings (similar to rumination), intermediate when they performed a strategy analogous to cognitive reappraisal, and lowest when they mentally distanced themselves from the event. This study illustrates that the successful regulation of a negative memory differs from the regulation of other stimuli in its dampening down of the medial prefrontal cortex (associated with self-referential processing). Interestingly, recent work further suggests that the direction of regulation may influence *when* regulation-related neural activity is engaged. Down-regulation via cognitive reappraisal appears to engage medial and lateral PFC and MTL activity as memories are initially being constructed and presumably being appraised as negative, whereas up-regulation engages similar regions as individuals prepare to recall events (i.e., prior to the presentation of a memory cue) and later as they elaborate upon the details of those memories (Holland & Kensinger, 2012). Taken together, this work suggests that the circuitry underlying emotion regulation during memory retrieval, and the time course over which it is engaged, can be dependent on the type of strategy invoked (see Cooney et al., 2007, for a similar discussion).

The Constructive Nature of Memory for Emotions

Up to this point, we have focused on the way that emotion and emotional goals can influence which details are encoded or later brought to mind. The implicit assumption throughout this discussion has been that these memories are fairly accurate representations. As we reviewed earlier, however, the constructive nature of memory leaves it susceptible to biases and distortions; these errors can be influenced by our emotional state or goals at encoding or retrieval. For example, although it often feels as though we will never forget the emotions associated with episodic events, a plethora of research has demonstrated that emotional details are subject to the same types of constructive processes (and therefore errors) as other episodic details (reviewed by Levine, Safer, & Lench, 2006). In particular, the emotions we remember feeling are often related more strongly to how we predicted we would feel before an event (Mitchell, Thompson, Peterson, & Cronk, 1997) and how we feel at the time of recall (Levine, 1997) than to how we reported feeling as the event was occurring. For example, the "rosy view" phenomenon has been used to describe the observation that individuals who expect an event like a vacation to be positive recall it that way, even if they actually experienced it as a mix of both positive and negative emotions (Mitchell et al., 1997). The same is true for events that we expect to be negative, such as Mondays: Even though individuals tend to experience these events as fairly neutral, they remember them as being negative (Areni & Burger, 2008). Cognitive reappraisal has also been associated with biases in memory for emotions. Indi-

viduals who reappraised their initial negative responses to the outcome of an election remembered feeling less negative about the election than those who had not reappraised their response (Levine, 1997). As we noted previously, older adults, a group that demonstrates enhanced emotion regulation and a positivity bias in attention and memory, also tend to remember the past as more positive than they experienced it (reviewed by Mather, 2006).

From a behavioral standpoint, the reconstructive nature of memory for emotions might stem from the same mechanisms that underlie the reconstructive nature of memory for other details. It would be inefficient to have a memory system that recorded and stored every detail that we encounter on a moment-by-moment basis. Perhaps for this reason, specific perceptual and conceptual details are forgotten relatively quickly after an episode ends (reviewed by Robinson & Clore, 2002) and are reconstructed based on heuristics. This heuristic information might include the peak and end moments of affective intensity during an episode (e.g., Frederickson, 2000). Alternatively, or in addition to the peak and end heuristic, our reconstructions can be guided by contextual information (e.g., remembering what we were thinking as an event occurred) or semantic information (e.g., knowing that vacations are usually positive; Robinson & Clore, 2002).

Just as with other types of details, the construction of emotional details might be quite functional in that the process allows for the updating of memory (Levine et al., 2006). Given that a key function of episodic memory construction is to create future simulations that will guide future behavior (Schacter & Addis, 2008), it is critical to understand the neural mechanisms that underlie the reconstruction of past emotions. Much of the evidence in this domain comes from neuropsychological patients and points to a distinction between memory systems for event details versus emotional details (reviewed by Conway & Pleydell-Pearce, 2000). Amnesics with medial temporal lobe damage demonstrate impaired memory for narrative details but spared memory for affective impressions of a person (Johnson, Kim, & Risse, 1985). The reverse can also be true for individuals with temporary or permanent cortical right-hemisphere lesions: These individuals report normal event-related details, but fail to report emotional details (see Conway & Pleydell-Pearce, 2000).

More recent research has honed in on the hippocampus, amygdala, and nearby cortical areas as potential supporters of the retrieval of negative emotional autobiographical memories (Buchanan, Tranel, & Adolphs, 2006). When damage occurs to the right-lateralized anteromedial temporal lobe (but not to the hippocampus alone), there is a decrease in the number of negative details and the reported emotional intensity associated with negative memories (Buchanan et al., 2006). These patient findings are in line with the evidence reviewed earlier that the amygdala is recruited during emotional memory retrieval and is associated with intensity during retrieval (Daselaar et al., 2008; Greenberg et al., 2005). Given that the retrieval of event-related details can occur without affective details (Conway & Pleydell-Pearce, 2000), it seems that the neural correlates of the reconstruction of event-related and emotional details may also be dissociable.

Flashbulb Memory

To this point, we have reviewed evidence that emotional events and emotional details are reconstructed at retrieval and therefore are susceptible to the same types of errors and biases as neutral information. There exists a special category of highly emotional, personally significant, and surprising events, termed "flashbulb memories" by Brown and Kulik (1977). Initially, it was believed that flashbulb memories were remembered more accurately (i.e., with fewer reconstructive errors) than other events. Brown and Kulik's (1977) seminal paper examined individuals' memories for a number of negative public events, the most cited being President John F. Kennedy's

assassination. The authors reported that the personally significant and surprising nature of the events led to memories that were vivid and highly detailed. The nature of the details was such that both event-related and seemingly unimportant personal context details (e.g., who I was with when I learned the news) were reported. Brown and Kulik (1977) hypothesized that the surprising and personally relevant nature of flashbulb events signals biological relevance to individuals, setting off a cascade of neural activation that results in a vivid snapshot of the details – even those idiosyncratic in nature – on first learning of the event.

Follow-up research confirmed that individuals can in fact form very vivid and detailed memories about flashbulb events (reviewed by Talarico & Rubin, 2003). However, investigations into the accuracy and consistency of these memories over time have revealed that flashbulb memories are subject to the same types of reconstructive errors as other neutral and emotional events. One of the first studies to demonstrate flashbulb memory inconsistencies over time examined individuals' memories for the personal details they experienced when they learned the news of the *Challenger* space shuttle explosion in 1986 (Neisser & Harsch, 1992). Participants' memories were examined shortly after the explosion and again 30 months later; even though participants believed their memories were vivid and accurate, they actually contained a number of distortions. Similar inconsistencies have been shown for people's memories for the outcome of the O. J. Simpson trial (Schmolck, Buffalo, & Squire, 2000) and the September 11 terrorist attacks (Pezdek, 2003).

Several lines of research may shed light on why there are inaccuracies and inconsistencies in even the most emotional of experiences. One line of research concerns what has been termed the emotional memory "tradeoff." Emotion does not enhance memory equally for all types of details. Instead, the details that are central to the emotional aspect of an event often receive a mnemonic benefit that comes at the cost of background or peripheral details (see Levine & Edelstein, 2009, for a review). The memory tradeoff has been illustrated in terms of the types of details – either those directly tied to the event or those tied to personal context – that are remembered most consistently or accurately. Pezdek (2003) queried individuals about the details of the September 11 terrorist attacks (e.g., What time did the first tower fall?) and about the personal details they experienced during the day (e.g., Who were you with when you learned about the attacks?). Those individuals who were located closest to the World Trade Centers on that day demonstrated the most accurate memory for event-related details when compared to participants in California and Hawaii. Despite this mnemonic benefit for the facts of the event, however, the Manhattan sample reported a relative paucity of personal details from the day compared to the more distant samples. These findings can be explained in terms of the tradeoff: The central details for the Manhattan sample were those tied to the event, which potentially had important implications for their own physical safety. The personal details of the day were likely remembered less well because they constituted the less critical, background information (Pezdek, 2003). Interestingly, Brown and Kulik (1977) alluded to this very phenomenon in their seminal paper when they noted that flashbulb memory is far from complete and misses details just as a camera misses information that falls outside of its focus. Therefore, the measured accuracy and consistency of flashbulb memories may depend on what information is being remembered.

The second factor that can influence the memory of flashbulb events is the perceived valence of the event. Most flashbulb memory studies have followed highly negative public events, like natural disasters, terrorist attacks, and the deaths of public figures. One way to examine how the valence of an event influences its later retrieval is to make use of events whose outcome can be perceived as either negative or positive,

such as a sporting event (Kensinger & Schacter, 2006) or a political election (Holland & Kensinger, 2012; Levine, 1997). These studies generally converge on the finding that negative emotion appears to confer a particular mnemonic benefit for the memory of that event's details above and beyond the mnemonic advantage evident when an event is viewed as positive. This valence-dependent difference in memory might be due to the mode of information processing that is induced by negative and positive emotions. Negative emotion is associated with detailed, item-specific processing that enhances attention to the details that might have led to the negative emotion. In contrast, positive emotion is associated with a greater reliance on heuristics and relational processing (reviewed by Kensinger, 2009), which may increase the number of reconstructive errors that are later made during retrieval.

The Confidence of Emotional Memories

The definition of episodic memory requires that an event be ascribed to one's personal past, and the hallmark of an episodic memory is the feeling of reexperience that accompanies the reconstruction of some of the features of the past event (Tulving, 1972). A number of studies have suggested that this feeling of reexperience may be particularly pronounced when information is emotional. People are more likely to claim that they vividly remember emotional experiences (e.g., Ochsner, 2000; Sharot et al., 2004), and as just discussed in relation to flashbulb memories, people often feel confident in their recollections of emotional events.

There has been much discussion as to whether these subjective reports reflect an accurate interpretation of the high fidelity with which an emotional event has been recorded or whether emotion may simply bias a person to believe that a vivid memory has been maintained (see Kensinger, 2009; Mather, 2007; Sharot et al., 2004). The findings with regard to the amygdala's role in emotional memory have been similarly mixed; some studies have revealed that amygdala activity during encoding or retrieval corresponds with the accuracy of a memory (e.g., Smith et al., 2006), whereas other studies have shown that its activity does not correspond with the ability to remember episodic detail (e.g., Sharot et al., 2004).

A recent neuroimaging study may help shed light on the reason for these conflicting findings. In this study (Kensinger, Addis, & Atapattu, 2011), participants viewed emotional objects and were later asked to report the vividness of their memory for the object, as well as to recall a number of contextual details associated with the object's presentation. The results revealed that amygdala activity corresponded with a parametric increase in the subjective vividness of a memory, but that its engagement only enabled individuals to encode the visual details of the object that had been presented, and not any other episodic details. These findings suggest that amygdala engagement corresponds with memory for only a select set of episodic details, but that it may be those details that people use to gauge the vividness of a memory. In other words, an emotional memory may be vivid not because lots of different details are remembered, but because a small set of details are remembered very well.

Conclusion

In this chapter, we reviewed evidence that the emotional content of information influences – and selectively enhances – each phase of episodic memory: encoding, consolidation, and retrieval. Our present emotional states and emotional goals can further modulate which information we are likely to encode or retrieve. Critically, neuroimaging evidence has elucidated that memory for emotional information relies on many of the same medial temporal lobe and prefrontal cortex structures as memory for neutral information, but that this memory network receives additional modulation from structures known to be associated with emotional processing.

Now that a solid foundation of neuroimaging research on emotional memory is being built, it appears that a particularly ripe area for future work will be examining not only how emotion affects each phase of memory but also how emotion influences the interaction among the different phases of memory and how our attempts to control or change those emotions might influence what is encoded or retrieved.

Outstanding Questions and Future Directions

• Through what mechanisms do different motivational states influence the encoding and retrieval of memories? Motivational states appear to influence attentional resources (e.g., narrowing or broadening attention) when information is being encoded and may modulate the accessibility of particular event details at retrieval. On a neural level, these changes are likely associated with interactions between the prefrontal cortex and medial temporal lobe. More work is needed to delineate how the connections between these regions may be affected by different motivational states, particularly those that are defined beyond the dimension of valence (e.g., discrete emotions). It has been suggested that specific, discrete emotions (i.e., sadness, happiness, anger, fear) are associated with unique motivational states such as approach and avoidance (reviewed by Levine & Edelstein, 2009), and so it is possible that these states might modulate the memory network in different ways. One study that contrasted the recall of negative and positive events demonstrated dissociable contributions of the prefrontal cortex, temporal lobe, and retrosplenial cortex to each (Piefke, Weiss, Ziller, Markowitsch, & Fink, 2003), but it is unclear whether effects like these are due to the emotional valence of the events or to the different motivations associated with each valence (e.g., approach vs. avoidance motivation for positive and negative valence, respectively). Examining events associated with different discrete emotions might further disentangle the contributions of valence and motivational goals on memory.

- How do our attempts to regulate emotion influence what is encoded or retrieved? Prior research has demonstrated the effects of emotional valence and intensity on memory encoding and retrieval, but investigations into how attempts to change such valence or intensity affect memory are in their infancy. Only a small subset of emotion regulation strategies in the context of memory retrieval has been examined so far, and it remains to be seen which neural structures are engaged by strategies that focus on the down-regulation of positive information, up-regulation of negative information, or suppression at retrieval. It is likely that emotion regulation influences both the content of an experience that is encoded and retrieved and the quality (e.g., vividness, accuracy) of that information. Understanding the effects of emotion regulation on memory may shed light on affective disorders associated with emotion dysregulation.
- How do encoding, consolidation, and retrieval processes interact to influence the retention of emotional experiences? Although most research has focused on each of these stages in isolation, there are likely to be many interactions among the phases. The details that are attended during encoding or the mood elicited during the initial experience of an event is likely to influence the dimensions of an event that become consolidated in memory or the efficacy with which retrieval processes guide the recovery of information. Now that we have a basic understanding of the way that emotional content or emotional state can modulate each individual phase of memory, future research will do well to consider each phase of memory in the context of the others.
- How is memory affected when the motivational goals present during encoding do

not match those invoked during retrieval? Examinations of how motivational goals influence memory have so far focused on goals present at either encoding or retrieval. However, motivational goals likely exist at both time points. As yet, it is unclear how goals and their associated neural activity at encoding *and* retrieval might interact. Erk et al. (2010) suggested that regulating emotional responses at encoding led individuals to "cognitivize" emotional images and subsequently rely on more prefrontal areas during retrieval when compared to the recognition of unregulated images. It remains to be seen what would happen if additional regulatory goals were invoked at retrieval or if incongruent goals were in place at each time (e.g., down-regulating a negative emotion at encoding but up-regulating a negative emotion at retrieval). Future research should investigate how the goals present at both encoding and retrieval might interact and influence the content and quality of the information retrieved, particularly if those goals are incongruent with one another.

Acknowledgments

Preparation of this chapter was supported by the National Institutes of Health (grant MH080833 to E. A. K.), the Searle Scholars Program (to E. A. K.), and a National Defense Science and Engineering Graduate Fellowship (to A. C. H.). We thank Donna Addis, Angela Gutchess, Brendan Murray, Jessica Payne, Christina Leclerc, Katherine Mickley Steinmetz, Maya Tamir, and Jill Waring for helpful discussion of the issues reviewed in this chapter.

References

Amaral, D., Price, J., Pitkanen, A., & Carmichael, S. (1992). The amygdala: Neurobiological aspects of emotion, memory, and mental dysfunction. In J. P. Aggleton (Ed.), *The amygdala: Neurobiological aspects of emotion, mem-*

ory, and mental dysfunction (pp. 1–66). New York: Wiley-Liss.

Areni, C., & Burger, M. (2008). Memories of "bad" days are more biased than memories of "good" days: Past Saturdays vary, but past Mondays are always blue. *Journal of Applied Social Psychology, 38,* 1395–1415.

Bartlett, F. C. (1932). Remembering: A study in experimental and social psychology Cambridge: Cambridge University Press.

Bluck, S., Alea, N., Habermas, T., & D. C. Rubin. (2005). A tale of three functions: The self-reported uses of autobiographical memory. *Social Cognition, 23,* 91–117.

Bower, G. H. (1981). Mood and memory, *American Psychologist, 36,* 129–48.

Brainerd, C.J., Stein, L.M., Silveira, R.A., Rohenkohl, G., & Reyna, V. F. (2008). Does negative emotion cause false memories?. *Psychological Science, 19,* 919–25.

Brown, R., & Kulik, J. (1977). Flashbulb memories. *Cognition, 5,* 73–99.

Buchanan, T.W. (2007). Retrieval of emotional memories. *Psychonomic Bulletin, 133,* 761–79.

Buchanan, T. W., Tranel, D., & Adolphs, R. (2006). Memories for emotional autobiographical events following unilateral damage to medial temporal lobe. *Brain, 129,* 115–27.

Cabeza, R., & St. Jacques, P. (2007). Functional neuroimaging of autobiographical memory. *Trends in Cognitive Sciences, 11,* 219–27.

Conway, M. A., & Pleydell-Pearce, C.W. (2000). The construction of autobiographical memories in the self-memory system. *Psychological Review, 107,* 261–88.

Cooney, R. E., Joormann, J., Atlas, L. Y., Eugène, F., & Gotlib, I. H. (2007). Remembering the good times: Neural correlates of affect regulation. *Neuroreport, 18,* 1771–74.

Daselaar, S. M., Rice, H. J., Greenberg, D. L., Cabeza, R., LaBar, K. S., & Rubin, D. C. (2008). The spatiotemporal dynamics of autobiographical memory: Neural correlates of recall, emotional intensity, and reliving. *Cerebral Cortex, 18*(1), 217–29.

Dillon, D. G., Ritchey, M., Johnson, B. D., & LaBar, K. S. (2007). Dissociable effects of conscious emotion regulation strategies on explicit and implicit memory. *Emotion, 7,* 354–65.

Dolan, R. J., Lane, R., Chua, P., & Fletcher, P. (2000). Dissociable temporal lobe activations during emotional episodic memory retrieval. *Neuroimage, 11,* 203–9.

Dolcos, F., LaBar, K. S., & Cabeza, R. (2004). Interaction between the amygdala and the medial temporal lobe memory system predicts better memory for emotional events. *Neuron, 42*(5), 855–63.

Dolcos, F., LaBar, K. S., & Cabeza, R. (2005). Remembering one year later: Role of the amygdala and the medial temporal lobe memory system in retrieving emotional memories. *Proceedings of the National Academy of Sciences, 102,* 2626–31.

Elliott, R., Rubinsztein, J. S., Sahakian, B. J., & Dolan, R. J. (2002). The neural basis of mood-congruent processing biases in depression. *Archives of General Psychiatry, 59,* 597–604.

Erk, S, von Kalckreuth, A., & Walter, H. (2010). Neural long-term effects of emotion regulation on episodic memory processes. *Neuropsychologia, 48,* 989–96.

Fredrickson, B. L. (2000). Extracting meaning from past affective experiences: The importance of peaks, ends, and specific emotions. *Cognition and Emotion: Special Issue: Emotion, Cognition, and Decision Making, 14*(4), 577–606.

Gallo, D. A., Foster, K. T. & Johnson, E. L. (2009). Elevated false recollection of emotional pictures in young and older adults. *Psychology and Aging, 24,* 981–88.

Goldin, P. R., McRae, K., Ramel, W., & Gross, J. J. (2008). The neural bases of emotion regulation: Reappraisal and suppression of negative emotion. *Biological Psychiatry, 63,* 577–86.

Greenberg, D. L., Rice, H. J., Cooper, J. J., Cabeza, R., Rubin, D. C., & LaBar, K. S. (2005). Coactivation of the amygdala, hippocampus, and inferior frontal gyrus during autobiographical memory retrieval. *Neuropsychologia, 43,* 659–74.

Gross, J. (1998). The emerging field of emotion regulation: An integrative review. *Review of General Psychology, 2,* 271–99.

Hayes, J. P., Morey, R. A., Petty, C. M., Seth, S., Smoski, M. J., McCarthy, G., & LaBar, K. S. (2010). Staying cool when things get hot: Emotion regulation modulates neural mechanisms of memory encoding. *Frontiers in Human Neuroscience, 4,* 1–10.

Hofstetter, C., Achaibou, A., & Vuilleumier, P. (2012). Reactivation of visual cortex during memory retrieval: Content specificity and emotional modulation. *Neuroimage, 60,* 1734–45. Holland, A. C., & Kensinger, E. A. (2012). The neural correlates of cognitive reappraisal during emotional autobiographical memory recall. *Journal of Cognitive Neuroscience.* doi:10.1162/jocn_a_00289

Holland, A. C., & Kensinger, E.A. (2012). Younger, middle-aged, and older adults' memories for the 2008 U.S. Presidential Election. *Journal of Applied Research in Memory and Cognition.* doi.org/10.1016/j.jarmac.2012.06.001

Holland, A. C., Tamir, M., & Kensinger, E. A. (2010). The effect of regulation goals on emotional event specific knowledge. *Memory, 18,* 504–18.

Isen, A. M. (1984). Toward understanding the role of affect in cognition. In R. S. Wyer & T. K. Srull (Eds.), *Handbook of social cognition* (pp. 179–236). Hillsdale, NJ: Erlbaum.

Johnson, M. K., Kim, J. K., & Risse, G. (1985). Do alcoholic Korsakoff's syndrome patients acquire affective reactions? *Journal of Experimental Psychology: Learning, Memory, and Cognition, 11*(1), 22–36.

Josephson, B. R., Singer, J. A., & Salovey, P. (1996). Mood regulation and memory: Repairing sad moods with happy memories. *Cognition and Emotion, 10,* 437–44.

Kapucu, A., Rotello, C. M., Ready, R. E., & Seidl, K. N. (2009). Response bias in "remembering" emotional stimuli: A new perspective on age differences. *Journal of Experimental Psychology: Learning, Memory, and Cognition, 34,* 703–11.

Kensinger, E. A. (2009). Remembering the details: Effects of emotion. *Emotion Review, 1,* 99–113.

Kensinger, E. A., Addis, D. R., & Atapattu, R. (2011). Amygdala activity at encoding corresponds with memory vividness and with memory for select episodic details. *Neuropsychologia, 49,* 663–73.

Kensinger, E. A., & Corkin, S. (2004). Two routes to emotional memory: Distinct neural processes for valence and arousal. *Proceedings of the National Academy of Sciences, 101,* 3310–15.

Kensinger, E. A., & Leclerc, C. M. (2009). Age-related changes in the neural mechanisms supporting emotion processing and emotional memory. *European Journal of Cognitive Psychology, 21*(2–3), 192–215.

Kensinger, E. A., & Schacter, D. L. (2006). When the Red Sox shocked the Yankees: Comparing negative and positive memories. *Psychonomic Bulletin and Review, 13,* 757–63.

Kensinger, E. A., & Schacter, D. L. (2007). Remembering the specific visual details of presented objects: Neuroimaging evidence for

effects of emotion. *Neuropsychologia, 45,* 2951–62.

Kern, R. P., Libkuman, T. M., Otani, H., & Holmes, K. (2005). Emotional stimuli, divided attention, and memory. *Emotion, 5,* 408–17.

Kiefer, M., Schuch, S., Schenck, W., & Fiedler, K. (2007). Mood states modulate activity in semantic brain areas during emotional word encoding. *Cerebral Cortex, 17,* 1516–30.

Kross, E., Davidson, M., Weber, J., & Ochsner, K. (2009). Coping with emotions past: The neural bases of regulating affect associated with negative autobiographical memories. *Biological Psychiatry, 65,* 361–66.

LaBar, K. S., & Cabeza, R. (2006). Cognitive neuroscience of emotional memory. *Nature Reviews Neuroscience, 7*(1), 54–64.

LaBar, K. S., & Phelps, E. A. (1998). Arousal-mediated memory consolidation: Role of the medial temporal lobe in humans. *Psychological Science, 9,* 490–93.

Leclerc, C. M., & Kensinger, E. A. (2008). Effects of age on detection of emotional information. *Psychology and Aging, 23,* 209–15.

Lench, H. C., & Levine, L. J. (2010). Motivational biases in memory for emotions. *Cognition and Emotion, 24,* 401–18.

Levine, L. J. (1997). Reconstructing memory for emotions. *Journal of Experimental Psychology: General, 126,* 165–77.

Levine, L. J., & Edelstein, R. S. (2009). Emotion and memory narrowing: A review and goal-relevance approach. *Cognition and Emotion, 23*(5), 833–75.

Levine, L. J., Safer, M. A., & Lench, H. C. (2006). Remembering and misremembering emotions. In L. J. Sanna & E. C. Chang (Eds.), *Judgments over time: The interplay of thoughts, feelings, and behaviors* (pp. 271–90). New York: Oxford University Press.

Lewis, P. A., & Critchley, H. D. (2003). Mood-dependent memory. *Trends in Cognitive Sciences, 7,* 431–33.

Lewis, P. A., Critchley, H. D., Smith, A. P., & Dolan, R. J. (2005). Brain mechanisms for mood congruent memory facilitation. *NeuroImage, 25,* 1214–23.

MacKay, D. G., Shafto, M., Taylor, J. K., Marian, D. E., Abrams, L., & Dyer, J. R. (2004). Relations between emotion, memory, and attention: Evidence from taboo Stroop, lexical decision, and immediate memory tasks. *Memory and Cognition, 32,* 474–88.

Maratos, E. J., Dolan, R. J., Morris, J. S., Henson, R. N., & Rugg, M. D. (2001). Neural activity associated with episodic memory for emotional context. *Neuropsychologia*, 39, 910–20.

Mather, M. (2006). Why memories may become more positive as people age. In B. Uttl, N. Ohta, & A. L. Siegenthaler (Eds.), *Memory and emotion: Interdisciplinary perspectives* (pp. 135–59). Oxford: Blackwell.

Mather, M. (2007). Emotional arousal and memory binding: An object-based framework. *Perspectives on Psychological Science*, 2, 33–52.

Mathews, A., & MacLeod, C. (2005). Cognitive vulnerability to emotional disorders. *Annual Review of Clinical Psychology*, 1, 167–95.

Matthews, G., & Margetts, I. (1991). Self-report arousal and divided attention: A study of performance operating characteristics. *Human Performance*, 4, 107–25.

McGaugh, J. L. (2004). The amygdala modulates the consolidation of memories of emotionally arousing experiences. *Annual Review of Neuroscience*, 27, 1–28.

Mickley Steinmetz, K. R., & Kensinger, E. A. (2009). The effects of valence and arousal on the neural activity leading to subsequent memory. *Psychophysiology*, 46, 1190–99.

Mitchell, T. R., Thompson, L., Peterson, E., & Cronk, R. (1997). Temporal adjustments in the evaluation of events: The "rosy view." *Journal of Experimental Social Psychology*, 33(4), 421–48.

Murty, V. P., Ritchey, M., Adcock, R. A., & LaBar, K. S. (2010). fMRI studies of successful emotional memory encoding: A quantitative meta-analysis. *Neuropsychologia*, 48, 3459–69.

Nadel, L., & Moscovitch, M. (1997). Memory consolidation, retrograde amnesia and the hippocampal complex. *Current Opinion in Neurobiology*, 7(2), 217–27.

Nashiro, K., Sakaki, M., & Mather, M. (2012). Age differences in brain activity during emotion processing: Reflections of age-related decline or increased emotion regulation? *Gerontology*, 58, 156–63.

Neisser, U., & Harsch, N. (1992). Phantom flashbulbs: False recollections of hearing the news about Challenger. In E. Winograd & U. Neisser (Eds.), *Affect and accuracy in recall: Studies of 'flashbulb' memories* (pp. 9–31). New York: Cambridge University Press.

Ochsner, K. N. (2000). Are affective events richly "remembered" or simply familiar? The experience and process of recognizing feelings past. *Journal of Experimental Psychology: General*, 129, 242–61.

Ochsner, K. N., Bunge, S. A., Gross, J. J., & Gabrieli, J. D. (2002). Rethinking feelings: An FMRI study of the cognitive regulation of emotion. *Journal of Cognitive Neuroscience*, 14, 1215–29.

Ochsner, K., & Gross, J. J. (2008). Cognitive emotion regulation: Insights from social cognitive and affective neuroscience. *Current Directions in Psychological Science*, 17, 153–58.

Paller, K. A., & Wagner, A. D. (2002). Observing the transformation of experience into memory. *Trends in Cognitive Sciences*, 6(2), 93–102.

Parrott, W. G., & Sabini, J. (1990). Mood and memory under natural conditions: Evidence for mood incongruent recall. *Journal of Personality and Social Psychology*, 59, 321–36.

Payne, J. D., & Kensinger, E. A. (2011). Sleep leads to changes in the emotional memory trace: Evidence from fMRI. *Journal of Cognitive Neuroscience*, 23, 1285–97.

Payne, J. D., Swanberg, K., Stickgold, R., & Kensinger, E. A. (2008). Sleep preferentially enhances memory for emotional components of scenes. *Psychological Science*, 19, 781–88.

Pezdek, K. (2003). Event memory and autobiographical memory for the events of September 11, 2001. *Applied Cognitive Psychology*, 17, 1033–45.

Philippot, P., Baeyens, C., Douilliez, C., & Francart, B. (2004). Cognitive regulation of emotion: Application to clinical disorders. In P. Philippot & R. S. Feldman (Eds.), *The regulation of emotion* (pp. 71–98). Mahwah, NJ: Erlbaum.

Piefke, M., Weiss, P. H., Zilles, K., Markowitsch, H. J., & Fink, G. R. (2003). Differential remoteness and emotional tone modulate the neural correlates of autobiographical memory. *Brain*, 126, 650–68.

Pottage, C. L., & Schaefer, A. (2012). Visual attention and emotional memory: Recall of aversive pictures is partially mediated by concurrent task performance. *Emotion*, 12, 33–38.

Ramel, W., Goldin, P. R., Eyler, L. T., Brown, G. G., Gotlib, I. H., & McQuaid, J. R. (2007). Amygdala reactivity and mood-congruent memory in individuals at risk for depressive relapse. *Biological Psychiatry*, 61, 231–39.

Richards, J. M., & Gross, J. J. (1999). Composure at any cost? The cognitive consequences of emotion suppression. *Personality and Social Psychology Bulletin*, 25, 1033–44.

Robbins, T. W., & Everitt, B. J. (1996). Neurobehavioural mechanisms of reward and motivation. *Current Opinion in Neurobiology*, 6, 228–36.

Robinson, M. D., & Clore, G. L. (2002). Belief and feeling: Evidence for an accessibility model of emotional self-report. *Psychological Bulletin*, 128, 934–60.

Rubin, D. C., & Kozin, M. (1984). Vivid memories. *Cognition*, 16(1), 81–95.

Rubin, D. C., Schrauf, R. W., & Greenberg, D. L. (2003). Belief and recollection of autobiographical memories. *Memory and Cognition*, 31, 887–901.

Russell, J. A. (1980). A circumplex model of affect. *Journal of Personality and social Psychology*, 39, 1161–78.

Rusting, C. L. (1998). Personality, mood, and cognitive processing of emotional information: Three conceptual frameworks. *Psychological Bulletin*, 124, 165–96.

Sander, D., Grafman, J., & Zalla, T. (2003). The human amygdala: An evolved system for relevance detection. *Reviews in the Neurosciences*, 14, 303–16.

Schacter, D. L., & Addis, D. R. (2008). The cognitive neuroscience of constructive memory: Remembering the past and imagining the future. In J. Driver, P. Haggard, & T. Shallice (Eds.), *Mental processes in the human brain* (pp. 27–47). Oxford: Oxford University Press.

Schmolck, H., Buffalo, E. A., & Squire, L. R. (2000). Memory distortions develop over time: Recollections of the O.J. Simpson trial verdict after 15 and 32 months. *Psychological Science*, 11, 39–45.

Sergerie, K., Lepage, M., & Armony, J. L. (2006). A process-specific functional dissociation of the amygdala in emotional memory. *Journal of Cognitive Neuroscience*, 18, 1359–67.

Sharot, T., Delgado, M. R., & Phelps, E. A. (2004). How emotion enhances the feeling of remembering. *Nature Neuroscience*, 12, 1376–80.

Sharot, T., & Yonelinas, A. P. (2008). Differential time-dependent effects of emotion on the recollective experience and memory for contextual information. *Cognition*, 106, 538–47.

Smith, A. P., Stephan, K. E., Rugg, M. D., & Dolan, R. J. (2006). Task and content modulate amygdala-hippocampal connectivity in emotional retrieval. *Neuron*, 49, 631–38.

Squire, L. R., & Zola, S. M. (1998). Episodic memory, semantic memory, and amnesia. *Hippocampus*, 8, 205–11.

Sterpenich, V., Albouy, G., Darsaud, A., Schmidt, C., Vandewalle, G., et al. (2009). Sleep promotes the neural reorganization of remote emotional memory. *Journal of Neuroscience*, 29, 5143–52.

Svoboda, E., McKinnon, M. C., & Levine, B. (2006). The functional neuroanatomy of autobiographical memory: A meta-analysis. *Neuropsychologia*, 44(12), 2189–2208.

Symons, C. S., & Johnson, B. T. (1997). The self-reference effect in memory: A meta-analysis. *Psychological Bulletin*, 121(3), 371–94.

Tabert, M. H., Borod, J. C., Tang, C. Y., Lange, G., Wei, T. C., Johnson, R., et al. (2001). Differential amygdala activation during emotional decision and recognition memory tasks using unpleasant words: An fMRI study. *Neuropsychologia*, 39, 556–73.

Talarico, J. M., & Rubin, D. C. (2003). Confidence, not consistency, characterizes flashbulb memories. *Psychological Science*, 14, 455–61.

Talmi, D., Anderson, A. K., Riggs, L., Caplan, J. B., & Moscovitch, M. (2008). Immediate memory consequences of the effect of emotion on attention to pictures. *Learning & Memory*, 15, 172–82.

Talmi, D., Luk, T. C. B., McGarry, L., & Moscovitch, M. (2007). Are emotional pictures remembered better just because they are semantically related and relatively distinct? *Journal of Memory and Language*, 56, 555–74.

Tamir, M., Mitchell, C., & Gross, J. J. (2008). Hedonic and instrumental motives in anger regulation. *Psychological Science*, 19, 324–28.

Tulving, E. (1972). Episodic and semantic memory. In E. Tulving & W. Donaldson (Eds.), *Organization of memory* (pp. 381–403). New York: Academic Press.

Wagner, U., Hallschmid, M., Rasch, B., & Born, J. (2006). Brief sleep after learning keeps emotional memories alive for years. *Biological Psychiatry*, 60, 788–90.

Walker, M. P., & Stickgold, R. (2006). Sleep, memory, and plasticity. *Annual Review of Psychology*, 57, 139–66.

Whalen, P. J., Kagen, J., Cook, R. G., Davis, F. C., Hackjin, K., et al. (2004). Human amygdala responsivity to masked fearful eye whites. *Science*, 306, 2061.

Whittlesea, B. W. A. (1993). Illusions of familiarity. *Journal of Experimental Psychology: Learning, Memory, and Cognition*, 19, 1235–53.

Williams, J. M. G., Barnhofer, T., Crane, C., Hermans, D., Raes, F., et al. (2007). Autobiographical memory specificity and emotional disorder. *Psychological Bulletin*, 133, 122–48.

Section VI

SOCIAL EMOTIONS

CHAPTER 21

Moral Emotions

Roland Zahn, Ricardo de Oliveira-Souza, & Jorge Moll

Moral feelings motivate humans to act on other people's needs (e.g. "giving money to a beggar") or on moral values (e.g. "generosity," "honesty"), even in the absence of negative consequences for not doing so, such as being punished by law enforcement systems. The importance of moral feelings has been highlighted by philosophers of the 18th-century Scottish enlightenment (Bishop, 1996): most prominently by Francis Hutcheson, Adam Smith, and David Hume. Adam Smith stated that the chief "moral sentiment" is "sympathy" (Lamb, 1974). The German philosopher Immanuel Kant opposed the idea that moral sentiments could be used as a principle of deciding between actions that are morally right and wrong. Nevertheless, he stressed the importance of moral feelings as motivational forces for moral behavior. In contrast to the Scottish school of philosophy, he highlighted "respect for the moral law" [Achtung vor dem Moralgesetz] as the only true "moral" motive (Kant, 1786, p. 17). This "respect" was, however, not a feeling generated from sensory experience, but was directly generated by the internalized

moral rules (Kant, 1786). This distinction was important, because feelings or sentiments as generated from the senses cannot have moral significance according to Kant, because they are not generated by free will – a prerequisite of moral motivation (pp. 15–17).

As recognized by philosophers early on, there is a close relationship between causal agency (i.e., willful action) and moral evaluation (Hume, 1777). If people have control over their actions and intentionally violate moral rules or act against other people's needs, we are more likely to blame them than when this is not the case. Equally, the quality of moral feelings changes depending on whether we direct blame toward ourselves (e.g., guilt, shame) or others (e.g., indignation). The same is true of praise for our own (e.g., pride) and other people's actions: gratitude when being the recipient and awe when being the observer. Sympathy (pity, compassion) is felt when observing other people's suffering and is usually stronger for people whom we perceive as victims rather than causal agents of their miserable situation. Some feelings, such as contempt, hate, disgust, and anger, can be directed both toward ourselves and others in a moral context.

Before we can decompose these complex moral feelings into cognitive components and investigate their neuroanatomical basis, we need a definition of what is a feeling and, more specifically, what is a moral feeling. We suggest a working definition here rather than presenting a definite answer, because there is too little direct evidence to settle disputes about the validity of different definitions of these terms. Here, we use the term "feelings" for complex subjective emotional experiences that people would label as "feelings" themselves. Thus the term "feelings" may refer to quite variable experiences. We use the term "sentiment" as synonymous with "feeling" and avoid using the term "emotion" as much as we can, because it often has the connotation of specific psychological or neuroanatomical models of feelings. We use the terms "moral feelings" and "sentiments" for those subjective experiences that enable us to be motivated by other people's needs (i.e., interpersonal altruism) or sociocultural norms (Moll, De Oliveira-Souza, & Zahn, 2008).

Moral motivations are defined here as consisting of (1) the motivational/emotional state/force (e.g., "anxiety") and (2) the goal with which this motivational state is associated ("soothing a child"). This definition highlights an important second ingredient for moral motivation: knowing about the needs of others and about sociocultural norms (i.e., social knowledge) that serve as the goals of moral actions. Social knowledge allows us not only to interpret people's actions and infer their needs but also to store more general social information such as action rules (e.g., "greeting a colleague at work") and social concepts describing values (e.g., "politeness"). One possibility is that moral feelings are evoked by social knowledge, but are themselves devoid of social knowledge content. Another possibility, which we consider to be more plausible, is that social knowledge is inextricably linked with moral feelings such that a moral

feeling always at least implicitly entails social knowledge (Moll, Zahn, de Oliveira-Souza, Krueger, & Grafman, 2005). One important argument for such an inextricable link is that moral feelings can be distinguished most clearly from each other by complex attributions of causal agency that imply social knowledge, as detailed later. We then briefly touch on evidence that abnormalities in the experience of moral sentiments are important symptoms of specific neuropsychiatric disorders. Subsequently, we review evidence on the neuroanatomical basis of moral sentiments and summarize opposing models of how to explain this evidence. We then address the question whether the brain has developed specialized systems for moral motivations (e.g., helping others or society) as opposed to selfish motivations (e.g., seeking monetary rewards). This chapter closes with a discussion on future directions for this challenging and promising field of research.

Causal Attribution and Moral Sentiments

Feelings are very tightly linked with motivations and volition. Motivation psychology has provided rich evidence that humans are motivated not only by simple conditioned learning of associations between actions or goals with pleasant or unpleasant valence, but that human motivation entails striving for understanding ourselves and the world around us (Weiner, 1992). Human motivation has been shown to critically depend on attributions of causal agency (i.e., the understanding of who carried out a social action and why she or he did so). Different qualities of moral sentiments can be directly linked with different types of causal attributions (Weiner, 1985). Table 21.1 illustrates how different moral sentiments can be distinguished on the basis of causal attributions. In addition to the valence of the feeling (positive or negative), one can distinguish moral sentiments on the basis of different types of agency roles (agent, recipient, observer) and causal attributions

Table 21.1: Association of Causal Attributions, Agency Role, and Valence with Different Qualities of Moral Sentiments

Valence	Agency Role of Subject of Sentiment	Directed toward	Causal Agency Attribution	Requires Observer of Oneself	Moral Sentiment
Positive	Observer	Other	Other had control	No	Awe/admiration
	Recipient	Other	Other had control	No	Gratitude
	Agent	Self	Self had control	No	Pride
Negative	Observer	Other	Other had no control	No	Pity/sympathy/compassion
	Recipient/observer	Other	Other had control	No	Indignation/anger towards others
			Other has character fault	No	Contempt/disgust towards others
	Agent	Self	Self had control	No	Guilt
			Self has character fault	At least imagined	Shame
			Self had no control	Yes	Embarrassment
			Self has character fault	No	Self-contempt/-disgust/-hate

Modified from Moll, Oliveira-Souza, Zahn, & Grafman (2007). Please note that not all the categorizations within this table are evidence-based yet, and that there exist discrepancies within the literature. (For further reading, we recommend Eisenberg, 2000; Fischer & Roseman, 2007; Haidt, 2003; Higgins, 1987; Tangney, Stuewig, & Mashek, 2007; Tracy & Robins, 2006; Tracy, Shariff, & Cheng, 2010; Weiner, 1985.)

of agency (controllable/uncontrollable, stable/unstable; Weiner, 1985). We have incorporated the distinction made by Janoff-Bulman between attributions of causality to a person's stable character fault versus those attributed to a controllable behavior in a specific situation (Janoff-Bulman, 1979). The former has been associated with shame and the latter with guilt (Tangney, Wagner, & Gramzow, 1992). Contempt was found to be associated more strongly with long-term social exclusion of others pointing to stable characterological attributions, whereas moral anger was associated with short-term attacks but long-term reconciliation pointing to behavioral attributions (Fischer & Roseman, 2007). Some feelings have been associated more strongly with internal moral duties (e.g., self-contempt); others are more strongly associated with being lowered in the esteem of others (shame; Higgins, 1987). All moral sentiments, except for pity/sympathy/compassion, seem to be associated with blaming or praising someone.

One important feature of other-directed moral sentiments is that they entail that the subject of the feeling has a different agency role from the person to whom the feeling is directed. For example, feeling pity for someone entails being an observer of someone who is a recipient/victim. In contrast, empathic simulation of others' feelings entails disregarding agency roles (de

Vignemont & Singer, 2006). Empathic simulation may be the prerequisite of pity, because we cannot feel pity for someone whose feelings we cannot read. However, being able to simulate other people's feelings does not necessarily result in feelings of pity; it can also result in withdrawal because of being distressed (Decety & Jackson, 2004). Other-critical (blaming) feelings such as indignation or contempt are important for the enforcement of sociocultural norms in societies, especially when law enforcement is absent or insufficient. It has been hypothesized that punishment of other members of a social group who violate moral rules while risking their own lives was of evolutionary importance in enhancing group survival in a competition between rival small groups (Gintis, Henrich, Bowles, Boyd, & Fehr, 2008). In the next section, we describe the importance of keeping the right balance between self- and other-blaming moral feelings for our mental health.

Psychopathology of Moral Sentiments

Psychopathology describes unusual experiences or behavior that cause suffering to an individual or society. A lack of remorse, guilt, and compassion has been described early on as a core feature of people with "moral insanity," as it was then called (Augstein, 1996; Cleckley, 1976). More recently, this disorder has been labeled as "psychopathy" and can be reliably assessed using psychometric scales that measure callousness as one important component (Hare, 2003). On the contrary, an exaggeration of guilt (overgeneralization of guilt to inappropriate contexts) and other types of self-blaming feelings are frequently observed in people with major depression (Berrios et al., 1992; O'Connor, Berry, Weiss, & Gilbert, 2002). Increased shame-proneness has been associated with depressive symptoms in people with no clinical diagnosis of depression (Tangney et al., 1992), but was not associated with the severity of depression in people with a clinical diagnosis of major depression in which abnor-

mal forms of guilt seem to be more prominent (Alexander, Brewin, Vearnals, Wolff, & Leff, 1999). Shame-proneness was found to be largely increased in people with emotionally unstable ("borderline") personality disorder (Rusch et al., 2007). Clinical descriptions of people with manic episodes as part of a bipolar disorder report increases in pride and anger or indignation. However, people with manic episodes may develop quite different types of behaviors, probably depending on their overall personality. For example, we observed a patient who gave all her money away to people in need during her manic phase, whereas others would spend it on shopping for themselves.

There is a great need for further experimental studies probing proneness to specific moral sentiments in different psychiatric disorders. Experimental investigations of disturbances of specific moral sentiments in affective disorders are scarce in comparison with those investigating disturbances of "basic" emotions (Elliott, Zahn, Deakin, & Anderson, 2010). Impairments of specific moral sentiments, however, are more likely to account for pathogenetic mechanisms specific to one affective disorder (e.g., major depression; Zahn, 2009) compared with others (e.g., panic disorder). The next section describes abnormalities in moral sentiments associated with structural brain lesions.

Neuroanatomical Basis of Moral Sentiments

Evidence from Patients with Brain Lesions

In 1888, Leonore Welt reviewed a series of her own as well as published cases with brain lesions, including the now famous one of Phineas Gage (Damasio, Grabowski, Frank, Galaburda, & Damasio, 1994), and concluded that the orbitofrontal cortex, especially its right medial aspect, was the most consistently affected region associated with changes in character while leaving general intelligence intact. The descriptions of character changes were mostly related to social behavior such as talking about intimate matters with strangers, or exhibiting jocular childish and aggressive behavior. In the 1980s, with the advent of computed tomography, renewed interest in linking specific brain lesions in humans with changes in social behavior was sparked by Eslinger and Damasio's description of a patient with a ventral frontal lesion (EVR) who had severe changes in everyday behavior and human relationships despite intact executive functioning (Eslinger & Damasio, 1985).

Another source of evidence came from patients with neurodegeneration of the ventral and anterior temporal cortex, called frontotemporal dementia (Neary et al., 1998): They consistently display a lack of empathic concern and inappropriate social behavior, which caregivers observe as a clear change from their premorbid character (e.g., one of our patients, a female 80-year-old woman, patted male strangers' bottoms when they bent over in the supermarket while expressing no increased sexual desire and actually being sexually inactive). Interestingly, these patients often show intact executive functions on standard tests such as the Wisconsin Card Sorting Test (Hodges, 2001).

Modern MRI and positron emission tomography make use of individual differences in the pattern of the regional distribution of pathology within groups of patients with frontotemporal dementia to tease apart the contributions of anterior temporal and ventral frontal regions to the degree of abnormal social behavior. It has been shown that both the right anterior temporal and ventromedial frontal cortex make independent contributions to inappropriate social behavior in these patients (Liu et al., 2004). Right superior anterior temporal atrophy has been further linked with a lack of cognitive and emotional empathy in frontotemporal dementia (Rankin et al., 2006). Acquired lesions of subcortical mesolimbic structures such as the amygdala, hypothalamus, septal area, and basal ganglia may also lead to antisocial behavior (reviewed in Moll, de Oliveira-Souza, & Eslinger, 2003).

Taken together, evidence from patients with brain lesions reveals that a network of specific fronto-temporo-mesolimbic areas is necessary for appropriate social behavior (Figure 21.1; Moll, Zahn, et al., 2005). Subtle volume reductions in this network are jointly associated with callousness in people with developmental psychopathy (de Oliveira-Souza et al., 2008). In contrast, patients with lesions to the lateral parietal lobes, precuneus, posterior cingulate cortex, and medial temporal lobe as occur in typical Alzheimer's disease early on (Herholz, 2003) do not display marked abnormalities of social behavior (Bozeat, Gregory, Ralph, & Hodges, 2000).

The challenge lies in identifying the different contributions that parts of this network are making to appropriate social behavior. Inappropriate social behavior could either result from the loss of or deficient access to knowledge of appropriate behavior (i.e., social knowledge), the loss of the motivation to act on this knowledge (i.e., moral motivation), or a combination of both. A third mechanism that is widely used to explain inappropriate social behaviour is the inability to control one's inappropriate urges. This "disinhibition" or "urge-suppression" model of inappropriate social behavior rests on the assumption that people have access to the knowledge of appropriate social behavior and have the motivation to act on it. Interestingly, the idea that the frontal cortex acts to inhibit subcortical limbic urges probably originated from conditioning experiments with nonhuman animals (Brutkowski, 1965); although this idea is widely propagated, we are unaware of compelling supporting anatomical evidence; namely, a solely inhibitory pathway from the frontal cortical areas to subcortical structures without additional evidence for excitatory or reciprocal connections between the same structures. A detailed discussion of frontolimbic suppression models is beyond the scope of this chapter, but we later discuss top-down frontal-subcortical control models that are much more in keeping with anatomical evidence, in that they do not claim frontal-subcortical

Social sensory features: face, voice, body posture, gestures, gaze, etc

Abstract conceptual knowledge of social behaviours: e.g. stingy, honourable qualities of behaviour

Sequences of actions/events (complex branching, long-term)

Sequential action-motivational state associations-aversion-related?

Motivational/ Emotional states: e.g. free-floating anger, anxiety, attachment, fear, hunger

Sequences of actions/events (complex branching, long-term)

Sequential action-motivational state associations-attachment-related?

moral sentiments, values, and "rational" beliefs

suppression as the sole mechanism of frontal control.

Evidence that inappropriate social behavior in patients with brain lesions may at least in part derive from the loss of social knowledge is the finding that neurodegeneration of the right superior anterior temporal lobe, recently shown to selectively represent conceptual knowledge of social behavior (e.g., what it means to act "stingily"; Zahn et al., 2007), leads to the selective loss of conceptual social knowledge while leaving other types of conceptual knowledge relatively intact (Zahn, Moll, Iyengar, et al., 2009). Moreover, patients with selective impairments of conceptual social knowledge exhibited higher degrees of inappropriate social behavior (i.e., "disinhibition") than patients without such deficits. These findings may also explain why patients with ventral frontal lesions appear to have intact social knowledge when the gist of the situation is summarized for them (Eslinger & Damasio, 1985; Saver & Damasio, 1991), because this gist description may allow their anterior temporal lobes to enable judging of the social appropriateness of behavior. The question remains whether ventral frontal regions store another type of social knowledge that is related more closely to the detailed knowledge of action sequences one needs for real-life decisions, as well as planning and executing social behavior, as proposed by Wood and Grafman (2003). An influential alternative explanation has been that the ventral frontal lobe only stores linkages between subcortical (hypothalamic) motivational states ("somatic markers") and social knowledge that is stored elsewhere (Bechara, Damasio, & Damasio, 2000).

Evidence directly probing the experience of different moral sentiments in patients with brain lesions is scarce, but recently the loss of guilt, embarrassment, and compassion has been specifically linked to frontopolar neurodegeneration in frontotemporal dementia (Moll et al., 2011). In addition, impairments of guilt and compassion were associated with neurodegeneration of the septal area. These effects were specific to these sentiments and contrasted with impaired disgust and anger being associated with amygdala and dorsomedial frontal neurodegeneration. Caregiver questionnaires indicate reduced feelings of guilt in people with ventromedial frontal lesions that also include damage to the frontopolar cortex (Koenigs et al., 2007). Functional neuroimaging data in keeping with this lesion evidence are reviewed in the next section.

Evidence from Functional Neuroimaging in Healthy Participants

Moral feelings were initially investigated in functional MRI studies using pictures or

---

Figure 21.1. Brain regions involved in moral functions based on evidence from brain lesions and functional neuroimaging (adapted from Moll, Zahn, de Oliveira-Souza, Krueger, & Grafman, 2005, & Moll & Schulkin, 2009). Cortical region: frontopolar cortex (FPC), medial and lateral ventral prefrontal cortex (PFC), right anterior dorsolateral PFC, anterior temporal lobes (aTL), and posterior superior temporal sulcus (pSTS). Subcortical structures include the extended amygdala, hypothalamus, basal forebrain (especially the preoptic and septal regions), basal ganglia, and midbrain regions. Integration across these corticolimbic structures gives rise to event-feature-emotion complexes (EFEC) by temporal binding according to the fronto-temporo-mesolimbic integration model (Moll, Zahn, de Oliveira-Souza, Krueger, & Grafman, 2005). The hypothesized cognitive-anatomical components are the following: (1) Sequential knowledge of actions/events represented within PFC subregions. FPC: complex branching of consequences of actions and ventral PFC regions representing associative knowledge of motivational/emotional states embedded into sequential event/action contexts; (2) social sensory features stored in pSTS and abstract (i.e. context-independent) conceptual knowledge of social behavior stored in the anterior temporal cortex, especially in the superior sectors; (3) central motive or basic emotional states, such as "free-floating" anger, attachment, sadness, and sexual arousal (represented by the subcortical limbic structures listed earlier).

short verbal statements of moral or no moral relevance as determined by rating scores obtained before the experiments. Brain activation patterns for morally relevant compared with morally irrelevant conditions were compared while controlling for emotional intensity. These studies used explicit moral judgments (morally right or wrong) or tasks without explicit moral decisions (i.e., implicitly moral tasks). Taken together, the evidence suggests involvement of frontopolar, ventral frontal, anterior temporal, posterior superior temporal sulcus, and mesolimbic regions in morally relevant tasks independent of task demands (reviewed in Moll, Zahn, et al., 2005).

Recently, studies have investigated differences in activation patterns associated with specific moral sentiments. Here, we only report brain regions that have been also associated with changes in moral behavior in patient lesion studies (see Figure 21.1) and that were systematically investigated in more than one study.

Guilt: Guilt, shame, and embarrassment may be quite different with regard to entailed causal attributions (Eisenberg, 2000; O'Connor et al., 2002; Tangney, Stuewig, & Mashek, 2007; Tracy & Robins, 2006; see Table 21.1). Most neuroimaging studies have focused on guilt, and activation of the frontopolar cortex is the most consistent finding across studies. This result is obtained when using different control conditions: other-critical feelings (e.g., indignation; Moll, Oliveira-Souza, Zahn, & Grafman, 2007; Zahn, Moll, Paiva, et al., 2009), embarrassment (Takahashi et al., 2004), or self-directed anger (Kedia, Berthoz, Wessa, Hilton, & Martinot, 2008). The first study that examined the neural correlates of guilt using functional imaging reported anterior cingulate activation dorsally to the genu of the corpus callosum in comparison with a neutral condition (Shin et al., 2000). The subgenual portion of the cingulate gyrus was detected as guilt-selective, but only when modeling individual differences in either the frequency of the guilt experience (Zahn, Moll, Paiva, et al., 2009) or empathic concern (Zahn, de Oliveira-Souza, Bramati,

Garrido, & Moll, 2009). Subgenual cingulate activation was selective for guilt versus other-critical feelings (indignation) when ensuring that both conditions were matched on negative valence and conceptual detail (Zahn, Moll, Paiva, et al., 2009).

Pity (compassion, sympathy): Pity is closely related to emotional empathy, which is, however, usually conceived as empathic simulation of other people's feelings rather than feeling pity (for the neural basis of emotional and cognitive empathy, see Decety & Jackson, 2004; de Vignemont & Singer, 2006; Eslinger, 1998; Shamay-Tsoory, Aharon-Peretz, & Perry, 2009; see Chapter 23). Frontopolar activation comparable to studies of guilt was found for compassion when compared with neutral conditions (Immordino-Yang, McColl, Damasio, & Damasio, 2009) and with control conditions evoking self-directed anger (Kedia et al., 2008) or indignation toward others (Moll et al., 2007). Interestingly, the ventral striatum and ventral tegmental area showed higher activity for empathic moral sentiments (compassion and guilt) than for other-critical feelings (disgust, indignation; Moll et al., 2007).

Other-critical (other-blaming) moral sentiments: Moral indignation/anger and contempt/disgust toward others led to overlapping patterns of activation in fMRI studies in the lateral orbitofrontal and anterior insular cortex (Zahn, Moll, Paiva, et al., 2009). Bilateral orbitofrontal cortex activation was stronger for indignation and moral disgust than for nonmoral disgust in one study that reported right amygdala activation to be more pronounced for nonmoral than moral disgust (Moll, de Oliveira-Souza, et al., 2005). Another study compared different forms of moral disgust and disgust for behaviors related to health risks for the agent (pathogen disgust) versus an emotionally and morally neutral condition. (Borg, Lieberman, & Kiehl, 2008). All disgust conditions shared the following activations: frontopolar cortices, anterior temporal lobes, left lateral orbitofrontal cortex, bilateral amygdala, and basal ganglia. There was no direct comparison with prosocial moral sentiments such as guilt to investigate whether frontopolar activation was specific for disgust. Another study also found frontopolar cortex activation for anger toward others, compared with a condition evoking anger toward oneself (Kedia et al., 2008). Further, left lateral orbitofrontal and right dorsolateral frontal activity have been shown in fMRI investigations of punishment for violating social norms relative to a condition in which participants did not expect punishment for those norm violations (Spitzer, Fischbacher, Herrnberger, Gron, & Fehr, 2007). These findings may be explained by shared lateral orbitofrontal representations of other people's indignation toward ourselves and our own indignation towards others.

Pride: Adam Smith saw pride as a self-interested feeling, postulating a separate striving for "dignity" as motivating "ethical improvement" (Lamb, 1974). David Hume recognized "good and bad forms of pride" (Hume, 1777). Neuroimaging studies of pride have aimed at the moral variant of pride. One study found pride-evoking stimuli to be related to right posterior superior temporal sulcus and left anterior temporal lobe activation relative to a neutral condition (Takahashi et al., 2008). Activations within the mesolimbic reward system (ventral tegmental area) with its projections to the basal forebrain (posterior septum) and within the ventral frontopolar cortex were reported for pride compared with gratitude and guilt (Figure 21.2; Zahn, Moll, Paiva, et al., 2009).

Taken together, these studies of specific moral sentiments point to certain fronto-mesolimbic subregions within the network being more preferentially activated for some moral sentiments relative to others. Frontopolar activations were probably the most consistent for moral sentiments in general (Moll, Zahn, et al., 2005). Those studies that compared prosocial moral sentiments (especially guilt, compassion) with other-critical moral sentiments have demonstrated selective activation for prosocial moral sentiments within the frontopolar cortex. Other-critical (other-blaming) moral sentiments were most invariably associated with lateral orbitofrontal and anterior insular activations when compared with prosocial moral sentiments. Few studies have investigated pride and gratitude, but activation of mesolimbic and basal forebrain regions was found in one study (Figure 21.2).

A recent fMRI study has shown that moral and social values are associated with the activation of fronto-temporo-mesolimbic networks representing the abstract context-independent conceptual detail (within the anterior temporal lobe) and context-dependent moral sentiments (within different fronto-mesolimbic subregions) tied to the same concept (Figure 21.2; Zahn, Moll, Paiva, et al., 2009). This neural architecture may enable us to communicate about moral values such as "honor" across sociocultural groups, even if the feelings and actions we associate with the same value vary. For example, an environmental activist may associate the action of blocking railways to stop transport of atomic waste with the moral values of "honor," "courage," and "dutifulness" and anticipate feeling pride, whereas a police officer may associate ensuring dissolution of the blockade despite adversity as an act of honor," "courage," and "dutifulness" and anticipate feeling pride as well. Some people may despise the values of honor," "courage," and "dutifulness" altogether and feel contempt for actions associated with these values. All these different individuals are nevertheless able to understand the common core (context-independent) meaning of the quality of honorable, courageous, or dutiful behavior. Communication between different sociocultural groups may be enhanced by finding common value dimensions on a more abstract level. Recent research shows that important dimensions of values are shared across cultures (Schwartz, 1992). Whereas this section has focused on possible neuroanatomical differences between different types of moral feelings, some would argue that the type of process or task is more important for understanding moral emotions and cognition than the content. This debate is summarized in the next section.

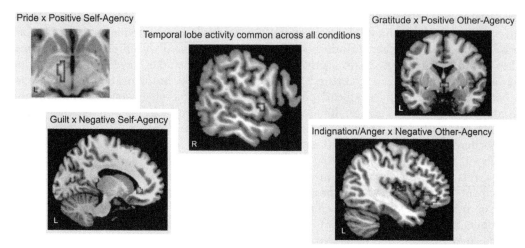

Figure 21.2. Using fMRI in healthy participants this study investigated the neuroanatomical basis of abstract moral and social values (figure adapted from Zahn, Moll, Paiva. et al., 2009). Participants had to imagine actions in accordance with or counter to a value described by a written sentence and to decide whether they would feel pleasantly or unpleasantly about the action. After the scan they rated the unpleasantness/pleasantness on a scale and chose labels that best described their feelings (the analysis compares each moral sentiment versus visual fixation and versus two other moral sentiments; only selective effects were reported). There were four experimental conditions: (1) positive self-agency: "Tom (first name of participant) acts generously toward Sam (first name of best friend)"– pride in this condition was associated with ventral tegmental, septal, and ventral medial FPC activation (not depicted); 2) positive other-agency: "Sam acts generously toward Tom" – gratitude in this condition was associated with hypothalamic activation; (3) negative self-agency: "Tom acts stingily toward Sam" – guilt in this condition was associated with subgenual cingulate cortex as well as ventral medial FPC activation (not depicted and only when modeling individual frequency of guilt trials); and (4) negative other-agency: "Sam acts stingily toward Tom" – indignation/anger in this condition was associated with lateral orbitofrontal/insular activation. In the center, one can see the right superior aTL region showing equally strong activation during all moral sentiment and agency contexts; this region showed increased activity with increasing richness of conceptual details describing social behavior and is identical to the activation found in a semantic judgment task (Zahn et al., 2007). These results confirmed the right superior anterior temporal lobe as a context-independent store of social conceptual knowledge that allows us to understand the core meaning of social and moral values regardless of what exact feelings or actions we tie to the value. See color plate 21.2.

Neuroanatomical Models of Moral Cognition-Emotion Interaction

Functional MRI studies of moral reasoning agree on the activation of anterior dorsolateral prefrontal cortex (PFC) and frontopolar cortex (Greene, Nystrom, Engell, Darley, & Cohen, 2004; Greene, Sommerville, Nystrom, Darley, & Cohen, 2001; Moll, Eslinger, & Oliveira-Souza, 2001). Disagreement, however, exists on how to interpret these activations and what functional role different frontal regions have in moral cognition and emotions. One view is that reasoning (assumed to be purely "cognitive")

and emotion (equated with the subjective experience of feelings) rely on anatomically separable systems (cognition in the dorsolateral PFC and parietal areas, and emotion in the ventromedial PFC and subcortical-limbic regions) and that cognition and emotion can be placed in conflict and compete with each other during decisions (McClure, Botvinick, Yeung, & Cohen, 2006).

Moral dilemmas are usually used to test the predictions of this dual-process model of moral cognition and emotion. One typical moral dilemma is the so-called trolley dilemma: having to decide to push an innocent man to death on the tracks of a runaway trolley to save five other individuals. When facing this decision, the emotional (intuitive) system is predicted to prefer avoiding this choice, whereas the cognitive system is predicted to favor this decision, because it is the "utilitarian" (i.e., the "rational") choice that leads to the maximum overall benefit (Greene et al., 2004). The dual-process model thus predicts that the decision to push the man on the tracks is the result of cognitive brain areas successfully overcoming or suppressing the emotional bias of refraining from this action – an extension of the influential cognitive control model (Miller & Cohen, 2001) of moral cognition.

In one study, patients with focal brain lesions that encompassed the ventral medial PFC bilaterally were exposed (Ciaramelli, Muccioli, Ladavas, & di Pellegrino, 2007; Koenigs et al., 2007) to "trolley-type" dilemmas. They made "utilitarian" decisions more often than healthy controls in high-conflict scenarios (highly emotionally aversive decisions that result in a greater overall benefit; for example, more lives saved). Several explanations have been offered for this increased bias toward "utilitarian" (rational) decisions in patients with ventral medial PFC lesions. One account is that general emotional blunting and reduced autonomic signaling due to ventral medial PFC damage may have led to an increased bias toward "rational" decisions – an interpretation favored by the somatic-marker hypothesis (Bechara et al., 2000). This explanation, however, is not supported by the results of another study (Koenigs & Tranel, 2007) investigating the same group of patients using the two-person ultimatum game. In the ultimatum game, participants anonymously interact only once with another player, and must decide between accepting an unfair but financially rewarding proposal (the economically "rational" choice) or rejecting the offer to punish the unfair player (the "emotional" choice; see Chapter 19). Patients with ventral medial PFC lesions made "emotional" decisions more often than controls, rejecting unfair offers more often. This response is normally accompanied by

anger. Thus, patients with lesions to the ventral medial PFC appeared to decide more "rationally" in moral dilemmas and more "emotionally" in economic interactions. Our view has therefore been that their performance can neither be accounted for by a single mechanism of overall emotional blunting, as predicted by the somatic marker model, nor by the dual-process model, in which dorsal cortical cognition suppresses ventral cortical-subcortical emotion (Greene et al., 2004); for a reply to our criticism, please see (Greene, 2007).

An alternative account of these findings can be made using a representational model of the frontal cortex (Wood & Grafman, 2003), which we adopted in our extension of this model to moral cognition (Moll, Zahn, et al., 2005). If the frontal cortex is conceived of as a store of information such as any other cortical area, then the prediction follows that there should be a topographic coding depending on the contents and/or format of represented information, as can be found for example in the motor cortex (Wood & Grafman, 2003). As summarized in the previous section, there is some evidence from fMRI studies to support the notion that the frontopolar cortex and the subgenual region (parts of the ventral medial PFC) are involved more strongly in prosocial moral sentiments (guilt, compassion) than other-critical moral feelings (indignation, contempt toward others). This could explain a selective decrease in the ability to experience guilt and compassion with preserved other-critical feelings in patients with ventral medial PFC lesions. It would account for increased anger in the context of unfair offers and decreased guilt/compassion when faced with moral dilemmas.

Our model of moral cognition has emphasized the functional integration of information between subcortical mesolimbic and frontotemporal cortical areas as the correlate of reasoning and emotion (Moll, Zahn, et al., 2005). According to this fronto-temporo-mesolimbic integration model of moral cognition, there is no opposition between "emotions" and "rational thoughts;" however, there is competition among different fronto-temporo-mesolimbic association complexes representing subjective experiences that we may sometimes call "feeling" or "rational thought," "rule," or "value" – depending on how vividly we have experienced emotional/motivational states represented in subcortical regions, how long we have activated this representation, or how detailed and vividly we have activated abstract rule and conceptual representations in frontotemporal cortical areas.

The fronto-temporo-mesolimbic integration view of moral cognition draws on research on the neural correlates of consciousness demonstrating that subjective experiences depend on the temporal binding of neural activity in large-scale distributed networks, rather than on activity in isolated areas (Tononi & Koch, 2008). We have argued that the subcortical mesolimbic system is most likely to represent motivational states, such as attachment or hunger, in a "free-floating" rather than in the contextualized fashion in which we almost always experience them (e.g., "attachment to our family members" or "or appetite for roast duck"). The contextualization of a motivational/emotional state with a goal is necessary to motivate behavior. There is rich electrophysiological evidence in non-human primates, as well as human neuroimaging evidence, that the orbitofrontal cortex represents reward and punishment values of specific goals (Kringelbach & Rolls, 2004; see Chapter 19). More complex goals such as moral values were shown to depend on anterior temporal lobe representations (Zahn, Moll, Paiva, et al., 2009). If goal representations require frontotemporal areas, motivations will be represented in fronto-temporo-mesolimbic circuits rather than solely in subcortical mesolimbic brain areas.

Despite the plausibility of this model, there is much more work needed to provide direct reproducible and unequivocal evidence supporting one model while excluding the other. A summary of the three alternative models on the role of the frontal cortex in moral and social behavior is shown in Table 21.2.

Neuroanatomical Separation of Moral and Selfish Motivations

The previous section laid out the controversial models on cognition-emotion interaction necessary to enable moral motivations. None clearly explains why patients with impaired moral behavior are often able to serve their own self-interest relatively well; this capacity is especially apparent in individuals with developmental psychopathy. Although some of these dissociations may be accounted for by the higher cognitive complexity of moral behavior, these observations strongly suggest at least partly separable correlates of moral and selfish motivations in the human brain.

Moral decision-making in real life is often about competition or choosing between one's self-interest and other people's needs or moral principles. Therefore the question is how competition between selfish and moral motivations is organized in our brains. Building on earlier work on cooperation in neuroeconomic games, the first study to probe moral motivations beyond the direct interpersonal sphere by using charity donation indeed demonstrated brain regions that were selectively activated for altruistic decisions to donate, compared with decisions leading to pure monetary gain for oneself (Figure 21.3; Moll et al., 2006). Two larger sectors, the septal-subgenual cingulate and the anterior orbitofrontal/frontopolar region, showed selectivity for altruistic decisions. Subsequent studies have confirmed activation of the septal region, a part of the basal forebrain, and the septal part of the nucleus accumbens for donation behavior (Harbaugh, Mayr, & Burghart, 2007; Hsu, Anen, & Quartz, 2008). This region has also been found to be activated for unconditional trust in economic interactions (Krueger et al., 2007). Future studies will have to confirm functional specializations within these brain networks and whether there are indeed selective subsectors for moral motivations.

One crude motivational ingredient of complex moral motivations is attachment. Attachment supports pair bonding and

Table 21.2. Alternative Models of the Role of Frontal Cortex in Social and Moral Behavior

Hypothesis Label	Main Claim
Top-down frontal cognitive control	Frontal cortex does not store linkages between stimulus and response, but it represents goals that control the information flow in other cortical and subcortical areas when an automatic response needs to be overcome (Miller & Cohen, 2001).
Bottom-up subcortical control	Ventral (medial) frontal cortex stores linkages of subcortical "somatic markers" and action knowledge in posterior brain areas. Explains problems with rapid and complex decision making after ventral (medial) frontal lesions (Bechara, Damasio, & Damasio, 2000).
Reciprocal fronto-temporo-subcortical integration	Context-dependent knowledge of sequences of social actions/events is stored in ventral frontal (and frontopolar) cortex necessary to enable context-appropriate social behavior (Moll, Zahn, de Oliveira-Souza, Krueger, & Grafman, 2005). In this model the frontal cortex stores sequential information linking stimuli and responses in different contexts.

mother-offspring bonding in human as well as nonhuman animal species (Insel & Young, 2001) and may be an evolutionary precursor to the motivational states enabling humans to act morally. Attachment has been shown to depend on oxytocin (Zak, Kurzban, & Matzner, 2004), opioidergic, and monoaminergic (Depue & Morrone-Strupinsky, 2005) neurochemistry and has been linked with a network of areas overlapping with the mesolimbic reward and basal forebrain system (Insel & Young, 2001). One hypothesis is that human moral motivation arises by binding attachment-related motivational states within the basal forebrain together with complex interpersonal goals and moral value representations in fronto-temporal circuits (Moll & Schulkin, 2009).

Conclusions and Future Directions

Taken together, there is considerable agreement that a fronto-temporo-mesolimbic network of brain regions is associated with moral feelings. Further it has been suggested that different types of moral feel-ings rely on parts of this network to different degrees. The frontopolar cortex may be more important for prosocial moral feelings (e.g., guilt) than for other-critical feelings (e.g., indignation toward others). Major controversies exist, however, with regard to the exact function of subregions of this network (especially regarding the role of the frontal cortex) and whether one should primarily study different types of moral processes (cognitive vs. emotional) or different types of moral feelings (e.g., guilt versus indignation). In addition, there is no agreement on how to subdivide the different types of moral feelings. Future studies will have to test more directly the predictions of alternative models of moral emotions (top-down frontal control, bottom-up subcortical control, fronto-temporo-mesolimbic integration).

To address these questions, one will need experiments in which psycholinguistic and other important differences between conditions are controlled, something that has not been done rigorously in many previous studies. Further, the field needs to work to develop criteria for the

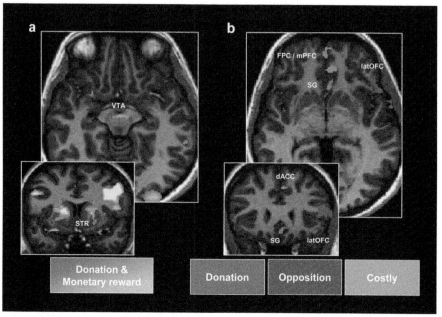

Figure 21.3. Brain regions activated when participants donated or were opposed to donate to charitable organizations during fMRI (Moll et al., 2006); figure adapted from Moll & Schulkin (2009). (a) Both pure monetary rewards and decisions to donate (with or without personal financial costs) activated the mesolimbic reward system, including the ventral tegmental area (VTA) and the ventral and dorsal striatum. (b) The septal-subgenual region (SG), however, was selectively activated by decisions to donate, as compared with pure monetary rewards (both by costly and noncostly decisions, conjunction analysis). The lateral orbitofrontal cortex (latOFC) was activated by decisions to oppose charities. This activation extended to the anterior insula and to the inferior dorsolateral PFC and was present both for costly and noncostly decisions (conjunction analysis). The FPC and ventral medial PFC (mPFC) were activated for costly decisions (when voluntarily sacrificing one's own money either to donate to a charity or to oppose it (conjunction analysis). See color plate 21.3.

neurobiological validity of cognitive models of moral functions. It is still unclear whether defining moral functions according to philosophical traditions (e.g., "utilitarian" or "non-utilitarian") is valid for neurobiological research or whether it is preferable to break down moral functioning into cognitive components derived from other fields of cognitive neuroscience, not all of which need to be specific to moral functions (e.g., "conceptual-semantic," "sensory-semantic," and so on). Further, it will be important to demonstrate process selectivity by showing common involvement of a brain region across two different types of contents/formats while being selective for one task over another. Conversely, content/format selectivity of a brain region could be concluded from involvement of that brain region regardless of task, but selec-

tively for one content/format over another. Reproducibility across different types of methods and populations including patients with brain lesions will be crucial for the validation of future models of moral cognitive neuroscience. Taken together, the study of moral brain functions will profit from the expertise of scientists who have worked in more traditional areas of cognitive neuroscience to improve the methodological and terminological rigor in the field and contribute to tackling the exciting experimental questions about one of the most evolutionarily recent functions of the human brain.

We are looking toward an exciting and stimulating future that allows investigations of one of the most sophisticated human abilities with ever more refined experimental rigor. Importantly, these new insights allow novel approaches to improving the prevention and treatment of neuropsychiatric disorders (Zahn, 2009), as well as balancing moral motivations in complex social systems.

Outstanding Questions and Future Directions

- Are there impairments of specific types of moral sentiments and judgments after dorsolateral and ventrolateral frontal lesions as compared with ventromedial frontal lesions?
- Do different sectors of the frontal cortex store different contents/formats of action/event sequences, or are these regions necessary for content/format-independent processing of action knowledge stored elsewhere in the brain?
- Are functional MRI associations of specific moral sentiments with specific brain regions reproducible?
- What is the specific functional contribution of particular brain areas in the moral cognition/emotion network?

References

Alexander, B., Brewin, C. R., Vearnals, S., Wolff, G., & Leff, J. (1999). An investigation of shame and guilt in a depressed sample. *British Journal of Medical Psychology*, 72, 323–38.

Augstein, H. F. (1996). J. C. Prichard's concept of moral insanity: A medical theory of the corruption of human nature. *Medical History*, 40(3), 311–43.

Bechara, A., Damasio, H., & Damasio, A. R. (2000). Emotion, decision making and the orbitofrontal cortex. *Cerebral Cortex*, 10(3), 295–307.

Berrios, G. E., Bulbena, A., Bakshi, N., Dening, T. R., Jenaway, F, Markar, H., et al. (1992). Feelings of guilt in major depression – conceptual and psychometric aspects. *British Journal of Psychiatry*, 160, 781–87.

Bishop, J. D. (1996). Moral motivation and the development of Francis Hutcheson's philosophy. *Journal of the History of Ideas*, 57(2), 277–95.

Borg, J. S., Lieberman, D., & Kiehl, K. A. (2008). Infection, incest, and iniquity: Investigating the neural correlates of disgust and morality. *Journal of Cognitive Neuroscience*, 20(9), 1529–46.

Bozeat, S., Gregory, C. A., Ralph, M. A., & Hodges, J. R. (2000). Which neuropsychiatric and behavioral features distinguish frontal and temporal variants of frontotemporal dementia from Alzheimer's disease? *Journal of Neurology, Neurosurgery, & Psychiatry*, 69(2), 178–86.

Brutkowski, S. (1965). Functions of prefrontal cortex in animals. *Physiological Reviews*, 45(4), 721–46.

Ciaramelli, E., Muccioli, M., Ladavas, E., & di Pellegrino, G. (2007). Selective deficit in personal moral judgment following damage to ventromedial prefrontal cortex. *Social Cognitive & Affective Neuroscience*, 2(2), 84–92.

Cleckley, H. M. (1976). *The mask of sanity* (5th ed.). St. Louis: Mosby.

Damasio, H., Grabowski, T., Frank, R., Galaburda, A. M., & Damasio, A. R. (1994). The return of Phineas Gage: Clues about the brain from the skull of a famous patient. *Science*, 264(5162), 1102–5.

Decety, J., & Grezes, J. (2006). The power of simulation: Imagining one's own and other's behavior. *Brain Research*, 1079, 4–14.

Decety, J., & Jackson, P. L. (2004). The functional architecture of human empathy. *Behavioral Cognitive Neuroscience Review*, 3, 71–100.

de Oliveira-Souza, R., Hare, R. D., Bramati, I. E., Garrido, G. J., Azevedo Ignácio, F., Tovar-Moll, F., et al. (2008). Psychopathy as a disorder of the moral brain: Fronto-temporo-limbic grey matter reductions demonstrated by voxel-based morphometry. *NeuroImage*, 40(3), 1202–13.

Depue, R. A., & Morrone-Strupinsky, J. V. (2005). A neurobehavioral model of affiliative bonding: Implications for conceptualizing a human trait of affiliation. *Behavioral and Brain Sciences*, 28(3), 313–350.

de Vignemont, F., & Singer, T. (2006). The empathic brain: How, when and why? *Trends in Cognitive Sciences*, 10(10), 435–41.

Eisenberg, N. (2000). Emotion, regulation, and moral development. *Annual Review of Psychology*, 51, 665–97.

Elliott, R., Zahn, R., Deakin, J. F., & Anderson, I. M. (2010). Affective cognition and its disruption in mood disorders. Neuropsychopharmacology. doi:10.1038/npp.2010.77

Eslinger, P. J. (1998). Neurological and neuropsychological bases of empathy. *European Neurology*, 39(4), 193–99.

Eslinger, P. J., & Damasio, A. R. (1985). Severe disturbance of higher cognition after bilateral frontal lobe ablation: patient EVR. *Neurology*, 35(12), 1731–41.

Fischer, A. H., & Roseman, I. J. (2007). Beat them or ban them: The characteristics and social functions of anger and contempt. *Journal of Personality and Social Psychology*, 93(1), 103–15.

Gintis, H., Henrich, J., Bowles, S., Boyd, R., & Fehr, E. (2008). Strong reciprocity and the roots of human morality. *Social Justice Research*, 21(2), 241–253.

Greene, J. D. (2007). Why are VMPFC patients more utilitarian? A dual-process theory of moral judgment explains. *Trends in Cognitive Sciences*, 11(8), 322–323.

Greene, J. D., Nystrom, L. E., Engell, A. D., Darley, J. M., & Cohen, J. D. (2004). The neural bases of cognitive conflict and control in moral judgment. *Neuron*, 44(2), 389–400.

Greene, J. D., Sommerville, R. B., Nystrom, L. E., Darley, J. M., & Cohen, J. D. (2001). An fMRI investigation of emotional engagement in moral judgment. *Science*, 293(5537), 2105–8.

Haidt, J. (2003). The moral emotions. In R. J. Davidson, K. R. Scherer, & H. H. Goldsmith (Eds.), *Handbook of affective sciences* (pp. 852–70). Oxford: Oxford University Press.

Harbaugh, W. T., Mayr, U., & Burghart, D. R. (2007). Neural responses to taxation and voluntary giving reveal motives for charitable donations. *Science*, 316(5831), 1622–25.

Hare, R. D. (2003). *The Hare Psychopathy Checklist-Revised* (2nd ed.). Toronto: Multi-Health Systems.

Herholz, K. (2003). PET studies in dementia. *Annals of Nuclear Medicine*, 17(2), 79–89.

Higgins, E. T. (1987). Self-discrepancy – a theory relating self and affect. *Psychological Review*, 94(3), 319–40.

Hodges, J. R. (2001). Frontotemporal dementia (Pick's disease): Clinical features and assessment. *Neurology*, 56(11 Suppl. 4), S6–10.

Hsu, M., Anen, C., & Quartz, S. R. (2008). The right and the good: Distributive justice and neural encoding of equity and efficiency. *Science*, 320(5879), 1092–95.

Hume, D. (1777). *An enquiry into the principles of morals*, Vol. 2. London: T. Cadell.

Immordino-Yang, M. H., McColl, A., Damasio, H., & Damasio, A. (2009). Neural correlates of admiration and compassion. *Proceedings of the National Academy of Sciences*, 106(19), 8021–26.

Insel, T. R., & Young, L. J. (2001). The neurobiology of attachment. *Nature Reviews Neuroscience*, 2(2), 129–36.

Janoff-Bulman, R. (1979). Characterological versus behavioral self-blame – inquiries into depression and rape. *Journal of Personality and Social Psychology*, 37(10), 1798–1809.

Kant, I. (1786). *Grundlegung zur Metaphysik der Sitten* (2nd ed.). Riga: Johann Friedrich Hartknoch.

Kedia, G., Berthoz, S., Wessa, M., Hilton, D., & Martinot, J. L. (2008). An agent harms a victim: A functional magnetic resonance imaging study on specific moral emotions. *Journal of Cognitive Neuroscience*, 20(10), 1788–98.

Koenigs, M., & Tranel, D. (2007). Irrational economic decision-making after ventromedial prefrontal damage: Evidence from the Ultimatum Game. *Journal of Neuroscience*, 27(4), 951–56.

Koenigs, M., Young, L., Adolphs, R., Tranel, D., Cushman, F., Hauser, M., et al. (2007). Damage to the prefrontal cortex increases utilitarian moral judgements. *Nature*, 446(7138), 908–11.

Kringelbach, M. L., & Rolls, E. T. (2004). The functional neuroanatomy of the human orbitofrontal cortex: Evidence from neuroimaging and neuropsychology. *Progress in Neurobiology*, 72(5), 341–72.

Krueger, F., McCabe, K., Moll, J., Kriegeskorte, N., Zahn, F, Strenziok, M., et al. (2007). Neural correlates of trust. *Proceedings of the National Academy of Sciences*, 104(50), 20084–89.

Lamb, R. B. (1974). Adam Smith's system: Sympathy not self-interest. *Journal of the History of Ideas*, 35(4), 671–82.

Liu, W., Miller, B. L., Kramer, J. H., Rankin, K., Wyss-Coray, C., Gearhart, R., et al. (2004). Behavioral disorders in the frontal and temporal variants of frontotemporal dementia. *Neurology*, 62(5), 742–48.

McClure, S. M., Botvinick, M. M., Yeung, J. D., & Cohen, J. D. (2006). Conflict monitoring in cognition-emotion competition. In J. J. Gross (Ed.), *Handbook of emotion regulation*. New Yor k Guilford Press.

Miller, E. K., & Cohen, J. D. (2001). An integrative theory of prefrontal cortex function. *Annual Review of Neuroscience*, 24, 167–202.

Moll, J., de Oliveira-Souza, R., & Eslinger, P. J. (2003). Morals and the human brain: A working model. *Neuroreport*, 14(3), 299–305.

Moll, J., de Oliveira-Souza, R., Garrido, G. J., Bramati, I. E., Caparelli-Daquer, E. M. A., Paiva, M. M. F., et al. (2007). The self as a moral agent: Linking the neural bases of social agency and moral sensitivity. *Social Neuroscience*, 2(3 & 4), 336–52.

Moll, J., de Oliveira-Souza, R., Moll, F. T., Ignacio, F. A., Bramati, I. E., Caparelli-Daquer, E. M., et al. (2005). The moral affiliations of disgust: A functional MRI study. *Cognitive & Behavioral Neurology*, 18(1), 68–78.

Moll, J., De Oliveira-Souza, R., & Zahn, R. (2008). The neural basis of moral cognition: Sentiments, concepts, and values. *Annals of the New York Academy of Sciences*, 1124(1), 161–80.

Moll, J., Eslinger, P. J., & Oliveira-Souza, R. (2001). Frontopolar and anterior temporal cortex activation in a moral judgment task: Preliminary functional MRI results in normal subjects. *Arquivos de Neuro-Psiuiatria*, 59(3-B), 657–64.

Moll, J., Krueger, F., Zahn, R., Pardini, M., de Oliveira-Souza, R., & Grafman, J. (2006). Human fronto-mesolimbic networks guide decisions about charitable donation. *Proceedings of the National Academy of Sciences*, 103(42), 15623–28.

Moll, J., Oliveira-Souza, R., Zahn, R., & Grafman, J. (2007). The cognitive neuroscience of moral emotions. In W. Sinnott-Armstrong (Ed.), Moral psychology, Vol. 3: *Morals and the brain*. Cambridge, MA: MIT Press.

Moll, J., & Schulkin, J. (2009). Social attachment and aversion in human moral cognition. *Neuroscience and Biobehavioral Reviews*, 33(3), 456–65.

Moll, J., Zahn, R., de Oliveira-Souza, R., Bramati, I. E., Krueger, F., Tura, B., et al. (2011). Impairment of prosocial sentiments is associated with frontopolar and septal damage in frontotemporal dementia. *Neuroimage*, 54(2), 1735–42.

Moll, J., Zahn, R., de Oliveira-Souza, R., Krueger, F., & Grafman, J. (2005). Opinion: The neural basis of human moral cognition. *Nature Reviews Neuroscience*, 6(10), 799–809.

Neary, D., Snowden, J. S., Gustafson, L., Passant, U., Stuss, D., Black, S., et al. (1998). Frontotemporal lobar degeneration: A consensus on clinical diagnostic criteria. *Neurology*, 51(6), 1546–54.

O'Connor, L. E., Berry, J. W., Weiss, J., & Gilbert, P. (2002). Guilt, fear, submission, and empathy in depression. *Journal of Affective Disorders*, 71(1–3), 19–27.

Rankin, K. P., Gorno-Tempini, M. L., Allison, S. C., Stanley, C. M., Glenn, S., Weiner, M. W., et al. (2006). Structural anatomy of empathy in neurodegenerative disease. *Brain*, 129(11), 2945–56.

Rusch, N., Lieb, K., Gottler, I., Hermann, C., Schramm, E., Richter, H., et al. (2007). Shame and implicit self-concept in women with borderline personality disorder. *American Journal of Psychiatry*, 164(3), 500–8.

Saver, J. L., & Damasio, A. R. (1991). Preserved access and processing of social knowledge in a patient with acquired sociopathy due to ventromedial frontal damage. *Neuropsychologia*, 29(12), 1241–49.

Schwartz, S. H. (1992). Universals in the content and structure of values – theoretical advances and empirical tests in 20 countries. *Advances in Experimental Social Psychology*, 25, 1–65.

Shamay-Tsoory, S. G., Aharon-Peretz, J., & Perry, D. (2009). Two systems for empathy: A double dissociation between emotional and cognitive empathy in inferior frontal gyrus versus ventromedial prefrontal lesions. *Brain*, 132, 617–27.

Shin, L. M., Dougherty, D. D., Orr, S. P., Pitman, R. K., Lasko, M., Macklin, M. L., et al. (2000). Activation of anterior paralimbic structures during guilt-related script-driven imagery. *Biological Psychiatry*, 48(1), 43–50.

Spitzer, M., Fischbacher, U., Herrnberger, B., Gron, G., & Fehr, E. (2007). The neural signature of social norm compliance. *Neuron*, 56(1), 185–96.

Takahashi, H., Matsuura, M., Koeda, M., Yahata, N., Suhara, T., Kato, M., et al. (2008). Brain activations during judgments of positive self-conscious emotion and positive basic emotion: Pride and joy. *Cerebral Cortex*, 18(4), 898–903.

Takahashi, H., Yahata, N., Koeda, M., Matsuda, T., Asai, K., & Okubo, Y. (2004). Brain activation associated with evaluative processes of guilt and embarrassment: an fMRI study. *Neuroimage*, 23(3), 967–74.

Tangney, J. P., Stuewig, J., & Mashek, D. J. (2007). Moral emotions and moral behavior. *Annual Review of Psychology*, 58, 345–72.

Tangney, J. P., Wagner, P., & Gramzow, R. (1992). Proneness to shame, proneness to guilt, and psychopathology. *Journal of Abnormal Psychology*, 101(3), 469–78.

Tononi, G., & Koch, C. (2008). The neural correlates of consciousness – An update. *Year in Cognitive Neuroscience, 1124,* 239–61.

Tracy, J. L., & Robins, R. W. (2006). Appraisal antecedents of shame and guilt: Support for a theoretical model. *Personality and Social Psychology Bulletin, 32*(10), 1339–51.

Tracy, J. L., Shariff, A. F., & Cheng, J. T. (2010). A naturalist's view of pride. *Emotion Review,* 163–77.

Weiner, B. (1985). An attributional theory of achievement-motivation and emotion. *Psychological Review, 92*(4), 548–73.

Weiner, B. (1992). *Human motivation: Metaphors, theories, and research.* Beverly Hills, CA: Sage.

Welt, L. (1888). Über Charakterveränderungen des Menschen. *Dtsch Arch Klin Med, 42,* 339–90.

Wood, J. N., & Grafman, J. (2003). Human prefrontal cortex: processing and representational perspectives. *Nature Reviews Neuroscience, 4*(2), 139–47.

Zahn, R. (2009). The role of neuroimaging in translational cognitive neuroscience. *Topics in Magnetic Resonance Imaging, 20*(5), 279–89.

Zahn, R., de Oliveira-Souza, R., Bramati, I., Garrido, G., & Moll, J. (2009). Subgenual cingulate activity reflects individual differences in empathic concern. *Neuroscience Letters, 457*(2), 107–10.

Zahn, R., Moll, J., Iyengar, V., Huey, E. D., Tierney, M., Krueger, F., et al. (2009). Social conceptual impairments in frontotemporal lobar degeneration with right anterior temporal hypometabolism. *Brain, 132*(Pt. 3), 604–16.

Zahn, R., Moll, J., Krueger, F., Huey, E. D., Garrido, G., & Grafman, J. (2007). Social concepts are represented in the superior anterior temporal cortex. *Proceedings of the National Academy of Sciences, 104*(15), 6430–35.

Zahn, R., Moll, J., Paiva, M. M. F., Garrido, G., Krueger, F., Huey, E. D., et al. (2009). The neural basis of human social values: Evidence from functional MRI. *Cerebral Cortex, 19*(2), 276–83.

Zak, P. J., Kurzban, R., & Matzner, W. T. (2004). The neurobiology of trust. *Annals of the New York Academy of Sciences, 1032,* 224–27.

CHAPTER 22

Social Stress and Social Approach

Markus Heinrichs, Frances S. Chen, Gregor Domes, &
Robert Kumsta

Psychobiology of Stress

Stress is an everyday phenomenon. Our organism is constantly challenged by internal and external forces, be they psychological or physiological, real or anticipated. Stress can be defined as an actual or anticipated disruption of homeostasis, which is defined as a dynamic and harmonious equilibrium. The stress response has evolved as a highly adaptive response, aimed at maintaining physiological integrity in the face of an anticipated threat to physiological or psychological well-being (Chrousos, 2009).

The effects of stress become manifest on multiple levels, including behavior, subjective experience, cognitive function, and physiology. There is a surge in arousal, focused attention, vigilance, alertness, and cognitive processing. Peripherally, physiological responses are aimed at reinstating homeostasis, reflected in activation of the autonomic nervous system (ANS) and of the hypothalamus-pituitary-adrenal (HPA) axis.

The two interlocked stress response systems are characterized by different response dynamics. The ANS provides a rapid response to stress through activation of its sympathetic and parasympathetic branches. The sympathetic activation represents the classic "fight-or-flight" response. Within seconds, the sympatho-adrenomedullary branch excites end organs and the adrenal medulla through neural innervation, which generally increases circulating levels of adrenaline (primarily from the adrenal medulla) and noradrenaline (primarily from sympathetic nerves), heart rate and force of contraction, peripheral vasoconstriction, and energy mobilization. Parasympathetic actions, also modulated during stress, are generally opposite to those of the sympathetic system. Owing to reflex parasympathetic activation, excitation of the ANS is characterized by short-lived responses.

The HPA axis is a hierarchical hormonal system that connects the central nervous system with the endocrine system; the hormonal mechanism is sluggish relative to the synaptic mechanisms that drive ANS activation. Regulation of the HPA axis is governed by hypothalamic circuits that integrate multiple inputs from limbic regions and the brainstem. Excitatory and

inhibitory inputs are integrated by corticotropin-releasing hormone (CRH) neurons
of the hypothalamic paraventricular nucleus
(PVN) into a net secretory signal at the pituitary gland. Release of CRH and the co-
expressed neuropeptide vasopressin (AVP)
are essential for coordinating the stress response and for governing HPA axis activity.
They trigger the release of adrenocorticotropic hormone (ACTH) from the pituitary into the general circulation, which acts on the
adrenal cortex to induce synthesis and increased secretion of glucocorticoids (GCs),
mainly cortisol in humans (Figure 22.1).

Cortisol acts at virtually all levels of the
body through binding to the glucocorticoid receptor (GR). The end effects of GCs
include energy mobilization, suppression
of several immune functions, potentiation
of sympathetic-nervous-system–mediated
vasoconstriction, and suppression of reproductive function. Another important function of cortisol is the exertion of negative
feedback at multiple brain sites to terminate
the release of CRH and ACTH (Sapolsky,
Romero, & Munck, 2000).

The HPA axis has two modes of operation. One is the regulation of the diurnal
rhythm of cortisol secretion, and the other
is the control of cortisol secretion following
stress. Under unstimulated, nonstress conditions, cortisol levels are highest in the morning followed by a decline throughout the
day until the nadir is reached around midnight. Interestingly, cortisol levels increase
about 50–75% within 30–45 minutes after
awakening, the so-called cortisol awakening response (CAR). Recent sleep laboratory research has shown that the awakening rise is a discrete entity superimposed on
the circadian cycle and can be regarded as
a response to awakening (Wilhelm, Born,
Kudielka, Schlotz, & Wüst, 2007).

With regard to stress responsivity, two
distinct realms of stress activation have
been proposed. Stimuli triggering "reactive"
responses represent genuine homeostatic
challenges recognized by somatic or visceral
sensory pathways. These stressors would
include pain, humoral homeostatic signals
(e.g., changes in glucose or insulin levels), or

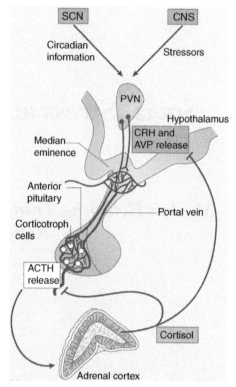

Figure 22.1. The hypothalamus-pituitary-adrenal
(HPA) axis is a key system in stress reactivity.
When a threat is detected, neurons in the
paraventricular nucleus of the hypothalamus
release corticotropin-releasing hormone (CRH)
and arginine vasopressin (AVP). This triggers
the subsequent secretion of adrenocorticotropic
hormone (ACTH) from the pituitary gland,
leading to increased production and release of
glucocorticoids (mainly cortisol in humans) by
the adrenal cortex. The HPA axis is controlled
by feedback loops involving pituitary,
hypothalamic, and hippocampal sites. Reprinted
by permission from Macmillan Publishers Ltd:
Nature Reviews Neuroscience, Lightman, S.L.
& Conway-Campbell, B.L. (2010). The crucial
role of pulsatile activity of the HPA axis for
continuous dynamic equilibration. Nat Rev
Neurosci 11 (10) pp. 710–8, © 2010, Nature
Publishing Group.

humoral inflammatory signals. These inputs
are mediated via direct innervations to the
PVN from regions known to receive first- or
second-order inputs from somatic nociceptors, visceral afferents, or humoral sensory
pathways and can therefore elicit rapid and
reflexive activation of the HPA axis.

Important for understanding physiological reactions to psychological or psychosocial stress is the fact that activation of the HPA axis can also occur in the absence of physiological challenge. These reactions are termed "anticipatory" responses and are centrally generated to mount a cortisol response in anticipation of, rather than in reaction to, homeostatic disruption. Anticipatory responses can be elicited either by classically or contextually conditioned stimuli (i.e., memory programs) or by innate species-specific predispositions. These innate programs include the recognition of predators or illuminated spaces for rodents, or social challenges and unfamiliar environments or situations in humans. In 1968, John Mason noted, "Psychological influences are among the most potent natural stimuli known to affect pituitary-adrenal cortical activity" (Mason, 1968, pp. 595–96). He proposed that situations characterized by novelty, uncontrollability and unpredictability, perception of threat, and ego involvement reliably elicit HPA axis responses. This has been confirmed by a recent meta-analysis showing that most pronounced cortisol responses are observed in situations that are uncontrollable and characterized by social-evaluative threat (Dickerson & Kemeny, 2004). Anticipatory responses are under control of limbic brain regions, which serve as the interface between the incoming sensory information and the appraisal process. Limbic regions known to influence the stress response include the hippocampus, nuclei of the amygdala, the lateral septum, and the medial prefrontal cortex. However, none of these regions send direct projections to the PVN. Modulation of PVN activity is achieved through interactions with "reactive" stress circuits in the brainstem, hypothalamic regions, and regions of the bed nucleus of the stria terminalis (BNST) that directly innervate the PVN. Thus, limbic input is superimposed onto brainstem and hypothalamic stress effectors, and a hierarchical system is formed capable of mediating both reactive and anticipatory stress responses (Ulrich-Lai & Herman, 2009).

Recent imaging studies using a stress paradigm for the fMRI environment (see the later discussion) have shown a specific brain activation pattern under stress, characterized by deactivation in limbic areas. In particular, the results indicated that deactivation of the hippocampus initiates the hormonal stress response (Pruessner et al., 2008). It was proposed that this set of limbic system structures shows high activity during baseline states, thereby serving as an alarm system. When signs of incoming danger or threat are detected, inhibition of stress systems is actively curtailed – "the foot is taken off the brake" – thereby initiating the adaptive responses to the threat.

Measuring Social Stress in the Laboratory: The Trier Social Stress Test

For the investigation of the stress response under controlled conditions, a research tool was needed capable of inducing significant increases of hormonal, cardiovascular, and subjective parameters in the majority of subjects. Almost 20 years ago, the Trier Social Stress Test (TSST) was developed (Kirschbaum, Pirke, & Hellhammer, 1993). Since 1993, more than 4,000 TSSTs have been performed in many laboratories around the world (Kudielka, Wüst, Kirschbaum, & Hellhammer, 2007). It is fair to say that the TSST has become the gold standard for the experimental induction of psychological stress.

How Does the TSST Work?

The TSST consists of a free speech and a mental arithmetic task performed in front of a panel of judges and a camera (for a detailed description, see Kudielka et al., 2007). Briefly, the participant is asked to take on the role of a job applicant who is invited for a personal interview. After a preparation period of 3 minutes, the participant is asked to introduce him- or herself to the panel and to convince them that he or she is the perfect applicant for the vacant position.

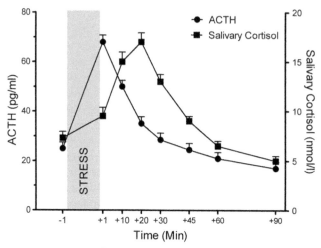

Figure 22.2. Typical ACTH (left y-axis) and salivary cortisol (right y-axis) profile in response to the TSST. ACTH levels typically reach their peak immediately after stress exposure, and for salivary cortisol levels, maximum levels are typically seen about 10 minutes after the cessation of stress.

Following 5 minutes of free speech, the participant is asked to perform an arithmetic task (repeatedly subtracting from a starting number, 2,023, in increments of 17), again for 5 minutes. The judges are introduced as experts in monitoring nonverbal behavior, and subjects are informed that the video recordings will be used to analyze their performance. The panel is composed of two or three confederates of the experimenter who are unacquainted with the subject. The judges are trained to communicate with the subject in an neutral manner and to withhold facial or verbal feedback.

Stress Measures

To capture the entire response dynamic of the selected outcome measure(s), multiple samples must be taken. These typically cover prestress levels, the initial stress response, peak level, and recovery. A typical response curve for ACTH and salivary cortisol is shown in Figure 22.2. ACTH levels peak immediately after stress, whereas cortisol shows slightly delayed responses with peak levels around 10–20 min after cessation of the task. About 70–80% of subjects respond to the TSST with increases of 50–200% in cortisol. In addition to HPA axis hormones, other outcome measures increase significantly and are often measured. These include adrenalin and noradrenalin, heart rate, systolic and diastolic blood pressure, growth hormone, prolactin, testosterone, and immune parameters.

TSST for Children and TSST for Groups

An adapted version of the TSST has been developed for children in the age range of 7–14 years. The TSST-C (Buske-Kirschbaum et al., 1997) also consists of a preparation period, a free speech, and mental arithmetic task. In contrast to a job interview, children receive the beginning of a story and are told to finish telling it and to make it as exciting as possible. The numbers of the mental arithmetic task are adapted to the performance level of the respective age group.

Recently, our laboratory has developed a group version of the TSST (TSST-G; von Dawans, Kirschbaum, & Heinrichs, 2011), in which up to six participants can be tested at a time. The procedure is comparable to the single-participant version. During stress exposure, participants are separated by dividing walls that prevent eye contact and interaction with the other participants.

Each participant is called on in random order to speak for 2 minutes. In the remaining 8 minutes, each participant is required to perform a mental arithmetic task for 80 seconds. Notably, the TSST-G also consists of a specific control condition containing all factors of the TSST-G (e.g., orthostasis, speech task, cognitive load, timeline), except for the psychosocially stressful components (i.e., social-evaluative threat and uncontrollability.

What Makes the TSST Stressful?

A meta-analysis of more than 200 studies using laboratory stress paradigms has delineated the situational elements capable of eliciting HPA axis responses (Dickerson & Kemeny, 2004). It was shown that robust cortisol responses are observed in the context of performance tasks that are (1) uncontrollable, (2) create a context of forced failure, or (3) are characterized by social-evaluative threat. In these tasks, subjects are unable to avoid negative consequences or cannot succeed despite their best efforts, and task performance can be negatively judged by others. Tasks containing both the components of uncontrollability and social-evaluative threat were associated with the largest HPA axis responses and the longest recovery times. The TSST is one of the few available protocols that satisfies the criteria of a motivated performance task that combines these two critical elements (Dickerson & Kemeny, 2004).

Stress in the fMRI Environment

The Montreal Imaging Stress Test

To investigate brain activation involved in stress responsivity and stress regulation, stress paradigms for the functional neuroimaging environment have been developed. As noted earlier, an important situational element to elicit HPA axis activation is social-evaluative threat (i.e., negative judgment of one's task performance by others). The Montreal Imaging Stress Task (MIST; Dedovic et al., 2005) was developed to create social-evaluative threat in a neu-

roimaging environment. The MIST combines mental arithmetic with an adaptive algorithm and a built-in social comparison component. The algorithm adjusts the difficulty of the arithmetic beyond the subject's capabilities, so that the subject obtains only 50% correct answers independent of math aptitude. Furthermore, with feedback, the subjects are made to believe that they are performing much poorer than the average subject. Between runs, subjects are told that they should try and improve their performance in subsequent runs.

Compared to laboratory stressors that include face-to-face interaction with an audience such as the TSST, the MIST has to be considered a less potent psychological stressor. About 50% of the subjects exposed to the MIST show significant increases in cortisol (responders), whereas nonresponders show the typical circadian decline of cortisol levels over the course of the experiment. Furthermore, in the responders, the overall increases in cortisol are, on average, 30–50%, compared to 50–200% in the TSST. The subgroups of responders and nonresponders also differ with respect to brain activation changes after MIST exposure. Distinct brain activation differences could be observed in the relevant contrast (mental arithmetic under social threat versus mental arithmetic under control conditions). In the responders, deactivation of specific parts of the limbic system, including the hypothalamus, hippocampus, amygdala, and medio-orbitofrontal cortex, were observed. Furthermore, the degree of deactivation in the hippocampus was correlated with the overall cortisol stress response (Pruessner et al., 2008; see also the earlier discussion).

Scanstress

Recently, a new stress paradigm for the fMRI environment was introduced with the goal of increasing the social-evaluative threat component during task performance. In the *ScanStress* test (Streit et al., in preparation), participants perform a mental arithmetic task and a mental rotation task.

Subjects are required to respond under time pressure, which is visualized by a countdown, while the software adapts task speed and difficulty to the individual's performance. Critically, during the scanning procedure as well between the sequences, an observer panel is presented to the subject though a live video stream, thereby inducing social-evaluative threat. Although observers remain passive in the control blocks, they give disapproving visual and verbal feedback during the task blocks and between the sequences. In a first evaluation study, ScanStress was shown to induce significant ACTH and cortisol responses, and on the neural level, a distinct pattern of activation and deactivation became evident (unpublished data). Recently, ScanStress and the MIST tests have been used in an investigation of the effects of city living and urban upbringing on stress processing. Urban upbringing affected the anterior cingulate cortex, a key region for regulation of amygdala activity, and current city living was associated with increased amygdala activity (Lederbogen et al., 2011).

Determinants of HPA Axis Reactivity

With the availability of standardized laboratory stress protocols, extensive phenotyping of HPA axis stress responses has been performed over the past years. Both from a basic research perspective and to obtain a better understanding of the mechanisms linking stress and mental health, knowledge of intervening and moderating variables that affect HPA axis responses is important. Research has shown that a consistent feature of HPA axis responses to psychosocial challenge is large intra- and interindividual variability. The identified factors include gender, age, endogenous and exogenous sex steroid levels, smoking, coffee and alcohol consumption, dietary energy supply, lactation and breastfeeding, and personality factors. Not all of these factors can be discussed here in detail, and the reader is referred to more comprehensive reviews (e.g., Kudielka, Hellhammer, & Wüst,

2009). Here, the focus is on genetic factors, including gene-environment interactions and epigenetics, and the influence of early life experience on HPA axis regulation in adulthood.

Genetic Factors

It is not the aim of this section to review in full all candidate gene association studies regarding HPA axis regulation. Instead, it provides a few examples of the most relevant candidates – glucocorticoid receptor (GR) and mineralocorticoid receptor (MR) – and of polymorphisms studied in other contexts of emotion regulation (5-HTTLPR, GABA, BDNF).

Twin studies have shown that HPA axis responses to acute challenge are significantly influenced by genetic factors (Wüst et al., 2004). Sequencing of the human genome has made it possible to associate polymorphisms in HPA axis-related genes with differences in HPA axis response patterns. Because the HPA axis is a complexly regulated system, multiple genes involved in different peripheral and central pathways contribute to interindividual response variability. Putative candidates are the genes coding for hormones and receptors implicated in the direct regulation of HPA axis activity (e.g., the glucocorticoid receptor) and those involved in indirect modulation (e.g., opioidergic, catecholaminergic, or GABAergic modulation). Other candidates are the genes coding for proteins or enzymes involved in cortisol biosynthesis, bioavailability (e.g., 11-beta hydroxysteroid dehydrogenases), transport (e.g., CBG), or systemic absorption (e.g., P-Glycoprotein) or factors playing a role in the cellular pathways transducing the cortisol signal (e.g., heat-shock proteins or cofactors).

The genes coding for the two receptors that mediate the effects of cortisol have been considered prime candidates for HPA axis regulation. Cortisol operates through a dual receptor system, which consists of the high-affinity mineralocorticoid receptor (MR) and the 10-fold lower affinity glucocorticoid receptor (GR). The GR modulates negative feedback regulation of the HPA axis (i.e., termination of the stress response; de Kloet, Joels, & Holsboer, 2005). The efficacy of cortisol in exerting its function is determined by a number of factors, including sensitivity of the GR, which in turn is influenced by common genetic variants.

GLUCOCORTICOID RECEPTOR GENE (GR, NR3C1)

Several common single nucleotide polymorphisms (SNPs) of the GR have been associated with ACTH and cortisol responses to psychosocial stress. Initially, the *Bcl*I C/G (rs41423247; located in intron B), and the N363S A/G (rs6195; located in exon 2) polymorphisms were studied. In response to the TSST, homozygous carriers of the *Bcl*I G allele showed decreased salivary cortisol levels, whereas N363S AG carriers displayed relatively increased levels. A follow-up study (Kumsta et al., 2007) included two additional GR SNPs – the R23K A/G (rs6190) SNP, located in exon 2, and the A3669G (rs6198) polymorphism in exon 9beta – in the analyses. Similar results were observed for the *Bcl*I polymorphism: Male *Bcl*I GG carriers showed the lowest serum cortisol levels compared to the remaining groups. Interestingly, the same genotype in women was associated with the highest serum cortisol levels, resulting in a sex by genotype interaction. The 9beta AG genotype was associated with higher ACTH and serum cortisol (but not salivary cortisol) responses in males compared to the remaining groups. Recently, an SNP in the promoter region of the GR (rs10482605 T/C; located in promoter of exon 1C) was shown to be in almost complete linkage disequilibrium with the 9beta A/G SNP (Kumsta et al., 2009). Therefore, the observed associations must in fact be attributed to a haplotype (a combinations of SNPs or alleles) harboring two functional SNPs. The third study investigating GR gene SNPs in relation to stress replicated the finding of a diminished serum cortisol reaction to the TSST in the *Bcl*I GG genotype; however, no sex by genotype interaction was observed (Ising et al., 2008).

MINERALOCORTICOID RECEPTOR GENE (MR, NR3C2)

In contrast to the GR, which suppresses the stress response, the MR maintains the basal HPA axis pulse and controls the neuroendocrine activation of the stress response (de Kloet, Fitzsimons, Datson, Meijer, & Vreugdenhil, 2009). The common MR I180V polymorphism (rs5522 A/G, located in exon 2) was associated with hormonal and cardiovascular responses to repeated TSST sessions (Derijk et al., 2006). Carriers of the 180V variant showed increased salivary and plasma cortisol responses as well as increased autonomic output as measured by heart beat across all three TSST sessions. Interestingly, the effects of this polymorphism seem to be specific to functions of the cortisol-responsive MR in limbic brain, because no associations were observed with aldosterone-dependent effects on sodium balance.

FK506-BINDING PROTEIN 51 GENE (FKBP5)

GR sensitivity is influenced by a multiprotein complex that mediates proper ligand binding and receptor activation. It consists of heat-shock proteins (Hsp) and several other chaperone proteins. Ising et al. (2008) studied polymorphisms within the FKBP5 gene, which codes for the FK506-binding protein 51 (FKBP51), a co-chaperone of Hsp 90 and negative regulator of glucocorticoid action. Homozygotes for the minor allele of three investigated SNPs (rs4713916, rs1360780, rs3800737) showed the highest plasma cortisol levels during the recovery periods of both TSST sessions, with almost identical results for all three SNPs. Self-reported anxiety during recovery after the second TSST was significantly elevated in rs4713916 AA and rs3800373 GG carriers. No effects were observed for ACTH responses. The three FKBP5 SNPs are located in noncoding regions, and no functional studies have been performed. However, the intronic rs1360780 polymorphism was previously associated with elevated FKBP5 protein levels, supporting the findings of delayed recovery after stress.

GABA$_A$$\alpha$6 SUBUNIT (GABRA6)

Inhibition of HPA axis activity is also exerted through γ-aminobutyric acid (GABA), the main inhibitory neurotransmitter in the central nervous system. CRH neurons within the PVN and noradrenalin-producing neurons within the locus coeruleus both express GABA receptors. After the TSST, individuals carrying a T allele of SNP rs3219151 had higher ACTH, cortisol, and blood pressure responses compared to those with the C/C genotype. Furthermore, subjects homozygous for the C allele had lower scores on the NEO Personality Inventory extraversion factor (Uhart, McCaul, Oswald, Choi, & Wand, 2004).

SEROTONIN TRANSPORTER GENE (5-HTT, SLC6A4)

There is a functional link between the serotonergic system and central HPA axis components. A common polymorphism in the promoter region of the 5-HTT gene, termed 5-HTTLPR (see also Chapter 25), has repeatedly been shown to moderate the influence of life stress on depression (Karg, Burmeister, Shedden, & Sen, 2011), and one possible mechanism underlying these findings involves differences in stress reactivity.

Gotlib and colleagues (2008) studied a sample of girls with either the presence or absence of a family history of depression. They assessed salivary cortisol in response to a test consisting of mental arithmetic and a semi-structured interview developed to induce emotional stress and arousal. Independently of mothers' or children's depression scores, girls homozygous for the s-allele showed a marked increase in cortisol levels after stress exposure. L-allele carriers, in contrast, did not show any cortisol response. In a nonclinical male adult sample, the interaction between stressful life events and endocrine responses to the TSST was tested. No main effect of the 5-HTTLPR genotype was observed; however, s-allele homozygotes with a history of stressful life events showed markedly elevated cortisol responses to the stressor compared to all other groups, indicating a significant gene-by-

environment interaction (Alexander et al., 2009).

BRAIN-DERIVED NEUROTROPHIC FACTOR

Animal studies have shown an involvement of brain-derived neurotrophic factor (BDNF) in the regulation of HPA axis activity. Acute and repeated immobilization stress and corticosterone administration have been shown to reduce BDNF expression in the rat hippocampus (Scaccianoce, Del Bianco, Caricasole, Nicoletti, & Catalani, 2003), and BDNF injection was shown to modify HPA axis activity in adult male rats (Givalois et al., 2004). A common polymorphism in the human BDNF gene (rs6265 G/A) has been identified, with the A allele producing an amino acid substitution (valine to methionine) at codon 66 (Val66Met). Functionality of this SNP is supported by in vitro and brain imaging studies (Hariri et al., 2003). Following the TSST, male val/val homozygotes showed a larger increase in salivary cortisol than val/met heterozygotes, whereas there was a trend for the opposite response in female subjects. The same sex-specific response patterns were observed for blood pressure, heart rate, and self-reported measures of stress (Shalev et al., 2009).

Early Life Experiences and Gene-Environment Interaction

Early life experiences can have profound lifelong consequences. Certain early childhood experiences are a major risk factor for mental and physical illnesses in adult life. These experiences include sexual and/or physical abuse, growing up in families characterized by overt family conflict, and family relationships that are cold, neglectful, and unsupportive (reviewed by Repetti, Taylor, & Seeman, 2002). Increased rates of major depressive disorder (Kendler, Kuhn, & Prescott, 2004), anxiety disorder (Young, Abelson, Curtis, & Nesse, 1997), posttraumatic stress disorder (PTSD; Bremner, Southwick, Johnson, Yehuda, & Charney, 1993), substance abuse (Kendler et al., 2000), and conduct disorder (Holmes, Slaughter, & Kashani, 2001) were found in adults with a history of childhood abuse. These observations raised the question of how the long-lasting health consequences of early adverse rearing conditions are sustained. Research on the biological mechanisms linking early adversity and poor health outcomes has shown an important mediating role of physiological stress response systems.

A number of studies have demonstrated an association between childhood trauma (neglect, sexual and physical abuse) and dysregulations of the HPA axis. The HPA axis has been suggested as both a target for environmental influences and a mediator of the relationship between early adversity and mental health in adulthood. The central hypothesis is that early trauma leads to dysregulations of the HPA axis and sensitization to the effects of acute stress (Heim & Nemeroff, 2001). Childhood trauma has been associated with alterations in HPA axis response dynamics. For instance, following the TSST, increased HPA axis responses were observed in women with abuse experience, most robustly in subjects with current symptoms of depression and anxiety (Heim et al., 2000). In response to different pharmacological provocation tests to assess HPA axis dynamics, dysregulations became evident on multiple regulatory levels (Heim, Newport, Mletzko, Miller, & Nemeroff, 2008), and the evidence suggests that childhood abuse leads to an increased drive of the HPA axis and associated disinhibition of central stress responses. However, Carpenter et al. (2009) found decreased cortisol levels and decreased ACTH responses to the TSST in a sample of men reporting childhood maltreatment. Furthermore, relative hypocortisolism has been observed in PTSD, reflected by low basal cortisol concentrations, low awakening cortisol response, and increased ACTH and cortisol suppression following low-dose dexamethasone administration (Yehuda, 2002).

Thus, trauma can produce both exaggerated or dampened stress system reactivity, and the nature of HPA axis dysregulation (i.e., hyper- versus hypo-reactivity) seems to be determined in part by the time that has elapsed since exposure to traumatic experience, as well as by the nature and chronicity of the stressful experience (Miller, Chen, & Zhou, 2007). Because control of the HPA axis involves multiple regulatory mechanisms allowing for counter-regulation at different levels, these observations are not surprising. The crucial points, however, are that adverse experiences lead to changes in HPA axis response dynamics and that both hyper- and hypo-reactivity have been associated with physical and mental illness.

Gene-Environment Interactions

Despite the strong link between early trauma and increased risk for psychopathology, there is extensive evidence of a huge heterogeneity in the response of individuals to all environmental hazard, both physical and psychosocial (Rutter, 2006). Accordingly, not all individuals with childhood adverse experiences develop mental health problems. One important part of the mechanism involved in outcome heterogeneity concerns gene-by-environment (GxE) interaction, observed when the effect of exposure to an environmental pathogen on health outcomes is moderated by genotype (Moffitt, Caspi, & Rutter, 2005). For instance, the common promoter polymorphism in the serotonin transporter gene (5-HTTLPR) has repeatedly been shown to moderate the likelihood of whether an individual develops depression following early life stress (Karg et al., 2011). Such findings for GxE are also emerging for HPA axis genes with regard to depression, PTSD, and HPA axis regulation in patients with a history of childhood trauma. For instance, Bradley, et al. (2008) studied 15 SNPs of the CRH1 receptor gene (total sample: n = 621) and identified an interaction between two *CRHR1* haplotypes and child abuse predicting both current depressive symptoms and lifetime diagnosis of major depression. The most significant association was found for the haplotype formed of the TCA alleles of SNPs rs7209436, rs4792887, and rs110402 spanning intron 1, which seems to confer relative protection in a dose-dependent manner.

Another example is provided by Binder et al. (2008), who tested the interacting effect between eight SNPs in the FKBP5 gene, child abuse, and adult trauma to predict PTSD symptom severity in an urban, low-income, and predominantly black sample (n = 762). No interacting effect was found between genotype and adult trauma; however, four FKBP5 SNPs (rs9296158, rs3800373, rs1360780, rs9470080) interacted with the severity of child abuse to predict the level of adult PTSD symptoms.

Epigenetics

A pivotal question is how psychosocial experiences, especially those acting early in life, "get under the skin" to alter physiology and eventually influence disease risk. This answer might be provided by epigenetics: mechanisms that control gene expression states independent of changes to the underlying DNA sequence. These include DNA methylation, histone and chromatin modification, and control of mRNA expression by noncoding RNAs (Jaenisch & Bird, 2003). It has been shown that HPA axis activity can be programmed by early life experience and that the underlying mechanism involves epigenetic modifications of the GR. In a series of elegant studies on rodents, Michael Meaney's group demonstrated a functional link between naturally occurring variations in maternal behavior, specific epigenetic modifications leading to changes in gene expression, and stable and life-long phenotypic differences in physiology and behavior, including HPA axis reactivity. As adults, the offspring of mothers with high maternal care (more licking and grooming of pups during the first 10 days of life) were less fearful and showed reduced HPA axis responses to stress, increased hippocampal GR mRNA expression, and enhanced glucocorticoid feedback sensitivity. Subsequent studies showed that variations in maternal care were associated with alterations in DNA methylation patterns. Low maternal care was associated with increased methylation of the nerve-growth-factor-inducible protein A (NGFI-A) binding site located in the GR gene exon 1_7 promoter, leading to decreased GR expression (Weaver et al., 2004). In a recent study, parallel results were found in humans. Meaney and colleagues (McGowan et al., 2009) investigated postmortem hippocampal tissue of 24 suicide subjects (12 with childhood abuse and 12 without childhood abuse) and of 12 control subjects without abuse experience who died suddenly of causes other than suicide. Childhood abuse was associated with decreased levels of hippocampal GR mRNA and a different methylation pattern of the exon 1_F promoter, corresponding to the promoter region of exon 1_7 investigated in the rat. Differences in methylation were limited to specific sites, including a noncanonical binding site for NGFI-A. In vitro studies with exon 1_F promoter constructs with a methylation status that mimicked the methylation patterns of abused suicide victims showed decreased binding of this transcription factor, associated with decreased NGFI-A inducible gene transcription. These observations provide (1) a mechanism by which early environmental stimuli can be transduced to a molecular level, (2) a biological explanation of how phenotypic outcomes retain their stability throughout life, and (3) evidence that programming of HPA axis activity via epigenetic modifications of the GR represents an important mediating factor between early adverse experience and psychopathology in later life.

Psychobiology of Social Approach Behavior

Few molecules could be more important for affective and social neuroscience than the neuropeptide oxytocin (OXT). OXT plays an important role in social approach behavior, social recognition, and attachment (Insel & Young, 2001), as well as in the regulation of other complex social behaviors (Heinrichs, von Dawans, & Domes, 2009; Meyer-Lindenberg, Domes, Kirsch, &

Heinrichs, 2011). Recent research also suggests that impaired functioning of the oxytocin system contributes to the difficulties associated with social approach behavior experienced by individuals with disorders such as autism and social anxiety disorder. OXT, especially in combination with psychotherapy, is emerging as a promising component of novel treatment approaches for these and other mental disorders characterized by social dysfunction.

Neurophysiological Bases

OXT is synthesized in magnocellular neurons in the paraventricular and supraoptic nuclei of the hypothalamus. It is processed along the axonal projections to the posterior lobe of the pituitary, where it is stored in secretory vesicles and released into peripheral circulation. It is released from both axonal terminals and dendrites into the extracellular space, resulting in both local action and diffusion to reach distant targets in the brain (Ludwig & Leng, 2006). In addition, smaller OXT-producing parvocellular neurons in the paraventricular nucleus project directly to other regions in the brain, including the amygdala, hippocampus, striatum, suprachiasmatic nucleus, bed nucleus of stria terminalis, and brainstem, where OXT acts as a neuromodulator or neurotransmitter. For example, OXT modulates neural populations in the central amygdala (Viviani et al., 2011). For an overview of studies on endogenous levels of OXT and human behavior, see Heinrichs et al. (2009). For an overview of the neurogenetic mechanisms of the OXT system including neuroimaging studies, see Kumsta & Heinrichs (2012).

Methodological Issues of Oxytocin Research in Humans

Researchers have used several methods to study the functioning of the oxytocin system in humans. The remainder of this chapter focuses on studies that have used the method of intranasal administration, which in recent years has been successfully combined with established behavioral and neuroimaging paradigms to clarify OXT's actions in the human brain. Intranasal administration provides a relatively noninvasive method for delivering OXT directly to the brain (Born et al., 2002; Heinrichs & Domes, 2008).

Peripheral levels of OXT can be measured through the plasma. Although these results are intriguing, the relationship between peripheral levels and CNS availability of OXT remains unclear (Anderson, 2006; Carter et al., 2007; Landgraf & Neumann, 2004). Therefore, further investigation of this issue will be necessary before conclusions can be drawn about a direct relationship between peripheral OXT levels and brain function.

A third approach to studying OXT effects involves the measurement of OXT levels in cerebrospinal fluid (CSF). The level of neuropeptides in CSF has been shown to reflect their immediate availability in the brain (Born et al., 2002), which is more directly relevant for behavioral effects or psychopathology than peripheral neuropeptide levels (Heinrichs & Domes, 2008). However, obtaining CSF samples involves an invasive methodology that cannot be easily used in routine human research.

Molecular genetic methods are well suited for investigating natural interindividual variations in the OXT system and their implications for human social behavior (Kumsta & Heinrichs, 2012). In several studies, a single nucleotide polymorphism (SNP) located in the third intron of the oxytocin receptor gene (*OXTR*), rs53576 (G/A), has been associated with socioemotional functioning. Specifically, the A allele of rs53576 has been associated with a larger startle response (Rodrigues, Saslow, Garcia, John, & Keltner, 2009) and reduced amygdala activation during emotional face processing (Inoue et al., 2010). It has also been linked to increased risk for autism (Lerer et al., 2008), reduced maternal sensitivity to child behavior (Bakermans-Kranenburg & van Ijzendoorn, 2008), lower empathy (Rodrigues et al., 2009) and, in men, reduced positive affect (Lucht et al., 2009).

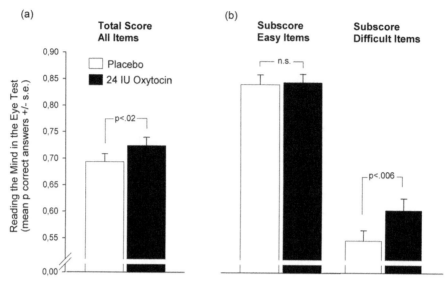

Figure 22.3. (A) Oxytocin improved performance in the Reading the Mind in the Eyes Test (RMET) compared to placebo. (B) Performance in the RMET as a function of item difficulty: Oxytocin improved performance on the difficult items and not on the easy items. Figure modified from Domes et al. (2007), with permission from © 2007, Society of Biological Psychiatry.

Oxytocin and Emotion Recognition

OXT has been found to play a role in the recognition of subtle social signals encoded in facial expressions, an ability with important implications for social approach behavior. In one study conducted on healthy men, intranasal OXT administration improved the performance in the "Reading the Mind in the Eyes" test (Domes, Heinrichs, Michel, Berger, & Herpertz, 2007), a measure developed to assess the social cognitive abilities of adults with autism spectrum disorder (ASD; Baron-Cohen, Wheelwright, Hill, Raste, & Plumb, 2001). Specifically, participants receiving OXT were more accurate than those receiving placebo in determining other individuals' emotional or mental states based on photos of those individuals' eyes (Figure 22.3).

OXT may also have a role in individual differences in emotion recognition accuracy (Bartz et al., 2010). In a task that measured "empathic accuracy" (operationalized as the ability to infer the emotions felt by another person as they are displayed in a film clip), intranasal OXT improved empathic accuracy only in individuals with high levels of autistic traits, who presumably have low baseline empathic abilities. These results are in line with research suggesting that empathic abilities are associated with genetic variation of the oxytocin system marked by *OXTR* rs53576 (Rodrigues et al., 2009).

The extent to which OXT selectively affects recognition of specific emotions remains unclear. Existing studies have yielded mixed results, with some suggesting that OXT specifically enhances processing of positive facial expressions (Di Simplicio, Massey-Chase, Cowen, & Harmer, 2009; Marsh, Yu, Pine, & Blair, 2010) or specifically decreases aversion to angry faces (Evans, Shergill, & Averbeck, 2010), and others suggesting that OXT specifically improves recognition of fearful faces (Fischer-Shofty, Shamay-Tsoory, Harari, & Levkovitz, 2010). In a visual search task, no effect of OXT on emotion recognition was observed (Guastella et al., 2010). A recent study suggests that during the early stages of visual processing (with faces presented for only 17 to 83 ms), OXT promotes recognition of both happy and angry faces (Schulze et al., 2011). Further research will be necessary to reconcile these findings.

Visual attention to neutral and emotional faces plays a critical role in the recognition of facial emotions (Adolphs, 2002). To date, four studies have examined the effects of OXT on patterns of visual attention to faces. With one exception (Domes et al., 2010), these studies have reported increased gazing time on the eye region compared to other parts of the face (Domes, Steiner, Porges, & Heinrichs, 2012). Although these results suggest that improved facial emotion recognition after OXT treatment might be due at least in part to increased eye gaze, this hypothesis has not yet been explicitly tested. Because several mental disorders involving social deficits have been linked to impaired or biased processing of emotional expressions as well as reduced or atypical gaze to the eye region, a more complete understanding of the conditions under which oxytocin can enhance emotion recognition and eye gaze will likely have translational implications for the treatment of these disorders.

Compared to studies investigating the effects of OXT on more cognitive aspects of empathy such as emotion recognition, research on OXT effects on emotional empathy (i.e., the vicarious feeling of an emotion) has been relatively rare to date (Hurlemann et al., 2010). Recent studies have begun to address this gap in the literature, with one study reporting positive effects of intranasal OXT on emotional empathy but not cognitive empathy (Hurlemann et al., 2010).

Oxytocin, Stress, and Social Support

A number of studies suggest that OXT dampens the typical endocrine response to stressful social interaction, which includes HPA axis activation and the secretion of CRH, ACTH and cortisol (see the earlier discussion). Breastfeeding, which is associated with endogenous secretion of OXT, has been associated with dampened cortisol responses to psychosocial stressors in women (Heinrichs et al., 2001). In another study, healthy males were randomly assigned to receive social support or no social support and OXT or placebo

during preparation for the Trier Social Stress Test (TSST). Subjects receiving social support and OXT showed the lowest cortisol response to the TSST, whereas subjects who received no social support and placebo showed the highest response (Figure 22.4; Heinrichs, Baumgartner, Kirschbaum, & Ehlert, 2003). Notably, subjects who received social support and OXT also reported the lowest levels of subjective stress (lower anxiety and higher calmness). The stress-buffering effect of OXT has been replicated in other recent studies (Quirin, Kuhl, & Dusing, 2011). Complementary interindividual differences in stress responses have been linked to the variation in the oxytocin receptor gene: The *OXTR* rs53576 AA genotype has been associated both with a reduced tendency to seek social support (Kim et al., 2010) and to reduced physiological and psychological responsivity to social support (Chen, Kumsta, von Dawans, Monakhov, Ebstein, & Heinrichs, 2011).

In a study on couples, OXT administration increased positive communication and reduced plasma cortisol levels in both men and women during a conflict (Ditzen et al., 2009), suggesting that central OXT facilitates human pair bonding in a manner parallel to that observed in prior animal studies. In men with an insecure attachment pattern, OXT enhanced secure interpretations of ambiguous attachment-related scenarios (Buchheim et al., 2009). Because secure attachment in humans is associated with lower stress reactivity and a better ability to interact socially (Ditzen et al., 2009), understanding the role of OXT in attachment may have clinical implications for several mental and developmental disorders associated with stress and impairments in social approach behavior.

These results suggest that OXT enhances the buffering effect of positive social interactions on stress responsivity, although the underlying biological and developmental mechanisms of this effect remain unclear (Gamer & Buchel, 2012). It is likely that the baseline sensitivity of the CNS to OXT is influenced by significant events occurring

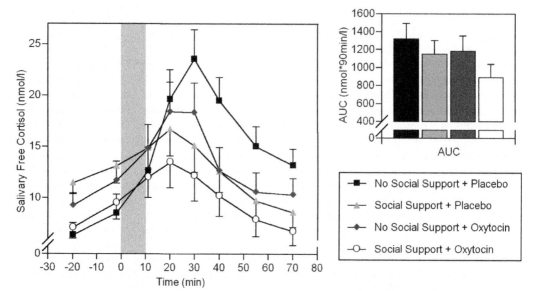

Figure 22.4. Mean salivary free cortisol concentrations (± SEM) during psychosocial stress exposure (Trier Social Stress Test). Participants were randomly assigned to receive intranasal oxytocin (24 IU) or placebo and either no social support or social support from their best friend before stress. The shaded area indicates the period of the stress tasks (public speaking followed by mental arithmetic in front of a panel of evaluators). The areas under the individual response curves (AUC) represent cumulative cortisol release (calculated by aggregating data from eight saliva sampling points) throughout the session. Significant interaction effects on cortisol were observed (social support by time effect, $p < .001$; social support by oxytocin by time effect, $p < .01$). Figure modified from Heinrichs et al. (2003), with permission from © 2003 Society of Biological Psychiatry.

early in life. Early parental separation stress, for example, has been shown to reduce the suppressive effect of OXT on cortisol levels (Meinlschmidt & Heim, 2007). Because stress increases risk for many psychiatric disorders, whereas positive social interactions decrease it, further research on these issues may enhance possibilities for treatment and early intervention for these disorders.

Oxytocin and Social Memory

In one early study, OXT was associated with an impairment of general semantic memory (Fehm-Wolfsdorf, Born, Voigt, & Fehm, 1984). However, more recent studies suggest that OXT selectively modulates social memory. In one study, intranasal OXT selectively reduced men's implicit memory of socially relevant (and not neutral) words (Heinrichs, Meinlschmidt, Wippich, Ehlert, & Hellhammer, 2004). In another study, intranasal OXT selectively

improved recognition memory for faces but not for nonsocial stimuli (Rimmele, Hediger, Heinrichs, & Klaver, 2009). In one study, intranasal OXT administered before a learning task enhanced memory for happy faces over angry and neutral faces (Guastella, Carson, Dadds, Mitchell, & Cox, 2009). Whether and how OXT administration influences memory for specific emotions remains unclear.

Oxytocin and Approach Behavior

In many mammalian species, OXT promotes social approach behavior and reduces the tendency to avoid proximity with unfamiliar others. In humans, OXT increases trust, which can be considered an indicator of psychological readiness for social approach. In the first study to investigate the role of OXT in interpersonal trust (Kosfeld, Heinrichs, Zak, Fischbacher, & Fehr, 2005), participants who had received OXT showed

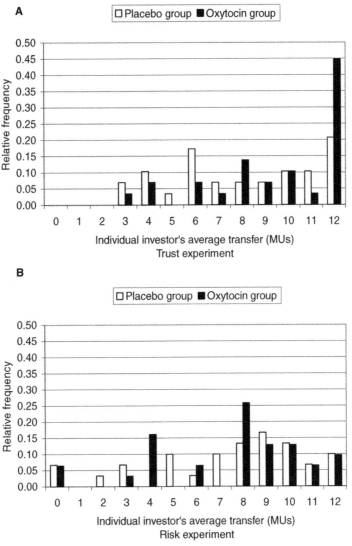

Figure 22.5. Transfers in the trust and risk experiments. Each observation represents the average transfer amount (in monetary units, MU) per investor across four transfer decisions. (A) Relative frequency of investors' average transfers in the oxytocin (filled bars) and placebo (open bars) groups in the trust experiment: Subjects given oxytocin showed significantly higher transfer levels. (B) Relative frequency of investors' average transfers in the oxytocin (filled bars) and placebo (open bars) groups in the risk experiment: Subjects in the oxytocin and the placebo group showed statistically identical transfer levels. Figure modified from Kosfeld, Heinrichs et al. (2005), with permission from © 2005, Nature Publishing Group.

greater willingness to take social risks in a trust game relative to the placebo group (Figure 22.5). Notably, OXT increased participants' willingness to take risks only when the interaction involved a social component.

Another study showed that OXT can sustain trusting behavior after a breach of trust (Baumgartner, Heinrichs, Vonlan-then, Fischbacher, & Fehr, 2008). After several rounds of a trust game, participants were informed that their social partners had made selfish decisions that were disadvantageous to the participant (i.e., betrayed the participant's trust). Whereas participants who had received placebo subsequently made decisions indicating reduced trust of the social partner, participants who had received intranasal OXT continued to make decisions indicating sustained trust. In another study, OXT increased motivation for continued social interaction following an experience of inclusion (in a virtual ball-tossing game, "cyberball"), although it did not buffer against the negative feelings associated with blunt social ostracism (Alvares, Hickie, & Guastella, 2010).

Evidence of OXT's effects on social approach-related behaviors and cognitions has been found in other domains. OXT has also been shown to enhance perceptions of facial trustworthiness and attractiveness (Theodoridou, Rowe, Penton-Voak, & Rogers, 2009). In one study, OXT positively affected the responsiveness of fathers toward their toddlers, thereby possibly promoting positive interactions (Naber, van Ijzendoorn, Deschamps, van Engeland, & Bakermans-Kranenburg, 2010). The social context appears to be a critical modulator of OXT's effects on social interaction: Brief prior face-to-face contact with a social partner has been found to enhance the effects of OXT on cooperative or prosocial behavior (Declerck, Boone, & Kiyonari, 2010), and ingroup versus outgroup membership modulates the effects of OXT on cooperation (Chen et al., 2011; De Dreu et al., 2010; De Dreu, Greer, Van Kleef, Shalvi, & Handgraaf, 2011).

In summary, OXT appears to increase motivation to engage in social interactions, enhance the ability to decode and recall key social cues such as facial expressions of emotion, and promote trusting behavior, cooperation, and willingness to take social risks. The few studies that have directly investigated the specificity of these effects through the inclusion of both social and nonsocial stimuli suggest that the effects are more pronounced for social stimuli (Norman et al., 2011; Rimmele et al., 2009).

Translational Perspectives for Social Neuropeptides

OXT's potential therapeutic value for social disorders is clearly evidenced by its effects on social behavior, links between atypical levels of endogenous oxytocin and mental disorders (for a review, see Heinrichs et al., 2009), associations between OXTR polymorphisms and social behavior, and associations between OXTR polymorphisms and risk for mental disorders characterized by severe social deficits (Kumsta & Heinrichs, 2012). Because only a small fraction of intravenously administered neuropeptide passes through the blood-brain barrier, the method of intravenous administration of OXT has limited applicability in clinical settings. Furthermore, intravenous infusion could potentially have side effects due to actions on hormone systems. Currently, the most promising clinical intervention method is intranasal administration, which affords a direct pathway to the human brain (Born et al., 2002; Heinrichs et al., 2009).

So far, no systematic, randomized control trials on the therapeutic effects of intranasal OXT treatment have been completed. To fully assess the therapeutic value of OXT, large-scale neuropharmacological studies on clinical samples that systematically manipulate neuropeptide availability in the CNS are necessary. However, preclinical studies in patients have demonstrated promising results of a single dose of intranasal OXT on various mental disorders. The following section reviews recent advances using OXT as part of a therapeutic program for psychopathological states.

In healthy individuals, intranasal administration of OXT improves social cognition, emotion recognition, secure attachment, and empathy (Buchheim et al., 2009; Ditzen et al., 2009; Domes, Heinrichs, Michel, et al., 2007; Guastella, Mitchell, & Dadds, 2008; Heinrichs et al., 2004; Rimmele et al., 2009), reduces physiological and psychological stress responses (Heinrichs et al., 2003), mediates stress-protective consequences of social support ("social buffering;" Heinrichs et al., 2003), and attenuates amygdala reactivity to social stimuli; Baumgartner et al., 2008; Domes, Heinrichs, Glascher, et al., 2007; Gamer et al., 2010; Kirsch et al., 2005. Pharmacological intervention in the OXT system represents a

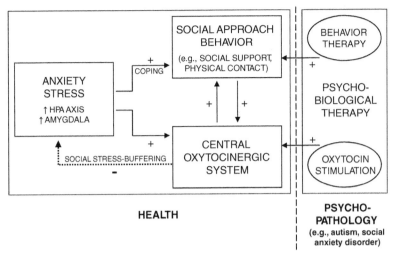

Figure 22.6. Integrative translational model of the interactions of the oxytocin system, social approach behavior, and social stress in humans. *Left*: Social stress and social anxiety stimulate the amygdala–cingulate circuit and the hypothalamic–pituitary–adrenal (HPA) axis. In healthy individuals, stress and anxiety encourage social approach behavior as a coping strategy. They also stimulate oxytocin release, which further promotes social approach behavior. Furthermore, positive social interaction (e.g., physical contact) is itself associated with OXT release and therefore promotes continued social approach behavior. OXT reduces amygdala and HPA axis reactivity to social stressors and as such serves as an important mediator of the anxiolytic and stress-protective effects of positive social interaction ("social buffering"). *Right*: Patients with mental and developmental disorders characterized by severe deficits in social interactions (e.g., autism, social anxiety disorder, borderline personality disorder) may benefit from novel "psychobiological therapy" approaches in which psychotherapy is combined with the administration of OXT or OXT receptor agonists. Figure modified from Heinrichs & Domes (2008), with permission from © 2008, Elsevier.

particularly promising new angle for treatment for those with pathologies in these domains (Figure 22.6). Especially in combination with interaction-based psychotherapy, administration of OXT or selective and longer acting OXTR agonists such as carbetocin may represent an effective treatment option for mental disorders characterized by extreme difficulties in social interactions and/or disrupted attachment relationships, such as social anxiety disorder and autism spectrum disorder (Meyer-Lindenberg et al., 2011). Initial results of experimental neuropeptide administration in these patient groups have been encouraging, especially given the fact that these "social disorders" are notoriously difficult to treat or as, in the case of autism, currently cannot be effectively treated at all.

Social anxiety disorder (SAD) is the third most common mental health disorder after depression and alcoholism (Kessler et al.,

1994) and thus represents a major public health issue. SAD is characterized by a fear of negative evaluation by others and extreme anxiety and discomfort before, during, and after exposure to social settings. In one study, patients with SAD were administered intranasal OXT and participated in five weekly sessions of brief exposure intervention (Guastella, Howard, Dadds, Mitchell, & Carson, 2009). OXT administration improved speech performance over the course of the exposure sessions; however, possibly because of the low frequency of sessions, a more generalized overall improvement in treatment outcome was not observed. In another study (Labuschagne et al., 2010), SAD patients and healthy controls were administered intranasal OXT or placebo and performed an emotional face matching task involving pictures of fearful, angry, and happy faces. In the placebo condition, patients with SAD showed a hyperactive amygdala response to fearful faces relative to the healthy control group. Although OXT administration did not change amygdala reactivity to emotional faces in the control group, it dampened amygdala reactivity to fearful faces in the SAD group (Labuschagne et al., 2010). These findings suggest that OXT has a specific effect on fear-related amygdala activity, particularly when the amygdala is hyperactive as in SAD.

Another disorder for which OXT shows therapeutic promise is autism spectrum disorder (ASD). ASD, a neurodevelopmental disorder, is characterized by severe deficits in social functioning, communication deficits, and repetitive or compulsive behaviors in combination with restricted interests. In a recent study (Guastella et al., 2010), adolescent males (aged 12 to 19) with ASD were treated with intranasal OXT or placebo. OXT administration improved performance on the "Reading the Mind in the Eyes" Task (Baron-Cohen et al., 2001). In another study (Andari et al., 2010) involving individuals with ASD, intranasal OXT increased social interactions and feelings of trust in a simulated ball game that involved interactions with fictitious partners (cyberball). In addition, OXT administration increased ASD patients' gazing time toward the eye region of facial photos. Intravenous infusion of OXT has also been shown to induce subtle behavioral and psychological effects in individuals with ASD, including enhanced understanding of emotional speech and decreased repetitive behaviors (Bartz & Hollander, 2008), although it should be noted that only a small fraction of intravenously administered OXT is thought to pass the blood-brain barrier. These studies, as a whole, suggest that OXT has therapeutic potential (especially when intervention occurs early in life) for the core deficits associated with ASD, by enhancing emotion recognition, reducing repetitive behaviors, and improving social behavior and responsiveness to others.

Several clinical trials are currently being carried out (see the list of projects in clinicaltrials.gov) to develop and evaluate new clinically relevant approaches for neuropeptide administration. Intranasal OXT treatment is expected to enhance patients' willingness to interact socially (e.g., in cognitive-behavioral group therapy) as well as to confront feared social situations outside of therapy sessions by dampening stress reactivity. Figure 22.6) presents an integrative model of the relationships among social anxiety and stress, social approach behavior, and the human central OXT system. This model highlights the importance of systematic inquiry into "propsychotherapeutic" neuropharmacology – an approach in which pharmacological intervention supports and enhances psychotherapeutic interventions rather than serving in isolation as an alternative route to a cure. We therefore propose the term "psychobiological therapy" for this novel integrative approach.

The model also calls attention to important topics for further research. For instance, more research is required to clarify the mechanisms by which OXT, receptor agonists, and antagonists reach the brain after different forms of administration, as well as to clarify the relationship between peripheral and central OXT levels. Such knowledge would promote the development of optimal strategies to manipulate neuropeptide availability or potentially to use them as markers of beneficial treatment. The development of specific radioactive labeling of neuropeptides in positron emission tomography would help clarify the precise location of OXT receptors in the human brain. In combination with in vitro studies identifying OXT binding sites in the human brain and fMRI studies identifying brain areas responsive to OXT administration (Heinrichs & Domes, 2008), positron emission tomography with OXT would provide much needed information about brain circuits involved in social information processing. The development of nonpeptidergic drugs acting on OXT receptors represents another significant research goal. Further studies on how specific genetic variants influence behavioral and brain response to OXT administration will be crucial for decoding individual differences in the functioning of the social brain and to tailor new treatment strategies sensitive to individual differences. These studies may also clarify how the neuroanatomical distribution and sensitivity of OXT receptors are influenced by variations in the regulatory regions of their respective genes. Overall, the tremendous growth in this research field offers not only a promising new path for exploring the neuroendocrinology of the social brain but also a translational perspective for developing novel treatment strategies for social disorders.

Outstanding Questions and Future Directions

- How could stress response measures (hormonal and/or neural) in combination with genetic information be used to tailor therapeutic approaches for stress-related disorders?
- Epigenetic mechanisms have been shown to influence HPA axis regulation; however, the effects seem to be tissue specific. It will be critical to investigate whether peripheral, easy-to-obtain markers in humans will be useful; that is, reflect epigenetic changes in central nervous tissue.
- Which methods of administration of neuropeptides that penetrate the brain are currently available? How could their effectiveness (e.g., half-life time, specificity) be improved?
- How could a combination of genotyping of neuropeptide receptor gene polymorphisms and neuropeptide administration improve potential clinical effects?

References

Adolphs, R. (2002). Recognizing emotion from facial expressions: psychological and neurological mechanisms. *Behavioral and Cognitive Neuroscience Review*, 1(1), 21–62.

Alexander, N., Kuepper, Y., Schmitz, A., Osinsky, R., Kozyra, E., & Hennig, J. (2009). Gene-environment interactions predict cortisol responses after acute stress: Implications for the etiology of depression. *Psychoneuroendocrinology*, 34(9), 1294–1303.

Alvares, G. A., Hickie, I. B., & Guastella, A. J. (2010). Acute effects of intranasal oxytocin on subjective and behavioral responses to social rejection. *Experimental and Clinical Psychopharmacology*, 18(4), 316–21.

Andari, E., Duhamel, J. R., Zalla, T., Herbrecht, E., Leboyer, M., & Sirigu, A. (2010). Promoting social behavior with oxytocin in high-functioning autism spectrum disorders. *Proceedings of the National Academy of Sciences*, 107(9), 4389–94.

Anderson, G. M. (2006). Report of altered urinary oxytocin and AVP excretion in neglected orphans should be reconsidered. *Journal of Autism and Developmental Disorders*, 36(6), 829–30.

Bakermans-Kranenburg, M. J., & van Ijzendoorn, M. H. (2008). Oxytocin receptor (OXTR) and serotonin transporter (5-HTT) genes associated with observed parenting. *Social, Cognitive & Affective Neurosciences*, 3(2), 128–34.

Baron-Cohen, S., Wheelwright, S., Hill, J., Raste, Y., & Plumb, I. (2001). The "Reading the Mind in the Eyes" Test revised version: A study with normal adults, and adults with Asperger syndrome or high-functioning autism. *Journal of Child Psychology and Psychiatry*, 42(2), 241–51.

Bartz, J. A., & Hollander, E. (2008). Oxytocin and experimental therapeutics in autism spectrum disorders. *Progress in Brain Research*, 170, 451–62.

Bartz, J. A., Zaki, J., Bolger, N., Hollander, E., Ludwig, N. N., Kolevzon, A., et al. (2010). Oxytocin selectively improves empathic accuracy. *Psychological Science*, 21(10), 1426–28.

Baumgartner, T., Heinrichs, M., Vonlanthen, A., Fischbacher, U., & Fehr, E. (2008). Oxytocin shapes the neural circuitry of trust and trust adaptation in humans. *Neuron*, 58(4), 639–50.

Binder, E. B., Bradley, R. G., Liu, W., Epstein, M. P., Deveau, T. C., Mercer, K. B., et al. (2008). Association of FKBP5 polymorphisms and childhood abuse with risk of posttraumatic stress disorder symptoms in adults. *Journal of the American Medical Association*, 299(11), 1291–1305.

Born, J., Lange, T., Kern, W., McGregor, G. P., Bickel, U., & Fehm, H. L. (2002). Sniffing neuropeptides: A transnasal approach to the human brain. *Nature Neuroscience*, 5(6), 514–16.

Bradley, R. G., Binder, E. B., Epstein, M. P., Tang, Y., Nair, H. P., Liu, W., et al. (2008).

Influence of child abuse on adult depression: Moderation by the corticotropin-releasing hormone receptor gene. *Archives of General Psychiatry*, 65(2), 190–200.

Bremner, J. D., Southwick, S. M., Johnson, D. R., Yehuda, R., & Charney, D. S. (1993). Childhood physical abuse and combat-related posttraumatic stress disorder in Vietnam veterans. *American Journal of Psychiatry*, 150(2), 235–39.

Buchheim, A., Heinrichs, M., George, C., Pokorny, D., Koops, E., Henningsen, P., et al. (2009). Oxytocin enhances the experience of attachment security. *Psychoneuroendocrinology*, 34(9), 1417–22.

Buske-Kirschbaum, A., Jobst, S., Wustmans, A., Kirschbaum, C., Rauh, W., & Hellhammer, D. (1997). Attenuated free cortisol response to psychosocial stress in children with atopic dermatitis. *Psychosomatic Medicine*, 59(4), 419–26.

Carpenter, L. L., Tyrka, A. R., Ross, N. S., Khoury, L., Anderson, G. M., & Price, L. H. (2009). Effect of childhood emotional abuse and age on cortisol responsivity in adulthood. *Biological Psychiatry*, 66(1), 69–75.

Carter, C. S., Pournajafi-Nazarloo, H., Kramer, K. M., Ziegler, T. E., White-Traut, R., Bello, D., et al. (2007). Oxytocin: behavioral associations and potential as a salivary biomarker. *Annals of the New York Academy of Sciences*, 1098, 312–22.

Chen, F. S., Kumsta, R., von Dawans, B., Monakhov, M., Ebstein, R. P., & Heinrichs, M. (2011). Common oxytocin receptor gene (*OXTR*) polymorphism and social support interact to reduce stress in humans. *Proceedings of the National Academy of Sciences of the United States of America (PNAS)*, 108, 19937–19942.

Chen, F. S., Kumsta, R., & Heinrichs, M. (2011). Oxytocin and intergroup relations: Goodwill is not a fixed pie. *Proceedings of the National Academy of Sciences*, 108(13), E45; author reply E46.

Chrousos, G. P. (2009). Stress and disorders of the stress system. *Nature Reviews: Endocrinology*, 5(7), 374–81.

Declerck, C. H., Boone, C., & Kiyonari, T. (2010). Oxytocin and cooperation under conditions of uncertainty: The modulating role of incentives and social information. *Hormones and Behavior*, 57(3), 368–74.

Dedovic, K., Renwick, R., Mahani, N. K., Engert, V., Lupien, S. J., & Pruessner, J. C. (2005). The Montreal Imaging Stress Task: Using functional imaging to investigate the effects of perceiving and processing psychosocial stress in the human brain. *Journal of Psychiatry & Neuroscience*, 30(5), 319–25.

De Dreu, C. K., Greer, L. L., Handgraaf, M. J., Shalvi, S., Van Kleef, G. A., Baas, M., et al. (2010). The neuropeptide oxytocin regulates parochial altruism in intergroup conflict among humans. *Science*, 328(5984), 1408–11.

De Dreu, C. K., Greer, L. L., Van Kleef, G. A., Shalvi, S., & Handgraaf, M. J. (2011). Oxytocin promotes human ethnocentrism. *Proceedings of the National Academy of Sciences*, 108(4), 1262–66.

de Kloet, E. R., Fitzsimons, C. P., Datson, N. A., Meijer, O. C., & Vreugdenhil, E. (2009). Glucocorticoid signaling and stress-related limbic susceptibility pathway: About receptors, transcription machinery and microRNA. *Brain Research*, 13(1293),129–41.

de Kloet, E. R., Joels, M., & Holsboer, F. (2005). Stress and the brain: From adaptation to disease. *Nature Reviews Neuroscience*, 6(6), 463–75.

Derijk, R. H., Wüst, S., Meijer, O. C., Zennaro, M. C., Federenko, I. S., Hellhammer, D. H., et al. (2006). A common polymorphism in the mineralocorticoid receptor modulates stress responsiveness. *Journal of Clinical Endocrinology and Metabolism*, 91(12), 5083–89.

Di Simplicio, M., Massey-Chase, R., Cowen, P., & Harmer, C. (2009). Oxytocin enhances processing of positive versus negative emotional information in healthy male volunteers. *Journal of Psychopharmacology*, 23(3), 241–48.

Dickerson, S. S., & Kemeny, M. E. (2004). Acute stressors and cortisol responses: A theoretical integration and synthesis of laboratory research. *Psychological Bulletin*, 130(3), 355–91.

Ditzen, B., Schaer, M., Gabriel, B., Bodenmann, G., Ehlert, U., & Heinrichs, M. (2009). Intranasal oxytocin increases positive communication and reduces cortisol levels during couple conflict. *Biological Psychiatry*, 65(9), 728–31.

Domes, G., Heinrichs, M., Glascher, J., Buchel, C., Braus, D. F., & Herpertz, S. C. (2007). Oxytocin attenuates amygdala responses to emotional faces regardless of valence. *Biological Psychiatry*, 62(10), 1187–90.

Domes, G., Heinrichs, M., Michel, A., Berger, C., & Herpertz, S. C. (2007). Oxytocin improves "mind-reading" in humans. *Biological Psychiatry*, 61(6), 731–33.

Domes, G., Lischke, A., Berger, C., Grossmann, A., Hauenstein, K., Heinrichs, M., et al. (2010). Effects of intranasal oxytocin on emotional face processing in women. *Psychoneuroendocrinology*, 35(1), 83–93.

Domes, G., Steiner, A., Porges, S. W., & Heinrichs, M. (2012). Oxytocin differentially modulates eye gaze to naturalistic social signals of happiness and anger. *Psychoneuroendocrinology*, in press (doi: 10.1016/j.psyneuen.2012.10.002).

Evans, S., Shergill, S. S., & Averbeck, B. B. (2010). Oxytocin decreases aversion to angry faces in an associative learning task. *Neuropsychopharmacology*, 35(13), 2502–9.

Fehm-Wolfsdorf, G., Born, J., Voigt, K. H., & Fehm, H. L. (1984). Human memory and neurohypophyseal hormones: Opposite effects of vasopressin and oxytocin. *Psychoneuroendocrinology*, 9(3), 285–92.

Fischer-Shofty, M., Shamay-Tsoory, S. G., Harari, H., & Levkovitz, Y. (2010). The effect of intranasal administration of oxytocin on fear recognition. *Neuropsychologia*, 48(1), 179–84.

Gamer, M., & Buchel, C. (2012). Oxytocin specifically enhances valence-dependent parasympathetic responses. *Psychoneuroendocrinology*, 37(1), 87–93.

Gamer, M., Zurowski, B., & Buchel, C. (2010). Different amygdala subregions mediate valence-related and attentional effects of oxytocin in humans. *Proceedings of the National Academy of Sciences*, 107(20), 9400–5.

Givalois, L., Naert, G., Rage, F., Ixart, G., Arancibia, S., & Tapia-Arancibia, L. (2004). A single brain-derived neurotrophic factor injection modifies hypothalamo-pituitary-adrenocortical axis activity in adult male rats. *Molecular and Cellular Neuroscience*, 27(3), 280–95.

Gotlib, I., Joormann, J., Minor, K., & Hallmayer, J. (2008). HPA axis reactivity: A mechanism underlying the associations among 5-HTTLPR, stress, and depression. *Biological Psychiatry*, 63(9), 847–51.

Guastella, A. J., Carson, D. S., Dadds, M. R., Mitchell, P. B., & Cox, R. E. (2009). Does oxytocin influence the early detection of angry and happy faces? *Psychoneuroendocrinology*, 34(2), 220–25.

Guastella, A. J., Einfeld, S. L., Gray, K. M., Rinehart, N. J., Tonge, B. J., Lambert, T. J., et al. (2010). Intranasal oxytocin improves emotion recognition for youth with autism spectrum disorders. *Biological Psychiatry*, 67(7), 692–94.

Guastella, A. J., Howard, A. L., Dadds, M. R., Mitchell, P., & Carson, D. S. (2009). A randomized controlled trial of intranasal oxytocin as an adjunct to exposure therapy for social anxiety disorder. *Psychoneuroendocrinology*, 34(6), 917–23.

Guastella, A. J., Mitchell, P. B., & Dadds, M. R. (2008). Oxytocin increases gaze to the eye region of human faces. *Biological Psychiatry*, 63(1), 3–5.

Hariri, A. R., Goldberg, T. E., Mattay, V. S., Kolachana, B. S., Callicott, J. H., Egan, M. F., et al. (2003). Brain-derived neurotrophic factor val66met polymorphism affects human memory-related hippocampal activity and predicts memory performance. *Journal of Neuroscience*, 23(17), 6690–94.

Heim, C., & Nemeroff, C. B. (2001). The role of childhood trauma in the neurobiology of mood and anxiety disorders: Preclinical and clinical studies. *Biological Psychiatry*, 49(12), 1023–39.

Heim, C., Newport, D. J., Heit, S., Graham, Y. P., Wilcox, M., Bonsall, R., et al. (2000). Pituitary-adrenal and autonomic responses to stress in women after sexual and physical abuse in childhood. *Journal of the American Medical Association*, 284(5), 592–97.

Heim, C., Newport, D. J., Mletzko, T., Miller, A. H., & Nemeroff, C. B. (2008). The link between childhood trauma and depression: Insights from HPA axis studies in humans. *Psychoneuroendocrinology*, 33(6), 693–710.

Heinrichs, M., Baumgartner, T., Kirschbaum, C., & Ehlert, U. (2003). Social support and oxytocin interact to suppress cortisol and subjective responses to psychosocial stress. *Biological Psychiatry*, 54(12), 1389–98.

Heinrichs, M., & Domes, G. (2008). Neuropeptides and social behavior: Effects of oxytocin and vasopressin in humans. *Progress in Brain Research*, 170, 337–50.

Heinrichs, M., Meinlschmidt, G., Neumann, I., Wagner, S., Kirschbaum, C., Ehlert, U., et al. (2001). Effects of suckling on hypothalamic-pituitary-adrenal axis responses to psychosocial stress in postpartum lactating women. *Journal of Clinical Endocrinology and Metabolism*, 86(10), 4798–4804.

Heinrichs, M., Meinlschmidt, G., Wippich, W., Ehlert, U., & Hellhammer, D. H. (2004). Selective amnesic effects of oxytocin on human memory. *Physiology and Behavior*, 83(1), 31–38.

Heinrichs, M., von Dawans, B., & Domes, G. (2009). Oxytocin, vasopressin, and human social behavior. *Frontiers in Neuroendocrinology*, 30(4), 548–57.

Holmes, S. E., Slaughter, J. R., & Kashani, J. (2001). Risk factors in childhood that lead to the development of conduct disorder and antisocial personality disorder. *Child Psychiatry and Human Development*, 31(3), 183–93.

Hurlemann, R., Patin, A., Onur, O. A., Cohen, M. X., Baumgartner, T., Metzler, S., et al. (2010). Oxytocin enhances amygdala-dependent, socially reinforced learning and emotional empathy in humans. *Journal of Neuroscience*, 30(14), 4999–5007.

Inoue, H., Yamasue, H., Tochigi, M., Abe, O., Liu, X., Kawamura, Y., et al. (2010). Association between the oxytocin receptor gene and amygdalar volume in healthy adults. *Biological Psychiatry*, 68(11), 1066–72.

Insel, T. R., & Young, L. J. (2001). The neurobiology of attachment. *Nature Reviews Neuroscience*, 2(2), 129–36.

Ising, M., Depping, A., Siebertz, A., Lucae, S., Unschuld, P., Kloiber, S., et al. (2008). Polymorphisms in the FKBP5 gene region modulate recovery from psychosocial stress in healthy controls. *European Journal of Neuroscience*, 28(2), 389–98.

Jaenisch, R., & Bird, A. (2003). Epigenetic regulation of gene expression: how the genome integrates intrinsic and environmental signals. *Nature Genetics*, 33(Suppl.), 245–54.

Karg, K., Burmeister, M., Shedden, K., & Sen, S. (2011). The serotonin transporter promoter variant (5-HTTLPR), stress, and depression meta-analysis revisited: Evidence of genetic moderation. *Archives of General Psychiatry*, 68(5), 444–54.

Kendler, K. S., Bulik, C. M., Silberg, J., Hettema, J. M., Myers, J., & Prescott, C. A. (2000). Childhood sexual abuse and adult psychiatric and substance use disorders in women: An epidemiological and co-twin control analysis. *Archives of General Psychiatry*, 57(10), 953–59.

Kendler, K. S., Kuhn, J. W., & Prescott, C. A. (2004). Childhood sexual abuse, stressful life events and risk for major depression in women. *Psychological Medicine*, 34(8), 1475–82.

Kessler, R. C., McGonagle, K. A., Zhao, S., Nelson, C. B., Hughes, M., Eshleman, S., et al. (1994). Lifetime and 12-month prevalence of DSM-III-R psychi-atric disorders in the United States. Results from the National Comorbidity Survey. *Archives of General Psychiatry*, 51(1), 8–19.

Kim, H. S., Sherman, D. K., Sasaki, J. Y., Xu, J., Chu, T. Q., Ryu, C., et al. (2010). Culture, distress, and oxytocin receptor polymorphism (OXTR) interact to influence emotional support seeking. *Proceedings of the National Academy of Sciences*, 107(36), 15717–21.

Kirsch, P., Esslinger, C., Chen, Q., Mier, D., Lis, S., Siddhanti, S., et al. (2005). Oxytocin modulates neural circuitry for social cognition and fear in humans. *Journal of Neuroscience*, 25(49), 11489–93.

Kirschbaum, C., Pirke, K. M., & Hellhammer, D. H. (1993). The "Trier Social Stress Test" – a tool for investigating psychobiological stress responses in a laboratory setting. *Neuropsychobiology*, 28(1–2), 76–81.

Kosfeld, M., Heinrichs, M., Zak, P. J., Fischbacher, U., & Fehr, E. (2005). Oxytocin increases trust in humans. *Nature*, 435(7042), 673–76.

Kudielka, B. M., Hellhammer, D. H., & Wust, S. (2009). Why do we respond so differently? Reviewing determinants of human salivary cortisol responses to challenge. *Psychoneuroendocrinology*, 34(1), 2–18.

Kudielka, B., Wüst, S., Kirschbaum, C., & Hellhammer, D. H. (Eds.). (2007). *Trier Social Stress Test*, Vol. 3. Oxford: Academic Press.

Kumsta, R., Entringer, S., Koper, J., Vanrossum, E., Hellhammer, D., & Wust, S. (2007). Sex specific associations between common glucocorticoid receptor gene variants and hypothalamus-pituitary-adrenal axis responses to psychosocial stress. *Biological Psychiatry*, 62(8), 863–69.

Kumsta, R., Moser, D., Streit, F., Koper, J. W., Meyer, J., & Wust, S. (2009). Characterization of a glucocorticoid receptor gene (GR, NR3C1) promoter polymorphism reveals functionality and extends a haplotype with putative clinical relevance. *American Journal of Medical Genetics B: Neuropsychiatric Genetic s*, 150B(4), 476–82.

Kumsta, R., & Heinrichs, M. (2012). Oxytocin, stress and social behavior: neurogenetics of the human oxytocin system. *Current Opinion in Neurobiology*, in press (doi: 10.1016/j.conb.2012.09.004).

Labuschagne, I., Phan, K. L., Wood, A., Angstadt, M., Chua, P., Heinrichs, M., et al.

(2010). Oxytocin attenuates amygdala reactivity to fear in generalized social anxiety disorder. *Neuropsychopharmacology*, 35(12), 2403–13.

Landgraf, R., & Neumann, I. D. (2004). Vasopressin and oxytocin release within the brain: A dynamic concept of multiple and variable modes of neuropeptide communication. *Frontiers in Neuroendocrinology*, 25(3–4), 150–76.

Lederbogen, F., Kirsch, P., Haddad, L., Streit, F., Tost, H., Schuch, P., et al. (2011). City living and urban upbringing affect neural social stress processing in humans. *Nature*, 474(7352), 498–501.

Lerer, E., Levi, S., Salomon, S., Darvasi, A., Yirmiya, N., & Ebstein, R. P. (2008). Association between the oxytocin receptor (OXTR) gene and autism: Relationship to Vineland Adaptive Behavior Scales and cognition. *Molecular Psychiatry*, 13(10), 980–88.

Lucht, M. J., Barnow, S., Sonnenfeld, C., Rosenberger, A., Grabe, H. J., Schroeder, W., et al. (2009). Associations between the oxytocin receptor gene (OXTR) and affect, loneliness and intelligence in normal subjects. *Progress in Neuropsychopharmacology and Biological Psychiatry*, 33(5), 860–66.

Ludwig, M., & Leng, G. (2006). Dendritic peptide release and peptide-dependent behaviors. *Nature Reviews Neuroscience*, 7(2), 126–36.

Marsh, A. A., Yu, H. H., Pine, D. S., & Blair, R. J. (2010). Oxytocin improves specific recognition of positive facial expressions. *Psychopharmacology (Berl)*, 209(3), 225–32.

Mason, J. W. (1968). A review of psychoendocrine research on the pituitary-adrenal cortical system. *Psychosomatic Medicine*, 30(5), 576–607.

McGowan, P. O., Sasaki, A., D'Alessio, A. C., Dymov, S., Labonte, B., Szyf, M., et al. (2009). Epigenetic regulation of the glucocorticoid receptor in human brain associates with childhood abuse. *Nature Neuroscience*, 12(3), 342–48.

Meinlschmidt, G., & Heim, C. (2007). Sensitivity to intranasal oxytocin in adult men with early parental separation. *Biological Psychiatry*, 61(9), 1109–11.

Meyer-Lindenberg, A., Domes, G., Kirsch, P., & Heinrichs, M. (2011). Oxytocin and vasopressin in the human brain: Social neuropeptides for translational medicine. *Nature Reviews Neuroscience*, 12(9), 524–38.

Miller, G. E., Chen, E., & Zhou, E. S. (2007). If it goes up, must it come down? Chronic stress and the hypothalamic-pituitary-adrenocortical axis in humans. *Psychological Bulletin*, 133(1), 25–45.

Moffitt, T. E., Caspi, A., & Rutter, M. (2005). Strategy for investigating interactions between measured genes and measured environments. *Archives of General Psychiatry*, 62(5), 473–81.

Naber, F., van Ijzendoorn, M. H., Deschamps, P., van Engeland, H., & Bakermans-Kranenburg, M. J. (2010). Intranasal oxytocin increases fathers' observed responsiveness during play with their children: A double-blind within-subject experiment. *Psychoneuroendocrinology*, 35(10), 1583–86.

Norman, G. J., Cacioppo, J. T., Morris, J. S., Karelina, K., Malarkey, W. B., Devries, A. C., et al. (2011). Selective influences of oxytocin on the evaluative processing of social stimuli. *Journal of Psychopharmacology*, 25(10), 1313–19.

Pruessner, J. C., Dedovic, K., Khalili-Mahani, N., Engert, V., Pruessner, M., Buss, C., et al. (2008). Deactivation of the limbic system during acute psychosocial stress: Evidence from positron emission tomography and functional magnetic resonance imaging studies. *Biological Psychiatry*, 63(2), 234–40.

Quirin, M., Kuhl, J., & Dusing, R. (2011). Oxytocin buffers cortisol responses to stress in individuals with impaired emotion regulation abilities. *Psychoneuroendocrinology*, 36(6), 898–904.

Repetti, R. L., Taylor, S. E., & Seeman, T. E. (2002). Risky families: Family social environments and the mental and physical health of offspring. *Psychological Bulletin*, 128(2), 330–66.

Rimmele, U., Hediger, K., Heinrichs, M., & Klaver, P. (2009). Oxytocin makes a face in memory familiar. *Journal of Neuroscience*, 29(1), 38–42.

Rodrigues, S. M., Saslow, L. R., Garcia, N., John, O. P., & Keltner, D. (2009). Oxytocin receptor genetic variation relates to empathy and stress reactivity in humans. *Proceedings of the National Academy of Sciences*, 106(50), 21437–41.

Rutter, M. (2006). Implications of resilience concepts for scientific understanding. *Annals of the New York Academy of Sciences*, 1094, 1–12.

Sapolsky, R. M., Romero, L. M., & Munck A. U. (2000). How do glucocorticoids influence stress responses? Integrating permissive, suppressive, stimulatory, and preparative actions. *Endocrine Review*, 21(1), 55–89.

Scaccianoce, S., Del Bianco, P., Caricasole, A., Nicoletti, F., & Catalani, A. (2003). Relationship between learning, stress and hippocampal brain-derived neurotrophic factor. *Neuroscience*, 121(4), 825–28.

Schulze, L., Lischke, A., Greif, J., Herpertz, S. C., Heinrichs, M., & Domes, G. (2011). Oxytocin increases recognition of masked emotional faces. *Psychoneuroendocrinology*, 36(9), 1378–82.

Shalev, I., Lerer, E., Israel, S., Uzefovsky, F., Gritsenko, I., Mankuta, D., et al. (2009). BDNF Val66Met polymorphism is associated with HPA axis reactivity to psychological stress characterized by genotype and gender interactions. *Psychoneuroendocrinology*, 34(3), 382–88.

Theodoridou, A., Rowe, A. C., Penton-Voak, I. S., & Rogers, P. J. (2009). Oxytocin and social perception: Oxytocin increases perceived facial trustworthiness and attractiveness. *Hormones and Behavior*, 56(1), 128–32.

Uhart, M., McCaul, M. E., Oswald, L. M., Choi, L., & Wand, G. S. (2004). GABRA6 gene polymorphism and an attenuated stress response. *Molecular Psychiatry*, 9(11), 998–1006.

Ulrich-Lai, Y. M., & Herman, J. P. (2009). Neural regulation of endocrine and autonomic stress responses. *Nature Reviews Neuroscience*, 10(6), 397–409.

Viviani, D., Charlet, A., van den Burg, E., Robinet, C., Hurni, N., Abatis, M., et al. (2011). Oxytocin selectively gates fear responses through distinct outputs from the central amygdala. *Science*, 333(6038), 104–7.

von Dawans, B., Kirschbaum, C., & Heinrichs, M. (2011). The Trier Social Stress Test for Groups (TSST-G): A new research tool for controlled simultaneous social stress exposure in a group format. *Psychoneuroendocrinology*, 36(4), 514–22.

Weaver, I. C., Cervoni, N., Champagne, F. A., D'Alessio, A. C., Sharma, S., Seckl, J. R., et al. (2004). Epigenetic programming by maternal behavior. *Nature Neuroscience*, 7(8), 847–54.

Wilhelm, I., Born, J., Kudielka, B. M., Schlotz, W., & Wust, S. (2007). Is the cortisol awakening rise a response to awakening? *Psychoneuroendocrinology*, 32(4), 358–66.

Wüst, S., Federenko, I. S., van Rossum, E. F., Koper, J. W., Kumsta, R., Entringer, S., et al. (2004). A psychobiological perspective on genetic determinants of hypothalamus-pituitary-adrenal axis activity. *Annals of the New York Academy of Sciences*, 1032, 52–62.

Yehuda, R. (2002). Post-traumatic stress disorder. *New England Journal of Medicine*, 346(2), 108–14.

Young, E. A., Abelson, J. L., Curtis, G. C., & Nesse, R. M. (1997). Childhood adversity and vulnerability to mood and anxiety disorders. *Depression and Anxiety*, 5(2), 66–72.

CHAPTER 23

Empathy from the Perspective of Social Neuroscience

Olga Klimecki & Tania Singer

Empathy, which can be broadly defined as the capacity to share and understand other people's emotions (for comprehensive reviews, see Batson, 2009a; Decety & Jackson, 2006; de Vignemont & Singer, 2006; Eisenberg, 2000; Hoffman, 2000; Singer & Lamm, 2009; Singer & Leiberg, 2009), has recently become an important focus of attention in the field of social neuroscience. What motivates the quest for the neural substrates underlying our understanding of emotions in others?

After many years in which neuroscientific research mainly focused on cognitive and sensory processing, attention has increasingly turned to understanding how the human brain tackles emotions and social interactions, which after all are both phenomena at the core of our existence as social beings. Thus, the field of social neuroscience has started to investigate the neural mechanisms underlying social cognition and emotions, such as our ability to empathize. In addition to the basic understanding of the biological mechanisms underlying social emotions and empathy in healthy individuals, research on the neural substrates of

empathy may also help us understand clinical phenomena related to a lack of affective and social skills such as autism, which is characterized by impairments in social interaction and communication (American Psychiatric Association, 2000), or alexithymia, a subclinical phenomenon associated with difficulties in identifying and describing emotions (Nemiah, Freyberger, & Sifneos, 1976).

The importance of empathy in our everyday lives becomes clear when we try to imagine what it would be like to live in a world completely devoid of empathy. Take the following scenario, for instance: A baby starts crying while her mother is reading a book. Without empathy, the mother would probably continue reading and not look after the baby. Her capacity to empathize, however, enables her to realize the baby's needs and react to them appropriately. As this example illustrates, empathy does not only motivate other-related prosocial behavior but also enables us to better predict the behavior of others and adapt our reactions accordingly. Finally, empathy also plays a crucial role in observational learning – by witnessing the emotional reaction of others in different circumstances, we learn which situations are good for us and which situations are better avoided.

In this chapter, we start out by revisiting the definition of empathy and delineating it from other routes to social understanding; namely, theory of mind and action understanding. We then examine the theoretical and neural underpinnings of concepts such as emotion contagion and mimicry, which can be thought of as antecedents of empathy, and compassion and empathic distress, which are introduced as consequences of empathy. Before turning our focus to how research in social neuroscience has advanced our understanding of empathy in the human brain, we review the major contributions of psychological research to our understanding of empathy and its relation to prosocial behavior. Because the neural underpinnings of empathy have been examined most prominently in the domain of empathy for pain, we begin by summarizing this line of research and discussing the reported results in light of the shared network hypothesis. In this context, we stress the specific role of the insula as a neural structure that processes both, interoception and empathy. Subsequently, we describe factors that modulate the experience of empathy for pain along with their neural underpinnings, before turning to neural correlates of empathy in other domains such as touch or smell. Finally, we show initial findings from social neuroscience research focusing on more positive aspects of empathy, such as compassion. We conclude the chapter by outlining outstanding questions in the field.

Defining Empathy and Related Concepts

Empathy is commonly defined as the human capacity to understand and share another person's emotion without confusing it with one's own emotional state (for comprehensive reviews, see Batson, 2009a; Decety & Jackson, 2006; de Vignemont & Singer, 2006; Eisenberg, 2000; Hoffman, 2000; Singer & Lamm, 2009; Singer & Leiberg, 2009). In

other words, we empathize with another human being when we vicariously share their affective state, but at the same time are aware that the other person's emotion is causing our response.

In this section, we first point out the conceptual difference among *empathy*, *mentalizing*, and *action understanding*, which can be conceived of as different routes to the understanding of others. After showing that the psychological distinction among these three concepts is paralleled by differences in the underlying neural networks, we take a closer look at the "sisters of empathy" – *emotion contagion, mimicry, sympathy and compassion* – all of which are concepts closely related to empathy.

Mentalizing and Action Understanding as Alternative Routes for Understanding Others

In addition to *empathy*, which can be seen as the emotional route for understanding others, there are at least two other ways of putting oneself into another person's shoes. On the one hand, we have the cognitive ability to understand the thoughts, beliefs, and intentions of others, which is called *mentalizing, perspective-taking,* or *theory of mind* (ToM; Frith and Frith, 2003; Premack and Woodruff, 1978). On the other hand, we have the capacity to understand the motor intentions of others, which has been associated with the discovery of mirror neurons (see Rizzolatti & Sinigaglia, 2010, for a review). Although all three often occur simultaneously in everyday social cognition, the psychological and neural processes underlying these distinct routes to understanding others can be clearly distinguished (for reviews, see de Vignemont & Singer, 2006; Preston & de Waal, 2002; Singer & Lamm, 2009). Cognitive processes related to theory of mind have been associated with activations in the medial prefrontal cortex (mPFC), superior temporal sulcus (STS), and the adjacent temporoparietal junction (TPJ; for reviews, see Amodio & Frith, 2006; Frith & Frith, 2006; Mitchell, 2009; Saxe, 2006; Saxe & Baron-Cohen, 2006), whereas the neural correlates of *action understanding* are found in a neural network spanning the inferior parietal lobe (IPL), the inferior frontal gyrus, and ventral premotor areas (see Rizzolatti & Sinigaglia, 2010, for a recent review). In monkeys, recordings from so-called *mirror neurons* in corresponding areas have revealed that these neurons encode both the execution of an action and the observation of the same action in others (Gallese et al., 1996; Rizzolatti, Fadiga, Gallese, & Fogassi, 1996). Paralleling the establishment of this mirror network in monkeys, recent research has extended these findings to humans by means of magnetoencephalography, (MEG; Hari et al., 1998), transcranial magnetic stimulation (TMS; Cattaneo, Sandrini, & Schwarzbach, 2010; Fadiga, Fogassi, Pavesi, & Rizzolatti, 1995) and functional magnetic resonance imaging (fMRI) studies (Iacoboni et al., 2005). Together, these studies suggest that monkeys as well as humans may use the same neural structures to encode their own actions and to understand the actions of others (for a review, see Rizzolatti & Craighero, 2004, or Rizzolatti & Sinigaglia, 2010). In a meta-analysis, Grèzes and Decety (2001) compared the activation foci of a variety of studies and found that overlapping activations for execution, simulation, and observation of actions are located in the supplementary motor area, dorsal premotor cortex, supramarginal gyrus, and superior parietal lobe. Finally, as discussed in detail later, the neural correlates of empathy are mainly observed in limbic and paralimbic areas such as the anterior insula (AI) and anterior cingulate cortex (ACC; for recent reviews, see Lamm & Singer, 2010; Singer & Lamm, 2009; Singer & Leiberg, 2009). Together, theory of mind, action understanding, and empathy allow us to infer the thoughts, motor intentions, and emotions of others, thereby facilitating social interactions.

Different Components of Empathy

After having introduced theory of mind, action understanding, and empathy as three complementary routes to the understanding of others relying on distinct neural networks, we now describe the different facets of empathy-related phenomena. They range from rather automatic and primitive reactions, such as mimicry and emotional contagion (which can be thought of as precedents of empathy), to states like compassion or empathic distress that follow from empathy and are, themselves, important determinants of behavior (Figure 23.1; Batson, 2009b; de Vignemont & Singer, 2006; Eisenberg, 2000; Goetz, Keltner, & Simon-Thomas, 2010; Klimecki & Singer, 2012; Singer & Lamm, 2009).

Mimicry and Emotional Contagion

Mimicry can be described as an automatically elicited response mirroring another person's emotional expression conveyed by facial, vocal, or postural expressions or by movements (see Hatfield, Rapson, & Li, 2009, for a recent review). In the domain of facial mimicry, for instance, electromyographic (EMG) recordings reveal that the visual presentation of emotional faces elicits corresponding emotional facial expressions in the observer (see Dimberg & Öhman, 1996, for a review); the perception of happy faces evokes increased activity in the zygomatic major muscle (which raises the corners of the mouth during smiling), whereas the perception of angry faces leads to increased activity in the corrugator supercilii muscle (which is associated with frowning). The short latency between stimulus onset and facial reaction (300–400 ms) supports the claim that facial mimicry is elicited automatically and occurs preattentively. Complementing these findings in the domain of facial mimicry, researchers observed that people also tend to synchronize their vocal expressions and adopt the postures and movements of others (reviewed, for example, by Hatfield et al., 2009).

Emotional contagion goes one step further than mimicry in that the automatic imitation and synchronization of displayed emotions – whether at the level of facial expressions, vocalizations, postures, or

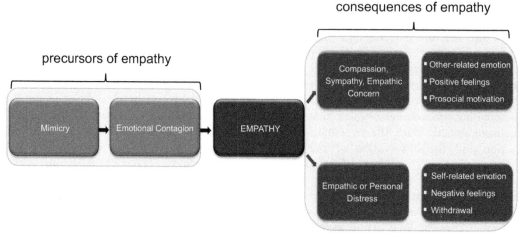

Figure 23.1. Schematic model showing the precursors and consequences of empathy.

movements – result in a convergence in the actual emotional experience (see Hatfield et al., 2009, for a recent review or Dimberg & Öhman, 1996). This is in line with the claim that peripheral-physiological feedback shapes our emotional experience (e.g., Adelmann & Zajonc, 1989) and the finding that perceiving another person in a certain emotional state can induce a congruent state in the observer (e.g., Gottman & Levenson, 1985; Harrison, Singer, Rotshtein, Dolan, & Critchley, 2006; Neumann & Strack, 2000). More concretely, this finding suggests that seeing another person smile makes us smile, which in turn makes us feel happy. Mimicry and emotional contagion can thus be regarded as precursors of empathy. In contrast to emotional contagion and mimicry, however, which can occur without self-other distinction, empathy crucially relies on the capacity to distinguish between oneself and the other. In other words, an empathic observer is aware that he or she is experiencing feelings vicariously and that these feelings were induced by emotions experienced by another person, not by his or her primary experience (de Vignemont & Singer, 2006).

Empathic Distress

Whereas mimicry and emotion contagion can be regarded as precursors of empathy, empathy may, in turn, lead to two opposing consequences: empathic distress and compassion. *Empathic distress*, which is also referred to as *personal distress*, is an aversive and self-oriented emotional response to the suffering of others. It often results in withdrawal behavior, which is motivated by the desire to protect oneself from negative emotions (Batson, O'Quin, Fultz, Vanderplas, & Isen, 1983; Eisenberg et al., 1989). In this light, empathic distress, although regarded as a consequence of empathy, falls somewhat between emotion contagion and empathy as the self-other distinction becomes blurred when the secondary empathic experience triggered by another person's suffering becomes so overwhelming that it turns into distress. This concept is particularly important for people working in health care sectors, where repeated encounters with suffering may lead to burnout (for a review, see Klimecki & Singer, 2012). Therefore, it is vital to find alternative ways of dealing with the suffering of others: Empathy does not necessarily have to take the route of empathic distress, but can instead lead to more adaptive positive emotions of compassion.

Compassion, Empathic Concern, and Sympathy

Compassion, empathic concern, and sympathy[1] all denote affective states that can be experienced as a consequence of empathy and that are not shared *with* someone, but felt *for* someone (Batson, 2009a; Singer & Lamm, 2009). Empathy or *"feeling with"* denotes a state in which the feelings of someone else are vicariously shared so that the empathizer feels an isomorphic state (de Vignemont & Singer, 2006): On witnessing a sad person, the empathizer becomes sad him- or herself. In contrast, *"feeling for"* someone refers to an emotional state that is not necessarily isomorphic to the target's affective state, but instead relies on feelings of concern for the other. More precisely, compassion can be defined as *"the emotion one experiences when feeling concern for another's suffering and desiring to enhance that individual's welfare"* (Keltner & Goetz, 2007). In other words, compassion consists of two main components. First, there is a caring feeling for the suffering of others that secondly motivates behavior aimed at relieving the other's suffering. As described in detail later, research in social and developmental psychology has demonstrated that empathic concern actually motivates prosociality and helping behaviors (see Batson, 2009b, or Eisenberg, 2000, for a review). In sum, whereas empathy is a vicarious emotion isomorphic to the emotional experience of the other, the experience of compassion, sympathy, or empathic concern denotes an affective state experienced with regard to the other that does not encompass the sharing of negative affect, but instead relies on a feeling of care and concern that motivates prosocial behavior. Before turning to empirical evidence for the promotion of prosocial behavior by compassion, we provide an overview of measures developed by psychologists to assess empathy and its different components.

Empathy Research in Psychology

Psychologists from various fields have investigated empathy and its relation to prosocial behavior. In this section, we first describe self-report, behavioral, and physiological measures of empathy before summarizing how research in developmental and social psychology established the link between empathy and prosocial behavior. Theodor Lipps (1903) first introduced the concept of empathy by proposing that we imitate the gestures and actions of others in order to understand their inner states. To measure empathy, Davis (1980) developed a questionnaire called the Interpersonal Reactivity Index (IRI) that includes four distinct components: perspective-taking, empathic concern, personal distress, and fantasy. Perspective-taking is very close to the earlier mentioned notion of theory of mind, because it measures the tendency of people to cognitively adopt the perspective of others. Empathic concern, however, is related more closely to the concept of sympathy or compassion as discussed earlier, whereas the personal distress subscale measures how prone individuals are to experiencing discomfort as a result of witnessing distress in others. Finally, the fantasy scale asks people how well they tend to identify with fictional characters in books or movies. The Balanced Emotional Empathy Scale (BEES; Mehrabian, 1997; Mehrabian & Epstein, 1972), which includes subscales such as "susceptibility to emotional contagion" or "sympathetic tendency," is another questionnaire that measures the emotional aspects of empathy.

These self-report measures are complemented by the assessment of empathic accuracy. Levenson and Ruef (1992), for instance, presented subjects with videotaped marital interactions. By comparing the subjects' ratings of positive and negative emotions displayed in the video with the self-report of the actual target, an empathy accuracy score is obtained that assesses the degree to which subjects correctly identify the emotional state of others. Additionally, physiological measures such as skin conductance and heart rate can be compared with respect to the level of physiological linkage between the target and the subject empathizing with the target (see also Gottman & Levenson, 1985). Ickes and colleagues (Ickes, 1993, for a review) used a similar approach to determine to what degree subjects succeed in inferring another person's thoughts and the content of their emotions.

Empathy and Its Relation to Prosocial Behavior

To establish the link between empathy and prosocial behavior, researchers in developmental and social psychology have conducted studies that suggest that empathy can have two opposing consequences depending on the nature of the empathic experience. In the field of social psychology, Batson and colleagues conducted several experiments (see Batson, Duncan, Ackerman, Buckley, & Birch, 1981; Batson, Fultz, & Schoenrade, 1987; Batson et al., 1983) that established that participants experiencing empathic concern feel the urge to help people in need, regardless of whether the adverse situation is easy or difficult to escape. On the contrary, participants suffering from empathic distress tend to be more self-oriented and to withdraw from negative experiences whenever possible; thus they only choose to help when the aversive situation is difficult to escape. This tendency to escape might result from aim to protect oneself by reducing one's own negative affect.

The link between empathic concern vs. empathic distress and prosocial behavior has been extended to children by research in developmental psychology, which, in addition, has established a relationship between the physiological correlates of emotional reactions and helping behavior (for a review, see Eisenberg, 2000). Eisenberg and colleagues (1989), for instance, found that adults' self-reports and facial display of sympathy predicted prosocial behavior. In children, however, the propensity to offer help was not predicted by their verbal reports of distress and sympathy. Instead, children's facial display of distress was negatively related to helping. This difference between adults and children may indicate that children's capacity to report their emotional experience reliably is underdeveloped. In sum, these results indicate that although there are differences between adults and children, empathic concern (or sympathy) promotes prosociality, whereas empathic distress is associated with withdrawal tendencies. Interestingly, a recent study revealed that prosocial behavior toward strangers can be increased by short-term training of compassion (Leiberg, Klimecki, & Singer, 2011). These findings have broad implications for the implementation of compassion training in schools and other public organizations, because compassion was shown to be a trainable and generalizable skill, motivating prosocial behavior that even extends toward strangers.

Empathy in Social Neuroscience

After having reviewed the various methods employed by social and developmental psychologists to study empathy and related concepts, we turn to the paradigms developed by social neuroscientists. Because a vast majority of empathy studies in the fMRI setting are based on variations of the empathy-for-pain paradigm, we begin this section by describing the main methods, findings, and implications of empathy-for-pain research. Subsequently, we integrate these findings with neuroscientific studies on empathy in various other domains.

Empathy for Pain

Given that empathy is a highly social phenomenon, researchers were (and still are) faced with the difficulty of coming up with a paradigm that is compatible with fMRI measurements while at the same time being ecologically valid. To reconcile both aims, Singer and colleagues (Singer et al., 2004) designed an empathy-for-pain paradigm in which two participants who are present in the same scanner environment alternately receive painful stimuli administered through electrodes attached to the back of their hand. More specifically, both the person lying in the scanner and the person sitting next to the scanner receive painful and nonpainful electric stimulation. This setup allows for the comparison between brain responses elicited when the scanned subjects experience painful stimulation versus neural activations related to witnessing another person experiencing pain. During the brain scan, arrows in different colors that can be seen by the participant through the help of a mirror system indicate who is going to be stimulated next and whether the stimulation is going to be painful or not. Under the assumption that people in a very close relation feel strong empathy for each other, Singer and colleagues (2004) started out by examining empathy for pain in couples. Intriguingly, the results of this study show that the neural signature of empathy for pain is very similar to the neural processes underlying the self-experience of pain (for brain circuits mediating pain perception, the so-called pain matrix, see Chapter 9). More specifically, empathy for pain activated selective parts of the neural pain matrix including the AI and the anterior cingulate cortex (ACC), which both are key regions in processing bodily and feeling states (see also Singer, Critchley, & Preuschoff, 2009, and Chapter 3). These findings have been replicated by several studies using similar paradigms (Bird et al., 2010; Hein, Silani, Preuschoff, Batson, & Singer, 2010; Singer et al., 2006, 2008). Converging evidence for the involvement of AI and, less consistently, the ACC in empathy for pain also has been obtained from several other studies (some of which are discussed in more detail later) using various paradigms ranging from simultaneous pain administration in the scanner to the presentation of photographs or videos depicting painful events (e.g., Botvinick et al., 2005; Cheng, Chen, Liu, Chou, & Decety, 2010; Chen et al., 2007; Danziger, Faillenot, & Peyron, 2009; Decety, Echols, & Correll, 2010; Gu & Han, 2007; Jackson, Brunet, Meltzoff, & Decety, 2006; Lamm, Batson, & Decety, 2007; Lamm & Decety, 2008; Lamm, Nusbaum, Meltzoff, & Decety, 2007; Moriguchi et al., 2007; Morrison, Lloyd, di Pellegrino, & Roberts, 2004; Ogino et al., 2007; Saarela et al., 2007; Zaki, Ochsner, Hanelin, Wager, & Mackey, 2007).

In support of the claim that the observed neural activation patterns are closely related to the concept of empathy developed by psychologists, Singer and colleagues (2004) showed that higher self-reports of empathy as measured by the BEES and the IRI were accompanied by increased neural activity during empathy for pain in the left AI and ACC, thereby supporting the external validity of the empathy-for-pain paradigm. Further evidence for the link between the observed brain responses and empathic experience stems from studies in which neural activation patterns in specific empathy-related regions were shown to correlate with self-reported impressions and actual helping behavior (Hein et al., 2010), as well as with individual unpleasantness ratings (e.g., Jabbi, Swart, & Keysers, 2007; Lamm, Nusbaum, et al., 2007; Saarela et al., 2007; Singer et al., 2008). Importantly, the existence of a shared neural network for self-experienced pain and empathy for pain is supported by a recent meta-analysis of Lamm, Decety, and Singer (2011), which showed consistent overlaps in AI and ACC across nine independent fMRI studies and is discussed in more detail later. Although the studies described here point to a shared neural representation of self-experienced and vicariously experienced pain, the question still remains whether activations in the AI and the ACC overlap on the level of neuronal subpopulations and single neurons (e.g., Singer & Lamm, 2009).

Shared and Distinct Neural Networks in Empathy for Pain

In addition to confirming an overlap between first-hand and vicarious pain experience in the AI and ACC, the meta-analysis of Lamm and colleagues (2011) suggests that this shared network can be accessed via several routes depending on the paradigm employed. Whereas the use of picture-based empathy paradigms is linked to additional activation increases in the inferior parietal, ventral premotor, and dorsomedial cortex (a neural circuitry typically observed in action understanding), cue-based paradigms induce activation in networks typically linked to theory of mind, such as the mPFC, precuneus, STS, and TPJ.

Distinct connectivity patterns of the AI and ACC with other brain regions during self-experienced pain versus empathy for pain have been examined by Zaki and colleagues (2007), who reported that self-experienced pain is associated with stronger connectivity between the AI and regions involved in the transmission of painful sensations, such as clusters in the midbrain, periaqueductal gray, and mid-insula. Conversely, empathy for pain has been shown to be associated with higher connectivity of the ACC and AI with brain regions implicated in social cognition and affect processing, such as the medial prefrontal cortex.

Converging evidence for the activation of sensory brain structures during self-pain stems from the earlier mentioned meta-analysis (Lamm et al., 2011), where the direct experience of pain recruited mid- and posterior insula, as well as primary sensory cortices in addition to the AI and ACC (see Figure 23.2 for illustration). The stronger involvement of brain regions processing sensory information in self-experienced pain suggests that we share the pain of others by accessing the neural structures representing our own affective states, while leaving aside sensory and nociceptive components.

Moreover, the meta-analysis on empathy for pain showed that contralateral primary somatosensory cortex (SI) activation, which most likely encodes somatosensory aspects of painful sensations, is restricted to self-experienced pain in cue-based studies. Picture-based studies, on the contrary, evoke bilateral SI activations during both empathy for painful and nonpainful situations, thus pointing to an unspecific role of the SI in empathy for pain that is presumably related to seeing body parts being touched. Interestingly, activity in somatosensory cortices can also be increased when subjects are instructed to evaluate the sensory consequences of painful stimuli, suggesting that attention can influence the quality of the empathic experience and that this shift in focus is accompanied by corresponding brain activations (Lamm, Nusbaum, et al., 2007). Complementing these findings, sensorimotor reso-

nance with empathy for visually depicted pain has been shown by studies using TMS (Avenanti, Bueti, Galati, & Aglioti, 2005; Avenanti, Pauuello, Bufalari, & Aglioti, 2006) and EEG (Bufalari, Aprile, Avenanti, Di Russo, & Aglioti, 2007; Valeriani et al., 2008). Taken together, these results point to a core shared network for self-experienced pain and empathy for pain in the ACC and AI that varies in its connectivity with other brain regions. Thus, the AI and ACC are coactivated with areas involved in processing self-related components of nociceptive experience when experiencing pain in oneself. However, when empathizing with others, the AI and ACC are co-activated with networks involved in social cognition (ToM and action observation). This finding suggests that the information available in the task and the situational demands determine which of the social cognition networks will be predominantly engaged.

With regard to the quality of the empathic experience, the reported studies suggest that we primarily share painful experiences by simulating the affective and not so much the sensory and nociceptive components of pain. Note, however, that there seems to be a graded activation of the neural pain matrix, such that activations in the posterior insula and secondary somatosensory cortex can be observed, even without the administration of pain, if subjects adopt a first-person perspective (Jackson et al., 2006) or simply imagine a painful event (Ogino et al., 2007). Because these activation patterns do not include the primary somatosensory cortex, there seems to be a continuum between directly and vicariously experienced pain that is reflected in the underlying neural substrates.

The Role of the Insula in Empathy and Interoception

The posterior-anterior gradient of the insula in self-experienced pain and empathy for pain is mirrored by research showing that primary nociceptive information is first processed in dorsal posterior parts of the insula

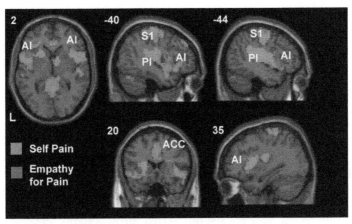

Figure 23.2. Shared and distinct neural networks for self-experienced pain and empathy for pain. Depicted functional neural activations are the result of a meta-analysis based on nine fMRI studies investigating empathy for pain (Lamm et al., 2011). Activations related to self-experienced pain (green) encompass a large portion of the insula, including the middle and posterior insular cortex, whereas activations related to empathy for pain (red) are restricted to the most anterior parts of AI, where they overlap with activations related to self-experienced pain. Functional activation maps are overlaid on a high-resolution structural MRI scan in standard stereotactic space (MNI space). White labels indicate slice number in stereotactic space, L = left hemisphere, AI = anterior insula, ACC = anterior cingulate cortex, PI = posterior insula, S1 = primary somatosensory cortex. With permission from Springer Science+Business Media: Brain Structure and Function, The role of anterior insular cortex in social emotions, 214, 2010, p. 581, Lamm, C., & Singer, T., Figure 1. See color plate 23.2.

before being remapped and integrated with other information in the AI where emotions access consciousness (Craig, 2002, 2009). These results fit into the general notion of the insula as a key player in processing interoceptive information from the body (Craig, 2002; Damasio, 1994; Ostrowsky et al., 2000, 2002; see Chapter 3) and emotions more generally (shown by a meta-analysis by Kober et al., 2008). Given these findings, Singer et al. (2004, 2009) proposed that the insula fulfills a dual role: (1) processing bodily information, such as heart beat or temperature-related sensations, which are then integrated into global feeling states, and (2) predicting the affective states of others in the process of empathizing. In other words, we use our own bodily and affective representation to understand the emotional experiences of others. This interpre-

tation implies that a deficit in understanding our own feelings should entail difficulties in empathizing with the feelings of others. Indeed, this claim was confirmed in studies focusing on people with alexithymia, a subclinical phenomenon characterized by difficulties in identifying and describing emotions (Nemiah et al., 1976). Silani and colleagues (2008) demonstrated that activity in the AI during interoception on emotional stimuli diminished with increasing alexithymia scores, whereas activation in the AI during interoception was positively related to trait empathy. Furthermore, this study showed that a higher degree of alexithymia was accompanied by lower levels of trait empathy. Extending these results, Bird and colleagues (2010), using the Singer et al. (2004) empathy-for-pain paradigm, found that AI activations also decrease when highly alexithymic participants are asked to empathize with others in pain.

Modulation of Empathy

In this section, we discuss findings indicating that empathic brain responses in the AI are not only modulated by person-specific characteristics, such as alexithymia, but can also be affected by the relation to the target (e.g., liking or disliking), contextual and attentional factors, and the appraisal of the situation (for recent reviews, see de Vignemont & Singer, 2006; Singer & Lamm, 2009). Several studies have shown that stimuli that under normal circumstances lead to empathic responses fail to induce empathy in certain situations and may even evoke the opposite; namely what has been referred to as "Schadenfreude" – the joy of witnessing another person's misfortune.

Relationship between Empathizer and Target

Singer and colleagues (2006) observed such a reversal of emotional response to the pain of others when they studied how perceived fairness affects empathy for pain. In their experiment, participants first played an economic game with two other volunteers, one of whom played fairly while the other played unfairly. When the participant was subsequently scanned, the fair and unfair players (who were actually confederates) were sitting next to the scanner, and all three alternately received painful or nonpainful stimulation on the back of their hands. In line with previous findings, Singer and colleagues observed that both the first-hand experience of pain and empathy for pain experienced for the fair person rely on shared neural representations in the AI and the ACC. However, when empathizing with the pain of the unfair player, only female subjects showed greater activations in these regions. Male subjects, by contrast, showed a decline in AI activation while witnessing the unfair, as opposed to the fair, player in pain. This reduction

in the men's neural empathy response was accompanied by increased activation in the nucleus accumbens – a region known to be crucially involved in reward processing (for recent reviews, see Knutson & Cooper, 2005; Schultz, 2000; Chapter 19). Moreover, the extent of nucleus accumbens activation was positively correlated to the subjectively expressed desire of revenge. In other words, activity in this reward-related brain structure was higher when men reported a stronger desire for revenge toward the unfair player. This activation pattern may imply that men actually experienced "Schadenfreude" when witnessing the unfair player being punished.

In another study, Hein and colleagues (2010) extended these findings by showing a relationship between empathy-related brain responses in the AI and subsequent prosocial behavior. The authors examined ingroup-outgroup biases in male soccer fans while they witnessed a fan of their favorite team (ingroup) or a fan of a rival team (outgroup) receiving painful electric shocks. As expected, the observation of ingroup members receiving pain was linked to greater AI activations. More importantly, the intensity of AI activation actually predicted the degree to which subjects would later help their ingroup member by taking the painful shocks themselves. In contrast, nucleus accumbens (NAcc) activation elicited by witnessing an outgroup member suffering predicted a refusal to help and reflected how negatively the subject evaluated the outgroup member. These findings imply that empathy-related insula activation drives altruistic behavior, whereas an antagonistic signal in the NAcc reduces the propensity to help. Other examples of factors that influence the nature of social relationships, and thereby the degree of empathy and its neural correlates, are ethnicity (Xu, Zuo, Wang, & Han, 2009) and closeness to the other person (Cheng et al., 2010).

Characteristics of the Empathizer

In a similar line as the earlier described alexithymia research, which established the link between high alexithymia (Silani et al., 2008) and low empathy, as well as the decrease of AI activations during empathy for pain in alexithymic participants (Bird et al., 2010), the characteristics of the empathizer have also been shown to influence empathic experiences in other domains. Cheng and colleagues (2007), for instance, showed that, when observing needles being inserted into different body parts, participants without experience in acupuncture showed activations in the neural network involved in empathy for pain, whereas physicians who practice acupuncture themselves did not show such a neural response.

Situational Context, Attention, and Appraisal

The role of contextual appraisal in relation to empathy has been examined in relation to the attribution of responsibility. Decety and colleagues (2010), for example, tested the degree to which empathic responses to videos of pain in AIDS patients differed as a function of the target's responsibility (infection through transfusion or drug taking). The self-report measures and the neural activations of the subjects both conveyed that attributed responsibility influences the extent of empathic response. Participants reported higher pain and empathy ratings toward the pain of transfusion targets as compared to drug targets, and these reports were accompanied by greater activation of the neural networks involved in processing pain (AI and ACC).

Another factor that has been shown to influence empathy is attention. Gu and Han (2007) reported lower ACC activity when participants were asked to count neutral stimuli in images displaying painful events compared to rating the intensity of the pain. Finally, Lamm, Nusbaum, et al. (2007) investigated the effects of cognitive appraisal and perspective-taking on empathic responses by presenting video clips of painful facial expressions during a medical treatment. Perspective-taking was varied by instructing the participants to imagine themselves in the depicted situation versus imagining the feelings of the patient during the medical treatment. To manipulate cognitive appraisal, subjects were told either that the medical treatment had been beneficial or unsuccessful. When subjects were told that the treatment had not been successful, they provided higher ratings of pain and unpleasantness than in the condition in which the treatment had been beneficial. Brain data corroborate these findings by showing stronger activations in the perigenual ACC for the ineffective treatment condition. With regard to the different perspectives adopted, results show that participants reported higher personal distress when they imagined themselves in the patient's situation (self-perspective), whereas participants reported more empathic concern when they cognitively differentiated between the patient and themselves (other-perspective). The observed increase in empathic distress when adopting a self-perspective fosters the claim that empathic distress arises due to an over-identification with the suffering of others. On the neural level, adopting a self-perspective was associated with increased activations of the neural pain matrix. This finding speaks for a stronger sharing of pain in distress and underscores the important distinction between empathic distress and empathic concern as two opposing outcomes of empathy associated with different qualities of emotional experience.

Empathy for Touch, Smell, and Taste

As reviewed earlier, a majority of neuroscience studies on empathy have focused on pain. However, an early study focused on the examination of shared representations for smell and disgust (Wicker et al., 2003). In their experiment, Wicker and colleagues studied how processing the actual experience of disgusting olfactory stimuli differs from processing others' visual display of disgust. The results of this fMRI study show that both self- and other-related disgust are accompanied by overlapping activation in the AI and ACC. Further support for this finding comes from a study by Jabbi and colleagues (2008), who showed AI activation regardless of whether subjects tasted an unpleasant substance, viewed disgusted facial expressions, or read disgusting scenarios. Finally, Keysers and colleagues (2004) reported that, whereas the sensory experience of being touched is specifically linked to activation in the contralateral primary somatosensory cortex, the neural signatures of being touched and observing touch overlap in the secondary somatosensory cortex. In summary, these studies parallel findings on empathy in the domain of pain by providing evidence for the involvement of a shared neural network underlying empathy in other modalities such as touch, smell, and taste.

The Compassionate Brain

Although social neuroscience has so far mostly focused on finding evidence for shared networks and their modulation, the field has recently moved forward to the investigation of positive consequences of empathy such as empathic concern, sympathy, or compassion. In a recent intervention study, Klimecki and colleagues (Klimecki, Leiberg, Lamm, & Singer, 2012) investigated how training compassion over several days changes neural function and subjective emotional experience. To this end, the researchers specifically developed a new paradigm, the Socio-affective Video Task (SoVT) in which participants witness the distress of others. At pre-training, this stimulus material elicited strong empathy and strong negative emotions. Consistent with findings from a recent empathy for pain meta-analysis (Lamm et al., 2011), empathy ratings in response to other's distress were accompanied by activations in anterior insula and ACC. Training compassion over several days changed this response pattern: participants reported feeling more positive emotions towards the suffering of others and showed increased activations in medial orbitofrontal cortex, ventral tegmental area/ substantia nigra (VTA/SN), putamen and pallidum. The involvement of

these brain areas in compassion is also supported by cross-sectional studies on compassion and love. Kim and colleagues (2009), for instance, showed that adopting a compassionate attitude towards pictures of sad faces augmented activations in ventral striatum and VTA/SN. Moreover, romantic as well as maternal love (Bartels and Zeki, 2000; 2004) have been associated to activations in the middle insula, the dorsal part of the ACC, and the striatum (comprised of the putamen, globus pallidus, and caudate nucleus). Similar results were reported by Beauregard and colleagues (2009) who observed increased activations of the middle insula, the dorsal ACC, the globus pallidus, and the caudate nucleus when their participants adopted a stance of unconditional love toward pictures of individuals with intellectual disabilities. Finally, a cross-sectional study revealed that expert meditators, but not novice meditators had augmented activations in middle insula when listening to distressing sounds (Lutz, Brefczynski-Lewis, Johnstone, & Davidson, 2008).Given that the observed regions are linked to reward processing and show a high density of oxytocin and vasopressin receptors – neuropeptides that play a crucial role in attachment and bonding (for a review, see Depue & Morrone-Strupinsky, 2005; Zeki, 2007), the described results might be interpreted as reflecting the rewarding nature of experiencing love and warmth, even when faced with the suffering of others.

Taken together, these results suggest that the previously introduced distinction between empathic distress and compassion as the two consequences of empathy is paralleled by the involvement of different neural substrates. Whereas distressing empathic experiences have been shown to be associated with the AI and ACC, compassionate or loving experiences seem to involve the medial orbitofrontal cortex, as well as mid-insular and striatal regions. Because of the scarcity of research in this field, many more studies are needed to refine the delineation of the neural networks involved in the positive emotions of compassion and love and to compare those in sharing negative feelings such as pain or unpleasant tastes and odors.

Conclusion

The field of social neuroscience is evolving quickly and the studies described in this chapter have (among others) greatly advanced our understanding of the neural bases of empathy. Most importantly, the development and use of ecologically valid paradigms could show that self-experienced and vicariously experienced pain rely on shared neural substrates in the AI and ACC. Together with the finding of distinct activation patterns in self-experienced affective states, this suggests that we understand the feelings of others by simulating the affective component of the observed states. In this context, the insula plays a specific role, because it generally serves as an interoceptive cortex supporting representations and predictions of feeling states for oneself and for others. Despite the major advances in our understanding of the empathic brain, many questions remain to be answered while at the same time new questions arise with newly gained insights.

Outstanding Questions and Future Directions

- In light of the findings speaking to a shared network for self-experienced and vicariously experienced emotions, how far are the neural substrates shared on the level of single neurons? Can these phenomena be distinguished by functional gradients in structures like the insula?
- By which mechanisms can empathic experiences be influenced so that, instead of resulting in empathic distress, empathy leads to compassion? Which neural changes accompany these interventions, and how do neural pathways underlying compassion differ from neural signatures of negative experiences associated with sharing someone else's pain?

- What role do neurotransmitters like oxytocin and vasopressin play in empathy, and how do they interact in the circuitry of emotion processing?
- Given that the acquisition of empathic and compassionate skills probably depends on the maturation of certain cortical structures, which neural changes accompany the development of empathy and related concepts from early childhood to adolescence? How do these findings tie in with emotional plasticity over the lifespan?

Acknowledgments

O. K. received funding from the University of Zurich (Forschungskredit). T. S. received grants from the Neuroscience Center Zurich, the Betty & David Koetser Foundation for Brain Research, and the European Research Council (ERC, Grant agreement no. 205557).

Notes

1 Because these three terms are often used to denote the same underlying concept (Batson, 2009a) – with Batson primarily using the term empathic concern (Batson, 2009b), whereas Eisenberg instead speaks of sympathy (Eisenberg, 2000) – we use these terms interchangeably throughout the chapter.

References

Adelmann, P. K., & Zajonc, R. B. (1989). Facial efference and the experience of emotion. *Annual Review of Psychology*, 40, 249–80.

American Psychiatric Association. (2000). *Diagnostic and statistical manual of mental disorders* (Revised 4th ed.). Washington, DC: Author.

Amodio, D. M., & Frith, C. D. (2006). Meeting of minds: The medial frontal cortex and social cognition. *Nature Reviews Neuroscience*, 7, 268–77.

Avenanti, A., Bueti, D., Galati, G., & Aglioti, S. M. (2005). Transcranial magnetic stimulation highlights the sensorimotor side of empathy for pain. *Nature Neuroscience*, 8, 955–60.

Avenanti, A., Paluello, I. M., Bufalari, I., & Aglioti, S. M. (2006). Stimulus-driven modulation of motor-evoked potentials during observation of others' pain. *Neuroimage*, 32, 316–24.

Bartels, A., & Zeki, S. (2000). The neural basis of romantic love. *Neuroreport*, 11, 3829–34.

Bartels, A., & Zeki, S. (2004). The neural correlates of maternal and romantic love. *Neuroimage*, 21, 1155–66.

Batson, C. D. (2009a). These things called empathy: Eight related but distinct phenomena. In J. Decety & W. Ickes (Eds.), *The social neuroscience of empathy* (pp. 3–15). Cambridge, MA: MIT Press.

Batson, C. D. (2009b). Empathy-induced altruistic motivation. In M. Mikulincer & P. R. Shaver (Eds.), *Prosocial motives, emotions, and behavior* (pp. 15–34). Washington, DC: American Psychological Association.

Batson, C. D., Duncan, B. D., Ackerman, P., Buckley, T., & Birch, K. (1981). Is empathic emotion a source of altruistic motivation? *Journal of Personality and Social Psychology*, 40, 290–302.

Batson, C. D., Fultz, J., & Schoenrade, P. A. (1987). Distress and empathy: Two qualitatively distinct vicarious emotions with different motivational consequences. *Journal of Personality*, 55, 19.

Batson, C. D., O'Quin, K., Fultz, J., Vanderplas, M., & Isen. A. (1983). Influence of self-reported distress and empathy on egoistic versus altruistic motivation to help. *Journal of Personality and Social Psychology*, 45, 706–18.

Beauregard, M., Courtemanche, J., Paquette, V., & St-Pierre, E. L. (2009). The neural basis of unconditional love. *Psychiatry Research*, 172, 93–98.

Bird, G., Silani, G., Brindley, R., White, S., Frith, U., & Singer, T. (2010). Empathic brain responses in insula are modulated by levels of alexithymia but not autism. *Brain*, 133, 1515–25.

Botvinick, M., Jha, A. P., Bylsma, L. M., Fabian, S. A., Solomon, P. E., & Prkachin, K. M. (2005). Viewing facial expressions of pain engages cortical areas involved in the direct experience of pain. *Neuroimage*, 25, 312–19.

Bufalari, I., Aprile, T., Avenanti, A., Di Russo, F., & Aglioti, S. M. (2007). Empathy for pain and touch in the human somatosensory cortex. *Cerebral Cortex*, 17, 2553–61.

Cattaneo, L., Sandrini, M., & Schwarzbach, J. (2010). State-dependent TMS reveals a hierarchical representation of observed acts in the temporal, parietal, and premotor cortices. *Cerebral Cortex*, bhp291.

Cheng, Y., Chen, C., Lin, C. P., Chou, K. H., & Decety, J. (2010). Love hurts: An fMRI study. *Neuroimage*, 51, 923–29.

Cheng, Y., Lin, C. P., Liu, H. L., Hsu, Y. Y., Lim, K. E., Hung, D., et al. (2007). Expertise modulates the perception of pain in others. *Current Biology*, 17, 1708–13.

Craig, A. D. (2002). How do you feel? Interoception: The sense of the physiological condition of the body. *Nature Reviews Neuroscience*, 3, 655–66.

Craig, A. D. (2009). How do you feel – now? The anterior insula and human awareness. *Nature Reviews Neuroscience*, 10, 59–70.

Damasio, A. R. (1994). Descartes' error and the future of human life. *Scientific American*, 271, 144.

Danziger, N., Faillenot, I., & Peyron, R. (2009). Can we share a pain we never felt? Neural correlates of empathy in patients with congenital insensitivity to pain. *Neuron*, 67, 203–12.

Davis, M. H. (1980). A multidimensional approach to individual differences in empathy. *JSAS Catalogue of Selected Documents in Psychology*, 10, 85.

Decety, J., Echols, S., & Correll, J. (2010). The blame game: The effect of responsibility and social stigma on empathy for pain. *Journal of Cognitive Neuroscience*, 22, 985–97.

Decety, J., & Jackson, P. L. (2006). A social-neuroscience perspective on empathy. *Current Directions in Psychological Science*, 15, 54–58.

Depue, R. A., & Morrone-Strupinsky, J. V. (2005). A neurobehavioral model of affiliative bonding: Implications for conceptualizing a human trait of affiliation. *Behavioral and Brain Sciences*, 28, 313–50.

de Vignemont, F., & Singer, T. (2006). The empathic brain: How, when and why? *Trends in Cognitive Sciences*, 10, 435–41.

Dimberg, U., & Öhman, A. (1996). Behold the wrath: Psychophysiological responses to facial stimuli. *Motivation and Emotion*, 20, 149–82.

Eisenberg, N. (2000). Emotion, regulation, and moral development. *Annual Review of Psychology*, 51, 665–97.

Eisenberg, N., Fabes, R. A., Miller, P. A., Fultz, J., Shell, R., Mathy, R. M., et al. (1989). Relation of sympathy and personal distress to prosocial behavior: A multimethod study. *Journal of Personality and Social Psychology*, 57, 55–66.

Fadiga, L., Fogassi, L., Pavesi, G., & Rizzolatti, G. (1995). Motor facilitation during action observation: A magnetic stimulation study. *Journal of Neurophysiology, 73*, 2608–11.

Frith, C., & Frith, U. (2006). The neural basis of mentalizing. *Neuron, 50*, 531–34.

Frith, U., & Frith, C. D. (2003). Development and neurophysiology of mentalizing. *Philosophical Transactions of the Royal Society of London. Series B: Biological Sciences, 358*, 459–73.

Gallese, V., Fadiga, L., Fogassi, L., & Rizzolatti, G. (1996). Action recognition in the premotor cortex. *Brain, 119* (Pt. 2), 593–609.

Goetz, J. L., Keltner, D., & Simon-Thomas, E. (2010). Compassion: An evolutionary analysis and empirical review. *Psychological Bulletin, 136*, 351–74.

Gottman, J. M., & Levenson, R. W. (1985). A valid measure for obtaining self-report of affect. *Journal of Consulting and Clinical Psychology, 53*, 151–60.

Grèzes, J., & Decety, J. (2001). Functional anatomy of execution, mental simulation, observation, and verb generation of actions: A meta-analysis. *Human Brain Mapping, 12*, 1–19.

Gu, X., & Han, S. (2007). Attention and reality constraints on the neural processes of empathy for pain. *Neuroimage, 36*, 256–67.

Hari, R., Forss, N., Avikainen, S., Kirveskari, E., Salenius, S., & Rizzolatti, G. (1998). Activation of human primary motor cortex during action observation: A neuromagnetic study. *Proceedings of the National Academy of Sciences, 95*, 15061–65.

Harrison, N. A., Singer, T., Rotshtein, P., Dolan, R. J., & Critchley, H. D. (2006). Pupillary contagion: Central mechanisms engaged in sadness processing. *Social Cognitive and Affective Neuroscience, 1*, 5–17.

Hatfield, E., Rapson, R. L., & Le, Y. L. (2009). Emotional contagion and empathy. In J. Decety & W. Ickes (Eds.), *The social neuroscience of empathy* (pp. 19–30) Cambridge, MA: MIT.

Hein, G., Silani, G., Preuschoff, K., Batson, C. D., & Singer, T. (2010). Neural responses to ingroup and outgroup members' suffering predict individual differences in costly helping. *Neuron, 68*, 149–60.

Hoffman, M. L. (2000). *Empathy and moral development*. Cambridge: Cambridge University Press.

Iacoboni, M., Molnar-Szakacs, I., Gallese, V., Buccino, G., Mazziotta, J. C., & Rizzolatti,

G. (2005). Grasping the intentions of others with one's own mirror neuron system. *PLoS Biology, 3*, e79.

Ickes, W. (1993). Empathic accuracy. *Journal of Personality, 61*, 587–610.

Jabbi, M., Bastiaansen, J., & Keysers, C. (2008). A common anterior insula representation of disgust observation, experience and imagination shows divergent functional connectivity pathways. *PLoS One, 3*, e2939.

Jabbi, M., Swart, M., & Keysers, C. (2007). Empathy for positive and negative emotions in the gustatory cortex. *Neuroimage, 34*, 1744–53.

Jackson, P. L., Brunet, E., Meltzoff, A. N., & Decety, J. (2006). Empathy examined through the neural mechanisms involved in imagining how I feel versus how you feel pain. *Neuropsychologia, 44*, 752–61.

Keltner, D., & Goetz, J. L. (2007). Compassion. In R. F. Baumeister & K. D. Vohs (Eds.), *Encyclopedia of social psychology* (pp. 159–60). Thousand Oaks, CA: Sage.

Keysers, C., Wicker, B., Gazzola, V., Anton, J. L., Fogassi, L., & Gallese, V. (2004). A touching sight: SII/PV activation during the observation and experience of touch. *Neuron, 42*, 335–46.

Klimecki, O.M., Leiberg, S., Lamm, C., & Singer, T. (2012). Functional Neural Plasticity and Associated Changes in Positive Affect After Compassion Training. *Cerebral Cortex*. doi: 10.1093/cercor/bhs142

Klimecki, O., & Singer, T. (2012). Empathic distress fatigue rather than compassion fatigue? Integrating findings from empathy research in psychology and social neuroscience. In B. Oakley, A. Knafo, G. Madhavan, & D. S. Wilson (Eds.), *Pathological altruism* (pp. 368–83). New York: Oxford University Press.

Knutson, B., & Cooper, J. C. (2005). Functional magnetic resonance imaging of reward prediction. *Current Opinion in Neurology, 18*, 411–17.

Kober, H., Barrett, L. F., Joseph, J., Bliss-Moreau, E., Lindquist, K., & Wager, T. D. (2008). Functional grouping and cortical-subcortical interactions in emotion: A meta-analysis of neuroimaging studies. *Neuroimage, 42*, 998–1031.

Lamm, C., Batson, C., & Decety, J. (2007). The neural substrate of human empathy: Effects of perspective-taking and cognitive appraisal. *Journal of Cognitive Neuroscience, 19*, 42–58.

Lamm, C., & Decety, J. (2008). Is the extrastriate body area (EBA) sensitive to the perception of pain in others? *Cerebral Cortex, 18*, 2369–73.

Lamm, C., Decety, J., & Singer, T. (2011). Meta-analytic evidence for common and distinct neural networks associated with directly experienced pain and empathy for pain. *Neuroimage*, *54*, 2492–2502.

Lamm, C., Nusbaum, H. C., Meltzoff, A. N., & Decety, J. (2007). What are you feeling? Using functional magnetic resonance imaging to assess the modulation of sensory and affective responses during empathy for pain. *PLoS One*, *2*, e1292.

Lamm, C., & Singer, T. (2010). The role of anterior insular cortex in social emotions. *Brain Structure and Function*, *214*, 579–91.

Leiberg, S., Klimecki, O. & Singer, T. (2011). Short-term compassion training increases prosocial behavior in a newly developed prosocial game. *PLoS One*, *6*, e17798.

Levenson, R. W., & Ruef, A. M. (1992). Empathy: A physiological substrate. *Journal of Personality and Social Psychology*, *63*, 234–46.

Lipps, T. (1903). Einfühlung, innere Nachahmung, und Organempfindungen [Empathy, inner imitation, and sense-feelings]. *Archiv für die gesamte Psychologie*, *1*, 185–204.

Lutz, A., Brefczynski-Lewis, J., Johnstone, T., & Davidson, R. J. (2008). Regulation of the neural circuitry of emotion by compassion meditation: Effects of meditative expertise. *PLoS One*, *3*, e1897.

Mehrabian, A. (1997). Relations among personality scales of aggression, violence, and empathy: Validational evidence bearing on the risk of eruptive violence scale. *Aggressive Behavior*, *23*, 433–45.

Mehrabian, A., & Epstein, N. (1972). A measure of emotional empathy. *Journal of Personality*, *40*, 525–43.

Mitchell, J. P. (2009). Inferences about mental states. *Philosophical Transactions of the Royal Society of London. Series B: Biological Sciences*, *364*, 1309–16.

Moriguchi, Y., Decety, J., Ohnishi, T., Maeda, M., Mori, T., Nemoto, K., et al. (2007). Empathy and judging other's pain: An fMRI study of alexithymia. *Cerebral Cortex*, *17*, 2223–34.

Morrison, I., Lloyd, D., di Pellegrino, G., & Roberts, N. (2004). Vicarious responses to pain in anterior cingulate cortex: Is empathy a multisensory issue? *Cognitive, Affective & Behavioral Neuroscience*, *4*, 270–78.

Nemiah, J. C., Freyberger, H., & Sifneos, P. E. (1976). Alexithymia: A view of the psychosomatic process. In O. W. Hill (Ed.), *Modern trends in psychosomatic medicine* (pp. 430–39). London: Butterworths.

Neumann, R., & Strack, F. (2000). "Mood contagion": The automatic transfer of mood between persons. *Journal of Personality & Social Psychology*, *79*, 211–23.

Ogino, Y., Nemoto, H., Inui, K., Saito, S., Kakigi, R., & Goto, F. (2007). Inner experience of pain: Imagination of pain while viewing images showing painful events forms subjective pain representation in human brain. *Cerebral Cortex*, *17*, 1139–46.

Ostrowsky, K., Isnard, J., Ryvlin, P., Guénot, M., Fischer, C., & Mauguière, F. (2000). Functional mapping of the insular cortex: Clinical implication in temporal lobe epilepsy. *Epilepsia*, *41*, 681–86.

Ostrowsky, K., Magnin, M., Ryvlin, P., Isnard, J., Guenot, M., & Mauguiere, F. (2002). Representation of pain and somatic sensation in the human insula: A study of responses to direct electrical cortical stimulation. *Cerebral Cortex*, *12*, 376–85.

Premack, D., & Woodruff, G. (1978). Does the chimpanzee have a theory of mind? *Behavioral and Brain Sciences*, *1*, 515–26.

Preston, S. D., & de Waal, F. B. M. (2002). Empathy: Its ultimate and proximate bases. *Behavioral and Brain Science*, *25*, 1–72.

Rizzolatti, G., & Craighero, L. (2004). The mirror neuron system. *Annual Review of Neuroscience*, *27*, 169–92.

Rizzolatti, G., Fadiga, L., Gallese, V., & Fogassi, L. (1996). Premotor cortex and the recognition of motor actions. *Brain Research: Cognitive Brain Research*, *3*, 131–41.

Rizzolatti, G., & Sinigaglia, C. (2010). The functional role of the parieto-frontal mirror circuit: Interpretations and misinterpretations. *Nature Reviews Neuroscience*, *11*, 264–74.

Saarela, M. V., Hlushchuk, Y., Williams, A. C., Schurmann, M., Kalso, E., & Hari, R. (2007). The compassionate brain: Humans detect intensity of pain from another's face. *Cerebral Cortex*, *17*, 230–37.

Saxe, R. (2006). Why and how to study Theory of Mind with fMRI. *Brain Research*, *1079*, 57–65.

Saxe, R., & Baron-Cohen, S. (2006). The neuroscience of theory of mind. *Social Neuroscience*, *1*, i–ix.

Schultz, W. (2000). Multiple reward signals in the brain. *Nature Reviews Neuroscience*, *1*, 199–207.

Silani, G., Bird, G., Brindley, R., Singer, T., Frith, C., & Frith, U. (2008). Levels of emotional awareness and autism: An fMRI study. *Social Neuroscience, 3*, 97–112.

Singer, T., Critchley, H. D., & Preuschoff, K. (2009). A common role of insula in feelings, empathy and uncertainty. *Trends in Cognitive Sciences, 13*, 334–40.

Singer, T., & Lamm, C. (2009). The social neuroscience of empathy. *Year in Cognitive Neuroscience 2009: Annals of the New York Academy of Sciences, 1156*, 81–96.

Singer, T., & Leiberg, S. (2009). Sharing the emotions of others: The neural bases of empathy. In M. S. Gazzaniga (Ed.), *The cognitive neurosciences IV* (pp. 971–84). Cambridge, MA: MIT.

Singer, T., Seymour, B., O'Doherty, J., Kaube, H., Dolan, R., & Frith, C. (2004). Empathy for pain involves the affective but not sensory components of pain. *Science, 303*, 1157–62.

Singer, T., Seymour, B., O'Doherty, J. P., Stephan, K. E., Dolan, R. J., & Frith, C. D. (2006). Empathic neural responses are modulated by the perceived fairness of others. *Nature, 439*, 466–69.

Singer, T., Snozzi, R., Bird, G., Petrovic, P., Silani, G., Heinrichs, M. et al. (2008). Effects of oxytocin and prosocial behavior on brain responses to direct and vicariously experienced pain. *Emotion, 8*, 781–91.

Valeriani, M., Betti, V., Le Pera, D., De Armas, L., Miliucci, R., Restuccia, D., et al. (2008). Seeing the pain of others while being in pain: A laser-evoked potentials study. *Neuroimage, 40*, 1419–28.

Wicker, B., Keysers, C., Plailly, J., Royet, J. P., Gallese, V., & Rizzolatti, G. (2003). Both of us disgusted in My insula: The common neural basis of seeing and feeling disgust. *Neuron, 40*, 655–64.

Xu, X., Zuo, X., Wang, X., & Han, S. (2009). Do you feel my pain? Racial group membership modulates empathic neural responses. *Journal of Neuroscience, 29*, 8525–29.

Zaki, J., Ochsner, K. N., Hanelin, J., Wager, T. D., & Mackey, S. C. (2007). Different circuits for different pain: Patterns of functional connectivity reveal distinct networks for processing pain in self and others. *Social Neuroscience, 2*, 276–91.

Zeki, S. (2007). The neurobiology of love. *FEBS Letters, 581*, 2575–79.

Section VII

INDIVIDUAL DIFFERENCES IN EMOTION

CHAPTER 24

Trait Anxiety, Neuroticism, and the Brain Basis of Vulnerability to Affective Disorder

Sonia Bishop & Sophie Forster

Studies of the brain basis of "normative" or "healthy" processing of emotionally salient stimuli have flourished over the last two decades. An initial focus on regions implicated in the detection of emotionally salient stimuli (Morris et al., 1996; Whalen et al., 1998) has broadened to include discussion of mechanisms supporting regulatory functions (Bishop, Duncan, Brett, & Lawrence, 2004; Davidson, 2002; Ochsner, Bunge, Gross, & Gabrieli, 2002; Kim, Somerville, Johnstone, Alexander, & Whalen, 2003; Phelps, Delgado, Nearing, & LeDoux, 2004). Running in parallel to this literature, psychiatric imaging studies have described alterations in brain function across a wide range of anxiety and depressive disorders (for reviews and meta-analyses see Etkin & Wager, 2007; Ressler & Mayberg, 2007; Shin & Liberzon, 2010; Stein 2009). The study of the brain mechanisms underlying vulnerability to disorder has, for some reason, fallen outside of the primary spotlight. We argue that work of this nature is critical to bridging studies in healthy volunteer and patient groups and to identifying the pathways through which risk to affective illness is conferred.

Understanding the brain basis of vulnerability to affective disorder goes hand in hand with a focus on individual variation and, in particular, trait differences in the mechanisms supporting the detection and controlled processing of emotional stimuli. How do we study trait differences in vulnerability to anxiety and depressive disorders and try to unpack the brain mechanisms though which these might act? A number of approaches have been adopted, with both shared and unique advantages and limitations.

Studies of the brain basis of vulnerability to affective disorders typically rely on recruiting nonclinical volunteer samples and then regressing scores on self-report measures of trait affect or experience of disorder-related symptomatology against indices of brain function or structure. It is important to remember that this approach is correlational in nature, and hence no conclusions can be drawn about the direction of causality. For example, if we find that, in a student population, elevated scores on a measure of neuroticism are linked to poor frontal recruitment, this could equally plausibly reflect individuals scoring high on neuroticism being less able to cope with environmental stress, resulting in diminished frontal function; individuals with compromised frontal function being more likely to develop a neurotic personality style; both elevated neuroticism and compromised frontal function stemming from a primary disruption to neurotransmitter function; or all of these factors in combination. There are also important methodological issues pertaining to good practice in conducting correlational analyses of brain activity, which are discussed briefly later in the chapter.

A shared positive feature of studies in this area is that constructs such as trait anxiety or neuroticism can be examined as continuous factors, facilitating exploration of their linear and nonlinear relationships with regional brain activity. This allows for a more complex and potentially accurate picture to be drawn than one that solely uses DSM categorical assessments of the binary presence or absence of a given disease state. The latter "diagnostic" approach faces limitations arising from difficulties in applying categorical cutoffs, high comorbidity between many anxiety and depressive disorders, and poor diagnostic reliability (Brown & Barlow, 2009).

Studies of the brain basis of vulnerability to affective disorder can be categorized according to the measure used to assess individual differences in trait affective style. Arguably there are three main categories. The first involves measures derived from the clinical literature and normed for use in nonclinical populations to assess individuals' tendency to show disorder-related symptomatology, affective and cognitive styles. A prominent example is the Spielberger State Trait Anxiety Inventory (STAI; Spielberger, Gorsuch, Lushene, Vagg, & Jacobs, 1983), widely used in studies of the cognitive correlates of trait anxiety within nonselected student samples. The second

category uses measures taken from the personality literature, such as the Neuroticism scale from either the Eysenck Personality Questionnaire (EPQ; Eysenck & Eysenck, 1975) or the NEO Personality Inventory (Costa & MacCrae, 1992). The third category focuses on genetic markers that differ among individuals (functional polymorphisms with two or more common variants) and that have been linked to differences in affect-related behaviors in humans and other species. In this chapter, we focus on the first two of these categories, commenting only briefly on the third (for further discussion, see Chapter 25). The majority of studies on the brain basis of vulnerability to affective disorder falling within these categories have used measures of trait anxiety (category 1) or neuroticism (category 2). We use these examples to explore the state of the field as it stands and to address outstanding questions for future research.

Trait Anxiety and Neuroticism: Indexing Vulnerability to Affective Disorders through Self-Report

The trait subscale of the Spielberger State Trait Anxiety Inventory (Spielberger et al., 1983) is a widely used measure of trait propensity to anxiety. It has been shown to have good concurrent validity, with patients with anxiety disorders (ADs) scoring higher on the STAI trait subscale than controls (Bieling, Antony, & Swinson, 1998). Although fewer studies have examined predictive validity, pretrauma STAI trait scores have been found to predict levels of posttraumatic stress disorder symptomatology after trauma (Weems et al., 2007). However, the STAI has been criticized for having poor discriminative validity, with individuals with major depressive disorder (MDD) also showing elevated scores on the trait subscale (Mathews, Ridgway, & Williamson, 1996). One possibility is that this low discriminant validity reflects a poor choice of anxiety-specific items for the scale. A second is that there is genuine shared variance underlying vulnerability to both ADs and MDD.

Not only are STAI trait scores elevated in patients with MDD but scores on this and other anxiety scales, such as the Taylor Manifest Anxiety Scale (Taylor, 1953), have also been found to correlate highly with scores on self-report measures of depressive symptomatology; for example, the Beck Depression Inventory (BDI; Beck Ward, Mendelson, Mock, & Erbaugh, 1961) and personality indices of neuroticism (Luteijn & Bouman, 1988). Neuroticism is characterized by a propensity for negative affect (Watson & Clark, 1984). This trait, measured by widely used instruments such as the NEO Personality Inventory and the Eysenck Personality Questionnaire, has emerged over the last century as one of the most widely studied personality traits (Costa & Mac-Crae, 1992; Eysenck & Eysenck, 1975; John, 1990). The relationship with vulnerability to affective disorder has arguably been investigated more thoroughly for neuroticism than for any other dimension of personality (Brown, 2007; Brown & Rosellini, 2011, Kendler, Gardner, Gatz, & Pedersen, 2007). There is strong evidence to support not only shared variance but also common genetic influences among neuroticism, anxiety disorders, and depressive disorders (Hettema et al., 2008; Kendler et al., 2007).

A likely interpretation of the high correlations observed among indices of anxiety, depression, and neuroticism is that they tap, at least in part, into a common underlying trait (Figure 24.1). According to the popular tripartite model, anxiety and depression not only have a shared component – a propensity to negative affect (which arguably maps on to the construct of neuroticism) – but also unique components of anxious arousal and anhedonia, respectively (Clark & Watson, 1991). This conception has led to the development of the Mood and Anxiety Symptoms Questionnaire (MASQ; Watson & Clark, 1991), which aims to measure both these shared and unique components. Unfortunately the MASQ focuses on "state"

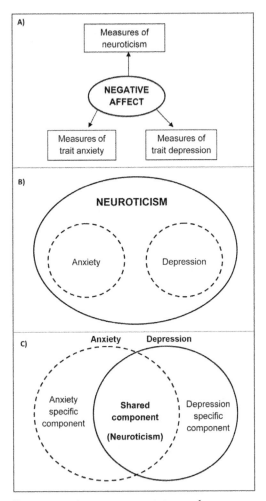

Figure 24.1. Anxiety, neuroticism and depression: overlapping constructs? Three alternate models. (A). Self-report measures of anxiety, depression, and neuroticism could potentially all be tapping the same single underlying trait. (B). Alternatively, anxiety and depression might be separate components of the broader trait of neuroticism. In keeping with this perspective, the NEO-PI-R includes anxiety and depression as subfactors, or "facets," of neuroticism (Costa & McCrae; 1995). (C). A third theoretical stance, represented by Clark and Watson's (1991) tripartite model, asserts that anxiety and depression not only have a shared component of negative affect or general distress (potentially corresponding to the construct of neuroticism) but also unique components of "anxious arousal" (autonomic hyperactivity) and "anhedonic depression" (low positive affect).

or current mood levels and not on trait differences between individuals. Indeed, the
scarcity of trait measures of propensity to
anxiety and depression poses a major difficulty for researchers aiming to investigate
the brain basis of these tendencies. Not only
the MASQ but also the major depressive
inventories – including both the BDI and the
Center for Epidemiologic Studies Depression Scale (CES-D; Radloff 1977) – focus on
current levels of symptomatology. This may
explain why several imaging studies have
used neuroticism as a proxy for vulnerability
to depression, but doing so inevitably hin-
ders attempts to disentangle the extent to
which neuroticism, trait anxiety, and trait
depression involve disruption to common or
unique mechanisms at either a cognitive or
systems (regional brain structure and function) level of analysis.

Studying Affective Trait-Related Differences in Cognitive and Brain Function: Lessons from the Last Decade

Over the last 10 years, much progress has
been made in using neuroimaging techniques to study individual differences in
neurocognitive function; recent challenges
and developments set the stage for equivalent progress over the next decade. In the
early 2000s, neuroimaging studies of personality led to a conceptual shift in the approach
to the investigation of human brain function. These studies argued that individual
variation need not simply be treated as a
source of noise in group studies of "normative" neurocognitive function but that
between-subject differences could be studied in their own right by examining associations between traits such as extraversion or
neuroticism and regional brain function (for
a review see Canli, 2004).

Although these studies were groundbreaking in advancing the investigation
of individual differences in neurocognitive
function, as with many first steps in a new
field, several of these studies have since been

subject to criticism (Vul, Harris, Winkielman, & Pashler, 2009). However, many of
the issues raised – pertaining to whole-brain
correlational analyses, insufficient correction for multiple comparisons, and biased
selection of regions of interest – can be
avoided if investigations of differences in
regional brain function associated with personality indices or trait affective style are
constrained to ones that specifically test theories derived from the cognitive or social
psychological literature. An elegant argument for this approach was initially made
by Kosslyn et al. (2002). In this article, Kosslyn and colleagues take the proposal put
forward by Underwood (1975) – that naturally occurring individual differences can
be used to test psychological theories and
to reveal the structure of psychological processes, potentially providing greater insights
than group-based methods – and argue that
the same logic can be applied to the use
of individual differences to investigate the
biological mechanisms that underpin cognitive processes. The authors make the case
that there is natural variation around every
central tendency, that individuals may differ
in the efficiency and recruitment of mechanisms (which can be studied at various levels including both regional brain activation
and cognitive processing), and that pooling
information across individuals may be unin-
formative or misleading. They also point out
that the main dangers of unguided correlational studies can be avoided by theoretically
grounding the study design and the analysis and interpretation of results, with alternate theoretical explanations of observed
correlations being used to generate further
hypotheses than can in turn be tested. In
the sections that follow, we illustrate how
the approach proposed by Kosslyn and colleagues can be applied, using the example of
studies that have investigated the brain basis
of the association between trait anxiety and
attentional capture by threat. In addition,
we explore if we can ascertain whether neuroticism shows a similar, potentially common, relationship to the function of these
mechanisms.

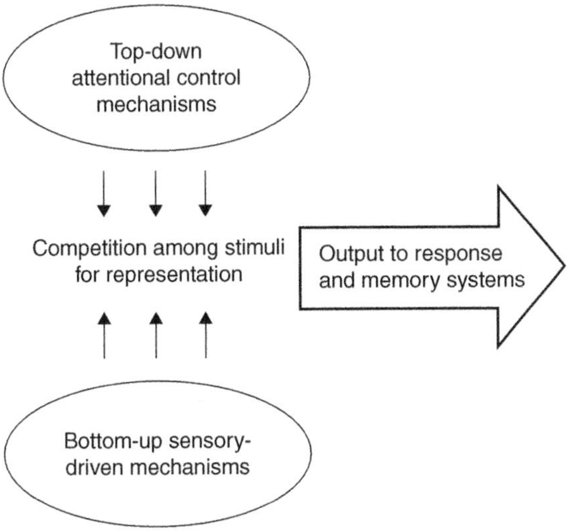

Figure 24.2. According to the biased-competition model of selective attention (Desimone & Duncan, 1995; Kastner & Ungerleider, 2000), top-down attentional control mechanisms, which favor task-relevant stimuli, and bottom-up sensory-driven mechanisms, sensitive to stimulus salience, jointly determine which stimuli are selected for further processing. Adapted from Bishop (2008) and Kastner and Ungerleider (2000), with permission.

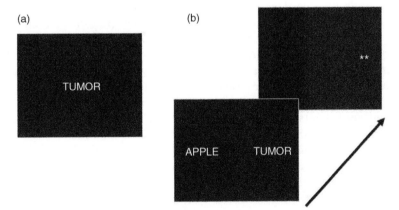

Figure 24.3. Two widely used tasks in the attention to threat literature. (A) In the Emotional Stroop task, participants are asked to name the font color of a word (here green/gray), ignoring its meaning, which can be either threat-related or neutral in valence. High trait anxious subjects show RT slowing for threat-related words. (B) In the Probe Detection task, participants are presented with two words, followed by a "probe" (the two asterisks presented here) in the location of one of the words. They are typically asked either to indicate when the probe appears or to specify its orientation. On key trials, one word is threat-related, and the other is neutral. High trait anxious individuals show RT speeding when the location of the probe was previously occupied by a threat word (as in the example here), suggesting that attention was allocated to the location of the threat word.

Trait Anxiety, Neuroticism, and Threat-Related Biases in Selective Attention: Cognitive Models and Findings

Both AD patients and high trait anxious participants show elevated attentional capture by threat-related stimuli (Mathews & Mackintosh, 1998). According to biased competition models of selective attention, attentional competition is influenced both by "bottom-up" sensory mechanisms that prioritize the processing of salient stimuli and by "top-down" attentional control mechanisms that support the processing of task-relevant stimuli (Figure 24.2; Desimone & Duncan, 1995; Kastner & Ungerleider, 2000). Stimulus valence – the extent to which a given stimulus is threat or reward related – is an important dimension of stimulus salience. A number of selective attention tasks have been adapted to examine how stimulus valence, especially threat-relatedness, influences attentional competition. Two notable examples are the Emotional Stroop and Probe Detection tasks (Figure 24.3). In the Emotional Stroop task, participants name the ink color of a stimulus word while ignoring its semantic content. On this task, high trait anxious individuals show slower color naming of threat-related words than emotionally neutral words; in low trait anxious individuals this slowing is reduced or absent (Richards & Millwood, 1989). In the Probe Detection task, participants are presented with two words or pictures (e.g. faces) followed by a single dot or pair of dots in the position previously occupied by one of the two stimuli. Here, high trait anxious individuals are faster to detect the presence of a single dot or to determine the orientation of a pair of dots, when the dot probe is presented in the position previously occupied by a threat-related stimulus (Macleod & Mathews, 1988).

These findings have informed cognitive models of anxiety that extend the biased competition model of selective attention to specifically deal with attentional capture by threat-related stimuli (Mathews & Mackintosh, 1998; Mogg & Bradley, 1998). These models typically propose that anxiety acts by amplifying the signal from a bottom-up preattentive threat detection mechanism that biases attentional competition in favor of threat-related stimuli. When these stimuli are distracters (non-task-relevant), this is held to interfere with the processing of target stimuli, as indexed by slowed reaction times (RTs) and/or elevated error rates. These models have not, in the most part, argued for disrupted top-down or controlled processing of threat-related stimuli in anxiety.

A number of studies have used variants of the Probe Detection task to examine whether attentional biases are also associated with elevated neuroticism ("N") scores. These have produced rather mixed results. Reed and Derryberry (1995) found evidence for a correlation between N scores and attentional bias toward negative trait adjectives previously rated as self-applicable. However, this correlation was only observed at one of three alternate adjective-probe stimulus onset asynchronies (500 ms, not 250 ms or 750 ms). In addition, Chan, Goodwin, and Harmer (2007) and Rijsdijk et al. (2009) failed to find any relationship between neuroticism and performance on probe detection tasks using social threat words and subliminally presented threat-related faces, respectively. Differences among these studies in the choice of stimuli, stimulus onset asynchrony, and neuroticism scale (EPQ versus NEO) further complicate interpretation of these findings.

Interestingly, the limited evidence for an association between neuroticism and attentional bias toward negatively valenced stimuli parallels similarly mixed findings within the subclinical depression literature. Here, two studies using the Emotional Stroop task have reported increased RT slowing for color naming of negatively valenced words as a function of scores on the Beck Depression Inventory (BDI). These effects were strongest in participants with elevated BDI scores at two time points a year apart (Williams & Nulty, 1986) and were not found when a depressed mood was induced in participants with low BDI scores (Gotlib &

McCann, 1984), potentially suggesting the role of an enduring trait conferring vulnerability to depression, rather than simply state affect. Other studies have found no relationship between individual differences in subclinical levels of depression and attentional bias toward negative or threat-related stimuli across both the Emotional Stroop and Probe Detection tasks (Bradley, Mogg, Falla, & Hamilton, 1998; Gotlib, MacLachan, & Katz, 1988; Hill & Dutton, 1989; Hill & Knowles, 1991; Macleod & Hagan, 1992).

One possibility is that a partial correlate of depression scores, such as trait anxiety levels, rather than depression itself, might be responsible for the intermittently reported attentional interference effects. A similar argument can be made for neuroticism. The NEO measure of neuroticism comprises different subfacets, one of which is especially related to anxiety and another to depression (Costa & MacCrae, 1992; see also Figure 24.1). Variability among studies in the items that high-N participants endorse might explain the occasional but inconsistent findings of attentional biases reported by studies using this measure.

It is also possible that multiple mechanisms contribute to attentional capture by threat stimuli – with trait anxiety, neuroticism, and depression potentially sharing a common relationship with one of these mechanisms but differing in their association with others. The most obvious candidate mechanisms are those involved in bottom-up responsivity to threat versus top-down attentional control. Investigation of the brain basis of these mechanisms opens up a new door for examining how different trait characteristics are linked to the function of these component processes. Specifically, it is possible to build on what is known about the function of different brain regions to explore whether trait anxiety is associated with increased activation of brain mechanisms involved in processing stimulus threat value, with impoverished recruitment of brain mechanisms involved in attentional control, or with altered function of both processes. We can also explore whether neuroticism is linked to a simi-

lar pattern of task-specific hyperactivity and hypo-recruitment. Studies that have begun to address this question are reviewed next.

From Networks to Modules and Back Again

The late 1930s through to the early 1950s saw the advent of theories that proposed that networks of brain regions including areas such as the hippocampus, cingulate gyrus, amygdala, and orbital frontal cortex were responsible for emotional processing (MacLean 1949; Papez, 1937). Support for the "Papez circuit" and "limbic system" was countered by criticisms that these accounts were more descriptive than functional and lacked a clear rationale for inclusion of certain regions and the exclusion of others (for more extensive discussion of these criticism, see Chapter 9 in Gazzaniga Ivry, & Mangun, 2009).

Early neuroimaging studies of emotion conducted in the late 1990s and early 2000s took a more modular approach. Much research was focused on the amygdala and its role in the detection or evaluation of threat (Morris et al., 1996; Vuilleumier, Armony, Driver, & Dolan, 2001; Whalen et al., 1998, 2004) Indeed, a number of studies from the later part of this era used scan parameters that focused data acquisition on a narrow slab of slices covering the amygdala but omitting much of the rest of the brain.

In contrast, within the last 5 to 10 years, there has been an increasing focus on the interplay of regions involved in the evaluation of threat stimuli with those that enable the regulation of emotional state and physiological fear responses, the (re)appraisal of stimuli, and the control of attentional focus (Bishop, Duncan, Brett, & Lawrence, 2004a; Kim et al., 2003; Ochsner et al., 2002; Phelps et al., 2004). This focus has been accompanied by a shift from examining brain regions in isolation and toward conceptualizing regions as nodes within interconnected networks, the activation of which varies with task engagement and may be meaningful even at "rest" (Deco, Jirso, &

McIntosh, 2011). Neuroimaging investigations of the association between trait anxiety and brain function and structure have similarly evolved across this time period. In the remaining sections of this chapter, we examine what these studies can tell us about the brain basis of the association between trait anxiety and attentional capture by threat, the shared or distinct relationship with neuroticism, and the potential common underpinning of function across other domains of emotional processing.

Amygdala and Frontal Mechanisms underlying Attentional Capture by Threat: Hyper- and Hypo-Activity Linked to Trait Anxiety

Based on findings from the basic neuroscience literature, a relatively widely held view (which has recently come under renewed scrutiny; Pessoa and Adolphs, 2010; see also Chapter 15) is that a direct subcortical thalamo-amygdala pathway facilitates the preattentive processing of threat-related stimuli (LeDoux, 2000; Tamietto & de Gelder, 2010). In line with this position, a number of neuroimaging studies conducted in the early 2000s reported that the amygdala response to threat-related stimuli such as fearful faces is not modulated by the focus of spatial attention (Anderson, Christoff, Panitz, De Rosa, & Gabrieli, 2003; Vuilleumier et al., 2001). These findings lent support to the proposition that the amygdala might provide the biological underpinning, or instantiation, of the preattentive threat detection mechanism described in cognitive models of anxiety. According to this proposal, amygdaloid activation might influence the competitive success of threat-related stimuli in winning attentional resources through a gain function analogous to that held to underlie the facilitation of the processing of targets by top-down attentional control (see Chapter 14).

Further support for this position appeared, initially, to be provided by findings that individuals with elevated anxiety levels show a stronger selective amygdala response to threat-related distracters (Bishop, Duncan, & Lawrence, 2004). However, in this study, it was state rather than trait anxiety that showed a relationship to the amygdala response to unattended threat stimuli. In addition, these results do not necessarily indicate that high anxious individuals show an increased *preattentive* amygdala response to threat-related distracters. An alternate possibility is that attentional resources may not have been fully occupied by the primary task, with attentional "spillover" facilitating the processing of threat-related distracters. Indeed, it has been demonstrated that when the perceptual demands or "load" of the main task is increased, a differential amygdala response to threat-related versus neutral distracters is no longer observed (Pessoa, McKenna, Gutierrez, & Ungerleider, 2002); between-participant differences in the amygdala response to threat distracters as a function of anxiety also being eliminated (Bishop, Jenkins, & Lawrence, 2007).

An interesting model, of value in conceptualizing these findings, is the load theory put forward by Lavie (e.g., Lavie, 2005). Lavie argues that the debate between "early" and "late" accounts of selective visual attention (i.e., whether or not the processing of certain stimulus characteristics is obligatory and unconstrained by attentional resources) may be resolved by taking into account the perceptual load of the task at hand and allowing for two separate stages of attentional competition. According to this model, there is, first, a stage of early perceptual competition. The processing of distracters terminates at this stage when the perceptual load of the primary task is high. Second, under conditions of low perceptual load, competition is held to occur for further processing resources, including the initiation of behavioral responses, with active recruitment of control mechanisms being required to inhibit the processing of salient distracters and support task-related processing. Lavie's hybrid early/late model has primarily been used to account for findings showing that increasing perceptual load reduces or eliminates the processing of affectively neutral salient distracters, such as moving dot patterns, lexical stimuli that promote competing responses to that required by the current target, and colorful or novel scenes (Lavie, 2005; Rees, Frith, & Lavie, 1997). It is, however, interesting to speculate whether the finding that the amygdala response to threat distracters is diminished under high load (Bishop et al., 2007; Pessoa et al., 2002) might be consistent with amygdaloid processing of threat-related stimuli being subject to similar perceptual processing limitations that have been found to affect the processing of other classes of salient visual stimuli.

An alternate theoretical stance to that put forward by Mathews and Mackintosh (1998) is that elevated trait anxiety is associated with impoverished recruitment of the frontal mechanisms required for task-focused attentional control. If high trait anxious participants show impaired recruitment of attentional control mechanisms, this could result in increased "capture" of attentional resources by threat-related distracters. As just outlined, Lavie argues that the active recruitment of attentional control mechanisms to support the processing of targets and inhibit the processing of distracters is particularly required under conditions of low perceptual load to prevent salient distracters from receiving further processing. In support of this claim, Lavie cites findings that groups characterized by weakened attentional control – specifically the elderly and children – show particularly large response competition effects under low perceptual load conditions (Huang-Pollock, Carr, & Nigg, 2002; Maylor & Lavie, 1998). In an interesting parallel, elevated trait anxiety was found to be associated with diminished activation of the dorsolateral prefrontal cortex (DLPFC), ventrolateral prefrontal cortex (VLPFC), and anterior cingulate cortex (ACC) in response to threat distracters under conditions of low but not high perceptual load (Bishop et al., 2007). This finding suggests that trait anxiety might be linked to impoverished recruitment of frontal regions required for

attentional control under task conditions where these mechanisms are needed to regulate trial-by-trial fluctuations in processing competition from emotionally salient distracters.

This raises two further questions. First, can we say anything about the relative attentional control functions of the lateral prefrontal and anterior cingulate cortical regions shown to be under-recruited by high trait anxious individuals? Second, if trait anxiety is linked to difficulties in the use of these frontal regions to regulate attention, will they also be apparent when distracter salience is unrelated to threat value? In regard to the former question, it has been suggested that specific subregions of the prefrontal cortex may play differing roles in top-down attentional control, with the ACC involved in detecting the presence of competition for processing resources and the lateral prefrontal cortex (LPFC) responding to increased expectation of processing competition by augmenting top-down control to support the processing of task-relevant stimuli (Botnivick, Cohen, & Carter, 2004; see Figure 24.4 for illustration of the regions concerned). Evidence for this account has primarily come from studies using response-competition tasks with affectively neutral stimuli (e.g., Carter et al., 2000; Macdonald, Cohen, Stenger, & Carter, 2000), including ones that manipulate the frequency, and hence the expectancy, of high competition trials (Carter et al., 2000). Through application of an equivalent frequency manipulation to a task requiring attentional control over threat distracters, it is possible to investigate whether ACC and LPFC regions show parallel differential responses to unexpected (infrequent) and expected (frequent) threat-related distracters, respectively. This was indeed found to be the case (Bishop, Duncan, Brett, & Lawrence, 2004). Further, the results of this study indicated that individuals with high levels of anxiety showed impoverished recruitment of both these mechanisms (state anxiety analyses were reported, similar results were observed with trait anxiety, unpublished data).

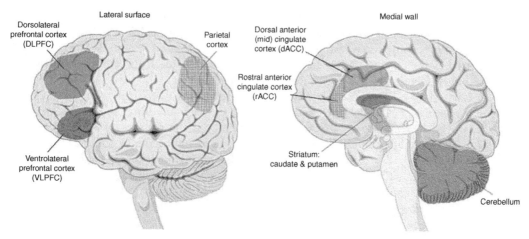

Figure 24.4. Frontal brain regions implicated in regulation of attention to emotionally and non-emotionally salient stimuli include the dorsolateral prefrontal cortex (DLPFC), ventrolateral prefrontal cortex, (VLPFC), rostral anterior cingulate cortex (rACC), and dorsal anterior (mid) cingulate cortex (dACC). Subgenual anterior cingulate cortex is not shown here. Adapted with permission from Bush, 2010.

Intriguingly, a more recent study has produced findings that are discrepant from both those of Bishop and colleagues (2004) and those from the earlier response-competition literature. Using a "face/word" version of the Stroop task, Etkin, Peraza, Kandel, and Hirsch (2006) asked volunteers to indicate whether faces showed fearful or happy expressions while ignoring the word "happy" or "fearful" superimposed on each face. They reported that activation of the ACC, rather than the LPFC, increased when processing competition was expected (frequent face/word incongruent trials) and that LPFC activity increased when processing competition was infrequent or unexpected. One interesting difference from the study by Bishop, Duncan, Brett, and Lawrence (2004) is that in Etkin"s task, both the distracters and targets were emotionally valenced, with the valence of targets and distracters being balanced across "high-conflict" and "low-conflict" trials; those conditions differed instead in face/word congruence. It is difficult to disentangle effects of emotional congruency from response congruency in this design. However, this still does not easily explain why the conditions under which the LPFC and ACC were activated differed from those previously observed in both emo-

tional distracter and response-competition paradigms. One hopes that these discrepant findings will spark further research that may help resolve and unite these results and advance our theoretical understanding of the role of the ACC and LPFC in the detection and resolution of different types of processing competition.

A further point worth considering here concerns the role of rostral versus dorsal subdivisions of the ACC (see Figure 24.4). Early studies reported dorsal ACC activity when processing competition arose from response competition, and rostral ACC activity when processing competition was caused by the presence of emotionally salient but task-irrelevant distracters (Bishop, Duncan, Brett, & Lawrence, 2004; Bush, Luu, & Posner, 2000). This distinction is also apparent within the psychiatric imaging literature (Bush et al., 1999; Shin et al., 2001). However, more recently this distinction has been challenged by a range of studies suggesting a role for the dorsal ACC in emotional processing – not only in emotional distracter tasks but also in studies investigating the anticipation and experience of pain and the expression of conditioned fear (Bishop et al., 2007; Milad, Quirk, et al., 2007; see Shackman et al., 2011, for a comprehensive review). This also calls for further investigation of the precise function of this region. The difference in nomenclature conventions used across groups and the changes in those terms across time complicate this investigation. In this chapter, we follow the nomenclature convention introduced by Mayberg and colleagues (1999) and adopted in our earlier work (Bishop, Duncan, Brett, & Lawrence, 2004 , 2007), whereby rostral ACC excludes subgenual ACC (the region ventral to the corpus callosum). The subdivision referred to here as the dorsal ACC or dACC (see Figure 24.4) has elsewhere been renamed the dorsal anterior mid-cingulate gyrus since this term arguably reflects more accurately the region under consideration (Bush, 2010).

The second question raised above concerns the nature of the association between trait anxiety and the deficient recruitment of frontal attentional control mechanisms. Is this association specific to attentional control over threat, perhaps being secondary to hyper-responsivity of the amygdala to threat-related stimuli? Or does it reflect a more general dysregulation of frontal attentional function that is independent of amygdala responsivity to threat? The cognitive literature provides some suggestion that the latter might be the case, with findings linking trait anxiety to impoverished or inefficient attentional control (Derryberry & Reed, 2002; Eysenck, Derakshan, Santos, & Calvo, 2007). In a test of the hypothesis that trait anxiety is associated with reduced recruitment of frontal attentional control mechanisms even in the absence of threat-related stimuli, Bishop (2009) examined DLPFC recruitment while volunteers performed a response-competition task under conditions of low versus high perceptual load. High trait anxious volunteers showed reduced DLPFC recruitment to high response-competition trials under conditions of low but not high perceptual load, in line with the Lavie model and consistent with trait-anxiety-related dysregulation of frontal attentional mechanisms extending beyond the specific case of attentional control over threat. Further support for a threat-

independent relationship between trait anxiety and impoverished recruitment of frontal attentional control mechanisms comes from the ERP literature. Using an antisaccade task (where volunteers must saccade away from the position in which a cue is presented), Ansari and Derakshan (2011) found that high trait anxious individuals showed longer antisaccade latencies together with reduced frontocentral activity during antisaccade preparation.

The studies discussed here provide some initial evidence that trait anxiety is linked to impoverished recruitment of frontal regions important for attentional control both when processing competition is caused by threat-related distracters and when it is caused by response conflict. This raises the question of whether this deficient recruitment can be remediated by cognitive interventions such as attentional training. A number of early trials provide some initial hope that this might indeed be the case (Amir, Weber, Beard, Bomyea, & Taylor, 2008; Hakamata et al., 2010).

Although work reviewed here suggests a relationship between trait anxiety and frontal dysfunction in the absence of task-related differences in amygdala activity (Bishop, 2009), this leaves open the question as to whether trait anxiety is also linked to amygdala hyper-responsivity to threat in the absence of differential activation of frontal mechanisms. To address this question, we need to turn to tasks that require the relatively passive processing of threat-related stimuli in the absence of demands on attention or other executive processes. Surprisingly few such studies exist that meet the constraints of having examined amygdala function and also having measured individual differences in trait anxiety. In one early study, Etkin et al. (2004) reported that trait anxiety was associated with elevated amygdala responsivity to masked threat-related faces, but not to unmasked threat-related faces. In a second study, Stein, Simmons, Feinstein, and Paulus (2007) reported that elevated STAI trait scores were linked to greater amygdala activity during conditions requiring matching of facial emotions than during conditions requiring matching of basic shapes.

One intriguing possibility is that an association between trait anxiety and amygdala responsivity to threat-related stimuli might primarily be seen when the stimuli are ambiguous or require some form of resolution of their threat value (Whalen, 2007). This is arguably more the case for masked than for unmasked threat-related faces and also potentially the case when different faces with varying emotional expressions need to be judged for their equivalence in expression. This is clearly a tentative hypothesis, and it remains to be more firmly established under precisely which conditions trait anxiety is linked to amygdala hyper-responsivity to threat. Furthermore, given the possibility that frontal mechanisms may be important for certain forms of ambiguity resolution (Kim et al., 2003; Nomura et al., 2003), it will also be important to confirm that trait-anxiety-related differences in amygdala responsivity to weak or ambiguous threat stimuli are not secondary to the differential recruitment of frontal mechanisms.

Neuroticism and the Brain Mechanisms Influencing Attentional Capture by Threat

As reviewed in the previous section of this chapter, in recent years an increasing number of studies have examined the relationship between trait anxiety and recruitment of the frontal and amygdaloid mechanisms implicated in attentional control over threat distracters. This makes it possible to start to ask relatively specific questions about which parts of the neural circuitry influencing attentional capture by threat show altered function in high trait anxious individuals. Although the corresponding literature on neuroticism is more limited, we can look at the initial studies available to begin to assess whether neuroticism and trait anxiety show similar relationships with regional brain function – as might be expected if they both represent the same single underlying construct – or whether neuroticism and

trait anxiety only partially covary in their relationship with the function of discrete brain mechanisms as might, for example, be predicted by Clark and Watson's tripartiate model (see Figure 24.1).

At the time of writing, three studies have examined the correlates of neuroticism while participants perform fMRI tasks involving manipulation of selective attention and emotional stimuli. Two of the three – one using the Emotional Stroop task and the other the Probe Detection task – reported no significant association between neuroticism scores and regional brain activity during conditions of attentional competition from emotional stimuli (Amin, Constable, & Canli, 2004; Canli, Amin, Haas, Omura, & Constable, 2004). However, given that the sample size in each case was fairly small for a correlational study (12 or fewer subjects), it is difficult to draw strong conclusions from these null results.

In a subsequent larger study (n = 36), Haas, Omura, Constable, and Canli (2007) administered a Stroop-like task, similar to that of Etkin et al. (2006), in which trials differed in the emotional congruence of target words and the expressions of background faces. In this study, the words did not map directly onto the names of the facial expressions, thereby reducing the association between emotional incongruency and response conflict. Individuals with high neuroticism levels were found to show increased amygdala and subgenual anterior cingulate activity to trials with emotionally incongruent face/word pairs (collapsing positive-face/negative-word and negative-face/positive-word trials). This result is intriguing, but difficult to relate to findings from imaging studies examining the influence of trait anxiety on the neural mechanisms regulating selective attention to threat, because the task manipulation used by Haas and colleagues (emotional congruency) is not one of distracter threat-relatedness, being orthogonal to distracter valence. One possibility is that the heightened amygdala responsivity to emotionally incongruent stimuli in high-N individuals reported here might primarily reflect sensitivity to stimuli that are ambiguous in their emotional significance, in line with the proposals put forward by Whalen and colleagues (Whalen, 2007).

To explore the "ambiguity sensitivity" hypothesis further, we review studies that have examined the influence of neuroticism on regional brain activity to emotional stimuli using passive viewing or cognitively undemanding tasks. Here, the question of interest is whether neuroticism is particularly linked to heightened amygdala responsivity to emotional stimuli when these stimuli are in some form ambiguous in their valence or threat-relatedness. Canli and colleagues reported that although the amygdala response to happy faces and positive images was predicted by extraversion, there was no relationship between neuroticism and amygdala responsivity to either negative emotional faces or negative emotional images (Canli et al. 2001, 2002). Similarly, Britton, Ho, Taylor, and Liberzon (2007) found no relationship between neuroticism and amygdala responsivity during the passive viewing of emotional images, facial expressions, and emotional films. Cremers et al. (2010) also found no relationship between neuroticism and the amygdala response to negative emotional faces during a gender discrimination task. The one exception is a study by Chan, Norbury, Goodwin, and Harmer (2009) that examined amygdala responsivity to fearful, happy, neutral, and morphed facial expressions during a gender discrimination task in individuals high and low in neuroticism. Here high N scores were associated with stronger amygdala activity to faces with expressions "morphed" partway between neutral and fear. It could be argued that these morphed facial stimuli are milder or more ambiguous in their threat value than the "fully" negative stimuli used in the other studies. However, this one finding does not permit any definitive conclusions to be drawn in favor of the "ambiguity" account without further empirical investigation.

It also remains to be established whether neuroticism is associated with impoverished recruitment of the frontal mechanisms supporting attentional control, during non-emotional task performance, in a similar manner to that observed for trait anxiety. There is little existing work that pertains to this issue. Using an oddball detection task, Eisenberger, Lieberman, and Satpute (2005) found that neuroticism was associated with reduced lateral prefrontal cortical and rostral ACC recruitment but increased dorsal ACC activity. Further detailed investigation of the relationship between neuroticism and recruitment of lateral frontal and anterior cingulate subregions is required to form a clearer picture of the commonalities and differences in the relationship between neuroticism and trait anxiety with regional brain function. In particular, as noted earlier, the precise role of the dorsal ACC in cognitive and emotional processing remains an issue under active debate.

It is hoped that this chapter has provided a flavor of how, in line with the case made by Kosslyn and colleagues, it is possible to conduct neuroimaging studies that may advance both our understanding of the brain mechanisms supporting attentional capture by threat and the relationship between trait anxiety and variation in the function of these mechanisms. Although there are fewer studies pertaining to neuroticism, the available studies serve to generate hypotheses that could form the basis of future research. The work reviewed here also raises questions as to the extent to which the association among trait predisposition to anxiety, amygdala hyperactivity, and frontal hypoactivity is dependent on task domain. Specifically, will the associations reported here also be observed in the context of performance of other tasks? Or even in the absence of any task? Studies pertaining to these questions are reviewed in the next two sections.

Trait Anxiety and Hyper-Amygdala and Hypo-Frontal Function: The Case of Fear Conditioning

The rodent fear conditioning literature provides strong evidence for the role of frontal inhibitory influences on the amygdala in the attenuation of physiological and behavioral fear responses. Findings indicate that the amygdala is involved in the acquisition and expression of cued fear, with medial prefrontal cortical inputs inhibiting amygdala responsivity to conditioned fear stimuli (CSs) following extinction training (Maren & Quirk, 2004; Sotres-Bayon, Bush, & LeDoux, 2004). Human studies of conditioned fear have implicated similar circuitry with ventral medial regions of prefrontal cortex (vmPFC) facilitating context-specific recall of "CS – unconditioned stimulus (UCS) absent" associations formed during extinction training (Milad, Wright, et al., 2007; Phelps et al., 2004). Disruption to this circuitry has been documented in adults with posttraumatic stress disorder (Milad et al., 2009) and has been proposed to be of potential relevance to other anxiety disorders.

Recently, a handful of studies have begun to address whether trait vulnerability to anxiety is linked to altered functioning of this circuitry. Two initial studies reported that high trait anxious individuals showed elevated amygdala activity during extinction (Barrett & Armony, 2009; Sehlmeyer et al., 2011). Associations of extinction-related ACC activity with trait anxiety were also reported, but the directionality and specific locus of these effects did not replicate across the two studies. In recent work from our own lab, we found that elevated amygdala activity to a CS that predicted an aversive stimulus (the UCS) mediated the relationship between trait anxiety and the strength of initial acquisition of skin conductance responses to the predictive CS (Indovina et al., 2011). We also found that trait anxiety was negatively related to recruitment of ventral frontal regions linked to context-appropriate down-regulation of both cued and contextual fear *prior* to omission of the UCS. Hierarchical regression revealed that the relationship between trait anxiety and amygdala responsivity to the predictive CS was independent of that between trait anxiety and context-appropriate ventral PFC recruitment. It is interesting to note

that the medial and lateral regions of ventral prefrontal cortex reported in this study, the activation of which was associated with lower cued and contextual fear responses, overlap with those reported elsewhere to be activated during deliberate emotion regulation and affective stimulus reappraisal (see Chapter 16). Delgado and colleagues have further reported that activation of similar ventral PFC regions accompanies a reduction in conditioned fear, regardless of whether it occurs due to extinction or emotion regulation (Delgado, Nearing, LeDoux, & Phelps, 2008).

Together with the work reviewed earlier, these findings raise the possibility that individual variation in the recruitment of different subregions of frontal cortex may influence volunteers' ability to regulate their emotional responses to the anticipation of aversive stimuli, as well as their locus of attention when threat-related visual stimuli are presented. It is important to note that characteristics such as trait anxiety may map onto individual differences not only in the ability to regulate responses to aversive stimuli but also in the nature of the regulation strategy selected. Initial studies have begun to examine the brain regions activated by different emotion regulation strategies (e.g., Vrtička, Sander, & Vuilleumier, 2011), but as yet this work has not been integrated with investigation of individual differences in strategy selection or success in implementation.

Trait Vulnerability to Affective Disorder: What Might We Learn from Resting State Studies?

Recently, there has been increasing interest in whether the structural and functional connectivity between different brain regions may be informative even in the absence of task performance. One high-profile example is the recently launched Human Connectome Project, which aims to "comprehensively map human brain circuitry... using cutting-edge methods of noninvasive neuroimaging... yield[ing] invaluable information about brain connectivity, its relationship to behavior, and the contributions of genetic and environmental factors to individual differences in brain circuitry" (http://humanconnectome.org/). This interest has been accompanied by a renewed emphasis on examining the function of brain regions in the context of the networks in which they are embedded as "nodes." It has also brought increased recognition of the need to study individual differences in order to understand normative brain function. It is beyond the scope of the current chapter to provide a comprehensive review of this literature (see Deco et al., 2011). We limit this section to a consideration of a few findings to date that may inform our understanding of the brain basis of trait vulnerability to affective disorder.

Roy et al. (2009) provided a detailed report of connectivity between the amygdala and other brain regions at rest. Positive correlations were found between resting state blood-oxygen-level-dependent (BOLD) activity in the amygdala and a number of brain regions, including the medial frontal gyrus, rostral ACC, dorsal ACC, insula, thalamus, and striatum. Negative correlations were also observed between the amygdala and areas, including the superior frontal gyrus, bilateral middle frontal gyrus, posterior cingulate cortex, precuneus, and parietal and occipital lobes. Further analyses were conducted to profile the connections of different amygdala subnuclei. These provided some suggestion of negative connectivity between the basolateral nucleus and central nucleus of the amygdala, as well as opposing patterns of connectivity between these subnuclei with the medial frontal gyrus and anterior cingulate cortex.

These findings are intriguing, but have several limitations. First, as noted by the authors, it is extremely difficult to specify amygdala subnuclei on echoplanar images. Although the probabilistic approach adopted by Roy and colleagues can provide an estimate, it is not clear if the level of accuracy achieved is sufficient for analyses

of this nature. Second, an issue that pertains to all resting state studies is that it is not clear how to interpret negative versus positive patterns of BOLD connectivity at rest. Are inhibitory connections at the neuronal level likely to be reflected as negative BOLD connectivity patterns? This is often assumed but far from established. A third problem is that it is unclear as to what criteria should be used for including or excluding regions in different "resting state" networks, raising spectra of the criticisms applied to the circuits of Papez (1937) and MacLean (1949). Specifically, with both seed-based and component-based approaches, the same question occurs as to what threshold to use – whether in terms of significance levels for whole-brain seed-driven analyses or the number of components for independent or principal-components-based analyses. As the field develops, the challenge will be to find ways to address these issues.

Building on the work by Roy and colleagues, Kim et al. (2011) examined the influence of individual differences in self-reported pre-scan anxiety on resting state functional connectivity. They reported that anxiety levels significantly modulated connectivity between the amygdala and only two regions. High state anxious individuals showed negative amygdala-vmPFC connectivity contrasting with positive functional connectivity between these regions in low state anxious individuals. In addition, they also showed an absence of the negative connectivity between the amygdala and dorsal medial PFC observed in low state anxious volunteers. The effects of anxiety in this study are particularly of interest because of their selectivity. In advancing our understanding of trait vulnerability to affective disorder, a limitation is that the primary analyses presented used state anxiety measures, with analyses using trait anxiety measures being described as showing similar but weaker trends. One hopes that future studies will further explore the extent to which anxiety-related variability in amygdala-frontal functional connectivity at rest reflects stable individual differences versus effects of a temporary mood state.

Trait Vulnerability to Affective Disorder: From Correlation to Causation?

If, based on the studies reviewed in this chapter, we come to the conclusion that there are stable trait-related differences in the function of amygdala-frontal circuitry, what might cause these differences? There are a number of possibilities, which are by no means mutually exclusive. These include structural or functional differences in one or both regions reflecting either genetic or environmental influences, differences in the integrity of tracts connecting these regions, and differences in neurochemical modulation of one or both regions, again potentially reflecting either genetic or environmental influences uniquely or in combination.

The evidence pertaining to these alternatives is relatively limited. Diffusion tensor imaging findings suggest that reduced integrity of white matter tracts (as indexed by fractional anisotrophy) that link the amygdala to vmPFC in humans may indeed be associated with trait vulnerability to anxiety (Kim & Whalen, 2009). Positron emission topography studies meanwhile point to a relationship between neuroticism and resting state frontal hypo-perfusion (Deckersbach et al., 2006). Arguably the most intriguing findings are those emerging from the rodent and human literature on the effects of stress and gene-environment interactions on amygdala-frontal circuitry (see Arnsten, 2009, and Chapters 22 and 25). Periods of acute stress are associated with neurochemical changes, including elevated levels of noradrenaline and dopamine release (Goldstein, Rasmusson, Bunney, & Roth, 1996). High levels of these catecholamines enhance amygdala function (Debiec & LeDoux, 2006), but undermine prefrontal cortical function (Arnsten, Mathew, Ubriani, Taylor, & Li, 1999). Chronic stress leads to long-term alterations in the frontal-

amygdala network, with contrasting patterns of dendritic change being reported in the frontal cortex and amygdala. Whereas amygdaloid dendrites increase (Vyas, Mitra, Shankaranarayano Rao, & Chattarji, 2002), neurons in the PFC show a reduction in dendritic branches, which appears linked to deficient performance on measures of executive control (see Holmes & Wellman, 2009, for a review). Genetic differences, including common genetic polymorphisms influencing catecholamine metabolism in the frontal cortex (e.g., the COMT val 158 met polymorphism), as well as ones affecting serotonergic modulation of amygdala activity (e.g., polymorphisms in the serotonin transporter gene), may well interact with such environmental influences (Hyde, Bogdan, & Hariri, 2011) and also with the effects of early life stress on gene expression (Francis, Champagne, Liu, & Meaney, 1999). Hence, a combination of genetic and environmental influences potentially leads to changes in both frontal and amygdala integrity and function. Increased integration of the stress, epigenetics, and functional genomics literatures with that reviewed in the earlier sections of this chapter may enable us to move beyond description of the cognitive and neural correlates of trait vulnerability to affective disorders to begin to outline causal trajectories underlying observed individual differences in affective style, disorder-related symptomatology, processing of emotionally salient stimuli, and associated brain function.

Conclusions

Studying trait vulnerability to affective disorder may both inform our understanding of healthy brain function and provide an important bridge to studies of psychiatric disorder. It may also enable us to establish markers of elevated risk for psychiatric illness that could be used to identify individuals who might benefit from preventive interventions (e.g., cognitive training) before a deepening spiral into clinically significant illness occurs. To date, cross-group studies of normative brain function and between-group studies of specific affective disorders far outnumber studies using continuous trait measures to study the brain basis of vulnerability to affective disorder. These latter studies face a number of challenges. In addition to the need for well-validated trait measures of affective style and vulnerability, rigor in neuroimaging design and analysis is likely to be an important determinant of progress in this field. Exciting advances are being made in the methods and techniques available, both within neuroimaging and converging approaches. By incorporating these advances and by drawing on models derived from both the human cognitive and basic neuroscience literatures, it will be possible to test increasingly sophisticated hypotheses regarding the brain basis of vulnerability to affective disorder.

Outstanding Questions and Future Directions

- How do different dimensions of personality relate to vulnerability to affective disorder?
- Are there multiple "pathways" by which dysregulation of amygdala/frontal circuitry confers vulnerability to affective disorder?
- To what extent does this dysregulation reflect genetic influences, the effects of early life stress on gene expression, or the direct effect of chronic or acute stress on this circuitry?
- On a methodological front, how can we best balance hypothesis-driven research with exploratory investigations? Within the area of neuroimaging, what are the respective limitations of different methods of data acquisition and styles of analysis (e.g., region-of-interest approaches versus whole-brain analyses)?
- If we seek to understand genetic influences on brain mechanisms implicated in vulnerability to affective disorder, how can we deal with the multiple comparisons problem due to both brain voxel and genetic polymorphism array size?

References

Amin, Z., Constable, R. T., & Canli, T. (2004). Attentional bias for valenced stimuli as a function of personality in the dot-probe task. *Journal of Research in Personality*, 38, 15–23.

Amir, N., Weber, G., Beard, C., Bomyea, J., & Taylor, C. T. (2008). The effect of a single-session attention modification program on response to a public-speaking challenge in socially anxious individuals. *Journal of Abnormal Psychology*, 117(4), 860–68.

Anderson, A. K., Christoff, K., Panitz, D., De Rosa, E., & Gabrieli, J.D. (2003). Neural correlates of the automatic processing of threat facial signals. *Journal of Neuroscience*, 23(13), 5627–33.

Ansari, T. L., & Derakshan, N. (2011). The neural correlates of impaired inhibitory control in anxiety. *Neuropsychologia*, 49(5), 1146–53.

Arnsten, A. F. T. (2009). Stress signaling pathways that impair prefrontal cortex structure and function. *Nature Reviews Neuroscience*, 10, 410–22.

Arnsten, A. F. T., Mathew, R., Ubriani, R., Taylor, J. R., & Li, B.-M. (1999). α-1 noradrenergic receptor stimulation impairs prefrontal cortical cognitive function. *Biological Psychiatry*, 45, 26–31.

Barrett, J., & Armony, J. L. (2009). Influence of trait anxiety on brain activity during the acquisition and extinction of aversive conditioning. *Psychological Medicine*, 39(2), 255–65.

Beck, A. X, Ward, C. H., Mendelson, M., Mock, J., & Erbaugh, J. (1961). An inventory for measuring depression. *Archives of General Psychiatry*, 4, 561–71.

Bieling, P. J., Antony, M. M., & Swinson, R. P. (1998). The state–trait anxiety inventory, trait version: Structure and content re-examined. *Behaviour Research and Therapy*, 36, 777–88.

Bishop, S. J. (2008). Neural mechanisms underlying selective attention to threat. *Annals of the New York Academy of Sciences*, 1129, 141–52.

Bishop, S. J. (2009) Trait anxiety and impoverished prefrontal control of attention. *Nature Neuroscience*, 12, 92–98.

Bishop, S. J., Duncan, J., Brett, M., & Lawrence, A. D. (2004). Prefrontal cortical function and anxiety: Controlling attention to threat-related stimuli. *Nature Neuroscience,* 7(2),184–88.

Bishop, S. J., Duncan, J., & Lawrence, A. (2004b). State anxiety modulation of the amygdala response to unattended threat-related stimuli. *Journal of Neuroscience,* 24, 10364–68.

Bishop, S. J., Jenkins, R., & Lawrence, A. (2007). The neural processing of task-irrelevant fearful faces: Effects of perceptual load and individual differences in trait and state anxiety. *Cerebral Cortex,* 17, 1595–1603.

Botvinick, M. M., Cohen, D. D., & Carter, C. S. (2004). Conflict monitoring and anterior cingulated cortex: An update. *Trends in Cognitive Sciences,* 12, 539–46.

Bradley, B. P., Mogg, K., Falla, S. J., & Hamilton, L. R. (1998). Attentional bias for threatening facial expressions in anxiety: Manipulation of stimulus duration. *Cognition Emotion,* 12, 737–53.

Britton, J. C., Ho, S. H., Taylor, S. F., & Liberzon, I. (2007). Neuroticism associated with neural activation patterns to positive stimuli. *Psychiatric Research – Neuroimaging,* 156(3), 263–67.

Brown, T. A. (2007). Temporal course and structural relationships among dimensions of temperament and DSM-IV anxiety and mood disorder constructs. *Journal of Abnormal Psychology,* 116, 313–28.

Brown, T. A., & Barlow, D. H. (2009). A proposal for a dimensional classification system based on the shared features of the DSM-IV anxiety and mood disorders: Implications for assessment and treatment. *Psychological Assessment,* 21(3), 256–71.

Brown, T. A., & Rosellini, A. J. (2011). The direct and interactive effects of neuroticism and life stress on the severity and longitudinal course of depressive symptoms. *Journal of Abnormal Psychology,* 120(4), 844–56

Bush, G. (2010). Attention-deficit/hyperactivity disorder and attention networks. *Neuropsychopharmacology,* 35, 278–300.

Bush, G., Frazier, J. A., Rauch, S. L., Seidman, L .J., Whalen, P. J., Jenike, M. A., & Biederman, J. (1999). Anterior cingulate cortex dysfunction in attention-deficit/hyperactivity disorder revealed by fMRI and the Counting Stroop. *Biological Psychiatry,* 45(12), 1542–52.

Bush, G., Luu, P., & Posner, M. I. (2000). Cognitive and emotional influences in anterior cingulated cortex. *Trends in Cognitive Sciences,* 4(6), 215–22.

Canli, T. (2004). Functional brain mapping of extraversion and neuroticism: Learning from individual differences in emotion processing. *Journal of Personality,* 72, 1105–32.

Canli, T., Amin, Z., Haas, B., Omura, K., & Constable, R. T. (2004). A double dissociation between mood states and personality traits in the anterior cingulate. *Behavioral Neuroscience,* 18, 897–904.

Canli, T., Sivers, H., Whitfield, S. L., Gotlib, I. H., & Gabrieli, J. D. (2002). Amygdala response to happy faces as a function of extraversion. *Science,* 296, 2191.

Canli, T., Zhao, Z., Desmond, J. E., Kang, E., Gross, J., & Gabrieli, J. D. E. (2001). An fMRI study of personality influences on brain reactivity to emotional stimuli. *Behavioral Neuroscence,* 115, 33–42.

Carter, C. S., Macdonald, A. M., Botvinick, M., Ross, L. L., Stenger, V. A., Noll, D., & Cohen, J. D. (2000). Parsing executive processes: Strategic vs. evaluative functions of the anterior cingulated cortex. *Proceedings of the National Academy of Sciences,* 97, 1944–48.

Chan, S. W., Goodwin, G. M., & Harmer, C. J. (2007). Highly neurotic never-depressed students have negative biases in information processing. *Psychological Medicine,* 37, 1281–91.

Chan, S. W. Y., Norbury, R., Goodwin, G. M., & Harmer C. J. (2009). Risk for depression and neural responses to fearful facial expressions of emotion. *British Journal of Psychiatry,* 194, 139–45.

Clark, L. A., & Watson D. (1991). Tripartite model of anxiety and depression: Psychometric evidence and taxonomic implications. *Journal of Abnormal Psychology,* 100(3), 16–36.

Costa, P. T, Jr., & McCrae, R. R. (1995). Domains and facets: Hierarchical personality assessment using the Revised NEO Personality Inventory. *Journal of Personality Assessment,* 64, 21–50.

Costa, P., & McCrae, R. R. (1992). Normal personality assessment in clinical practice: The NEO Personality Inventory. *Psychological Assessment,* 4, 5–13.

Cremers, H. R., Demenescu, L. R., Aleman, A., Renken, R., van Tol, M.J., van der Wee, N. J., & Roelofs, K. (2010). Neuroticism modulates amygdala-prefrontal connectivity in response to negative emotional facial expressions. *Neuroimage,* 49, 963–70.

Davidson, R. J. (2002). Anxiety and affective style: Role of prefrontal cortex and amygdala. *Biological Psychiatry*, 51(1), 68–80.

Debiec, J., & LeDoux, J. E. (2006). Noradrenergic signaling in the amygdala contributes to the reconsolidation of fear memory: Treatment implications for PTSD. *Annals of the New York Academy of Sciences*, 1071, 521–24.

Deckersbach, T., Miller, K. K., Klibanski, A., Fischman, A., Dougherty, D. D., Blais, M. A., & Rauch, S. L. (2006). Regional cerebral brain metabolism correlates of neuroticism and extraversion. *Depression and Anxiety*, 23(3), 133–38.

Deco, G., Jirsa, V. K., & McIntosh, A. R. (2011). Emerging concepts for the dynamical organization of resting-state activity in the brain. *Nature Reviews Neuroscience*, 12(1), 43–56.

Delgado, M. R., Nearing, K. I., Ledoux, J. E., & Phelps, E. A. (2008). Neural circuitry underlying the regulation of conditioned fear and its relation to extinction. *Neuron.*, 59(5), 829–38.

Derryberry, D., & Reed, M .A. (2002). Anxiety-related attentional biases and their regulation by attentional control. *Journal of Abnormal Psychology*, 111, 225–36.

Desimone, R., & Duncan, J. (1995). Neural mechanisms of selective attention. *Annual Review of Neuroscience*, 18, 193–222.

Eisenberger, N. I., Lieberman, M. D., & Satpute, A. B. (2005). Personality from a controlled processing perspective: An fMRI study of neuroticism, extraversion, and self-consciousness. *Cognitive Affective & Behavioral Neuroscience*, 5, 169–81.

Etkin, A., Egner, T., Peraza, D. M., Kandel, E. R., & Hirsch, J. (2006). Resolving emotional conflict: A role for the rostral anterior cingulate cortex in modulating activity in the amygdala. *Neuron*, 51, 871–82.

Etkin, A., Klemenhagen, K. C., Dudman, J. T., Rogan, M. T., Hen, R., Kandel, E. R., & Hirsch, J. (2004). Individual differences in trait anxiety predict the response of the basolateral amygdala to unconsciously processed fearful faces. *Neuron*, 44(6), 1043–55.

Etkin, A., & Wager, T. D. (2007) Functional neuroimaging of anxiety: A meta-analysis of emotional processing in PTSD, social anxiety disorder, and specific phobia. *American Journal of Psychiatry*, 164(10), 1476–88.

Eysenck, H. J., & Eysenck, S. B. G. (1975). *Eysenck Personality Questionnaire manual*. San Diego: Educational and Industrial Testing Service.

Eysenck, M. W., Derakshan, N., Santos, R., & Calvo, M. G. (2007). Anxiety and cognitive performance: Attentional control theory. *Emotion*, 7, 336–53.

Francis, D. D., Champagne, F. A., Liu, D., & Meaney, M. J. (1999). Maternal care, gene expression, and the development of individual differences in stress reactivity. *Annals of the New York Academy of Sciences*, 896, 66–84.

Gazzaniga, M. S. Ivry, R. B., & Mangun, G. R. (2009). Emotion. In M.S. Gazzaniga, R. B. Ivry, & G. R. Mangun (Eds.), *Cognitive neuroscience – the biology of the mind* (3rd ed., pp. 364–281). New York: Norton.

Goldstein, L. E., Rasmusson, A. M., Bunney, S. B., & Roth, R. H. (1996). Role of the amygdala in the coordination of behavioral, neuroendocrine and prefrontal cortical monoamine responses to psychological stress in the rat. *Journal of Neuroscience*, 16, 4787–98.

Gotlib, I. H., MacLachlan, A., & Katz, A. (1988). Biases in visual attention in depressed and nondepressed individuals. *Cognition Emotion*, 2, 185–200.

Gotlib, I. H., & McCann, C. D. (1984). Construct accessibility and depression: An examination of cognitive and affective factors, *Journal of Personality and Social Psychology*, 47, 427–39.

Haas, B. W., Omura, K., Constable, R. T., & Canli, T. (2007). Emotional conflict and neuroticism: Personality-dependent activation in the amygdala and subgenual anterior cingulate. *Behavioral Neuroscience*, 121, 249–56.

Hakamata, Y., Lissek, S., Bar-Haim, Y., Britton, J. C., Fox, N. A., Leibenluft, E., & Pine, D. S. (2010). Attention bias modification treatment: A meta-analysis toward the establishment of novel treatment for anxiety. *Biological Psychiatry*, 68(11), 982–90.

Hettema, J. M., An, S. S., Bukszar, J., van den Oord, E. J., Neale, M. C., Kendler, K. S., & Chen, X. (2008). Catechol-O-methyltransferase contributes to genetic susceptibility shared among anxiety spectrum phenotypes. *Biological Psychiatry*, 64(4), 302–10.

Hill, A. B., & Dutton, F. (1989). Depression and selective attention to self-esteem threatening words. *Personality and Individual Differences*, 10, 915–17.

Hill, A. B., & Knowles, T. H. (1991). Depression and the emotional Stroop effect. *Personality and Individual Differences*, 12, 481–85.

Holmes, A., & Wellman, C. L (2009). Stress-induced prefrontal reorganization and executive dysfunction in rodents. *Neuroscience and Biobehavioral Reviews*, 33, 773–83.

Huang-Pollock, C. L., Carr, T. H., & Nigg, J. T. (2002). Development of selective attention: Perceptual load influences early versus late attentional selection in children and adults. *Developmental Psychology*, 38, 363–75.

Hyde, L. W., Bogdan, R., & Hariri, A. R. (2011). Understanding risk for psychopathology through imaging gene-environment interactions. *Trends in Cognitive Sciences*, 15(9), 417–27.

Indovina, I., Robbins, T. W., Núñez-Elizalde, A. O., Dunn, B. D., Bishop, S. J. (2011). Fear-conditioning mechanisms associated with trait vulnerability to anxiety in humans. *Neuron*, 69(3), 563–71.

John, O. P. (1990). The "Big Five" factor taxonomy: Dimensions of personality in the natural language and in questionnaires. In L. A. Pervin (Ed.), *Handbook of personality theory and research* (pp. 66–100). New York: Guilford Press.

Kastner, S., & Ungerleider, L.G. (2000). Mechanisms of visual attention in the human cortex. *Annual Review of Neuroscience*, 23, 315–41.

Kendler, K. S., Gardner, C. O., Gatz, M., & Pedersen, N. L. (2007). The sources of comorbidity between major depression and generalized anxiety disorder in a Swedish national twin sample. *Psychological Medicine*, 37(3), 453–62.

Kim, M. J., Gee, D. G., Loucks, R. A., Davis, F. C., & Whalen, P. J. (2011). Anxiety dissociates dorsal and ventral medial prefrontal cortex functional connectivity with the amygdala at rest. *Cerebral Cortex*, 21(7), 1667–73.

Kim, H., Somerville, L. H., Johnstone, T., Alexander, A. L., & Whalen, P. J. (2003). Inverse amygdala and medial prefrontal cortex responses to surprised faces. *Neuroreport*, 14(18), 2317–22.

Kim, M. J., & Whalen, P. J. (2009). The structural integrity of an amygdala-prefrontal pathway predicts trait anxiety. *Journal of Neuroscience*, 29(37), 11614–18.

Kosslyn, S. M., Cacioppo, J. T., Davidson, R.J., Hugdahl, K., Lovallo, W. R., Spiegel, D., & Rose, R.(2002). Bridging psychology and biology. *American Psychologist*, 57, 341–51.

Lavie, N. (2005). Distracted and confused?: Selective attention under load. *Trends in Cognitive Sciences*, 9, 75–82.

LeDoux, J. E. (2000). Emotion circuits in the brain. *Annual Review of Neuroscience*, 23, 155–84.

Luteijn, F., & Bouman, T. K. (1988). The concepts of depression, anxiety, and neuroticism in questionnaires. *European Journal of Personality*, 2, 113–20.

MacDonald, A. W., Cohen, J. D., Stenger, V. A., & Carter, C. S. (2000). Dissociating the role of dorsolateral prefrontal cortex and anterior cingulate cortex in cognitive control. *Science*, 288, 1835–38.

MacLean, P. D. (1949). Psychosomatic disease and the "visceral brain": Recent developments bearing on the Papez theory of emotion. *Psychosomatic Medicine*, 11, 338–53

MacLeod, C., & Hagan, R. (1992). Individual differences in the selective processing of threatening information, and emotional responses to a stressful life event. *Behaviour Research and Therapy* , 30, 151–61.

MacLeod, C., & Mathews, A. (1988). Anxiety and the allocation of attention to threat. *Quarterly Journal of Experimental Psychology*, 40, 653–70.

Maren, S., & Quirk, G. J. (2004). Neuronal signaling of fear memory. *Nature Reviews Neuroscience*, 5, 844–52.

Mathews, A., & Mackintosh, B. (1998). A cognitive model of selective processing in anxiety. *Cognitive Therapy Research*, 22, 539–60.

Mathews, A., Ridgeway, V., & Williamson, D. A., (1996). Evidence for attention to threatening stimuli in depression. *Behaviour Research and Therapy*, 34, 695–705.

Mayberg, H. S., Liotti, M., Brannan, S. K., McGinnis, S., Mahurin, R. K., Jerabek, P. A., & Fox, P. T. (1999). Reciprocal limbic-cortical function and negative mood: Converging PET findings in depression and normal sadness. *American Journal of Psychiatry*, 156, 675–82.

Maylor, E., & Lavie, N. (1998). The influence of perceptual load on age differences in selective attention. *Psychology and Aging*, 13, 563–73.

Milad, M. R., Pitman, R. K., Ellis, C. B., Gold, A. L., Shin, L. M., Lasko, N. B., & Rauch, S. L. (2009). Neurobiological basis of failure to recall extinction memory in posttraumatic stress disorder. *Biological Psychiatry*, 66(12), 1075–82.

Milad, M. R., Quirk, G. J., Pitman, R. K., Orr, S. P., Fischl, B., & Rauch, S.L. (2007). A role for the human dorsal anterior cingulate cortex in fear expression. *Biological Psychiatry*, 62(10), 1191–94.

Milad, M. R, Wright, C. I., Orr, S. P., Pitman, R. K., Quirk, G. J., & Rauch, S. L. (2007). Recall of fear extinction in humans activates the ventromedial prefrontal cortex and hippocampus in concert. *Biological Psychiatry*, 62(5), 446–54.

Mogg, K., & Bradley, B. P. (1998). A cognitive-motivational analysis of anxiety. *Behaviour Research and Therapy*, 36, 809–48.

Morris, J. S., Frith, C. D., Perrett, D. I., Rowland, D., Young, A. W., Calder, A. J., & Dolan, R. J. (1996). A differential neural response in the human amygdala to fearful and happy facial expressions. *Nature*, 383(6603), 812–15.

Nomura, M., Iidaka, T., Kakehi, K., Tsukiura, T., Hasegawa, T., Maeda, Y., & Matsue, Y. (2003). Frontal lobe networks for effective processing of ambiguously expressed emotions in humans. *Neuroscience Letters*, 348(2), 113–16.

Ochsner, K. N., Bunge, S. A., Gross, J. J., & Gabrieli, J. D. (2002). Rethinking feelings: An FMRI study of the cognitive regulation of emotion. *Journal of Cognitive Neuroscience*, 14(8), 1215–29.

Papez, J. W. (1937). A proposed mechanism of emotion. *Archives of Neurology and Psychiatry*, 38, 725–74.

Pessoa, L., & Adolphs, R. (2010). Emotion processing and the amygdala: From a "low road" to "many roads" of evaluating biological significance. *Nature Reviews Neuroscience*, 11(11), 773–83.

Pessoa, L., McKenna, M., Gutierrez, E., & Ungerleider, L.G. (2002). Neural processing of emotional faces requires attention. *Proceedings of the National Academy of Sciences*, 99(17), 11458–63.

Phelps, E. A., Delgado, M.R., Nearing, K. I., & LeDoux, J. E. (2004). Extinction learning in humans: Role of the amygdala and vmPFC. *Neuron*, 43(6), 897–905.

Radloff, L. S. (1977). The CES-D Scale: A self-report depression scale for research in the general population. *Applied Psychological Measurement*, 1, 385–401.

Reed, M. A., & Derryberry, D. (1995). Temperament and attention to positive and negative trait information. *Personality and Individual Differences*, 18, 135–47.

Rees, G, Frith, C. D., & Lavie, N. (1997). Modulating irrelevant motion perception by varying attentional load in an unrelated task. *Science*, 278(5343), 1616–19.

Ressler, K. J., & Mayberg, H.S. (2007). Targeting abnormal neural circuits in mood and anxiety disorders: From the laboratory to the clinic. *Nature Neuroscience*, 10, 1116–24.

Richards, A., & Millwood, B. (1989). Colour-identification of differentially valenced words in anxiety. *Cognition Emotion*, 3, 171–76.

Rijsdijk, F. V., Riese, H., Tops, M., Snieder, H., Brouwer, W. H, Smid, H. G. O. M., & Ormel, J. (2009). Neuroticism, recall bias and attention bias for valenced probes: A twin study. *Psychological Medicine*, 39(1), 45–54.

Roy, A .K., Shehzad, Z., Margulies, D. S., Kelly, A. M., Uddin, L. Q., Gotimer, K., Biswal, B. B., & Milham, M. P. (2009). Functional connectivity of the human amygdala using resting state fMRI. *Neuroimage*, 45(2), 614–26.

Sehlmeyer, C., Dannlowski, U., Schöning, S., Kugel, H., Pyka, M., Pfleiderer, B., Zwitserlood, P., & Konrad, C. (2011). Neural correlates of trait anxiety in fear extinction. *Psychological Medicine*, 41(4), 789–98.

Shackman, A. J., Salomons, T. V., Slagter, H. A., Fox, A. S., Winter, J. J., & Davidson, R. J. (2011). The integration of negative affect, pain and cognitive control in the cingulate cortex. *Nature Reviews Neuroscience*, 12(3), 154–67.

Shin, L .M., & Liberzon, I. (2010). The neurocircuitry of fear, stress, and anxiety disorders. *Neuropsychopharmacology*, 35(1), 169–91.

Shin, L. M., Whalen, P. J., Pitman, R. K., Bush, G., Macklin, M. L., Lasko, N. B., Orr, S. P., & Rauch, S. L. (2001). An fMRI study of anterior cingulate function in posttraumatic stress disorder. *Biological Psychiatry*, 50(12), 932–42.

Sotres-Boyen, F., Bush, D. E. A., & LeDoux, J. E. (2004). Emotional perseveration: An update on prefrontal–amygdala interactions in fear extinction. *Learning and Memory*, 11, 525–35.

Spielberger C. D., Gorsuch R. L., Lushene P. R., Vagg P. R., & Jacobs, A. G. (1983). *Manual for the State-Trait Anxiety Inventory (Form Y)*. Palo Alto, CA: Consulting Psychologists Press.

Stein, M. B. (2009). Neurobiology of generalized anxiety disorder. *Journal of Clinical Psychiatry*, 70(Suppl. **2**), 15–19.

Stein, M. B., Simmons, A. N., Feinstein, J. S., & Paulus, M. P. (2007). Increased amygdala and insula activation during emotion processing in anxiety-prone subjects. *American Journal of Psychiatry*, 164(2), 318–27.

Tamietto, M., & de Gelder, B. (2010). Neural bases of the non-conscious perception of emotional signals. *Nature Reviews Neurosciences*, 11(10), 697–709.

Taylor, J. A. (1953). A personality scale of manifest anxiety. *Journal of Abnormal and Social
Psychology*, 48, 285–90.

Underwood, B. J. (1975). Individual differences
as a crucible in theory construction. *American
Psychologist*, 30, 128–34.

Vrtička, P., Sander, D., & Vuilleumier, P. (2011).
Effects of emotion regulation strategy on brain
responses to the valence and social content of
visual scenes. *Neuropsychologia*, 49(5), 1067–
82.

Vuilleumier, P., Armony, J. L, Driver, J., &
Dolan, R. J. (2001). Effects of attention and
emotion on face processing in the human
brain: An event-related fMRI study. *Neuron*,
30, 829–41.

Vul, E., Harris, C., Winkielman, P., & Pashler, H.
(2009). Puzzlingly high correlations in fMRI
studies of emotion, personality, and social cognition. *Perspectives on Psychological Science*, 4,
274–290.

Vyas, A., Mitra, R., Shankaranarayana Rao,
B. S., & Chattarji, S. (2002). Chronic
stress induces contrasting patterns of dendritic remodeling in hippocampal and amygdaloid neurons. *Journal of Neuroscience*, 22,
6810–18.

Watson, D., & Clark, L. A. (1984). Negative affectivity: The disposition to experience

aversive emotional states. *Psychological Bulletin*, 96, 465–90.

Watson, D., & Clark, L. A. (1991). *The Mood and
Anxiety Symptom Questionnaire*. Iowa City:
University of Iowa.

Weems, C. F., Pina, A. A., Costa, N. M., Watts, S.
E., Taylor, L. K., & Cannon, M. F. (2007). Pre-
disaster trait anxiety and negative affect predict posttraumatic stress in youth after Hurri-
cane Katrina. *Journal of Consulting and Clinical Psychology*, 75, 154–59.

Whalen, P. J. (2007). The uncertainty of it all.
Trends in Cognitive Sciences, 11(12), 499–500.

Whalen, P. J., Kagan, J, Cook, R. G., Davis, F. C.,
Kim, H., Polis, S., McLaren, D. G., & Johnstone, T. (2004). Human amygdala responsivity to masked fearful eye whites. *Science*,
306(5704), 2061.

Whalen, P. J., Rauch, S. L., Etcoff, N. L., McInerney, S. C., Lee, M. B., & Jenike, M. A
(1998). Masked presentations of emotional
facial expressions modulate amygdala activity
without explicit knowledge. *Journal of Neuroscience*, 18(1), 411–18.

Williams, J. M. G., & Nulty, D.D. (1986). Construct accessibility, depression and the emotional Stroop task: Transient mood or stable
structure? *Personality and Individual Differences*, 7, 485–491.

CHAPTER 25

Mapping Neurogenetic Mechanisms of Individual Differences in Affect

Ahmad R. Hariri

Individual differences in trait affect, personality, and temperament are critical in shaping complex human behaviors, successfully navigating social interactions, and overcoming challenges from our ever changing environments. Such individual differences may also serve as important predictors of vulnerability to neuropsychiatric disorders including depression, anxiety, and addiction, especially after exposure to environmental adversity. Accordingly, identifying the biological mechanisms that give rise to trait individual differences affords an unique opportunity to develop a deeper understanding of complex human behaviors, disease liability, and treatment. Having established multiple modal neural processes supporting specific aspects of complex behavioral processes, human neuroimaging studies – especially those employing blood-oxygen-level-dependent (BOLD) fMRI – have now begun to reveal the neural substrates of interindividual variability in these and related constructs. Moreover, recent studies have established that BOLD fMRI measures represent temporally stable and reliable indices of brain function (see

Chapter 5). Thus, much like their behavioral counterparts, patterns of brain activation represent enduring, trait-like phenomena that in and of themselves may serve as important markers of individual differences as well as disease liability and pathophysiology.

As neuroimaging studies continue to illustrate the predictive relationship between regional brain activation and trait-like behaviors (e.g., increased amygdala reactivity predicts trait anxiety; see Chapter 24), an important next step is to systematically identify the underlying mechanisms driving variability in brain circuit function. In this regard, recent neuroimaging studies employing pharmacological challenge paradigms, principally targeting monoamine neurotransmission, have revealed that even subtle alterations in dopaminergic, noradrenergic, and serotonergic signaling can have a profound impact on the functional response of brain circuitries supporting affect, personality, and temperament. Similarly, multimodal neuroimaging approaches have provided evidence for directionally specific relationships between key components of monoaminergic signaling cascades, assessed with radiotracer positron emission tomography (PET), and brain function, assessed with BOLD fMRI. Collectively, pharmacological challenge neuroimaging and multimodal PET/fMRI are revealing how variability in behaviorally relevant brain activation emerges as a function of the underlying variability in key brain signaling pathways (e.g., increased serotonin signaling predicts increased amygdala reactivity). The next logical step is to identify the sources of interindividual variability in these key neurochemical signaling mechanisms.

In the modern era of human molecular genetics, this step is firmly planted in the direction of identifying common variation in the genes that influence the functioning or availability of components in these pathways. Because DNA sequence variation across individuals represents the ultimate wellspring of variability in emergent molecular, neurobiological, and related behavioral processes, understanding the relationships among genes, brain, and behavior is important for establishing a mechanistic foundation for individual differences in behavior and related psychiatric disease. Moreover, such genetic polymorphisms can be readily identified from DNA collected via cells from individual blood or even saliva samples using relatively well-tolerated, inexpensive, and standardized laboratory protocols. Once collected and isolated, an individual's DNA can be amplified repeatedly, providing an almost endless reservoir of material for genotyping of additional candidate polymorphisms as they are identified. When a precise cascade of related neurobiological and behavioral effects is clearly established, common polymorphisms can represent incredibly powerful predictive markers of such emergent properties that are more readily accessible (e.g., samples can be collected in doctor's offices), applicable (e.g., even newborns can be genotyped), and economical (e.g., costing only tens of dollars per sample in comparison to the hundreds and even thousands required for fMRI and PET) than their technological counterparts in neuroimaging and neuropharmacology.

Of course, arriving at this ultimate reduction requires intensive and expansive efforts in which all these technologies as well as epidemiological and clinical studies are first brought to bear on explicating the detailed biological mechanisms mediating individual differences in trait behaviors and the related risk for neuropsychiatric disease.

In the last 5 years, significant progress has been made in describing the contributions of multiple common genetic polymorphisms to individual differences in complex behavioral phenotypes and disease liability – in particular, by identifying effects of functional genetic variation on the neural processes that mediate behavioral responses to environmental challenge (Brown & Hariri, 2006; Caspi & Moffitt, 2006). This chapter reviews how the integration of psychology, neuroimaging, neuropharmacology, and molecular genetics can work toward the ultimate goal of understanding the detailed mechanisms mediating individual differences in human behavior and, in turn, the establishment of predictive makers of disease vulnerability. I highlight the vast potential of such an integrated approach by reviewing recent studies whose collective results demonstrate that common sequence variation in human genes that bias key components of molecular signaling cascades results in altered brain circuit function that mediates individual differences in complex behavioral traits such as temperamental anxiety and impulsivity (Figure 25.1). With increased use and continued expansion, each level of analysis in this integrative strategy – brain circuit function, neural signaling cascades, and molecular genetics – also has the potential to uniquely illuminate clinically relevant information that can be used in efforts to devise individually tailored treatment regimes and establish predictive disease markers. Instead of describing a general framework, I use three examples to illustrate the effectiveness of this integrated strategy to parse biological mechanisms mediating individual differences in complex behaviors. In each example, subjects were retrospectively genotyped for the candidate functional polymorphisms of interest from

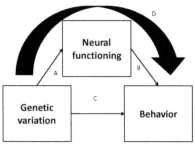

Figure 25.1. Genetic variation in individuals leads to individual variability in neural functioning (path A), and individual variability in neural functioning leads to differences in behavior or psychopathology (path B). Genetic variation might or might not have a direct impact on distal complex behavior (path C). Genetic variation has an indirect or mediated effect on behavior via its effect on neural functioning (path D).

stored samples of DNA, and this information was used to group them based on their individual genotypes. Notably, the behavioral assessments in all three examples were conducted as a component of a larger parent protocol that preceded measurement of task-related regional brain function with BOLD fMRI by an average interval of 29 weeks. The fact that robust brain-behaviors correlations were observed despite the separation in time is consistent with the suggestion that both metrics (i.e., brain function and behavior) are remarkably stable, possibly indicative of trait-related variation. Such a relationship further underscores the likelihood that interindividual variability in brain-behavior associations is influenced by genetic polymorphism affecting the functioning of signaling pathways that modulate underlying neural circuitries.

Multiple mechanisms involving de novo biosynthesis, vesicular release, active reuptake, metabolic degradation, and a myriad of both pre- and postsynaptic receptors contribute to the regulation of neurotransmission and its subsequent modulation of brain function. In general, component processes that affect the magnitude of signaling (e.g., biosynthesis, reuptake, autoregulation, degradation) rather than localized effects on target neurons (e.g., postsynaptic receptors)

represent key bottlenecks in neurotransmitter regulation of neural circuit function. To illustrate the powerful capacity of functional genetic polymorphisms to model emergent variability in signaling pathways, each of the three exemplars focuses on a different critical node in regulating the magnitude of neurotransmission; namely, autoregulatory negative feedback, active synaptic reuptake, and enzymatic degradation. In the first example, individual differences in trait anxiety are mapped onto threat-related amygdala reactivity. Variability in amygdala reactivity is, in turn, mapped to serotonin signaling. Finally, variability in serotonin signaling is mapped to a common functional polymorphism affecting the capacity for negative feedback inhibition of serotonergic neurons in the midbrain. The second example presents a similar relationship among variability in impulsivity, reward-related ventral striatum reactivity, dopamine signaling, and a polymorphism affecting the synaptic clearance of striatal dopamine. In the third and last example, a common polymorphism affecting the enzymatic degradation of endocannabinoids is linked to divergent effects on threat-related amygdala reactivity and reward-related ventral striatum reactivity.

Trait Anxiety, the Amygdala, and Serotonin

The experience of anxiety is commonplace among both human and nonhuman primates as well as other highly social animals. In the context of social interactions, especially within delimited social hierarchies consisting of dominant and subordinate individuals, anxiety serves to shape appropriate and often opposing responses to precipitating events such as competition for limited resources (e.g., food, water, reproductive partners). Sensitivity to potentially threatening social cues (e.g., affective facial expressions) varies considerably among individuals and represents a core component of commonly employed constructs representing trait anxiety (see Chapter 24).

Individuals with high trait anxiety exhibit a propensity to more frequently appraise situations as more threatening than do others and are generally more sensitive to social cues, including those representing both explicit and implicit threat (e.g., angry and fearful facial expressions). In turn, these individuals are at increased risk for developing neuropsychiatric disorders characterized by abnormal social and emotional behaviors such as depression and that are often precipitated by exposure to chronic or severe stressors. Examining the neural correlates of individual variability in dispositional temperament such as trait anxiety represents an important step in understanding key socioemotional behaviors, as well as an effective means of elucidating pathophysiological processes contributing to related disordered states.

Converging evidence from animal and human studies clearly demonstrates that the amygdala is centrally involved in mediating both physiological (e.g., autonomic reactivity) and behavioral (e.g., reallocation of attentional resources) effects that allow an individual to respond adaptively to varied environmental and social challenges. A large corpus of human neuroimaging research reveals that the amygdala is robustly engaged by varied biologically salient stimuli, most notably emotional facial expressions representing threat (see Chapter 7). However, individuals differ appreciably in the magnitude of amygdala activation on exposure to emotionally expressive facial expressions, and these individual differences appear to be stable over time (David et al., 2005; Manuck, Brown, Forbes, & Hariri, 2007). Thus, they may contribute to the emergence of stable differences in temperament such as trait anxiety.

Recent neuroimaging studies have reported positive relationships between the magnitude of amygdala reactivity to affective, especially threatening, stimuli and interindividual variability in indices of trait and state anxiety. In one study, Stein and colleagues reported that high trait anxiety is associated with greater amygdala reactivity not only to angry and fearful but also to happy facial expressions (Stein, Simmons, Feinstein, & Paulus, 2007). Consistent with this pattern of normal variability, various mood and anxiety disorders (e.g., unipolar and bipolar depression, generalized anxiety disorder, social phobia) have been linked with greater amygdala responses to facial expressions depicting fear and anger, as well as sadness and disgust, and, more variably, to emotionally neutral facial expressions. Such findings demonstrate that anxiety-related psychopathology is associated with a heightened amygdala response to diverse affective stimuli. More importantly, in the absence of such disorders, variability in the magnitude of threat-related amygdala reactivity is an important predictor of individual differences in trait anxiety.

Having first established a predictive link between amygdala reactivity and trait anxiety, factors that drive such behaviorally relevant variability in brain function can be now be identified in the broader context of detailing the biological mechanisms mediating individual differences in temperamental anxiety. Converging preclinical and clinical evidence indicates that amygdala functioning is sensitive to the effects of central serotonin, whose principal forebrain innervation is provided by the midbrain dorsal raphe nuclei (DRN). Available data from animal studies indicate that relative increases in local 5-HT result in potentiation of amygdala activation and associated behavioral phenomena, such as fear conditioning (Amat, Matus-Amat, Watkins, & Maier, 1998; Amat et al. 2004; Burghardt, Sullivan, McEwen, Gorman, & LeDoux, 2004; Forster et al., 2006; Maier & Watkins, 2005).

As presented in the introduction of this chapter, recent neuroimaging studies using multimodal PET/fMRI or pharmacological challenge BOLD fMRI have provided direct evidence for parallel effects of 5-HT in humans. Specifically, in vivo PET has revealed that decreased endogenous capacity for local 5-HT reuptake (Rhodes et al., 2007) is associated with relatively increased amygdala reactivity. Acute IV administration of a selective serotonin reuptake inhibitor, which reduces the capacity for 5-HT reuptake, during BOLD fMRI is likewise associated not only with increased amygdala reactivity but also with decreased habituation of amygdala reactivity over time (Bigos et al., 2008). These data clearly indicate that variability in the regulation of 5-HT signaling is an important source of individual differences in amygdala reactivity.

Crucial among components regulating 5-HT neurotransmission and its subsequent modulation of brain function is the activation of somatodendritic 5-HT$_{1A}$ autoreceptors, which mediate negative feedback on DRN neurons resulting in decreased 5-HT release at postsynaptic targets in the forebrain. Using multimodal PET/fMRI, we previously reported that the density of 5-HT$_{1A}$ autoreceptors accounts for 30–44% of the variability in amygdala reactivity in healthy adults (Fisher et al., 2006), confirming the important role of 5-HT$_{1A}$ autoreceptors in modulating the activity of serotonergic target regions. Given the critical role of 5-HT$_{1A}$ autoreceptors in regulating 5-HT signaling and its resulting influence on the functioning of major brain targets, such as the amygdala, as well as complex behavioral processes, it is important to identify sources of emergent variability in 5-HT$_{1A}$ function.

Common sequence variation in the human 5-HT$_{1A}$ gene (HTR1A) represents one potential source of such interindividual variability. Recently, a relatively frequent single nucleotide polymorphism, C(-1019)G, in the promoter region of HTR1A was demonstrated to affect transcriptional regulation of the gene through altered binding of the transcription factors. Specifically, the -1019G allele abolishes or impairs transcriptional repression of the promoter and, as a consequence, is associated with increased 5-HT$_{1A}$ expression (Lemonde et al., 2003), a phenomenon that appears to be specific to autoreceptors (Czesak, Lemonde, Peterson, Rogaeva, & Albert, 2006). Consistent with this finding, in vivo human PET has revealed specifically increased 5-HT$_{1A}$ autoreceptor density in both healthy adults and depressed patients

carrying the -1019G allele (Parsey et al., 2006). However, a similar effect was not observed in an earlier PET study (David et al., 2005). Regardless, the in vitro effects of the HTR1A -1019G allele and the more general relationship documented between increased 5-HT$_{1A}$ autoreceptor density and decreased amygdala reactivity (Fisher et al., 2006) suggest that this common functional genetic variation may contribute significantly to the emergence of interindividual variability in serotonin signaling that, in turn, biases amygdala reactivity.

Consistent with the existing data (i.e., increased 5-HT$_{1A}$ autoreceptors leading to increased negative feedback inhibition of DRN and decreased 5-HT release), we recently demonstrated that the HTR1A -1019G allele is associated with significantly decreased threat-related amygdala reactivity (Fakra et al., 2009). In addition, we found that HTR1A genotype effects on trait anxiety were mediated through its impact on threat-related amygdala reactivity, which presumably reflects the genotype's modulation of postsynaptic 5-HT release. Specifically, although path models revealed no significant direct genotype effect on trait anxiety, they demonstrated that HTR1A C(-1019)G and amygdala reactivity indirectly predicted a significant proportion (9.2%) of individual differences in trait anxiety through their respective indirect and direct paths. The data from this study are remarkably consistent with that reported for other common functional polymorphisms that are also associated with relatively increased 5-HT signaling, most notably the 5-HTTLPR short allele (Hariri, Mattay, Tessitore, Kolachana, et al., 2002; Munafo, Brown, & Hariri, 2008). These findings represent an important step in this avenue of research by providing empirical documentation for the basic premise that genetic variation in neural signaling cascades indirectly affects emergent behavioral processes by biasing the response of underlying neural circuitries. More generally, however, the predictive links among genes, amygdala function, and anxiety will require further investigations, including the elucidation of developmental effects of genetically driven variability in serotoninergic signaling on amygdala reactivity, as well as patterns of structural and functional connectivity between the amygdala and regulatory regions of prefrontal cortex (see Chapter 24).

Impulsivity, the Ventral Striatum, and Dopamine

Discounting future outcomes underlies much of human decision making (see Chapter 17) and figures prominently in several overlapping psychological constructs, such as self-regulation, impulse-control, delay of gratification, and intertemporal choice (Manuck, Flory, Muldoon, & Ferrell, 2003). Moreover, individuals who strongly prefer immediate over deferred rewards of larger nominal value are often generally impulsive or lacking in self-control and at risk for addictive disorders, such as pathological gambling, cigarette smoking, and drug and alcohol abuse (Alessi & Petry, 2003; Bickel, Odum, & Madden, 1999; Kirby, Petry, & Bickel, 1999; Madden, Petry, Badger, & Bickel, 1997). In experimental research on intertemporal choice, discounting of future rewards or delay discounting (DD) is a well-characterized behavioral measure of preference for immediate over delayed rewards and provides an index of impulsive tendencies in humans. Behavioral tests used to derive estimates of DD commonly ask participants to choose between multiple immediate rewards that vary in value and a constant, larger reward available after varying intervals of delay. In such tasks, rates of discounting often differ appreciably and consistently among individuals. Thus, DD represents a potentially important psychometric index of individual differences in present-versus future-oriented tendencies.

Similar to the research on trait anxiety and amygdala reactivity, explication of the underlying neural processes that give rise to such interindividual variability has the potential to allow for a more comprehensive understanding of the mechanisms leading not only to normal variability in such behaviors but also the pathophysiology of addiction and related disorders. Through reciprocal cortical and subcortical connections, the nucleus accumbens (NAcc) and, more broadly, the ventral striatum (VS) contribute to the motivational salience of stimuli and abet appetitive or reward-dependent behaviors. Activity of the VS increases in response to both the anticipation and receipt of rewarding stimuli, including primary (e.g., food) and secondary (e.g., money) reinforcers (see Chapter 19). Moreover, in addiction, craving and compulsive drug seeking and sensitivity to drug cues are associated with dysregulated increases in VS activity (Kalivas & Volkow, 2005). Because the response of the VS involves an immediate response to rewards, the magnitude of VS activity may contribute to individual differences in a relative preference for immediate, compared to delayed, rewards.

Using BOLD fMRI, we have demonstrated that the magnitude of VS reactivity predicts individual differences in a simple laboratory measure of DD (Hariri et al., 2006). Our analyses revealed that individual differences in DD correlate positively with the magnitude of VS activation in response to both positive and negative feedback, as well as with differential reward-related VS activation in response to positive compared with negative feedback. Consistent with the strong general correlation between DD and traditional self-report measures of impulsivity (de Wit, 2009), we have also found that reward-related VS reactivity is positively correlated with scores from the Barratt Impulsiveness Scale (Forbes et al., 2009). Collectively, our results suggest that increased self-reported impulsivity and the preference for smaller immediate over larger delayed rewards reflect both a relatively indiscriminate and hyper-reactive VS circuitry. Similar variability in VS function has also been associated with more complex measures of incentive-based decision making (Knutson, Rick, Wimmer, Prelec, & Loewenstein, 2007). Moreover, dysregulation of the VS contributes to addiction, perhaps by affecting impulsive decision making (Kalivas & Volkow, 2005). As such, interindividual variability in VS reactivity to reward-related stimuli likely contributes to the emergence of differences in the intermediate behavioral risk factors for and the clinical expression of, addiction. Identifying variability in neural signaling pathways that contributes to individual differences in VS function offers additional traction in the search for underlying biological mechanisms.

Dopamine (DA) modulation of neuronal activity, especially in the VS (i.e., mesolimbic system), serves as a nexus for the expression of DA signaling at the level of reward-related behaviors. Functioning of the DA system has been linked to normal individual differences in reward-related traits, and disorders involving enhanced reward-seeking, such as addiction, have been hypothesized to reflect maladaptive alterations of this mesolimbic reward system (Hyman, Malenka, & Nestler, 2006; Volkow, Fowler, & Wang, 1999). Multimodal and pharmacological neuroimaging studies of DA effects on brain function again offer a unique opportunity to more directly evaluate underlying molecular mechanisms regulating this circuitry. A recent in vivo human study reported a direct relationship between striatal DA synthesis, assessed with PET, and brain activity, assessed with BOLD fMRI (Siessmeier et al., 2006). An acute increase in DA release via oral amphetamine has also been linked with a relatively increased extent of BOLD-fMRI-assessed VS activity (Menon et al., 2007). More generally, the acute pharmacological increase of DA in both healthy volunteers (Hariri, Mattay, Tessitore, Fera, et al., 2002) and patients with Parkinson's disease (Tessitore et al., 2002) results in relatively increased BOLD-fMRI-assessed activity in closely related limbic brain regions, namely the amygdala. Given the importance of DA in modulating this behaviorally relevant neural circuitry, identifying factors that determine interindividual variability in DA signaling and its related impact on the reactivity of the VS will facilitate our understanding of the neurobiological mechanisms governing reward-related behaviors and augment efforts to improve the treatment and even prevention of patho-

logical behaviors such as drug abuse and addiction.

We have explored the role of altered DA signaling, resulting from a common functional polymorphism affecting active synaptic reuptake in the striatum, in determining interindividual variability in reward-related VS reactivity and the correlated variability in behavioral impulsivity. Consistent with the research on serotonin signaling, amygdala reactivity, and trait anxiety, the selection of our candidate polymorphism was driven by available in vitro and/or in vivo assays demonstrating significant impact of the variant on aspects of biological function related to DA neurotransmission – and not on available data from association studies with behavioral (e.g., impulsivity) or clinical (e.g., alcoholism) phenotypes. Although association studies are necessary for understanding the ultimate contribution of genetic polymorphisms to variability in behavioral and clinical phenomena, they do not readily allow for inferences regarding polymorphic effects on gene or protein function. Such inferences are instrumental for the development of biologically plausible and tractable hypotheses regarding the impact of genetic variation on interindividual variability in brain function and associated behaviors such as those pursued in our current work.

The dopamine transporter is responsible for the active clearance of synaptic DA and thus plays a critical role in regulating the duration of postsynaptic DA signaling, especially in the striatum. Accumulating evidence indicates that a 40-base pair variable number of tandem repeats (VNTR) polymorphism in the 3' untranslated region of the DAT gene (DAT1) affects the expression and availability of DAT (Bannon, Michelhaugh, Wang, & Sacchetti, 2001). Although a genotype effect has not been consistently observed across all studies, several studies suggest that, in comparison to the 9-repeat allele, the 10-repeat is associated with relatively increased levels of DAT both in vivo (Cheon, Ryu, Kim, & Cho, 2005; Heinz et al., 2000) and in vitro (Mill, Asherton, Browes, D'Souza, & Craig, 2002;

VanNess, Owens, & Kilts, 2005). We hypothesized that there would be relatively
greater VS reactivity associated with the
9-repeat allele, which is linked with reduced
DAT expression and presumably greater
striatal synaptic DA, in comparison with the
10-repeat allele. Consistent with our hypothesis, the DAT1 9-repeat allele was associated with relatively greater VS reactivity and
accounted for nearly 12% of the interindividual variability. In contrast, genetic variation
directly affecting DA signaling only in the
prefrontal cortex (i.e., COMT Val158Met)
was not associated with variability in VS
reactivity. These results highlight an important role for a genetic polymorphism
affecting striatal DA neurotransmission in
mediating interindividual differences in
reward-related VS reactivity. They further
suggest that altered VS reactivity may represent a key neurobiological pathway through
which these polymorphisms contribute to
variability in behavioral impulsivity and the
related risk for substance use disorders.

Endocannabinoids, Threat-, and Reward-Related Brain Function

Modern neuroscience methodologies have
greatly advanced our understanding of the
intrinsic mechanisms mediating and regulating endogenous cannabinoid or endocannabinoid (eCB) signaling in the CNS
(Piomelli, 2003). Such eCB signaling has
emerged as a potent modulator of neural circuitries mediating both basic physiological
and advanced behavioral responses. Experimental manipulation of these mechanisms
has revealed significant behavioral effects,
especially in threat- and reward-related
domains, which are generally consistent
with the effects of *Cannabis* intoxication, which are largely driven by the constituent chemical Δ^9-tetrahydrocannabinol.
The elucidation of molecular mechanisms
regulating eCB signaling, akin to that for
serotonin and dopamine, has motivated
attempts to understand its possible contribution to the emergence of variability in
brain circuit function and related individ-

ual differences in behavioral attributes (e.g.,
anxious or impulsive temperament) associated with an increased risk for psychiatric
disorders.

After their biosynthesis from arachidonic
acid, eCBs such as anandamide (AEA)
and 2-arachidonoylglycerol (2-AG), typically modulate synaptic neurotransmission
through stimulation of CB1, the principal
CNS cannabinoid receptor widely expressed
on multiple neuronal subtypes and their distributed circuitries. In turn, the duration
and intensity of eCB signaling, especially
for AEA, are regulated by two complementary mechanisms: enzymatic degradation via
fatty acid amide hydrolase (Cravatt et al.,
1996) and active synaptic clearance via the
AEA transporter (Piomelli et al., 1999). The
psychotropic and THC-like effects of AEA,
however, appear to be coupled with fatty
acid amide hydrolase (FAAH), but not AEA
transporter function (Solinas, Tanda. et al.,
2007). Thus, FAAH, an integral membrane
enzyme, may uniquely regulate behaviorally
relevant eCB signaling by mediating the
hydrolytic breakdown of AEA into arachidonic acid and ethanolamine.

Again, common genetic variation (i.e.,
polymorphisms) affecting the functioning of
components involved in eCB neurotransmission (e.g., AEA, CB1, FAAH) may represent
a significant potential source of interindividual variability in eCB signaling that mediates emergent differences in emotion- and
reward-related behaviors. Because of its critical role in regulating the signaling duration
and intensity of AEA, and its selective contribution to AEA's psychotropic effects, we
examined the neurobiological and behavioral effects of a common functional nonsyn-
onymous single nucleotide polymorphism
(SNP) resulting in the conversion of a con-
served proline residue to threonine (P129T)
in the amino acid sequence of FAAH (Hariri
et al., 2009). In vitro, *FAAH* 385A is associated with normal catalytic properties, but
reduced cellular expression of FAAH, possibly through enhanced sensitivity to prote-
olytic degradation (Chiang, Gerber, Sipe, &
Cravatt, 2004; Sipe, Chiang, Gerber, Beutler, & Cravatt, 2002). Moreover, the C385A

is the only common mutation in *FAAH* (Flanagan, Gerber, Cadet, Beutler, & Sipe, 2006), and the 385A, which putatively augments AEA signaling via decreased enzymatic degradation, has been associated with reward-related pathologies including street drug use and problem drug/alcohol abuse, as well as being overweight and obese (Flanagan et al., 2006; Sipe et al., 2002).

In animal models, both pharmacological and genetic disruption of FAAH function result in *decreased* anxiety-like behaviors, as well as *increased* consumption and preference for ethanol (Basavarajappa, Yalamanchili, Cravatt, Cooper, & Hungund, 2006; Blednov, Cravatt, Boehm, Walker, & Harris, 2007; Kathuria et al., 2003; Moreira, Kaiser, Monory, & Lutz, 2008; Solinas, Yasar, & Goldberg, 2007). Moreover, a recent pharmacological fMRI study in human subjects has reported that acute oral administration of THC is associated with reduced amygdala reactivity to threat-related facial expressions of emotion (Phan et al., 2008). Consistent with these effects, we hypothesized that the *FAAH* 385A would be associated with relatively *decreased* threat-related amygdala reactivity, but *increased* reward-related reactivity in the ventral striatum (VS). Analyses revealed that carriers of the *FAAH* 385A, associated with reduced enzyme expression and, presumably, increased AEA signaling, have decreased threat-related amygdala reactivity. In contrast, carriers of the *FAAH* 385A exhibited increased reward-related VS reactivity in comparison to C385 homozygotes. Moreover, divergent effects of the *FAAH* C385A genotype on brain function were manifest in a consistent manner at the level of brain-behavior relationships. Relative to C385 homozygotes, *FAAH* 385A carriers showed a diminished relationship between amygdala reactivity and trait anxiety. In contrast, they exhibited a markedly increased relationship between VS reactivity and delay discounting, a behavioral index of impulsivity and reward sensitivity.

It is important to note that there were no direct associations between *FAAH* genotype and behavioral phenotypes (i.e., anxiety or impulsivity) in this study, a common occurrence when working with relatively small samples; it possibly reflects the minimal effect that a proximal biological impact associated with any genotype has on any distal behavioral phenotype, as well as the importance of environmental stressors in unmasking genetically driven effects on behavior (Caspi & Moffitt, 2006). However, there were robust differences in the relationships between regional brain function and complex behaviors as a function of the *FAAH* C385A genotype. These observed brain-behavior patterns may reflect the influence of *FAAH* C385A-associated differences in endogenous eCB tone on stimulus-driven neural circuit function mediating complex behavioral processes. Relatively higher levels of AEA in the amygdala of *FAAH* 385A carriers may reduce the responsiveness of this structure to salient input (possibly through CB1-mediated potentiation of local GABAergic interneurons) and, as a consequence, lead to reduced anxiety-like behaviors predicted by amygdala function. In contrast, higher levels of AEA may increase the responsiveness of the VS in *FAAH* 385A carriers (possibly through CB1-mediated increased dopamine release and potentiation of VS neuron activity), leading to increased reward-sensitivity predicted by VS function. Support for this speculation exists in studies reporting a failure of restraint stress to effect changes in amygdala activation in knockout mice lacking FAAH or animals treated with FAAH inhibitors (Patel, Cravatt, & Hillard, 2005), and increased food intake as a result of local FAAH inhibition in the nucleus accumbens (Sorice-Gomez et al., 2007). Thus, the endogenous state of eCB signaling associated with either constitutive genetic variation such as the FAAH C385A or acute pharmacological manipulation likely biases the responsiveness of neural circuits to behaviorally relevant information and their subsequent regulation of complex behaviors.

Decreased threat-related amygdala reactivity and associated trait anxiety may contribute to the emergence of pathologies such as addiction and obesity, previously associated with the *FAAH* 385A genotype

(Flanagan et al., 2006; Sipe et al., 2002; Tyndale, Payne, Gerber, & Sipe, 2007), by reducing the sensitivity of these individuals to potential environmental threat or harm. In fact, blunted amygdala reactivity has been reported in individuals at high familial risk for alcoholism and has been interpreted as possibly contributing to decreased threat sensitivity and subsequently increased risk-taking behaviors in these genetically predisposed individuals (Glahn, Lovallo, & Fox, 2007). An increase in reward-related VS reactivity and associated impulsivity (e.g., steeper discounting of future relative to immediate rewards) may likewise contribute to disinhibitory psychopathologies through heightened reward sensitivity and impulsive decision making. Studies in addicted patients have generally reported a sensitization of the neural circuitry for reward, including the VS (Kalivas & Volkow, 2005). And increased behavioral impulsivity and reward sensitivity are significant risk factors for addiction (de Wit & Richards 2004). Thus, through divergent effects on both threat- and reward-related brain function, the influence of *FAAH* C385A on eCB signaling may have a compound and accelerated effect on risk for related pathologies.

Conclusions and Future Directions

As detailed in this chapter, neuroimaging technologies, especially BOLD fMRI, have begun to identify how variability in neural substrates associated with processing specific forms of information contribute to emergent individual differences in stable and enduring aspects of human behaviors such as personality and temperament. In parallel, the application of pharmacological fMRI and multimodal PET/fMRI is allowing for an understanding of how variability in specific molecular signaling pathways influences individual differences in the function of these behaviorally relevant brain circuitries. Moreover, information on DNA sequence variation in humans and the related identification of functional

genetic polymorphisms are now being used to understand the biological origins of variability in component processes of molecular signaling pathways and to efficiently model how such emergent variability affects behaviorally relevant brain function. Such ongoing efforts to understand the detailed mechanisms that mediate individual differences in complex behavioral traits and related neuropsychiatric diseases at the level of brain circuit function, molecular signaling pathways, and functional genetic polymorphisms have the potential to inform clinically relevant issues and provide guiding principles for the development of more effective and individually tailored treatment regimes. In addition, the elucidation of such mechanisms, especially those mapped to functional genetic polymorphisms, can lead to identification of predictive risk markers that interact with unique environmental factors to precipitate disease.

Although the three examples highlighted in this chapter are evidence for the potential of an informed and integrated research strategy to identify the neurobiology of individual differences in complex behavioral traits and their related clinical endpoints, much work remains to be done. First, to allow for tractable experimental designs and testable hypotheses in existing samples, the studies highlighted here have focused on the effects of a single signaling pathway on behaviorally relevant brain circuitry. Of course, it is very clear that are numerous complex interactions between signaling pathways and that more than one pathway contributes to the regulation of any brain circuitry. For example, we know that DA plays an important role in modulating amygdala function and anxiety (Hariri, Mattay, Tessitore, Fera, et al., 2002; Tessitore et al., 2002) and that 5-HT can influence reward-related brain circuitry and impulsivity (Manuck et al., 1998). However, existing studies lack the power and sophistication to model such complex interactions while effectively controlling for other important modulatory factors (e.g., age, gender) in the context of BOLD fMRI, pharmacological MRI, or multimodal PET/fMRI protocols.

To do so, we must aggressively expand the scale and scope of our studies to include hundreds and, preferably, thousands of subjects. This will afford opportunities to effectively examine interactions between signaling pathways (e.g., 5-HT and DA) on brain function and behavior through modeling of multiple functional polymorphisms (e.g., *HTR1A* -1019 and DAT1) and thereby examine the effects of genetically driven variation in signaling pathways on multiple behaviorally relevant brain circuitries.

A second important consideration is that existing studies have been largely conducted in ethnically and racially homogeneous populations. Thus, the observed effects may not generalize to other populations. This is especially true of studies using functional genetic polymorphisms because the potential effect of any single genetic variant on a complex biological and behavioral phenotype is likely small against the background of the approximately 20,000–25,000 human genes and the multitude of other neurobiologically relevant functional variants they likely harbor. In fact, we have already seen that the well-replicated effects of a common functional polymorphism affecting 5-HT signaling on amygdala reactivity in Caucasian subjects may be reversed in those of Asian ancestry (Munafo et al., 2008). Importantly, our most recent studies have experimentally controlled for occult genetic stratification (i.e., differences in the genetic backgrounds of individuals who superficially appear similar), regardless of self-reported race or ethnicity, as well as the independence of the target genotype from other functional polymorphisms affecting the brain functions under study. Although such efforts allow for the attribution of emergent variability in brain and behavior to the candidate variant of interest and not to other possible polymorphisms or more general differences between genotype groups in genetic background, it is important to explicitly test the independence of functional polymorphisms through rigorous statistical modeling in larger samples and also to test the validity of any associations derived in one sample population (e.g., Caucasian) to populations with different genetic backgrounds (e.g., Asian).

A third important consideration for the future of this research is the need to conduct large-scale prospective studies beginning in childhood to determine any developmental shifts in neurogenetic pathways mediating individual differences in behavior, as well as their predictive utility in identifying neuropsychiatric disease risk as a function of environmental or other stressors (see also Chapter 27). All of the studies described in this chapter and most of the studies available in the literature have been conducted in adults carefully screened for the absence of psychopathology. Therefore, these findings identify mechanisms contributing to variability only in the normative range of behavior. The utility of these markers of individual differences in behavior – be they neural, molecular, or genetic – in predicting vulnerability to neuropsychiatric disorder is unclear. Such predictive utility is ideally tested through prospective studies beginning with premorbid populations that account for the moderating effects of environmental stress in the emergence of clinical disorder over time (Caspi & Moffitt, 2006; Viding, Williamson, & Hariri, 2006).

A fourth issue is the need to further integrate pharmacological challenge protocols with multimodal PET/fMRI to determine if variability in molecular components of signaling pathways mediates the effects of specific neurotransmitters or neuromodulators on individual differences in behaviorally relevant brain circuit function. For example, despite the remarkable convergence of findings implicating variability in eCB signaling in threat- and reward-related brain function, the exact nature of the downstream signaling pathways through which *FAAH* C385A may modulate neuronal and neural circuit function cannot be determined from the available results. FAAH catalyzes the hydrolysis of other biologically active endogenous fatty acid amides (e.g., oleamide & oleoylethanolamide), which affect threat- and reward-related behaviors independently of AEA. Although, FAAH has high selectivity for AEA (Desarnaud,

Cadas, & Piomelli, 1995) the effects of *FAAH* C385A cannot be specifically linked to AEA neurotransmission without additional data. If the neural and behavioral effects of *FAAH* C385A are mediated by genotype-driven differential availability of AEA, then these effects should be sensitive to manipulation of CB1 receptors. An interesting test of this putative mechanism would be to examine the impact of CB1 antagonists, such as rimonabant, on neural phenotypes associated with the *FAAH* C385A genotype using pharmacological fMRI. The availability of a PET radiotracer for CB1 (Burns et al., 2007) also allows for the determination of any *FAAH* C385A effects on endogenous receptor concentrations. If this polymorphism biases brain function through AEA stimulation of CB1, then antagonism of the receptor should eliminate the divergent effects on amygdala and VS reactivity documented here. Any genotype-related alterations in AEA concentrations may also be reflected in relative up- or down-regulation of CB1 receptors assayed via PET. If CB1 antagonism fails to abolish the differential effects of *FAAH* C385A on brain function or if there are no differences in CB1 concentrations based on the genotype, then the existing effects are likely mediated by non-eCB fatty acid amides. In addition to testing this mechanistic hypothesis with pharmacological fMRI and multimodal PET/fMRI, future studies with substantially increased sample sizes can model allele load effects of *FAAH* 385A, as well as potential *FAAH* interactions with functional genetic polymorphisms affecting other components of eCB neurotransmission.

Finally, there is tremendous potential in developing large databases (again preferably with thousands of subjects) with detailed measures of behavioral traits, neuroimaging-based measures of multiple brain circuitries, and extensive genotyping. One of the most exciting applications of molecular genetics is in identifying novel biological pathways contributing to the emergence of complex traits. The continued refinement of a detailed map of sequence variation across the entire human genome (i.e., SNPs that "tag" every

gene) and the production of technologies supporting efficient high-throughput identification of such variation in individuals have dramatically accelerated the discovery of genes involved in the emergence of complex disease processes (Fellay et al., 2007; Link et al., 2008) as well as normal variability in continuous traits (Lettre et al., 2008). Many of the genes identified in such studies have illuminated novel pathways not previously implicated in these processes or traits, spurring intensive efforts to understand the potential biological effects of the proteins produced by these genes.

As such, these "genome-wide" screens represent an opportunity to leap forward beyond the available pool of candidate molecules and pathways in parsing the mechanisms of complex biological processes. Because neuroimaging-based measures of brain function reveal key mechanisms involved in the emergence of individual differences in behavioral traits and are closer to the biological effects of functional genetic polymorphisms, they are ideal substrates for genome-wide screens. For example, BOLD fMRI estimates of amygdala reactivity predicting variability in temperamental anxiety can be used as the continuous trait in a genome-wide screen. Any significant associations that emerge between genetic variation and amygdala reactivity may confirm existing relationships (e.g., the importance of genes biasing 5-HT signaling) or, more importantly, reveal unexpected candidate molecules or pathways (e.g., a gene producing a molecule that is expressed in the brain and may function in second-messenger signaling cascades). Once identified and, ideally, replicated in large-scale databases that effectively address confounds common to genome-wide screens (e.g., controlling for multiple comparisons resulting from testing the association of a phenotype with hundreds of thousands or millions of SNPs), the impact of variation in novel genes associated with amygdala reactivity can be explored at each level of the biological cascade leading to trait anxiety (i.e., be fed back into the discovery loop outlined in Figure 25.1). In addition to exponentially improving our understanding of neurobiological pathways leading to individual differences in complex behavioral traits, these efforts may lead to the discovery of novel therapeutic strategies targeting related disease processes.

Outstanding Questions and Future Directions

- Are studies finding relationships between single brain areas (e.g., the amygdala) and behavior that are the result of more complex interactions among multiple brain structures that we do not yet understand?
- To what extent do genetic variants affect behavior through their influence on function versus structure versus connectivity in the brain?
- When and how do most genes of interest have their effect on brain and behavior?
- Are there experiences that interact differently with genetic polymorphisms depending on when they occur?
- Can intermediate neural phenotypes and, ultimately, the genetic polymorphisms by which they are predicted usefully inform diagnosis and treatment?

Acknowledgments

This chapter is largely based on Hariri, *Annual Review of Neuroscience*, 2009. Some material is also based on Hyde, Bogdan, & Hariri, *Trends in Cognitive Sciences*, 2011.

References

Alessi, S. M., & Petry, N. M. (2003). Pathological gambling severity is associated with impulsivity in a delay discounting procedure. *Behavioral Processes*, 64, 345–54.

Amat, J., Matus-Amat, P., Watkins, L. R., & Maier, S. F. (1998). Escapable and inescapable stress differentially alter extracellular levels of 5-HT in the basolateral amygdala of the rat. *Brain Research*, 812, 113–20.

Amat, J., Tamblyn, J. P., Paul, E. D., Bland, S. T., Amat, P., et al. (2004). Microinjection of uro-cortin 2 into the dorsal raphe nucleus activates serotonergic neurons and increases extracellular serotonin in the basolateral amygdala. *Neuroscience*, 129, 509–19.

Bannon, M. J., Michelhaugh, S. K., Wang, J., & Sacchetti, P. (2001). The human dopamine transporter gene: gene organization, transcriptional regulation, and potential involvement in neuropsychiatric disorders. *European Neuropsychopharmacology*, 11, 449–55.

Basavarajappa, B. S., Yalamanchili, R., Cravatt, B. F., Cooper, T. B., & Hungund, B. L. (2006). Increased ethanol consumption and preference and decreased ethanol sensitivity in female FAAH knockout mice. *Neuropharmacology*, 50, 834–44.

Bickel, W. K., Odum, A. L., & Madden, G. J. (1999). Impulsivity and cigarette smoking: Delay discounting in current, never, and ex-smokers. *Psychopharmacology (Berl)*, 146, 447–54.

Bigos, K. L., Pollock, B. G., Aizenstein, H., Fisher, P. M., Bies, R. R., & Hariri, A. R. (2008). Acute 5-HT reuptake blockade potentiates human amygdala reactivity. *Neuropsychopharmacology*, 33(13), 3221–25.

Blednov, Y. A., Cravatt, B. F., Boehm, S. L., 2nd, Walker, D., & Harris, R. A. (2007). Role of endocannabinoids in alcohol consumption and intoxication: studies of mice lacking fatty acid amide hydrolase. *Neuropsychopharmacology*, 32, 1570–82.

Brown, S. M., & Hariri, A. R. (2006). Neuroimaging studies of serotonin gene polymorphisms: Exploring the interplay of genes, brain, and behavior. *Cognitive, Affective, & Behavioral Neuroscience*, 6, 44–52.

Burghardt, N. S., Sullivan, G. M., McEwen, B. S., Gorman, J. M., & LeDoux, J. E. (2004). The selective serotonin reuptake inhibitor citalopram increases fear after acute treatment but reduces fear with chronic treatment: A comparison with tianeptine. *Biological Psychiatry*, 55, 1171–78.

Burns, H. D., Van Laere, K., Sanabria-Bohorquez., S., Hamill, T. G., Bormans, G., et al. (2007). [18F]MK-9470, a positron emission tomography (PET) tracer for in vivo human PET brain imaging of the cannabinoid-1 receptor. *Proceedings of the National Academy of Sciences*, 104, 9800–5.

Caspi, A., & Moffitt, T. E. (2006). Gene-environment interactions in psychiatry: Joining forces with neuroscience. *Nature Reviews Neuroscience*, 7, 583–90.

Cheon, K. A., Ryu, Y. H., Kim, J. W., & Cho, D. Y. (2005). The homozygosity for 10-repeat allele at dopamine transporter gene and dopamine transporter density in Korean children with attention deficit hyperactivity disorder: Relating to treatment response to methylphenidate. *European Neuropsychopharmacology, 15*, 95–101.

Chiang, K. P., Gerber, A. L., Sipe, J. C., & Cravatt, B. F. (2004). Reduced cellular expression and activity of the P129T mutant of human fatty acid amide hydrolase: Evidence for a link between defects in the endocannabinoid system and problem drug use. *Human Molecular Genetics, 13*, 2113–19.

Cravatt, B. F., Giang, D. K., Mayfield, S. P., Boger, D. L., Lerner, R. A., & Gilula, N. B. (1996). Molecular characterization of an enzyme that degrades neuromodulatory fatty-acid amides. *Nature, 384*, 83–87.

Czesak, M., Lemonde, S., Peterson, E. A., Rogaeva, A., & Albert, P. R. (2006). Cell-specific repressor or enhancer activities of Deaf-1 at a serotonin 1A receptor gene polymorphism. *Journal of Neuroscience, 26*, 1864–71.

David, S. P., Murthy, N. V., Rabiner, E. A., Munafo, M. R., Johnstone, E. C., et al. (2005). A functional genetic variation of the serotonin (5-HT) transporter affects 5-HT1A receptor binding in humans. *Journal of Neuroscience, 25*, 2586–90.

de Wit, H. 2009. Impulsivity as a determinant and consequence of drug use: A review of underlying processes. *Addictive Biology, 14*: 22–31.

de Wit, H., & Richards, J. B. (2004). Dual determinants of drug use in humans: Reward and impulsivity. *Nebraska Symposium on Motivation, 50*, 19–55.

Desarnaud, F., Cadas, H., & Piomelli, D. (1995). Anandamide amidohydrolase activity in rat brain microsomes. *Journal of Biological Chemistry, 270*, 6030–35.

Fakra, E., Hyde, L. W., Gorka, A., Fisher, P. M., Munoz, K. E., et al. (2009). Effects of HTR1A C(-1019)G on amygdala reactivity & trait anxiety. *Archives of General Psychiatry, 66*(1), 33–40.

Fellay, J., Shianna, K. V., Ge, D., Colombo, S., Ledergerber, B., et al. (2007). A whole-genome association study of major determinants for host control of HIV-1. *Science, 317*, 944–47.

Fisher, P. M., Meltzer, C. C., Ziolko, S. K., Price, J. C., & Hariri, A. R.. (2006). Capacity for 5-HT$_{1A}$-mediated autoregulation predicts amygdala reactivity. *Nature Neuroscience, 9*. 1362–63.

Flanagan, J. M., Gerber, A. L., Cadet, J. L., Beutler, E., & Sipe, J. C. (2006). The fatty acid amide hydrolase 385 A/A (P129T) variant: haplotype analysis of an ancient missense mutation and validation of risk for drug addiction. *Human Genetics, 120*, 581–58.

Forbes, E. E., Brown, S. M., Kimak, M., Ferrell, R. E., Manuck, S. B., & Hariri, A. R. (2009). Genetic variation in components of dopamine neurotransmission impacts ventral striatal reactivity associated with impulsivity. *Molecular Psychiatry, 14*, 60–70.

Forster, G. L., Feng, N., Watt, M. J., Korzan, W. J., Mouw, N. J., et al. (2006). Corticotropin-releasing factor in the dorsal raphe elicits temporally distinct serotonergic responses in the limbic system in relation to fear behavior. *Neuroscience, 141*, 1047–55.

Glahn, D. C., Lovallo, W. R., & Fox, P. T. (2007). Reduced amygdala activation in young adults at high risk of alcoholism: Studies from the Oklahoma family health patterns project. *Biological Psychiatry, 61*, 1306–9.

Hariri, A. R., Brown, S. M., Williamson, D. E., Flory, J. D., de Wit, H., & Manuck, S. B. (2006). Preference for immediate over delayed rewards is associated with magnitude of ventral striatal activity. *Journal of Neuroscience, 26*, 13213–17.

Hariri, A. R., Gorka, A., Hyde, L. W., Kimak, M., Halder, I., et al. (2009). Divergent effects of genetic variation in endocannabinoid signaling on human threat- and reward-related brain function. *Biological Psychiatry, 66*, 9–16.

Hariri, A. R., Mattay, V. S., Tessitore, A., Fera, F., Smith, W. G., & Weinberger, D. R. (2002a). Dextroamphetamine modulates the response of the human amygdala. *Neuropsychopharmacology, 27*, 1036–40.

Hariri, A. R., Mattay, V. S., Tessitore, A., Fera, F., Smith, W. G., & Weinberger, D. R. (2002b). Serotonin transporter genetic variation and the response of the human amygdala. *Science, 297*, 400–3.

Heinz, A., Goldman, D., Jones, D. W., Palmour, R., Hommer, D., et al. (2000). Genotype influences in vivo dopamine transporter availability in human striatum. *Neuropsychopharmacology, 22*, 133–39.

Hyman, S. E., Malenka, R. C., & Nestler, E. J. (2006). Neural mechanisms of addiction: the role of reward-related learning and memory. *Annual Review of Neuroscience, 29,* 565–98.

Kalivas, P. W., & Volkow, N. D. (2005). The neural basis of addiction: A pathology of motivation and choice. *American Journal of Psychiatry, 162,* 1403–13.

Kathuria, S., Gaetani, S., Fegley, D., Valino, F., Duranti, A., et al. (2003). Modulation of anxiety through blockade of anandamide hydrolysis. *National Medicine, 9,* 76–81.

Kirby, K. N., Petry, N. M., & Bickel, W. K. (1999). Heroin addicts have higher discount rates for delayed rewards than non-drug-using controls. *Journal of Experimental Psychology: General, 128,* 78–87.

Knutson, B., Rick, S., Wimmer, G. E., Prelec, D., & Loewenstein, G. (2007). Neural predictors of purchases. *Neuron, 53,* 147–56.

Lemonde, S., Turecki, G., Bakish, D., Du, L., Hrdinam P. D., et al. (2003). Impaired repression at a 5-hydroxytryptamine 1A receptor gene polymorphism associated with major depression and suicide. *Journal of Neuroscience, 23,* 8788–99.

Lettre, G., Jackson, A. U., Gieger, C., Schumacher, F. R., Berndt, S. I., et al. (2008). Identification of ten loci associated with height highlights new biological pathways in human growth. *Nature Genetics, 40,* 584–91.

Link, E., Parish, S., Armitage, J., Bowman, L., Heath, S., et al. (2008). SLCO1B1 variants and statin-induced myopathy – a genomewide study. *New England Journal of Medicine, 359,* 789–99.

Madden, G. J., Petry, N. M., Badger, G. J., & Bickel, W. K. (1997). Impulsive and self-control choices in opioid-dependent patients and non-drug-using control participants: Drug and monetary rewards. *Experimental and Clinical Psychopharmacology, 5.* 256–62.

Maier, S. F., & Watkins, L. R. (2005). Stressor controllability and learned helplessness: The roles of the dorsal raphe nucleus, serotonin, and corticotropin-releasing factor. *Neuroscience and Biobehavioral Reviews, 29,* 829–41.

Manuck, S. B., Brown, S. M., Forbes, E. E., & Hariri, A. R. (2007). Temporal stability of individual differences in amygdala reactivity. *American Journal of Psychiatry, 164,* 1613–14.

Manuck, S. B., Flory, J. D., McCaffery, J. M., Matthews, K. A., Mann, J. J., & Muldoon, M. F. (1998). Aggression, impulsivity, and central nervous system serotonergic responsivity in a nonpatient sample. *Neuropsychopharmacology, 19,* 287–99.

Manuck, S. B., Flory, J. D., Muldoon, M. F., & Ferrell, R. E. (2003). A neurobiology of intertemporal choice In G. Loewenstein, D. Read, & R. F. Baumeister (Eds.), *Time and decision: Economic and psychological perspectives on intertemporal choice* (pp. 139–72). New York: Sage.

Menon, M., Jensen, J., Vitcu, I., Graff-Guerrero, A., Crawley, A., et al. (2007). Temporal difference modeling of the blood-oxygen level dependent response during aversive conditioning in humans: Effects of dopaminergic modulation. *Biological Psychiatry, 62(7),* 765–72.

Mill, J., Asherson, P., Browes, C., D'Souza, U., & Craig, I. (2002). Expression of the dopamine transporter gene is regulated by the 3' UTR VNTR: Evidence from brain and lymphocytes using quantitative RT-PCR. *American Journal of Medical Genetics, 114,* 975–99.

Moreira, F. A., Kaiser, N., Monory, K., & Lutz, B. (2008). Reduced anxiety-like behaviour induced by genetic and pharmacological inhibition of the endocannabinoid-degrading enzyme fatty acid amide hydrolase (FAAH) is mediated by CB1 receptors. *Neuropharmacology, 54,* 141–50.

Munafo, M. R., Brown, S. M., & Hariri, A. R. (2008). Serotonin transporter (5-HTTLPR) genotype and amygdala activation: A meta-analysis. *Biological Psychiatry, 63,* 852–57.

Parsey, R. V., Oquendo, M. A., Ogden, R. T, Olvet, D. M., Simpson, N., et al. (2006). Altered serotonin 1A binding in major depression: A [carbonyl-C-11]WAY100635 positron emission tomography study. *Biological Psychiatry, 59,* 106–13.

Patel, S., Cravatt, B. F., & Hillard, C. J. (2005). Synergistic interactions between cannabinoids and environmental stress in the activation of the central amygdala. *Neuropsychopharmacology, 30,* 497–507.

Phan, K. L., Angstadt, M., Golden, J., Onyewuenyi, I., Popovska, A., & de Wit, H. (2008). Cannabinoid modulation of amygdala reactivity to social signals of threat in humans. *Journal of Neuroscience, 28,* 2313–19.

Piomelli, D. (2003). The molecular logic of endocannabinoid signalling. *Nature Reviews Neuroscience, 4,* 873–84.

Piomelli, D., Beltramo, M., Glasnapp, S., Lin, S. Y., Goutopoulos, A., et al. (1999). Structural determinants for recognition and translocation by the anandamide transporter.

Proceedings of the National Academy of Sciences, 96, 5802–7.

Rhodes, R. A., Murthy, N. V., Dresner, M. A., Selvaraj, S., Stavrakakis, N., et al. (2007). Human 5-HT transporter availability predicts amygdala reactivity in vivo. *Journal of Neuroscience*, 27, 9233–37.

Siessmeier, T., Kienast, T., Wrase, J., Larsen, J. L., Braus, D. F., et al. (2006). Net influx of plasma 6-[18F]fluoro-l-DOPA (FDOPA) to the ventral striatum correlates with prefrontal processing of affective stimuli. *European Journal of Neuroscience*, 24, 305–13.

Sipe, J. C., Chiang, K., Gerber, A. L., Beutler, E., & Cravatt, B. F. (2002). A missense mutation in human fatty acid amide hydrolase associated with problem drug use. *Proceedings of the National Academy of Sciences*, 99: 8394–99.

Solinas, M., Tanda, G., Justinova, Z., Wertheim, C. E., Yasar, S., et al. (2007). The endogenous cannabinoid anandamide produces delta-9-tetrahydrocannabinol-like discriminative and neurochemical effects that are enhanced by inhibition of fatty acid amide hydrolase but not by inhibition of anandamide transport. *Journal of Pharmacology and Experimental Therapy*, 321, 370–80.

Solinas, M., Yasar, S., & Goldberg, S. R. 2007. Endocannabinoid system involvement in brain reward processes related to drug abuse. *Pharmacological Research*, 56, 393–405.

Sorice-Gomez, E., Matias, I., Rueda-Orozco, P. E., Cisneros, M., Petrosino, S., et al. (2007). Pharmacological enhancement of the endo- cannabinoid system in the nucleus accumbens shell stimulates food intake and increases c-Fos expression in the hypothalamus. *British Journal of Pharmacology*, 151, 1109–16.

Stein, M. B., Simmons, A. N., Feinstein, J. S., & Paulus, M. P. (2007). Increased amygdala and insula activation during emotion processing in anxiety-prone subjects. *American Journal of Psychiatry*, 164, 318–27.

Tessitore, A., Hariri, A. R., Fera, F., Smith, W. G., Chase, T. N., et al. (2002). Dopamine modulates the response of the human amygdala: A study in Parkinson's disease. *Journal of Neuroscience*, 22, 9099–1003.

Tyndale, R. F., Payne, J. I., Gerber, A. L, & Sipe, J. C. (2007). The fatty acid amide hydrolase C385A (P129T) missense variant in cannabis users: Studies of drug use and dependence in Caucasians. *American Journal of Medical Genetics B: Neuropsychiatric Genetics*, 144, 660–66.

VanNess, S. H., Owens, M. J., & Kilts, C. D. (2005). The variable number of tandem repeats element in DAT1 regulates in vitro dopamine transporter density. *BMC Genetics*, 6, 55.

Viding, E., Williamson, D. E., & Hariri, A. R. 2006. Developmental imaging genetics: Challenges and promises for translational research. *Developmental Psychopathology*, 18, 877–92.

Volkow, N. D., Fowler, J. S., & Wang, G. J. (1999). Imaging studies on the role of dopamine in cocaine reinforcement and addiction in humans. *Journal of Psychopharmacology*, 13, 337–45.

CHAPTER 26

Sex Differences in Emotion

Annett Schirmer

"Women are never disarmed by compliments. Men always are. That is the difference between the sexes."

–Oscar Wilde

Among the existing stereotypes, those regarding sex differences appear to be most pervasive. Across time and culture, women are typically viewed as the fairer but also the weaker sex. Emotional sensitivity and empathy are more readily ascribed to women than to men, who in turn are perceived as more knowledgeable and competent (Kimmel, 2000). Moreover, whereas sex-specific behavioral norms endorse socially responsible and accommodating interaction styles in women, they endorse dominant and assertive interaction styles in men.

In line with these popular perceptions, and possibly because of them, women and men differ in their temperament. Across different geographical regions, women are found to be more depressive, anxious, and cyclothymic than men, who in contrast are found to be more irritable and hyper-

thymic than women (Figueira et al., 2008; Pompili et al., 2008). These temperamental differences emerge in infancy, where girls are typically less active and novelty seeking than boys (Maccoby & Jacklin, 1974). As children, girls are better than boys in inhibiting inappropriate responses and behaviors, but tend to show more fear (Else-Quest, Hyde, Goldsmith, & Van Hulle, 2006). As a consequence, stressful life events more readily evoke internalizing problems, marked by withdrawal, somatic complaints, fear, or sadness, in girls, whereas boys tend to show more externalizing problems, marked by delinquent or aggressive behavior (Crijnen, Achenbach, & Verhulst, 1997). In adulthood, this translates into sex differences in the prevalence of psychiatric disorders. Specifically, anxiety and depression occur about twice as often in women than in men (Hamann, 2005; Nolen-Hoeksema, 2001). Conversely, conduct disorder and psychopathy are more prevalent and severe in men (Rogstad & Rogers, 2008; Simonoff et al., 1997).

Both female and male typical psychiatric conditions have marked social and economic consequences not only for the affected individuals but also for their immediate social circle and society at large. Therefore, it is very important to characterize sex-specific vulnerabilities and their development. In this chapter, I first review research that addresses such sex-specific vulnerabilities through the investigation of emotional responses, emotion regulation strategies, and influences of emotion on cognition in healthy women and men. I then discuss the biological and environmental factors that produce sex-specific resources and challenges and consider how these resources and challenges engender male and female minds.

Emotional Perception and Expression

As apparent from the different temperaments, behavioral problems, and psychiatric conditions of men and women, emotional differences between the sexes are not one-dimensional. Rather than being simply "more emotional," women differ qualitatively from men in their emotional experiences. Moreover, certain emotions, such as fear, sadness, and happiness, appear to play a greater role in women, whereas others, such as anger, contempt, and disgust, play a greater role in men. Researchers have categorized these emotions as prosocial or powerless and antisocial or powerful emotions, respectively (Hess, Adams, & Kleck, 2005; Safdar et al., 2009). Expressions of fear, sadness, and happiness are thought to appeal to others and to communicate dependency or a willingness to cooperate and, in that sense, can be considered as "prosocial." Expressions of anger, contempt, and disgust, in contrast, signal the rejection of something or someone and a willingness to defend one's own interests, thus having more "antisocial" functions. As seen later, this classification fails to fully map onto existing sex differences: Women do not consistently score higher on prosocial and lower on antisocial emotions than men. Nevertheless, this classification represents a useful approach for the analysis of sex differences

in emotional processing and behavioral patterns, allowing us to link these differences to psychopathology.

Prosocial Emotions

Fear

Fear is an emotion felt in response to threats that, if confronted, entail a great risk of immediate physical or social damage. Frightened individuals appraise these threats as more powerful than themselves and thus seek to avoid them. The brain system supporting threat appraisal has been studied extensively. From these studies, the amygdala has emerged as a key structure. Located in the medial temporal lobe, the amygdala receives sensory information from cortical and subcortical structures and modifies activity in these and other brain regions according to appraisal outcomes. Appraisal by the amygdala is believed to be automatic and may thus occur independently of cognitive or reflective processes (see Chapters 14 and 15 for reviews). However, such processes, if they occur, can influence amygdala function (see Chapter 16 for a review).

Once activated by threat, the amygdala initiates a cascade of physiological and cognitive responses aimed at escaping or minimizing damage. The sympathetic adrenal medullary system and the hypothalamic-pituitary-adrenal (HPA) axis become activated and issue the release of adrenaline/noradrenaline and corticosteroids, respectively. These hormones then attach to target receptors, thereby regulating activity of the autonomous nervous system, the metabolic system, and the immune system. In the short term, they prepare the body for action by facilitating physiological processes such as heart rate, blood pressure, and sweating. In the long term, they deplete the body's energy stores and weaken the immune system. In addition to these physiological effects, the release of stress hormones feeds back to the central nervous system and modulates brain activity. Among other regions, this feedback reaches the amygdala, thereby influencing the effect of amygdala activity on cognition (McGaugh, 2004). At the cost of other ongoing processes, the amygdala facilitates attention to threatening stimuli and, together with peripheral feedback, makes their representation and evaluation a priority (McGaugh, 2004; see also Chapter 14). Thus, threat typically "pops out" and is retained more easily in memory than other mundane information (see Chapter 20 for a review).

Although neural, physiological, and cognitive responses associated with fear are largely comparable in women and men, differences nevertheless exist and translate into behavioral differences. At the neural level, sex differences have been observed for both structure and function. Specifically, structural studies have found the amygdala to be smaller in women than in men (when controlled for total brain size; Goldstein et al., 2001). Additionally, there are differences in the structural covariation of the amygdala and other brain regions. Gray matter density of the left amygdala and the right angular gyrus is more positively correlated in women than in men, whereas gray matter density of the left amygdala and bilateral anterior inferior temporal cortex is more positively correlated in men than in women (Mechelli, Friston, Frackowiak, & Price, 2005). Furthermore, during the resting state, amygdala functional connectivity with other brain structures is left-lateralized in women but right-lateralized in men (Kilpatrick, Zald, Pardo, & Cahill, 2006).

Given these structural and functional differences, it is not surprising that brain responses to threat differ between women and men. Threat perceived from angry (McClure et al., 2004) or frightened faces (Williams et al., 2005) elicits greater amygdala activity in women than in men. Likewise, vocal threat has been shown to excite greater neural responses in women as compared with men (Schirmer, Simpson, & Escoffier, 2007; Figure 26.1). Conversely, pictures portraying physical threat from human or animal attack elicit lower amygdala and fusiform activity in women as compared to men, despite women's greater self-reported fear (Schienle, Schäfer, Stark, Walter, &

Vaitl, 2005). Thus, it seems that information relating to physical combat may have more implicit relevance for men, whereas social threat outside of combat has more relevance for women. This accords with the roles of men and women in hunter/gatherer societies and the proposed sex differences in the nature of the threat response: Whereas this response has been associated with fight-or-flight in men, recent evidence suggests a greater significance of tend-and-befriend behavior in women (Taylor et al., 2000). According to this evidence, women, because of their reproductive responsibilities, are less willing to engage in physical combat. Instead they engage in nurturing activities protecting the self and offspring and form alliances with other women and, to a lesser extent, men that can be tapped on in times of need.

As mentioned earlier, once activated, the amygdala triggers a cascade of physiological, cognitive, and behavioral responses; again these responses are qualified by sex. In particular, physiological indices of defensive activation to threat, such as heart rate deceleration, startle reflex, or facial muscle activity, are greater in women than in men (Anokhin & Golosheykin, 2010; Bradley, Codispoti, Cuthbert, & Lang, 2001). At a cognitive level, women more readily notice threat – particularly if it is social in nature (Schirmer et al., 2005, 2007). Additionally, there are sex differences in the relationship between threat and learning. After a stressor, learning in males is enhanced, whereas learning in females is impaired (Wood & Shors, 1998). Nonhuman animal studies, furthermore, have revealed that males fear-condition more readily if freezing is used as the dependent measure, whereas females fear-condition more readily if the startle reflex is used as the dependent measure (for a review see Dalla & Shors, 2009). This finding, as well as that females learn more readily to avoid a footshock, has been taken to imply baseline behavioral differences that propagate sex-specific fear responses. Greater baseline activity levels may make defensive or avoidance behaviors more accessible in females as compared with males (Dalla & Shors, 2009).

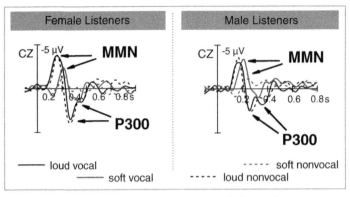

Figure 26.1. Auditory deviants in an unattended sound sequence elicit an event-related potential component termed mismatch negativity (MMN). Illustrated here are the results from a study in which participants listened to sound sequences composed of spoken syllables (vocal) or synthetic sounds (nonvocal; Schirmer et al., 2007). MMN responses to intensity changes in spoken syllables (reflective of increases or decreases in negative emotional arousal) differed between men and women. Only women showed a larger MMN to increases (loud) relative to decreases (soft) in sound amplitude, suggesting that they perceived an increase in negative vocal arousal as more salient than a decrease. No sex differences were observed for the processing of intensity changes in synthetic sounds. Reprinted from Brain Research, 1174, Schirmer et al., Listen up! Processing of intensity change differs for vocal and nonvocal sounds, 103–112, Copyright (2007), with permission from Elsevier.

Sadness

Significant losses, perceived as irrevocable, elicit sadness. Typically, such losses are of social relevance, as when a person loses a job or a partner. They are therefore difficult to enact within the laboratory, which has created challenges for the investigation of brain circuits supporting sadness. Moreover, the approach adopted from research on threat has been futile. Neuroimaging studies presenting sad pictures or facial expressions revealed inconsistent results likely because these stimuli failed to reliably evoke sadness in the observer (Eugène et al., 2003). Unlike threat, for which an automatic fear response is adaptive, sadness may not be evoked automatically when detected in someone else. What would the benefits be if we felt sad on observing something or someone sad? We would become inactive and withdrawn and make matters worse rather than improve them. Thus, evoking sadness in a research environment likely requires

that events experienced or imagined have some personal significance (see Chapter 23). A neuroimaging study by Eisenberg and colleagues (2003) created such significance by engaging participants in a cyberball game with two other players. In one condition, these players passed the ball to the participant, whereas in another condition they excluded the participant from the game. This exclusion was associated with heightened social distress, and the rating of distress correlated positively with activity in the anterior cingulate. The role of the anterior cingulate also emerged in a study using positron emission tomography (PET). In this study, participants were asked to recall sad events; this recall was associated with increased mu-opioid receptor availability in the anterior cingulate (Zubieta et al., 2003). Given the role of the anterior cingulate and the mu-opioid system in pain, these results suggest a close relationship between pain and sadness. Moreover, they advance the notion that sadness piggybacked onto the evolutionary older pain system.

Sex differences in pain and sadness can again be observed at different levels of analysis. Research comparing the morphology of the anterior cingulate found it to be larger in women than in men (Goldstein et al., 2001). Furthermore, both pain and sadness recruit this structure in sex-specific ways. Activation of the anterior cingulate by noxious stimuli is more likely in women than in men (Paulson, Minoshima, Morrow, & Casey, 1998) and is associated with sex-specific patterns of regional connectivity (Labus et al., 2008). Women also activate this structure more automatically than men when perceiving someone else who is in pain (Singer et al., 2006). Activation of the anterior cingulate by social exclusion does not differ between the sexes. However, only in women does this activation correlate with increased immune system activity (Eisenberger, Inagaki, Rameson, Mashal, & Irwin, 2009). The absence of such a correlation in men has been linked to potentially stronger regulatory activity aimed at reducing social distress. Such activity may buffer against the coupling between social exclusion, social pain, and immune system activity and thus reduce the risk for depression.

Given the lower perceptual and neural thresholds for pain and possibly sadness in women (Paulson et al., 1998), it is not surprising that they differ from men in a key physiological response: crying. Compared to men, women cry more frequently, longer, and more intensely, especially in situations involving "tender feelings," criticisms from or disputes with others, and problems at work (Williams & Morris, 1996). This is also true for depressed women relative to depressed men (Romans, Tyas, Cohen, & Silverstone, 2007) and appears to emerge early in infancy (Fuller, 2002). A survey across 33 countries revealed that female crying increases during the luteal phase of the menstrual cycle, when estrogen is high (but note cultural differences; see van Tilburg, Becht, & Vingerhoets, 2003). Likewise, pain perception increases during the luteal phase, again corroborating the link between sadness and pain and implicating sex steroids in the moderation or mediation of sex differences (Martin, 2009).

Happiness and Attraction

Like other emotions, the positive feelings evoked when anticipating or obtaining something longed for are fundamental motivators of behavior. Unlike other emotions, however, they are critical in giving life a sense of meaning or fulfillment. The brain system that mediates positive feelings is commonly referred to as the reward system and overlaps with the dopaminergic system (for a review, see Chapter 19). The dopaminergic system originates in the midbrain, where neurons in the ventral tegmental area and substantia nigra project upward to subcortical and cortical targets. Most important for reward is the mesolimbic pathway projecting to the nucleus accumbens and with more recently identified projections to the amygdala. Once activated, these projections trigger the release of dopamine, which binds to receptors located in various parts of the brain. Dopamine activity, particularly in the nucleus accumbens, is associated with several life-sustaining activities like eating or reproduction. It creates pleasurable feelings and thereby makes these activities rewarding (Wise, 2004). Pleasurable feelings can also be elicited through the stimulation of dopaminergic structures via implanted electrodes or the application of drugs that act as dopaminergic agonists. However, whether experienced through the consumption of natural rewards, electrical stimulation, or drugs, pleasurable feelings entice humans and nonhuman animals to repeat temporally linked behaviors and therefore contribute to the development of addiction.

As already mentioned, a morphometric analysis identified the amygdala as being larger in men than in women. Analysis of the nucleus accumbens, however, failed to reveal gross morphological differences (Goldstein et al., 2001). Nevertheless, sexual dimorphisms in these and other dopaminergic structures have been identified at a smaller level in nonhuman animal models.

Here, females have been shown to differ from males in the number of dopaminergic neurons and receptors and in the amount of dopamine released during activation. For example, females, compared to males, demonstrate a chronically lower dopaminergic tone and a smaller number of D_1 receptors in the striatum and nucleus accumbens (for a review, see Becker, 2009). Researchers use these and similar observations to explain why women and men differ in their response to rewarding stimuli. Such differences have been documented for addiction. Although more men than woman are drug abusers and have addictions, women, if exposed to drugs, become addicted more easily (for a review, see Kuhn et al., 2010). This finding has been replicated in rodent models and linked to both dopamine and estrogen. In particular, the addictive effect of drugs and sexual dimorphisms in the dopamine system increases with increasing levels of estrogen. Sex differences in addictive behaviors emerge during adolescence, when gonadal hormones bring about sexual maturation and introduce females to heightened and cyclically modulating levels of estrogen (Kuhn et al., 2010).

Of course, the human reward system evolved not for our appreciation of recreational drugs, but as a means to motivate self-sustenance. Through this system, the approach or consumption of stimuli that serve the purpose of self-sustenance becomes rewarding. Among others, such stimuli include food, peaceful nature scenes, other, positively spirited humans, and opportunities for reproduction. Given the effects observed for drug addiction, one may venture that the response to these evolutionary more appropriate rewards differs between women and men. However, studies investigating brain activation patterns to positive scenes or faces failed to find sex differences (e.g., Sabatinelli, Flaisch, Bradley, Fitzsimmons, & Lang, 2004). Yet, such differences were observed for vocal expressions of happiness (Schirmer et al., 2005), with greater neuronal responses in women relative to men. Sex differences also exist for responses to erotica. Although

erotica activates the nucleus accumbens regardless of sex, men show enhanced activity in an extended network including the visual cortex (Sabatinelli et al., 2004) and the sexually dimorphic amygdala (Hamann, Herman, Nolan, & Wallen, 2004). Thus, this evidence suggests that, whereas certain affiliative cues from other humans may be more important for women, cues related to sexual intercourse may be more important for men. Given the role of female gonadal hormones in reward, these effects are likely to vary across the menstrual cycle, which may explain why some sex differences have not been reported consistently.

Among the behaviors that are associated with happiness, one has emerged as being markedly different between women and men. Despite similarities in the reported feelings of happiness, across different cultures women smile more frequently than men (Safdar et al., 2009). Facial displays, similar to the human smile, exist in other primates and play a role in regulating social intercourse by signaling appeasement or submission. It is believed that these functions are still preserved to some extent in the human smile, and that it thus reflects an individual's power (LaFrance & Henley, 1994). This belief, however, has received mixed support, and more recent evidence points to a relationship between smiling and affiliation: Compared to nonsmiling individuals, smiling individuals are perceived as more affiliative rather than less dominant (Hess et al., 2005). Thus, women's greater propensity to smile might reflect their greater interest in affiliation. Notably, a recent study identified another contributing factor to women's greater frequency of smiles (Becker, Kenrick, Neuberg, Blackwell, & Smith, 2007). In a clever series of experiments it was demonstrated that female faces differ from male faces in looking happier – even without a smile (Figure 26.2). Thus, one may speculate that this sexual dimorphism of the face evolved to make females look more approachable and males look less approachable, thereby facilitating different interactional styles.

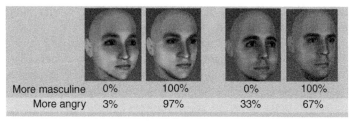

| More masculine | 0% | 100% | 0% | 100% |
| More angry | 3% | 97% | 33% | 67% |

Figure 26.2. Male and female faces differ in their structure, and this difference correlates with how happy or angry they are perceived. Illustrated here are stimuli and results employed by a study by Becker and colleagues (2007). In their study, more masculine faces were rated as angrier and as less happy than more feminine faces. Masculinity and anger ratings are presented in the first and second data row, respectively. Reprinted from Journal of Personality and Social Psychology, 92, Becker et al., The confounded nature of angry men and happy women, 179–190, Copyright (2007), with permission from the American Psychological Association.

Antisocial Emotions

Anger

Anger is elicited when our rights or those of important others are inappropriately curtailed. For example, we may become angry when a parking spot, for which we have signaled and which we are slowly approaching, is quickly taken by someone else. Feelings of anger are more likely when acts such as these are perceived as intentional and performed by an individual with equal or lower social standing or power. Thus, we may react angrily if the offender had noted but ignored our parking intention and/or is subordinate to us in the company we are working for. In contrast, any anger might be subdued if we are the subordinate, and/or the parking thief approached from a direction that prevented him or her from noticing our intention.

The brain systems subserving human anger have remained largely elusive. As with sadness, it has been difficult to devise experimental paradigms that successfully (and repeatedly) elicit anger in research participants without violating human subject rights. Moreover, the presentation of anger-related stimuli, such as angry faces or violent scenes, is probably more threatening than anger provoking in a typical neuroimaging experiment. In such an experiment, participants are prevented from or constrained in

their movement, which likely biases avoidance over approach motivational tendencies (Harmon-Jones & Peterson, 2009). A popular solution to this problem has been to study the effect of brain lesions, sex hormones, and other neurochemical manipulations on aggressive behaviors outside an imaging context. However, because aggressive behaviors are not necessarily reflective of anger, this approach also has its problems. Certain forms of aggression are instrumental or calculated and can even be linked to pleasurable feelings. For example, anyone experienced with cats will confirm that they thoroughly enjoy hunting smaller animals such as birds.

With these caveats in mind, we may now consider the findings from research on anger and aggression. This research has revealed that lesions in several structures influence aggressive behaviors in rodents, nonhuman primates, and humans. For example, across species, lesions to the amygdala have been shown to decrease aggression, whereas lesions to the orbitofrontal cortex have been shown to increase aggression, suggesting that aggressive acts arise from a combination of excitatory and inhibitory mechanisms (for a review see Nelson & Trainor, 2007). In line with this claim, several neurochemicals have been implicated in aggression. Increased serotonergic activity has been linked to a decrease in aggression, whereas increased levels of dopamine and testosterone have been linked to an increase in aggression. For example, the anticipation of a fight has been show to reduce serotonin secretion (Ferarri, Van Erp, Tornatzky, & Miczek, 2003) while enhancing both testosterone (Oliveira et al., 2001) and dopamine secretion (Ferarri et al., 2003).

Research on the neural underpinnings of anger and aggression has revealed sex differences at various levels. For one, there are sex differences in brain structure. In addition to the previously mentioned larger amygdala, men have on average smaller orbitofrontal cortices relative to women (Goldstein et al., 2001). Furthermore, women and men differ in the neurochemical systems implicated in aggression, such as the dopamine system (see preceding section). Additionally, there are sex differences in circulating testosterone levels at different stages of development. As such, testosterone has both sexually dimorphic organizational and activational effects. Early surges of testosterone in males effect neuronal changes that promote later aggressive behavior (Bronson & Desjardin, 1968). In adulthood, increases in testosterone have been shown to down-regulate GABAergic activity, thereby reducing the brain's main inhibitory mechanism and increasing the immediate likelihood of physical attack (Pinna, Costa, & Guidotti, 2005). Additionally, testosterone levels appear to be linked to differences in the activation of brain structures implicated in aggression. Whereas in women testosterone is unrelated to the activation of brain regions in the context of angry faces, such a relationship exists in men. Non-intuitively, however, testosterone in men correlates positively with vmPFC activation and negatively with amygdala activation as evoked by angry faces (Stanton, Wirth, Waugh, & Schultheiss, 2009). One possible explanation for this might be that these faces indeed trigger anger-related patterns of processing more readily with increasing levels of testosterone. However, the constrained situation in the fMRI scanner and/or the realization that these are only pictures and not real interaction partners may induce men to down-regulate their anger feelings (see Chapter 16).

Research studying the emotional and behavioral consequences of sex-specific brain mechanisms for aggression and anger has found that women are similar to men in the former but not the latter. In particular, surveys assessing felt anger found that this emotion is experienced equally often and intensely across the sexes (Archer, 2004). Nevertheless, one may argue that this finding cannot fully discount the possibility of sex differences in feeling anger. Because many emotions are elicited automatically and may be experienced without conscious reflection, explicit emotion judgments may be difficult and unreliable. For example, researchers have observed sex differences in cardiac responses to emotion induction in the absence of sex differences in self-report (Labouvie-Vief, Lumley, Jain, & Heinze, 2003). Moreover, there is some evidence that men control their anger more frequently than women, suggesting the possibility that anger may be perceived more frequently and/or more intensely by men relative to women (Doster, Purdum, Martin, Goven, & Moorefield, 2009).

Although the jury is still out on sex differences in the feelings of anger, there is unanimous support for sex differences in aggression. In the United States, men commit 10 times more murders than women and are 5 times more likely to receive "correctional supervision" (Craig & Halton, 2009). Similar statistics have been observed in other nations and suggest a greater readiness of men to engage in violent acts. Given the lack of self-reported differences in anger, these findings have been linked to men's smaller orbitofrontal cortex and attributed to a greater difficulty in inhibiting aggressive impulses (Jones, 2008). Nevertheless, it is possible that such impulses are up-regulated by sex-specific dopaminergic and testosterone activity.

Disgust and Contempt

Disgust is experienced in response to repulsive objects whose presence may be revealed by their sight, smell, taste, touch, or sound. Thus, although disgust, like anger, is a negative emotion, it is tied more closely to the various senses and promotes avoidance rather than approach. Researchers believe disgust to be an adaptive response to disease-salient stimuli (Curtis, Aunger, & Rabie, 2004). It prevents us from contaminating ourselves with viruses, bacteria, or parasites that feast on bad food, cadavers, and the sick. The notion of contamination has been extended to foul acts performed by individuals with whom we share a social circle. Noticing such acts is believed to elicit a social variant of disgust referred to as contempt.

Of the senses tied to the experience of disgust, the sense of taste is particularly important. Even if experienced from a distance, disgusting stimuli activate a region in the anterior insula called the primary gustatory cortex and may thus literally leave a bad taste in one's mouth. Brain imaging studies find that the anterior insula is activated more strongly to disgusting stimuli or human nonverbal signals of disgust than to neutral information (Wicker et al., 2003). Additional evidence comes from neurological patients. For example, NK, a patient with a lesion to the insula extending into the basal ganglia, was no longer disgusted by normally repulsive, disease-salient stimuli. He also had difficulties recognizing expressions of disgust in other individuals (Calder, Keane, Manes, Antoun, & Young, 2000).

Gross morphometric analysis of the insula and basal ganglia found no meaningful sex differences (Goldstein et al., 2001; but see Welborn et al., 2009, who found a larger putamen and globus pallidus in women). Nevertheless, there appear to exist sex differences in function. Several neuroimaging studies revealed greater neuronal activity in response to disgust-relevant images in female relative to male participants. These activity differences have been reported in the bilateral insula and frontal and temporal cortex (Aleman & Swart, 2008). Interestingly, facial expressions of contempt elicit less activity in female as compared to male participants (Aleman & Swart, 2008) sug-

gesting a dissociation between disgust and its social counterpart, contempt.

These neuroimaging results nicely align with self-reported disgust sensitivity. Across several cultures, women feel greater disgust than men, and this difference appears to be relatively consistent across the lifespan (Curtis et al., 2004). Comparatively little research is available on subjective experiences of contempt. What is available, however, suggests a greater role of this emotion for men. Observers perceive a man more readily as contemptuous than a woman, particularly if he is also perceived as high in dominance and low in affiliation (Hess et al., 2005). Moreover, self-reported social dominance has been shown to correlate with brain responses to contemptuous faces, leading researchers to speculate that social dominance mediates greater contempt sensitivity in men relative to women (Aleman & Swart, 2008).

Emotion Regulation

Emotions are fundamental motivators of behavior. If we do not feel, we do not act. Sometimes, however, a full-blown emotional response may be inappropriate and even impair behavioral outcomes. For example, being overwhelmed by fear may prevent individuals from succeeding in a job interview. Being overwhelmed by anger may cause people to turn small disputes into physical violence. Thus, although nature designed emotions to trigger important behavioral impulses, it also built in a brake to stop these impulses from running unchecked.

Researchers refer to nature's brake as emotion regulation (see Chapter 16). In the past decade, they identified numerous mechanisms through which emotion regulation may be achieved and developed a range of classification systems. Two of the best studied mechanisms with respect to their neural underpinnings are (1) cognitive reappraisal, an emotion regulation strategy that moderates attention and/or knowledge, thereby reevaluating an emotional event in a goal-oriented manner, and (2) emotion expression suppression, an emotion regulation strategy that has bodily targets such as the facial muscles and, like cognitive reappraisal, may serve a situational goal (Welborn et al., 2009).

Research investigating both regulation strategies suggests the existence of two dedicated brain systems (Ochsner & Gross, 2005). A ventral system situated in the orbitofrontal cortex is believed to support the implicit and context-sensitive appraisal of emotional stimuli and the selection of an appropriate response. A dorsal system situated in the dorsal PFC presumably supports explicit reasoning about an event and may affect emotion through influencing the ventral system or through biasing perceptual and memory systems. As with other functions that rely on the dorsal prefrontal cortex, with practice or experience explicit regulation attempts may become implicit, and the contribution of the dorsal system to emotion regulation may decrease.

Of the brain systems implicated in emotion regulation, the ventral system has been repeatedly shown to differ between men and women. Across several morphometric studies, men were found to have smaller orbitofrontal cortices than women, particularly in the right lateral and ventromedial aspects (Goldstein et al., 2001; Welborn et al., 2009). Furthermore, the volume of the vmPFC correlates negatively with the self-reported frequency of using expression suppression in emotionally challenging situations and as such may mediate the sex differences that have been observed for the latter measure (Gross & John, 2003). Men report using expression suppression more frequently than women, and this difference can be explained by differences in the size of the vmPFC (Welborn et al., 2009).

In addition to differences in size, research suggests that the ventral system is differently engaged by men and women during emotion regulation. In men, lesions to this system result in decreased stress responses as measured by blood levels of cortisol during a stress challenge task. In contrast, comparable lesions in women increase the blood level of cortisol (Buchanan et al., 2010). Sex differences have also been observed for measures of brain activity during emotion regulation tasks. For example, Mak and colleagues (2009) found that men engage the dorsal emotion regulation system to a greater extent than women, who engaged the ventral system more strongly. Unfortunately, this study and the earlier mentioned brain lesion study failed to specify which regulation strategy participants should use during the task. It is hence possible that the observed sex differences reflect differences in the strategies typically used by men and women. For example, men, being more likely to engage in expression suppression, may more strongly rely on the dorsal system. Moreover, regulation through this system may become easier with impairment to the potentially competing ventral system. In contrast, women may gravitate to emotion regulation via the ventral system. When this system is impaired, emotional challenges may be experienced as more intense.

Studies investigating sex differences for a specified emotion regulation strategy are scarce. In one such study, McRae and colleagues (2008) presented participants with negative pictures and asked them to either "look" or "regulate" their emotional response. In the look condition, participants passively viewed the pictures. In the regulate condition, participants were asked to reduce a potentially negative response using cognitive reappraisal. Compared to the look condition, the regulate condition elicited greater activity in the ventral and dorsal system and reduced activity in the amygdala. Sex differences were observed in both the ventral and dorsal system, with greater activity in women as compared to men. In the amygdala, the effect was reversed. Here men but not women showed the reported reduction of activity as a function of regulation. Notably, women showed an effect of emotion regulation in the ventral striatum that was absent in men. The authors thus speculated that women, instead of down-regulating a negative emotional response, reappraise events to elicit a positive emotional response. Although highly speculative, this interpretation accords with evidence on self-reported emotion regulation. Although women are more likely than men to dwell on negative events by ruminating or catastrophizing (Garnefski, Teerds, Kraaij, Legerstee, & van den Kommer, 2004), they are also more likely to use positive refocusing. That is, if they have the intention to change their emotion for "the better," they are apparently more likely than men to think about joyful experiences (Garnefski et al., 2004).

As is apparent from the preceding discussion, women and men differ in whether and how they engage in emotion regulation. One may thus ask to what extent these differences explain the sex differences observed in the experience and neural correlates of basic emotions. Researchers have demonstrated a relationship between habitual emotion regulation and emotional processing. For example, individuals who report frequent use of reappraisal in everyday life show reduced amygdala and increased PFC activation relative to individuals who use reappraisal less frequently (Drabant, McRae, Manuck, Hariri, & Gross, 2009). It is thus possible for sex-specific emotion regulation strategies to produce sex-specific emotional responses.

Although we may want to keep this possibility in mind when considering sex differences in emotional processing, the following observation qualifies such an emotion regulation confound. Generally, women experience prosocial emotions more strongly than men, whereas men experience antisocial emotions more strongly than women. Thus, sex differences in emotional processing are not unidirectional, but emerge from the social function of the experienced emotion. Because there currently is no evidence to suggest that emotion regulation mechanisms and associated sex differences are likewise emotion specific, the existing work fails to fully account for the sex differences we see in emotional responding. However, because assumptions founded on the absence of evidence are problematic, future research will have to tackle this issue.

Sex Differences in the Effects of Emotion on Cognition

So far, we have reviewed the many ways in which men and women differ in their response to emotional events. Part and parcel of this response are cognitive processes that arise from the events and that influence both immediate and future behavior of the individual. In the following section I briefly describe a subset of cognitive processes that were shown to vary as a function of emotion and for which emotional variation differs as a function of sex.

The first processes presented here relate to attention. It is now well established that emotional events capture and hold attention more effectively than neutral events. Moreover, there is some indication that women and men differ in this regard. For example, women appear more likely to notice emotional information that is presented outside the focus of attention. Specifically, women are more likely than men to show an increased mismatch negativity – an event-related potential marker for auditory change detection – when an unattended auditory sequence is suddenly interrupted by an emotional as compared to a neutral deviant (Schirmer et al., 2005; Figure 26.1). That this effect was found for vocal but not nonvocal deviants (Schirmer et al., 2007) supports the notion that social relevance is critical in explaining emotion-related sex differences. Men and women also differ in the influence of emotions on language processing. Among other findings, there is evidence that women more readily integrate contextual emotional information during language comprehension (Schirmer, Kotz, & Friederici, 2002). As a consequence they have less difficulty processing words related to that context. Moreover, for women, more than men, positive mood facilitates the processing of distantly related concepts (Federmeier, Kirson, Moreno, & Kutas, 2001). Activations in the semantic network of happy women seem to spread farther, making it easier to link and possibly generate ideas.

Finally, there are well-established sex differences in the relationship between emotions and memory. Although emotions benefit subsequent memory in both men and women, there are different mechanisms underlying this benefit. Across several functional imaging studies, emotion effects during memory encoding elicited right-lateralized amygdala activity in men and left-lateralized amygdala activity in women (Cahill et al., 2001). These differences have been linked to differences in amygdala connectivity during rest (Kilpatrick et al., 2006) and to differential forms of memory. With respect to the forms of memory, beta-blockers administered to men and women prior to an emotional memory task were found to impair the subsequent retrieval of global/gist and local/detail information, respectively (Cahill & van Stegeren, 2003). Thus, it has been proposed that right amygdala recruitment in men supports the storage of global/gist information, whereas left amygdala recruitment in women supports the storage of local/detail information. These and other memory effects have been shown to depend on the female menstrual cycle (Andreano & Cahill, 2008), suggesting hormonal mediation.

Factors Contributing to Sexual Differentiation

Scientists and philosophers have long debated the cause of sex differences in emotion and other aspects of the human mind. For example, Aristotle argued that "women are [generally] defective by nature" (Whitback, 1976). In contrast, his mentor, Plato, held that, despite their physical inferiority, women may not be intellectually inferior and, if instructed in the same way as men, may be capable of similar pursuits (Plato, 2000). The idea of natural gender equality was also popular in Western cultures of the 20th century. With the emergence of behaviorism as a school of thought, researchers interpreted apparent differences between men and women as the result of the different environments in which they are placed. The more responsible and authoritative positions that men held were thought to

nurture responsibility and authority in men and to curtail similar aptitudes in women. The assertion "Give me a child and I'll shape him into anything," famously attributed to B. F. Skinner, nicely reflects these sentiments.

As scientists overcame the dogmas of behaviorism and started to explore the human mind and its substrate, the brain, several biological differences between men and women emerged. As reviewed earlier, both structural and functional brain differences were discovered that could be linked to differences in mental processes and behavior. Yet, these discoveries failed to fully convince of the importance of nature. After all, gendered environments provide different challenges and resources to developing girls and boys, thereby shaping their brains differently (Kimmel, 2000). Moreover, skeptics held that differences between the sexes are negligible at birth and that if boys and girls were treated in the same way the differences would remain negligible into adulthood.

That this belief is wrong became clear when researchers identified cases in which the environment failed to successfully shape male and female typical behaviors. One such case is that of Bruce Reimer (Colapinto, 2000). As an infant, he lost his genitals during circumcision, and his parents, following medical advice at the time, raised Bruce as a girl. Despite this upbringing and female hormonal treatments, however, Bruce experienced difficulties with his gender identity. When his parents later revealed his biological sex to him, he decided to return to being a male and underwent the necessary medical treatments. Yet, his childhood experiences left a deep mark, and he failed to achieve life satisfaction as an adult. The resulting psychological difficulties were so strong that, even though he had become a husband and adoptive father, he took his life at the age of 38.

Other observations that underline the role of nature have been made in children with congenital adrenal hyperplasia (CAH). CAH is a genetic disorder that affects the enzymes responsible for the production of

Figure 26.3. Vervet monkeys (Cercopithecus aethiops sabaeus) show sex-specific toy preferences (Alexander & Hines, 2002). Female monkeys spend more time with toys that are typically preferred by girls (e.g., dolls), whereas male monkeys spend more time with toys typically preferred by boys (e.g., cars). Reprinted from Evolution and Human Behavior, 23, Alexander & Hines, Sex differences in response to children's toys in nonhuman primates (Cercopithecus aethiops sabaeus), 467–479, Copyright (2002), with permission from Elsevier.

cortisol by the adrenal gland. One of the consequences of this disorder is the hyper- or hypo-production of sex steroids. CAH girls with increased concentration of androgens, the male sex steroid, show more male-typical preferences for toys than girls without the disorder. When given a choice, they select building blocks or guns over dolls and beauty items. Importantly, they make these selections despite parental encouragement to play with female-typical toys (Pasterski et al., 2005). The fact that such toy preferences can also be observed in male and female nonhuman primates further underlines the importance of nature in determining sex-specific behaviors (Alexander & Hines, 2002; Figure 26.3).

Finally, evidence is accumulating for a role of gonadal hormones in the emotional responses of healthy human adults. Several of the emotion phenomena described earlier depend on the levels of testosterone, estrogen, and progesterone, which vary across the day and an individual's lifetime and in women across the menstrual cycle. For example, early cortical responses to unattended vocal deviants differ as a function of emotion and estrogen (Schirmer et al., 2008). Moreover, estrogen and progesterone seem to enhance amygdala and hippocampus activation to negative images (Andreano & Cahill, 2010). Together with testosterone, these hormones also affect emotion regulation. Among others, a review by van Wingen and colleagues (2011) suggests that progesterone enhances connectivity between the amygdala and the medial prefrontal cortex, whereas testosterone decreases connectivity between the amygdala and the orbitofrontal cortex, thus potentially promoting emotion regulation and interfering with behavioral inhibition, respectively. Lastly, there is evidence for gonadal hormones influencing the learning that results from an emotional event (Milad et al., 2006, 2010). Importantly, women are more likely to show spontaneous recovery after fear conditioning and extinction when estrogen is low as compared to high. Researchers speculate that such hormonal modulation of learning could be implicated in the high incidence of anxiety disorders in women.

Despite the overwhelming evidence for organizational and activational effects of gonadal hormones, it would be inappropriate to conclude that they as opposed to environmental influences fully explain sex differences in emotions. Instead, it appears that sex differences result from both innate biological mechanisms *and* the environments that these mechanisms meet. Evidence for this claim comes from a research field called epigenetics, which investigates gene expression as a function of the information that is stored together with the genome. Methylation is one such type of information. It refers to the methyl groups that bind to parts of a cell's DNA, thereby regulating transcription factor binding and cell-specific protein synthesis.

Research has demonstrated that methylation changes as a function of environmental conditions. Important for the present discussion is evidence from nonhuman animals that parental care affects brain function through gene expression. Early tactile interactions between mother and her offspring have been shown to affect the expression of glucocorticoid receptors in the hippocampus. Offspring experiencing frequent licking and grooming from their biological or surrogate mothers develop a greater number of glucocorticoid receptors in the hippocampus than offspring experiencing little licking and grooming (Zhang & Meaney, 2010). The hippocampus plays a critical role in regulating activity of the HPA axis, because it receives feedback about the level of glucocorticoids released from the adrenal gland. A greater number of glococorticoid receptors therefore translates into a greater dampen-

ing of HPA activity following initial encounters with a stressor. Licking and grooming have also been demonstrated to influence the expression of estrogen receptors in the medial preoptic area and the associated development of oxytocin receptors (Zhang & Meaney, 2010). Female offspring experiencing frequent licking and grooming show a greater number of oxytocin receptors and more readily and intensely care for pubs that are not their own (Zhang & Meaney, 2010).

These effects are remarkable because they demonstrate sustained changes in brain function that result from experiences during the first days of life. Moreover, recent evidence of such experiences influencing methylation and gene expression in the human brain indicates that the epigentic effects observed in nonhuman animals are also present in humans (McGowan et al., 2009). It is thus reasonable to consider environmental factors, such as parental care, as crucial variables in the emergence of sex differences. In particular, there is abundant evidence that parents interact differently with boys and girls. For example, some researchers found that parents talk less about feelings with boys than with girls and restrict the expression of sadness more strongly in boys than in girls (Maccoby, 1998). Others reported that women tend to smile more at female as compared to male infants, select different toys (Will, Self, & Datan, 1976), and touch them in different ways (Fleishman, 1983). Compared with infant girls, infant boys receive less ventral-to-ventral contact with their mothers. However, during the first 3 months of life, they receive more general touch than infant girls. At the age of 6 months, the pattern reverses. From then on into adulthood, girls engage in tactile contact more frequently than boys (for a review, see Fleishman, 1983).

Given the role of early tactile experiences for gene expression, it is easy to conceive that sex-specific parenting affects brain development. Moreover, one may speculate that greater tactile stimulation of girls promotes the development of the brain's social system and associated prosocial emotions. Conversely, a restriction of tactile contact with boys may curtail their social development. Thus, together nature and nurture shape the human mind and create two individuals with different emotional dispositions.

Conclusions

The emotions of men and women differ in many ways. For some emotions, men show stronger subjective feelings, cognitive, and/or behavioral effects than women (e.g., anger, contempt), whereas for others we find the opposite (e.g., sadness, fear, disgust). Moreover, we also observe sex differences for a range of emotions that depend not so much on the emotion itself but on the eliciting stimulus (e.g., social vs. nonsocial). Different emotion regulation mechanisms in men and women further contribute to this sexual specialization.

Although the sex differences reported here are highly complex, an organizing principle may be inferred from other aspects of sexual differentiation. Specifically, humans like most animals show sexual dimorphisms that go together with sex-specific roles in reproduction and the care of offspring. In human evolution, these dimorphisms potentially assisted in the emergence of different lifestyles and the inception of the division of labor – a key feature of modern human societies. According to some, the propensity of early human males to engage in hunting and for early human females to engage in food gathering and child care developed into a more diversified division of labor that eventually enabled modern humans to domesticate animals, cultivate plants, and create what we call "civilization" (Kuhn & Stiner, 2006).

The evidence reviewed in this chapter suggests that emotional specialization could have been part and parcel of this development. Moreover, one may speculate that the emergence of male and female typical tasks leveraged on sex-specific emotional dispositions. For example, hunting, particularly of large game, required a certain readiness to engage in aggression and to tolerate poten-

tial harm to one's life. The same applies to territorial behavior, which in humans and other primates is more strongly developed in males. Thus, emotional responses that facilitated aggression (e.g., anger/contempt) may have been of greater benefit to males than emotions that reduced aggression (e.g., fear/sadness). Conversely, early female typical tasks such as food gathering and child care were less confrontational and dangerous. Hence, here aggression may not have been as important and potentially impeded group cohesion. Given their lesser physical strength and greater investment in reproduction, females likely relied more than males on social bonds for protection (Taylor et al., 2000). As such, emotional responses linked to self-preservation (e.g., fear/disgust) and the facilitation of prosocial behavior (e.g., fear/sadness/happiness) may have been of greater benefit to women than emotional responses that triggered aggressive impulses.

One consequence of such an emotional specialization is that men and women positioned themselves at different points on different "basic emotion continua." Thus, if they present with an emotional disturbance, they are more likely to be considered abnormal when they digress away from the mean of both sexes as compared to when they digress away from the mean of their own sex toward the mean of the other sex (Figure 26.4). Therefore, the diagnosis of emotional disorders may vary between the sexes. Women present more often than men with disorders of prosocial emotions. That is they are more likely than men to suffer from intense and prolonged feelings of fear or sadness. Men, in contrast, present more often with disorders of antisocial emotions. They are more likely than women to be diagnosed with sociopathy or contact disorder. To deal successfully with these conditions, it is important to understand healthy emotional processing and its variants in men and women. Although for a long time emotion research disregarded sex as an important variable, this position has changed significantly in the last decade. During this time, researchers have identified chemical,

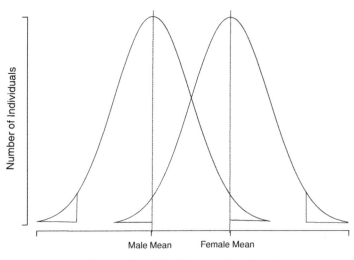

Figure 26.4. Men and women differ in how frequently they are diagnosed for specific socioemotional disorders. This likely reflects sex differences in the responsiveness/sensitivity of emotion systems implicated in these disorders. Women show a greater readiness to feel socially relevant emotions (e.g., sadness, happiness, fear), whereas men show a greater readiness to feel emotions associated with social conflict (e.g., anger, contempt). Sex-specific biases in the diagnoses of psychological disorders likely result from disorders being diagnosed in reference to normal behavior as defined by the mean of both sexes, rather than sex-specific means.

cellular, gross structural, and functional differences between male and female brains and shed light on the interplay between nature and nurture. From this evidence, we now know that both innate mechanisms and environmental conditions shape the human mind in a sex-specific manner. Although interactions between both determinants have been reported primarily for early developmental periods, there is indication that they remain active throughout the lifespan (Weaver, Meaney, & Szyf, 2006). Thus, a better understanding of the nature-nurture interplay promises new perspectives on the prevention and treatment of both child and adult psychopathology.

Outstanding Questions and Future Directions

- This chapter suggests that different emotions produce qualitatively different sex differences. Moreover, it is proposed that one principle underlying these differences is whether an emotion biases pro- versus antisocial behavior. Whether this

is a valid principle and whether there are other principles contributing to sex differences are still open questions.

- Currently we do not understand the relationship between sex differences in gross brain morphology and brain function. Moreover, we know little about sex differences in neuronal connectivity and neurochemical signaling. These issues need to be addressed before we can fully appreciate why men and women feel differently.

- Our capacity to automatically regulate emotions based on goals or situational constraints creates a major challenge for the investigation of emotions and associated sex differences. Future research on emotional processing needs to consider emotion regulation effects and find means to model their influence.

References

Abler, B., Hofer, C., & Viviani, R. (2008). Habitual emotion regulation strategies and baseline brain perfusion. *Neuroreport, 19,* 21–24.

Andreano, J. M., & Cahill, L. (2008). Menstrual cycle modulation of the relationship between cortisol and long-term memory. *Psychoneuroendocrinology, 33,* 874–82.

Andreano, J. M., & Cahill, L. (2010). Menstrual cycle modulation of medial temporal activity evoked by negative emotion. *Neuroimage, 53,* 1286–93.

Aleman, A., & Swart, M. (2008). Sex differences in neural activation to facial expressions denoting contempt and disgust. *PLoS One, 3,* e3622.

Alexander, G. M., & Hines, M. (2002). Sex differences in response to children's toys in nonhuman primates (Cercopithecus aethiops sabaeus). *Evolution and Human Behavior, 23,* 467–79.

Archer, J. (2004). Sex differences in aggression in real-world settings: A meta-analytic review. *Review of General Psychology, 8,* 291–322.

Anokhin, A. P., & Golosheykin, S. (2010). Startle modulation by affective faces. *Biological Psychology, 83,* 37–40.

Becker, D. V., Kenrick, D. T., Neuberg, S. L., Blackwell, K. C., & Smith, D. M. (2007). The confounded nature of angry men and happy women. *Journal of Personality and Social Psychology, 92,* 179–90.

Becker, J. B. (2009). Sexual differentiation of motivation: A novel mechanism? *Hormones and behavior, 55,* 646–54.

Bradley, M. M., Codispoti, M., Cuthbert, B. N., & Lang, P. J. (2001). Emotion and motivation I: Defensive and appetitive reactions in picture processing. *Emotion, 1,* 276–98.

Bronson, F. H., & Desjardins, C. (1968). Aggression in adult mice: Modification by neonatal injections of gonadal hormones. *Science, 161,* 705–6.

Buchanan, T. W., Driscoll, D., Mowrer, S. M., Sollers III, J. J., Thayer, J. F., Kirschbaum, C., et al. (2010). Medial prefrontal cortex damage affects physiological and psychological stress responses differently in men and women. *Psychoneuroendocrinology, 35,* 56–66.

Cahill, L., Haier, R. J., White, N. S., Fallon, J., Kilpatrick, L., Lawrence, C., et al. (2001). Sex-related difference in amygdala activity during emotionally influenced memory storage. *Neurobiology of Learning and Memory, 75,* 1–9.

Cahill, L., & van Stegeren, A. (2003). Sex-related impairment of memory for emotional events with ß-adrenergic blockade. *Neurobiology of Learning and Memory, 79,* 81– 88.

Calder, A. J., Keane, J., Manes, F., Antoun, N., & Young, A. W. (2000). Impaired recognition and experience of disgust following brain injury. *Nature Neuroscience, 3,* 1077–78.

Colapinto, J. (2000). *As nature made him: The boy who was raised as a girl.* New York: HarperCollins.

Craig, I. W., & Halton, K. E. (2009). Genetics of human aggressive behaviour. *Human Genetics, 126,* 101–13.

Crijnen, A. A. M., Achenbach, T. M., & Verhulst, F. C. (1997). Comparisons of problems reported by parents of children in 12 cultures: Total problems, externalizing, and internalizing. *Journal of the American Academy of Child and Adolescent Psychiatry, 36,* 1269–77.

Curtis, V., Aunger, R., & Rabie, T. (2004). Evidence that disgust evolved to protect from risk of disease. *Proceedings of the Royal Society of London, 271,* 131–33.

Dalla, C., & Shors, T. J. (2009). Sex differences in learning processes of classical and operant conditioning. *Physiology & Behavior, 97,* 229–38.

Doster, J. A., Purdum, M. B., Martin, L. A., Goven, A. J., & Moorefield, R. (2009). Gender differences, anger expression, and cardiovascular risk. *Journal of Nervous and Mental Disease, 197,* 552–54.

Drabant, E. M., McRae, K., Manuck, S. B., Hariri, A. R., & Gross, J. J. (2009). Individual differences in typical reappraisal use predict amygdala and prefrontal responses. *Biological Psychiatry, 65,* 367–73.

Eisenberger, N. I., Inagaki, T. K., Rameson, L. T., Mashal, N. M., & Irwin, M. R. (2009). An fMRI study of cytokine-induced depressed mood and social pain: The role of sex differences. *NeuroImage, 47,* 881–90.

Eisenberger, N. I., Lieberman, M. D., & Williams, K. D. (2003). Does rejection hurt? An fMRI study of social exclusion. *Science, 302,* 290–92.

Else-Quest, N. M., Hyde, J. S., Goldsmith, H. H., & Van Hulle, C. A. (2006). Gender differences in temperament: A meta-analysis. *Psychological Bulletin, 132,* 33–72.

Eugène, F., Lévesque, J., Mensour, B., Leroux, J. M., Beaudoin, G., Bourgouin, P., et al. (2003). The impact of individual differences on the neural circuitry underlying sadness. *Neuroimage, 19,* 354–64.

Federmeier, K. D., Kirson, D. A., Moreno, E. M., & Kutas, M. (2001). Effects of transient, mild mood states on semantic memory organization and use: An event-related potential investigation in humans. *Neuroscience Letters, 305*(3), 149–52.

Ferrari, P. F., Van Erp, A. M. M., Tornatzky, W., & Miczek, K. A. (2003). Accumbal dopamine and serotonin in anticipation of the next aggressive episode in rats. *European Journal of Neuroscience*, 17, 371–78.

Figueira, M. L., Caeiro, L., Ferro, A., Severino, L., Duarte, P. M., Abreu, M., et al. (2008). Validation of the Temperament Evaluation of Memphis, Pisa, Paris and San Diego (TEMPS-A): Portuguese-Lisbon version. *Journal of Affective Disorders*, 111(2–3), 193–203.

Fleishman, E. G. (1983). Sex-role acquisition, parental behavior, and sexual orientation: Some tentative hypotheses. *Sex Roles*, 9, 1051–59.

Fuller, B. F. (2002). Infant gender differences regarding acute established pain. *Clinical Nursing Research*, 11, 190–203.

Garnefski, N., Teerds, J., Kraaij, V., Legerstee, J., & van den Kommer, T. (2004). Cognitive emotion regulation strategies and depressive symptoms: Differences between males and females. *Personality and Individual Differences*, 36, 267–76.

Goldstein, J. M., Seidman, L. J., Horton, N. J., Makris, N., Kennedy, D. N., Caviness Jr, V. S., et al. (2001). Normal sexual dimorphism of the adult human brain assessed by in vivo magnetic resonance imaging. *Cerebral Cortex*, 11, 490–97.

Gross, J. J., & John, O. P. (2003). Individual differences in two emotion regulation processes: Implications for affect, relationships, and well-being. *Journal of Personality and Social Psychology*, 85, 348–62.

Hamann, S. (2005). Sex differences in the responses of the human amygdala. *Neuroscientist*, 11, 288–93.

Hamann, S., Herman, R. A., Nolan, C. L., & Wallen, K. (2004). Men and women differ in amygdala response to visual sexual stimuli. *Nature Neuroscience*, 7, 411–16.

Harmon-Jones, E., & Peterson, C. K. (2009). Supine body position reduces neural response to anger evocation. *Psychological Science*, 20, 1209–10.

Hess, U., Adams Jr, R., & Kleck, R. (2005). Who may frown and who should smile? Dominance, affiliation, and the display of happiness and anger. *Cognition & Emotion*, 19, 515–36.

Jones, D. (2008). Killer instincts: What can evolution say about why humans kill – and about why we do so less than we used to? *Nature* 451, 512–15.

Kilpatrick, L. A., Zald, D. H., Pardo, J. V., & Cahill, L. (2006). Sex-related differences in amygdala functional connectivity during resting conditions. *Neuroimage*, 30, 452–61.

Kuhn, C., Johnson, M., Thomae, A., Luo, B., Simon, S. A., Zhou, G., et al. (2010). The emergence of gonadal hormone influences on dopaminergic function during puberty. *Hormones and Behavior*, 58, 122–37.

Kuhn, S. L., & Stiner, M. C. (2006). What's a mother to do? The division of labor among Neandertals and modern humans in Eurasia. *Current Anthropology*, 47, 953–80.

Kimmel, M. S. (2000). *The gendered society*. New York: Oxford University Press.

Labouvie-Vief, G., Lumley, M. A., Jain, E., & Heinze, H. (2003). Age and gender differences in cardiac reactivity and subjective emotion responses to emotional autobiographical memories. *Emotion*, 3, 115–26.

Labus, J. S., Naliboff, B. N., Fallon, J., Berman, S. M., Suyenobu, B., Bueller, J. A., et al. (2008). Sex differences in brain activity during aversive visceral stimulation and its expectation in patients with chronic abdominal pain: A network analysis. *Neuroimage*, 41, 1032–43.

LaFrance, M., & Henley, N. M. (1994). On oppressing hypotheses: Or differences in nonverbal sensitivity revisited. In H. L. Radtke & H. J. Stam (Eds.), *Power/gender: Social relations in theory and practice. Inquiries in social construction* (pp. 287–311). London: Sage.

Maccoby, E. E. (1998). The socialization component. In E. E. Maccoby (Ed.), *The two sexes: Growing up apart, coming together* (pp. 118–52). Cambridge, MA: Belknap Press.

Maccoby, E. E., & Jacklin, C. N. (1974). *The psychology of sex differences*. Stanford, CA: Stanford University Press.

Mak, A. K., Hu, Z., Zhang, J. X., Xiao, Z., & Lee, T. M. (2009). Sex-related differences in neural activity during emotion regulation. *Neuropsychologia*, 47, 2900–08.

Martin, V. T. (2009). Ovarian hormones and pain response: A review of clinical and basic science studies. *Gender Medicine: Official Journal of the Partnership for Gender-Specific Medicine at Columbia University*, 6(Suppl. 2), 168–92.

McClure, E. B., Monk, C. S., Nelson, E. E., Zarahn, E., Leibenluft, E., Bilder, R. M., et al. (2004). A developmental examination of gender differences in brain engagement during evaluation of threat. *Biological Psychiatry*, 55, 1047–55.

McGaugh, J. L. (2004). The amygdala modulates the consolidation of memories of emotionally arousing experiences. *Annual Review of Neuroscience*, 27, 1–28.

McGowan, P. O., Sasaki, A., D'Alessio, A. C., Dymov, S., Labonté, B., Szyf, M., et al. (2009). Epigenetic regulation of the glucocorticoid receptor in human brain associates with childhood abuse. *Nature Neuroscience*, 12, 342–48.

McRae, K., Hughes, B., Chopra, S., Gabrieli, J. D., Gross, J. J., & Ochsner, K. N. (2010). The neural bases of distraction and reappraisal. *Journal of Cognitive Neuroscience*, 22, 248–62.

McRae, K., Ochsner, K. N., Mauss, I. B., Gabrieli, J. J., & Gross, J. J. (2008). Gender differences in emotion regulation: An fMRI study of cognitive reappraisal. *Group Processes & Intergroup Relations*, 11, 143–62.

Mechelli, A., Friston, K. J., Frackowiak, R. S., & Price, C. J. (2005). Structural covariance in the human cortex. *Journal of Neuroscience*, 25, 8303–10.

Milad, M. R., Goldstein, J. M., Orr, S. P., Wedig, M. M., Klibanski, A., Pitman, R. K., & Rauch, S. L. (2006). Fear conditioning and extinction: Influence of sex and menstrual cycle in healthy humans. *Behavoural Neuroscience*, 120, 1196–1203.

Milad, M. R., Zeidan, M. A., Contero, A., Pitman, R. K., Klibanski, A., Rauch, S. L., & Goldstein, J. M. (2010). The influence of gonadal hormones on conditioned fear extinction in healthy humans. *Neuroscience*, 168, 652–58.

Nelson, R. J. & Trainor, B. C. (2007). Neural mechanisms of aggression. *Nature Reviews Neuroscience*, 8, 536–46.

Nolen-Hoeksema, S. (2001). Gender differences in depression. *Current Directions in Psychological Science*, 10, 173–76.

Ochsner, K. N., & Gross, J. J. (2005). The cognitive control of emotion. *Trends in Cognitive Sciences*, 9, 242–49.

Oliveira, R. F., Lopes, M., Carneiro, L. A., & Canário, A. V. (2001). Watching fights raises fish hormone levels. *Nature*, 409, 475.

Pasterski, V. L., Geffner, M. E., Brain, C., Hindmarsh, P., Brook, C., & Hines, M. (2005). Prenatal hormones and postnatal socialization by parents as determinants of male-typical toy play in girls with congenital adrenal hyperplasia. *Child Development*, 76, 264–78.

Paulson, P. E., Minoshima, S., Morrow, T. J., & Casey, K. L. (1998). Gender differences in pain perception and patterns of cerebral activation during noxious heat stimulation in humans. *Pain*, 76, 223–29.

Pinna, G., Costa, E., & Guidotti, A. (2005). Changes in brain testosterone and allopregnanolone biosynthesis elicit aggressive behavior. *Proceedings of the National Academy of Sciences*, 102, 2135–40.

Plato (2000). *The republic*. Mineola, NY: Dover Publications

Pompili, M., Girardi, P., Tatarelli, R., Iliceto, P., De Pisa, E., Tondo, L., et al. (2008). TEMPS-A (Rome): Psychometric validation of affective temperaments in clinically well subjects in mid- and south Italy. *Journal of Affective Disorders*, 107, 63–75.

Rogstad, J. E., & Rogers, R. (2008). Gender differences in contributions of emotion to psychopathy and antisocial personality disorder. *Clinical Psychology Review*, 28, 1472–84.

Romans, S. E., Tyas, J., Cohen, M. M., & Silverstone, T. (2007). Gender differences in the symptoms of major depressive disorder. *Journal of Nervous and Mental Disease*, 195, 905–11.

Sabatinelli, D., Flaisch, T., Bradley, M. M., Fitzsimmons, J. R., & Lang, P. J. (2004). Affective picture perception: gender differences in visual cortex? *Neuroreport*, 15, 1109–12.

Safdar, S., Matsumoto, D., Kwantes, C.T., Friedlmeier, W., Yoo, S.H., Kakai, H., et al. (2009). Variations of emotional display rules within and across cultures: A comparison between Canada, USA, and Japan. *Canadian Journal of Behavioural Science*, 41, 1–10.

Schienle, A., Schäfer, A., Stark, R., Walter, B., & Vaitl, D. (2005). Gender differences in the processing of disgust- and fear-inducing pictures: An fMRI study. *Neuroreport*, 16, 277–80.

Schirmer, A., Escoffier, N., Li, Q. Y., Li, H., Strafford-Wilson, J., & Li, W.-I. (2008). What grabs his attention but not hers? Estrogen correlates with neurophysiological measures of vocal change detection. *Psychoneuroendocrinology*, 33, 718–27.

Schirmer, A., Kotz, S. A., & Friederici, A. D. (2002). Sex differentiates the role of emotional prosody during word processing. *Cognitive Brain Research*, 14, 228–33.

Schirmer, A., Simpson, E., & Escoffier, N. (2007). Listen up! Processing of intensity change differs for vocal and nonvocal sounds. *Brain Research*, 1176, 103–12.

Schirmer, A., Striano, T., & Friederici, A.D. (2005). Sex differences in the pre-attentive processing of vocal emotional expressions. *Neuroreport*, 16, 635–39.

Simonoff, E., Pickles, A., Meyer, J. M., Silberg, J. L., Maes, H. H., Loeber, R., et al. (1997). The Virginia Twin Study of Adolescent Behavioral Development: Influences of age, sex, and impairment on rates of disorder. *Archives of General Psychiatry*, 54, 801–8.

Singer, T., Seymour, B., O'Doherty, J. P., Stephan, K. E., Dolan, R. J., & Frith, C. D. (2006). Empathic neural responses are modulated by the perceived fairness of others. *Nature*, 439, 466–69.

Stanton, S. J., Wirth, M. M., Waugh, C. E., & Schultheiss, O. C. (2009). Endogenous testosterone levels are associated with amygdala and ventromedial prefrontal cortex responses to anger faces in men but not women. *Biological Psychology*, 81, 118–22.

Taylor, S. E., Klein, L. C., Lewis, B. P., Gruenewald, T. L., Gurung, R. A. R., & Updegraff, J. A. (2000). Biobehavioral responses to stress in females: Tend-and-befriend, not fight-or-flight. *Psychological Review*, 107, 411–29.

van Tilburg, M. A., Becht, M. C., & Vingerhoets, A. J. (2003). Self-reported crying during the menstrual cycle: Sign of discomfort and emotional turmoil or erroneous beliefs? *Journal of Psychosomatic Obstetrics and Gynaecology*, 24, 247–55.

van Wingen, G.A., Ossewaarde, L., Bäckström, T., Hermans, E. J., Fernández, G. (2011). Gonadal hormone regulation of the emotion circuitry in humans. *Neuroscience*, 191, 38–45.

Weaver, I. C., Meaney, M. J., & Szyf, M. (2006). Maternal care effects on the hippocampal transcriptome and anxiety-mediated behaviors in the offspring that are reversible in adulthood. *Proceedings of the National Academy of Sciences*, 103, 3480–85.

Welborn, B. L., Papademetris, X., Reis, D. L., Rajeevan, N., Bloise, S. M., & Gray, J. R. (2009). Variation in orbitofrontal cortex volume: Relation to sex, emotion regulation and affect. *Social Cognitive and Affective Neuroscience*, 4, 328–39.

Whitbeck, C. (1976). Theories of sex difference. In C. C. Gould, & M. W. Wartofsky (Eds.), *Women and philosophy: Toward a theory of liberation* (pp. 54–80). New York: Putnam.

Wicker, B., Keysers, C., Plailly, J., Royet, J. P., Gallese, V., & Rizzolatti, G. (2003). Both of us disgusted in My insula: The common neural basis of seeing and feeling disgust. *Neuron*, 40, 655–64.

Will, J. A., Self, A., & Datan, N. Maternal behavior and perceived sex of infant. *American Journal of Orthopsychiatry*, 46(1), 135–39.

Williams, D. G., & Morris, G. H. (1996). Crying, weeping or tearfulness in British and Israeli adults. *British Journal of Psychology*, 87, 479–505.

Williams, L. M., Barton, M. J., Kemp, A. H., Liddell, B. J., Peduto, A., Gordon, E., et al. (2005). Distinct amygdala-autonomic arousal profiles in response to fear signals in healthy males and females. *Neuroimage*, 28, 618–26.

Wise, R. A. (2004). Dopamine, learning and motivation. *Nature Reviews Neuroscience*, 5, 483–94.

Wood, G. E., & Shors, T. J. (1998). Stress facilitates classical conditioning in males, but impairs classical conditioning in females through activational effects of ovarian hormones. *Proceedings of the National Academy of Sciences*, 95, 4066–71.

Zhang, T.Y. & Meaney, M. J. (2010). Epigenetics and the environmental regulation of the genome and its function. *Annual Review of Psychology*, 61, 439–66.

Zubieta, J. K., Ketter, T. A., Bueller, J. A., Xu, Y., Kilbourn, M. R., Young, E. A., et al. (2003). Regulation of human affective responses by anterior cingulate and limbic mu-opioid neurotransmission. *Archives of General Psychiatry*, 60, 1145–53.

CHAPTER 27

Development of Affective Circuitry

Essi Viding, Catherine L. Sebastian, & Eamon J. McCrory

This chapter provides an overview of research into development of those neural structures and neurocognitive functions implicated in emotion perception and regulation. To provide the context for specific findings in developmental affective neuroscience, we start with a brief review of emotional brain systems that have been the focus of developmental research with children. We then review affective neuroscience findings from studies of typically developing children. In particular, we focus on emotion and emotion regulation circuitry during infancy, early childhood, and adolescence, highlighting the challenges in this field and outlining several outstanding research questions. In the final section of this chapter, we focus on individual differences in emotional development in childhood. We also highlight genetic and environmental factors that may account for individual differences in the development of the brain's affective circuitry (in particular, childhood maltreatment) and the utility of a developmental affective neuroscience framework in advancing our understanding of the mechanisms underpinning childhood disorders.

We use conduct disorder as a case study to illustrate the potential contribution of affective neuroscience within an interdisciplinary context. We conclude that affective neuroscience can shed light on only one part of the developmental puzzle and needs to be considered in the context of additional information from other fields such as genetics and developmental psychopathology. Several avenues for future research are also suggested.

Core Circuitry Implicated in Affective Processing and Regulation

Most of the developmental research in affective neuroscience can be crudely divided into two areas: the development of basic affective processing (including processing of reward) and the development of emotion regulation. Before we review findings relating to typically developing children, we briefly outline those parts of the core emotion circuitry that have been investigated in affective neuroscience studies with child participants. Because a thorough coverage of the emotion brain systems can be found in Chapters 19 (striatum), 18 (amygdala), 16, and 24 (prefrontal cortex), this section provides only a schematic overview for the purposes of anchoring the developmental findings presented in this chapter.

The Amygdala

The amygdala is a subcortical region that is important for processing the current value of stimul (Adolphs, 2010). This structure has a critical role in several affective processes, such as mediating conditioned emotional responses, responding to various emotional stimuli (including facial expressions of emotion), and influencing social behavior toward conspecifics (see, e.g., Adolphs, 2010; Sergerie, Chochol, & Armony, 2008; and Chapter 1).

The Striatum

The striatum is a subcortical region that plays a role in modulating behavior toward potentially rewarding stimuli, particularly stimuli that hold a high subjective reward value to an individual (see, e.g., Peters & Buchel, 2010; Rosen & Levenson, 2009; and Chapter 19).

The Anterior Cingulate Cortex

The anterior cingulate cortex (ACC) is thought to play a distinct role in complex aspects of emotion, such as processing moral emotions (e.g., guilt), self-regulation of negative emotions, and action reinforcement (the route by which reward history influences action choice; see, e.g., Kédia, Berthoz, Wessa, Hilton, & Martinot, 2008; Levesque et al., 2004; Rushworth, Behrens, Rudebeck & Walton, 2007; and Chapters 16 and 24).

The Prefrontal Cortex

Various sectors of the prefrontal cortex (PFC) have been implicated in emotion (see e.g., Davidson, Jackson, & Kalin, 2000; Vuilleumier & Pourtois, 2007; and Chapters

16 and 24). The areas that have received most attention in affective neuroscience studies of children include the orbitofrontal cortex (OFC); ventromedial prefrontal cortex (vmPFC); ventrolateral prefrontal cortex (VLPFC); and dorsolateral prefrontal cortex (DLPFC). The OFC is thought to implement rapid stimulus-reinforcement associations and the correction of these associations when the contingencies of reinforcement change (e.g., Mitchell, Richell, Pine, & Blair, 2008; O'Doherty, 2004; Rolls & Grabenhorst, 2008), whereas the vmPFC is thought to, among other functions, represent the elementary positive and negative affective states in the absence of immediately present incentives, as well as being important for encoding outcome expectations (e.g., Davidson & Irwin, 1999; Mitchell, 2011). A more rostral region of the medial PFC has been implicated in the processing of more complex social emotions such as guilt and embarrassment (Burnett, Bird, Moll, Frith, & Blakemore, 2009; Takahashi et al., 2004). Current research suggests that the VLPFC integrates affective information and supports response selection by increasing the salience of alternative motor response option representations through interactions with the striatum (e.g., Mitchell, 2011; Mitchell et al., 2008). It is also associated with effortful regulation of negative affect via connections with subcortical structures including the amygdala (Ochsner & Gross, 2005; Wager, Davidson, Hughes, Lindquist, & Ochsner, 2008). The DLPFC, in turn, is thought to increase attentional control of task-relevant stimulus features and represent goal states toward which more elementary positive and negative affective states are directed (Mitchell, 2011).

This, of course, represents only an extremely succinct overview of the brain areas (and their putative functions) that form the brain's affective circuitry. We alluded only briefly to the phenomenon of connectivity in the PFC section. However, most of the brain's affective processes are achieved by functional integration across several brain areas. That is, although this section has presented broad functions for individual brain areas, many of these areas work together to achieve an appropriate behavioral outcome for the individual. For example, the amygdala, together with the PFC and ventral striatum, forms a network of structures involved in processing the current value of stimuli, and various PFC/ACC regions are connected either directly or indirectly with the amygdala to achieve emotion regulation via numerous mechanisms, such as reappraisal.

Typical Development of Affective Circuitry

There is now a wide body of evidence to suggest that the development of affective circuitry is relatively protracted (Paus, Keshavan, & Giedd, 2008). In particular, it has been proposed that bidirectional connections between the amygdala and regulatory regions in PFC continue to develop into the second decade of life (Nelson, Leibenluft, McClure, & Pine, 2005). The PFC undergoes a particularly drawn-out development, with reductions in gray matter volume and thickness continuing into adolescence and the early twenties (Shaw et al., 2008). Subcortical emotion-processing structures, such as the amygdala, are functional at birth and play a part in emotional face processing from the early postnatal period (Johnson, 2005). The amygdala has also been shown to increase in volume between 7.5 and 18.5 years (Schumann et al., 2004), suggesting that even subcortical structures continue to mature in adolescence. Across all lobes of the brain, white matter volume continues to increase during childhood and adolescence (Giedd et al., 1999), which may reflect continuing axonal myelination, thereby increasing the efficiency of neurotransmission between brain regions.

Development of Affective Processing and Its Neural Bases

Much of the work investigating the development of affect perception has focused on

social signals such as emotional facial expressions (Leppanen & Nelson, 2009). Other people's facial expressions can provide both salient social communication and vital clues about the nature of the surrounding environment (see Chapter 7). For example, someone displaying a fearful expression might signal to an observer the presence of a potential and previously unnoticed threat. Being able to detect and attach appropriate valence to such cues is likely to have strong adaptive value (Leppanen & Nelson, 2009).

Infancy

Converging evidence suggests that our ability to discriminate facial expressions emerges early in infancy. By 5 months, infants habituate to faces showing the same expression across differing identities (Bornstein & Arterberry, 2003). By 7 months, infants can discriminate a habituated facial expression (happy) from fearful and angry faces, but only when faces are upright, not inverted (Kestenbaum & Nelson, 2010). This suggests that an adult-like configural strategy for emotion recognition is already in place at this stage. An adult-like preference for looking at fearful faces compared with happy faces also emerges by 7 months (Nelson, Morse, & Leavitt, 1979). This suggests enhanced attention to fearful faces, with one recent study showing that 7-month-olds are less able to disengage attention from a fearful face than a neutral or happy face in the presence of a peripheral distracter (Peltola, Leppanen, Palokangas, & Hietanen, 2008).

Although methods with good spatial specificity such as fMRI are less practical for use with young infants, methods such as EEG/ERP and near-infrared spectroscopy (NIRS) have been widely used to investigate emotion processing in this age group. Several ERP studies have shown that by 7 months (but not at 5 months), infants display an enhanced negativity at frontocentral electrodes in response to fearful expressions relative to happy ones (Nelson & de Haan, 1996). This "negative central" or Nc component occurs 400–800 ms after stimulus onset and is thought to reflect enhanced attention, possibly generated within the ACC (Reynolds & Richards, 2005).

Although most studies have focused on the high salience of fearful faces, the neural response to positive facial expressions in infancy has also been investigated. A recent NIRS study found an OFC response to happy facial expressions in infants aged 9–13 months (Minagawa-Kawai et al., 2009). This response was greatest when infants saw their mother, relative to both familiar and unfamiliar others. The authors suggested that OFC activation in this context may represent a neural substrate for attachment to the primary caregiver, via the elicitation of a shared affective response. Thus, even a rudimentary understanding of different facial expressions provides both a cue as to the external environment and a basis of shared communication with caregivers.

Despite this growing body of data, we still have much to learn about the neurocognitive and functional systems implicated in emotion perception in infancy. First, it is unclear whether the amygdala, so central to affect perception in adulthood, contributes to effects such as enhanced attention to fearful faces. Given that the amygdala is thought to be functional at birth and may orient infants toward salient social stimuli such as faces (Johnson, 2005), this role seems likely, but there is still a lack of direct evidence. Another question is the extent to which perception of an emotional expression leads to the production of a similar affective state. As noted earlier, an attentional bias toward fearful faces from an early age may confer a survival advantage (Leppanen & Nelson, 2009). Only with experience, however, is the link made between a facial expression cue and the infant's own affective response (i.e., learning what a facial expression really means). Further work is needed to determine how this link may develop and at what age.

Childhood and Adolescence

Although behavioral and neural responses to emotional stimuli are in place within the first year of life, they are refined over the course of childhood and adolescence. Behavioral studies investigating accuracy rates for recognizing different expressions suggest that accuracy improves with age during childhood, but does so at different rates for different expressions. In the preschool years, the ability to recognize happiness develops first, followed by sadness/anger, and finally by surprise and fear (see Herba & Phillips, 2004, for a review). It is possible that the identification of more nuanced expressions, such as embarrassment, takes still longer to develop, perhaps because insight into one's own and others' capacity to feel mixed emotional states emerges only in mid- to late childhood (Larsen, To, & Fireman, 2007). In addition, we know that the ability to label complex emotional states depends on a certain level of verbal competence.

To investigate the development of more subtle emotion recognition abilities in late childhood and adolescence, one recent study used morphed faces that varied along continua from neutral to fear, neutral to anger, and fear to anger (Thomas, De Bellis, Graham, & LaBar, 2007). Across all expression morphs, adults were more accurate than children (aged 7–13) and adolescents (aged 14–18). However, the developmental trajectory for fear differed from that for anger. Accuracy for fear recognition showed a linear improvement across the three age groups, whereas that for anger showed a quadratic trend, with a sharp improvement between adolescence and adulthood. The authors suggested that this variation might reflect different neural correlates for the detection of these two expressions. This suggestion is at least partially supported by evidence from fMRI studies in adults, with one recent meta-analysis showing that, relative to neutral faces, fear was associated with responses in the bilateral amygdala, fusiform, and medial frontal gyri, whereas anger elicited responses in the left insula and right occipital gyrus (Fusar-Poli et al., 2009).

As described, this study (Thomas et al., 2007) found that adolescents were more accurate than younger children. However, McGivern, Andersen, Byrd, Mutter, and Reilly (2002) found evidence for a "pubertal dip" in performance on a match-to-sample task in which participants had to match emotional faces to words. Reaction times were 10–20% longer at the onset of puberty for both males and females than in younger children. Performance only regained its pre-pubertal level at 16–17 years. This dip may be caused by neural reorganization occurring around the onset of puberty. However, the pubertal dip effect has not been replicated with simple emotion expression recognition, and the differential effects of puberty and chronological age on the development and functioning of emotional brain circuitry in humans are not yet known.

Several recent studies have used fMRI to identify the neural substrates associated with affective processing in children and adolescents. One of the first studies compared young adolescents (mean age 11 years) with adults using fMRI during the passive viewing of fearful and neutral faces (Thomas et al., 2001). It was found that, whereas adults activated the amygdala more in response to fearful faces than neutral ones, adolescents showed the opposite response. This was possibly because neutral faces were interpreted as more ambiguous and therefore more threatening in the adolescent group or possibly because the amygdala is less selective earlier in development. However, there are inconsistent findings regarding amygdala response in adolescence. For example, Guyer and colleagues found greater amygdala activation to fearful faces in adolescents (aged 9–17 years) compared to adults (Guyer et al. 2008). This finding is in line with recent theories of adolescent neurocognitive development that suggest that activity in subcortical structures such as the amygdala and ventral striatum are not adequately regulated by prefrontal structures during early and mid-adolescence (e.g., Nelson et al., 2005).

It should be noted that task demands influence the nature of differential responses between adolescents and adults during facial expression processing (Monk et al., 2003). During passive viewing of fearful faces (relative to neutral faces), adolescents (aged 9–17) activated the amygdala, ACC, and OFC more than did adults (aged 25–36). Similarly, when participants were asked to attend to a nonemotional aspect of the stimuli (e.g., "how wide is the nose?"), ACC activation was greater in the adolescents than in the adults. However, when participants were instructed to rate how afraid they felt on viewing each face, adults activated the right OFC more than adolescents. The authors suggested that adults were able to modulate their neural responses based on task demands, with the OFC selectively engaged in response to the requirement to focus on emotional content. By contrast, adolescents' responses were modulated by the emotional nature of the stimulus across tasks, suggesting that this age group may find it harder to disengage from affectively salient information, regardless of task demands. These findings highlight the importance of considering the context in which an emotional response is measured, because different task demands may differentially engage subcortical and cortical affective structures.

Sex differences further complicate the emerging picture of emotional brain development (see Chapter 26). At a behavioral level, there is a small female advantage in emotional expression recognition across development, from infancy to adolescence (McClure, 2000). Some studies have found evidence of a differential response to emotional faces between the sexes in the amygdala and PFC, although they disagree on the precise nature of these differences and the timing with which they emerge. For example, one study reported an increase in PFC response to fearful faces with age in girls aged 9 to 17, but no relationship with age in boys (Killgore, Oki, & Yurgelun-Todd, 2001). Another study found no differences in the neural response to facial expressions between adolescent girls and boys aged 9–17, but did find a greater response to angry faces in adult females relative to males in the OFC and amygdala (McClure et al., 2004), suggesting that sex differences emerge between adolescence and adulthood. Studying the possible neural basis of sex differences in facial emotion perception across the entire developmental time course and how it relates to behavioral performance is an important task for future research.

The majority of fMRI studies on emotional processing in childhood and adolescence have used emotional faces. This is partly because the neural circuitry associated with responses to emotional faces is well established in adults, and partly because understanding facial expressions is less dependent on verbal ability than are alternative kinds of emotional stimuli (Herba & Phillips, 2004). However, studies that have used nonface stimuli can provide complementary evidence via the use of richly detailed and/or ecologically valid emotional stimuli. Guyer and colleagues, for example, used a chat-room paradigm to investigate neural responses to anticipated peer evaluation in adolescents aged 9–17. When viewing peers of high interest to the participant, relative to low, there was increasing activation with age in regions involved in affective processing, including the nucleus accumbens, hypothalamus, hippocampus, and insula in females, but there were no age-related changes in males (Guyer, McClure-Tone, Shiffrin, Pine, & Nelson, 2009).

Another recent study (Burnett et al., 2009) used emotional vignettes with fMRI and found that the development of neural circuitry underpinning responses to social emotions such as embarrassment may be more protracted than that underpinning responses to basic emotions such as fear, continuing into late adolescence in regions such as the medial PFC. Using a cartoon vignette paradigm, Sebastian et al. (2012) found differences in response between adolescents and adults in a more ventral region of the medial PFC – but only when understanding the cartoon scenarios required a combination of affective processing and theory of mind ("affective ToM") relative to a physical causality control condition, as opposed to theory of mind alone ("cognitive ToM"; Figure 27.1). These kinds of studies are helping advance our understanding of the development of responses to more complex emotions embedded within a social context. Such approaches are of particular

relevance in the study of adolescence where social and peer influences play an increasingly important role.

In this section we have largely focused on fMRI studies, given the increasingly widespread use of this technique in the study of emotional processing in child and adolescent populations. fMRI is particularly useful for elucidating the response of individual neural structures, such as the amygdala, across development. However, because fMRI is correlational (see Chapter 5), it cannot be used to investigate potential change in the causal contribution of a given brain region to a cognitive process during development. Therefore, complementary methods such as developmental lesion studies (see Chapter 6) are important. However, there have been a limited number of such studies; we briefly highlight some findings here.

One study showed that bilateral amygdala damage sustained early in life can cause fear recognition deficits (Adolphs, Tranel, Damasio, & Damasio, 1994), whereas similar damage sustained in adulthood may not (Hamann et al., 1996). Thus, it may be that the amygdala supports learning of a connection between what fear is and what a fearful expression looks like. Once established, fear recognition can occur without the amygdala, although this recognition may not be accompanied by a subjective fear response. A similar pattern of findings has been demonstrated in patients with prefrontal damage including to portions of the OFC (Anderson, Bechara, Damasio, Tranel, & Damasio, 1999). This study found that two patients with damage to these regions before the age of 16 months showed impaired social and moral reasoning resembling psychopathy and demonstrated considerably more antisocial behavior than a similar group of patients with adult-onset lesions.

The studies reviewed here indicate the degree to which there is considerable ongoing development in the neural circuitry subserving emotion processing during childhood and adolescence. Future studies should interrogate emotion processing at different age points using the same task parameters,

a) Condition by Group interaction in ventromedial PFC for Affective ToM relative to Physical Causality

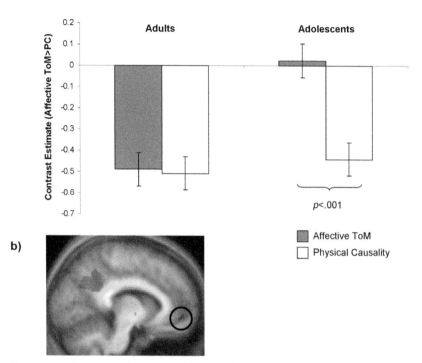

b)

Figure 27.1. Recent studies suggest that development of the functional neural bases of complex affective processing continues between adolescence and adulthood. This figure shows a region of the ventromedial prefrontal cortex (peak voxel: −10 46 8) that responded to a greater extent in adolescent males (mean age 14.1 years; n = 15) than in matched adult controls during the presentation of cartoon scenarios requiring affective Theory of Mind (understanding emotions in a social context) relative to those requiring cause-and-effect reasoning (physical causality). Group differences in this region were not seen in response to scenarios requiring cognitive Theory of Mind (mentalizing), suggesting that integrating affective and social cognition may represent a unique challenge for the developing adolescent brain. Figure adapted from Sebastian et al. (2011). See color plate 27.1.

as well as broaden the range of paradigms that are used; for example, to routinely include stimuli from a wide range of modalities (such as emotional voices and body postures). Increasing use should be made of ecologically valid paradigms measuring social interaction. Furthermore, most functional studies have tended to be cross-sectional in nature; future work should include longitudinal studies that are able to chart the development of emotion processing within an individual over time. It is also necessary to investigate developmental changes in connectivity between affective brain regions, and not just regional differences with age. One area of research in which this approach will be particularly informative is that of

affect regulation, because it depends on connectivity between subcortical and cortical structures, such as the amygdala and prefrontal cortex.

Development of Neural Circuitry Subserving Affect Regulation

It has been suggested that "emotion regulation consists of the extrinsic and intrinsic processes responsible for monitoring, evaluating and modifying emotional reactions" (Thompson, 1994, p. 27). As such, it is somewhat artificial to separate a discussion of emotion regulation from that of emotion itself, because these processes "co-evolve" via bidirectional connections between limbic and cortical regions (Lewis & Stieben, 2004). The following section explores the development of emotion regulation, from the inflexible automatic resources available to the infant to the emergence of more effortful and consciously directed cognitive strategies that can modulate affective responses (for a fuller discussion of emotion regulation in adults, see Chapters 16 and 24).

Infancy

In terms of the definition of emotion regulation just stated, infants are more dependent on extrinsic compared with intrinsic resources than at any other point in the lifespan. It therefore follows that the relationship between the infant and the primary caregiver is likely to play a critical role, with the primary caregiver helping to "scaffold" the development of the infant's affective and regulatory circuitry (Fonagy, Gergely, Jurist & Target, 2002). For example, a caregiver may be able to reduce distress by holding or rocking the infant or by distracting his or her attention away from the cause of distress. With time, the infant builds on this training and is able to self-sooth, possibly via the development of a mid-frontal cognitive control system (Posner & Rothbart, 2000). Thus, the quality of the infant-caregiver relationship is typically crucial to the successful early development of affect regulation systems. Future research should be tailored to explicitly test, as well as advance, our current models of attachment, reflective functioning, affect mirroring, and agency to provide a coherent framework within which we can make sense of the neurobiological correlates of affective response and regulation (Fonagy et al., 2002).

By the middle of the first year, there is evidence of a rudimentary system for orienting attention to salient affective stimuli. The evidence we have cited in relation to affective processing in infancy suggests that, by the age of 7 months, cognitive control regions such as the ACC (as indexed by the Nc component) seem to be engaged in the preferential allocation of attention to fear-ful faces, which may signify threat (Nelson & de Haan, 1996). However, this component reflects only an automatic response to potential threat. It has been argued that deliberate self-regulation does not develop until the third year of life and that it depends to a large extent on the development of effortful control, or the ability to inhibit a prepotent response in order to achieve a goal (Posner & Rothbart, 2000). Tasks that require conflict resolution, such as the Stroop task or the go/no-go task, are commonly used as an index of inhibitory control. Successful performance on age-appropriate versions of these tasks emerges at around 30 months and is associated with lower negative affect even at this early age (Gerardi-Caulton, 2000). The next section focuses on two key approaches to emotion regulation: the development of inhibitory control and its neural bases, and the use of explicit emotion regulation strategies in childhood and adolescence.

Childhood and Adolescence

Inhibitory control is mediated by a number of prefrontal structures including the dorsolateral, ventrolateral, and ventromedial PFC and the ACC. Behavioral and neuroimaging studies demonstrate that inhibitory control continues to develop throughout childhood and adolescence (e.g., Davidson, Amso, Anderson, & Diamond, 2006) and that the prefrontal response during inhibitory tasks becomes more efficient between childhood and adolescence (Lewis, Lamm, Segalowitz, Stieben, & Zelazo, 2006) and then between adolescence and adulthood (Luna et al., 2001). However, there is some debate as to the trajectory of this development. Studies using standard inhibitory control tasks without an affective component, such as the go/no-go and Simon tasks, have demonstrated a linear improvement with age (Davidson et al., 2006). However, as discussed later, there is evidence that a linear trend may not adequately describe the developmental trajectory of inhibitory control of affect, particularly in paradigms designed to emulate emotionally charged situations with "real-world" validity (Somerville & Casey, 2010).

Recent models of adolescence suggest that development of prefrontal regulatory structures lags behind that of the limbic structures that mediate an initial affective response (e.g., Nelson et al., 2005). These models would predict that inhibitory control of an affective response follows a U-shaped trajectory, with less effective PFC regulation of subcortical structures such as the amygdala in adolescence relative to childhood and adulthood. One recent fMRI study investigated age-related differences in PFC and amygdala function while participants (aged 7–32) completed an emotional go/no-go task involving fearful, happy, and calm facial expressions (Hare et al., 2008). Amygdala reactivity to fearful faces was greater in adolescents than in children or adults, and it correlated with reaction time delays to fearful relative to happy expressions. Activity in the ventral PFC, a regulatory region, was negatively correlated with reaction time difference, but did not vary with age. The authors suggested that increased limbic activation relative to ventral PFC regulation could contribute to the increased emotional reactivity and poor decision making associated with adolescence.

Similar conclusions have been reached by studies that have used gambling tasks to investigate the striatal response to reward across development. One such study (Van Leijenhorst et al., 2010) found an exaggerated response to anticipated reward in the striatum in 14–15 year olds, relative to both 10–12 year olds and 18–23 year olds. Another study found that this increased striatal response was driven by greater prediction error signals in the striatum in adolescents relative to children or adults (Cohen et al., 2010). The authors suggested that this increased response may render adolescents more sensitive to potentially positive outcomes (or less sensitive to potentially negative outcomes) and thus may motivate them to take more risks than at other ages. The pattern emerging from these studies is that of an increased subcortical response to emotion-eliciting stimuli during adolescence, in the absence of a similarly up-regulated response in regulatory regions. These data are complemented by studies that have shown a decreased regulatory response in prefrontal regions during affective tasks in adolescents relative to adults. Both Eshel, Nelson, Blair, Pine, and Ernst (2007) and Sebastian et al. (2011) have found evidence for a reduced response in ventrolateral PFC in adolescents compared with adults: the former during a gambling task and the latter during a task measuring neural responses to social rejection.

These studies have focused on the prefrontal modulation of subcortical structures during tasks requiring effortful control in the presence of affective stimuli. Although participants must explicitly direct their attention to a particular aspect of the stimuli to successfully complete these tasks, regulation of their own affective response is an implicit requirement. Individuals are also able to consciously engage these neural systems for the explicit purpose of emotion regulation: Learning to consciously modulate an emotional response is vital for successful socialization (Posner & Rothbart, 2000). According to Gross's (1998) process-oriented approach, a number of strategies for emotion regulation are available, of which two, suppression and reappraisal, have received considerable empirical attention. Suppression involves directly inhibiting an emotional response, whereas reappraisal involves interpreting an emotion-eliciting experience in a more positive light and is thought to be more successful in repairing negative moods than suppression.

Developmentally, the use of a suppression strategy has been shown to decrease with age between 9 and 15 (Gullone, Hughes, King, & Tonge, 2010), in line with the idea that more adaptive emotion regulation strategies are employed with increasing maturation. Surprisingly, Gullone and colleagues found that self-reported use of reappraisal also decreased over this same age range. It may be that such strategies become more automatic and less effortful with age and therefore become less readily amenable to investigation with self-report measures. Few studies have investigated neurocognitive development of these strategies. One fMRI study by Levesque et al. (2004) investigated the neural response to sad film clips in 8- to 10-year-old girls during both passive viewing and under instructions to use a reappraisal strategy. Reappraisal was associated with greater recruitment of several prefrontal loci, including the lateral, ventrolateral, orbital, and medial PFC, as well as ACC. A similar earlier study involving adult women found that fewer prefrontal loci were active in this contrast (Levesque et al., 2003), and it may be that this more widespread response in the developmental sample reflects immaturity of prefrontal control.

In summary, there is evidence for protracted behavioral and neural development of affective processing and emotion regulation. The following section explores individual differences in affective processing during development and discusses how vulnerabilities in these systems may give rise to developmental disorders of affective circuitry, with special reference to conduct disorder and anxiety.

Individual Differences in Affective Development

Clearly there are individual differences in emotion processing and regulation styles and abilities and in how these styles and abilities develop (e.g., Braver, Cole, & Yarkoni, 2010). Disturbances in emotion processing and regulation and in the related circuitry are also a hallmark of many forms of developmental psychopathology. In this section, we first discuss how genetic and environmental risk factors can alter the development of those brain areas involved in affect processing and regulation. We also outline periods of vulnerability within different parts of the affective circuitry – to the extent that they are known for humans. Antisocial behavior in childhood is used as an example of how affective neuroscience research can inform the developmental psychopathology evidence base, particularly when combined with other levels

of analyses (see the case study in the next section). Finally, we consider how affective neuroscience can have a translational impact in the field of developmental psychopathology.

The Impact of Genotype Differences

In the context of individual differences in typical development, as well as in developmental psychopathology, genes represent the cornerstone of mechanisms that either directly or in concert with environmental events ultimately result in disease (see Chapter 25). It is thought that these genetic variants act across the lifespan by biasing the functioning of several brain and hormonal circuits that are crucial for effecting a stress response. Although most human behaviors cannot be explained by genes alone, and certainly much variance in aspects of affective processing is not genetically determined directly, it is anticipated that variations in the genetic sequence that affect gene function will contribute an appreciable amount of variance to these resultant complex behavioral phenomena. This conclusion is implicit in the results of studies of twins that have revealed heritabilities ranging from 40 to 70% for various aspects of cognition, temperament, and personality. Gene effects on behavior are mediated by their molecular and cellular effects on information processing in the brain. Thus, examining gene effects on the brain represents a critical step in understanding their ultimate contribution to variability in behavior and in the development of psychopathology.

Because genes are directly involved in the development and function of brain regions subserving specific cognitive and emotional processes, functional polymorphisms in genes may be strongly related to the function of these specific neural systems and in turn, may mediate/moderate their involvement in behavioral outcomes. This is the underlying assumption of investigations examining the relation between genes and neural systems, known as "imaging genetics" (see Chapter 25). Imaging genetics within the context of a candidate gene association approach provides an ideal opportunity to further our understanding of biological mechanisms that potentially contribute to individual differences in behavior and the development of psychopathology.

Imaging genetics is still a relatively young field. Although adult studies have now gained momentum and provided several replicated findings of genetic polymorphisms that have an effect on the structure and functioning of affective neural circuitry (e.g., serotonin transporter polymorphism [5-HTT], monoamine oxidase-A [MAOA], cathecol methyl o-transferase [COMT], and several hypothalamus-pituitary-adrenal [HPA] axis polymorphisms), only few published studies to date have investigated child samples. Our own recent study examined the effects of the COMT valine (val) 158 methionine (met) (val158met) polymorphism – which has been shown to moderate predisposition to negative mood and affective disorders in adults – on brain structure and function in children between 10 and 12 years of age (Mechelli, A., Tognin, S., McGuire, P. K., Prata, D., Sartori, G., Fusar-Poli, P., De Brito, S., Hariri, A. R., Viding, E. 2009). In line with adult data we found that the met 158 allele was positively associated with gray matter volume in the left hippocampal head, where the genotype accounted for 59% of interindividual variance. In addition, the met158 allele was positively associated with neuronal responses to fearful relative to neutral facial expressions in the right parahippocampal gyrus, where the genotype accounted for 14% of the interindividual variance. These preliminary findings suggest that the met158 allele is associated with increased gray matter volume and heightened reactivity during emotional processing within the limbic system in children as young as 10 to 12 years of age. These findings are also consistent with the notion that, from childhood, genetic factors affect brain function to moderate vulnerability to affective psychopathology.

To provide another example, a study by Lau and colleagues (Lau et al., 2009) examined the effects of 5-HTT polymorphism and developmental psychopathology (depression and anxiety in adolescents) on amygdala responses to emotional faces. This study reported that, consistent with healthy adult data, healthy adolescents with at least one copy of the short allele (or functional equivalent, Lg) exhibited stronger amygdala responses to fearful faces than healthy adolescents with the long allele of 5-HTT. However, the opposite pattern was found for adolescents with mood disorders. All genotype effects emerged when the participants were specifically asked to be in an attentive state in which they monitored fear. The authors demonstrated that some emotion processing biases associated with anxiety show developmental differences. For example, although anxious adults exhibit selective attention toward threat stimuli, anxious adolescents shift attention *away* from these stimuli. Whether these types of emotion processing differences reflect distinct biases or compensatory responses in adults vs. adolescents is unclear. However, such findings are in line with the notion of developmental differences, and variable effects of certain polymorphisms across development will probably be found in other studies as well.

Collectively, these studies highlight the utility of using genotype information when studying the development (and individual differences therein) of the brain's affective circuitry. Although investigations of localized structural and functional abnormalities have provided insights about individual differences in the affective neurocognitive functioning as well as in behavioral outcomes, it is critical to conduct developmentally relevant work at the level of dynamically interacting neural systems. The study of such relationships has the ability to capture more proximally the functional consequences of genetically influenced neurodevelopmental processes, which alter circuitry function implicated in human temperament and psychiatric disorders.

We hypothesize that findings from adult imaging genetic studies represent windows into systems whose current structure and function resulted from developmental alterations during unique periods of plasticity, long before the physiological associations were captured via neuroimaging in adulthood (i.e., they represent "ghosts in the machine"). One avenue of fruitful research into these developing systems is the use of longitudinal studies beginning in childhood. This approach represents an ideal way to examine the impact of genetic and environmental effects on the developing neural circuitry that supports behavior and confers risk for psychopathology (environmental effects on affective circuitry are reviewed in the next section of the chapter). Such an approach allows for the determination of genetically driven variation on structural and functional brain development during windows of time that reflect critical maturational processes (e.g., myelination, synaptic pruning).

A study by Shaw et al. (2009) examined the effects of the 7-repeat microsatellite in the dopamine receptor 4 (DRD4) gene on clinical outcome and cortical development in ADHD throughout childhood and adolescence. They found that possession of the DRD4 7-repeat allele was associated with a thinner right OFC/inferior prefrontal and posterior parietal cortex. Among the children with ADHD, those carrying the DRD4 7-repeat allele had a better clinical outcome and a distinct trajectory of cortical development. They showed normalization of the right parietal cortical region, a pattern that has been linked with better clinical outcome in earlier studies. The authors concluded that the DRD4 7-repeat allele, which has been associated with a diagnosis of ADHD and better clinical outcome, is associated with cortical thinning in regions important in attentional control. This regional thinning was most apparent in childhood and largely resolved during adolescence. Although it did not directly assess the development of neural circuitry supporting affective processing or affect regulation, this study highlighted the wealth of information that can be gleaned from longitudinal imaging genetic data.

Developmental imaging genetic approaches hold substantial promise in increasing our understanding of individual differences in the development of affective circuits and consequent individual differences in vulnerability to affective psychopathology. They may be particularly useful in providing a better understanding of "dormant vulnerabilities" and how such vulnerabilities may expose an individual to a maladaptive outcome when he or she experiences environmental risk.

A Case Study: Childhood Antisocial Behavior

Differences in several brain areas and information-processing functions associated with perception and the regulation of emotions have been implicated in adult populations with antisocial behavior (Blair, 2010). In particular, the OFC/ventral PFC, ACC, amygdala, and interconnected regions have shown both structural and functional abnormalities in these individuals (Blair, 2010). These abnormalities likely reflect both genetic vulnerability and environmental risk for antisocial behavior.

In children, both structural MRI and fMRI have only been available relatively recently for the study of antisocial behavior; as a result, only a handful of developmentally informative studies have been conducted to date. Findings from these studies are generally in line with studies of adult antisocial populations and indicate that abnormalities in several regions, including the amygdala, ACC, and OFC, are already observable in childhood (Sterzer & Stadler, 2009).

Imaging genetic research on adults suggests that genetic variants known to predispose to antisocial behavior, such as MAOA, also influence the structure and functioning of several key areas in the emotion processing circuitry, including the amygdala, ACC, and OFC (Buckholtz & Meyer-Lindenberg, 2009). In addition, research with child samples suggests that environmental risk factors known to predispose to antisocial behavior, such as maltreatment, also affect the structural development of the brain's affective circuitry, including the OFC (McCrory, DeBrito, & Viding, 2010).

It is clear from behavioral data that children who display antisocial behavior cannot be regarded as a homogeneous group (Viding, McCrory, Blakemore, & Frederickson, 2011). Affective neuroscience research can help establish whether there are distinct trajectories to antisocial behavior and whether they are underpinned by different neurocognitive vulnerabilities. Such research has the genuine scope to provide researchers and practitioners with a developmentally informed model of persistent antisocial behavior that can in turn shape approaches to intervention (Viding et al., 2011).

The current evidence base suggests that at least two subgroups of children with early-onset antisocial behavior can be delineated on the basis of their affective processing style; one characterized by emotional under-reactivity (callous-unemotional; CU+) and another by emotional over-reactivity (non-callous, CU−; Viding et al., 2011). Existing neuroimaging studies provide tentative support for this distinction (Sterzer & Stadler, 2009; Viding et al., 2011). A selective overview of some findings relating to amygdala functioning in children with antisocial behavior illustrates the current state of the field. Sterzer et al. (2005) were the first to conduct fMRI research in youth with antisocial behavior. They reported that as a group youth with antisocial behavior showed amygdala hypo-reactivity to passively viewed negative and threatening pictures, but this result emerged only when anxiety scores were used as a covariate. Another fMRI study using a similar paradigm found increased amygdala activation, partly related to comorbid anxiety, in children with antisocial behavior (Herpertz et al., 2008). A more recent study using emotional face stimuli found evidence of amygdala hypo-reactivity to sad, but hyper-reactivity to neutral faces in adolescents and young adults with antisocial behavior (Passamonti et al., 2010). In addition to these studies focusing on antisocial behavior in general, two studies to date have explicitly recruited antisocial children with CU+ and tested the hypothesis that this group would show amygdala hypo-reactivity

to others' distress (Jones, Laurens, Herba, Barker, & Viding, 2009; Marsh et al., 2008). Both studies employed an implicit emotion-processing task (gender recognition) and indeed found amygdala hypo-reactivity to fearful faces in antisocial children with CU+ compared to typically developing children and/or children with ADHD. This variable pattern of findings across studies and stimulus types warrants further investigation and may partly reflect the heterogeneous nature of the samples that have been studied. A recent study from our group demonstrated that amygdala activity to emotional stimuli can vary as a function of CU traits in children with antisocial behavior (Sebastian et al., 2012).

These preliminary findings from brain imaging studies are promising because they help illuminate the neurological basis of some of the affective differences found across the different developmental pathways to antisocial behavior (e.g., CU+ and CU−). For example, they can help make sense of the different patterns of antisocial behavior seen in the CU+ and CU− groups, with the CU+ group showing significantly more premeditated aggression and the CU− group having a predominant problem in controlling reactive aggression (Viding et al., 2011). Refining the affective neuroscience phenotypes for different subtypes of antisocial behavior is important in understanding the neurocognitive mechanisms through which inherited predispositions and environmental adversity can place a child at risk for the development of antisocial traits. Combining affective neuroscience data with other levels of analyses (e.g., genetics and the environment) and using longitudinal data offer great promise for advancing our knowledge of the different pathways to the same diagnostic outcome.

Environmental Influences on Affective Development

It is now well established from both animal and human studies that psychosocial stress and poor caregiving can have a significant impact on the developmental of stress regulatory systems and the affective circuitry (McCrory, De Brito & Viding, 2010). A growing body of research has investigated a number of environmental stressors, including experiences of physical, sexual, and emotional abuse as well as periods of extended maternal separation. This work highlights the key role that the caregiver plays in establishing the context in which the child's affective system develops. Indeed, the caregiver arguably acts as a scaffold to support the infant in monitoring and regulating the stress response and, over time, shapes how the infant calibrates his or her response to social affective cues. For example, studies have investigated how maltreatment and poor parental care can impact on the HPA axis and in turn increase an individual's vulnerability to later psychopathology. We review this evidence briefly, before considering how maltreatment might also lead to changes in those brain structures implicated in affective processing. We place particular emphasis on the importance of timing, highlighting how the affective circuitry may show differential vulnerability depending on when any maltreatment is experienced. Finally, we describe how physical abuse, as one example of an adverse environmental experience, can influence the functioning of the affective system. We suggest that, although adaptation of the affective system to early stress may be functional in the short term, such adaptation may have longer term costs leading to changes in the affective system that act to increase an individual's risk of psychopathology.

Stress, the HPA System, and Risk for Psychopathology

The HPA axis, a part of the neuroendocrine system, mediates the impact of stress on the affective circuitry (see Lupien, McEwen, Gunnar, & Heim, 2009, for a review). On detection of a threat, corticotrophin-releasing hormone (CRH) is released from the hypothalamus. This hormone targets the pituitary gland, which then releases adrenocorticotropic hormone (ACTH). This then stimulates the production of glucocorticoids (cortisol in humans) from the adrenal cortex. Feedback loops are present at a number of levels to modulate responsiveness of the HPA axis and return the system to homeostasis (Lupien et al., 2009).

Although adaptive in the short term, the chronic release of cortisol caused by long-term stressors can have maladaptive consequences. Peripheral cortisol is able to pass through the blood-brain barrier (Zarrow, Philpott, & Denenberg., 1970), meaning it is able to exert modulatory effects on neural circuitry. Regions such as the amygdala and hippocampus have a high density of glucocorticoid receptors and are therefore particularly responsive to fluctuating cortisol levels. For a full discussion of the effects of cortisol on these structures at different stages of development, see Tottenham and Sheridan (2010).

Evidence from animal studies are consistent in reporting atypical HPA axis functioning (either attenuated or exaggerated activity) after repeated or extended periods of maternal separation (Francis, Caldji, Champagne, Plotsky, & Meaney, 1999; Sanchez, Ladd, & Plotsky, 2001). However, studies with children and adolescents investigating the impact of maltreatment on HPA functioning are mixed (McCrory et al., 2010, for a review). For example, in one study of HPA axis response to CRH stimulus, Kaufman et al. (1997) reported ACTH hyper-responsiveness, but only among a subsample of maltreated children who were depressed and still exposed to a stressful home environment; no differences were found in cortisol measures. By contrast, Hart et al. (1995), in a study of preschoolers who had experienced maltreatment, reported a pattern of cortisol suppression in situations of stress that was associated with social competence. It is possible that hyper-responsivity is contingent on the presence of a current threatening environment.

It should also be noted that several studies of children with antisocial behavior have reported reduced basal cortisol concentrations and lower cortisol levels when exposed to stress (see van Goozen & Fairchild,

2008, for a comprehensive review). One possibility is that exposure to early adversity in these children is associated with stress habituation over time, a pattern that may be linked to their difficulties in emotional and behavioral regulation; equally, reduced stress responsivity may emerge as a result of genetic factors or gene–environment interactions (van Goozen & Fairchild, 2008). A recent meta-analysis has suggested that patterns of diurnal and morning cortisol levels may vary depending on the type of antisocial behavior, patterns of internalizing comorbidity, and early environmental adversity (Hawes, Brennan, & Dadds, 2009). In instances when parenting is compromised but where there is no maltreatment – for example, in the context of maternal depression – there appears to be a link with atypical HPA activity. Halligan and colleagues found that morning salivary cortisol in adolescents who had been exposed to maternal postnatal depression was elevated and more variable compared to nonexposed peers, a pattern associated with an increased risk of depression (Halligan, Herbert, Goodyer, & Murray, 2004).

There is now increasing support for the hypothesis that that the association between early adversity (in the form of compromised maternal care, including maltreatment) and a heightened risk for later psychopathology is associated with atypical HPA functioning (McCrory et al., 2010). For example, Heim and colleagues in a convincing review of the evidence make a strong case that childhood maltreatment increases the risk of developing depression in adulthood due to the sensitization of the HPA system (Heim, Newport, Mletzko, Miller, & Nemeroff, 2008). By contrast, increased risk for posttraumatic stress disorder (PTSD) may be associated with hypocortisolism; Meewisse and colleagues noted the relationship between lower cortisol levels and PTSD in the context of physical and sexual forms of abuse (Meewisse, Reitsma, De Vries, Gersons, & Olff, 2007). These findings indicate a possible dissociation, with HPA hypo-activity in those with maltreatment-related PTSD, but hyper-activity of the HPA system in maltreated individuals presenting with depression. Both effects may reflect adaptations of the HPA axis in response to different forms of maltreatment and perhaps different periods of onset and chronicity.

Maltreatment and Brain Structure: the Importance of Timing

A growing number of MRI and DTI studies have now been conducted both in children who have experienced maltreatment and in adults with histories of childhood abuse; this work, reviewed more fully elsewhere, provides evidence of measurable changes in both gray and white matter in these groups (McCrory et al., 2010, 2011). There is now reliable evidence that a reduction in the volume of the corpus callosum is associated with maltreatment; this white matter structure controls interhemispheric communication of a host of processes, including, but not limited to, arousal, emotion, and higher cognitive abilities (Giedd et al., 1996). Findings for the amygdala are more mixed. Although two recent studies have reported an increase in amygdala volumes (Mehta et al., 2009; Tottenham et al., 2010) a meta-analysis of children with maltreatment-related PTSD did not find significant differences between maltreated and non-maltreated children (Woon & Hedges, 2008). It is notable that increased amygdala volume has been reported in the context only of institutional rearing in infancy before being adopted into normative environments (Tottenham et al., 2010). These children were therefore likely to have been exposed to very early experiences of stress at a time when the amygdala was still structurally immature. This interpretation is consistent with findings from the animal literature. For example, in monkeys, maternal separation at 1 week of age had differential effects on behavior and gene expression patterns in the amygdala compared with maternal separation at 1 month (Sabatini et al., 2007), although both groups of separated monkeys showed aberrant social and emotional behavior relative to nonseparated monkeys. This finding suggests not only that the amygdala is sensitive to stress early in life but also that even a difference in timing of a few weeks is enough to produce measurable effects on its integrity. It is possible that such experience-dependent alterations to the amygdala's structure early in life play an adaptive role in preparing an individual for future adverse environments (Tottenham & Sheridan, 2010).

Evidence for structural differences in the prefrontal cortex after early adversity or maltreatment is more mixed (see McCrory et al., 2010, for a review). One study reported decreased volume of the OFC in a group of children and young adolescents who had experienced physical abuse, possibly over an extended time period (Hanson et al., 2010). Notably, smaller volumes in the right OFC observed in the physically abused children predicted greater problems in children's functioning across a range of social domains. This finding suggests that environmental adversity in the form of physical abuse is associated with structural changes in the affective circuitry and that these in turn have implications for the child's social and emotional functioning.

Each of these structures – the corpus callosum, the amygdala, and the OFC – are likely to be differentially susceptible to maltreatment and psychosocial stress depending on when the environmental stressor was experienced (e.g., Tottenham & Sheridan, 2010). We already know that the experience of maltreatment at different ages is likely to be associated with heightened risk for different forms of later psychopathology. In a study of adults who had experienced abuse or neglect in childhood, Kaplow and Widom (2007) reported that, whereas earlier maltreatment was associated with increased anxiety and depression in adulthood, later maltreatment was associated with increased behavioral problems. Although this study did not look at the neural underpinnings of these effects, it is likely that these differential outcomes are at least in part accounted for by the differential impact of psychosocial stress on brain development at different ages.

In other words, there is a strong likelihood that neural systems have sensitive peri-ods in development; that is, a time when a neural system or brain region is especially plastic and therefore more susceptible to environmental influence (Tottenham & Sheridan, 2010). Previously we noted that the impact of amygdala damage on affect perception was associated with the developmental timing of the lesion; the experience of maltreatment and environmental stress is likely to have a similar differential impact on brain development depending on the child's stage of development. A recent MRI study, for example, investigated the effects of sexual abuse on brain structure in women who had experienced abuse at varying ages (Andersen et al., 2008). Relative to controls, reduced hippocampal volumes were seen in young adult women who had experienced sexual abuse between the ages of 3 and 5 years, whereas frontal cortex volumes were reduced in those who had experienced abuse between the ages of 11 and 13 years of age. This finding fits with evidence regarding the developmental trajectories of these regions, with the hippocampus thought to be largely mature by age 4 (Giedd et al., 1996), whereas the PFC continues to develop into adolescence (Giedd et al., 1999; Gogtay et al., 2004). No group differences were seen in the amygdala, which is consistent with the view that the amygdala is particularly susceptible to environmental stress very early in life. By contrast, regions with a longer developmental trajectory such as the prefrontal cortex appear most susceptible later in development, such as during adolescence. This is one of the first studies to directly show unique windows of vulnerability for different brain regions following a common environmental stressor, in this case, sexual abuse.

A complicating factor in investigating the effects of stress at different ages is that they may not be immediately apparent and instead may emerge only later in development. For example, although most developmental indices improve once a child is adopted away from institutional care, one study found that children who had been adopted in infancy showed increased emotional problems at age 11 than at age 6 (Colvert et al., 2008). Another study showed that, although clinical depression is common in individuals who have experienced sexual abuse, the average length of time between the onset of abuse and the onset of depression is 11.5 years, with most cases of depression occurring during adolescence (Widom, DuMont, & Czaja, 2007). It may be that stress modifies the trajectory of connections during an "incubation period," after which the effects of stress are seen (Lupien et al. 2009). This line of argument might account for the discrepancy between a consistent pattern of reduced hippocampal volume in adults with maltreatment-related PTSD and the absence of such a pattern in children. In other words, it is possible that the hippocampal volume reduction evident in adults with histories of maltreatment is a delayed consequence of a chronic period of stress during childhood. Consistent with this hypothesis, Carrion and colleagues (2007) reported that cortisol levels and PTSD symptoms at baseline predicted the degree of hippocampal volume reduction over an ensuing 12- to 18-month interval in 15 maltreated children with PTSD (Carrion, Weems, & Reiss, 2007). Alternatively, it is possible that a smaller hippocampal volume is a predisposing risk factor for PTSD that is present in some individuals prior to any traumatic experience (Gilbertson et al., 2002). Longitudinal studies or studies taking advantage of identical twins discordant for maltreatment exposure are required to provide empirical support for incubation effects at the neural level and distinguish these kind of competing accounts.

Maltreatment and the Functioning of the Affective System

In addition to investigating the neuroendocrine and structural correlates of early adversity and maltreatment, researchers have studied how such experiences may lead to functional differences in the way that the affective system responds to social cues that vary in emotional valence. Children who have experienced physical abuse in particular have been reported to show a consistent pattern of facilitated or enhanced processing of anger. For example the work of

Pollak and colleagues has demonstrated that these children develop broader perceptual boundaries for categorizing anger (Pollak & Kistler, 2002), are able to identify angry facial expressions with less perceptual information than their peers, and accord greater attentional resources to the processing of angry faces (Pollak, Klorman, Thatcher, & Cicchetti, 2001). A recent fMRI study from our group has demonstrated that children who have experienced family violence show amygdala and anterior insula hyper reactivity to angry faces (McCrory et al., 2011). It is suggested that this pattern of differential responsiveness to anger may reflect an adaptation to an environment where these threat signals predict harm (Shackman, Shackman & Pollak, 2007). It is known that experiences of maltreatment are associated with a general increase in risk for psychopathology, including anxiety disorders. One possibility is that a pattern of hyper-vigilance to social threat cues in the environment (such as anger) may, at least in part, mediate the relationship between physical abuse and anxiety symptoms.

Pollak and colleagues have used event-related potentials (ERPs) to investigate this possibility. They examined the extent to which early traumatic experiences were associated with children's ability to regulate voluntary and involuntary attention to threat and how this in turn could account for levels of anxiety symptoms (Shackman et al., 2007). Relative to controls, abused children were found to over-attend to visual and auditory anger cues. For example, the presence of a task-irrelevant vocal anger cue (but not happiness or sadness) elicited a negative frontal ERP component, occurring at approximately 400 ms, that was larger in abused children than in controls. The N2 component has typically been interpreted to reflect enhanced cognitive control; therefore it is possible that, as a consequence of greater processing of auditory anger cues, abused children must exert greater cognitive control to resolve conflicting signals and maintain their attention on the task. Abused children also showed a greater 3Pb response to their mother's angry face and voice, which likely indexes greater voluntary processing of these potentially threatening cues. These higher 3Pb amplitudes were associated with higher levels of anxiety symptoms and in fact significantly mediated the relationship between the children's abuse experience and anxiety symptoms. This finding is important because it demonstrates that not only does early environmental adversity lead to an adaptation of the affective processing system at both the neural and behavioral levels but also that adaptation contributes directly to a heightened vulnerability for psychopathology.

In summary, there is accumulating evidence pointing to a variety of neurobiological changes associated with childhood maltreatment. Such changes can, on the one hand, be viewed as a cascade of deleterious effects that are harmful for the child; however, a more evolutionary and developmentally informed view would suggest that such changes are in fact adaptive responses to an early environment characterized by threat. If a child is to respond optimally to the challenges posed by his or her surroundings then early stress-induced changes in affective systems can be seen as a means of "programming" or calibrating those systems to match the demands of a hostile environment. From a clinical perspective, such adaptation may heighten vulnerability to psychopathology later in life, partly due to the changes in how emotional and cognitive systems mediate social interaction. For example, early-established patterns of hyper-vigilance, although adaptive in an unpredictable home environment, may be maladaptive in other settings, thus increasing vulnerability for behavioral, emotional, and social difficulties. Investigation of atypical affective neural development in populations of children exposed to such aversive early stress experiences provides one way to advance our understanding of the role and importance of early caregiving in shaping a child's affective development.

Conclusions

The neural circuitry associated with affective processing in children is becoming increasingly well delineated. This circuitry overlaps to a great extent with neural regions implicated in affective processing in adults; however, we have seen that affective processing and regulation tasks can elicit different patterns of activation depending on age. This is to be expected. There is now an extensive social and experimental psychological literature documenting the development of social and emotional processing across infancy, childhood, and adolescence. Integrating these data with emerging evidence from affective neuroscience research represents a core task for the next decade of research. We hope that this endeavor will not simply be characterized by the search for "neural correlates" of specific cognitive processes, but rather will reflect a mutual exchange of ideas and questions, with affective neuroscience serving to generate novel developmental hypotheses about how emotional capacities change across childhood. Conduct disorder is an example where neuroimaging is helping shed new light on an old problem. Specifically, the neuroimaging findings of atypical amygdala activation to distress in a subgroup of children with conduct problems are helping inform psychological and clinical models of antisocial behavior, including the emergence of psychopathy. However, further questions are raised by this research, including the degree to which any atypical patterns of activation reflect functional impairments or atypical processing styles that are capable of change.

The range of research in the field of developmental affective neuroscience increasingly acknowledges the complex interplay among genetic, neural, and environmental factors and the need to bear in mind that these interactions may vary depending on the age of the child. For example, we have seen that the impact of sexual abuse on neural structures may be contingent on the age at which it was experienced. Neural systems not only show global maturation across development but also there are regional variations in the rates of maturation of different brain regions, and specific environmental influences are likely to affect this maturation in different ways. This interaction in turn will be shaped by individual differences in genetic factors, such that not all children exposed to the same experience at the same time will be influenced in the same way.

It is worth noting the increasing emphasis on the functional integration of neural systems, rather than the functioning of specific regions. A more sophisticated model of how limbic and frontal systems interact, for example, is essential if we are to interpret our functional imaging findings in a more meaningful way. Research in the field of emotion regulation is pertinent in this regard, given that the concept of emotion regulation necessarily requires a consideration of regions that support both bottom-up and top-down processes.

Future research in this field faces several significant challenges. First, there is a need to develop a much more detailed "developmental map" of how affect processing and regulation typically change across development and how such maturational changes interface with the development of other cognitive and social processes. This work has started, but there is much still to do in relation to nearly all stages of development. Second, we need to develop a more sophisticated, ecologically valid, and relational set of paradigms. To date many studies have simply used visual stimuli to look at evocative effects of different forms of emotion. Although helpful in mapping the basic bottom-up processes, this approach tells us little about how affect is regulated and may be influenced by context, including the influence of current (and past) social interactions. Finally, we suggest the need for more longitudinal studies to examine the possible causal role that regions may play in relation to child functioning. Such longitudinal research has the potential to open up new approaches to intervention and indeed to prevention.

Outstanding Questions and Future Directions

- What are the developmental trajectories of affect processing and affect regulation? Longitudinal research on functional brain development is needed to better understand brain correlates of emotional development.
- What are the neural correlates of complex social interactions that often have considerable affective content? For example, we know relatively little about "real-life" affect regulation in children.
- Do atypical patterns of neural structure or function at one stage of development predict later impaired functioning or psychopathology? We currently have very limited information about "affective biomarkers" that may be important for understanding developmental vulnerability to psychopathology.

Acknowledgments

This work was supported by ESRC (RES-062–23-2202) and British Academy (BARDA 53229) grants to E. V. and an ESRC grant (RES-061–25-0189) to E. M. C. We thank Patricia Lockwood for her assistance in preparing this manuscript.

References

Adolphs, R. (2010). What does the amygdala contribute to social cognition? *Annals of the New York Academy of Sciences*, 1191, 42–61.

Adolphs, R., Tranel, D., Damasio, H., & Damasio, A. (1994). Impaired recognition of emotion in facial expressions following bilateral damage to the human amygdala. *Nature*, 372, 669–72.

Andersen, S. L., Tomada, A., Vincow, E. S., Valente, E., Polcari, A., & Teicher, M. H. (2008). Preliminary evidence for sensitive periods in the effect of childhood sexual abuse on regional brain development. *Journal of Neuropsychiatry and Clinical Neuroscience*, 20, 292–301.

Anderson, S. W., Bechara, A., Damasio, H., Tranel, D., & Damasio, A. R. (1999). Impairment of social and moral behavior related to early damage in human prefrontal cortex. *Nature Neuroscience*, 2, 1032–37.

Blair, R. J. (2010). Neuroimaging of psychopathy and antisocial behavior: A targeted review. *Current Psychiatry Reports*, 12, 76–82.

Bornstein, M. H., & Arterberry, M. E. (2003). Recognition, discrimination and categorization of smiling by 5-month-old infants. *Developmental Science*, 6, 585–99.

Braver, T. S., Cole, M. W., & Yarkoni, T. (2010). Vive les differences! Individual variation in neural mechanisms of executive control. *Current Opinions in Neurobiology*, 20(2), 242–50.

Buckholtz, J. W., & Meyer-Lindenberg, A. (2009) Gene-brain associations: The example of MAOA. In S. Hodgins & E. Viding (Eds.), *Persistent violent offenders: Neuroscience and rehabilitation* (pp. 265–86). Oxford: Oxford University Press.

Burnett, S., Bird, G., Moll, J., Frith, C., & Blakemore, S. J. (2009). Development during adolescence of the neural processing of social emotion. *Journal of Cognitive Neuroscience*, 21, 1736–50.

Carrion, V. G., Weems, C. F., & Reiss, A. L. (2007). Stress predicts brain changes in children: A pilot longitudinal study on youth stress, posttraumatic stress disorder, and the hippocampus. *Pediatrics*, 119, 509–16.

Cohen, J. R., Asarnow, R. F., Sabb, F. W., Bilder, R. M., Bookheimer, S. Y., Knowlton, B. J., & Poldrack, R. A. (2010). A unique adolescent response to reward prediction errors. *Nature Neuroscience*, 13, 669–71.

Colvert, E., Rutter, M., Kreppner, J., Beckett, C., Castle, J., Groothues, C., Hawkins, A.,...Sonuga-Bark, J. S. (2008). Do theory of mind and executive function deficits underlie the adverse outcomes associated with profound early deprivation? Findings from the English and Romanian adoptees study. *Journal of Abnormal Child Psychology*, 36(7), 1057–68.

Davidson, M. C., Amso, D., Anderson, L. C., & Diamond, A. (2006). Development of cognitive control and executive functions from 4 to 13 years: Evidence from manipulations of memory, inhibition, and task switching. *Neuropsychologia*, 44, 2037–78.

Davidson, R., & Irwin, W. (1999). The functional neuroanatomy of emotion and affective style. *Trends in Cognitive Sciences*, 3(1), 11–21.

Davidson, R. J., Jackson, D. C., & Kalin, N. H. (2000). Emotion, plasticity, context, and regulation: Perspectives from affective neuroscience. *Psychological Bulletin*, 126(6), 890–909.

Eshel, N., Nelson, E. E., Blair, R. J., Pine, D. S., & Ernst, M. (2007). Neural substrates of choice selection in adults and adolescents: Development of the ventrolateral prefrontal and ante-

rior cingulate cortices. *Neuropsychologia*, 45, 1270–79.

Fonagy, P., Gergely, G., Jurist, E., & Target, M. (2002). *Affect regulation, mentalization and the development of the self.* New York: Other Press

Francis, D. D., Caldji, C., Champagne, F., Plotsky, P. M., & Meaney, M. J. (1999). The Role of corticotrophin-releasing factor–norepinepherine systems in mediating the effects of early experience on the development of behavioral and endocrine Responses to stress. *Biological Psychiatry*, 46(9), 1153–66.

Fusar-Poli, P., Placentino, A., Carletti, F., Landi, P., Allen, P., Surguladze, S.,...Politi, P. (2009). Functional atlas of emotional faces processing: A voxel-based meta-analysis of 105 functional magnetic resonance imaging studies. *Journal of Psychiatry and Neuroscience*, 34, 418–32.

Gerardi-Caulton, G. (2000). Sensitivity to spatial conflict and the development of self-regulation in children 24–36 months of age. *Developmental Science*, 3, 397–404.

Giedd, J. N., Blumenthal, J., Jeffries, N. O., Castellanos, F. X., Liu, H., Zijdenbos, A.,...Rapoport, J. L. (1999). Brain development during childhood and adolescence: A longitudinal MRI study. *Nature Neuroscience*, 2, 861–63.

Giedd, J. N., Rumsey, J. M., Castellanos, F.X., Rajapakse, J.C., Kaysen, D., Vaituzis, A. C.,...Rapoport, J. L. (1996). A quantitative MRI study of the corpus callosum in children and adolescents. *Developmental Brain Research*, 91, 274–80.

Gilbertson, M. W., Shenton, M. E., Ciszewski, A., Kasai, K., Lasko, N. B., Orr, S. P., & Pitman, R. K. (2002). Smaller hippocampal volume predicts pathologic vulnerability to psychological trauma. *Nature Neuroscience*, 5, 1242–47.

Gogtay, N., Giedd, J. N., Lusk, L., Hayashi, K. M., Greenstein, D., Vaituzis, A. C.,...Thompson, P. M. (2004). Dynamic mapping of human cortical development during childhood through early adulthood. *Proceedings of the National Academy of Sciences*, 101, 8174–79.

Gross, J. J. (1998). The emerging field of emotion regulation: An integrative review. *Review of General Psychology*, 2, 271–299.

Gullone, E., Hughes, E. K., King, N. J., & Tonge, B. (2010). The normative development of emotion regulation strategy use in children and adolescents: A 2-year follow-up study.

Journal of Child Psychology and Psychiatry, 51, 567–74.

Guyer, A. E., McClure-Tone, E. B., Shiffrin, N. D., Pine, D. S., & Nelson, E. E. (2009). Probing the neural correlates of anticipated peer evaluation in adolescence. *Child Development*, 80(4), 1000–15.

Guyer, A. E., Monk, C. S., Clure-Tone, E. B., Nelson, E. E., Roberson-Nay, R., Adler, A. D.,... Ernst, M. (2008). A developmental examination of amygdala response to facial expressions. *Journal of Cognitive Neuroscience*, 20, 1565–82.

Halligan, S. L., Herbert, J., Goodyer, I. M., & Murray, L. (2004). Exposure to postnatal depression predicts elevated cortisol in adolescent offspring. *Biological Psychiatry*, 55(4), 376–81.

Hamann, S. B., Stefanacci, L., Squire, L. R., Adolphs, R., Tranel, D., Damasio, H., & Damasio, A. (1996). Recognizing facial emotion. *Nature*, 379, 497.

Hanson, J. L., Chung, M. K., Avants, B. B., Shirtcliff, E. A., Gee, J. C., Davidson, R. J., & Pollak, S. D. (2010). Early stress is associated with alterations in the orbitofrontal cortex: A tensor-based morphometry investigation of brain structure and behavioral risk. *Journal of Neuroscience*, 30, 7466–72.

Hare, T. A., Tottenham, N., Galvan, A., Voss, H. U., Glover, G. H., & Casey, B. J. (2008). Biological substrates of emotional reactivity and regulation in adolescence during an emotional go-no go task. *Biological Psychiatry*, 63, 927–34.

Hart, J., Gunnar, M., & Cicchetti, D. (1995). Salivary cortisol in maltreated children: evidence of relations between neuroendocrine activity and social competence. *Development and Psychopathology*, 7, 11–26.

Hawes, D. J., Brennan, J., & Dadds, M. R. (2009). Cortisol, callous-unemotional traits, and pathways to antisocial behavior. *Current Opinion in Psychiatry*, 22(4), 357–62.

Heim, C., Newport, D. J., Mletzko, T., Miller, A. H., & Nemeroff, C. B. (2008). The link between childhood trauma and depression: Insights from HPA axis studies in humans. *Psychoneuroendocrinology*, 33, 693–710.

Herba, C., & Phillips, M. (2004). Annotation: Development of facial expression recognition from childhood to adolescence: Behavioral and neurological perspectives. *Journal of Child Psychology and Psychiatry*, 45, 1185–98.

Herpertz, S. C., Huebner, T., Marx, I., Vloet, T. D., Fink, G. R., Stoecker, T., Shah, N.

J.,... Herpertz-Dahlmann, B. (2008). Emotional processing in male adolescents with childhood-onset conduct disorder. *Journal of Child Psychology and Psychiatry*, 49(7), 781–91.

Johnson, M. H. (2005). Subcortical face processing. *Nature Reviews Neuroscience*, 6, 766–74.

Jones, A. P., Laurens, K. R., Herba, C. M., Barker, G. J., & Viding, E. (2009). Amygdala hypoactivity to fearful faces in boys with conduct problems and callous-unemotional traits. *American Journal of Psychiatry*, 166(1), 95–102.

Kaplow, J. B. & Widom, C. S. (2007) Age of onset of child maltreatment predicts long-term mental health outcomes. *Journal of Abnormal Psychology*, 116(1), 176–87.

Kaufman, J., Birmaher, B., Perel, J., Dahl, R. E., Moreci, P., Nelson, B.,... Ryan, N. D. (1997). The corticotropin-releasing hormone challenge in depressed abused, depressed nonabused, and normal control children. *Biological Psychiatry*, 42(8), 669–79.

Kédia, G., Berthoz, S., Wessa, M., Hilton, D., & Martinot, J.-L. (2008). An agent harms a victim: A functional magnetic resonance imaging study on specific moral emotions. *Journal of Cognitive Neuroscience*, 20(10), 1788–98.

Kestenbaum, R., & Nelson, C. A. (2010). The recognition and categorization of upright and inverted emotional expressions by 7-month-old infants. *Infant Behavior and Development*, 13, 497–511.

Killgore, W. D., Oki, M., & Yurgelun-Todd, D. A. (2001). Sex-specific developmental changes in amygdala responses to affective faces. *Neuroreport*, 12, 427–33.

Larsen, J. T., To, Y. M., & Fireman, G. (2007). Children's understanding and experience of mixed emotions. *Psychological Science*, 18, 186–91.

Lau, J. Y. F., Goldman, D., Buzas, B., Fromm, S. J., Guyer, A. E., Monk, C. S., Nelson, E. E.,... Ernst, M. (2009). Amygdala function and 5-HTT gene variants in adolescent anxiety and major depressive disorder. *Anxiety*, 65(4), 349–55.

Leppanen, J. M., & Nelson, C. A. (2009). Tuning the developing brain to social signals of emotions. *Nature Reviews Neuroscience*, 10, 37–47.

Levesque, J., Eugene, F., Joanette, Y., Paquette, V., Mensour, B., Beaudoin, G.,... Beauregard, M. (2003). Neural circuitry underlying voluntary suppression of sadness. *Biological Psychiatry*, 53, 502–10.

Levesque, J., Joanette, Y., Mensour, B., Beaudoin, G., Leroux, J. M., Bourgouin, P. &

Beauregard, M. (2004). Neural basis of emotional self-regulation in childhood. *Neuroscience*, 129, 361–69.

Lewis, M. D., Lamm, C., Segalowitz, S. J., Stieben, J., & Zelazo, P. D. (2006). Neurophysiological correlates of emotion regulation in children and adolescents. *Journal of Cognitive Neuroscience*, 18, 430–43.

Lewis, M. D., & Stieben, J. (2004). Emotion regulation in the brain: Conceptual issues and directions for developmental research. *Child Development*, 75, 371–76.

Luna, B., Thulborn, K. R., Munoz, D. P., Merriam, E. P., Garver, K. E., Minshew, N. J., . . . Sweeney, J. A. (2001). Maturation of widely distributed brain function subserves cognitive development. *Neuroimage*, 13, 786–93.

Lupien, S. J., McEwen, B. S., Gunnar, M. R., & Heim, C. (2009). Effects of stress throughout the lifespan on the brain, behavior and cognition. *Nature Reviews. Neuroscience*, 10(6), 434–45.

Marsh, A. A., Finger, E. C., Mitchell, D. G. V., Reid, M. E., Sims, C., Kosson, D. S., Towbin, K. E., et al. (2008). Reduced amygdala response to fearful expressions in children and adolescents with callous-unemotional traits and disruptive behavior disorders. *American Journal of Psychiatry*, 165(6), 712–20.

McClure, E. B. (2000). A meta-analytic review of sex differences in facial expression processing and their development in infants, children, and adolescents. *Psychological Bulletin*, 126, 424–53.

McClure, E. B., Monk, C. S., Nelson, E. E., Zarahn, E., Leibenluft, E., Bilder, R. M., . . . Pine, D. S. (2004). A developmental examination of gender differences in brain engagement during evaluation of threat. *Biological Psychiatry*, 55, 1047–55.

McCrory, E. J., De Brito, S. A., Sebastian, C. L., Mechelli, A., Bird, G., Kelly, P. A., & Viding, E. (2011). Heightened neural reactivity to threat in child victims of family violence. *Current Biology*, 21(23), R947–R948.

McCrory, E., De Brito, S. A., & Viding, E. (2010). Research review: The neurobiology and genetics of maltreatment and adversity. *Journal of Child Psychology and Psychiatry*, 10, 1079–95.

McCrory, E., De Brito, S. A., & Viding, E. (2011). The impact of childhood maltreatment: A review of neurobiological and genetic factors. *Frontiers in Psychiatry*, 2, 48.

McGivern, R. F., Andersen, J., Byrd, D., Mutter, K. L., & Reilly, J. (2002). Cognitive efficiency on a match to sample task decreases at the onset of puberty in children. *Brain and Cognition*, 50, 73–89.

Mechelli, A., Tognin, S., McGuire, P. K., Prata, D., Sartori, G., Fusar-Poli, P., De Brito, S., Hariri, A. R., Viding, E. (2009). Genetic Vulnerability to Affective Psychopathology in Childhood: A Combined Voxel-Based Morphometry and Functional Magnetic Resonance Imaging Study. *Biol Psychiatry* 66(3), 231–237.

Meewisse, M. L., Reitsma, J. B., De Vries, G. J., Gersons, B. P. R., & Olff, M. (2007). Cortisol and post-traumatic stress disorder in adults: Systematic review and metaanalysis. *British Journal of Psychiatry*, 191, 387–92.

Mehta, M. A, Golembo, N. I., Nosarti, C., Colvert, E., Mota, A., Williams, S. C., . . . Sonuga-Barke, E. (2009). Amygdala, hippocampal and corpus callosum size following severe early institutional deprivation: The English and Romanian Adoptees study pilot. *Journal of Child Psychology and Psychiatry*, 50(8), 943–51.

Mitchell, D. G. V. (2011). The nexus between decision making and emotion regulation: A review of convergent neurocognitive substrates. *Behavioral Brain Research*, 217(1), 215–31.

Mitchell, D. G. V., Richell, R. A., Pine, D., & Blair, R. J. R. (2008). The contribution of ventrolateral and dorsolateral prefrontal cortex to response reversal. *Behavioral Brain Research*, 187(1), 80–87.

Minagawa-Kawai, Y., Matsuoka, S., Dan, I., Naoi, N., Nakamura, K., & Kojima, S. (2009). Prefrontal activation associated with social attachment: Facial-emotion recognition in mothers and infants. *Cerebral Cortex*, 19, 284–92.

Monk, C. S., McClure, E. B., Nelson, E. E., Zarahn, E., Bilder, R. M., Leibenluft, E., et al. (2003). Adolescent immaturity in attention-related brain engagement to emotional facial expressions. *Neuroimage*, 20, 420–28.

Nelson, C. A., & de Haan. M. (1996). Neural correlates of infants' visual responsiveness to facial expressions of emotion. *Developmental Psychobiology*, 29, 577–95.

Nelson, C. A., Morse, P. A., & Leavitt, L. A. (1979). Recognition of facial expressions by seven-month-old infants. *Child Development*, 50, 1239–42.

Nelson, E. E., Leibenluft, E., McClure, E. B., & Pine, D. S. (2005). The social re-orientation of adolescence: A neuroscience perspective on the process and its relation to psychopathology. *Psychological Medicine*, 35, 163–74.

Ochsner, K. N., & Gross, J. J. (2005). The cognitive control of emotion. *Trends in Cognitive Sciences*, 9, 242–49.

O'Doherty, J. P. (2004). Reward representations and reward-related learning in the human brain: Insights from neuroimaging. *Current Opinions in Neurobiology*, 14(6), 769–76.

Passamonti, L., Fairchild, G., Goodyer, I. M., Hurford, G., Hagan, C. C., Rowe, J. B., & Calder, A. J. (2010) Neural abnormalities in early-onset and adolescence-onset conduct disorder. *Archives of General Psychiatry*, 67(7), 729–38.

Paus, T., Keshavan, M., & Giedd, J. N. (2008). Why do many psychiatric disorders emerge during adolescence? *Nature Reviews Neuroscience*, 9, 947–57.

Peltola, M. J., Leppanen, J. M., Palokangas, T., & Hietanen, J. K. (2008). Fearful faces modulate looking duration and attention disengagement in 7-month-old infants. *Developmental Science*, 11, 60–68.

Peters, J., & Büchel, C. (2010). Episodic future thinking reduces reward delay discounting through an enhancement of prefrontal-medio-temporal interactions. *Neuron*, 66(1), 138–48.

Posner, M. I., & Rothbart, M. K. (2000). Developing mechanisms of self-regulation. *Development and Psychopathology*, 12, 427–41.

Pollak, S. D., Cicchetti, D., Klorman, R., & Brumaghim, J. T. (1997). Cognitive brain event-related potentials and emotion processing in maltreated children. *Child Development*, 68, 773–87.

Pollak, S. D., & Kistler, D. J. (2002). Early experience is associated with the development of categorical representations for facial expressions of emotion. *Proceedings of the National Academy of Sciences*, 99, 9072–76.

Pollak, S. D., Klorman, R., Thatcher, J. E., & Cicchetti, D. (2001). P3b reflects maltreated children's reactions to facial displays of emotion. *Psychophysiology* 38, 267–74.

Reynolds, G. D., & Richards, J. E. (2005). Familiarization, attention, and recognition memory in infancy: An event-related potential and cortical source localization study. *Developmental Psychology*, 41, 598–615.

Rolls, E. T., & Grabenhorst, F. (2008). The orbitofrontal cortex and beyond: From affect to decision-making. *Progress in Neurobiology*, 86(3), 216–44.

Rosen, H. J., & Levenson, R. W. (2009). The emotional brain: Combining insights from patients and basic science. *Neurocase*, 15(3), 173–81.

Rushworth, M. F. S., Behrens, T. E. J., Rudebeck, P. H., & Walton, M. E. (2007). Contrasting roles for cingulate and orbitofrontal cortex in decision and social behavior. *Trends in Cognitive Sciences*, 11, 168–76.

Sabatini, M. J., Ebert, P., Lewis, D. A, Levitt, P., Cameron, J. L., & Mirnics, K. (2007). Amygdala gene expression correlates of social behavior in monkeys experiencing maternal separation. *Journal of Neuroscience*, 27(12), 3295–3304.

Sánchez, M. M., Ladd, C. O., & Plotsky, P. M. (2001). Early adverse experience as a developmental risk factor for later psychopathology: Evidence from rodent and primate models. *Development and Psychopathology*, 13, 419–49.

Schumann, C. M., Hamstra, J., Goodlin-Jones, B. L., Lotspeich, L. J., Kwon, H., Buonocore, M. H., ... Amaral, D. G. (2004). The amygdala is enlarged in children but not adolescents with autism; the hippocampus is enlarged at all ages. *Journal of Neuroscience*, 24, 6392–6401.

Sebastian, C. L., Fontaine, N. M. G., Bird, G., Blakemore, S.-J., De Brito, S. A., McCrory, E. J. P., & Viding, E. (2012). Neural processing associated with cognitive and affective Theory of Mind in adolescents and adults. *Social Cognitive and Affective Neuroscience*, 7(1), 53-63. doi: 10.1093/scan/nsr023

Sebastian, C. L., McCrory, E. J., Cecil, C. A., Lockwood, P. L., De Brito, S. A., Fontaine, N. M., & Viding, E. (2012). Neural responses to affective and cognitive theory of mind in children with conduct problems and varying levels of callous-unemotional traits. *Archives of General Psychiatry*, 69(8), 814–22.

Sebastian, C. L., Tan, G. C. Y., Roiser, J. P., Viding, E., Dumontheil, I., & Blakemore, S. J. (2011). Developmental influences on the neural bases of responses to social rejection: Implications of social neuroscience for education. *Neuroimage*, 57(3), 686–94.

Sergerie, K., Chochol, C., & Armony, J. L. (2008). The role of the amygdala in emotional processing: A quantitative meta-analysis of functional neuroimaging studies. *Neuroscience and Biobehavioral Reviews*, 32(4), 811–30.

Shackman, J. E., Shackman, A. J., & Pollak, S. D. (2007). Physical abuse amplifies attention to threat and increases anxiety in children. *Emotion*, 7(4), 838–52.

Shaw, P., Kabani, N. J., Lerch, J. P., Eckstrand, K., Lenroot, R., Gogtay, N.,... Wise, S. P. (2008). Neurodevelopmental trajectories of the human cerebral cortex. *Journal of Neuroscience*, 28, 3586–94.

Shaw, P., Lalonde, F., Lepage, C., Rabin, C., Eckstrand, K., Sharp, W., Greenstein, D.,... Rapoport, J. (2009). Development of cortical asymmetry in typically developing children and its disruption in attention-deficit/hyperactivity disorder. *Archives of General Psychiatry*, 66(8), 888–96.

Somerville, L. H., & Casey, B. J. (2010). Developmental neurobiology of cognitive control and motivational systems. *Current Opinions in Neurobiology*, 20, 236–41.

Sterzer, P., & Stadler, C. (2009). Neuroimaging of aggressive and violent behavior in children and adolescents. *Frontiers in Behavioral Neuroscience*, 3(35), 1–8.

Sterzer, P., Stadler, C., Krebs, A., Kleinschmidt, A., & Poustka, F. (2005). Abnormal neural responses to emotional visual stimuli in adolescents with conduct disorder. *Biological Psychiatry*, 57(1), 7–15.

Takakahashi, H., Yahata, N., Koeda, M., Matsuda, T., Asai, K., & Okubo, Y. (2004). Brain activation associated with evaluative processes of guilt and embarrassment: An fMRI study. *Neuroimage*, 23, 967–74.

Thomas, K. M., Drevets, W. C., Whalen, P. J., Eccard, C. H., Dahl, R. E., Ryan, N. D., et al. (2001). Amygdala response to facial expressions in children and adults. *Biological Psychiatry*, 49, 309–16.

Thomas, L. A., De Bellis, M. D., Graham, R., & LaBar, K. S. (2007). Development of emotional facial recognition in late childhood and adolescence. *Developmental Science*, 10, 547–58.

Thompson, R. (1994). Emotion regulation: A theme in search of a definition. In N. A. Fox (Ed.), *Emotion regulation: Biological and behavioral considerations. Monographs of the Society for Research in Child Development* (pp. 25–52). Chicago: University of Chicago Press.

Tottenham, N., Hare, T. A., Quinn, B. T., McCarry, T. W., Nurse, M., Gilhooly, T.,... Casey, B. J. (2010). Prolonged institutional rearing is associated with atypically large amygdala volume and difficulties in emotion regulation. *Developmental Science*, 13(1), 46–61.

Tottenham, N., & Sheridan, M. A. (2010). A review of adversity, the amygdala and the hippocampus: A consideration of developmental timing. *Frontiers in Human Neuroscience*, 3(68), 1–18.

van Goozen, S. H. M., & Fairchild, G. (2008). How can the study of biological processes help design new interventions for children with severe antisocial behavior? *Development and Psychopathology*, 20(3), 941–73.

Van Leijenhorst, L., Zanolie, K., Van Meel, C. S., Westenberg, P. M., Rombouts, S. A. R. B., & Crone, E. A. (2010). What motivates the adolescent? Brain regions mediating reward sensitivity across adolescence. *Cerebral Cortex*, 20, 61–69.

Viding, E., McCrory, E. J., Blakemore, S.-J., & Frederickson, N. (2011). Behavioral problems and bullying at school: Can cognitive neuroscience shed new light on an old problem? *Trends in Cognitive Sciences*, 15(7), 289–91.

Vuilleumier, P., & Pourtois, G. (2007). Distributed and interactive brain mechanisms during emotion face perception: Evidence from functional neuroimaging. *Neuropsychologia*, 45(1), 174–94.

Wager, T. D., Davidson, M. L., Hughes, B. L., Lindquist, M. A., & Ochsner, K. N. (2008). Prefrontal-subcortical pathways mediating successful emotion regulation. *Neuron*, 59, 1037–50.

Widom, C. S., DuMont, K., & Czaja, S. J. (2007). A prospective investigation of major depressive disorder and comorbidity in abused and neglected children grown up. *Archives of General Psychiatry*, 64(1), 49–56.

Woon, F. L., & Hedges, D. W. (2008). Hippocampal and amygdala volumes in children and adults with childhood maltreatment-related posttraumatic stress disorder: A meta-analysis. *Hippocampus*, 18, 729–36.

Zarrow, M. X., Philpott, J. E., & Denenberg, V. H. (1970). Passage of 14-C-4 corticosterone from the rat mother to the fetus and neonate. *Nature*, 226, 1058–59.

CHAPTER 28

Emotion and Aging

Linking Neural Mechanisms to Psychological Theory

Peggy L. St. Jacques, Amy Winecoff, & Roberto Cabeza

As we age, our cognitive abilities decline steadily, in parallel with the gradual deterioration of brain anatomy and physiology (Dennis & Cabeza, 2008). Yet, there is at least one domain in which healthy older adults can match or even surpass younger adults: emotional well-being. Despite mounting challenges in many domains – including deficits in vision, audition, and memory; reduced mobility and physical health; and the death of relatives and friends – most healthy elderly are surprisingly well adjusted at the emotional level. Several psychological theories have been proposed to account for this counterintuitive phenomenon, and they have inspired a substantial amount of behavioral research (for a review, see Scheibe & Carstensen, 2010). More recently, age-related changes in emotional processing have become the focus of an increasing number of functional neuroimaging studies, which have identified substantial differences between the neural mechanisms of how young and older individuals perceive, remember, make decisions about, and regulate emotional materials. The goal of this chapter is to review the main findings of these functional neuroimaging studies and to link them to theories regarding aging effects on emotional processing.

The chapter has three main sections. The first section summarizes evidence for two cognitive neuroscience accounts of preserved emotional processing in old age: anatomical preservation and functional compensation. The second section, which is the core of the chapter, reviews behavioral and functional neuroimaging studies on the effects of aging in the domains of emotional perception, emotional memory, emotional decision making, and emotion regulation. Despite different paradigms and stimuli, these studies show a consistent pattern whereby aging is associated with an increase in frontal activity that is sometimes coupled with decreases in amygdalar responses to negative stimuli. We call this pattern the *frontoamygdalar age-related differences in emotion* (FADE) and suggest possible interpretations of this pattern. The final section of the chapter considers the links between functional neuroimaging findings and psychological theories regarding older adults' emotional well-being.

Two Accounts of Spared Emotional Processing in Old Age

The fact that emotional processing is relatively spared by aging is surprising,. given evidence of substantial neural decline in healthy aging (for a review, see Dennis & Cabeza, 2008). One possible explanation is that age-related anatomical deterioration is less pronounced in the brain regions mediating emotional processing (*anatomical preservation hypothesis*). Another possible explanation is that age-related anatomical and physiological decline is partly counteracted by compensatory increases in brain activity (*functional compensation hypothesis*). Evidence for these two hypotheses, which are not incompatible with each other, is reviewed next.

Anatomical Preservation

Age-related anatomical decline is most pronounced in the lateral prefrontal cortex (PFC). The lateral PFC shows the steepest rate of age-related atrophy (Raz et al., 2005), and this atrophy has been linked to cognitive deficits, particularly in executive functions (Gunning-Dixon & Raz, 2003). Age-related atrophy is also substantial in the hippocampus (e.g., Raz, 2005), which also shows age-related reductions in memory-related brain activity (for a review, see Dennis et al., 2008). In contrast with the decline of regions mediating executive and memory functions, brain regions supporting emotional and reward processing, such as the amygdala, ventral striatum, and the medial PFC (O'Doherty, 2004; Phan, Wager, Taylor, & Liberzon, 2002) are relatively well preserved in healthy older adults.

AMYGDALA
The amygdala has been associated with the automatic detection of emotions, as well as with the generation of emotion and associated physiological responses (Phelps, 2006). It is also assumed to mediate emotional modulation of perception, emotion, and decision making, an idea consistent with dense anatomical connections between this

structure and visual cortex, the medial temporal lobes, and the frontal lobes (Amaral & Price, 1984).

The structural integrity of the amygdala remains relatively preserved in aging (Brabec et al., 2010; Cherubini, Peran, Caltagirone, Sabatini, & Spalletta, 2009). Although a few studies have reported age-related volume reductions (Mu, Xie, Wen, Weng, & Shuyun, 1999), this effect has been attributed to the inclusion of white matter within the amygdalar region of interest (Brabec et al., 2010). In contrast with healthy aging, substantial amygdalar atrophy has been found in individuals with Alzheimer's disease (AD) or at genetic risk for AD (Honea, Vidoni, Harsha, & Burns, 2009).

STRIATUM
The striatum can be divided into the dorsal striatum, which includes the caudate and putamen nuclei, and the ventral striatum, which includes the nucleus accumbens. In addition to important contributions to motor and executive functions, the striatum has been associated with the processing of reward (see Chapter 19). Unlike the amygdala, striatal nuclei have been associated with substantial atrophy in healthy aging (Cherubini et al., 2009). Whereas the dorsal striatum, particularly the caudate, shows substantial shrinkage as a function of aging (Raz et al., 2003), there is evidence that the ventral striatum shows very little age-related atrophy (Cherubini et al., 2009).

It is worth noting, however, that the striatum is affected by considerable age-related decline in dopamine function, including reductions in dopamine receptors (e.g., Antonini & Leenders, 1993; Wang et al., 1998) and dopamine transporter (e.g., van Dyck et al., 1995). Dopamine decline plays a major role in age-related cognitive deficits and has been strongly linked to reductions in episodic memory and executive function (e.g., Erixon-Lindroth et al., 2005). Substantial decline in dopamine function leads to the prediction that striatal contributions to reward processing are likely to be disrupted by aging (Mohr, Li, & Heekeren, 2009), even if the anatomical integrity of the ventral striatum is relatively well preserved in older adults.

MEDIAL PREFRONTAL CORTEX

In contrast with more automatic emotional processing in the amygdala and striatum, the PFC is assumed to mediate emotional control processes (Ochsner & Gross, 2005; Chapter 16). Lateral PFC regions (Brodmann's areas – BAs 44/46, 46/9), which are strongly associated with executive functions (Miller & Cohen, 2001), have been linked to deliberate emotion regulation strategies, such as reappraisal (Ochsner & Gross, 2005). For example, ventrolateral PFC (VLPFC) regions tend to be recruited when participants try to down-regulate emotions using semantic elaboration strategies (Ochsner, Bunge, Gross, & Gabrieli, 2002). In contrast, medial PFC regions (BA 10) – which, for simplicity in this chapter, we consider as comprising also the most anterior aspect of the anterior cingulate cortex (ACC; BA 32, 24) – are assumed to be involved in less deliberate forms of emotional control (Ochsner & Gross, 2007). Within the medial PFC, BA 10 has been associated with *self-referential processing* (Amodio & Frith, 2006), which refers to relating information to one's self, such as internal feelings and thoughts. For example, this region shows greater activity when participants judge themselves or close others than when they judge other people (Krienen, Tu, & Buckner, 2010), or when participants process event information from the perspective of the self versus the other (St. Jacques, Conway, Lowder, & Cabeza, 2011). The medial PFC is part of the default network, which is a set of regions that tend to be deactivated during attention-demanding tasks and have been attributed to inward-direct attention, such as emotions and memories (Andrews-Hanna, Reidler, Sepulcre, Poulin, & Buckner, 2010).

Whereas lateral PFC regions shows substantial decline in older adults, some evidence suggests that some medial PFC regions are relatively well preserved in old age (e.g., Salat, Kaye, & Janowsky, 2001). If the relative preservation of the medial PFC is confirmed, it would be consistent with the evidence reviewed later that older adults rely more on these regions than young adults during emotional processing. At any rate, emotional and reward processing in older adults reflects not only the anatomical and physiological integrity of various brain regions but also older adults' ability to recruit these regions or to compensate for their anatomical and physiological decline by relying on different strategies and over-recruiting other brain regions.

Functional Compensation

In addition to the relative preservation of some regions such as the amygdala, ventral striatum, and medial PFC, another factor explaining spared emotional processing in healthy aging is functional compensation. Functional neuroimaging studies have shown that, whereas some brain regions tend to show weaker activity in older than younger adults, other brain regions, such as the PFC, often show increased activity with aging (Dennis & Cabeza, 2008). Several researchers have proposed that age-related PFC over-recruitment could help counteract neural decline (Cabeza et al., 1997; Grady et al., 1994; Reuter-Lorenz et al., 2000). Rather than focusing on functional compensation in the emotion domain, which is considered later in the chapter, the following subsections focus on two forms of PFC over-recruitment in older adults that have been observed in many cognitive domains and linked to functional compensation: the posterior-anterior shift with aging (PASA) and the hemispheric asymmetry reduction in older adults (HAROLD). These two domain-general patterns provide a useful background for evaluating the possible compensatory role of PFC over-recruitment in the emotion domain (i.e., FADE).

POSTERIOR-ANTERIOR SHIFT IN AGING

The *posterior-anterior shift in aging* or PASA (Davis, Dennis, Daselaar, Fleck, & Cabeza, 2008; Dennis & Cabeza, 2008) refers to age-related decreases in occipital activity coupled with an age-related increase in PFC activity. This pattern has been observed in many cognitive domains, including perception, attention, working memory, problem solving, and episodic memory encoding and memory retrieval (Dennis & Cabeza, 2008). PASA was first reported by Grady et al. (1994), who suggested that older adults compensated for visual processing deficits (occipital decrease) by recruiting higher order cognitive processes (PFC increase). Consistent with the compensation hypothesis, there is evidence that the PFC increase in older adults is positively correlated with cognitive performance and negatively correlated with the occipital decrease (Davis et al., 2008).

HEMISPHERIC ASYMMETRY REDUCTION IN OLDER ADULTS (HAROLD)

The second brain activity pattern in older adults found consistently across cognitive domains is a more bilateral (less asymmetric) pattern of PFC activity. This pattern, which is known as the *hemispheric asymmetry reduction in OLDer adults* (HAROLD) has been reported in the domains of perception, attention, working memory, episodic memory encoding and memory retrieval, and inhibitory control (Cabeza, 2002) The HAROLD pattern was originally described by Cabeza et al. (1997) and was also attributed to a compensatory mechanism. This *compensation account* is consistent with evidence that bilateral activity in older adults is positively correlated with successful cognitive performance (Reuter-Lorenz et al., 2000) and is found in high-performing rather than in low-performing older adults (Cabeza, 2002). The alternative *dedifferentiation account* is that HAROLD reflects an age-related difficulty in engaging specialized neural mechanisms (e.g., Logan, Sanders, Snyder, Morris, & Buckner, 2002). In general, the available evidence tends to be more consistent with the compensation than with the dedifferentiation account (Dennis & Cabeza, 2008).

Summary of Current Accounts

In this first section, we considered evidence for two cognitive neuroscience accounts of

spared emotional processing in old age: the anatomical preservation hypothesis and the functional compensation hypothesis. Both hypotheses have some empirical support. The anatomical preservation hypothesis is consistent with evidence that, in contrast with substantial atrophy in lateral PFC regions, the structural integrity of emotional processing regions such as the amygdala, ventral striatum, and medial PFC is relatively well maintained in older adults. The anatomical preservation hypothesis is less consistent with dorsal striatal atrophy and declines in dopamine function, as well as with the atrophy of the lateral PFC, which plays a role in some forms of emotion regulation. The functional compensation hypothesis is indirectly supported by evidence that age-related neural decline can be partly counteracted by changes in brain activity, such as PFC over-recruitment. Two patterns of PFC over-recruitment – the posterior-anterior shift with aging (PASA) and the hemispheric asymmetry reduction in older adults (HAROLD) – have been linked to improved cognitive performance, opening the possibility that PFC over-recruitment could also explain spared emotional processing in old age. More direct evidence for the contribution of functional compensation to improved emotional processing in aging is provided by functional neuroimaging studies in the emotion domain, as reviewed in the next section.

Behavioral and Functional Neuroimaging Studies of Emotion and Aging

The following sections review behavioral and functional neuroimaging studies on the effects of aging on emotional processing in different domains, including emotional perception, emotional episodic memory, emotional decision making, and emotion regulation. The most consistent pattern is an increase in frontal activity that is sometimes coupled with decreases in amygdalar responses to negative stimuli; that is, the pattern we have called *frontoamygdalar age-related differences in emotion* (FADE;

St. Jacques, Bessette-Symons, & Cabeza, 2009). The nature of this pattern will become clear when illustrated by specific findings in the following sections. One question to keep in mind is whether age-related PFC increases could partly account for spared emotional processing in older adults (functional compensation hypothesis).

Emotional Perception: Behavior

In young adults, emotional stimuli are more salient such that they are perceived and attended to with greater ease and fluency when compared to neutral stimuli (for a review, see Kensinger, 2004, and Chapter 14). Older adults also benefit from emotion during emotional perception, such that emotional salience remains relatively stable with age (for a meta-analysis, see Murphy & Isaacowitz, 2008). For example, compared to young adults, older adults perform similarly on attention (Mather & Knight, 2006; Samanez-Larkin, Robertson, Mikels, Carstensen, & Gotlib, 2009) and perception of emotional stimuli (for a review, see Kensinger, 2009). These results suggest that the automatic processing of emotion remains relatively intact with age (for reviews, see Kensinger & Leclerc, 2009; Mather, 2006).

Subtle age-related effects on emotional perception, however, might emerge depending on the particular quality and type of emotional stimulus. Compared to young adults, older adults have greater difficulty perceiving negative stimuli, but their perception of positive stimuli is less impaired. The age-related reduction for negative stimuli and the increase or comparable performance for positive stimuli are known as the *positivity effect* (for a review, see Mather & Carstensen, 2005). For example, in a recent meta-analysis examining age-related differences in emotional perception, Ruffman, Henry, Livingston, and Phillips (2008) found that older adults had impaired recognition of angry and sad faces compared to young adults, but were less impaired during the recognition of happy faces. These results are similar to age-related effects observed for other emotional stimuli such as pic-

tures. For example, older adults tend to rate positive pictures as more positive when compared to young adults and to standardized ratings (e.g., Gruhn & Scheibe, 2008). In sum, although emotional salience might generally remain intact during healthy aging, there are some age-related differences in the perception of negative versus positive emotions.

EMOTIONAL PERCEPTION: FUNCTIONAL NEUROIMAGING

The majority of functional neuroimaging studies on the effects of aging on emotional processing have focused on perception of emotional stimuli. One of the most consistent findings from functional neuroimaging studies of emotional perception is an age-related reduction in amygdalar activation for negative stimuli (see Table 28.1). For example, in the first fMRI study of emotion and aging, Iidaka et al. (2002) found less left amygdalar activity for negative faces in older adults when compared to young adults, and other studies have observed similar findings for both emotional faces and pictures (Fischer et al., 2005; Gunning-Dixon et al., 2003; Leclerc & Kensinger, 2011; Tessitore et al., 2005). However, in some of the aforementioned studies (Gunning-Dixon et al., 2003; Iidaka et al., 2002; Tessitore et al., 2005) older adults' reported negative stimuli valence ratings that were less negative than the ones given by young adults, consistent with the behavioral findings showing age-related reductions in the recognition of negative faces. Thus, one potential interpretation is that the age-related reduction in amygdala activity reflects an inability of these types of stimuli to elicit strong negative emotions in older adults, rather than a deficit in amygdala function per se. Consistent with this idea, we and others have found that amygdala activity can be as strong in older as in younger adults when stimuli were classified according to participants' own ratings (Leclerc & Kensinger, 2008; Mather et al., 2004; Ritchey, Bessette-Symons, Hayes, & Cabeza, 2011; St. Jacques, Dolcos, & Cabeza, 2010; Wright, Wedig, Williams, Rauch, & Albert, 2006) or when there were no age-related differences in emotional

Table 28.1. Results of Functional Neuroimaging Studies of Aging and Emotion

Author Year	Val	Stimuli	Contrast & Scanning Task	PFC Lat	PFC Med	Amygdala	Striatum Dors	Striatum Vent
Perception								
Iidaka 02	Neg	faces	neg (a, s) > control; gender discrimiation			•		
Mather 04*	Neg	pictures	neg vs baseline; emotion rating			•		
Fischer 05	Neg	faces	neg(a) > neut; passive viewing			•		
Tessitore 05	Neg	faces	neg (a, afr) > control; perceptual matching	○		•		
Williams 06*	Neg	faces	neg (f) > neut; passive viewing		○	•	•	
Wright 06*	Neg	faces	neg (f) +novel > neut; passive viewing			❖		
Wright 07*	Neg	faces	neg (f) + novel > neut; passive viewing			❖		
St.Jacques 10	Neg	pictures	neg > neut; emotion rating	○	○	❖		○
LeClerc 08	Neg	objects	neg > pos; semantic rating	•				•
Iidaka 02	Pos	faces	pos (h) > control; gender discrimiation					
Mather 04*	Pos	pictures	neg vs baseline; emotion rating			❖		
Williams 06*	Pos	faces	pos (f) > neut; passive viewing		•	•	•	
LeClerc 08	Pos	objects	pos > neg; semantic rating	○	○	❖		
Gutchess 07	Pos	words	(pos self>pos other)>(neg self>neg other); self/other rating	○	○			
Episodic Memory								
Fischer 10	Neg	faces	neg (f) > neut; emotion rating	○		•		
St. Jacques 09	Neg	pictures	neg vs. neut; emotion rating	○		❖	•	
Murty 09	Neg	pictures	neg vs. neut; semantic rating		○			
Murty 09	Neg	pictures	neg > neut; old/new recognition	○	○	•		
Kensinger 08	Neg	objects	neg > pos & neut; semantic rating					

Author Year	Val	Stimuli	Contrast & Scanning Task	PFC		Amygdala	Striatum	
				Lat	Med		Dors	Vent
Kensinger 08	Pos	objects	pos > neg & neut; semantic rating	❖	○			❖
Decision Making & Reward								
Samanez-Larkin 07	Neg	money	anticipation: loss (large, small) > none; emotion rating	●			●	
Jacobson 10	Neg	taste	outcome (taste during satiety)	○	○		●	
Schott 07	Pos	points	anticipation: reward > none	●	○		●	●
Dreher 08	Pos	money	outcome: gain > none		○		●	●
Jacobson 10	Pos	taste	outcome: (taste during hunger)	○			○	
Samanez-Larkin 07	Pos	money	outcome: none > loss (large, small)		●		●	
Samanez-Larkin 10	Pos	money	outcome: gain > loss	○				
Emotional Regulation								
Winecoff 10	Neg	pictures	neg reappraise > neg experience	●				
Winecoff 10	Pos	pictures	pos reappraise > pos experience					

● Young > older; ○ older > young; ❖ young = older.

Contrast: neg: negative, pos: postive, neut: neutral; h: happy, a: angry, s: sad, d: disgust, f: fear, afr: afraid

Brain regions: Lat: lateral; Med: medial; Amy: amygdala:

*Region-of-interest analysis.

ratings (Fischer et al., 2005). Furthermore, we (St. Jacques et al., 2010) found that amygdala activity was indeed reduced for negative stimuli that older adults subjectively rated as neutral. Interestingly, age-invariant activity in the amygdala is typically observed for positive stimuli (Gutchess, Kensinger, Yoon, & Schacter, 2007; Leclerc & Kensinger, 2011; Mather et al., 2004; although see Williams et al., 2006) and might reflect a shift in the preference of amygdala activation in aging (Mather et al., 2004; also see Wright et al., 2006). In sum, amygdalar responses to negative stimuli tend to be reduced by aging, but this reduction may reflect a failure of the stimuli to elicit strong negative emotions in older adults.

In contrast with the amygdala, functional neuroimaging studies of emotional perception have generally found an age-related increase in PFC recruitment. This effect is often more pronounced in the medial PFC (see Table 28.1), but it can be also observed in lateral PFC regions (Gunning-Dixon et al., 2003; Gutchess, Kensinger, & Schacter, 2007; Tessitore et al., 2005). Some studies have observed an age-related increase in the recruitment of the medial PFC during the perception of negative versus neutral pictures (Leclerc & Kensinger, 2011; St. Jacques,

Dolcos, & Cabeza, 2010; Williams et al., 2006), whereas other studies have observed that the age-related increases in medial PFC recruitment are greater for positive versus negative stimuli (Gutchess, Kensinger, & Schacter, 2007; Leclerc & Kensinger, 2008, 2011; Ritchey, Bessette-Symons, Hayes, & Cabeza, 2011; also see Leclerc & Kensinger, 2010). These apparent differences might be due to the dissociable effects of arousal and valence in dorsal versus ventral aspects of the medial PFC (e.g., Dolcos, LaBar, & Cabeza, 2004). For example, Leclerc and Kensinger (2008) found age-invariant activity in dorsomedial regions reflecting emotional arousal, whereas the age-related differences observed in ventromedial regions (specifically ventral ACC) reflected differences in positive versus negative valence. Additional research is needed to tease apart potential age-related differences in the neural correlates subserving emotional arousal and valence.

The age-related increase in PFC activity may reflect greater recruitment of controlled processes during emotional perception. Evidence for this hypothesis was recently provided by Ritchey et al. (2011). First, they found that age-related increases in medial PFC and ventrolateral PFC activity depended on the engagement of controlled processes during perception. Second, they found that individual differences in executive function predicted the recruitment of these PFC regions. The increased recruitment of controlled processes could potentially explain age-related differences in the perception of emotional stimuli. Consistent with this idea, we (St. Jacques et al., 2010) found that negative to neutral shifts in older adults' ratings of pictures modulated the involvement of the medial PFC and its coupling with the amygdala.

In sum, consistent with FADE, emotional perception studies of aging converge on the observation of an age-related reduction in amygdala activation for negative stimuli coupled with an increase in PFC activation for both negative and positive stimuli. The latter effect suggests that older adults engage more controlled processing during

the perception of emotional stimuli. The fMRI studies reviewed here suggest that perceptual differences for positive versus negative valence in aging are sometimes observed because these tasks rely on controlled processes associated with the PFC that are preferentially engaged in older adults.

Emotional Episodic Memory: Behavior

In young adults, memory is typically better for emotional than neutral stimuli (emotionally enhanced memory, EEM; see Chapter 20). Although EEM is relatively preserved in healthy aging there is an age-related alteration in the extent of EEM, especially for negative information (for a meta-analysis, see Murphy & Isaacowitz, 2008). Some studies have reported that EEM in older adults is similar for positive and negative emotions (e.g., Gruhn, Smith, & Baltes, 2005; St. Jacques & Levine, 2007), whereas, others have reported differential effects of valence (e.g., Mather & Carstensen, 2003). One interpretation of the different findings is that age-related effects on valence are only evident under certain conditions. According to Mather (2006) the positivity effect is less likely to be generated when there are tasks during encoding that interfere with older adults' ability to direct limited cognitive resources to emotional stimuli. In a series of experiments, Mather and Knight (2005) demonstrated that older adults engage in greater elaborative processing for positive than negative stimuli, that the positivity bias is correlated with performance on cognitive control, and that older adults who are distracted during the encoding of emotional stimuli do not show a preference in memory for positive items. Similarly, Emery and Hess (2008) manipulated viewing instructions during encoding and found that older adults' emotional memory was better when stimuli were processed in an emotionally meaningful way compared to perceptual processing or to passive viewing. Taken together these results suggest that age-related differences in memory for positive and negative stimuli are less likely to occur when encoding places greater demands on cognitive resources that reduce attention to emotionally salient aspects of the stimuli.

Alternatively, the mixed findings regarding the positivity effect in aging could be due to differential levels of arousal elicited across studies (cf. Gruhn et al., 2005). Online ratings of arousal are sometimes not acquired in studies, or they are not analyzed with respect to potential age-related interactions with valence when obtained. Kensinger (2008) showed that the positivity effect is more likely for low-arousing words compared to high-arousing stimuli. In sum, interpretations of a positivity effect or negative reduction in episodic memory are problematic without a careful consideration of task demands and the amount of arousal elicited by emotional stimuli.

EMOTIONAL MEMORY: FUNCTIONAL NEUROIMAGING

Only recently have functional neuroimaging studies begun to explore the neural bases of the age-related changes in EEM. Despite differences in methodology, functional neuroimaging studies of memory encoding generally show increases in PFC activity and alterations in the amygdala. For example, we (St. Jacques, Dolcos, & Cabeza, 2009) found that amygdala activity predicted subsequent memory of negative versus neutral pictures in both young and older adults, but that older adults recruited additional frontal activity to support memory formation as visual cortex activity declined. Recently, Fischer (2010) observed age-related increases in left dorsolateral PFC (DLPFC) for subsequent memory of fearful versus neutral faces. Although both age groups recruited bilateral amygdala during successful encoding of fearful faces, young adults recruited greater right amygdala. Similarly, Murty et al. (2009) found age-related increases in the recruitment of left DLPFC during the encoding of negative versus neutral picture blocks, but they did not observe age-related differences in recruitment of the amygdala. Complementing these findings, Kensinger and Schacter (2008) observed age-invariant recruitment of the amygdala during success-

ful memory encoding of objects, regardless of the particular negative or positive valence, but older adults elicited greater medial PFC activity during the successful encoding of positive objects.

Furthermore, we and others have observed an age-related decrease in functional connectivity between the amygdala and the areas that typically support memory formation (i.e., the hippocampus) for negative stimuli, but an age-related increase in functional connectivity with PFC areas involved in controlled processing (Murty et al., 2009; St. Jacques, Dolcos, & Cabeza, 2009; although see Addis, Leclerc, Muscatell, & Kensinger, 2010). Thus, increased frontal recruitment could reflect compensatory processes that support successful memory formation. Based on age-related reductions in EEM observed in these studies, however, this age-related frontal shift is less effective compared to the modulation of the hippocampus by the amygdala, which boosts consolidation processes and is likely to persist over time (Ritchey, Dolcos, & Cabeza, 2008).

Addis et al. (2010) recently showed that the pattern of connectivity during the formation of positive memories also differs in older adults. Using a structural equation model to examine the effective connectivity in the emotional network, they found that older adults had stronger positive connections in the top-down influence of the amygdala and ventromedial PFC on the hippocampus, whereas in young adults these same regions had a negative influence on the hippocampus. Further, young adults had greater positive influence of the thalamus on the hippocampus. Addis and colleagues suggested that the age-related changes in effective connectivity during successful encoding of positive memories might reflect greater self-referential processing in the older adults, which could also explain their increased memory for these same stimuli.

Currently, only one study has examined age-related effects during memory retrieval. The aforementioned study by Murty et al. (2009) found that older adults showed a reduction in the recruitment of the amygdala during memory retrieval of negative versus neutral blocks, but an age-related increase in the right DLPFC. Further, older adults had greater amygdalar-DLPFC coupling, but less amygdalar-hippocampal coupling during negative retrieval blocks, suggesting a possible compensatory mechanism to aid memory retrieval or potentially the engagement of controlled processes that regulate emotional responses during retrieval.

In sum, the results of these initial fMRI studies suggest that aging leads to an increased reliance on controlled processes in the PFC that support and maintain enhanced memory for emotional materials. These results are in line with the behavioral studies reviewed earlier that suggest that age-related changes in memory for emotion stimuli depend on the recruitment of controlled processes that influence emotion. Future research will need to more closely examine how both valence and arousal contribute to potential age-related differences in the neural mechanisms supporting successful memory encoding and retrieval.

Affective Decision Making: Behavior

Information processing during decision making has often been characterized as relying on two separate systems: one deliberative and cognitive, and the other affective and experiential (Peters, Hess, Västfjäll, & Auman, 2007; see Chapter 17). Changes in both deliberative and affective aspects of information processing in decision making occur with age (Kennedy & Mather, 2007); however, the degree to which these changes act in concert to produce maladaptive choices may depend on a number of contextual factors (Peters et al., 2007). Nonetheless, age-related differences in emotional processing may result in suboptimal real-world financial behavior in older adults (Weierich et al., 2011). Thus, characterizing the ways in which aging affects affective processing is critical to understanding decision making in older adulthood.

Consistent with studies of emotion perception and memory, older adults' decisions are differentially influenced by positive versus negative information. For example,

older adults are susceptible to framing effects when gains are emphasized but not when losses are emphasized (Mikels & Reed, 2009), and they spend more time reviewing positive relative to negative information when making decisions about physicians and health care plans than do young adults (Lockenhoff & Carstensen, 2007). These results suggest that older adults' decisions are influenced by goals to actively manage their emotional experiences. In line with this idea, although young and older adults seek similar levels of variety in choices for current consumption, older adults' choices for future consumption show less variety. By selecting options that are known to be preferred, older adults may be attempting to regulate their future emotional experiences (Novak & Mather, 2007). Given that emotion regulatory processes can be used to reduce behavioral reports and physiological metrics of loss (Sokol-Hessner et al., 2009) and risk aversion (Heilman, Crisan, Houser, Miclea, & Miu, 2010), the motivation to regulate emotions during decision making may not necessarily produce poorer decision outcomes in older adults in all contexts.

Motivational influences play a critical role in decision making. As a result, several studies have investigated age-related differences in decision making by examining how older adults learn the associations between particular stimuli and rewarding or punishing outcomes (e.g., Denburg, Recknor, Bechara, & Tranel, 2006); however, it is not exactly clear how aging affects information processing in reinforcement learning. On the one hand, older adults sometimes show preferential learning from positive rewards. For example, Denburg et al. (2006) found that high-performing older adults were more likely to generate anticipatory skin conductance responses when selecting from advantageous decks on the Iowa Gambling Task, whereas low-performing older adults did not show differential anticipatory responses between advantageous and disadvantageous decks. This finding suggests that older adults potentially learn better from positive than negative reinforcement, perhaps representing an age-related shift consistent with changes in emotional focus in later life (Denburg et al.,

2006). On the other hand, older adults may be biased toward negative outcomes in some contexts. Using a probabilistic learning task, Frank and Kong (2008) assessed whether older adults' initial learning was guided by approach or avoidance strategies and found that the oldest group of participants learned more from negative than positive outcomes. However, this age-related increase in avoidance learning does not appear to hold for younger samples of older adults, suggesting that the effect may not generalize to all older adults.

In sum, like young adults, older adults' decisions are biased by emotional information; however, the valence and nature of emotional information in decision making and reward tasks may have different impacts on behavior in later adulthood. Similar to studies examining age-related changes in emotional perception and memory, this research suggests that older adults potentially prefer positive information and reinforcers when making and processing emotional decisions; however, the influence of context and the extent to which an emotional bias is present during decision making in older adults are not yet fully elucidated.

AFFECTIVE DECISION MAKING:
FUNCTIONAL NEUROIMAGING

Consistent with age-related declines in dopaminergic function and the volume of the dorsal striatum, as reviewed earlier, functional neuroimaging studies have reported reduced striatal activity in older adults during reward processing while learning associations (Mell et al., 2009) and when anticipating rewards (Dreher et al., 2008; Schott et al., 2007; although see Samanez-Larkin et al., 2007). For example, Mell et al. (2009) found differential age effects during early versus late stages of reward learning from feedback on a probabilistic object reversal task. During the late phase of learning, older adults showed reduced activation in the striatum to rewards compared to young adults. In the early learning stage, however, older adults showed greater ventral striatal response to reward processing. Given that behavioral performance in older adults was worse overall,

these findings were interpreted as evidence that older adults do not activate the striatum in a systematic way to guide subsequent reward learning. This is consistent with the hypothesis that, although older adults do not show deficits in the processing of reward outcomes, they do not effectively integrate this information into predictions about future rewards (Schott et al., 2007). Similarly, increased temporal variability in signals arising from the nucleus accumbens in older adults predicts poorer decision performance (Samanez-Larkin, Kuhnen, Yoo, & Knutson, 2010). Thus, differences in striatal functioning in older adults are consistent with deficits in reinforcement learning processes that rely on reward-signal processing in the basal ganglia.

Some evidence, however, points to a valence-specific shift in neural reward processing in older adulthood, providing consistency with findings in the domains of perception and memory. When anticipating monetary gains, older adults demonstrate preserved striatal responses to gains but diminished responses to losses (Samanez-Larkin et al., 2007). Also, although older adults show similar striatal responses to the presentation of monetary outcomes when the entire outcome period is modeled (Cox, Aizenstein, & Fiez, 2008; Samanez-Larkin et al., 2007), they show a reduced effect of negative outcomes on striatal signaling initially after outcomes are presented (Cox et al., 2008). Together, these results are suggestive of the role of altered affective processing during decision making in later adulthood, particularly when older adults are considering potential economic losses.

Consistent with evidence of altered PFC function during affective processing in later life, older adults show changes in the PFC during reward learning and decision making. In one investigation, older adults showed decreased activation of the DLPFC, but less deactivation in the medial PFC during the receipt of reward, compared to younger adults (Dreher et al., 2008). Along the same lines, older adults showed greater activation in the DLPFC during decision making when reward contingencies were already well learned, which potentially suggests that older adults over-recruit dorsolateral aspects of the PFC to maintain and monitor performance even after learning has already taken place (Mell et al., 2009). Because in vivo positron emission tomography research has shown that the relationship between mesolimbic and prefrontal dopamine systems is altered in aging, these differences may reflect age-related dopaminergic decline (Dreher et al., 2008), which could account for age-related alterations in the reward system as well as in the PFC. Interestingly, one study has linked changes in the PFC during hedonic processing to experience of gustatory stimuli. Regardless of the specific taste, older adults showed greater responses not only in brain circuitry involved in affective processing, such as the caudate and amygdala, but also in the anterior cingulate and medial prefrontal cortex (Jacobson, Green, & Murphy, 2010). These results suggest that age affects the processing of motivational stimuli both in limbic and prefrontal regions.

In sum, the handful of neuroimaging studies of reward processing and decision making in later life show that older adults demonstrate altered patterns of reward processing and that these patterns may result not only from dopaminergic decline but also from altered emotional functioning in aging. Although studies of reward learning and decision making in older adults have typically interpreted findings of differential PFC recruitment as representing cognitive decline, these studies cannot rule out the potential influence of altered emotional control processes acting during decision making as a source of PFC engagement. It will be important in future research to dissociate the effects of declining cognitive and neural function from changes in emotional biases in later life because they may affect decision making in older adults in different ways.

Emotion Regulation: Behavior

Emotion regulation is a process by which individuals attempt to manage their emotional experiences by altering which specific emotion is experienced, when an emotion is experienced, or how an emotion is expressed (Gross, 1998b; Chapter 16). Aging is associated with increased control over emotional experiences in everyday life (Gross et al., 1997). Within laboratory settings, older adults differentially employ both relatively automatic and controlled forms of emotion regulation. First, older adults seem to automatically engage emotional regulation strategies when not instructed to do so. For example, studies of spatial attention have shown that, despite a preserved ability to perceive threat-related stimuli more quickly than neutral stimuli (Mather & Knight, 2006), older adults are less likely to attend to faces displaying negative emotion (Isaacowitz, Wadlinger, Goren, & Wilson, 2006; Mather & Carstensen, 2003) and more likely to attend to faces displaying positive emotion (Isaacowitz et al., 2006), when compared to young adults. This *attention deployment* to positive versus negative stimuli is a type of antecedent-focused emotion regulation strategy (Gross, 1998b), in which older adults seem to be experts (Charles & Carstensen, 2007).

Older adults also differ in their implementation of controlled emotion regulation. However, the age-related differences in emotion regulation under explicit instructions are not fully understood. For example, contrary to studies in which they deploy automatic emotion regulation, older adults show a decreased ability to emotionally detach themselves from negative stimuli (Shiota & Levenson, 2009; Winecoff, LaBar, Madden, Cabeza, & Huettel, 2011). Despite this finding, older adults also show a preserved ability to suppress behavioral responses to emotional stimuli (Kunzmann, Kupperbusch, & Levenson, 2005; Shiota & Levenson, 2009) and an enhanced ability to regulate emotions by creating more positive interpretations of negative stimuli compared to younger adults (Shiota & Levenson, 2009). Some researchers have speculated that emotionally detaching from stimuli relies more on fluid intelligence, whereas creating positive reinterpretations of stimuli relies more on expertise, which potentially explains the age-related variance in performance based on emotion regulation strategy (Shiota & Levenson, 2009); however, this idea does not account for the finding that older adults are equally as effective as younger adults in emotionally detaching themselves from positive stimuli (Winecoff et al., 2011). Thus, the relationship between age and controlled emotion regulation is not yet fully elucidated.

The engagement of both automatic and controlled forms of emotional regulation may also depend on the availability of cognitive resources. For example, although selective attention is not very cognitively taxing (e.g., Allard & Isaacowitz, 2008), whether older adults use selective attention as an emotional regulation strategy may depend on intact cognitive resources (Mather & Carstensen, 2005). This poses an interesting problem for the study of aging: To the extent that emotion regulatory strategies rely on cognitive resources, how is emotional functioning maintained in later life? Because functional neuroimaging allows for the investigation of the underlying mechanisms of emotion regulation, it provides one promising avenue for answering this question. In particular, functional neuroimaging studies can help us understand how the neural mechanisms of automatic versus controlled regulation differ across the lifespan.

EMOTIONAL REGULATION: FUNCTIONAL NEUROIMAGING

Functional neuroimaging studies provide some evidence that older adults may automatically engage emotional regulation strategies although not instructed to do so. Consistent with FADE, in many studies, the age-related increase in frontal activity was coupled with a reduction in amygdala activity during perception (Gunning-Dixon et al., 2003; Tessitore et al., 2005; also see Fischer et al., 2005; Iidaka et al., 2002; Samanez-Larkin et al., 2007; St. Jacques et al., 2010; although see Williams et al., 2006) and retrieval (Murty et al., 2009) of negative stimuli. Thus, one possibility is that older adults' enhanced emotion regulation strategies lead to the recruitment of PFC-mediated control processes that dampen

amygdala responses for negative stimuli. For example, we examined age-related differences in the functional connectivity with the amygdala and found an age-related increase in the functional connectivity between the ventral ACC and the amygdala (St. Jacques et al., 2010). Importantly, we found a negative correlation between these regions during the perception of negative pictures that older adults subjectively rated as neutral and also a subsequent decrease in amygdala activity, which suggests the engagement of emotion regulation.

Implementing emotion regulation strategies via increased PFC recruitment (Ochsner & Gross, 2005) can also reduce striatal activation to anticipated gains (Delgado, Gillis, & Phelps, 2008). A clear link between altered striatal function and automatic forms of emotion regulation in aging has not yet been established. However, in one recent investigation using emotional images, young adults showed increased functional connectivity between the medial PFC and the striatum during the presentation of negative stimuli, whereas older adults showed greater functional connectivity between these regions during the presentation of positively valenced stimuli (Ritchey et al., 2011). Though this study did not focus on reward processing or decision making per se, it suggests that a FADE-like pattern might extend more widely to reward regions of the brain.

Functional neuroimaging studies have also begun to investigate age-related changes during controlled emotion regulation. One form of emotion regulation that has been studied extensively in young adults is reappraisal, whereby the emotional meaning of a stimulus is transformed through the use of some cognitive strategy. This antecedent-focused emotion regulation strategy, as does attentional deployment, operates early in the emotion-generation period (Gross, 1998b) and is therefore more likely to reduce emotionally evoked physiological arousal (Gross, 1998a). Given that older adults show declines in cognitive control but preserved or improved emotional functioning (Mather & Carstensen, 2005), one hypothesis might be that older adults rely on different neural networks for voluntary emotion regulation than younger adults; however, preliminary data suggest that this is not the case. In one study of reappraisal in an older cohort, older adults engaged diverse aspects of the PFC during emotion regulation, and participants showing the greatest reappraisal-related decreases in amygdala activation showed increased activation in the medial PFC relative to those who did not show this effect (Urry et al., 2006). Similarly, in a study directly comparing older and young adults' neural responses to reappraisal, few age-related differences emerged (Winecoff et al., 2011). In both young and older adults, cognitive reappraisal recruited PFC regions previously observed in emotion regulation (Kim & Hamann, 2007; Ochsner et al., 2002; Ochsner et al., 2004), whereas the experience of emotion recruited the amygdala. Further, across age groups, task-related decreases in amygdala activation were functionally coupled with increased activation in the dorsolateral prefrontal cortex during reappraisal. The only age-related differences to emerge were in the left inferior frontal gyrus and left medial and superior temporal sulcus, where older adults showed reduced recruitment when actively attempting to regulate responses to negative (but not positive) stimuli. Consistent with the suggestion that cognitive control is necessary for emotion regulation (Mather & Knight, 2005), higher performance on a battery of cognitive tests predicted greater reappraisal-related decreases in the amygdala even after controlling for the effects of age (Winecoff et al., 2011; also see Ritchey et al., 2011).

Collectively, these results suggest that automatic engagement of emotional regulation strategies may underlie some of the age-related changes in the neural correlates supporting emotional processing, whereas controlled emotion regulation relies on generally similar brain systems across the lifespan. Future research is needed to better understand the boundary conditions of these effects in order to reconcile discrepancies in the neural mechanisms supporting age-related changes in automatic versus controlled forms of emotion regulation, as

well as potential age-invariant or age-related differences in the emotion regulation of positive and negative valence.

Frontoamygdalar Age-Related Differences in Emotion (FADE) Evidence from age-related functional neuroimaging studies across emotional perception, memory, and emotional regulation domains generally shows the activity pattern we called FADE; namely, age-related increases in PFC activity that are sometimes coupled with decreases in amygdalar responses to negative stimuli. Few functional neuroimaging studies have investigated age-related changes in decision making and reward; however, the available evidence points to a similar age-related increase in frontal recruitment and reduced function in the striatum, suggesting a more general pattern of age-related cortical increases and subcortical decreases (Samanez-Larkin & Carstensen, 2011). Although FADE refers to functional changes in brain activity, it can also be related to structural changes in anatomy. Thus, FADE can be linked to both the anatomical preservation hypothesis and the functional compensation hypothesis, as described in the following two subsections.

FADE AND THE ANATOMICAL PRESERVATION HYPOTHESIS

Although findings of age-related reductions in amygdalar activity during perception (Fischer et al., 2005; Iidaka et al., 2002; Tessitore et al., 2005) and memory (Fischer, 2010; Murty et al., 2009) involving negative emotions may appear as inconsistent with evidence of little age-related atrophy in the amygdala, the anatomical preservation of the amygdala can explain why activity reductions can vary as a function of stimulus type and are less frequent for positive stimuli. The fact that age-related atrophy is minimal in the amygdala supports the idea that age-related reductions in amygdala activity for negative stimuli reflect a change in emotional-processing strategies rather than simple anatomical deterioration.

A similar argument can be made about age-related increases in PFC activity. The fact that these increases occur both in lateral PFC regions that show substantial age-related atrophy and in medial PFC regions that show relatively less atrophy suggests that these increases reflect a change in the way older adults process emotions, rather than a simple reflection of anatomical preservation vs. decline.

Finally, the anatomical preservation hypothesis cannot easily account for age effects on striatal activity, which often shows reductions in both dorsal and ventral regions, despite anatomical evidence that age-related atrophy is minimal in ventral regions. Although global striatal reductions could be attributed to age-related dopamine deficits, the latter cannot explain why some studies (e.g., Jacobson et al., 2010; Samanez-Larkin et al., 2007) found age-related increases in striatal activity in some conditions.

In sum, age-related changes in neural activity during emotional processing cannot be simply attributed to anatomical preservation or decline. To better link changes in anatomy to the functional changes described by FADE, future studies could investigate the relationship between volumetric changes in regions of interest with changes in the activity of these regions.

FADE AND THE FUNCTIONAL COMPENSATION HYPOTHESIS

The PFC component of FADE is clearly consistent with evidence of age-related PFC increases in various cognitive domains, as summarized by the posterior-anterior shift in aging (PASA) and hemispheric asymmetry reduction in older adults (HAROLD) patterns (Dennis & Cabeza, 2008). FADE fits particularly well with the PASA pattern, which comprises not only age-related increases in anterior brain regions but also age-related decreases in posterior brain regions. Although it is tempting to see the age-related amygdalar reductions in FADE as an example of the posterior reductions in PASA, there is an important difference in how these reductions are conceptualized. In PASA, PFC increases are interpreted as compensating for the posterior reductions, whereas FADE does not assume that

PFC increases compensate for the amygdalar decreases. In fact, if one interprets FADE in terms of emotion regulation, the effect would be in the opposite direction, with PFC-mediated control processes dampening amygdala-mediated processing of negative emotions. At any rate, further research is required to determine if the FADE pattern within the emotion domain fits with global age-related activation patterns observed in other cognitive domains, such as PASA.

As noted earlier, the fact that age-related PFC increases during emotional processing occur both in regions showing substantial age-related atrophy, such as the lateral PFC, and in regions showing relatively less anatomical decline, such as the medial PFC, suggests that these increases reflect changes in processing strategies rather than anatomical changes. What is unclear is what these processing strategy changes are.

One possibility is that age-related PFC increases could reflect emotion regulation. Emotional well-being in aging has been associated with a shift from automatic processing to more controlled processing of emotions via the recruitment of the medial PFC (Williams et al., 2006). As reviewed earlier, the pattern of activation across a number of studies suggests that older adults potentially engage automatic emotion regulation strategies when processing emotional stimuli by recruiting frontal control regions that may dampen emotional responses mediated by the amygdala. Interestingly, when the differential engagement of these strategies is equated across age groups via explicit instructions, few age-related differences are observed (Winecoff et al., 2011).

Second, the frontal increase could be an instance of PASA, which is frequently observed in nonemotional domains (Dennis & Cabeza, 2008) and thus could reflect a compensatory strategy. Consistent with this idea, we and others have found that the increase in PFC activity during emotional processing was coupled with a decrease in the recruitment of posterior regions (St. Jacques, Dolcos, et al. 2009; St. Jacques et al., 2010; Tessitore et al., 2005; also see Gunning-Dixon et al., 2003; Iidaka et al.,

2002). Further, in keeping with the compensatory account of PASA, we also found a significant correlation between the age-related increase in frontal activity and the reduction in visual cortex activity during emotional perception (St. Jacques et al., 2010) and that the age-related frontal increase was predictive of subsequent memory for negative stimuli (St. Jacques, Dolcos, et al., 2009).

Another possibility is that age-related increases in the medial PFC could reflect an augmentation of self-referential processes (Kensinger & Leclerc, 2009). One line of evidence supporting this interpretation is that medial PFC recruitment in older adults has been shown to vary as a function of valence (Kensinger & Schacter, 2008; Leclerc & Kensinger, 2008). For example, Leclerc and Kensinger (2008) found an age-related reversal in the medial PFC, such that older adults recruited this region more for positive stimuli and less for negative stimuli (although see Williams et al., 2006). They suggested that older adults might interpret positive stimuli in a more self-relevant way. In keeping with this interpretation, a study directly interrogating age-related differences in self-referential processing for emotional stimuli found that older adults recruited medial PFC regions to a greater extent for self-related positive words (Gutchess, Kensinger, & Schacter, 2007). Given that older adults tend to engage the default network more during cognitive tasks (Grady, Springer, Hongwanishkul, McIntosh, & Winocur, 2006), one possibility is that the positivity shift observed in perception and memory studies might result from an age-related increase in the tendency to interpret information in a self-relevant manner (cf. Kensinger & Leclerc, 2009).

It is worth noting that emotion regulation, compensation, and self-referential processing accounts are not incompatible with each other. In fact, emotional regulation could be seen as a form of compensation (St. Jacques et al., 2010), and self-referential processing could be seen as an emotion regulation strategy (Kensinger & Leclerc, 2009). Yet, not all forms of emotion regulation are beneficial for performance (i.e., compensatory), and self-referential processing is not

necessarily an effective regulation strategy. Thus, understanding the specific contributions of each of these processes and their interactions is a major challenge for future research.

Linking Brain Data to Theories of Emotional Aging

The number of functional neuroimaging studies of emotion and aging is growing rapidly; however, many of the aforementioned studies do not directly link age-related changes in neural activation to cognitive and social theories of emotional aging. There are at least four different theories of emotional changes in aging: the socioemotional selectivity theory (Carstensen, Mikels, & Mather, 2006), dynamic integration theory (Labouvie-Vief, 2003, 2009), learning and practice theory (Blanchard-Fields, 2007), and the byproduct of biological decline theory (Cacioppo, Berntson, Bechara, Tranel, & Hawkley, 2011). Several of these theories were originally proposed to account for behavioral data, and hence, they do not include assumptions about brain mechanisms and cannot make predictions for functional neuroimaging. However, using current knowledge regarding the neural bases of various cognitive and emotional processes, one may expand these theories with assumptions about neural mechanisms and derive predictions for functional neuroimaging. We next describe each of these theories, how they could be expanded to incorporate hypotheses regarding brain function, and whether the derived predictions fit available functional neuroimaging evidence.

Socioemotional Selectivity Theory

BASIC THEORY AND EXPANDED THEORY
WITH NEURAL ASSUMPTIONS AND
PREDICTIONS
Socioemotional selectivity theory (SST) postulates that aging is associated with a limited perspective on time, which leads to motivational differences in allocating attention to information (Carstensen, Fung, & Charles, 2003; Mather & Carstensen,

2005). Specifically, the theory has two predictions: (1) Aging involves the greater allocation of cognitive resources to emotional stimuli, and (2) older adults are more likely to allocate these limited resources to information that enhances their mood and well-being. Because of this mood-enhancing goal, older adults are expected to be more sensitive to positive information and less sensitive to or avoidant of negative information, a phenomenon known as the *positivity effect* (Carstensen & Mikels, 2005; Carstensen et al., 2006). In the context of studies comparing attention, memory, or decisions involving positive versus negative stimuli, the positivity effect is defined as an age-related shift in the overall ratio of positive-to-negative material attended to, remembered, or selected (Scheibe & Carstensen, 2010). Further, SST proposes that the positivity effect is more likely to occur on tasks that require greater controlled emotional processing and less so on more automatic emotional tasks (Mather, 2006). In sum, SST suggests that older adults are more likely to allocate cognitive resources to regulate their emotions.

The fact that functional neuroimaging studies of emotional aging frequently discuss the popular SST suggests that this theory is amenable to brain-based interpretations (for related reviews, see Knight & Mather, 2006; Mather, 2006; Samanez-Larkin & Carstensen, 2011; Scheibe & Carstensen, 2010). Given that SST assumes that older adults use controlled processes to up-regulate responses to positive stimuli and/or down-regulate responses to negative stimuli, this theory predicts that during emotional processing older adults should show (1) increased control-related PFC activity and (2) the effects of this control in the form of shifts in amygdalar responses to positive vs. negative stimuli or in striatal responses to gains vs. losses.

FUNCTIONAL NEUROIMAGING EVIDENCE
Consistent with the expanded SST, several functional neuroimaging studies of emotional aging have found the FADE pattern: an age-related increase in frontal recruitment and altered amygdala recruitment

(also see Samanez-Larkin & Carstensen, 2011; St. Jacques, Bessette-Symons, et al., 2009). Emerging findings from the domain of decision making suggest that a more general pattern of age-related reduction in subcortical activation and increase in cortical activation could explain both the amygdalar and striatal findings (Samanez-Larkin & Carstensen, 2011). These studies are in line with the expanded SST, which suggests that older adults' enhanced emotion regulation strategies lead to the recruitment of PFC-mediated control processes that dampen amygdala or striatal responses for negative stimuli and losses. Further supporting this idea are studies that have examined coupling between frontal and amgydalar regions (Murty et al., 2009; St. Jacques et al., 2010; St. Jacques, Dolcos, et al., 2009). Some of the studies that have explicitly queried emotion regulation are also consistent with the expanded SST. For example, Urry et al. (2006) directly asked older adults to regulate emotions while viewing negative pictures and found that, compared to passive viewing, when older adults were asked to decrease their emotional responses they recruited greater vmPFC activity coupled with a reduction in the recruitment of the amygdala. In fact, emotional well-being in aging has been associated with a shift from automatic processing to more controlled processing of emotions via the recruitment of the medial PFC (Williams et al., 2006). Moreover, consistent with predictions from SST, the frontal over-recruitment may occur only on controlled emotional tasks but not on automatic ones (Ritchey et al., 2011).

Dynamic Integration Theory

BASIC THEORY AND EXPANDED THEORY WITH NEURAL ASSUMPTIONS AND PREDICTIONS
According to dynamic integration theory (DIT; Labouvie-Vief, 2009) age-related changes in emotional processing depend on the interaction between situational circumstances and individual differences, which determines the effectiveness of emotion regulation. DIT suggests that the level of

emotional activation, emotional complexity, and individual differences in cognitive functioning are important factors contributing to emotional changes in aging. At low levels of activation, aging involves differentiation and complexity in emotional experience; for example, blending positive and negative elements of emotions, as in bittersweet. Because differentiation and complexity involve elaborative processes, higher levels of activation yield greater difficulties with aging, especially in the face of increasing cognitive demands and/or reduced cognitive functioning. Thus, at high levels of activation older adults will compensate by relying on less effortful optimization strategies that involve minimizing negative affect and increasing positive affect (i.e., the positivity effect). In contrast with SST, DIT contends that the age-related positivity effect does not reflect increased emotional resiliency, but is in fact due to a decline in emotional complexity involving reduced integration and tolerance of negative emotions (Labouvie-Vief, 2003).

DIT emphasizes that prefrontal-amygdalar function is critical for implementing emotion regulation in aging (Labouvie-Vief, 2009), but does not explicitly provide hypotheses regarding the pattern of age-related changes in functional activations. The expanded DIT incorporating brain mechanisms predicts differential age effects at low vs. high demanding emotional tasks. At low levels, DIT predicts an age-related increase in controlled prefrontal recruitment and a subsequent decrease in emotional responses in the amygdala; at high levels DIT predicts dysfunctional frontoamygdalar function involving a heightened amygdalar response coupled with reduced or ineffective control-related frontal activation. Further, the expanded DIT predicts that individual differences in cognitive function mediate this frontal-amgydalar pattern.

FUNCTIONAL NEUROIMAGING EVIDENCE
Many of the studies reviewed here have noted a FADE pattern, observing an age-related increase in frontal recruitment and

age-related reductions in the amgydala, which would seem to fit the predictions of the expanded DIT for less demanding emotional tasks. However, it is important to point out that the majority of these studies do not incorporate varying levels of emotional activation or complexity, which are necessary to determine the validity of the expanded DIT. For example, it is possible that older adults relied on well-developed emotion regulation strategies or that these tasks did not involve high levels of complexity (cf. Labouvie-Vief, 2009). There is some initial evidence to support the expanded DIT with respect to emotional activation and cognitive demand. For example, we (St. Jacques et al., 2010) found an age-related positive coupling between the medial PFC and the amygdala for the most negatively valenced pictures in our sample based on the standardized International Affective Picture System (IAPS) ratings, which presumably engaged greater emotional activation. The medial PFC-amygdalar coupling shifted to negative for the less negatively valenced pictures, which were also rated in the neutral direction by older adults. We interpreted these findings in terms of the success of emotion regulation, which tended to be greater at low levels of emotional activation. Thus, these results are consistent with the expanded DIT, which suggests that prefrontal-amygdalar regulatory function is preserved at lower levels of emotional activation but not at higher levels. An additional study provides partial evidence for the expanded DIT predictions concerning cognitive demands and individual differences. Ritchey et al. (2011) found that individual differences in executive function were positively related to the recruitment of medial PFC when emotional picture processing required greater elaboration. Thus, consistent with the expanded DIT, the recruitment of frontal regions for cognitively demanding tasks was only evident in older adults with high levels of cognitive resources.

None of the previous studies reviewed here can directly test the complete predictions of the expanded DIT. However, fully considering the link between brain mechanisms and DIT leads to some novel questions for future research. In particular, a greater number of studies are needed to examine the influence of emotional activation, emotional complexity, cognitive demands, and individual differences in performance, which are critical for understanding age-related differences in the neural correlates of emotion.

Learning and Practice Theory

BASIC THEORY AND EXPANDED THEORY WITH NEURAL ASSUMPTIONS AND PREDICTIONS

According to the theory of learning and practice, older adults have developed expertise in emotion regulation through substantial experience across the lifespan (Blanchard-Fields, 2007; Hess, 2005). Older adults' expertise in dealing with socioemotional situations results in more complex, flexible, and mature emotion regulation strategies compared to young adults. The increasing ease with which older adults apply emotion regulation strategies in their daily lives potentially underlies age-related reductions in the perceptions of stress due to health problems, bereavement, and environmental catastrophes (for reviews see Charles & Carstensen, 2007, 2010).

Given the emphasis on experience, the learning and practice theory suggests that older adults will be most effective in applying emotion regulation strategies to familiar situations. Thus, the expanded learning and practice theory predicts that older adults should show (1) increased control-related PFC activity and (2) the effects of this control in the form of up- or down-regulation of amygdala or striatal activity to a greater extent in familiar versus unfamiliar situations.

FUNCTIONAL NEUROIMAGING EVIDENCE

To date there is little functional neuroimaging evidence supporting the expanded theory of learning and practice because very few studies have examined age-related differences during emotional processing for familiar versus novel situations. In one potentially

relevant fMRI study, Gutchess, Kensinger, and Schacter (2007) asked young and older adults to judge whether positive and negative adjectives described themselves or Albert Einstein. Both the self and other conditions are relatively familiar situations; however, presumably referencing the self is more familiar than referencing Einstein. The fMRI results revealed that, compared to young adults, older adults engaged a region in the dorsal medial PFC to a greater extent for positive versus negative self-referencing, but there was no interaction with valence when making a judgment about another person. The Gutchess et al. (2007) findings provide preliminary partial support for the expanded learning and practice theory, in that they suggest that older adults potentially engage increased controlled processing for more familiar positive versus negative stimuli. However, this same contrast revealed no activation in subcortical regions; thus, it is not clear whether the recruitment of controlled processes was in the service of emotion regulation. Further research is needed to directly test age-related differences in emotional processes of familiar versus unfamiliar situations.

Byproduct of Biological Decline Theory

BASIC THEORY AND EXPANDED THEORY WITH NEURAL ASSUMPTIONS AND PREDICTIONS

Unlike the previous cognitive and social theories of emotional aging, biological decline theories directly link age-related differences to brain function. According to one such theory, the aging-brain model (Cacioppo et al., 2011), age-related changes in emotion are the byproduct of biological decline. The aging-brain model postulates that there is a valence shift in the response of amygdala activation due to age-related attenuations in arousal for negative stimuli. The age-related reduction in arousal response to negative stimuli reduces the emotional enhancement of memory (EEM) for negative stimuli, but increases subjective well-being. Further, the aging-brain model suggests that attenuation in arousal responses to negative stimuli potentially impairs decision-making processes that rely on negative feedback. Proponents of the aging-brain model suggest that the pattern of age-related changes in emotion is similar to that in patients with selective amygdala lesions, implying that amygdala dysfunction is the basis of emotional changes in aging.

Taking directly from the aging-brain model hypothesis, there will be age-related reductions in amygdala activation for negative stimuli, but not for positive stimuli. Unlike the previous theories, the aging-brain model is agnostic with respect to age-related changes in the PFC because it posits that the attenuation of arousal responses to negative stimuli are due to dysfunction of the amygdala. The aging-brain model relies on the assumption that arousal drives age-related changes; thus, one additional hypothesis is that age-related differences in the amygdalar responses for low-arousing emotional stimuli will be minimal.

FUNCTIONAL NEUROIMAGING EVIDENCE
Several functional neuroimaging studies have observed age-related reductions in the recruitment of the amygdala for negative stimuli. Although very few studies have examined age-related changes for positively valenced stimuli, the handful of studies to date generally show age-invariant recruitment for positive stimuli (e.g., Leclerc & Kensinger, 2008; Mather et al., 2004). Contrary to the aging-brain model, however, several studies have also observed age-invariant activation in the amygdala for negative stimuli (e.g., Ritchey et al., 2011; St. Jacques et al., 2010). Based on the aging-brain model one explanation of these discrepant findings is that the level of arousal differed in studies that failed to find an age-related difference in amygdala response for negative stimuli. According to the aging-brain model, age-related differences in the recruitment of the amygdala should be minimal when emotional stimuli are low arousing. Thus, studies that did not find age-related differences in amygdalar responses for negative stimuli may have included

lower arousing emotional stimuli. However, we (St. Jacques et al., 2010) showed that amygdala activation was reduced in older adults for the subset of less arousing negative stimuli, but not for more arousing negative stimuli, which is the exact opposite of the aging-brain model hypothesis. Further, as suggested earlier, age-related differences in the amygdalar response to negative stimuli tended to occur when there were also age-related differences in behavioral ratings for negative stimuli, suggesting that these stimuli were ineffective in engendering a strong emotional response in older adults (although see Ritchey et al., 2011). It will be important for future research to test the brain hypotheses of the aging-brain model using a range of arousing stimuli.

The current research does not appear to provide much support for the hypothesis that age-related changes in the neural mechanisms of emotional aging are merely a byproduct of biological decline (Scheibe & Carstensen, 2010). Cacioppo et al. (2011) argue that patients with amygdalar lesions seem to show similar findings to those of older adults, suggesting a possible link between amygdalar damage and age-related changes in emotional processing. However, the studies reviewed here generally suggest that the structure and function of the amygdala remain relatively intact across the lifespan, although there is some debate regarding the preference of this region for positive versus negative stimuli. Further, let us consider the findings from patients with Alzheimer's disease, a neurodegenerative disease that affects the structure and function of the amygdala (for a review, see Chow & Cummings, 2000). In contrast with healthy older adults, patients with Alzheimer's disease show a disruption of emotional processes (for a review, see Kensinger, 2009). In sum, these findings bring into question whether emotional changes in healthy aging are due to biological decline in emotional regions such as the amygdala. It is possible that future research will reveal subtle differences in age-related biological decline that could account for the findings in emotional processes.

Summary of the Theoretical Models and Brain Substrates

Expanding cognitive and social theories of emotional aging to incorporate brain mechanisms yields specific predictions regarding functional neuroimaging that are generally supported by the available evidence. Interestingly, a recent theory of emotional well-being in aging, the strength and vulnerability theory (Charles, 2010), incorporates aspects of each of the aforementioned theories by positing when and why emotional regulation will be successful in older adults. Consequently, the expanded theories should not be viewed as opposing but as complementary components that determine the ease and frequency of emotion regulation strategy engagement in aging and related changes in functional activations. In sum, considering the expanded versions of these psychological theories leads to novel predictions that will be fruitful for future functional neuroimaging investigations.

Conclusions

We started this chapter by noting that, unlike executive and memory functions, emotional processing is well preserved in healthy aging. The preservation of emotional processing in older adults is remarkable given that healthy aging is associated with substantial anatomical decline in several brain regions. We considered two possible explanations: Emotional processing regions are relatively resistant to anatomical decline, and anatomical decline is counteracted by increased PFC activity. A brief review of age-related changes in brain anatomy and brain activity provided support for both hypotheses. Consistent with the anatomical preservation hypothesis, age-related atrophy is relatively modest in three regions important for emotional processing: the amygdala, medial PFC, and the ventral striatum; consistent with the functional compensation hypothesis, there is evidence that PFC over-recruitment in age-related activated patterns like PASA and HAROLD is asso-

ciated with enhanced performance in older adults.

More direct evidence for the functional compensation hypothesis was provided by our review of functional neuroimaging studies of emotional processing. In the domains of perception, episodic memory, decision making, and emotion regulation, older adults often showed increased PFC responses to emotional stimuli, which were sometimes coupled with reduced amygdala responses, particularly to negative stimuli. We called this pattern frontoamygdalar age-related differences in emotion or FADE. The PFC component of FADE may reflect functional compensation, similar to PFC over-recruitment in the domain-independent age-related activations patterns known as PASA and HAROLD. In the case of emotion studies, age-related PFC increases could reflect greater reliance on emotion regulation or self-referential processing. These accounts are not incompatible and could be integrated.

Finally, we considered how functional neuroimaging findings fit with psychological theories of age-related emotional changes: the socioemotional selectivity theory (SST), dynamic integration theory (DIT), learning and practice theory, and the byproduct of biological decline theory. Given that most of these theories do not include specific assumptions about brain mechanisms, we expanded them with additional neural assumptions. SST fits generally well with the FADE pattern if one interprets age-related PFC increases and amygdalar decreases for negative stimuli as reflecting emotion regulation. DIT is difficult to assess because few studies have manipulated emotional complexity, but there is evidence that PFC-amygdalar coupling in older adults varies with the level of emotional activation (St. Jacques et al., 2010), which is a finding consistent with DIT. Learning and practice theory is consistent with evidence that medial PFC recruitment in older adults varies with whether they are judging themselves vs. less familiar others (Gutchess, Kensinger, & Schacter, 2007). Finally the byproduct of biological decline theory cannot easily account for the fact that activation findings do not fit well with patterns of anatomical decline in healthy aging. In general, these various theories have complementary strengths and weaknesses and could in principle be integrated to achieve a more complete account of age-related changes in emotional processing. The challenge for future research will be to incorporate psychological theories into cognitive neuroscience accounts of emotional processing in old age.

Outstanding Questions and Future Directions

- How do valence and arousal interact and influence age-related differences in the neural correlates supporting emotional perception, emotional memory, emotional decision making, and emotion regulation?
- What is the relationship between anatomy and functional changes described by the frontoamygdalar age-related differences in emotion (FADE) pattern?
- Are age-related increases in prefrontal cortex recruitment during emotional processing related to different processing strategies? Do age-related increases in the prefrontal cortex account for spared emotional processing in older adults (functional compensation hypothesis)?
- What are the neural mechanisms supporting automatic versus controlled deployment of emotion regulation in aging? How can we reconcile discrepancies in the age-related differences supporting these different emotion regulation strategies?
- Linking age-related changes in neural activation to cognitive and social theories of emotional aging generates several topics for future research on the neural basis of emotion and aging, including the influence of emotional activation, emotional complexity, familiarity, cognitive demands, and individual differences in cognitive performance.

Acknowledgments

This work was supported by grants AG19731 and AG34580 (RC), a postdoctoral NRSA AG038079, and the L'Oreal USA for Women in Science Fellowship (PLS). We thank Dr. Scott Huettel for helpful comments on an earlier draft.

References

Addis, D. R., Leclerc, C. M., Muscatell, K. A., & Kensinger, E. A. (2010). There are age-related changes in neural connectivity during the encoding of positive, but not negative, information. *Cortex*, 46(4), 425–33.

Allard, E., & Isaacowitz, D. (2008). Are preferences in emotional processing affected by distraction? Examining the age-related positivity effect in visual fixation within a dual-task paradigm. *Aging, Neuropsychology, and Cognition*, 15(6), 725–43.

Amaral, D. G., & Price, J. L. (1984). Amygdalo-cortical projections in the monkey (Macaca fascicularis). *Journal of Comparative Neurology*, 230(4), 465–96.

Amodio, D. M., & Frith, C. D. (2006). Meeting of minds: The medial frontal cortex and social cognition. *Nature Reviews Neuroscience*, 7(4), 268–77.

Andrews-Hanna, J. R., Reidler, J. S., Sepulcre, J., Poulin, R., & Buckner, R. L. (2010). Functional-anatomic fractionation of the brain's default network. *Neuron*, 65(4), 550–62.

Antonini, A., & Leenders, K. L. (1993). Dopamine D2 receptors in normal human brain: Effect of age measured by positron emission tomography (PET) and [11C]-raclopride. *Annals of the New York Academy of Sciences*, 695, 81–85.

Blanchard-Fields, F. (2007). Everyday problem solving and emotion: An adult developmental perspective. *Current Directions in Psychological Science*, 16(1), 26–31.

Brabec, J., Rulseh, A., Hoyt, B., Vizek, M., Horinek, D., Hort, J., et al. (2010). Volumetry of the human amygdala – an anatomical study. *Psychiatry Research*, 182(1), 67-72.

Cabeza, R. (2002). Hemispheric asymmetry reduction in older adults: The HAROLD model. *Psychology and Aging*, 17(1), 85–100.

Cabeza, R., Grady, C. L., Nyberg, L., McIntosh, A. R., Tulving, E., Kapur, S., et al. (1997).

Age-related differences in neural activity during memory encoding and retrieval: A positron emission tomography study. *Journal of Neuroscience*, 17(1), 391–400.

Cacioppo, J. T., Berntson, G. G., Bechara, A., Tranel, D., & Hawkley, L. C. (2011). Could an aging brain contribute to subjective well-being?: The value added by a social neuroscience perspective. In A. Tadorov, S. T. Fiske, & D. Prentice (Eds.), *Social neuroscience: Towards understanding the underpinnings of the social mind* (pp. 249–62). New York: Oxford University Press.

Carstensen, L. L., Fung, H. H., & Charles, S. T. (2003). Socioemotional selectivity theory and the regulation of emotion in the second half of life. *Motivation and Emotion*, 27(2), 103–23.

Carstensen, L. L., & Mikels, J. A. (2005). At the intersection of emotion and cognition: Aging and the positivity effect. *Current Directions in Psychological Science*, 14, 117–21.

Carstensen, L. L., Mikels, J. A., & Mather, M. (2006). Aging and the intersection of cognition, motivation and emotion. In J. Birren & K. W. Schaie (Eds.), *Handbook of the psychology of aging* (pp. 343–62). San Diego: Academic Press.

Charles, S. T. (2010). Strength and vulnerability integration: A model of emotional well-being across adulthood. *Psychological Bulletin*, 136(6), 1068–91.

Charles, S. T., & Carstensen, L. L. (2007). Emotion regulation and aging. In J. J. Gross (Ed.), *Handbook of emotion regulation* (pp. 307–27). New York: Guilford.

Charles, S. T., & Carstensen, L. L. (2010). Social and emotional aging. *Annual Review of Psychology*, 61, 383–409.

Cherubini, A., Peran, P., Caltagirone, C., Sabatini, U., & Spalletta, G. (2009). Aging of subcortical nuclei: Microstructural, mineralization and atrophy modifications measured in vivo using MRI. *Neuroimage*, 48(1), 29–36.

Chow, T.W., & Cummings, J. L. (2000). The amygdala and Alzheimer's disease. In J. Aggleton (Ed.), *The amygdala – A functional analysis* (pp. 655–80). Oxford: Oxford University Press.

Cox, K., Aizenstein, H., & Fiez, J. (2008). Striatal outcome processing in healthy aging. *Cognitive, Affective, & Behavioral Neuroscience*, 8(3), 304.

Davis, S. W., Dennis, N. A., Daselaar, S. M., Fleck, M. S., & Cabeza, R. (2008). Que PASA? The posterior-anterior shift in aging. *Cerebral Cortex*, 18(5), 1201–9.

Delgado, M., Gillis, M., & Phelps, E. (2008). Regulating the expectation of reward via cognitive strategies. *Nature Neuroscience*, 11(8), 880–81.

Denburg, N., Recknor, E., Bechara, A., & Tranel, D. (2006). Psychophysiological anticipation of positive outcomes promotes advantageous decision-making in normal older persons. *International Journal of Psychophysiology*, 61(1), 19–25.

Dennis, M., Farrell, K., Hoffman, H. J., Hendrick, E. B., et al. (1988). Recognition memory of item, associative and serial-order information after temporal lobectomy for seizure disorder. *Neuropsychologia*, 26(1), 53–65.

Dennis, N. A., & Cabeza, R. (2008). Neuroimaging of healthy cognitive aging. In F. I. M. Craik & T. A. Salthouse (Eds.), *The handbook of aging and cognition* (3rd ed., pp. 1–54). Mahwah, NJ: Erlbaum.

Dennis, N. A., Hayes, S. M., Prince, S. E., Madden, D. J., Huettel, S. A., & Cabeza, R. (2008). Effects of aging on the neural correlates of successful item and source memory encoding. *Journal of Experimental Psychology: Learning, Memory & Cognition*, 34(4), 791–808.

Dolcos, F., LaBar, K. S., & Cabeza, R. (2004). Dissociable effects of arousal and valence on prefrontal activity indexing emotional evaluation and subsequent memory: An event-related fMRI study. *Neuroimage*, 23(1), 64–74.

Dreher, J., Meyer-Lindenberg, A., Kohn, P., & Berman, K. (2008). Age-related changes in midbrain dopaminergic regulation of the human reward system. *Proceedings of the National Academy of Sciences*, 105(39), 15106.

Emery, L., & Hess, T. M. (2008). Viewing instructions impact emotional memory differently in older and young adults. *Psychology and Aging*, 23(1), 2–12.

Erixon-Lindroth, N., Farde, L., Wahlin, T. B., Sovago, J., Halldin, C., & Bäckman, L. (2005). The role of the striatal dopamine transporter in cognitive aging. *Psychiatry Research: Neuroimaging*, 138(1), 1–12.

Fischer, H. (2010). Age-related differences in brain regions supporting successful encoding of emotional faces. *Cortex*, 46, 490–97.

Fischer, H., Sandblom, J., Gavazzeni, J., Fransson, P., Wright, C. I., & Backman, L. (2005). Age-differential patterns of brain activation during perception of angry faces. *Neuroscience Letters*, 386(2), 99–104.

Frank, M., & Kong, L. (2008). Learning to avoid in older age. *Psychology and Aging*, 23(2), 392–98.

Grady, C. L., Maisog, J. M., Horwitz, B., Ungerleider, L. G., Mentis, M. J., Salerno, J. A., et al. (1994). Age-related changes in cortical blood flow activation during visual processing of faces and location. *Journal of Neuroscience*, 14(3, Pt. 2), 1450–62.

Grady, C. L., Springer, M. V., Hongwanishkul, D., McIntosh, A. R., & Winocur, G. (2006). Age-related changes in brain activity across the adult lifespan. *Journal of Cognitive Neuroscience*, 18(2), 227–41.

Gross, J. (1998a). Antecedent-and response-focused emotion regulation: Divergent consequences for experience, expression, and physiology. *Journal of Personality and Social Psychology*, 74, 224–37.

Gross, J. (1998b). The emerging field of emotion regulation: An integrative review. *Review of General Psychology*, 2(3), 271–99.

Gross, J., Carstensen, L., Pasupathi, M., Tsai, J., Skorpen, C., & Hsu, A. (1997). Emotion and aging: Experience, expression, and control. *Psychology and Aging*, 12, 590–99.

Gruhn, D., & Scheibe, S. (2008). Age-related differences in valence and arousal ratings of pictures from the International Affective Picture System (IAPS): Do ratings become more extreme with age? *Behavioral Research Methods*, 40(2), 512–21.

Gruhn, D., Smith, J., & Baltes, P. B. (2005). No aging bias favoring memory for positive material: Evidence from a heterogeneity-homogeneity list paradigm using emotionally toned words. *Psychology and Aging*, 20(4), 579–88.

Gunning-Dixon, F. M., Gur, R. C., Perkins, A. C., Schroeder, L., Turner, T., Turetsky, B. I., et al. (2003). Age-related differences in brain activation during emotional face processing. *Neurobiology of Aging*, 24(2), 285–95.

Gunning-Dixon, F. M., & Raz, N. (2003). Neuroanatomical correlates of selected executive functions in middle-aged and older adults: A prospective MRI study. *Neuropsychologia*, 41(14), 1929–41.

Gutchess, A. H., Kensinger, E. A., & Schacter, D. L. (2007). Aging, self-referencing, and medial prefrontal cortex. *Social Neuroscience*, 2(2), 117–33.

Gutchess, A. H., Kensinger, E. A., Yoon, C., & Schacter, D. L. (2007). Ageing and the self-reference effect in memory. *Memory*, 15(8), 822–37.

Heilman, R., Crisan, L., Houser, D., Miclea, M., & Miu, A. (2010). Emotion regulation and decision making under risk and uncertainty. *Emotion*, 10(2), 257–65.

Hess, T. M. (2005). Memory and aging in context. *Psychological Bulletin*, 131(3), 383–406.

Honea, R. A., Vidoni, E., Harsha, A., & Burns, J. M. (2009). Impact of APOE on the healthy aging brain: A voxel-based MRI and DTI study. *Journal of Alzheimers Disease*, 18(3), 553–64.

Idika, T., Okada, T., Murata, T., Omori, M., Kosaka, H., Sadato, N., et al. (2002). Age-related differences in the medial temporal lobe responses to emotional faces as revealed by fMRI. *Hippocampus*, 12(3), 352–62.

Isaacowitz, D., Wadlinger, H., Goren, D., & Wilson, H. (2006). Is there an age-related positivity effect in visual attention? A comparison of two methodologies. *Emotion*, 6(3), 511–16.

Jacobson, A., Green, E., & Murphy, C. (2010). Age-related functional changes in gustatory and reward processing regions: An fMRI study. *Neuroimage*, 53, 602–10.

Kennedy, Q., & Mather, M. (2007). Aging, affect and decision making. In R. Baumeister & G. Lowenstein (Eds.), *Do emotions help or hurt decision making? A hedgefoxian perspective* (pp. 245–65). New York: Russel Sage Foundation.

Kensinger, E. A. (2004). Remembering emotional experiences: The contribution of valence and arousal. *Reviews of Neuroscience*, 15(4), 241–51.

Kensinger, E. A. (2008). Age differences in memory for arousing and nonarousing emotional words. *Journal of Gerontology Series B: Psychological and Social Sciences*, 63(1), P13–18.

Kensinger, E. A. (2009). *Emotional memory across the adult lifespan*. New York: Taylor & Francis.

Kensinger, E. A., & Leclerc, C. M. (2009). Age-related changes in the neural mechanisms supporting emotion processing and emotional memory. *European Journal of Cognitive Psychology*, 21, 192–215.

Kensinger, E. A., & Schacter, D. L. (2008). Neural processes supporting young and older adults' emotional memories. *Journal of Cognitive Neuroscience*, 20(7), 1161–73.

Kim, S., & Hamann, S. (2007). Neural correlates of positive and negative emotion regulation. *Journal of Cognitive Neuroscience*, 19(5), 776–98.

Knight, M., & Mather, M. (2006). The affective neuroscience of aging and its implications for cognition. In T. Canli (Ed.), *The biological bases of personality and individual differences* (pp. 159–183). New York: Guilford Press.

Krienen, F. M., Tu, P. C., & Buckner, R. L. (2010). Clan mentality: Evidence that the medial prefrontal cortex responds to close others. *Journal of Neuroscience*, 30(41), 13906–15.

Kunzmann, U., Kupperbusch, C. S., & Levenson, R. W. (2005). Behavioral inhibition and amplification during emotional arousal: A comparison of two age groups. *Psychology & Aging*, 20(1), 144–58.

Labouvie-Vief, G. (2003). Dynamic integration: Affect, cognition and the self in adulthood. *Current Directions in Psychological Science*, 12(6), 201–6.

Labouvie-Vief, G. (2009). Dynamic integration theory: Emotion, cognition and equilibrium in later life. In V. L. Bengtson, D. Gans, N. M. Putney, & M. Silverstein (Eds.), *Handbook of theory of aging* (2nd ed., pp. 277–93). New York: Springer.

Leclerc, C. M., & Kensinger, E. A. (2008). Age-related differences in medial prefrontal activation in response to emotional images. *Cognitive, Affective, & Behavioral Neuroscience*, 8(2), 153–64.

Leclerc, C. M., & Kensinger, E. A. (2010). Age-related valence-based reversal in recruitment of medial prefrontal cortex on a visual search task. *Social Neuroscience*, 5(5–6), 560–76.

Leclerc, C. M., & Kensinger, E. A. (2011). Neural processing of emotional pictures and words: A comparison of young and older adults. *Developmental Neuropsychology*, 36, 519–38.

Lockenhoff, C., & Carstensen, L. (2007). Aging, emotion, and health-related decision strategies: Motivational manipulations can reduce age differences. *Psychology and Aging*, 22(1), 134–46.

Logan, J. M., Sanders, A. L., Snyder, A. Z., Morris, J. C., & Buckner, R. L. (2002). Under-recruitment and nonselective recruitment: Dissociable neural mechanisms associated with aging. *Neuron*, 33, 827–40.

Mather, M. (2006). Why memories may become more positive as people age. In B. Uttl & A. L. Ohta (Eds.), *Memory and emotion: Interdisciplinary perspectives* (pp. 135–57). Malden, MA: Blackwell.

Mather, M., Canli, T., English, T., Whitfield, S., Wais, P., Ochsner, K., et al. (2004). Amygdala responses to emotionally valenced stimuli in older and younger adults. *Psychological Science*, 15(4), 259–63.

Mather, M., & Carstensen, L. L. (2003). Aging and attentional biases for emotional faces. *Psychological Science*, 14(5), 409–15.

Mather, M., & Carstensen, L. L. (2005). Aging and motivated cognition: The positivity effect in attention and memory. *Trends in Cognitive Sciences*, 9(10), 496–502.

Mather, M., & Knight, M. (2005). Goal-directed memory: The role of cognitive control in older adults' emotional memory. *Psychology and Aging*, 20(4), 554.

Mather, M., & Knight, M. (2006). Angry faces get noticed quickly: Threat detection is not impaired among older adults. *Journals of Gerontology Series B: Psychological Sciences and Social Sciences*, 61(1), P54.

Mell, T., Wartenburger, I., Marschner, A., Villringer, A., Reischies, F., & Heekeren, H. (2009). Altered function of ventral striatum during reward-based decision making in old age, *Frontiers in Human Neuroscience*, 3, 34.

Mikels, J. A., & Reed, A. E. (2009). Monetary losses do not loom large in later life: Age differences in the framing effect. *Journals of Gerontology Series B: Psychological Sciences and Social Sciences*, 64B(4), 457–60.

Miller, E. K., & Cohen, J. D. (2001). An integrative theory of prefrontal cortex function. *Annual Reviews in Neuroscience*, 24, 167–202.

Mohr, P.N., Li, S. C., & Heekeren, H. R. (2009) Neuroeconomics and aging: Neuromodulation of economic decision making in old age. *Neuroscience & Biobehavioral Reviews*, 34, 6878–88.

Mu, Q., Xie, J., Wen, Z., Weng, Y., & Shuyun, Z. (1999). A quantitative MR study of the hippocampal formation, the amygdala, and the temporal horn of the lateral ventricle in healthy subjects 40 to 90 years of age. *American Journal of Neuroradiology*, 20(2), 207–11.

Murphy, N. A., & Isaacowitz, D. M. (2008). Preferences for emotional information in older and younger adults: A meta-analysis of memory and attention tasks. *Psychology and Aging*, 23(2), 263–86.

Murty, V. P., Sambataro, F., Das, S., Tan, H. Y., Callicott, J. H., Goldberg, T. E., et al. (2009). Age-related alterations in simple declarative memory and the effect of negative stimulus valence. *Journal of Cognitive Neuroscience*, 21(10), 1920–33.

Novak, D., & Mather, M. (2007). Aging and variety seeking. *Psychology and Aging*, 22(4), 728.

Ochsner, K., Bunge, S., Gross, J., & Gabrieli, J. (2002). Rethinking feelings: An fMRI study of the cognitive regulation of emotion. *Journal of Cognitive Neuroscience*, 14(8), 1215–29.

Ochsner, K., & Gross, J. (2005). The cognitive control of emotion. *Trends in Cognitive Sciences*, 9(5), 242–49.

Ochsner, K. N., & Gross, J. J. (2007). The neural architecture of emotional regulation. In J. J. Gross & R. Buck (Eds.), *The handbook of emotion regulation* (pp. 87–109). New York: Guilford Press.

Ochsner, K. N., Ray, R. D., Cooper, J. C., Robertson, E. R., Chopra, S., Gabrieli, J. D., et al. (2004). For better or for worse: Neural systems supporting the cognitive down- and up-regulation of negative emotion. *Neuroimage*, 23(2), 483–99.

O'Doherty, J. P. (2004). Reward representations and reward-related learning in the human brain: Insights from neuroimaging. *Current Opinions in Neurobiology*, 14(6), 769–76.

Peters, E., Hess, T. M., Västfjäll, D., & Auman, C. (2007). Adult age differences in dual information processes: Implications for the role of affective and deliberative processes in older adults' decision making. *Perspectives on Psychological Science*, 2(1), 1–23.

Phan, K. L., Wager, T., Taylor, S. F., & Liberzon, I. (2002). Functional neuroanatomy of emotion: A meta-analysis of emotion activation studies in PET and fMRI. *Neuroimage*, 16(2), 331–48.

Phelps, E. A. (2006). Emotion and cognition: Insights from studies of the human amygdala. *Annual Review of Psychology*, 57, 27–53.

Raz, N. (2005). The aging brain observed in vivo: Differential changes and their modifiers. In R. Cabeza, L. Nyberg, & D. C. Park (Eds.), *Long-term memory and aging: A cognitive neuroscience perspective* (pp. 19–57). New York: Oxford University Press.

Raz, N., Lindenberger, U., Rodrigue, K. M., Kennedy, K. M., Head, D., Williamson, A., et al. (2005). Regional brain changes in aging healthy adults: General trends, individual differences and modifiers. *Cerebral Cortex*, 15(11), 1676–89.

Raz, N., Rodrigue, K. M., Kennedy, K. M., Head, D., Gunning-Dixon, F., & Acker, J. D. (2003). Differential aging of the human striatum: Longitudinal evidence. *American Journal of Neuroradiology*, 24(9), 1849–56.

Reuter-Lorenz, P. A., Jonides, J., Smith, E. E., Hartley, A., Miller, A., Marshuetz, C., et al. (2000). Age differences in the frontal lateralization of verbal and spatial working memory revealed by PET. *Journal of Cognitive Neuroscience*, 12(1), 174–87.

Ritchey, M., Bessette-Symons, B., Hayes, S., & Cabeza, R. (2011). Emotion processing in the aging brain is modulated by semantic elaboration. *Neuropsychologia*, 49, 640–50.

Ritchey, M., Dolcos, F., & Cabeza, R. (2008). Role of amygdala connectivity in the persistence of emotional memories over time: An event-related FMRI investigation. *Cerebral Cortex*, 18(11), 2494–2504.

Ruffman, T., Henry, J. D., Livingstone, V., & Phillips, L. H. (2008). A meta-analytic review of emotion recognition and aging: Implications for neuropsychological models of aging. *Neuroscience & Biobehavioral Reviews*, 32(4), 863–81.

Salat, D. H., Kaye, J. A., & Janowsky, J. S. (2001). Selective preservation and degeneration within the prefrontal cortex in aging and Alzheimer disease. *Archives of Neurology.*, 58(9), 1403–8.

Samanez-Larkin, G. R., & Carstensen, L. L. (2011). Socioemotional functioning and the aging brain. In J. Decety & J. T. Cacioppo (Eds.), *The handbook of social neuroscience* (pp. 507–21). New York: Oxford University Press.

Samanez-Larkin, G., Gibbs, S., Khanna, K., Nielsen, L., Carstensen, L., & Knutson, B. (2007). Anticipation of monetary gain but not loss in healthy older adults. *Nature Neuroscience*, 10(6), 787–91.

Samanez-Larkin, G. R., Kuhnen, C. M., Yoo, D. J., & Knutson, B. (2010). Variability in nucleus accumbens activity mediates age-related suboptimal financial risk taking. *Journal of Neuroscience*, 30(4), 1426–34.

Samanez-Larkin, G. R., Robertson, E. R., Mikels, J. A., Carstensen, L. L., & Gotlib, I. H. (2009). Selective attention to emotion in the aging brain. *Psychology and Aging*, 24(3), 519–29.

Scheibe, S., & Carstensen, L. L. (2010). Emotional aging: Recent findings and future trends. *Journal of Gerontology Series B: Psychological Sciences and Social Sciences*, 65, 135–44.

Schott, B., Niehaus, L., Wittmann, B., Schtze, H., Seidenbecher, C., Heinze, H., et al. (2007). Ageing and early-stage Parkinson's disease affect separable neural mechanisms of mesolimbic reward processing. *Brain*, 130(9), 2412.

Shiota, M., & Levenson, R. (2009). Effects of aging on experimentally instructed detached reappraisal, positive reappraisal, and emotional behavior suppression. *Psychology and Aging*, 24(4), 890–900.

Sokol-Hessner, P., Hsu, M., Curley, N., Delgado, M., Camerer, C., & Phelps, E. (2009). Thinking like a trader selectively reduces individuals' loss aversion. *Proceedings of the National Academy of Sciences*, 106(13), 5035.

St. Jacques, P. L., Bessette-Symons, B., & Cabeza, R. (2009). Functional neuroimaging studies of aging and emotion: fronto-amygdalar differences during emotional perception and episodic memory. *Journal of the International Neuropsychological Society*, 15(6), 819–25.

St. Jacques, P. L., Conway, M. A., Lowder, M. W., & Cabeza, R. (2011). Watching my mind unfold versus yours: An fMRI study using a novel camera technology to examine neural differences in self-projection of self versus other perspectives. *Journal of Cognitive Neuroscience*, 23, 1275–84.

St. Jacques, P. L., Dolcos, F., & Cabeza, R. (2009). Effects of aging on functional connectivity of the amygdala for subsequent memory of negative pictures: A network analysis of fMRI data. *Psychological Science*, 20(1), 74–84.

St. Jacques, P., Dolcos, F., & Cabeza, R. (2010). Effects of aging on functional connectivity of the amygdala during negative evaluation: A network analysis of fMRI data. *Neurobiology of Aging*, 31(2), 315–27.

St. Jacques, P. L., & Levine, B. (2007). Ageing and autobiographical memory for emotional and neutral events. *Memory*, 15(2): 129–44.

Tessitore, A., Hariri, A. R., Fera, F., Smith, W. G., Das, S., Weinberger, D. R., et al. (2005). Functional changes in the activity of brain regions underlying emotion processing in the elderly. *Psychiatry Research*, 139(1), 9–18.

Urry, H., van Reekum, C., Johnstone, T., Kalin, N., Thurow, M., Schaefer, H., et al. (2006). Amygdala and ventromedial prefrontal cortex are inversely coupled during regulation of negative affect and predict the diurnal pattern of cortisol secretion among older adults. *Journal of Neuroscience*, 26(16), 4415.

van Dyck, C. H., Seibyl, J. P., Malison, R. T., Laruelle, M., Wallace, E., Zoghbi, S. S., et al. (1995). Age-related decline in striatal dopamine transporter binding with iodine-123-beta-CITSPECT. *Journal of Nuclear Medicine*, 36(7), 1175–81.

Wang, Y., Chan, G. L., Holden, J. E., Dobko, T., Mak, E., Schulzer, M., et al. (1998). Age-dependent decline of dopamine D_1 receptors in human brain: A PET study. *Synapse*, 30(1), 56–61.

Weierich, M., Kensinger, E., Munnell, A., Sass, S., Dickerson, B., Wright, C., et al. (2011). Older and wiser? An affective science perspective on age-related challenges in financial decision making, *Social Cognitive & Affective Neuroscience*, 6, 195–206.

Williams, L. M., Brown, K. J., Palmer, D., Liddell, B. J., Kemp, A. H., Olivieri, G., et al. (2006). The mellow years? Aeural basis of improving emotional stability over age. *Journal of Neuroscience*, 26(24), 6422–30.

Winecoff, A., LaBar, K. S., Madden, D. J., Cabeza, R., & Huettel, S. A. (2011). Cognitive and neural contributors to emotion regulation in aging. *Social Cognitive and Affective Neuroscience*, 6, 165–76.

Wright, C. I., Wedig, M. M., Williams, D., Rauch, S. L., & Albert, M. S. (2006). Novel fearful faces activate the amygdala in healthy young and elderly adults. *Neurobiology of Aging*, 27(2), 361–74.

Index